RRB ALP

Basic Science & Electronics Engineering

for

Indian Railways (RRB)

ASSISTANT LOCO PILOT

Recruitment Examination 2024-2025

(Stage II)

Title : RRB - ALP : Basic Science & Electronics Engineering (Assistant Loco Pilot Stage II)

Language : English

Editor's Name : GKP Editorial Team

Typeset & Published by :

Career Launcher Infrastructure (P) Ltd.

A-45, Mohan Cooperative Industrial Area, Near Mohan Estate Metro Station, New Delhi - 110044

Marketed by :

G.K. Publications (P) Ltd.

Plot No. 63, Sector-27A, Near Sector - 28 Metro Station, Faridabad, Haryana-121003

ISBN : **978-93-56813-65-6**

Printer's Details: Printed in India, New Delhi.

For product information :

Visit ***www.gkpublications.com*** or email to ***gkp@gkpublications.com***

CONTENTS

Basic Science

Electronics

Basic Science

Engineering Drawing

ENGINEERING DRAWING

Engineering drawing is a graphical representation of an object or a system that is created by engineers to communicate design and technical information. It serves as a precise and detailed visual reference that provides information about the size, shape, dimensions, and other geometric characteristics of a component, structure, or machine.

Engineering drawings are typically created using computer-aided design (CAD) software or drawn manually using traditional drafting techniques. They include various types of views, such as orthographic views (top, front, side), isometric views, sectional views, and auxiliary views. These views allow engineers, designers, and manufacturers to understand the object or system from different angles and perspectives.

The information conveyed in an engineering drawing includes dimensions, tolerances, materials, surface finishes, assembly instructions, and other specifications necessary for manufacturing, construction, or fabrication. Drawings also include symbols, notations, and annotations to indicate important features, such as holes, threads, welds, and part numbers.

Engineering drawings follow internationally recognized standards and conventions, such as those established by the American National Standards Institute (ANSI) or the International Organization for Standardization (ISO). These standards ensure consistency, clarity, and accuracy in communicating design intent across different industries and countries.

Overall, engineering drawings play a vital role in the design and production process, facilitating clear communication between engineers, manufacturers, and other stakeholders involved in the realization of a product or system.

Engineering drawings common features:

Engineering drawings typically include several common features to convey information accurately and consistently. Here are some of the common features found in engineering drawings:

1. Title Block: The title block is located in the lower right-hand corner of the drawing and contains important information about the drawing, such as the title, drawing number, revision status, scale, date, and the name of the drafter or designer.
2. Views: Engineering drawings feature different views of the object or system being represented. The most common views are orthographic views (top, front, side) that provide a 2D representation of the object from different perspectives. Other views, such as isometric views or sectional views, may also be included to provide additional clarity.
3. Dimensions: Dimensions are numerical values that specify the size, shape, and location of features on the object or system. Linear dimensions indicate lengths, while angular dimensions specify angles. Dimensions are typically shown with lines, arrows, and text indicating the measurement.
4. Geometric Tolerances: Geometric tolerances define the allowable variations in size, form, orientation, and location of features. These tolerances ensure that the manufactured component meets the design requirements. Geometric tolerances are represented using symbols and are usually accompanied by specific values or limits.
5. Sectional Views: Sectional views are used to reveal the internal structure or hidden details of an object. These views are obtained by cutting a part of the object and showing the internal features beyond the cutting plane. Sectional views are helpful for understanding the inner workings or complex arrangements within an object.
6. Symbols and Notations: Engineering drawings utilize a variety of symbols and notations to represent specific features or characteristics. For example, symbols can indicate surface finishes, welding, fasteners, electrical connections, or specific types of components. Notations may provide additional information or instructions related to the design or manufacturing process.
7. Assembly Information: In drawings for assemblies, there is often information regarding the relationship between different components, including how they fit together and how they are fastened or joined. This information helps in the assembly and manufacturing process.

8. Bill of Materials (BOM): A Bill of Materials lists all the components and parts required for manufacturing or assembling the object. It provides a comprehensive inventory of the materials needed, including part numbers, quantities, and sometimes additional specifications.

These are just a few common features found in engineering drawings. Depending on the specific application and industry, additional features and information may be included to ensure clear communication and accurate manufacturing or construction.

Examples of engineering drawings:

1. Mechanical Drawing: This type of drawing represents mechanical components and assemblies. It may include detailed views, dimensions, and annotations. For example, a mechanical drawing can show the exploded view of a gearbox, with all the individual parts labeled and dimensioned.
2. Electrical Schematic: An electrical schematic is a diagram that represents the electrical connections and components in a system. It uses standardized symbols to illustrate circuits and their interconnections. For instance, an electrical schematic can depict the wiring and connections of a control panel for a motor.
3. Civil Engineering Plan: A civil engineering plan is used in civil engineering projects, such as road construction or building design. It shows the layout, dimensions, and details of various elements like roads, buildings, drainage systems, and utilities. An example could be a site plan for a housing development, illustrating lot boundaries, roads, and utility connections.
4. Architectural Floor Plan: An architectural floor plan is a drawing that represents the layout of a building at the ground level. It typically shows the walls, doors, windows, and major fixtures within a building. For instance, an architectural floor plan could show the layout of rooms, corridors, and common areas in a house or office building.
5. Structural Drawing: A structural drawing provides details about the structural components of a building or infrastructure project. It includes information about beams, columns, foundations, and other load-bearing elements. For example, a structural drawing can illustrate the reinforcement details for a concrete beam.
6. Piping and Instrumentation Diagram (P&ID): A P&ID is a schematic representation of a process system, indicating the piping, instruments, valves, and equipment used in the system. It is commonly used in industries such as chemical plants or oil refineries. A P&ID could show the flow of fluids, the location of pumps and valves, and the instrumentation used for process control.

These are just a few examples of engineering drawings, and there are many other types depending on the specific field and purpose. Engineering drawings serve as communication tools, providing precise information to engineers, technicians, and manufacturers for the design, construction, and operation of various systems and structures.

Types of drawing

There are several types of drawings, each serving a different purpose and catering to various fields. Here are some common types of drawings:

1. Engineering Drawing: Engineering drawings are used to communicate technical details and specifications for the design, construction, and operation of various engineering systems. They can include mechanical drawings, electrical schematics, civil engineering plans, structural drawings, and more.
2. Architectural Drawing: Architectural drawings are created by architects to represent the design and construction of buildings and structures. They include floor plans, elevations, sections, and details that show the layout, dimensions, and materials used in architectural projects.
3. Technical Drawing: Technical drawings are detailed and precise drawings that provide specific instructions for the manufacturing, assembly, or installation of a product or system. They often include dimensions, annotations, and symbols to convey information clearly to technicians and manufacturers.
4. Perspective Drawing: Perspective drawings are used to represent three-dimensional objects or scenes on a two-dimensional surface, creating an illusion of depth and space. They are commonly used in architectural design, art, and illustration to provide a realistic representation of objects or spaces.
5. Isometric Drawing: Isometric drawings are a type of technical drawing that represents three-dimensional objects using a 30-degree angle. They show the object's height, width, and depth without distortion, making them useful for conveying the shape and layout of objects in engineering and design.
6. Exploded View Drawing: An exploded view drawing shows the individual components of an assembly separated and positioned in a way that illustrates how they fit together. It is commonly used in engineering and manufacturing to demonstrate the assembly process and to aid in understanding the relationship between different parts.
7. Conceptual Drawing: Conceptual drawings are often freehand sketches or illustrations used in the early stages of the design process to explore and communicate ideas. They are less detailed and more focused on conveying the overall concept or artistic vision.
8. Topographical Drawing: Topographical drawings, also known as contour maps, depict the elevation and features of a specific area of land. They are used in various fields, including civil engineering, urban planning, and environmental studies.

These are just a few examples of the types of drawings that exist. Different industries and disciplines may have their own specific types of drawings based on their requirements and purposes.

Types of Drawings

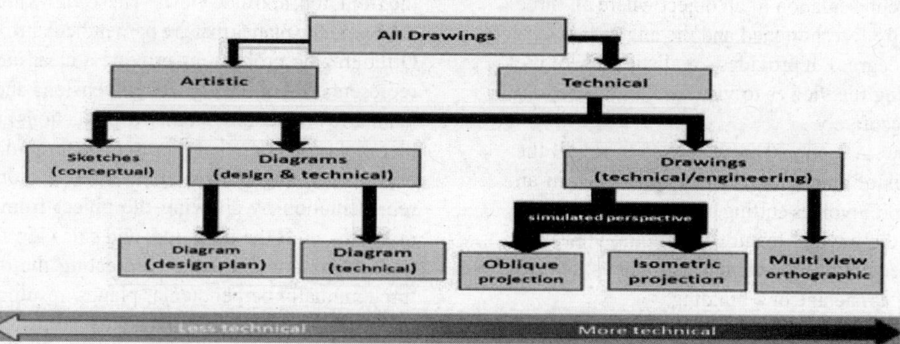

Dimensioning in engineering drawing:

Dimensioning in engineering drawing refers to the process of adding precise measurements, symbols, and notes to convey the size, location, and tolerances of features on a drawing. It is a crucial aspect of technical communication in engineering, as it provides clear instructions to manufacturers, fabricators, assemblers, and inspectors for the production and quality control of a design. Here are some key considerations for dimensioning in engineering drawing:

1. Types of Dimensions:
   - Linear Dimensions: Represent the length, width, and height of features using numerical values.
   - Angular Dimensions: Specify angles between lines, surfaces, or features.
   - Radial Dimensions: Indicate the radius or diameter of arcs, circles, or rounded features.
2. Placement of Dimensions:
   - Dimensions should be placed outside the outline of the object or feature, avoiding overcrowding or overlapping.
   - Use extension lines with arrowheads to indicate precisely where the dimensions apply.
   - Group related dimensions together and align them for clarity and ease of reading.
3. Dimensioning Techniques:
   - Aligned Dimensions: Dimensions are placed parallel to the feature being measured.
   - Baseline Dimensions: Dimensions are referenced from a common baseline or datum line.
   - Chain Dimensions: Dimensions are shown in a continuous chain, reducing the number of dimension lines.
   - Ordinate Dimensions: Dimensions are measured from a common reference point or coordinate system.
4. Dimensioning Standards:
   - Follow relevant standards such as ASME Y14.5 or ISO 129-1 to ensure consistency and compatibility with other drawings.
   - Use appropriate dimensioning symbols, line types, and text styles as per the chosen standards.
5. Tolerancing:
   - Specify tolerances to indicate allowable variations in dimensions.
   - Use appropriate tolerance notations, such as "+" or "-" signs, limit dimensions, or geometric tolerancing symbols.
   - Clearly communicate tolerance requirements for critical dimensions to ensure proper functionality and fit.
6. Units of Measurement:
   - Clearly specify the units of measurement (e.g., millimeters, inches) for each dimension.
   - Ensure consistency throughout the drawing, using a single unit system.
7. Clear Communication:
   - Dimensioning should be clear, concise, and unambiguous, leaving no room for misinterpretation.
   - Use clear and readable text, appropriate font sizes, and proper line weights.
8. Critical Dimensions:
   - Focus on dimensioning features that are critical to the design's functionality, form, or fit.
   - Clearly indicate which dimensions are critical by providing specific notes or callouts.

Dimensioning in engineering drawing plays a vital role in accurately conveying design intent, ensuring proper manufacturing, assembly, and inspection of components and products. By providing precise and clear dimensioning information, engineering drawings facilitate effective communication and collaboration between design teams and various stakeholders involved in the production process.

Views of engineering drawing:

Engineering drawings are essential tools used in various fields of engineering to communicate and document design information. Here are some common views used in engineering drawing:

1. Orthographic projection view: This is the most common method used to represent three-dimensional objects on a two-dimensional plane. Orthographic projection involves creating multiple views of an object from different directions, typically front, top, and right-side views. These views provide a comprehensive representation of the object's shape and dimensions.

2. Isometric View: Isometric projection is a three-dimensional representation of an object where all three axes are equally foreshortened and the angles between them are 120 degrees. It provides a realistic view of the object, allowing the viewer to visualize the shape and proportions accurately.
3. Sectional View: A sectional view is used to reveal the internal details of an object that cannot be seen in an external view. It involves cutting a portion of the object and showing the internal features. Sectional views are commonly used to illustrate complex structures, such as the interior of a machine or a building.
4. Exploded View: An exploded view is a pictorial representation that shows how various components of an object fit together and interact. The individual parts are separated and spaced apart to provide a clear understanding of their relationship and assembly sequence.
5. Auxiliary View: An auxiliary view is used to show features of an object that are not parallel to the principal views. It is created by projecting the object onto a plane that is perpendicular to the feature of interest. Auxiliary views are particularly useful when detailing inclined or oblique surfaces.
6. Detail View: A detail view is an enlarged portion of a larger drawing, providing a close-up view of a specific area or feature. It allows for a more detailed examination of intricate parts or areas that require additional attention.
7. Perspective View: Perspective views are used to represent objects as they appear in three-dimensional space. They provide a more realistic and natural representation by incorporating vanishing points and foreshortening. Perspective views are often used in architectural and industrial design presentations.
8. Cross-sectional views: Cross-sectional views are a type of view used in engineering drawings to show the internal features and structures of an object. They are created by cutting or slicing through an object and then revealing the resulting section. Cross-sectional views are particularly useful for illustrating the interior details, hidden components, and complex geometries of objects.

These different views help engineers, designers, and manufacturers communicate design intent, dimensions, and construction details accurately. They play a crucial role in ensuring that a product or structure is properly understood and manufactured according to specifications.

Projections of engineering drawing:

Projections in engineering drawing are graphical representations of objects in different views to accurately communicate their shape, size, and features. There are several types of projections commonly used, including orthographic projections, isometric projections, and perspective projections. Here's a brief overview of each:

1. Orthographic Projections: Orthographic projections are the most common type of projection used in engineering drawing. They show the object as a series of two-dimensional views from different directions, typically the front, top, and side views. These views are projected onto separate planes that are perpendicular to each other. Orthographic projections provide a clear and accurate representation of the object's dimensions and features.
2. Isometric Projections: Isometric projections are a type of pictorial projection that represents a three-dimensional object in a single view. It provides a more realistic representation by showing the object from an angle, rather than just the front, top, and side views. Isometric projections are created by projecting the object onto three mutually perpendicular planes, resulting in equal foreshortening along each axis. This creates an illusion of depth and helps visualize the object in three dimensions.
3. Perspective Projections: Perspective projections create a realistic representation of an object by simulating how it appears to the human eye. In perspective projections, the object is shown as it would be seen from a specific viewpoint. Unlike orthographic and isometric projections, perspective projections use vanishing points and converging lines to create depth and a sense of scale. Perspective projections are often used in architectural drawings or when a more lifelike representation is desired.
4. Oblique Projections: Oblique projections are another type of axonometric projection that shows an object with one face parallel to the picture plane and the other faces at an angle. In oblique projections, the receding lines are parallel, and the depth of the object is typically represented at a 45-degree angle. Oblique projections are often used when a quick and simple representation of an object is needed.
5. Auxiliary projections: Auxiliary projection, also known as auxiliary view, is a technique used in engineering drawing to show an object in a new view that is not one of the standard orthographic views (front, top, side). It is used to represent features of an object that are not easily visible or accurately shown in the standard views.

In engineering drawing, projections are typically created using drafting techniques or computer-aided design (CAD) software. They are essential for accurately communicating design intent, dimensions, and details of an object to manufacturers, fabricators, and other stakeholders involved in the production process.

Isometric projection:

Isometric projection is a type of graphical representation that depicts three-dimensional objects in a two-dimensional space. It is commonly used in engineering and technical drawings to provide a clear and accurate representation of objects from multiple angles.

In isometric projection, two isometric axes are held at an angle of 30 with the horizontal plane. While the third axis forms an angle of 90 with the horizontal plane. And all three principal axes of the object are equally foreshortened at a 120-degree angle, resulting in a three-dimensional appearance.

ISOMETRIC PROJECTION

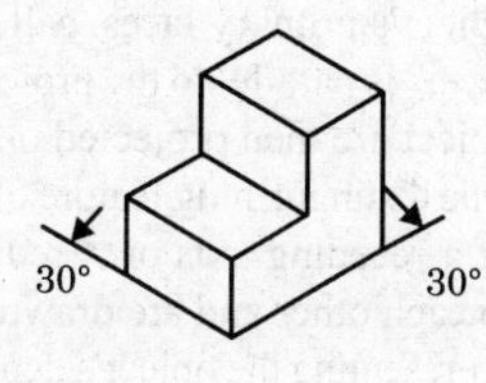

Here are some key features and characteristics of isometric projection:

1. Equal foreshortening: In isometric projection, all three dimensions (length, width, and height) of an object are equally reduced or foreshortened. This means that the angles between any two axes are 120 degrees.
2. Fixed angles: Isometric projection maintains fixed angles between lines parallel to each of the three axes. Horizontal lines are inclined at **30 degrees** to the horizontal axis, while vertical lines remain parallel to the vertical axis.
3. Orthogonal lines: In isometric projection, lines parallel to the three principal axes (x, y, and z) are always mutually perpendicular.
4. No vanishing points: Unlike perspective projections, which have vanishing points and convey depth perception, isometric projection does not represent depth or distance and all dimensions appear uniformly scaled.
5. Easy measurement: Isometric drawings allow for accurate measurements along each axis, making it easier to determine the size and positioning of objects.

Isometric projection is widely used in various fields, including mechanical engineering, architecture, industrial design, and manufacturing, to represent objects and assemblies in a clear and understandable manner. It helps convey the spatial relationships and proportions of objects without the need for complex perspective calculations.

Orthographic projection:

Orthographic projection is a technique used in engineering and technical drawing to represent a three-dimensional object in two dimensions. It provides multiple views of an object from different angles to convey its shape, size, and details accurately. Here are the main types of orthographic projections:

1. Front View: The front view, also known as the elevation view or the front orthographic projection, shows the object as if it is viewed directly from the front. It provides a flat representation of the object's front face, displaying its width and height.
2. Top View: The top view, also called the plan view or the overhead orthographic projection, shows the object as if it is viewed directly from above. It provides a flat representation of the object's top face, displaying its length and width.
3. Side View: The side view, also known as the profile view or the side orthographic projection, shows the object as if it is viewed directly from one of its sides. It provides a flat representation of the object's side face, displaying its length and height.

ORTHOGRAPHIC PROJECTIONS

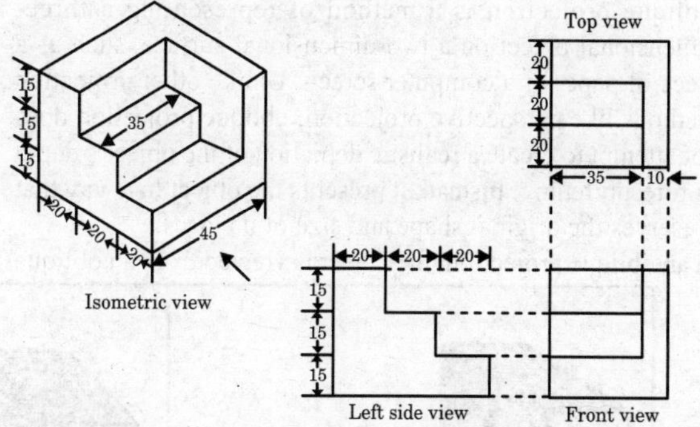

These three views (front, top, and side) are the fundamental projections used in orthographic drawings. By combining these views, a complete understanding of the object's shape and dimensions can be achieved. These views are typically placed orthogonally (at right angles) to each other, with each view representing a different perspective.

In addition to these primary views, orthographic projections may include other views to provide further details or specific information about the object. These can include sectional views, auxiliary views, or detail views, which show specific parts or aspects of the object in more detail.

Orthographic projections are an essential tool in engineering and technical drawing, allowing designers, engineers, and manufacturers to accurately represent and communicate the shape, size, and geometry of objects. They provide a clear and standardized representation of objects, aiding in the design, analysis, and fabrication processes.

Perspective projection:

In perspective projection the **center of projection** is at finite distance from **projection plane**. This projection produces realistic views but does not preserve relative proportions of an object dimensions. Projections of distant object are smaller than projections of objects of same size that are closer to projection plane.

The distance and angles are not preserved and parallel lines do not remain parallel. Instead, they all converge at a single point called **center of projection** or **projection reference point**. There are 3 types of perspective projections which are shown in the following chart.

- **One point** perspective projection is simple to draw.
- **Two point** perspective projection gives better impression of depth.
- **Three point** perspective projection is most difficult to draw.

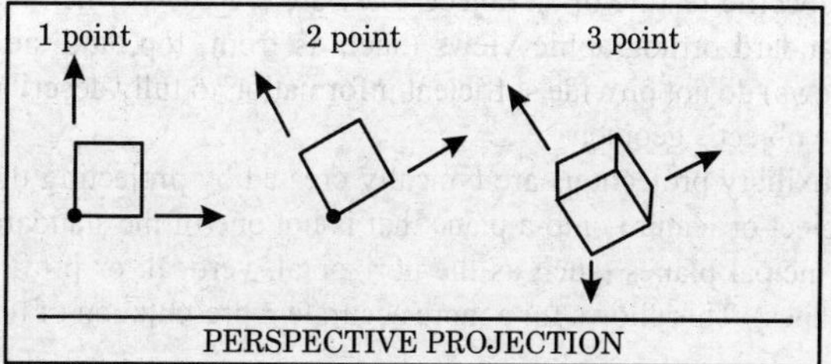

Oblique Projections:

Oblique projection is a method of representing a three-dimensional object on a two-dimensional surface, such as a piece of paper or a computer screen. Unlike other projection methods like perspective projection, oblique projection does not attempt to create a realistic depiction of the object's depth or foreshortening. Instead, it presents the object in a way that preserves the original shape and size of its faces.

In an oblique projection, the object is viewed from an oblique angle relative to the projection plane. Typically, one of the object's primary faces, called the "frontal face" or "principal face," is parallel to the projection plane. The other faces of the object are then projected onto the plane using parallel lines. One distinguishing feature of oblique projection is the inclusion of a receding axis or receding lines. These lines are parallel to each other and are drawn at an angle from the frontal face, representing the object's depth. The angle at which the receding lines are drawn determines the type of oblique projection.

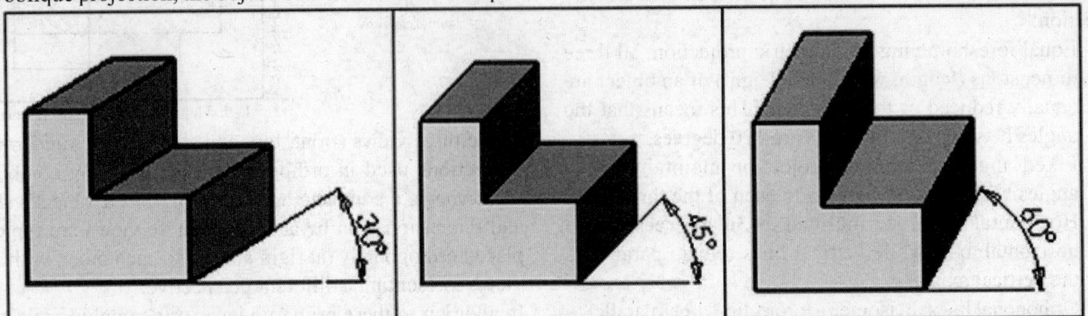

There are different types of oblique projections, but the two most common ones are:

1. **Cavalier Oblique Projection:** In a cavalier oblique projection, the receding lines are drawn at a 45-degree angle relative to the frontal face. This means that the depth of the object is represented at its full scale. However, this type of projection does not provide a realistic sense of depth.
2. **Cabinet Oblique Projection:** In a cabinet oblique projection, the receding lines are drawn at a lesser angle, usually 30 degrees, relative to the frontal face. This reduces the scale of the depth, making the object appear somewhat compressed or foreshortened along the depth axis. Cabinet oblique projection provides a more aesthetically pleasing representation while still maintaining a clear view of the object's faces.

Oblique projection is commonly used in technical drawings, architecture, engineering, and computer graphics when a simplified representation of an object is sufficient and maintaining accurate proportions is important. It is relatively easy to construct and can be a useful tool for conveying the basic form and dimensions of an object.

Auxiliary projections

Auxiliary projections, also known as auxiliary views or secondary views, are graphical techniques used in technical drawing to represent the true shape and size of an object or a specific feature of an object. They are employed when the standard orthographic views (such as front, top, and side views) do not provide sufficient information to fully describe the object's geometry.

Auxiliary projections are typically created by projecting the object or feature onto a plane that is not one of the standard principal planes (such as the horizontal, vertical, or profile planes). This allows for a more accurate representation of the object's true shape, eliminating the distortions that can occur in the standard orthographic views.

In this case, the drawing is prepared by placing the plane parallel to the inclined surface. Such a plane is called **Auxiliary Plane.** The drawing made on this plane is called **Auxiliary View.**

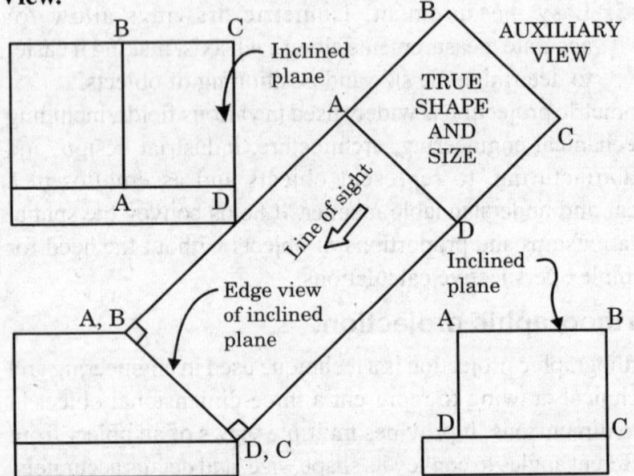

The process of creating an auxiliary projection involves the following steps:

1. Determine the plane of projection: Select a plane that will provide the most useful and informative view of the object or feature. This plane should be oriented in a way that showcases the desired details.
2. Establish reference lines: Draw reference lines between the object or feature and the plane of projection. These lines indicate the direction of the projection.
3. Project the points: Transfer the points from the object or feature along the reference lines onto the plane of projection. This is done by drawing perpendicular lines from the object to the reference lines and extending them until they intersect the projection plane.

4. Complete the projection: Connect the projected points on the projection plane to form the desired auxiliary view. This view can be used in conjunction with the other orthographic views to provide a comprehensive representation of the object.

Auxiliary projections are particularly useful when representing complex features, such as inclined surfaces, oblique planes, or irregular shapes that cannot be easily captured in the standard orthographic views. They provide additional clarity and help communicate the object's geometry more accurately, aiding in manufacturing, construction, and other technical processes.

Drawing instruments/tools:

Drawing instruments refer to tools and materials used for creating artwork, sketches, technical drawings, or illustrations. They can vary depending on the artist's preference, style, and the specific purpose of the drawing. Here are some commonly used drawing instruments:

1. Pencils: Pencils are versatile drawing tools and come in different grades, ranging from hard (H) to soft (B). They allow for precise lines and shading techniques.
2. Pens: Pens provide a consistent and permanent line. They come in various types, such as ballpoint, rollerball, gel, or fountain pens. Each type offers different line widths and ink characteristics.
3. Charcoal: Charcoal is a soft and dark drawing medium that produces rich, dramatic lines. It comes in various forms, including vine charcoal, compressed charcoal, and charcoal pencils.
4. Graphite Sticks: Graphite sticks are solid chunks of graphite that can be used for expressive and large-scale drawings. They allow for bold, dark lines and can be blended or smudged for shading.
5. Ink: Inks, available in bottles or cartridges, are used with dip pens or fountain pens. They offer a range of colors and can create fine lines or bold strokes.
6. Pastels: Pastels are sticks of pigment mixed with a binder. They come in soft pastels (chalk-like) and oil pastels (waxy). Pastels are known for their vibrant colors and are commonly used for drawing and painting.
7. Markers: Markers are popular for their bright and vivid colors. They come in various types, such as alcohol-based markers, water-based markers, or brush markers. Markers are often used for illustrations and graphic design.
8. Brushes: Brushes are used with various drawing mediums, including watercolors, inks, or acrylics. They come in different shapes, sizes, and bristle types, allowing for a wide range of brush strokes and textures.
9. Rulers and Compasses: These tools help artists and designers create precise lines, circles, angles, and geometric shapes. They are essential for technical drawings and architectural illustrations.
10. Erasers: Erasers are used to correct or remove unwanted lines, smudges, or marks from the drawing surface. Different types of erasers, such as kneaded erasers or vinyl erasers, are suitable for different drawing mediums.
11. Blending Tools: Blending tools, such as tortillons, blending stumps, or smudge sticks, are used to smudge or blend pencil, charcoal, or pastel lines to create smooth transitions and gradients.

These are just a few examples of drawing instruments. Artists often combine multiple tools and techniques to achieve their desired effects and styles. The choice of drawing instruments depends on personal preference, the intended artwork, and the artist's skill level.

LINE:

Lines in engineering drawing are fundamental graphical elements used to represent various features, dimensions, and relationships between objects or components. They play a crucial role in communicating information and conveying the design intent in a clear and standardized manner. Lines in engineering drawing can be categorized into different types, each serving a specific purpose.

Types of Lines:

Following are the different **types of lines** used in engineering drawing:

Type A -Continuous Thick (Visible Outline of Parts):

Outline of Parts type lines represent the visible edges of the objects, hence should be outstanding in appearance and therefore, are drawn as bold i.e., thick continuous lines.

Type B- Continuous Thin (Dimension, Projection, Leader, Hatching Lines):

Dimension, Projection, Leader, Hatching type lines must be drawn thin and continuous. The extension lines for dimensioning should run from the outlines without leaving a gap and extend beyond the dimension lines. This type is also used to draw outlines of adjacent and revolved sections.

Type C- Continuous Thin Freehand (Limits or Boundaries of Partial or Interrupted Views):

Limits or Boundaries of Partial or Interrupted Views type lines are drawn as continuous, thin, wavy, freehand lines to represent limits or boundaries of partial or interrupted views.

Type D- Break Lines- (Zig-Zag):

Break Lines type lines are ruled, short, zig-zag thin lines drawn to represent the breaks.

Type E-Hidden Lined (Dashes Thick):

Hidden Lined (Thick) type lines consist of thick short dashes, closely and evenly spaced. These lines are drawn to represent hidden or invisible edges of the objects.

Type F-Hidden Lines (Dashes Thin):

Hidden Lines (Thin) type lines consist of thin short dashes, closely and evenly spaced. These lines are drawn to represent hidden or invisible edges of the objects. Although THICK lines of Type-E are recommended for representing the hidden edges, THIN lines of Type-F are preferred.

Type G-Centre lines, Lines of Symmetry, Trajectories, and Pitch Circles (Chain Thin):

Centre lines, Lines of Symmetry, Trajectories, and Pitch Circles type of lines are long, thin, chain lines with alternately long and short dashes of proportion ranging from 6:1 to 4:1 and evenly spaced. The proportion once selected should be maintained throughout the drawing. The center lines are extended by a short distance beyond the outline. These lines are also drawn to represent the lines of symmetry, trajectories, pitch circles, etc.

Type H- Cutting Plane Lines (Cutting Plane):

Cutting Plane Lines are long lines, thickened ar ends and thin elsewhere, with alternately long and short dashes of proportion ranging from 4:1 to 6:1 and evenly spaced. The corners where the section plane charges the direction are made thick for a short length.

Type J-(Lines to indicate Surfaces which require Additional Treatment):

These are long thick lines with alternatively long and short dashes of proportion ranging from 6:1 to 4:1 and evenly spaced. These lines are drawn to indicate surfaces, to receive additional treatment like anodizing, plating, etc.

Type K-(Chain Thin).

Lines to indicate Outlines of Adjacent parts, Extreme positions of Movable Parts, Centroidal lines, Parts situated in front of the Cutting Planes, Initial outlines prior to forming. These are thin lines with a long and two short dashes alternately and evenly placed in the proportion ranging from 6:1 to 4:1. These lines are used to represent the outlines of adjacent parts, extreme positions of movable parts in the assembly drawings, parts situated in front of the cutting planes, initial outlines prior to forming, centroidal lines etc.

Type	Line	Description	Application
A		Continuous THICK	Visible outlines, Visible edges.
B		Continuous THIN	Dimension lines, Projection lines, Leader lines, Imaginary lines of intersections, Outlines of revolved sections.
C		Continuous THIN Freehand	Boundaries of Limits of Partial or Interrupted views.
D		Continuous THIN Zig-Zag	Long break lines
E		Dashed THICK	Hidden outlines, Hidden edges.
F		Dashed THIN	
G		Chain THIN	Centre lines, Lines of Symmetry, Trajectories.
H		Chain THIN and THICK at ends & Changes of Direction	Cutting Planes
J		Chain THICK	Indication of lines or surfaces to which special treatment required.
K		Chain THIN Double Dash	Outlines of adjacent parts, Alternate and Extreme positions of movable parts, Centroidal lines, Initial outlines, Prior to forming.

1. Visible Lines: These lines are solid, continuous lines that represent the visible edges or outlines of objects in the drawing.
2. Hidden Lines: Hidden lines are used to represent features that are not visible from the current viewing angle. They are often depicted as short dashes or evenly spaced dots.
3. Centerlines: Centerlines are used to indicate the center of a cylindrical or symmetrical object. They consist of long and short dashes alternately repeated.
4. Extension Lines: Extension lines are thin lines that extend from the object's outline and have arrowheads at the end. They indicate the boundaries or endpoints for dimensioning.
5. Dimension Lines: Dimension lines are used to specify the size, length, and location of features in the drawing. They are thin, continuous lines with arrowheads at each end and measurements placed in between.
6. Section Lines: Section lines are used in sectional views to indicate the material or internal features of an object. They are evenly spaced, thin lines that are usually inclined at a 45-degree angle.
7. Break Lines: Break lines are used to shorten long objects or to indicate that a section of an object is not shown in the drawing. They consist of a series of zigzag lines with two short parallel lines at the beginning and end.
8. Phantom Lines: Phantom lines are used to represent alternate positions, repeated detail, or temporary structures. They are composed of long dashes alternately interrupted by pairs of short dashes.
9. Construction Lines: Construction lines are lightly drawn lines used as guides to help in the construction or layout of the drawing. They are usually drawn using a dashed or dotted line style.
10. Leader Lines: Leader lines are used to connect notes, labels, or dimensions to specific features in the drawing. They are straight lines with an arrow or dot at one end and a text or symbol at the other end.

Scales in engineering drawing:

In engineering drawing, scales are used to represent the size of objects and the distances between them accurately. They are essential tools for communicating dimensions and proportions in technical drawings. Here are some common types of scales used in engineering drawings:

1. **Architect's Scale:** This type of scale is commonly used in architectural drawings. It typically consists of three scales: 1:1, 1:50, and 1:100. The 1:1 scale represents the actual size of the object, while the other scales represent a reduced size of the object.
2. **Engineer's Scale**: Engineer's scales are used in civil and mechanical engineering drawings. They are typically triangular in shape and have multiple scales on each edge. The most common engineer's scale is the 1:10 scale, which allows for larger objects to be drawn while still fitting on standard-sized paper.
3. **Metric Scale**: Metric scales are used in engineering drawings that adhere to the metric system. They are typically labeled with metric units such as millimeters (mm) or centimeters (cm) and represent the actual size of the object.
4. **Inch Scale**: Inch scales are used in engineering drawings that follow the imperial system. They are labeled with inches (in) and fractions of an inch (e.g., 1/2 inch, 1/4 inch) and represent the actual size of the object.

When using scales in engineering drawings, it's important to ensure that all objects are drawn to the correct proportion and that the dimensions are accurately conveyed.

Drawing standards:

Drawing standards in engineering refer to a set of guidelines and conventions that define how technical drawings should be created, interpreted, and communicated within the engineering field. These standards ensure consistency, clarity, and accuracy in engineering drawings, allowing engineers, designers, manufacturers, and other stakeholders to understand and work with the drawings effectively. Here are some key aspects of drawing standards in engineering:

1. Dimensioning and Tolerancing: Drawing standards specify the methods and conventions for dimensioning and tolerancing, including the placement, style, and format of dimensions, tolerances, and geometric symbols. This ensures that the dimensions and tolerances are clearly defined and can be interpreted correctly.
2. Line Types and Weights: Drawing standards define the different line types and weights used in technical drawings. For example, different line types may be used to represent visible edges, hidden lines, centerlines, and section lines. Consistent line weights help in differentiating between different features and provide visual clarity.
3. Title Blocks and Borders: Engineering drawings typically include a title block and border, which contain important information such as the drawing title, scale, author, revision history, and company details. Drawing standards provide guidelines for the placement and format of these elements, ensuring that the necessary information is included and easily accessible.
4. Symbols and Notations: Various symbols and notations are used in engineering drawings to represent features, materials, surface finishes, welding specifications, and other important information. Drawing standards specify the appropriate symbols and notations to be used, ensuring consistency and proper communication of technical details.
5. Drawing Views and Projections: Drawing standards define the types of views and projections that should be used to represent objects in different orientations. This includes orthographic projections (e.g., front view, top view, side view) and isometric or perspective views when necessary. The standards provide guidelines for the arrangement and alignment of views to accurately represent the object's shape and dimensions.
6. File Formats and Data Exchange: With the advancement of computer-aided design (CAD) software, drawing

standards also encompass guidelines for file formats, layering, naming conventions, and data exchange protocols. These standards facilitate the exchange of drawings and data between different software platforms and ensure compatibility and consistency in digital workflows.

Common drawing standards used in engineering include ASME Y14.5 for dimensioning and tolerancing, ISO 128 for general principles of presentation, and ANSI/ASME Y14.100 for engineering drawing practices. However, specific industries or organizations may have their own additional standards or variations to meet their unique requirements.

Adhering to drawing standards is crucial in engineering as it enables clear communication, promotes interoperability, and ensures that drawings are easily understood and accurately interpreted by all stakeholders involved in the design, manufacturing, and inspection processes.

Drawing sheet:

In engineering, drawing sheets are used to create detailed technical drawings and plans for various purposes, such as architectural design, mechanical engineering, civil engineering, and more. These drawings serve as a visual representation of the design and provide important information for the construction or manufacturing process. Here are some key aspects of drawing sheets in engineering:

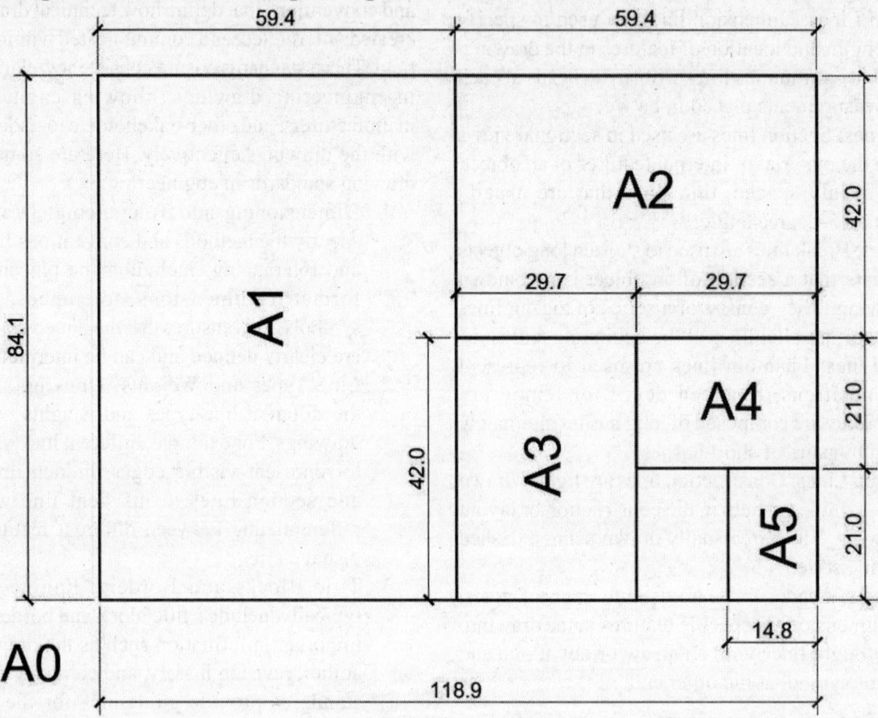

1. Paper Size: Drawing sheets typically follow standard paper sizes, such as ISO sizes (A0, A1, A2, A3, A4, etc.) or ANSI sizes (ANSI A, ANSI B, ANSI C, etc.). The choice of paper size depends on the scale and complexity of the drawing.

   The most common ISO sizes for engineering drawings are:
   - A0: 841 mm × 1189 mm (33.1 in × 46.8 in)
   - A1: 594 mm × 841 mm (23.4 in × 33.1 in)
   - A2: 420 mm × 594 mm (16.5 in × 23.4 in)
   - A3: 297 mm × 420 mm (11.7 in × 16.5 in)
   - A4: 210 mm × 297 mm (8.3 in × 11.7 in)

   ANSI sizes for engineering drawings are:
   - ANSI A: 216 mm × 279 mm (8.5 in × 11 in)
   - ANSI B: 279 mm × 432 mm (11 in × 17 in)
   - ANSI C: 432 mm × 559 mm (17 in × 22 in)
   - ANSI D: 559 mm × 864 mm (22 in × 34 in)
   - ANSI E: 864 mm × 1118 mm (34 in × 44 in)
2. Title Block: The title block is an area located at the bottom or right-hand side of the drawing sheet. It contains essential information about the drawing, including the title, drawing number, revision history, scale, date, and the name of the drafter.
3. Border and Frame: The drawing sheet is usually surrounded by a border or frame, which provides a clear boundary for the drawing. The border may include reference information, such as project name, company logo, and other relevant details.
4. Drawing Views: The main portion of the drawing sheet is dedicated to drawing views, which represent different aspects or sections of the design. These views can include orthographic projections (front, top, side views), isometric views, exploded views, and cross-sections.
5. Dimensions and Annotations: Dimensions and annotations are essential elements of engineering drawings. They provide precise measurements,

tolerances, and additional information about features, materials, and assembly instructions. Dimensions are typically shown using lines, arrows, and numerical values, while annotations include notes, symbols, and labels.

6. Scales: Drawings often require scaling to accurately represent the design within the available drawing space. Scales can be expressed as a ratio (e.g., 1:50) or represented graphically using a scale bar. The scale allows measurements on the drawing to be converted into real-world dimensions.
7. Layers and Line Types: Engineering drawings often utilize layers and different line types to distinguish various components or features. Different colors or line weights may be used to differentiate between object lines, hidden lines, centerlines, dimensions, and annotations.
8. Drawing Standards: Engineering drawings should adhere to specific standards, which vary depending on the industry and country. Common standards include ISO (International Organization for Standardization) and ASME (American Society of Mechanical Engineers) standards, among others.

It's important to note that with the advancement of computer-aided design (CAD) software, traditional drawing sheets are increasingly being replaced by digital formats. CAD software allows for easier editing, storage, and sharing of drawings, and provides additional tools for 3D modeling, simulations, and rendering.

Technical Lettering:

Technical lettering in engineering drawing refers to the process of creating clear and consistent letterforms on drawings to convey information effectively. It involves using specific guidelines and techniques to ensure legibility, uniformity, and accuracy in the lettering.

Here are some key aspects of technical lettering in engineering drawing:

1. Lettering Style: In technical drawing, a standardized lettering style is often used to maintain consistency and clarity. The most commonly used style is the Gothic style, which features block letters with uniform stroke widths.

   Lettering and numbering should be in a perfect manner style. The upper, lower case letters and numbers are neatly drawn in the below figure:

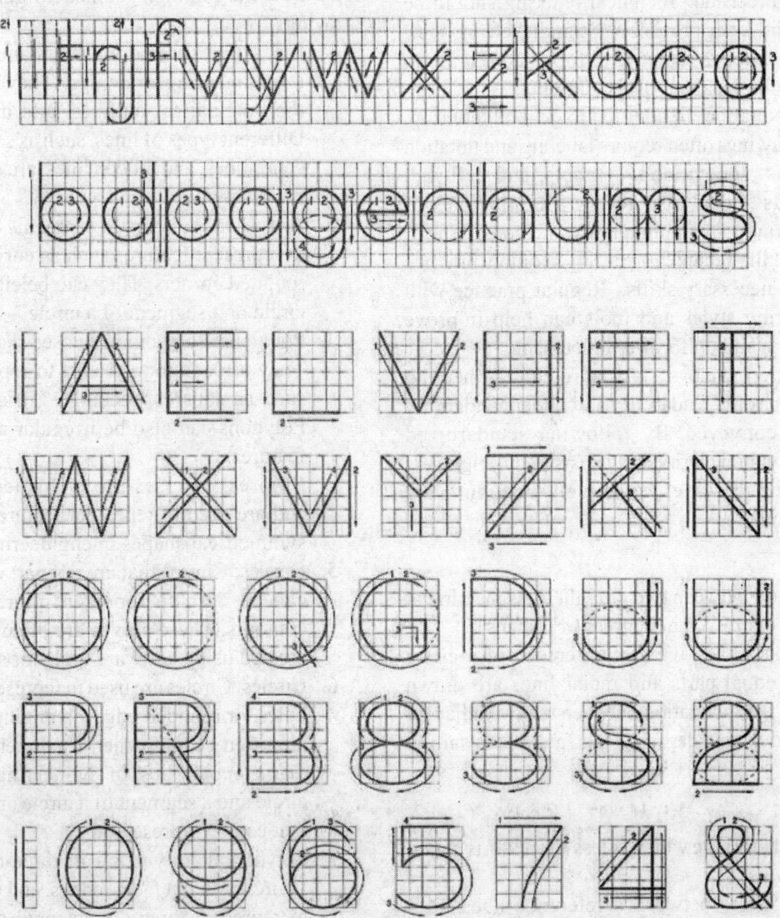

2. Lettering Tools: Technical lettering can be done using various tools, including mechanical pencils, technical pens, or lettering stencils. The choice of tool depends on personal preference and the level of precision required.
3. Lettering Height: The height of the letters is typically determined based on the scale of the drawing. It is essential to select a lettering size that ensures readability while also fitting within the available space.
4. Stroke Width: Consistent stroke widths are crucial for legible technical lettering. The strokes should be even and uniform throughout each letter. This can be achieved by maintaining a consistent pressure while lettering or using pens with fixed stroke widths.
5. Spacing: Proper spacing between letters, words, and lines is essential for readability. Adequate spacing ensures that the text does not appear cluttered or crowded. Generally, the spacing between letters is approximately equal to the width of the letter "I."
6. Alignment: The letters should be aligned vertically and horizontally. Horizontal alignment ensures that the baseline of each letter is consistent, while vertical alignment ensures that the letters are positioned correctly in relation to each other.
7. Neatness and Precision: Technical lettering should be done neatly and with precision. Straight, clean lines, sharp corners, and consistent letterforms contribute to the overall professionalism of the drawing.
8. Labeling and Notation: In addition to general lettering, engineering drawings often require labeling and notation for dimensions, annotations, symbols, and callouts. These elements should also follow the principles of technical lettering to maintain clarity and consistency.
9. Practice and Skill: Technical lettering requires practice to develop the necessary skills. Regular practice with different lettering styles and tools can help improve speed, accuracy, and uniformity in lettering.

Overall, technical lettering plays a crucial role in engineering drawings as it enhances the readability and understandability of the information conveyed. By following standardized guidelines and focusing on clarity and consistency, engineers can ensure that their drawings effectively communicate important details to others.

Angles:

Angle is the inclination between two straight lines meeting at a point. The angle is expressed in degrees or radians.

Concept of a degree: When the circumference of a circle is divided into 360 equal parts and radial lines are drawn through these points, the inclination between the two adjacent radia lines is defined as one degree. Thus, a circle is said to contain 360°.

Types of angles:

- **Acute angle:** If an angle which is **less than 90°** is called an acute angle.
- **Right angle:** Angle between a reference line and a perpendicular line is called right angle. A right angle is an **inclination between two perpendicular lines**.
- **Obtuse angle:** This refer to an angle between 90° and 180°
- **Straight angle:** This refers to an angle of 180°. This is also called as the angle of a straight line.
- Reflex angle: It is the angle which is more than 180° (two right angles).
- **Adjacent angles:** These are the **angles lying on either side of a line**.
- **Complementary angles:** The complementary angles are those when two angles together make 90°.
- **Supplementary angle:** The supplementary angles are those when two anglles together make 180°.

Geometric figures in engineering drawing:

In engineering drawing, geometric figures refer to precise mathematical entities that have well-defined properties, dimensions, and relationships. These figures are typically represented using specific geometric constructions, equations, or formulas. Geometric figures in engineering drawing include points, lines, curves, circle, arcs, polygons, and other shapes that can be precisely defined. They serve as the building blocks for creating accurate and detailed representations of objects in technical drawings.

Here are some common geometric figures used in engineering drawings:

1. Lines: Lines are the most fundamental geometric figures in engineering drawings. They are used to represent the boundaries, outlines, and dimensions of objects. Different types of lines, such as solid lines, dashed lines, centerlines, and hidden lines, are used to convey specific information.
2. Arcs: Arcs are curved segments of circles and are used to represent features such as curved surfaces, fillets, or rounded corners. They can be either part of a complete circle or a segment of a circle.
3. Polygons: Polygons are closed shapes with straight sides. They are commonly used to represent regular shapes, such as squares, rectangles, triangles, and hexagons. Polygons can also be irregular and represent complex features.
4. Ellipses: Ellipses are elongated or flattened circles and are used to represent features like holes, bores, or symmetrical shapes in engineering drawings.
5. Curves: Curves that are not part of a circle or an ellipse can be used to represent more complex shapes or contours. These curves are often sketched manually or created using software tools for smooth representation.
6. Circles: Circles are used to represent cylindrical features, holes, or rounded edges in engineering drawings. They are often accompanied by dimensions indicating their diameter or radius. In engineering drawing, a sector of a circle and a segment of a circle are two common shapes that can be represented.
7. Polyhedral: Polyhedral are three-dimensional geometric figures with flat faces, edges, and vertices. They are used to represent three-dimensional objects in engineering drawings. Common examples include cubes, pyramids, prisms, and cylinders.

8. Splines: Splines are smooth curves that are often used to represent complex or irregular shapes. They can be used to define contours or irregular profiles.
9. Solids: Solids, such as cubes, cylinders, and spheres, are used to represent three-dimensional objects in engineering drawings. They can represent components or provide a visual representation of the design.
10. Geometric Tolerances: Geometric tolerances, such as concentricity, parallelism, and perpendicularity, are used to specify the acceptable variation in dimensions and orientations of features. These geometric symbols are used alongside the geometric shapes to define the tolerance requirements.
11. Geometric Constructions: Geometric constructions are special figures created using specific rules or methods. These constructions may involve intersecting lines, perpendicular bisectors, parallel lines, or any other geometric relationships.

These geometric figures, along with appropriate annotations, dimensions, and symbols, help communicate the design intent, shapes, and sizes of objects in engineering drawings.

GEOMETRIC SHAPES

In engineering drawing, the term "shape" is used to describe the overall form or external appearance of an object. It focuses on the visual characteristics and outlines of an object rather than its precise mathematical properties. Shapes are commonly described using common geometric terms like squares, rectangles, triangles, or other irregular forms. They are often used to convey the general form or outline of an object in a drawing, providing a visual representation that aids in understanding without requiring precise measurements or calculations. Geometric shapes play a crucial role in engineering drawing as they form the basis for representing various components and features. Here are some common geometric shapes used in engineering drawing:

Types of Geometric Shapes

Quadrilaterals and their properties

Quadrilateral is a plane figure bounded by four sides and four angles. Sum of the four angles in a quadrilateral is of interior angles is equal to 360°. The side joining opposite corners is called diagonal. To construct a quadrilateral out of four sides, four angles and two diagonals a minimum of five dimensions are required of which two must be sides. Quadrlilaterals are also referred as Trapezoid.

Types of quadrilaterals: Square, Rectangle, Rhombus, Rhomboid/ Paralllelogram, Trapezoid, Trapezium

Square:

- In a square all the **four sides are equal**, and **its four angles are right angles.**
- The **two diagonals are equal and perpendicular** to each other.
- To construct a square, we need to know (a) length of the side or (b) length of the diagonal.

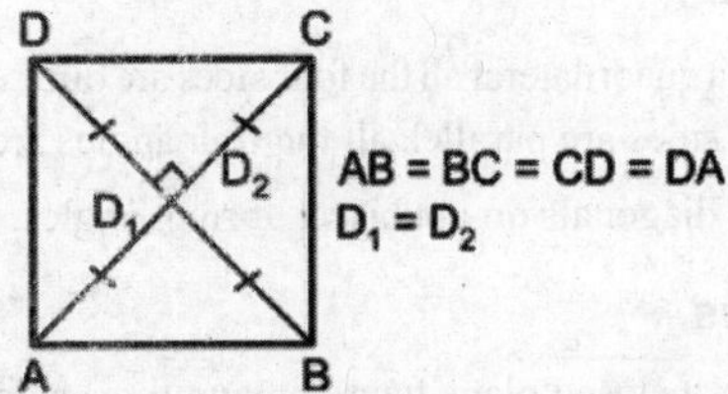

Rectangle:

- In a rectangle, opposite sides are equal and parallel, and all four angles are right angles.
- Diagonals AC and BD are equal, bisect but not at right angles.
- To construct a rectangle, we need to know the length (a) two adjacent sides or (b) diagonal and one side.

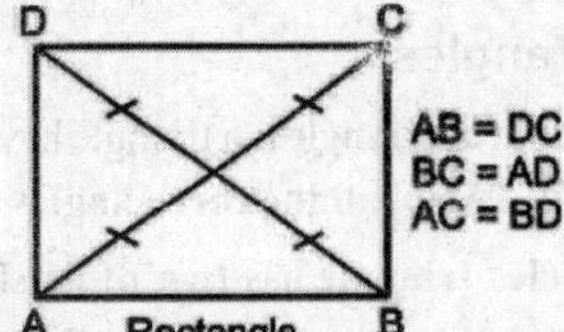

Rectangle

Rhombus:

- In rhombus all the **four sides are equal** but **only the opposite angles are equal.**
- **Diagonals AC and BD are not equal but bisecting at right angles.**
- To construct a rhombus, we need to know (a) two diagonals (b) one diagonal and an opposite angle or (c) one side and its adjacent angle.

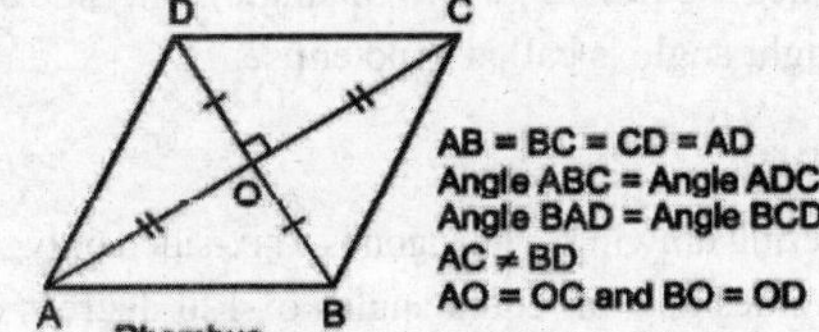

Rhombus

Rhomboid/Parallelogram:

- In a parallelogram **opposite sides are equal and parallel. Opposite angles are also equal.**
- **Diagonals are not equal but bisect each other.**
- Parallelogram is also known as rhomboid.
- To construct a parallelogram, we need (a) two adjacent sides and an angle between them or (b) one side, diagonal, and an angle between them or (c) two adjacent sides and perpendicular distance between the opposite sides.

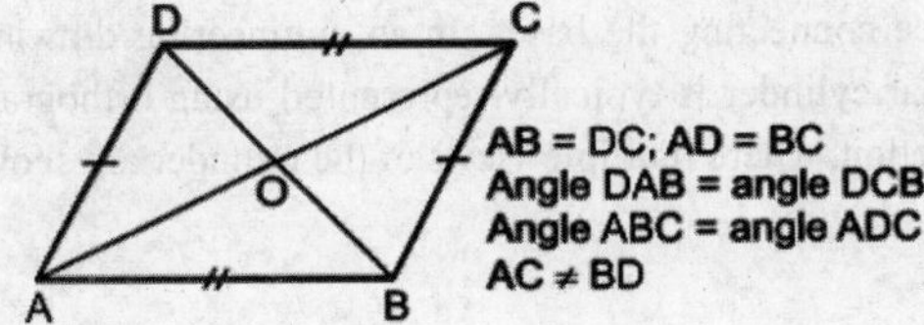

Trapezoid:

- It is a quadrilateral all the four sides are different and only two sides are parallel, all the four angles are different.
- The diagonals do not bisect at right angles.

Triangles

Triangle is a closed plane figure having three sides and three angles. The sum of the three angles always equals to 180°. The sum of any two sides is more than the third side. To define a triangle, we need to have a mmimum of three measurements as follows:

- 3 sides
- 2 sides and one angle
- 2 angles and one side

Types of tri'angles

- **An equilateral triangle** is a triangle having all the **three sides equal. Also, all the three angles are equal (60°)**
- **An isosceles triangle** has **two of its sides equal.** The angles opposite to the two equal sides are also equal.
- **A scalene triangle** has all the three sides unequal in lengths. All the three angles are also unequal.
- **An acute-angled triangle** is one in which **all the three angles are less than 90°.**
- **An obtuse-angled triangle** has **one of the angles as more than 90°.**
- **A right-angled triangle** is the one in which one of the angiles is **equal to 90°** (Right angle). The side opposite to right angle is called hypotenuse.

Hexagon:

In engineering drawing, a hexagon is a six-sided polygon with six equal sides and six equal angles of 120 degrees each. It is a commonly used shape in engineering and is often used to represent bolts, nuts, or other fasteners. When drawing a hexagon in engineering, we can use various methods depending on the requirements and the tools available.

Circular Cylinder & Cone

In engineering drawing, a circular cylinder and a cone are two common geometric shapes that are often represented. Here's a brief explanation of how they are typically depicted in engineering drawings:

Circular Cylinder: A circular cylinder is a three-dimensional shape with two parallel circular bases and a curved lateral surface connecting the bases. In an engineering drawing, a circular cylinder is typically represented using orthographic projection, where multiple views of the cylinder are shown.

To depict a circular cylinder, at least two orthographic views are commonly used: the front view and the top view. The front view shows the cylinder as a rectangle with circular arcs at the top and bottom, representing the bases. The top view displays the circular bases as complete circles, while the sides of the cylinder are not visible in this view.

Cone: A cone is a three-dimensional shape with a circular base and a curved lateral surface tapering to a point called the apex. Similar to a circular cylinder, a cone is represented using orthographic projection in engineering drawings.

To depict a cone, again, at least two orthographic views are generally used: the front view and the top view. The front view shows the cone as a triangle with a circular arc at the bottom, representing the base. The top view displays the circular base as a complete circle, while the tapering sides of the cone are not visible in this view.

In addition to the front and top views, engineering drawings may also include other views such as the side view or isometric view to provide a more comprehensive representation of the cylinder or cone.

Sphere:

In engineering drawing, a sphere is a three-dimensional shape that is often represented using orthographic projection. A sphere is a perfectly round geometrical object with all points on its surface equidistant from its center.

When depicting a sphere in an engineering drawing, multiple views are typically used to provide a comprehensive representation. The most common views used are the front view and the top view, similar to other geometric shapes.

The front view of a sphere shows a circle, representing the cross-section of the sphere. The circle should be drawn in a way that it appears tangent to the edges of the drawing frame. The top view displays a complete circle, representing the full extent of the spherical shape.

To provide a more accurate representation of the sphere, other views can be included, such as the side view or isometric view. The side view will show a semicircle, while the isometric view will display the sphere as an ellipse.

It's important to note that in engineering drawings, the diameter of the sphere is typically indicated for dimensional purposes. This information can be added to the drawing through dimensioning techniques, such as placing a linear dimension between two points on the sphere's circle.

As always, it is crucial to consult and adhere to applicable standards and guidelines when creating engineering drawings to ensure accurate and standardized representation of a sphere or any other geometric shape.

Symbolic representation in engineering drawing:

Symbolic representation in engineering drawing refers to the use of standardized symbols to represent different elements, features, and characteristics of a design or a component in a technical drawing. These symbols are typically used to convey information about dimensions, materials, surface finishes, tolerances, and other specifications related to the design.

Here are some commonly used symbolic representations in engineering drawing:

1. Geometric Symbols: These symbols represent basic geometric shapes such as lines, circles, arcs, and polygons. They are used to define the outline and shape of a component.
2. Dimensioning Symbols: These symbols indicate the size and location of features on a drawing. They include arrows, extension lines, dimension lines, and tolerance symbols.
3. Surface Finish Symbols: These symbols represent the desired surface texture or finish of a component. They provide information about parameters such as roughness, waviness, and lay.
4. Material Symbols: These symbols indicate the type of material to be used for a specific component. Common material symbols include letters or abbreviations representing different materials like steel, aluminum, plastic, or wood.
5. Welding Symbols: These symbols are used to represent different types of welds and welding operations. They provide information about the specific welding process, joint configuration, and additional requirements.
6. Electrical Symbols: In electrical engineering drawings, various symbols represent different electrical components such as resistors, capacitors, switches, and transformers. These symbols help in understanding the electrical connections and circuits.
7. Piping and Instrumentation Symbols: These symbols are used in piping and instrumentation diagrams (P&IDs) to represent different components and instruments in industrial processes, such as valves, pumps, tanks, and sensors.
8. Assembly Symbols: These symbols depict how multiple components fit together to form an assembly. They include exploded views, section views, and detail views to show the relationship and arrangement of parts.

It is important to note that there are several standardized symbol libraries, such as ANSI (American National Standards Institute) and ISO (International Organization for Standardization), which provide guidelines for symbolic representation in engineering drawings. These standards ensure clear and consistent communication of design intent across different engineering disciplines and industries.

Objective Type Questions

1. Which of the following is NOT a common feature found in engineering drawings?
   (a) Dimension lines (b) Section lines
   (c) Centerlines (d) Title blocks
2. Which feature is used to represent the contour of a cylindrical object on an engineering drawing?
   (a) Section lines (b) Hidden lines
   (c) Dimension lines (d) Centerlines
3. What is the purpose of a title block in an engineering drawing?
   (a) To provide information about the part being represented
   (b) To indicate the scale of the drawing
   (c) To show the overall dimensions of the part
   (d) To specify the material used for the part
4. Which type of line is used to represent hidden features in an engineering drawing?
   (a) Solid line (b) Dashed line
   (c) Dotted line (d) Centerline
5. What do dimension lines in an engineering drawing indicate?
   (a) The overall size of the part
   (b) The location of hidden features
   (c) The shape of the part
   (d) The material used for the part
6. Which feature is used to represent the symmetry of a part in an engineering drawing?
   (a) Dimension lines (b) Section lines
   (c) Hidden lines (d) Centerlines
7. What information is typically included in a revision block on an engineering drawing?
   (a) The title of the drawing
   (b) The name of the drafter
   (c) The date of the revision
   (d) The overall dimensions of the part
8. Which feature is used to represent a break in a long object on an engineering drawing?
   (a) Hidden lines (b) Dimension lines
   (c) Centerlines (d) Break lines
9. What does a section line indicate in an engineering drawing?
   (a) The location of hidden features
   (b) The material used for the part
   (c) The overall size of the part
   (d) The shape of the part in a specific section
10. Which feature is used to represent the center of a hole or a circle on an engineering drawing?
    (a) Hidden lines (b) Dimension lines
    (c) Centerlines (d) Break lines
11. Which type of drawing focuses on depicting the external appearance of an object or structure?
    (a) Isometric drawing
    (b) Perspective drawing
    (c) Orthographic drawing
    (d) Technical drawing
12. Which type of drawing represents a three-dimensional object on a two-dimensional surface using parallel lines that converge at a vanishing point?
    (a) Isometric drawing
    (b) Perspective drawing
    (c) Orthographic drawing
    (d) Technical drawing
13. Which type of drawing is commonly used in engineering and architecture to represent a three-dimensional object using three mutually perpendicular planes?
    (a) Isometric drawing
    (b) Perspective drawing
    (c) Orthographic drawing
    (d) Technical drawing
14. Which type of drawing shows the object as it appears when viewed from the top, front, and right side?
    (a) Isometric drawing
    (b) Perspective drawing
    (c) Orthographic drawing
    (d) Technical drawing
15. Which type of drawing is used to represent the exact dimensions, specifications, and construction details of an object?
    (a) Isometric drawing
    (b) Perspective drawing
    (c) Orthographic drawing
    (d) Technical drawing
16. Which type of drawing uses geometric shapes, lines, and patterns to create an abstract or non-representational artwork?
    (a) Sketching
    (b) Technical drawing
    (c) Perspective drawing
    (d) Graphic design

17. Which type of drawing involves creating a preliminary, rough representation of an object or idea?
(a) Sketching (b) Technical drawing
(c) Perspective drawing (d) Graphic design

18. Which type of drawing is often used in comic books and animations to tell a story or convey a sequence of events?
(a) Sketching (b) Technical drawing
(c) Storyboarding (d) Graphic design

19. Which type of drawing is used to create detailed, realistic representations of human figures or portraits?
(a) Sketching (b) Technical drawing
(c) Illustration (d) Graphic design

20. Which type of drawing focuses on capturing the essence or basic shapes of an object rather than its details?
(a) Sketching (b) Technical drawing
(c) Illustration (d) Graphic design

21. What is the purpose of dimensioning in engineering drawing?
(a) To make the drawing look visually appealing
(b) To provide instructions for manufacturing and inspection
(c) To indicate the scale of the drawing
(d) To showcase the artistic skills of the drafter

22. Which of the following is NOT a commonly used type of dimension line?
(a) Continuous thin line (b) Chain line
(c) Dotted line (d) Phantom line

23. What is the purpose of extension lines in dimensioning?
(a) To connect the dimension line with the object being dimensioned
(b) To indicate the centerline of a cylindrical feature
(c) To show hidden features in the object
(d) To mark the limits of the drawing sheet

24. Which of the following dimensioning systems allows for the most precise measurements?
(a) Decimal-inch system
(b) Fractional-inch system
(c) Metric system
(d) Engineering scale system

25. What is a tolerance in dimensioning?
(a) The allowable variation in the size of a feature
(b) The number of decimal places used in a dimension
(c) The distance between extension lines and dimension lines
(d) The thickness of the dimension lines

26. Which of the following is true about baseline dimensioning?
(a) It uses a common baseline for all dimensions in a group
(b) It places dimensions randomly throughout the drawing
(c) It is used only for circular features
(d) It is not a recognized dimensioning method

27. What is the purpose of a leader line in dimensioning?
(a) To indicate the overall size of the drawing
(b) To connect extension lines to dimension lines
(c) To highlight important dimensions
(d) To separate different sections of the drawing

28. What is the purpose of a centerline in dimensioning?
(a) To indicate symmetry in the object
(b) To represent hidden features in the object
(c) To provide a reference for measuring dimensions
(d) To mark the center of the drawing sheet

29. Which of the following is an example of a direct dimensioning method?
(a) Coordinate dimensioning
(b) Chain dimensioning
(c) Ordinate dimensioning
(d) Baseline dimensioning

30. When should a limit dimension be used?
(a) When the exact size is critical for functionality
(b) When the dimension is large and difficult to measure precisely
(c) When the drawing needs additional decorative elements
(d) When the dimension exceeds the size of the drawing sheet

31. Which of the following is NOT a commonly used view in engineering drawing?
(a) Isometric view (b) Front view
(c) Side view (d) Top view

32. What is the purpose of an auxiliary view in engineering drawing?
(a) To represent an object in a three-dimensional perspective
(b) To show hidden features that cannot be seen in the primary views
(c) To provide additional dimensions for complex features
(d) To indicate the scale of the drawing

33. Which view is typically used to depict the true shape and size of circular features?

(a) Front view (b) Side view
(c) Isometric view (d) Auxiliary view

34. What is the purpose of section views in engineering drawing?

(a) To represent an object in a three-dimensional perspective
(b) To show hidden features that cannot be seen in the primary views
(c) To provide additional dimensions for complex features
(d) To display internal details of an object

35. Which view is typically used to provide an overall representation of an object?

(a) Front view (b) Side view
(c) Isometric view (d) Top view

36. Which of the following views is typically used to show the depth of an object?

(a) Front view (b) Side view
(c) Isometric view (d) Top view

37. Which view is used to represent the topmost surface of an object?

(a) Front view (b) Side view
(c) Isometric view (d) Top view

38. What is the purpose of an isometric view in engineering drawing?

(a) To show hidden features that cannot be seen in other views
(b) To provide an overall representation of the object
(c) To depict the true shape and size of circular features
(d) To represent an object in a three-dimensional perspective

39. Which view is typically used to represent the front face of an object?

(a) Front view (b) Side view
(c) Isometric view (d) Auxiliary view

40. When is a detailed view used in engineering drawing?

(a) To represent an object in a three-dimensional perspective
(b) To show hidden features that cannot be seen in the primary views
(c) To provide an enlarged view of a specific area
(d) To indicate the scale of the drawing

41. In engineering drawing, a projection is a technique used to:

(a) Create 3D models
(b) Convert 2D views into 3D views
(c) Represent objects on a 2D surface
(d) Visualize engineering concepts

42. Which of the following is NOT a type of projection commonly used in engineering drawing?

(a) Isometric projection
(b) Orthographic projection
(c) Perspective projection
(d) Oblique projection

43. In orthographic projection, the object is represented using:

(a) One view (b) Two views
(c) Three views (d) Four views

44. Isometric projection is a type of projection that:

(a) Shows the object as it appears to the human eye
(b) Represents the object using only vertical and horizontal lines
(c) Uses three angles of 30° with respect to each other
(d) Represents the object in a distorted manner

45. The purpose of using auxiliary views in engineering drawing is to:

(a) Show hidden details that cannot be seen in the standard views
(b) Represent the object from different angles
(c) Highlight specific features of the object
(d) Create a 3D model of the object

46. In engineering drawing, the term "projection plane" refers to:

(a) The surface on which the projection is made
(b) The position from which the object is viewed
(c) The distance between the object and the viewer
(d) The line connecting the object to the viewer

47. Which of the following projections shows the true shape and size of the object's features?

(a) Front view (b) Side view
(c) Top view (d) Isometric view

48. The term "multiview projection" refers to:

(a) A technique that combines multiple projections of an object
(b) A projection that shows multiple objects simultaneously
(c) A projection technique used for complex objects only
(d) A projection that requires special equipment

49. A section view is used in engineering drawing to:

(a) Show the object in its entirety
(b) Highlight specific features of the object
(c) Represent the object in a 3D format
(d) Create a mirror image of the object

50. Which of the following projections provides the most realistic representation of an object?
(a) Isometric projection
(b) Orthographic projection
(c) Perspective projection
(d) Oblique projection

51. Which drawing instrument is commonly used to measure angles?
(a) Compass (b) Protractor
(c) T-square (d) French curve

52. Which drawing instrument is used to create circles and arcs?
(a) Compass (b) Protractor
(c) T-square (d) French curve

53. Which drawing instrument is primarily used for parallel line construction?
(a) Compass (b) Protractor
(c) T-square (d) French curve

54. Which drawing instrument is utilized to draw irregular curves?
(a) Compass (b) Protractor
(c) T-square (d) French curve

55. Which drawing instrument is employed to create straight horizontal and vertical lines?
(a) Compass (b) Protractor
(c) T-square (d) French curve

56. Which drawing instrument is commonly used to measure angles?
(a) Compass (b) Protractor
(c) T-square (d) French curve

57. Which drawing instrument is used to create circles and arcs?
(a) Compass (b) Protractor
(c) T-square (d) French curve

58. Which drawing instrument is primarily used for parallel line construction?
(a) Compass (b) Protractor
(c) T-square (d) French curve

59. Which drawing instrument is utilized to draw irregular curves?
(a) Compass (b) Protractor
(c) T-square (d) French curve

60. Which drawing instrument is employed to create straight horizontal and vertical lines?
(a) Compass (b) Protractor
(c) T-square (d) French curve

61. Which drawing instrument is used to create shading and blending in pencil drawings?
(a) Eraser (b) Smudge stick
(c) Ruler (d) Drawing compass

62. Which drawing instrument is used to remove graphite or charcoal marks from the drawing surface?
(a) Pencil sharpener (b) Eraser
(c) T-square (d) Compass

63. Which drawing instrument is used to measure and transfer proportions accurately?
(a) Compass (b) Ruler
(c) Divider (d) French curve

64. Which drawing instrument is used to create precise geometric shapes such as squares and rectangles?
(a) Protractor (b) T-square
(c) French curve (d) Compass

65. Which drawing instrument is used to create smooth and flowing curves?
(a) Compass (b) Protractor
(c) French curve (d) Smudge stick

66. What type of line is typically used to represent visible edges or outlines of an object in an engineering drawing?
(a) Hidden line (b) Centerline
(c) Object line (d) Extension line

67. Which type of line is used to represent edges or features that cannot be seen in the current view but are necessary for the complete understanding of the object?
(a) Hidden line (b) Centerline
(c) Phantom line (d) Section line

68. What type of line is used to indicate the axis of symmetry or centerline of a symmetrical object?
(a) Hidden line (b) Centerline
(c) Object line (d) Extension line

69. Which type of line is used to indicate the dimension of a feature or the distance between two points?
(a) Hidden line (b) Centerline
(c) Object line (d) Extension line

70. What type of line is used to represent alternate positions of a moving part in an assembly drawing?
(a) Hidden line (b) Centerline
(c) Phantom line (d) Section line

71. Which type of line is used to indicate the imaginary line along which a section view is cut?
(a) Hidden line (b) Break line
(c) Cutting plane line (d) Section line

72. What type of line is used to indicate a change in the surface contour or shape of an object in an engineering drawing?
(a) Hidden line (b) Centerline
(c) Break line (d) Section line

73. Which type of line is used to represent an imaginary line indicating the path of a cutting plane in a sectional view?
(a) Hidden line (b) Centerline
(c) Phantom line (d) Section line

74. What type of line is used to indicate the limit or boundary of a part or object in an engineering drawing?
(a) Hidden line (b) Dimension line
(c) Object line (d) Leader line

75. Which type of line is used to show the path of motion or movement in a mechanical drawing?
(a) Hidden line (b) Centerline
(c) Leader line (d) Dimension line

76. Which scale is commonly used to represent large objects or structures, such as buildings or bridges?
(a) Architectural scale (b) Engineering scale
(c) Metric scale (d) Isometric scale

77. Which scale is typically used in mechanical engineering drawings to represent precise measurements and dimensions?
(a) Architectural scale (b) Engineering scale
(c) Metric scale (d) Isometric scale

78. Which scale is commonly used in international standards and represents measurements in millimeters?
(a) Architectural scale (b) Engineering scale
(c) Metric scale (d) Isometric scale

79. Which scale is used to represent three-dimensional objects and shows all three principal axes in equal measure?
(a) Architectural scale (b) Engineering scale
(c) Metric scale (d) Isometric scale

80. Which scale is used to represent objects or structures in terms of their actual size?
(a) Architectural scale (b) Engineering scale
(c) Metric scale (d) Full-scale

81. Which scale would be appropriate for representing a building floor plan where 1 inch on the drawing represents 10 feet in real life?
(a) 1:10 (b) 1:20
(c) 1/8" = 1' (d) 1/4" = 1'

82. Which scale would be suitable for representing a small mechanical component where 1 cm on the drawing represents 2 mm in real life?
(a) 1:10 (b) 1:20
(c) 1:50 (d) 1:100

83. Which scale is commonly used in civil engineering drawings to represent large areas, such as maps or site plans?
(a) Architectural scale (b) Engineering scale
(c) Metric scale (d) Topographic scale

84. Which scale is used to represent objects or structures at a reduced size, where the ratio is less than 1?
(a) Enlarged scale (b) Reduced scale
(c) Fractional scale (d) Representative scale

85. Which scale is typically used in architectural drawings to represent the overall layout of a building or a floor plan?
(a) Architectural scale (b) Engineering scale
(c) Metric scale (d) Plotting scale

86. Which scale would be appropriate for representing a large machine or equipment in a technical drawing?
(a) 1:10 (b) 1:50
(c) 1:100 (d) 1:500

87. Which scale is commonly used in electrical engineering drawings to represent wiring diagrams or circuit layouts?
(a) Architectural scale (b) Engineering scale
(c) Metric scale (d) Electrical scale

88. Which scale would be suitable for representing a detailed part or component in an engineering drawing?
(a) 1:2 (b) 1:5
(c) 1:10 (d) 1:20

89. Which scale would be appropriate for representing a site plan where 1 inch on the drawing represents 50 feet in real life?
(a) 1:50 (b) 1:100
(c) 1:200 (d) 1:500

90. Which scale is commonly used in mechanical engineering drawings to represent assembly drawings or exploded views?
(a) Architectural scale (b) Engineering scale
(c) Metric scale (d) Assembly scale

91. Which scale is typically used in surveying and mapping to represent large areas, such as cities or regions?
(a) Architectural scale (b) Engineering scale
(c) Metric scale (d) Cartographic scale

92. Which scale would be suitable for representing a small electronic component with intricate details in an engineering drawing?
(a) 1:1000 (b) 1:2000
(c) 1:5000 (d) 1:10000

93. Which organization is responsible for developing and maintaining international drawing standards?
(a) ISO (International Organization for Standardization)
(b) ANSI (American National Standards Institute)
(c) ASME (American Society of Mechanical Engineers)
(d) DIN (Deutsches Institut für Normung)

94. Which type of line weight is typically used for object lines in engineering drawings?
(a) Thin line weight (b) Medium line weight
(c) Thick line weight (d) Variable line weight

95. Which unit of measurement is commonly used for dimensions in engineering drawings?
(a) Inches (b) Feet
(c) Millimeters (d) Meters

96. What does the abbreviation "GD&T" stand for in the context of engineering drawings?
(a) General Dimensioning and Text
(b) Geometric Design and Testing
(c) Geometric Dimensioning and Tolerancing
(d) Global Drafting Techniques

97. Which type of projection is commonly used in engineering drawings to represent three-dimensional objects on a two-dimensional plane?
(a) Orthographic projection
(b) Isometric projection
(c) Perspective projection
(d) Oblique projection

98. Which line type is used to indicate the dimension lines in engineering drawings?
(a) Hidden line (b) Centerline
(c) Extension line (d) Dimension line

99. Which standard format is commonly used for engineering drawings in the United States?
(a) ANSI A (8.5" x 11")
(b) ANSI B (11" x 17")
(c) ANSI C (17" x 22")
(d) ANSI D (22" x 34")

100. Which symbol is typically used to indicate a surface finish requirement on an engineering drawing?
(a) Diameter symbol (⌀)
(b) Concentricity symbol (⊗)
(c) Perpendicularity symbol (⊥)
(d) Roughness symbol (∇)

101. Which type of line is used to represent hidden or invisible edges in engineering drawings?
(a) Phantom line (b) Construction line
(c) Centerline (d) Section line

102. Which drawing view is typically used to represent an object as it would be seen by looking directly at one of its sides?
(a) Isometric view (b) Auxiliary view
(c) Section view (d) Front view

103. What is the standard size of an A4 drawing sheet?
(a) 210 mm × 297 mm (b) 297 mm × 420 mm
(c) 420 mm × 594 mm (d) 594 mm × 841 mm

104. Which type of drawing sheet is commonly used for architectural plans?
(a) A0 (b) A1
(c) A2 (d) A3

105. Which of the following is NOT a type of drawing sheet orientation?
(a) Landscape (b) Portrait
(c) Square (d) None of the above

106. What is the purpose of a title block on a drawing sheet?
(a) To indicate the type of drawing
(b) To provide information about the scale used
(c) To display the name of the drafter
(d) All of the above

107. Which type of line is typically used to indicate the visible edges of an object in a drawing?
(a) Solid line (b) Dashed line
(c) Dotted line (d) Wavy line

108. What is the purpose of drawing border lines on a drawing sheet?
(a) To frame the drawing
(b) To provide a clean edge
(c) To establish the drawing's boundary
(d) All of the above

109. Which of the following is NOT a common drawing sheet material?
(a) Paper (b) Vellum
(c) Tracing cloth (d) Aluminum

110. What does the term "scale" refer to in relation to a drawing sheet?
(a) The size of the drawing relative to the actual object
(b) The type of pencil used for drawing
(c) The thickness of the drawing sheet
(d) The color palette used in the drawing

111. Which type of drawing sheet is the largest in size?
(a) A0 (b) A1
(c) A2 (d) A3

112. Which of the following is a common unit of measurement used on drawing sheets?
(a) Meters (b) Centimeters
(c) Inches (d) All of the above

113. In engineering drawing, technical lettering is primarily used for:

(a) Adding decorative elements to the drawing
(b) Enhancing the aesthetics of the drawing
(c) Communicating important information clearly
(d) Providing a signature of the drafter

114. Which of the following is a commonly used lettering style in engineering drawing?

(a) Roman (b) Gothic
(c) Italic (d) Cursive

115. In engineering drawing, which type of lettering is typically used for dimensions, notes, and labels?

(a) Uppercase lettering (b) Lowercase lettering
(c) Capitalized lettering (d) Script lettering

116. The recommended letter height for uppercase letters in engineering drawing is generally:

(a) 1/8 inch (b) 1/4 inch
(c) 1/2 inch (d) 1 inch

117. Which of the following statements about technical lettering in engineering drawing is true?

(a) Lettering should always be done by hand.
(b) Mechanical or digital lettering is recommended for accuracy.
(c) Engineering drawing software automatically generates technical lettering.
(d) Technical lettering is not necessary in engineering drawing.

118. In engineering drawing, what is the purpose of using guidelines for technical lettering?

(a) To ensure consistent letter height
(b) To maintain uniform spacing between letters
(c) To align the baseline of the letters
(d) All of the above

119. Which of the following tools is commonly used for technical lettering in engineering drawing?

(a) Technical pens (b) Pencil
(c) Highlighters (d) Fountain pens

120. When creating uppercase letters in engineering drawing, the correct order of strokes is typically:

(a) Vertical strokes, horizontal strokes, and diagonal strokes
(b) Horizontal strokes, vertical strokes, and diagonal strokes
(c) Diagonal strokes, vertical strokes, and horizontal strokes
(d) Horizontal strokes, diagonal strokes, and vertical strokes

121. Which of the following fonts is commonly used for technical lettering in engineering drawings?

(a) Arial (b) Times New Roman
(c) Helvetica (d) Comic Sans

122. The recommended height for uppercase letters in technical lettering is typically:

(a) 4 mm (b) 6 mm
(c) 8 mm (d) 10 mm

123. Which of the following is the correct order for drawing a lowercase letter "a" in technical lettering?

(a) Vertical line, horizontal line, curved line
(b) Curved line, horizontal line, vertical line
(c) Horizontal line, vertical line, curved line
(d) Curved line, vertical line, horizontal line

124. In technical lettering, the space between characters is typically:

(a) Equal to the width of a character
(b) Half the width of a character
(c) One-third the width of a character
(d) Double the width of a character

125. When labeling dimensions in engineering drawings, which of the following should be used for fractions?

(a) Decimal format
(b) Decimal format with a slash (/) symbol
(c) Decimal format with parentheses ()
(d) Stacked fractions

126. Which of the following is the recommended method for emphasizing text in technical lettering?

(a) Underlining
(b) Italicizing
(c) Using a heavier stroke
(d) Capitalizing the letters

127. True or False: In technical lettering, the letters should be drawn with a consistent stroke width throughout the text.

(a) True (b) False

128. Which of the following is the correct order for drawing a number "9" in technical lettering?

(a) Curved line, vertical line, curved line
(b) Vertical line, curved line, horizontal line
(c) Horizontal line, vertical line, curved line
(d) Curved line, horizontal line, vertical line

129. Which of the following is NOT a characteristic of good technical lettering in engineering drawings?

(a) Legibility (b) Consistency
(c) Artistic flair (d) Uniformity

130. Which of the following is the recommended method for correcting errors in technical lettering?

(a) Erasing and redrawing the entire letter

(b) Using correction fluid

(c) Crossing out the error and writing the correct letter above or beside it

(d) Ignoring the error and moving on

131. Which geometric figure is commonly used to represent a hole in engineering drawings?

(a) Circle (b) Square

(c) Triangle (d) Rectangle

132. What is the name of the geometric figure used to represent a bolt or screw head in engineering drawings?

(a) Circle (b) Square

(c) Triangle (d) Hexagon

133. In engineering design, a cross-sectional view of a cylindrical object would appear as a:

(a) Circle (b) Square

(c) Triangle (d) Rectangle

134. Which geometric figure is commonly used to represent a gear in engineering drawings?

(a) Circle (b) Square

(c) Triangle (d) Hexagon

135. In engineering drawings, what geometric figure is used to represent a fillet or rounded corner?

(a) Circle (b) Square

(c) Triangle (d) Arc

136. A dimension line in an engineering drawing is typically represented by a:

(a) Straight line (b) Curved line

(c) Dotted line (d) Zigzag line

137. What geometric figure is used to represent an electrical connector or terminal in engineering drawings?

(a) Circle (b) Square

(c) Triangle (d) Rectangle

138. In engineering drawings, what geometric figure is commonly used to represent a chamfer or beveled edge?

(a) Circle (b) Square

(c) Triangle (d) Line segment

139. What is the name of the geometric figure used to represent a weld in engineering drawings?

(a) Circle (b) Square

(c) Triangle (d) Weld symbol

140. In engineering drawings, a hidden line is typically represented by a:

(a) Solid line (b) Dashed line

(c) Dotted line (d) Zigzag line

141. What is the definition of a circle?

(a) A polygon with six sides

(b) A closed curve with no straight sides

(c) A quadrilateral with opposite sides parallel

(d) A three-dimensional object with flat faces

142. What is the formula to calculate the circumference of a circle?

(a) $C = 2\pi r$ (b) $C = \pi d$

(c) $C = \pi r^2$ (d) $C = 4\pi r$

143. Which of the following is an example of a regular polygon?

(a) Rectangle (b) Triangle

(c) Pentagon (d) Trapezoid

144. What is the name of a three-dimensional shape with six rectangular faces?

(a) Cylinder (b) Pyramid

(c) Cube (d) Cone

145. Which of the following statements is true about an isosceles triangle?

(a) It has three equal sides

(b) It has three right angles

(c) It has two equal sides

(d) It has no equal sides

146. What is the formula to calculate the area of a rectangle?

(a) $A = \pi r^2$ (b) $A = l \times w$

(c) $A = 2\pi r$ (d) $A = bh$

147. Which of the following is a characteristic of a parallelogram?

(a) All sides are equal

(b) All angles are right angles

(c) Opposite sides are parallel and equal in length

(d) It has a curved shape

148. What is the name of a three-dimensional shape with a circular base and a curved surface that tapers to a point?

(a) Cylinder (b) Cone

(c) Sphere (d) Pyramid

149. Which of the following statements is true about a trapezoid?

(a) It has two pairs of parallel sides

(b) It has four equal sides

(c) It has three right angles

(d) It has no equal sides

150. What is the formula to calculate the volume of a sphere?

(a) $V = \pi r^2$ (b) $V = 2\pi r$

(c) $V = 4/3\pi r^3$ (d) $V = l \times w \times h$

151. In engineering drawing, what does a filled triangle symbol represent?
(a) Datum feature (b) Surface roughness
(c) Perpendicularity (d) Concentricity

152. What does a circle with two parallel lines passing through its center signify in engineering drawing?
(a) Position (b) True profile
(c) Concentricity (d) Circular runout

153. What does an 'R' with a circle around it stand for in engineering drawing?
(a) Radius (b) Roughness
(c) Runout (d) Right-hand thread

154. In engineering drawing, what does a perpendicular line with two small outward arrows at its end depict?
(a) Angularity (b) Perpendicularity
(c) Symmetry (d) Parallelism

155. What is the purpose of a diamond symbol in engineering drawing?
(a) Maximum material condition
(b) Center of gravity
(c) Dimension origin
(d) Flatness

156. What does a square symbol with an 'A' inside signify in engineering drawing?
(a) Area (b) Angularity
(c) Surface finish (d) Chamfer

157. In engineering drawing, what does an 'M' with a circle around it denote?
(a) Material thickness
(b) Surface roughness
(c) Maximum material condition
(d) Minimum material condition

158. What does a straight line with one long arrow and one short arrow signify in engineering drawing?
(a) Symmetry (b) Profile of a surface
(c) Position (d) Parallelism

159. What does a series of evenly spaced short lines on an engineering drawing denote?
(a) Surface roughness (b) Counterbore
(c) Tolerance zone (d) Symmetry

160. In engineering drawing, what does an 'X' symbol inside a circle represent?
(a) Center of gravity (b) Counterbore
(c) Spotface (d) Hole callout

Answers

1. (d) **2.** (d) **3.** (a) **4.** (b) **5.** (a) **6.** (d) **7.** (c) **8.** (d) **9.** (d) **10.** (c)
11. (d) **12.** (b) **13.** (a) **14.** (c) **15.** (d) **16.** (d) **17.** (a) **18.** (c) **19.** (c) **20.** (a)
21. (b) **22.** (b) **23.** (a) **24.** (c) **25.** (a) **26.** (a) **27.** (b) **28.** (a) **29.** (c) **30.** (a)
31. (a) **32.** (b) **33.** (d) **34.** (d) **35.** (a) **36.** (b) **37.** (d) **38.** (d) **39.** (a) **40.** (c)
41. (c) **42.** (d) **43.** (c) **44.** (c) **45.** (a) **46.** (a) **47.** (a) **48.** (a) **49.** (b) **50.** (c)
51. (b) **52.** (a) **53.** (c) **54.** (d) **55.** (c) **56.** (b) **57.** (a) **58.** (c) **59.** (d) **60.** (c)
61. (b) **62.** (b) **63.** (c) **64.** (b) **65.** (c) **66.** (c) **67.** (a) **68.** (b) **69.** (d) **70.** (c)
71. (c) **72.** (c) **73.** (d) **74.** (c) **75.** (c) **76.** (a) **77.** (b) **78.** (c) **79.** (d) **80.** (d)
81. (c) **82.** (d) **83.** (d) **84.** (b) **85.** (a) **86.** (b) **87.** (d) **88.** (c) **89.** (a) **90.** (d)
91. (d) **92.** (a) **93.** (a) **94.** (b) **95.** (c) **96.** (c) **97.** (a) **98.** (d) **99.** (b) **100.** (d)
101. (a) **102.** (d) **103.** (a) **104.** (b) **105.** (c) **106.** (d) **107.** (a) **108.** (d) **109.** (d) **110.** (a)
111. (a) **112.** (d) **113.** (c) **114.** (b) **115.** (a) **116.** (b) **117.** (b) **118.** (d) **119.** (a) **120.** (b)
121. (c) **122.** (b) **123.** (b) **124.** (a) **125.** (d) **126.** (c) **127.** (true) **128.** (a) **129.** (c) **130.** (c)
131. (a) **132.** (d) **133.** (a) **134.** (a) **135.** (d) **136.** (c) **137.** (a) **138.** (d) **139.** (d) **140.** (b)
141. (b) **142.** (b) **143.** (c) **144.** (c) **145.** (c) **146.** (b) **147.** (c) **148.** (b) **149.** (a) **150.** (c)
151. (a) **152.** (c) **153.** (a) **154.** (b) **155.** (c) **156.** (d) **157.** (c) **158.** (b) **159.** (a) **160.** (c)

Explanations

1. Title blocks are actually a common feature found in engineering drawings and are typically located in the lower right corner of the drawing. They contain information such as the title of the drawing, the name of the company or organization, the drawing number, the scale of the drawing, and other relevant details.
2. Centerlines are used to represent the contour of a cylindrical object on an engineering drawing. They indicate the center axis of the cylindrical feature and are typically drawn as long, dashed lines.
3. To provide information about the part being represented. The purpose of a title block in an engineering drawing is to provide essential information about the part or assembly being represented in the drawing. This information may include the part name, the drawing title, the drawing number, the date of creation, the scale of the drawing, and other pertinent details.
4. Dashed lines are commonly used to represent hidden features in an engineering drawing. These hidden features are typically those that cannot be seen in the current view but exist in the part or assembly.
5. The overall size of the part. Dimension lines in an engineering drawing indicate the overall size of the part. They are used to specify the lengths, widths, diameters, and other measurements of the features represented in the drawing.
6. Centerlines are used to represent the symmetry of a part in an engineering drawing. They are drawn as long, dashed lines and indicate the center axis or symmetry line of a feature or part.
7. A revision block on an engineering drawing typically includes information about the revisions made to the drawing. This information often includes the revision number, the date of the revision, the name or initials of the person who made the revision, and a brief description of the changes made.
8. Break lines are used to represent a break in a long object on an engineering drawing. They indicate that a portion of the object has been intentionally omitted for the purpose of clarity and to save space on the drawing.
9. A section line in an engineering drawing is used to indicate a specific section plane through the part or assembly. It represents the shape of the part when cut along that section plane.
10. Centerlines are used to represent the center of a hole or a circle on an engineering drawing. They indicate the exact center position of the feature and are typically drawn as long, dashed lines.
11. Technical drawing is a type of drawing that focuses on accurately representing the external appearance of an object or structure, usually with precise measurements and annotations.
12. Perspective drawing is a technique used to represent a three-dimensional object on a two-dimensional surface by creating the illusion of depth and space through the use of converging parallel lines that meet at a vanishing point.
13. Isometric drawing is commonly used in engineering and architecture to represent a three-dimensional object using three mutually perpendicular planes. The object is displayed without perspective and with all lines parallel to the three principal axes of the object.
14. Orthographic drawing, also known as multiview projection, shows the object as it appears when viewed from the top, front, and right side. It represents the object in two dimensions and provides multiple views to accurately depict its shape and features.
15. Technical drawing is used to represent the exact dimensions, specifications, and construction details of an object. It provides comprehensive and precise information for manufacturing, construction, or other technical purposes.
16. Graphic design uses geometric shapes, lines, and patterns to create visually appealing and communicative designs. While graphic design may incorporate elements of drawing, it is a broader field that encompasses various visual communication techniques, including digital media, typography, and layout design.
17. Sketching involves creating a preliminary, rough representation of an object or idea. It is often done quickly and freely to capture initial concepts, explore different possibilities, or communicate basic visualizations.
18. Storyboarding is a type of drawing used in comic books, animations, and filmmaking to visually plan and sequence a story or a series of events. It involves creating a series of rough sketches or panels that depict key moments and actions to guide the overall narrative.
19. Illustration is a type of drawing that is used to create detailed, realistic representations of human figures, portraits, or other subjects. It often focuses on capturing the likeness and characteristics of the subject matter, and it can be used in various contexts, including books, magazines, advertisements, and digital media.
20. Sketching often emphasizes capturing the essence or basic shapes of an object rather than its intricate details. It is a freehand technique that allows for a more spontaneous and expressive approach to drawing, often used for quick studies, brainstorming, or creating loose visual representations.
21. To provide instructions for manufacturing and inspection. Dimensioning in engineering drawing is essential to communicate the size, shape, and other geometric characteristics of the object being represented. It provides precise measurements and tolerances necessary for manufacturing and inspection processes.

22. Chain lines are not typically used for dimensioning purposes. Continuous thin lines, dotted lines, and phantom lines are commonly used to indicate dimensions, extension lines, and hidden features, respectively.

23. To connect the dimension line with the object being dimensioned. Extension lines are drawn from the object's edges to the dimension lines, indicating which part of the object is being measured.

24. The metric system is widely used in engineering and provides a decimal-based measurement system, allowing for more precise and consistent measurements compared to the fractional-inch and decimal-inch systems.

25. The allowable variation in the size of a feature. Tolerance specifies the acceptable range of variation in the dimensions of a part. It ensures that the manufactured part falls within the acceptable limits for functionality and fit.

26. It uses a common baseline for all dimensions in a group. Baseline dimensioning is a method where a single baseline is established, and all dimensions are measured from that line. It is commonly used for organizing dimensions in a group or when multiple features share a common measurement reference.

27. To connect extension lines to dimension lines. A leader line is a thin line with an arrowhead at one end. It is used to connect the extension lines to the dimension lines and point to the specific location on the object where the measurement applies.

28. To indicate symmetry in the object. A centerline is a thin, long-dashed line used to represent the axis of symmetry in an object. It helps to locate and dimension features symmetrically and accurately.

29. Ordinate dimensioning is a direct dimensioning method where each feature is dimensioned from a common baseline or origin. It involves using X and Y coordinates to specify the location of features, simplifying the dimensioning process.

30. When the exact size is critical for functionality. A limit dimension specifies the upper and lower acceptable limits for a feature's size. It is used when precise sizing is crucial to ensure the functionality, interchangeability, or fit of the part.

31. While isometric views are used to represent objects in a three-dimensional perspective, they are not typically used as the primary views in engineering drawings. Front view, side view, and top view are commonly used orthographic views.

32. To show hidden features that cannot be seen in the primary views. An auxiliary view is used to display a particular part or feature of an object that is not visible or fully understandable in the primary views. It provides a more detailed and accurate representation of the hidden features.

33. An auxiliary view is commonly used to show the true shape and size of inclined or oblique surfaces, as well as circular features such as holes, arcs, or cylinders. It provides a view perpendicular to the inclined or oblique surface, resulting in an accurate representation of the feature.

34. To display internal details of an object. Section views are used to reveal the internal structure, hidden parts, or complex features of an object. By cutting or slicing the object, the internal details become visible, aiding in understanding its construction and functionality.

35. The front view provides the principal view of an object and represents its external shape and features. It is usually the most descriptive and detailed view and serves as the starting point for creating other views.

36. The side view, also known as the profile view, provides a representation of an object from the side, showing its depth or thickness. It helps in understanding the overall shape and proportions of the object.

37. The top view, also known as the plan view, provides a representation of the object as seen from above. It shows the shape and arrangement of the object's top surface and is particularly useful for understanding the layout or arrangement of components.

38. To represent an object in a three-dimensional perspective. An isometric view is a pictorial representation that shows an object in a three-dimensional form. It provides a realistic view of the object by showing all three dimensions—length, width, and height—at the same time.

39. The front view is a two-dimensional representation that shows the object as viewed from the front or primary viewing direction. It provides a detailed representation of the object's external features, such as its contours, holes, or cutouts.

40. To provide an enlarged view of a specific area. A detailed view is used to magnify and show specific regions or features of an object that require more detailed representation. It allows for a closer examination of intricate areas without having to enlarge the entire drawing.

41. Projections in engineering drawing are used to represent three-dimensional objects on a two-dimensional surface, such as a piece of paper or a computer screen. It allows engineers to visualize and communicate the shape, size, and features of objects accurately.

42. Oblique projection is a type of projection commonly used in engineering drawing. It involves projecting the object onto the drawing plane at an oblique angle, typically 45 degrees. Orthographic projection, isometric projection, and perspective projection are other commonly used types.

43. Orthographic projection represents the object using three mutually perpendicular views: front view, top view, and side view. Each view shows the object from a different direction, providing a comprehensive representation of its shape and features.

44. Isometric projection is a type of projection that uses three angles of 30° with respect to each other. It provides a three-dimensional representation of an object with equal foreshortening along each of the three axes. This projection is commonly used to create technical illustrations.

45. Auxiliary views are additional views used in engineering drawing to show hidden details that cannot be adequately represented in the standard views (front, top, and side views). They provide a more detailed representation of specific features or surfaces of the object.

46. The projection plane in engineering drawing refers to the surface on which the projection is made, typically a flat surface such as a sheet of paper or a computer screen. It is where the views of the object are projected and drawn.

47. The front view in orthographic projection shows the true shape and size of the object's features that are parallel to the projection plane. It provides a two-dimensional representation of the object as it would appear when viewed directly from the front.

48. Multiview projection is a technique in engineering drawing that involves combining multiple projections of an object, such as front, top, and side views, to provide a comprehensive representation of its shape and features from different perspectives.

49. A section view in engineering drawing is used to highlight specific features of an object that are not easily visible in the standard views. It involves cutting a portion of the object and showing the internal details or hidden surfaces, providing a clearer understanding of its construction.

50. Perspective projection provides the most realistic representation of an object as it appears to the human eye.

51. A protractor is a drawing instrument specifically designed to measure angles. It typically consists of a semicircular or circular tool with degree markings. By aligning the protractor with the lines or edges on a drawing, you can accurately measure and draw angles.

52. A compass is a drawing instrument that consists of two adjustable arms joined at a pivot point. One arm holds a pencil or pen, while the other arm has a pointed end. By adjusting the arms, you can create circles or arcs of various sizes by rotating the compass around the pivot point while keeping the pointed end fixed.

53. A T-square is a drawing instrument with a long, straightedge and a perpendicular crosspiece. It is used to draw straight horizontal and vertical lines. By aligning the T-square's straightedge with the drawing surface's edge, you can create parallel lines by sliding the T-square along the edge while drawing.

54. A French curve is a flexible, curved tool made of plastic or metal. It is used to draw smooth and irregular curves in freehand drawing. The French curve comes in various shapes, allowing artists and designers to create a wide range of curved lines by tracing along its edges.

55. As mentioned earlier, a T-square is the drawing instrument used to draw straight horizontal and vertical lines. Its straightedge is aligned with the drawing surface's edge to ensure precise and straight lines are drawn at right angles.

56. A protractor is a drawing instrument specifically designed to measure angles. It typically consists of a semicircular or circular tool with degree markings. By aligning the protractor with the lines or edges on a drawing, you can accurately measure and draw angles.

57. A compass is a drawing instrument that consists of two adjustable arms joined at a pivot point. One arm holds a pencil or pen, while the other arm has a pointed end. By adjusting the arms, you can create circles or arcs of various sizes by rotating the compass around the pivot point while keeping the pointed end fixed.

58. A T-square is a drawing instrument with a long, straightedge and a perpendicular crosspiece. It is used to draw straight horizontal and vertical lines. By aligning the T-square's straightedge with the drawing surface's edge, you can create parallel lines by sliding the T-square along the edge while drawing.

59. A French curve is a flexible, curved tool made of plastic or metal. It is used to draw smooth and irregular curves in freehand drawing. The French curve comes in various shapes, allowing artists and designers to create a wide range of curved lines by tracing along its edges.

60. As mentioned earlier, a T-square is the drawing instrument used to draw straight horizontal and vertical lines. Its straightedge is aligned with the drawing surface's edge to ensure precise and straight lines are drawn at right angles.

61. A smudge stick, also known as a blending stump or tortillon, is a cylindrical tool made of tightly rolled paper or soft fabric. It is used to create shading and blending effects in pencil drawings. By gently rubbing the smudge stick over graphite or charcoal, artists can achieve smooth transitions and gradients.

62. An eraser is a drawing instrument used to remove unwanted graphite or charcoal marks from the drawing surface. It is available in various types, including kneaded erasers, vinyl erasers, and electric erasers. Erasers allow artists to correct mistakes or lighten areas of their drawings.

63. A divider is a drawing instrument with two pointed legs joined by a pivot. It is used to measure and transfer proportions accurately in drawings. By adjusting the distance between the legs and then transferring that measurement elsewhere on the drawing, artists can ensure consistent proportions.

64. A T-square is a drawing instrument consisting of a long, straightedge with a perpendicular crosspiece. It is primarily used to draw straight horizontal and vertical lines, but it can also be used to create precise geometric shapes such as squares and rectangles by aligning the T-square's straightedge with the drawing surface's edges.
65. As mentioned earlier, a French curve is a flexible, curved tool used to draw smooth and irregular curves. It is particularly useful for creating flowing curves in freehand drawing or when precision is required for repetitive curves.
66. Object lines are thick, continuous lines used to represent visible edges or outlines of an object in an engineering drawing. They define the shape and form of the object being represented.
67. Hidden lines are used to represent edges or features that are not visible in the current view but are necessary for a complete understanding of the object. They are typically drawn using a series of short dashes.
68. Centerlines are thin, alternating long and short dashes used to indicate the axis of symmetry or centerline of a symmetrical object. They are used to show the location of holes, slots, or other features that are symmetrical about a centerline.
69. Extension lines are thin lines used to indicate the dimension of a feature or the distance between two points. They extend from the object line to the dimension line and are typically terminated with an arrowhead.
70. Phantom lines are used to represent alternate positions of a moving part in an assembly drawing. They are drawn using long dashes alternating with pairs of short dashes and are used to indicate the possible positions of a component when it is in different operating modes or configurations.
71. Cutting plane lines are used to indicate the imaginary line along which a section view is cut. They are typically represented as a series of short dashes and two long dashes.
72. Break lines are used to indicate a change in the surface contour or shape of an object in an engineering drawing. They consist of a series of zigzag lines and are used to shorten the length of a long continuous line without changing its basic meaning.
73. Section lines are used to represent an imaginary line indicating the path of a cutting plane in a sectional view. They consist of evenly spaced thin lines and are used to distinguish the material that has been cut by the cutting plane.
74. Object lines are used to indicate the limit or boundary of a part or object in an engineering drawing. They are thick, continuous lines that define the shape and form of the object being represented.
75. Leader lines are used to show the path of motion or movement in a mechanical drawing. They consist of a thin solid line with an arrowhead and are typically used to connect notes, dimensions, or other annotations to specific features on the drawing.
76. Architectural scales are commonly used to represent large objects or structures, such as buildings or bridges. They typically use ratios like 1:50 or 1:100, where one unit on the drawing represents 50 or 100 units in real life.
77. Engineering scales are typically used in mechanical engineering drawings to represent precise measurements and dimensions. They use ratios such as 1:10 or 1:20, where one unit on the drawing represents 10 or 20 units in real life.
78. Metric scales are commonly used in international standards and represent measurements in millimeters. They use ratios such as 1:100 or 1:1000, where one unit on the drawing represents 100 or 1000 units in real life.
79. Isometric scales are used to represent three-dimensional objects and show all three principal axes in equal measure. They are often used in technical illustrations or drawings where a 3D representation is required.
80. Full-scale is used to represent objects or structures in terms of their actual size. It means that one unit on the drawing represents one unit in real life, without any scaling factor.
81. In the given scenario, the scale 1/8" = 1' would be appropriate. This means that one-eighth of an inch on the drawing represents one foot in real life.
82. In the given scenario, the scale 1:100 would be suitable. This means that one unit on the drawing represents 100 units in real life, so 1 cm on the drawing would represent 2 mm
83. Topographic scales are commonly used in civil engineering drawings to represent large areas, such as maps or site plans. They typically use ratios like 1:10,000 or 1:50,000, where one unit on the drawing represents 10,000 or 50,000 units in real life.
84. Reduced scale is used to represent objects or structures at a reduced size, where the ratio is less than 1. It means that the drawing is smaller than the actual size, and the dimensions are proportionally reduced.
85. Architectural scales are typically used in architectural drawings to represent the overall layout of a building or a floor plan. They use ratios such as 1/8" = 1' or 1/4" = 1', where one unit on the drawing represents a specific length in real life.
86. In the given scenario, the scale 1:50 would be appropriate for representing a large machine or equipment. This means that one unit on the drawing represents 50 units in real life, allowing for a detailed representation.

87. Electrical scales are commonly used in electrical engineering drawings to represent wiring diagrams or circuit layouts. They are specialized scales that allow for accurate representation of electrical components and connections.

88. In the given scenario, the scale 1:10 would be suitable for representing a detailed part or component. This means that one unit on the drawing represents 10 units in real life, allowing for a larger and more detailed representation.

89. In the given scenario, the scale 1:50 would be appropriate for representing a site plan. This means that one unit on the drawing represents 50 units in real life, allowing for a comprehensive representation of the site and its features.

90. Assembly scales are commonly used in mechanical engineering drawings to represent assembly drawings or exploded views. These scales are specific to the assembly or exploded view and may vary based on the level of detail required.

91. Cartographic scales are typically used in surveying and mapping to represent large areas, such as cities or regions. These scales are designed to accurately represent geographical features and distances.

92. In the given scenario, the scale 1:1000 would be suitable for representing a small electronic component with intricate details. This means that one unit on the drawing represents 1000 units in real life, allowing for a highly detailed and accurate representation.

93. ISO is responsible for developing and maintaining international drawing standards, such as ISO 128 for technical drawings.

94. Object lines in engineering drawings are typically represented using a medium line weight, which ensures clear visibility without excessive boldness.

95. Millimeters are commonly used as the unit of measurement for dimensions in engineering drawings, especially in international standards.

96. GD&T (Geometric Dimensioning and Tolerancing) is a system used to specify and control the geometric features of a part in engineering drawings.

97. Orthographic projection is commonly used in engineering drawings to represent three-dimensional objects accurately. It uses multiple views (top, front, side) to show different aspects of the object.

98. Dimension lines are used to indicate the measurements or dimensions in engineering drawings. They are usually represented using a thin, continuous line.

99. ANSI B (11" x 17") is a commonly used standard format for engineering drawings in the United States, especially for smaller-sized drawings.

100. The roughness symbol (∇) is used to indicate surface finish requirements on an engineering drawing, providing information about the desired texture or smoothness of a surface.

101. Phantom lines are used to represent hidden or invisible edges, such as edges obscured by other objects or features, in engineering drawings.

102. The front view is typically used to represent an object as it would be seen by looking directly at one of its sides in engineering drawings. It provides the most detailed and accurate representation of the object's shape and features from a specific orientation.

103. The standard size of an A4 drawing sheet is 210 mm × 297 mm. A4 is a widely used size for drawings, documents, and printouts.

104. The type of drawing sheet commonly used for architectural plans is A1. A1 sheets are larger than A4 and provide ample space for detailed architectural drawings.

105. The type of drawing sheet orientation that is NOT commonly used is Square. Drawing sheets are typically oriented in either landscape (wider than tall) or portrait (taller than wide) format.

106. The purpose of a title block on a drawing sheet is the title block contains important information about the drawing, such as the type of drawing, scale used, drafter's name, date, etc.

107. The type of line typically used to indicate the visible edges of an object in a drawing is Solid line. Solid lines are used to represent visible lines, while dashed or dotted lines are used for hidden or construction lines.

108. The purpose of drawing border lines on a drawing sheet is All the given options. Drawing border lines frame the drawing, provide a clean edge, and establish the drawing's boundary.

109. The material that is NOT a common drawing sheet material is Aluminum. Drawing sheets are commonly made of paper, vellum (a translucent material), or tracing cloth.

110. The term "scale" refers to the size of the drawing relative to the actual object. Scale indicates the ratio between the dimensions of the drawing and the actual object it represents.

111. The largest size of drawing sheet is A0. A0 sheets are the largest in the A-series of drawing sheet sizes, with dimensions of 841 mm × 1189 mm.

112. The common units of measurement used on drawing sheets are all the given options. Only depending on the region and industry, measurements can be expressed in meters, centimeters, or inches on drawing sheets.

113. Technical lettering in engineering drawing is used to convey essential details, such as labels, dimensions, notes, and other textual information, in a clear and legible manner.

114. Gothic lettering is widely used in engineering drawing due to its clear, uniform strokes and easy readability.

115. Uppercase letters are commonly used for dimensions, notes, and labels in engineering drawing because they provide clarity and distinction in the text.

116. In engineering drawing, the recommended letter height for uppercase letters is often around 1/4 inch (6.35 mm). This size ensures legibility without compromising the available drawing space.

117. Mechanical or digital lettering is recommended for accuracy. While hand-lettering is still common, mechanical or digital lettering methods are often recommended in engineering drawing to ensure precise and consistent letterforms

118. Guidelines are used in technical lettering to ensure consistent letter height, maintain uniform spacing between letters, and align the baseline of the letters. This helps in creating neat and well-organized lettering.

119. Technical pens, known for their consistent ink flow and fine lines, are commonly used for technical lettering in engineering drawing. They allow for precise and controlled strokes.

120. The correct answer is (b) Horizontal strokes, vertical strokes, and diagonal strokes. When creating uppercase letters, it is generally recommended to start with horizontal strokes, followed by vertical strokes, and then diagonal strokes. This stroke order helps maintain consistent letterforms and uniformity.

121. Helvetica is a widely used font for technical lettering in engineering drawings due to its simplicity, legibility, and uniform stroke width.

122. The 6 mm height ensures that the letters are clear and readable while allowing sufficient space for annotations and dimensions.

123. The correct answer is (b) Curved line, horizontal line, vertical line. This sequence accurately represents the shape of the letter "a" in most technical lettering styles.

124. The correct answer is (a) Equal to the width of a character. This spacing ensures proper readability and consistency throughout the text.

125. Stacked fractions are easier to read and interpret compared to other formats such as decimal format with a slash or parentheses.

126. Applying a slightly heavier stroke to certain letters or words helps to make them stand out without compromising overall legibility.

127. The statement is true. In technical lettering, maintaining a consistent stroke width throughout the text is crucial for uniformity and professional appearance.

128. The correct order for drawing a number '9' Curved line, vertical line, curved line. This sequence accurately represents the shape of the number "9" in most technical lettering styles.

129. Technical lettering focuses on clarity, legibility, and precision rather than artistic embellishments.

130. The correct answer is (c) Crossing out the error and writing the correct letter above or beside it. This approach ensures that the correct information is clearly conveyed and avoids confusion caused by erasures or correction fluid.

131. In engineering drawings, a hole is typically represented by a circle with specific dimensions indicating its diameter.

132. Bolt or screw heads are often represented by hexagons in engineering drawings, as they are typically designed to be tightened or loosened using a hexagonal wrench or socket.

133. When looking at a cylindrical object from a cross-sectional view, such as cutting it in half, the resulting shape is a circle.

134. Gears are typically represented by circles in engineering drawings, with additional details such as teeth and dimensions to indicate their specific design.

135. A fillet or rounded corner is represented by an arc in engineering drawings. The arc connects the straight lines of the intersecting surfaces, creating a smooth transition.

136. Dimension lines in engineering drawings are commonly represented by dotted lines. They indicate the distance or size of an object or feature.

137. Electrical connectors or terminals are often represented by circles in engineering drawings. The specific details and symbols within the circle indicate the type and characteristics of the connector.

138. A chamfer or beveled edge is represented by a line segment in engineering drawings. The line is typically drawn at an angle to indicate the specific bevel.

139. A weld is represented by a specific symbol in engineering drawings, typically consisting of a triangle or other shapes with specific details indicating the type and characteristics of the weld.

140. Hidden lines, which represent features that are not visible from a particular view, are typically represented by dashed lines in engineering drawings. The dashed lines help differentiate them from visible lines.

141. A closed curve with no straight sides. A circle is a geometric shape that consists of all points in a plane that are equidistant from a fixed center point. It is a curved shape with no straight sides.

142. The circumference of a circle is calculated by multiplying the diameter (d) of the circle by π (pi). So, $C = \pi d$.

143. A regular polygon is a polygon with equal-length sides and equal internal angles. A pentagon is a polygon with five sides, and if it is regular, then all five sides and angles are equal.

144. A cube is a three-dimensional shape with six rectangular faces, all of which are congruent squares.

145. An isosceles triangle is a triangle with at least two sides of equal length. The angles opposite the equal sides are also equal.

146. The area of a rectangle is calculated by multiplying the length (l) of one side by the width (w) of the rectangle $A = l \times w$.

147. Opposite sides are parallel and equal in length. A parallelogram is a four-sided polygons in which opposite sides are parallel and equal in length.

148. A cone is a three-dimensional shape with a circular base and a curved surface that tapers to a point called the apex.

149. It has two pairs of parallel sides. A trapezoid is a quadrilateral with at least one pair of parallel sides.

150. The volume of a sphere is calculated by multiplying $4/3\pi$ (pi) by the cube of the radius (r). The correct answer is (c) $V = 4/3\pi r^3$.

151. A filled triangle symbol is used to represent a datum feature. Datum features are reference surfaces or points used in the GD&T (Geometric Dimensioning and Tolerancing) system to establish a datum reference frame for dimensional control.

152. The circle with two parallel lines passing through its center represents concentricity. Concentricity is a GD&T tolerance that ensures the axis of a cylindrical feature is centered and aligned with a datum axis.

153. An 'R' with a circle around it represents the radius of a curved feature on the drawing. It indicates the dimension of the circular arc.

154. A perpendicular line with two small outward arrows at its end represents perpendicularity. It shows that the referenced surface or line is perpendicular to the datum reference.

155. A diamond symbol indicates the dimension origin point on the drawing, from which other measurements are taken. It is usually used as a reference point for locating other features.

156. A square symbol with an 'A' inside represents a chamfer. It indicates that the specified edges or corners should be beveled or rounded.

157. An 'M' with a circle around it represents the maximum material condition. It is used in GD&T to indicate that the referenced feature has the maximum amount of material within its tolerance zone.

158. A straight line with one long arrow and one short arrow indicates the profile of a surface. It represents the allowable variations in the shape of the surface within specified tolerances.

159. A series of evenly spaced short lines, often referred to as "finish marks," represents surface roughness. They provide information about the surface texture and the manufacturing process required for the specific part.

160. An 'X' symbol inside a circle indicates a spotface. A spotface is a flat, machined surface around a hole to provide a consistent seating area for fasteners.

Please note that engineering drawing practices may vary slightly depending on the standards and conventions followed in different countries and industries. The explanations provided above are based on general practices.

CHAPTER

2

Units and Measurements

PHYSICAL QUANTITIES

All the quantities in terms of which laws of physics can be expressed, described and can be measured directly or indirectly, caused physical quantities.

Physical quantities are classified as follows :

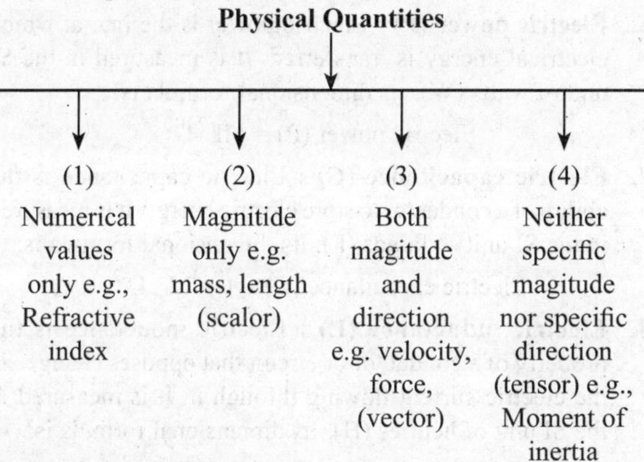

Its mainly two types.

Fundamental Quantity

Types of physical quantities :

Some fundamental quantities are given below.

S. No.	Quantity	SI Unit	Symbol
(i)	Length	metre	m
(ii)	Mass	kilogram	kg
(iii)	Time	second	s
(iv)	Electric current	ampere	A
(v)	Thermodynamic temperature	kelvin	K
(vi)	amount of substance	mole	mol
(vii)	Luminous intensity	candela	cd

Two supplementary units namely plane angle and solid angle are also defined. Their units are radian (rad) and steradian (st) respectively.

- To measure a physical quantity we need some standard, called units.
- Magnitude of physical quantity = Numerical value × System of units in which physical quantity is to be measured. (nu).

Derived unit : The physical quantities where unit can be derived from fundamental unit is called derived unit and quantities is said to be derived physical quantities e.g., force, young's modulum etc.

Dimensional equation and Dimensional formulae

Dimensional equations:

When a dimensional formula is equated to its physical quantity then the equation is called dimensional equation.

A dimensional equation is an equation that shows the relationship between the dimensions of physical quantities. It is a way of expressing the units of a physical quantity in terms of the fundamental units of measurement.

For example, the dimensional equation for velocity is:

$$[v] = [L]\,[T]^{-1}$$

This means that velocity is measured in units of length (L) divided by units of time (T). In other words, velocity has the dimensions of length per time.

Dimensional equation of force:

The dimensional equation of force can be derived from the formula for force,

which is F = m*a. In this formula, F is the force, m is the mass, and a is the acceleration.

The dimension of mass is M, the dimension of length is L, and the dimension of time is T. Therefore, the dimension of m is M, the dimension of a is T^{-2}, and the dimension of F is MLT^{-2}. So the dimensional equation of force is $M^1 L^1 T^{-2}$.

Dimensional equation of energy :

By, E = W = force* displacement.

The dimensional equation of energy (E) is $[M^1 L^1 T^{-2}]$ $[L^1] = M^1 L^2 T^{-2}$. This means that energy is a quantity that has the dimensions of mass, length, and time, and that it is measured in units of Joules (J). One Joule is equal to one kilogram-meter squared per second squared ($kg\text{-}m^2/s^2$). The kinetic energy of an object is given by the formula KE = 1/2 mv^2, where KE is the kinetic energy, m is the mass of the object, and v is the velocity of the object. The dimension of kinetic energy is $M^1 L^2 T^{-2}$.

Dimensions in heat quantities :

Dimensions in heat quantities can be expressed in terms of the fundamental dimensions of mass, length, and time, denoted by M, L, and T, respectively. Here are some common heat quantities and their dimensional formulas:

1. **Heat (Q) :** Heat is a form of energy that is transferred between objects due to a temperature difference. Its dimensional formula is :

   Heat (Q) = MLT^{-2}

2. **Specific heat capacity (c) :** Specific heat capacity is the amount of heat energy required to raise the temperature of one unit mass of a substance by one degree Celsius or Kelvin. Its dimensional formula is :

   Specific heat capacity (c) = $ML^{-2}T^{-2}K^{-1}$

3. **Latent heat of fusion (L_f) :** Latent heat of fusion is the amount of heat energy required to change one gram of a solid substance to its liquid state at its melting point. Its dimensional formula is:

   Latent heat of fusion (L_f) = $ML^{-2}T^{-1}K^{-1}$

4. **Latent heat of vaporization (L_v) :** Latent heat of vaporization is the amount of heat energy required to change one gram of a liquid substance to its vapor state at its boiling point. Its dimensional formula is :

   Latent heat of vaporization (L_v) = $ML^{-2}T^{-1}K^{-1}$

5. **Thermal conductivity (k) :** Thermal conductivity is the ability of a material to conduct heat. It is defined as the amount of heat energy flowing through a unit area of a material per unit time per unit temperature gradient. Its dimensional formula is :

   Thermal conductivity (k) = $ML^{-2}T^{-3}K^{-1}$

6. **Heat transfer coefficient (h) :** Heat transfer coefficient is a measure of the efficiency of heat transfer between a fluid and a solid surface. Its dimensional formula is:

   Heat transfer coefficient (h) = $ML^{-2}T^{-3}K^{-1}$

7. **Heat flux (q) :** Heat flux is the rate of heat transfer per unit area. Its dimensional formula is:

   Heat flux (q) = $ML^{-2}T^{-3}K^{-1}$

Dimensions in electricity quantities:

Dimensions in electricity quantities can be expressed in terms of the fundamental dimensions of mass, length, and time, denoted by M, L, and T, respectively. Here are some common electrical quantities and their dimensional formulas:

1. **Electric charge (Q) :** Electric charge is a fundamental property of matter that determines its electromagnetic interactions. It is measured in the SI unit of coulombs (C). Its dimensional formula is:

   Electric charge (Q) = IT

   Where I represents electric current and T represents time.

2. **Electric current (I) :** Electric current is the flow of electric charge through a conductor. It is measured in the SI unit of amperes (A). Its dimensional formula is :

   Electric current (I) = CT^{-1}

3. **Electric potential (V) :** Electric potential is the electrical energy per unit charge. It is measured in the SI unit of volts (V). Its dimensional formula is:

   Electric potential (V) = $ML^{2}I^{-1}T^{-3}$

4. **Electric field (E) :** Electric field is the force per unit charge experienced by a small charged particle in the vicinity of other charged particles or electric fields. It is measured in the SI unit of volts per meter (V/m). Its dimensional formula is:

   Electric field (E) = $ML^{-2}I^{-3}T^{-1}$

5. **Electric resistance (R) :** Electric resistance is the opposition to the flow of electric current in a conductor. It is measured in the SI unit of ohms (Ω). Its dimensional formula is:

   Electric resistance (R) = $ML^{2}I^{-2}T^{-3}$

6. **Electric power (P) :** Electric power is the rate at which electrical energy is transferred. It is measured in the SI unit of watts (W). Its dimensional formula is:

   Electric power (P) = $ML^{2}T^{-3}$

7. **Electric capacitance (C) :** Electric capacitance is the ability of a conductor to store electric energy. It is measured in the SI unit of farads (F). Its dimensional formula is:

   Electric capacitance (C) = $I^{2}T^{4}M^{-1}L^{-2}$

8. **Electric inductance (L) :** Electric inductance is the property of a conductor or circuit that opposes changes in the electric current flowing through it. It is measured in the SI unit of henries (H). Its dimensional formula is:

   Electric inductance (L) = $ML^{2}I^{-2}T^{-2}$

Dimensions of magnetic quantities:

Dimensions in magnetic quantities can be expressed in terms of the fundamental dimensions of mass, length, and time, denoted by M, L, and T, respectively. Here are some common magnetic quantities and their dimensional formulas:

1. **Magnetic field (B) :** The magnetic field is a vector quantity that describes the force exerted on a moving charged particle. Its SI unit is the tesla (T). The dimensional formula for the magnetic field is:

   Magnetic field (B) = $MLT^{-1}C^{-1}$

2. **Magnetic flux (Φ) :** Magnetic flux is the amount of magnetic field passing through a surface. Its SI unit is the weber (Wb). The dimensional formula for magnetic flux is:

   Magnetic flux (Φ) = $MLT^{-1}C^{-1}L^{2}$

3. **Magnetomotive force (MMF) :** Magnetomotive force is a measure of the ability of a source to produce a magnetic field. Its SI unit is the ampere-turn (AT). The dimensional formula for magnetomotive force is:

   Magnetomotive force (MMF) = IT

4. **Magnetic permeability (μ):** Magnetic permeability is a measure of the ability of a material to be magnetized. Its SI unit is the henry per meter (H/m). The dimensional formula for magnetic permeability is :

$$\text{Magnetic permeability } (\mu) = MLT^{-2}I^{-1}$$

5. **Magnetic reluctance (R_m) :** Magnetic reluctance is a measure of the opposition to magnetic field lines passing through a material. Its SI unit is the ampere-turn per weber (AT/Wb). The dimensional formula for magnetic reluctance is:

$$\text{Magnetic reluctance } (R\_m) = T^2I$$

6. **Magnetic induction (B) :** Magnetic induction is the total magnetic field, including both the external magnetic field and the field produced by magnetization of the material. Its SI unit is the tesla (T). The dimensional formula for magnetic induction is:

$$\text{Magnetic induction } (B) = MLT^{-1}C^{-1}$$

7. **Magnetization (M) :** Magnetization is a measure of the alignment of magnetic moments within a material. Its SI unit is the ampere per meter (A/m). The dimensional formula for magnetization is:

$$\text{Magnetization } (M) = ITL^{-3}$$

8. **Magnetic susceptibility (χ_m):** Magnetic susceptibility is a measure of the ease with which a material can be magnetized. It is a dimensionless quantity. The dimensional formula for magnetic susceptibility is:

$$\text{Magnetic susceptibility } (\chi\_m) = L^3$$

Dimensionless quantity:

A dimensionless quantity is a quantity to which no physical dimension is assigned. Dimensionless quantities are widely used in many fields, such as mathematics, physics, chemistry, engineering, and economics.

Examples of dimensionless quantities include :

- The ratio of two lengths. For example, the aspect ratio of a rectangle is the ratio of its length to its width.
- The ratio of two areas. For example, the coverage ratio of a paint is the ratio of the area it covers to the area of the surface it is applied to.
- The ratio of two volumes. For example, the volume fraction of a solution is the ratio of the volume of one component of the solution to the total volume of the solution.

Dimensionless quantities can also be ratios of physical quantities that have different dimensions. For example, the Reynolds number is the ratio of the inertial forces to the viscous forces in a fluid. It is a dimensionless quantity that is used to characterize the flow of fluids.

Dimensionless quantities are useful because they are independent of the system of units that is used. This means that they can be compared directly, even if the measurements were made in different units. For example, the aspect ratio of a rectangle is the same, regardless of whether it is measured in meters, centimeters, or inches.

Another advantage of dimensionless quantities is that they can be used to simplify complex equations. For example, the Navier-Stokes equations, which describe the motion of fluids, can be simplified by introducing dimensionless variables. This can make it easier to solve the equations and to understand the behavior of fluids.

Overall, dimensionless quantities are a powerful tool that can be used to solve problems in a wide variety of fields.

Here are some additional examples of dimensionless quantities:

- The angle between two lines.
- The frequency of a wave.
- The efficiency of a machine.
- The probability of an event occurring.
- The correlation coefficient between two variables.

Dimensionless quantity:

A dimensionless quantity is a quantity to which no physical dimension is assigned. Dimensionless quantities can be ratios of two physical quantities that have different dimensions. For example, the Reynolds number is the ratio of the inertial forces to the viscous forces in a fluid. It is a dimensionless quantity that is used to characterize the flow of fluids.

Dimensionless quantities are often used to measure the efficiency of a process or the similarity between two objects. For example, the Froude number is a dimensionless quantity that is used to measure the hydrodynamic similarity of two objects.

Dimensionless quantities are also often used to define physical constants. For example, the fine-structure constant is a dimensionless quantity that is defined as the ratio of two fundamental physical constants: the electric charge and the Planck constant.

Dimensionless quantities are a powerful tool that can be used to solve problems in a wide variety of fields. They are often used to simplify complex equations and to make it easier to compare different systems.

Here are some examples of dimensionless quantities :

- The aspect ratio of a rectangle.
- The coverage ratio of paint.
- The volume fraction of a solution.
- The Reynolds number.
- The Froude number.
- The fine-structure constant.
- The angle between two lines.
- The frequency of a wave.
- The efficiency of a machine.
- The probability of an event occurring.
- The correlation coefficient between two variables.

Principle of homogeneity :

The principle of homogeneity states that the dimensions of all the terms in an equation must be the same. This principle is used to check the validity of physical equations and to convert units.

For example, in the equation F = ma, where F is force, m is mass, and a is acceleration, the dimension of all the terms must be the same. The dimension of force is MLT^{-2}, the dimension of mass is M, and the dimension of acceleration is LT^{-2}. Therefore, the equation F = ma is dimensionally correct.

The principle of homogeneity can also be used to convert units. For example, if we want to convert the velocity of an object from meters per second to kilometers per hour, we can use the following equation:

v = frac{d}/{t}

Where, v is the velocity, d is the distance traveled, and t is the time.

The dimension of velocity is LT^{-1}, the dimension of distance is L, and the dimension of time is T.

Therefore, the equation v = d/t, is a dimensionally correct.

The principle of homogeneity is a fundamental principle of physics. It is used to ensure that the laws of physics are consistent and to make it easier to solve problems.

Application of dimensional analysis:

Dimensional analysis is a powerful technique in physics that is used to derive relationships between physical quantities and to check the consistency of dimensional equations. It is based on the principle that physical quantities with the same dimensions can be added, subtracted, or multiplied.

Here are some of the applications of dimensional analysis :

- Deriving relationships between physical quantities. For example, dimensional analysis can be used to derive the relationship between the acceleration of a falling object and its mass and time of flight.
- Checking the consistency of dimensional equations. For example, dimensional analysis can be used to check whether the units of an equation are consistent. This is important because an equation with inconsistent units is meaningless.
- Converting units. For example, dimensional analysis can be used to convert units from one system to another. This is useful for solving problems in physics and engineering.
- Estimating values of physical quantities. For example, dimensional analysis can be used to estimate the value of a physical quantity that is difficult to measure directly.
- Understanding the nature of physical quantities. For example, dimensional analysis can be used to understand the relationship between the dimensions of a physical quantity and its physical properties.

Dimensional analysis is a valuable tool for physicists and engineers. It is a simple technique that can be used to solve a wide variety of problems.

Limitation of dimensional analysis:

Dimensional analysis is a powerful tool for understanding the relationships between physical quantities. However, it is important to be aware of its limitations.

1. **Cannot determine dimensionless constants :** Dimensional analysis is unable to determine the numerical values of dimensionless constants in an equation. For example, it can be used to determine that the period of oscillation of a pendulum is proportional to the square root of its length, but it cannot determine the exact value of the constant of proportionality.
2. **Cannot be used to derive relations with more than one term on one side :** Dimensional analysis is only able to derive relations between quantities that have the same dimensions. For example, it can be used to determine that the velocity of an object is proportional to the distance it travels divided by the time it takes to travel that distance, but it cannot be used to derive a relation between the velocity of an object, the force acting on it, and its mass.
3. **Cannot be used to derive relations with trigonometric functions, exponential functions, or logarithmic functions :** Dimensional analysis is only able to derive relations between quantities that can be expressed as products of powers of fundamental dimensions. For example, it can be used to determine that the kinetic energy of an object is proportional to its mass times its velocity squared, but it cannot be used to derive a relation between the kinetic energy of an object, its mass, and its velocity that includes a trigonometric function, exponential function, or logarithmic function.
4. **Cannot determine the vector vs scalar nature of a quantity :** Dimensional analysis can only determine the dimensions of a quantity, not whether it is a scalar or a vector. For example, it can determine that the velocity of an object has dimensions of length divided by time, but it cannot determine whether the velocity of an object is a scalar or a vector.
5. **Cannot determine the specific form of a relation :** Dimensional analysis can only determine the general form of a relation between quantities, not the specific form of the relation. For example, it can determine that the period of oscillation of a pendulum is proportional to the square root of its length, but it cannot determine the exact form of the proportionality constant.

Dimensions of a physical quantity are the powers to which the fundamental quantities must be raised to represent the given physical quantity.

For example,

$$\text{Density} = \frac{\text{mass}}{\text{volume}} = \frac{[M]}{[L^3]} = [ML^{-3}]$$

MEASUREMENT

(i) Least count of vernier callipers

= [value of 1 part of main scale (s)] – [value of 1 part of vernier scale (v)]

$\Rightarrow$ least count of vernier callipers = 1 MSD – 1 VSD

where MSD = Main Scale Division

VSD = Vernier Scale Division

(ii) Least count

$$= \frac{\text{Value of 1 part on main scale}(s)}{\text{Number of parts on vernier scale } (n)}$$

$$1 \text{ VSD} = \frac{9}{10} \text{ MSD} = 0.9 \text{ mm}$$

$$\begin{aligned} VC &= 1 \text{ MSD} - 1 \text{ VSD} \\ &= 1 \text{ mm} - 0.9 \text{ mm} \\ &= 0.1 \text{ mm} \\ &= 0.01 \text{ cm} \end{aligned}$$

(iii) Least count of screw gauge

$$= \frac{\text{Pitch } (p)}{\text{No. of division on circular path } (n)}$$

If pitch is 1 mm and there are 100 divisions on circular scale then

$$LC = \frac{1\text{mm}}{100} = 0.01 \text{ mm} = 0.001 \text{ cm} = 1 \mu\text{m}.$$

- Smaller the least count, higher is the accuracy of measurement.
- Larger the number of significant figures after the decimal in a measurement, higher is the accuracy of measurement.
- Significant figures retained after mathematical operations (like addition, subtraction, multiplication and division) should be equal to the minimum, significant figures involved in any physical quantity in the given operation.

Measurement of large distance :

Large distances, such as the distances between planets, stars, and galaxies, are measured using a variety of methods, including :

- **Parallax method :** This method uses the apparent shift in the position of an object when viewed from two different locations. The parallax angle is the angle between the two lines of sight to the object. The parallax angle is inversely proportional to the distance to the object, so the larger the parallax angle, the closer the object. The parallax method is used to measure the distances to nearby stars.
- **Triangulation :** This method uses the angles between three known points to determine the distance to a fourth point. Triangulation is used to measure the distances to distant stars and galaxies.
- **Standard candles :** These are objects with known brightness, such as certain types of stars. By comparing the brightness of a standard candle to its apparent brightness, astronomers can determine its distance.
- **Redshift :** This is the shift in the wavelength of light from an object due to the object's motion away from the observer. The greater the redshift, the faster the object is moving away and the further away it is. Redshift is used to measure the distances to distant galaxies.

The units used to measure large distances include:

- **Astronomical unit (AU) :** The average distance between the Earth and the Sun (about 93 million miles).
- **Light-year :** The distance that light travels in one year (about 6 trillion miles).
- **Parsec (pc) :** A unit of distance used to measure distances to astronomical objects outside the solar system. One parsec is about 3.26 light-years.

Accuracy, precision, and errors in measurement :

Accuracy, precision, and errors in measurement are three important concepts in science and engineering. They are all related to the quality of a measurement.

Accuracy is how close a measured value is to the true value of the quantity being measured. It is a measure of how systematic the errors are in a measurement.

Precision is how close repeated measurements of the same quantity are to each other. It is a measure of how random the errors are in a measurement.

Errors in measurement are the differences between the measured value and the true value of the quantity being measured. They can be caused by a variety of factors, such as the limitations of the measuring instrument, environmental conditions, and human error.

Combination of errors :

The combination of errors in measurement is a fundamental aspect of scientific experimentation. It is important to understand how errors are combined in order to make accurate and reliable measurements.

There are two main types of errors in measurement: random errors and systematic errors. Random errors are caused by factors that are beyond the control of the experimenter, such as variations in the environment or fluctuations in the instrument. Systematic errors are caused by factors that are within the control of the experimenter, such as improper calibration of the instrument or a mistake in the experimental procedure.

The combination of errors in measurement depends on the type of operation being performed. For example, the combination of errors in addition and subtraction is different from the combination of errors in multiplication and division.

Here are the rules for combining errors in measurement :

- For addition and subtraction, the absolute errors are added.
- For multiplication and division, the relative errors are added.
- For a quantity raised to a power, the relative error is multiplied by the power.

For example, if you measure the length of a box to be 10.0 cm with an error of 0.1 cm, and you measure the width of the box to be 5.0 cm with an error of 0.05 cm, then the area of the box is 50.0 cm^2 with an error of 0.3 cm^2.

The combination of errors in measurement is an important part of data analysis. By understanding how errors are combined, you can make more accurate and reliable conclusions about your data.

Here are some additional tips for combining errors in measurement :

- Always use the same units of measurement when combining errors.
- Be aware of the magnitude of the errors when combining them.
- When possible, use a more precise instrument to reduce the error.

Significant figures:

Significant figures are the digits in a number that are relevant to its accuracy. They are important in scientific measurements because they allow scientists to express the precision of their results.

The number of significant figures in a number depends on the following rules :

- All non-zero digits are significant.
- Zeros between non-zero digits are significant.
- Zeros to the right of the decimal point and to the left of the first non-zero digit are significant if they are written behind a decimal point.
- Zeros to the left of the decimal point and to the right of the last non-zero digit are not significant.

For example, the number 0.00123 has four significant figures: 0, 0, 1, and 2. The number 1200 has four significant figures : 1, 2, 0, and 0. The number 0.00012 has two significant figures: 1 and 2.

Significant figures are important when adding, subtracting, multiplying, and dividing numbers. When performing these operations, the number of significant figures in the result is equal to the smallest number of significant figures in any of the numbers being added, subtracted, multiplied, or divided.

For example, when adding the numbers 1.23 and 0.0012, the result is 1.2312. This number has four significant figures because 0.0012 has only four significant figures.

When multiplying the numbers 2.34 and 1.2, the result is 2.808. This number has three significant figures because 1.2 has only three significant figures.

When dividing the number 12.34 by the number 0.0012, the result is 10290. This number has four significant figures because 0.0012 has only four significant figures.

Significant figures are an important part of scientific measurement and should be used carefully when reporting results.

Rounding off rules of rounding off uncertain digits:

When rounding off numbers, it is important to follow a consistent set of rules to ensure accuracy and consistency. The following are the rules for rounding off uncertain digits:

Rule 1 : If the uncertain digit is less than 5, do not change the preceding digit. For example, 2.34 rounded off to two decimal places is 2.34.

Rule 2 : If the uncertain digit is 5 or greater, add 1 to the preceding digit. For example, 2.35 rounded off to two decimal places is 2.35, and 3.75 rounded off to two decimal places is 3.80.

Rule 3 : If the uncertain digit is 5 and the preceding digit is even, do not change the preceding digit. For example, 2.45 rounded off to two decimal places is 2.45.

Rule 4 : If the uncertain digit is 5 and the preceding digit is odd, add 1 to the preceding digit. For example, 3.45 rounded off to two decimal places is 3.45, and 5.45 rounded off to two decimal places is 5.50.

These rules are essential for maintaining precision and accuracy in calculations and measurements. By following these rules, you can ensure that your results are consistent and reliable.

Errors in Measurement

(i) Let the measured values of a physical quantity be $a_1, a_2, \ldots, a_n$. The arithmetic mean of the values is

$$a_{\text{mean}} = \frac{a_1 + a_2 + \ldots + a_n}{n}$$

(ii) Mean absolute error

$$\Delta a_{\text{mean}} = \frac{|\Delta a_1| + |\Delta a_2| + \ldots + |\Delta a_n|}{n}$$

(iii) Fractional or relative error $= \dfrac{\Delta a_{\text{mean}}}{a_{\text{mean}}}$

(iv) Percentage error $= \dfrac{\Delta a_{\text{mean}}}{a_{\text{mean}}} \times 100$

Errors in some or difference

$$\Delta x = \pm(\Delta a + \Delta b)$$

Errors in product

$$\frac{\Delta x}{x} = \pm\left(\frac{\Delta a}{a} + \frac{\Delta b}{b}\right)$$

Errors in division

$$\frac{\Delta x}{x} = \pm\left(\frac{\Delta a}{a} + \frac{\Delta b}{b}\right)$$

Errors in quantity raised to some power

$$\frac{\Delta x}{x} = \pm\left(n\frac{\Delta a}{a} + m\frac{\Delta b}{b}\right) \text{ where, } x = \frac{a^n}{b^m}$$

Erros's can be classified as follow :

Errors

Based on cause of error	Based on magnitude of error
(1) Systematic error (where causy one known) to us	(1) Absolute error (2) Mean absolute error (3) Relative error
(2) Random error where causes one not know flous.	(4) Puntage error

So it can be minimixed by taking lange number of obsurvation and taking arithmatic mean of all the observations.

UNITS

A unit of measurement is a definite magnitude of a quantity, defined and adopted by convention or by law that is used as a standard for measurement of the same kind of quantity. Any other quantity of that kind can be expressed as a multiple of the unit of measurement. Units are used to make it possible to compare quantities that are of different magnitudes.

Some important properties of units are:

- **Units must be consistent :** This means that the same unit must be used to measure the same quantity throughout a calculation. For example, if you are measuring the length of a table in meters, you cannot suddenly switch to using centimeters in the middle of the calculation.
- **Units must be accurately defined :** This means that the definition of a unit must be clear and unambiguous. For example, the definition of a meter is "the distance traveled by light in a vacuum in 1/299,792,458 of a second."
- **Units must be reproducible :** This means that the same unit can be reproduced anywhere in the world with the same accuracy. For example, a meter is defined in terms of the speed of light, which is a universal constant.
- **Units must be universally recognized :** This means that the same unit must be accepted and used by scientists and engineers around the world. For example, the SI system of units is the most widely used system of units in the world.

Types of Units :

There are many types of units, including :

- **Base units :** Base units are the fundamental units of a system of units. They are not defined in terms of any other units. For example, the meter, kilogram, second, ampere, Kelvin, candela, and mole are the seven base units of the International System of Units (SI).
- **Derived units :** Derived units are units that are defined in terms of base units. For example, the unit of velocity is meters per second (m/s), which is derived from the base units of meters (m) and seconds (s).
- **SI prefixes :** SI prefixes are used to represent multiples and submultiples of base units. For example, the prefix kilo- (k) represents 1,000, so one kilometer (km) is equal to 1,000 meters (m).
- **Non-SI units :** Non-SI units are units that are not part of the SI system. Some examples of non-SI units include the inch, pound, and degree Fahrenheit.
- **Natural units :** Natural units are units that are based on fundamental constants of nature. For example, the unit of time in natural units is the Planck time, which is the time it takes for light to travel one Planck length.

Units of Some Physical Quantities in Different Systems

	Physical quantity	System		
		CGS	**MKS**	**FPS**
Fundamental	Length Mass Time	cm g s	m kg s	ft lb s
Derived	Four power impulse	N J/S N-s		

Some Practical Units are

(i) 1 fermi = 1 fm = 10^{-15} m

(ii) 1 X-ray unit = 1 XU = 10^{-13} m

(iii) 1 angstrom = 1Å = 10^{-10} m

(iv) 1 micron = 1 μm = 10^{-6} m

(v) 1 astronomical unit = 1 AU = 1.49×10^{11} m

[Average distance between sun and earth *i.e.,* radius of earth's orbit]

(vi) 1 light year = 1 ly = 9.46×10^{15} m

[distance that light travels in 1 year in vacuum]

(vii) 1 parsec = 1 pc = 3.08×10^{16} m = 3.26 light year

[The distance at which a star subtends an angle of parallex of 1 sec at an arc of 1 AU]

Objective Type Questions

1. An experiment measures quantities a, b and c and x is calculated from the formula

$$X = \frac{ab^2}{c^3}$$

If the percentage error in a, b and c are $\pm 1\% \pm 3\%$ and $\pm 2\%$ respectively. The percentage error in X will be

(a) $\pm 13\%$ (b) $\pm 7\%$
(c) $\pm 4\%$ (d) $\pm 1\%$

2. If radius of the sphere is (5.3 ± 0.1) cm. Then percentage error in its volume will be

(a) $3 + 6.01 \times \frac{100}{5.3}$ (b) $\frac{1}{3} \times 0.01 \times \frac{100}{5.3}$
(c) $\left(\frac{3 \times 0.1}{5.3}\right) \times 100$ (d) $\frac{0.1}{5.3} \times 100$

3. If voltage $V = (100 \pm 5)$ volt and current $I = (10 \pm 0.2)$ A, the percentage error in resistance R is

(a) 5.2% (b) 25%
(c) 7% (d) 10%

4. The values of two resistors are $R_1 = (6 \pm 0.3)$ kΩ and $R_2 = (10 \pm 0.2)$ kΩ. The percentage error in the equivalent resistance when they are connected in parallel is

(a) 5.125% (b) 2%
(c) 10.125% (d) 7%

5. The frequency of vibration of string is given by

$$v = \frac{p}{2l}\left[\frac{F}{m}\right]^{1/2}$$

Here p is number of segments in the string and l is the length. The dimensional formula for m will be

(a) $[M^0LT^{-1}]$ (b) $[ML^0T^{-1}]$
(c) $[ML^{-1}T^0]$ (d) $[M^0L^0T^0]$

6. The dimensions of $\frac{a}{b}$ in the equation $P = \frac{a - t^2}{bx}$, where P is pressure, x is distance and t is time are

(a) $[M^2LT^{-3}]$ (b) $[MT^{-2}]$
(c) $[LT^{-3}]$ (d) $[ML^3T^{-1}]$

7. $[ML^2T^{-3}I^{-1}A^{-1}]$ is the dimension of

(a) electric field (b) capacity
(c) potential (d) permittivity

8. A gas bubble formed from an explosion under water oscillates with a period T proportional to $p^a d^b E^c$, where p is pressure, d is the density of water and E is the total energy of explosion. The value of a, b, c are

(a) $a = 1, b = 1, c = 2$
(b) $a = 1, b = 2, c = 1$
(c) $a = \frac{5}{6}, b = \frac{1}{2}, c = \frac{1}{3}$
(d) $a = -\frac{5}{6}, b = \frac{1}{2}, c = \frac{1}{3}$

9. The physical quantities not having same dimensions are

(a) Torque and work
(b) Momentum and Planck's constant
(c) Stress and Young's modulus
(d) Speed and $(\mu_0\varepsilon_0)^{-1/2}$

10. Dimensions of $\frac{1}{\mu_0\varepsilon_0}$, where symbols have their usual meaning are:

(a) $[L^{-1}T]$ (b) $[L^2T^2]$
(c) $[L^2T^{-2}]$ (d) $[LT^{-1}]$

11. Which one of the following represents the correct dimensions of the coefficient of viscosity?

(a) $[ML^{-1}T^{-2}]$ (b) $[MLT^{-1}]$
(c) $[ML^{-1}T^{-1}]$ (d) $[ML^{-2}T^{-2}]$

12. Identify the pair whose dimensions are equal

(a) Torque and work (b) Stress and energy
(c) Torce and stress (d) force and work

13. Which of the following units denotes the dimensions $[ML^2/Q^2]$, where Q denotes the electric charge?

(a) Wb/m^2 (b) henry (H)
(c) H/m^2 (d) Weber (Wb)

14. Out of the following pairs which one does not have identical dimensions?

(a) Angular momentum and Plank's constant
(b) Impulse and momentum
(c) Moment of inertia and moment of a force
(d) Work and torque

15. A body of mass m = 3.513 kg is moving along the x-axis with a speed of 5.00 ms^{-1}. The magnitude of its momentum is recorded as:

(a) 17.6 kg ms^{-1} (b) 17.565 kg ms^{-1}
(c) 17.56 kg ms^{-1} (d) 17.57 kg ms^{-1}

16. Two full turns of the circular scale of a screw gauge cover a distance of 1 mm on its main scale. The total number of divisions on the circular scale is 50. Further, it is found that screw gauge has zero error of – 0.03 mm. While measuring the diameter of a thin wire, a student notes the main scale reading of 3 mm and the number of circular scale divisions in line with main scale as 35. The diameter of wire is:

(a) 3.32 mm (b) 3.73 mm
(c) 3.67 mm (d) 3.38 mm

17. In an experiment the angles are required to be measured using an insrtument 29 divisions of the main scale exactly coincide with the 30 divisions of the vernier scale. If the smallest divisions of the main scale is hay-a-degree (= 0.5°) then the least count of the instrument is

(a) hay minute (b) one degree
(c) hay degree (d) one minute

18. The respective number of significant figures for the numbers 23.023; 0.0003 and 2.1×10^{-3} are:

(a) 4, 4, 2 (b) 5, 1, 2
(c) 5, 1, 5 (d) 5, 5, 2

19. A screw gauge gives the following reading when used to measure the diameter of a wire.

Main scale reading: 0 mm
Circular scale reading : 52 divisions
Given that 1 mm on main scale corresponds to 100 divisions of the circular scale. The diameter of wire from the above data is:

(a) 0.005 cm (b) 0.52 cm
(c) 0.052 cm (d) 0.026 cm

20. The dimensions of magnetic field in M, L, T and C(coulomb) is given by:

(a) $MLT^{-1} C^{-1}$ (b) $MT^2 C^{-2}$
(c) $MT^{-1} C^{-1}$ (d) $MT^{-2} C^{-1}$

21. In the formula $X = 3YZ^2$, X and Z have dimensions of capacitance and magnetic induction respectively. What are the dimensions of Y in MKSQ system?

(a) $[M^{-3}L^{-1}T^3Q^4]$ (b) $[M^{-3}L^{-2}T^4Q^4]$
(c) $[M^{-2}L^{-2}T^4Q^4]$ (d) $[M^{-3}L^{-2}T^4Q^1]$

22. The dimensions of $\left(\frac{1}{2}\right)\varepsilon_0 E^2$ is:

(ε_0 – permittivity of free space, E – electric field)

(a) $[MLT^{-1}]$ (b) $[ML^2T^{-2}]$
(c) $[ML^{-1}T^{-2}]$ (d) $[ML^2T^{-1}]$

23. A cube has a side of length 1.2×10^{-2} m. Calculate its volume.

(a) 1.7×10^{-6} m^3 (b) 1.73×10^{-6} m^3
(c) 1.70×10^{-6} m^3 (d) 1.732×10^{-6} m^3

24. Let $[\varepsilon_0]$ denote of the permittivity of the vacuum, and $[\mu_0]$ denote the permeability of the vacuum. If M = mass, L = length, T = time and I = electric current, then the dimensional formulae of ε_0 and μ_0 are:

(a) $[\varepsilon_0] = [M^{-1}L^{-3}T^2I]$ (b) $[\varepsilon_0] = [M^{-1}L^{-3}T^4I^2]$
(c) $[\mu_0] = [MLT^2I^{-2}]$ (d) $[\mu_0] = [ML^2T^{-1}I]$

25. The pair of physical quantities that have the same dimensions is:

(a) Reynolds number and coefficient of friction
(b) Curie and frequency of a light wave
(c) Latent heat and gravitational potential
(d) Planck's constant and torque

26. The dimensions of length are expressed as $G^x c^y h^z$. where G, c and h are the universal gravitational constant, speed of light and Planck's constant respectively, then:

(a) $x = (1/2), y = (1/2)$ (b) $x = (1/2), z = (1/2)$
(c) $y = (-3/2), z = (1/2)$ (d) $y = (1/2), z = (3/2)$

27. The SI unit of inductance, the henry can be written as:

(a) weber/ampere (b) volt-sec/amp
(c) joule/(ampere)^2 (d) ohm-second

Directions (Q. 28 to 30) : Consider C as velocity of light, the constant of gravitation G and Plank's constant h, be chosen as fundamental unit. Answer the following:

28. Find the value of a gram in new unit of mass, length and time.

(a) 1.8355×10^5 (b) 1.5×10^5
(c) 18.35×10^5 (d) 15×10^5

29. Find the value of a centimeter in the above units.

(a) 743×10^{42} (b) 7.43×10^{42}
(c) 74.3×10^{42} (d) 743.25×10^{42}

30. Find the value of a second in the above unit.

(a) 24.76×10^{32} (b) 2.476×10^{32}
(c) 2.476×10^{32} (d) 24×10^{32}

Directions (Q.31 to 33) : The van-der Waals equation is

$$\left(P + \frac{a}{V^2}\right)(V\text{-}b) = RT,$$

where P is pressure, V is molar volume and T is the temperature of the given sample of gas. R is called molar gas constant, a and b are called vander Waal constants.

31. The dimensional formula for b is same as that for

(a) P (b) V
(c) PV^2 (d) RT

32. The dimensional formula for a is same as that for

(a) V^2 (b) P
(c) PV^2 (d) RT

33. Which of the following does not possess the same dimensional formula as that for RT?

(a) PV (b) Pb
(c) a/V^2 (d) ab/V^2

Directions (Q. 34 to 36) : In the study of physics, we often have to measure the physical quantities. The numerical value of a measured quantity can only be approximate as it depends upon the least count of the measuring instrument used. The number of significant figures in any measurement indicates the degree of precision of that measurement. The importance of significant figures lies in calculation. A mathematical calculation cannot increase the precision of a physical measurement. Therefore, the number of significant figures in the sum or product of a group of numbers cannot be greater than the number that has the least of significant figures. A chain cannot be stronger than its weakest link.

34. A bee of mass 0.000087 kg sits on a flower of mass 0.0123 kg. What is the total mass supported by the stem of the flower upto appropriate significant figures?

(a) 0.012387 kg (b) 0.01239 kg
(c) 0.0124 kg (d) 0.012 kg

35. The radius of a uniform wire is $r = 0.021$ cm. The value π is given to be 3.142. What is the area of cross-section of the wire upto appropriate significant figures?

(a) 0.0014 cm^2 (b) 0.00139 cm^2

(c) 0.001386 cm^2 (d) 0.0013856 cm^2

36. A man runs 100.5 m in 10.3 s. His average speed upto appropriate significant figures is

(a) 9.76 ms^{-1} (b) 9.757 ms^{-1}

(c) 9.7573 ms^{-1} (d) 9.8 ms^{-1}

37. In SI units, the dimensions of $\sqrt{\frac{\varepsilon_0}{\mu_0}}$ is

(a) $AT^{-3}ML^{3/2}$ (b) $A^{-1}TML^3$

(c) $AT^2M^{-1}L^{-1}$ (d) $A^2T^3M^{-1}L^{-2}$

38. Let $[\varepsilon_0]$ denote the dimensional formula of the permittivity of vacuum. If M = mass, L = Length, T = Time and A = electric current, then

(a) $[\varepsilon_0] = [M^{-1}L^{-3}T^2A]$

(b) $[\varepsilon_0] = [M^{-1}L^{-3}T^4A^2]$

(c) $[\varepsilon_0] = [M^{-2}L^2T^{-1}A^{-2}]$

(b) $[\varepsilon_0] = [M^{-1}L^2T^{-1}A^2]$

39. Which of the following sets have different dimensions?

(a) Pressure, Young's modulus, Stress

(b) Emf, Potential difference, Electric potential

(c) Heat, Work done, Energy

(d) Dipole moment, Electric flux, Electrict field

40. In the relation,

$$p = \frac{\alpha}{\beta} e^{-\frac{\alpha Z}{k\theta}}$$

p is pressure, Z is distance, k is Boltzmann's constant and θ is the temperature. The dimensional formula of β will be

(a) $[M^0L^2T^0]$ (b) $[ML^2T]$

(c) $[ML^0T^{-1}]$ (d) $[M^0L^2T^{-1}]$

Directions (Q. 41 to 42) : In electromagnetic theory, the electric and magnetic phenomena are related to each other. Therefore, the dimensions of electric and magnetic quantities must also be related to each other. In the question below, [E] and [B] stand for dimensions of electric and magnatic fields respectively, while $[\varepsilon_0]$ and $[\mu_0]$ stand for dimensions of the permittivity and permeability of free space respectively. [L] and [T] are dimensions of length and time respectively. All the quantities are given in SI units.

41. The relation between [E] and [B] is

(a) [E] = [B] [L] [T] (b) [E] = [B] $[L]^{-1}$ [T]

(c) [E] = [B] [L] $[T]^{-1}$ (d) [E] = [B] $[L]^{-1}$ $[T]^{-1}$

42. The relation between $[\varepsilon_0]$ and $[\mu_0]$ is

(a) $[\mu_0] = [\varepsilon_0] [L]^2 [T]^{-2}$

(b) $[\mu_0] = [\varepsilon_0] [L]^{-2} [T]^2$

(c) $[\mu_0] = [\varepsilon_0]^{-1} [L]^2 [T]^{-2}$

(d) $[\mu_0] = [\varepsilon_0]^{-1} [L]^{-2} [T]^2$

Directions (Q. 43 to 44) : If the measurement errors in all the independent quantities are known, then it is possible to determine the error in any dependent quantity. This is done by the use of series expansion and truncating the expansion at the first power of the error. For example, consider the relation $z = x/y$. If the errors in x, y and z are Δx, Δy and Δz, respectively, then

$$z \pm \Delta z = \frac{x \pm \Delta x}{y \pm \Delta y} = \frac{x}{y}\left(1 \pm \frac{\Delta x}{x}\right)\left(1 \pm \frac{\Delta y}{y}\right)^{-1}$$

The series expansion for $\left(1 \pm \frac{\Delta y}{y}\right)^{-1}$, to first power in $\Delta y/y$, is $1 \mp (\Delta y/y)$. The relative errors in independent variables are always added. So the error in z will be $\Delta z = z\left(\frac{\Delta x}{x} + \frac{\Delta y}{y}\right)$.

The above derivation makes the assumption that $\Delta x/x \ll 1$, $\Delta y/y \ll 1$. Therefore, the higher powers of these quantities are neglected.

43. Consider the ratio $r = \frac{(1-a)}{(1+a)}$ to be determined by measuring a dimensionless quantity a. If the error in the measurement of a is Δa ($\Delta a/a \ll 1$), then what is the error Δr in determining r?

(a) $\frac{\Delta a}{(1+a)^2}$ (b) $\frac{2\Delta a}{(1+a)^2}$

(c) $\frac{\Delta a}{(1-a^2)}$ (d) $\frac{2a\Delta a}{(1-a^2)}$

44. In an experiment the initial number of radioactive nuclei is 3000. It is found that 1000 ± 40 nuclei decayed in the first 1.0 s. For $|x| \ll 1$, $\ln(1 + x) = x$ up to first power in x. The error $\Delta\lambda$, in the determination of the decay constant λ, in s^{-1}, is

(a) 0.04 (b) 0.03

(c) 0.02 (d) 0.01

45. The density of a material in the shape of a cube is determined by measuring three sides of the cube and its mass. If the relative errors in mesuring in mass and length are respectively 1.5% and 1% the maximum error in determining the density is:

(a) 4.5% (b) 6%

(c) 2.5% (d) 3.5%

46. A person measures the depth of a well by measuring the time interval between dropping a stone and receiving the sound of impact with the bottom of the well. The error in his measurement of time is $\delta T = 0.01$s and he measures the depth of the well to be $L = 20$ m. Take the acceleration due to gravity $g = 10$ ms^{-2} and the velocity of sound is 300 ms^{-1}. Then the fractional error in the measurement, $\frac{\delta L}{L}$, is closest to

(a) 1% (b) 5%
(c) 3% (d) 0.2%

47. A Screw gauge with a pitch of 0.5 mm and a circular scale with 50 divisions is used to measure the thickness of a thin sheet of aluminium. Before starting the measurement, it is found that when the two jaws of the screw gauge are brought in contact, the 45th division coincides with the main scale line and that the zero of the main scale is barely visible. What is the thickness of the sheet, if the main scale reading is 0.5 mm and the 25th division coincides with the main scale line?

(a) 0.75 mm (b) 0.80 mm
(c) 0.70 mm (d) 0.50 mm

48. There are two vernier calipers both of which have 1 cm divided into 10 equal divisions on the main scale. The vernier scale of one of the calipers (C_1) has 10 equal divisions that correspond to 9 main scale divisions.

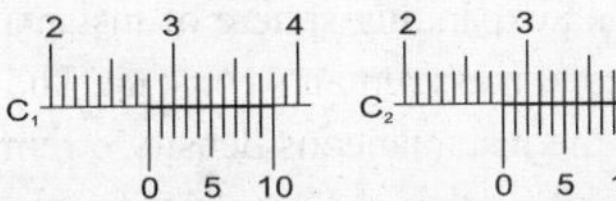

The vernier scale of the other caliper (C_2) has 10 equal divisions that correspond to 11 main scale divisions. The reading of the two calipers are shown in the figure. The measured values (in cm) by calipers C_1 and C_2 respectively, are

(a) 2.87 and 2.87 (b) 2.87 and 2.83
(c) 2.85 and 2.82 (d) 2.87 and 2.86

49. The period of oscillation of a simple pendulum is $T = 2\pi\sqrt{\frac{L}{g}}$. Measured value of L is 20.0 cm known to 1 mm accuracy and time for 100 oscillations of the pendulum is found to be 90 s using a wrist watch of 1s resolution. The accuracy in the determination of g is

(a) 3% (b) 2%
(c) 1% (d) 5%

50. The current voltage relation of diode is given by $I = (e^{1000V/T} - 1)$mA, where the applied voltage V is in volt and the temperature T is in kelvin. If a student makes an error measuring $\pm$ 0.01 V while measuring the current of 5 mA at 300 K, what will be the error in the value of current in mA?

(a) 0.2 mA (b) 0.02 mA
(c) 0.5 mA (d) 0.05 mA

51. A student measured the length of a rod and wrote it as 3.50 cm. Which instrument did he use to measure it?

(a) A meter scale
(b) A vernier caliper where 10 divisions in vernier scale matches with 9 divisions in main scale and main scale has 10 divisions in 1 cm
(c) A screw gauge having 100 divisions in the circular scale and pitch as 1 mm and pitch as 1 mm
(d) A screw gauge having 50 divisions in the circular scale

52. The diameter of a cylinder is measured using a vernier calipers with no zero error. It is found that the zero of the vernier scale lies between 5.10 cm and 5.15 cm of the main scale. The vernier scale has 50 division equivalent to 2.45 cm. The 24th division of the vernier scale exactly coincides with one of the main scale divisions. The diameter of the cylinder is

(a) 5.112 cm (b) 5.124 cm
(c) 5.136 cm (d) 5.148 cm

53. In the determination of Young's modulus $\left(Y = \frac{4MLg}{\pi l d^2}\right)$ by using Searle's method, a wire of length $L = 2$ m and diameter $d = 0.5$ mm is used. For a load $M = 2.5$ kg, an extension $l = 0.25$ mm in the length of the wire is observed. Quantities d and l are measured using a screw gauge and a micrometer, respectively. They have the same pitch of 0.5 mm. The number of divisions on their circular scale is 100. The contributions to the maximum probable error of the Y measurement is

(a) due to the errors in the measurements of d and l are the same
(b) due to the error in the measurement of d is twice that due to the error in the measurement of l
(c) due to the error in the measurement of l is twice that due to the error in the measurement of d
(d) due to the error in the measurement of d is four times that due to the error in the measurement of l

54. The density of a solid ball is to be determined in an experiment. The diameter of the ball is measured with a screw gauge, whose pitch is 0.5 mm and there are 50 divisions on the circular scale. The reading on the main scale is 2.5 mm and that on the circular scale is 20 divisions. If the measured mass of the ball has a relative error of 2%, the relative percentage error in the density is

(a) 0.9% (b) 2.4%
(c) 3.1% (d) 4.2%

55. A vernier calipers has 1 mm marks on the main scale. It has 20 equal divisions on the vernier scale which match with 16 main scale divisions. For this vernier calipers, the least count is

(a) 0.02 mm (b) 0.05 mm
(c) 0.1 mm (d) 0.2 mm

56. Students I, II and III perform an experiment for measuring the acceleration due to gravity (g) using a simple pendulum. They use different lengths of the pendulum and/or record time for different number of oscillations. The observations are shown in the table.

Least count for length = 0.1 cm, Least count for time = 0.1s.

Student	Length of the pendulum (cm)	Number of oscillations (n)	Total time for (n) oscillations (s)	Time period (s)
I	64.0	8	128.0	16.0
II	64.0	4	64.0	16.0
III	20.0	4	36.0	9.0

If E_I, E_{II} and E_{III} are the percentage errors in g, i.e. $\left(\frac{\Delta g}{g} \times 100\right)$ for students I, II and III, respectively.

(a) $E_I = 0$
(b) E_I is minimum
(c) $E_I = E_{II}$
(d) E_{II} is maximum

57. In the experiment to determine the speed of sound using a resonance column

(a) prongs of the tuning fork are kept in a vertical plane
(b) prongs of the tuning fork are kept in a horizontal plane
(c) in one of the two resonances observed, the length of the resonating air column is close to the wavelength of sound in air
(d) in one of the two resonances observed, the length of the resonating air column is close to half of the wavelength of sound in air

58. A student performs an experiment to determine the Young's modulus of a wire, exactly 2 m long, by Searle's method. In a particular reading, the student measures the extension in the length of the wire to be 0.8 mm with an uncertainty of ± 0.05 mm at a load of exactly 1.0 kg. The student also measures the diameter of the wire to be 0.4 mm with an uncertainty of ± 0.01 mm. Take g = 9.8 m/s^2 (exact? The Young's moduls obtained from the reading is close to

(a) $(2.0 \pm 0.3)\ 10^{11}$ N/m^2
(b) $(2.0 \pm 0.2) \times 10^{11}$ N/m^2
(c) $(2.0 \pm 0.1) \times 10^{11}$ N/m^2
(d) $(2.0 \pm 0.05) \times 10^{11}$ N/m^2

59. The circular scale of a screw gauge has 50 divisions and pitch of 0.5 mm. Find the diameter of sphere. Main scale reading is 2.

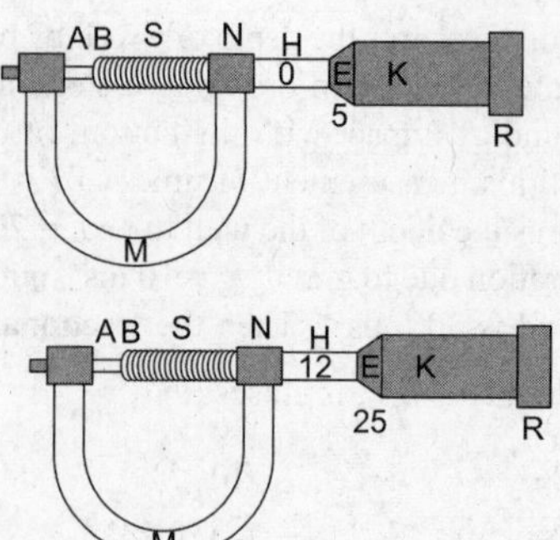

(a) 1.2 mm (b) 1.25 mm
(c) 2.20 mm (d) 2.25 mm

60. A wire has a mass (0.3 ± 0.003) g, radius (0.5 ± 0.005) mm and length (6 ± 0.06) cm. The maximum percentage error in the measurement of its density is

(a) 1 (b) 2
(c) 3 (d) 4

61. The density of a material in SI units is 128 kg m^{-3}. In certain units in which the unit of length in 25 cm and the unit of mass is 50 g, the numerical value of density of the material is :

(a) 40 (b) 16
(c) 640 (d) 410

62. Consider an expanding sphere of instantaneous radius R whose total mass remains constant. The expansion is such that the instantaneous density ρ remains uniform throughout the volume. The rate of fractional change in density $\left(\frac{1}{p}\frac{d\rho}{dt}\right)$ is constant. The velocity v of any point of the surface of the expanding sphere is proportional to

(a) R (b) $\frac{1}{R}$
(c) R^3 (d) $R^{\frac{2}{3}}$

63. Three vectors **P/Q** and **R** are shown in the figure. Let S be any point on the vector **R**. The distance between the points P and S is b [**R**]. The general relation among vectors **P**, **Q** and **S** is

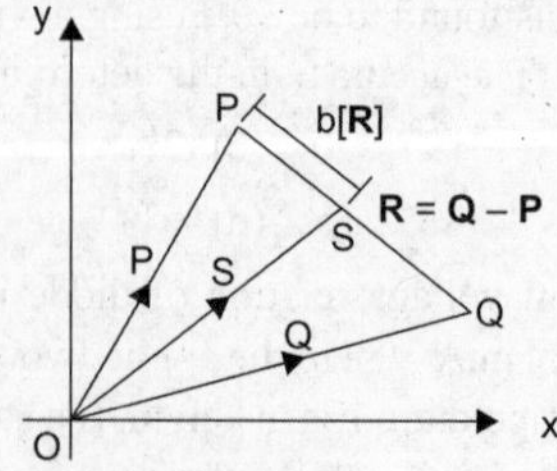

(a) $\mathbf{S} = (1 - b^2)\mathbf{P} + b\mathbf{Q}$
(b) $\mathbf{S} = (b - 1)\mathbf{P} + b\mathbf{Q}$
(c) $\mathbf{S} = (1 - b)\mathbf{P} + b\mathbf{Q}$
(d) $\mathbf{S} = (1 - b)\mathbf{P} + b^2\mathbf{Q}$

Directions (Q. 64 to 65) : A dense collection of equal number of electrons and positive ions is called neutral plasma. Certain solids containing fixed positive ions surrounded by free electrons can be treated as neutral plasma. Let N be the number density of free electrons, each of mass m. When the electrons are subjected to an electric field, they are displaced relatively away from the heavy positive ions. If the electric field becomes zero, the electrons begin to oscillate about the positive ions with a natural angular frequency ω_p, which is called the plasma frequency.

To sustain the oscillations, a time varying electric field needs to be applied that has an angular frequency ω, where a part of the energy is absorbed and a part of it is reflected. As ω approaches ω_p, all the free electrons are set to resonance together and all the energy is reflected. This is the explanation of high reflectivity of metals.

64. Taking the electronic charge as e and the permittivity as ε_0, use dimensional analysis to determine the correct expression for ω_p.

(a) $\sqrt{\dfrac{Ne}{m\varepsilon_0}}$

(b) $\sqrt{\dfrac{m\varepsilon_0}{Ne}}$

(c) $\sqrt{\dfrac{Ne^2}{m\varepsilon_0}}$

(d) $\sqrt{\dfrac{m\varepsilon_0}{Ne^2}}$

65. Estimate the wavelength at which plasma reflection will occur for a metal having the density of electrons $N \approx 4 \times 10^{27}$ m^{-3}. Take $\varepsilon_0 \approx 10^{-11}$ and $m \approx 10^{-30}$, where these quantities are in proper SI units.

(a) 800 nm

(b) 600 nm

(c) 300 nm

(d) 200 nm

Directions (Q. 66 to 68) : Phase space diagrams are useful tools in analysing all kinds of dynamical problems. They are especially useful in studying the changes in motion as initial position and momentum are changed. Here we consider some simple dynamical systems in one dimension. For such systems, phase space is a plane in which position is plotted along horizontal axis and momentum is plotted along vertical axis. The phase space diagram is $x(t)$ *vs* $p(t)$ curve in this plane. The arrow on the curve indicated the time flow. For example, the phase space diagram for a particle moving with constant velocity is a straight line as shown in the figure. We use the sign convention in which position or momentum upwards (or to right) is positive and downwards (or to left) in negative.

66. The phase space diagram for a ball thrown vertically up from ground is

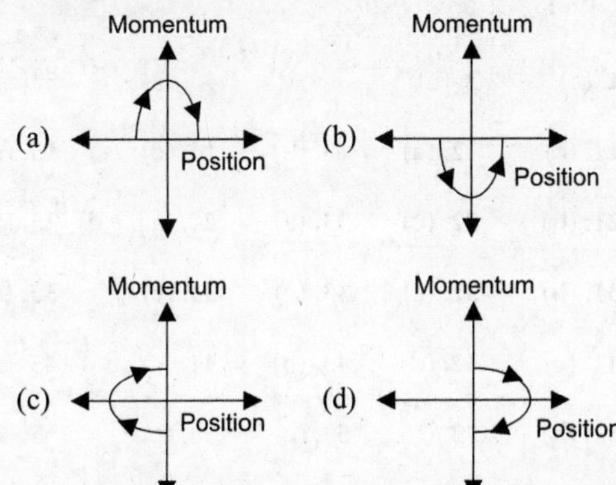

67. The phase space diagram for simple harmonic motion is a circle centered at the origin. In the figure, the two circles represent the same oscillator but for different initial conditions, and E_1 and E_2 are the total mechanical energies respectively. Then,

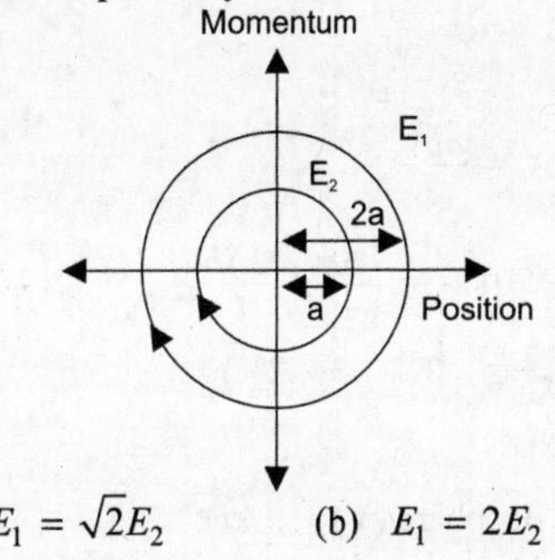

(a) $E_1 = \sqrt{2}E_2$ (b) $E_1 = 2E_2$

(c) $E_1 = 4E_2$ (d) $E_1 = 16E_2$

68. Consider the spring mass system, with the mass submerged in water, as shown in the figure. The phase space diagram for one cycle of this system is

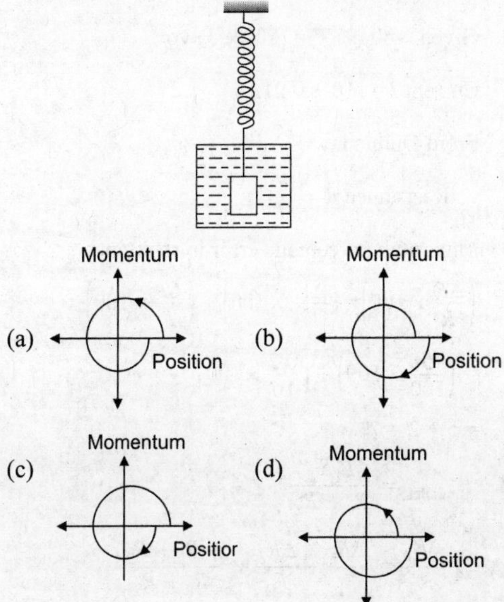

Answers

1. (a)	**2.** (c)	**3.** (c)	**4.** (c)	**5.** (c)	**6.** (b)	**7.** (c)	**8.** (d)	**9.** (b)	**10.** (c)
11. (c)	**12.** (a)	**13.** (b)	**14.** (c)	**15.** (a)	**16.** (d)	**17.** (d)	**18.** (b)	**19.** (c)	**20.** (c)
21. (b)	**22.** (c)	**23.** (a)	**24.** (a,b,c,d)	**25.** (b,c)	**26.** (a,b,c)	**27.** (b,c)	**28.** (a)	**29.** (b)	**30.** (c)
31. (b)	**32.** (c)	**33.** (c)	**34.** (c)	**35.** (a)	**36.** (a)	**37.** (d)	**38.** (b)	**39.** (d)	**40.** (a)
41. (c)	**42.** (d)	**43.** (b)	**44.** (c)	**45.** (a)	**46.** (a)	**47.** (b)	**48.** (b)	**49.** (a)	**50.** (a)
51. (b)	**52.** (b)	**53.** (c)	**54.** (c)	**55.** (d)	**56.** (b)	**57.** (a)	**58.** (b)	**59.** (a)	**60.** (d)
61. (a)	**62.** (a)	**63.** (c)	**64.** (c)	**65.** (b)	**66.** (d)	**67.** (c)	**68.** (d)		

Explanations

1. Given, $X = \dfrac{ab^2}{c^3}$

$$\therefore \frac{\Delta X}{X} \times 100 = \pm\left(\frac{\Delta a}{a} + \frac{2\Delta b}{b} + \frac{3\Delta c}{c}\right) \times 100$$

$= \pm (1\% + 2 \times 3\% + 3 \times 2\%)$

$= \pm 13\%$

2. Volume of sphere (V) = $\dfrac{4}{3}\pi r^3$

Percentage error in volume = $\dfrac{3 \times \Delta r}{r} \times 100$

$= \left(\dfrac{3 \times 0.1}{5.3}\right) \times 100$

3. Given, voltage $V = (100 \pm 5)$ volt,

Current $I = (10 \pm 0.2)$ A

From Ohm's law $V = IR$

$\therefore$ Resistance $R = \dfrac{V}{I}$

Maximum percentage error in resistance

$$\left(\frac{\Delta R}{R} \times 100\right) = \left(\frac{\Delta V}{V} \times 100\right) + \left(\frac{\Delta I}{I} \times 100\right)$$

$$= \left(\frac{5}{100} \times 100\right) + \left(\frac{0.2}{10} \times 100\right)$$

$= 5 + 2 = 7\%$

4. $R_{\text{parallel}} = \dfrac{R_1 R_2}{R_1 + R_2}$

$$\Rightarrow \frac{\Delta R_p}{R_p} = \frac{\Delta R_1}{R_1} + \frac{\Delta R_2}{R_2} + \frac{\Delta(R_1 + R_2)}{R_1 + R_2}$$

$$\Rightarrow \frac{\Delta R_p}{R_p} = \frac{0.3}{6} + \frac{0.2}{10} + \frac{0.3 + 0.2}{10 + 6}$$

$$\therefore \frac{\Delta R_p}{R_p} \times 100 = 10.125\%$$

5. Given $\quad v = \dfrac{p}{2l}\left[\dfrac{F}{m}\right]^{1/2}$

Squaring the equation on either side, we have

$$v^2 = \frac{p^2}{4l^2}\left[\frac{F}{m}\right]$$

$$\Rightarrow m = \frac{p^2 F}{4l^2 v^2}$$

or $[m] = \dfrac{[\text{MLT}^{-2}]}{[\text{L}^2][\text{T}^{-1}]^2} = [\text{ML}^{-1}\text{T}^0]$

6. Given, $p = \dfrac{a - t^2}{bx}$ or $pbx = a - t^2$

By the law of homogenity of dimensions

Dimensions of a = dimensions of $t^2 = [\text{T}^2]$

Dimensions of b = dimensions of $\dfrac{t^2}{px}$

$= [\text{M}^{-1}\text{T}^4]$

So, dimensions of $\dfrac{a}{b}$ is $[\text{ML}^{-2}]$

7. $[\text{ML}^2\text{T}^{-3}\text{A}^{-1}]$ are the dimensions of potential

Because, potential = $\dfrac{\text{energy}}{\text{charge}}$

$$= \frac{[ML^2T^{-2}]}{[AT]} = [\text{ML}^2\text{T}^{-3}\text{A}^{-1}]$$

8. Given $T \alpha p^a d^b E^c$

We have $[M^0L^0T] = k\,[ML^{-1}T^{-2}]^a\,[ML^{-3}]^b\,[ML^2T^{-2}]^c$

where k is a constant.

Comparing dimensions of similar terms, we have

$[M^0L^0T] = k\,[M^{a+b+c}L^{-a-3b+2c}T^{-2a-2c}$

Comparing powers of M, we have

$0 = a + b + c$ ....(i)

Comparing powers of L, we have

$0 = -a - 3b + 2c$ ....(ii)

Comparing powers of T, we have

$1 = -2a - 2c$ .....(iii)

Solving Eqs. (i), (ii) and (iii), we have

$a = -\frac{5}{6}, b = \frac{1}{2}, c = \frac{1}{3}$

9. [Momentum] = $[MLT^{-1}]$

Planck's constant = $[ML^2T^{-1}]$

Not same

Rest all are same.

10. $c^2 = \frac{1}{\mu_0\varepsilon_0}$ [where c is the speed of light]

Dimensions of $\frac{1}{\mu_0\varepsilon_0}$ is (velocity)^2

i.e., $[LT^{-1}]^2 = [L^2T^{-2}]$

11. The correct dimensions of viscosity is $[ML^{-1}T^{-1}]$

12. Out of the following pair, torque and work have same dimensions.

13. Dimensions of inductance, *i.e.*, henry are $[ML^2/Q^2]$.

14. Moment of inertia and moment of a force do not have same dimensions.

15. Magnitude of momentum

$P = mV = 3.513 \times 5.00 \approx 17.6$

Because in both the parameters least significant figure are 3.

16. Diameter of wire

= (main scale reading) + (circular scale reading) × (least count) + zero error

$= 3 + 35 \times \left(\frac{0.5}{50}\right) + 0.03 = 3.38$ mm

17. 30 VSD = 29 MSD

$1\text{ VSD} = \frac{29}{30}\text{MSD}$

$1\text{MSD} - 1\text{ VSD} = 1 - \frac{29}{30} = \frac{1}{30}\text{MSD}$

Least count = $\frac{1}{30} \times 0.5$

$= \frac{1}{60}$ degree or one minute

18. Number of significant figures in 23.023 are 5. Number of significant figures in 0.0003 are 1. Number of significant figures in 2.1×10^{-3} are 2.

19. Least count of screw gauge $= \frac{1}{100}$ mm = 0.01 mm

diameter of the wire = Divisions on circular scale × Least count + main scale reading

$= 52 \times 0.01 + 0$

$= 0.52$ mm $= 0.052$ cm

20. Magnetic field (B) $= \frac{F}{qv} = \frac{[MLT^{-2}]}{[C][LT^{-1}]}$

$= [MC^{-1}T^{-1}]$

21. The quantity $Y = \frac{X}{3Z^2}$

Thus, $[Y] = \frac{[M^{-1}L^{-2}T^2Q^2]}{[MT^{-1}Q^{-1}]^2}$

$[Y] = [M^3L^{-2}T^4Q^4]$

22. This physical quantity is energy per unit volume. Thus, its dimensions are

$\frac{ML^2T^{-2}}{L^3} = [ML^{-1}T^{-2}]$

23. volume (V) $= (1.2 \times 10^{-2})^3 = 1.728 \times 10^{-6}$ m^3 but since side length is having only two significant figure. Hence, volume will also contain two significant figures.

Thus, $V = 1.7 \times 10^{-6}$ m^3

24. $|\varepsilon_0| = \frac{[IT]^2}{[MLT^{-2}][L^2]}$

$[\varepsilon_0] = [M^{-1}L^{-3}T^4I^2]$

$\frac{1}{\sqrt{\mu_0\varepsilon_0}} = c$

$[\mu_0] = \frac{1}{\varepsilon_0 c^2}$

$\therefore$ Dimensions of $[\mu_0] = [MLT^{-2}I^{-2}]$

Thus, (b) and (c) are correct choices.

25. Reynolds number $= \frac{\text{Inertial force}}{\text{Viscous force}}$ = Dimensionless

Curie = No. of atoms/time = $|T^{-1}|$

Frequency = $|T^1|$

Latent heat $= \frac{\text{Energy}}{\text{Mass}}$

Gravitational potential $= \frac{\textit{Energy}}{\textit{Mass}}$

Thus, only (a), (b), (c) are correct.

26. $[M^0L^1T^0] = [G]^x\,[c]^y\,[h]^z$

$[M^0L^1T^0] = [M^{-1}L^3T^{-2}]^x\,[LT^{-1}]^y\,[ML^2T^{-1}]^z$

Thus, $z - x = 0$

$3x + y + 2z = 1$

$-2x - y - z = 0$

Solving, we get $\begin{cases} x = 1/2 \\ y = -3/2 \\ z = 1/2 \end{cases}$

27. (a), (b), (c) and (d) all are correct

$\phi = L.I \quad \Rightarrow [L] = \dfrac{\text{weber}}{\text{ampere}}$

$e = L\dfrac{dI}{dt} \quad \Rightarrow [L] = \left(\dfrac{\text{volt - second}}{\text{ampere}}\right)$

$U = \dfrac{1}{2}LI^2 \Rightarrow [L] = \dfrac{\text{joule}}{\text{ampere}^2}$

$e = L^2\dfrac{\Delta t}{t} \Rightarrow [L] = \left(\dfrac{e}{\Delta i}\right).(\Delta t)$

= (Resistance) × (Time) = (ohm × second)

28. 1.8355×10^5

29. 7.43×10^{42}

30. 2.476×10^{32}

31. Principle of homogenity to identify the answer

32. as $\rho = \dfrac{a}{V^2} = a = \rho V^2$

33. From homogenity principle

$a = ML^5T^{-2}, b = L^3$

$\therefore \dfrac{a}{v^2} = \dfrac{ML^5T^{-2}}{L^6} \neq ML^{-2}T^{-2}$

34. Total mass = 0.000087 + 0.0123 = 0.012387 kg. The mass of the bee is accurate upto sixth decimal place in kg, whereas the mass of the flower is accurate only upto the fourth decimal place. Hence the sum must be rounded off to the fourth decimal place. Therefore the correct choice is (c).

35. $A = \pi r^2 = 3.142 \times (0.021)^2 = 0.00138562\ \text{cm}^2$. Now, there are only two significant figures in 0.021 cm. Hence the result must be rounded off to two significant figure as $A = 0.0014\ \text{cm}^2$, which is choice (a).

36. Average speed $= \dfrac{100.5\ \text{m}}{10.3\ \text{s}} = 9.7573\ \text{ms}^{-1}$

The distance has four significant figures but the time has only three. Hence, the result must be rounded off to three significant figure to $9.76\ \text{ms}^{-1}$. Thus the correct choice is (a).

37. $\overline{P_1}\sqrt{\dfrac{\epsilon_0}{\mu}} = \dfrac{1}{z}$ = Impedence

$A^2T^3M^{-1}L^{-2}$

38. By Coulomb's law, we have

$F = \dfrac{1}{4\pi\varepsilon_0}\dfrac{q_1q_2}{R^2}$

$\varepsilon_0 = \dfrac{q_1q_2}{4\pi FR^2}$

On putting the units, we have

$\varepsilon_0 = N - m^2 = \dfrac{[AT]^2}{[MLT^{-2}][L^2]} = [M^{-1}L^{-3}T^4A^2]$

39. Dipole moment = (charge) × (distance)

Electric flux = (electric field) × (area)

Hence, the correct option is (d).

40. $\left[\dfrac{\alpha Z}{k\theta}\right] = [M^0L^0T^0]$

$[\alpha] = \left[\dfrac{k\theta}{Z}\right]$

Now

$[P] = \left[\dfrac{\alpha}{\beta}\right]$

$[\beta] = \left[\dfrac{\alpha}{P}\right] = \left[\dfrac{k\theta}{Zp}\right]$

As Dimensions of $k\,\theta$ represents energy. Hence,

$[\beta] = \left[\dfrac{ML^2T^{-2}}{LML^{-1}T^{-2}}\right] = [M^0L^2T^0]$

41. As $\dfrac{E}{B} = v$

So $\dfrac{E}{B} = \left[LT^{-1}\right]$

$[E] = [B]\,[L]\,[T]^{-1}$

42. $C = \dfrac{1}{\sqrt{\mu_0\varepsilon_0}} \Rightarrow C^2 = \dfrac{1}{\mu_0\varepsilon_0}$

$L^2T^{-2} = \dfrac{1}{\mu_0\varepsilon_0}$

$[\mu_0] = [\varepsilon_0]^{-1}\,[L]^{-2}\,[T]^2$

43. $r = \dfrac{(1-a)}{(1+a)}$

$\ln r = \ln(1-a) - \ln(1+a)$

So $\dfrac{\Delta r}{r} = \dfrac{\Delta a}{1-a} + \dfrac{\Delta a}{1+a}$

$\dfrac{\Delta r}{r} = \dfrac{2\Delta a}{1-a^2}$

$(1+a)\dfrac{\Delta r}{(1-a)} = \dfrac{2(\Delta a)}{(1-a^2)}$

So $\Delta r = \dfrac{2\Delta a}{(1+a)^2}$

44. Let number of nuclei decayed be N.

As we know that

$N = N_0(1 - e^{-\lambda t})$

$\lambda t = \ln\left(\frac{N_0}{N_0 - N}\right)$

$\lambda t = \ln N_0 - \ln(N_0 - N)$

$(\Delta\lambda)t = \frac{dN}{(N_0 - N)}$

$(\Delta\lambda) = \frac{40}{(3000 - 1000)} = 0.02\ s^{-1}$

45. Percentage error in m an $\frac{\Delta m}{m} \times 100 = 1.5$

Percentage error in length $\frac{\Delta \ell}{\ell} \times 100 = 1$

density is given by $d = \frac{m}{\ell^3}$

Now $\Rightarrow \frac{\Delta d}{d} \times 100 = \frac{\Delta m}{m} \times 100 + \frac{3\Delta \ell}{\ell} \times 100$

$= 1.5 + 3 = 4.5\%$

46. Distance moved by the stone

$L = \frac{1}{2}gt^2 = \frac{1}{2} \times 10 \times t^2$

$t_1 = \sqrt{\frac{L}{5}}$

$\therefore$ Time interval between dropping a stone and splash here is.

$dt = \frac{1}{\sqrt{5}}\frac{1}{2}L^{-1/2}dL + \left(\frac{1}{300}dL\right)$

$dt = \frac{1}{2\sqrt{5}}\frac{1}{\sqrt{20}}dL + \frac{dL}{300} = 0.01$

$dL\left(\frac{1}{20} + \frac{1}{300}\right) = 0.01$

$dL\left[\frac{15}{300}\right] = 0.01,\ dL = \frac{3}{16}$

$\frac{dL}{L} \times 100 = \frac{3}{16} \times \frac{1}{20} \times 100 = \frac{15}{16} \simeq 1\%$

47. As Least count of the instrument

$= \frac{\text{Pitch}}{\text{Number of Divisions on circular scale}} = \frac{0.5\text{mm}}{50}$

$\therefore$ LC = 0.01

Negative zero error = –5× LC = –0.005 mm

Measured value = main scale reading (M.S.R) + screw gauge reading – zero error

= 0.5 mm + {25 × 0.01 – (–0.05)} mm = 0.8 mm

48. For vernier C_1

10 VSD = 9 MSD = 9 mm

1 VSD = 0.9 mm

$\Rightarrow$ LC = 1 MSD – 1 VSD = 1mm – 0.9 mm = 0.1 mm

Reading of C_1 = MSR + (VSR) (LC)

= 28 mm + (7) (0.1)

Reading of C_1 = 28.7 mm = 2.87 cm

For vernier C_2 : the vernier C_2 is abnormal

So, we have to find the reading from basics.

The point where both of the marks are matching:

Distance measured from main scale = distance measured from vernier scale

28 mm + (1 mm) (8) = (28 mm + x) + (1.1 mm) (7)

on, Solving we get, x = 0.3 mm

Hence reading of C_2 = 28 mm + 0.3 mm = 2.83 cm

49. Time period is given by, $T = \frac{t}{n}$

As we know, $T = 2\pi\sqrt{\frac{L}{g}}$, $T^2 = 4\pi^2\frac{L}{g}$

$\Rightarrow g = \frac{(4\pi^2)L}{T^2} = \frac{(4\pi^2)(L)}{\left(\frac{t}{n}\right)^2} = (4\pi^2 n^2)\frac{L}{t^2}$

Percentage error in the value of 'g' will be

$\frac{\Delta g}{g} \times 100 = \left(\frac{\Delta L}{L}\right) \times 100 + 2\left(\frac{\Delta t}{t}\right) \times 100$

$= \frac{0.1}{20} \times 100 + 2 \times \left(\frac{1}{90}\right) \times 100$

$= 2.72\%$

$\therefore$ The nearest answer is 3%

50. Here Given that, $I = (e^{1000V/T} - 1)$ mA, $dV = \pm 0.01$V

$T = 300$ K

So, $I = e^{1000V/T} - 1$

$I + 1 = e^{1000V/T}$

Taking log on both sides, we get

$\log(I + 1) = \frac{1000V}{T}$

On differentiating, $\frac{dI}{I+1} = \frac{1000}{T}dV$

$dI = \frac{1000}{T} \times (I + 1)dV$

$\Rightarrow \quad dI = \frac{1000}{300} \times (5 + 1) \times 0.01 = 0.2$ mA

So, error in the value of current is 0.2 mA.

51. If student measures 3.50 cm, it means that there is an uncertainly of the order 0.01 cm.

For vernier scale with 1 MSD = $\frac{1}{10}$ cm

and 9 MSD = 10 VSD

LC of vernier caliper is given by = 1MSD – 1VSD

$= \frac{1}{10}\left(1-\frac{9}{10}\right)=\frac{1}{100}$ cm = 0.01 cm

52. Here 1 MSD = 5.15 cm – 5.10 cm = 0.05 cm

So 1 VSD = $\frac{2.45}{50}$ cm = 0.049 cm

∴ LC = 1 MSD – 1 VSD = 0.01 cm

Hence, diameter of cylinder = (Main scale reading) + (Vernier scale reading) (LC)

= 5.10 + (24) (0.001) = 5.124 cm

53. Here $\Delta d = \Delta l = \frac{0.5}{100}$ mm = 0.005 mm

As we know that young's modulus is given by

$$Y = \frac{MLg}{\pi l d^2} \Rightarrow \left(\frac{\Delta Y}{Y}\right)_{\max} = \left(\frac{\Delta l}{l}\right) + 2\left(\frac{\Delta d}{d}\right)$$

Hence percentage error in length

$$\left(\frac{\Delta l}{l}\right) = \frac{0.5/100}{0.25} = 0.02 \text{ and } \frac{2\Delta d}{d} = \frac{(2)(0.5/100)}{0.5} = 0.02$$

or $\frac{\Delta l}{l} = 2\frac{\Delta d}{d}$

54. Here L.C of screw gauge = $\frac{0.5}{50}$ = 0.01 mm = Δr

Diameter, r = 2.5 mm + 20 × $\frac{0.5}{50}$ = 2.70 mm

$\frac{\Delta r}{r} = \frac{0.01}{2.70}$ or $\frac{\Delta r}{r} \times 100 = \frac{1}{2.7}$

Now, density, $d = \frac{m}{V} = \frac{m}{\frac{4}{3}\pi\left(\frac{r}{2}\right)^3}$

Here, r is the diameter.

Percentage error in diameter will be

$$\frac{\Delta d}{d} \times 100 = \left\{\frac{\Delta m}{m} + 3\left(\frac{\Delta r}{r}\right)\right\} \times 100$$

$$= \frac{\Delta m}{m} \times 100 + 3 \times \left(\frac{\Delta r}{r}\right) \times 100$$

$$= 2\% + 3 \times \frac{1}{2.7} = 3.11\%$$

55. LC of vernier calipers

LC = 1 MSD – 1 VSD

$= \frac{\text{Smallest division on main scale}}{\text{Number of divisions on vernier scale}}$

20 divisions of vernier scale = 16 divisions of main scale

∴ 1 VSD = $\frac{16}{20}$ mm = 0.8 mm

Hence, LC = 1MSD – 1VSD = 1 mm – 0.8 mm = 0.2 mm

56. $T = 2\pi\sqrt{\frac{l}{g}}$ or $\frac{t}{n} = 2\pi\sqrt{\frac{l}{g}}$

$$\therefore\ g = \frac{(4\pi^2)(n^2)l}{t^2}$$

% error in $g = \frac{\Delta g}{g} \times 100 = \left(\frac{\Delta l}{l} + \frac{2\Delta t}{t}\right) \times 100$

$$E_I = \left(\frac{0.1}{64} + \frac{2 \times 0.1}{128}\right) \times 100 = 0.3125\%$$

$$E_{II} = \left(\frac{0.1}{64} + \frac{2 \times 0.1}{64}\right) \times 100 = 0.46875\%$$

$$E_{III} = \left(\frac{0.1}{20} + \frac{2 \times 0.1}{36}\right) \times 100 = 1.055\%$$

Hence E_I is minimum.

57. Length of air column in resonance is odd integer multiple of $\lambda/4$.

58. Young's modulus of elasticity $Y = \frac{FL}{Al} = \frac{4FL}{\pi d^2 l}$

$$= \frac{(4)(1.0 \times 9.8)(2)}{\pi(0.4 \times 10^{-3})^2(0.8 \times 10^{-3})}$$

= 2.0 × 10^{11} N/m^2

Further $\frac{\Delta Y}{Y} = 2\left(\frac{\Delta d}{d}\right) + \left(\frac{\Delta l}{l}\right)$

So ∴ $\Delta Y = \left\{2\left(\frac{\Delta d}{d}\right) + \left(\frac{\Delta l}{l}\right)\right\} Y$

$$= \left\{2 \times \frac{0.01}{0.4} + \frac{0.05}{0.8}\right\} \times 2.0 \times 10^{11}$$

= 0.225 × 10^{11} N/m^2 = 0.2 × 10^{11} N/m^2

On rounding off

or $(Y \pm \Delta Y) = (2 \pm 0.2) \times 10^{11}$ N/m^2

59. As Least count (LC)

$$= \frac{\text{Pitch}}{\text{Number of divisions on circular scale}}$$

$$= \frac{0.5}{50} = 0.01 \text{ mm}$$

Now, diameter of ball

= (2 × 0.5 mm) + (25 – 5) (0.01)

= 1.2 mm

60. As Density, $\rho = \frac{m}{\pi r^2 L}$

So percentage error in density.

$$\therefore\ \frac{\Delta\rho}{\rho} \times 100 = \left(\frac{\Delta m}{m} + 2\frac{\Delta r}{r} + \frac{\Delta L}{L}\right) \times 100$$

On putting the values, we get the maximum percentage error in density = 4%

Hence, the correct option is (d).

61. Given density = 128 Kgm^{-3}

$$= 128(20 \times 50g)\left(\frac{1}{4 \times 25}\right)^3 = \frac{128 \times 20}{4^3}(50g)\left(\frac{1}{25\text{cm}}\right)^3$$

$$= 40(50g)\left(\frac{1}{25\text{cm}}\right)^3$$

62. Mass $m = \frac{4\pi R^3}{3} \times \rho$

On taking log both sides, we have

$$\text{In}(m) = \text{In}\left(\frac{4\pi}{3}\right) + \text{In}(\rho) + 3\text{In}(R)$$

On differentiating with respect to time, we get

$$0 = 0 + \frac{1 d\rho}{\rho\, dt} + \frac{3}{R}\frac{dR}{dt}$$

$$\Rightarrow \left(\frac{dR}{dt}\right) = -R \times \frac{1}{\rho}\left(\frac{d\rho}{dt}\right)$$

$$\because \frac{dR}{dt} = v$$

$$\therefore v = -R \propto \frac{1}{\rho}\left(\frac{d\rho}{dt}\right)$$

$$\therefore v \propto R$$

63. $\mathbf{S} = \mathbf{P} + b\mathbf{R} = \mathbf{P} + b(\mathbf{Q} - \mathbf{P}) = \mathbf{P}(1 - b) + b\mathbf{Q}$

64. N = Number of electrons per unit volume

$\therefore$ [N] = [L^{-3}], [e] = [q] = [It] = [AT]

[ε_0] = [$M^{-1}L^{-3}T^4A^2$]

Putting the dimensions, we can see that

$$\left[\sqrt{\frac{Ne^2}{m\varepsilon_0}}\right] = [T^{-1}]$$

Angular frequency has also the dimension [T^{-1}]

65. As we know $\omega = \frac{2\pi}{T} = 2\pi f = \omega = 2\pi f = \frac{2\pi c}{\lambda}$

$$\therefore \lambda = \frac{2\pi c}{\omega} = \frac{2\pi c}{\sqrt{\frac{Ne^2}{m\varepsilon_0}}}$$

On putting the values, we get $\lambda \simeq$ 600 nm.

66. Momentum is first positive but decreasing. Displacement (or say position) is initially zero. It will first increase. At highest point, momentum is zero and displacement is maximum. After that momentum is downwards (negative) and increasing but displacement is decreasing. Only (d) option satisfies these conditions.

67. $E = \frac{1}{2} m\omega^2 A^2$ or $E \propto A^2$,

$$\frac{E_2}{E_1} = \left(\frac{A_2}{A_1}\right)^2 = \left(\frac{a}{2a}\right)^2 \text{ or } E_1 = 4E_2$$

68. In all the given four figure, at mean position, the position coordinate is zero.

At the same time, mass is starting from the extreme position in all four cases. In Fig. (c) and (d), extreme position is more than the initial extreme position. But due to viscosity opposite should be the case.

Hence, the answer should be either option (a) or option (b).

Correct answer is (b), because mass starts from positive extreme position (from uppermost position). Then, it will move downwards or momentum should be negative.

3

CHAPTER

Mass, Weight and Density

MASS

Mass is a fundamental property of matter that measures the quantity of matter contained within objects and it represents the inherent resistance of an object to changes in its state of motion and is often considered a measure of the amount of substance present. Mass is an intrinsic property and remains constant regardless of an object's location or the presence of gravity. It also represents the quantity of matter an object possesses and remains constant regardless of its location. The SI unit for mass is the kilogram (kg).

Mass can be measured using various units, including grams (g), metric tons (t), and ounces (oz). The conversion between units is as follows: 1 kg = 1000 g, 1 kg = 0.001 (t), 1 kg ≈ 35.27 (oz)

In simpler terms mass can be thought of as the "stuff" or material that makes up an object. It is the measure of how much matter an object contains. The greater the mass of an object, the more matter it possesses.

According to the law of conservation of mass, mass cannot be created or destroyed but can only be converted from one form to another. In any physical or chemical process, the total mass of the system remains constant.

Property of Mass:

Mass is a fundamental property of matter with several key characteristics:

1. Inertia: Mass is closely related to an object's inertia, which is the tendency of an object to resist changes in its state of motion. Objects with greater mass have greater inertia, meaning they require more force to accelerate or decelerate. This property is described by Newton's first law of motion, often referred to as the law of inertia.
2. Scalar Quantity: Mass is a scalar quantity, meaning it is described only by its magnitude and does not have a specific direction. The mass of an object is always positive and cannot be negative.
3. Additive Mass: When multiple objects are combined, the total mass is equal to the sum of the individual masses. For example, if two objects have masses m_1 and m_2, respectively, the total mass when they are combined is $m_1 + m_2$.
4. Conservation: According to the law of conservation of mass, mass is conserved in any isolated system. This means that in a closed system, the total mass before and after any physical or chemical process remains the same. Mass cannot be created or destroyed, only rearranged or converted into different forms.
5. Universal Gravitational Interaction: Mass interacts with other masses through gravitational forces. Every object with mass exerts a gravitational pull on other objects, and this force is proportional to the product of their masses and inversely proportional to the square of the distance between them. The universal law of gravitation, formulated by Sir Isaac Newton, describes this interaction.
6. Measurement: Mass is typically measured using the International System of Units (SI), specifically in kilograms (kg) or its multiples such as grams (g) or metric tons (t). Mass can also be measured using other units like ounces (oz) or pounds (lb) in non-SI systems.
7. Independence from Location: Mass is an intrinsic property of matter that remains constant regardless of an object's location or the presence of gravity. It is the same on Earth, in space, or on any other planet. Mass is different from weight, which is the force of gravity acting on an object and can vary with the strength of gravity.

Application of Mass:

Mass plays a crucial role in various scientific disciplines and has numerous practical applications. Here are a few examples and applications of mass:

1. Newton's Second Law of Motion: Mass is a key component of Newton's second law, which states that the acceleration of an object is directly proportional to the net force applied to it and inversely proportional to its mass. This law is fundamental in understanding and predicting the motion of objects under the influence of forces.
2. Engineering and Construction: Mass is a critical factor in designing structures, vehicles, and machines. Engineers must consider the mass of materials and components to ensure structural integrity, stability, and performance.

For example, when designing bridges or buildings, engineers need to calculate the mass of the structure to determine the appropriate materials and support systems.

3. Aerospace and Aviation: In the aerospace industry, mass plays a vital role in spacecraft and aircraft design. Engineers need to carefully calculate and distribute the mass of various components to ensure proper balance, stability, and fuel efficiency. Determining the mass of payloads, fuel, and equipment is crucial for successful missions.
4. Medicine and Pharmacology: Mass is essential in pharmaceutical research and dosage calculations. The mass of active ingredients in medications must be accurately measured and controlled to ensure the desired therapeutic effects and minimize potential side effects. Pharmacists and medical professionals rely on precise mass measurements to determine appropriate drug dosages for patients.
5. Environmental Sciences: Mass measurements are crucial in environmental sciences to assess pollution levels and monitor environmental impacts. For example, scientists measure the mass of pollutants in air, water, and soil samples to determine contamination levels and develop mitigation strategies. Mass measurements of greenhouse gases also help in understanding climate change.
6. Astrophysics and Cosmology: Mass plays a central role in astrophysics and cosmology, helping scientists understand the formation and evolution of celestial objects. The mass of stars, planets, galaxies, and black holes is measured and used to study gravitational interactions, stellar evolution, and the large-scale structure of the universe.

WEIGHT

Weight is a concept in physics that refers to the force exerted on an object due to gravity. It is a measure of how heavy an object is and is often represented by the symbol "W" or "Fg" (force of gravity). Weight is distinct from mass, although the two terms are often used interchangeably in everyday language.

1. Definition of Weight: Weight is defined as the force experienced by an object due to the gravitational attraction between the object and the Earth (or any other celestial body). It is a vector quantity, meaning it has both magnitude and direction. The magnitude of the weight is equal to the force of gravity acting on the object, while the direction is towards the center of the Earth.
2. Relationship between Weight and Mass: Mass and weight are related but different physical quantities. Mass refers to the amount of matter present in an object and is a scalar quantity. It remains constant regardless of the location of the object. Weight, on the other hand, depends on the gravitational field strength and varies with the location of the object.

   The relationship between weight and mass is given by Newton's second law of motion:

   $$F = m \times a$$

   where F is the force, m is the mass of the object, and a is the acceleration. In the case of weight, the force is the weight (W), mass (m) is the mass of the object, and the acceleration (a) is the acceleration due to gravity (g). Therefore, we have:

   $$W = m \times g$$

   Where, g is the acceleration due to gravity. On Earth's surface, the standard value for g is approximately 9.8 m/s^2. This equation shows that weight is directly proportional to the mass of an object. Consequently, if the mass increases, the weight also increases proportionally.
3. Units of Weight: The SI unit for weight is the Newton (N), named after Sir Isaac Newton. One Newton is defined as the force required to accelerate a one-kilogram mass by one meter per second squared. In everyday usage, weight is often expressed in pounds (lb) or kilograms (kg). For example, a person weighing 150 pounds has a weight of approximately 680 Newton's.
4. Weight and Gravitational Field Strength: Weight depends on the strength of the gravitational field acting on the object. The gravitational field strength varies depending on the distance from the center of the massive body. On Earth, the gravitational field strength is approximately constant near its surface but decreases with increasing distance from the surface (such as at higher altitudes or in outer space).

   As a result, an object will weigh less when moved to a location where the gravitational field strength is weaker. For example, an object on the Moon would weigh approximately one-sixth of its weight on Earth due to the Moon's weaker gravity.
5. Weightlessness: In situations where an object or a person experiences negligible gravitational forces, such as during free fall or in orbit around a planet, the sensation of weightlessness occurs. Weightlessness does not mean the absence of mass but rather the absence of a sensation of weight. Astronauts in space experience weightlessness because they are in a state of continuous free fall around the Earth.

The property of weight:

The property of weight refers to the measure of the gravitational force exerted on an object due to its mass. Weight is a vector quantity, which means it has both magnitude and direction. Weight is often confused with mass, but they are different concepts. Mass is a measure of the amount of matter in an object and is a scalar quantity, whereas weight depends on both the mass of an object and the acceleration due to gravity. The weight of an object can vary depending on the gravitational field strength, whereas its mass remains constant.

Applications of Weight:

The concept of weight has numerous practical applications across various fields. Here are some common applications of weight:

1. Engineering and Construction: Weight plays a crucial role in designing structures and determining load capacities. Engineers consider the weight of materials, equipment, and occupants to ensure the stability and integrity of buildings, bridges, and other structures.
2. Transportation and Logistics: Weight is essential in determining the maximum load capacity of vehicles such as trucks, airplanes, and ships. It is used to calculate payload capacity, fuel efficiency, and distribution of weight for safe transportation.
3. Product Design and Manufacturing: Weight is a critical factor in designing and manufacturing products, especially those involving safety, ergonomics, or portability. For example, the weight of a car affects its performance and fuel efficiency, while the weight of a handheld device influences its user-friendliness.
4. Health and Medicine: Weight is an essential measurement in the field of medicine. It is used to monitor patient health, calculate medication dosages, assess nutritional requirements, and diagnose conditions such as obesity. Body mass index (BMI), a weight-to-height ratio, is widely used to evaluate the overall health and risk factors associated with weight.
5. Agriculture and Food Industry: Weight is critical in agricultural practices, including the weighing of crops, livestock, and machinery. In the food industry, weight is used to measure ingredients, portion sizes, and packaging quantities to ensure consistency and quality control.
6. Astronomy and Space Exploration: Understanding the concept of weight is crucial in studying celestial bodies. Weight plays a role in calculating gravitational forces between objects, determining the trajectories of spacecraft, and analyzing the effects of gravity on astronauts during space missions.

DENSITY

Density is a physical property that measures how much mass is contained within a given volume. It is a fundamental property of matter and is often used to characterize and compare different substances.

Density can vary widely depending on the material or substance being considered. For example, substances like lead and gold are dense, meaning they have a high mass in a given volume. On the other hand, substances like air or helium are less dense, as they have a low mass in a given volume.

Density is often used to identify and classify materials. For instance, it can help differentiate between solids, liquids, and gases, as they have different densities due to the arrangement and spacing of their particles. Density can also be used to determine the purity or composition of a substance, as different materials typically have different densities.

One practical application of density is buoyancy. In fluids, an object will float or sink depending on its density relative to the density of the fluid. If the object is less dense than the fluid, it will float; if it is denser, it will sink. This principle is why objects made of wood or foam float on water, while metals sink.

The relationship between weight and density can be understood by considering the formula:

Weight = Mass × Acceleration due to gravity

Density is calculated by dividing the mass of an object or substance by its volume. The formula for density is:

Density = Mass / Volume

The standard SI unit for density is kilograms per cubic meter (kg/m^3), but other units such as grams per cubic centimeter (g/cm^3) or pounds per cubic inch (lb/in^3) are also commonly used.

From these formulas, we can see that weight depends on both mass and the acceleration due to gravity, while density depends on mass and volume.

The property of density:

Density is a fundamental property of matter that describes how much mass is contained within a given volume. It is commonly denoted by the symbol "ρ" (rho) and is calculated by dividing the mass of an object or substance by its volume. Density is a useful property because it helps us compare and classify different materials based on how closely their atoms or molecules are packed together. Materials with higher density have more mass in a given volume and are generally considered denser than materials with lower density.

Different states of matter have different average densities. Generally, solids are denser than liquids, and liquids are denser than gases. For example, water is denser in its liquid state compared to its solid (ice) or gaseous (water vapor) states.

Density is affected by temperature and pressure. As temperature increases, most substances expand and become less dense, while cooling them down usually increases their density. Similarly, increasing pressure can compress materials and increase their density, while decreasing pressure can cause them to expand and decrease in density.

Applications of density:

Density has numerous applications across various fields. Here are some common applications of density:

1. Identification of substances: Density is often used as a characteristic property to identify and classify substances. By measuring the density of an unknown material and comparing it to known densities of different substances, scientists can determine the composition and purity of the material.
2. Material selection: Density plays a crucial role in material selection for different applications. For example, in construction, the density of materials like concrete, wood, and steel is considered to ensure structural integrity and load-bearing capacity.

3. Buoyancy and flotation: Density is essential in understanding buoyancy and flotation. Objects with a lower density than the fluid they are immersed in will float, while those with a higher density will sink. This principle is utilized in designing ships, submarines, and flotation devices like life jackets and buoys.
4. Fluid mechanics: Density is a key parameter in fluid mechanics, where it affects fluid flow, pressure, and viscosity. It is used in calculations related to fluid dynamics, including the design of pipelines, pumps, and hydraulic systems.
5. Pharmaceutical industry: Density is crucial in the pharmaceutical industry for drug formulation and dosage calculations. It helps determine the concentration of active ingredients in a medication and ensures accurate dosing.
6. Environmental monitoring: Density measurements are employed in environmental monitoring to assess water quality. Changes in water density can indicate variations in temperature, salinity, or pollutant levels, providing valuable information for ecological studies.
7. Geology and mineralogy: Density is used to identify and classify minerals and rocks in geology. It helps determine the composition and type of geological formations, aiding in mineral exploration and resource evaluation.
8. Food and beverage industry: Density measurements are used in quality control and process monitoring within the food and beverage industry. It helps assess the concentration of ingredients, monitor fermentation processes, and ensure product consistency.

Types of density:

Density is a physical property that measures the amount of mass per unit volume of a substance. There are several types of density that are commonly referred to:

1. Energy density: Energy density refers to the amount of energy stored in a given volume or mass of a substance. It is commonly used in fields such as physics, engineering, and materials science. The unit for energy density depends on the context and can be expressed in joules per cubic meter (J/m^3), watt-hours per kilogram (Wh/kg), or other appropriate units.
2. Charge density: Charge density is a measure of the electric charge per unit volume of a material or a system. It is commonly used in physics and electrical engineering to describe the distribution of electric charge. The unit for charge density is coulombs per cubic meter (C/m^3).
3. Linear density: Linear density refers to the mass per unit length of a one-dimensional object, such as a string, wire, or thread. It is calculated by dividing the mass of the object by its length. The unit for linear density depends on the system of measurement used, such as kilograms per meter (kg/m) or grams per centimeter (g/cm)..
4. Mass density: Mass density, as mentioned earlier, is the most common type of density and is applicable to fluids as well. It represents the mass per unit volume of the fluid. The mass density of a fluid determines its inertia and is often used to characterize the fluid's behavior. The standard unit for mass density of fluids is kilograms per cubic meter (kg/m^3) in the SI system.
5. Fluid density: Fluid density specifically refers to the mass density of a fluid, such as a liquid or a gas. It represents how much mass is contained within a given volume of the fluid. Fluid density is an important property in fluid mechanics and is often used in calculations involving fluid flow, buoyancy, and pressure.
6. Weight density: Weight density, also known as gravitational density, is the force per unit volume exerted by a substance due to gravity. It is calculated by multiplying the mass density by the acceleration due to gravity (g). The units of weight density depend on the units used for mass density and acceleration due to gravity. For example, if mass density is given in kg/m^3 and g is approximately 9.8 m/s^2, then the weight density would be expressed in newton's per cubic meter (N/m^3).
7. Relative density: Relative density, also called specific gravity, compares the density of a substance to the density of a reference substance, usually water. It is a dimensionless quantity and is calculated by dividing the density of the substance by the density of the reference substance. Since water is commonly used as the reference substance, the relative density of water is typically 1. Relative density is often used to determine the purity or composition of a substance by comparing it to a known standard.
8. Volumetric density: Volumetric density, also known as volume density, is the reciprocal of the specific volume of a fluid. It represents the volume occupied by a unit mass of the fluid. Volumetric density is the inverse of mass density and is often used in thermodynamics and fluid mechanics. The unit for volumetric density is cubic meters per kilogram (m^3/kg).
9. Number density: Number density, as mentioned earlier, is a measure of the number of particles per unit volume. In the context of fluids, number density refers to the concentration of particles, such as molecules or ions, in the fluid. It is particularly relevant in studies involving gases or solutions. The unit for number density is particles per cubic meter (particles/m^3).
10. Partial density: Partial density refers to the density of a specific component or species within a mixture or solution. It represents the mass per unit volume of that particular component. Partial density is commonly used in chemical engineering and environmental science to analyze the composition and properties of mixtures. The unit for partial density is typically the same as mass density (kg/m^3).

Measurement of density

The density at any point of a homogeneou object equals its total mass divided by its total volume. The mass is normally measured with an appropriate scale or balance; the volume may be measured directly from the geometry of the object) or by the displarement of a fluid. Hydrostatic weighing, for instance uses, the displaoement of water due to a submerged object to determine the density of the object.

If the body is not homogeneous, then the density is a function of the position. In that case the density around any given location is determined by calculating the density of a small volume around that location. In the limit of an infinitesimal vohlme the density of an inhomogeneous object at a point becomes: $\rho(r)=dm/dV$, where dV is an elementary volume at position r. The mass of the body then can be expressed as

$$m = \int_V \rho(r)\, dV.$$

The density of granular material can be ambiguous depending on exactly how its volume is defined, and this may cause confusion in measurement. A common example is sand: if it is gently poured into a container, the density, will be low; if the same sand is then compacted it will occupy less volume and consequently exhibit a greater density. This is because sand, like all powders and granular solids, contains a lot of air space in between individual grains. The density of the material including the air spaces is the bulk density which differs significantly from the density of an individual grain of sand with no air in.eluded.

Specific gravity for measure the density:

Specific gravity is a relative measure of density that compares the density of a substance to the density of water at a specified temperature and pressure. It is a dimensionless quantity and is often used in industries such as mining and metallurgy to determine the concentration of minerals in ores or the purity of metals.

Mathematically, the specific gravity of a substance is measure by dividing its density by the density of the reference substance. Since water is commonly used as the reference substance, the specific gravity of a material is often a comparison of its density to that of water.

The formula for specific gravity (SG) is:

S.G = density of substance / density of water

Since water has a density of 1 gram per cubic centimeter (g/cm^3) or 1000 kilograms per cubic meter (kg/m^3), the specific gravity of a substance is numerically equivalent to its density in relation to water.

For example, if the specific gravity of a substance is 2, it means that the substance is twice as dense as water. If the specific gravity is less than 1, it means the substance is less dense than water.

Changes of density

In general, density can be changed by changing either the pressure or the temperature. Increasing the pressure always increases the density of a materal. Increasing the temperature generally decreases the density but there are notable exception to this generalization. For example, the density of water increases between its melting point at 0 °C and 4 °C; similar behavior is observed in silicon at low temperatures.

The effect of pressure and temperature on the densities of liquids and solids is small. The compressibility for a typical liquid or solid is 10^{-6} bar^{-1} (1 bar = 0.1 MPa) and a typical thermal expansivity is 10^{-5} K^{-1}. This roughly translates into needing around ten thousand times atmospheric pressure to reduce the volume of a substance by one percent. Although the pressures needed may be around a thousand times smaller for sandy soil and some clays.) A one percent expansion of volume typically requires a tempernture increase on the order of thousands of degrees Celsius.

In contrast, the density of gases is strongly affected by pressure. The density of an ideal gas is

$$\rho = \frac{MP}{RT},$$

where M is the molar mass, P is the pressure R is the universal gas constant, and T is the absolute temperature. This means that the density of an ideal gas can be doubled by doubling the pressure, or by halving the absolute temperature.

Density of solutions

The density of a solution is the sum of mass (massic) concentrations of the components of that solution. Mass (massic) concentration of a given component ρ_i in a solution can be called partial density of that component.

$$\rho = \sum_i \rho_i$$

Expressed as a function of the densities of pure components of the mixture and their volume participation it read:

$$\rho = \sum_i \rho_{0}i \frac{V_0 i}{V}$$

Densities of Various Materials

Material	ρ in kg/m^3	Notes
Interstellar medium	10^{-25} – 10^{-15}	Assuming 90% H, 10% He; variable T
Earth's atmosphere	1.2	At sea level
Aerogel	1 – 2	
Styrofoam	30 – 120[6]	
Cork	220 – 260[6]	
Potassium	860[]	At STP
Sodium	970	At STP
Ice	916.7	
Water (fresh)	1000	At STP
Water (salt)	1030	
Plastics	850 – 1400	For polypropylene and PETE/PVC
Magnesium	1740	At STP

Gold	19320	At STP
Plutonium	19840	At STP
Platinum	21450	At STP
Iridium	22420	At STP
Osmium	22570	At STP
The core of the Sun	~150000	
White dwarf star	1×10^{9}[9]	
Atomic nuclei	2.3×10^{17} [10]	Does not depend strongly on size of nucleus

Neutron star	8.4×10^{16} – 1×10^{18}	
Black hole	4×10^{17}	Mean density inside the Schwarzschild radius of an Earth-mass black hole (theoretical)

Beryllium	1850	At STP
Glycerol[7] [8]	1261	
Silicon	2330	At STP
Aluminium	2700	At STP
Titanium	4540	At STP
Selenium	4800	At STP
The Earth	5515.3	Mean density
Vanadium	6100	At STP
Antimony	6690	At STP
Zinc	7000	At STP
Chromium	7200	At STP
Manganese	7210 - 7440	At STP
Tin	7310	At STP
Iron	7870	At STP
Niobium	8570	At STP
Cadmium	8650	At STP
Cobalt	8900	At STP
Nickel	8900	At STP
Copper	8920 – 8960	Near room temperature
Bismuth	9750	At STP
Molybdenum	10220	At STP
Silver	10500	At STP
Lead	11340	Near room temperature
Thorium	11700	At STP
Rhodium	12410	At STP
The Inner Core of the Earth	~13000	As listed in Earth
Mercury	13546	At STP
Tantalum	16600	At STP
Uranium	18800	At STP
Tungsten	19300	At STP

Objective Type Questions

1. Which of the following best defines mass?
   (a) The force exerted on an object
   (b) The amount of matter in an object
   (c) The volume occupied by an object
   (d) The speed at which an object moves
2. What is the SI unit of mass?
   (a) Kilogram (kg) (b) Meter (m)
   (c) Second (s) (d) Newton (N)
3. Which of the following statements is true about mass?
   (a) It depends on the gravitational field.
   (b) It changes with temperature.
   (c) It is a vector quantity.
   (d) It is conserved in all physical processes.
4. Which property of mass determines the amount of gravitational force between two objects?
   (a) Inertia (b) Weight
   (c) Volume (d) Density
5. Which of the following is an example of an extensive property of mass?
   (a) Density (b) Weight
   (c) Volume (d) Inertia
6. Which principle states that the acceleration of an object is directly proportional to the force acting on it and inversely proportional to its mass?
   (a) Newton's first law (b) Newton's second law
   (c) Newton's third law (d) Archimedes' principle
7. The inertia of an object is directly related to its:
   (a) Acceleration (b) Mass
   (c) Weight (d) Volume
8. Which property of mass determines how difficult it is to change the state of motion of an object?
   (a) Inertia (b) Weight
   (c) Volume (d) Density
9. Which of the following statements is true about the gravitational force acting on an object?
   (a) It depends on the mass of the object.
   (b) It depends on the shape of the object.
   (c) It depends on the volume of the object.
   (d) It depends on the density of the object.
10. Which of the following is an application of mass spectrometry?
    (a) Determining the volume of an object
    (b) Measuring the mass of celestial bodies
    (c) Calculating the density of a liquid
    (d) Studying the properties of electromagnetic waves
11. Which property of mass is used in the equation $E = mc^2$?
    (a) Density (b) Weight
    (c) Inertia (d) Energy equivalence
12. Which of the following devices measures the mass of an object?
    (a) Thermometer (b) Barometer
    (c) Spectrometer (d) Balance
13. Which property of mass is used to determine the purity of a substance?
    (a) Inertia (b) Weight
    (c) Density (d) Melting point
14. Which of the following statements is true about the relationship between mass and acceleration?
    (a) Greater mass always leads to greater acceleration.
    (b) Greater mass always leads to smaller acceleration.
    (c) Mass and acceleration are unrelated.
    (d) The relationship between mass and acceleration depends on the force applied.
15. Which property of mass determines the amount of matter contained within a given volume?
    (a) Inertia (b) Weight
    (c) Density (d) Kinetic energy
16. Which of the following is an application of mass balance?
    (a) Measuring the speed of an object
    (b) Determining the volume of a gas
    (c) Measuring the force exerted by an object
    (d) Quantifying the mass of a substance
17. Which property of mass plays a crucial role in the formation of stars and galaxies?
    (a) Inertia (b) Weight
    (c) Volume (d) Gravitational attraction
18. Which of the following is an example of a macroscopic application of mass?
    (a) Atomic mass spectroscopy
    (b) Gravitational wave detection
    (c) Particle accelerator experiments
    (d) Measurement of drug doses
19. Which property of mass determines the gravitational potential energy of an object?
    (a) Inertia (b) Weight
    (c) Volume (d) Height
20. Which of the following is an example of an application of mass in engineering?
    (a) Determining the color of an object
    (b) Designing structures to withstand forces
    (c) Measuring the acidity of a solution
    (d) Studying the behavior of subatomic particles

21. What is weight?
(a) The amount of matter in an object
(b) The force of gravity acting on an object
(c) The measure of an object's size
(d) The density of an object

22. Which of the following is not a property of weight?
(a) Weight is a vector quantity.
(b) Weight depends on the mass of an object.
(c) Weight is measured in kilograms.
(d) Weight can change with location.

23. When you travel to the Moon, your weight will:
(a) Increase (b) Decrease
(c) Remain the same (d) Become zero

24. The weight of an object can be determined by:
(a) Measuring its mass
(b) Measuring its volume
(c) Using a spring scale
(d) Counting the number of atoms in the object

25. Which of the following statements about weight is true?
(a) Weight and mass are the same thing.
(b) Weight is a scalar quantity.
(c) Weight can be negative.
(d) Weight depends on the shape of an object.

26. Which of the following objects will have the greatest weight on Earth?
(a) A 1 kg iron ball
(b) A 1 kg feather
(c) A 1 kg piece of wood
(d) They will all have the same weight.

27. The weight of an object is least on which of the following planets?
(a) Earth (b) Mars
(c) Jupiter (d) Venus

28. Which of the following factors does not affect the weight of an object?
(a) Mass of the object
(b) Distance from the center of the Earth
(c) Altitude above sea level
(d) Temperature of the object

29. The weight of an object on the Moon is approximately:
(a) One-sixth of its weight on Earth
(b) One-fourth of its weight on Earth
(c) Half of its weight on Earth
(d) The same as its weight on Earth

30. Which property allows weight to be measured using a balance scale?
(a) Inertia (b) Density
(c) Volume (d) Mass

31. The weight of an object in free fall is:
(a) Zero (b) Constant
(c) Increasing (d) Decreasing

32. Which of the following is an application of weight measurement?
(a) Determining the volume of an object
(b) Calculating the density of a substance
(c) Balancing chemical equations
(d) Measuring the force exerted by an object

33. The weight of an object is directly proportional to its:
(a) Density (b) Volume
(c) Mass (d) Temperature

34. Which of the following materials would have the greatest weight for the same volume?
(a) Wood (b) Plastic
(c) Steel (d) Aluminum

35. Which instrument is commonly used to measure weight?
(a) Barometer (b) Thermometer
(c) Hydrometer (d) Spring scale

36. Which property of weight allows objects to sink or float in a fluid?
(a) Buoyancy (b) Elasticity
(c) Viscosity (d) Cohesion

37. Weight is a measure of an object's:
(a) Speed (b) Size
(c) Force (d) Temperature

38. The weight of an object can be calculated using the formula:
(a) Weight = Mass × Volume
(b) Weight = Mass ÷ Volume
(c) Weight = Mass × Acceleration
(d) Weight = Mass × Gravity

39. Which of the following is not an example of weight conversion?
(a) Pounds to kilograms (b) Ounces to grams
(c) Newtons to pounds (d) Inches to meters

40. The weight of an object on the surface of the Earth is approximately:
(a) 9.8 N/kg (b) 1 N
(c) 9.8 kg (d) 1 kg

41. Which of the following statements about weight and mass is correct?
(a) Weight and mass are the same thing.
(b) Weight is a measure of the amount of matter in an object.
(c) Mass is a measure of the force of gravity acting on an object.
(d) Weight and mass have different units of measurement.

42. Which of the following is not a unit of weight?
(a) Newton (N) (b) Kilogram (kg)
(c) Pound (lb) (d) Gram (g)

43. Weightlessness occurs when:
(a) An object is in free fall
(b) An object is at rest on a surface
(c) The weight of an object is zero
(d) An object is in equilibrium

44. Which of the following is an example of weight being balanced by another force?
(a) A book resting on a table
(b) A car accelerating on a road
(c) A balloon floating in the air
(d) A person standing on the ground

45. The weight of an object is greatest at:
(a) The North Pole (b) The Equator
(c) Sea level (d) High altitudes

46. Which of the following is not a property of weight?
(a) Weight is a vector quantity.
(b) Weight depends on the location.
(c) Weight is independent of the mass of an object.
(d) Weight can be measured using a spring scale.

47. Weight plays a significant role in which of the following sports?
(a) Basketball (b) Gymnastics
(c) Swimming (d) Chess

48. Which property allows weight to be used in determining the stability of an object?
(a) Inertia (b) Elasticity
(c) Friction (d) Momentum

49. Which of the following industries relies heavily on weight measurement?
(a) Automotive (b) Information technology
(c) Fashion (d) Entertainment

50. Which property of weight allows it to be used in determining the mass of an object?
(a) Inertia (b) Buoyancy
(c) Gravitational force (d) Surface area

51. What is the definition of density?
(a) The amount of matter in an object
(b) The mass of an object divided by its volume
(c) The weight of an object divided by its volume
(d) The size of an object divided by its weight

52. Which of the following units is used to measure density?
(a) Newton (b) Joule
(c) Pascal (d) Kilogram per cubic meter

53. Which of the following substances has the highest density?
(a) Air (b) Water
(c) Gold (d) Aluminum

54. Which property does not affect the density of an object?
(a) Temperature (b) Pressure
(c) Shape (d) Mass

55. Which of the following substances has the lowest density?
(a) Lead (b) Iron
(c) Styrofoam (d) Copper

56. What happens to the density of a substance as its temperature increases?
(a) Density increases
(b) Density decreases
(c) Density remains constant
(d) Density depends on the substance

57. Which property allows objects with greater density to float on objects with lower density?
(a) Buoyancy (b) Gravity
(c) Viscosity (d) Inertia

58. Which instrument is used to measure the density of a liquid?
(a) Barometer (b) Hydrometer
(c) Thermometer (d) Manometer

59. Which property of density enables the layering of different liquids?
(a) Viscosity (b) Surface tension
(c) Refractive index (d) Relative density

60. Which property of density is used in medical imaging techniques like X-rays?
(a) Absorption (b) Reflection
(c) Refraction (d) Dispersion

61. Which property of density is used to separate substances in centrifugation?
(a) Viscosity (b) Solubility
(c) Buoyancy (d) Magnetic susceptibility

62. Which property of density is utilized in flotation devices?
(a) Viscosity (b) Compressibility
(c) Buoyancy (d) Refraction

63. Which factor has the most significant influence on the density of an object?
(a) Volume (b) Mass
(c) Temperature (d) Pressure

64. What is the density of an object that has a mass of 500 grams and a volume of 100 cubic centimeters?
(a) 5 g/cm³ (b) 50 g/cm³
(c) 100 g/cm³ (d) 500 g/cm³

65. Which property of density is used in the production of alloys?
(a) Reactivity (b) Ductility
(c) Malleability (d) Solubility

66. Which property of density is important in the design of skyscrapers and bridges?
(a) Elasticity (b) Tensile strength
(c) Hardness (d) Brittleness

67. Which property of density is responsible for the greenhouse effect?
(a) Absorption (b) Reflection
(c) Refraction (d) Scattering

68. Which property of density is used in the production of batteries?
(a) Conductivity (b) Elasticity
(c) Hardness (d) Solubility

69. Which property of density is used in geology to identify and classify minerals?
(a) Color (b) Hardness
(c) Luster (d) Specific gravity

70. Which property of density is used in the determination of alcohol content in beverages?
(a) Refractive index (b) Viscosity
(c) Density (d) Surface tension

71. Which property of density is utilized in the operation of hot air balloons?
(a) Viscosity (b) Buoyancy
(c) Surface tension (d) Refractive index

72. Which property of density is used in the flotation process to extract minerals from ore?
(a) Magnetic susceptibility
(b) Conductivity
(c) Surface tension
(d) Frothability

73. Which property of density is important in the selection of materials for shipbuilding?
(a) Ductility (b) Elasticity
(c) Compressibility (d) Buoyancy

74. Which property of density is used in the measurement of blood sugar levels?
(a) Conductivity (b) Refractive index
(c) Viscosity (d) Optical density

75. Which property of density is used in the production of plastics and polymers?
(a) Elasticity (b) Solubility
(c) Viscosity (d) Melt flow index

76. Which property of density is used in the determination of the purity of precious metals?
(a) Hardness (b) Conductivity
(c) Reactivity (d) Luster

77. Which property of density is used in the design of building insulation materials?
(a) Thermal conductivity
(b) Viscosity
(c) Surface tension
(d) Elasticity

78. Which property of density is utilized in the operation of air conditioning and refrigeration systems?
(a) Surface tension (b) Viscosity
(c) Latent heat (d) Thermal expansion

79. Which property of density is used in the analysis of petroleum products?
(a) Viscosity (b) Flash point
(c) Pour point (d) API gravity

80. Which property of density is important in the design of lightweight construction materials?
(a) Hardness
(b) Brittleness
(c) Compressive strength
(d) Specific strength

81. Which property of density is used in the determination of air pollution levels?
(a) Reflectivity (b) Transparency
(c) Absorption (d) Scattering

82. Which property of density is important in the field of aerodynamics?
(a) Surface tension (b) Viscosity
(c) Drag coefficient (d) Elastic modulus

83. Which property of density is used in the determination of groundwater levels?
(a) Permeability (b) Porosity
(c) Capillarity (d) Specific yield

84. Which property of density is utilized in the design of soundproofing materials?
(a) Elasticity
(b) Conductivity
(c) Absorption coefficient
(d) Malleability

85. Which property of density is used in the analysis of soil composition?
(a) pH level
(b) Particle size distribution
(c) Organic matter content
(d) Bulk density

86. Which property of density is important in the selection of materials for radiation shielding?
(a) Absorption coefficient
(b) Transparency
(c) Conductivity
(d) Damping coefficient

87. Which property of density is used in the measurement of fluid flow rates?
(a) Viscosity (b) Pressure
(c) Surface tension (d) Flow velocity

88. Which property of density is important in the design of vehicle safety features?
(a) Friction coefficient (b) Impact resistance
(c) Surface tension (d) Yield strength

89. Which property of density is utilized in the analysis of air quality?
(a) Reflectivity (b) Transparency
(c) Absorption (d) Scattering

90. Which property of density is important in the design of filtration systems?
(a) Porosity (b) Surface tension
(c) Permeability (d) Optical density

91. Which property of density is used in the measurement of soil moisture content?
(a) Conductivity (b) Capillarity
(c) Permeability (d) Water holding capacity

92. Which property of density is utilized in the design of optics and lenses?
(a) Refractive index (b) Elasticity
(c) Viscosity (d) Surface tension

93. Which property of density is used in the determination of water purity?
(a) pH level (b) Electrical conductivity
(c) Turbidity (d) Hardness

94. Which property of density is important in the design of packaging materials?
(a) Biodegradability (b) Elastic modulus
(c) Flexibility (d) Specific volume

95. Which property of density is utilized in the analysis of air humidity?
(a) Viscosity (b) Dew point
(c) Vapor pressure (d) Relative humidity

96. Which property of density is used in the determination of soil compaction?
(a) Permeability (b) Particle size distribution
(c) Bulk density (d) Organic matter content

97. Which property of density is important in the design of heat exchangers?
(a) Thermal conductivity
(b) Thermal expansion
(c) Specific heat capacity
(d) Thermal diffusivity

98. Which property of density is utilized in the determination of the concentration of solutions?
(a) pH level (b) Molarity
(c) Viscosity (d) Freezing point depression

99. Which property of density is important in the selection of materials for aerospace applications?
(a) Ductility (b) Thermal expansion
(c) Specific strength (d) Reflectivity

100. Which property of density is used in the determination of the sugar content in fruits and beverages?
(a) Refractive index (b) Viscosity
(c) Solubility (d) Optical density

Answers

1. (b)	**2.** (a)	**3.** (d)	**4.** (b)	**5.** (c)	**6.** (b)	**7.** (b)	**8.** (a)	**9.** (a)	**10.** (b)
11. (c)	**12.** (d)	**13.** (c)	**14.** (b)	**15.** (c)	**16.** (d)	**17.** (d)	**18.** (d)	**19.** (b)	**20.** (b)
21. (b)	**22.** (c)	**23.** (b)	**24.** (c)	**25.** (c)	**26.** (d)	**27.** (b)	**28.** (d)	**29.** (a)	**30.** (d)
31. (a)	**32.** (d)	**33.** (c)	**34.** (c)	**35.** (d)	**36.** (a)	**37.** (c)	**38.** (d)	**39.** (d)	**40.** (a)
41. (d)	**42.** (b)	**43.** (a)	**44.** (a)	**45.** (a)	**46.** (c)	**47.** (c)	**48.** (a)	**49.** (a)	**50.** (a)
51. (b)	**52.** (d)	**53.** (c)	**54.** (c)	**55.** (c)	**56.** (b)	**57.** (a)	**58.** (b)	**59.** (d)	**60.** (a)
61. (c)	**62.** (c)	**63.** (b)	**64.** (a)	**65.** (c)	**66.** (a)	**67.** (a)	**68.** (a)	**69.** (d)	**70.** (c)
71. (b)	**72.** (d)	**73.** (d)	**74.** (d)	**75.** (d)	**76.** (b)	**77.** (a)	**78.** (c)	**79.** (d)	**80.** (d)
81. (c)	**82.** (c)	**83.** (d)	**84.** (c)	**85.** (d)	**86.** (a)	**87.** (a)	**88.** (b)	**89.** (c)	**90.** (a)
91. (d)	**92.** (a)	**93.** (b)	**94.** (d)	**95.** (d)	**96.** (c)	**97.** (a)	**98.** (b)	**99.** (c)	**100.** (a)

Explanations

1. The amount of matter in an object. Mass is a fundamental property of matter that represents the quantity of matter in an object.
2. The kilogram is the base unit of mass in the International System of Units (SI).
3. Mass is a conserved quantity, meaning it remains constant regardless of changes in gravitational field or temperature. It is conserved in all physical processes.
4. Weight is the force experienced by an object due to the gravitational attraction of another object and is directly proportional to mass.
5. Extensive properties depend on the amount of substance present, and volume is an example of such a property.
6. Newton's second law of motion states that the acceleration of an object is directly proportional to the net force acting on it and inversely proportional to its mass.
7. Inertia is the resistance of an object to changes in its motion and is directly related to the mass of the object.
8. Inertia is the property of mass that determines how difficult it is to change the state of motion of an object.
9. The gravitational force acting on an object is directly proportional to its mass. It depends on the mass of the object.
10. Mass spectrometry is a technique used to measure the masses and relative abundances of atoms and molecules, and it has applications in various fields, including astronomy. So, it measuring the mass of celestial bodies.
11. The equation $E = mc^2$, derived by Einstein, relates energy (E) to the mass (m) of an object and the speed of light (c). It highlights the equivalence of mass and energy.
12. A balance is a device used to measure the mass of an object by comparing it with known masses.
13. The density of a substance can be used to determine its purity since impurities can affect the density.
14. According to Newton's second law of motion, for a given force, the acceleration is inversely proportional to the mass. Therefore, greater mass results in smaller acceleration and smaller acceleration.
15. Density is the ratio of mass to volume and provides information about the amount of matter contained within a given volume.
16. The mass of a substance. A mass balance is a device used to measure the mass of an object or substance accurately.
17. The mass of celestial bodies, such as stars and galaxies, determines the strength of their gravitational attraction, which plays a crucial role in their formation and behavior.
18. While the other options involve studying or measuring properties at the atomic or subatomic level, the measurementof drug doses involves the macroscopic application of mass.
19. The gravitational potential energy of an object is determined by its weight, which is directly related to its mass.
20. Designing structures to withstand forces. In engineering, knowledge of mass is essential for designing structures that can withstand the forces acting on them, ensuring their stability and safety.
21. Weight is the force of gravity acting on an object, so the correct answer is (b).
22. Weight is actually measured in newtons, not kilograms. So, the correct answer is (c).
23. Your weight will decrease on the Moon because the Moon has less gravitational force than Earth. So, the correct answer is (b).
24. The weight of an object can be determined by using a spring scale, which measures the force of gravity acting on the object. So, the correct answer is (c).
25. Weight and mass are not the same thing. Weight is a vector quantity, and it can never be negative. So, the correct answer is (c).
26. The weight of an object depends on its mass and the force of gravity. Since all the objects have the same mass (1 kg) and are on Earth, they will all have the same weight. So, the correct answer is (d).
27. The weight of an object is least on Mars because Mars has less gravitational force compared to Earth. So, the correct answer is (b).
28. The temperature of an object does not affect its weight. Weight depends on the mass of the object and the distance from the center of the Earth. So, the correct answer is (d).
29. The weight of an object on the Moon is approximately one-sixth of its weight on Earth because the Moon has approximately one-sixth of the gravitational force of Earth. So, the correct answer is (a).
30. Weight cannot be directly measured using a balance scale. Instead, a balance scale measures mass, which is indirectly related to weight. So, the correct answer is (d).
31. In free fall, the weight of an object is zero because there is no support force acting on it. So, the correct answer is (a).
32. Measuring the force exerted by an object is an application of weight measurement. So, the correct answer is (d).

33. The weight of an object is directly proportional to its mass. So, the correct answer is (c).

34. The weight of an object depends on its mass, not its volume. Therefore, the material with the highest density would have the greatest weight for the same volume. In this case, steel typically has a higher density than wood, plastic, and aluminum. So, the correct answer is (c).

35. A spring scale is commonly used to measure weight. So, the correct answer is (d).

36. Buoyancy, which is the upward force exerted on an object submerged in a fluid, determines whether an object will sink or float. So, the correct answer is (a).

37. Weight is a measure of the force of gravity acting on an object. So, the correct answer is (c).

38. The weight of an object can be calculated using the formula Weight = Mass × Gravity, where gravity is the acceleration due to gravity. So, the correct answer is (d).

39. Converting inches to meters is a conversion of length, not weight. So, the correct answer is (d).

40. The weight of an object on the surface of the Earth is approximately 9.8 N/kg, which is the acceleration due to gravity. So, the correct answer is (a).

41. Weight and mass are not the same thing. Mass is a measure of the amount of matter in an object, while weight is the force of gravity acting on an object. They have different units of measurement as well. So, the correct answer is (d).

42. Kilogram (kg) is not a unit of weight; it is a unit of mass. So, the correct answer is (b).

43. Weightlessness occurs when an object is in free fall and there is no support force acting on it. So, the correct answer is (a).

44. A book resting on a table is an example of weight being balanced by the support force exerted by the table. So, the correct answer is (a).

45. The weight of an object is greatest at the poles because the Earth's gravitational force is slightly stronger there due to the shape of the Earth. So, the correct answer is (a).

46. Weight is dependent on the mass of an object, so weight is not independent of mass. So, the correct answer is (c).

47. Weight plays a significant role in swimming because buoyancy and the weight of the swimmer affect their ability to float and move through the water. So, the correct answer is (c).

48. Inertia, which is the resistance of an object to changes in its motion, is related to weight and can be used to determine the stability of an object. So, the correct answer is (a).

49. The automotive industry relies heavily on weight measurement for purposes such as determining fuel efficiency, load capacity, and vehicle safety. So, the correct answer is (a).

50. Inertia, which is the resistance of an object to changes in its motion, is related to mass and can be used to determine the mass of an object indirectly. So, the correct answer is (a).

51. Density is the measure of how much mass is contained in a given volume. So, the mass of an object divided by its volume.

52. Density is typically measured in kilograms per cubic meter (kg/m^3) in the International System of Units (SI).

53. Gold has a higher density than air, water, and aluminum. Its high atomic mass and compact structure contribute to its high density.

54. The shape of an object does not affect its density. Density depends on the mass and volume of the object.

55. Styrofoam is a lightweight material with low density, whereas lead, iron, and copper have higher densities.

56. As temperature increases, most substances expand and become less dense.

57. Objects with greater density than the surrounding fluid will sink, while objects with lower density will float due to the upward buoyant force.

58. A hydrometer is a device that measures the density or specific gravity of a liquid. It typically consists of a weighted glass tube.

59. The relative density of liquids determines the order in which they will layer when different liquids are carefully poured into a container.

60. X-rays are absorbed by different tissues in the body based on their density, allowing for the creation of images.

61. Centrifugation uses the differences in densities of substances to separate them based on their buoyant forces in a rotating container.

62. Flotation devices like life jackets work by providing enough buoyant force to keep a person afloat due to the density difference between their body and water.

63. The mass of an object has the greatest influence on its density, as density is calculated by dividing mass by volume.

64. Density is calculated by dividing the mass (500 g) by the volume (100 cm^3), resulting in 5 g/cm^3.

65. Malleability, the ability of a substance to be hammered into thin sheets, is important in the production of alloys with desired densities and properties.

66. Elasticity, the ability of a material to regain its shape after being deformed, is crucial in ensuring the stability and safety of structures under varying loads.

67. Greenhouse gases like carbon dioxide absorb and re-emit infrared radiation, contributing to the greenhouse effect and the warming of the Earth's atmosphere.

68. The density of conductive materials, such as metals, is important in the production of batteries to ensure efficient flow of electrical charges.

69. Specific gravity, a measure of the density of a substance relative to the density of water, is often used to identify and classify minerals.

70. The density of a beverage is used to determine its alcohol content. Alcohol has a lower density than water, so the density measurement can indicate the alcohol concentration.

71. Hot air balloons work based on the principle of buoyancy, where the hot air inside the balloon is less dense than the surrounding air, causing it to rise.

72. Froth flotation relies on the property of density to separate minerals from ore. The minerals attach to bubbles with lower density and rise to the surface.

73. The buoyancy of materials is crucial in shipbuilding to ensure that a ship can float and carry its intended load without sinking.

74. Optical density, also known as absorbance, is used in measuring blood sugar levels through spectrophotometry, where the density of glucose affects the absorption of light.

75. Melt flow index is a measure of the flowability of plastics and polymers and is influenced by their density, molecular weight, and processing conditions.

76. The electrical conductivity of precious metals is used to determine their purity, as impurities can affect their conductivity and, thus, their density.

77. The thermal conductivity of insulation materials affects their ability to resist heat transfer, which is crucial for maintaining energy efficiency in buildings.

78. Latent heat, the heat absorbed or released during phase changes, is utilized in air conditioning and refrigeration systems to cool or heat air or fluids.

79. API gravity is a measure of the density of petroleum products relative to the density of water. It helps classify and compare different petroleum fractions.

80. Specific strength, the strength of a material relative to its density, is important in designing lightweight construction materials that can maintain structural integrity.

81. The absorption of light by air pollutants is used to determine their concentrations and measure air pollution levels in the atmosphere.

82. The drag coefficient, which is influenced by the shape and density of an object, is crucial in understanding and optimizing aerodynamic performance.

83. Specific yield is the ratio of the volume of water that drains from an aquifer to the decrease in its water level, which is used to estimate groundwater levels.

84. The absorption coefficient of materials affects their ability to absorb sound energy, making it an important property in soundproofing applications.

85. Bulk density, the mass of soil per unit volume, is used in analyzing soil composition, assessing soil health, and determining its suitability for various applications.

86. The absorption coefficient of materials determines their ability to attenuate or absorb radiation, making it crucial for radiation shielding applications.

87. Viscosity, a measure of a fluid's resistance to flow, is used in determining fluid flow rates and designing systems such as pumps and pipelines.

88. The impact resistance of materials is crucial in designing vehicle safety features, such as bumpers and crumple zones, to protect occupants in collisions.

89. The absorption of light by air pollutants is used to analyze air quality and determine the presence and concentration of specific pollutants.

90. The porosity of filtration materials affects their ability to allow fluid flow while retaining particles of certain sizes, making it important in filtration system design.

91. Water holding capacity is the ability of a soil to retain water and is influenced by its density and porosity, making it a measure of soil moisture content.

92. The refractive index, a measure of how light is bent when passing through a medium, is crucial in designing optics and lenses with specific properties.

93. The electrical conductivity of water is influenced by dissolved ions and impurities, making it a measure of water purity and its mineral content.

94. Specific volume, the reciprocal of density, is used in the design of packaging materials to optimize space utilization and reduce transportation costs.

95. Relative humidity is a measure of the amount of water vapor present in the air compared to the maximum amount it can hold at a given temperature, influencing density.

96. Bulk density, the mass of soil per unit volume, is used in determining soil compaction levels and assessing the suitability of soil for plant growth.

97. The thermal conductivity of materials affects their ability to transfer heat and is crucial in the design of efficient heat exchangers for various applications.

98. Molarity is a measure of the concentration of a solution, expressed as the number of moles of solute per liter of solution, which is influenced by density.

99. Specific strength, the strength of a material relative to its density, is crucial in aerospace applications where weight reduction and structural integrity are important.

100. The refractive index of liquids is influenced by their density and is used to measure the sugar content in fruits and beverages, such as refractometers.

4

CHAPTER

Speed and Velocity

KINEMATICS

It deals with the motion of particles and rigid bodies without accounting for the forces responsible for their motion.

Motion: When the body changes position *w.r.t.* observer, the body is said to be in motion. If the body doesn't change position then it is said to be at rest *w.r.t.* observer.

Rectilinear Motion: If the body is, however, of a small size such that its motion can be described by a point mass moving along a straight line, such a motion is called rectilinear motion or motion in one dimension.

Distance and Displacement: Distance is the actual length covered along the path, while displacement is the difference between the final and initial positions of the particle. The position of a particle is given by a position vector drawn from the origin to the particle.

The figure illustrates the difference between distance and displacement. The curve length AB is called the distance; the vector $r_{AB} = r_B - r_A$ is called the displacement.

(a) Distance is a scalar; displacement is vector.

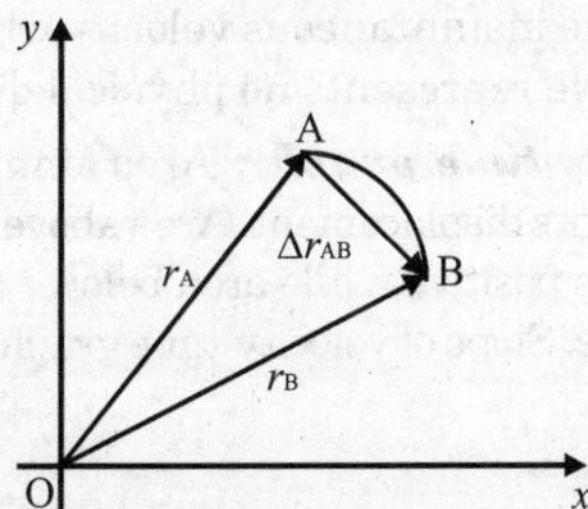

(b) The magnitude of displacement is always less than or equal to distance.

(c) For a moving body, displacement can be zero but distance cannot be zero.

Average Speed and Average Velocity

The average speed in a time interval is defined as the total distance travelled by the particle divided by the time interval.

$$\text{Average speed} = \frac{\text{Total distance travelled}}{\text{Total time taken}}$$

The average velocity is defined as

$$V_{av} = \frac{\text{displacement}}{\text{time elapsed}}$$

$$\text{or } \quad v = \frac{r_B - r_A}{t_B - t_A} = \frac{\Delta r_{AB}}{\Delta t}$$

(a) Average speed is a scalar quantity; average velocity is a vector quantity. Both are expressed in ms^{-1} or kmh^{-1}.

(b) Average velocity can be zero but average speed cannot be zero.

(c) The magnitude of average velocity is always less than or equal to the average speed.

$$|v_{av}| \le v \text{ or } \left|\frac{\text{displacement}}{\text{time elapsed}}\right| \le \frac{\text{distance}}{\text{time elapsed}}$$

thus $|\text{displacement}| \le \text{distance}$

(d) Average speed does not mean the magnitude of the average velocity vector.

(e) Consider a body moving on the straight line having the initial position A at time t_i at a distance x_i from the origin. It travels a distance x_1 to reach B and thereafter travels a distance x_2 from B to C reaching at time t_f. C is the final position is at a distance x_f from the origin. The average speed will be equal to ratio of total distance covered to the total time.

$$\therefore \quad \text{Average speed} = \frac{x_1 + x_2}{t_f - t_i}$$

$$\text{Average velocity} = \frac{x_f - x_i}{t_f - t_i}$$

Instantaneous Speed and Instantaneous Velocity

The instantaneous speed and velocity are the respective average speed and velocity for the infinitesimally small time interval (*i.e.* $\Delta t \to 0$). Thus

$$\text{Instantaneous speed } v = \lim_{\Delta t \to 0} \frac{\Delta r}{\Delta t} = \frac{dr}{dt}$$

$$\text{Instantaneous velocity } v = \lim_{\Delta t \to 0} \frac{\Delta r}{\Delta t} = \frac{dr}{dt}$$

(a) The instantaneous velocity direction is always tangential to the path followed by the particle.

(b) The instantaneous speed is equal to the magnitude of the instantaneous velocity.

(c) A particle may have constant speed but variable velocity.

(d) For a particle moving with constant velocity, its average velocity and instantaneous velocity are always equal.

Average Acceleration and Instantaneous Acceleration: The acceleration is defined as the time rate of change of velocity. The average acceleration is defined as

$$a_{av} = \frac{v_2 - v_1}{t_2 - t_1} = \frac{\Delta v}{\Delta t}$$

The instantaneous acceleration is defined as

$$a = \lim_{\Delta t \to 0} \frac{\Delta v}{\Delta t} = \frac{dv}{dt}$$

(a) Acceleration is a vector quantity with S.I. units ms^{-2}.

(b) The direction of average acceleration vector is the direction of the change in velocity vector.

(c) There is no definite relation between the direction of velocity vector and the direction of acceleration vector.

(d) If the magnitude of velocity is constant and only its direction changes with time, then acceleration is perpendicular to the velocity vector.

(e) If a body is moving on a straight line with uniform acceleration, for such a body, average acceleration and instantaneous acceleration will be the same.

Types of Motion:

Motion can be broadly classified into three types

(a) **Uniform Motion :** The acceleration is zero. So the velocity remains constant.

displacement = velocity*time

(b) **Uniformly Accelerated Motion :** The acceleration of the body remains constant. The motion is described by sets of equation called as Equation of Motion.

Equation of Motion

$$v = u + at$$

$$s = ut + \frac{1}{2}at^2$$

$$v^2 = u^2 + 2as$$

Also, we have an equation for distance travelled in n^{th} second given by

$$x_n = u + \frac{a}{2}(2n-1)$$

Sign Convention: We need to use sign convention while using Equation of motion. Generally, upward direction is taken as positive and downward direction is taken as negative. While direction along right is taken as positive and direction along left is taken as negative.

Non-Uniformly Accelerated Motion : The acceleration of the body is variable with time and position. Differentiation and Integration is used to solve such questions. We apply the following equations.

$$\frac{dv}{dt} = a \quad \text{...(i)}$$

$$\frac{dx}{dt} = v \quad \text{...(ii)}$$

Graphs:

(a) ***Position-time graph*** **:** The slope of $x - t$ curve gives the instantaneous velocity while area under the curve represents no physical quantity.

(b) ***Velocity-time graph*** **:** Area under $v - t$ curve represents displacement. Area above the time axis is taken as positive while area below t axis is taken as negative. Slope of velocity-time graph is accelertaion.

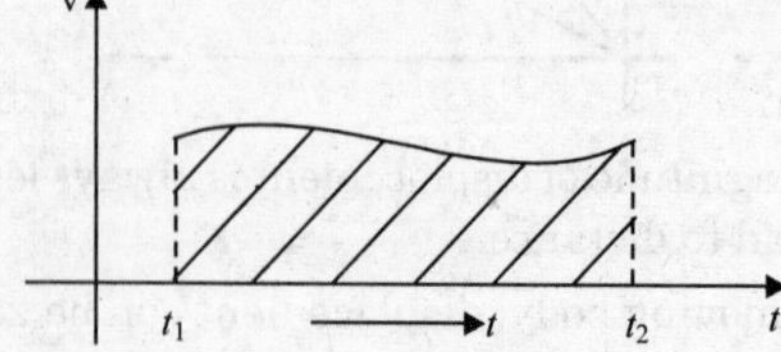

Total distance travelled is given by sum of magnitude of areas calculated in different time intervals.

(c) ***Acceleration time graph*** **:** Slope at any point gives no physical quantity.

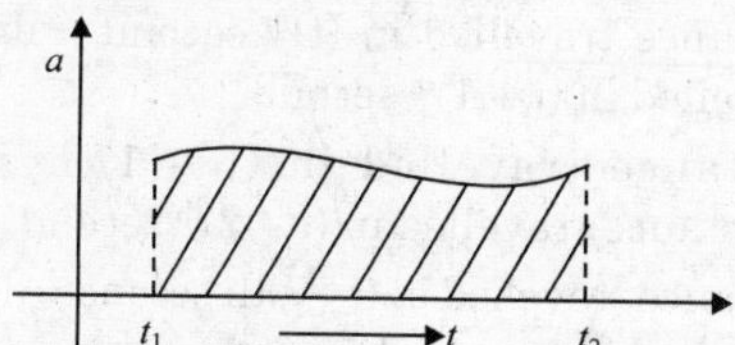

Area under the curve is equal to the change in velocity in time interval under consideration. Area above the time axis is taken as positive while area below *t* axis is taken as negative.

Important Points

1. If a body covers s_1 distance with speed v_1, s_2 with speed v_2, then its average speed is

$$V_{av} = \frac{s_1 + s_2}{\frac{s_1}{v_1} + \frac{s_2}{v_2}} = \frac{\sum s}{\sum \frac{s}{v}}$$

2. If a body coves first half distance with speed v_1 and next half with speed v_2, then Average speed

$$= \frac{2v_1v_2}{v_1 + v_2} \text{ (Harmonic mean)}$$

3. If a body travels with uniform speed v_1 time v_1 and with uniform speed v_2 for time t_2, then average speed

$$= \frac{v_1t_1 + v_2 + t_2}{t_1 + t_2} = \frac{\sum vt}{\sum t}.$$

If $t_1 = t_2 = \frac{T}{2}$ then $v_{av} = \frac{v_1 + v_2}{2}$

[T = time of journey] (Arithmetic mean)

4. If body covers first one third with speed v_1, next one third with speed v_2 and remaining one third with speed

v_3 then $v_{av} = \frac{3v_1v_2v_3}{v_1v_2 + v_2 + v_3 + v_3 + v_1}$

5. If a body moves from one point (A) to another point (B) with speed v_1 and returns back (from B to A) with speed v2 then average velocity is 0 but

average speed $= \frac{2v_1v_2}{v_1 + v_2}$

6. Slope of the chord joining two points on the displacement-time graph gives there average velocity during the time interval between those points.

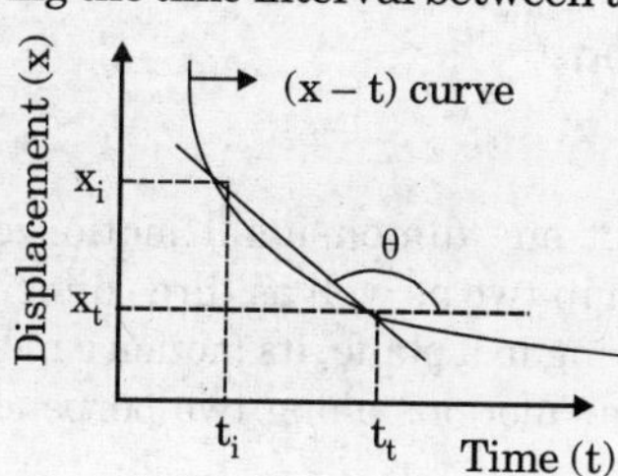

$$\tan\theta = \frac{x_f - x_i}{t_f - t_i} = V_{av}$$

7. Slope of the chord joining two points on the velocity-time graph gives the average acceleration during the time between those points.

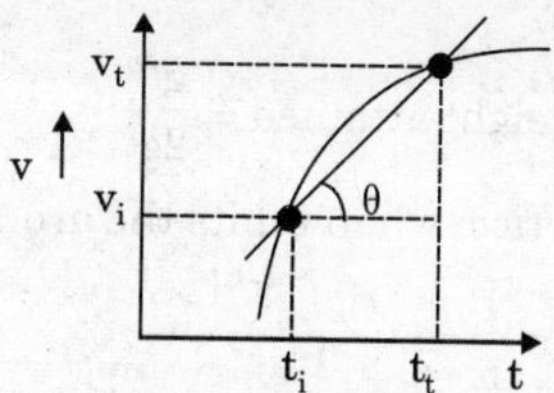

$$\tan\theta = \frac{x_f - x_i}{t_f - t_i} = V_{av}$$

= Average acceleration in time interval $t_f - t_i$.

8. The displacement-time graph cannot sharp turns because it gives two different velocities at that point.
9. The displacement-time graph cannot be symmetric about the time-axis because at an instant a particle cannot have two displacements, but the graph may be symmetric about the displacement-axis.
10. The distance-time graph is always an increasing curve for a moving body.
11. The displacement-time graph does not show the trajectory of the particle.
12. If a particle is moving with uniform acceleration and have velocity V_A at A and V_B at B, then velocity of particle midway on line AB is $V = \sqrt{\frac{V_A^2 + V_B^2}{2}}$.
13. If a body starts rest with acceleration α and then retards to rest with retardation β, such that total time of journey is T, then

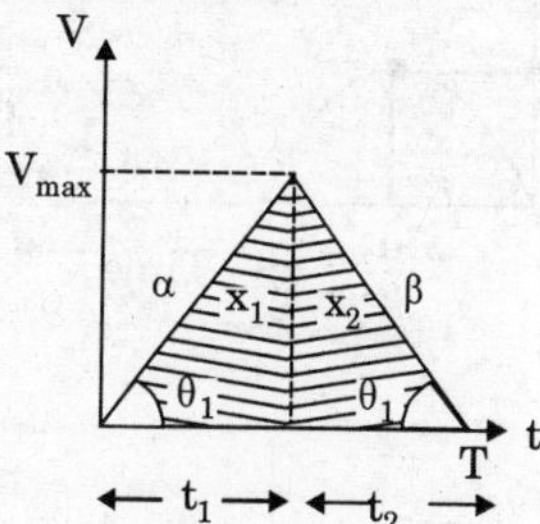

(a) Maximum velocity during the trip

$$v_{max} = \left(\frac{\alpha\beta}{\alpha + \beta}\right).T$$

(b) Length of the journey $L = \frac{1}{2}\left(\frac{\alpha\beta}{\alpha + \beta}\right)T^2$

(c) Average velocity of the trip

$$= \frac{v_{max}}{2} = \frac{\alpha\beta T}{2(\alpha + \beta)} \text{ \&}$$

(d) $\frac{x_1}{x_2} = \frac{\beta}{\alpha} = \frac{t_1}{t_2}$.

14. A particle is projected from ground with velocity u in vertically upward direction then

(a) Time of ascent = Time of descent

$$= \frac{\text{Time of flight}}{2} = \frac{T}{2} = \frac{u}{g}$$

(b) Maximum height attained = $\frac{u^2}{2g}$

(c) Speed of particle when it hits the ground = u

(d) Graphs

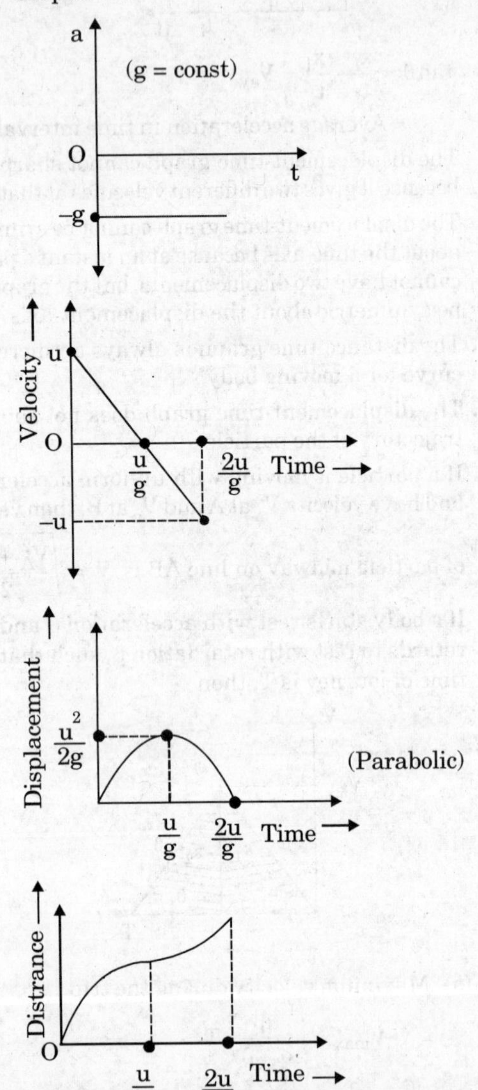

(e) Displacement of particle in complete journey = zero ⇒ average velocity $v_{av} = 0$

(f) Distance covered by particle journey = $\frac{u^2}{g}$

⇒ Average speed in complete journey = $\frac{u}{g}$

15. A body is thrown upward such that it takes t seconds to reach its highest point.

(a) Distance travelled in $(t)^{th}$ second = distance travelled in $(t + 1)^{th}$ second.

(b) Distance travelled in (t – 1)th second = distance travelled in $(t + 2)^{th}$ second.

(c) Distance travelled in (t – r)th second = distance travelled in $(t + r + 1)^{th}$ second.

16. From the top of a tower a body is projected upward with a certain speed, 2nd body is thrown downward with same speed and 3rd is let to fall freely from same point then

$$t_3 = \sqrt{t_1 t_2}$$

where, t_1 = Time of flight of body projected upward
t_2 = Time of flight of body thrown downward
t_3 = Time of flight of body dropped.

17. If u and v are velocity of particle at $t = t_1$ and $t = t_2$, which is moving with uniform acceleration, then average velocity of particle during time interval $(t_2 - t_1)$ is $V_{av} = \frac{u + v}{2}$.

18. For a body starting from rest and moving with uniform acceleration, the ratio of distances covered in 1s, 2s, 3s, etc. is $1^2 : 2^2 : 3^2$ etc., 1 : 4 : 9 etc

19. A body starting from rest and moving with uniform acceleration has distances covered by it in 1st, 2nd and 3rd seconds in the ratio 1 : 3 : 5 etc. i.e., odd numbers only.

20. A body moving with a velocity v is stopped by application of brakes after covering a distance s. If the same body moves with a velocity nv, it stops after covering a distance n^2s by the application of same brake force.

21. In the absence of air resistance, the velocity of projection is equal to the velocity with which the body strikes the ground.

22. In case of air resistance, the time of ascent is less than time of descent for a body projected vertically upward.

23. For a body projected vertically upwards, the magnitude of velocity at any given point on the path is same whether the body is moving in upwards or downward direction.

Projectile Motion

Motion In a Plane:

The kinematics of one dimensional motion can be applied for motion in two as well as three dimensions. If a particle is moving in a plane, its motion can be split into two rectilinear motions along two perpendicular directions which are called the rectangular components for the displacement, velocity and acceleration for the two dimensional motion.

If a particle is moving along the path AB in XY plane, then at any time t, it reaches point $P(x,y)$ where its radius vector $\mathbf{r}$ makes an angle ϕ with x-axis.

Then its component are $x = r\cos\phi$, $y = r\sin\phi$, $r = \sqrt{x^2 + y^2}$ and $\tan\phi = \frac{y}{x}$.

If the velocity vector $\mathbf{v}$ at P makes an angle θ with the x-direction, its rectangular component will be given by $v_x = v\cos\theta$, $v_y = v\sin\theta$, $v = \sqrt{v_x^2 + v_y^2}$ and $\tan\theta = \frac{v_y}{v_x}$.

Similarly the acceleration a at any time can be split up into components $\mathbf{a}_x$ and $\mathbf{a}_y$ along respective x and y directions.

In vectorial notation, the two dimensional motion can be described as per the following relations :

$$\boldsymbol{r} = x\mathbf{i} + y\mathbf{j}, \quad \boldsymbol{v} = v_x\mathbf{i} + v_y\mathbf{j}, \quad \boldsymbol{a} = a_x\mathbf{i} + a_y\mathbf{j}$$

Projectile Motion: When a body is projected at an angle in uniform force field(like uniform gravitational field), with the direction of force. The path followed by the body is known as projectile path.

If a particle is projected at origin O with velocity u, (called as velocity of projection) at angle θ (called as angle of projection)to the horizontal, its horizontal component $u\cos\theta$ remains constant whereas its vertical component $u\sin\theta$ changes continuously because of acceleration due to gravity which acts in the downward direction.

The vertical velocity decreases due to retardation g and becomes zero at the highest point at height H.

The vertical speed then increases when the body moves downwards until it reaches the x-axis covering a distance R in the horizontal direction which is called the horizontal range.

If v_x and v_y are the horizontal and the vertical components of velocity u after time t, then $v_x = u\cos\theta$, $v_y = u\sin\theta - gt$. If α is the angle subtended by v with horizontal,

$$\tan\alpha = \frac{v_y}{v_x} = \frac{u\sin\theta - gt}{u\cos\theta}$$

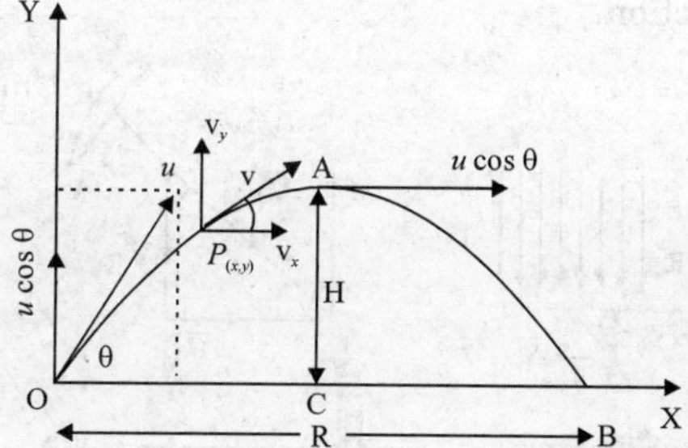

Maximum Height

If H is maximum height of the projectile, its velocity in the vertical direction is zero at this height.

$$H = \frac{u^2\sin^2\theta}{2g}$$

Time of Flight

If T is time of flight from O to B, for which vertical displacement $y = 0$, then

$$T = \frac{2u\sin\theta}{g}$$

Time to reach maximum height $= \frac{T}{2} = \frac{u\sin\theta}{g}$. It is called as time of ascent. The time taken to reach ground from maximum height is called as time of descent . Time of ascent is equal to time of descent

Range

$$R = \frac{u^2\sin 2\theta}{g}$$

The range R of a particle is maximum when $\sin 2\theta = 1$ or $2\theta = \frac{\pi}{2}$ or $\theta = \frac{\pi}{4} = 45°$.

Maximum value of horizontal range $= \frac{u^2}{g}$

There are two angles of projection *i.e.,* θ or $\frac{\pi}{2} - \theta$ for which the horizontal range of a particle is equal provided the initial velocity u is same in each case. This is called as *complemetry angle of projection*

Projectile thrown Horizontally from height : If a body is thrown horizontally from a height h with an initial speed u, its horizontal velocity remains unchanged whereas its vertical component increases due to acceleration of gravity in the downward direction. If a particle is projected from a height h with horizontal velocity u, its velocity v at any point B after time t has component $v_x = v\cos\theta = u$ and $v_y = v\sin\theta = gt$ where θ is the angle made by instantaneous velocity *w.r.t.* horizontal direction given then $\tan\theta = \frac{gt}{u}$.

$$v = \sqrt{u^2 + g^2t^2}$$

Horizontal distance travelled by the particle, $x = ut$

Vertical distance travelled by the particle, $y = \frac{1}{2}gt^2$

Equation of trajectory $y = \left(\frac{g}{2u^2}\right)x^2$

The resultant path or trajectory of the particle is a parabola. If T is the time taken by the particle to reach the ground from height h, then $h = \frac{1}{2}gT^2$ or $T = \sqrt{\frac{2h}{g}}$. The horizontal distance OC, covered to reach the ground, is called the horizontal range, R.

$$R = uT = u\sqrt{\frac{2h}{g}}$$

Projection on an Inclined Plane

Consider a particle projected with the velocity u at an angle θ to the horizontal on a plane inclined at angle β to the horizontal. The particle strikes the plane at point $P(x,y)$ having range $R = OP$ on the plane. The initial velocity of projection will have two components

(a) $u\cos(\alpha - \beta)$ along the plane

(b) $u\sin(\alpha - \beta)$ perpendicular to the plane.

Similarly, the acceleration $g\sin\beta$ is acceleration along the negative x axis and $g\cos\beta$ as acceleration perpendicular to theplane in negative y axis. Let t be the time taken by the particle to reach from O so that the P. Displacement perpendicular to OP is equal to zero.

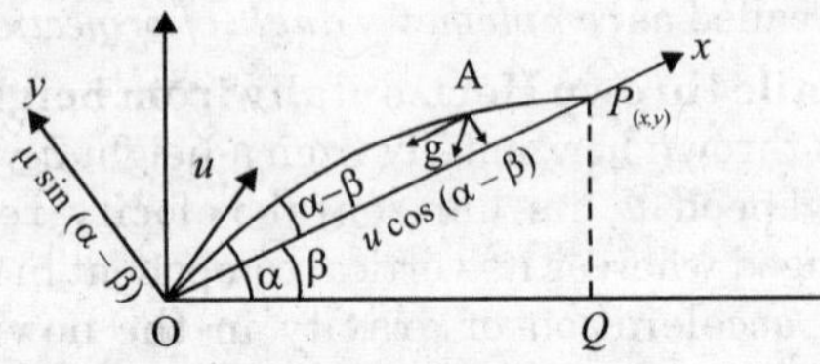

Time of Flight $= t = \frac{2u\sin(\alpha-\beta)}{g\cos\beta}$

$$\text{Range} = \frac{OQ}{\cos\beta} = \frac{2u^2\sin(\alpha-\beta)\cos\alpha}{g\cos^2\beta}$$

If it is down the incline plane just replace the negative sign everywhere with positive sign.

Relative Motion in One Dimension

1. If two bodies A and B are moving in straight line same direction with velocity V_A and V_B, then relative velocity of A with respect to B is $V_{AB} = V_A - V_B$. Similarly $V_{BA} = V_B - V_A$.

A ——→ V_A B ——→ V_B

2. If two bodies A and B are moving in straight line in opposite direction then

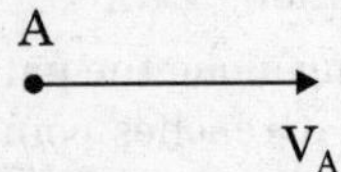

$$V_{AB} = V_A + V_B \text{ (towards B)}$$

$$V_{BA} = V_B + V_A \text{ (towards A)}$$

$$V_{AB} = -V_{BA}$$

Same concept is used for acceleration also.

3. If two cars A and B are moving in same direction with velocity V_A and V_B ($V_A > V_B$) when A is behind B at a distance d, driver in car A applies brake which causes retardation a in car A, then minimum value of d to avoid collision is

$$\frac{(V_A = -V_B)^2}{2a} \text{ i.e, } d > \frac{(V_A - V_B)^2}{2a}$$

4. A particle is dropped and another particle is thrown downward with initial velocity u, then
   (a) Relative acceleration is always zero
   (b) Relative velocity is always u.
   (c) Time at which their separation is x is $\frac{x}{u}$.

5. Two bodies are thrown upwards with same initial velocity with time gap τ. They will meet after a time t from projection of first body.

$$t = \frac{\tau}{2} + \frac{u}{g}$$

Relative Motion in Two Dimensions

Relative velocity :

Velocity of object A w.r.t object B is

$$\vec{V}_{AB} = \vec{V}_A - \vec{V}_B, \ \vec{V}_{BA} = \vec{V}_B - \vec{V}_A$$

1. **Direction of Umbrella** : A person moving one straight road has to hold his umbrella opposite to direction of relative velocity of rain. The angle θ is given by $\tan\theta = \frac{v_M}{v_R}$ with vertical in forward direction.

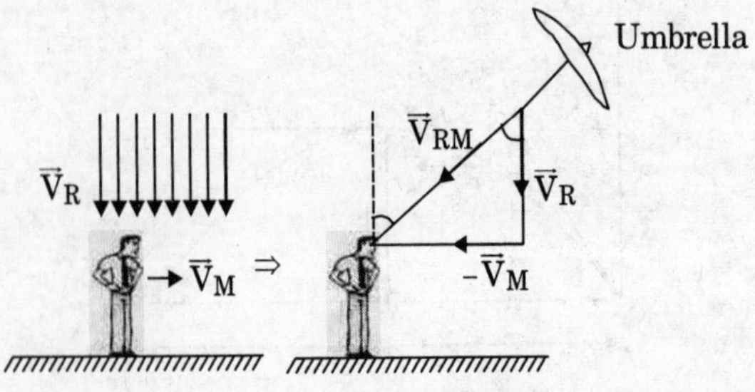

2. **Closest approach :** Two objects A and B having velocities $\vec{v}_A$ and $\vec{v}_B$ at separation x are shown in figure

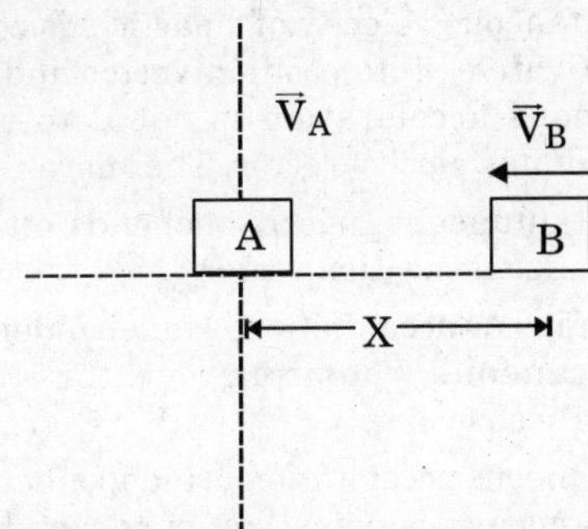

The relative velocity of A with respect to B is given by

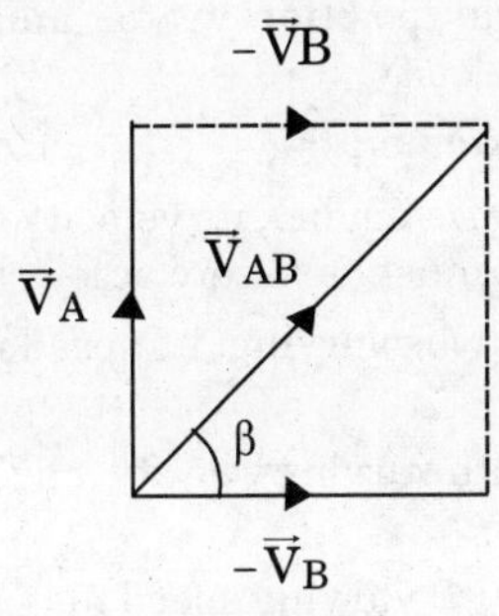

$\vec{v}_{AB} = \vec{v}_A - \vec{v}_B$

$\tan\beta = \frac{v_A}{v_B}$

The above situation is similar to figure given below y is the distance of closest approach.

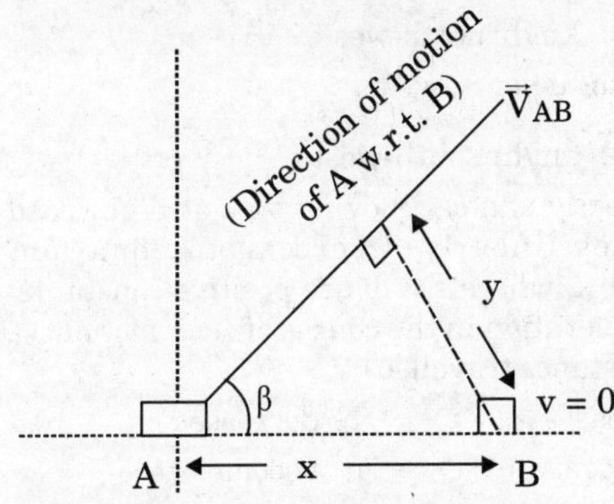

Now, $\sin\beta = \frac{y}{x}$

$\Rightarrow y = x\sin\beta$

$$y = \frac{x\tan\beta}{\sqrt{1+\tan^2\beta}} = \frac{xV_A}{\sqrt{V_B^2 + V_A^2}}$$

3. **Crossing a river** :

v = velocity of the man in still water

(also called velocity of swimmer wrt river = v_{SR})

θ = angle of which man swims w.r.t. normal to bank such that

$vx = -v\sin\theta,\ v_y = v\cos\theta.$

$v_R = U$

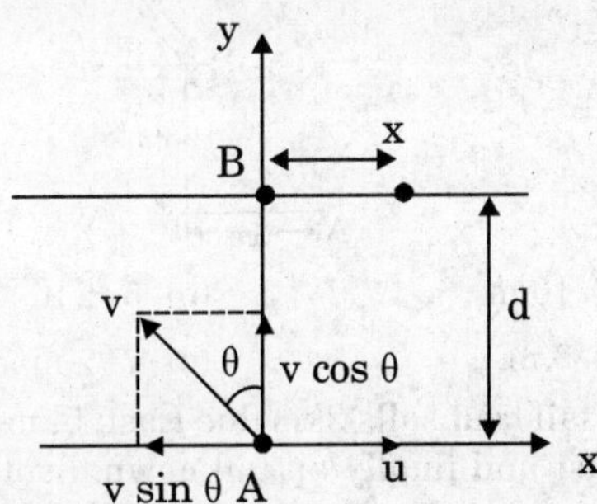

Velocity along the river

$v'_x = u - v\sin\theta$

Distance drifted along the river = $D = tv'_x$

$$x = \frac{d}{v\cos\theta}(u - v\sin\theta)$$

Case I :

The minimum time to cross the river is given by

$$\tau_{min} = \frac{d}{v} \text{ (when } \cos\theta = 1, \theta = 0°, u \perp v)$$

Distance drifted is given by

$$D = \frac{d}{v} \times u$$

Case II :

To cross the river straight

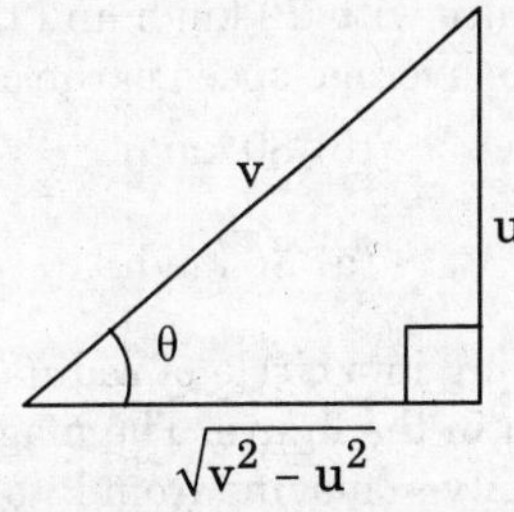

drift $x = 0 \Rightarrow u - v\sin\theta = 0$

$$\sin\theta = \frac{u}{v} \Rightarrow (v > u)$$

Time to cross the river straight across is given by

$$t = \frac{d}{v\cos\theta} = \frac{d}{\sqrt{v^2 - u^2}}$$

Objective Type Questions

1. A particle moves along a path ABCD as shown in the figure. Then the magnitude of net displacement of the particle from position A to D is :

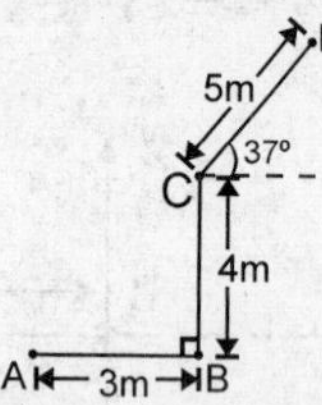

(a) 10 m (b) $5\sqrt{2}$ m
(c) 9 m (d) $7\sqrt{2}$ m

2. A sail boat sails 2km due East, 5km 37° South of East and finally an unknown displacement . If the final displacement of the boat from the starting point is 6km due East, the third displacement is
(a) 3 km (b) 4 km
(c) 5 km (d) 2 km

3. A body goes 10 km north and 20 km east. What will be the displacement from initial point ?
(a) 22.36 km (b) 2 km
(c) 5 km (d) 30 km

4. A particle starts from rest with uniform acceleration a. Its velocity after 'n' second is 'v'. The displacement of the body in the last two second is
(a) $\frac{2v(n-1)}{n}$ (b) $\frac{v(n-1)}{n}$
(c) $\frac{v(n+1)}{n}$ (d) $\frac{2v(2n+1)}{n}$

5. One car moving on a straight road covers one third of the distance with 20 km/h and the rest with 60 km/h. The average speed of the car is
(a) 40 km/h (b) 80 km/h
(c) $46\frac{2}{3}$ km/h (d) 36 km/h

6. A particle is moving in a circle of radius r with speed v as shown in the figure. The magnitude of change in velocity in moving from P to Q is:

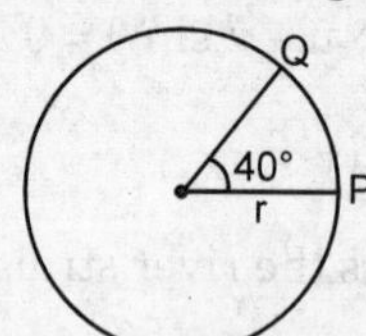

(a) 2 v cos 40° (b) 2 v sin 20°
(c) 2 v cos 20° (d) none of these

7. The instantaneous velocity of a particle is equal to time derivative of its position vector and the instantaneous acceleration is equal to time derivative of its velocity vector. Therefore:
(a) the instantaneous velocity depends on the instantaneous position vector
(b) instantaneous acceleration is independent of instantaneous position vector and instantaneous velocity
(c) instantaneous acceleration is independent of instantaneous position vector but depends on the instantaneous velocity
(d) instantaneous acceleration depends both on the instantaneous position vector and the instantaneous velocity.

8. Mark the correct statement(s).
(a) If speed of a body is varying, its velocity must be varying and it must have zero acceleration
(b) If velocity of a body is varying, its speed must be varying
(c) A body moving with varying velocity may have constant speed
(d) A body moving with varying speed may have constant velocity if its direction of motion remains constant.

9. A truck travelling due north at 50 km/hr turns west and travels at the same speed. What is the change in velocity.
(a) 50 km/hr north-west
(b) $50\sqrt{2}$ km/hrnorth-west
(c) 50 km/hr south-west
(d) $50\sqrt{2}$ km/hr south-west

10. The velocity of a car moving on a straight road increases linearly according to equation, v = a + bx, where a & b are positive constants. The acceleration in the course of such motion: (x is the distance travelled)
(a) increases (b) decreases
(c) stay constant (d) becomes zero

11. The speed v of a car moving on a straight road changes according to equation, $v^2 = a + bx$, where a & b are positive constants. Then the magnitude of acceleration in the course of such motion: (x is the distance travelled)
(a) increases
(b) decreases
(c) stay constant
(d) first decreases and then increases

12. Sign of acceleration tells us : (for rectilinear motion)
   (a) whether the particle's speed is increasing or decreasing
   (b) about change in speed depending on the choice of the positive direction of the velocity
   (c) both of the above (a) & (B)
   (d) none of the above (a) & (B)

13. The position vector of a particle is given as $\vec{r} = (t^2 - 4t + 6)\hat{i} + (t^2)\hat{j}$. The time after which the velocity vector and acceleration vector becomes perpendicular to each other is equal to
   (a) 1sec (b) 2 sec
   (c) 1.5 sec (d) not possible

14. A particle of mass m moves along a curve $y = x^2$. When particle has x – co-ordinate as 1/2m and x-component of velocity as 4m/s then.
   (a) the magnitude of velocity at that instant is 4 m/s
   (b) the magnitude of velocity at that instant is $2\sqrt{2}$ m/s
   (c) the magnitude of velocity at that instant is $4\sqrt{2}$ m/s
   (d) the magnitude of velocity at that instant is 2 m/s

15. The position of a particle moving rectilinearly is given by $x = t^3 - 3t^2 - 10$. Find the distance travelled by the particle in the first 4 seconds starting from t = 0.
   (a) 24 units (b) 12 units
   (c) 48 units (d) 6 units

16. Following statements are given for the motion of a particle along the straight line. Choose correct statement out of these :
   (a) Magnitude of the average velocity is equal to the average speed.
   (b) Distance travelled by the particle is always greater than magnitude of the displacement.
   (c) A particle having negative acceleration may speed up.
   (d) A particle having its velocity equal to zero at any instant of the motion, then its acceleration is also zero at that instant.

17. Each of the four particles move along an x axis. Their coordinates (in metres) as function of time (in seconds) are given by
   Particle 1 : $x(t) = 3.5 - 2.7t^3$
   Particle 2 : $x(t) = 3.5 + 2.7t^3$
   Particle 3 : $x(t) = 3.5 + 2.7t^2$
   Particle 4 : $x(t) = 3.5 - 3.4t - 2.7t^2$
   which of these particles is speeding up for t > 0?
   (a) All four (b) only 1
   (c) only 1, 2 and 3. (d) only 2, 3 and 4.

18. For a particle moving along a straight line, the displacement x depends on time t as $x = \alpha t^3 + \beta t^2 + \gamma t + \delta$. The ratio of its initial acceleration to its initial velocity depends:
   (a) only on α & β (b) only on β & γ
   (c) only on α & γ (d) only on α

19. A man moves on his motorbike with 54 km/h and then takes a u turn (180°) and continues to move with same speed. The time of u turn is 10 s. Find the average acceleration during u turn.
   (a) 0 (b) 3 ms^{-2}
   (c) $1.5\sqrt{2}$ ms^{-2} (d) none of these

20. A particle moves in x-y plane according to equations, $x = 4t^2 + 5t + 16$ & $y = 5t$. The acceleration of the particle will be:
   (a) 8 m/sec² (b) 13 m/sec²
   (c) 14 m/sec² (d) none of these

21. If $v = x^2 - 5x + 4$, find the acceleration of the particle when velocity of the particle is zero.
   (a) 0 (b) 2
   (c) 3 (d) none of these

22. The displacement of a body from a reference point is given by, $\sqrt{x} = 2t - 3$, where 'x' is in metres and t in seconds. This shows that the body:
   (a) rest at t = 3/2 (b) is accelerated
   (c) is decelerated (d) is in uniform motion

23. A car of mass *m*, travelling at speed *v*, stops in time *t* when maximum braking force is applied. Assuming the braking force is same for both cases, what time would be required to stop a car of mass *2m* travelling at speed *v*?
   (a) $\frac{1}{2}t$ (b) t
   (c) $\sqrt{2}t$ (d) $2t$

24. A particle is moving eastward with a velocity of 5m/s. In 10 seconds the velocity changes to 5m/s northwards. The average acceleration $(\Delta\vec{v}/\Delta t)$ in this time is
   (a) zero
   (b) $1/\sqrt{2}$ m/s² towards north-west
   (c) $1/\sqrt{2}$ m/s² towards north-east
   (d) $1/\sqrt{2}$ m/s² towards north

25. A particle P is moving with a constant speed of 6m/s in a direction $2\hat{i}-\hat{j}-2\hat{k}$. When t = 0, P is at a point whose position vector is $3\hat{i}+4\hat{j}-7\hat{k}$. Find the position vector of the particle P after 4 seconds.

(a) $\vec{r}=19\hat{i}-4\hat{j}-23\hat{k}$ (b) $\vec{r}=19\hat{i}-4\hat{j}-23\hat{k}$

(c) $\vec{r}=19\hat{i}-4\hat{j}-23\hat{k}$ (d) $\vec{r}=19\hat{i}-4\hat{j}-23\hat{k}$

26. The velocity of a particle moving along a straight line is given by the equation $v = t^2 - 2t - 3$ where 't' is time. The minimum velocity of the particle is (Assume all are in S.I. unit)

(a) 4 m/s (b) – 1 m/s

(c) zero (d) – 4 m/s

27. A body travelling with uniform acceleration crosses two points A and B with velocities 20 m s^{-1} and 30 m s^{-1} respectively. The speed of the body at the mid-point of A and B is

(a) 24 m s^{-1} (b) 25 m s^{-1}

(c) 25.5 m s^{-1} (d) $10\sqrt{6}$ m s^{-1}

28. The velocity - time graph of a particle is as shown in figure

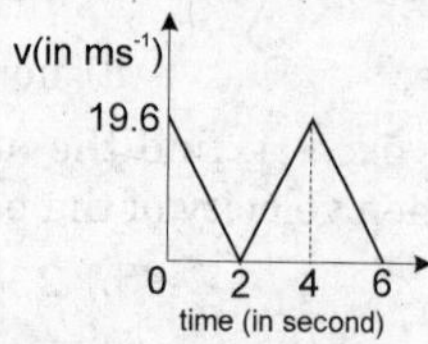

(a) It moves with a constant acceleration throughout

(b) It moves with an acceleration of constant magnitude but changing direction at the end of every two second

(c) The displacement of the particle is zero

(d) The velocity becomes zero at t = 4 second

29. A car starts from rest and moves with constant acceleration. The ratio of the distance covered in the nth second to that covered in n seconds is:

(a) $\frac{2}{n^2}-\frac{1}{n}$ (b) $\frac{2}{n^2}+\frac{1}{n}$

(c) $\frac{2}{n}-\frac{1}{n^2}$ (d) $\frac{2}{n}+\frac{1}{n^2}$

30. A particle is moving with initial velocity $\vec{u}=\hat{i}-\hat{j}+\hat{k}$. What should be its acceleration so that it can remain moving in the same straight line ?

(a) $\vec{a}=2\hat{i}-2\hat{j}+2\hat{k}$ (b) $\vec{a}=-2\hat{i}+2\hat{j}-2\hat{k}$

(c) $\vec{a}=3\hat{i}+3\hat{j}+-3\hat{k}$ (d) $\vec{a}=1\hat{i}-1\hat{j}$

31. A train is moving at speed of 40 km/h.As soon as another train going in the opposite direction passes by the window, the passenger of the first train started his stopwatch and noted that other train passedthe window in 3 s. Find the speed of the train going in the opposite direction if its length is 75 m.

(a) 25km/h (b) 50km/h

(c) 75km/h (d) 40km/h

Direction (Q. 32 to 35) : Following are three functions which relates the parameters of motion.

$$S(t) = ut + \frac{1}{2}at^2 \quad v(s) = \sqrt{u^2 + 2as} \quad v(t) = u + at$$

Where ; S, u, t, a, v are respectively the displacement (dependent variable), initial velocity (constant), time taken (independent variable), acceleration (constant) and final velocity (dependent variable) of the particle after time t.

32. Find displacement of a particle after 10 seconds starting from rest with an uniform acceleration of $2m/s^2$.

(a) 10 m (b) 100 m

(c) 50 m (d) 200 m

33. Find the velocity of the particle after 100 m –

(a) 10 m/s (b) 20 m/s

(c) 30 m/s (d) 0 m/s

34. Find the velocity of the particle after 10 seconds if its acceleration is zero in interval (0 to 10 s) –

(a) 10 m/s (b) 20 m/s

(c) 30 m/s (d) 0 m/s

35. Find the displacement of the particle when its velocity becomes 10 m/s if acceleration is 5 m/s^2 all through–

(a) 50 m (b) 200 m

(c) 10 m (d) 100 m

36. A body thrown vertically up from the ground passes the height 10.2 m twice at an interval of 10 sec. What was its initial velocity. [g = 10 m/s^2]

(a) 52 m/s (b) 26 m/s

(c) 35 m/s (d) none of these

37. A balloon is ascending vertically with an acceleration of 0.4 m/s^{-2}. Two stones are dropped from it at an interval of 2 sec. Find the distance between them 1.5 sec. after the second stone is released. (g = 10 m/sec^2)

(a) 26 m (b) 52m

(c) 78m (d) 13 m

38. Two bodies are thrown vertically upward, with the same initial velocity of 98 m/s, but the second one is thrown 4 sec. after the first is thrown. At what time after the first particle is thrown will both of them meet ? [g = 9.8 m/s2]

(a) 8 s (b) 10 s

(c) 6 s (d) 12 s

39. A particle moves rectilinearly with a constant acceleration 1 m/s^2. Its speed after 10 seconds is 5 m/s. The distance covered by the particle in this duration is (Initial & final velocities are in opposite direction)

(a) 20 m (b) 25 m

(c) 30 m (d) 50 m

40. A particle is moving along a straight line with constant acceleration. At the end of tenth second its velocity becomes 20 m/s and in tenth second it travels a distance of 10 m. Then the acceleration of the particle will be-

(a) 10 m/s^2 (b) 20 m/s^2

(c) $\frac{1}{5}$ m/s^2 (d) 3.8 m/s^2

41. A balloon is moving along with constant upward acceleration of 1 m/s^2. A stone is thrown from the balloon downwards with speed 10 m/s with respect to the balloon. At the time of projection balloon is at height 120 m from the ground and is moving with speed 20 m/s. The time required to fall on the ground by the stone after the projection will be -

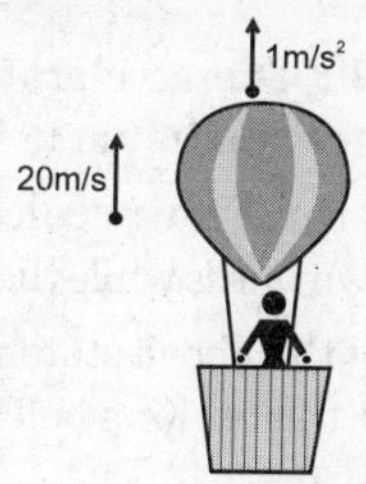

(a) 4 sec. (b) 5 sec.

(c) 6 sec. (d) None of these

42. A particle is moving along x axis with constant acceleration. At t = 0 sec. the particle is at x = 3 m and v = + 4 m/s. The maximum value of x coordinate of the particle is observed 2 sec. later. Starting fromt = 0 sec after what time particle reaches its initial position again

(a) 4 sec.

(b) 6 sec.

(c) 8 sec.

(d) 12 sec.

43. From the top of a tower a stone is dropped. If it covers 24.5 m in the last second of its motion, find the height of the tower.

(a) 40.1 m. (b) 42.1 m.

(c) 46.1 m. (d) 44.1 m.

44. A particle is thrown upwards from ground. It experiences a constant air resistance force which can produce a retardation of 2 m/s^2. The ratio of time of ascent to the time of descent is : [g = 10 m/s^2]

(a) 1 : 1 (b) $\sqrt{\frac{2}{3}}$

(c) $\frac{2}{3}$ (d) $\sqrt{\frac{3}{2}}$

45. A stone is dropped from the top of a tower. When it has fallen by 5m from the top, another stone is dropped from a point 25m below the top. If both stones reach the ground at the same moment, then height of the tower from ground is : (take g = 10m/s^2)

(a) 45 m (b) 50m

(c) 60m (d) 65m

46. A ball is thrown vertically upwards in air. If the air resistance cannot be neglected (assume it to be directly proportional to velocity), then the acceleration of the ball at the highest point will be:

(a) 0 (b) g

(c) > g (d) < g

47. If a body starts with initial velocity 'u' with a constant acceleration 'a' then find out the increase in velocity after 't' seconds :

(a) u–at (b) u

(c) u + at (d) at

48. A stone thrown upwards, has its equation of motion s = 490 t - 4.9 t^2 where 's' in metres and t in seconds respectively. What is the maximum height reached by it ?

(a) 12000 m (b) 12250 m

(c)11000 m (d) 11250 m

49. The displacement of a body at any time t after starting is given by s = 15t – 0.4t^2. The velocity of the body will be 7 ms^{-1} after time :

(a) 20 s (b) 15 s

(c) 10 s (d) 5 s

50. The displacement of a body at any time t after starting is given by $s = 10t - \frac{1}{2}(0.2)t^2$. The velocity of the body is zero after :

(a) 50 s (b) 100 s

(c) 80 s (d) 40 s

51. A particle is moving in a straight line with initial velocity u and uniform acceleration f. If the sum of the distances travelled in t^{th} and $(t+1)^{th}$ seconds is 100 cm, then its velocity after t seconds, in cm s, is

(a) 20 (b) 30

(c) 50 (d) 80

52. The displacement of a body is given to be proportional to the cube of time elapsed. Acceleration of the body is proportional to:

(a) t^4 (b) t^3

(c) t^2 (d) t

53. The velocity of a particle moving on the x-axis is given by $v = x^2 + x$ where v is in m/s and x is in m. Find its acceleration in m/s^2 when passing through the point x = 2 m

(a) 0 (b) 5

(c) 11 (d) 30

54. Two particles, one with constant velocity 50m/s and the other with uniform acceleration 10m/s^2, start moving simultaneously from the same position in the same direction. They will be at a distance of 125m from each other after

(a) 5 sec. (b) $5(1+\sqrt{2})$ sec.

(c) Both A and B (d) None of these

55. A body moving with constant acceleration travels 200 cm in the first two seconds and 220 cm in the next four seconds. What will be the velocity at the end of 7 second from start?

(a) 12 cm s^{-1} (b) 8 cm s^{-1}

(c) 11 cm s^{-1} (d) 10 cm s^{-1}

56. A parachutist drops freely from an aeroplane for 10 s before the parachute opens out. Then he descends with a net retardation of 2.5 ms^{-2}. If he bails out of the plane at a height of 2495 m and g = 10 ms^{-2}, his velocity on reaching the ground will be :

(a) 2.5 ms^{-1} (b) 7.5 ms^{-1}

(c) 5 ms^{-1} (d) 10 ms^{-1}

57. A ball is thrown vertically upwards from the ground. It crosses a point at the height of 25 m twice at an interval of 4 secs. The ball was thrown with the velocity of

(a) 20 m/sec. (b) 25 m/sec.

(c) 30 m/sec. (d) 35 m/sec.

58. The distance travelled by a freely falling body is proportional to

(a) the mass of the body

(b) the square of the acceleration due to gravity

(c) the square of the time of fall

(d) the time of fall

59. A body is projected vertically downwards from A, the top of the tower reaches the ground in t_1 seconds. If it is projected upwards with same velocity it reaches the ground in t_2 seconds. At what time it will reach the ground if it is dropped from A.

(a) $\sqrt{t_1/t_2}$ (b) $\sqrt{t_2/t_1}$

(c) $\sqrt{t_1 t_2}$ (d) $t_1 t_2$

60. A stone is dropped from the top of building and at the same time a second stone is thrown vertically upward from the bottom of the building with a speed of 20 ms^{-1}. They pass each other 3 seconds later. Find the height of the building.

(a) 20 m (b) 25 m

(c) 30 m (d) 60 m

61. A stone is dropped from the top of a tall tower and after one second another stone is dropped from a balcony 20 m below the top. If both the stones reach the ground at the same instant, calculate the height of the tower.

(a) 30.25 m (b) 31.25 m

(c) 32.25 m (d) 36.25 m

62. A person throws a ball vertically up in air. The ball rises to maximum height and then falls back down such that the person catches it. Neglect the friction due to air. While the ball was in air, three statements are given below. (g = 9.8 m/s^2)

Statement 1 : Just after the ball leaves the persons hand, the direction of its acceleration is upwards.

Statement 2 : The acceleration of ball is zero when it reaches maximum height.

Statement 3 : The acceleration of ball is g = 9.8 m/s^2 downwards while the ball is falling down.

Then which of the above statement or statements are correct in the options below.

(a) Statement 1 only

(b) Statement 2 only

(c) Statement 3 only

(d) Both statement 2 and statement 3

63. For the graph shown in the fig. the distance covered by the body in the first 12 seconds is :

(a) 360 m

(b) 240 m

(c) 285 m

(d) none of these

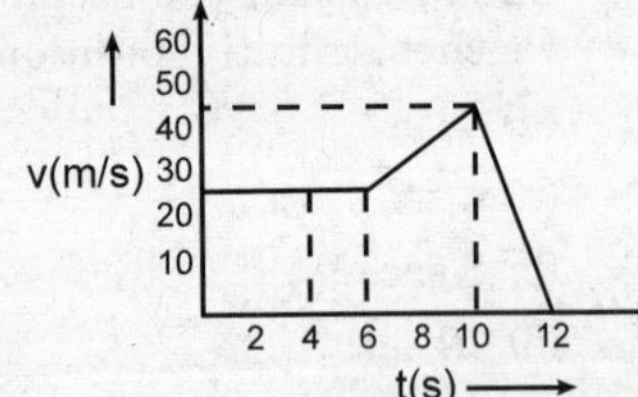

64. The acceleration time graph of a particle moving along a straight line is as shown in the figure. At what time the particle acquires its velocity equal to initial velocity?

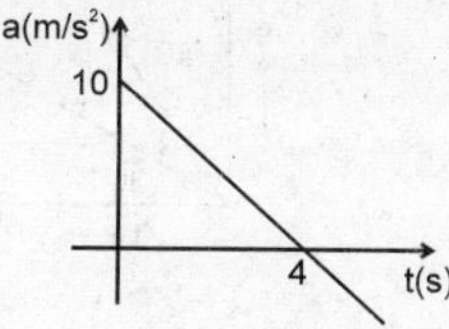

(a) 12 sec (b) 5 sec
(c) 8 sec (d) none of these

65. On a displacement/time graph, two straight lines make angles at 30° & 60° with the time axis. The ratio of the velocities represented by them is:

(a) 1 : 2 (b) 1 : 3
(c) 2 : 1 (d) 3 : 1

66. Figure shows the velocity time graph of a particle moving along straight line (v is m/s and t is in seconds). Its average velocity in 20 seconds will be:

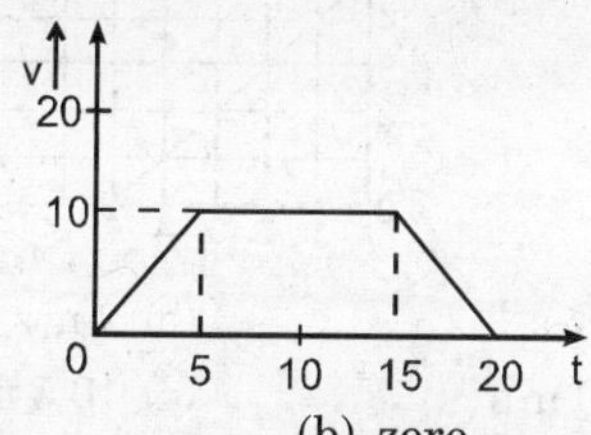

(a) 10 m/s (b) zero
(c) 3.75 m/s (d) 7.5 m/s

67. The velocity time graph of a linear motion is shown in the figure. The distance from the starting point after 8 seconds will be:

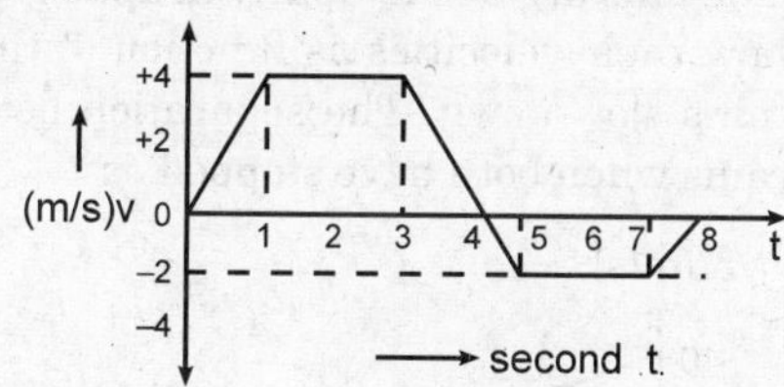

(a) 18 m (b) 6 m
(c) 8 m (d) none of these

68. A lift starts from rest. Its acceleration is plotted against time in the following graph. When it comes to rest its height above its starting point is:

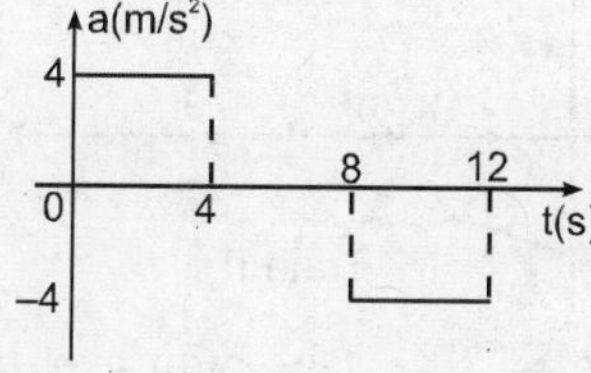

(a) 20 m (b) 64 m
(c) 32 m (d) 128 m

69. A particle can travel from point A to B from two different paths 1 and 2, as shown, in same interval of time. Then which of the following is incorrect?

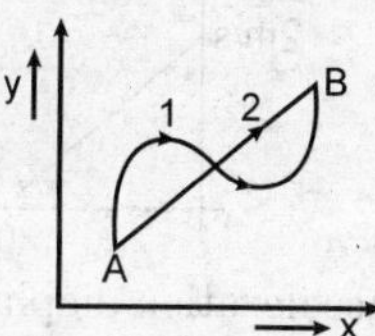

(a) Average velocity along the two paths must be equal
(b) The particle may travel along both the paths unaccelerated
(c) The direction of instantaneous velocity along the path 1 & 2 can be same for a maximum of two point on the paths.
(d) The average and instantaneous velocity along path 1 can have same direction.

70. Initially car A is 10.5 m ahead of car B. Both start moving at time t = 0 in the same direction along a straight line. The velocity time graph of two cars is shown in figure. The time when the car B will catch the car A, will be

(a) t = 21 sec
(b) $t = 2\sqrt{5}$ sec
(c) t = 20 sec.
(d) None of these

V
car B
10m/s
car A
45°
t

71. For which of the following graphs the average velocity of a particle moving along a straight line for time interval (0, t) must be negative

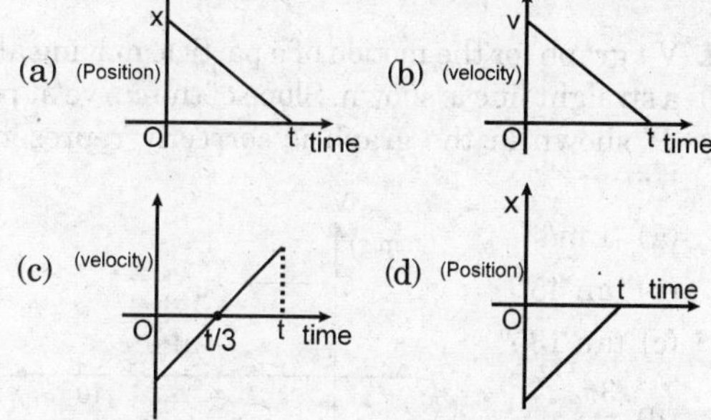

72. A person starts from origin and for his linear motion velocity is given as shown in figure. Find maximum displacement of the person.

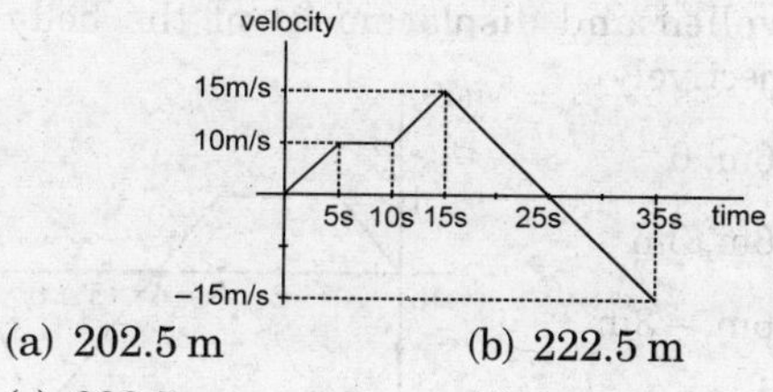

(a) 202.5 m (b) 222.5 m
(c) 232.5 m (d) 212.5 m

73. The velocity displacement graph of a particle moving along a straight line is shown in figure.

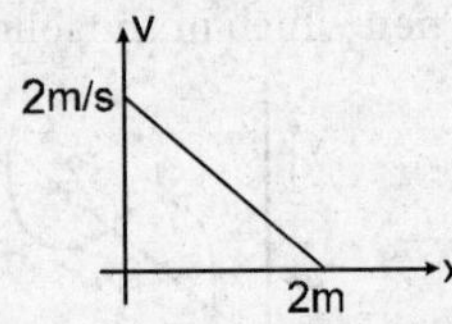

Then the acceleration displacement graph is.

(a)

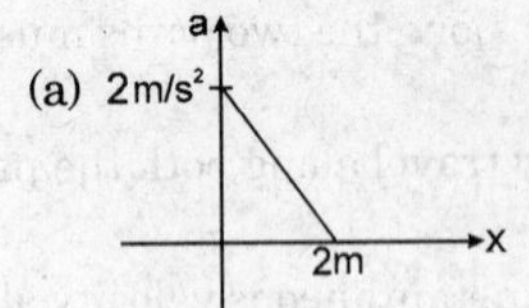

(b)

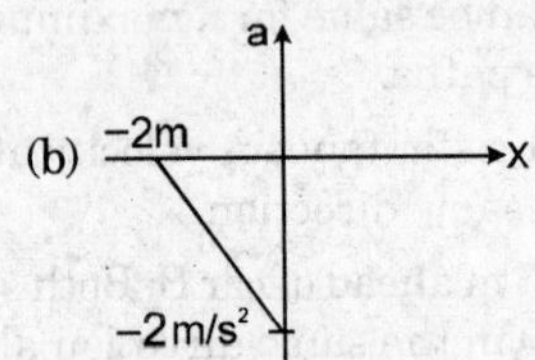

(c)

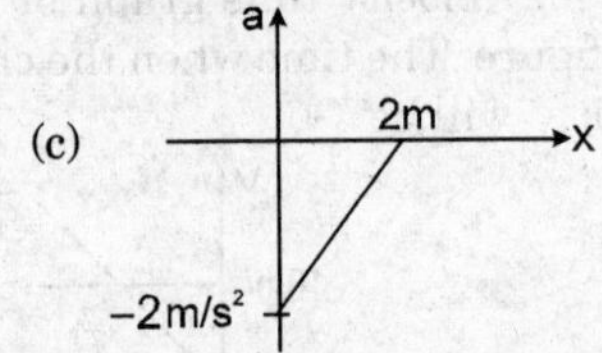

(d)

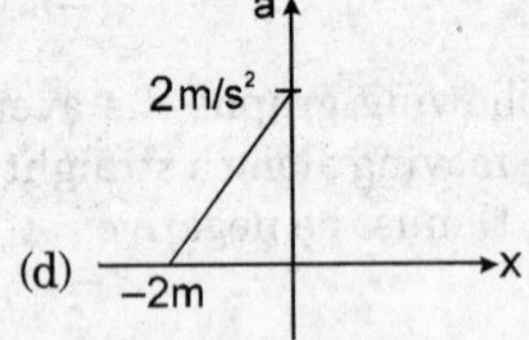

74. V-t graph for the motion of a particle moving along a straight line is shown. Slope of the curve at point 'P' shown in the graph is correctly represented by:

(a) -1 m/s^2

(b) tan 45°

(c) tan 135°

(d) $\frac{3\pi}{4}$

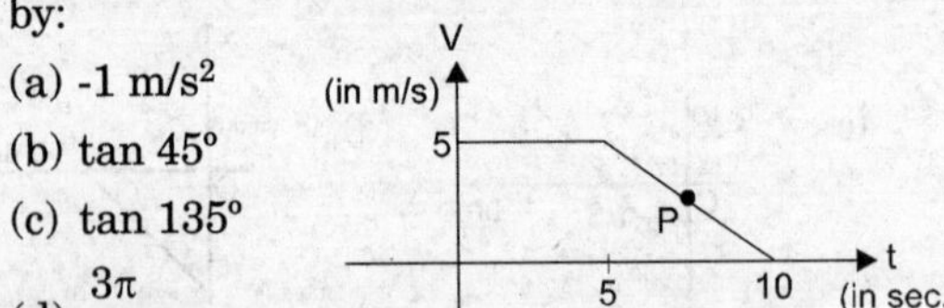

75. The velocity time graph of a body travelling along a straight line is given below. The distance travelled and displacement of the body are respectively

(a) 6m, 0

(b) 6m, 3m

(c) 6m, – 3m

(d) 0, 0

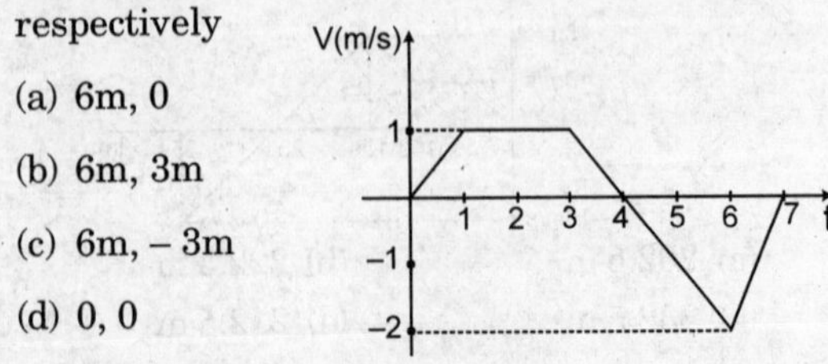

76. The displacement time graphs of two bodies A and B are shown in figure. The ratio of velocity of A, v_A to velocity of B, v_B is :

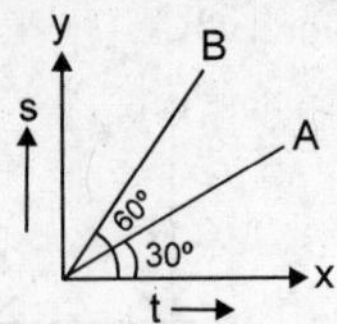

(a) $\frac{1}{\sqrt{3}}$ (b) $\sqrt{3}$

(c) $\frac{1}{3}$ (d) 3

77. Starting from rest at t = 0, a car moves in a straight line with an acceleration given by the accompanying graph. The speed of the car at t = 3 s is :

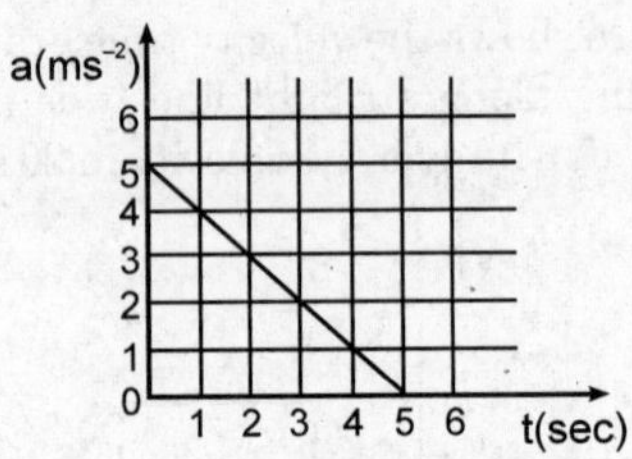

(a) 1 m s^{-1} (b) 2 m s^{-1}

(c) 6.0 m s^{-1} (d) 10.5 m s^{-1}

78. Two trains, which are moving along different tracks in opposite directions, are put on the same track due to a mistake. Their drivers, on noticing the mistake, start slowing down the trains when the trains are 300 m apart. Graphs given below show their velocities as function of time as the trains slow down. The separation between the trains when both have stopped, is :

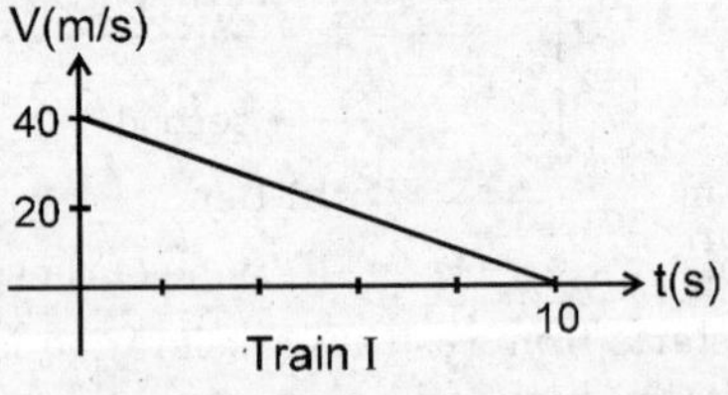

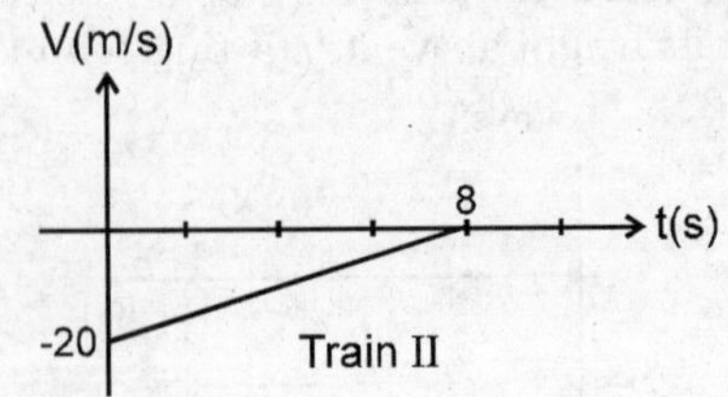

(a) 120 m (b) 280 m

(c) 60 m (d) 20 m.

79. Position (Km) - Time (min.) graph is shown for two cars 'A' and 'B'. Both collide at time t = 150 minute. Then the distance of position 'R' of accident from the starting point 'Q' of car A will be. (Initial distance between the two cars is 500 km) (Position in the graph shows the distance of the two cars from the point 'Q') -

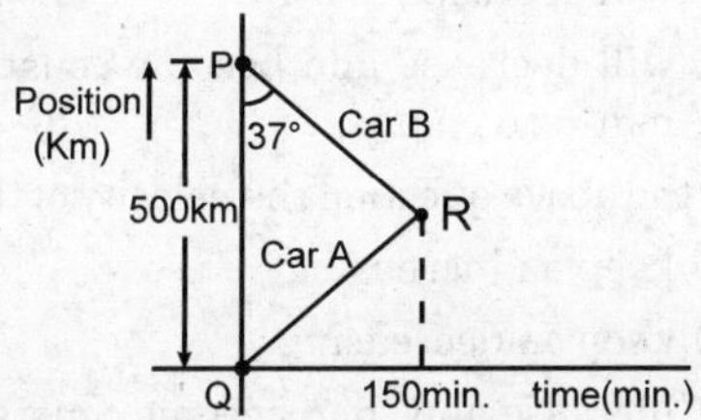

(a) 200 km (b) 300 km
(c) 250 km (d) 400 km

80. The velocity time graph of a particle moving in a straight line starting from a point *P* is shown in figure.

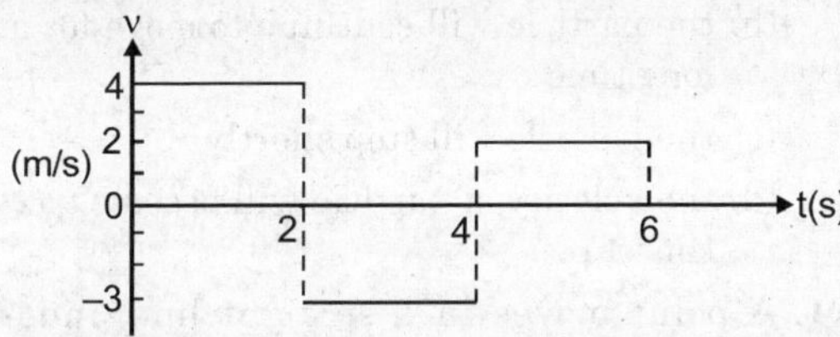

The distance of particle from *P* at the end of 6 seconds is :

(a) 6 m (b) 8 m
(c) 12 m (d) 18 m

81. The graph shown in the figure shows the velocity v versus time t of a body. Which of the graphs shown in figure represents the corresponding acceleration versus time graphs?

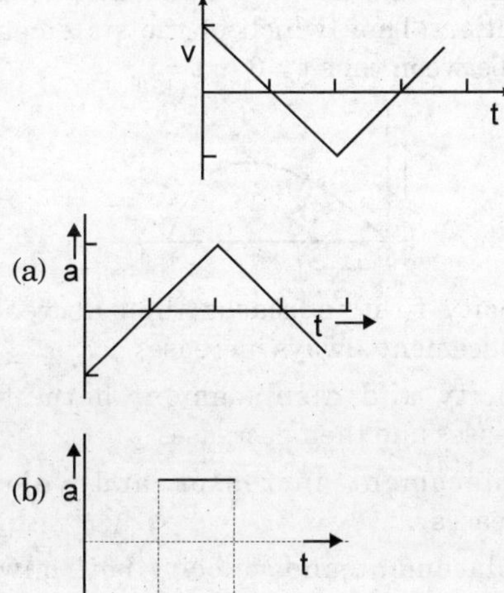

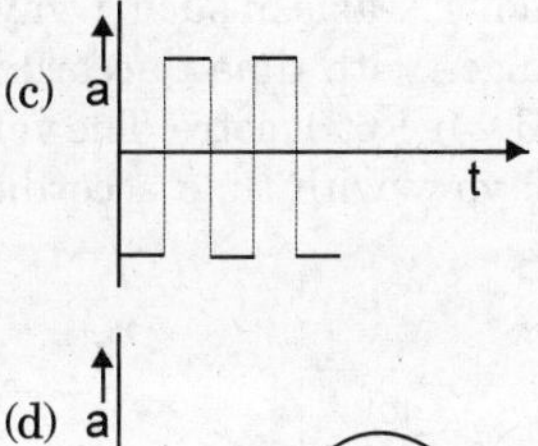

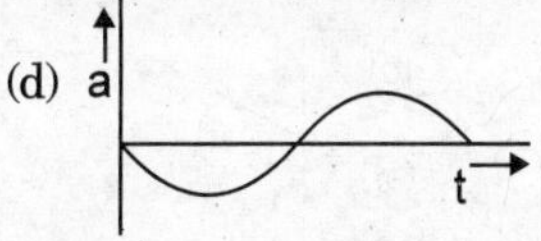

82. The diagram shows the velocity time graph for a particle moving in a straight line. The sum of the magnitudes of two shaded areas represents :

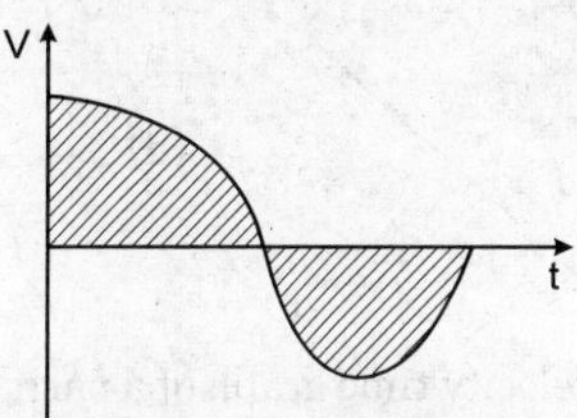

(a) displacement of the particle
(b) average velocity of the particle
(c) distance moved by the particle
(d) average speed of the particle.

83. The acceleration–time graph of a particle moving on a straight line is as shown in figure. The velocity of the particle at time t = 0 is 2m/s. The velocity after 2 seconds will be

a(m/s^2)
4
1
2 t(s)

(a) 6 m/s
(b) 4 m/s
(c) 2 m/s
(d) 8 m/s

84. The displacement-time graph of a moving object is shown in figure. The velocity-time graph representing the motion of the same body is :

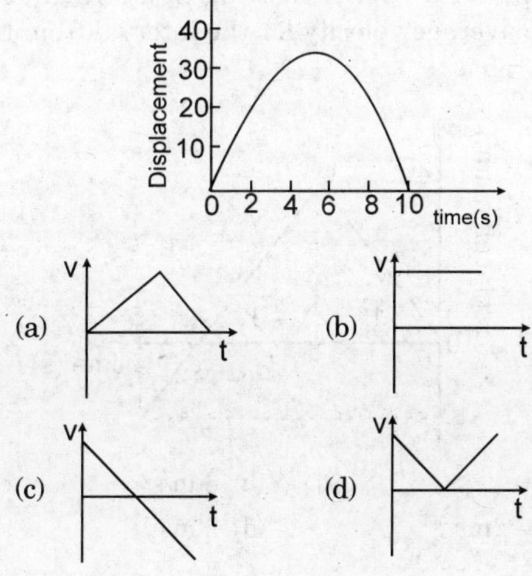

85. A particle moves along X-axis in such a way that its x-coordinate varies with time t according to the equation : $x = (6 - 4t + 6t^2)$ metre. The velocity of the particle will vary with time according to the graph

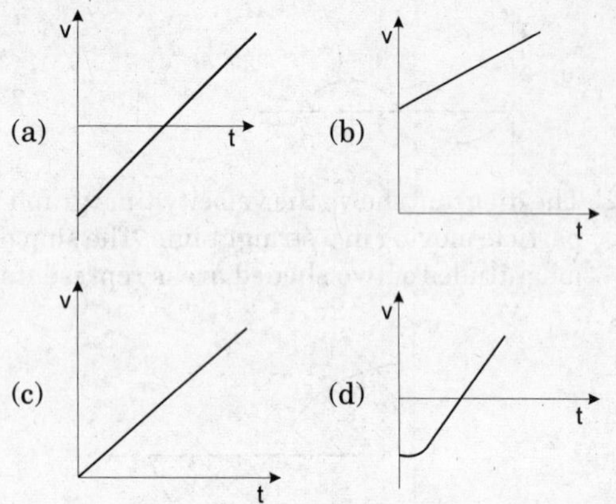

86. The velocity time graph of a particle moving along a straight line in a given time interval is as shown in figure. Then the particle (with increase in time starting from t = 0 sec.)

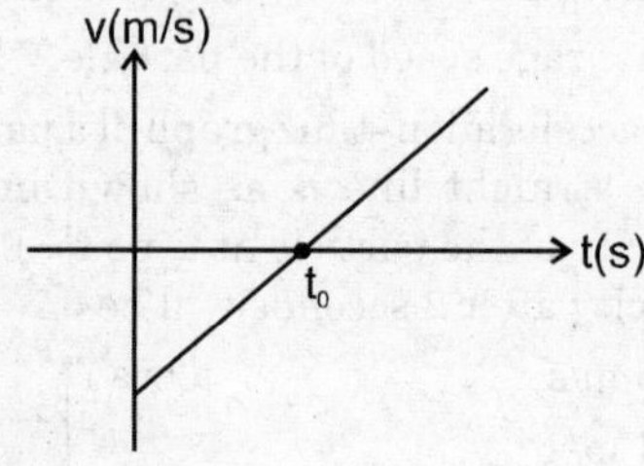

(a) speeds up

(b) speeds down

(c) first speeds down and then speeds up

(d) first speeds up and then speeds down

87. The diagram shows the displacement-time graph for a particle moving in a straight line. The average velocity for the interval from t = 0 to t = 5 is :

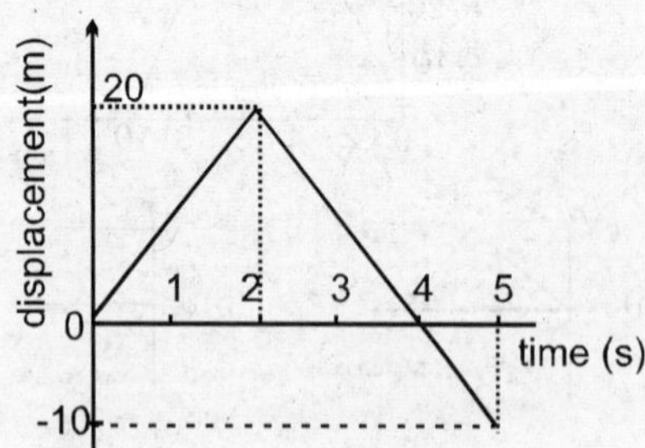

(a) 0 (b) 6 m/s^{-1}

(c) – 2ms^{-1} (d) 2 ms^{-1}

88. A particle initially at rest is subjected to two forces; one is constant, the other is a retarding force proportional to the particle velocity. In the subsequent motion of the particle, the acceleration:

(a) will increase then decrease

(b) will decrease than increase

(c) will decrease to zero

(d) will decrease and become constant at some non zero value.

89. In the above question the velocity of the block will:

(a) keep on increasing

(b) keep on decreasing

(c) increase and then become constant

(d) increase and then decrease

90. A particle moves with an initial velocity v_0 and retardation βv, where v is its velocity at any time t (β is a positive constant).

(a) the particle will cover a total distance of $2v_0/\beta$

(b) the particle will continue to move for a very long time

(c) the particle will stop shortly

(d) the velocity of particle will become $v_0/2$ after time $1/\beta$.

91. A point moves in a straight line under the retardation a v^2, where 'a' is a positive constant and v is speed. If the initial velocity is u, the distance covered in 't' seconds is :

(a) a u t (b) $\frac{1}{a}\log(a\,u\,t)$

(c) $\frac{1}{a}\log(1 + a\,u\,t)$ (d) a log (a u t)

92. A particle is moving in a straight line whose acceleration versus time graph is given. Assume that initial velocity is in the direction of acceleration. Then which of the statement is correct between time t = 0 to t = t_0.

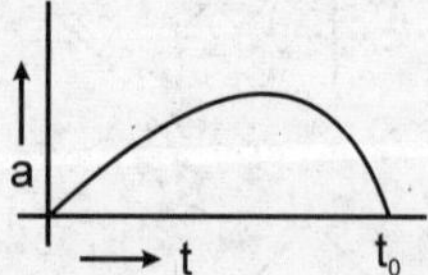

(a) Velocity first increases then decreases, displacement always increases

(b) Velocity and displacement both, first increases and then decreases

(c) Displacement increases and velocity decreases

(d) Displacement and velocity both always increases

93. A point moves in a straight line under the retardation kv^2. If the initial velocity is u, the distance covered in t seconds is:

(a) kut (b) $(1/k)\log_e(1+kut)$

(c) $(1/k)\log_e kut$ (d) $k\log_e kut$

94. A particle is moving rectilinearly so that its acceleration is given as $a = 3t^2+1$ m/s^2. Its initial velocity is zero.

(a) The velocity of the particle at t=1 sec will be 2m/s.

(b) The displacement of the particle in 1 sec will be 2m.

(c) The particle will NOT continue to move in positive direction.

(d) The particle will come back to its starting point after some time.

For Q. No. 95 to 97 :

If a man has a velocity varying with time given as $v = 3t^2$, then :

95. Find out the velocity of the man after 3 sec.

(a) 18 m/s (b) 9 m/s

(c) 27 m/s (d) 36 m/s

96. Find out his displacement after 2 seconds of his start :

(a) 10 m (b) 6 m

(c) 12 m (d) 8 m

97. Find out his acceleration after 3 seconds:

(a) 9 m/s^2 (b) 18 m/s^2

(c) 12 m/s^2 (d) 6 m/s^2

98. An aeroplane is flying in a horizontal direction with a velocity of 600 km/hour and at a height of 1960 m. When it is vertically below the point A on the ground a body is dropped from it. The body strikes the ground at point B. Calculate the distance AB.

(a) 3233 m (b) 3033 m

(c) 3433 m (d) 3333 m

99. Acceleration of a particle under projectile motion at the highest point of its trajectory is :

(a) g

(b) zero

(c) less than g

(d) dependent upon projection velocity

100. An object is thrown from a point 'A' horizontally from a tower and hits the ground 3s later at B. The line from 'A' to 'B' makes an angle of 30° with the horizontal. The initial velocity of the object is : (take g = 10 m/s^2)

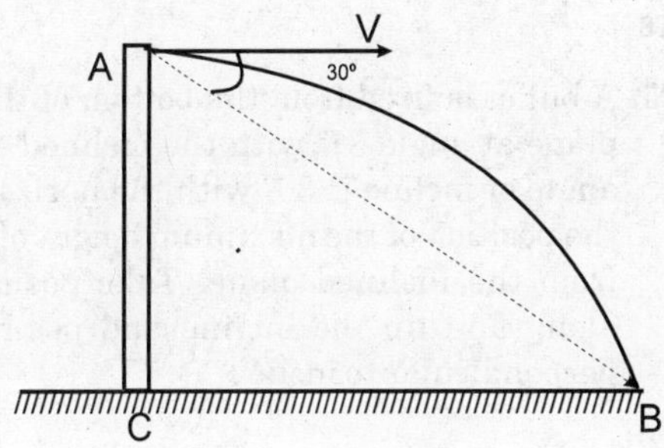

(a) $15\sqrt{3}$ m/s (b) 15 m/s

(c) $10\sqrt{3}$ m/s (d) $25/\sqrt{3}$ m/s

101. A partical A is projected with speed V_A from a point making an angle 60° with the horizontal. At the same instant, a second particle B is thrown vertically upwards from a point directly below the maximum height point of parabolic path of A, with velocity V_B. If the two particles collide then the ratio of V_A/V_B should be ;

(a) 1 (b) $2/\sqrt{3}$

(c) $\sqrt{3}/2$ (d) $\sqrt{3}$

102. A particle is projected at an angle of 60° from a horizontal plane. Then the path of projectile cannot appear a straight line to an observer:

(a) moving with constant acceleration in horizontal direction

(b) moving with constant velocity in horizontal direction

(c) moving downwards with constant acceleration 'g'

(d) none of these.

103. A particle is projected from a horizontal floor with speed 10 m/s at an angle 30° with the floor and striking the floor after sometime. State which is correct.

(a) Velocity of particle will be perpendicular to initial direction two seconds after projection.

(b) Minimum speed of particle will be 5 m/sec.

(c) Displacement of particle after half second will be 35/4 m.

(d) None of these

104. A particle is projected up the incline such that its component of velocity along the incline is 10 m/s. Time of flight is 2 sec and maximum height above the incline is 5 m. Then velocity of projection will be:

(a) 10 m/s (b) $10\sqrt{2}$ m/s

(c) $5\sqrt{5}$ m/s (d) none

105. A bullet is fired from the bottom of the inclined plane at angle 37° with the inclined plane. The angle of incline is 30° with the horizontal. Find the position of the maximum height of the bullet from the inclined plane. Take positive x-axis along and up the incline and positive y-axis perpendicular to incline.

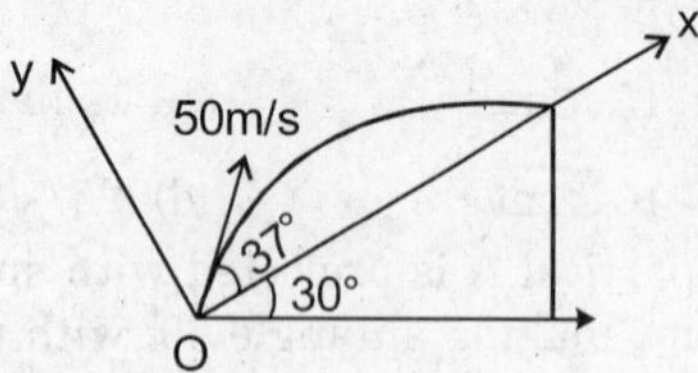

(a) $80\sqrt{3}, 30\sqrt{3}$) (b) $80\sqrt{3}-30, 30\sqrt{3}$)

(c) $80\sqrt{3}+30, 30\sqrt{3}$) (d) none

106. Velocity of a stone projected, 2 second before it reaches the maximum height, makes angle 53° with the horizontal then the velocity at highest point will be

(a) 20 m/s (b) 15 m/s

(c) 25 m/s (d) 80/3 m/s

107. A pebble is thrown horizontally from the top of a 20 m high tower with an initial velocity of 10 m/s. The air drag is negligible. The speed of the pebble when it is at the same distance from top as well as base of the tower (g = 10 m/s²)

(a) $10\sqrt{2}$ m/s (b) $10\sqrt{3}$ m/s

(c) 20 m/s (d) 25 m/s

108. A particle is projected from the inclined plane at angle 37° with the inclined plane in upward direction with speed 10 m/s. The angle of inclined plane with horizontal is 53°. Then the maximum height attained by the particle from the incline plane will be -

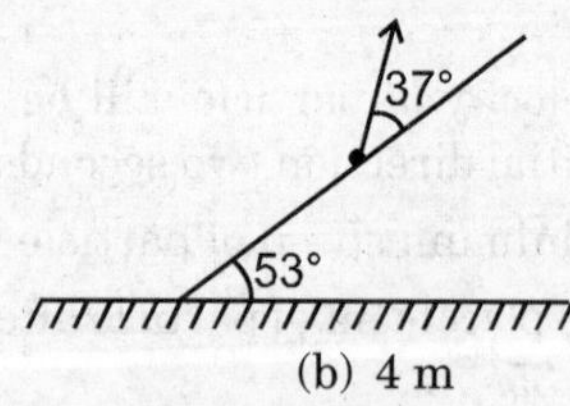

(a) 3m (b) 4 m

(c) 5 m (d) zero

109. A stone projected at angle 53° attains maximum height 25 m during its motion in air. Then its distance from the point of projection where it will fall is -

(a) 75 m (b) $\frac{400}{3}$ m

(c) 50 m (d) 60 m

110. A stone projected at angle 'θ' with horizontal from the roof of a tall building falls on the ground after three second. Two second after the projection it was again at the level of projection. Then the height of the building is-

(a) 5 m (b) 25 m

(c) 20 m (d) 15 m

111. A very broad elevator is going up vertically with a constant acceleration 1 ms^{-2}. At the instant when the velocity of the lift is 2 m/s, a stone is projected from the floor of the lift with a speed of 20 m/s relative to the floor at an elevation 30°. Find the time taken by the stone to return to the floor.

(a) 5/11 sec (b) 4/11 sec

(c) 3/11 sec (d) 2/11 sec

112. In the previous question find the range of the stone over the floor of the lift.

(a) $\frac{2}{11}$ m (b) $\frac{2\sqrt{3}}{11}$ m

(c) $\frac{2\sqrt{2}}{11}$ m (d) None of these

113. Ram can throw a ball on a horizontal surface upto a maximum distance of 50 m. The maximum height upto which he can throw the ball is

(a) 50 m (b) 25 m

(c) 12.5 m (d) 100 m

114. A ball is projected with velocity u at right angle to the slope down the incline which is inclined at an angle α with the horizontal. The distance 'x' along the inclined plane that it will travel before again striking the slope is -

(a) $\frac{2u^2}{g}\cos\alpha$ (b) $\frac{2u^2}{g}\tan\alpha$

(c) $\frac{2u^2}{g}\frac{\tan\alpha}{\cos\alpha}$ (d) $\frac{2u^2}{g}\frac{\tan\alpha}{\sin\alpha}$

115. Two bodies are thrown with the same speed at angles α and 90–α to the horizontal. Ratio of maximum heights reached by the bodies is -

(a) tan α (b) $\tan^2\alpha$

(c) $\cot^2\alpha$ (d) cot α

116. For two projection angles θ_1 and θ_2 (at the same speed), the range of a projectile is the same and time of flights are t_1 and t_2. If the range isR then the product $t_1 t_2$ is proportional to :

(a) R (b) R^2

(c) 1/R (d) $1/R_2$

117. The velocity at the maximum height of a projectile is half of its initial velocity u. Its range on the horizontal plane is:

(a) $\frac{2u^2}{3g}$ (b) $\frac{\sqrt{3}u^2}{2g}$

(c) $\frac{u^2}{3g}$ (d) $\frac{u^2}{2g}$

118. A cricket ball is hit for a six leaving the bat at an angle of 45° to the horizontal with kinetic energy k. At the top of trajectory the kinetic energy of the ball is :

(a) zero (b) k

(c) $\frac{k}{\sqrt{2}}$ (d) $\frac{k}{2}$

119. The trajectory of a projectile fired horizontally with velocity v is a parabola given by :

(a) $y = \frac{g}{2v^2}x^2$ (b) $y = -\frac{g}{2v^2}x^2$

(c) $x = \frac{g}{2v^2}y^2$ (d) $x = -\frac{g}{2v^2}y^2$

120. A body is projected with a speed u at an angle to the horizontal to have maximum range. At the highest point the velocity is:

(a) zero (b) $u\sqrt{2}$

(c) u (d) $\frac{u}{\sqrt{2}}$

121. Two particles are projected from the same point with the same speed at different angles θ_1 & θ_2 to the horizontal. They have the same range. Their times of flight are t_1 & t_2 respectively.

(a) $\theta_1 = 90 - \theta_2$ (b) $\frac{t_1}{\sin\theta_1} = \frac{t_2}{\sin\theta_2}$

(c) $\frac{t_1}{t_2} = \tan\theta_1$ (d) $\frac{t_1}{t_2} = \tan\theta_2$

122. Two balls are thrown from an inclined plane at angle of projection α with the plane one up the incline plane and other down the incline as shown in the figure. If R_1 & R_2 be their respective ranges, then which of the following is incorrect:

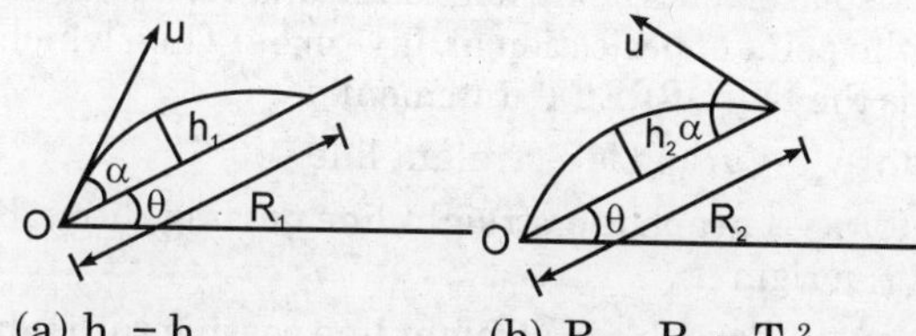

(a) $h_1 = h_2$ (b) $R_2 - R_1 = T_1^2$

(c) $R_2 - R_1 = g\sin\theta\, T_2^2$ (d) $R_2 - R_1 = g\sin\theta\, T_1^2$

[here T_1 & T_2 are times of flight in the two cases respectively]

123. A ball rolls off the top of a stair way with a horizontal velocity u m/s. If the steps are h metre high and b metres wide, the ball will hit the edge of the nth step if:

(a) $n = 2hu/gb^2$ (b) $n = 2hu^2/gb^2$

(c) $n = 2hu^2/gb$ (d) $n = hu^2/gb^2$

124. A particle has a range R on the horizontal plane. If h and h′ are the greatest heights in the two possible paths for this range and a given speed, then :

(a) $R = 4\sqrt{(h h')}$ (b) $R = \frac{4h}{h'}$

(c) $R = 4hh'$ (d) $R = \sqrt{hh'}$

125. A body is projected at time (t = 0) from a certain point on a planet's surface with a certain velocity at a certain angle with the planet's surface (assumed horizontal). The horizontal and vertical displacements x & y (in metre) respectively vary with time t in second as, $x = 10\sqrt{3}\ t$ & $y = 10t - t^2$. Then the max. height attained by the body is

(a) 200 m (b) 100 m

(c) 50 m (d) 25 m

126. A shell fired from a heavy gun at sea level rises to a maximum height of 5 km when fired at a ship 20 km away. The muzzle velocity (velocity relative to gun) should be:

(a) 7 m/sec (b) 14 m/s

(c) 28 m/sec (d) $200\sqrt{5}$ m/s

127. A particle is thrown from a platform with velocity v at an angle of 60° with the horizontal. The range obtained is R. If the platform moves horizontally in the direction of target with velocity v/2, the range will increase to :

(a) 3R/2 (b) 5R/2

(c) 2 R (d) 3 R

128. A ball is thrown upward at an angle of 30° with the horizontal and lands on the top edge of a building that is 20 m away. The top edge is 5m above the throwing point. The initial speed of the ball in metre/second is (take g = 10 m/s²) :

(a) 10 m/s (b) 20 m/s

(c) 25 m/s (d) 30 m/s

129. A ball is thrown from bottom of an incline plane at an angle α from the inclined surface up the plane. Another ball is thrown from a point on the inclined plane with same speed and at same angle α from the inclined surface down the plane. If in the two cases, maximum height attained by the balls with respect to the inclined surface during projectile motion are h_1 and h_2 then :

(a) $h_1 > h_2$ (b) $h_1 < h_2$

(c) $h_1 = h_2$ (d) All of these

130. A particle is projected with a velocity $10\sqrt{2}$ m/s making an angle 45° with the horizontal. Neglect the effect of air friction. Then after 1 seconds of projection. Take g=10 m/s²

(a) the height of the particle above the point of projection is 5 m.

(b) the height of the particle above the point of projection is 10 m.

(c) the horizontal distance of the particle from the point of projection is 5 m.

(d) the horizontal distance of the particle from the point of projection is 15 m.

131. An aircraft moving with a speed of 1000 km/h is at a height of 6000 m, just overhead of an anti-aircraft gun. If the muzzle velocity of the gun is 540 m/s, the firing angle θ for the bullet to hit the aircraft should be

(a) 73^0

(b) 30^0

(c) 60^0

(d) 45^0

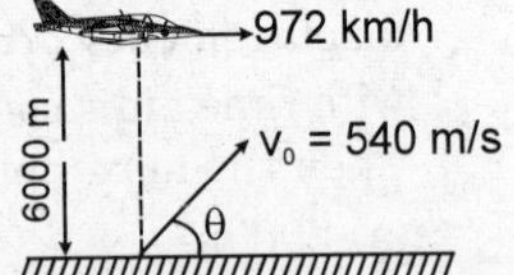

132. The vertical height of the projectile at time t is given by $y = 4t - t^2$ and the horizontal distance covered is given by $x = 3t$. What is the angle of projection with the horizontal?

(a) $\tan^{-1} 3/5$ (b) $\tan^{-1} 4/5$

(c) $\tan^{-1} 4/3$ (d) $\tan^{-1} 3/4$

133. A body is projected horizontally from the top of a tower with initial velocity 18 ms^{-1}. It hits the ground at angle 45°. What is the vertical component of velocity when it strikes the ground?

(a) $18\sqrt{2}$ ms^{-1} (b) 18 ms^{-1}

(c) $9\sqrt{2}$ ms^{-1} (d) 9 ms^{-1}

134. The equation of motion of a projectile is $y = 12x - 3/4\,x^2$. Given that g = 10 ms^{-2}. What is the range of the projectile?

(a) 36 m (b) 30.6 m

(c) 16 m (d) 12.4 m

135. An athlete runs with a speed 12 ms^{-1}. Determine the longest jump he can undertake.

(a) 14.4 (b) 12 m

(c) 12.1 m (d) 16.2 m

136. The maximum height attained by a projectile and its horizontal range are equal to each other if the projectile is projected at an angle θ given by

(a) $\theta = \tan^{-1}(2)$ (b) $\theta = \tan^{-1}(3)$

(c) $\theta = \tan^{-1}(4)$ (d) $\theta = \tan^{-1}(5)$

137. A bomb is dropped from an aeroplane when it is at a height h directly above the target. If the aeroplane is moving horizontally with a speed v, the distance by which the bomb will miss the target is given by

(a) $2v\sqrt{\dfrac{h}{g}}$ (b) $v\sqrt{\dfrac{h}{g}}$

(c) $v\sqrt{\dfrac{2h}{g}}$ (d) $v\sqrt{\dfrac{h}{2g}}$

138. A body is projected with kinetic energy k at angle ϕ with the vertical. Neglecting friction, its potential energy at the highest point will be

(a) $k\cos^2\phi$ (b) $k\sin^2\phi$

(c) k (d) zero

139. Distance between a frog and an insect on a horizontal plane is 10 m. Frog can jump with a maximum speed of $\sqrt{10}$ m/s. g =10 m/s². Minimum number of jumps required by the frog to catch the insect is:

(a) 5 (b) 10

(c) 100 (d) 50

140. A stone is projected from level ground such that its horizontal and vertical components of initial velocity are u_x = 10 m/s and u_y = 20 m/s respectively. Then the angle between velocity vector of stone one second before and one second after it attains maximum height is :

(a) 30° (b) 45°

(c) 60° (d) 90°

141. A stone is projected from point A with speed u making an angle 60° with horizontal as shown. The fixed inclined surface makes an angle 30° with horizontal. The stone lands at B after time t. Then the distance AB is equal to.

(a) $\dfrac{ut}{\sqrt{3}}$

(b) $\dfrac{\sqrt{3}ut}{2}$

(c) $\sqrt{3}ut$

(d) 2 ut

142. A stone is projected from level ground at time t=0. Let v_x and v_y are the horizontal and vertical components of velocity at any time t ; x and y are displacements along horizontal and vertical from the point of projection at any time t. Then which is the INCORRECT statement

(a) $v_y - t$ graph is a straight line

(b) $x - t$ graph is a straight line passing through origin

(c) $y - t$ graph is a straight line passing through origin

(d) $v_x - t$ graph is a straight line

143. A boat is rowed across a river at the rate of 4.5 km/hr. The river flows at the rate of 6 km/hr. The velocity of boat in m/s is:

(a) 3.1 (b) 2.1

(c) 2.9 (d) 5

144. A boat which can move with a speed of 5 m/s relative to water crosses a river of width 480 m flowing with a constant speed of 4 m/s. Find the time taken by the boat to cross the river along the path which is shortest.

(a) 160s (b) 80s

(c) 100s (d) 40s

145. Find also the length of shortest path in the previous question

(a) 160m (b) 400m

(c) 240m (d) 480m

146. The driver in a running car is at _________with respect to the person in the back seat of the car but is in _________with respect to a pedestrian on the road. Fill in the blanks

(a) rest, rest (b) motion, motion

(c) motion, rest (d) rest, motion

147. Man A is sitting in a car moving with a speed of 54 km/hr observes a man B in front of the car crossing perpendicularly a road of width 15 m in three seconds. Then the velocity of man B (in m/s) will be:

(a) $5\sqrt{10}$ towards the car at some angle

(b) $5\sqrt{10}$ away from the car at some angle

(c) 5 perpendicular to the road

(d) 15 along the road

148. A boat is moving towards east with velocity 4 m/s with respect to still water and river is flowing towards north with velocity 2 m/s and the wind is blowing towards north with velocity 6 m/s. The direction of the flag blown over by the wind hoisted on the boat is:

(a) north-west (b) south-east

(c) $\tan^{-1}\frac{1}{2}$ with east (d) north

149. A train is standing on a platform , a man inside a compartment of a train drops a stone . At the same instant train starts to move with constant acceleration . The path of the particle as seen by the person who drops the stone is :

(a) parabola

(b) straight line for sometime & parabola for the remaining time

(c) straight line

(d) variable path that cannot be defined

150. A man wearing a hat of extended length 12 cm is running in rain falling vertically downwards with speed 10 m/s. The maximum speed with which man can run, so that rain drops do not fall on his face (the length of his face below the extended part of the hat is 16 cm) will be :

(a) 7.5 m/s (b) 13.33 m/s

(c) 10 m/s (d) zero

151. A man holding a flag is running in North-East direction with speed 10 m/s. Wind is blowing in east direction with speed $5\sqrt{2}$ m/s. Find the direction in which flag will flutter.

(a) south (b) east

(c) north (d) west

152. A coin is released inside a lift at a height of 2 m from the floor of the lift. The height of the lift is 10 m. The lift is moving with an acceleration of 9 m/s^2 downwards. The time after which the coin will strike with the lift is : (g = 10 m/s^2)

(a) 4 s (b) 2 s

(c) $\frac{4}{\sqrt{21}}$ s (d) $\frac{2}{\sqrt{11}}$ s

153. A man in a balloon, throws a stone downwards with a speed of 5 m/s with respect to balloon. The balloon is moving upwards with a constant acceleration of 5 m/s^2. Then velocity of the stone relative to the man after 2 second is :

(a) 10 m/s (b) 30 m/s

(c) 15 m/s (d) 35 m/s

154. A boat is rowing in a river at the rate of 4.8 km/hr with respect to river. The river flows at the rate of 6 km/hr. The speed of boat in m/s can be :

(a) 3.1 (b) 2.1

(c) 4.5 (d) 5

155. P is a point moving with constant speed 10 m/s such that its velocity vector always maintains an angle 60° with line OP as shown in figure (O is a fixed point in space). The initial distance between O and P is 100 m. After what time shall P reach O.

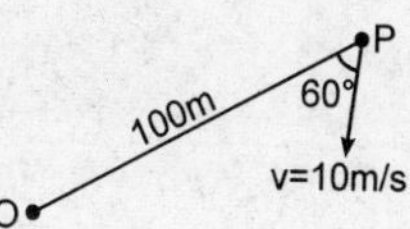

(a) 10 sec.

(b) 15 sec.

(c) 20 sec.

(d) $20\sqrt{3}$ sec

156. A man is sitting inside a moving train and observes the objects outside of the train. Then choose the single correct choice from the following statements -

(a) all stationary objects outside the train will move with same velocity in opposite direction of the train with respect to the man.

(b) stationary objects near the train will move with greater velocity & object far from train will move with lesser velocity with respect to the man.

(c) large objects like moon or mountains will move with same velocity as that of the train.

(d) all of these.

157. When two bodies move uniformly towards each other, the distance between them diminishes by 16 m every 10 s. If bodies move with velocities of the same magnitude and in the same direction as before the distance between then will decrease 3 m every 5 s. The velocity of each body is

(a) $v_1 = 1$ m/s and $v_2 = 0.5$ m/s.

(b) $v_1 = 0.1$ m/s and $v_2 = 0.5$ m/s.

(c) $v_1 = 1.1$ m/s and $v_2 = 1.5$ m/s.

(d) $v_1 = 1.1$ m/sand $v_2 = 0.5$ m/s.

158. Two particles are moving along a straight line as shown. The velocity of approach between A and B is

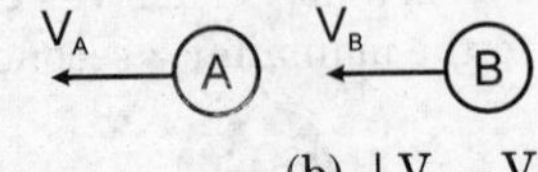

(a) $V_A + V_B$ (b) $|V_A - V_B|$

(c) $V_A - V_B$ (d) $V_B - V_A$

159. A truck is moving with a velocity of 5 m/s. A man at the rear end of the truck throws a ball with a velocity 10 m/s at an angle of 60° with horizontal with respect to the truck and in the opposite direction to the direction of truck. Then the path (w.r.t. ground) of the particle is:

(a) a parabola

(b) linear motion in horizontal motion

(c) vertical linear motion

(d) none of these.

160. A train is standing on a platform, a man inside a compartment of a train drops a stone. At the same instant train starts to move with constant acceleration. The path of the particle as seen by the person who drops the stone is :

(a) parabola

(b) straight line for sometime & parabola for the remaining time

(c) straight line

(d) variable path that cannot be defined

161. A jet airplane travelling from east to west at a speed of 500 km h^{-1} ejected out gases of combustion at a speed of 1500 km h^{-1} with respect to the jet plane. What is the elocity of the gases with respect to an observer on the ground ?

(a) 1000 km h^{-1} in the direction west to east

(b) 1000 km h^{-1} in the direction east to west

(c) 2000 km h^{-1} in the direction west to east

(d) 2000 km h^{-1} in the direction east to west

162. Rain is falling vertically with a velocity of 3 kmh^{-1}. A man walks in the rain with a velocity of 4 kmh^{-1}. The rain drops will fall on the man with a velocity of

(a) 5 kmh^{-1} (b) 4 kmh^{-1}

(c) 3 kmh^{-1} (d) 1 kmh^{-1}

163. To a man running on level horizontal ground at a speed of 5 m/sec, rain drops appear to be falling at an angle of 45° from the vertical. If the rain drops are actually falling vertically downwards, then find the velocity of rain drops relative to ground?

(a) 4 m/s (b) 3 m/s

(c) 6m/s (d) 5m/s

164. A man who can swim at the rate of 2 km/hr (in still river) crosses a river to a point exactly opposite on the other bank by swimming in a direction of 120° to the flow of the water in the river. The velocity of the water current in km/hr is

(a) 1

(b) 2

(c) 1/2.

(d) 3/2

Answers

1. (*d*)	**2.** (*a*)	**3.** (*a*)	**4.** (*a*)	**5.** (*d*)	**6.** (*b*)	**7.** (*b*)	**8.** (*c*)	**9.** (*d*)	**10.** (*a*)
11. (*c*)	**12.** (*b*)	**13.** (*a*)	**14.** (*c*)	**15.** (*a*)	**16.** (*c*)	**17.** (*a*)	**18.** (*b*)	**19.** (*b*)	**20.** (*a*)
21. (*a*)	**22.** (*b*)	**23.** (*d*)	**24.** (*b*)	**25.** (*d*)	**26.** (*c*)	**27.** (*c*)	**28.** (*b*)	**29.** (*c*)	**30.** (*a*)
31. (*b*)	**32.** (*b*)	**33.** (*b*)	**34.** (*d*)	**35.** (*c*)	**36.** (*a*)	**37.** (*b*)	**38.** (*d*)	**39.** (*b*)	**40.** (*b*)
41. (*c*)	**42.** (*a*)	**43.** (*d*)	**44.** (*b*)	**45.** (*a*)	**46.** (*b*)	**47.** (*d*)	**48.** (*d*)	**49.** (*c*)	**50.** (*a*)
51. (*c*)	**52.** (*d*)	**53.** (*d*)	**54.** (*c*)	**55.** (*d*)	**56.** (*c*)	**57.** (*c*)	**58.** (*c*)	**59.** (*c*)	**60.** (*c*)
61. (*b*)	**62.** (*c*)	**63.** (*c*)	**64.** (*c*)	**65.** (*b*)	**66.** (*d*)	**67.** (*b*)	**68.** (*d*)	**69.** (*b*)	**70.** (a)
71. (*a*)	**72.** (*d*)	**73.** (*c*)	**74.** (*a*)	**75.** (*a*)	**76.** (*c*)	**77.** (*d*)	**78.** (*d*)	**79.** (*b*)	**80.** (*a*)
81. (*b*)	**82.** (*c*)	**83.** (*a*)	**84.** (*c*)	**85.** (*a*)	**86.** (*d*)	**87.** (*c*)	**88.** (*c*)	**89.** (*c*)	**90.** (*b*)
91. (*c*)	**92.** (*d*)	**93.** (*b*)	**94.** (*a*)	**95.** (*c*)	**96.** (*d*)	**97.** (*b*)	**98.** (*d*)	**99.** (*a*)	**100.** (*a*)
101. (*b*)	**102.** (*d*)	**103.** (*d*)	**104.** (*b*)	**105.** (*b*)	**106.** (*b*)	**107.** (*b*)	**108.** (*a*)	**109.** (*a*)	**110.** (*d*)
111. (*d*)	**112.** (*b*)	**113.** (*b*)	**114.** (*c*)	**115.** (*b*)	**116.** (*a*)	**117.** (*b*)	**118.** (*d*)	**119.** (*b*)	**120.** (*d*)
121. (*a*)	**122.** (*b*)	**123.** (*b*)	**124.** (*a*)	**125.** (*d*)	**126.** (*b*)	**127.** (*c*)	**128.** (*b*)	**129.** (*c*)	**130.** (*a*)
131. (*c*)	**132.** (*c*)	**133.** (*b*)	**134.** (*c*)	**135.** (*a*)	**136.** (*c*)	**137.** (*c*)	**138.** (*a*)	**139.** (*b*)	**140.** (*d*)
141. (*a*)	**142.** (*c*)	**143.** (*b*)	**144.** (*a*)	**145.** (*d*)	**146.** (*d*)	**147.** (*b*)	**148.** (*a*)	**149.** (*c*)	**150.** (*a*)
151. (*a*)	**152.** (*b*)	**153.** (*d*)	**154.** (*b*)	**155.** (*c*)	**156** (*a*)	**157.** (*d*)	**158.** (*d*)	**159.** (*c*)	**160.** (*c*)
161. (*a*)	**162.** (*a*)	**163.** (*d*)	**164.** (*a*)						

Explanations

1. As can be seen from the figure

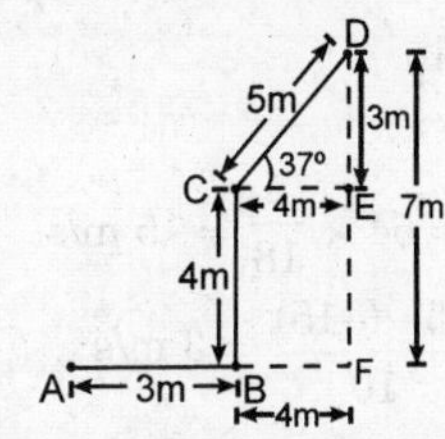

the displacement is $\sqrt{(AF)^2 + (FD)^2} = 7\sqrt{2}$ m

2. $\vec{d}_i = 2\hat{i}$

$\vec{d}_2 = 2\hat{i}$

$\vec{d}_2 = 5\cos 37\hat{i} - 5\sin 37\hat{j}$

$\vec{d}_3 = ?$

$\vec{d} = 6\hat{i}$

$\vec{d} = \vec{d}_1 + \vec{d}_2 + \vec{d}_3$

$\vec{d}_3 = 6\hat{i} - 2\hat{i} - 4\hat{i} + 3\hat{j} = 3\hat{j}$

3. $\vec{d} = \vec{d}_1 + \vec{d}_2$ where $\vec{d}_1 = 10\hat{j}$ and $\vec{d}_2 = 20\hat{i}$

$\vec{d} = 10\hat{j} + 20\hat{i}$

$|\vec{d}| = \sqrt{500} = 22.36$ km.

4. $S_2 = S_n - S_{n-2}$.

$$S_2 = \frac{1}{2}an^2 - \frac{1}{2}a(n-2)^2 \quad ....(1)$$

$$\text{and } v = an = a = \frac{v}{n} \quad ....(2)$$

5. $$v_{an} = \frac{\text{displacement}}{\text{time}} = \frac{x}{\frac{x}{3(20)} + \frac{2x}{3(60)}} = 36$$

6. $\vec{v}_i = v\hat{j}$

$\vec{v}_f = -v\sin\hat{i} + v\cos\theta\hat{j}$

$|\Delta\vec{V}| = |\vec{v}_F - \vec{v}_I| = |-(v + v\sin\theta)\hat{i} + v\cos\theta\,\hat{j}|$

$\Delta\vec{v} = \sqrt{(v + v\sin\theta)^2 + (v\cos\theta)^2} = 2v\sin 20°$

8. For example uniform circular motion.

9. $V_1 = 50\hat{j}$

$V_2 = -50\hat{i}$

$\Delta V = -50\hat{i} - 50\hat{j}$

10. $V = a + bx$

(V increases as x increases)

$\frac{dV}{dt} = b\frac{dx}{dt} = bV$

hence acceleration increases as V increases with x.

11. $v^2 = a + bx$

v increases as x increases

$a = v\frac{dv}{dx} = \frac{1}{2}\frac{d}{dx}(v^2) = \frac{b}{2}$

hence acceleration is constant.

12. About change in speed depending on the choice of the positive direction of the velocity

13. $\vec{r} = (t^2 - 4t + 6)\hat{i} + t^2\hat{j}$;

$\vec{v} = \frac{d\vec{r}}{dt} = (2t-4)\hat{i} + 2t\hat{j}$,

$\vec{a} = \frac{d\vec{v}}{dt} = 2\hat{i} + 2\hat{j}$

if $\vec{a}$ and $\vec{v}$ are perpendicular

$\vec{a}\cdot\vec{v} = 0$

$(2\hat{i} + 2\hat{j}).((2t-4)\hat{i} + 2t\hat{j}) = 0$

$8t - 8 = 0$, $t = 1$ sec.

14. On the curve

$y = x^2$ at $x = 1/2$

$y = \frac{1}{4}$

Hence the coordinate $\left(\frac{1}{2},\frac{1}{4}\right)$

Differentiating : $y = x^2$

$v_y = 2xv_x$

$v_y = 2\left(\frac{1}{2}\right)(4) = 4$ m/s

Which satisfies the line

$4x - 4y - 1 = 0$(tangent to the curve)

& magnitude of velocity :

$|\vec{v}| = \sqrt{v_x^2 + v_y^2} = 4\sqrt{2}$ m/s

15.

x_2: from −14 to 6; x_1: from −14 to −10

−14 (t = 2 sec.), −10 (t = 0 sec.), 0, 6 (t = 4 sec.)

$x = t^3 - 3t^2 - 10$

$v = \frac{dx}{dt} = 3t^2 - 6t$

v = 0; gives t = 0

and t = 2 sec.

Velocity will become zero at t = 2 sec., so particle will change direction after t = 2 sec.

At t = 0

$x_{(0\ sec)} = -10$

At t = 2 sec.

$x_{(2\ sec)} = 2^3 - 3(2)^2 - 10$

$= 8 - 12 - 10 = -14$

At t = 4 sec.

$x_{(4\ sec)} = 4^3 - 3(4)^2 - 10 = 64 - 48 - 10 = 6$

Distance travelled $= x_1 + x_2$

$= |-14-(-10)| + |6-(-14)|$

$= 4 + 20 = 24$

16. If the velocity is in the direction of acceleration it will speed up.

17. At t = 0

$\frac{dx}{dt} = 0$ for particles 1,2 and 3 and $\left|\frac{d^2x}{dt^2}\right| > 0$ for $t > 0$

and= − 3.4 m/s for particle 4 and $\frac{d^2x}{dt^2}$ is negative for $t > 0$

Therefore for $t > 0$; $\left|\frac{dx}{dt}\right|$ is increasing in all.

18. $v_p = \left.\frac{dx}{dt}\right|_{t=0} = \gamma$ and $a_i = \left.\frac{d^2x}{dt^2}\right|_{t=0} = 2\beta$

$\Rightarrow \frac{a_i}{v_i} = \frac{2\beta}{\gamma}$

19. $54\ km/h = 54 \times \frac{5}{18} = 15$ m/s

$\langle a \rangle = \frac{15-(-15)}{10} = 3\ m/s^2$.

20. $a_x = \frac{d^2x}{dt^2} = 8m/s^2$

$a_y = \frac{d^2x}{dt^2} = 0$

21. $v = 0 \Rightarrow x^2 - 5x + 4 = 0$

x = 1m & 4m

$\frac{dv}{dt} = (2x-5)v = (2x-5)(x^2 - 5x + 4)$

at x = 1 m and 4m ; $\frac{dv}{dt} = 0$

22. $\sqrt{x} = (2t-3)$

$x = (2t-3)^2$

$\frac{dx}{dt} = 2(2t-3)(2) = 4(2t-3)$

$V = 4(2t-3) = 0$

rest at $t = 2/3$

$a = 8$ m/s.

23. Let the acceleration of first car be a, then acceleration of second car is $\frac{a}{2}$.

For first car $\Rightarrow O = v - at$

or $t = \frac{v}{a}$

for second car $\Rightarrow O = v - \frac{a}{2}t'$ or $t' = \frac{2v}{a} = 2t$

24. $\vec{a}_{av} = \frac{\Delta\vec{v}}{\Delta t} = \frac{5\hat{j} - 5\hat{i}}{10} = \frac{1}{2}\hat{j} - \frac{1}{2}\hat{i}$

So $\frac{1}{\sqrt{2}} m/s^2$ is 2nd Quadrant

25. $\vec{V} = 6\frac{2\hat{i} - \hat{j} - 2\hat{k}}{3}$

$\vec{r} = \vec{r}_0 + \vec{v}t = 3\hat{i} + 4\hat{j} - 7\hat{k} + 4 \times 2(2\hat{i} - \hat{j} - 2\hat{k})$

$\Rightarrow \vec{r} = 19\hat{i} - 4\hat{j} - 23\hat{k}$

26. V_{min} when acceleration is zero

$\frac{dv}{dt} = 0 = 2t - 2 \Rightarrow t = 1\text{sec}$

$\Rightarrow V_{min} = 1^2 - 2 \times 1 - 3 = 0$

27.

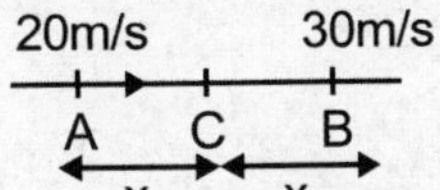

20m/s 30m/s

A C B

x x

$a = \frac{V_B^2 - V_A^2}{2 \times 2x} = \frac{900 - 400}{4x} = \frac{125}{x}$

$\therefore V_C = \sqrt{V_B^2 + 2ax}$

$= \sqrt{400 + 2 \times \frac{125}{x} \times x} = \sqrt{650} = 25.5$ m/s.

28. Magnitude of slope is same but sign is opposite.

29. $\frac{S_{nth}}{S_n} = \frac{\frac{a}{2}(2n-1)}{\frac{a}{2}n^2} = \frac{2}{n} - \frac{1}{n^2}$

30. To move in a straight line

$\vec{a} \,||\, \vec{u}$

31. $\text{time} = \frac{75/1000}{40 + v} = \frac{3}{3600} = v = 50\text{km/h}.$

32. $S = \frac{1}{2} \times 2 \times 10^2 = 100\text{m}$

33. $v = \sqrt{u^2 + 2as}$

$= \sqrt{0^2 + 2 \times 2 \times 100} = 2 \times 10 = 20$ m/sec.

34. Since acceleration is zero, and final velocity is dependent variable on a and u

So, $v = 0$ m/sec.

35. $V^2 = u^2 + 2as$

$(10)^2 = 0 + 2 \times 5 \times S$

$\Rightarrow S = 10$ m.

36. $10.2 = vt - \frac{1}{2}gt^2$

$gt^2 - 2vt + 20.4 = 0$

The difference of root is 10s

$\Rightarrow \frac{\sqrt{v^2 - 4 \times 10.2 \times 5}}{5} = 10$

$\Rightarrow v = 52$ m/s.

37. At position A balloon drops first particle

So, $u_A = 0$, $a_A = -g$, $t = 3.5$ sec.

$S_A = \left(\frac{1}{2}gt^2\right)$ ....(i)

Balloon is going upward from A to B in 2 sec.so distance travelled by balloon in 2 second.

$\left(S_B = \frac{1}{2}a_B t^2\right)$ ....(ii)

$a_B = 0.4\ m/s^2, t = 2$ sec.

$S_1 = BC = (SB + SA)$ ....(iii)

Distance travell by second stone which is droped from balloon at B

$u_2 = u_B = a_B t = 0.4 \times 2 = 0.8$ m/s $t = 1.5$ sec.

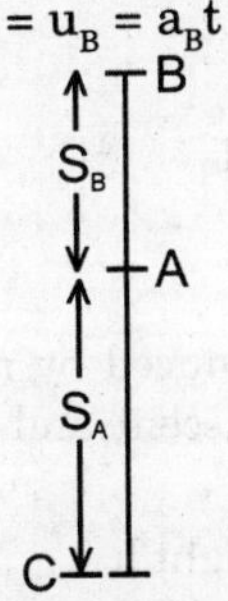

B

S_B

A

S_A

C

$\left(S_2 = u_2 t - \frac{1}{2}gt^2\right)$ ....(iv)

Distance between two stone

$\Delta S = S_1 - S_2$.

38. if they meet position is same

$$x_1 = 98t - \frac{1}{2}(9.8)t^2$$

$$x_2 = 98(t-4) - \frac{1}{2}(9.8)(t-4)^2$$

$\Rightarrow x_1 = x_2 \Rightarrow t = 12s.$

39.

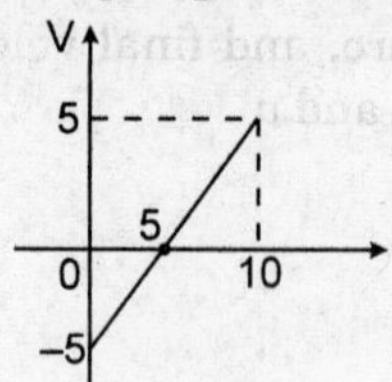

From the graph distance $= 2\left(\frac{1}{2}\times 5\times 5\right) = 25$ m

40. $v = u + at \Rightarrow 20 = u + a \times 10$ ....(1)

$s_n = u + \frac{a}{2}(2n-1)$

$\Rightarrow 10 = u + \frac{a}{2}(2 \times 10 - 1)$ ....(2)

On solving (1) and (2) we get

$a = 20$ m/s²

41. $V_{SB} = 10$(down)

$V_B = 20$(up)

$\vec{V}_S = \vec{V}_{SB} + \vec{V}_B = -10\hat{j} + 20\hat{j} = 10\hat{j}$

$120 = 10t = \frac{1}{2} \times 10t^2 \Rightarrow t = 6 \text{ or } -4$

42. At maximum displacement velocity is zero.

$0 = 4 + a(2) \Rightarrow = -2$ m/s²

For displacement to be zero

$0 = 4(t) - \frac{1}{2}(2)t^2 \Rightarrow t = 4s.$

43. $t = \sqrt{\frac{2h}{g}}$

$$S_{n_{th}} = 0 + \frac{g}{2}\left(2\sqrt{\frac{2h}{g}} - 1\right) = 24.5$$

$\Rightarrow h = 44.1$ M

44. Let a be the retardation produced by resistive force, t_a and t_d be the time ascent and descent respectively.

If the particle rises upto a height h

then $h = \frac{1}{2}(g + a)t_a^2$ and $h = \frac{1}{2}(g - a)t_d^2$

$$\therefore \frac{t_a}{t_d} = \sqrt{\frac{g-a}{g+a}} = \sqrt{\frac{10-2}{10+2}} = \sqrt{\frac{2}{3}}$$

45. el. of Ist stone when passing at A →

$V^2 = 0 + 2.10.5$

$V = 10$ m/s

$S_1 - S_2 = 20$ m.

$$\Rightarrow \left(10.t + \frac{1}{2}10.t^2\right) - \left(\frac{1}{2}.10.t^2\right) = 20$$

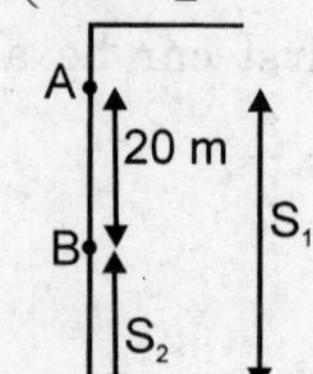

$t = 2s$

$S_2 = \frac{1}{2}.10.4 = 20$ m

Ht = 25 + 20 = 45 m.

46. At the highest point v = 0, so acceleration due to air to air resistance is zero.

47. $v = u + at$

$v - u = at$

48. $\frac{ds}{dt} = 490 - 9.8\,t = 0$

$\Rightarrow t = \frac{490}{9.8} = 50$

Maximum height reached = 490 × 50 – 4.9 × 50²

= 12250 m.

49. Velocity of the body at any time t

$v = \frac{ds}{dt} = 15 - 0.8\,t$

when v = 7

$\Rightarrow 15 - 0.8\,t = 7$

$\Rightarrow t = \frac{15-7}{0.8} = 10$

50. Velocity of the body at any time t is

$v = \frac{ds}{dt} = 10 - 0.2\,t$

when v = 0

$t = \frac{10}{0.2} = 50$ s.

51. Sum of distance travelled in t^{th} & $(t+1)^{th}$ Seconds = 100 cm

$\Rightarrow u + \frac{a}{2}(2t-1) + u + \frac{a}{2}(2(t+1)-1) = 100$

$\Rightarrow 2u + 2ft = 100$

$\Rightarrow u + ft = 100/2$

$\Rightarrow v = 50$ cm/s.

52. $x \propto t^3 \Rightarrow x = ct^3$ (say)

Then, $\frac{dx}{dt} = 3ct^2$

and, $\frac{d^2x}{dt^2} = a = 6ct$

$\therefore a \propto t.$

53. $V = x^2 + x$

$\Rightarrow \frac{dv}{dt} = 2x\frac{dx}{dt} + \frac{dx}{dt}$

$\Rightarrow a = (2x + 1)V = (2x + 1)(x^2 + x)$

$\therefore$ When x = 2m

$a = (2 \times 2 + 1)(2^2 + 2) = 5 \times 6 = 30 \text{ m/s}^2.$

54. Displacement of particle 1 after time t,

$x_1 = 50\,t$

Displacement of particle 2 after time t,

$x_2 = \frac{1}{2} \times 10 \times t^2 = 5t^2$

According to question,

$5t^2 - 50t = 125$ or $50t - 50t^2 = 125$

$\Rightarrow t^2 - 10t - 25 = 0$ or $t^2 - 10t + 25 = 0$

$\Rightarrow t = 5(1 + \sqrt{2})$s or $t^2 = 5$ sec.

55. According to question,

Displacement in 2 s = 200 cm

Displacement in 6 s = 200 + 220 = 420 cm

$\therefore 2u + \frac{1}{2} \times a \times 2^2 = 200$

$\Rightarrow 2u + 2a = 200$

$\Rightarrow u + a = 100$ ....(i)

$6u + \frac{1}{2} \times a \times 6^2 = 420$

$\Rightarrow 6u + 18a = 420$

$\Rightarrow u + 3a = 70$ ....(ii)

Solving equation, (i) & (ii)

$u = 115$ cm/s, $a = -15 \text{ cm/s}^2$

$\therefore v = u + at = 115 - 15 \times 7 = 115 - 105 = 10$ cm/s.

56. At B parachute opens out & he falls with a retardation of 2.5 m/s².

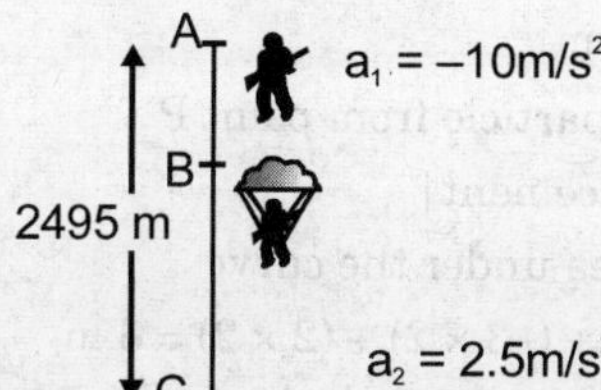

$\therefore AB = \frac{1}{2} \times 10 \times 10^2 = 500$ m

$\therefore BC = AC - AB = 2495 - 500 = 1995$ m.

Velocity at B,

$V_B = gt = 10 \times 10 = 100$ m/s $\downarrow$

Velocity at C,

$V_C = \sqrt{V_B^2 + 2ay} = \sqrt{100^2 + 2 \times 2.5 \times (-1995)}$

$= \sqrt{25} = 5$ m/s $\downarrow$

57. Let initial velocity of the ball = u

$\therefore 25 = ut - \frac{1}{2}gt^2 = ut - 5t^2$

$\Rightarrow 5t^2 - ut + 25 = 0$

If t_1 and t_2 are the two solutions,

Then, $t_2 - t_1 = \sqrt{(t_2 + t_1)^2 - 4t_1t_2}$

58. Distance travelled by a freely falling body

$y = v\frac{1}{2}gt^2$

$\therefore y \propto t^2$.

59. For downward motion,

$h = ut_1 + \frac{1}{2}gt_1^2$ ....(i)

For upward motion,

$h = -ut_2 + \frac{1}{2}gt_2^2$ ....(ii)

From (1) & (2)

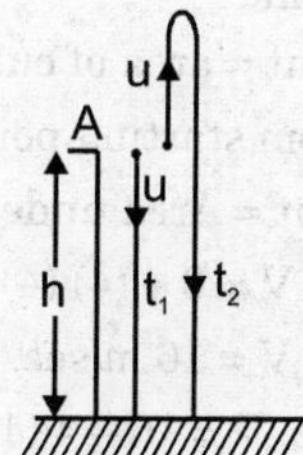

$ut_1 + \frac{1}{2}gt_1^2 = -ut_2 + \frac{1}{2}gt_2^2$

$\Rightarrow u(t_1 + t_2) = \frac{1}{2}g(t_2^2 - t_1^2)$

$\therefore h = \frac{g}{2}(t_1 - t_1)t_1 + \frac{g}{2}gt_1^2 = \frac{gt_2t_1}{2}$

$\therefore$ Reguired time $t = \sqrt{\frac{2h}{g}} = \sqrt{t_1t_2}$.

60.

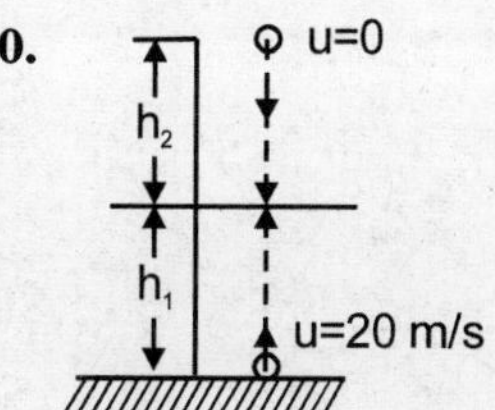

Height of the building

$H = h_1 + h_2 = \frac{1}{2}gt^2 + ut - \frac{1}{2}gt^2 = ut = 60$ m.

61. According to the question :

$$\sqrt{\frac{2h}{g}}-\sqrt{\frac{2(h-20)}{g}}=1$$

$$\Rightarrow \frac{2h}{g}+\frac{2(h-20)}{g}=2\sqrt{\frac{4(h-20)}{g^2}}$$

$$\Rightarrow \frac{4h}{g}-\frac{40}{g}-1=\frac{4}{g}\sqrt{h(h-20)}$$

Solving we get, $h=\frac{125}{4}=31.25$ m.

62. The acceleration of ball during its flight is $g = 9.8 m/s^2$ downwards.

63. Distance = sum of modulus of displacement
Displacement = Area under v-t graph

64. $\frac{dv}{dt}=a=-2.5t+1$

$$\int_U^U dV=\int_0^t(-2.5t+10)\,dt$$

$$0=-2.5\frac{t^2}{2}+10t\Rightarrow t=8s$$

65. Slope of displacement time graph is velocity

66. $V_{av}=\frac{\text{Displacement}}{\text{time}}$

Displacement = area of curve

67. Distance from starting point is displacement = Area under v-t graph

68. At t = 4 sec, V = 0 + (4) (4) = 16 m/sec.
At t = 8 sec, V = 16 m/sec.
At t = 12 sec, V = 16 – 4 (12 – 8) = 0
For 0 to 4 sec $s_1 = ½ at^2 = ½ (4) (4)^2 = 32$ m
For 4 to 8 sec $s_2 = 16 (8 – 4) = 64$ m
For 8 to 12 sec $s_3 = 16 (4) – ½ (4) (4)^2 = 32$ m
So $s_1 + s_2 + s_3 = 32 + 64 + 32 = 128$ m

69. Along a curved path direction will continuously change. So velocity cannot be same.

70. $x_A = x_B$

$$10.5+10t=\frac{1}{2}at^2$$

a = tan45° = 1

$t^2 – 20t – 21 = 0$

$$t=\frac{20\pm\sqrt{400+84}}{2}$$

t = 21 sec.

71. In (A) $x_f – x_2$
0 – x = – x = – ve
So average velocity is – ve.

72. Maximum displacement is a 25 sec. displacement = 25 + 50 + 62.5 + 75 = 212.5 m.

73.

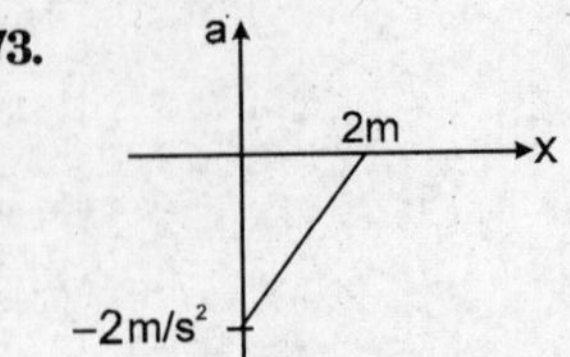

From the graph, we can write

v = – x + 2

$$a=\frac{dv}{dt}=-\frac{dx}{dt}$$

$$=-v=-(-x+2)=x-2$$

74. Slope of V-t graph = acceleration.

$$=-\frac{5}{10-5}=-1\ m/s^2.$$

75. Area under velocity-time graph

76. For A, $\frac{ds}{dt}=V_A=\frac{1}{\sqrt{3}}$

For B, $\frac{ds}{dt}=V_B=\sqrt{3}$

$$\frac{V_A}{V_B}=\frac{1}{3}$$

77. $V_{t=3}-V_{t=0}$ = area under a – t curve

$\therefore V_{t=3}=10.5$ m/s

78. Area under velocity-time graph

79.

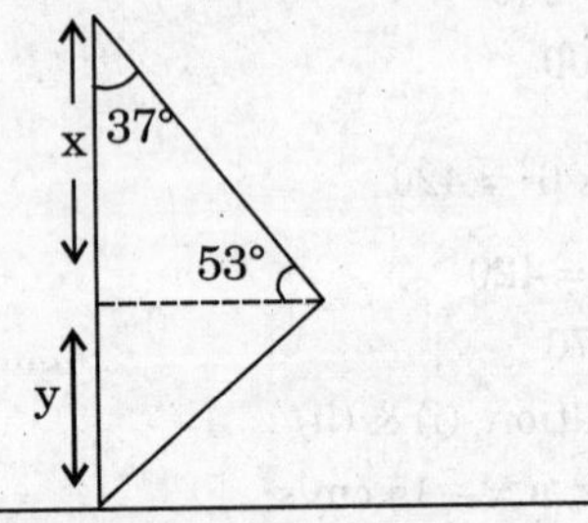

$$\tan 53°=\frac{x}{150}\ \text{km/min}$$

$\Rightarrow$ x = 200 km

$\Rightarrow$ y = 300 km

80. Distance of particle from point P
= |displacement|
= Net Area under the curve
= (4 × 2) + (–3 × 2) + (2 × 2) = 6 m

81. For half of the time velocity is decreasing at a constant rate or $\frac{dv}{dt}$ is –ve, so acceleration will be –ve & similarly for the rest half acceleration will be +ve.

82. Sum of magnitude of displacement is distance

83. Area under a – t graph = Δv = 4 m/s

$\Delta v = v_f - v_i = 4$

$\Rightarrow v_f = 4 + v_i = 4 + 2 = 6$ m/s

84. velocity is slope of k – t graph and acceleration is slope of v – t graph.

85. $\frac{dx}{dt} = -4 + 12t$ straight line with –ve intercept.

86. From t = 0 sec. to $t = t_0$ second, the speed decreases and after $t = t_0$ second the speed increases. Hence particle first decelerates and then accelerates

87. Displacement from t = 0 to t = 5 second is = – 10 m

$\therefore$ Average velocity = $\frac{\text{Total displacement}}{\text{Total time}}$

$= -\frac{10}{5} = -2$ m/s

88. As velocity increases variable force will become equal to constant force. And thus net force will become zero.

89. So initially.

$a = F_c = F_v (F_c > F_v)$

So velocity will increase

after some time

$F_c = F_v = 0$

So velocity will become constant

90. (i) $V\frac{dv}{dx} = -\beta V$

(ii) $a = -\beta V$

$dv = -\beta dx \frac{dv}{dt} = -\beta V$

$$\int_{v_0}^{0} dv = \beta \int_0^x dx$$

$$\int_{v_0}^{v} \frac{dv}{v} = -\beta \int_0^t dt$$

$-v_0 = -\beta x$

$\ell n\left(\frac{V}{V_0}\right) = -\beta t$

$x = \frac{v_0}{\beta}$ $\quad V = V_0 e^{-\beta t}$

$V = \frac{V_0}{e^{\beta t}}$

at $t \to \infty$ V = 0.

$\therefore$ A & B are correct answer

91. The retardation is given by

$\frac{dv}{dt} = -av^2$

Integrating between proper limits

$\Rightarrow -\int_u^v \frac{dv}{v^2} = \int_0^t a\,dt$ or

$\frac{1}{v} = at + \frac{1}{u}$

$\Rightarrow \frac{dt}{dx} = at + \frac{1}{u} \Rightarrow dx = \frac{u\,dt}{1+aut}$

Integrating between proper limits

$\Rightarrow \int_0^s dx = \int_0^t \frac{u\,dt}{1+aut}$

$\Rightarrow S = \frac{1}{a}\lambda n(1+aut)$

92. It is clear from the figure that acceleration does not change sign, i.e., does not change in direction. Only the magnitude of acceleration first increases and then decreases.

$\therefore$ Velocity keeps on increasing.

Hence displacement also keeps on increasing.

93. The retardation is given by $\frac{dv}{dt} = -av^2$

Integrating between proper limits

$\Rightarrow -\int_u^v \frac{dv}{v^2} = \int_0^t a\,dt$ or $\frac{1}{v} = at + \frac{1}{u}$

$\Rightarrow \frac{dt}{dx} = at + \frac{1}{u} \Rightarrow dx = \frac{u\,dt}{1+aut}$

$\int_0^s dx = \int_0^t \frac{u\,dt}{1+aut} \Rightarrow S = \frac{1}{a}\lambda n(1+aut)$

94. $a = 3t^2 + 1$

$\frac{dv}{dt} = 3t^2 + 1 \Rightarrow \int_0^v dv = \int_0^1 (3t^2+1)dt$

$v = (t^3+t)_0^1 = 2$ m/s. $\Rightarrow v = t^3 + t$

$\therefore \int_0^s ds = \int_0^1 (t^3+t)dt \Rightarrow S = \frac{1}{4} + \frac{1}{2} = 0.75$

95. $v = 3t^2$

v = 3(3)2 = 2.7 m/s

96. $\int_0^s dS = \int_0^2 3t^2 dt$

$S = \left[t^3\right]_0^2 = 8$

97. $f = 6t$

$f = 6 \times 3 = 18\ m/s^2$

99. Time of flight $= \sqrt{\frac{2H}{g}} = 20$ s

$\therefore$ AB $= U_x T = 3333.3$ m $= 3.333$ km.

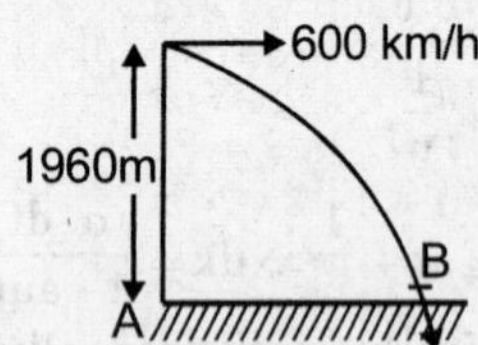

99. Gravitational acceleration is constant near the surface of the earthGravitational acceleration is constant near the surface of the earth

100. $AC = \frac{1}{2}\ gt^2 = 45$ m

$BC = 45\sqrt{3}$ m $= u.t$

$u = \frac{45}{\sqrt{3}} = 15\sqrt{3}$ m/s.

101. $\frac{(V_A \sin\theta)^2}{2g} = \frac{V_B{}^2}{2g}$

$\Rightarrow \frac{V_A}{V_B} = \frac{1}{\sin\theta} = \frac{2}{\sqrt{3}}$

104.

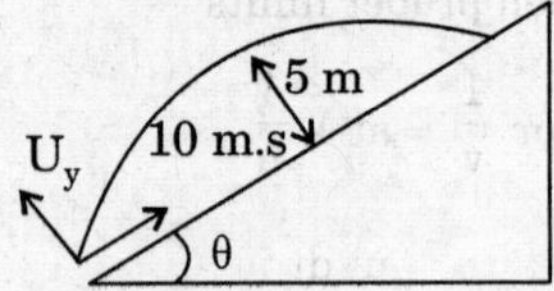

$T_f = 2$ sec

$a_x = -g\sin\theta,\ a_y = -g\cos\theta$

$T_f = \frac{2U_y}{ay} = 2$ .....(1)

$H = \frac{U_y{}^2}{2ay} = 5$ ....(2)

105.

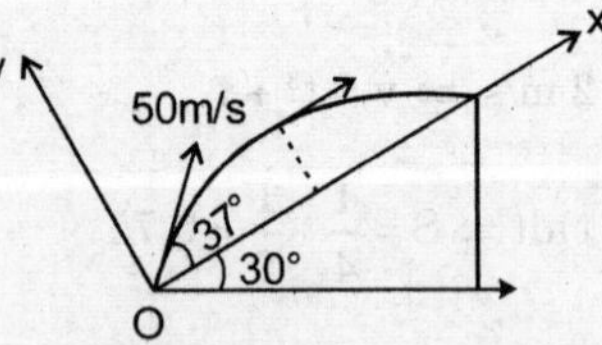

By taking axis system as shown in figure

At highest point $V_y = 0$

$V_y^2 = U_y^2 + 2a_y y$

$0 = (30)^2 - 2g\cos30^\circ y$

$y = 30\sqrt{3}$ ....(1)

Again for x coordinate

$V_y = U_y + a_y t$

$0 = 30 - g\cos30^\circ \times t$

$t = 2\sqrt{3}$

$x = U_x t + \frac{1}{2} a_x t^2$

$x = 40 \times \frac{1}{2} g\sin30^\circ \times (2\sqrt{3})^2$

$x = 80\sqrt{3} - 30$

106.

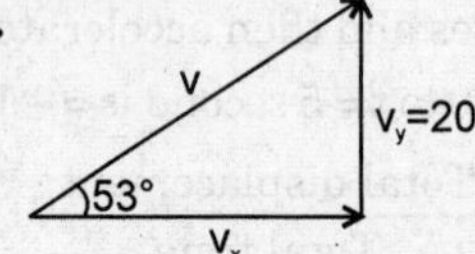

Two second before maximum height

$v_y = g \times 2 = 20$ cm/s

$\tan 53^\circ = \frac{20}{v_x}$ $v_x = 15$ m/s

107.

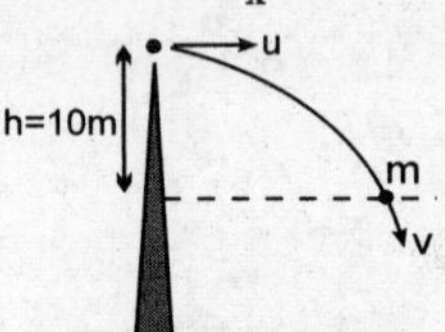

The pebble is at same distance from top and base of the tower after it falls down by a distance h = 10 m.

Applying conservation of energy.

$\frac{1}{2}\ mv^2 = \frac{1}{2}\ mu^2 + mgh$

or $v^2 = u^2 + 2gh = 100 + 2 \times 10 \times 10 = 300$

$\therefore$ $v = 10\sqrt{3}$ m/s.

108. Maximum height from inclined plane is

$H = \frac{u_\perp^2}{2a_\perp} = \frac{(10\sin37^\circ)^2}{2g\cos53^\circ} = 3$ m

109. $H = \frac{U_y{}^2}{2g}$, $R = \frac{2U_x U_y}{g}$ and

$\frac{U_y}{U_x} = \tan53^\circ$

$\frac{H}{R} = \frac{U_y^2 / 2g}{2U_x U_y / g}$

$= \frac{U_y}{4U_x} = \frac{\tan53^\circ}{4}$

$\Rightarrow R = 75$ m

110.

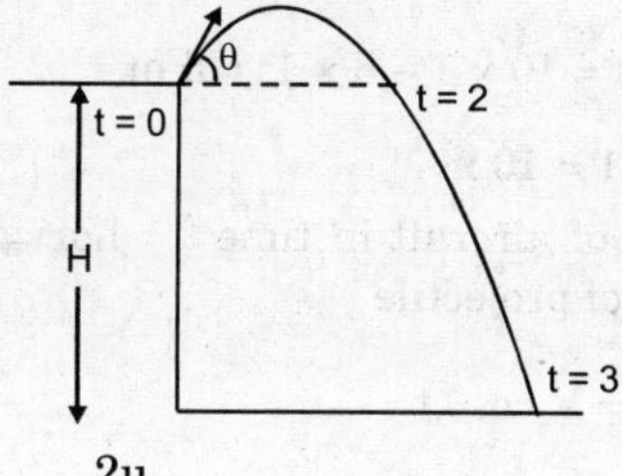

$2 = \frac{2u_y}{g} \Rightarrow u_y = 10$ m/s

Now, $H = -u_y t + \frac{1}{2} gt^2 = -30 + 45 = 15$ m.

111. Initial velocity of stone w.r.t. lift = 20 sin 30° $\hat{j}$ + 20 cos 30° $\hat{i}$ = $(10\sqrt{3}\,\hat{i} + 10\,\hat{j})$ m/s

Initial velocity of stone w.r.t. ground

$= \left(10\sqrt{3}\,\hat{i} + 10\hat{j}\right)$ m/s

The initial position of stone & lift are same and when they again meet their final positions will also be same. So both will have same displacement in vertical direction in same time

Displacement of lift = $2(t) + \frac{1}{2} \times 1 \times t^2 = 2t + \frac{t^2}{2}$

Displacement of stone = $12(t) - \frac{1}{2} \times 10 \times t^2$

$= 12t - 5t^2$

so $2t + \frac{t^2}{2} = 12t - 5t^2$

$\frac{11t^2}{2} = 10t \Rightarrow t = \frac{20}{11}$ sec.

113. $R_{max} = \frac{u^2}{g} = 50 \Rightarrow u^2 = 500$

Maximum height he can throw is

$H_{max.} = \frac{u^2}{2g} = \frac{500}{20} = 25$ m

114. Equation for motion perpendicular to the incline

$\Rightarrow u.t - \frac{1}{2} g \cos\alpha . t^2 \Rightarrow t = \frac{2u}{g\cos\alpha}$

Along incline $x = 0 + \frac{1}{2} \times (g \sin\alpha) \left(\frac{2u}{g\cos\alpha}\right)^2$

115. $$\frac{H_1}{H_2} = \frac{\frac{V_0^2 \sin^2\alpha}{2g}}{\frac{V_0^2 \sin^2(90-\alpha)}{2g}} = \tan^2\alpha$$

116. $t_1 = \frac{2u\sin\theta}{g}$

$t_2 = \frac{2u\sin(90-\theta)}{g} = \frac{2u\cos\theta}{g}$

$t_1 t_2 = \frac{4u^2 \sin\theta\cos\theta}{g^2} = \frac{2}{g}R$

$t_1 t_2 \propto R$

117. At maximum height v = u cosθ

$\frac{u}{2} = v \Rightarrow \cos\theta = \frac{1}{2} \Rightarrow \theta = 60°$

$R = \frac{u^2 \sin 2\theta}{g} = \frac{u^2 \sin(120°)}{g} = \frac{u^2 \cos 30°}{g} = \frac{\sqrt{3}u^2}{2g}$

118. At the top of trajectory,

$K' = \frac{1}{2} m(u\cos\theta)^2 = \frac{1}{2} mu^2 . \cos^2 45° = \frac{k}{2}$.

119.

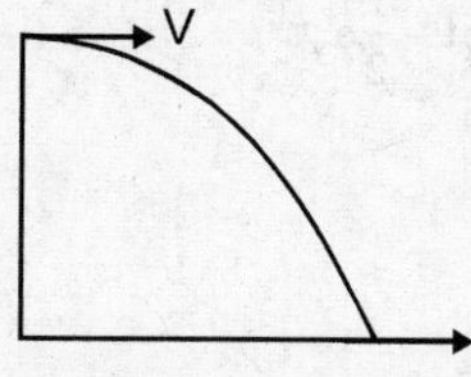

x = vt

$y = -\frac{1}{2} gt^2 = -\frac{1}{2} g . \frac{x^2}{v^2}$

$\therefore\ y = \frac{-g}{2v^2} x^2$

120. For maximum range, θ = 45°

At the highest point, $v = u\cos\theta = \frac{u}{\sqrt{2}}$

121. $R = \frac{u^2 \sin 2\theta}{g}$ is same for angles θ & 90° – θ.

$t_1 = \frac{2u\sin\theta_1}{g} = \frac{2u\sin(90° - \theta_2)}{g}$

$t_2 = \frac{2u\sin\theta_2}{g} = 2u \sin\frac{(90° - \theta_1)}{g}$

122. $R_1 = \frac{24^2 \sin\alpha \cos(\alpha + \theta)}{g\cos^2\theta}$

$R_2 = \frac{24^2 \sin\alpha \cos(\alpha - \theta)}{g\cos^2\theta}$

$R_1 - R_2 = g \sin\theta\, T_2^2$

$R_1 - R_2 = g \sin\theta\, T_1^2$

123.

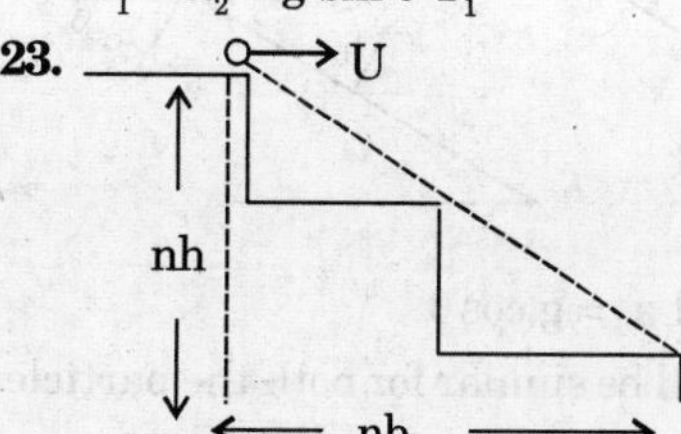

$R = nb$

$H = nh$

$t = \sqrt{\dfrac{2H}{g}}, R = Ut$

$\Rightarrow (nb)^2 = U^2 \dfrac{2}{g}(nh)$

124. $h = \dfrac{u^2 \sin^2 \theta_1}{2g}$ $h' = \dfrac{u^2 \sin^2(90° - \theta_1)}{g}$;

$R = \dfrac{u^2 \sin 2\theta_1}{g} \Rightarrow R = 4\sqrt{hh'}$

125. $x = u_x t$ and $y = y = U_x t - \dfrac{1}{2} a_y t^2$

$\Rightarrow U_x = 10\sqrt{3}$ m/s

$U_y = 10$ m/s

$a_y = 2$ m/s

$H = \dfrac{Uy^2}{2a_y} = \dfrac{(10)^2}{2 \times 2} = 25$m.

126. R = 20 km, H = 5 km

127. $R = U_x T_f = (v \cos 60) T_f$

$R' = \left(v \cos 60 + \dfrac{v}{2}\right) T_f$

$\Rightarrow \dfrac{R}{R'} = \dfrac{1}{2} \Rightarrow R' = 2R$

128.

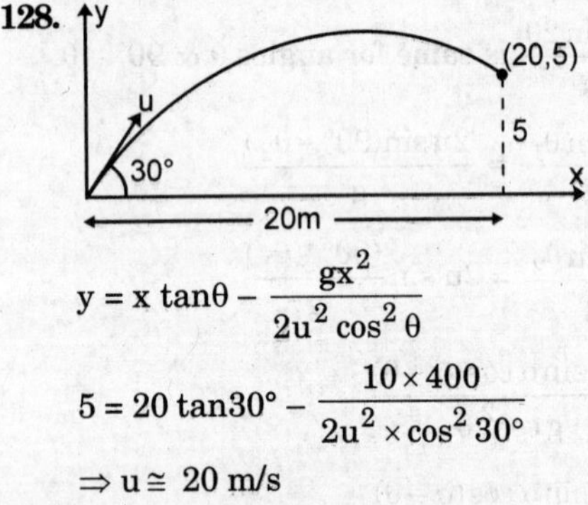

$y = x \tan\theta - \dfrac{gx^2}{2u^2 \cos^2 \theta}$

$5 = 20 \tan 30° - \dfrac{10 \times 400}{2u^2 \times \cos^2 30°}$

$\Rightarrow u \cong 20$ m/s

129. For both the particles

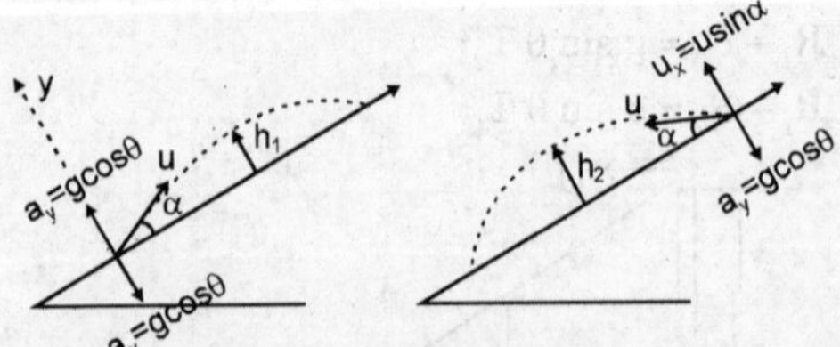

$u_y = u\sin\theta$ and $a_y = g\cos\theta$

So y motion will be similar for both the particles.

$\Rightarrow$ Maximum height and time of flight will be same for the both. $\Rightarrow h_1 = h_2$

130. $y = u_x t - \dfrac{1}{2} . g t^2 = 10 \times 1 - 5 \times 1^2 = 5$ m

$x = u_x t = 10 \times 1 = 10$ m

131. Displacement of aircraft in time t = horizontal displacement of projectile

$\Rightarrow 972 \times \dfrac{5}{18} t = V_0 \cos\theta . t$

$\Rightarrow \cos\theta = \dfrac{54 \times 5}{540} = \dfrac{1}{2}$

$\Rightarrow \theta = 60°$.

132.

$y = 4t - t^2$, $x = 3t$

$Vy = \dfrac{dy}{dt} = 4 - 2t$, $Vx = \dfrac{dy}{dt} = 3$

$\Rightarrow uy = vy\big|_{t=0} = 4$, $u_x = v_x\big|_{t=0}$

The angle of projection :

$\tan\theta = \dfrac{4y}{4x} = \dfrac{4}{3} \Rightarrow \theta = \tan^{-1}\left(\dfrac{4}{3}\right)$ **Ans.**

133. $an45° = \dfrac{V_y}{V_x}$

$\Rightarrow v_y = v_x = 18$m/s Ans.

134. $y = 12 \times \left(-\dfrac{3}{4}\right) x^2 = 12 \times \left(1 - \dfrac{x}{16}\right)$

$\Rightarrow$ Range = **16 m Ans.**

135. u = 12 m/s for longest jump; the range should be max.

i.e. $R_{max} = \dfrac{u^2}{g} = 14.4$ m

136. H = R

$\dfrac{U_y^2}{2g} = \dfrac{2U_x U_y}{g}$

$\dfrac{U_y}{U_x} = 4\tan\theta$

137. $R = U_x T_f = v\sqrt{\dfrac{2h}{g}}$

138. ϕ is with vertical $\Rightarrow H = \dfrac{U_y^2}{2g} = \dfrac{(U\cos\phi)^2}{2g}$

$U = mgH = mg\dfrac{(U\cos\theta)}{2g}$

$K = \dfrac{1}{2}nU^2$

139. Maximum distance covered in one jump

$= \dfrac{u^2}{g} = 1\text{ m}$

So minimum no. of jumps = 10

140. $T_F = \dfrac{2U_y}{g} = \dfrac{2\times 20}{10} = 4\,\text{sec}$

$V_y = U_y - gt = 20 - 10\times 1 = 10\text{ m/s}$

$\Rightarrow \tan\theta_1 = \dfrac{10}{10} = 1 \Rightarrow \theta_1 = 45°$

also $\tan\theta_2 = 1 \Rightarrow \theta_2 = 45°$

$\Rightarrow$ angle is $\theta_1 + \theta_2 = 90°$

141. The horizontal displacement in time t is

$AC = u\cos 60°\, t = \dfrac{ut}{2}$

$\therefore$ Range on inclined plane $= \dfrac{AC}{\cos 30} = \dfrac{ut}{\sqrt{3}}$

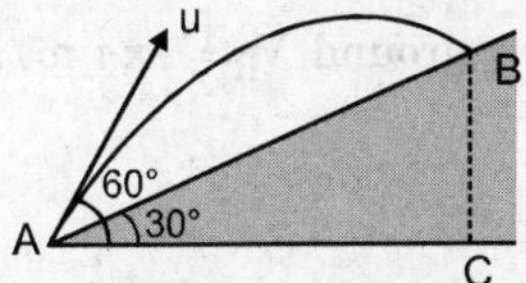

143. V_{boat}, river = 4.5 km/m

V_{rim}, ground = 6 km/hr.

V_{boat}, ground $= (6\hat{i}+4.5\hat{j})$ km/m

$= (6\hat{i}+4.5\hat{j}) \times \dfrac{5}{18}$ m

V_{boat}, ground $= \sqrt{6^2+4.5^2} \times \dfrac{5}{18}$

$= 1.5 \times 5 \times \dfrac{5}{18} = \dfrac{37.5}{18} = 2.1$ m/sec.

147.

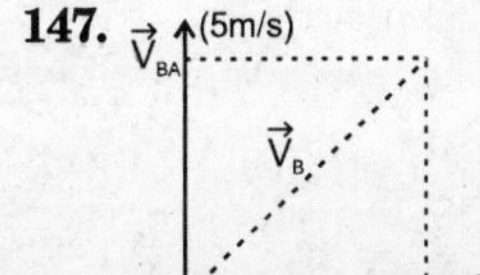

Velocity of A and velocity of B relative to A are as shown.

$\therefore\ \vec{V}_B = \vec{V}_{BA} + \vec{V}_A \Rightarrow V_0 = \sqrt{5^2+15^2} = 5\sqrt{12}$

and direction of $\vec{V}_B$ is away from $\vec{V}_A$.

148. Vboat , river $= 4\hat{i}$

Vriver , ground $= 2\hat{i}$

Vwind , ground $= 6\hat{j}$

$\vec{V}$ wind, boat $= \vec{V}_{wg} + \vec{V}_{gr} + \vec{V}_{rb} = 6\hat{j} - 2\hat{j} - 4\hat{i}$

$= -4\hat{i} + 4\hat{j}$

So flag blown in north west.

149. Relative to the person in the train, acceleration of the stone is 'g' downward, a (acceleration of train) backwards.

According to him : $x = \dfrac{1}{2}at^2,\ Y = \dfrac{1}{2}gt^2$

$\Rightarrow \dfrac{X}{Y} = \dfrac{a}{g} \Rightarrow Y = \dfrac{g}{a}x \Rightarrow$ straight line.

150. $V_{R/G(x)} = 0,\ V_{R/G(y)} = 10$ m/s

Let, velocity of man = v

$\tan\theta = \dfrac{16}{12} = \dfrac{4}{3}$

then, $v_{R/man} = v$ (opposite to man)

For the required condition :

$\tan\theta = \dfrac{V_{R/M(y)}}{V_{R/M(x)}} = \dfrac{10}{v} = \dfrac{4}{3}$

$\Rightarrow V = \dfrac{10\times 3}{4} = 7.5$ **Ans.**

151. From given data

$\vec{V}_M = 5\sqrt{2}\,\hat{i} + 5\sqrt{2}\,\hat{j}$

velocity of man

Velocity of wind

$\vec{V}_W = 5\sqrt{2}\,\hat{i}$

The flag will flutter in the direction in which wind is blowing with respect to the man holding the flag.

$\Rightarrow \vec{V}_{WM} = \vec{V}_W - \vec{V}_M$

$\vec{V}_{WM} = 5\sqrt{2}\,\hat{i} - (5\sqrt{2}\,\hat{i} + 5\sqrt{2}\,\hat{j})$

$\vec{V}_{WM} = -5\sqrt{2}\,\hat{j} = 5\sqrt{2}(-\hat{j})$

This implies direction of wind with respect to man in south.

152. Relative to lift initial velocity and acceleration of coin are 0 m/s and 1 m/s² downward

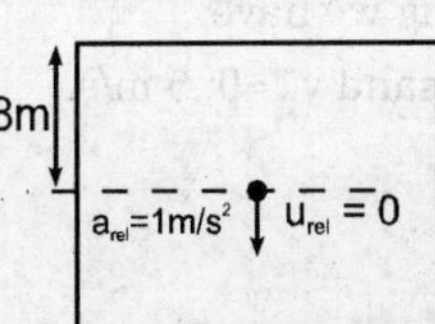

$\therefore\ 2 = \dfrac{1}{2}(1)\,t^2$ or t = 2 second

153. Relative velocity of stone = 5 m/s

Relative acceleration of stone = 10 + 5 = 15 m/s²

$\therefore$ v = u + at = 5 + 15 × 2 = 35 m/s

$\therefore$ Relative velocity after t = 2 second is 35 m/s

154. $\vec{V}_{BG} = \vec{V}_{BR} + \vec{V}_{RG}$

$\therefore |\vec{V}_{BG}| = \sqrt{V_{BR}^2 + V_{RG}^2 + 2V_{BR}V_{RG}\cos\theta}$

$\because \theta$ is unknown $\therefore 6 - 4.8 \le |\vec{V}_{BG}| \le (6 + 4.8)$

$\Rightarrow 1.2 \le |\vec{V}_{BG}| \le 10.8$

155.

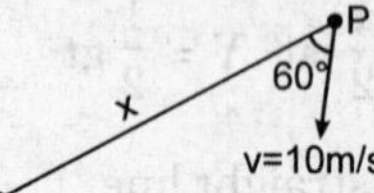

Velocity of approach of P and O is

$-\frac{dx}{dt} = v\cos 60° = 5$ m/s

It can be seen that velocity of approach is always constant.

$\therefore$ P reaches O after $= \frac{100}{5} = 20$ sec.

156. $\vec{V}_{O,M} = \vec{V}_O - \vec{V}_M$

$\vec{V}_{O,M} = \vec{V}_O - \vec{V}_{Train}$

$V_{O,M}$ = velocity of object with respect to man

V_O = velocity of object

V_M = velocity of man

Here velocity of object is zero.

So, $\vec{V}_{O,M} = -\vec{V}_M$

157. Let velocity of bodies be v_1 and v_2.

in first case

$u_1 = v_1 + v_2$ .... (i)

in second case

$u_2 = v_1 - v_2$ .... (i)

$\therefore v_1 = \frac{u_1 + u_2}{2}$ and $v_2 = \frac{u_1 + u_2}{2}$

Here $u_1 = \frac{16}{10}$ m/s and $u_2 = \frac{3}{5}$

After solving we have

$v_1 = 1.1$ m/sand $v_2 = 0.5$ m/s.

158. Velocity of approach = $\vec{V}_B - \vec{V}_A$.

159. Vertical Linear Motion

160. Relative to the person in the train, acceleration of the stone is 'g' downward, a (acceleration of train) backwards.

According to him : $x = \frac{1}{2}at^2$, $Y = \frac{1}{2}gt^2$

$\frac{X}{Y} = \frac{a}{g} \Rightarrow Y = \frac{g}{a}x \Rightarrow$ straight line.

161. W ← → E

$\vec{V}_A = -500\hat{i} \Rightarrow \vec{V}_{GA} + \vec{V}_A = V_{GAS}$

$\vec{V}_{GA} = 1500\hat{i} \Rightarrow 1500\hat{i} - 500\hat{i} = 1000\hat{i}$

162. $\vec{V}_{RG} = 3\hat{j} - 4\hat{i}$

$\vec{V}_{mg} = 4\hat{i}$

$\vec{V}_{RG} = 3\hat{j}$

$V_{RG} = 5$ km/sec.

163. Then velocity of man w.r.t. ground $\vec{V}_M = 5\hat{i}$ m/s

velocity of rain w.r.t. ground $\vec{V}_R = -x\hat{j}$ m/s

$\vec{V}_{RM} = x\hat{j} - 5\hat{i}$,

$\tan 45° = \frac{x}{5}$

164.

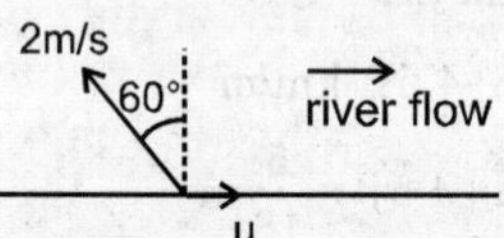

Let speed of current be u.

For net velocity of man to be normal to river flow.

2 cos 60° = u

or u = 1 km/hr.

5

CHAPTER

Work, Energy and Power

WORK

In Physics, the term work is used in a specific sense which involves the displacement of a particle or a body under the action of force. It is measured by the product of force and displacement. It is scalar quantity with unit joule.

Work on an object is defined as the magnitude of the force multiplied by the distance moved by the object in the direction of the applied force.

Work done = force × distance = F × s

1 Joule = 1 Newton × 1 metre.

The unit of work is joule.

- Work done by a force acting obliquely is equal to W = F cos θ × s
- Work done on a body moving in circular path is zero.

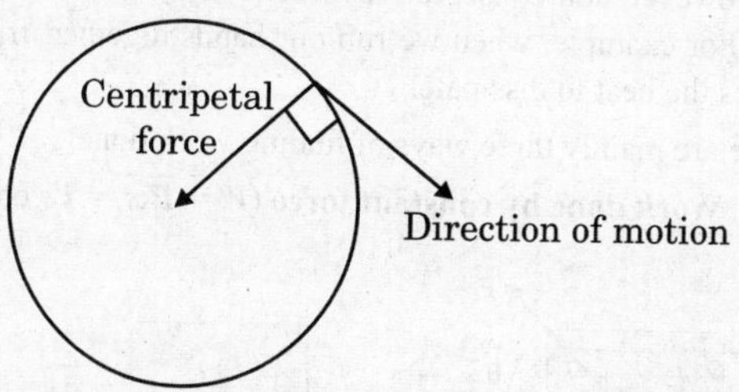

Units of Work:

The SI unit of work is the joule (J), which is defined as the work done by a force of one newton (N) causing a displacement of one meter (m).

Other units of work include:

- **Newton-meter (N·m) :** This unit is sometimes used as the measuring unit for work, but it can be confused with the measurement unit of torque.
- **Kilowatt-hour :** This unit is used to measure electrical energy and is equal to 3600 J.
- **Horsepower-hour :** This unit is used to measure the work done by a motor and is equal to 746 J.

Which unit of work is used depends on the context. For example, joules are typically used in physics and engineering, while horsepower-hours are typically used in mechanics and thermodynamics.

Dimensions of Work:

The dimensions of work are $[M^1 L^2 T^{-2}]$, where:

- M is mass
- L is length
- T is time

This can be derived from the following equation:

Work = Force * Displacement

Force has the dimensions $[M^1 L^1 T^{-2}]$ and displacement has the dimensions $[L^1]$, so work must have the dimensions $[M^1 L^1 T^{-2}] * [L^1] = [M^1 L^2 T^{-2}]$.

The SI unit of work is the joule (J).

Work done in pulling and pulling and pushing an object:

The work done in pulling and pushing an object is the same, as long as the force applied and the distance moved are the same. However, there may be some differences in how much effort is required to pull versus push an object, depending on the object's weight, the surface it is moving on, and the angle at which it is being moved.

For example, it is generally easier to pull a heavy object on a smooth surface than it is to push it on a rough surface. This is because the frictional force between the object and the surface is lower when the object is being pulled.

It is also easier to push an object at a slight angle upwards than it is to pull it at the same angle. This is because the component of the force that is parallel to the ground is greater when the object is being pushed.

In general, the amount of work done in pulling and pushing an object can be calculated using the following equation:

Work = Force * Displacement

where:

- Force is the force applied to the object
- Displacement is the distance moved by the object

For example, if you pull a 100 kg object 10 meters, you will do 1000 joules of work. The same amount of work would be done if you pushed the object 10 meters.

However, if you were to push the object up a ramp at a 30 degree angle, you would do more work than if you pulled it on a level surface. This is because the displacement of the object is greater when it is being pushed up the ramp.

Work done by external force when spring is elongated from x_1 to x_2 :

The work done by an external force when a spring is elongated from x_1 to x_2 is given by the following equation:

$W = \int x_2 x_1 F(x)\, dx$

where :

- W is the work done by the external force (in joules)
- F(x) is the force exerted by the spring on the external force (in newtons)
- x_1 and x_2 are the initial and final elongations of the spring (in meters)

The force exerted by the spring on the external force is given by Hooke's law :

$F(x) = -kx$

where :

- k is the spring constant (in newtons per meter)

Therefore, the work done by the external force can be written as follows:

$W = \int x_2 x_1 (-kx)\, dx$

$W = k(x_2^2 - x_1^2)/2$

This equation shows that the work done by the external force is proportional to the square of the change in elongation of the spring.

For example, if a spring with a spring constant of 100 N/m is elongated from 10 cm to 20 cm, the work done by the external force would be 500 J.

$W = k(x_2^2 - x_1^2)/2$

$= (100\text{ N/m}) * ((0.2\text{ m})^2 - (0.1\text{ m})^2)/2 = 500\text{ J}.$

Conservative & non conservative force :

Conservative forces are forces for which the work done is independent of the path taken. This means that the work done by a conservative force to move an object from one point to another is the same, regardless of the route taken.

Non-conservative forces are forces for which the work done depends on the path taken. This means that the work done by a non-conservative force to move an object from one point to another can vary depending on the route taken.

Examples of conservative forces include:

- Gravitational force
- Spring force
- Electric force
- Magnetic force

Examples of non-conservative forces include:

- Friction
- Air resistance
- Tension

Conservative forces can be associated with a potential energy function. The potential energy function is a function of the position of the object and gives the amount of work that a conservative force can do to move the object from one point to another.

The work done by a conservative force can be calculated by taking the negative of the change in potential energy of the object.

$W = -\Delta U$

Where;

- W is the work done by the conservative force
- ΔU is the change in potential energy of the object

Non-conservative forces do not have a potential energy associated with them. This is because the work done by a non-conservative force cannot be completely recovered as potential energy.

The work done by a non-conservative force is dissipated as heat, sound, or other forms of energy.

Conservative forces are important in physics because they allow us to conserve energy. For example, if we lift an object up in the air, we are doing work against the gravitational force. The work that we do is stored as potential energy in the object. When we let the object go, the potential energy is converted back into kinetic energy and the object falls back to the ground.

Non-conservative forces can also be useful. For example, friction allows us to walk and drive. Air resistance allows us to fly. However, non-conservative forces can also lead to energy loss. For example, when we rub our hands together, friction causes the heat to dissipate.

There are mainly three ways of finding work done.

1. **Work done by constant force** ($W = \vec{F}.\vec{s} = Fs\cos\theta$)

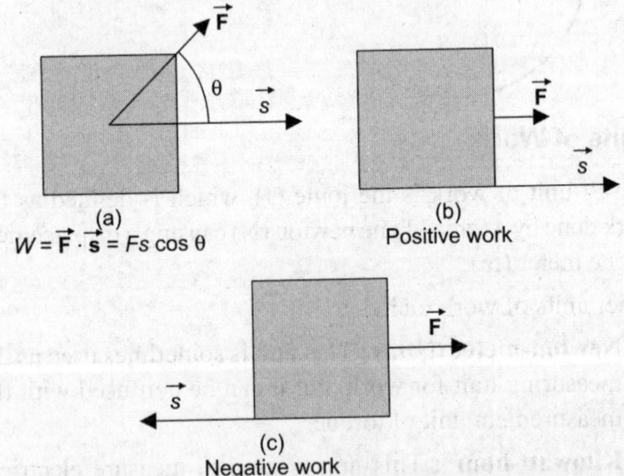

(a) $W = \vec{F}\cdot\vec{s} = Fs\cos\theta$ (b) Positive work (c) Negative work

- Work can be positive or negative or zero as θ is acute (< 90°) or obtuse (> 90°) or right (θ = 90°): positive work means that force (or its component) is parallel to displacement while negative work means that force (or its component) is opposite to displacement. Zero work done signify that force and displacement are perpendicular to each other.

- Work depends on frame of reference. With change of frame of reference inertial force does not change while displacement may change. So, the work done by a force will be different in different frames. For example, if a person is pushing a box inside a moving train, then work done as seen from the frame of reference of train is $\vec{F}.\vec{S}$ while as seen from the ground it is $\vec{F}.(\vec{S}+\vec{S}_0)$. Here $\vec{S}_0$ is the displacement of train relative to ground.

2. **Work done by variable force** When the force is variable, work obtained by integrating $\vec{F}.\vec{dx}$. Thus $W = \int \vec{F}.\vec{dx}$.

If the work done by a force field along a closed path is zero, then force is said to be conservative otherwise it is called non-conservative. Under such forces, the work done depends only upon the initial and final positions and is path independent.

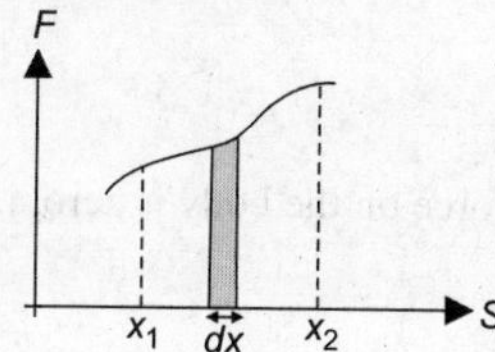

If number of forces act on a body or particle then, work is calculated by using

$$W = W_1 + W_2 + W_3 + \ldots\ldots$$

or $W = \int \vec{F_1} \cdot \vec{ds} + \int \vec{F_2} + \ldots \vec{ds}$

or $W = \int (\vec{F_1} + \vec{F_2} + \ldots) \cdot \vec{ds}$

or $W = \int \vec{F_R} \cdot \vec{ds}$ [as $\vec{F}_R = \Sigma \vec{F}$]

3. **Work done by F-S graph:** This is applicable in one dimensional motion. When force and displacement are parallel or anti-parallel to each other, then work done is obtained by area under F - S graph W = Area under F - S graph.

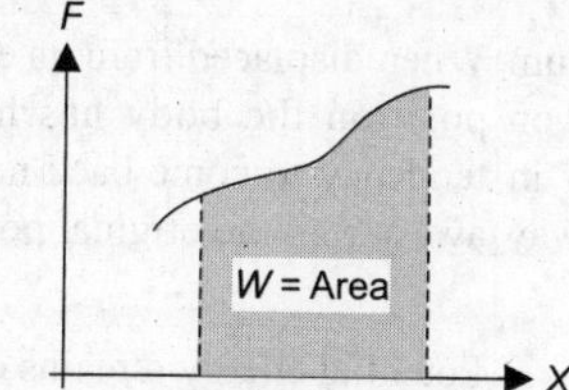

ENERGY

Energy is that physical quantity which enables a system to do work. In this section, we restrict ourselves to mechanical energy which consists of two forms:

(i) Kinetic energy

(ii) Potential energy

Kinetic Energy

The kinetic energy of a body is the energy possessed by the body by virtue of its motion. Mathematically, it is equal to $\frac{1}{2}mv^2$ where m is the mass of the body and v is the speed of the body.

$$K.E = \frac{1}{2}mv^2 = \frac{p^2}{2m}$$

Hence, a body cannot have kinetic energy without having momentum and vice-versa.

Work-Energy Theorem

The increase in kinetic energy of a body is equal to the sum of the work done by all the forces acting on the body. In another words, we can say work done is always equal to change in kinetic energy

$$W = \frac{1}{2}mv^2 - \frac{1}{2}mu^2 = K_F - K_i = \Delta KE$$

Points to Remember:

- If work is positive, $K_f > K_i$, so, the kinetic energy will increase while if work is negative, $K_f < K_i$, so, the kinetic energy will decrease.
- This theorem is also valid for a system in presence of all types of forces (external or internal, conservative or nonconservative).

Potential Energy

The energy stored in a body or system by virtue of its configuration or its position in a field is called potential energy.

In case of conservative force as:

$F = -(dU/dr)$ i.e., $dU = -F\,dr$

So, $\int_{U_1}^{U_2} dU = -\int_{r_1}^{r_2} \mathbf{F} \cdot \vec{\mathbf{dr}}$

i.e., $U_2 - U_1 = -\int_{r_1}^{r_2} \mathbf{F} \cdot \vec{\mathbf{dr}} (= -W)$ ...(1)

Whenever and wherever possible, we generally take the reference point at ∞ and assume potential energy to be zero there, i.e., if we take $r_1 = \infty$ and $U_1 = 0$

$U = -\int_{\infty}^{r} \mathbf{F} \cdot \vec{dr} = -W$ ...(2)

Potential energy can be defined only for conservative forces. It does not exists for non-conservative forces. Potential energy can be positive or negative.

Law of Conservation of Mechanical Energy

The sum of potential energy and the kinetic energy is called mechanical energy:

From work-energy theorem

$$K_f - K_i = W$$

From definition of potential energy in a conservative field

$$U_f - U_i = -\int \vec{F}\vec{dr} = -W$$

$$\Rightarrow U_f - U_i = -(K_f - K_i) \Rightarrow U_f + K_f = U_i + K_i$$

$$\Rightarrow K + U = \text{constant}$$

Hence, total mechanical energy of a system always remains constant, if only conservative forces are acting on the system.

Energy of Spring

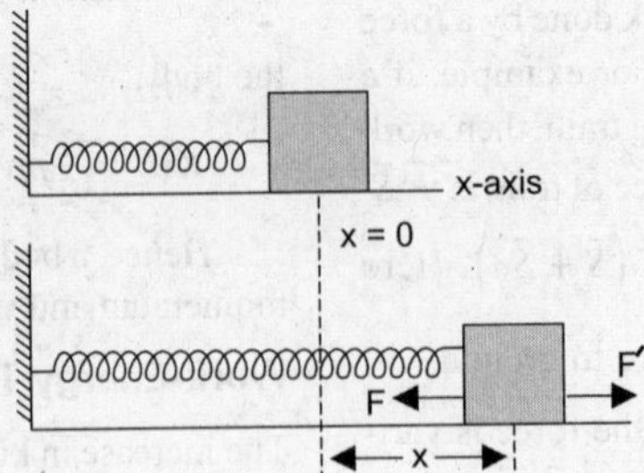

It is evident that the work done in compressing the spring by an amount x is given by $W = \frac{1}{2}kx^2$. The work done in stretching or compressing a spring is stored in it in the form of potential energy which is due to the changed configuration of the coils of the spring. Hence the potential energy of a massless elastic spring of force constant k when it is stretched or compressed by an amount x is given by

$$U = W = \frac{1}{2}kx^2$$

Equilibrium

When several forces act on a body simultaneously in such a way that the resultant force on the body is zero, i.e.,

$$\vec{\mathbf{F}} = 0 \text{ with } \vec{\mathbf{F}} = \Sigma \vec{\mathbf{F}}_i$$

then the body is said to be in equilibrium. So for equilibrium $\vec{\mathbf{F}}_{\text{net}} = 0$.

If the forces are conservative $F = -\frac{dU}{dr}$

For equilibrium $F = 0$, $\frac{-dU}{dr} = 0, \frac{dU}{dr} = 0$

Types of equilibrium are given in tabular form as given below.

Table 1: Types of Equilibrium

S.No.	Stable Equilibrium	Unstable Equilibrium	Neutral Equilibrium
1.	Net force is zero.	Net force is zero.	Net force is zero.
2.	$\frac{dU}{dr} = 0$ or slope of U-r graph is zero.	$\frac{dU}{dr} = 0$ or slope of U-r graph is zero.	$\frac{dU}{dr} = 0$ or slope of U-r graph is zero.
3.	When displaced from its equilibrium position a net restoring force starts acting on the body which has a tendency to bring the body back to its equilibrium position.	When displaced from its equilibrium position, a net force starts acting on the body which moves the body in the direction of displacement or away from the equilibrium position.	When displaced from its equilibrium position the body has neither the tendency to come back nor to move away from the original position.
4.	Potential energy in equilibrium position is minimum as compared to its neighbouring points. Or $\frac{d^2U}{dr^2}$ = positive	Potential energy in equilibrium position is maximum as compared to its neighbouring points. Or $\frac{d^2U}{dr^2}$ = negative	Potential energy remains constant even if the body is displaced from its equilibrium position. Or $\frac{d^2U}{dr^2} = 0$
5.	When displaced from equilibrium position the centre of gravity of the body goes up.	When displaced from equilibrium position the centre of gravity of the body comes down.	When displaced from equilibrium position the centre of gravity of the body remains at the same level.

POWER

Rate of doing work is called power. By definition, work done by a force does not depend on the time taken for a given displacement, i.e., work is independent of time. The time rate of doing work is defined as power and is given by

$$(\text{Power})_{\text{inst.}} = P = \frac{dW}{dt}$$

and $(\text{Power})_{\text{av.}} = \dfrac{W}{t}$

$$\text{Power } P = \frac{dW}{dt} = \frac{\vec{F}\cdot\vec{ds}}{dt} \quad [\text{as } dW = \vec{F}\cdot\vec{ds}]$$

i.e., $P = \vec{F}\cdot\vec{v}$ [as $\vec{ds}/dt = \vec{v}$]

i.e., power is equal to the scalar product of force and velocity.

Power is a scalar quantity with dimensions [ML^2T^{-3}]. The SI unit of power is J/s and is called watt (W). Practical unit of power is horse power with

1 hp = 746 watt = 550 ft-lb/s

> **Note**: If force is variable, we calculate the average power as $P_{av} = \dfrac{\int_o^t P dt}{\int_o^t dt}$

COLLISION

Collision is an isolated event in which a strong force acts between two or more bodies for a short time. The collision is infact a redistribution of total momentum of the particles.

Types of Collision

(a) **Elastic Collision**: Collision is elastic i.e., = 1, where e = coefficient of restitution.

For elastic collision:

(i) Impulse of deformation = Impulse of reformation

(ii) Velocity of separation = Velocity of approach

(iii) KE before collision = KE after collision

(iv) Momentum before collision = Momentum after collision.

$\Rightarrow m_1u_1 + m_2u_2 = m_1v_1 + m_2v_2$

Total energy before collision = Total energy after collision.

(v) $\frac{1}{2}m_1u_1^2 + \frac{1}{2}m_2u_2^2 = \frac{1}{2}m_1v_1^2 + \frac{1}{2}m_2v_2^2$

(vi) $v_1 = \dfrac{(m_1 - m_2)u_1}{m_1 + m_2} + \dfrac{2m_2u_2}{m_1 + m_2}$

(vii) $v_2 = \dfrac{2m_1u_1}{m_1 + m_2} + \dfrac{(m_2 - m_1)u_2}{m_1 + m_2}$

(b) **Inelastic Collision:** For $0 < e < 1$, collision is inelastic where e = coefficient of restitution

(i) Impluse of reformation < Impluse of deformation

(ii) Velocity of separation < Velocity of approach

(iii) KE is not conserved.

(iv) TE conserved. Momentum remains conserved.

(v) For e = 0, completely inelastic collision.

(vi) Impulse of reformation = 0

(vii) Velocity of separation = 0

(viii) KE in not conserved in inelastic collision

(ix) $v_1 = \left(\dfrac{m_1 - em_2}{m_1 + m_2}\right)u_1 + \left(\dfrac{(1+e)m_2}{m_1 + m_2}\right)u_2$

(x) $v_2 = \left(\dfrac{(1+e)m_1}{m_1 + m_2}\right)u_1 + \left(\dfrac{m_2 - em_1}{m_1 + m_2}\right)u_2$

(xi) In perfectly elastic collision both colliding bodies stick together and move with a common velocity

$$v = \frac{m_1u_1 + m_2u_2}{m_1 + m_2}$$

(c) **Head on collision or oblique collision**: Consider oblique collision of two particles as shown below here we have

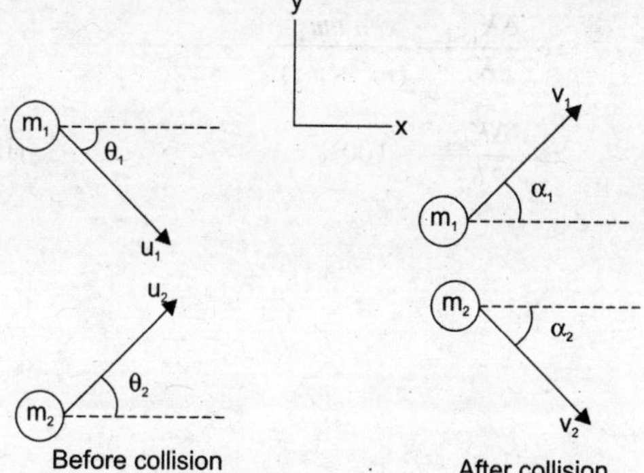

(i) Momentum conservation along c-axis :

$$m_1u_1 \cos\theta + m_2u_2 \cos\theta_1 + m_2u_2 \cos\theta_2 = m_1v_1 \cos\alpha_1 + m_2v_2 \cos\alpha_2$$

(ii) Momentum conservation of y-axis :

$$-m_1u_1 \sin\theta_1 + m_2u_2 \sin\theta_2 = m_1v_1 \sin\alpha_1 - m_2v_2 \sin\alpha_2$$

(iii) Velocity of approach = $u_1 \cos\theta_1 - u_2 \cos\theta_2$

(iv) Velocity of separation = $v_2 \cos\alpha_2 - v_1 \cos\alpha_1$

$$\therefore \quad e = \frac{v_2 \cos\alpha_2 - v_1 \cos\alpha_1}{u_1 \cos\theta_1 - u_2 \cos\theta_2}$$

Consider the oblique collision as shown below. Here we have:

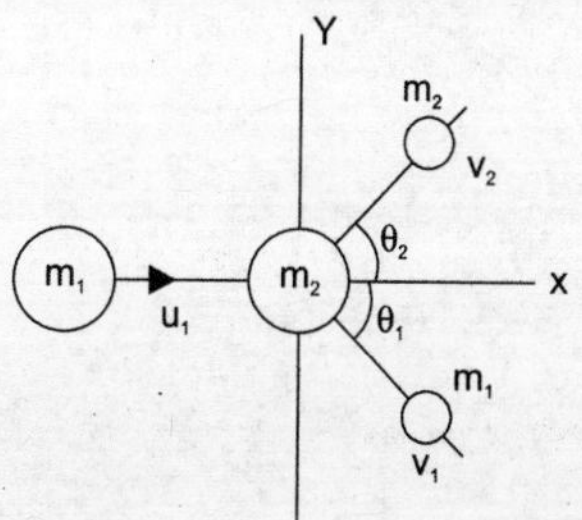

(i) $m_1u_1 = m_1v_1 \cos\theta_1 + m_2v_2 \cos\theta_2$ (along x-axis)

(ii) $m_1v_1 \sin\theta_1 - m_2v_2 \sin\theta_2 = 0$ (along Y-axis)

(iii) Momentum of the system is conserved along x-axis

(iv) Relative speed of separation = e (relative speed of approch)

Coefficient of restitution, $e = \dfrac{|v_2 - v_1|}{|u_1 - u_2|}$

$e = 1$ for elastic collision

$e = 0$ for completely inelastic collision.

$0 \le e \le 1$ for inelastic collision.

Energy Loss in Collision

(i) Elastic collision, for first (incident) particle

$$\frac{K_f}{K_i} = \left(\frac{m_1 - m_2}{m_1 + m_2}\right)^2$$

$$\Rightarrow \frac{\Delta K_{\text{lost}}}{K_i} = \frac{4m_1m_2}{(m_1 + m_2)^2}$$

$$\Rightarrow \frac{\Delta K_{\text{lost}}}{K_i} = 100\% \qquad (\text{if } m_1 = m_2)$$

(ii) Inelastic collision, loss in KE

$\Delta K_{\text{lost}} = K_i - K_f$

$$\frac{1}{2}\frac{m_1m_2}{m_1 + m_2}(u_1 - u_2)^2(1 - e^2)$$

On putting $e = 0$

$$\Delta K_{\text{lost}} = \frac{m_1m_2(u_1 - u_2)^2}{2(m_1 + m_2)}$$

Rebounding of a ball on Collision with Floor

(i) Speed of ball after nth rebound.

$v_n = e^n vo = e^n\sqrt{2gh}$

(ii) Height covered by the ball after nth rebound

$h_n = e^{2n} . h_o$

(iii) Total distance covered by the ball before comes to rest

$$h_0 = \left(\frac{1 + e^2}{1 - e^2}\right)$$

Objective Type Questions

1. A ball falling freely from height of 4.9 m hits a floor. If e = 3/4 then the ball will hit the surface second time after.
   (a) 2.5 sec (b) 1.5 sec
   (c) 3.5 sec (d) 3.6 sec

2. A body of mass m is moving towards east and another body of equal mass is moving towards north. If after collision both stick together, their speed after collision would be
   (a) v (b) $v/2$
   (c) $\sqrt{2}v$ (d) $v/\sqrt{2}$

3. A body of mass M moves with velocity v and collides elastically with another body of mass m ($M >> m$) at rest, then the velocity of body of mass m is
   (a) v (b) $2v$
   (c) $v/2$ (d) zero

4. An electron with kinetic 5 eV is incident on a H-atom in its ground state. The collision
   (a) must be elastic
   (b) may be partially elastic
   (c) may be completely elastic
   (d) may be completely inelastic

5. A bomb of mass 30 kg at rest explodes into two pieces of masses 18 kg and 12 kg. The velocity of 18 kg mass is 6 ms^{-1}. The kinetic energy of the other mass is
   (a) 256 J (b) 486 J
   (c) 524 J (d) 324 J

6. A ball is dropped from a height h. If the coefficient of restitution is e then to what height will it rise after jumping twice from the ground?
   (a) $\frac{eh}{2}$ (b) $2eh$
   (c) eh (d) e^4h

7. A particle of mass m moving with velocity v collides with a stationary particle of mass $2m$. The speed of the system, will be
   (a) $3v$ (b) $v/2$
   (c) $v/3$ (d) $2v$

8. A neutron makes a head-on elastic collision with a stationary deuteron. The fractional energy loss of the neutron in the collision is
   (a) 16/81 (b) 8/9
   (c) 8/27 (d) 2/3

9. A spring of force-constant k is cut into two pieces such that one piece is double the length of the other. Then the long piece will have a force-constant of:
   (a) $\left(\frac{2}{3}\right)k$ (b) $\left(\frac{3}{2}\right)k$
   (c) $3k$ (d) $6k$

10. A particle of mass m is moving in a circular path of constant radius r such that its centripetal acceleration a_c is varying with time t as $a_c = k^2 rt^2$ where k is a constant. The power delivered to the particle by the force acting on it is:
    (a) $2\pi mk^2 r^2 t$ (b) $mk^2 r^2 t$
    (c) $\frac{(mk^4 r^2 t^5)}{3}$ (d) zero

11. A force $F = -K(y\hat{i} + x\hat{j})$ (where K is a positive constant) acts on a particle moving in the xy-plane. Starting from the origin, the particle is taken along the positive x-axis to the point $(a, 0)$ and then parallel to the y-axis to the point (a, a). The total work done by the force F on the particle is:
    (a) $-2Ka^2$ (b) $2Ka^2$
    (c) $-Ka^2$ (d) Ka^2

12. A wind powered generator converts wind energy into electrical energy. Assume that the generator converts a fixed fraction of the wind energy intercepted by its blades into electrical energy. For wind speed v, the electrical power output will be proportional to:
    (a) v (b) v^2
    (c) v^3 (d) v^4

13. At time $t = 0$ s, a particle starts moving along the x-axis. If its kinetic energy increases uniformly with time t, the net force acting on it must be proportional to:
    (a) t (b) $1/\sqrt{t}$
    (c) $\sqrt{t}$ (d) Constant

14. The potential energy function for a particle executing linear SHM is given by $V(x) = \frac{1}{2}kx^2$

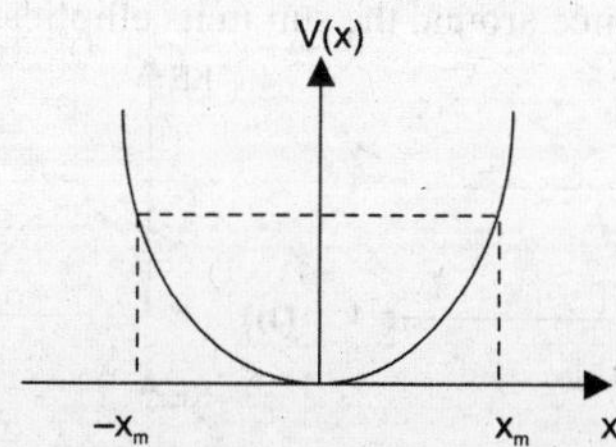

where k is the force constant of the oscillator. For $k = 0.5$ Nm^{-1}, the graph of $V(x)$ versus x is shown in the figure.

A particle of total energy E turns back when it reaches $x = \pm x_m$. If V and K indicate the potential energy and kinetic energy, respectively of the particle at $x = \pm x_m$, then which of the following is correct?

(a) $V = 0, K = E$ (b) $V = E, K = 0$

(c) $V < E, K = 0$ (d) $V = 0, K < E$

15. A body of mass m is accelerated uniformly from rest to a speed v in a time T. The instantaneous power delivered to the body as a function of time, is given by:

(a) $\frac{mv^2}{T^2} \cdot t$ (b) $\frac{mv^2}{T^2} \cdot t^2$

(c) $\frac{1}{2}\frac{mv^2}{T^2} \cdot t$ (d) $\frac{1}{2}\frac{mv^2}{T^2} \cdot t^2$

16. The potential energy of a 1 kg particle free to move along the x-axis is given by $V(x) = \left(\frac{x^4}{4} - \frac{x^2}{2}\right)$ J. The total mechanical energy of the particle is 2 J. Then, the maximum speed (in m/s) is:

(a) $\frac{3}{\sqrt{2}}$ (b) $\sqrt{2}$

(c) $\frac{1}{\sqrt{2}}$ (d) 2

17. Which of the diagrams shown in figure represents variation of total mechanical energy of a pendulum oscillating in air as function of time?

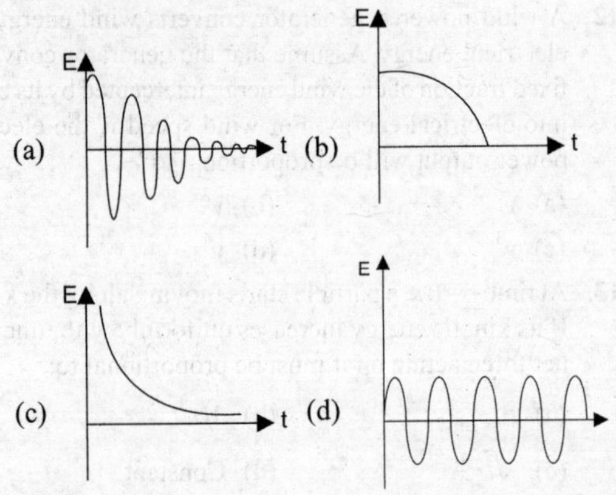

18. Which of the diagrams shown in figure most closely shows the variation in kinetic energy of the earth as it moves once around the sun in its elliptical orbit?

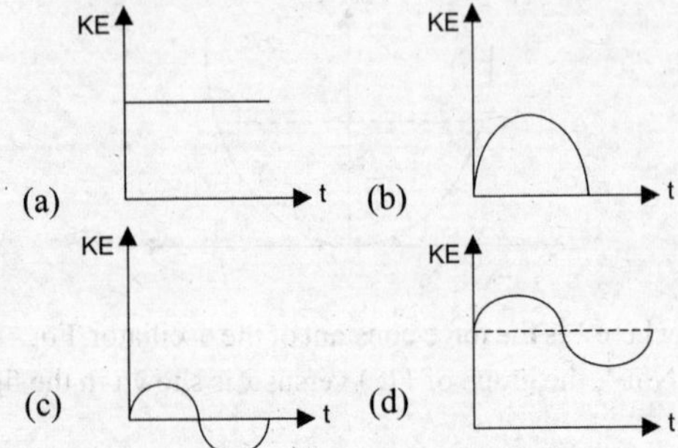

19. A body is moving unidirectionally under the influence of a source of constant power supplying energy. Which of the diagrams shown in figure correctly shows the displacement time curve for its motion?

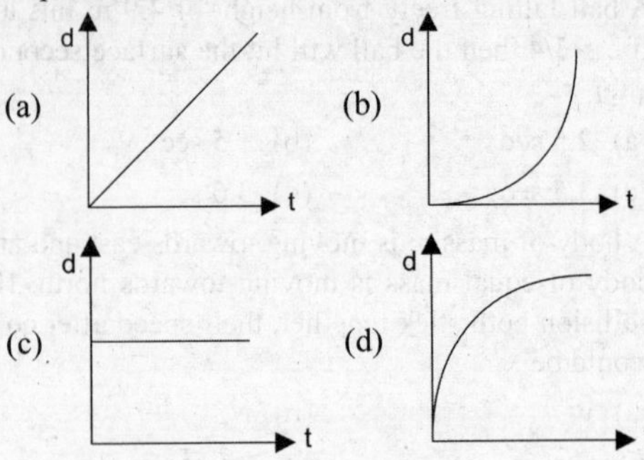

20. A raindrop falling from a height h above ground, attains a near terminal velocity when it has fallen through a height $\left(\frac{3}{4}\right)h$. Which of the diagrams shown in figure correctly shows the change in kinetic and potential energy of the drop during its fall up to the ground?

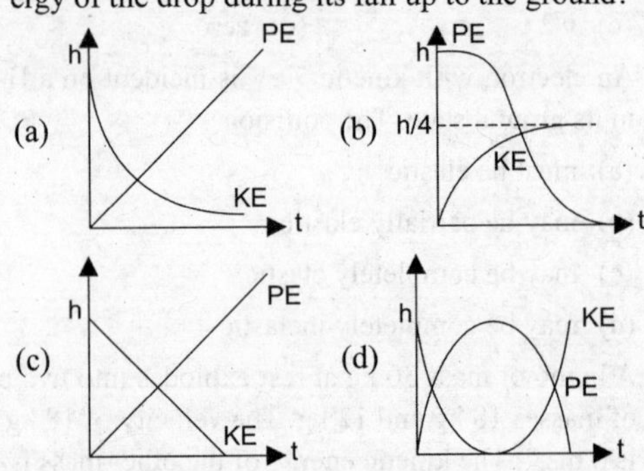

21. A uniform chain of length L and mass M is lying on a smooth table and one-third of its length is hanging vertically down over the edge of the table. If g is acceleration due to gravity, the work required to pull the hanging part on to the table is

(a) MgL

(b) $MgL/3$

(c) $MgL/9$

(d) $MgL/18$

22. A force $\mathbf{F} = -k(y\hat{\mathbf{i}} + x\hat{\mathbf{j}})$ (where k is a positive constant) acts on a particle moving in the x - y plane. Starting from the origin, the particle is taken along the positive x-axis to the point $(a, 0)$ and then parallel to the Y-axis to the point (a, a). The total work done by the force F on the particle is

(a) $-2ka^2$ (b) $2ka^2$

(c) $-ka^2$ (d) ka^2

23. A mass of M kg is suspended by a weightless string. The horizontal force that is required to displace it until the string makes an angle of 45° with the initial vertical direction is:

(a) $Mg(\sqrt{2}+1)$ (b) $Mg\sqrt{2}$

(c) $\frac{Mg}{\sqrt{2}}$ (d) $Mg(\sqrt{2}-1)$

24. A particle, which is constrained to move along the x-axis, is subjected to a force in the same direction which varies with the distance x of the particle from the origin as $F(x) = -kx + ax^3$. Here k and a are positive constants. For $x \geq 0$, the functional graphically form of the potential energy $U(x)$ of the particle is:

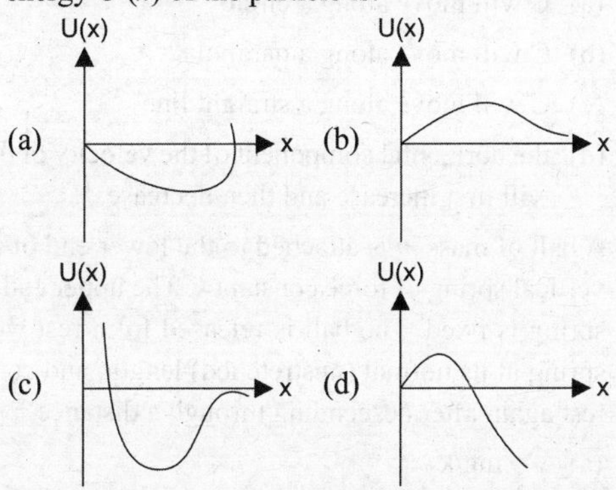

25. A smooth sphere of radius R is made to translate in a straight line with a constant acceleration $a = g$. A particle kept on the top of the sphere is released from there at zero velocity with respect to the sphere. The speed of the particle with respect to sphere as a function of θ as it slides down is

(a) $\sqrt{Rg(\sin\theta + \cos\theta)}$ (b) $\sqrt{Rg(1 + \cos\theta - \sin\theta)}$

(c) $\sqrt{4Rg\sin\theta}$ (d) $\sqrt{2Rg(1 + \sin\theta - \cos\theta)}$

26. A force $F = -k(y\hat{i} + x\hat{j})$, where k is a positive constant, acts on a particle moving in the xy plane. Starting from the origin, the particle is taken along the positive x-axis to the point $(a, 0)$, and the parallel to the y-axis to the point (a, a). The total work done by the force on the particle is

(a) $-2ka^2$ (b) $2ka^2$

(c) $-ka^2$ (d) ka^2

27. A stone tied to a string of length L is whirled in a vertical circle with the other end of the string at the centre. At a certain instant of time, the stone is at its lowest position, and has a speed u. The magnitude of the change in its velocity as it reaches a position where the string is horizontal is:

(a) $\sqrt{u^2 - 2gL}$ (b) $\sqrt{2gL}$

(c) $\sqrt{u^2 - 2gL}$ (d) $\sqrt{2(u^2 - gL)}$

28. A particle of mass m is moving in a circular path of constant radius r such that its centripetal acceleration a_c is varying with time as $a_c = k^2rt^2$, where k is a constant. The power delivered to the particle by the forces acting on it is

(a) $2\pi mk^2r^2t$ (b) mk^2r^2t

(c) $\frac{1}{3}mk^4r^2t^5$ (d) 0

29. A particle, which is constrained to move along the x-axis, is subjected to a force in the same direction which varies with the distance x of the particle from the origin as $F(x) = -kx + ax^3$. Here k and a are positive constants. For $x \geq 0$, the functional form of the potential energy $U(x)$ of particle is

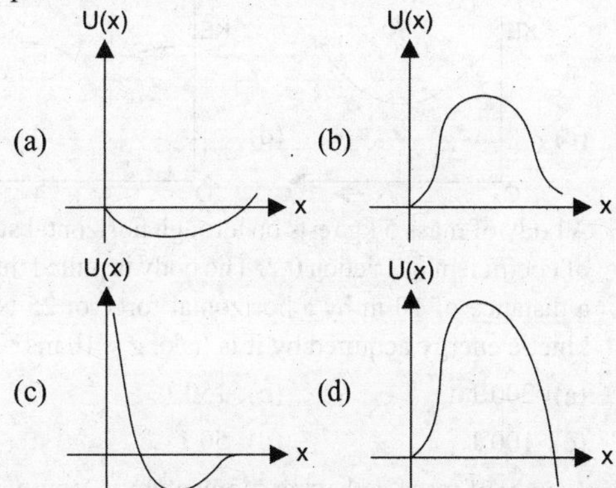

30. A wind – powered generator converts wind energy into electric energy. Assume that the generator converts a fixed fraction of the wind energy intercepted by its blades into electric energy. For wind speed V, the electrical power output will be proportional to

(a) V (b) V^2

(c) V^3 (d) V^4

31. A body is moved along a straight line by a machine delivering constant power. The distance moved by the body in time t is proportional to

(a) $t^{1/2}$ (b) $t^{3/4}$

(c) $t^{3/2}$ (d) t^2

32. A particle is acted by a force $F = kx$, where k is a positive constant. Its potential energy at $x = 0$ is zero. Which curve correctly represents the variation of potential energy of the block with respect to x?

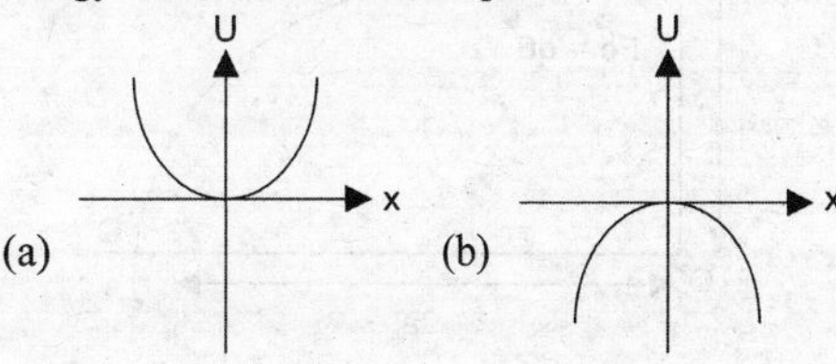

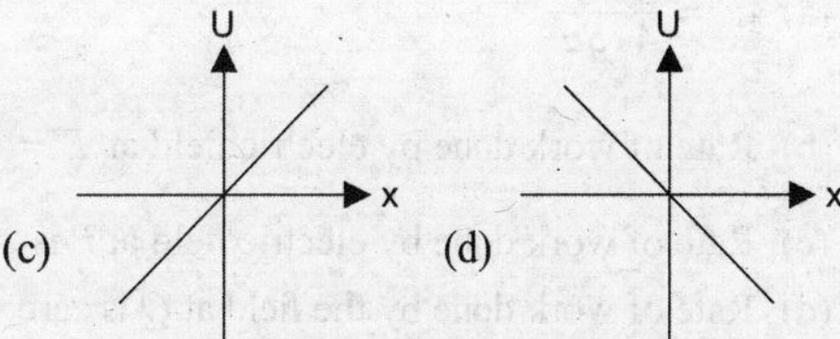

33. A ball is thrown up with a certain velocity at angle θ to the horizontal. The kinetic energy KE of the ball varies with horizontal displacement x as:

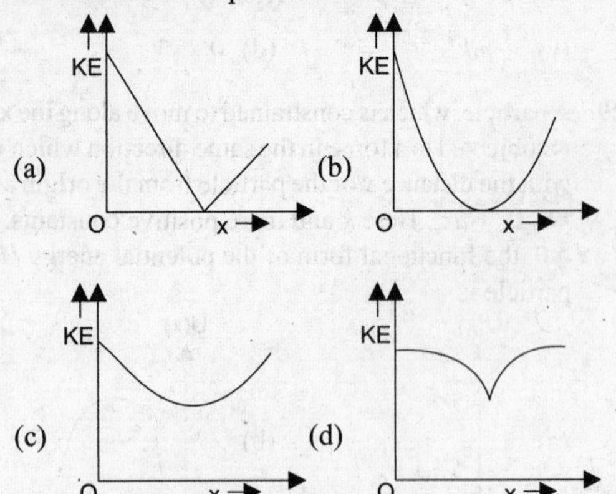

34. A body of mass 5 kg rests on a rough horizontal surface of coefficient of friction 0.2. The body is pulled through a distance of 10 m by a horizontal force of 25 N. The kinetic energy acquired by it is (take $g = 10$ ms^{-2})

(a) 200 J (b) 150 J

(c) 100 J (d) 50 J

35. A body of mass m, having momentum p, is moving on a rough horizontal surface. If it is stopped in a distance x, the coefficient of friction between the body and the surface is given by

(a) $\mu = \dfrac{p^2}{2gm^2x}$ (b) $\mu = \dfrac{p^2}{2gmx}$

(c) $\mu = \dfrac{p}{2gmx}$ (d) $\mu = \dfrac{p}{2gm^2x}$

36. A particle of charge +q and mass m, moving under the influence of uniform electric field $E\hat{i}$ and a uniform magnetic field $B\hat{k}$ follows a trajectory from P to Q as shown in figure. The velocity at P and Q are $\mathrm{V}\hat{i}$ and $-2\mathrm{v}\,\hat{j}$. Choose the correct statement.

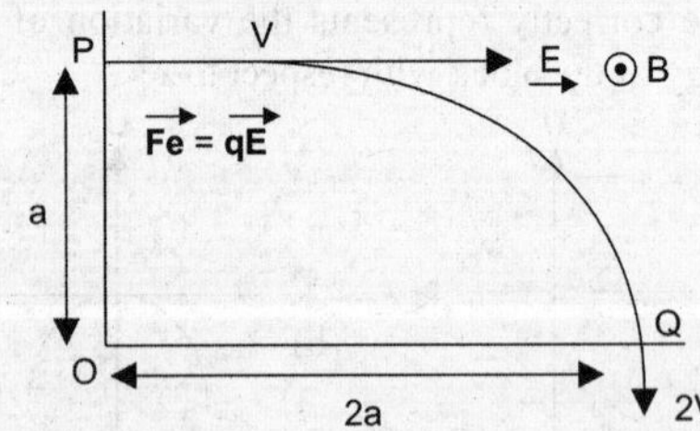

(a) $E = \dfrac{3}{4}\dfrac{mv^2}{qa}$

(b) Rate of work done by electric field at $P = \dfrac{3}{4}\dfrac{mv^3}{a}$

(c) Rate of work done by electric field at P is zero.

(d) Rate of work done by the field at Q is zero.

37. A small ball is connected to a block by light string of length l. Both are initially on the ground. There is sufficient friction on the ground to prevent the block from slipping. The ball is projected vertically up

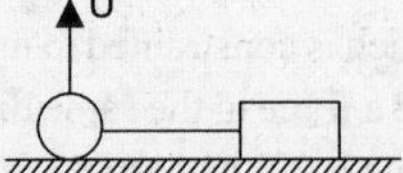

with a velocity u, where $2gl < u^2 < 3gl$. The centre of mass of the 'block + ball' system is C

(a) C will move along a circle

(b) C will move along a parabola

(c) C will move along a straight line

(d) the horizontal component of the velocity of the ball will first increase and then decrease.

38. A ball of mass m is attached to the lower end of a light vertical spring of force constant k. The upper end of the spring is fixed. The ball is released from rest with the spring at its normal (unstretched) length, and comes to rest again after descending through a distance x.

(a) x = mg/k

(b) x = 2mg/k

(c) The ball will have no acceleration at the position where it has descended through $x/2$

(d) The ball will have an upward acceleration equal to g at its lowermost position.

39. A long block A is at rest on a smooth horizontal surface. A small block B, whose mass is half of A, is placed on A at one end and projected along A with some velocity u. The coefficient of friction between the blocks is μ.

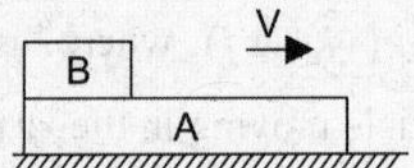

(a) the blocks will reach a final common velocity $\dfrac{u}{3}$

(b) the work done against friction is two-third of the initial kinetic energy of B.

(c) before the blocks reach a common velocity, the acceleration of A relative to B is $\dfrac{2}{3}\mu g$

(d) before the blocks reach a common velocity the acceleration of A relative to B is $\dfrac{3}{2}\mu g$

40. A particle is acted upon by a constant force which is always perpendicular to the velocity of the particle. The motion of the particle takes in a plane it follows that

(a) its velocity is constant

(b) its acceleration is constant

(c) its K.E is constant

(d) its moves in a circular path

41. A pendulum is released from point A as shown in figure. At some instant net force on the bob is making an angle θ with the string:

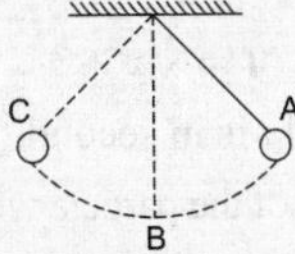

(a) for $\theta = 90°$ particle is at A

(b) for $\theta = 0°$ particle is at B

(c) for $\theta = 90°$ particle at the position where string is horizontal

(d) For $\theta = 0°$ particle is at A

42. A body of mass 1 kg is suspended from an inextensible string of length 1 m. When the string makes an angle 60° with vertical, speed of the bob is 4 m/s.

(a) net acceleration of the bob at the instant is 10 m/s^2.

(b) net acceleration of the bob at the instant is 18.2 m/s^2.

(c) the bob will rise to a maximum height with respect to bottom most point > 1.3 m

(d) the bob will rise to a maximum height with respect to bottom most point < 1.3m

43. A body is moved along a straight line by a machine delivering a power proportional to time t, then

(a) velocity is proportional to t

(b) displacement is proportional to t^3

(c) work done is proportional to t^2

(d) velocity is proportional to t^2

44. In the figure shown upper block is given a velocity of 6 m/s and lower block 3 m/s. When relative motion between them is stopped.

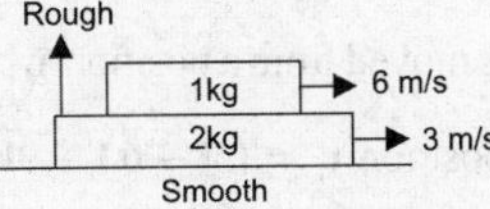

(a) work done by friction on upper block is negative

(b) work done by friction on both blocks is positive

(c) work done by friction on upper block is – 10 J

(d) net work done by friction is zero.

45. $U(r) = \frac{A}{r^2} - \frac{B}{r}$ where r is the distance from the centre of the force and A and B are positive constants then

(a) the equilibrium distance is given by $\frac{2A}{B}$

(b) the work required to move the particle from equilibrium distance to infinity is $\frac{B^2}{4A}$

(c) the work required to move the particle from equilibrium position to infinity is $\frac{B}{4A}$

(d) equilibrium distance is given by $\frac{B}{2A}$

46. Power of a force acting on a block varies with time t as shown in the figure. The angle between force acting on the block and its velocity is:

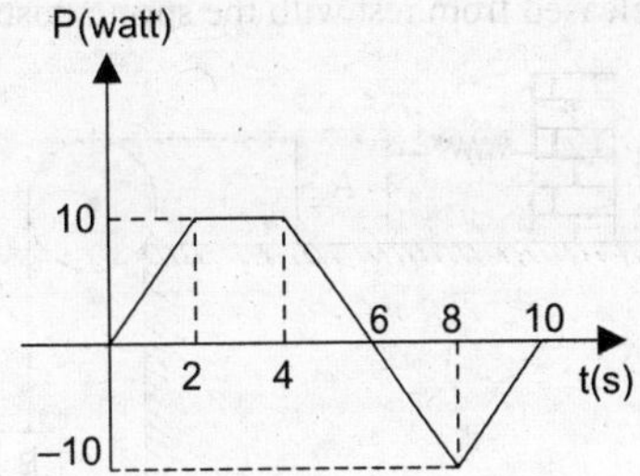

(a) acute at $t = 1$s

(b) 90° at $t = 3$ s

(c) obtuse at $t = 7$ s

(d) change in kinetic energy from $t = 0$, to $t = 10$ s is 20 J.

47. Displacement time graph of a particle moving in a straight line is as shown in figure. Select the correct alternative(s):

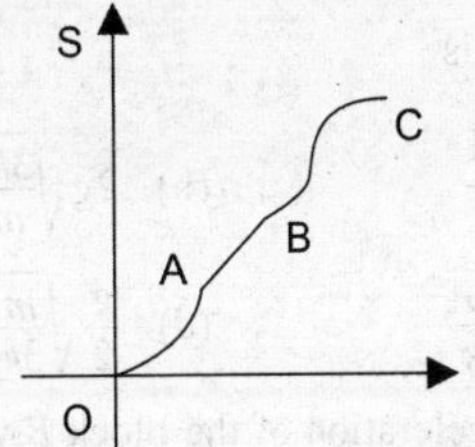

(a) Work done by all the forces in region OA and BC is positive

(b) Work done by all the forces in region AB is zero

(c) Work done by all the forces in region BC is negative

(d) Work done by all forces in region OA is negative

48. A block of mass 2 kg is hanging over a smooth and light pulley through a light string. The other end of the string is pulled by a constant force $F = 40$ N. The kinetic energy of the particle increases 40 J in a given interval of time. Then, (g = 10m/s^2)

(a) tension in the string is 40 N

(b) displacement of the block in the given interval of time is 2 m

(c) work done by gravity is –20 J

(d) work done by tension is 80 J.

49. Select the correct alternatives:

(a) work done by static friction is always zero

(b) work done by kinetic friction can be positive also

(c) kinetic energy of a system can not be increased without applying any external force on the system

(d) work energy theorem is valid in non-inertial frames also.

Directions (Q. 50 to 52) : Consider the situation shown in figure. Mass of block A is m and that of block B is $2\ m$. The force constant of spring is K. Friction is absent everywhere. System is released from rest with the spring unstretched.

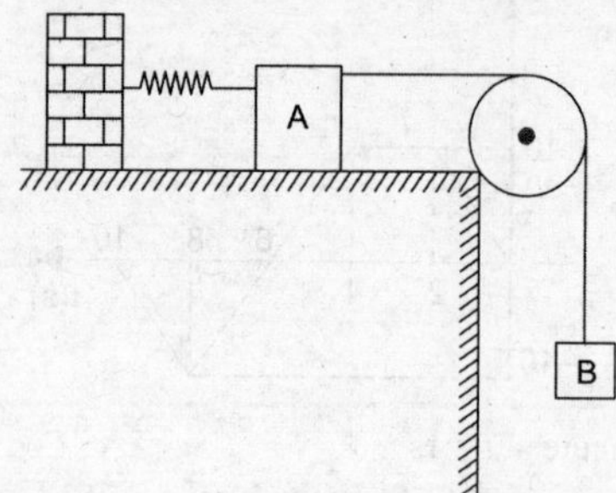

50. The maximum extension of the spring will be

(a) $\frac{mg}{k}$ (b) $\frac{2mg}{k}$

(c) $\frac{3mg}{k}$ (d) $\frac{4mg}{k}$

51. The speed of block A when the extension in the spring is $x = \frac{xm}{2}$ is

(a) $\frac{g}{2}\sqrt{\frac{3k}{m}}$ (b) $2g\sqrt{\frac{3k}{m}}$

(c) $2g\sqrt{\frac{m}{3k}}$ (d) $\frac{g}{2}\sqrt{\frac{m}{3k}}$

52. The net acceleration of the block B when extension in the spring is $x = \frac{xm}{4}$ is

(a) $\frac{g}{2}$ downward (b) $\frac{g}{3}$ upward

(c) $\frac{g}{2}$ upward (d) $\frac{g}{3}$ downward

Directions (Q. 53 to 55) : In a spring gun having spring constant 100 N/m, a small ball of mass 0.1 kg is put in its barrel by compressing the spring through 0.05 m as shown in figure.

53. The velocity of the ball when the spring is released will be

(a) $\sqrt{5/2}$ m/s (b) $\sqrt{2/5}$ m/s

(c) $5/2$ m/s (d) $2/5$ m/s

54. The time taken by the ball to reach the ground will be

(a) $2/5$ sec (b) $\sqrt{\frac{2}{5}}$ sec

(c) $5/2$ sec (d) $\sqrt{5/2}$ sec

55. Where should a box be placed on the ground so that the ball fall in it, if the ball leaves the gun horizontally at a height of 2 m above the ground is

(a) 0.5 m (b) 1 m

(c) 1.5 m (d) 2.0 m

Directions (Q. 56 to 58) : The displacement x of a particle moving in one dimension, under the action of a constant force is varying according to relation

$$t = \sqrt{x} + 3$$

where x is in metre and t is in second.

56. The displacement of the particle when its velocity is zero is

(a) zero (b) 1 m

(c) 2 m (d) 3 m

57. The acceleration of the particle

(a) increases with time

(b) decreases with time

(c) increases with time up to $t = 3$ s and then decreases with time.

(d) remains constant at 2 ms^{-2}

58. The work done by the force in first 6 s is

(a) 1 J (b) 3 J

(c) 6 J (d) zero

Directions (Q. 59 to 62) : The work done by a constant force acting on a body is given by

$$W = \mathbf{F}\cdot\mathbf{r}$$

where **F** is the force vector and **r** is displacement vector. The displacement vector $\mathbf{r} = \mathbf{r}_2 - \mathbf{r}_1$ where $\mathbf{r}_1$ is the initial position vector and $\mathbf{r}_2$ is the final position vector.

If the force is variable, the work done in moving a body from a position r_1 to a position $\mathbf{r}_2$ is given by

$$W = \int_{r_1}^{r_2} \mathbf{F}.\mathbf{dr}$$

where **dr** is an infinitesimally small displacement.

59. A particle is moved from a position $\mathbf{r}_1 = (3\hat{\mathbf{i}} + 2\hat{\mathbf{J}} + 4\hat{\mathbf{k}})$ metre to a position $\mathbf{r}_1 = (5\hat{\mathbf{i}} + 6\hat{\mathbf{J}} + 9\hat{\mathbf{k}})$ metre under the action of a force $\mathbf{F} = (\hat{\mathbf{i}} + 3\hat{\mathbf{J}} + \hat{\mathbf{k}})$ newton. The work done is

(a) zero (b) 13 J

(c) 27 J (d) 35 J

60. A body of mass m is projected from a tower of height h at an angle θ above the horizontal. The work done by the gravitational force during the time it takes to hit the ground is

(a) $mgh\ (1 + \cos\theta)$ (b) $mgh\ (1 + \sin\theta)$

(c) mgh (d) zero

61. A body of mass m is projected from the ground with a velocity u at an angle θ above the horizontal. The work done by the gravitational force in time $t = \frac{u\sin\theta}{g}$ is

(a) $2mu^2\sin^2\theta$ (b) $mu^2\sin^2\theta$

(c) $\frac{mu^2\sin^2\theta}{2}$ (d) zero

62. If $\theta = 45°$, the work done by gravitational force in above question in time $t = \frac{2\mu \sin\theta}{g}$

(a) $\frac{mu^2}{4}$ (b) $\frac{mu^2}{2}$

(c) mu^2 (d) zero

Directions (Q. 63 to 65) : Work done by a constant force acting on a particle is defined as $W = \vec{F}.\Delta\vec{r}$ where $\Delta\vec{r} = \vec{r}_f - \vec{r}_i, \vec{r}_f$ is the final position of particle and $\vec{r}_i$ is the initial position of particle. If the force is variable work done is defined as $W = \int_{r_i}^{r_f} \vec{F}.d\vec{r}$, where $\vec{F}$ is the force at any general position $\vec{r}$ between $\vec{r}_i$ and $\vec{r}_f$ and $d\vec{r}$ is representing infinitely small displacement of particle. $\vec{dr} = dx\hat{\mathbf{i}} + dy\hat{\mathbf{j}} + dz\hat{\mathbf{k}}$.

63. A particle is thrown from a tower of height h at an angle θ above horizontal. Work done by gravity during its time of flights is (mass of particle is m)

(a) 0 (b) $mgh \cos\theta$

(c) $mgh \sin\theta$ (d) mgh

64. Given: $\vec{F} = 2\hat{i}+4\hat{j}$, $\vec{r}_i = 2\hat{i} + 3\hat{j}$ and $\vec{r}_f = 3\hat{i} + 4\hat{j}$ work done is (use SI units)

(a) 4 J (b) 6 J

(c) 10 J (d) zero

65. A particle thrown from ground with a velocity v at an angle θ above horizontal. Work done by gravity in $t = \frac{2v\sin\theta}{g}$ equals

(a) $\frac{mgv^2 \sin^2\theta}{2g}$ (b) $\frac{mgv^2 \sin^2\theta}{g}$

(c) zero (d) $\frac{2mgv^2 \sin^2\theta}{g}$

Directions (Q. 66 to 69) : A block of mass 0.5 kg is taken from the bottom of an inclined plane to its top and then allowed to slide down to the bottom. The length of the inclined plane is 2.5 m and its height is 1.5 m. The coefficient of friction between the block and the plane is 0.2.

66. Work done by the gravitational force over the round trip is

(a) 0 J (b) 0.5J

(c) 1 J (d) 1.5J

67. Work done by the applied force over the upward journey

(a) 0 J (b) 5.5 J

(c) 9.5 J (d) 8.5 J

68. Work done by the frictional force over the round trip

(a) 4.5 J (b) – 4 J

(c) – 4.5 j (d) 4 J

69. The kinetic energy of the block when it reaches the bottom of the plane is.

(a) 5.5 J (b) 6.5 J

(c) 4.5 J (d) 3.5 J

Directions (Q. 70 to 71) : An elastic ball of mass $\left(\frac{1}{2}\right)$ kg slides down along a smooth inclined plane having inclination angle 37° for a distance of $\left(\frac{100}{3}\right)$ m along the incline and collides with a similar ball elastically, which is at rest on a horizontal smooth plane as shown in the figure. Then,

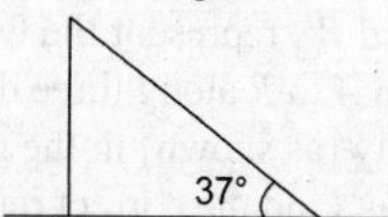

70. The velocity of two ball after collision will be.

(a) $v_1 = 0$, $v_2 = 10$ m/s

(b) $v_1 = 5$ m/s, $v_2 = 10$ m/s

(c) $v_1 = 0$ m/s, v2 = 20 m/s

(d) $v_1 = 10$ m/s, v2 = 0 m/s

71. Impulsive reaction produced on the second ball by the first ball will be.

(a) 10 N-s (b) 5 N-s

(c) 20 N-s (d) 2.5 N-s

72. A block of mass m is kept on a platform which starts from rest with constant acceleration g/2 upward, as shown in figure. Work done by normal reaction on block in time t is :

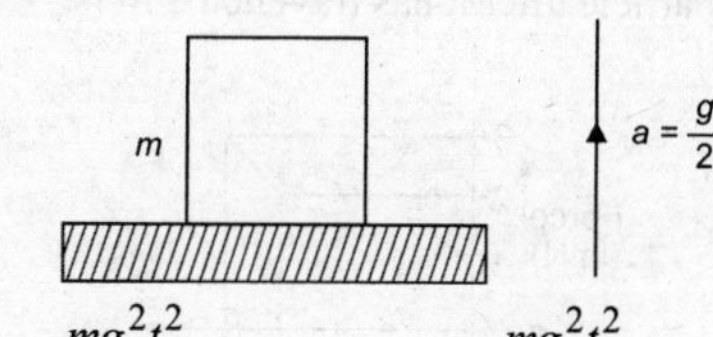

(a) $-\frac{mg^2t^2}{8}$ (b) $\frac{mg^2t^2}{8}$

(c) 0 (d) $\frac{3mg^2t^2}{8}$

73. A time dependent force $F = 6t$ acts on a particle of mass 1 kg. If the particle starts from rest, the work done by the force during the first 1 s will be

(a) 22J (b) 9 J

(c) 18 J (d) 4.5 J

74. When a rubber band is stretched by a distance x, it exerts a restoring force of magnitude $F = ax + bx^2$, where a and b are constants. The work done in stretching the unstretched rubber band by L is

(a) $aL^2 + bL^3$ (b) $\frac{1}{2}(aL^2 + bL^3)$

(c) $\frac{aL^2}{2} + \frac{bL^3}{3}$ (d) $\frac{1}{2}\left(\frac{aL^2}{2} + \frac{bL^3}{3}\right)$

75. The work done on a particle of mass m by a force, $K\left[\frac{x}{(x^2+y^2)^{3/2}}\hat{i}+\frac{y}{(x^2+y^2)^{3/2}}\hat{j}\right]$ (K being a constant of appropriate dimensions), when the particle is taken from the point $(a, 0)$ to the point $(0, a)$ along a circular path of radius a about the origin in the x - y plane is

(a) $\frac{2k\pi}{a}$ (b) $\frac{k\pi}{a}$

(c) $\frac{k\pi}{2a}$ (d) 0

76. If W_1, W_2 and W_3 represent the work done in moving a particle from A to B along three different paths 1, 2 and 3 respectively (as shown) in the gravitational field of a point mass m. Find the correct relation between W_1, W_2 and W_3

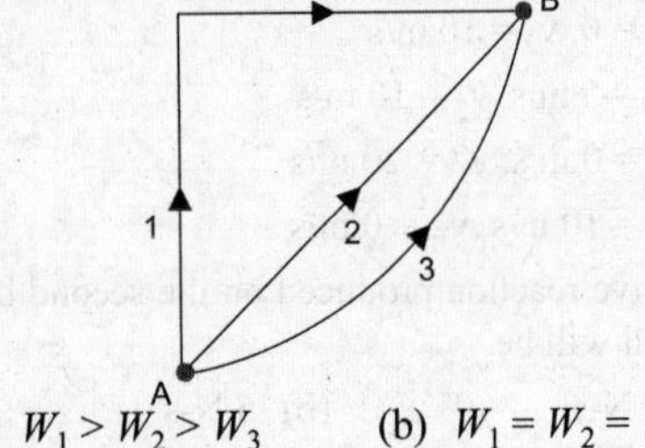

(a) $W_1 > W_2 > W_3$ (b) $W_1 = W_2 = W_3$

(c) $W_1 < W_2 < W_3$ (d) $W_2 < W_1 > W_3$

77. A particle moves in one dimension from rest under the influence of a force that varies with the distance travelled by the particle as shown in the figure. The kinetic energy of the particle after it has travelled 3 m is:

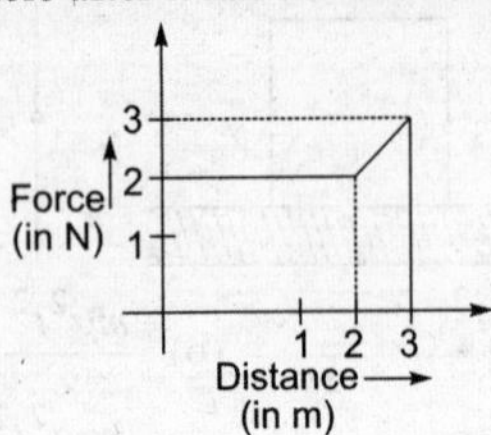

(a) 5 J

(b) 6.5 J

(c) 4 J

(d) 2.5 J

78. A particle is moving in a circular path of radius a under the action of an attractive potential $U = \frac{-k}{2r^2}$ its total energy is:

(a) zero

(b) $-\frac{3k}{2a^2}$

(c) $-\frac{K}{4a^2}$

(d) $\frac{K}{2a^2}$

79. A body of mass $m = 10^{-2}$ kg is moving in a medium and experiences a frictional force $F = -kv^2$. Its initial speed is $v_0 = 10\ \text{ms}^{-1}$. If, after 10 s, its energy is $\frac{1}{8}mv_0^2$, the value of k will be

(a) $10^{-3}\ \text{kgs}^{-1}$

(b) $10^{-4}\ \text{kgm}^{-1}$

(c) $10^{-1}\ \text{kgm}^{-1}\ \text{s}^{-1}$

(d) $10^{-3}\ \text{kgm}^{-1}$

80. A block of mass 2 kg is free to move along the x-axis. It is at rest and from $t = 0$ onwards it is subjected to a time dependent force $F(t)$ in the x-direction. The force $F(t)$ varies with t as shown in the figure. The kinetic energy of the block after 4.5 s is

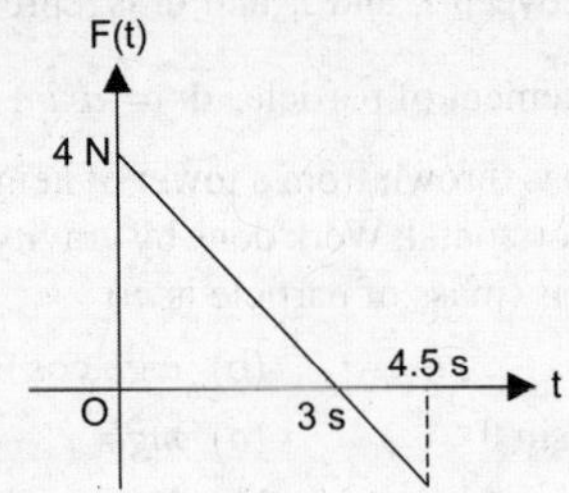

(a) 4.50 J

(b) 7.50 J

(c) 5.06 J

(d) 14.06 J

81. A block (B) is attached to two unstretched springs S_1 and S_2 with spring constants k and $4k$, respectively. The other ends are attached to two supports M_1 and M_2 not attached to the walls. The springs and supports have negligible mass. There is no friction anywhere.

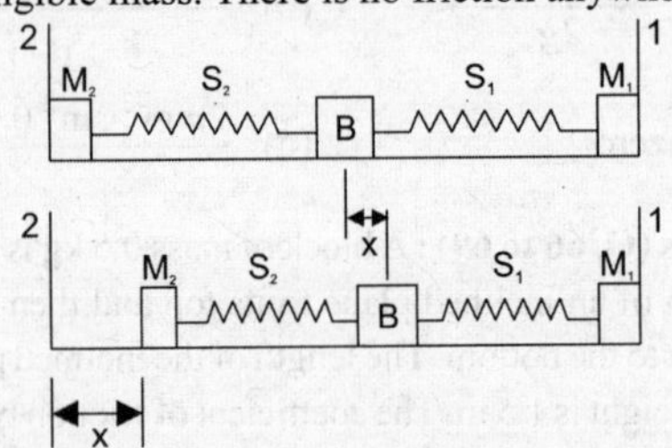

The block B is displaced towards wall 1 by a small distance x and released. The block returns and moves a maximum distance y towards wall 2. Displacements x and y are measured with respect to the equilibrium position of the block B. The ratio $\frac{y}{x}$ is

(a) 4

(b) 2

(c) $\frac{1}{2}$

(d) $\frac{1}{4}$

82. An ideal spring with spring constant k is hung from the ceiling and a block of mass M is attached to its lower end. The mass is released with the spring initially unstretched. Then the maximum extension in the spring is

(a) $\frac{4Mg}{k}$

(b) $\frac{2Mg}{k}$

(c) $\frac{Mg}{k}$

(d) $\frac{Mg}{2k}$

83. A particle is placed at the origin and a force $F = kx$ is acting on it (where, k is a positive constant). If $U(0) = 0$, the graph of $U(x)$ *versus* x will be (where, U is the potential energy function)

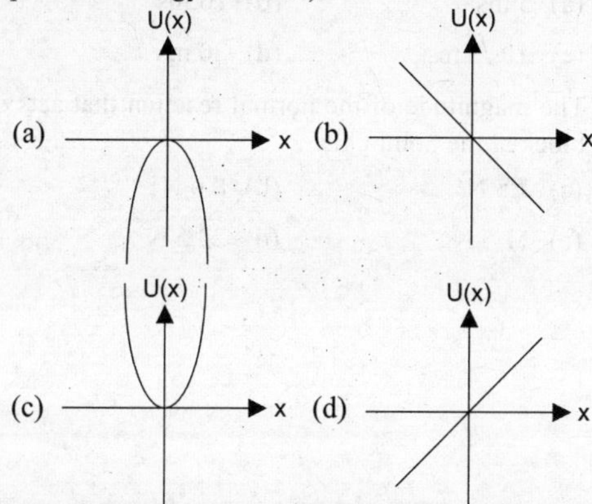

84. A particle of mass m is initially at rest at the origin. It is subjected to a force and starts moving along the x-axis. Its kinetic energy K changes with time as $dK/dt = \gamma t$, where γ is a positive constant of appropriate dimensions. Which of the following statements is (are) true?

(a) The force applied on the particle is constant

(b) The speed of the particle is proportional to time

(c) The distance of the particle from the origin increases linearly with time

(d) The force is conservative.

85. A person trying to loose weight by burning fat lifts a mass of 10 kg upto a height of 1 m 1000 times. Assume that the potential energy lost each time he lowers the mass is dissipated. How much fat will he use up considering the work done only when the weight is lifted up? Fat supplies 3.8×10^7 J of energy per kg which is converted to mechanical energy with a 20% efficiency rate. (Take, $g = 9.8$ ms^{-2})

(a) 2.45×10^{-3} kg

(b) 6.45×10^{-3} kg

(c) 9.89×10^{-3} kg

(d) 12.89×10^{-3} kg

86. It is found that if a neutron suffers an elastic collinear collision with deuterioum at rest, fractional loss of its energy is p_d, while for its similar collision with carbon nucleus at rest, fractional loss of energy is p_c. The value of p_d and p_c are respectively.

(a) (0, 0) (b) (0, 1)

(c) (0.89, 0.28) (d) (0.28, 0.89)

87. In a collinear collision, a particle with an initial speed v_0 strikes a stationary particle of the same mass. If the final kinetic energy 50% greater than the original kinetic energy, the magnitude of the relative velocity between the two particles, after collision, is

(a) $\frac{v_0}{2}$ (b) $\frac{v_0}{\sqrt{2}}$

(c) $\frac{v_0}{4}$ (d) $\sqrt{2}v_0$

88. A point particle of mass m, moves along the uniformly rough track PQR as shown in the figure. The coefficient of friction, between the particle and the rough track equals μ. The particle is released from rest, from the point P and it comes to rest at a point R. The energies lost by the ball, over the parts PQ and QR of the track, are equal to each other, and no energy is lost when particle changes direction from PQ to QR. The values of the coefficient of friction μ and the distance x (= QR), are respectively close to

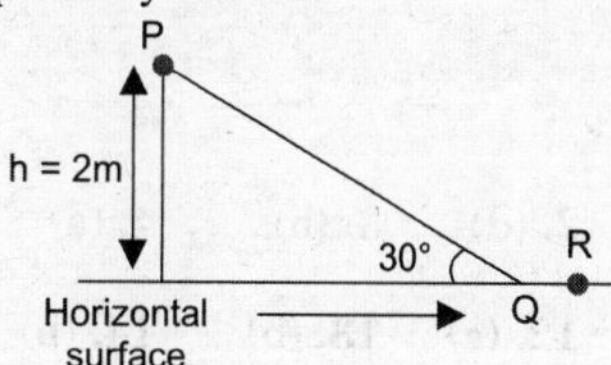

(a) 0.2 and 6.5 m

(b) 0.2 and 3.5 m

(c) 0.29 and 3.5 m

(d) 0.29 and 6.5 m

89. A wire, which passes through the hole in a small bead, is bent in the form of quarter of a circle. The wire is fixed vertically on ground as shown in the figure. The bead is released from near the top of the wire and it slides along the wire without friction. As the bead moves from A to B, the force it applies on the wire is

(a) always radially outwards

(b) always radially inwards

(c) radially outwards initially and radially inwards later

(d) radially inwards initially and radially outwards later

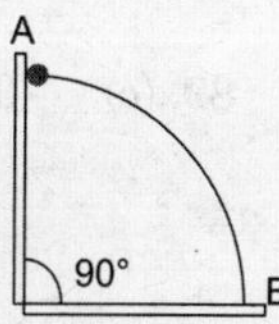

90. A bob of mass M is suspended by a massless string of length L. The horizontal velocity v at position A is just sufficient to make it reach the point B. The angle θ at which the speed of the bob is half of that at A, satisfies

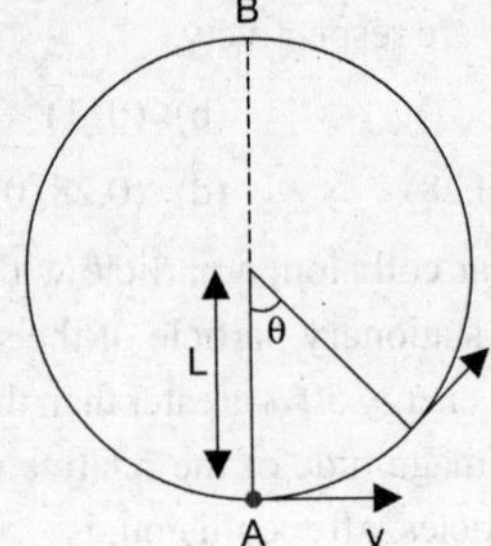

(a) $\theta = \frac{\pi}{4}$

(b) $\frac{\pi}{4} < \theta < \frac{\pi}{2}$

(c) $\frac{\pi}{2} < \theta < \frac{\pi}{4}$

(d) $\frac{3\pi}{4} < \theta < \pi$

Directions (Q. 91 to 92) :

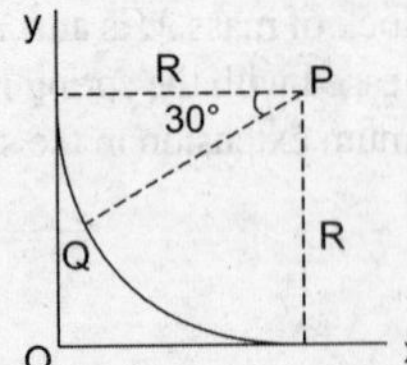

A small block of mass 1 kg is released from rest at the top of a rough track. The track is a circular arc of radius 40 m. The block slides along the track without toppling and a frictional force acts on it in the direction opposite to the instantaneous velocity. The work done in overcoming the friction up to the point Q, as shown in the figure, is 150 J. (Take the acceleration due to gravity, $g = 10\ \text{ms}^{-2}$)

91. The speed of the block when it reaches the point Q is

(a) $5\ \text{ms}^{-1}$ (b) $10\ \text{ms}^{-1}$

(c) $10\sqrt{3}\ \text{ms}^{-1}$ (d) $20\ \text{ms}^{-1}$

92. The magnitude of the normal reaction that acts on the block at the point Q is

(a) 7.5 N (b) 8.6 N

(c) 11.5 N (d) 22.5 N

Answers

1. (b)	**2.** (d)	**3.** (b)	**4.** (a)	**5.** (b)	**6.** (d)	**7.** (c)	**8.** (b)	**9.** (b)	**10.** (b)
11. (c)	**12.** (c)	**13.** (b)	**14.** (b)	**15.** (a)	**16.** (a)	**17.** (c)	**18.** (d)	**19.** (b)	**20.** (b)
21. (d)	**22.** (c)	**23.** (d)	**24.** (d)	**25.** (d)	**26.** (c)	**27.** (d)	**28.** (b)	**29.** (d)	**30.** (c)
31. (c)	**32.** (d)	**33.** (c)	**34.** (b)	**35.** (a)	**36.** (a,b,d)	**37.** (a,d)	**38.** (b,c,d)	**39.** (a,b,d)	
40. (c,d)	**41.** (a,b,c)		**42.** (b,d)	**43.** (a,c)	**44.** (a,c)	**45.** (a,b)	**46.** (a,c,d)	**47.** (b,d)	**48.** (a,b,d)
49. (b,d)	**50.** (d)	**51.** (c)	**52.** (a)	**53.** (a)	**54.** (b)	**55.** (b)	**56.** (a)	**57.** (d)	**58.** (d)
59. (c)	**60.** (c)	**61.** (c)	**62.** (d)	**63.** (d)	**64.** (b)	**65.** (c)	**66.** (a)	**67.** (c)	**68.** (b)
69. (a)	**70.** (c)	**71.** (a)	**72.** (d)	**73.** (d)	**74.** (c)	**75.** (d)	**76.** (b)	**77.** (b)	**78.** (a)
79. (b)	**80.** (c)	**81.** (c)	**82.** (b)	**83.** (a)	**84.** (a,b,c)	**85.** (d)	**86.** (c)	**87.** (d)	**88.** (c)
89. (c)	**90.** (d)	**91.** (b)	**92.** (a)						

Explanations

1. Where v is final velocity, u is initial velocity and h is height.

   Given $h = 4.9\text{m}$, $g = 9.8\ \text{ms}^{-2}$, $u = 0$

   $\therefore\ v = \sqrt{2gh} = \sqrt{2 \times 9.8 \times 4.9} = 9.8\ \text{ms}^{-1}$

   Coefficient of restitution (e) of an object is a unit fraction value representing the ratio of velocities before and after an impact.

   $v' = \frac{3}{4} \times 9.8$

   Time taken from first bounce to second bounce is

   $t = \frac{2v^1}{g} = 2 \times \frac{3}{4} \times 9.8 \times \frac{1}{9.8} = 1.5\ \text{sec}$

2. In inelastic collision most of the kinetic energy of the body is lost in other form of heat. Thus, in inelastic collision kinetic energy is not conserved but total energy and momentum are still conserved.

   Hence, we have

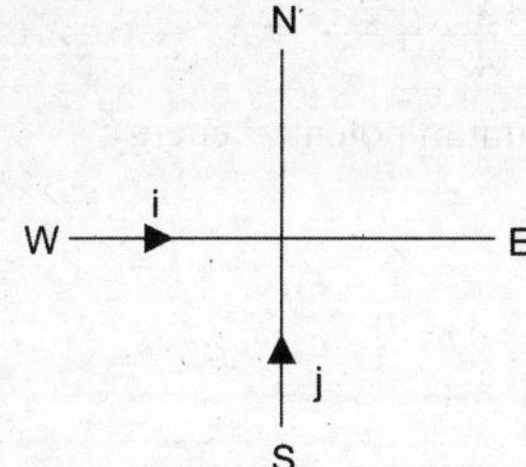

   $mvi + mvj = 2mv'$

   $\Rightarrow |2mv'| = m|vi + vj|$

   $\Rightarrow 2mv' = m\sqrt{v^2 + v^2}$

   $\Rightarrow v' = \frac{v\sqrt{2}}{2} = \frac{v}{\sqrt{2}}$

   From equation of motion

   $$v^2 = u^2 + 2gh$$

3. From law of conservation of linear momentum

   $m_1u_1 + m_2u_2 = m_1v_1 + m_2v_2$

   $M \times v + \text{m} \times 0 = M \times v_1 + mv_2$

   $Mv = Mv_1 + mv_2$ .....(i)

   $M(v - v_1) - mv_2$

   In elastic collision kinetic energy is also conserved

   $\frac{1}{2}m_1u_1^2 + \frac{1}{2}m_2u_2^2 = \frac{1}{2}m_1v_1^2 + \frac{1}{2}m_2v_2^2$

   $Mv^2 = Mv_1^2 = mv_2^2$

   $M(v + v_1)(v - v_1) = mv_2^2$ .....(ii)

   Dividing Eq. (ii) by Eq. (i) we get

   $v + v_1 \approx v_2$ as $M >> m$

   So, $v_1 = v$

   $\therefore\ v_2 = 2v$

4. In hydrogen atom $E_2 - E_1 = 10.2$ eV. Since, energy difference is 10.2 eV, which is greater that kinetic energy 5 eV the electron excites the hydrogen atom, hence collision is elastic.

5. Applying conservation of linear momentum, we write,

   $m_1u_1 = m_2u_2$

   here $m_1 = 18$ kg, $m_2 = 12$ kg

   $u_1 = 6\ \text{ms}^{-1}$, $u_2 = ?$

   $\therefore\ 18 \times 6 = 12u_2$

   $\Rightarrow\ u_2 = \frac{18 \times 6}{12} = 9\ \text{ms}^{-1}$

   Thus, kinetic energy of 12 kg mass

   $K_2 = \frac{1}{2}m_2u_2^2 = \frac{1}{2} \times 12 \times (9)^2 = 6 \times 81 = 486\ \text{J}$

6. Since, $e^n = \left(\frac{h_n}{h_0}\right)^{1/2}$

   $\therefore\ h_n = e^{2n}h_0 = e^2 \times e^2h = e^4h$

7. According to conservation of momentum

   $m_1v_1 + m_2v_2 = (m_1 + m_2)v'$

   $\therefore\ mv + m_2 \times 0 = (m + 2m)v'$

   or $v' = \frac{v}{3}$

8. Let the two balls of mass m_1 and m_2 collide each other elastically with velocities u_1 and u_2. Their velocities become v_1 and v_2 after the collision.

   Applying conservation of linear momentum, we get

   $$m_1u_1 + m_2u_2 = m_1v_1 + m_2v_2 \quad \text{...(i)}$$

   Also from conservation of kinetic energy

   $$\frac{1}{2}m_1u_1^2 + \frac{1}{2}m_2u_2^2 = \frac{1}{2}m_1v_1^2 + \frac{1}{2}m_2v_2^2 \quad \text{...(ii)}$$

   Solving Eqs. (i) and (ii), we get

   $$v_1 = \left(\frac{m_1 - m_2}{m_1 + m_2}\right)u_1 + \left(\frac{2m_2}{m_1 + m_2}\right)u_2 \quad \text{...(iii)}$$

   and $$v_2 = \left(\frac{m_2 - m_1}{m_1 + m_2}\right)u_2 + \left(\frac{2m_2}{m_1 + m_2}\right)u_1 \quad \text{...(iv)}$$

   On taking approximate value the mass of deuteron is twice the mass of neutron.

   Given $u_1 = u$, $u_2 = 0$, m_1, $m_2 = 2m$

   Velocity of neutron $v_1 = \left(\frac{m - 2m}{m + 2m}\right)u = -\frac{u}{3}$

   Velocity of deuteron $v_2 = \frac{2mu}{m + 2m} = \frac{2}{3}u$

   Fractional energy loss $= \dfrac{\frac{1}{2}mu^2 - \frac{1}{2}\left(-\frac{u}{3}\right)^2}{\frac{1}{2}mu^2}$

   $= 1 - \frac{1}{9} = \frac{8}{9}$

9. For a spring $k \propto \frac{1}{L}$. Thus we can say $k \times L$ = constant.

$$k \times L = k' \times \frac{2L}{3}$$

$$\therefore \quad k' = \left(\frac{3k}{2}\right)$$

10. $a_c = k^2 rt^2$ Hence, $\frac{v^2}{r} = k^2 rt^2 \Rightarrow v^2 = k^2 r^2 t^2$

The kinetic energy $= \frac{1}{2}mv^2 = \frac{1}{2}mk^2r^2t^2$

The rate of change of kinetic energy is the power developed by all the forces.

$$\frac{d}{dt}(\text{KE}) = \frac{1}{2}mk^2r^2(2t) = mk^2 r^2 t$$

11. $F = -K(y\hat{i} + x\hat{j})$

$$\overrightarrow{ds} = dx(\hat{i}) + dy(\hat{j}) + dz(\hat{k})$$

$$dw = \vec{F}.\overrightarrow{ds} = -K[y\hat{i} + x\hat{j}].[dx\,\hat{i} + dy\,\hat{j} + dz\,\hat{k}]$$

$$= -K\,[y.dx + x.\,dy] = -K\,d\,(xy)$$

$$\therefore \quad w = \int dw$$

$$w = -K\int_{(0,0)}^{(a,a)} d(xy)$$

$$w = -Ka^2$$

12. $P = mv$

$$F = \frac{dP}{dt} = m\frac{dv}{dt} + v\frac{dm}{dt}$$

$$\because \frac{dv}{dt} = 0$$

$$F = v.\frac{dm}{dt} = (v).\ \{\text{Mass flow rate}\}$$

$$F = (\text{v}).(\rho A\text{v})$$

$$F = \rho A\text{v}^2$$

Power = Force × Velocity

Power = $\rho A\text{v}^3$

Hence, Power $\propto \text{v}^3$

13. $K \propto t$

$$\frac{P^2}{2m} \propto t$$

$P^2 = (2cm)\,t$ (where c is the constant of proportionality)

$$P = \sqrt{2cm}\,t^{1/2}$$

$$\frac{dp}{dt} = F = \sqrt{2cm}\,\frac{1}{2}(t^{\frac{1}{2}-1})$$

$$F = \sqrt{2cm}\,\frac{1}{2}t^{-\frac{1}{2}}$$

$$F = \sqrt{\frac{cm}{2}}\,\frac{1}{\sqrt{t}}$$

$$F \propto \frac{1}{\sqrt{t}}$$

14. At any instant, the total energy of an oscillator is the sum of kinetic energy and potential energy.

Total energy, $E = K + V$

$$E = \frac{1}{2}mv^2 + \frac{1}{2}kx^2$$

At $x = +x_m$ the particle turns back, therefore its velocity at this point is zero, i.e., v = 0

$$\therefore K = 0$$

$$\therefore \quad E = \frac{1}{2}kx^2 = V$$

15. We know that

$$P = FV = mav = ma\,(at)$$

$$P = ma^2\,t = \left(\frac{mv^2}{T^2}\right)t$$

As $a = \frac{v}{t}$

16. $V_{(x)} = \left(\frac{X^4}{4} - \frac{X^2}{2}\right)$ J

$$\frac{dV}{dX} = \frac{4X^3}{4} - \frac{2X}{2} = X^3 - X = X(X^2 - 1)$$

For minimum potential energy

$$\frac{dV}{dX} = 0$$

$$\therefore X(X^2 - 1) = 0$$

$$X = 0, \pm 1$$

To check maxima or minima

$$\frac{d^2V}{dX^2} = 3X^2 - 1$$

Putting $X = 0$

$$\frac{d^2V}{dX^2} = -1 \text{ (it is maxima)}$$

Putting $X = 1$ or -1

$$\frac{d^2V}{dX^2} = +2 \text{ (this is minima)}$$

$$\therefore \text{Minimum PE } V_{\text{min}} = \frac{1}{4} - \frac{1}{2} = -\frac{1}{4}\text{ J}$$

$$\text{KE}_{\text{max}} = E_M - V_{\text{min}} = 2 - \left[-\frac{1}{4}\right] = \frac{9}{4}\text{ J}$$

$$\text{KE}_{\text{max}} = \frac{1}{2}MV_{\text{max}}^2$$

$$V_{\text{max}}^2 = \frac{2 \times 9}{4} = \frac{9}{2}$$

$$V_{\text{max}} = \frac{3}{\sqrt{2}}\text{ m/s}$$

17. When a pendulum is oscillating in air, its total mechanical energy decreases exponentially with time. Hence, option (c) represents correct diagram.

18. As the earth moves once around the sun in its elliptical orbit, its kinetic energy is maximum when it is closest to the sun and minimum when it is farthest from the sun. As kinetic energy is never zero during its motion, hence option (d) is correct.

19. For constant power, displacement $\propto t^{3/2}$.

20. At a height h above the gound, PE of raindrop is maximum and $KE = 0$. As the raindrop falls its PE goes on decreasing and KE goes on increasing upto a point $\frac{h}{4}$ above the gound. At this stage, rain drop has acquired near terminal velocity (= constant). Therefore, at this stage, KE tends to be constant. PE becomes zero when raindrop falls to the ground. Hence, option (b) is most appropriate.

21. Mass of hanging portion is $M/3$ (one - third) and centre of mass c, is at a distance $h = \frac{L}{6}$ below the table top. Therefore the required work done is,

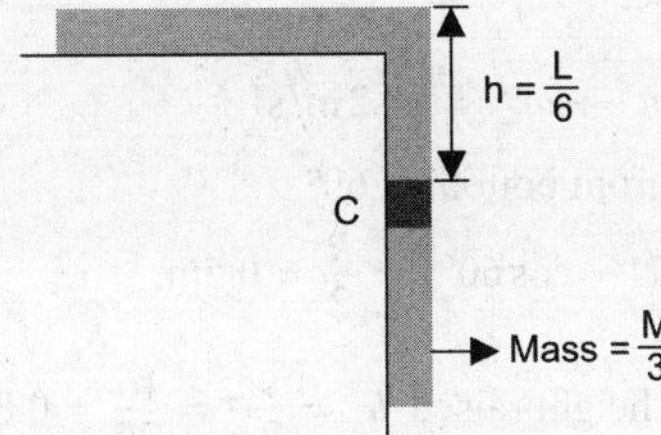

$$W = mgh = \left(\frac{M}{3}\right)(g)\left(\frac{L}{6}\right) = \frac{MgL}{18}$$

22. $dW = F.ds$, where $ds = dx\hat{i} + dy\hat{j} + dz\hat{k}$

and $F = -k(y\hat{i} + x\hat{j})$

$\therefore dW = -k\,(ydx + xdy)$

$= -kd\,(xy)$

$\therefore \quad W = \int_{0,0}^{a,a} dW = -k\int_{0,0}^{a,a} d(xy)$

$= -k[xy]_{0,0}^{a,a}$

$W = -ka^2$

23. On applying work-energy theorem

Work done by F from A to B = work done by Mg from A to B

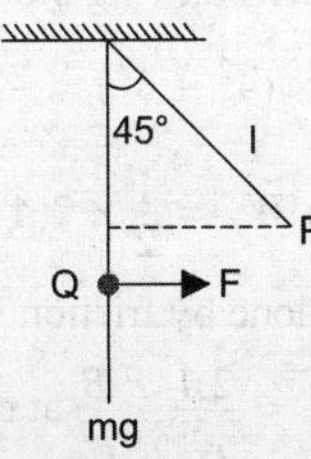

$Fl \sin 45° = mg\,[1 - \cos 45°]$

$F = mg\left(\sqrt{2} - 1\right)$

24. $F = -\frac{dU}{dx}$

$\therefore dU = -F.\,dx$

or $U(x) = -\int_0^x (-kx + ax^3)dx$

$U(x) = \frac{kx^2}{2} - \frac{ax^4}{4}$

$U(x) = 0$ at $x = 0$ and $x = \sqrt{\frac{2k}{a}}$

$U(x)$ = negative for $x > \sqrt{\frac{2k}{a}}$

From the given function, we can see that $F = 0$ at $x = 0$ i.e., slope of $U - x$ graph is zero at $x = 0$

25. $maR \sin\theta + mgR\,(1 - \cos\theta) = \frac{1}{2}mv^2$

On solving we get, $v = \sqrt{2Rg(1 + \sin\theta - \cos\theta}$

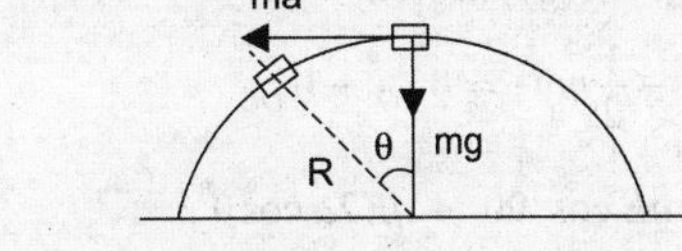

26. $W = -\int_{(0,0}^{(a,a)}\left(y\hat{i} + xy\hat{j}\right)\left(dx\hat{i} + dy\hat{i}\right)$

$= -k\int_{(0,0)}^{(a,a)}((ydx + xdy)$

$= -kxy\int_{(0,0)}^{(a,a)} d(xy) = -K[xy]_{(0,0)}^{(a,a)}$

27. Initial velocity = u. Final velocity = $\sqrt{u^2 - 2gl}$

So $|\Delta v| = \sqrt{u^2 + u^2 - 2gl} = \sqrt{2(u^2 - gl)}$

28. $P = F_t.v = ma_t.v; a_t = \frac{d|v|}{dt}; a_c = k^2rt^2$

$\Rightarrow \frac{v^2}{r} = k^2rt^2$

$v = krt \Rightarrow \frac{d|v|}{dt} = kr;$

$a_t = kr\; P = mkr.krt = mk^2r^2t$

29. $F(x) = -kx + ax^3$; $F(x) = 0$ for $x = 0$

$\Rightarrow x = \sqrt{\frac{k}{a}};$

so slope is zero at $x = 0$ $x = \sqrt{\frac{k}{a}}$

30. $P_{wind} = F.v = \rho Av^2.v \;\; P \propto v^3$

31. $P = Fv = mv\frac{dv}{dt}$

$v^2 \propto t$ or $v \propto t^{1/2}$

$\frac{dx}{dt} \propto t^{1/2}$ or $x \propto t^{3/2}$

32. $U = -\int Fdx \;\; = -\frac{1}{2}kx^2$

33. Velocity is minimum but not zero at max. height also $\frac{dv}{dx} = 0$ hence $\frac{dk}{dx} = 0$

34. Friction force = $\mu mg = 0.2 \times 5 \times 10 = 10$ N. Effective force F = applied force – frictional force = 25 – 10 = 15 N. Kinetic energy = work done by force F in pulling the body through a distance S (= 10 m) = 15 × 10 = 150 J, which is choice (b).

35. Force of friction = μmg. Therefore, retardation $a = \mu mg/m = \mu g$ Also $2ax = v^2$ or $2am^2x = m^2v^2$.

But $p = mv$. Therefore, $2am^2 x = p^2$. But $a = \mu g$. Therefore, $2\mu g^2x = p^2$ or $\mu = \frac{p^2}{2gm^2x}$

Hence the correct choice is (a)

36. Work done in magnetic field is always zero as force is perpendicular to the field.

From work energy theorem

$$\frac{1}{2}m(2v)^2 - \frac{1}{2}mv^2 = W_{PO} + W_{OQ}$$

$$\frac{3}{2}mv^2 = qE\cos 90^\circ + qE2a\cos 0^\circ$$

$$2qEa = \frac{3}{2}mv^2 \text{ or } E = \frac{3}{4}\left(\frac{3v^2}{qa}\right) \text{ and } p = \text{F.v} = \text{qEv}$$

$$= qv\frac{3}{4}\frac{mv^2}{qa} = \frac{3}{4}\frac{mv^3}{a}$$

So (a, b, d) are correct.

37. As the block does not move, the ball moves along a circular path of radius l. The centre of mass of the system always lies some where on the string.

Let v = speed of the ball when the string makes an angle θ with the horizontal.

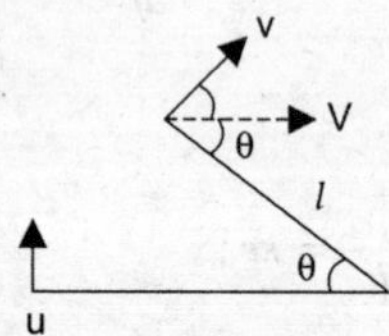

$$\frac{1}{2}mv^2 = \frac{1}{2}mu^2 - mgl\sin\theta$$

The horizontal component of

$$v = V = v\sin\theta = \sin\theta\sqrt{u^2 - 2gl\sin\theta}$$

For V to be maximum, $\frac{dV}{d\theta} = 0$,

which gives $\sin\theta = \frac{u^2}{3gl}$

38. $mgx = \frac{1}{2}kx^2$ or $x = \frac{2mg}{k}$

When the ball is at its lowest position, string force = kx = $2mg$

39. mu = $(m + 2m)$ v, v is the final common velocity

$$\frac{1}{2}mu^2 - \frac{1}{2}(3m) - \frac{1}{2}(3m)\frac{u^2}{9}$$

$$= \frac{1}{2}mu^2\left[1 - \frac{1}{3}\right] = \frac{2}{3} \times \frac{1}{2}mu^2$$

The force of friction between the blocks is μmg.

Acceleration of A (to the right) = $a_1 = \frac{\mu mg}{2m} = \frac{\mu g}{2}$

Acceleration of B (to the left) = $a_2 = \frac{\mu mg}{m} = \mu g$

Acceleration of A relative to $B = a_1 - (-a_2) = \frac{3}{2}\mu g$.

40. Here velocity and acceleration keep on changing their direction. Their magnitude remains constant. KE remains constant.

41. (a, b, c)

42. $at = g\sin 60^\circ = 5\sqrt{3}\ \text{m/s}^2$

$$ar = \frac{v^2}{r} = 16\,\text{m/s}$$

$$a = \sqrt{at^2 + ar^2} = 18.2\,\text{m/s}^2$$

Height from bottom at 60°

$$h_1 = R(1 - \cos 60^\circ) = \frac{R}{2} = 0.5\text{m}$$

Further height raised $h_2 = \frac{v^2}{2g} = \frac{16}{20} = 0.8\,\text{m}$

Now $h_1 + h_2 = 1.3$ m > R

The bob will raise to $\theta = 90^\circ$

But there string will slack and height will be < 1.3 m.

43. $P \propto t$ $W = \int P dt = \int \propto t\, dt$ or $W \propto t^2$

Hence, $v^2 \propto t^2$ or $v \propto t$ further, $v = \frac{ds}{dt}$

$$\therefore \frac{ds}{dt} \propto t$$

$ds \propto t\, dt$, $s \propto t^2$

44. From conservation of linear momentum (1 + 2)

$v = (6 \times 1) + (2 - 3)$

$\therefore$ v = 4 m/s (of both the blocks)

From work energy theorem

i.e., $W_{\text{total}} = \Delta$KE on 1 kg block,

$$W_f = \frac{1}{2} \times 1 \times (4^2 - 6^2) = -10\text{J}$$

on 2 kg block $W_f = \frac{1}{2} \times 2(4^2 - 3^2) = +7\text{J}$

$\therefore$ Net work done by friction is – 3 J.

45. $\because F = -\frac{dU}{dr} = \frac{2A}{r^3} - \frac{B}{r^2}$ at equilibrium $f = 0$, or

$$r = \frac{2A}{B}$$

At infinity $U = 0$, $r = \frac{2A}{B}$, $U = -\frac{B^2}{4A}$ $\Delta U = \frac{B^2}{4A}$

46. Power is the dot product of velocity. At 1s and 3s, power is positive. Hence, angle is acute. At 7s power is negative. Hence angle is obtuse.

47. In region *OA* particle is accelerated, in region *AB* particle has uniform velocity while in region *BD* particle is deceleration. Therefore, work done is positive in region *OA*, zero in region *AB* and negative in region *BC*.

48. $W_{net} = \Delta$ KE or $(40 - 20)\, s = 40$

$\therefore s = 2$m

Work done by gravity is $- 20 \times 2 = - 40$ J

and work done by tension is $40 \times 2 = 80$ J

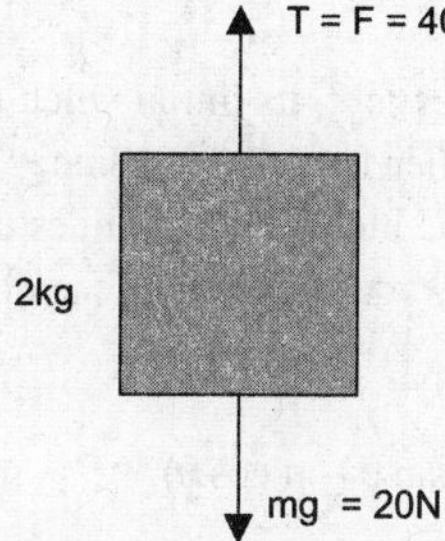

49. [b, d]

50. At maximum extension in the spring

$$v_A = v_B = 0 \text{ (momentarily)}$$

Therefore, applying conservation of mechanical energy: Decrease in gravitational potential energy of block *B* = increase in elastic potential energy of spring.

or $$m_B g x_m = \frac{1}{2} K x_m^2$$

or $$2mgx_m = \frac{1}{2} K x_m^2$$

$$\therefore \quad x_m = \frac{4mg}{K}$$

51. At $x = \dfrac{x_m}{2} = \dfrac{2mg}{K}$

Let $v_A = v_B = v$ (say)

Then, decrease in gravitational potential energy of block *B* = increase in elastic potential energy of spring + increase in kinetic energy of both the blocks.

$$\therefore \quad m_B g x = \frac{1}{2} K x^2 + \frac{1}{2}(m_A + m_B) v^2$$

or $$(2m)(g)\left(\frac{2gm}{K}\right) = \frac{1}{2} K \left(\frac{2mg}{K}\right)^2 + \frac{1}{2}(m + 2m) v^2$$

$$\therefore \quad v = 2g\sqrt{\frac{m}{3K}}$$

52. At $x = \dfrac{x_m}{4} = \dfrac{mg}{K}$, net upward force on block *B* is *Kx* or *mg* and net downward force on block *B* is 2 *mg*

$\therefore \quad F_{net} = 2\, mg - mg = mg$ (downwards)

$$\therefore \quad a = \frac{F_{net}}{m_B} = \frac{mg}{2m} = \frac{g}{2} \text{ downwards}$$

53. When the spring is released its elastic potential energy $(1/2)\, kx^2$ is converted into kinetic energy $(1/2) mv^2$ of the ball; so, by conservation of ME, $\frac{1}{2} mv^2 = \frac{1}{2} kx^2$

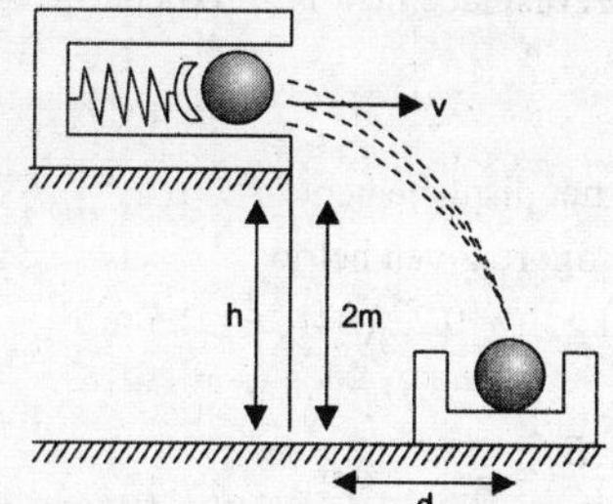

$$v = x\sqrt{\frac{k}{m}}$$

So $v = 0.05\sqrt{\dfrac{100}{0.1}}$ m/s $= \sqrt{\left(\dfrac{5}{2}\right)}$ m/s

54. As vertical component of velocity of ball is zero, time taken by the ball to reach the ground,

$$t = \sqrt{\frac{2h}{8}} = \sqrt{\frac{2 \times 2}{10}} = \sqrt{\frac{2}{5}} \text{ s}$$

55. So the horizontal distance travelled by the ball in this time

$$d = vt = \sqrt{\frac{5}{2}} \times \sqrt{\frac{2}{5}} = 1 \text{ m}$$

56. Given $t = \sqrt{x} + 3$ or $\sqrt{x} = t - 3$

or $x = (t - 3)^2$ ...(i)

Differentiating (i) with respect to *t*, we get

$$\frac{dx}{dt} = 2(t - 3) \quad \text{...(ii)}$$

or $v = 2\,(t - 3)$

From (ii) it follows that v = 0 at $t = 3$ s. Using $t = 3$ s (ii) in (i), we get $x = 0$. Thus, the displacement of the particle is zero when its velocity is zero. Thus, the correct choice is (a).

57. From Eq. (2), we have

$$a = \frac{dv}{dt} = \frac{d}{dt}[2(t - 3)] = 2\,\text{ms}^{-2}$$

Hence the correct choice is (d).

58. From Eq. (2), the initial velocity, i.e., velocity at $t = 0$ is $V_0 = 2\,(0 - 3) = 6$ m/s^2

At $t = 6$ sec

$V = 2\,(6 - 3) = 6$ m/s

W.D = Final KE – Initial KE

$$= \frac{1}{2} mv^2 - \frac{1}{2} mv_0^2 = \frac{1}{2} m(v^2 - v_0^2)$$

$$= \frac{1}{2} m\left[(6)^2 - (-6)^2\right] = 0$$

59. (c) W = $F.\,(r_2 - r_1)$

$= (\hat{i} + 3\hat{j} + \hat{k}).(2\hat{i} + 4\hat{j} + 13\hat{j})$

$= 2 + 12 + 13 = 27$ J.

60. (c) W = mgh

61. (c) W = $mgh_{max} = \frac{mu^2 \sin^2\theta}{2}$

62. (d) As net displacement is zero hence W = 0

63. (d) mgh

64. (b) 6 J

65. (c) 0 As net displacement is zero

Refer to figure given below.

$m = 0.5$ kg, $\mu = 0.2$, $l(= AC) = 2.5$ m

and $h\ (= AB) = 1.5$ m

$$\sin\theta = \frac{AB}{AC} = \frac{1.5}{2.5} = 0.6$$

$$\therefore \quad \cos\theta = \sqrt{1 - \sin^2\theta} = 0.8$$

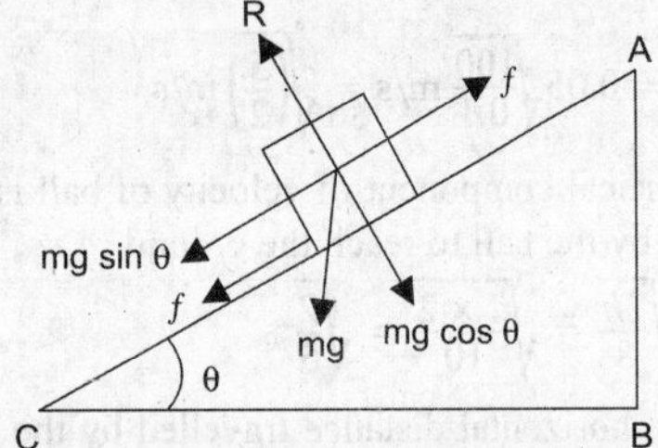

66. Work done by gravitational force to take the block from C to A is

$W_1 = (-\ mg \sin\theta)l$

The negative sign indicates that the gravitational force $mg \sin\theta$ is opposite to the displacement which is from C to A. Work done by the gravitational force to move the block from A to C is (because now the gravitational force is in the direction of the displacement)

$W_2 = (+\ mg \sin\theta)l$

$\because$ Total work done by the gravitational force over the round trip is

$W_G = W_1 + W_2 = 0$

This shows that gravitational force is conservative.

67. Frictional force $f = \mu R = \mu mg \cos\theta$. The applied force to move the block from C to A is

$F = mg \sin\theta + f = mg \sin\theta + \mu mg \cos\theta$

$= mg\ (\sin\theta + \mu\cos\theta)$

Work done by applied force to move the block from C to A is

$W_a = F \times AC = mg\ (\sin\theta + \mu\cos\theta) \times l$

$= 0.5 \times 10\ (0.6 + 0.2 \times 0.8) \times 2.5$

$= 9.5$ J

68. Friction always opposes motion. When the block is moved from C to A, frictional force f is opposite to direction. Hence work done by frictional force in the upward journey is

$W_3 = -fl$

When the block slides from A to C, f acts upwards along the plane and is opposite to the displacement. Hence, work done by frictional force in the downward journey is

$W_4 = -fl$

$\therefore$ Total work done by frictional force over the round trip is

$Wf = W_3 + W_4 = -2fl$

$= -\ 2\ \mu mg \cos\theta \times l$

$= -\ 2 \times 0.2 \times 0.5 \times 10 \times 0.8 \times 2.5$

$= -\ 4$ J

69. When the block is A, its initial velocity $u = 0$. Let v be the velocity when it reaches C. Since f acts upwards, the net force on the block when it slides down is

$F' = mg \sin\theta - f = mg\ (\sin\theta - \mu \cos\theta)$

$\therefore$ Acceleration

$$a = \frac{F'}{m} = g(\sin\theta - \mu\cos\theta)$$

$= 10\ (0.6 - 0.2 \times 0.8) = 4.4\ \text{ms}^{-2}$

From

$v^2 - u^2 = 2as$, we have

$v^2 - 0 = 2 \times 4.4 \times 2.5$

$\Rightarrow v^2 = 22\ \text{m}^2\ \text{s}^{-2}$

$\therefore$ Kinetic energy at $C = \frac{1}{2}mv^2$

$= \frac{1}{2} \times 0.5 \times 22 = 5.5$ J

70. (c) Applying COE,

$$mgh = \frac{1}{2}mv^2$$

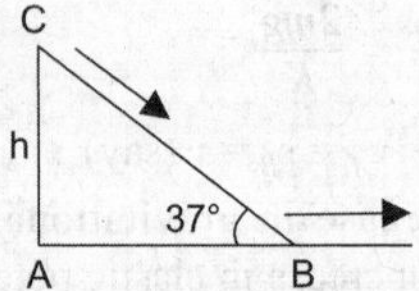

$v = \sqrt{2gh}$ ....(i)

But $\sin 37° = \frac{h}{100/3}$

$\frac{3}{5} = \frac{3h}{100} \Rightarrow h = 20$ m

Velocity before collision

$\therefore$ From Eq. (i)

$v = \sqrt{2(10(20)} = \sqrt{400} = 20$ m/s

Velocity after collision

$$e = -\frac{(v_2 - v_1)}{(u_2 - u_1)}; 1 = \frac{v_2 - v_1}{20 - 0}$$

$\Rightarrow v_2 - v_1 = 20$ ....(ii)

Applying COLM

$m(20) + 0 = mv_1 + mv_2$

$v_1 + v_2 = 20$ .....(iii)

From Eqs. (ii) and (iii),

$2v_2 = 40 \Rightarrow v_2 = 20$ m/s $\quad \therefore v_1 = 0$ m/s

71. (a) Impulse on the second ball $= m(v_2 - u_2)$

$= \frac{1}{2}(20 - 0) = 10$ N-s

72. Extension in spring will be

$$x_0 = \frac{mg}{k+k} = \frac{mg}{2k}$$

$$\Delta W = (\Delta E) = mg\left(\frac{mg}{4k}\right) + \frac{1}{2}k\left[\left(\frac{mg}{4k}\right)^2 - \left(\frac{mg}{2k}\right)^2\right] \times 2$$

$$\Delta W = \frac{m^2g^2}{16k}$$

On comparing given parameter we get $n = 4$.

73. As $N - mg = \frac{mg}{2}$

Normal force is given by $\frac{3mg}{2}$

Displacement of block is 't' sec is $\frac{1}{2}\frac{g}{2}t^2$

Work done by normal force is $\frac{3mg^2t^2}{8}$

74. From Newton's second law we get, $\frac{\Delta p}{\Delta t} = F$

$\Rightarrow \Delta p = F\Delta t$

$\therefore \quad p = \int dp = \int_0^1 F \; dt$

$\Rightarrow \quad p = \int_0^1 6t\, dt = 3\,\text{kg}\left(\frac{\text{m}}{\text{s}}\right)$

Also, $\Delta k = \frac{\Delta p^2}{2m} = \frac{3^2}{2 \times 1} = 4.5$

So, work done $= \Delta k = 4.5$ J

75. We know that change in potential energy of a system corresponding to a conservative internal force as

$U_f - U_i = -W = -\int_i^f \text{F}.dr$

Given, $\quad F = ax + bx^2$

We know that work done in stretching the rubber band by L is $|dW| = |Fdx|$

$$|W| = \int_0^L \left(ax + bx^2\right)dx = \left[\frac{ax^2}{2}\right]_0^L + \left[\frac{bx^3}{3}\right]_0^L$$

$$= \left[\frac{aL^2}{2} - \frac{a \times (0)^2}{2}\right] + \left[\frac{b \times L^3}{3} - \frac{b \times (0)^3}{3}\right]$$

$$= |W| = \frac{aL^2}{2} + \frac{bL^3}{3}$$

76. As, $r = OP = x\hat{i} + y\hat{j}$

$\therefore \quad$ Force, $\mathbf{F} = \frac{k}{(x^2 + y^2)^{3/2}}(x\hat{\mathbf{i}} + y\hat{\mathbf{j}}) = \frac{k}{r^3}(\mathbf{r})$

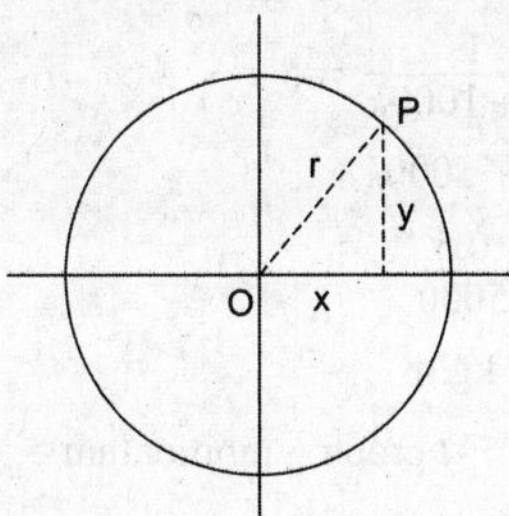

Since, **F** is along **r** or in radial direction. Therefore, work done is zero.

77. Gravitational field is a conservative force field. In a conservative force field work done is path independent

$\therefore W_1 = W_2 = W_3$

78. $W = (2 \times 2) + \frac{1}{2}(1)(5) = 6.5$ J

Final K.E. = 6.5 J

79. $\text{U} = -\frac{K}{2r^3}$

$$\text{F} = -\frac{du}{dr} = \left(-\frac{K}{2}\left(-\frac{2}{r^3}\right)\right) = -\frac{K}{r^3}$$

$$\frac{K}{r^3} = \frac{mv^2}{r}$$

$$\Rightarrow mv^2 = \frac{K}{r^2}$$

$$\text{K.E.} = \frac{1}{2}mv^2 = \frac{K}{2r^2}$$

E = P.E. + K.E. = 0

80. Since, force, $F = -kv^2$

$\therefore \quad$ Acceleration, $a = \frac{-k}{m}v^2$

or $\quad \frac{dv}{dt} = \frac{-k}{m}v^2$

$\Rightarrow \quad \frac{dv}{v^2} = -\frac{k}{m}.dt$

Now, with limits, we have

$$\int_{10}^{v}\frac{dv}{v^2} = -\frac{k}{m}\int_0^t dt$$

$$\Rightarrow \quad \left(-\frac{1}{v}\right)_{10}^{v} = -\frac{k}{m}t$$

$$\Rightarrow \quad \frac{1}{v} = 0.1 + \frac{kt}{m}$$

$$\Rightarrow \quad v = \frac{1}{0.1 + \frac{kt}{m}} = \frac{1}{0.1 + 1000k}$$

$$\Rightarrow \frac{1}{2} \times m \times v^2 = \frac{1}{8} \times v_0^2$$

$$\Rightarrow \quad v = \frac{v_0}{2} = 5$$

$$\Rightarrow \quad \frac{1}{0.1 + 1000k} = 5$$

$$\Rightarrow 1 = 0.5 + 5000k$$

$$\Rightarrow \quad k = \frac{0.5}{5000}$$

$$\Rightarrow k = 10^{-4} \text{ kg/m}$$

81. Area under F-t graph = momentum = $p = \sqrt{2km}$

$$\therefore \quad k = \frac{A^2}{2m} \quad (A = \text{net area of } F\text{-}t \text{ graph})$$

$$= \frac{\left\{\left(\frac{4 \times 3}{2}\right) - \left(\frac{1.5 \times 2}{2}\right)\right\}^2}{2 \times 2}$$

$$= 5.0625 \text{ J}$$

82. Using energy conservation we get,

$$\frac{1}{2}kx^2 = \frac{1}{2}(4k)y^2$$

$$\therefore \quad \frac{y}{x} = \frac{1}{2}$$

83. If x be the maximum extension of the spring, then from conservation of mechanical energy we get,

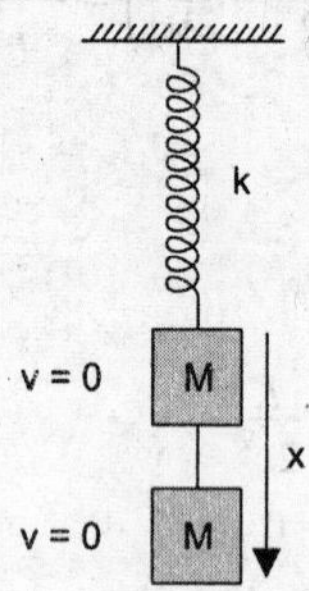

Decrease in gravitational potential energy = increase in elastic potential energy

$$\therefore \quad Mg\ x = \frac{1}{2}kx^2 \quad \text{or} \quad x = \frac{2Mg}{k}$$

84. From $F = -\dfrac{dU}{dx}$

$$\int_0^{U(x)} dU = -\int_0^x F dx = -\int_0^x (kx)\, dx$$

$$\therefore \quad U(x) = -\frac{kx^2}{2} \quad \text{as } U(0) = 0$$

85. As, $K = \dfrac{1}{2}mv^2$

$$\Rightarrow \quad \frac{dK}{dt} = mv\frac{dv}{dt}$$

given, $\dfrac{dK}{dt} = \gamma t$

$$\Rightarrow \quad mv\frac{dv}{dt} = \gamma t$$

$$\Rightarrow \int_0^v v dv = \int_0^t \frac{\gamma}{m} t dt$$

$$\Rightarrow \frac{v^2}{2} = \frac{\gamma}{m}\frac{t^2}{2}$$

$$\Rightarrow \boxed{v = \sqrt{\frac{\gamma}{m}}\, t}$$

$$\Rightarrow a = \frac{dv}{dt} = \sqrt{\frac{\gamma}{m}}$$

$$F = ma = \sqrt{\gamma m} = \text{constant}$$

$$\frac{dS}{dt} = \sqrt{\frac{\gamma}{m}}\, t$$

$$\Rightarrow \boxed{S = \sqrt{\frac{\gamma}{m}}\frac{t^2}{2}}$$

86. Work done in lifting mass = (10 × 9.8 × 1) × 1000

If m is mass of fat burnt, then energy

$$= m \times 3.8 \times 10^7 \times \frac{20}{100}$$

Equating the two, we get

$$\therefore \quad m = \frac{49}{3.8} \approx 12.89 \times 10^{-3} \text{kg}$$

87. Case I:

JBC

m → V   2m

JAC

V_1 ← m   2m → V_2

$$2V_2 - V_1 = V$$

$$V_2 + V_1 = V$$

$$3V_2 = 2V$$

$$V_2 = \frac{2V}{3}$$

$$V_1 = \frac{V}{3}$$

$$P_d = \frac{\frac{1}{2}mV^2 - \frac{1}{2}mV_1^2}{\frac{1}{2}mV^2} = \frac{1 - \frac{1}{9}}{1} = \frac{8}{9} = 0.89$$

Case II:

JBC

m → V   12m

JAC

V_1 ← m   12m → V_2

$$12V_2 - V_1 = V$$

$$V_2 + V_1 = V$$

$$13V_2 = 2V$$

$$V_2 = \frac{2V}{13}$$

$$V_1 = V - \frac{2V}{13} = \frac{11V}{13}$$

$$\Rightarrow P_c = \frac{\frac{1}{2}mV^2 - \frac{1}{2}mV_1^2}{\frac{1}{2}mV^2} = \frac{1 - \frac{121}{169}}{1} = \frac{48}{169} = 0.28$$

88. Applying conservation of linear momentum

$$mv_0 + 0 = mv_1 + mv_2$$

$$v_0 = v_1 + v_2 \quad \text{...(i)}$$

$$\frac{3}{2}\left[\frac{1}{2}mv_0^2\right] = \frac{1}{2}mv_1^2 + \frac{1}{2}mv_2^2$$

$$\frac{3}{2}v_0^2 = v_1^2 + v_2^2 \quad \text{...(ii)}$$

Solving equation (i) and (ii)

$$v_1 = \frac{v_0}{2}\left(1 + \sqrt{2}\right)$$

$$v_2 = \frac{v_0}{2}\left(1 - \sqrt{2}\right)$$

$$\vec{v}_{rel} = \vec{v}_1 - \vec{v}_2$$

$$\frac{v_0}{2}\left[1 + \sqrt{2} - 1 + \sqrt{2}\right] = \frac{v_0}{2} \times 2\sqrt{2} = \sqrt{2}v_0$$

89. Since energy loss is same, thus

$$\mu\, mg \cos\theta.\,(PQ) = \mu mg\,.\,(QR)$$

$$\therefore QR = (PQ)\cos\theta$$

$$\Rightarrow \quad QR = 4 \times \frac{\sqrt{3}}{2}$$

$$= 2\sqrt{3} \approx 3.5\text{m}$$

Further, decrease in potential energy = loss due to friction

$$\therefore mgh = (\mu mg \cos\theta)\, d_1 + (\mu mg)\, d_2$$

$$m \times 10 \times 2 = \mu \times m \times 10 \times \frac{\sqrt{3}}{2} \times 4 + \mu \times m \times 10 \times 2\sqrt{3}$$

$$\Rightarrow \quad 4\sqrt{3}\mu = 2$$

$$\Rightarrow \quad \mu = \frac{1}{2\sqrt{3}} = 0.288 = 0.29$$

90. We have, $h = R - R\cos\theta$

Using conservation of energy

$$mgR\,(1 - \cos\theta) = \frac{1}{2}mv^2$$

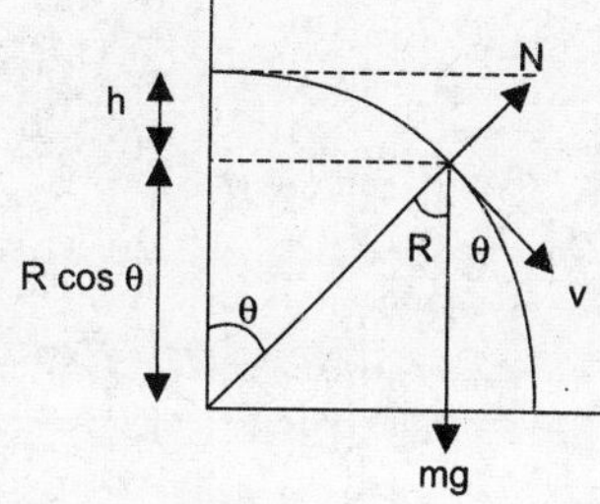

Radial force equation is

$$mg\cos\theta - N = \frac{mv^2}{R}$$

Here, N = nornal force on bead by wire

$$N = mg\cos\theta - \frac{mv^2}{R} = mg\,(3\cos\theta - 2)$$

$$N = 0 \text{ at } \cos\theta = \frac{2}{3}$$

⇒ Normal force act radially outward on bead, if $\cos\theta > \frac{2}{3}$ and normal force act radially inward on bead, if $\cos\theta < 2/3$

∴ Force on ring is opposite to normal force on bead.

91. As, $v = \sqrt{5gL}$ ...(i)

$$\left(\frac{v}{2}\right)^2 = v^2 - 2gh \quad \text{... (ii)}$$

$$h = L(1 - \cos\theta) \quad \text{...(iii)}$$

Solving Eqs. (i), (ii) and (iii), we get

$$\cos\theta = -\frac{7}{8}$$

$$\text{or } \theta = \cos^{-1}\left(-\frac{7}{8}\right) = 151^\circ$$

92. Height fallen up to point Q

$$h = R\sin 30^\circ = 40 \times \frac{1}{2} = 20\,\text{m}$$

Work done against friction = Initial mechanical energy – Final mechanical energy

$$= mgh - \frac{1}{2}mv^2$$

Putting the values, we get

$$150 = 1 \times 10 \times 20 - \frac{1}{2} \times 1 \times v^2$$

$$\Rightarrow v = 10 \text{ m/s}$$

CHAPTER 6

Heat and Temperature

HEAT & TEMPERATURE

According to kinetic theory "Heat is a form of energy possess by a body due to motion of molecules.

Heat is measured in calorie or in kilocalorie.

It is the thermal state of body which determines the direction of flow of heat. Temperature can be regarded as the effect of cause of heat. If the bodies are at same temperature then they are said to be in thermal equilibrium.

Temperature Measuring Scales

Production and measurement of very low temperature (below B.P of liquid nitrogen i.e., 77°C) is called cryogenics. While measurement of very high temperature near about more than 1000 K is called pyrometry. Temperature is expressed by °C in Celsius, °F in Fahrenheit and K in Kelvin scale. While change in temperature is expressed by °C in Celsius and F° in Fahrenheit Scale. We don't use degree while reporting Kelvin temperature.

Temperature measuring scales are related as

$$\frac{C-0}{100-0} = \frac{F-32}{212-32} = \frac{R-0}{80-0} = \frac{K-273}{373-273}$$

$$\Rightarrow \frac{C}{100} = \frac{F-32}{180} = \frac{R}{80} = \frac{K-273}{100}$$

Thermometers

These are temperature measuring devices. All thermometers are based on the principle that some physical properties of a system change with change in temperature. For example

(i) The volume of liquid.

(ii) Pressure of gas at constant volume.

(iii) Volume of gas at constant pressure.

(iv) Length of solid.

(v) Resistance of conductor etc.

Thermometric property is the property that can be used to measure the temperature. It is represented by any physical quantity such as length, volume, pressure, resistance etc.

Let x represents the thermometric of a physical quantity and x_0, x_{100} and x_t are its values at 0°C, 100°C and t°C respectively then

$$t = \left(\frac{x_t - x_0}{x_{100} - x_0}\right) \times 100$$

Hence,

(i) for constant volume gas thermometer we have to use

$$t = \left(\frac{p_t - p_0}{p_{100} - p_0}\right) \times 100$$

(ii) for platinum resistance thermometer we should use

$$t = \left(\frac{R_t - R_0}{R_{100} - R_0}\right) \times 100$$

(iii) and for mercury thermometer $t = \left(\frac{l_t - l_0}{l_{100} - l_0}\right) \times 100$

Apart from these, there are two more thermometers which are commonly used which are thermocouple thermometer and radiation thermometer.

Range of Thermometer

Thermometer	Lower Limit	Upper Limit
Radiation Thermometer	800°C	No limit
Thermocouple thermometer	- 200 °C	1600 °C
Platinum resistance thermometer	- 200 °C	1200 °C
Gas thermometer	- 268 °C	1500 °C
Mercury thermometer	- 30°C	300 °C

Triple Point

A substance is found to exists in three states solid, liquid and gas. For each substance there is a set of temperature and pressure at which all the three states may co-exists. This is known as triple point of substance. For water, the values of pressure and temperature corresponding to triple point are 4.58 mm of Hg and 273.15 K.

Thermal expansion

Every substance expands on heating, more or less depending on temperature and nature of substance.

Thermal expansion in solids can be classified in three ways.

(i) Linear expansion
(ii) Superficial expansion
(iii) Cubical expansion.

Linear Expansion

It is expressed as,

$$\alpha = \frac{\Delta L}{L} \times \frac{1}{\Delta \theta}$$

Here, L = original length

ΔL = change in length

$\Delta \theta$ = change in temperature

Coefficient of linear expansion is defined as fractional increase in length per C° increase in temperature.

Actually 'α' is the average value of coefficient of linear expansion over the temperature range θ °C to (θ + Δθ) so

$$\alpha = \lim_{\Delta\theta \to 0} \frac{1}{L}\frac{\Delta L}{\Delta \theta} = \frac{1}{L}\frac{dL}{d\theta}$$

S.I unit of α = K^{-1} or $°C^{-1}$

Superficial Expansion

It is defined as fractional increase in area per °C increase in temperature.

$$\therefore \quad \beta = \frac{\Delta S}{S \Delta \theta}$$

$$\Rightarrow \quad \Delta S = \beta S \Delta \theta$$

$$\Rightarrow \quad S = S_0(1 + \beta \Delta \theta)$$

S.I. unit of β is $°C^{-1}$ or K^{-1}

Cubical Expansion

It is defined as fractional increase in volume per °C increase in temperature.

$$\therefore \quad \gamma = \frac{\Delta V}{V \Delta \theta}$$

$$\Delta V = \gamma V \Delta \theta$$

$$\Rightarrow \quad V = V_0(1 + \gamma \Delta \theta)$$

S.I. unit = $°C^{-1}$ or K^{-1}

Relation Between α, β and γ

These are related as

$\alpha : \beta : \gamma :: 1 : 2 : 3$

For Isotropic solid

$$\alpha = \frac{\beta}{2} = \frac{\gamma}{3}$$

$$\Rightarrow \quad \beta = 2\alpha; \gamma = 3\alpha$$

For anisotropic solids

$\beta_{12} = \alpha_1 + \alpha_{21}$, $\beta_{23} = \alpha_2 + \alpha_3$ and $\beta_{31} = \alpha_1 + \alpha_3$

where β_{12}, β_{23} and β_{31} are coefficients of superficial expansions in *XY*, *YZ* and *ZX* plane and $\gamma = \alpha_1 + \alpha_2 + \alpha_3$.

Bimetallic Strip

If two strips of equal length but of different materials are placed on each other and riveted to form single strip. This arrangement is called bimetallic strip. This strip will bend with metal of greater co-efficient of linear expansion on outside i.e., convex side. These strips are used in auto-cut or thermostat in electric heating circuits.

The radius (R) of arc of bimetallic strip is given by

$$l_0(1 + \alpha_1 \Delta\theta) = \left(R - \frac{d}{2}\right)\theta$$

For lower strip

$$l_0(1 + \alpha_2 \Delta\theta) = \left(R + \frac{d}{2}\right)\theta$$

For upper strip

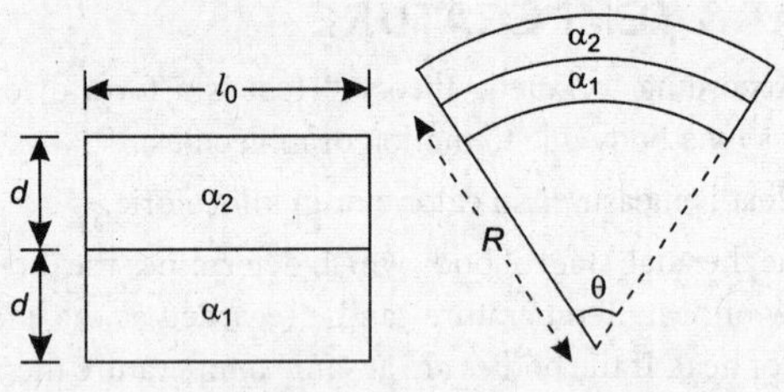

$$\Rightarrow \quad \frac{1 + \alpha_2 \Delta\theta}{1 + \alpha_1 \Delta\theta} = \frac{R + d/2}{R - d/2}$$

$$\Rightarrow \quad R = \frac{d}{(\alpha_2 - \alpha_1)\Delta\theta}$$

where, $\Delta\theta$ = Change in temperature.

Effect of Temperature on Scale Reading

(i) When only object expands

$l_2 = l_1[1 + \alpha(\theta_2 - \theta_1)]$

where l_1 = actual length of the object at θ_1 °C

l_2 = actual length of the object at θ_2 °C

α = co-efficient of linear expansion.

(ii) When only measuring instrument expands

In this situation scale reading = $l_1[(1 - \alpha_s)(\theta_2 - \theta_1)]$

where α_s = Co-efficient of linear expansion of measuring instrument.

(iii) When both an object and measuring instrument, a scale expands simultaneously.

In this situation scale reading = $l_1\{1 + (\alpha - \alpha_s)(\theta_2 - \theta_1)\}$

Now if, $\alpha > \alpha_s$ then scale reading is more than actual value at θ_1 °C and if $\alpha < \alpha_s$ the scale reading is less than actual value.

Hence time reading = scale reading $[1 + \alpha(\theta - \theta_0)]$

If $\theta > \theta_0$, time reading > scale reading

$\theta < \theta_0$, time reading < scale reading

Expansion of Liquid

In case of volume expansion of liquid.

$V_L = V(1 + \gamma_L \Delta\theta)$

whereas for volume expansion of container

$V_C = V(1 + \gamma_C \Delta\theta)$

So, change in volume of liquid relative to container

$V_L - V_C = V(\gamma_L - \gamma_C)\Delta\theta$

So, coefficient of apparent expansion of liquid, w.r.t container $\gamma_{app} = \gamma_L - \gamma_C$

$\Rightarrow \quad \Delta V_{app} = V\gamma_{app}\Delta\theta$ with $V_L - V_C = V_{app}$

Now following cases arises

(i) If $\gamma_L > \gamma_C$, $\gamma_{app} > 0$ so ΔV_{app} will be positive so level of liquid in container will rise on heating.

(ii) If $\gamma_L < \gamma_C$, $\gamma_{app} < 0$ so ΔV_{app} will be negative therefore level of liquid in the container will fall on heating.

(iii) If $\gamma_L = \gamma_C$, $\gamma_{app} = 0$ so ΔV_{app} will zero, hence level of liquid in container will be unchanged on heating. Therefore increase in height of liquid level is calculate by

$$h = \frac{\text{Volume of liquid over flow}}{\text{Area of container}}$$

$$= \frac{V_o(\gamma_L - \gamma_C)\Delta\theta}{S_o(1 + 2\alpha_C\Delta\theta)}$$

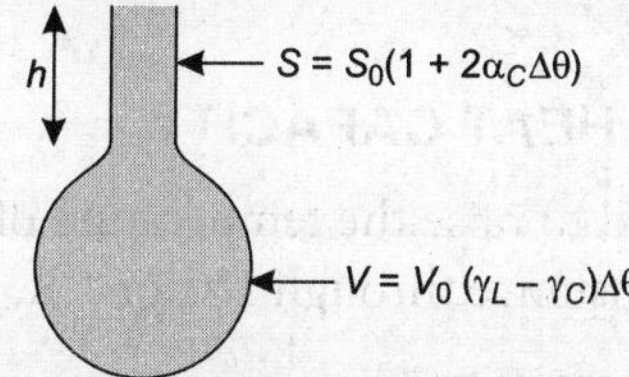

where α_c = linear expansion of container.

Variation in Density with Temperature

We know that density, $\rho = \dfrac{\text{Mass}}{\text{Volume}}$ or $\rho \propto \dfrac{1}{V}$

$$\frac{\rho'}{\rho} = \frac{V}{V'} = \frac{V}{V + \Delta V} = \frac{V}{V + \gamma V\Delta\theta} = \frac{1}{1 + \gamma\Delta\theta}$$

$$\Rightarrow \quad \rho' = \frac{\rho}{1 + \gamma\Delta\theta}$$

$$\Rightarrow \quad \rho' = \rho(1 + \gamma\Delta\theta)^{-1}$$

$$\Rightarrow \quad \rho' \approx \rho(1 - \gamma\Delta\theta)$$

Hence, with increase in temperature, density (ρ) of liquid decrease.

Effect of Temperature on Upthrust

When a solid body is completely immersed in a liquid, then there is apparent loss in its weight due to upthrust acting on it by the liquid. The apparent weight is given by $W - F$ where F = upthrust = $V_S \rho_L g$

Now with increase in temperature V_S increase while ρ_L decrease. So F may increase or decrease or remains same depending on the condition that which factor dominates on the other.

Here V_S = volume of solid.

ρ_L = density of liquid.

Now again $F \propto V_S \rho_L$

$$\Rightarrow \quad \frac{F'}{F} = \frac{V'_S\rho'_L}{V_S\rho_L} = \frac{V_S + \Delta V_S}{V_S} \cdot \left(\frac{1}{1 + \gamma_L\Delta\theta}\right)$$

$$= \left(\frac{V_S + \gamma_S V_S\Delta\theta}{V_S}\right)\left(\frac{1}{1 + \gamma_L\Delta\theta}\right)$$

$$\Rightarrow \quad F' = F\left(\frac{1 + V_S\Delta\theta}{1 + \gamma_L\Delta\theta}\right)$$

So if $\gamma_S > \gamma_L$, $F' > F$, $W_{app} < W_{app}$, fraction will increase.

If $\gamma_S < \gamma_L$, $F' < F$, $W'_{app} > W_{app}$

If $\gamma_S = \gamma_L$ $F' = F$, $W'_{app} = W_{app}$

Thus, immersed fraction will remain same.

Simply we can say

if $F' > F$, body will move down

$F' < F$, body will move up

$F' = F$, body will remains at same position

Effect of Temperature on Time Period of Simple Pendulum

Let $T = 2\pi\sqrt{\dfrac{L}{g}}$ at a temperature θ and $T' = 2\pi\sqrt{\dfrac{L'}{g'}}$ at a temperature θ'.

$$\Rightarrow \quad \frac{T'}{T} = \sqrt{\frac{L'}{L}} = \sqrt{\frac{L(1 + \alpha\Delta\theta)}{L}}, (\theta' > \theta)$$

$$\Rightarrow \quad \frac{T'}{T} = (1 + \alpha\Delta\theta)^{1/2}$$

$$\Rightarrow \quad \frac{T'}{T} \approx 1 + \frac{1}{2}\alpha\Delta\theta$$

Therefore change (loss or gain) in time per unit time lapsed will be

$$\frac{T' - T}{T} = \frac{1}{2}\alpha\Delta\theta$$

Gain or loss is time, is duration of time period with $\Delta t = \dfrac{1}{2}\alpha\Delta\theta$ if T is the correct time period, so

(i) if $\theta' < \theta$, $T' < T$, clock becomes faster and there is gain in time

(ii) if $\theta' > \theta$, $T' > T$, clock will become slower and there is loss in time

Thermal Stress

We know that thermal strain = $\dfrac{\Delta L}{L} = \alpha\Delta\theta$

So, thermal stress = $Y\alpha\Delta\theta$ as $Y = \dfrac{\text{Stress}}{\text{Strain}}$

Also, $F = YA\alpha\Delta\theta$ as stress = $\dfrac{\text{Force}}{\text{Area}}$

Anomalous Expansion of Water

Water expands on heating if its temperature is greater than 4°C. In the range 0°C to 4°C water contracts on heating and expands on cooling as co-efficient of volume expansion is negative. Such a behaviour of water in the range of 0°C to 4°C is called anomalous expansion. This anomalous behaviour is due to presence of three types of molecules H_2O, $(H_2O)_2$, and $(H_2O)_3$ having different volume/mass at different temperatures. This anamalous behavior of water causes ice to form first at the surface of lake in cold weather. Different graphs related to variation of volume and density of water with temperature is shown in figures given below.

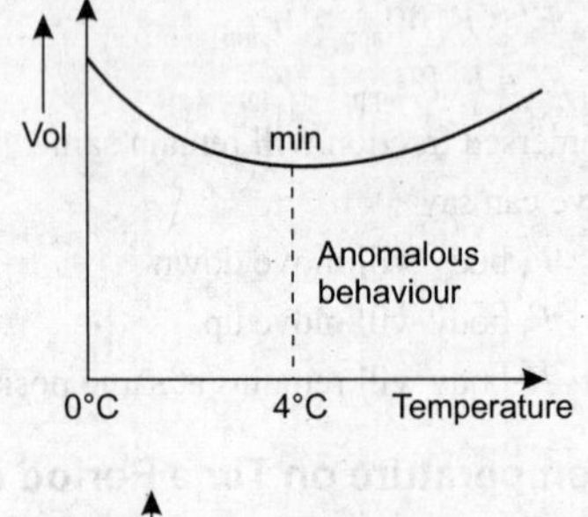

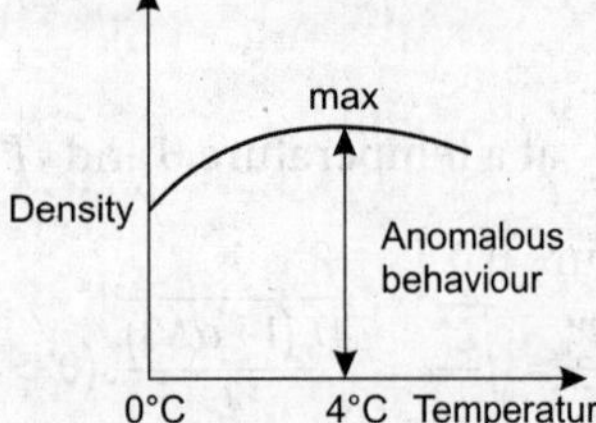

Points to Remember

(i) If α_x, α_y and α_z are co-efficients of linear expansions along x-axis, y-axis and z-axis (for anisotropic body) respectively then $\gamma = \alpha_x + \alpha_y + \alpha_z$

(ii) For water γ is negative between 0°C and 4°C.

(iii) Coefficient of apparent expansion (γ_a)

$$= \frac{\text{Apparent change in volume}}{\text{Initial vol.} \times \text{rise in temp.}}$$

In apparent expansion change in volume of container is not considered.

(iv) Coefficient of real expansion (γ_r)

$$= \frac{\text{Real change in volume}}{\text{Initial volume} \times \text{rise in temp}}$$

$$\gamma_r = \gamma_a + \gamma_c$$

(v) Increase in height of liquid level in container.

$$h = \frac{\text{Apparent change in volume of liquid}}{\text{Area of container}}$$

$$= \frac{V_0(\gamma_L - \gamma_C)\Delta\theta}{A_0(1 + 2\alpha_c \Delta\theta)}$$

(vi) Density of water is maximum at 4°C. Therefore water at the bottom of lake in winter is warmer than that at the surface.

(vii) The two rods of lengths L_1 and L_2 are placed side by side (one after other). If with increase in temperature, the difference in their lengths does not change i.e.

$$L_2' - L_1' = L_2 - L_1 \text{ where } L_1' = L_1(1 + \alpha_1 \Delta\theta)$$

and $$L_2' = L_2(1 + \alpha_2 \Delta\theta)$$

L_1, α_1

L_2, α_2

then $$L_1\alpha_1 = L_2\alpha_2$$

or $$\frac{L_1}{L_1 + L_2} = \frac{\alpha_2}{\alpha_2 - \alpha_1}$$

(viii) Coefficient of volume expansion of gas at constant temperature vary as $\gamma \propto \frac{1}{T}$

(ix) Let a solid body has a hole in it. Now if the temperature of the body increases, the size of hole also increases i.e., hole will expand, as every linear dimension of the body changes in the same way when the temperature changes.

SPECIFIC HEAT CAPACITY

Heat required to raise the temperature of unit mass of a substance through 1°C or 1 K, is called specific heat capacity, $C = \frac{1}{m} \cdot \frac{d\theta}{dt}$

Solid and liquid have single specific heat but gases has different specific heats ranging from negative to infinity (–ve, 0, +ve, ∞).

SI unit of specific heat is J/kg-K while practical unit is cal/gm °C.

Molar Specific Heat Capacity

It is given by, (C) $= \frac{1}{n} \cdot \frac{d\theta}{dt}$, where n = no. of moles with

$n = \frac{m}{M}$, where m = mass of substance, M = Molar mass of substance.

SI unit of Molar heat capacity is J/mol-K.

Some Important Terms Related to Specific Heat Capacity

(i) Specific heat of a substance depends on temperature.

(ii) Variation of specific heats with temperatures are shown in fig. (for water and metal).

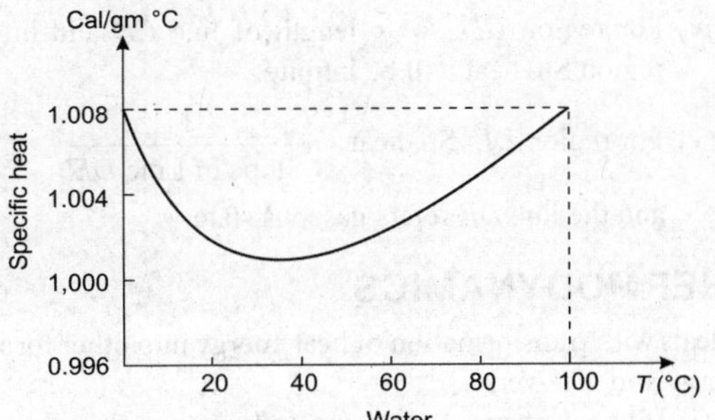

For metal

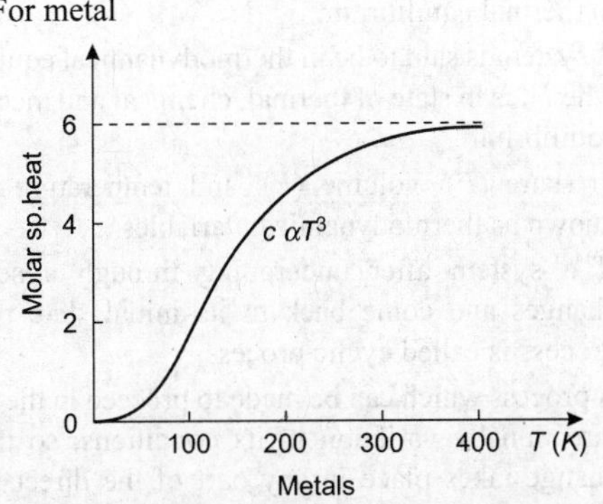

(iii) Specific heat is maximum for Hydrogen (3.5 cal/gm °C) then for water 1 cal/gm °C = 4200 J/kg K) and minimum for Radon and Actinium. For all other substances specific heat is less than 1 cal/gm °C.

(iv) Specific heat for ice (Solid) is 2100 J/kg K, for water (liquid) 4200 J/kg K and for steam (gas) it is 1970 J/kg K.

(v) For isothermal change, specific heat of gas is infinite while for adiabatic change it is zero.

(vi) If thermal capacity of a body is expressed in terms of mass of water it is called water equivalent of the body. If instead of unit mass we consider the mass of whole body then specific heat is termed as thermal capacity and is defined as amount of heat required to increase the temperature of a given body by 1°C is called its thermal capacity.

$$\text{Thermal capacity} = mc = nc = \frac{Q}{\Delta T}$$

Water-Equivalent = $(m \times c)$.

(vii) Gases has two specific heats one is specific heat at constant volume (C_V) and second is specific heat at constant pressure (C_P), such that

$C_P - C_V = R$ where R = Molar gas constant.

Note: The word capacity is misnomer as it is used for heat required per degree change in temperature and not the total amount of heat that a body can hold.

Heat of transformation

Amount of heat (Q) required to change the state of unit mass of a substance at a constant temperature is called the heat of transformation or latent heat i.e., $L = Q/m$ or $Q = mL$.

Here m = mass of the substance.

The heat of transformation during melting or freezing is called heat of fusion (L_F) while during boiling or condensation is called heat of vaporization (L_V).

It's SI unit is J/kg while practical unit is cal/gm.

Heat of transformation depends on nature and state of substance.

L_V = 540 cal/gm in C.G.S/practical units while in SI it is 2256×10^3 J/kg.

L_F = 80 cal/gm in C.G.S/practical while in SI it is 333×10^3 J/kg.

Heat of Evaporation

The amount of heat required to change unit mass of liquid into vapour at a given temperature is called heat of evaporation at that temperature. Liquid converts into gaseous phase (Vapour). Due to large heat of evaporation, water on sprinkling, produces cooling effect in a closed room.

Heat of sublimation

If a solid directly converts into gaseous phase at all temperatures then heat associated with the process is called heat of sublimation

Hoar Frost

If a vapour by releasing heat, directly comes to solid state without going through liquid phase, then the process is called Hoar Frost. Formation of snow by freezing water vapour in low temperature zone of atmosphere is an example of Hoar Frost. It is the reverse process of sublimation.

Change of state

In change of state, intermolecular distance changes. Also work is done against intermolecular force. If the molecules come closer in condensation, energy will be released and if go apart, energy will be absorbed (in boiling).

Clausius and clapeyron equations

It is given by $\dfrac{dp}{dT} = \dfrac{JL}{T_K(V_f - V_i)}$ where V_i and V_f are initial and final specific volume (cc/gm).

Important Conclusions

(i) Boiling point of every liquid rises with increase in pressure as $\dfrac{dp}{dT}$ is positive due to $V_f > V_i$.

(ii) Melting point of every substance which expands on melting (like sulphur, wax …) increases with increase in pressure as $V_f > V_i$.

(iii) Melting point of every substance which contracts on melting (Like rubber, ice….) decreases with increase in pressure as $\dfrac{dp}{dT}$ is negative due to $V_f < V_i$.

(iv) Melting of ice under the pressure and Its resolidification when pressure is released is called regelation.

CalorimetrY

It means measurement of heat. When a body is at higher temperature it releases heat while the body at lower temperature absorbs heat such that Heat lost = Heat gained.

Some Important Points

(i) Principle of calorimetry is the another form of conservation of heat energy.

(ii) Temperature of a mixture (T) can never be lesser than lower temperature (T_L) and greater than higher temperature (T_H).

$$T_L \leq T \leq T_H$$

(iii) The heat absorbed or released by a body of mass (m) is given by $Q = mC\Delta T$

where C = specific heat of body

ΔT = change in temperature in °C or K.

(iv) When state of a body changes, change of state takes place at constant temperature and heat absorbed or released is given by $Q = mL$, where L = latent heat

(v) If solid converts in liquid, heat is absorbed and if liquid converts in solid or vapour converts in liquid, heat is released.

(vi) No transfer of heat is possible if two bodies are at same temperature.

(vii) By calorimetry we are able to find specific heat and latent heat.

Heat Curve

Temperature time graph of a body as shown below is known as heat curve.

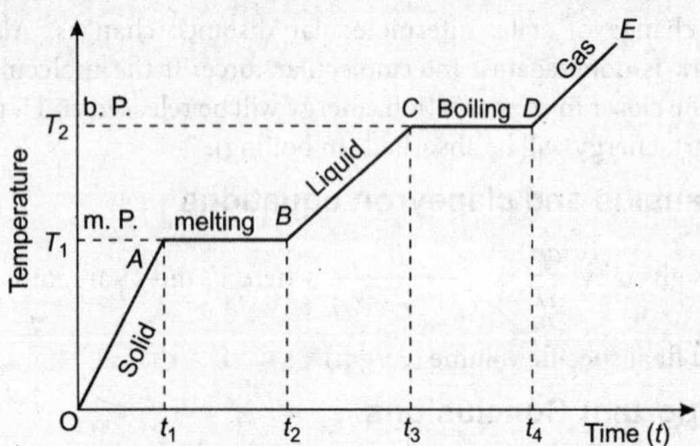

From the above graph we have

(i) For region OA,

$$C_S \propto \frac{1}{\text{Slope of Line } OA}$$ where C_S = specific heat of solid.

(ii) For region AB,

$L_F \propto$ Length of line AB. In this region specific heat will be infinite.

(iii) For region BC, $C_L \propto \dfrac{1}{\text{Slope of Line } BC}$ where C_L = specific heat of liquid.

(iv) For region CD, $L_V \propto$ length of line CD and in this region Sp. heat will be infinite.

(v) For region DE: Sp. heat $\propto \dfrac{1}{\text{Slope of Line } DE}$

and the line DE refers gaseous state.

THERMODYNAMICS

It deals with transformation of heat energy into other form of energy and vice-versa.

(i) If two systems are at same temperature, then they are in thermal equilibrium.

(ii) A system is said to be in thermodynamical equilibrium when it is in state of thermal, chemical and mechanical equilibrium.

(iii) Pressure (P), volume (V), and temperature (T) are known as thermodynamical variables.

(iv) If a system after undergoing through a series of changes and come back to its initial state then the process is called cyclic process.

(v) A process which can be made to proceed in the reverse direction by variation in its conditions, so that any change takes place in any part of the direct process are exactly reversed in the reverse process, called reversible process. Condensation and very slow evaporation are the examples of reversible process.

Conditions for Reversibility

(i) The direct and reverse processor must take place infinitely slow.

(ii) The temperature of system should not differ appreciably from its surroundings.

(iii) The dissipative forces such as friction, viscosity should be absent.

Thermodynamic Sign Conventions for Heat and Work

(i) Heat added to the system is positive ($Q > 0$).

(ii) Heat removed from the system is negative ($Q < 0$)

(iii) Work done by the system is positive ($W > 0$)

(iv) Work done on the system is negative ($W < 0$)

Zeroth law of thermodynamics

According to this law "If systems A and B are each in thermal equilibrium with a third system C separately, then A and B are also in thermal equilibrium with each other". It defines temperature as the property of the system which if equals to that of another system then two systems are in thermal equilibrium. Zeroth law of thermodynamics came to light in 1930. Later than Ist and IInd law of thermodynamics. Because the temperature is a fundamental concept for both laws, the laws that establishes temperature as a valid concept should have placed before Ist and IInd laws and hence it is called zeroth law of thermodynamics.

First Law of Thermodynamics

If we supply some heat (dQ) to a system so that the system may perform work (dW) then supplied heat is utilized in two ways, a part of supplied heat is consumed in increase the internal energy (dU, temperature) and remaining in performing work done such that,

$dQ = dU + dW$ (Heat supplied = increase in internal energy + work done by the gas)

Properties of Heat (dQ)

(i) It is path dependent.

(ii) It is the energy that is transfered between a system and its environment because of temperature difference.

(iii) It is a scalar quantity (Macroscopic).

(iv) It is taken to be positive if the system absorbs heat and negative if releases it.

(v) For solid and liquid $dQ = mL$ if there is a change of state and $dQ = mCdT$ if there is a change in temperature.

(vi) For gases when heat is absorbed and temperature changes $(dQ)_V = nC_VdT$, if volume is constant.

$(dQ)_P = nC_PdT$, if pressure is constant.

Internal Energy

It is the energy possessed by the system due to molecular motion (U_K) and molecular configuration (U_P). $U = U_K + U_P$.

Some properties of internal energy

These are

(i) Change in internal energy is path independent.

(ii) Change in internal energy depends only on the initial and final states of the system.

i.e., $dU = U_f - U_i$

(iii) For a gas $dU = nC_VdT = \frac{nRdT}{\gamma - 1}$ as $C_V = \frac{R}{\gamma - 1}$ whatever be the process no matter.

(iv) Change in internal energy of a cyclic process is always zero as for cyclic process $U_f = U_i$.

(v) As in ideal gas there is no intermolecular attraction so $U_P = 0$.

Therefore $U = U_K = \frac{3}{2}nRT$ with $\Delta U = \frac{3}{2}nRdT$

where R = molar gas constant, n = number of moles.

(vi) Change is internal energy dU of a system in case of gain is taken to be positive while it is taken to be negative if there is loss of energy.

(vii) For gas, $dU = nC_VdT = \frac{nRdT}{\gamma - 1} = \frac{P_fV_f - P_iV_i}{\gamma - 1}$

(viii) U (of an ideal gas) $= K_T + K_R$, at room temperature.

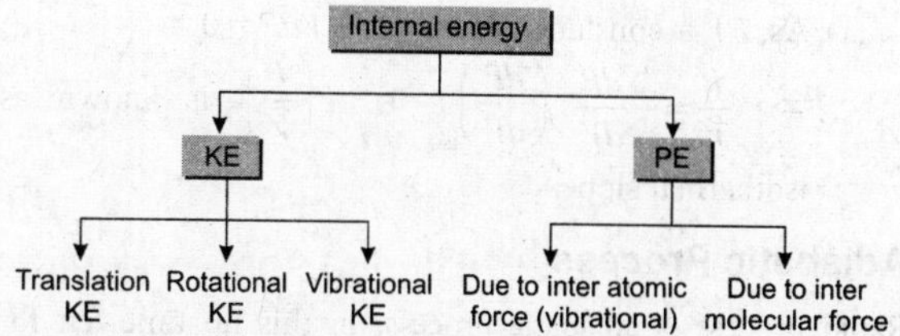

Work done (dW)

Work done by a system as it expands or contracts is given by

$W = \int dW = \int_{V_i}^{V_f} PdV$

(i) Work is path independent.

(ii) It is macroscopic and scalar quantity.

(iii) Work done by the system is taken to be positive while work done by the gas is taken to be negative.

(iv) For cyclic process, work done is equal to the area under the cycle and is positive if the cycle is clockwise and negative if anticlockwise.

THERMODYNAMICAL PROCESS

If state of a system changes in such a way that any of pressure (P), volume (V), temperature (T) changes, the process is called thermodynamical process.

It takes place, if the thermodynamic variables changes with time due to its interaction with its surroundings.

Isothermal Process

(i) In this, exchange of heat between system and surrounding is allowed.

(ii) Temperature remains constant or $dT = 0$.

(iii) Internal energy remain unchanged $dU = 0$.

(iv) As, $P \propto \frac{1}{V}$ or PV = constant, $P_iV_i = P_fV_f$.

(v) P-V graph is rectangular hyperbola.

(vi) Extremely very slow process is isothermal process.

(vii) As $dQ = dU + dW$ and here $dU = 0$ so $dQ = dW$.

(viii) $W_{iso} = nRT \log_e \frac{V_f}{V_i} = nRT \log_e \frac{P_i}{P_f}$

(ix) Heat supplied in an isothermal process is used to do work against external surroundings. Its PV-diagram is as shown below.

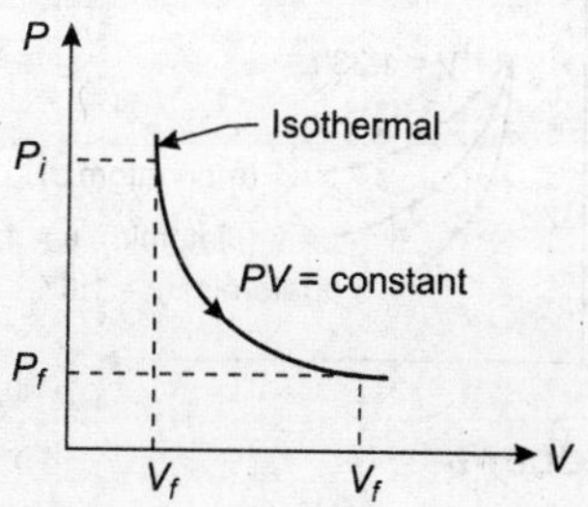

(x) As, PV = constant $\Rightarrow$ $PdV + VdP = 0$,

$\Rightarrow \frac{P}{V} = -\frac{dP}{dV}, \left(\frac{dP}{dV}\right)_{iso} = -\left(\frac{P}{V}\right)$ is known as isothermal slope.

Adiabatic Process

Rapid process is adiabatic process. In this no time left for exchange of heat between system and surroundings ($dQ = 0$).

As $dQ = dU + dW$, and $dQ = 0$. So $dU = -dW$

$\therefore$ Work done in adiabatic process,

$$W_{ad} = \frac{nR}{\gamma - 1}(T_i - T_f) = \frac{P_iV_i - P_fV_f}{\gamma - 1}$$

State equations

These are

(i) PV^γ = constant with $\gamma = \frac{C_P}{C_V}$

(ii) $TV^{\gamma-1}$ = constant, $T_1V_1^{\gamma-1} = T_2V_2^{\gamma-1}$

(iii) $\frac{P^{\gamma-1}}{T^\gamma}$ constant, $T_1V_1^{\gamma-1} = T_2V_2^{\gamma-1}$

$\Rightarrow \frac{P_1^{\gamma-1}}{T_1^\gamma} = \frac{P_2^{\gamma-1}}{T_2^\gamma}$ where $\gamma = \frac{C_P}{C_V}$

or $T_1^\gamma P_1^{1-\gamma} = T_2^\gamma P_2^{1-\gamma}$

Slope of PV graph

These are

(i) Adiabatic slope $= -\gamma\left(\frac{P}{V}\right)$

(ii) Adiabatic curve is steeper than isothermal.

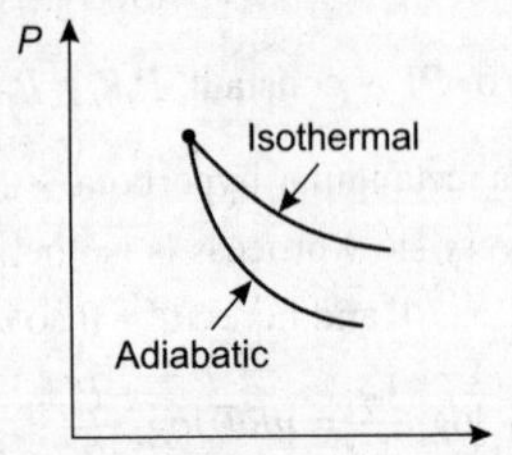

(iii) Adiabatic expansion for monoatomic, diatomic, and triatomic gases are shown in fig.

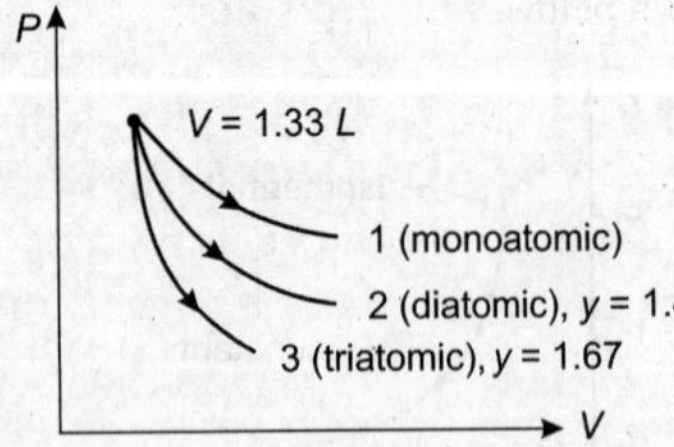

Isobaric Process

In this process, pressure is constant or $dp = 0$ (physical change at constant pressure)

State equations and work done

These are

(i) As, $V \propto T$ or $\frac{V}{T}$ = constant $\Rightarrow \frac{V_1}{T_1} = \frac{V_2}{T_2}$

(ii) V-T graph is straight line passing through origin.

$$\therefore \quad W_{isobaric} = \int_{V_i}^{V_f} PdV = P(V_f - V_i)$$

$$= nR(T_f - T_i)$$

As the temperature of the gas changes, so its internal energy also changes. Hence, in an isobaric process, the absorbed heat is utilized partly to increase internal energy and partly to do work.

Also, $dQ = nC_pdT$, $dU = nC_VdT$, $W = p(V_f - V_i)$

PV diagram

Isobaric expansion of a gas by PV diagram is shown in fig. given below.

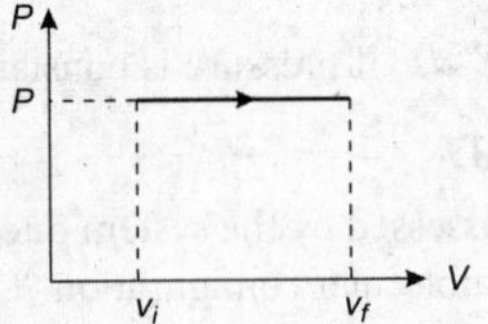

Isochoric Process

In this process volume is constant or $dV = 0$.

$\Rightarrow P \propto T$ or $\frac{P}{T}$ = constant $\Rightarrow \frac{P_1}{T_1} = \frac{P_2}{T_2}$

Work done and Graph

(i) P-T graph is straight line passing through origin.

(ii) As volume is constant so work done = 0, and $dQ = dU$. It means heat energy absorbed by the system goes entirely to change its internal energy. So $dQ = dU = nC_VdT$.

i.e., $W = 0$

$\Rightarrow dQ = dU = nC_VdT$.

(iii) Thermodynamical processes are shown in fig.

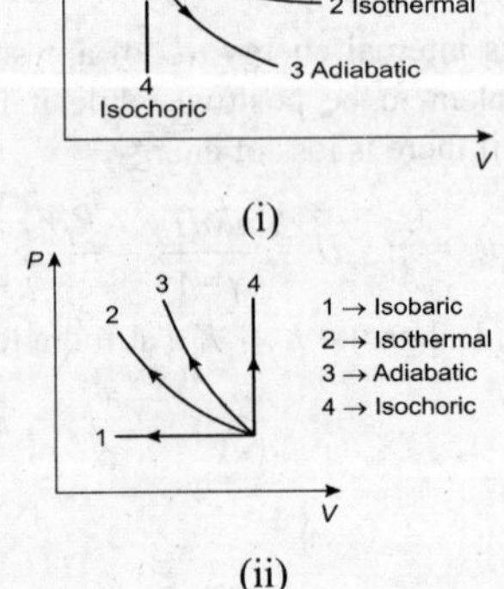

Cyclic Process

In a cyclic process, the system returns to its initial state

$\therefore \quad U_f = U_i$

$\Rightarrow \quad U_f - U_i = 0$

As $dQ = dU + dW$ and $dU = 0$ so $dQ = dW$ (heat supplied is equal to work done)

Work done

For cyclic process $W_{clockwise}$ = +ve (Shaded area)

$W_{anticlockwise}$ = –ve (Shaded area)

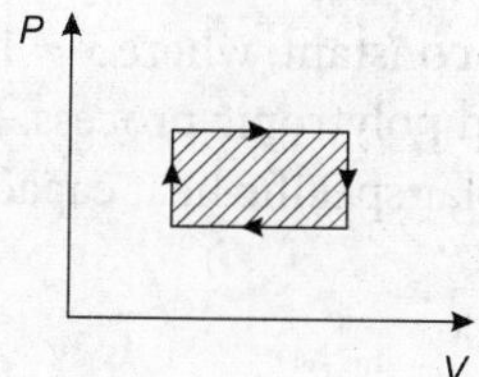

Second Law of Thermodynamics

Kelvin-Plank's Statement

It is impossible to construct an engine operating in a cyclic process to extract heat from a reservoir and convert it completely into work. In another words, whole heat can never be converted into work.

In simple way, it is not possible for an engine whose sole result is the absorption of heat from a reservoir and complete conversion of the heat into work.

Clausius Statement

It is impossible for a self acting engine unaided by any external agency to transfer heat from a cold reservoir to a hot reservoir. Simply we can say heat by itself cannot flow from a body at low temperature to a body at high temperature.

Heat engine

It is a device which converts heat into work continuously through a cyclic process. It consists of source of heat, working substance and sink as shown below.

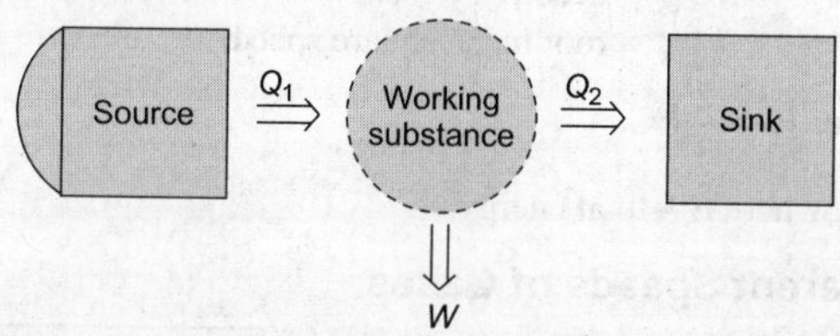

Efficiency of this engine, $\eta = 1 - \dfrac{Q_2}{Q_1}$

or $\eta = \dfrac{\text{Work done}}{\text{Heat obsorbed}} = \dfrac{W}{Q_1} = \dfrac{Q_1 - Q_2}{Q_1}$

PMM1 and PMM2

Any device (Machine) which violates the first law of thermodynamics (by creating energy) is called a perpetual motion machine of first type (PMM1) while the machine that violates the second law of thermodynamics by converting 100% of heat in work is called perpetual motion machine of second type (PMM2).

Types of Heat Engine

External combustion engine: Fuel is burnt outside the working substance. Steam engine is an example of external combustion engine. Efficiency of this engine is 12% to 20%.

Internal combustion engine: Fuel is burnt within the working substance. Diesel and petrol engines are examples of internal combustion engine. Efficiency of this engine is upto 52%.

Carnot engine

Essential parts of this engine are, source, working substance (cylinder) with perfectly non conducting wall, perfectly conducting fitted with non conducting friction-less piston. Sink and insulated pad.

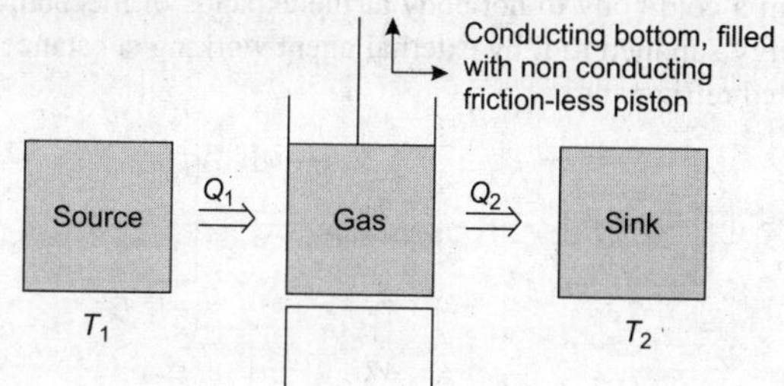

Work done

Carnot engine is taken through a reversible cyclic process through four steps as shown in figure.

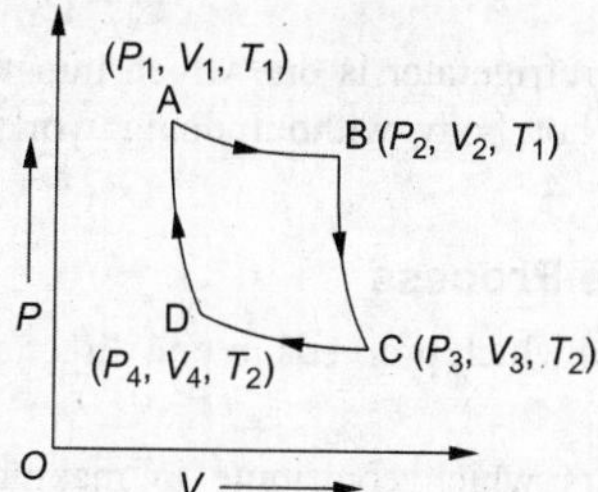

Work done during isothermal expansion (*AB*),

$$W_1 = Q_1 = nRT_1 \log_e \frac{V_2}{V_1} \text{ (Positive)}$$

Work done during adiabatic expansion (*BC*),

$$W_2 = -\Delta U = \frac{nR\Delta T}{1-\gamma}$$

Work done during isothermal compression (*CD*),

$$W_3 = Q_2\, nRT_2 \log_e\left(\frac{V_4}{V_3}\right) \text{ (– ve)}$$

Work done during adiabatic compression (DA),

$$W_4 = -\Delta U = \frac{nR\Delta T}{1-\gamma}$$

Efficiency

Efficiency of carnot engine $= 1 - \frac{T_2}{T_1}$

Also, Efficiency

$$= \frac{\text{Work done by working substance}}{\text{Heat supplied during the cycle}} \times 100$$

$$\Rightarrow \quad \eta = \frac{W_{\text{Total}}}{Q_{+\text{ve}}} \times 100$$

REFRIGERATOR

Refrigerator is also called heat pump. It is basically a heat engine runs in reverse direction.

In refrigerator working substance takes heat from a cold body (sink) and has a net amount of work done on it by an external agent (usually compressor) and gives large amount of heat to a hot body (usually atmosphere). It transfer heat from a cold body to hot body at the expands of mechanical energy supplied to it by external agent working substance is called refrigerant.

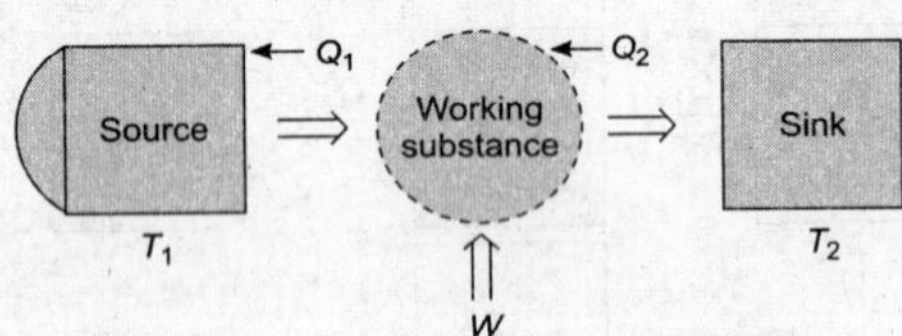

Coefficient of performance $= \frac{\text{heat external}}{\text{W.D}}$

Coefficient of performance $(k) = \frac{Q_2}{Q_1 - Q_2}$

A perfect refrigerator is one which transfers heat from cold body to hot body without doing work. i.e., $w = 0$ so $Q_1 = Q_2$, $K = \infty$

IRreversible Process

It is the process which proceeds in one direction and cannot be reversed.

The factors which contribute in making the process irreversible are friction, heat transfer through a finite temperature difference, mixing of two different substances and unrestrained expansion of fluid.

Thermodynamic parameters for a mixture of gases

(i) When n_1 moles of a gas with molar mass M_1 are mixed with n_2 moles of a gas with molar mass M_2 then equivalent molar mass will be

$$M = \frac{n_1 M_1 + n_2 M_2}{n_1 + n_2}$$

(ii) Internal energy of mixture $U = U_1 + U_2$

(iii) C_V of mixture $= \frac{n_1 C_{V_1} + n_2 C_{V_2}}{n_1 + n_2}$

(iv) C_P of mixture $= \frac{n_1 C_{P_1} + n_2 C_{P_2}}{n_1 + n_2}$

(v) γ of mixture will be

$$\gamma_{\text{mix}} = \frac{n_1 + n_2}{\gamma - 1} = \frac{n_1}{\gamma_1 - 1} + \frac{n_2}{\gamma_2 - 1}.$$

Polytropic process

When pressure (P) and volume (V) bears the relation PV^x = constant, where $x \neq 1$ then the process is called polytropic process. For polytropic process the molar specific heat capacity $C = C_V + \frac{R}{1-x} = \frac{R}{\gamma - 1} + \frac{R}{1-x}$.

Kinetic theory of gases

Assumptions of an ideal gas

(i) The number of particles in the gas is very large which are tiny, spherical, neutral and elastic.

(ii) Gaseous molecules are free to more in all possible directions, as intermolecular force is negligible.

(iii) Inter molecular distance is much larger as compared to their size.

(iv) The pressure of gas is due to the elastic collision of gas molecules with the wall of container.

(v) The gaseous molecules are identical in all respect.

(vi) The volume occupied by the gaseous molecules is much smaller than the volume of the gas.

Pressure of an Ideal Gas

Pressure of an ideal gas is given by,

$$P = \frac{1}{3}\frac{mN}{V} = \frac{1}{3}\frac{M}{V} V_{\text{rms}}^2$$

$$\Rightarrow \quad P = \frac{1}{3}\rho . V_{\text{rms}}^2$$

where M = Mass of the enclosed gas.

V = volume of container.

ρ = density of gas.

V_{rms}^2 = root mean square speed.

Note: $P = \frac{2}{3}E$

where E = total energy

Different Speeds of Gases

(i) Root mean square speed $V_{\text{rms}} = \sqrt{\frac{V_1^2 + V_2^2 + \cdots V_n^2}{n}}$

$$\Rightarrow \quad V_{\text{rms}} = \sqrt{\frac{3RT}{M}} = \sqrt{\frac{3P}{\rho}} = \sqrt{\frac{3K_BT}{m}} \text{ as } M = N_A \cdot m$$

(ii) Average speed (V_{av}) = $\dfrac{V_1+V_2+\cdots+V_n}{n}$

According to kinetic theory of gas.

$$V_{av} = \sqrt{\frac{8RT}{\pi M}} = \sqrt{\frac{8P}{\pi\rho}} = \sqrt{\frac{8K_BT}{\pi m}}$$ where, K_B = Boltzman's constant ; $V_{av} = 0.92\, V_{rms}$.

(iii) Most probable speed (V_{mp}) – It is the speed possessed by maximum number of gas molecules.

$$V_{mp} = \sqrt{\frac{2P}{\rho}} = \sqrt{\frac{2K_BT}{m}} = \sqrt{\frac{2RT}{M}} = \sqrt{\frac{2}{3}}\, V_{rms}$$

$$\Rightarrow \quad V_{rms} : V_{av} : V_{mp} = \sqrt{3} : \sqrt{\frac{8}{\pi}} : \sqrt{2}$$

$$\therefore \quad V_{rms} > V_{av} > V_{mp}.$$

Ideal gas equation

It is given by

$PV = RT$ for 1 mole

$\Rightarrow$ $PV = nRT$ for n moles

$PV = NK_BT$ for N moles of gas.

Values of few constants for an ideal gas

Name of Constant	Relation	Value	Dimension
(Molar gas constant)	$R = \dfrac{PV}{nT}$	8.31 J/mol-K	$[ML^2T^{-2}k^{-1}\mu^{-1}]$
Boltzman Constant (K_B)	$\dfrac{R}{N_A}$	1.38×10^{-23} J/K	$[ML^2T^{-2}k^{-1}]$
Avogadro's Number	$\dfrac{R}{K_B}$	6.023×10^{23} mol^{-1}	μ^{-1}

Kinetic Energy of an Ideal Gas

(i) Translational KE of molecules = $\dfrac{3}{2}K_BT$

(ii) KE of 1 mole of gas = $\dfrac{3}{2}RT$

(iii) KE of 1 gm of gas = $\dfrac{3}{2}\dfrac{R}{M}T$; where M = Molar mass of gas in gram.

Degree of freedom

(i) The total number of co-ordinates required to completely specify the position and configuration of a dynamical system is called degree of freedom (DF).

(ii) The total number of independent ways in which the position and configuration of a mechanical system may change is called degree of freedom.

(iii) The total number of independent ways in which the particle of a system can take up energy is called degree of freedom.

(iv) For 1-D motion DF will be one, For 2-D motion DF will be two and For 3-D motion DF will be three.

(v) Degree of freedom is given by $N = 3A - R$, where N = no. of degree of freedom, A = no. of atom, and R = no. of independent relation between them.

(vi) For mono atomic DF = 3

For diatomic DF = 5

For triatomic linear DF = 7

For triatomic non linear DF = 6

Note: No rotational motion is associated with point mass.

Law of Equipartion of Energy

For a dynamical system in thermal equilibrium, the energy of the system in equally distributed amongst the various degrees of freedom and the energy associated with each degree of freedom per molecule is $\frac{1}{2}K_BT$ when K_B is Boltzman constant.

Various parameters in tabular form

S.No.	Physical quantity	Monoatomic gas	Diatomic gas	Triatomic gas	
				Liners	Non-liners
1.	Atomicity	1	2	3	3
2.	Relations	0	1	2	3
3.	Degree of freedom N = $3A - R$	3	5	7	6
4.	C_V	3/2R or 2.97 cal/mol K.	5/2R or 4.95 cal/mol K.	7/2R or 6.92 cal/mol K.	3R or 5.91 cal/mol K.
5.	C_P	5/2R or 4.95 cal/mol K.	7/2R or 6.92 cal/mol K.	9/2R or 8.86 cal/mol K.	4R 7.88 cal/mol K.
6.	$\gamma = \frac{C_P}{C_V}$	5/3 = 1.67	7/5 = 1.4	9/7 = 1.2	4/3 = 1.33

Note: For Polyatomic $C_V = \frac{n}{2}R$

$$C_P = \left(\frac{n}{2}+1\right)R$$

$$\gamma = \frac{C_P}{C_V} = 1+\frac{2}{n}.$$

Mean free path

It is the distance travelled by molecules on an average between two successive collision of a gas molecules Mean free path is given by $\lambda = \frac{1}{\sqrt{2}\pi d^2 n}$ where d = diameter of molecules and n = no. of molecules/volume. Mean free path is also given by

$$\lambda = \frac{1}{\sqrt{2}}.\frac{K_BT}{\pi d^2 P}$$

As $PV = nRT = n\,NK_BT$

So $n = \frac{N}{V} = \frac{P}{K_BT}$

$\therefore \quad \lambda \propto \frac{1}{p} \Rightarrow \lambda \propto T \Rightarrow \lambda \propto \frac{1}{p}.$

Points to Remember

1. The mean free path depends on nature of molecules
2. With increase in n, l decrease
3. At NTP mean free path for air molecules is 0.01 μm.

Gas law

(i) Boyle's law $V \propto \frac{1}{p}$, T is constant

(ii) Charle's law $V \propto T$, P is constant

Gas equation $PV = RT$, at constant volume $P \propto T$.

(iii) *Avogadro's law*: Equal volume of all the gases under the same condition of temperature and pressure contains the same number of molecules.

From this law $V \propto n$, P and T are constants.

(iv) *Avogadro's number* $(N_A) = 6.023 \times 10^{23}\ \text{mol}^{-1}$

(v) *Grahm's law of diffusion*: According to this law relative rates of diffusion of gases are inversely proportional to square root of their densities.

i.e., $r \propto \frac{1}{\sqrt{\rho}}$

$\Rightarrow \quad \frac{r_1}{r_2} = \sqrt{\frac{\rho_2}{\rho_1}}$

(vi) *Dalton's law of partial pressure*: The total pressure exerted by a mixture of non-reacting gases occupying a vessel is equal to sum of the individual partial pressure which each gas exerts, if it alone occupied that volume.

$\therefore \quad P = P_1 + P_2 + P_3 + \ldots + P_n$

where P = Pressure exerted by mixture and $P_1, P_2 \ldots$ are partial pressures of individual gases.

Van der waal's equation

It is given by,

$$\left(P + \frac{a}{V^2}\right)(v - b) = RT$$

Here a and b are positive constants.

Critical Temperature, Pressure and Volume

(i) Gases can't be liquified above a temperature called critical temperature (T_C) how large the pressure be no matter.

(ii) The pressure required to liquified the gas at critical temperature is called critical pressure (P_C)

(iii) The volume of gas at critical temperature and pressure is called critical volume (V_C)

(iv) The values of critical constant in terms of Vander-waal's constants a and b is given by

$$V_C = 3b,\ P_C = \frac{a}{27b^2} \text{ and } T_C = \frac{8a}{27Rb}.$$

Also, $\frac{RT_C}{P_C V_C} = 8/3$ are called critical co-efficients and is same for all gases.

Heat transfer

Heat can be transferred from one place to other by three different process namely conduction, convection and radiation. Conduction usually takes place in solid, convection in fluid (liquid and gases) and no medium is required for radiation.

Heat Conduction

In this heat conduction in conductors takes place due to molecular collisions. Consider conductor through a thermal conducting rod as shown below.

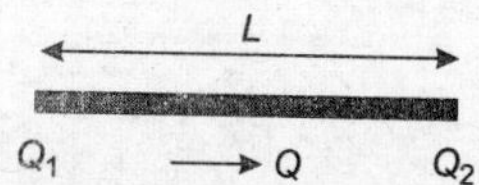

(i) In steady state $Q = \frac{KA(Q_1 - Q_2)}{L} t$

(ii) Rate of flow $\frac{dQ}{dt} = -KA\frac{dQ}{dx}$

(iii) Thermometric conductivity $(D) = \frac{K}{\rho_C}$, where

K = thermal conductivity, ρ_C = thermal capacity

(iv) According to Wiedemann-Franz law, $\frac{K}{\sigma T}$ = constant.

where K = thermal conductivity

σ = electrical conductivity.

This law signifies that a substance which is good conductor of heat is also a good conductor of electricity and a substance which is bad conductor of heat is also a bad conductor of electricity.

(v) Thermal resistance $R = \frac{L}{KA}$

(vi) Greater the thermal resistance, better will be the insulation and poorer will be the conduction.

(vii) For thermal resistances in series $R = R_1 + R_2$ with

$$R = \frac{L}{KA} \text{ and } H = \frac{Q_1 - Q_2}{R}$$

(viii) For thermal resistances in parallel

$$\frac{1}{R} = \frac{1}{R_1} + \frac{1}{R_2}$$

and $\quad H = \frac{Q_1 - Q_2}{R}$

(*ix*) Time taken by ice to grow a thickness x,

$$t = \frac{\rho L}{K\theta}\int_0^x x\,dx = \frac{1}{2}\frac{\rho L}{K\theta}.x^2$$

where L = Latent heat.

(*x*) Time taken to double and triple the thickness will be in the ratio of $t_1 : t_2 : t_3 :: 1^2 : 2^2 : 3^2$

Convection

(i) In this, rate of flow of heat, $\left(\frac{dQ}{dt}\right)_{\text{Convection}} = hAd\theta$

where h = constant of proportionality called convection coefficient.

(ii) Natural convection plays an important role in ventilation, in changing climate and weather and in forming land and sea breezes and trade wind.

(iii) Forced convection of blood in our body by the pump (heart) helps in keeping the temperature of body constant.

Radiation

(i) In this heat is transferred directly from one body to another without requiring any medium.

(ii) It is the fastest mode of heat transfer.

(iii) Absorptive power (a) = $\frac{\text{Energy absorbed}}{\text{Energy incident}}$

$a \le 1$, $a = 1$ for perfectly black body.

(iv) Spectral absorptive power

$$a_\lambda = \int_0^\infty a_\lambda d_\lambda$$

$$a_\lambda \le 1$$

$$a_\lambda = 1 \text{ for perfectly black body}$$

(v) Emissive power (e) is energy radiated per unit area per unit time is called emissive power with SI unit wm^{-2}

(vi) Spectral emissive power (e)

$$e = \int_0^\infty e_\lambda d_\lambda$$

(vii) According to Kirchoff's law the ratio of emissive power to absorptive power is same for all surfaces at the same temperature and is equal to the emissive power of a perfectly black body at that temperature.

$$\frac{e}{a} = \frac{E}{A}$$

For perfectly black body $A = 1$

$$\Rightarrow \quad \frac{e}{a} = E.$$

(viii) According to Stefan's law

$$E = e\sigma T^4$$

where σ = Stefan's constant = 5.67×10^{-8} W/m^2 K^4

(ix) Total energy radiated is given by

$$E = eA\sigma T^4$$

(x) Cooling by radiation is given by

$$-\frac{dT}{dt} = \frac{eA\sigma}{mc}\left(T^4 - T_0^4\right)$$

Wein's Displacement Law

According to this law the wavelength (λ_m) corresponding to the maximum intensity radiated is inversely proportional to the absolute temperature (T).

i.e. $\lambda_m \propto \frac{1}{T}$

$\Rightarrow \quad \lambda_m = \frac{b}{T}$, where $b = 2.89 \times 10^{-3}$ m-K

Variation of intensity

Intensity variation of radiation with wavelength is shown below.

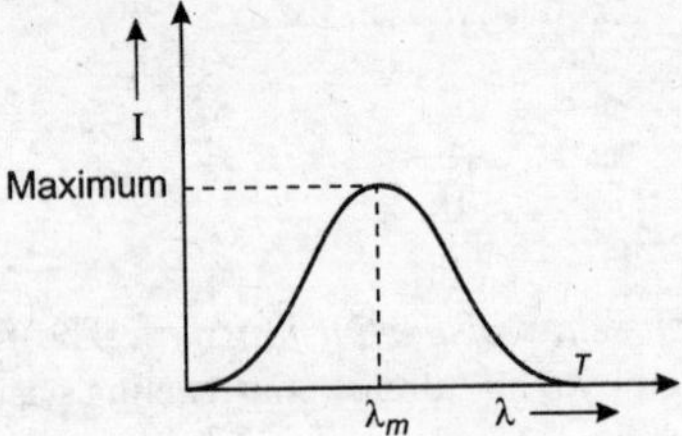

At the given wavelength (λ_m) the radiated intensity is maximum.

Newton's Law of Cooling

According to this law rate of cooling is directly proportional to the temperature difference between body and surroundings provided temperature difference should be small.

Mathematically $\frac{d\theta}{dt} \propto (\theta - \theta_0)$

$$\Rightarrow \quad \frac{\theta_1 - \theta_2}{t} = \left(\frac{\theta_1 + \theta_2}{2} - \theta_0\right)$$

Fall of temperature

The rate of fall of temperature (θ) is graphically shown below.

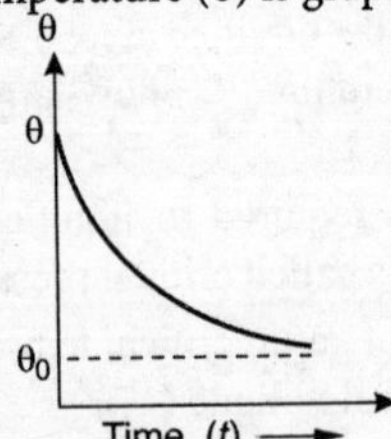

Objective Type Questions

1. Two rigid boxes containing different ideal gases are placed on a table. Box A contains one mole of nitrogen at T_0. While box B contain one mole of He at 7/3 T_0. The boxes are then put into thermal contact with each other and heat flows between them till the gases reach a common final temperature T_f. Ignore the heat capacity of boxes. Then T_f in terms of T_0 is

   (a) $T_f = \frac{7}{3} T_0$ (b) $T_f = \frac{5}{2} T_0$

   (c) $T_f = \frac{14}{9} T_0$ (d) $Tf = \frac{3}{2} T_0$

2. The molar specific heat at constant pressure of an ideal gas is (7/2 R). The ratio of specific heat at constant pressure to that at constant volume is

   (a) 9/7 (b) 7/5

   (c) 5/7 (d) 8/7

3. At what temperature is the rms velocity of a hydrogen molecule equal to that of an oxygen molecule at 47°C?

   (a) 80 K (b) –73 K

   (c) 3 K (d) 20 K

4. The average translational kinetic energy of O_2 (molar mass 32) molecules at a particular temperature is 0.048 eV. The translational kinetic energy of N_2 (molar mass 28) molecules in eV at the same temperature is

   (a) 0.0015 (b) 0.003

   (c) 0.048 (d) 0.768

5. A vessel contains 1 mole of O_2 gas (molar mass 32) at a temperature T. The pressure of the gas is P. An identical vessel containing one mole of He gas (relative molar mass 4) at a temperature $2T$ has a pressure of

   (a) $P/8$ (b) P

   (c) $2P$ (d) $8P$

6. Given is the graph between $\frac{PV}{T}$ and P for 1 gm of oxygen gas at two different temperatures T_1 and T_2, as shown in fig. Given, density of oxygen = 1.427 kg m^{-3}. The value of PV/T at the point A and the relation between T_1 and T_2 are respectively :

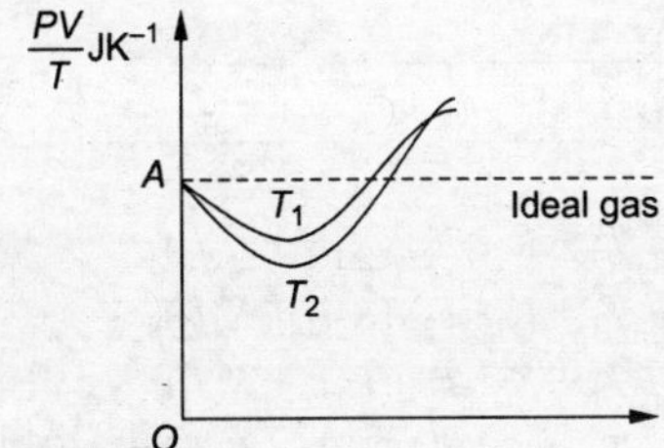

   (a) 0.256 JK^{-1} and $T_1 < T_2$

   (b) 8.314 J mol^{-1} K^{-1}and $T_1 > T_2$

   (c) 0.256 JK^{-1} and $T_1 > T_2$

   (d) 4.28 JK^{-1} and $T_1 < T_2$

7. A gas mixture consists of 2 mole of oxygen and 4 mole of argon at temperature T. Neglecting all vibrational modes, the total internal energy of the system is

   (a) $4RT$ (b) $15RT$

   (c) $9RT$ (d) $11RT$

8. The average translational kinetic energy and the root mean square speed of molecules in a sample of oxygen gas at 300 K are 6.21 × 10^{-21} J and 484 m/s respectively. The corresponding values at 600 K are nearly (assuming ideal gas behaviour)

   (a) 12.42 × 10^{-21} J, 968 m/s

   (b) 8.78 × 10^{-21} J, 684 m/s

   (c) 6.21 × 10^{-21} J, 968 m/s

   (d) 12.42 × 10^{-21} J, 684 m/s

9. A container with insulating walls is divided into two equal parts by a partition fitted with a valve. One part is filled with an ideal gas at *a* pressure P and temperature T, whereas the other part is completely evacuated. If the valve is suddenly opened, the pressure and temperature of the gas will be:

   (a) P, T (b) $P, \frac{T}{2}$

   (c) $\frac{P}{2}, T$ (d) $\frac{P}{2}, \frac{T}{2}$

10. A cylinder of radius R made of a material of thermal conductivity K_1 is surrounded by a cylindrical shell of inner radius R and outer radius $2R$ made of a material of thermal conductivity K_2. The two ends of the combined system are maintained at two different temperatures. There is no loss of heat across the cylindrical surface and the system is in steady state. The effective thermal conductivity of the system is

    (a) $K_1 + K_2$ (b) $K_1K_2/(K_1 + K_2)$

    (c) $(K_1 + 3K_2)/4$ (d) $(3K_1 + K_2)/4$

11. Three rods of identical cross-sectional area and made from the same metal from the sides of an isosceles triangle ABC, right angled at B. The points A amd B are maintained at temperatures T and $(\sqrt{2})T$ respectively. In the steady state, the temperatures of the point C is T_C/T. Assuming that only heat conduction takes place, T_C/T is

(a) $\frac{1}{2(\sqrt{2}-1)}$ (b) $\frac{3}{\sqrt{2}+1}$

(c) $\frac{1}{\sqrt{3}(\sqrt{2}-1)}$ (d) $\frac{1}{(\sqrt{2}-1)}$

12. Two metallic spheres S_1 and S_2 are made of the same material and have got identical surface finish. The mass of S_1 is thrice that of S_2. Both the spheres are heated to the same high temperature and placed in the same room having lower temperature but are thermally insulated from each other. The ratio of the initial rate of cooling of S_1 to that of S_2 is

(a) $\frac{1}{3}$ (b) $\frac{1}{\sqrt{3}}$

(c) $\frac{\sqrt{3}}{1}$ (d) $\left(\frac{1}{3}\right)^{1/3}$

13. A spherical black body with a radius of 12 cm radiates 450 W power at 500 K. If the radius were halved and the temperature doubled, the power radiated in watt would be

(a) 225 (b) 450

(c) 900 (d) 1800

14. A black body is at a temperature of 2880 K. The energy of radiation emitted by this body with wavelength between 499 nm and 500 nm is U_1, between 999 nm and 1000 nm is U_2 and between 1499 nm and 1500 nm is U_3. The Wien constant $b = 2.88 \times 10^6$ nm-K. Then,

(a) $U_1 = 0$ (b) $U_3 = 0$

(c) $U_1 > U_2$ (d) $U_2 > U_1$

15. The intensity of radiation emitted by the sun has its maximum value at a wavelength of 510 nm and that emitted by north star has the maximum value at 350 nm. If these stars behave like black bodies, then the ratio of the surface temperature of the sun and the north star is

(a) 1.46 (b) 0.69

(c) 1.21 (d) 0.83

16. Which one of the following is $\nu_m - T$ graph for perfectly black body? ν_m is the frequency of radiation with maximum intensity. T is the absolute temperature

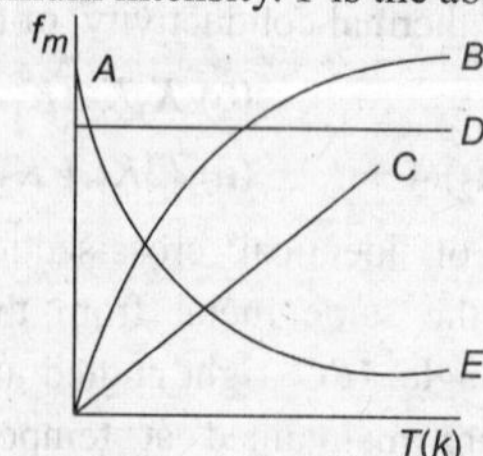

(a) A (b) B

(c) C (d) D

17. The plots of intensity (I) of radiation versus wavelength (λ) of three black bodies at temperatures T_1, T_2 and T_3 are shown in Fig. Then,

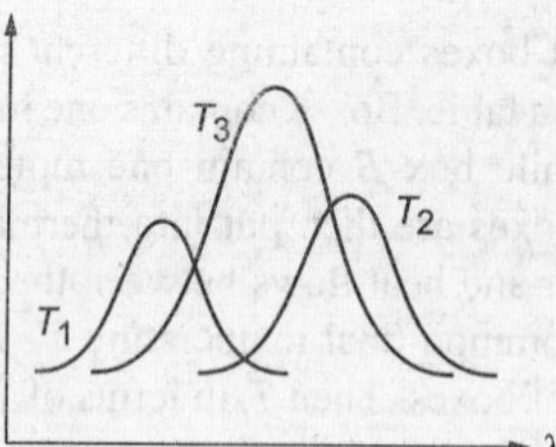

(a) $T_3 > T_2 > T_1$ (b) $T_1 > T_2 > T_3$

(c) $T_2 > T_3 > T_1$ (d) $T_1 > T_3 > T_2$

18. A black body at 1227°C emits radiation with maximum intensity at a wavelength of 5000 Å. If the temperature of the body is increased by 1000°C, the maximum intensity will be observed at

(a) 3000 Å (b) 4000 Å

(c) 5000 Å (d) 6000 Å

19. Three identical rods A, B and C are placed end to end. A temperature difference is maintained between the free ends of A and C. The thermal conductivity of B is thrice that of C and half that of A. The effective thermal conductivity of the system will be (K_A is the thermal conductivity of rod A)

(a) $\frac{1}{3} K_A$ (b) $3 K_A$

(c) $2 K_A$ (d) $\frac{2}{3} K_A$

20. Three identical thermal conductors are connected as shown in Fig. Considering no heat is lost due to radiation, the temperature of the junction is

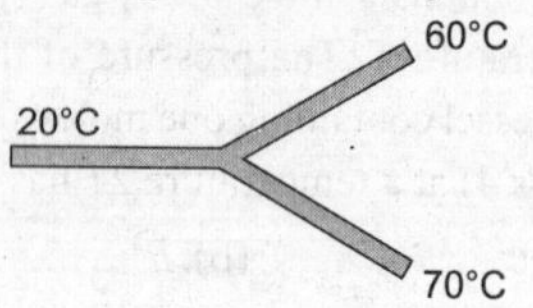

(a) 60°C (b) 20°C

(c) 50°C (d) 10°C

21. One end of a thermally insulated rod is kept at a temperature T_1 and the other at T_2. The rod is composed of two sections of lengths l_1 and l_2 and thermal conductivities K_1 and K_2 respectively. The temperature at the interface of the two sections is :

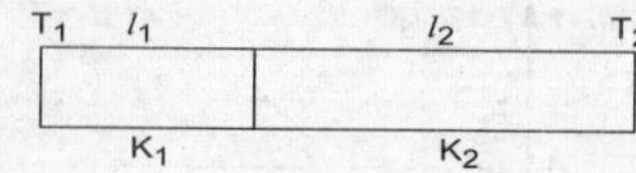

(a) $(K_2 l_2 T_1 + K_1 l_1 T_2)/(K_1 l_1 + K_2 l_2)$

(b) $(K_2 l_1 T_1 + K_1 l_2 T_2)/(K_2 l_1 + K_1 l_2)$

(c) $(K_1 l_2 T_1 + K_2 l_1 T_2)/(K_1 l_2 + K_2 l_1)$

(d) $(K_1 l_1 T_1 + K_2 l_2 T_2)/(K_1 l_1 + K_2 l_2)$

22. A long metallic bar is carrying heat from one of its ends to the other end under steady-state. The variation of temperature θ along the length x of the bar from its hot end is best described by which of the following figures?

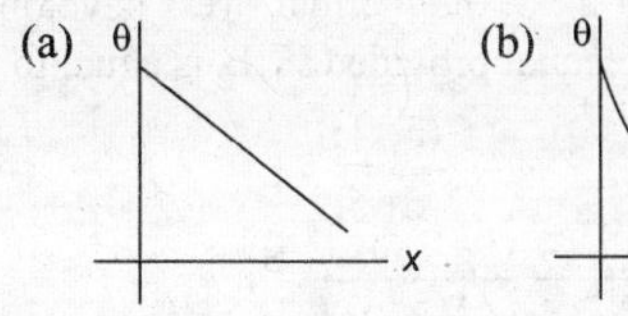

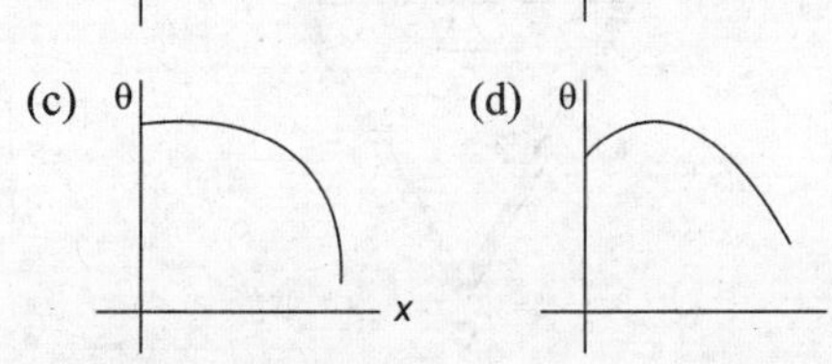

23. A Carnot engine takes 3×10^6 cal of heat from reservoir at 627°C and it to a sink at 27°C.
The work done by the engine is
(a) 4.2×10^6 J (b) 8.4×10^6 J
(c) 16.8×10^6 J (d) 2×10^6 J

24. The temperature inside and outside of a refrigerator are 273 K and 303 K respectively Assuming that the refrigerator cycle is reversible the heat delivered to surround for every joule of work done will be
(a) 20.1 J (b) 5.1 J
(c) 10.1 J (d) 30.1 J

25. The specific heat capacity of a metal at low temperature (T) is given as
$$C_P\,(\text{kJK}^{-1}\,\text{kg}^{-1}) = 32\left(\frac{T}{400}\right)^3$$
A 100 gram vessel of this metal is to be cooled from 20° K to 4° K by a special refrigerator operating at room temperature (27°C). The amount of work required to cool the vessel is
(a) equal to 0.002 kJ (b) greater than 0.148 kJ
(c) between 0.148 kJ and 0.028 kJ
(d) less than 0.028 kJ

26. Stream at 100°C is passed into 20 g of water at 10°C. When water acquires a temperature of 80°C, the mass of water present will be [Take specific heat of water = cal g^{-1}°C^{-1} and latent heat of steam = 540 cal g^{-1}]
(a) 24 g (b) 31.5 g
(c) 42.5 g (d) 22.5 g

27. A diatomic ideal gas is used in a Carnot engine as the working substance. If during the adiabatic expansion part of the cycle the volume of the gas increases from V to 32 V, the efficiency of the engine is :
(a) 0.25% (b) 0.5%
(c) 0.75% (d) 0.99%

28. 100 g of water is heated from 30°C to 50°C. Ignoring the slight expansion of the water, the change in its internal energy is (Specific heat of water is 4184 J/kg/K):
(a) 2.1 KJ (b) 4.2 KJ
(c) 8.4 KJ (d) 84 KJ

29. A Carnot engine operating between temperature T_1 and T_2 has efficiency $\frac{1}{6}$. When T_2 is lowered by 62 K its efficiency increases to $\frac{1}{3}$.
Then T_1 and T_2 are, respectively :
(a) 310 K and 248 K (b) 372 K and 310 K
(c) 372 K and 330 K (d) 330 K and 268 K

30. A thermally insulated vessel contains an ideal gas of molecular mass M and ratio of specific heats γ. It is moving with speed v and is suddenly brought to rest. Assuming no heat is lost to the surroundings, its temperature increases by:
(a) $\frac{(\gamma-1)}{2R}Mv^2K$ (b) $\frac{(\gamma-1)}{2(\gamma+1)R}Mv^2K$
(c) $\frac{(\gamma-1)}{2\gamma R}Mv^2K$ (d) $\frac{\gamma Mv^2}{2R}K$

31. If 4 gram of hydrogen and 4 gram of helium are mixed and given a heat of 32 calories, such that their volume does not change. The rise in temperature of the mixture will be
(a) 1°C (b) 2°C
(c) 3°C (d) 4°C

32. A Carnot engine, having an efficiency of $\eta = \frac{1}{10}$ as heat engine, is used as a refrigerator. If the work done on the system is 10 J, the amount of energy absorbed from the reservoir at lower temperature is :
(a) 99 J (b) 90 J
(c) 1 J (d) 100 J

33. A rod of length 20 cm made of metal A expands by 0.075 cm when its temperature is raised from 0°C to 100°C. Another rod of a different metal B having the same length expands 0.045 cm for the same change in temperature. A third rod of the same length is composed of two parts, one of metal A and other of metal B. This rod expands by 0.065 cm for the same change in temperature. They portion made of metal A has the length
(a) 10 cm (b) 13.3 cm
(c) 15 cm (d) 6.7 cm

34. A pendulum clock (fitted with small heavy bob that is connected with metal rod) is 5 seconds fast each day at a temperature of 30°C and 10 seconds slow each day at temperature of 15°C . The temperature at which it is designed to give correct time is
(a) 18°C (b) 20°C
(c) 24°C (d) 25°C

35. A sphere of radius 0.049 m and mass 0.596 kg floats in a liquid bath at 0°C. The density of liquid is 1.25×10^3 kg/m^3. Assume that the sphere does not expand. If the temperature of 30°C. The temperature of the bath is raised to 40°C, the sphere just begins to sink. The volume coefficient of liquid is

(a) 8.1×10^{-4}/°C (b) 1.3×10^{-4}/°C
(c) 4.15×10^{-4}/°C (d) 2.8×10^{-4}/°C

36. A steel tape measured the length of copper rod as 90.00 cm when both are 10°C, the calibration temp-erature, for the tape. When both are at 30°C given, $\alpha_{steel} = 1.2 \times 10^{-5}$/°C and $\alpha_{Cu} = 1.7 \times 10^{-5}$/°C

(a) 89.00 cm (b) 90.21 cm
(c) 89.90 cm (d) 90.01 cm

37. A brass wire 2 m long at 27°C is held taut with negligible tension between two rigid supports If the wire is cooled to a temperature of –33°C, the tension developed in the wire, its diameter being 2 mm, will be (coefficient of linear expansion of brass = 2.0×10^{-5}C^{-1} and Young's modulus of brass = 0.91×10^{11} pa

(a) 680 N (b) 3400 N
(c) 6800 N (d) 340 N

38. A pendulum clock, made of a material having coefficient of linear expansion $\alpha = 9 \times 10^{-7}$/°C has a period of 0.500 sec at 20°C. If the clock is used in a climate where temperature average 30°C, what correction is necessary at the end of 30 days to the time given by clock.

(a) 11.6 s (b) 3.88 s
(c) 0.100 s (d) 2.0 s

39. An iron tyre to be fitted on a wooden wheel 1.0 m in diameter. The diameter of the tyre is 6 mm smaller than that of the wheel. The tyre should be heated by a temperature of (coefficient of volume expansion of iron is 3.6×10^{-5}/°C)

(a) 400°C (b) 500°C
(c) 350°C (d) 250°C

40. A composite bar of length $L = L_1 + L_2$ is made up from a rod materials 1 and of length L_1 attached to a rod of material 2 and of length L_2 as shown. If α_1 and α_2 are their respective coefficient of linear expansion, then equivalent coefficient of linear expansion of the composite rod is

(a) $\frac{\alpha_1 L_2 + \alpha_2 L_1}{L}$ (b) $\frac{\alpha_1 L_2^2 + \alpha_2 L_1^2}{L^2}$

(c) $\frac{\alpha_1 L_1 + \alpha_2 L_2}{L}$ (d) $\frac{\alpha_1 \alpha (L_1^2 + L_2^2)}{(\alpha_1 L_1 + \alpha_2 L_2)}$

41. Two rods of different materials having coefficients of linear expansion α_1, α_2 and Young's modulii Y_1 and Y_2 respectively are fixed between two rigid massive walls. The rods are heated such that they undergo the same increase in temperature. There is no bending of rods. If $\alpha_1 : \alpha_2 = 2 : 3$, the thermal stress developed in the two rods are equal provided $Y_1 : Y_2$ is equal to.

(a) 2:3 (b) 1:1
(c) 3:2 (d) 5:9

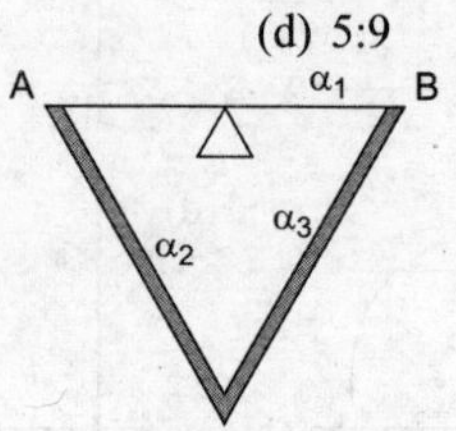

42. A vessel of volume V and linear coefficient of expansion α contains a liquid. The level of liquid does not change on heating. The volume coefficient of real expansion of the liquid is

(a) $\frac{V+\alpha}{V}$ (b) $\frac{V-\alpha}{V}$

(c) $\frac{V}{V-\alpha}$ (d) 3α.

43. A faulty Celsius thermometer has its fixed points marked at 5°C and 95°C respectively. What is the actual temperature of a liquid, if this thermometer reads 59°C?

(a) 64°C (b) 54°C
(c) 60°C (d) 68°C

44. The Fahrenheit and Kelvin scales in temperature will give the same reading at

(a) –40 (b) 313
(c) 574.25 (d) 732.75

45. Two thermometers, one and the other Fahrenheit are put in a hot bath. The reading on Fahrenheit thermometer is just three times the reading on Celsius thermometer. The temperature of the bath

(a) 100°C (b) (80/3)°C
(c) 80°C (d) 70°C

46. At a certain temperature dependent property of y varies according to law $y = \frac{\alpha(t_2 - t_1)}{1 + \alpha t_2}$ where t is in °C and α is constant, and $y > 1$ is not permitted. Then the absolute zero of temperature scale based on this property in °C is

(a) $\frac{1}{\alpha}$ (b) 0

(c) $\frac{\alpha}{1+\alpha}$ (d) $-\frac{1}{\alpha}$

47. Three rods of equal length are joined to form an equilateral triangle ABC as shown in figure. D is the midpoint of AB. The coefficient of linear expansion is α_1 for AB, and α_2 for AC and BC.
If the distance DC remains constant for small change in temperature, then

(a) $\alpha_1 = \alpha_2$ (b) $\alpha_1 = 2\,\alpha_2$

(c) $\alpha_1 = 4\alpha_2$ (d) $\alpha_1 = \frac{1}{2}\alpha_2$

48. In a vertical U–tube containing a liquid the two arms are maintained at different temperatures, t_1 and t_2. The liquid columns in the two arms have height l_1 and l_2 respectively. The coefficient of volume expansion of the liquid is equal to

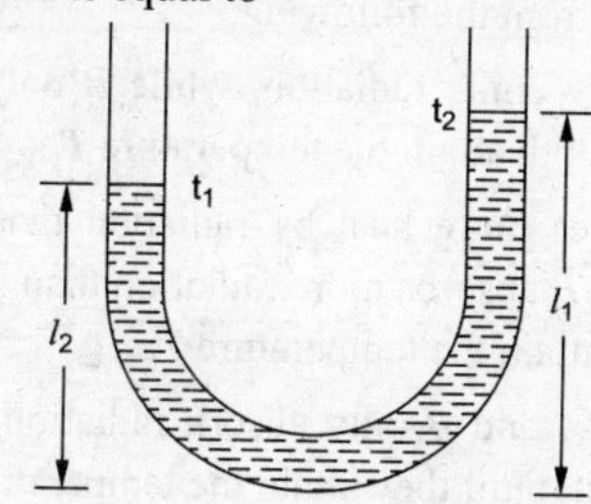

(a) $\frac{l_1 - l_2}{l_2t_1 - l_1t_2}$ (b) $\frac{l_1 + l_2}{l_2t_1 + l_1t_2}$

(c) $\frac{l_1 - l_2}{l_1t_1 - l_2t_2}$ (d) $\frac{l_1 + l_2}{l_1t_1 + l_2t_2}$

49 When a block of iron floats in mercury at 0°C, a fraction k_1 of its volume is submerged, while at the temperature 60°C, a fraction k_2 is seen to be submerged. if the coefficient of volume expansion of iron is γ_{Fe} and that of mercury is γ_{Hg}, then the ratio k_1/k_2 can be expressed as

(a) $\frac{1+60\gamma_{Fe}}{1+60\gamma_{Hg}}$ (b) $\frac{1-60\gamma_{Fe}}{1+60\gamma_{Hg}}$

(c) $\frac{1+60\gamma_{Fe}}{1-60\gamma_{Hg}}$ (d) $\frac{1+60\gamma_{Hg}}{1+60\gamma_{Fe}}$

50 The volume thermal expansion coefficient of an ideal gas at constant pressure is

(a) T (b) T^2

(c) $\frac{1}{T}$ (d) $\frac{1}{T^2}$

51. A cylindrical metal rod of length Lo is shaped into a ring with a small gap as shown. On heating the system

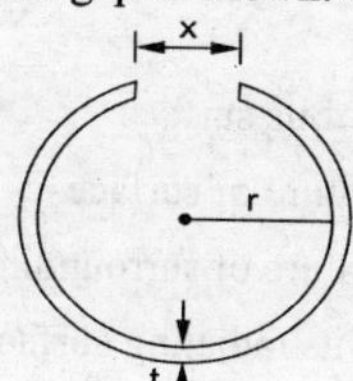

(a) x decreases, r and t increase

(b) x and r increase, t decrease

(c) x, r and t all increase

(d) data insufficient to arrive at a conclusion

52 The radius of ring is R and its coefficient of linear expansion is α. If the temperature of ring increases by θ, then its circumference will increase by.

(a) $\pi R\alpha\theta$ (b) $2\pi R\alpha\theta$

(c) $\pi R\alpha\theta/2$ (d) $\pi R\alpha\theta/4$

53. Two rods of length l_1 and l_2 are made of materials whose coefficients of linear expansion are α_1 and α_2. If the difference between the two lengths is independent of temp., then

(a) $\frac{l_1}{l_2} = \frac{\alpha_1}{\alpha_2}$ (b) $\frac{l_1}{l_2} = \frac{\alpha_2}{\alpha_1}$

(c) $l_2^2\alpha_2 = l_1^2\,\alpha_2$ (d) $\frac{\alpha_1^2}{l_1} = \frac{\alpha_2^2}{l_2}$

54. Two iron spheres of the same diameter are heated to the same temperature. One is solid and other is hollow. Which will expand more

(a) hallow

(b) Solid

(c) Same for hollow and solid

(d) data insufficient

55. An ideal gas is taken from the state A (P, V) to the state B (P/2, 2V) along a straight line path as shown in fig. Choose the correct option

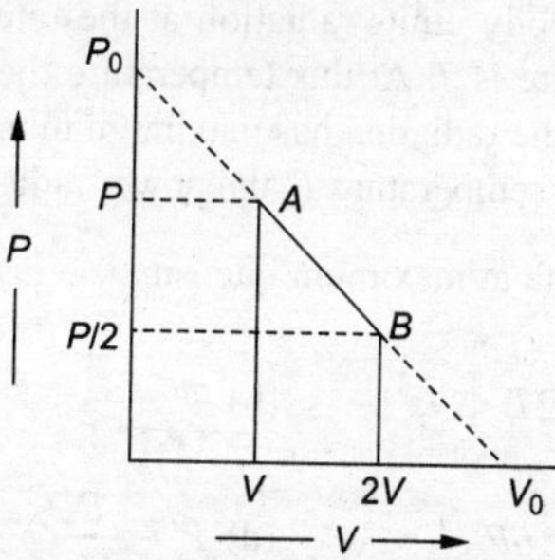

(a) In the T-V diagram, Path AB would becomes a Parabola

(b) In tP-T diagram, path would be part of hyperbola

(c) In going from A to B the temperature T of gas first increase to maximum value and then decreases.

(d) Work done by the gas in going from A to B exceeds the work done in going from A to B under constant temperature

56. Which of the following diagrams, depicts ideal gas behaviour?

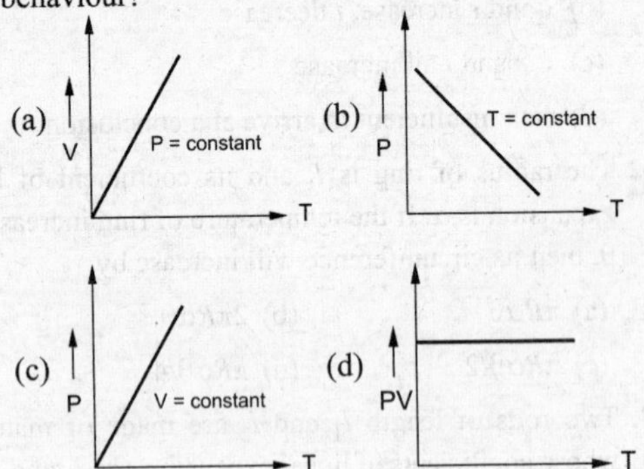

57. *ABCDEFGH* is a hollow cube made of an insulator, in the given figure. Face *ABCD* has positive charge on it. Inside the cube, we have ionized hydrogen.

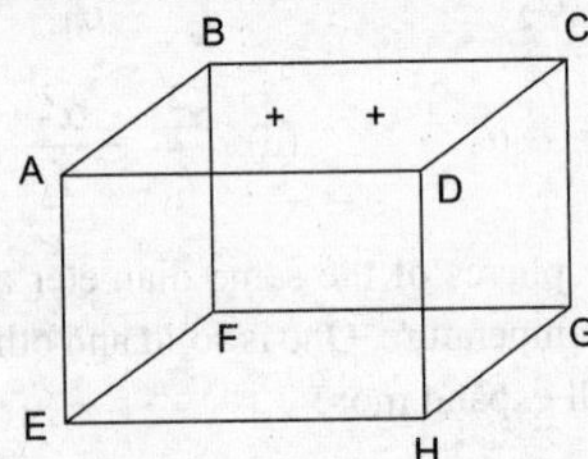

The usual kinetic theory expression for pressure

(a) will be valid.

(b) will not be valid since the ions would experience forces other than due to collision with the walls.

(c) will not be valid since collisions with walls would not be elastic.

(d) will not be valid because isotropy is lost.

58. A black body emits radiation at the rate *P* when its temperature is *T*. At this temperature the wavelength at which the radiation has maximum intensity is λ_0. If at another temperature *T'* the power radiated is *P'* and wavelength at maximum intensity is $\frac{\lambda_0}{2}$ then :

(a) $T' = 2T$ (b) $T' = \frac{T}{2}$

(c) $P' = 16P$ (d) $P' = \frac{P}{16}$

59. A black body is at a temperature of 2880 K. The energy of radiation emitted by this object between wavelength 4990 Å and 5000 Å is U_1, between 9990 Å and 10000 Å is U_2 and between 14990 Å and 15000 Å is U_3. The Wien's constant $b = 2.88 \times 10^{-3}$ mK, then

(a) $U_2 > U_1$ (b) $U_2 > U_3$

(c) $U_1 = U_3 < U_2$ (d) $U_1 < U_2 < U_3$

60. A hot body emits radiation which has maximum intensity at frequency ν_m. If the temperature of the body is doubled.

(a) the maximum intensity radiation will be at frequency $2\nu_m$

(b) the maximum intensity radiation will be at frequency $(1/2)\,\nu_m$

(c) the total emitted energy will increase by a factor 16

(d) the total emitted energy will increase by a factor 2

61. Two identical objects *A* and *B* are at temperature T_A and T_B respectively. Both objects are placed in a room with perfectly absorbing walls maintained at temperature T ($T_A > T > T_B$). The objects *A* and *B* attain the temperature *T* eventually. Select the correct statement from the following.

(a) *A* only emits radiation, while *B* only absorbs it until both attain the temperature *T*.

(b) *A* loses more heat by radiation than it absorbs while *B* absorbs more radiation than it emits until they attain the temperature *T*.

(c) Both *A* and *B* only absorb radiation, but do not emit it, until they attain the temperature *T*.

(d) Each objects continues to emit and absorb radiation even after attaining the temperature *T*.

62. Two Plates *A* and *B* of equal surface area are placed one on top of the other to form a composite plate of the same surface area. The thickness of *A* and *B* are 4.0 cm and 6.0 cm respectively. The temperature of the exposed surface of plate *A* is –10°C and that of the exposed surface of plate *B* is 10°C. Neglect heat loss from the edges of the composite plate, the temperature of the contact surface is T_1 if the plates *A* and *B* are made of the same material and T_2 if their thermal conductivities are in the ratio 2 : 3 then

(a) $T_1 = -4°C$ (b) $T_1 = -2°C$

(c) $T_2 = -3°C$ (d) $T_2 = 0$

63. A star appears red if the wavelength of maximum emission is in the range 620 nm to 780 nm. The corresponding temperatures of the star for maximum emission are T_1 and T_2 respectively. If Wien's constant is $b = 2.9 \times 10^{-3}$ m-K, then

(a) $T_1 = 3718$ K (b) $T_1 = 2690$ K

(c) $T_2 = 2318$ K (d) $T_2 = 4677$ K

64. The rate at which energy is radiated by hot body depends on

(a) The nature of its surface

(b) The temperature of surface

(c) The temperature of surroundings

(d) The area of its radiating surface

65. Two bodies A and B have thermal emissivities of 0.01 and 0.81 respectively. The outer surface areas of the two bodies are the same. The two bodies emit total radiant power of the same rate. The wavelength λ_B corresponding to maximum spectral radiancy in the radiation from B shifted from the wavelength corresponding to maximum spectral radiancy in the radiation from A, by 1.00 μm. If the temperature of A is 5802 K.

(a) the temperature of B is 1934 K

(b) $\lambda_B = 1.5$ μm

(c) the temperature of B is 11604 K

(d) the temperature of B is 2901 K.

66. Two spheres A and B have same radius but heat capacity of A is greater than that of B. The surface of both one painted black. They are heated to the same temperature and allowed to cool then

(a) A cools faster than B

(b) Both A and B cools at the same rate

(c) B cools faster than A

(d) at any temperature the ratio of their rates of cooling is a constant.

67. A Spherical black body of radius 'r' radiates power 'P' and its rate of cooling is R then

(a) $P \propto r$ (b) $P \propto r^2$

(c) $R \propto r^2$ (d) $R \propto \frac{1}{r}$

68. A vessel is partly filled with a liquid. When the vessel is heated, the space in the vessel, unoccupied by the liquid remains constant. The volume of the liquid (V_L), Volume of the vessel (V_V), the coefficient of cubical expansion of the material of the vessel (γ_V) and of the liquid (γ_L) are related as

(a) $\gamma_L > \gamma_V$ (b) $\gamma_L < \gamma_V$

(c) $\gamma_V/\gamma_L = V_V/V_L$ (d) $\gamma_V/\gamma_L = \gamma_L/V_V$

69. Three bars each of length L are connected with the help of three springs as shown in fig. Coefficients of linear expansion of A,B and C are 2α, α and 4α respectively. The surface on which the arrangement is kept is smooth. If the temperature of rods have been increased by ΔT (assume there is no effect of change in temperature on springs), then mark out the correct statement (Assume that thermal stress is negligible

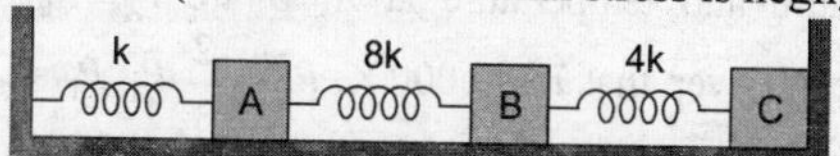

(a) The compression in spring having spring constant 8k is $(7/11)\alpha\, L\Delta T$

(b) The force exerted by C on the wall is $(56/11)\alpha k\, L\Delta T$

(c) The compression in all the three springs are different

(d) The compression in all the three springs is same.

70. A bimetallic strip is formed out two identical strips one of copper and the other of brass. The coefficient of linear expansion of the two metals are α_C and α_B. On heating, the temperature of the strip goes up by ΔT and the strip bends to form an arc of radius of curvature R. Then R is

(a) proportional to ΔT

(b) inversely proportional to ΔT

(c) proportional to $|\alpha_B - \alpha_C|$

(d) inversely proportional to $|\alpha_B - \alpha_C|$

71. When the temperature of a copper coin is raised by 80°C, its diameter increase by 0.2% Then.

(a) percentage rise in the area of a face is 0.4%

(b) percentage rise in the thickness is 0.4%

(c) percentage rise in the volume is 0.6%

(d) coefficient of linear expansion of copper is 0.25×10^{-4}/°C.

72. The temperature of an isotropic cubical solid of length L, density d and coefficient of expansion α per degree kelvin is raised by 10°C. Then, at this temperature, to good approximation

(a) length is $L(1 + 10\alpha)$

(b) total surface area is $6L_2(1 + 20\alpha)$

(c) density is $d(1 + 30\alpha)$

(d) density is $d/(1 + 30\alpha)$.

73. A metallic circular disc having a circular hole at its centre rotates about an axis is passing through its centre and perpendicular to its plane. When the disc is heated

(a) its angular velocity will decrease

(b) its diameter will decrease

(c) its moment of inertia will increase

(d) its speed will increase.

74. Due to thermal expansion with rise in temperature,

(a) metallic scale reading becomes less than the actual value

(b) pendulum clock becomes slow

(c) a floating body may sink if $\gamma_{liquid} > \gamma_{body}$

(d) a floating body may sink if $\gamma_{liquid} < \gamma_{body}$

Directions (Q. 75 to 77) : Solids and liquids both expand on heating. The density of substance decreases on expanding according to the relation $\rho_2 = \frac{\rho_1}{1+\gamma(T_2 - T_1)}$ where, ρ_1 and ρ_2 are the densities of substance at temperatures T_1 and T_2 respectively, when a solid is submerged in a liquid, the liquid exerts an upward force on solid which is equal to the weight of liquid displaced by submerged part of solid. Solid will float or sink depends on relative densities of solid and liquid.

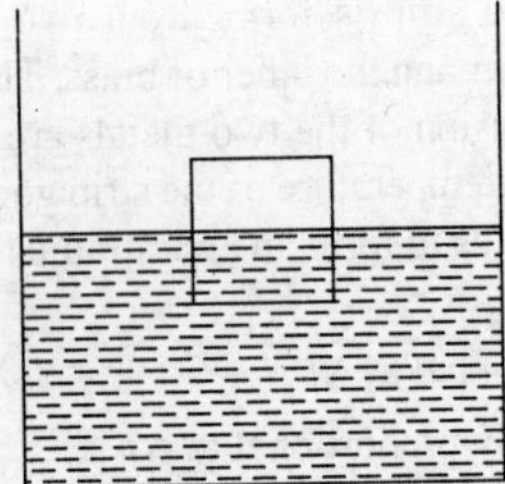

A cubical block of solid at temperature T floats in a liquid with half of its volume submerged in liquid as shown in figure. It is given that

α_s = coefficient of linear expansion of solid

γ_L = coefficient of volume expansion of solid

ρ_s = density of solid at temperature T

ρ_L = density of liquid at temperature T

75. The relation between densities of solid and liquid at temperature T is

(a) $\rho_s = 2\rho_L$ (b) $\rho_s = (1/2)\rho_L$

(c) $\rho_s = \rho_L$ (d) $\rho_s = (1/4)\rho_L$

76. If temperature of system increases, then fraction of solid submerged in liquid.

(a) increases (b) decreases

(c) remains unchanged (d) insufficient information

77. Imagine fraction submerged does not both change on increasing temperature. The relation between γ_L and α_s is.

(a) $\gamma_L = 3\alpha_s$ (b) $\gamma_L = 2\alpha_s$

(c) $\gamma_L = 4\alpha_s$ (d) $\gamma_L = (3/2)\alpha_s$.

Directions (Q. 78 to 79) : An ideal gas (monoatomic) is confined in a cylinder by a spring loaded piston of cross-section 8×10^{-3} m^2. Initially the gas is at 300 K and occupies a volume of 2.4×10^{-3} m^3 and spring is in its relaxed position. The gas is heated by a small electric heater until the piston moves out slowly by 0.1m force constant of spring is 8000 N/m and atmospheric pressure is 1×10^5 N/m^2.

78. The final temperature of the gas is

(a) 400 K (b) 350 K

(c) 800 K (d) 700 K

79. The heat supplied by the heater in joule is

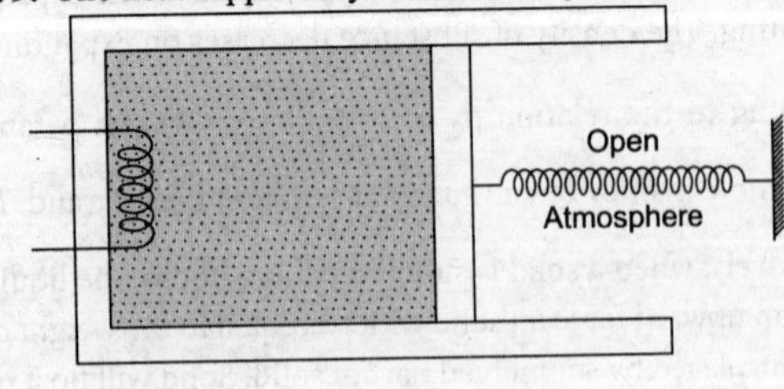

(a) 720 J (b) 520 J

(c) 620 J (d) 320 J

Directions (Q. 80 to 82) : Two moles of helium gas ($\gamma = 5/3$) are initially at temperature 27°C and occupy a volume 20 litre, The gas is first expanded at constant pressure until its volume is doubled. Now it undergoes an adiabatic change until the temperature back to its initial value.

80. The process on $P - V$ diagram is

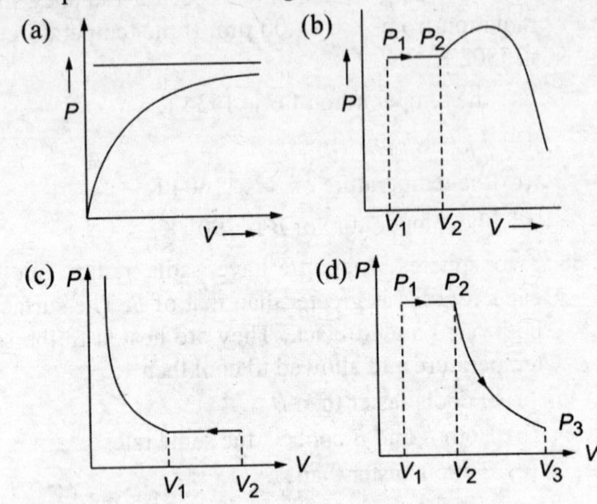

81. The final volume of gas will be

(a) 210.12×10^{-3} m^3 (b) 113.12×10^{-3} m^3

(c) 213.4×10^{-3} m^3 (d) 2.13×10^{-3} m^3

82. The find pressure of the gas will be.

(a) 0.11×10^5 N/m^2 (b) 0.22×10^5 N/m^2

(c) 0.33×10^5 N/m^2 (d) 0.44×10^5 N/m^2

Directions (Q. 83 to 85) : One mole of monoatomic ideal gas is taken through a cyclic process as shown in fig.

$A \to B$ adiabatic expansion

$B \to C$ Cooling at constant Volume

$C \to D$ adiabatic compression

$D \to A$ heating at constant volume.

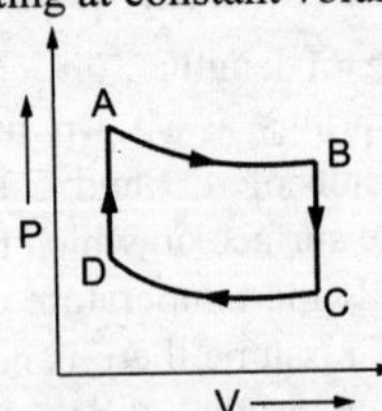

The pressure and temperature at A, B are P_A, T_A, P_B, T_B respectively. Given that $T_A = 1000$ K, $P_B = \frac{2}{3} P_A$, $P_C = \frac{1}{3} P_A$.

$(2/3)^{2/5} = 0.85$ and $R = 8.31$ J/mol K.

83. The work done by the gas in the process $A \to B$ will be

(a) 1869.75 J (b) 1069.75 J

(c) 1569.75 J (d) 1950.75 J

84. The heat lost by the gas in the process $B \to C$ will be.

(a) 5367.6 J (b) 5297.6 J

(c) 4237.6 J (d) 830.6 J

85. The temperature at D will be

(a) 400 K (b) 300 K

(c) 500 K (d) 200 K

Directions (Q. 86 to 89) : Two moles of an ideal monoatomic gas is taken through cyclic process ($ABCA$) such that pressure is inversely proportional to temperature.

The temperature $T = 300$ k.

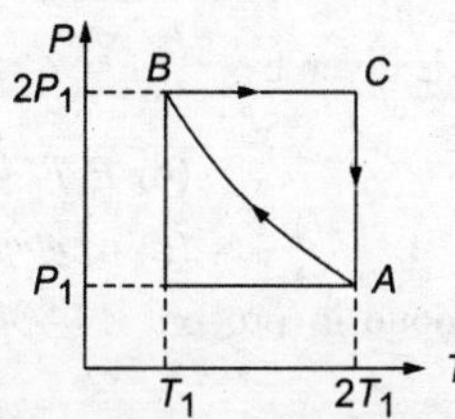

86. The work done on the gas in the process AB will be

(a) –1200 R (b) –600 R

(c) 1200 R (d) 600 R

87. Heat energy absorbed or released by the gas during the process AB will be

(a) –2100 R (b) 2100 R

(c) 1450 R (d) –1450 R

88. Heat energy absorbed or released by the gas during the process BC will be

(a) 300 R (b) 600 R

(c) 900 R (d) 1500 R

89. Heat energy absorbed or released during the process CA will be

(a) 831.6 R (b) 931.6 R

(c) 10.31 R (d) –831.6 R

Directions (Q. 90 to 92) : Two moles of a monoatomic ideal gas occupy a volume V at 27°C. The gas is expanded adiabtically to volume $2\sqrt{2}\ V$. Gas constant $R = 8.3\ \text{JK}^{-1}\ \text{mol}^{-1}$.

90. The final temperature of the gas is

(a) $\frac{150}{\sqrt{2}}$ K (b) 150 K

(c) 150°C (d) 13.6°C

91. The change in the internal energy of the gas in this process is

(a) –3735 J (b) 1245 J

(c) –2490 J (d) +3735 J

92. The work done by the gas during the process is

(a) 1245 J

(b) 1660 J

(c) 2490 J

(d) 3735 J

Directions (Q. 93 to 95) : A sample of 2 kg of monoatomic helium (assumed ideal) is taken through the process ABC and another sample of 2 kg of the same gas is taken through the process ADC as shown in Fig. The molecular mass = 4 and R = 8.3 J K^{-1} mol^{-1}.

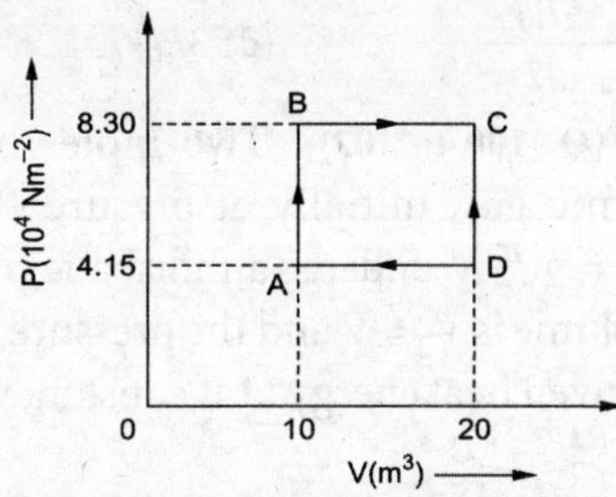

93. The temperature of state A is

(a) 100 K (b) 200 K

(c) 300 K (d) 415 K

94. The temperature state B is

(a) 150 K (b) 200 K

(c) 415 K (d) 830 K

95. The temperature of state C is

(a) 150 K (b) 300 K

(c) 400 K (d) 415 K

Directions (Q. 96 to 99) : One mole of an ideal monoatomic gas is taken round the cyclic process $ABCA$ as shown in fig.

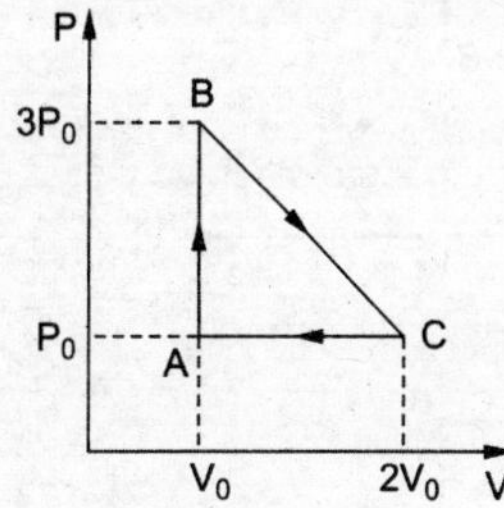

96. The work done by the gas is

(a) P_0V_0 (b) $2P_0V_0$

(c) $3P_0V_0$ (d) $4P_0V_0$

97. The heat energy rejected by the gas in the process $C \rightarrow A$ is

(a) $-\frac{P_0V_0}{2}$ (b) $-\frac{3P_0V_0}{2}$

(c) $-\frac{5P_0V_0}{2}$ (d) $-3P_0V_0$

98. The heat energy absorbed by the gas in the process $A \rightarrow B$ is

(a) P_0V_0 (b) $\frac{3P_0V_0}{2}$

(c) $\frac{5P_0V_0}{2}$ (d) $3P_0V_0$

99. The net heat energy rejected or absorbed by the gas in the process $B \to C$ is

(a) $\frac{P_0V_0}{2}$ (b) $-2P_0V_0$

(c) $-\frac{5P_0V_0}{2}$ (d) $3P_0V_0$

Directions (Q. 100 to 102) : Two moles of an ideal monoatomic gas, initially at presure $P_1 = P$ and volume $V_1 = 2\sqrt{2}\ V$, undergo an adiabatic compression until its volume is $V_2 = V$ and the pressure is P_2. Then the gas is given heat energy Q at constant volume V_2.

(a)

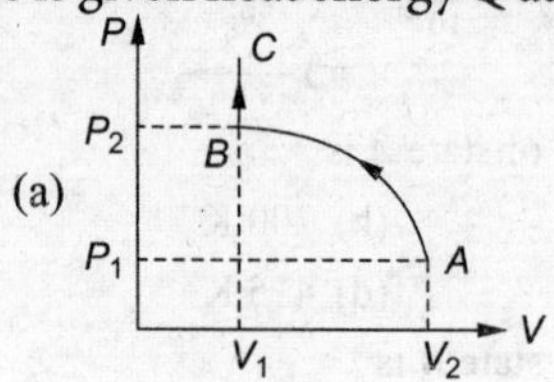

(b)

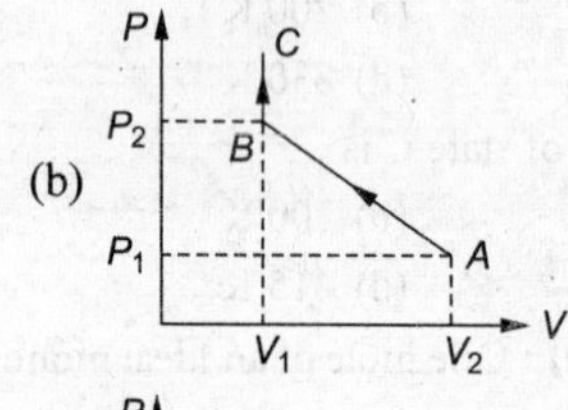

(c)

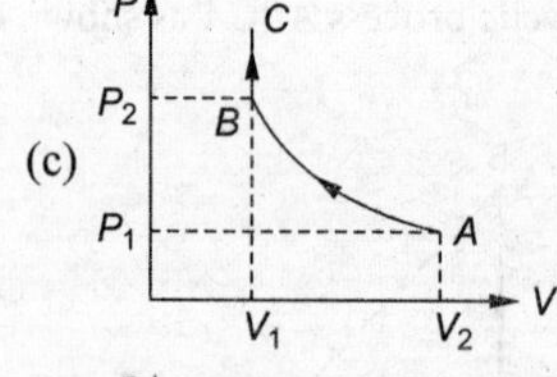

(d)

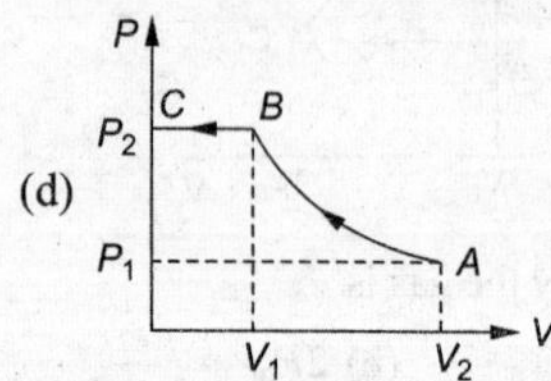

100. Which of the graphs shown in Fig. represents the $P-V$ diagram of the complete process.

101. Pressure P_2 is

(a) $\sqrt{2}\ P$ (b) $2\ P$

(c) $2\sqrt{2}\ P$ (d) none of these

102. The total work done by the gas is

(a) $-PV$ (b) $-2\sqrt{2}\ PV$

(c) $-3\sqrt{2}\ PV$ (d) $-3PV$

Directions (Q. 103 to 105) : Two moles of an ideal mono-atomic gas is taken through cycle $ABCA$ as shown in the P-T diagram During the process AB, pressure and temperature of the gas vary such that $PT = K$, where K is constant.

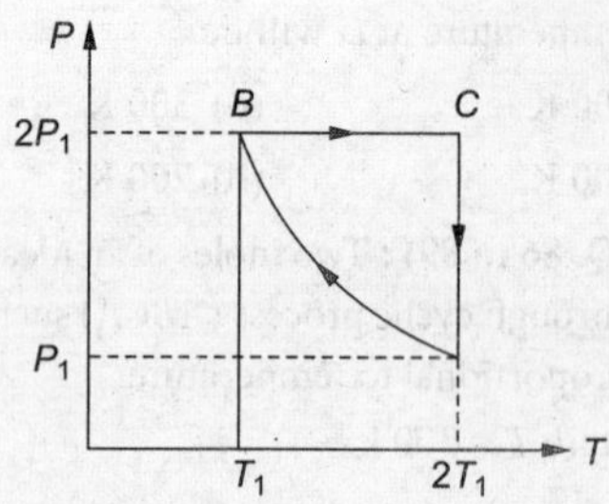

103. Constant K is given by

(a) $\frac{P_1T_1}{2}$ (b) P_1T_1

(c) $2P_1T_1$ (d) $\sqrt{2}P_1T_1$

104. The work done in process $A \to B$ is (R is the gas constant)

(a) $-RT_1$ (b) $-2RT_1$

(c) $-3RT_1$ (d) $-4RT_1$

105. The heat energy released in process $A \to B$ is

(a) $-3RT_1$ (b) $-5RT_1$

(c) $-7RT_1$ (d) $-9RT_1$

Directions (Q. 106 to 108) :

Stellar Spectra: Like the solar spectrum, the spectra of stars show a continuous spectrum on which dark aborption lines are superimposed. The inner layer (called the photosphere) of the star emits radiations of all wavelengths, producing a continuous spectrum. When these radiations pass through the outer, relatively cooler, layer of the star, the radiations of certain wavelength are selectively absorbed by this layer. This explains the dark lines in the spectrum of a star. The dark lines are characteristics of the substance present in the outer layer of the star.

The surface temperature T of a star can be estimated by measuring the wavelengths λ_m at which the intensity of the emitted radiation is maximum and then using Wien's displacement law which states that

$$\lambda_m \times T = b$$

where b is a constant called Wien's constant and the above relation is called Wien's Displacement Law which states that as the temperature increases, the maximum intensity of emission shifts (or is displaced) towards the shorter wavelengths. The value of constant b has been found experimentally to be 2.89×10^{-3} mK.

106. The spectrum of light received from a star is a

(a) continuous emission spectrum

(b) emission line spectrum

(c) emission band spectrum

(d) absorption line spectrum

107. The dark lines in the solar spectrum are due to the

(a) absence of corresponding wavelength from the light emitted by the core of the sun

(b) absorption of corresponding wavelengths by the outer layers of the sun

(c) absorption of corresponding wavelengths by the prism used in the spectrograph

(d) destructive interference between waves of certain definite wavelengths

108. The study of dark lines in the spectra of stars has revealed that the atmospheres of stars contains

(a) oxygen (b) nitrogen

(c) uranium (d) helium

Directions (Q. 109 to 111) : Three cylindrical rods *A*, *B* and *C* of equal lengths and equal diameters are joined in series as shown in the following figure. Their thermal conductivities are 2 *k*, *k* and 0.5 *k* respectively.

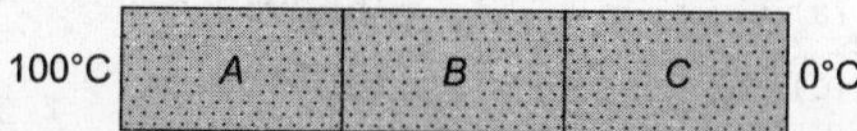

In the steady state, the free ends of rods *A* and *C* are at 100°C and 0°C respectively. Neglect loss of heat from the curved surfaces of rods.

109. The temperature of the junction between rods *A* and *B* is

(a) 55.7°C (b) 65.7°C

(c) 75.7°C (d) 85.7°C

110. The temperature of the junction between rods *B* and *C* is

(a) 57.1°C (b) 47.1°C

(c) 37.1°C (d) 27.1°C

111. The equivalent thermal conductivity of the combination is

(a) $\frac{7k}{3}$ (b) $\frac{2k}{7}$

(c) $\frac{5k}{3}$ (d) $\frac{3k}{5}$

112. An external pressure p is applied on a cube at 0°C so that it is equally compressed from all sides. K is the bulk modulus of the material of the cube and α is its coefficient of linear expansion. Suppose we want to bring the cube to its original size by heating. The temperature should be raised by

(a) $\frac{p}{\alpha K}$ (b) $\frac{3\alpha}{pK}$

(c) $3pK\alpha$ (d) $\frac{p}{3\alpha K}$

113. A pendulum clock loses 12 s a day if the temperature is 40°C and gains 4 s a day if the temperature is 20°C. The temperature at which the clock will show correct time, and the coefficient of linear expansion α of the metal of the pendulum shaft are, respectively.

(a) 25°C, $\alpha = 1.85 \times 10^{-5}$/°C

(b) 60°C, $\alpha = 1.85 \times 10^{-4}$/°C

(c) 30°C, $\alpha = 1.85 \times 10^{-3}$/°C

(d) 55°C, $\alpha = 1.85 \times 10^{-2}$/°C

114. The ends Q and R of two thin wires, PQ and RS, are soldered (joined) together. Initially, each of wire has a length of 1 m 10°C. Now, the end P is maintained at 10°C, while the end S is heated and maintained at 400°C. The system is thermally insulated from its surroundings. If the thermal conductivity of wire PQ is twice that of the wire RS and the coefficient of linear thermal expansion of PQ is 1.2×10^{-5}K^{-1}, the change in length of the wire PQ is

(a) 0.78 mm (b) 0.90 mm

(c) 1.56 mm (d) 2.34 mm

115. Two identical beakers *A* and *B* contain equal volumes of two different liquids at 60°C each and left to cool down. Liquid in *A* has density of 8×10^2 kg/m^3 and specific heat of 2000J kg^{-1} k^{-1} while liquid in *B* has density of 10^3 kg m^{-3} and specific heat of 4000J kg^{-1} k^{-1}. Which of the following beat describes their temperature vtersus time graph schematically? (Assume the emissivity of both the beakers to be the same)

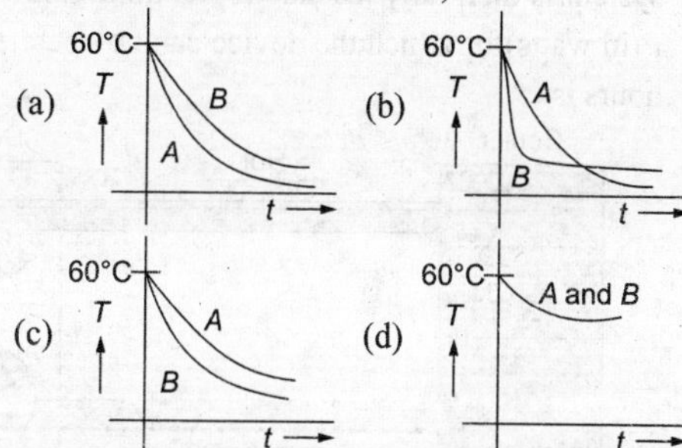

116. A thermally insulated vessel contains 150 g of water at 0°C. Then the air from the vessel is pumped out adiabatically. A fraction of water turns into ice and the rest evaporates at 0°C itself. The mass of evaporated water will be closest to :

(Latent heat of vaporization of water = 2.10×106 J kg^{-1})

(a) 35 g (b) 20 g

(c) 130 g (d) 150 g

117. Two moles of an ideal monoatomic gas occupies a volume V at 27°C. The gas expands adiabatically to a volume $2V$. Calculate (a) the final temperature of the gas and (b) change in its internal energy.

(a) (i) 189 K (ii) – 2.7 K

(b) (i) 195 K (ii) – 2.7 kJ

(c) (i) 189 K (ii) 2.7 kJ

(d) (i) 195 K (ii) – 2.7 kJ

118. C_p and C_v are specific heats at constant pressure and constant volume, respectively. It is observed that $C_p - C_v = a$ for hydrogen gas $C_p - C_v = b$ for nitrogen gas. The correct relation between a and b is

(a) $a = b$ (b) $a = 14b$

(c) $a = 28b$ (d) $a = \frac{1}{14}b$

119. A copper ball of mass 100 g is at a temperature *T*. It is dropped in a copper calorimeter of mass 100 g, filled with 170 g of water at room temperature. Subsequently, the temperature of the system is found to be 75°C. *T* is (Given, room temperature = 30°C, specific heat of copper = 0.1 cal/g°C)

(a) 885°C (b) 1250°C

(c) 825°C (d) 800°C

120. A water cooler of storage capacity 120 litres can cool water at a constant rate of *P* watts. In a closed circulation system (as shown schematically in the figure), the water from the cooler is used to cool an external device that generates constantly 3 kW of heat (thermal load). The temperature of water fed into the device cannot exceed 30°C and the entire stored 120 litres of water is initially cooled to 10°C. The entire system is thermally insulated. The minimum value of *P*(in watts)for which the device can be operated for 3 hours is

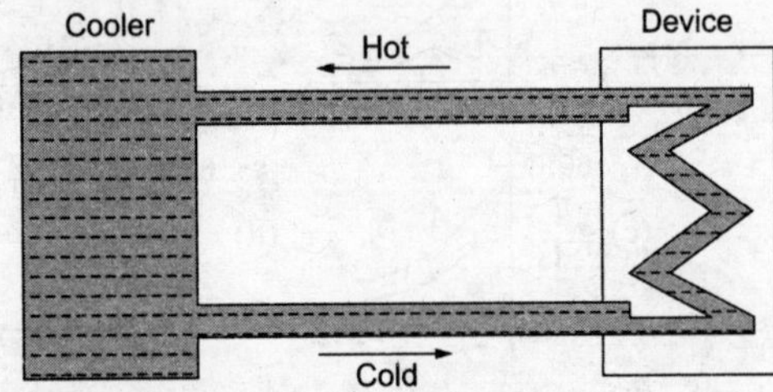

(Specific heat of water is 4.2 kJ kg^{-1}K^{-1} and the density of water is 1000 kg m^{-3})

(a) 1600 (b) 2067

(c) 2533 (d) 3933

121. *n* moles of an ideal gas undergoes a process *A* and *B* as shown in the figure. The maximum temperature of the gas during the process will be

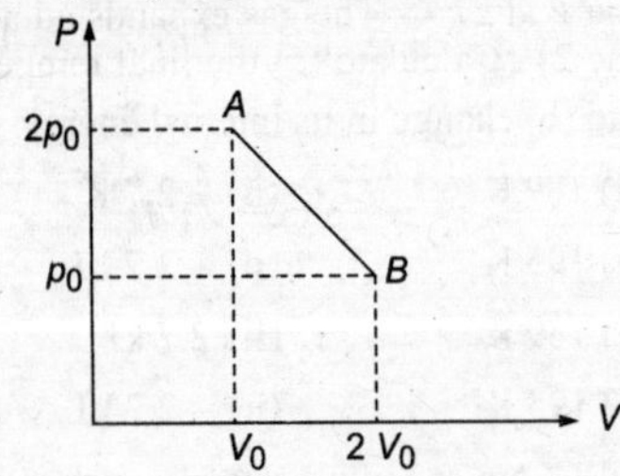

(a) $\frac{9p_0v_0}{4nR}$ (b) $\frac{3p_0v_0}{2\,nR}$

(c) $\frac{9p_0v_0}{2\,nR}$ (d) $\frac{9p_0v_0}{nR}$

122. A gas is enclosed in a cylinder with a movable frictionless piston. Its initial thermodynamic state at pressure p_i = 10^5 pa and volume V_1 = 10^{-3} m^3 changes to a final state at P_f = (1/32) × 10^5 pa and V_f = 8 × 10^{-3}m^3 in adiabatic Quasi–static process, such that p^3V^5 = constant. Consider another thermodynamic process that brings the system from the same initial state to the same final state in two steps: an isobaric expansion at p_i followed by an isochoric (isovolumetric) process at volume V_f. The amount of heat supplied to the system in the two-step process is approximately

(a) 112 J (b) 294 J

(c) 588 J (d) 813 J

123. Consider a spherical shell of radius *R* at temperature *T*. The black body radiation inside it can be considered as an ideal gas of photons with internal energy per unit volume $u = \frac{U}{V} \propto T^4$ and pressure $p = \frac{1}{3}\left(\frac{U}{V}\right)$.

If the shell now undergoes an adiabatic expansion, the relation between *T* and *R* is

(a) $T \propto e^{-R}$ (b) $T \propto \frac{1}{R}$

(c) $T \propto e^{-3R}$ (d) $T \propto \frac{1}{R^3}$

124. A solid body of constant heat capacity 1 J/°C being heated by keeping it in contact with reservoirs in two ways

(i) Sequentially keeping in contact with 2 reservoirs such that each reservoir supplies same amount of heat

(ii) Sequentially keeping in contact with 8 reservoirs such that each reservoir supplies same amount of heat.

In both the cases, body is brought from initial temperature 100°C to final temperature 200°C. Entropy change of the body in the two cases respectively, is

(a) In (2), In 2 (b) In 2, 2 In 2

(c) 2 In 2, 8 In 2 (d) In 2, 4 In 2

125. One mole of diatomic ideal gas undergoes a cyclic process *ABC* as shown in figure. The process *BC* is adiabatic. The temperature at *A*, *B* and *C* are 400 K, 800 K and 600 K respectively. Choose the correct statement.

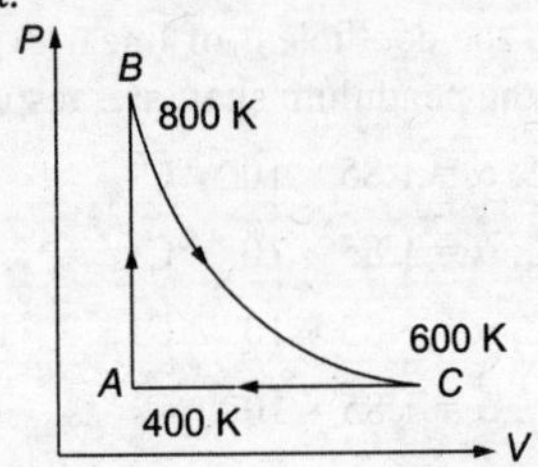

(a) The change in internal energy in whole cyclic process is 250 R

(b) The change in internal energy in the process CA is 700 R

(c) The change in internal energy in the process AB is –350 R

(d) The change in internal energy in the process BC is – 500 R

126. The shown p-V diagram represents the thermodynamic cycle of an engine, operating with an ideal monoatomic gas. The amount of heat, extracted from the source in a single cycle is

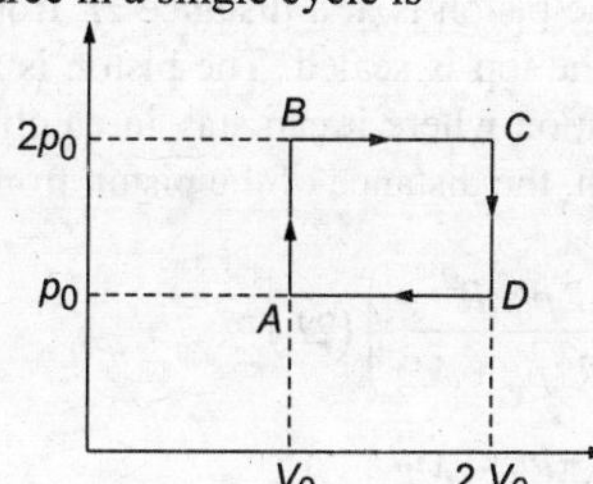

(a) p_0V_0 (b) $\left(\frac{13}{2}\right) p_0V_0$

(c) $\left(\frac{11}{2}\right) p_0V_0$ (d) $4\,P_0V_0$

127. One mole of a monoatomic ideal gas is taken along two cyclic processes $E \to F \to G \to E$ and $E \to F \to H \to E$ as shown in the p–V diagram.

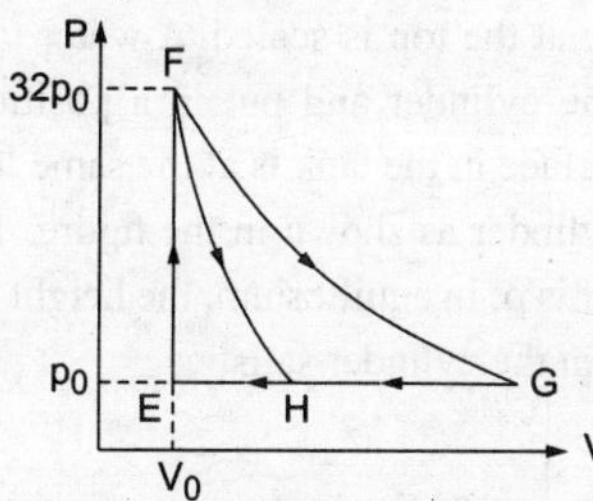

The processes involved are purely isochoric, isobaric, isothermal or adiabatic.

Match the paths in List I with the magnitudes of the work done in List II and select the correct answer using codes given below lists.

List I		List II	
P.	$G \to E$	1.	$160\, p_0V_0$ In 2
Q.	$G \to H$	2.	$36\, p_0V_0$
R.	$F \to H$	3.	$24\, p_0V_0$
S.	$F \to G$	4.	$31\, p_0V_0$

Codes

	P	Q	R	S
(a)	4	3	2	1
(b)	4	3	1	2
(c)	3	1	2	4
(d)	1	3	2	4

128. Two moles of ideal helium gas are in a rubber balloon at 30°C. The balloon is expandable and can be assumed to require no energy in its expansion. The temperature of the gas in the balloon is slowly changed to 35°C. The amount of heat required in raising the temperature is nearly (take R = 8.31 J/mol-K)

(a) 62 J (b) 104 J

(c) 124 J (d) 208 J

129. 5.6 L of helium gas at STP is adiabatically compressed to 0.7 L. Taking the initial temperature to T_1, the work done in the process is

(a) $\frac{9}{8}RT_1$ (b) $\frac{3}{2}RT_1$

(c) $\frac{15}{8}RT_1$ (d) $\frac{9}{2}RT_1$

130. Calorie is defined as the amount of heat required to raise temperature of 1 g of water by 1°C and it is defined under which of the following conditions?

(a) From 14.5°C to 15.5°C at 760 mm of Hg

(b) From 98.5°C to 99.5°C at 760 mm of Hg

(c) From 13.5°C to 14.5°C at 76 mm of Hg

(d) From 3.5°C to 4.5°C at 76 mm of Hg

131. Water of volume 2 L in a container is heated with a coil of 1 kW at 27°C. The lid of the container is open and energy dissipates at rate of 160 J/s. In how much time temperature will rise from 27°C to 77°C?

[Specific heat of water is 4.2 kJ/kg]

(a) 8 min 20 s

(b) 6 min 2 s

(c) 7 min

(d) 14 min

132. Liquid oxygen at 50 K is heated to 300 K at constant pressure of 1 atm. The rate of heating is constant. Which of the following graphs represent the variation of temperature with time?

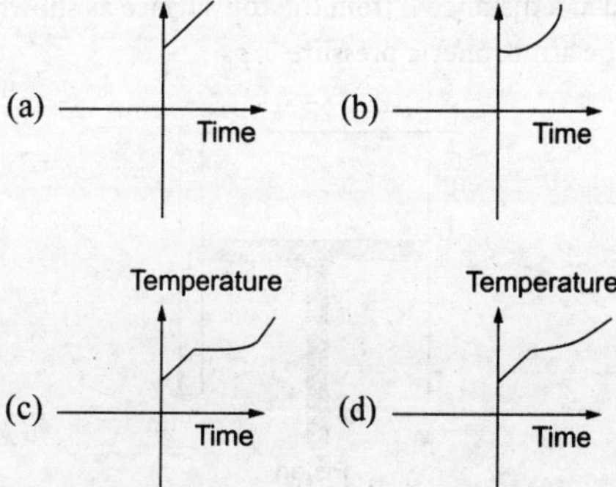

Directions (Q. 210 to 211)

In the figure a container is shown to have a movable (without friction) piston on top. The container and the piston are all made of perfectly insulating material allowing no heat transfer between outside and inside the container. The container is divided into two compartments by a rigid partition made of a thermally conducting material that allows slow transfer of heat.

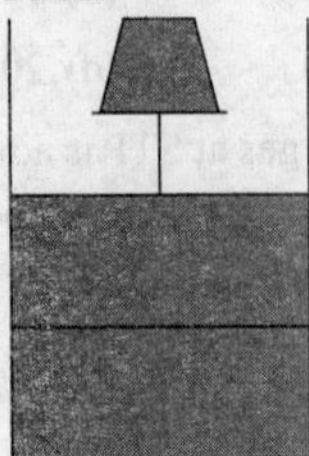

The lower compartment of the container is filled with 2 moles of an ideal monoatomic gas at 700 K and the upper compartment is filled with 2 moles of an ideal diatomic gas at 400 K. The heat capacities per mole of an ideal monoatomic gas are $C_v = \frac{3}{2}R$, $C_p = \frac{5}{2}R$, and those for ideal diatomic gas are $C_v = \frac{5}{2}R$, $C_p = \frac{7}{2}R$.

133. Consider the partition to be rigidly fixed so that it does not move. When equilibrium is achieved, the final temperature of the gases will be

(a) 550 K (b) 525 K

(c) 513 K (d) 490 K

134. Now consider the partition to be free to move without friction so that the pressure of gases in both compartments is the same. Then total work done by the gases till the time they achieve equilibrium will be

(a) 250 R (b) 200 R

(c) 100 R (d) – 100 R

Directions (Q. 212 to 214) : A fixed thermally conducting cylinder has a radius R and height L_0. The cylinder is open at its bottom and has a small hole at its top. A piston of mass M is held at a distance L from the top surface as shown in the figure. The atmospheric pressure is p_0.

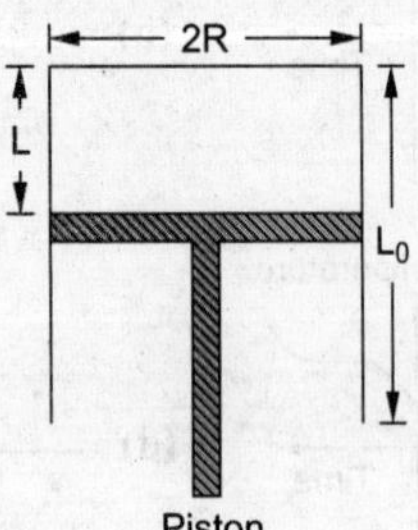

135. The piston is now pulled out slowly and held at a distance $2L$ from the top. The pressure in the cylinder between its top and the piston will then be

(a) p_0

(b) $\frac{p_0}{2}$

(c) $\frac{p_0}{2} + \frac{Mg}{\pi R^2}$

(d) $\frac{p_0}{2} - \frac{Mg}{\pi R^2}$

136. While the piston is at a distance $2L$ from the top, the hole at the top is sealed. The piston is then released, to a position where it can stay in equilibrium. In this condition, the distance of the piston from the top is

(a) $\left(\frac{2p_0\pi R^2}{\pi R^2 p_0 + Mg}\right)(2L)$

(b) $\left(\frac{p_0\pi R^2 - Mg}{\pi R^2 p_0}\right)(2L)$

(c) $\left(\frac{p_0\pi R^2 + Mg}{\pi R^2 p_0}\right)(2L)$

(d) $\left(\frac{p_0\pi R^2}{\pi R^2 p_0 - Mg}\right)(2L)$

137. The piston is taken completely out of the cylinder. The hole at the top is sealed. A water tank is brought below the cylinder and put in a position so that the water surface in the tank is at the same level as the top of the cylinder as shown in the figure. The density of the water is ρ. In equilibrium, the height H of the water column in the cylinder satisfies

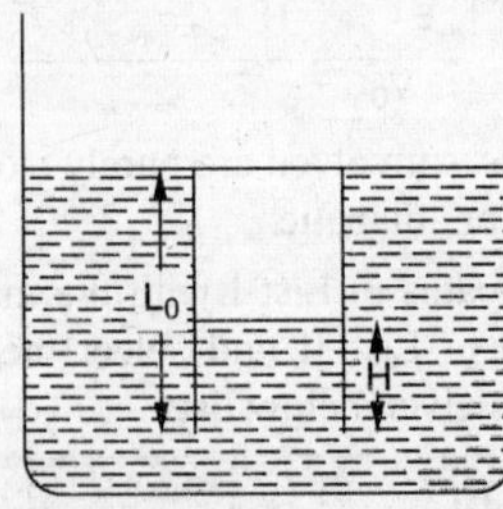

(a) $\rho g(L_0 - H)^2 + p_0(L_0 - H) + L_0 p_0 = 0$

(b) $\rho g(L_0 - H)^2 - p_0(L_0 - H) - L_0 p_0 = 0$

(c) $\rho g(L_0 - H)^2 + p_0(L_0 - H) - L_0 p_0 = 0$

(d) $\rho g(L_0 - H)^2 - p_0(L_0 - H) + L_0 p_0 = 0$

Directions (Q. 216 to 218) : An ideal gas undergoing a cyclic thermodynamic process in different ways as shown in the corresponding p–V diagrams in column 3 of the table. Consider only the path from state 1 to state 2. W denotes the corresponding work done on the system. The equations and plots in the table have standards notations and used in thermodynamic processes. Here γ is the ratio of heat capacities at constant pressure and constant volume. The number of moles in the gas is n.

Column 1		Column 2		Column 3	
(i)	$W_{1\to 2} = \frac{1}{\gamma - 1}(P_2V_2 - P_1V_1)$	(i)	Isothermal	(P)	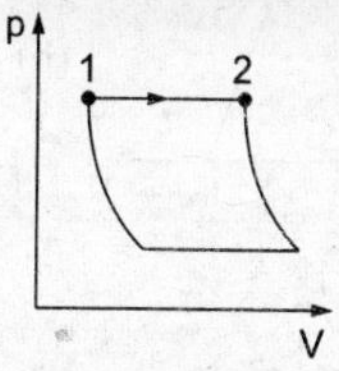
(ii)	$W_{1\to 2} = -pV_2 + pV_1$	(ii)	Isochoric	(Q)	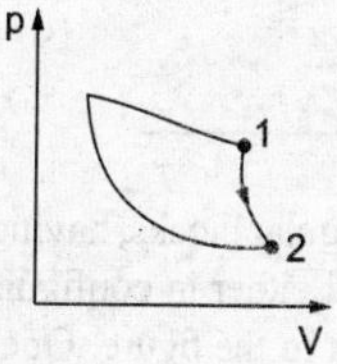
(iii)	$W_{1\to 2} = 0$	(iii)	Isobaric	(R)	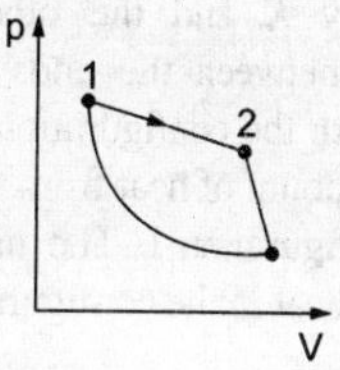
(iv)	$W_{1\to 2} = -nRT\ln\left(\frac{V_2}{V_1}\right)$	(iv)	Adiabatic	(S)	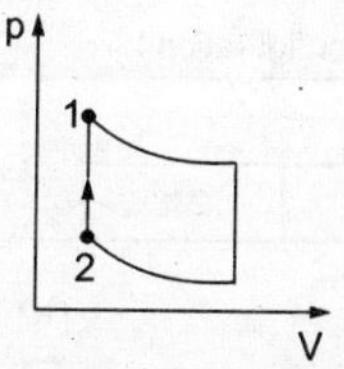

138. Which one the following options correctly represents a thermodynamic process that is used as a correction in the determination of the speed of sound in an ideal gas?

(a) (iv) (ii) (R) (b) (i) (ii) (Q)

(c) (i), (iv) (Q) (d) (iii) (iv) (R)

139. Which of the following options is the only correct representation of a process in which $\Delta U = \Delta Q - p\Delta V$?

(a) (ii) (iii) (S) (b) (ii) (iii) (S)

(c) (iii), (iii) (P) (d) (ii) (iv) (R)

140. Which one of the following options is the correct combination?

(a) (ii) (iv) (P) (b) (iii) (ii) (S)

(c) (ii) (iv) (R) (d) (iv) (ii) (S)

141. A heat source at $T = 10^3$ K is connected to another heat reservoir at $T = 10^2$ K by a copper slab which is 1 m thick. Given that the thermal conductivity of copper is 0.1 WK^{-1}m^{-1}, the energy flux through it in the steady state is :

(a) 90 Wm^{-2} (b) 120 Wm^{-2}

(c) 65 Wm^{-2} (d) 200 Wm^{-2}

142. Parallel rays of light of intensity $I = 912$ Wm^{-2} are incident on a spherical black body kept in surroundings of temperature 300 K. Take stefan constant $\sigma = 5.7 \times 10^{-8}$ Wm^{-2} K^{-4} and assume that the energy exchange with the surroundings is only through radiation. The final steady state temperature of black body is close to

(a) 330 K (b) 660 K

(c) 990 K (d) 1550 K

143. Three rods of copper, brass and steel are welded together to form a Y–shaped structure. Area of cross-section of each rod is 4 cm^2. End of copper rod is maintained at 100°C whereas ends of brass and steel are kept at 0°C. Lengths of the copper, brass and steel rods are 46, 13 and 12 cm respectively.

The rods are thermally insulated from surroundings except at ends. Thermal conductivities of copper, brass and steel are 0.92, 0.26 and 0.12 in CGS units, respectively. Rate of heat flow through copper rod is

(a) 1.2 cal/s (b) 2.4 cal/s

(c) 4.8 cal/s (d) 6.0 cal/s

144. If a piece of metal is heated to temperature θ and then allowed to cool in a room which is at temperature θ_0. The graph between the temperature T of the metal and time t will be closed to

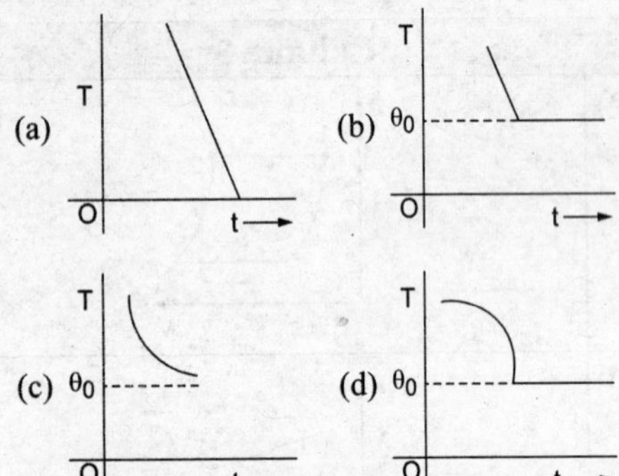

145. Two rectangular blocks, having identical dimensions, can be arranged either in configuration I or in configuration II as shown in the figure. One of the blocks has thermal conductivity K and the other $2K$. The temperature difference between the ends along the X-axis is the same in both the configurations. It takes 9 s to transport a certain amount of heat from the hot end to the cold end in the configuration I. The time to transport the same amount of heat in the configuration II is

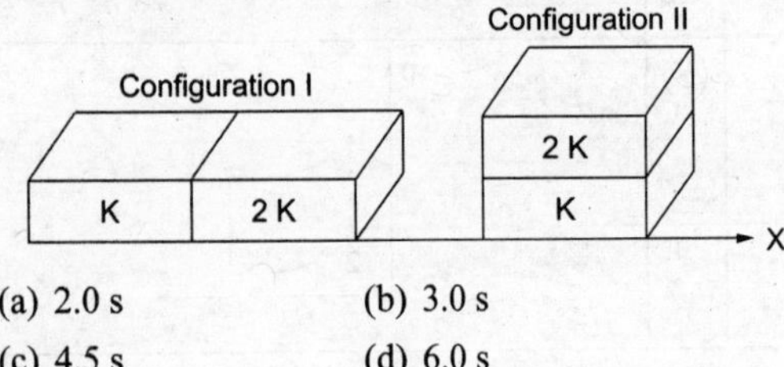

(a) 2.0 s (b) 3.0 s

(c) 4.5 s (d) 6.0 s

146. Three very large plates of same area kept parallel and close to each other. They are considered as ideal black surfaces and have very high thermal conductivity. The first and the third plates are maintained at temperature $2T$ and $3T$ respectively. The temperature of the middle (i.e. second) plate under steady state condition is

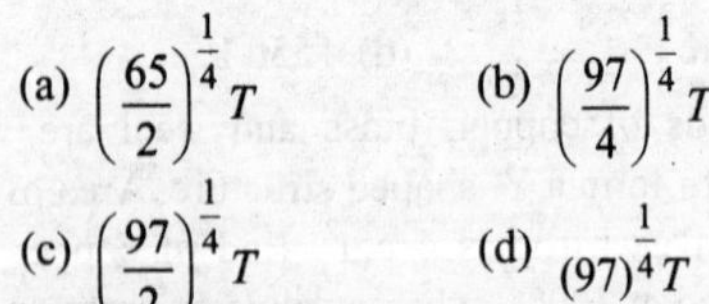

(a) $\left(\frac{65}{2}\right)^{\frac{1}{4}} T$ (b) $\left(\frac{97}{4}\right)^{\frac{1}{4}} T$

(c) $\left(\frac{97}{2}\right)^{\frac{1}{4}} T$ (d) $(97)^{\frac{1}{4}} T$

147. Variation of radiant energy emitted by sun, filament of tungsten lamp and welding arc as a function of its wavelength is shown in figure. Which of the following option is the correct match?

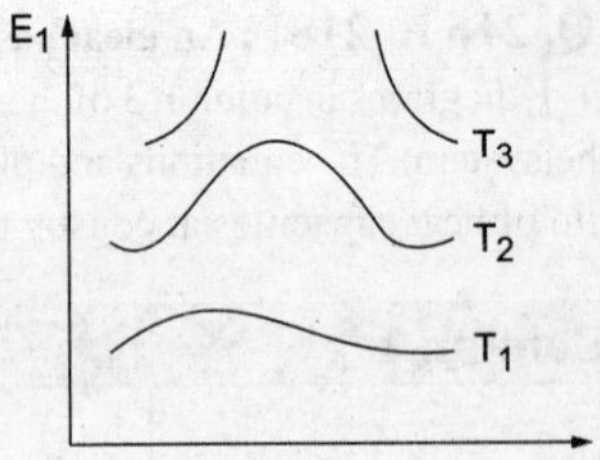

(a) Sun–T_1, tungsten filament–T_2, welding arc–T_3

(b) Sun–T_2, tungsten filament–T_1, welding arc–T_3

(c) Sun–T_3, tungsten filament–T_2, welding arc–T_1

(d) Sun–T_1, tungsten filament–T_3, welding arc–T_2

148. In which of the following process, convection does not take place primarily?

(a) Sea and land breeze

(b) Boiling of water

(c) Warming of glass of bulb due to filament

(d) Heating air around a furnace

149. Three discs, A, B and C having radii 2 m, 4 m and 6 m respectively are coated with carbon black on their outer surfaces. The wavelengths corresponding to maximum intensity are 300 nm, 400 nm and 500 nm, respectively. The power radiated by them are Q_A, Q_B and Q_C respectively

(a) Q_A is maximum (b) Q_B is maximum

(c) Q_C is maximum (d) $Q_A = Q_B = Q_C$

150. Two identical conducting rods are first connected independently to two vessels, one containing water at 100°C and the other containing ice at 0°C. In the second cases, the rods are joined end to end and connected to the same vessels. Let q_1 and q_2 gram per second be the rate melting of ice in the two cases respectively. The ratio $\frac{q_1}{q_2}$ is

(a) $\frac{1}{2}$ (b) $\frac{2}{1}$

(c) $\frac{4}{1}$ (d) $\frac{1}{4}$

151. If 10^{22} gas molecules each of mass 10^{-26} kg collide with a surface (perpendicular to it) elastically per second over an area 1 m^2 with a speed 10^4 m/s, the pressure exerted by the gas molecule will be of the order of :

(a) 4 N/m^2 (b) 2 N/m^2

(c) 3 N/m^2 (d) 6 N/m^2

152. The temperature of an open room of volume 30 m^3 increases from 17°C to 27°C due to the sunshine. The atmospheric pressure in the room of remains 1×10^5 pa. If n_i and n_f are the number of molecules in the room before and after heating, then $n_f - n_i$ will be

(a) 1.38×10^{23} (b) 2.5×10^{25}

(c) -2.5×10^{25} (d) -1.61×10^{23}

153. An ideal gas undergoes a quasi-static, reversible process in which its molar heat capacity C remains constant. If during this process the relation of pressure P and volume V is given by pV^n = constant, then n is given by (Here, C_p and C_v are molar specific heat at constant pressure and constant volume, respectively)

(a) $n = \frac{C_p}{C_v}$ (b) $n = \frac{C - C_p}{C - C_v}$

(c) $n = \frac{C_p - C}{C - C_v}$ (d) $n = \frac{C - C_v}{C - C_p}$

154. Two non-reactive monoatomic ideal gases have their atomic masses in the ratio 2 : 3. The ratio of their partial pressures, when enclosed in a vessel kept at a constant temperature, is 4 : 3. The ratio of their densities is

(a) 1 : 4 (b) 1 : 2

(c) 6 : 9 (d) 8 : 9

155. An ideal gas enclosed in a vertical cylindrical container supports a freely moving piston of mass M. The piston and the cylinder have equal cross–sectional area A. When the piston is in equilibrium the volume of the gas in V_0 and its pressure is p_0.The piston is slighting displaced from the equilibrium position and released. Assuming that the system is completely isolated from its surrounding, the piston executes a simple harmonic motion with frequency

(a) $\frac{1}{2\pi}\frac{A\gamma p_0}{V_0 M}$ (b) $\frac{1}{2\pi}\frac{V_0 M p_0}{A^2\gamma}$

(c) $\frac{1}{2\pi}\sqrt{\frac{A^2\gamma p_0}{MV_0}}$ (d) $\frac{1}{2\pi}\sqrt{\frac{MV_0}{A\gamma p_0}}$

156. A mixture of 2 moles of helium gas (atomic mass = 4 amu) and 1 mole of argon gas (atomic mass = 40 amu) is kept at 300 K in a container. The ratio of the rms speeds $\left(\frac{v_{\text{rms}}(\text{helium})}{v_{\text{rms}}(\text{argon})}\right)$ is

(a) 0.32 (b) 0.45

(c) 2.24 (d) 3.16

157. A real gas behaves like an ideal gas if its

(a) Pressure and temperature are both high

(b) Pressure and temperature are both low

(c) Pressure is high and temperature is low

(d) Pressure is low and temperature is high

158. An ideal gas is expanding such that pT^2 = constant. The coefficient of volume expansion of the gas is

(a) $\frac{1}{T}$ (b) $\frac{2}{T}$

(c) $\frac{3}{T}$ (d) $\frac{4}{T}$

Answers

1. (c)	**2.** (b)	**3.** (d)	**4.** (c)	**5.** (c)	**6.** (c)	**7.** (d)	**8.** (d)	**9.** (c)	**10.** (c)
11. (b)	**12.** (d)	**13.** (b)	**14.** (d)	**15.** (d)	**16.** (c)	**17.** (d)	**18.** (a)	**19.** (a)	**20.** (c)
21. (c)	**22.** (a)	**23.** (b)	**24.** (c)	**25.** (a)	**26.** (d)	**27.** (c)	**28.** (c)	**29.** (b)	**30.** (b)
31. (a)	**32.** (b)	**33.** (b)	**34.** (b)	**35.** (a)	**36.** (d)	**37.** (d)	**38.** (a)	**39.** (b)	**40.** (c)
41. (c)	**42.** (d)	**43.** (c)	**44.** (c)	**45.** (b)	**46.** (d)	**47.** (c)	**48.** (a)	**49.** (a)	**50.** (c)
51. (c)	**52.** (b)	**53.** (b)	**54.** (c)	**55.** (a,d)	**56.** (a,c)	**57.** (b,d)	**58.** (a,c)	**59.** (a,d)	**60.** (a,c)
61. (b,d)	**62.** (b,d)	**63.** (a,b)	**64.** (a,b,c,d)		**65.** (a,b)	**66.** (c,d)	**67.** (b,d)	**68.** (a,d)	**69.** (a,b,d)
70. (a,c)	**71.** (a,b,c)		**72.** (a,b,c)	**73.** (a,b,c)	**74.** (a,b,c)	**75.** (b)	**76.** (d)	**77.** (a)	**78.** (c)
79. (a)	**80.** (d)	**81.** (b)	**82.** (d)	**83.** (a)	**84.** (b)	**85.** (c)	**86.** (a)	**87.** (a)	**88.** (d)
89. (a)	**90.** (b)	**91.** (a)	**92.** (d)	**93.** (a)	**94.** (b)	**95.** (c)	**96.** (a)	**97.** (c)	**98.** (d)
99. (a)	**100.** (c)	**101.** (d)	**102.** (c)	**103.** (c)	**104.** (c)	**105.** (d)	**106.** (d)	**107.** (b)	**108.** (d)
109. (d)	**110.** (a)	**111.** (b)	**112.** (d)	**113.** (a)	**114.** (a)	**115.** (a)	**116.** (b)	**117.** (a)	**118.** (b)
119. (a)	**120.** (b)	**121.** (a)	**122.** (c)	**123.** (b)	**124.** (a)	**125.** (d)	**126.** (b)	**127.** (a)	**128.** (d)
129. (a)	**130.** (a)	**131.** (a)	**132.** (c)	**133.** (d)	**134.** (d)	**135.** (a)	**136.** (d)	**137.** (c)	**138.** (c)
139. (b)	**140.** (b)	**141.** (a)	**142.** (c)	**143.** (c)	**144.** (a)	**145.** (c)	**146.** (c)	**147.** (c)	**148.** (b)
149. (c)	**150.** (d)	**151.** (c)	**152.** (b)	**153.** (d)	**154.** (c)	**155.** (d)	**156.** (d)	**157.** (c)	**158.** (b,c,d)

Explanations

1. Here, $n_1 = 1$ mole, $n_2 = 1$ mole

For nitrogen, $C_{p_1} = \frac{7}{2}R$

For helium, $C_{p_2} = \frac{5}{2}R$

$$T_1 = T_0, T_2 = \frac{7}{3}T_0, T_f = ?$$

When gases are put into thermal contact, heat is exchanged between them till final temperature T_f is reached.

Now as we know that heat gain by Nitrogen = heat lost by helium

So, $n_1 C_{p_1}(T_f - T_i) = n_2 C_{p_2}(T_2 - T_f)$

$(n_1 C_{p_1} + n_2 C_{p_2}) T_f = n_2 C_{p_2} T_2 + n_1 C_{p_1} T_1$

$(1 \times \frac{7}{2}R + 1 \times \frac{5}{2}R) T_f$

$$= 1 \times 5/2\, R\, \frac{7}{3}T_0 + 1 \times \frac{7}{2}RT_0$$

$$6RT_f = \left(\frac{35}{6} + \frac{7}{2}\right) RT_0$$

$$T_f = \frac{56}{36}T_0 = \frac{14}{9}T_0$$

2. $C_p = \frac{7}{2}R$

$$C_v = C_p - R = \frac{7}{2}R - R = \frac{5}{2}R$$

$$\Upsilon = \frac{C_p}{C_v} = \frac{7/2R}{5/2R} = \frac{7}{5}$$

3. $v_{rms} = \sqrt{\frac{3RT_H}{M_H}} = \sqrt{\frac{3RT_{OXY}}{M_{OXY}}}$

$$\frac{T_H}{M_H} = \frac{T_{OXY}}{M_{OXY}}$$

or $T_H = T_{OXY}\frac{M_H}{M_{OXY}}$

$$= (47 + 273)\frac{2}{32} = \frac{320}{16} = 20 \text{ K}$$

4. Average $K.E.$ $(\bar{K}) = kT$

It depends on temperature and does not depend on molar mass.

$\therefore$ For both the gases, average translational kinetic energy will be same viz 0.048 eV.

5. $PV = nRT$

$$\frac{P_1}{P_2} = \frac{T_1}{T_2} \quad (\because V, n \text{ and } R \text{ are same})$$

$$\frac{P}{P_2} = \frac{T}{2T} \text{ or } P_2 = 2P$$

6. $PV = nRT = \frac{m}{M}RT$

where m = mass of the gas

and $\frac{m}{M} = n$ = number of moles.

$$\frac{PV}{T} = nR = a \text{ constant for all values of } P.$$

That is why, ideally it is a straight line.

$$\therefore \frac{PV}{T} = \frac{1\text{gm}}{32\text{gm}} \times 8.31 \text{ J mol}^{-1}\text{ K}^{-1}$$

$= 0.256$ JK^{-1}. Also, $T_1 > T_2$

7. Internal energy $= \frac{nfRT}{2}$

where n = number of mole of the gas

f = number of degree of freedom

$\therefore$ For 2 mole of oxygen, $U_0 = \frac{2 \times 5 \times RT}{2} = 5RT$

Again for 4 mole of argon, $U_a = \frac{4 \times 3 \times RT}{2} = 6RT$

$\therefore$ Total internal energy $= U_0 + U_a = 5RT + 6RT$

8. Average $K.E(\bar{K}) = \frac{3}{2}kT$

$$\frac{\bar{K_1}}{\bar{K_2}} = \frac{T_1}{T_2} \text{ or } \bar{K_2} = \frac{T_2}{T_1} \times \bar{K_1}$$

$$= \frac{600}{300} \times (6.21 \times 10^{-21})$$

or $\bar{K_2} = 12.42 \times 10^{-21}$ J ...(i)

$$v_{rms} = \sqrt{\frac{3kT}{m}}, \frac{v_2}{v_1} = \sqrt{\frac{T_2}{T_1}}$$

or $v_2 = \sqrt{\frac{T_2}{T_1}} \times v_1 = \sqrt{\frac{600}{300}} \times 484$

$= \sqrt{2} \times 484 = 1.414 \times 484$

$= 684$ m/s ...(ii)

$= 11RT$

9. Since on the other side of the partition vacuum is present offering no pressure; hence no work is done.

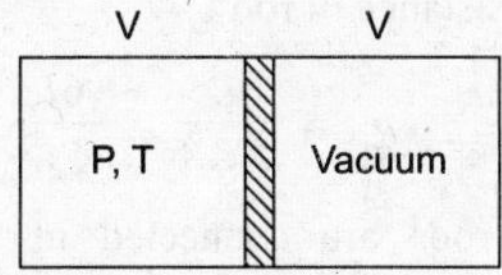

So, Heat supplied $\Delta\theta = 0$ [As vessel is insulating]

Work done $\Delta W = 0$

Hence $\Delta U = 0$

$$U_i = U_f$$

$$MC_V T_i = nC_V T_f$$

$$T_{\text{final}} = T_{\text{initial}}$$

Also $P_1V_1 = P_2V_2$

$$P_2 = \frac{P_1V_1}{V_2} = \frac{P_1V_1}{2V_1} = \frac{P_1}{2}$$

$$P_f = \frac{P_i}{2};\ T_f = T_i$$

10. Let R_1 and R_2 be the thermal resistance of inner and outer portions. Since, temperature difference at both ends is same, the resistance are in parallel. Hence,

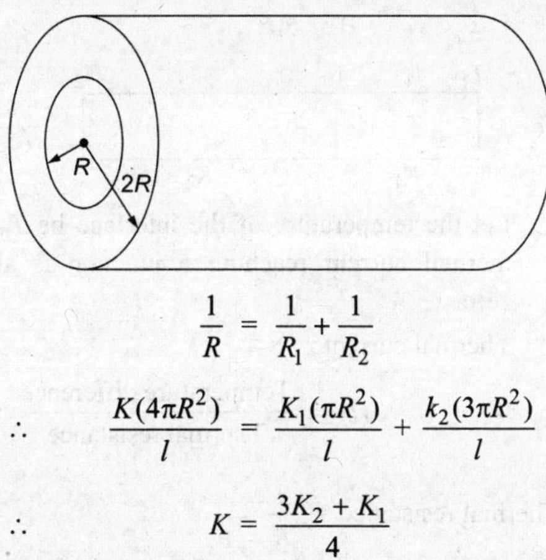

$$\frac{1}{R} = \frac{1}{R_1} + \frac{1}{R_2}$$

$$\therefore \quad \frac{K(4\pi R^2)}{l} = \frac{K_1(\pi R^2)}{l} + \frac{k_2(3\pi R^2)}{l}$$

$$\therefore \quad K = \frac{3K_2 + K_1}{4}$$

11. The diagrammatic representation of the given problem is shown in figure. Since, $T_B > T_A$ the heat will flow from B to A.

Similarly, heat will also flow from B to C and C to A.

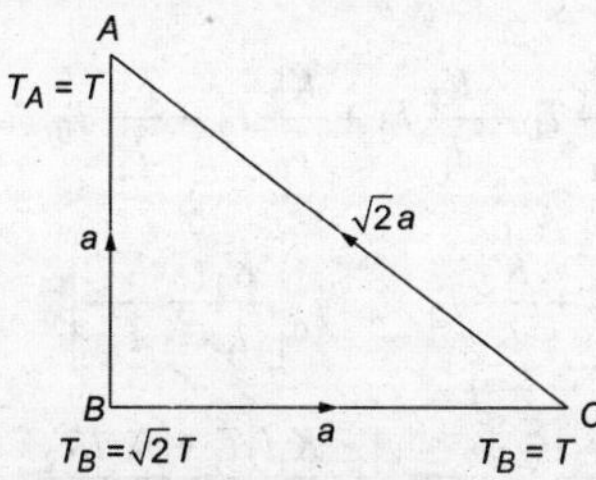

Applying the conduction formula

$$\frac{\Delta Q}{\Delta t} = \frac{KA}{l}(\Delta T)$$

$$= \left(\frac{\Delta T}{\sqrt{2}a}\right)_{CA} = \left(\frac{\Delta T}{a}\right)_{BC}$$

$$\Rightarrow \quad \frac{T_C - T}{\sqrt{2}a} = \frac{\sqrt{2}T - T_C}{a}$$

$$\Rightarrow \quad 3T = T_C(\sqrt{2} + 1)$$

$$\Rightarrow \quad \frac{T_C}{T} = \frac{3}{(\sqrt{2}+1)}$$

12. The rate at which energy radiates from the object is

$$\frac{\Delta Q}{\Delta t} = e\sigma AT^4$$

Since, $\Delta Q = mc\Delta T$, we get

$$\frac{\Delta T}{\Delta t} = \frac{e\sigma AT^4}{mc}$$

Also, since $m = \frac{4}{3}\pi r^3\rho$ for a sphere, we get

$$A = 4\pi r^2 = 4\pi\left(\frac{3m}{4\pi\rho}\right)^{2/3}$$

Hence, $\dfrac{\Delta T}{\Delta t} = \dfrac{e\sigma T^4}{mc}\left[4\pi\left(\dfrac{3m}{4\pi\rho}\right)^{2/3}\right] = K\left(\dfrac{1}{m}\right)^{1/3}$

For the given two bodies

$$\frac{(\Delta T/\Delta t)_1}{(\Delta T/\Delta t)_2} = \left(\frac{m_2}{m_1}\right)^{1/3} = \left(\frac{1}{3}\right)^{1/3}$$

13. From Wein's displacement law

$$\lambda_m T = \text{constant}$$

or $\quad T = \dfrac{1}{\lambda_m}$

$$\therefore \quad \frac{T_{\text{sun}}}{T_{\text{north star}}} = \frac{(\lambda_m)_{\text{north star}}}{(\lambda_m)_{\text{sun}}}$$

$$= \frac{350}{510} \approx 0.69$$

14. Power radiated (surface area) $(T)^4$. Thus radius is halved, hence, surface area will become $\frac{1}{4}$ times. Temperature is doubled, therefore, T^4 becomes 16 times.

New power = $(450)\left(\frac{1}{4}\right)(16) = 1800$ W.

15. Wien's displacement law is

$$\lambda_m T = b \qquad (b = \text{Wien's constant})$$

$$\lambda_m = \frac{b}{T} = \frac{2.88 \times 10^6 \text{ nm-K}}{2800 \text{ K}}$$

$$\lambda = 1000 \text{ nm}$$

Energy distribution with wavelength will be as follows:

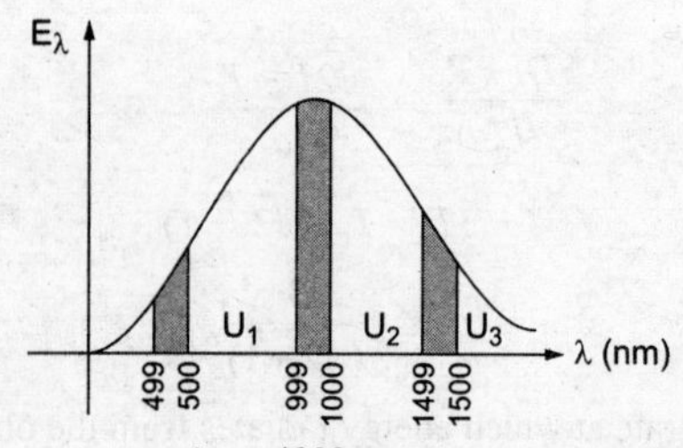

$\lambda_m = 1000$ nm

From the graph it is clear that

$$U_2 > U_1 \quad \text{(In fact } U_2 \text{ is maximum)}$$

16. According to Wein's displacement law

$$\lambda_m T = b = \text{Wein constant}$$

If v_m is the frequency corresponding to wavelength

λ_m then $\left(\dfrac{c}{v_m}\right) T = b$ or $v_m = \dfrac{c}{b} T$, i.e., $v_m \propto T$

$\therefore$ $v_m - T$ graph is a straight line shown by line C.

Thus, option (c) is true.

17. For black body radiation, $\lambda_m T$ = a constant = b or $\lambda_m \propto \dfrac{1}{T}$. The wavelength λ_m is less for curve T_1, more for curve T_3 and maximum for curve T_2.

Hence, $T_1 > T_3 > T_2$

18. According to Wein's displacement law

$$\lambda_m T = \text{a constant}$$

$$\therefore \quad \lambda_{m_2} T_2 = \lambda_{m_1} T_1$$

or

$$\lambda_{m_2} = \lambda_{m_1} \frac{T_1}{T_2}$$

$$= \frac{5000 \times (1227 + 273)}{(1500 + 1000)}$$

$$= 3000 \text{ Å}$$

19. Let L be the length and A be the area of cross-section of each rod. Given

$$K_B = 3K_c, K_B = \frac{1}{2} K_A$$

$$\therefore \quad K_C = \frac{1}{3} K_B = \frac{1}{3} \times \frac{1}{2} K_A = \frac{1}{6} K_A$$

Thermal resistance of rod A,

$$R_A = \frac{L}{K_A A}$$

Thermal resistance of rod B,

$$R_B = \frac{L}{K_B A} = \frac{2L}{K_A A}$$

Thermal resistance of rod C,

$$R_C = \frac{L}{K_C A} = \frac{6L}{K_A A}$$

Here, the rods are connected in series. If K is effective thermal conductivity of the system, and R_S is the total thermal resistance of the system then $R_S = R_A + R_B + R_C$

$$\therefore \quad \frac{3L}{KA} = \frac{L}{K_A A} + \frac{2L}{K_A A} + \frac{6L}{K_A A}$$

$$= \frac{9L}{K_A A}$$

or

$$\frac{3}{K} = \frac{9}{K_A} \text{ or } K = \frac{K_A}{3}$$

20. Let θ be the temperature of junction

$$\frac{KA(60° - \theta)}{x} + \frac{KA(70° - \theta)}{x} = \frac{KA(\theta - 20°)}{x}$$

$$60° - \theta + 70° - \theta = \theta - 20°$$

$$\theta = 50°$$

21.

T_1 l_1 T_0 l_2 T_2

K_1 K_2

Let the temperature of the interface be T_0. The thermal current reaching a junction is always zero.

Thermal current

$$(I) = \frac{\text{Temperature difference}}{\text{Thermal resistance}}$$

$$\text{Thermal resistance} = \frac{1}{K} \frac{1}{A}$$

Applying it on the interface T_0, we get

$$\frac{T_1 - T_0}{\frac{1}{K_1} \frac{l_1}{A}} + \frac{T_2 - T_0}{\frac{1}{K_2} \frac{l_2}{A}} = 0$$

$$\Rightarrow \quad \frac{K_1}{l_1} T_1 - \frac{K_1}{l_1} T_0 + \frac{K_2}{l_2} T_2 - \frac{K_2}{l_2} T_0 = 0$$

$$\Rightarrow \quad \frac{K_1}{l_1} T_1 + \frac{K_2}{l_2} T_2 = T_0 \left[\frac{K_1}{l_1} + \frac{K_2}{l_2} \right]$$

$$\Rightarrow \quad T_0 = \frac{K_1 l_2 T_1 + K_2 l_1 T_2}{K_1 l_2 + K_2 l_1}$$

22. In steady state, the rate of flow of heat is constant and it is given as

$$\frac{dQ}{dt} = -KA \frac{d\theta}{dx}$$

$$\Rightarrow \quad \frac{d\theta}{dx} = \frac{1}{-KA}\left(\frac{dQ}{dt}\right)$$

Let $\frac{1}{KA}\left(\frac{dQ}{dt}\right) = B = A$ constant

$$\Rightarrow \quad \frac{d\theta}{dx} = -B$$

$$\Rightarrow \quad \int_{\theta_1}^{\theta_2} d\theta = -B\int_0^x dx$$

$$\Rightarrow \quad \theta_2 - \theta_1 = -Bx$$

$$\Rightarrow \quad \theta_2 = \theta_1 - Bx$$

$$\Rightarrow \quad \theta_2 = -Bx + \theta_1$$

The θ vs x graph will be a straight line with negative slope and positive intercept on y-axis.

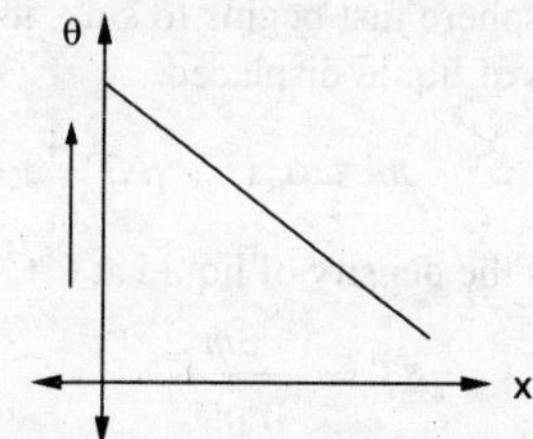

23. $\eta = \frac{W}{Q_1} = 1 - \frac{T_2}{T_1} \Rightarrow W = \left(\frac{T_1 - T_2}{T_1}\right)Q_1$

$$W = \frac{(627+273)-(27+273)}{(627+273)} \times 3\times10^6$$

$$= \frac{600}{900}\times3\times10^6 \text{cal} = 2\times10^6 \text{ cal}$$

$$= 8.4\times10^6 \text{J}$$

24. Coefficient of performance of Carnot refrigerator is given

by $\beta = \frac{Q_2}{W} = \frac{T_2}{T_1 - T_2}$

So $\frac{Q_2}{1} = \frac{273}{303-273}$

$$= \frac{273}{30} = 9.1 \text{ J}$$

Heat delivered to the surrounding

$$Q = Q_2 + W = 9.1 + 1 = 10.1 \text{ J}$$

25. $W = \int_{20}^{4} mCpdT = \int_{20}^{4} 0.1\left(32\frac{T^3}{400^3}\right)dT = 0.002$ kJ.

26. Heat gain by water = heat lost by steam

$$20\times1\times(80-10) = m\times540 + m\times1\times(100-80)$$

$$1400 = 560 \text{ m}$$

or $m = 2.5$ gm

Total mass of water = 20 + 2.5 = 22.5 gm

27. $\gamma_{\text{diatomic molecule}} = \frac{7}{5}$

Applying the adiabatic equation, i.e.,

$$T_1V_1^{\gamma-1} = T_2V_2^{\gamma-1}$$

$$T_1V^{2/5} = T_2(32V)^{2/5}$$

$$\frac{T_1}{T_2} = (32)^{2/5} = 4$$

Efficiency of a Carnot engine

$$= 1 - \frac{T_2}{T_1} = 1 - \frac{1}{4} = \frac{3}{4} = 0.75\%$$

28. As the question assumes no expansion, hence heat is supplied at constant volume; So heat supplied = change in internal energy.

Change in internal energy = $mS\Delta T$

$$= 0.1\times4184\times(50-30)$$

$$= 2\times4184 = 8368\text{J} = 8.4 \text{ kJ}$$

29. Let η is the efficiency of heat engine and β is the corresponding coefficient of performance of a refrigerator working between the same temperatures. The relation between η and β is

$$\beta = \frac{1}{\eta} - 1 = 10 - 1 = 9$$

Also $\beta = \frac{\text{Output}}{\text{Input}}$

$$= \frac{\text{Energy absorbed from the reservoir at lower temp.}}{\text{Work done on the system}}$$

$$\beta = 9 = \frac{\text{Energy absorbed}}{10 \text{ J}}$$

Hence, energy absorbed = 90 J

30. $\eta_1 = \frac{1}{6} = 1 - \frac{T_2}{T_1}$

$$\Rightarrow \quad \frac{T_2}{T_1} = 1 - \frac{1}{6} = \frac{5}{6} \qquad \text{...(i)}$$

$$\eta_2 = \frac{1}{3} = 1 - \frac{(T_2 - 62)}{T_1}$$

$$\Rightarrow \quad \frac{T_2 - 62}{T_1} = 1 - \frac{1}{3} = \frac{2}{3} \qquad \text{...(ii)}$$

On dividing equation (ii) by equation (i); we get

$$\frac{T_2 - 62}{T_2} = \frac{2}{3}\times\frac{6}{5} = \frac{4}{5}$$

$$5T_2 - 310 = 4T_2$$

$$T_2 = 310 \text{ K}$$

On replacing T_2 in equation number (i); we get

$$\frac{T_2}{T_1} = \frac{5}{6}$$

$$T_1 = \frac{6}{5}T_2 = \frac{6}{5} \times 310$$
$$= 6 \times 62 = 372 \text{ K}$$
$$T_1 = 372 \text{ K}$$
$$T_2 = 310 \text{ K}$$

31. Molecular mass of gas = M

Let these are N number of molecules;

Hence, total mass of the gas = NM

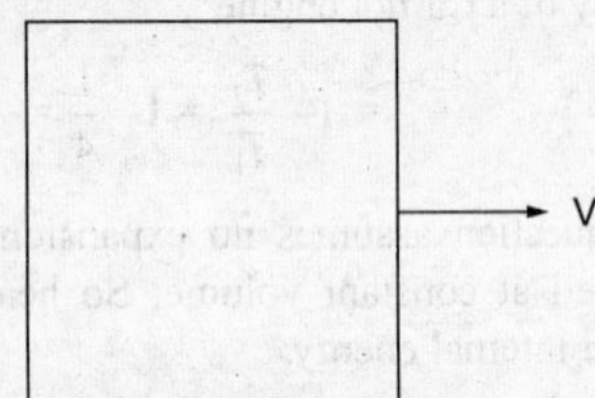

As the vehicle is brought to rest; the orderly kinetic energy for the gas becomes the disorderly kinetic energy of the molecules. It is this disorderly kinetic energy of the molecules which increases the temperature the gas.

Hence, $\frac{1}{2}(NM)v^2 = n\,C_v(\Delta T)$

$$\frac{1}{2}(NM)\,v^2 = \frac{N}{N_A}\left(\frac{R}{\gamma-1}\right)\Delta T$$

$$\Delta T = \left[\frac{1}{2}\frac{Mv^2(\gamma-1)}{R}\right]N_A$$

32. As C_V for hydrogen = $\frac{5}{2}R$ (diatomic)

C_V for helium = $\frac{3}{2}R$ (monoatomic)

$$C_V \text{ of mixture} = \frac{\frac{4}{2}\times\frac{5}{2}R+\frac{4}{2}\times\frac{3}{2}R}{4/2+4/2}$$
$$= \frac{(5+3)R}{4} = 2R$$
$$= 2 \times 2 \text{ cal/mol}$$

Hence, rise in temperature T will be

$$32 = 4 \times 4 \times T$$
$$T = 2°\text{C}$$

33. $\Delta LA = \alpha_A L\Delta T$ and $\Delta L_B = \alpha_B L\Delta T$

Let x be the length of metal A in the composite rod. Then, $\Delta L = \alpha_A x\,\Delta T + \alpha_B\,(L-x)\Delta T$

$$\Rightarrow \quad \Delta L = \frac{x\Delta L_A}{L}+(L-x)\frac{\Delta L_B}{L}$$

$$\Rightarrow \quad 0.065 \times 20 = x\,(0.075) + (20-x) \times 0.045$$

$$\therefore \quad x = 13.3 \text{ cm}$$

34. If n is number of seconds in a day and T is the time period of pendulum, then nT = constant.

$$\Rightarrow \quad n \times 2\pi\sqrt{\frac{1}{g}} = \text{constant}$$

$$\Rightarrow \quad \frac{\Delta n}{n}+\frac{1}{2}\frac{\Delta l}{l} = 0$$

$$\frac{\Delta n}{n} = -\frac{1}{2}\frac{\Delta l}{l} = -\frac{1}{2}\alpha\Delta\theta$$

Let θ be the temperature at which the clock gives correct time. Then, we have

$$\Rightarrow \quad \frac{5}{n} = -\frac{1}{2}\alpha(15-\theta)$$

$$\text{and} \quad \frac{-10}{n} = -\frac{1}{2}\alpha(30-\theta)$$

$$\Rightarrow \quad \frac{5}{-10} = \frac{15-\theta}{30-\theta}$$

$$\therefore \quad \theta = 20°\text{C}$$

35. When the sphere just begins to sink, its mass is equal to the mass of liquid displaced.

$$\Rightarrow \quad m = \rho_0\,(1-\gamma\Delta T)\frac{4}{3}\pi r^3$$

where ρ_0 is the density of liquid at 0°C temperature

$$\Rightarrow \quad 1-\gamma\Delta T = \frac{3m}{4\pi\rho_0 r^3}$$
$$= \frac{3+0.596}{4\pi\times(1.25\times10^3)\times0.049^3}$$
$$= 0.9675$$

$$\therefore \quad \gamma = \frac{1-0.9675}{40} = 8.1\times10^{-4}/°\text{C}$$

36. The apparent increase in length of the rod is

$$\Delta L = (\alpha_{cu}-\alpha_{steel})L\Delta T$$
$$= (1.7\times10^{-5}-1.2\times10^{-5}) \times 90 \times 20$$
$$= 9\times10^{-3} \text{ cm}$$
$$L + \Delta L = 90 + 0.009 = 90.009 \text{ cm}$$

Therefore, tape will read 90.01 cm

37. $$Y = \frac{F/A}{\Delta L/L}$$

$$\Rightarrow \quad F = AY\frac{\Delta L}{L} = AY\alpha\Delta T$$

$$F = \pi \times (10^{-3})^2 \times (0.91 \times 10^{11}) \times (2 \times 10^{-5}) \times 60$$
$$= 340 \text{ N}$$

38. $$T = 2\pi\sqrt{\frac{1}{g}}$$

$$\Rightarrow \quad \frac{\Delta T}{T} = -\frac{\Delta l}{l} = \frac{1}{2}\alpha\Delta\theta$$

If n is the number of second in 30 days,

$$\text{then} \quad nT = \text{constant} \; \frac{\Delta n}{n}+\frac{\Delta T}{T} = 0$$

$$\Delta n = -n\frac{\Delta T}{T} = -\frac{n}{2}a\Delta\theta$$

$$= -\frac{(30\times24\times3600)}{2}\times(\times10^{-7})\times10$$

$= -11.66$ sec.

39. The diameter (d) of iron tyre must be expanded by 6 mm.

Now, $Dd = adDT = (g/3)dDT.$

$$\Delta T = \frac{3\Delta d}{\gamma d} = \frac{3\times6\times10^{-3}}{3.6\times10^{-5}\times1} = 500°C$$

40. $\Delta L = \Delta L_1 + \Delta L_2$

$$\alpha(L_1+L_2)\Delta T = \alpha_1L_1\Delta T + \alpha_2L_2\Delta T$$

$$\alpha = \frac{\alpha_1L_1+\alpha_2L_2}{L}$$

41. $$Y = \frac{\sigma}{\Delta L/L} = \frac{\sigma}{\alpha\Delta T}$$

$$\Rightarrow \frac{Y_1}{Y_2} = \frac{a_2}{a_1} = \frac{3}{2}$$

42. Since the level does not change on heating

$$\gamma_{liquid} = \gamma_{vessel} = 3\alpha$$

43. (c) Let the actual temperature be T.

Then, $$\frac{T-0}{100-0} = \frac{59-5}{95-5}$$

$\therefore$ $T = 60°C$

44. (c): Let the actual temperature (x) $K = (x)°F$

Then, $\frac{5}{9}(x-32) + 273 = x$

$\therefore$ $x = 574.25$

45. Let the temperature of bath be x°C

Then, $3x = \frac{9}{5}x + 32$

$x = 80/3$

46. As $y > 1$ is not allowed so maximum value of γ should be 1

$$\gamma_{max} = 1$$

$$\gamma = \frac{\alpha(t_2-t_1)}{1+\alpha t_2} = 1$$

$$\alpha(t_2-t_1) = 1+\alpha t_2$$

$$\Rightarrow \alpha t_2 - \alpha t_1 = 1 + \alpha t_2$$

$$t_1 = -\frac{1}{\alpha}$$

47. $$\Delta C^2 = l^2 - \left(\frac{l}{2}\right)^2$$

$$= l^2(1+\alpha_2 t)^2 - \left[\frac{l}{2}(1+\alpha_1 t)\right]^2$$

Neglecting α_2^2 and α_1^2 and solving above we get $\alpha_1 = 4\alpha_2$

48. Let ρ_0, ρ_1 and ρ_2 be the densities of the liquid at temperatures t_0, t_1 and t_2 respectively.

To balance Pressure, $P_1l_1g = P_2l_2g$

or $$\left(\frac{\rho_o}{1+\gamma t_1}\right)l_1 = \left(\frac{\rho_o}{1+\gamma t_2}\right)t_2$$

$$l_1 + l_1\gamma t_2 = l_2 + l_2\gamma t_1$$

$$\gamma = \left(\frac{l_1-l_2}{l_2t_1-l_1t_2}\right)$$

49. $$K_1 = \frac{(d_{Fe})_0}{(d_{Hg})_0}$$

$$K_2 = \frac{(d_{Fe})_{60°}}{(d_{Hg})_{60°}} = \frac{\frac{(d_{Fe})_0}{1+\gamma_{Fe}60}}{\frac{(d_{Hg})_0}{1+\gamma_{Hg}60}}$$

$$\therefore \frac{K_1}{K_2} = \frac{1+60\gamma_{Fe}}{1+60\gamma_{Hg}}$$

50. $PV = nRT$

$PdV = nRdT$ (P = constant)

$$dV = \left(\frac{nR}{P}\right)dT$$

$$dV = \left(\frac{V}{T}\right)dT \quad ...(i)$$

Further $dV = \gamma V dt$ ...(ii)

From equation (i) and (ii) we get $\gamma = \frac{1}{T}$

51. x, r and t all increase.

52. If new radius is R'

then $R' = R(1+\alpha\theta)$

$$2\pi R' = 2\pi R + 2\pi R\alpha\theta$$

$\therefore$ Change in circumference $= 2\pi R' - 2\pi R = 2\pi R\alpha\theta$

53. $$L_1 = l_1[1+\alpha_1\Delta T]$$

$$L_2 = l_2[1+\alpha_2\Delta T]$$

$$L_1 - L_2 = (l_1 - l_2) + (\Delta T)(l_1\alpha_1 - l_2\alpha_2)$$

If $L_1 - L_2$ is to be independent of ΔT, then

$$l_1\alpha_1 - l_2\alpha_2 = 0$$

$$\Rightarrow \frac{l_1}{l_2} = \frac{\alpha_2}{\alpha_1}$$

54. Both will shown same expansion. Expansion of sphere does not depend on internal construction.

55. Isothermal curve from A to B will be parabolic with lesser area under the curve than the area under st. line AB. Therefore, work done by the gas in going straight from A to B is more. If P_o, V_o be the intercepts of the curve on P or V axis then from $y = mx + c$

$$p = \frac{P_o}{V_o}V + p_o$$

or $$\frac{RT}{V} = \frac{p_o V}{V_o} + p_o$$

$$T = \frac{p_o}{V_o R} V^2 + \frac{p_o V}{R}.$$

Hence $V - T$ curve is Parabola.

56. In an ideal gas, when P is constant, $V \propto T$ (Charle's Law) Choice (a) is correct.
Again, when V is constant, $P \propto T$ (Regnault's Law) Choice (c) is correct.

57. As face $ABCD$ has positive charge on it and the gas consists of ionized hydrogen, therefore, isotropy is lost. The usual expression for pressure on the basis of kinetic theory will not be valid as ions would also experience forces other than the forces due to collisions with the walls of container. Choices (b) and (d) are correct.

58. Since wavelength $|\lambda_0|$ becomes half, temperature will become double and power radiated will become 16 times

$\therefore \quad T = 2T$ and $P' = 16P$

59. $\lambda m = \frac{b}{T} = \frac{2.88 \times 10^{-3}}{2880} = 10{,}000$ Å, So maximum emission corresponds to wavelength around 10,000 Å

60. (a) According to Wien's displacement law ($\lambda_m T$ = Constant),
When temperature is made double, the wavelength corresponding to maximum emission becomes half and, therefore, frequency corresponding to maximum emission becomes double (i.e., $2V_m$).

61. (b) As $T_A > T$, the body A loses more heat than it absorbs. As $T > T_B$, the body B absorb more radiation then it emits.
(d) Even if the two bodies acquire temperature T, each body continues to emit and absorb heat.

62. Let T be the temperature of the contact surface
Then, in the steady state, we have

$$\frac{Q}{t} = \frac{K_A A(-10 - T)}{4.0} = \frac{K_B A(T - 10)}{6.0}$$

or $$\frac{K_A A(-10 - T)}{4} = \frac{K_B A(T - 10)}{6} \quad ...(1)$$

(a) If $K_A = K_B$, Eq. (1) gives $T_1 = -2°C$

(b) If $\frac{K_A}{K_B} = \frac{2}{3}$, Eq. (1) gives $T_2 = 0°C$

Thus the Correct choices are (b) and (d).

63. From Wein's law, $\lambda_{max}\, T = b$, Thus

$$T_1 = \frac{2.9 \times 10^{-3}}{7.8 \times 10^{-7}} = 3718 \text{ K}$$

$$T_2 = \frac{2.9 \times 10^{-3}}{6.2 \times 10^{-3}} = 4677 \text{ K}$$

So, the correct choice are (a) and (b)

64. To calculate temperature of B
Power of body $A = e_A \sigma T_A^4 \times$ (area)
Power of body $B = e_B \sigma T_B^4 \times$ (area)
The two powers are equal.

$\therefore \quad e_B \sigma T_B^4 \times \text{(area)} = e_A \sigma T_A^4 \times \text{(area)}$

or $$T_B^4 = \left(\frac{e_A}{e_B}\right) T_A^4$$

or $$T_B^4 = \left(\frac{0.01}{0.81}\right) \times (5802)^4$$

or $$T_B^4 = \left(\frac{1}{3}\right)^4 \times (5802)^4$$

or $$T_B = \left(\frac{5802}{3}\right)$$

or $T_B = 1934$ K Option (a) is correct.

(d) According to Wein's displacement law,

$$\lambda T = \text{constant } \lambda_A T_A = \lambda_B T_B$$

$$\frac{\lambda_A}{\lambda_B} = \frac{T_B}{T_A} = \frac{1934}{5802}$$

or $$\frac{\lambda_A}{\lambda_B} = \frac{1}{3} \text{ or } \lambda_B = 3\lambda_A$$

Given: $\lambda_B - \lambda_A = 1.0 \times 1.0^{-6}$ m

$3\lambda_A - \lambda_A = 10^{-6}$

or $2\lambda_A = 10^{-6}$ m

or $\lambda_A = 0.5 \times 10^{-6}$

and $\lambda_B = 3 \times 0.5 \times 10^{-6}$

or $\lambda_B = 1.5 \times 10^{-6}$ m.

Hence option (b) is correct
Options (c) and (d) are incorrect as option (a) is correct
Hence option (a) and (b) are correct.

65. At any temperature, they lose heat at the same rate

So $$\left(\frac{-d\theta}{dt}\right)_A = \left(\frac{-d\theta}{dt}\right)_B$$

or $$\frac{\left(\frac{-d\theta}{dt}\right)_A}{\left(\frac{-d\theta}{dt}\right)_B} = \text{Constant}$$

66. $$P = 4\pi r^2 \sigma T^4 = -mc\left(\frac{dT}{dt}\right)$$

$$= \frac{-4}{3} \pi r^3 \rho s \frac{dT}{dt}$$

Given $R = \frac{dT}{dt}$

$\therefore \quad P \propto r^2$ and $R \propto \frac{1}{r}$

67. If the space unoccupied by liquid remains the same, it means the expansion of both liquid and vessel is same at all temperature.

$\Rightarrow \quad \gamma_L V_L \Delta T = \gamma_V V_V \Delta T$

$\therefore \quad \gamma_V/\gamma_L = V_L/V_V$

Also since $V_V > V_L$, we have $\gamma_L > \gamma_L$

68. Let the springs of constant k,$8k$ and $4k$ be compressed by x_1, x_2 and x_3 respectively.

Then $x_1 + x_2 + x_3 = 2\alpha L\Delta T + \alpha L\Delta T + 4\alpha L\Delta T = 7\alpha L\Delta T$

The force F exerted by block C on the wall and force developed in all the springs in equal.

$\Rightarrow \quad kx_1 = 8kx_2 = 4kx_3$

$\Rightarrow \quad \frac{x_1}{8} = x_2 = \frac{x_3}{2} = C \text{ (say)}$

Then, $\quad x_1 = 8C, x_2 = C, x_3 = 2C$

$\Rightarrow \quad 8C + C + 2C = 7\alpha L\Delta T$

$\Rightarrow \quad C = \frac{7\alpha L\Delta T}{11}$

$\therefore \quad x_1 = \frac{56\,\alpha L\Delta T}{11}$

$x_2 = \frac{7\alpha L\Delta T}{11}$

$x_3 = \frac{28L\Delta T}{11}$

$F = kx_1 = \frac{56\,\alpha KL\Delta T}{11}$

69.

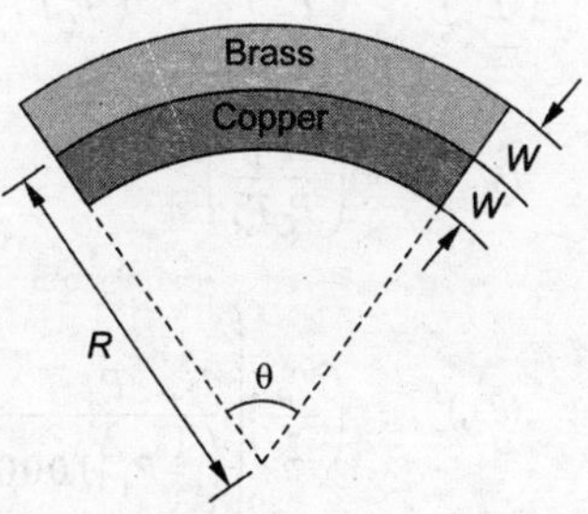

If W is the width of each strip and L_0 is their original length, then

$$\left(R + \frac{W}{2}\right)\theta = L_0(1 + \alpha_B \Delta T)$$

$$\left(R - \frac{W}{2}\right)\theta = L_0(1 + \alpha_C \Delta T)$$

On subtracting 2nd equation from 1st equation, we get

$$W\theta = L_0(\alpha_B - \alpha_C)\Delta T$$

Since, $\theta = L_0/R$, where have $R = \frac{W}{(\alpha_B - \alpha_C)\Delta T}$

$\therefore R \propto \frac{1}{|\alpha_B - \alpha_C|}$ and $R \propto \frac{1}{\Delta T}$

70. $\frac{\Delta d}{d} = \alpha\Delta T = 0.2\%$

$\therefore \quad \alpha = \frac{0.2}{100} \times \frac{1}{80}$

$= 0.25 \times 10^{-4}/°C$

$\frac{\Delta A}{A} = 2\alpha\Delta T = 0.4\%$

$\frac{\Delta V}{V} = 3\alpha\Delta T = 0.6\%$

71. New length $L' = L(1 + \alpha\Delta T) = L(1 + 10\alpha)$

New surface are, $A' = A(1 + 2\alpha\Delta T) = 6L^2\,(1 + 20\alpha)$

New density. $\quad d' = \frac{d}{1 + 3\alpha\Delta T} = \frac{d}{1 + 30\alpha}$

72. On heating, diameter will increase.

Hence, moment of inertia will increase.

Since, $I\omega$ = constant angular velocity will decreased

75. $\rho_s Vg = \rho_L(V/2) \quad \therefore g\rho_s(1/2)\rho_L$

76. The fraction of solid submerged in liquid depends on whether $\gamma_L > 3\alpha_s$ or $\gamma_L < 3\alpha_s$

77. If $\gamma_L = 3\alpha_s$, there is no change in fraction submerged.

78. $P_I = P_0 = 1 \times 10^5\ \text{N/m}^2$,

$V_I = V_0 = 2.4 \times 10^{-3}\ \text{m}^3$,

$T_I = T_0\ 300\ \text{k}$.

Finally, $\quad P_F = P_0 + \frac{Kx}{A}$

$= 1 \times 10^5 + \frac{8000 \times 0.1}{8 \times 10^{-3}}$

$= 2 \times 10^5\ \text{N/m}^2$

$V_F = V_0 + Ax$

$= 2.4 \times 10^{-3} + 0.1 \times 8 \times 10^{-3}$

$= 3.2 \times 10^{-3}\ \text{m}^3$.

Now from gas equation

$$\frac{P_I V_I}{T_I} = \frac{P_F V_F}{T_F}$$

$$T_F = \frac{P_F}{P_I} \times \frac{V_F}{V_I} \times T_I$$

$$= \frac{2 \times 10^5}{1 \times 10^5} \times \frac{3.2 \times 10^{-3}}{2.4 \times 10^{-3}} \times 300$$

$= 800\ \text{K}$

79. We known that $dw = \int PdV, P = P_0 + \frac{Kx}{A}$

$$dw = \int_0^{0.1} \left(P_0 + \frac{kx}{A}\right) A\,dx = \int_0^{0.1} (P_0 A + Kx)\,dx$$

$$= P_0Ax + \frac{1}{2}Kx^2$$

$$= 10^5 \times 8 \times 10^{-3} \times 0.1 + \frac{1}{2} \times 8000 \times (0.1)$$

$$= 80 + 40 = 120 \text{ J.}$$

Here 80 J of work is done against atmosphere and 40 J against spring

Now, $dU = nc_v\, dT$

$$= \frac{nRdT}{y-1} = \frac{P_FV_F - P_IV_I}{y-1}$$

$$= \frac{(2\times10^5)(3.2\times10^{-3})-(1\times10^5)\times(2.4\times10^{-3})}{5/3-1}$$

$$\Delta U = \frac{3}{2}\times10\,[6.4-2.4] = 600 \text{ J}$$

Hence total heat supplied

$$Q = dU + dW$$

$$= 600+120 = 720 \text{ J}$$

80. As the process is partly isobaric expansion and partly adiabatic

81. As for isobaric process P = constant

$$\frac{T_2}{T_1} = \frac{V_2}{V_1} = \frac{2V}{V} = 2$$

$$T_2 = 2T_1 = 2\times300 = 600\ k \quad ...(1)$$

Now $T_2V_2^{\gamma-1} = T_3V_3^{\ \gamma-1}$

$T_3 = T_1\ 300$ K, $T_2 = 600$ K, $V_2 = 40\times10^{-3}\text{m}^3$

$$V_3 = 40\times10^{-3}\times\left(\frac{600}{300}\right)^{3/2} = 113.12\times10^{-3}\ \text{m}^3.$$

82. $P_3V_3 = nRT_3$

So, $$P_3 = \frac{2\times8.3\times300}{113.12\times10^{-3}}$$

$$= 0.44\times10^5\ \text{N/m}^2$$

83. As we know that adiabatic relation between pressure and temperature is $\frac{T^\gamma}{P^{\gamma-1}}$ = constant

So, $\left(\frac{T_B}{T_A}\right)^\gamma = \left(\frac{P_B}{P_A}\right)^{\gamma-1}$ with $\gamma = 5/3$

$$T_B = T_A\left(\frac{2}{3}\right)^{1-\frac{1}{\gamma}}$$

$$= 1000\left(\frac{2}{3}\right)^{2/5} = 850 \text{ K} \quad ...(i)$$

Hence, work done $= \frac{nR(T_I - T_F)}{\gamma-1}$

$$= \frac{1\times8.31\,(1000-850)}{5/3-1}$$

$$= \frac{3}{2}\times8.31\times150 = 1869.75 \text{ J}$$

84. For the process $B \to C$, V = Constant, So $dW = 0$

Now from first law of thermodynamics

$$dQ = dU + dW = nC_VdT + 0$$

$$dQ = 1\times\frac{3}{2}R(T_C - 850)$$

Here, $P \propto T$

$$\frac{P_C}{P_B} = \frac{T_C}{T_B}$$

$$\therefore \quad T_C = \frac{\frac{1}{3}P_A}{(2/3)P_A}\times T_B = \frac{T_B}{2}$$

$$= \frac{850}{2} = 425 \text{ K} \quad ...(ii)$$

$$dQ = 1\times\frac{3}{2}\times8.31\,(425-850)$$

$$= -5297.6 \text{ J.}$$

Negative sign refers that heat is lost.

85. Here A and D lie at same isochoric

So, $\frac{P_D}{P_A} = \frac{T_D}{T_A}$, $P_D = P_A\times\frac{T_D}{T_A}$

B and C lie on the same adiabatic

$$\left(\frac{T_D}{T_C}\right)^y = \left(\frac{P_D}{P_C}\right)^{y-1} = \left(\frac{P_AT_D}{P_CT_A}\right)^{y-1}$$

$$(T_D)^{1/y} = \left(\frac{P_A}{P_CT_A}\right)^{1-\frac{1}{y}}$$

$$(T_D)^{3/5} = \left(\frac{T_B}{2}\right)\left(\frac{P_A}{\left(\frac{1}{3}P_A\right)1000}\right)^{2/5}$$

$$(T_D)^{3/5} = \frac{1}{2}\left(\frac{2}{3}\right)^{2/5}\times1000\times\left(\frac{3}{1000}\right)^{2/5},$$

$$T_D = 500 \text{ K}$$

86. $W = \int PdV$

$$PV = nRT$$

On differentiating

$$PdV + VdP = nRdT$$

According to question along AB

$$PT = \text{constant}$$

So, $PdT + TdP = 0$

$$dP = -\frac{PdT}{T}$$

$$\text{Hence, } PdV + V\left(-\frac{PdT}{T}\right) = nRdT$$

$$PdV + \left(\frac{-nRTdT}{T}\right) = nRdT$$

$$PdV = 2nRdT$$

$$W_{AB} = \int_{2T_1}^{T_1} 2nRdT = -2nRT_1$$

$$= -2 \times 2R \times 300 = -1200R \text{ Joule}$$

87. $$(dQ)_{AB} = dU + dW = nC_V dT + dW$$

$$= -2 \times \frac{3R}{2} \times 300 - 1200R = -2100R$$

88. $$dQ = 2 \times \frac{3R}{2} \times 300 + 2P_1(V_C - V_B)$$

$$V_C = \frac{nR_2T_1}{2P_1},\ V_B = \frac{nRT_1}{2P_1}$$

$$V_C - V_B = \frac{nR2T_1}{2P_1}$$

$$(dQ)_{BC} = 900R + 2P_1 \times \frac{nRT_1}{2P_1}$$

$$= 900R + 2 \times R \times 300 = 1500R$$

89. $$(dQ)C_A = 2 \times \frac{3R}{2} \times 0 + nR(2T_1)\log e^{V_A/V_C}$$

$$= 2nRT_1 \log e \frac{P_C}{P_A} = 2nRT_1 \log e^2$$

$$= 2 \times 2 \times 2 \times 300 \times 0.693 = 831.6R$$

90. $T_1 = 300$ K, $V_1 = V$, $V_2 = 2\sqrt{2}\,V$.

Let T_2 be the final temperature of the gas. T_2 is obtained from the adiabatic relation

$$T_1V_1^{\gamma-1} = T_2V_2\,(\gamma-1)$$

or $$T_2 = T_1 \times \left(\frac{V_1}{V_2}\right)^{(\gamma-1)}$$

For a monoatomic gas, $\gamma = \frac{5}{3}$. Therefore,

$$T_2 = 300 \times \left(\frac{1}{2\sqrt{2}}\right)^{2/3} = 150 \text{ K}$$

So, the correct choice is (b).

91. $U = nC_v(T_2 - T_1)$

For a monoatomic gas $C_v = \frac{3R}{2}$. Therefore,

$$\Delta U = 2 \times \frac{3}{2} \times 8.3 \times (150 - 300) = -3735 \text{ J}$$

The negative sign implies that the internal that the internal energy decreases in this process. So, the correct choice is (a).

92. For a adiabatic process, $\Delta Q = 0$, Hence $\Delta W = -\Delta U =$ 3735 J, which is choice (d).

93. Number of moles of helium is

$$n = \frac{\text{mass in gram}}{\text{molecular mass}} = \frac{2000}{4} = 500$$

From eqution state at A,

$$P_AV_A = nRT_A$$

$$T_A = \frac{P_AV_A}{nR} = \frac{4.15 \times 10^4 \times 10}{500 \times 8.3} = 100 \text{ K}$$

So, the correct choice is (a).

94. For isobaric process $A \to B$,

$$\frac{T_B}{T_A} = \frac{P_B}{P_A} = \frac{8.3 \times 10^4}{4.15 \times 10^4} = 2$$

Thus, $T_B = 2\,T_A = 200$ K, which is choice (b).

95. For isobaric process $B \to C$,

$$\frac{T_C}{T_B} = \frac{V_C}{V_B} = \frac{20}{10} = 2$$

Thus, $T_C = 2\,T_B = 400$ K which is choice (c)

96. Work done by the gas in the cyclic process $ABCA$ is W = area enclosed in the $P - V$ diagram

$$= \text{area of triangle } ABC$$

$$= \frac{1}{2} \times AB \times AC$$

$$= \frac{1}{2}(3P_0 - P_0) \times (2V_0 - V_0)$$

$$= P_0V_0.$$

which is choice (a).

97. In the isobaric process CA, the heat energy rejected by the gas is given by

$$Q_{CA} = nC_\pi\Delta T = n(T_A - T_C) \quad ...(1)$$

Using ideal gas equation $PV = nRT$ for points A and C, we have

$$P_AV_A = nRT_A \text{ or } P_0V_0 = nRT_A \quad ...(2)$$

and $$P_CV_C = nRT_C \text{ or } P_0(2V_0) = nRT_C \quad ...(3)$$

Subtracting (2) and (3), we have

$$P_0V_0 = nR(T_C - T_A)$$

or $$T_A - T_C = -\frac{P_0V_0}{nR} \quad ...(4)$$

Using (4) in (1), we get

$$Q_{CA} = -\frac{C_pP_0V_0}{R}, \text{ which is choice (c).} \quad ...(5)$$

98. The heat energy absorbed in the isochoric process AB is given by

$$Q_{AB} = nC_v\Delta T = nC_v(T_B - T_A) \quad ...(6)$$

Using the ideal gas equation for points A and B, we have

$$P_AV_A = nRT_A \text{ or } P_0V_0 = nRT_A$$

and $$P_BV_B = nRT_B \text{ or } (3\,P_0)V_0 = nRT_B$$

which give $T_B - T_A = \dfrac{2P_0V_0}{nR}$ ...(7)

Using (7) in (6), we get

$$Q_{AB} = \frac{2C_vP_0V_0}{R}$$

Now, for a monoatomic gas,

$$C_v = \frac{3R}{2}\text{. Therefore}$$

$$Q_{AB} = 3P_0V_0\text{, which is choice (d)} \quad ...(8)$$

99. From the first law of thermodynamics, the heat energy absorbed by the gas is given by

$$\Delta Q = \Delta U + \Delta W$$

where $\Delta W = W =$ work done by the gas $= P_0V_0$.

Since the process is cyclic, there is no change in the internal energy of the gas, i.e., $\Delta U = 0$. Hence

$$\Delta Q = \Delta W = P_0V_0 \quad ...(9)$$

If Q_{BC} is the heat absorbed the process BC, then

$$Q = Q_{AB} + Q_{BC} + Q_{CA} \quad ...(10)$$

Using (5), (8) and (9) in (10), we have

$$P_0V_0 = 3P_0V_0 + Q_{BC} - \frac{5P_0V_0}{2}$$

or $$Q_{BC} = \frac{P_0V_0}{2}$$

$\therefore$ Correct choice is (a)

100. The correct choice is (c).

101. For an adiabatic change, $P_1V_1 = P_2V_2$. Therefore

$$P_2 = P_1\left(\frac{V_1}{V_2}\right)^{\gamma}$$

For a monoatomic gas, $\gamma = 5/3$. Hence

$$P_2 = P\left(\frac{2\sqrt{2}V}{V}\right)^{5/3} = P(2\sqrt{2})^{5/3}.$$

So, the correct choice is (d).

102. In an adiabatic process, $\Delta Q = 0$. Hence from the first law of thermodynamics, we have

$$W = -\Delta U_1 = -nC_v\Delta T$$

$$= -2\,C_v \times (T_2 - T_1) \quad (\because n = 2)$$

Now for 2 moles $P_1V_1 = 2RT_1$ and $P_2V_2 = 2RT_2$

Thus, $$T_1 = \frac{P_1V_1}{2R} \text{ and } T_2 = \frac{P_2V_2}{2R}$$

Using these, we have

$$W = -\frac{C_v}{R}(P_2V_2 - P_1V_1)$$

$$= -\frac{C_v}{R}\left(\frac{P_1V_1^{\gamma}}{V_2^{\gamma}} \times V_2 - P_1V_1\right)$$

$$= -\frac{C_v}{R} \times P_1V_1\left[\left(\frac{V_1}{V_2}\right)^{\gamma-1} - 1\right]$$

$$= \frac{3P_1V_1}{2}\left[\left(\frac{V_1}{V_2}\right)^{2/3} - 1\right] \quad \left(\because C_v = \frac{3R}{2}\right)$$

$$= -\frac{3P \times 2\sqrt{2}V}{2}[(2\sqrt{2})^{2/3} - 1]$$

$$= -3\sqrt{2}\,PV$$

The work done at constant volume = 0. Hence the correct choices is (c).

103. Using the ideal gas equation $PV = nRT$, the volumes of the gas is states A, B and C are

$$V_A = \frac{nRT_A}{P_A} = \frac{nR(2T_1)}{P_1} = \frac{2nRT_1}{P_1} \quad ...(1)$$

$$V_B = \frac{nRT_B}{P_B} = \frac{nR(T_1)}{2P_1} = \frac{1}{2}\frac{n\,RT_1}{P_1} \quad ...(2)$$

and $$V_C = \frac{nRT_C}{P_C} = \frac{nR(2T_1)}{2P_1} = \frac{nR2T_1}{P_1} \quad ...(3)$$

It is given that in the process $A \to B$, the pressure and temperature of the gas such that

$$PT = K$$

where K is a constant. Thus for point A, we have

$$K = P_AT_A = P_1(2T_1) = 2\,P_1T_1 \quad ...(4)$$

So, the correct choice is (c).

104. For the process $A \to B$, we have

$$PV = nRT \quad ...(5)$$

$$PT = K \quad ...(6)$$

Eliminating T from (5) and (6) we get

$$PV = nR \times \frac{K}{P} \text{ or } P^2V = nRK \quad ...(7)$$

or $$P = \left(\frac{nRK}{V}\right)^{1/2} \quad ...(8)$$

The work done in process $A \to B$ is given by

$$W_{AB} = \int_{V_A}^{V_B} PdV = \int_{V_A}^{V_B}\left(\frac{nRK}{V}\right)^{1/2} dV$$

$$= \sqrt{nRK}\int_{V_A}^{V_B}\frac{dV}{\sqrt{V}} = 2\sqrt{nRK}\,(\sqrt{V_B} - \sqrt{V_A})$$

Using (1), (2) and (4), we get

$$W_{AB} = 2\sqrt{nR(2P_1T_1)}\left[\sqrt{\frac{1}{2}\frac{nRT_1}{P_1}} - \sqrt{\frac{2nRT_1}{P_1}}\right]$$

$$= 2\sqrt{2}\,nRT_1\left(\frac{1}{\sqrt{2}} - \sqrt{2}\right)$$

$$= -2nRT_1 = -4RT_1$$

The negative sign indicates that heat is absorbed in this process. The correct choice is (d)

105. For a monoatomic gas $C_v = 3R/2$. The internal energy of the gas in the process $A \to B$ is

$$(\Delta U)_{AB} = nC_v\Delta T = nC_v(T_B - T_A)$$

$$= 2 \times \frac{3R}{2} \times (T_1 - 2T_1)$$

$$= 3R \times (-T_1) = -3RT_1$$

From the first law of thermodynamics.

$$Q_{AB} = (\Delta U)AB + W_{AB}$$

$$= -3RT_1 - 4RT_1 = -7\,RT_1$$

which is choice (c).

109. In the steady state, the rate of flow of heat is the same for all rods. If T_1 and T_2 are the temperatures at the junction points between A and B and between B and C respectively, then

$$\frac{Q}{t} = \frac{k_A A(100 - T_1)}{d} = \frac{k_B A(T_1 - T_2)}{d}$$

$$= \frac{k_C A(T_2 - 0)}{d}$$

Given $k_A = 2k,\ k_B = \text{k}$

and $k_c = 0.5\ k$. Hence

$$2(100 - T_1) = (T_1 - T_2) = 0.5(T_2 - 0)$$

which gives $200 - 2T_1 = T_1 - T_2$ (1)

and $T_1 - T_2 = 0.5\ T_2$ (2)

Equation (1) and (2) gives $T_1 = 85.7°\text{C}$. So the correct choice is (d).

110. Putting $T_1 = 85.7°\text{C}$ in Eq. (1) or (2), we get $T_2 = 57.1°\text{C}$, which is choice (a).

111. Since the rods have the same lengths and the same diameters, the equivalent thermal conductivity of the series combination is given by

$$\frac{1}{k_e} = \frac{1}{k_A} + \frac{1}{k_B} + \frac{1}{k_C} = \frac{1}{2k} + \frac{1}{k} + \frac{1}{0.5k}$$

which gives $k_e = \frac{2k}{7}$. So, the correct choice is (b).

112.
$$K = \frac{p}{(-\Delta V/V)} \Rightarrow \frac{\Delta V}{V} = \frac{p}{K}$$

$$\Rightarrow \quad -\Delta V = \frac{pV}{K}$$

$$\Rightarrow \quad \frac{pV}{K} = V(3\alpha)\,\Delta T$$

$$\therefore \quad \Delta T = \frac{p}{3\alpha K}$$

113.
$$T_0 = 2\pi\sqrt{\frac{L}{g}}$$

$$T' = T_0 + \Delta T = 2\pi\sqrt{\frac{L + \Delta L}{g}}$$

$$\therefore \quad T' = T_0 + \Delta T$$

$$= 2\pi\sqrt{\frac{L(1 + \alpha\,\Delta\theta)}{g}}$$

$$= \left\{2\pi\sqrt{\frac{L}{g}}\right\}(1 + \alpha\Delta\theta)^{\frac{1}{2}}$$

$$\approx T_0\left(1 + \frac{\alpha\Delta\theta}{2}\right)$$

$$\therefore \quad \Delta T = T' - T_0 = \frac{\alpha\Delta\theta T_0}{2} \quad \text{...(i)}$$

$$\text{or} \quad \frac{\Delta T_1}{\Delta T_2} = \frac{\alpha\Delta\theta_1 T_0}{\alpha\Delta\theta_2 T_0}$$

$$\Rightarrow \quad \frac{12}{4} = \frac{40 - \theta}{\theta - 20}$$

$$\Rightarrow \quad 3(\theta - 20) = 40 - \theta$$

$$\Rightarrow \quad 4\theta = 100$$

$$\Rightarrow \quad \theta = 25°\text{C}$$

Time gained or lost is given by

$$\Delta T = \left(\frac{\Delta T}{T_0 + \Delta T}\right) t \approx \frac{\Delta t}{T_0} t$$

From Eq. (i), $\frac{\Delta T}{T_0} = \frac{\alpha\Delta\theta}{2}$

$$\therefore \quad \Delta t = \frac{\alpha(\Delta\theta)t}{2}$$

$$12 = \frac{\alpha(40 - 25)(24 \times 3600)}{2}$$

$$\therefore \quad \alpha = 1.85 \times 10^{-5}/°\text{C}$$

114.

P S Q, R 10°C 2K K 400°C 1 m 1 m

Rate of heat flow from P to Q

$$\frac{dQ}{dt} = \frac{2KA(T - 10)}{1}$$

Rate of heat flow from Q to S

$$\frac{dQ}{dt} = \frac{KA(4000 - T)}{1}$$

At steady state rate of heat flow is same

$$\therefore \quad \frac{2KA(T - 10)}{1} = KA(400 - T)$$

$$\text{or} \quad 2T - 20 = 400 - t \quad \text{or} \quad 3T = 420$$

$$\therefore \quad T = 140°$$

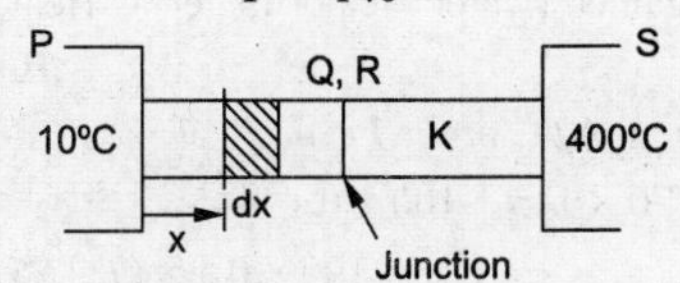

Temperature of junction is 140°C

Temperature at a distance x from end P is

$Tx = (130x + 10°)$

Change in length dx is suppose dy

Then, $dy = \alpha dx\,(Tx - 10)$

$$\int_0^{\Delta y} dy = \int_0^1 \alpha dx\,(130x + 10 - 10)$$

$$\Delta y = \left[\frac{\alpha x^2}{2} \times 130\right]_0^1$$

$$\Delta y = 1.2 \times 10^{-5} \times 65$$

$$\Delta y = 78.0 \times 10^{-5}\ \text{m} = 0.78\ \text{mm}$$

115. By using stefan's law

$$\frac{-dT}{dt} = \frac{\sigma A(T^4 - T_0^4)}{ms} = \frac{\sigma A(T^4 - T_0^4)}{V(\rho s)}$$

ρs is more for B.

116. $mL_v = (150 - m)L_f$

$m \times 2.1 \times 10^6 = (150 - m)(3.36 \times 10^5)$

$m \approx 20$ g

117. For adiabatic process

$$T_1 V_1^{\gamma-1} = T_2 V_2^{\gamma-1}$$

$$\gamma = \frac{5}{3}$$

$$\Rightarrow\ 300(V)^{2/3} = T_2(2V)^{2/3}$$

$$\Rightarrow\ T_2 = \frac{300}{2^{2/3}} \approx 189\ \text{K}$$

$$\Delta U = \frac{f}{2} nR\Delta T = \frac{3}{2}.2\frac{25}{3}(189 - 300)$$

$$= -2.7\ \text{kJ}$$

118. By Mayor's relation for 1 g mole of a gas,

$$C_p - C_v = R$$

So, when n gram moles are given

$$C_p - C_v = \frac{R}{n}$$

As per given question,

$$a = C_p - C_v = \frac{R}{2};\ \text{for H}_2$$

$$b = C_p - C_v = \frac{R}{28};\ \text{for N}_2$$

$$a = 14b$$

119. Heat gained (water + calorimeter) = Heat lost copper ball

$$\Rightarrow\ m_w s_w \Delta T + m_c s_c \Delta T = m_B s_B \Delta T$$

$$\Rightarrow\ 170 \times 145 + 100 \times 0.1 \times 45 = 100 \times 0.1 \times (T - 75)$$

$$\therefore\ T = 885°\text{C}$$

120. Heat generated in device 3 h = time × power = 3 × 3600 × 3 × 10^3 = 324 × 10^5 J

Heat used to heat water = $ms\Delta\theta$

$= 120 \times 1 \times 4.2 \times 10^3 \times 20$ J

Heat absorbed by coolant = Pt

$= 324 \times 10^5 - 120 \times 1 \times 4.2 \times 10^3 \times 20$ J

$= (325 - 100.8) \times 10^5$ J

$$P = \frac{223.2 \times 10^8}{3600} = 2067\ \text{W}$$

121. p–V equation for path AB

$$p = -\left(\frac{p_0}{V_0}\right)V + 3p_0$$

$$\Rightarrow\ pV = 3p_0V - \frac{p_0}{V_0}V^2$$

$$\text{or}\quad T = \frac{pV}{nR} = \frac{1}{nR}\left(3p_0V - \frac{p_0}{V_0}V^2\right)$$

For maximum temperature,

$$\frac{dT}{dV} = 0$$

$$\Rightarrow\ 3p_0 - \frac{2p_0V}{V_0} = 0$$

$$\Rightarrow\ V = \frac{3}{2}V_0$$

$$\text{and}\quad p = 3p_0 - \frac{p_0}{V_0} = \frac{3p_0}{2}$$

Therefore, at these values:

$$\therefore\ T_{\max} = \frac{\left(\frac{3p_0}{2}\right)\left(\frac{3V_0}{2}\right)}{nR} = \frac{9p_0V_0}{4nR}$$

122. In the first process: $p_i V_i^\gamma = p_f V_f^\gamma$

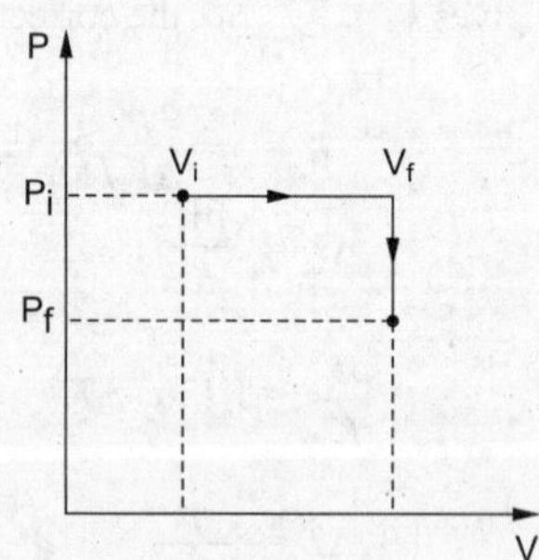

$$\Rightarrow\ \frac{p_i}{p_f} = \left(\frac{V_f}{V_i}\right)^\gamma$$

$$\Rightarrow\ 32 = 8^\gamma$$

$$\gamma = \frac{5}{3} \quad \text{...(i)}$$

For the two step process

$$W = p_i(V_f - V_i) = 10^5(7 \times 10^{-3})$$

$$W = 7 \times 10^2 \text{ J}$$

$$\Delta U = \frac{f}{2}(p_f V_f - p_i V_i)$$

$$= \frac{1}{\gamma - 1}\left(\frac{1}{4} \times 10^2 - 10^2\right)$$

$$\Delta U = -\frac{3}{2}\cdot\frac{3}{4} \times 10^2 = -\frac{9}{8} \times 10^2 \text{ J}$$

$$Q - W = \Delta U$$

$$\Rightarrow \quad Q = 7 \times 10^2 - \frac{9}{8} \times 10^2$$

$$= \frac{47}{8} \times 10^2 \text{ J} = 588 \text{ J}$$

123. Given, $\frac{U}{V} \propto T^4$

$$\frac{U}{V} = \alpha T^4$$

It is also given that, $P = \frac{1}{3}\left(\frac{U}{V}\right)$

$$\Rightarrow \quad \frac{nR_0 T}{V} = \frac{1}{3}(\alpha T^4) \quad (R_0 = \text{Gas constant})$$

$$\text{or} \quad VT^3 = \frac{3nR_0}{\alpha} = \text{constant}$$

$$\therefore \quad \left(\frac{4}{3}\pi R^3\right) T^3 = \text{constant or } RT = \text{constant}$$

$$\therefore \quad T \propto \frac{1}{R}$$

124. Entropy is a state functions. Therefore in both cases answer should be same.

125. According to first law of thermodynamics, we get

(i) Change in internal energy from A to B i.e. ΔU_{AB}

$$\Delta U_{AB} = nC_v(T_B - T_A) = 1 \times \frac{5R}{2}(800 - 400) = 1000 \text{ R}$$

(ii) Change in internal energy from B to $\Delta U_{BC} = nC_v$ $(T_c - T_B) = 1 \times \frac{5R}{2}(600 - 800) = -500 \text{ R}$

(iii) $\Delta U_{\text{isothermal}} = 0$

(iv) Change in internal energy from C to A i.e.

$$\Delta U_{CA}\ \Delta U_{CA} = nC_v(T_A - T_C)$$

$$= 1 \times \frac{5R}{2}(400 - 600) = -500 \text{ R}$$

126. Heat is extracted from the source means heat is given to the system (or gas) or Q is positive. This is positive only along the path ABC.

$\therefore$ Heat supplied,

$$Q_{ABC} = \Delta U_{ABC} + W_{ABC}$$

$$= nC_v(T_f - T_i) + \text{Area under } p\text{–}V \text{ graph}$$

$$= n\left(\frac{3}{2}R\right)(T_C - T_A) + 2p_0V_0$$

$$= \frac{3}{2}(nRT_C - nRT_A) + 2p_0V_0$$

$$= \frac{3}{2}(p_CV_C - P_AV_A) + 2p_0V_0$$

$$= \frac{3}{2}(4p_0V_0 - p_0V_0) + 2p_0V_0$$

$$= \frac{13}{2}p_0V_0$$

127.

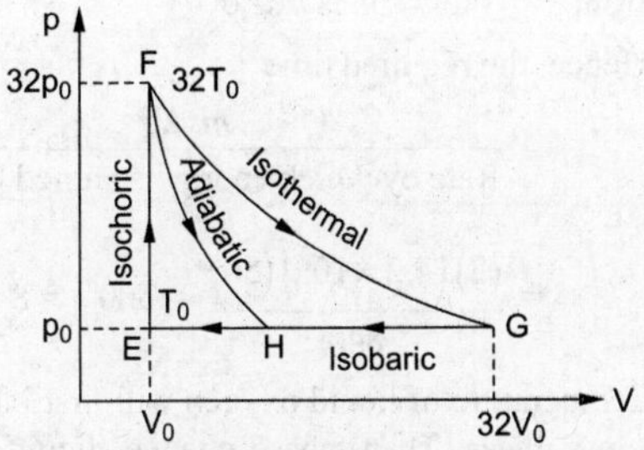

p, V, 32p₀, F, 32T₀, Isochoric, Adiabatic, Isothermal, T₀, p₀, E, H, G, Isobaric, V₀, 32V₀

In $F \to G$ work done in isothermal process is nRT In $\left(\frac{V_f}{V_i}\right) = 32\,p_0V_0 \ln\left(\frac{32V_0}{V_0}\right)$

$$= 32\,p_0V_0 \ln 2^5 = 160\,p_0V_0 \ln 2$$

In $G \to E$, $\Delta W = p_0\Delta V = p_0(31V_0) = 31\,p_0V_0$

In $G \to H$ work done is less than $31\,p_0V_0$ i.e., $24\,p_0V_0$

In $F \to H$ work done is $36\,p_0V_0$

128. The process may be assumed to be isobaric.

$$\therefore \quad Q = nC_p\Delta T = (2)\left(\frac{5}{2}R\right)(5)$$

$$= 5 \times 8.31 \times 5 = 207.75 \text{ J} \approx 208 \text{ J}$$

129. At STP. 22.4 L of any gas is 1 mole.

$$\therefore\ 5.6 \text{ L} = \frac{5.6}{22.4} = \frac{1}{4} \text{ moles} = n$$

In adiabatic process,

$$TV^{\gamma-1} = \text{constant}$$

$$\therefore \quad T_2V_2^{\gamma-1} = T_1V_1^{\gamma-1}$$

$$\text{or} \quad T_2 = T_1\left(\frac{V_1}{V_2}\right)^{\gamma-1}$$

$$\gamma = \frac{C_p}{C_v} = \frac{5}{3} \text{ for monoatomic He gas.}$$

$$\therefore \quad T_2 = T_1\left(\frac{5.6}{0.7}\right)^{\frac{5}{3}-1} = 4T_1$$

Further in adiabatic process, $Q = 0$

$$\therefore \quad W + \Delta U = 0$$

$$\text{or} \quad W = -\Delta U = -nC_v\Delta T$$

$$= -n\left(\frac{R}{\gamma - 1}\right)(T_2 - T_1)$$

$$= -\frac{1}{4}\left(\frac{R}{\frac{5}{3}-1}\right)(4T_1 - T_1) = -\frac{9}{8}RT_1$$

130. 1 calorie is the heat required to raise the temperature of 1 g of water from 14.5°C to 15.5°C at 760 mm of Hg.

Hence correct option is (a).

131. Energy gained by water (in 1 s) = energy supplied – energy lost = 1000 J – 160 J = 840 J

Total heat required to raise the temperature of water from 27°C to 77°C is $ms\Delta\theta$

Hence, the required time

$$t = \frac{ms\Delta\theta}{\text{Rate by which energy is gained by water}}$$

$$= \frac{(2)(4.2\times10^3)(50)}{840} = 500 \text{ s} = 8 \text{ min } 20 \text{ s}$$

132. Temperature of liquid oxygen will first increase in the same phase. Then, phase change (liquid to gas) will take place. During which temperature will remain constant. After that temperature of oxygen in gaseous state will further increase.

133. Let final equilibrium temperature of gases in T

Heat rejected by gas by lower compartment

$$= nC_V\Delta T = 2\times\frac{3}{2}R(700-T)$$

Heat received by the gas in above compartment

$$= nC_P\Delta T = 2\times\frac{7}{2}R(T-400)$$

Equating the two, we get

$$2100 - 3T = 7T - 2800$$

$$\Rightarrow \quad T = 490 \text{ K}$$

134.

$$\Delta W_1 + \Delta U_1 = \Delta Q_1 \quad \text{(i)}$$

$$\Delta W_2 + \Delta U_2 = \Delta Q_2 \quad \text{(ii)}$$

$$\Delta Q_1 + \Delta Q_2 = 0$$

$$\therefore \quad (nC_P\Delta T)_1 + (nC_P\Delta T)_2 = 0$$

But $\quad n_1 = n_2 = 2$

$$\therefore \quad \frac{5}{2}R(T-700)+\frac{7}{2}R(T-400) = 0$$

Solving, we get $T = 525$ K

Now, from Eqs. (i) and (ii), we get

$$\Delta W_1 + \Delta W_2 = -\Delta U_1 - \Delta U_2$$

as $\quad \Delta Q_1 + \Delta Q_2 = 0$

$$\therefore \quad \Delta W1 + \Delta W_2 = -[(nC_V\Delta T)_1 + (nC_V\Delta T)_2]$$

$$= -\left[2\times\frac{3}{2}R\times(525-700)+2\times\frac{5}{2}R\times(525-400)\right]$$

$$= -100 \text{ R}$$

135. Since it is open from top, pressure will be p_0

136. Let p be the pressure in equilibrium.

Then, $\quad pA = p_0A - Mg$

$$p = p_0 - \frac{Mg}{A} = p_0 - \frac{Mg}{\pi R^2}$$

Applying, $\quad p_1V_1 = p_2V_2$

$$\therefore \quad p_0(2AL) = (p)(AL')$$

$$\therefore \quad L' = \frac{2p_0L}{p} = \left(\frac{p_0}{p_0 - \frac{Mg}{\pi R^2}}\right)(2L)$$

$$= \left(\frac{p_0\pi R^2}{\pi R^2 p_0 - Mg}\right)(2L)$$

$\therefore$ Correct option is (d).

137. $p_1 = p_2$

$$p_0 + \rho g(L_0 - H) = p \quad \text{...(i)}$$

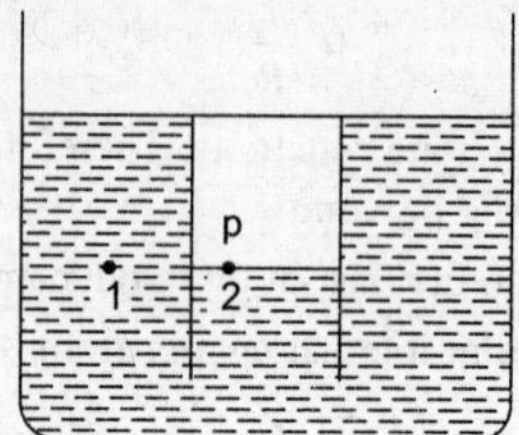

Now, applying $p_1V_1 = p_2V_2$ for the air inside the cylinder,

we have $\quad p_0(L_0) = p(L_0 - H)$

$$\therefore \quad p = \frac{p_0L_0}{L_0 - H}$$

Substituting in Eq. (i), we have

$$p_0 + \rho g(L_0 - H) = \frac{p_0L_0}{L_0 - H}$$

or $\quad \rho g(L_0 - H)^2 + p_0(L_0 - \text{H}) - p_0L_0 = 0$

$\therefore$ correct option is (c).

138. $v_{\text{sound}} = \sqrt{\frac{\gamma RT}{M}}$. As the sound wave propagates, the air in a chamber undergo compression and rarefaction very fastly hence undergo a adiabatic process.

So curves are steeper than isothermal.

$$\left(\frac{dp}{dV}\right)_{Adi} = -\gamma\left(\frac{p}{V}\right) \quad ...(i)$$

$$\left(\frac{dp}{dV}\right)_{Iso} = -\left(\frac{p}{V}\right) \quad ...(ii)$$

Graph 'Q' satisfies Eq. (i)

139. $\Delta U = \Delta Q - p\Delta V$; $\Delta U + p\Delta V = \Delta Q$

As $\Delta U \neq 0$, $W \neq 0$, $\Delta Q \neq 0$. The process represents, isobaric process

$$W_{gas} = -p(\Delta V) = -p(V_2 - V_1) = pV_2 + pV_1$$

Graph 'P' satisfies isobaric process.

140. Work done in isochoric process is zero.

$$W_{12} = 0 \text{ as } \Delta V = 0$$

Graph 'S' represents isochoric process.

141. Heat flow rate $= KA\dfrac{\Delta T}{l}$

Heat flux $= K\left(\dfrac{\Delta T}{l}\right)$

142. In steady state

Energy incident per second

= Energy radiated per second

$\therefore \quad I\pi R^2 = \sigma(T^4 - T_0^4)4\pi R^2 \Rightarrow I = \sigma(T^4 - T_0^4)4$

$\Rightarrow \quad T_4 = 121 \times 10^8 \Rightarrow T = 300$ K

143. In thermal conduction

$$\frac{\Delta G}{\Delta t} = \frac{KA(T_1 - T_2)}{x}$$

$$\frac{dQ_1}{dt} = \frac{dQ_2}{dt} + \frac{dQ_3}{dt}$$

$$\frac{0.92(100 - T)}{46} = \frac{0.26(T - 0)}{13} + \frac{0.12(T - 0)}{12}$$

$\Rightarrow \quad T = 40°C$

$$\frac{dQ_1}{dt} = \frac{0.92 \times 4(100 - 40}{40} = 4.8 \text{ cal/s.}$$

145. Since thermal resistance R_{II} is 4.5 less than thermal resistance R_I.

$$\therefore \quad t_{II} = \frac{t_I}{4.5} = \frac{9}{4.5} \text{ s} = 2 \text{ s}$$

146. Let temperature of middle plate in steady state is T_0

$$Q_1 = Q_2$$

Q = net rate of heat flow

$\therefore \sigma A(3T)^4 - \sigma A{T^4}_0 = \sigma A{T^4}_0 - \sigma A\,(2T)^4$

Solving this equation, we get

$$T_0 = \left(\frac{97}{2}\right)^{1/4} T$$

147. $\lambda_m T$ = constant

From the graph $T_3 > T_2 > T_1$

Temperature of sun will be maximum.

Therefore, (c) is the correct option.

148. Glass of bulb heats due to filament by radiation.

149. $Q \propto AT^4$ and λmT = constant

Hence, $\quad Q \propto \dfrac{A}{(\lambda_m)^4} \propto \dfrac{r^2}{(\lambda_m)^4}$

$$Q_A{:}Q_B{:}Q_C = \frac{(2)^2}{(3)^4}:\frac{(4)^2}{(4)^4}:\frac{(6)^2}{(5)^4} = \frac{4}{18}:\frac{1}{16}:\frac{36}{625}$$

$= 0.05{:}0.0625{:}\ 0.05$

i.e. Q_B is maximum.

150. $\dfrac{dQ}{dt} = L\left(\dfrac{dm}{dt}\right)$

or $\quad \dfrac{\text{Temperature difference}}{\text{Thermal resistance}} = L\left(\dfrac{dm}{dt}\right)$

or $\quad \dfrac{dm}{dt} \propto \dfrac{1}{\text{Thermal resistance}} \propto \dfrac{1}{R}$

In the first case rods are in parallel and thermal resist $\dfrac{R}{2}$ while in second case rods are in series and t resistance is $2R$.

$$\therefore \quad \frac{q_1}{q_2} = \frac{2R}{R/2} = \frac{4}{1}$$

151. As we know force

$$F = 2\frac{dN}{dt} \times mv = 2 \times 10^{22} \times 10^{-26} \times 10^4 = 2N$$

Pressure = 2 Nm^{-2}

152. From $pV = nRT = \dfrac{N}{N_A}RT$

We have, $n_f - n_i = \dfrac{pVN_A}{RT_f} - \dfrac{pVN_A}{RT_i}$

$$n_f - n_i = \frac{10^5 \times 30}{8.3} \times 6.02 \times 10^{23}\left(\frac{1}{300} - \frac{1}{290}\right)$$

$= -2.5 \times 10^{25}$

$\therefore \quad \Delta n = -2.5 \times 10^{25}$

153. $\Delta Q = \Delta U + \Delta W$

In the precess pV^n = constant, molar heat capacity is given by

$$C = \frac{R}{\gamma - 1} + \frac{R}{1 - n} = C_v + \frac{R}{1 - n}$$

$$\Rightarrow \quad 1 - n = \frac{C_p - C_v}{C - C_v}$$

$$\Rightarrow \quad n = 1 - \left(\frac{C_p - C_v}{C - C_v}\right) = \frac{C - C_p}{C - C_v}$$

154. $\rho = \dfrac{pM}{RT}$ $\rho \propto p_M$

or $\dfrac{\rho_1}{\rho_2} = \left(\dfrac{p_1}{P_2}\right)\left(\dfrac{M_1}{M_2}\right) = \left(\dfrac{2}{3}\right)\left(\dfrac{4}{3}\right) = \dfrac{8}{9}$

155. In equilibrium,

$$p_0 A = Mg \quad \text{...(i)}$$

when slightly displayed downwards,

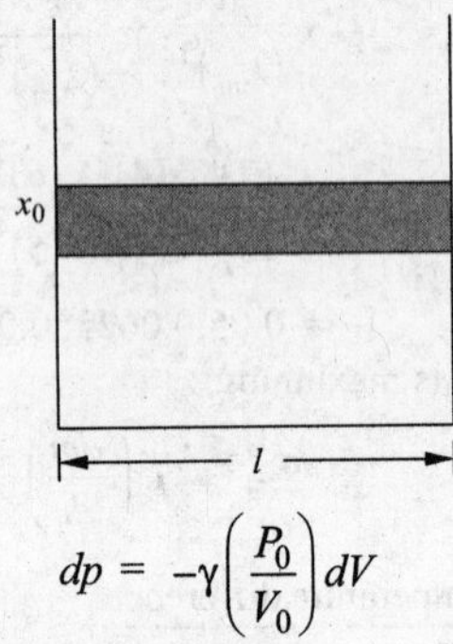

$$dp = -\gamma\left(\frac{P_0}{V_0}\right)dV$$

(As in adiabatic process,

$$\frac{dp}{dV} = -\gamma\frac{P}{V})$$

$\therefore$ Restoring force,

$$F = (dp)A = -\left(\frac{\gamma P_0}{V_0}\right)(A)(Ax)$$

$$F \propto -x$$

Therefore, motion is simple harmonic comparing with $F = -kx$ we have

$$k = \frac{\gamma p_0 A^2}{V_0} \quad \therefore f = \frac{1}{2\neq}\sqrt{\frac{k}{m}} = \frac{1}{2\pi}\sqrt{\frac{\gamma p_0 A^2}{MV_0}}$$

156. $v_{rms} = \sqrt{\dfrac{3RT}{M}}$ or $v_{rms} \propto \dfrac{1}{\sqrt{M}}$

$$\therefore \frac{(v_{rms})_{He}}{(v_{rms})_{Ar}} = \sqrt{\frac{M_{Ar}}{M_{He}}} = \sqrt{\frac{40}{4}} = \sqrt{10} \approx 3.16$$

157. A real gas behaves like an ideal gas at low pressure high temperature.

158. pT^2 = constant

$$\therefore \left(\frac{nRT}{V}\right)T^2 = \text{constant or } T^3V^{-1} = \text{constant}$$

Differentiating the equation, we get

$$\frac{3T^2}{V}.dT - \frac{T^3}{V^2}dV = 0 \text{ or } 3dT = \frac{T}{V}.dV \quad \text{...(i)}$$

From the equation

$$dV = V\gamma dT$$

γ =coefficient of volume expansion of gas $= \dfrac{dV}{V.dT}$

From Eq. (i) $\gamma = \dfrac{dV}{V.dT} = \dfrac{3}{T}$

7 CHAPTER

Basic Electricity

ATOM

An atom is a particle of matter that uniquely defines a chemical element. An atom consists of a central nucleus that is surrounded by one or more negatively charged electrons. The nucleus is positively charged and contains one or more relatively heavy particles known as protons and neutrons.

Atoms are the basic building blocks of matter. Anything that takes up space and anything with mass is made up of atoms. Protons and neutrons are subatomic particles that make up the center of the atom, or its atomic nucleus.

- A **proton** is positively charged. The number of protons in the nucleus of an atom is the atomic number for the chemical element. Different elements' atomic numbers are found in the Periodic Table of Elements. For example, sodium has 11 protons, and its atomic number is 11. A proton has a rest mass, denoted mp, of approximately 1.673 x 10-27 kilogram (kg).
- A **neutron** is electrically neutral and has a rest mass, denoted mn, of approximately 1.675 x 10-27.

The mass of a proton or neutron increases when the particle attains extreme speed, for example in a cyclotron or linear accelerator.

The structure of an atom:

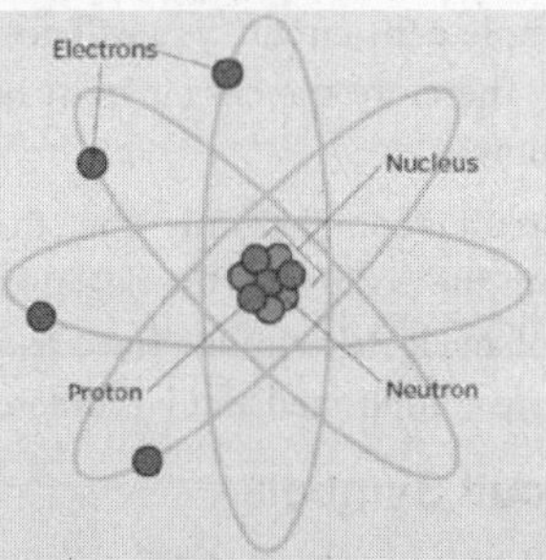

The total mass of an atom, including the protons, neutrons and electrons, is the atomic mass or atomic weight. The atomic mass or weight is measured in atomic mass units. Electrons contribute only a tiny part to the mass of the atomic structure; however, they play an important role in the chemical reactions that create molecules. For most purposes, the atomic weight can be thought of as the number of protons plus the number of neutrons. Because the number of neutrons in an atom can vary, there can be several different atomic weights for most elements. Protons and electrons have equal and opposite charges. Protons have a positive charge and electrons a negative charge. Normally, atoms have equal numbers of protons and electrons, giving them a neutral charge. An ion is an atom with a different number of electrons than protons and is electrically charged. An ion with extra electrons has a negative charge and is called an anion and an ion deficient in electrons has a positive charge and is called a cation. Atoms having the same number of protons but different numbers of neutrons represent the same element and are known as isotopes of that element. An isotope for an element is specified by the sum of the number of protons and neutrons.

Electricity:

Electricity is a fundamental property of matter that is the source of many physical phenomena, including electromagnetic fields, magnetism, and light. It is also the basis for a wide range of technological applications, including power generation, transmission, and distribution.

Electricity is produced by the movement of charged particles, such as electrons. When an object is charged, it has either an excess or a deficiency of electrons. If two objects with opposite charges are brought close together, the electrons will flow from the object with the excess electrons to the object with the deficiency. This flow of electrons is what we call electricity.

Electricity can be generated in a number of ways, including :

- **Chemical reactions:** Batteries generate electricity by using chemical reactions to create a flow of electrons.
- **Mechanical energy:** Generators convert mechanical energy into electrical energy by turning a coil of wire in a magnetic field.
- **Solar energy:** Solar panels convert sunlight into electrical energy using the photovoltaic effect.

- **Wind energy:** Wind turbines generate electricity by converting the kinetic energy of the wind into electrical energy.

Electricity is transmitted and distributed through a network of power lines. Power lines are made of conductive materials, such as copper or aluminum, that allow electrons to flow freely. The electrons are pushed through the power lines by an electric field, which is created by a voltage difference between the two ends of the line. The voltage difference is what we call electricity.

Electricity is used in a wide variety of applications, including :

- **Power generation :** Electricity is the primary source of power for most of the world's homes and businesses.
- **Transportation :** Electric vehicles are becoming increasingly popular as a way to reduce pollution from gasoline-powered vehicles.
- **Lighting :** Electric lights are the most common type of lighting in the world.
- **Communication :** Electricity is used to power a wide variety of communication devices, such as telephones, computers, and televisions.
- **Manufacturing :** Electricity is used to power a wide variety of manufacturing processes, such as metal working, plastics production, and food processing.

Electricity is a powerful and versatile form of energy that is essential to our modern way of life. As we continue to develop new technologies, electricity will continue to play an even more important role in our lives.

Basic electricity concepts:

Here are some basic electricity concepts that you should know:

- **Electric charge :** Electric charge is a property of matter that determines its electromagnetic interactions. There are two types of electric charge: positive and negative. Objects with the same charge repel each other, while objects with opposite charges attract each other.
- **Electric field :** An electric field is a region of space that is influenced by the presence of electric charges. Electric fields exert forces on charged particles.
- **Electric potential :** Electric potential is the amount of work that must be done to move a unit of electric charge from one point to another in an electric field. Electric potential is measured in volts (V).
- **Electric current :** Electric current is the flow of electric charge. Electric current is measured in amperes (A).
- **Resistance :** Resistance is a measure of how difficult it is for electric charge to flow through a material. Resistance is measured in ohms (Ω).
- **Voltage :** Voltage is the difference in electric potential between two points in an electric circuit. Voltage is measured in volts (V).
- **Ohm's law :** Ohm's law is a fundamental principle of electricity that states that the current flowing through a conductor between two points is directly proportional to the voltage difference across the two points and inversely proportional to the resistance between the two points.
- **Power :** Power is the rate at which energy is transferred. Power is measured in watts (W).
- **Circuits :** A circuit is a closed loop of conductors through which electric current flows. Circuits can be series circuits, parallel circuits, or combinations of both.
- **Batteries :** Batteries are devices that store chemical energy and convert it into electrical energy. Batteries are used to power a wide variety of devices, from portable electronics to electric vehicles.
- **Generators :** Generators are devices that convert mechanical energy into electrical energy. Generators are used to produce electricity for power grids.

Electric Circuits :

The electric circuits are closed-loop or paths, forming a network of electrical components where electrons can flow. This path is made using electrical wires and is powered by a source, like a battery. The start of the point from where the electrons start flowing is called the source, whereas the point where electrons leave the electrical circuit is called the return. Let's conduct a small experiment; you would need the following; Electric bulb, Wire, Electrical tape and a battery.

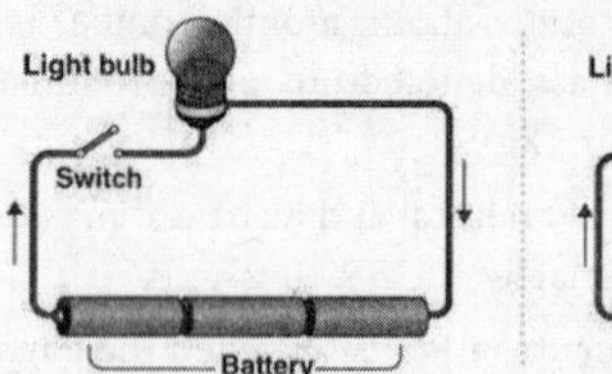

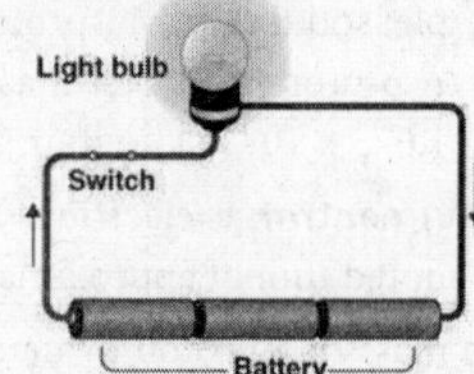

Connect the wires to the bulb and connect one end of the wire to the battery. Notice what happens, there won't be any change in the bulb, but when you connect the free wire to the battery and complete the circuit, you will notice that the bulb starts glowing. Therefore the circuit must be completed for the current to flow.

An electrical circuit is complete only when there is at least one closed loop from the positive to the negative end. This is the simplest form of an electric circuit. The circuit found inside a television is more complicated and has different components.

Electric Circuit Symbols

Every component and product of the electric circuit contains a symbol. The symbols represent parts of the circuit in a circuit diagram. Beneath are the basic set of symbols that are present in a circuit diagram.

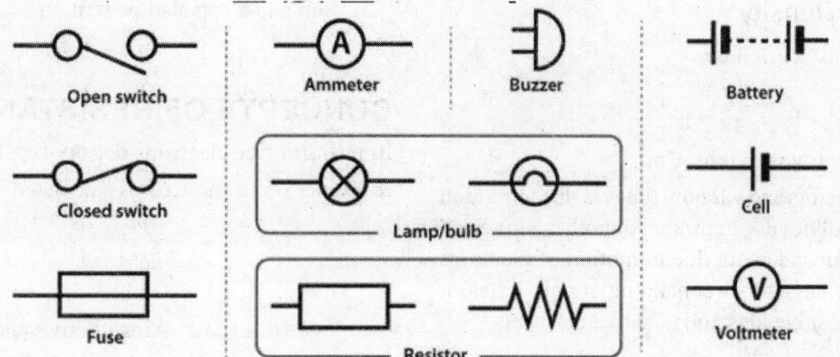

Basic components of an electrical circuit :

An electrical circuit is a closed loop path that allows electrons to flow continuously. It contains a source of electromotive force (EMF), such as a battery or generator, which drives current through the circuit.

The basic components of an electrical circuit are:

- **Source of EMF :** This provides the energy to drive the current in the circuit.
- **Conductor :** This is a material that allows electrons to flow freely through it.
- **Load :** This is a device that consumes electrical energy, such as a light bulb or motor.
- **Control devices :** These are devices that can switch or regulate the flow of current in the circuit, such as switches, relays, and transistors.

There are two main types of electrical circuits:

- **Series circuits :** In a series circuit, all the components are connected in a single loop, so the current must flow through each component in succession.
- **Parallel circuits :** In a parallel circuit, the components are connected in multiple branches, so the current can flow through each branch independently.

Electrical circuits are used in a wide variety of applications, including:

- **Power generation and transmission :** Electrical circuits are used to generate, transmit, and distribute electricity to homes and businesses.
- **Electronics :** Electrical circuits are used to create a wide variety of electronic devices, such as computers, smartphones, and televisions.
- **Industrial control :** Electrical circuits are used to control machinery and equipment in industrial settings.
- **Transportation :** Electrical circuits are used to power electric vehicles and trains.
- **Communication :** Electrical circuits are used to transmit and receive communication signals, such as telephone calls and internet traffic.
- **Medical devices :** Electrical circuits are used to power a wide variety of medical devices, such as pacemakers and MRI machines.

ELECTRIC CURRENT

The time rate of flow of charge through any cross-section is called current. So through a cross-section, Δq charge passes in time Δt is

$$\therefore \quad I_{av} = \frac{\Delta q}{\Delta t}$$

And hence instantaneous current

$$I = \lim_{\Delta t \to 0} \frac{\Delta q}{\Delta t} = \frac{dq}{dt}$$

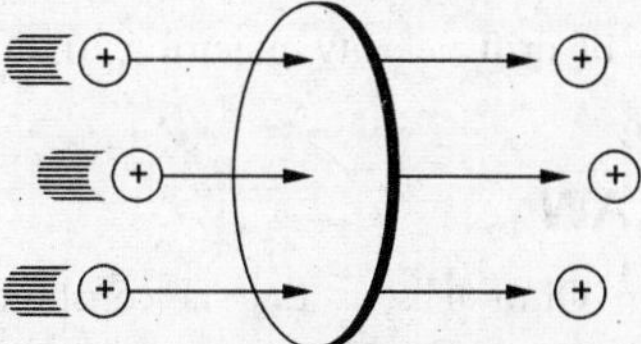

SI unit of electric current is Ampere.

Electric Current for Different Situations

(i) If there are n-particles, each of charge q passing through given area in time t then $I = \frac{\Delta q}{\Delta t} = \frac{nq}{t}$.

(ii) If n particles, each having a charge q, pass per sec per unit area, the current associated with cross-sectional area A is

$$I = \frac{\Delta Q}{\Delta t} = nqA$$

(iii) If there are n particles per unit volume, each having a charge q and moving with velocity v, the current through cross-sectional area A is

$$I = \frac{\Delta Q}{\Delta t} = nqA\frac{\Delta}{\Delta t} = nqvA \quad \text{...(i)}$$

(iv) Electric current due to rotational motion is given by, $\frac{qv}{2\pi r} = qf$.

Electric Current Density

Electric current density is given by,

$$J = \frac{I}{A}$$

It is a vector quantity with unit A/m^2.

Current in conductors and vacuum tubes is due to motion of electrons, in electrolytes due to motion of both positive and negative ions, in semiconductors due to motion of electrons and holes and in discharge tube (containing atomic gases) it is due to motion of positive ions and negative electrons.

DRIFT VELOCITY

It is the average velocity acquired by free electrons inside a metal under the influence of electric field which is responsible for current through it.

i.e., $$V_d = \frac{-eE}{m}\tau$$

$\Rightarrow$ $$V_d \propto E$$

where τ = Relaxation time and defined as the time interval between two successive collisions.

m = mass of electron

and e = elementary charge

Drift velocity per unit electric field is called mobility of electron (μ_e)

i.e., $$\mu_e = \frac{e}{m}\tau \text{ as } \mu_e = \frac{V_d}{E}$$

In terms of drift velocity, electric current is calculated by $I = AneV_d$.

OHM'S LAW

Georg Simon Ohm tells us that at constant temperature potential difference (V) across a conductor is directly proportional to its resistance (R).

i.e., $$V = IR$$

Conductors obeying Ohm's law are called ohmic conductors for example metal and their alloys. V-I graph for ohmic conductor is straight line as shown below.

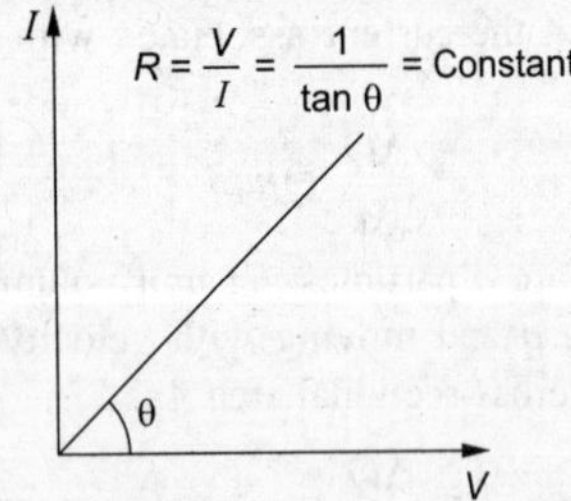

Conductivity or resistivity of a material is independent of the electric field existing in the material.

Conductors which do not obey Ohm's law are non ohmic conductors for example, electrolytes, gases thermionic tubes, transistors, rectifiers etc. V-I graphs for these materials are non-linear.

Ohm's law can also be written as

$$\vec{J} = \sigma\vec{E}$$

CONCEPTS OF RESISTANCE

In terms of free electrons density (n), relaxation time (τ) the resistance of a conductor is calculated by

$$R = \frac{m}{ne^2\tau}\cdot\frac{L}{A}$$

Here L = length of the conductor

A = Area of cross-section of the conductor

In terms of free electrons density and relaxation time resistivity of material is $\rho = \frac{m}{ne^2\tau}$

$$\therefore \quad J = \sigma E = \frac{1}{\rho}E = \frac{ne^2\tau E}{m}$$

Resistance and resistivity increases with increase in temperature according to relation

$$R_t = R_0(1 + \alpha\Delta\theta)$$
$$\rho_t = \rho_0(1 + \alpha\Delta\theta)$$

Here α = temperature coefficient

and $\Delta\theta$ = increase in temperature

Grouping of Resistance; Resistances in Series

Series combination of resistances is shown below:

R_1 R_2 R_3

V_1 V_2 V_3

For this combination equivalent resistance

$R_{eq} = R_1 + R_2 + R_3$

Voltages are in the ratio

$V_1 : V_2 : V_3 :: R_1 : R_2 : R_3$

(i) $V_1 = \frac{V R_1}{R_1 + R_2 + R_3}$, (ii) $V_2 = \frac{V R_2}{R_1 + R_2 + R_3}$,

(iii) $V_3 = \frac{V R_3}{R_1 + R_2 + R_3}$

Resistances in Parallel

Parallel combination of resistances is shown below:

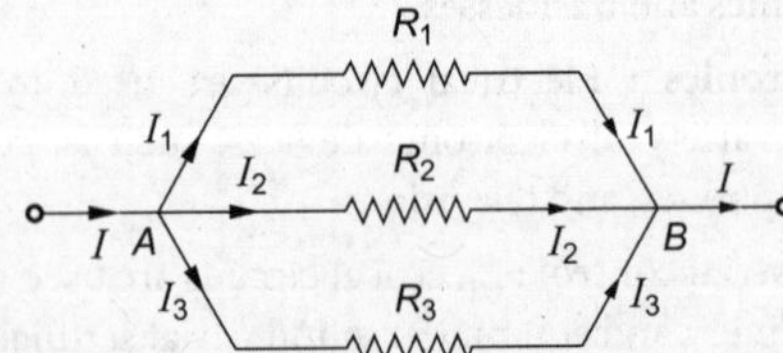

For this combination equivalent resistance is,

$$\frac{1}{R_{eq}} = \frac{1}{R_1} + \frac{1}{R_2} + \frac{1}{R_3}$$

Ratio of currents, $I_1 : I_2 : I_3 :: \frac{1}{R_1} : \frac{1}{R_2} : \frac{1}{R_3}$

When two resistors are in parallel then

$$I_1 = \frac{IR_2}{R_1 + R_2}$$

and $$I_2 = \frac{IR_1}{R_1 + R_2}$$

Points to Remember

(i) Ratio of equivalent resistances of series and parallel combinations of equal resistance, $\frac{R_s}{R_p} = n^2$

(ii) If a skeleton cube is made with 12 equal resistances, each having a resistance R, then the net resistance across

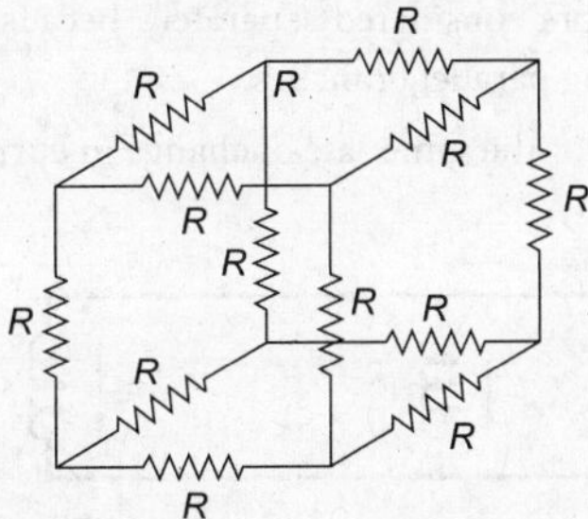

(a) the diagonal of cube = $\frac{5}{6}R$,

(b) the diagonal of a face = $\frac{3}{4}R$, and

(c) along a side = $\frac{7}{12}R$.

CONCEPTS OF CAPACITOR

Capacitors are passive electronic components that store electrical energy in the form of an electric field. They are used in a wide variety of applications, including filtering, timing, and energy storage.

A capacitor consists of two conducting plates separated by a dielectric material. The dielectric material can be a solid, liquid, or gas. When the plates are charged, an electric field is created between them. This electric field stores energy. The capacitance of a capacitor is the amount of charge it can store per unit of voltage. The capacitance of a capacitor is measured in farads (F).

The capacitance of a capacitor is calculated using the following formula:

$$C = \varepsilon A/d$$

where :

- C is the capacitance in farads (F)
- ε is the permittivity of the dielectric material in farads per meter (F/m)
- A is the area of each plate in square meters (m^2)
- d is the distance between the plates in meters (m)

The permittivity of a dielectric material is a measure of its ability to store electrical energy. The permittivity of free space is approximately 8.85 × 10-12 F/m. The permittivity of a dielectric material is always greater than the permittivity of free space.

Grouping of Capacitors:

Capacitors can be grouped together in two ways: in series and in parallel.

Series Capacitors:

Capacitors are connected in series when their terminals are connected together in a chain. The equivalent capacitance of a series combination of capacitors is calculated using the following formula :

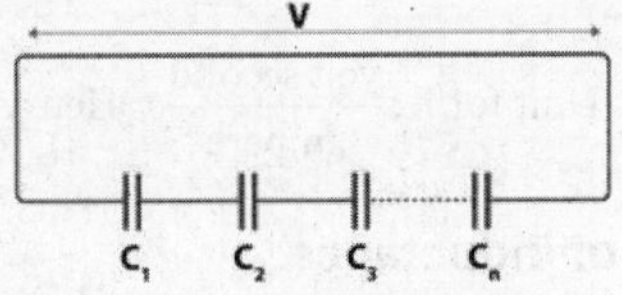

$$1/C_{eq} = 1/C_1 + 1/C_2 + ... + 1/C_n$$

Where, C_{eq} is the equivalent capacitance of the series combination $C_1, C_2, ..., C_n$ are the capacitances of the individual capacitors.

Parallel Capacitors:

Capacitors are connected in parallel when their plates are connected together. The equivalent capacitance of a parallel combination of capacitors is calculated using the following formula:

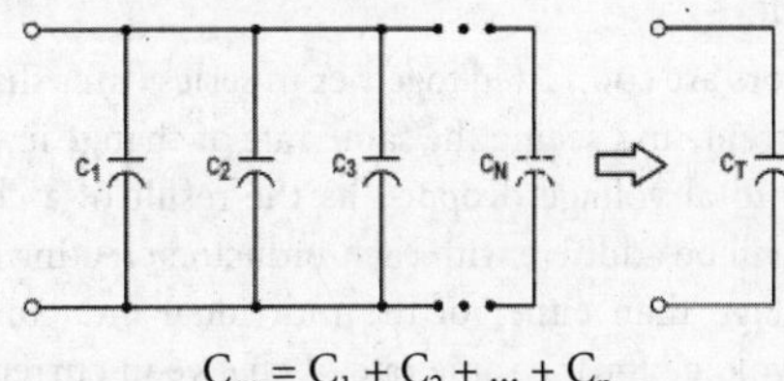

$$C_{eq} = C_1 + C_2 + ... + C_n$$

The equivalent capacitance of a group of capacitors is the capacitance of a single capacitor that would store the same amount of energy at the same voltage.

Applications of Capacitors

Capacitors are used in a wide variety of applications, including:

- **Filtering :** Capacitors can be used to remove unwanted frequencies from a signal. This is because capacitors block alternating current (AC) but allow direct current (DC) to pass through.
- **Timing :** Capacitors can be used to create time delays. This is because it takes time for a capacitor to charge and discharge.
- **Energy storage :** Capacitors can be used to store electrical energy. This is because capacitors can store an electric field.
- **Power factor correction :** Capacitors can be used to improve the power factor of a load. This is because capacitors reduce the amount of reactive power that a load consumes.

- **Coupling and decoupling :** Capacitors can be used to couple two circuits together or to decouple two circuits from each other. This is because capacitors block DC but allow AC to pass through.
- **Tuning :** Capacitors can be used to tune circuits. This is because capacitors can change the resonant frequency of a circuit.

CONCEPTS OF INDUCTANCE

Inductance is typified by the behavior of a coil of wire in resisting any change of electric current through the coil. Arising from Faraday's law, the inductance L may be defined in terms of the emf generated to oppose a given change in current :

$$\text{Emf} = -L\frac{\Delta I}{\Delta t}$$

$$\text{Unit for L}: \frac{\text{volt second}}{\text{ampere}} = \text{Henry}$$

Grouping of inductance:

Inductors can be grouped together in two ways: in series and in parallel.

Series inductors :

When inductors are connected in series, the total inductance is the sum of the individual inductors' inductances. To understand why this is so, consider the following: the definitive measure of inductance is the amount of voltage dropped across an inductor for a given rate of current change through it.

If inductors are connected together in series (thus sharing the same current, and seeing the same rate of change in current), then the total voltage dropped as the result of a change in current will be additive with each inductor, creating a greater total voltage than either of the individual inductors alone. Greater voltage for the same rate of change in current means greater inductance.

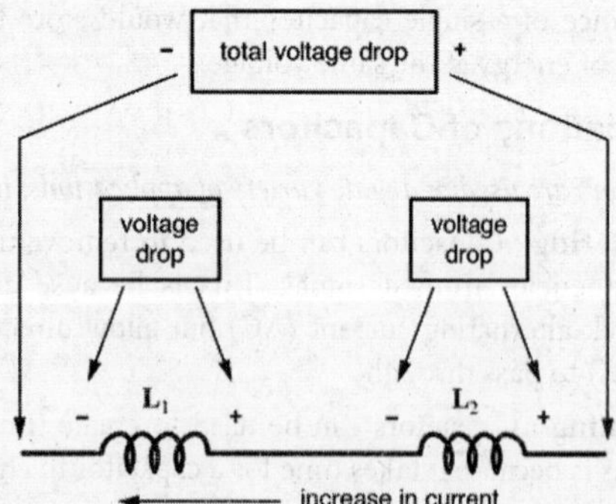

Thus, the total inductance for series inductors is more than any one of the individual inductors' inductances. The formula for calculating the series total inductance is the same form as for calculating series resistances :

$$L_{total} = L_1 + L_2 + \dots L_n$$

Parallel inductors :

When inductors are connected in parallel, the total inductance is less than any one of the parallel inductors' inductances. Again, remember that the definitive measure of inductance is the amount of voltage dropped across an inductor for a given rate of current change through it.

Since the current through each parallel inductor will be a fraction of the total current, and the voltage across each parallel inductor will be equal, a change in total current will result in less voltage dropped across the parallel array than for any one of the inductors considered separately. In other words, there will be less voltage dropped across parallel inductors for a given rate of change in current than for any of those inductors considered separately, because total current divides among parallel branches.

Less voltage for the same rate of change in current means less inductance.

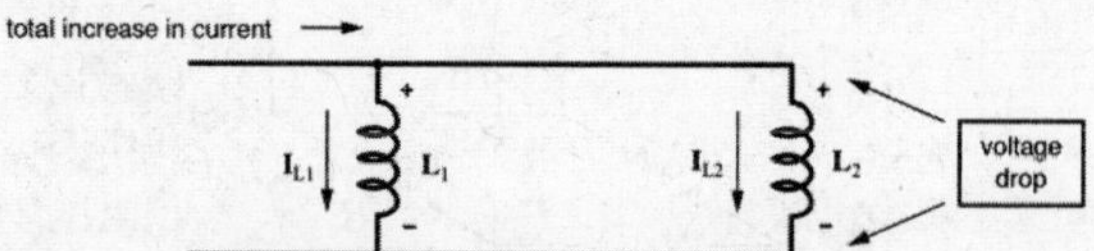

Thus, the total inductance is less than any one of the individual inductors' inductances. The formula for calculating the parallel total inductance is the same form as for calculating parallel resistances:

Parallel Inductances

$$L_{total} = \frac{1}{\frac{1}{L_1} + \frac{1}{L_2} + \dots \frac{1}{L_n}}$$

Electric voltage:

Electric voltage, also known as electric pressure, electric tension, or (electric) potential difference, is the difference in electric potential between two points. In a static electric field, it corresponds to the work needed per unit of charge to move a test charge between the two points.

Voltage is typically provided by a power source, such as a battery or a generator, and it is distributed through electrical circuits to power various devices and systems. In an electrical circuit, voltage is often represented by the symbol "V," and it is measured in volts (V).

Ohm's Law is a fundamental principle in electrical circuits that relates voltage (V), current (I), and resistance (R). The relationship is given by the formula:

$$V = I \cdot R$$

Where;

- V is the voltage (in volts),
- I is the current (in amperes), and
- R is the resistance (in ohms).

This formula indicates that voltage is equal to the product of current and resistance. Understanding voltage is crucial for designing and analyzing electrical circuits.

Voltage is often measured with a voltmeter. A voltmeter is a device that measures the potential difference between two points in a circuit. Voltmeters can be either analog or digital. Analog voltmeters have a needle that moves along a scale, while digital voltmeters display the voltage on a screen.

Voltage is an important concept in electronics. It is used to drive current through a circuit, and it is also used to measure the amount of energy that is transferred by a circuit.

There are two types of voltage: AC voltage and DC voltage. AC voltage is an alternating voltage, which means that it changes direction periodically. DC voltage is a direct voltage, which means that it does not change direction.

Most household appliances use AC voltage. This is because AC voltage can be easily transmitted over long distances. DC voltage is often used in electronic devices, such as computers and cell phones. This is because DC voltage is more stable than AC voltage.

RMS Voltage equation:

Root Mean Square (RMS) voltage is a measure of the effective voltage of an alternating current (AC) waveform. For a sinusoidal waveform, the RMS voltage is related to the peak voltage (V_peak) by the following equation :

$$V_{RMS} = \frac{V_{peak}}{\sqrt{2}}$$

Where :

- V_{RMS} is the RMS voltage,
- V_{peak} is the peak voltage.

For example, if you know the peak voltage of a sinusoidal AC waveform, you can use this formula equivalent basis. Note that this formula specifically applies to sinusoidal waveforms.

The RMS voltage is a useful concept in electrical engineering because it is a measure of the average power that a sinusoidal AC waveform can deliver to a load.

Power calculations :

The RMS voltage is used to calculate the power delivered to a load by an AC circuit. The formula for power is:

$$P = VI$$

where:

- P is the power,
- V is the RMS voltage,
- I is the current.
- **Voltage ratings :** The RMS voltage is used to rate the voltage of AC circuits and devices. For example, a household AC outlet is rated at 120 V RMS.
- **AC circuit analysis :** The RMS voltage is used to analyze AC circuits. For example, the impedance of an AC circuit can be calculated using the formula:

$$Z = V/I$$

Where;

- Z is the impedance,
- V is the RMS voltage,
- I is the current.

Basic circuit:

A basic circuit is a closed loop that allows electricity to flow from one point to another. It consists of a power source, a conductor, and a load. The power source provides the electrical energy to drive the current through the circuit. The conductor is a material that allows electricity to flow through it. The load is the device that uses the electrical energy to do work.

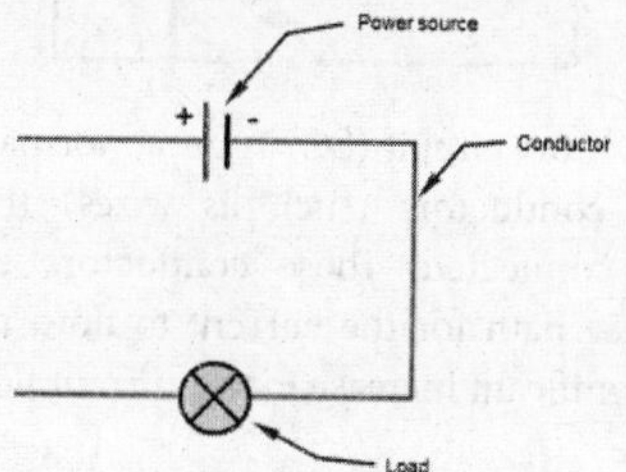

There are two types of basic circuits: series and parallel. In a series circuit, the components are connected in a single line, so the current has only one path to flow through. In a parallel circuit, the components are connected in separate branches, so the current can flow through multiple paths.

Basic circuits are used in a wide variety of applications, from household appliances to electronic devices. They are the building blocks of more complex circuits, and they are essential for understanding the principles of electricity.

Here are some examples of basic circuits :

- **A light switch :** A light switch is a series circuit that consists of a switch, a light bulb, and a power source. When the switch is turned on, the current flows from the power source to the light bulb, and the light bulb turns on.
- **A battery :** A battery is a series circuit that consists of two or more cells. Each cell contains a chemical reaction that produces electricity. The cells are connected in series so that the voltage of the battery is equal to the sum of the voltages of the cells.
- **A fuse :** A fuse is a series circuit that consists of a fuse wire and a power source. The fuse wire is made of a material that melts when the current through it exceeds a certain limit. If the current through the circuit is too high, the fuse wire will melt and open the circuit, protecting the other components from damage.
- **A transistor :** A transistor is a semiconductor device that can be used to amplify or switch electronic signals. Transistors are the building blocks of integrated circuits, which are used in a wide variety of electronic devices.

- **A light-emitting diode (LED) :** An LED is a semiconductor device that emits light when an electric current is passed through it. LEDs are used in a wide variety of applications, including displays, lighting, and communications.

These are just a few examples of the many different types of basic circuits. Basic circuits are an essential part of our everyday lives, and they are used in a wide variety of applications.

Short circuit :

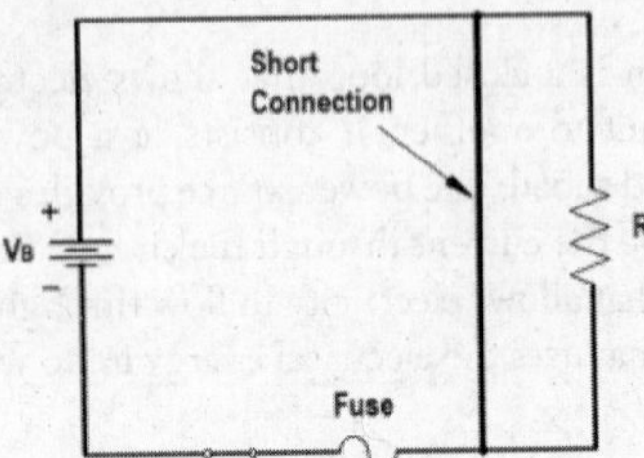

In a circuit, a short circuit (SC) is an abnormal connection between two conductors (such as wires) that normally shouldn't be connected. These conductors then provide a low-resistance path for the current to flow, resulting in a sudden and significant increase in the current flow beyond its intended value.

Short circuits can cause serious damage to electrical equipment and even start fires. They are often caused by accidental wire damage or by faulty insulation.

Here are some of the dangers of short circuits :

- Overheating: The sudden increase in current flow can cause the wires and other components in the circuit to overheat. This can lead to insulation failure, which can in turn cause fires.
- Electrical shock: The high current flow can also create a dangerous electrical shock hazard.
- Damage to equipment: The excessive current can damage electrical equipment, such as motors, transformers, and appliances.

There are a number of things that can be done to prevent short circuits, including :

- Using properly insulated wires: Proper insulation will prevent wires from touching each other and causing a short circuit.
- Inspecting wires regularly: Regularly inspecting wires for damage can help to identify potential problems before they cause a short circuit.
- Using fuses and circuit breakers: Fuses and circuit breakers are designed to protect circuits from short circuits. They will trip and cut off the power to the circuit if the current flow exceeds a certain limit.

By following these safety precautions, you can help to prevent short circuits and protect your electrical equipment from damage.

Here are some examples of how short circuits can occur :

- **A frayed wire :** A frayed wire can touch another wire or a grounded object, causing a short circuit.
- **A loose connection :** A loose connection can create a spark, which can ignite nearby flammable materials.
- **A nail or screw driven through a wire :** A nail or screw can pierce the insulation of a wire, causing a short circuit.
- **Water or other liquids :** Water or other liquids can conduct electricity and cause a short circuit if they come into contact with exposed wires.

Circuit protection :

Circuit protection is a crucial aspect of electrical engineering, as it safeguards electrical circuits from potential damage caused by overcurrent, overvoltage, or ground faults. By implementing appropriate protective devices, one can prevent electrical fires, equipment malfunctions, and personal injuries.

Types of Circuit Protection Devices:

1. **Fuses :** Fuses are among the oldest and most basic circuit protection devices. They consist of a thin metal wire that melts when the current exceeds a predetermined threshold, interrupting the circuit and preventing further damage.
2. **Circuit Breakers :** Circuit breakers operate on a similar principle to fuses, but they are resettable. When an overcurrent occurs, a circuit breaker trips, cutting off the power to the circuit. Once the fault is cleared, the circuit breaker can be manually reset to restore power.
3. **GFCIs (Ground Fault Circuit Breakers) :** GFCIs are specifically designed to protect against ground faults, which occur when electrical current leaks to the ground instead of following its intended path. GFCIs are particularly important in areas where electrical equipment is exposed to water, such as kitchens, bathrooms, and outdoor outlets.
4. **RCDs (Residual Current Devices) :** RCDs, also known as earth leakage protection (ELP), are similar to GFCIs but offer a higher level of sensitivity. They can detect even small leakage currents, providing protection against both ground faults and electrical shocks.
5. **Surge Protectors :** Surge protectors safeguard electrical devices from damage caused by power surges, which are sudden spikes in voltage. These spikes can be caused by lightning strikes, utility switching operations, or other events.
6. **Overcurrent Protection Relays :** Overcurrent protection relays are used in industrial settings to protect large electrical circuits. They monitor the current flow and trip when it exceeds a safe level, preventing damage to expensive equipment.

In addition to these devices, there are various other circuit protection methods employed in specific applications, such as thermal fuses, motor protection relays, and arc flash protection systems.

Selecting Appropriate Circuit Protection :

The choice of circuit protection devices depends on several factors, including the type of circuit, the current rating, the potential hazards, and the desired level of protection. Electrical engineers carefully consider these factors when designing and installing electrical systems to ensure the safety and reliability of electrical installations.

ELECTROCHEMICAL CELL

An electrochemical cell is a device which, by converting chemical energy into electrical energy, maintains the flow of charge in a circuit. It consists of two electrodes of different materials and an electrolyte. The electrode at higher potential is called positive terminal, or anode while at lower potential negative terminal, or cathode. When a cell is in use, i.e., discharging, current outside the cell is from anode to cathode while inside it from cathode to anode as shown in Fig.

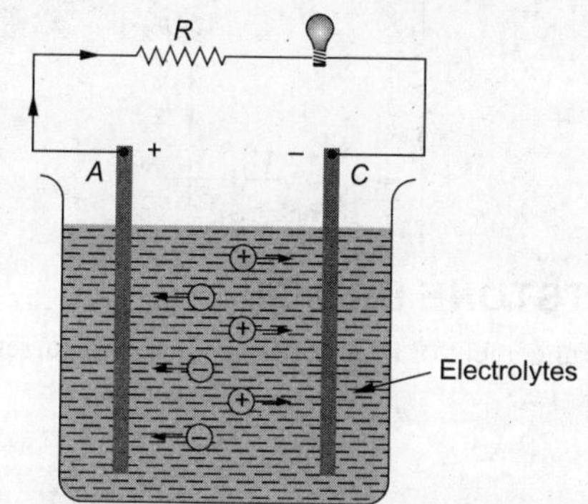

Some important terms related to the cell are:

(i) E.m.f of cell is $\frac{W}{q}$ with unit J/C, called volt.

$E = E_1 + E_2$ $\quad E = E_1 - E_2$ $\quad E = E_2 - E_1$

(ii) Internal resistance of cell is given by

$$r = \left(\frac{E - V}{V}\right) R$$

(iii) When cell is charging terminal potential difference, $V = E - Ir$

(iv) When cell is discharging $V = E + Ir$.

GROUPING OF CELLS

(a) In series as shown above,

(i) $E_{eq} = nE$

(ii) $r_{eq} = nr$

(iii) $I = \frac{nE}{R + nr}$.

(iv) If in series grouping of 'n' cells, 'm' cells are reversed then $I = \frac{(n - 2m) E}{R + nr}$

(v) If the cells are not identical then $I = \frac{\Sigma E_i}{R + \Sigma r_i}$

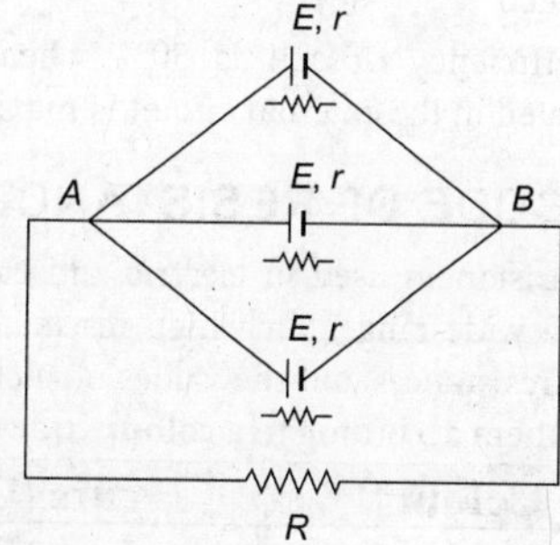

(b) In parallel as shown above,

(i) $r_{eq} = \frac{r}{n}$

(ii) $E_{eq} = E$

(iii) $I = \frac{E}{R + \frac{r}{n}}$

If the cells are not identical then

$$I = \frac{\frac{E_1}{r_1} - \frac{E_2}{r_2} + \frac{E_3}{r_3}}{1 + R\left(\frac{1}{r_1} + \frac{1}{r_2} + \frac{1}{r_3}\right)}$$

(c) In mixed grouping

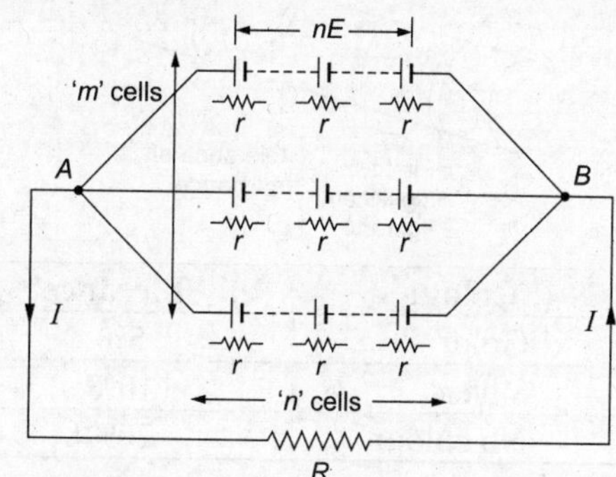

(i) $E_{eq} = nE$

(ii) $r_{eq} = \frac{nr}{m}$

(iii) $I = \frac{nE}{R + \frac{nr}{m}} = \frac{mnE}{mR + nr}$

(iv) For maximum current in circuit $\frac{m}{n} = \frac{r}{R}$.

Points to Remember

(i) Charging current for a secondary cell

$$= \frac{\text{emf of charge} - \text{emf of cell}}{\text{total resistance of the circuit}}$$

(ii) Efficiency of a cell is given by $\eta = \frac{R}{r+R}$

where R is external resistance and r is internal resistance.

(iii) The efficiency of cell is 50% when the power dissipated in the external circuit is maximum.

COLOUR CODE OF RESISTANCES

The value of resistances used in electric and electronic circuit vary over a wide range. Such high resistances used are usually carbon resistances and the values of such resistances are marked on them according to a **colour code** given below.

Colour	Figure (Code)
Black	0
Brown	1
Red	2
Orange	3
Yellow	4
Green	5
Blue	6
Violet	7
Grey	8
White	9

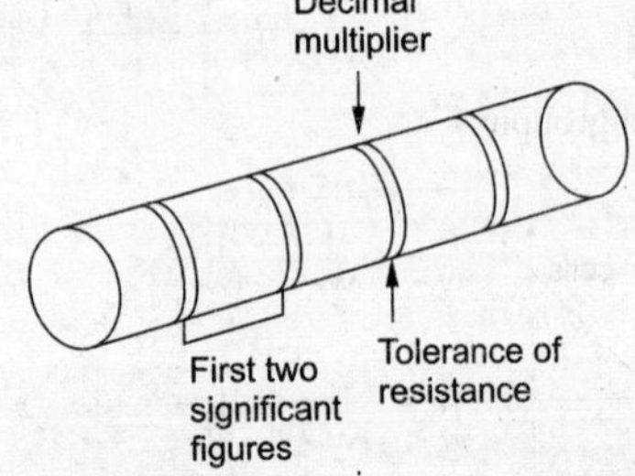

Colour	Tolerance
Gold	5%
Silver	10%
No colour	20%

KIRCHOFF'S LAW

First law (Junction law): The algebraic sum of currents meeting at a junction is zero.

i.e., $\Sigma I = 0$

$\Rightarrow \quad I_1 - I_2 - I_3 = 0$

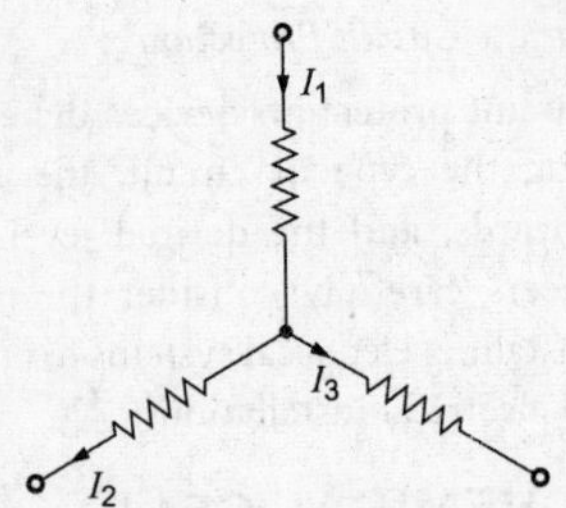

This law is based on conservation of charge.

Second law (loop law): The algebraic sum of all the potentials in a loop is zero.

i.e., $I_1R_1 + I_2R_2 - E_1 + I_3R_3 - I_4R_4 + E_2 = 0.$

This law is based on conservation of energy.

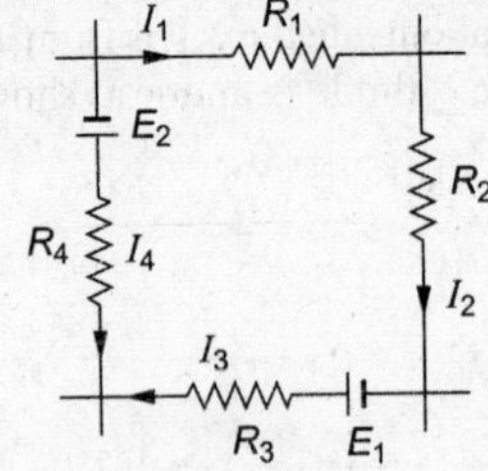

WHEATSTONE BRIDGE

In this arrangement of resistors (as shown), no current flows through R_0 i.e.,

$$V_A = V_B, \text{ if } \frac{P}{Q} = \frac{R}{S}$$

AMMETER

This instrument is used for measuring current in a circuit. In an ammeter, a resistor having a small resistance (r) is connected in parallel with the coil (R_c). This resistor is called the shunt.

$$R_{eq} = \frac{R_c \cdot r}{R_c + r}$$

Conversion of a Galvanometer into Ammeter

A galvanometer may be converted into an ammeter by connecting a suitable low resistance (known as shunt S) in parallel with the galvanometer. Value of shunt resistance is

$$S = \frac{GI_g}{I - I_g}$$

where I_g = maximum safe current (full scale deflection current) which can be passed through galvanometer, I = range of ammeter, G = resistance of galvanometer.

VOLTMETER

This instrument is used for measuring potential difference in a circuit.

In a voltmeter a resistor having a high resistance (R) is connected in series with the coil (R_c).

$$R_{eq} = R_c + R$$

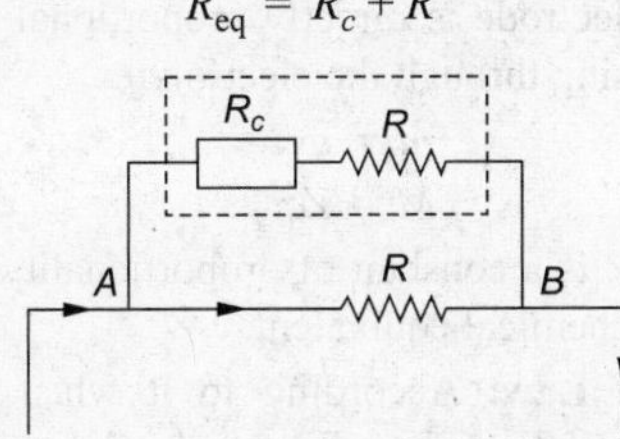

Conversion of Galvanometer into Voltmeter

A galvanometer may be converted into a voltmeter by connecting a suitable high resistance R in series with galvanometer.

Value of series resistance $R = \frac{V}{I_g} - G$

where V = range of voltage.

POTENTIOMETER

It is a device which does not draw any current from the given circuit and still measures the potential difference. Thus, it is equivalent to an ideal voltmeter.

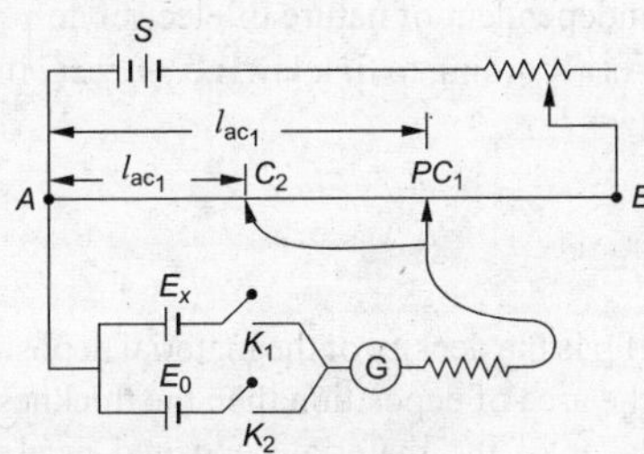

Let $\quad AP = x$ and $AB = L$

Then, $\quad V_{AB} = \frac{I}{L} E_0$

The potentiometer can be used to measure:

(i) internal resistance of a cell.

(ii) to compare emf's of two cells.

(iii) internal resistance of a cell is $\left(\frac{l_1}{l_2} - 1\right) R$,

emf's can be compared by using $\frac{E_1}{E_2} = \frac{l_1}{l_2}$

METRE BRIDGE

It is based on Practical applications of a wheatstone bridge.

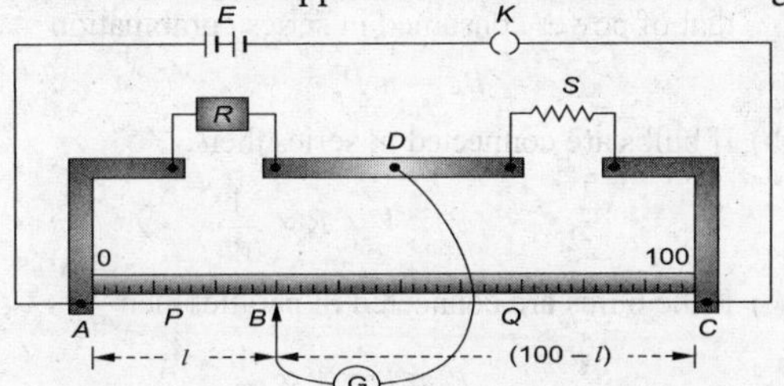

Unknown resistance is calculated by $S = \left(\frac{100 - l}{l}\right) R$

HEAT AND POWER

(a) The amount of energy dissipated as heat in a conductor in time t is

$$H = VIt = I^2Rt \text{ Joule} = \frac{V^2t}{R} \text{ Joule}$$

or $$H = \frac{VIt}{4.18} \text{ cal} = \frac{I^2Rt}{4.18} \text{ cal}$$

$$= \frac{V^2t}{4.18\,R} \text{ cal}$$

These equations are known as **Joule's law of heating.**

(b) The equation : $W = VIt$ is applicable to the conversation of electrical energy into any other form, but the equation: $H = I^2Rt$ is applicable only to the conversion of electrical energy into heat energy in an ohmic resistor.

(c) Joule's law of heating effect holds good even for AC circuits. Only current and voltage have to be replaced by their rms values.

(d) The maximum current that can pass through the fuse wire without melting is called safe current.

The safe current $i \propto r^{3/2}$

where r = radius of the wire

or $\quad i \propto A^{3/4} \quad (\because A \propto r^2)$

Safe current is independent of the length of the wire.

(e) An electric appliance consumes the specified power W only if it runs at the specified voltage V_S. If the applied voltage V_A is greater than specified voltage the appliance will get damaged, as in this situation $I = (V_A/R)$ will exceed its current capacity $I_C = (V_S/R)$. Further if an appliance is made to run at a lower voltage than specified value, then the true power consumption will be

$$P = \frac{V_A^2}{R} = \left(\frac{V_A}{V_S}\right)^2 W \qquad \left[\text{as } R = \frac{V^2{}_S}{W}\right]$$

(f) Necessary series resistance to glow a bulb if $V_{\text{applied}} > V_{\text{rated}}$ is $R = \left(\frac{V_{\text{applied}} - V_{\text{rated}}}{P_R}\right) \times V_R$

$$P_R = \text{Rated Power}$$

(g) Power Consumed in parallel combination is n^2 times that of power consumed in series combination

$$P_P = n^2 P_s$$

(h) If bulbs are connected in series then

$$P \propto V \propto R \propto \frac{1}{W}$$

(i) If the bulbs are connected in parallel then

$$P \propto I \propto W \propto \frac{1}{R}$$

The actual power consumed by an appliance of W watt meant to operate on voltage V_S, at voltage V_A is

$$P = \frac{V_A^2}{R}$$

$$= \left(\frac{V_A}{V_S}\right)^2 W \qquad \left[\text{as } R = \frac{V_s^2}{W}\right]$$

For a given appliance, if V_s and W are the specified voltage and wattage respectively:

$$I_C = \frac{W}{V_S}$$

and $$R = \frac{V_S}{I_C} = \frac{V_S^2}{W}$$

i.e., I_C is the maximum current which can be passed through the appliance safely and R is the resistance of the appliance which is constant for a given appliance and does not change with change in V or I.

(j) When a heavy current appliance such as motor, heater or geyser is switched on, it will draw a heavy current from the source so that terminal voltage of source decreases. Hence power consumed by the bulb decreases, so the light of bulb becomes less.

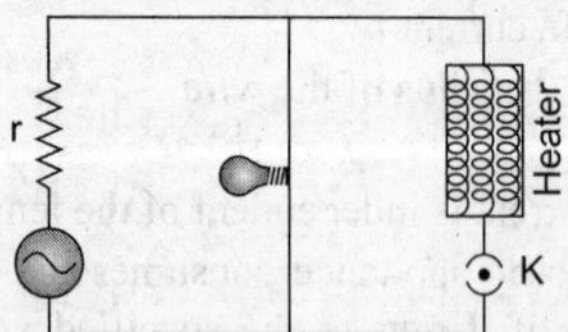

THERMOCOUPLE AND THERMO-EMF*

(a) Thermocouple can be compared to a heat engine. It absorbs heat at the junction (source), converts heat into electric energy (which appears as the circulating electric current) and rejects the remaining heat to cold junction (sink).

Thermo electric emf is given by the equation

$$E = \alpha t + \frac{1}{2}\beta t^2$$

where α and β are thermo electric constants having units volt/°C and volt/°C^2 respectively.

For E to be maximum (at $t = t_n$)

$$\frac{dE}{dt} = 0$$

i.e., $$\alpha + \beta t_n = 0$$

$$\Rightarrow \qquad t_n = -\frac{\alpha}{\beta}$$

(b) The temperature of hot junction at which thermo emf becomes maximum is called neutral temperature (t_n).

FARADAY'S LAWS OF ELECTROLYSIS*

(a) **First Law:** The mass (m) of ions liberated or deposited at an electrode is directly proportional to the charge (q) passing through the electrolyte.

i.e., $$m \propto q$$

or $$M = Zq$$

where Z is a constant of proportionality and is called electrochemical equivalent.

(b) **Second Law:** According to it when same charge is passed through different electrolytes, the masses of substances deposited or liberated are directly proportional to their chemical equivalents, i.e.,

$$\frac{m_1}{m_2} = \frac{E_1}{E_2} \text{ if } Q_1 = Q_2$$

(i) As from first law for $Q_1 = Q_2$, $(m_1/m_2) = (z_1 = z_2)$, second law becomes

$$\frac{z_1}{z_2} = \frac{E_1}{E_2}$$

i.e., $$\frac{E_1}{z_1} = \frac{E_2}{z_2} = \ldots = \frac{E}{z} = \text{Constt.}$$

i.e., in case of electrolysis the ratio of CE to EC E is constant and same for all electrolytes, i.e., is independent of nature of electrolyte.

(ii) As according to first law, i.e., $m = zQ$ if $m = E$ with $Q = F$

$$E = zf$$

i.e., $$\frac{E}{z} = F$$

(iii) If ρ is the density of the material deposited and A is the area of deposition then the thickness (d) of the layer of the material deposited in electroplating process is

$$d = \frac{m}{\rho A} = \frac{Zit}{\rho A};$$

where m = deposited mass, Z = electrochemical equivalent, i = electric current.

Objective Type Questions

1. In producing chlorine by electrolysis 100 kW power at 125 V is being consumed. How much chlorine per minute is liberated (ECE of chlorine is 0.367×10^{-6} kgC^{-1})

(a) 1.76×10^{-3} kg (b) 9.67×10^{-3} kg

(c) 17.61×10^{-3} kg (d) 3.67×10^{-3} kg

2. When a copper voltmeter is connected with a battery of emf 12 V. 2 g of copper is deposited in 30 min. If the same voltmeter is connected across a 6 V battery then the mass of copper deposited in 45 min would be

(a) 1 g (b) 1.5 g

(c) 2 g (d) 2.5 g

3. The negative Zn pole of Daniell cell, sending a constant current through a circuit, decreases in mass by 0.13 g in 30 min. If the electrochemical equivalent of Zn and Cu are 32.5 and 31.5 respectively, the increase in the mass of the position Cu pole in this time is

(a) 0.180 g (b) 0.141 g

(c) 0.126 g (d) 0.242 g

4. When 1 A of current is passed through $CuSO_4$ solution for 10 s, then the number of copper ions deposited at the cathode will be

(a) 1.6×10^{19} (b) 3.1×10^{19}

(c) 4.8×10^{19} (d) 6.2×10^{19}

5. The thermo-emf (E) of a certain thermocouple is found to vary with temperature t (in°C) in accordance with the relation

$$E = 40t - \frac{t^2}{20}$$

where t is the temperature of the hot junction, the cold junction being kept at 0°C. The neutral temperature of the couple is

(a) 100°C (b) 200°C

(c) 300°C (d) 400°C

6. The neutral temperature of a thermocouple is 300°C. What is the inversion temperature, if the temperature of cold junction is 10°C?

(a) 590°C (b) 610°C

(c) 310°C (d) 290°C

7. The thermo-emf of a thermocouple is 25μ V/°C at room temperature. A galvanometer of 40 Ω resistance capable of detecting current as low as 10^{-1}A, is connected with the thermocouple. The smallest temperature difference that can be detected by this system is

(a) 16°C (b) 12°C

(c) 8°C (d) 20°C

8. The inversion temperature of a copper-iron thermocouple is 540°C when the cold junction temperature is 0°C. If the cold junction temperature is increased by 10°C, then the inversion temperature and the neutral temperature of the thermocouple respectively are

(a) 270°C and 530°C (b) 270°C and 550°C

(c) 280°C and 530°C (d) 280°C and 550°C

9. A voltmeter has resistance of G ohm and range of V volt. The resistance required in series to convert it into a voltmeter of range nV volt is

(a) $(n-1)G$ (b) nG

(c) $\frac{G}{n}$ (d) $\frac{G}{(n-1)}$

10. Two bulbs 100 W, 250 V and 200 W, 250 V are connected in parallel across a 500 V line. Then

(a) 100 W bulb will be fused

(b) 200 W bulb will be fused

(c) both bulbs will be fused

(d) no bulb will be fused

11. A 2 kW boiler used for 1h/day consumes the following electrical energy in thirty days

(a) 60 unit

(b) 120 unit

(c) 15 unit

(d) 6×10^4 unit

12. The effective resistance between points P and Q of the electrical circuit shown in the figure is

(a) $\frac{2Rr}{R+r}$

(b) $\frac{8R(R+r)}{3R+r}$

(c) $2r + 4R$

(d) $\frac{5R}{2} + 2r$

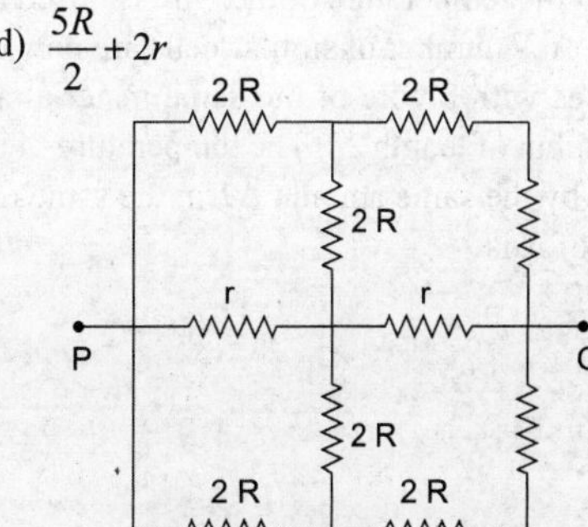

13. In the given circuit, it is observed that the current I is independent of the value of the resistance R_6. Then the resistance values must satisfy.

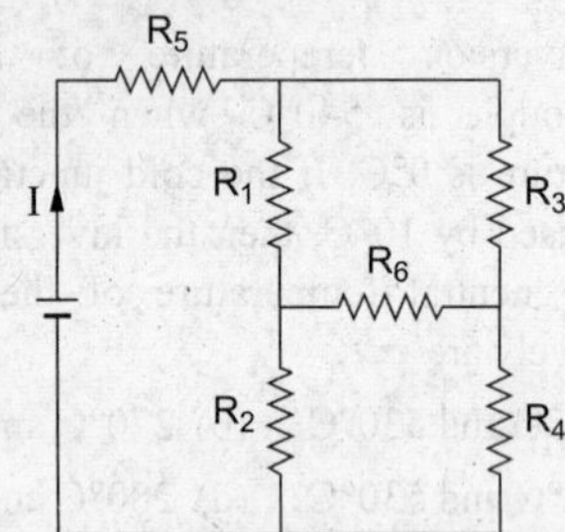

(a) $R_1R_2R_5 = R_3R_4R_6$

(b) $\frac{1}{R_5} + \frac{1}{R_6} = \frac{1}{R_1 + R_2} + \frac{1}{R_3 + R_4}$

(c) $R_1R_4 = R_2R_3$

(d) $R_1R_3 = R_2R_4 = R_4R_6$

14. A steady current flows in a metallic conductor of non-uniform cross-section. The quantity/quantities constant along the length of the conductor is/are

(a) current, electric field and drift speed

(b) drift speed only

(c) current and drift speed

(d) current only

15. In the circuit $P \neq R$, the reading of the galvanometer is same with switch S open or closed. Then

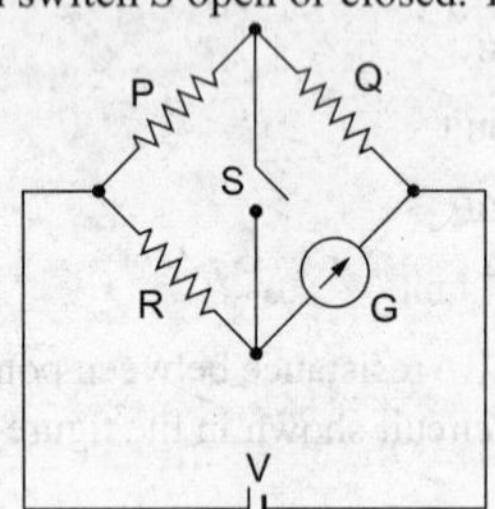

(a) $I_R = I_G$ (b) $I_P = I_G$

(c) $I_Q = I_G$ (d) $I_Q = I_R$

16. A wire of length L and three identical cells of negligible internal resistances are connected in series. Due to the current the temperature of the wire is raised by ΔT in a time t. A N number of similar cells are now connected in series with a wire of the same material and cross-section but of length $2L$. The temperature of the wire is raised by the same amount ΔT in the same time t. The value of N is

(a) 4

(b) 6

(c) 8

(d) 9

17. In the given circuit with steady current, the potential drop across the capacitor must be

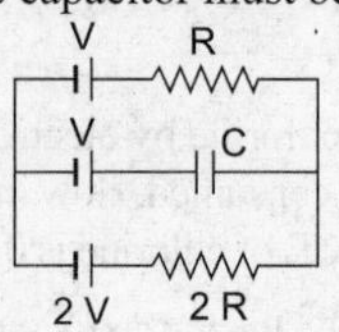

(a) V (b) $V/2$

(c) $V/3$ (d) $2V/3$

18. Three resistance of equal value are arranged in the different combinations as shown below. Arrange them in increasing order of power dissipation.

(I) 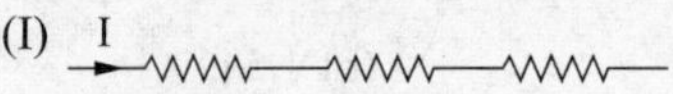

(II) 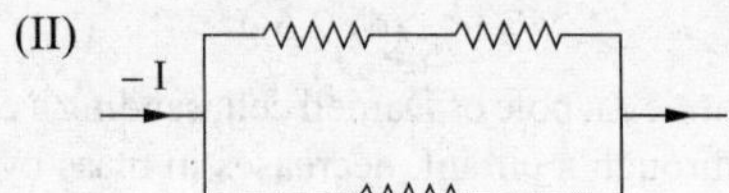

(III) 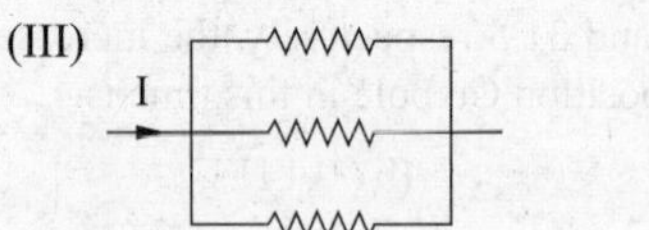

(IV) 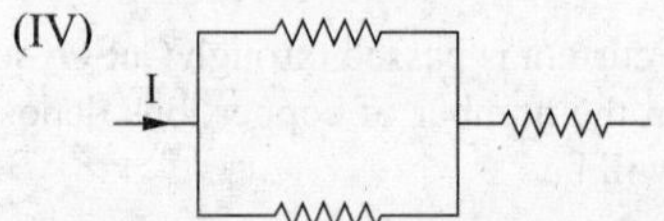

(a) III < II < IV < I (b) II < III < IV < I

(c) I < IV < III < II (d) I < III < II < IV

19. The temperature coefficient of resistance of a wire is 0.00125 per °C. At 300 K, its resistance is 1 ohm.

This resistance of the wire will be 2 ohm at

(a) 1154 K (b) 1100 K

(c) 1400 K (d) 1127 K

20. In the circuit shown in fig, the heat produced in the 5 ohm resistor due to the current flowing through it is 10 calorie per second. The heat generated in the 4 ohm resistor is

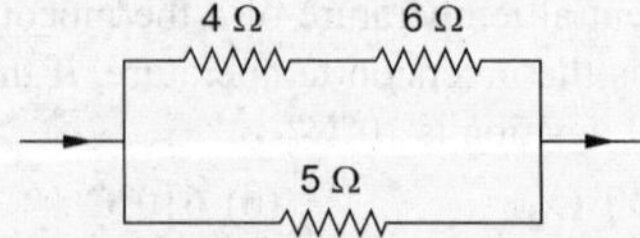

(a) 1 calorie/sec (b) 2 calorie/sec

(c) 3 calorie/sec (d) 4 calorie/sec

21. A 100 W bulb B_1 and two 60 W bulbs B_2 and B_3, are connected to a 250 V source, as shown in figure. Now W_1, W_2 and W_3 are the output powers of the bulbs B_1, B_2 and B_3, respectively.

Then

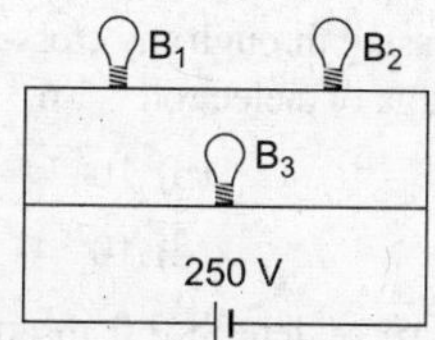

(a) $W_1 > W_2 = W_3$ (b) $W_1 > W_2 > W_3$
(c) $W_1 < W_2 = W_3$ (d) $W_1 < W_2 < W_3$

22. Express which of the following set ups can be used to verify Ohm's law?

(a)

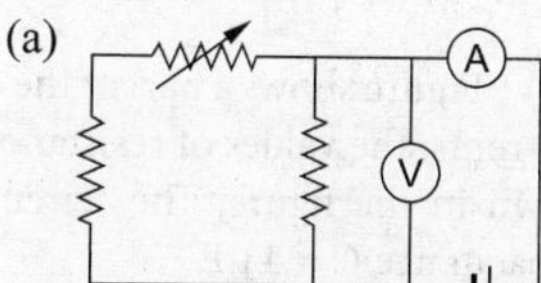

(b)

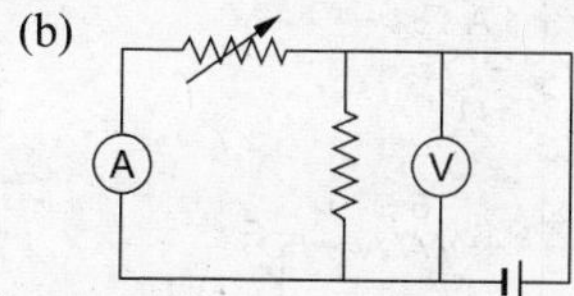

(c)

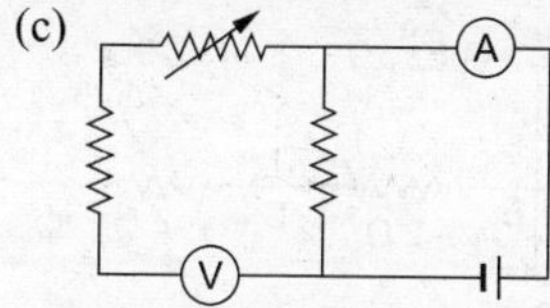

(d)

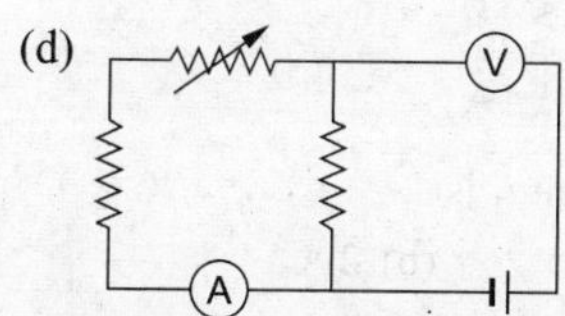

23. In the shown arrangement of the experiment of the meter bridge if AC corresponding to null deflection of galvanometer is x, what would be its value if the radius of the wire AB is doubled?

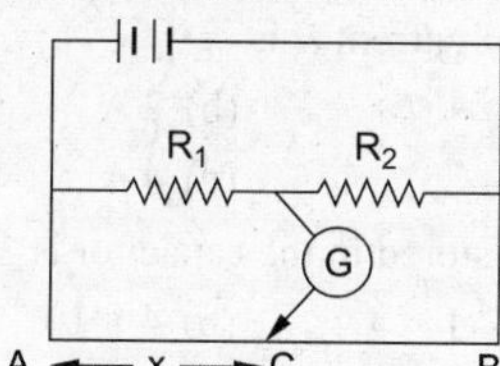

(a) x
(b) $x/4$
(c) $4x$
(d) $2x$

24. A battery of internal resistance 4 Ω is connected to the network of resistances as shown in the figure. In order that the maximum power can be delivered to the network, the value of R in Ω should be

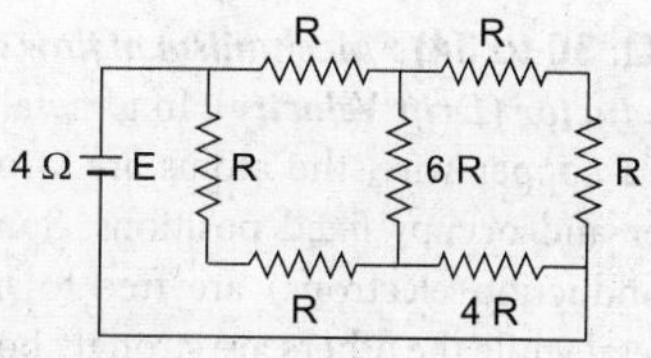

(a) 4/9 (b) 2
(c) 8/3 (d) 18

25. The thermo-emf of a thermocouple is 25μ V/°C at room temperature. A galvanometer of 40 Ω resistance, capable of detecting current as low as 10^{-5} A, is connected with the thermocouple. The smallest temperature difference that can be detected by this system is:

(a) 16°C (b) 12°C
(c) 8°C (d) 20°C

26. The length of a given cylindrical wire is increased by 100%. Due to the consequent decrease in diameter the change in the resistance of the wire will be:

(a) 200% (b) 100%
(c) 50% (d) 300%

27. The thermo emf of a thermocouple varies with the temperature θ of the hot junction as $E = a\theta + b\theta^2$ in volts where the ratio $\frac{a}{b}$ is 700°C. If the cold junction is kept at 0°C, then the neutral temperature is:

(a) 700°C
(b) 350°C
(c) 1400°C
(d) no neutral temperature is possible for this thermocouple

28. A wire when connected to 220 V mains supply has power dissipation P_1. Now, the wire is cut into two equal pieces which are connected in parallel to the same supply. Power dissipation in this case is P_2. Then P_2:P_1 is:

(a) 1 (b) 4
(c) 2 (d) 3

29. The total current supplied to the circuit by the battery is:

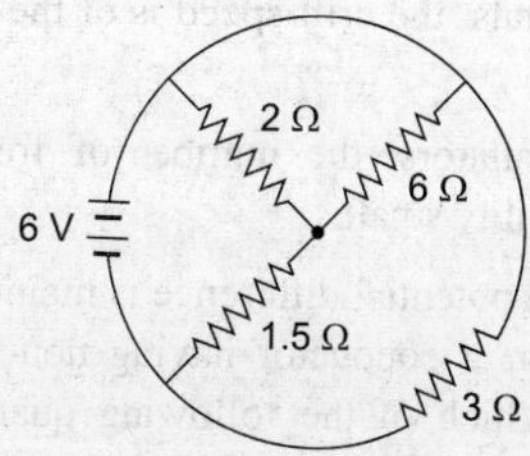

(a) 1 A (b) 2 A
(c) 4 A (d) 6 A

Directions (Q. 30 to 34) : ***Mechanism of flow of current in a metallic conductor (Drift Velocity):*** In a metal in the solid state, such as a copper wire, the atoms are strongly bound to one another and occupy fixed positions. Some electrons (called the conduction electrons) are free to move in the body of the metal while the others are strongly bound to their atoms. In good conductors, the number of free electrons is very large–of the order of 10^{28} electrons per cubic metre in copper. The free electrons are in random motion and keep colliding with atoms. At room temperature, they move with velocities of the order of 10^5 ms^{-1}. These velocities are completely random and there is no net flow of charge in any direction. If a potential difference is maintained between the ends of the metal wire (by connecting it across a battery), an electric field is set up which accelerates the free electrons. These accelerated electrons frequently collide with the atoms of the conductor, as a result, they acquire a constant speed called the drift speed which is given by

$$v_d = \frac{I}{enA}$$

where I = current in the conductor due to drifting electrons, e = charge of an electron, n = number of free electrons per unit volume of the conductor and A = area of cross-section of the conductor,

30. If no potential difference is maintained between the ends of a conductor,

(a) The free electrons are at rest

(b) The free electrons move randomly in all directions

(c) The rate at which electrons pass through a certain cross-section from right to left is equal to the rate at which electrons pass through it from left to right.

(d) No current flows through the conductor.

31. Choose the correct statements from the following.

(a) In copper, the number of free electrons is of the order of 10^{22} electrons per cubic centimetre.

(b) At room temperature, the free electrons move with very small velocities in the absence of an electric field.

(c) In metals, the drift speed is of the order of a few mms^{-1}.

(d) In insulators, the number of free electrons is negligibly small.

32. A constant potential difference is maintained between the ends of a conductor having non-uniform cross-section. Which of the following quantities will not change along the length of the conductor?

(a) Drift speed   (b) Electric field

(c) Resistance   (d) Current

33. A current of 1 A flows through a copper wire. The number of electrons passing through any cross-section of the wire in 1.6 s is (charge of a electron = 1.6×10^{-19}C)

(a) 10^{19} (b) 10^{22}

(c) 10^{25} (d) 10^{28}

34. A uniform wire of length 2.0 m and cross-sectional area 10^{-7} m^2 carries a current of 1.6 A. If there are 10^{28} free electrons per m^3 in copper, the drift speed of electrons in copper is

(a) 2 mms^{-1} (b) 5 mms^{-1}

(c) 10 mms^{-1} (d) 1 ms^{-1}

Directions (Q. 35 to 38) : Figure shows a part of the circuit in the steady state. The currents, the values of resistances and emfs of the cells are shown in the figure. The circuit also contains a capacitor of capacitance $C = 4$ μF.

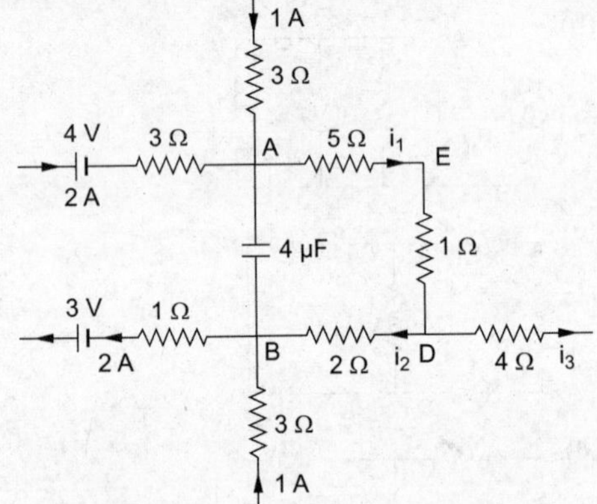

35. The value of current i_1 is

(a) 1 A   (b) 2 A

(c) 3 A   (d) 4 A

36. The value of current i_2 is

(a) 1 A   (b) 2 A

(c) 3 A   (d) 4 A

37. The value of current i_3 is

(a) 1 A   (b) 2 A

(c) 3 A   (d) 4 A

38. The energy stored in the capacitor is

(a) 2×10^{-4} J   (b) 4×10^{-4} J

(c) 6×10^{-4} J   (d) 8×10^{-4} J

Directions (Q. 39 to 42) ***Joule's Law:*** Consider a conductor having a finite resistance. A steady potential difference V is maintained between the ends A and B of the conductor. The end A of the conductor is connected to the positive terminal of the battery and is at a higher potential than end B which is connected to the negative terminal of the battery. A steady current I flows through the conductor. When a charge q moves from A to B in time t, the current in the conductor is

$$I = \frac{q}{t}$$

In moving from A to B, the charge has to do work which (from the definition of potential difference V) is given by

$$W = qV$$

This work represents the decrease in the electrical potential energy of the charge. The principle of conservation of energy tells us that this energy is transformed from electrical energy to some other form of energy. If the conductor is a metal (pure resistor), then the energy appears as heat in the metal, which is given by

$$H = qV = It\,V = I^2 Rt = \frac{V^2 t}{R} \qquad (\because V = IR)$$

The power P associated with transfer of heat is

$$P = \frac{H}{t} = IV = I^2 R = \frac{V^2}{R}$$

39. The end A of a metallic conductor is connected to the positive terminal and end B of conductor is connected to the negative terminal of a battery. Then

(a) The free electrons move from A to B

(b) The free electrons move from B to A

(c) The electrons lose potential energy as they move in the conductor.

(d) The electrons gain potential energy as they move in the conductor.

40. A constant potential difference is maintained between the ends of a metallic conductor. As the electrons move from one end of the conductor to the other,

(a) Their kinetic energy increases and potential energy decreases.

(b) Their kinetic energy decreases and potential energy increases.

(c) Their kinetic energy increases but potential energy remains unchanged.

(d) Their potential energy decreases but kinetic energy remains unchanged.

41. A potential difference V applied across a resistance R causes A current I to flow through the resistance. In which of the following cases is the rate at which electrical energy is converted to thermal energy the maximum?

(a) V is doubled with R unchanged

(b) R is doubled with V unchanged

(c) R is doubled with I unchanged

(d) Both R and V are doubled

42. A uniform wire is connected across the mains. It dissipates power P. The wire is now cut into two equal pieces which are then joined in parallel. If this combination is connected across the mains, the power dissipated will be

(a) $\frac{P}{4}$ (b) $\frac{P}{2}$

(c) $2P$ (d) $4P$

Directions (Q. 43 to 45) : In the circuit shown in a figure, the 5 Ω resistance develops 45 Js^{-1} of heat due to the flow of current through it.

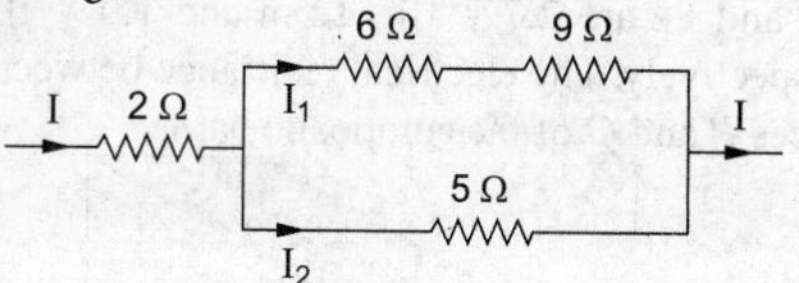

43. The value of current I is

(a) 1 A (b) 2 A

(c) 3 A (d) 4 A

44. The power dissipated in the 2 Ω resistor is

(a) 96 W (b) 48 W

(c) 32 W (d) 16 W

45. The potential difference across the 6 Ω resistor is

(a) 2 V (b) 4 V

(c) 6 V (d) 9 V

Directions (Q. 46 to 49) : Figure shows four resistances $R_1 = 4\ \Omega$, $R_2 = 6\ \Omega$, $R_3 = 12\ \Omega$ and $R_4 = 10\ \Omega$ connected with a 120 V battery and a capacitor of capacitance $C = 500\ \mu F$, by means of two switches S_1 and S_2. Switch S_1 is closed so that the capacitor is fully charged. Switch S_1 is then opened and switch S_2 is closed.

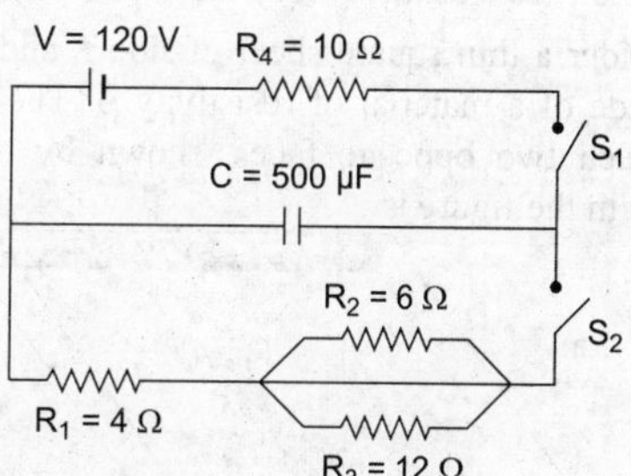

46. The power developed in resistor R_1 is

(a) 1.8 W (b) 3.6 W

(c) 5.4 W (d) 7.2 W

47. The power developed in resistor R_2 is

(a) 0.3 W (b) 0.6 W

(c) 0.9 W (d) 1.2 W

48. The power developed in resistor R_3 is

(a) 0.2 W (b) 0.4 W

(c) 0.6 W (d) 0.8 W

49. The power developed in resistor R_4 is

(a) 3.6 W (b) 1.2 W

(c) 0.4 W (d) Zero

50. A uniform metallic wire has a resistance of 18 Ω and is bent into an equilateral triangle. Then, the resistance between any two vertices of the triangle is :

(a) 4 Ω (b) 8 Ω

(c) 12 Ω (d) 2 Ω

51. In an aluminium (Al) bar of square cross-section, a square hole is drilled and is filled with iron (Fe) as shown in the figure. The electrical resistivities of Al and Fe are 2.7×10^{-8} Ω m and 1.0×10^{-7} Ω m, respectively. The electrical resistance between the two faces P and Q of the composite bar is

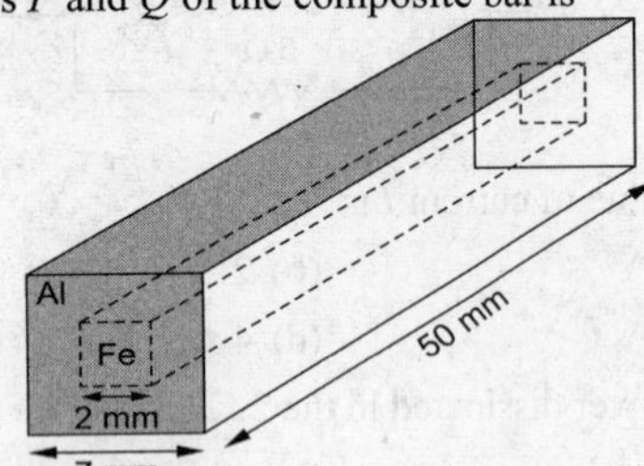

(a) $\frac{2475}{64} \mu \Omega$ (b) $\frac{1875}{64} \mu \Omega$

(c) $\frac{1875}{49} \mu \Omega$ (d) $\frac{2475}{132} \mu \Omega$

52. When 5 V potential difference is applied across a wire of length 0.1 m, the drift speed of electrons is 2.5×10^{-4} ms^{-1}. If the electron density in the wire is 8×10^{28} m^{-3} the resistivity of the material is close to

(a) 1.6×10^{-8} Ωm (b) 1.6×10^{-7} Ωm

(c) 1.6×10^{-5} Ωm (d) 1.6×10^{-6} Ωm

53. Consider a thin square sheet of side L and thickness t, made of a material of resistivity ρ. The resistance between two opposite faces, shown by the shaded areas in the figure is

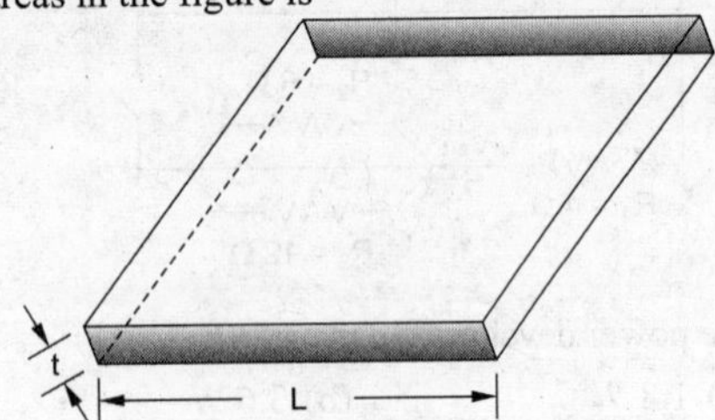

(*a*) directly proportional to L

(*b*) directly proportional to t

(c) independent of L

(d) independent of t

54. Six equal resistances are connected between points P, Q and R as shown in the figure. Then, the net resistance will be maximum between

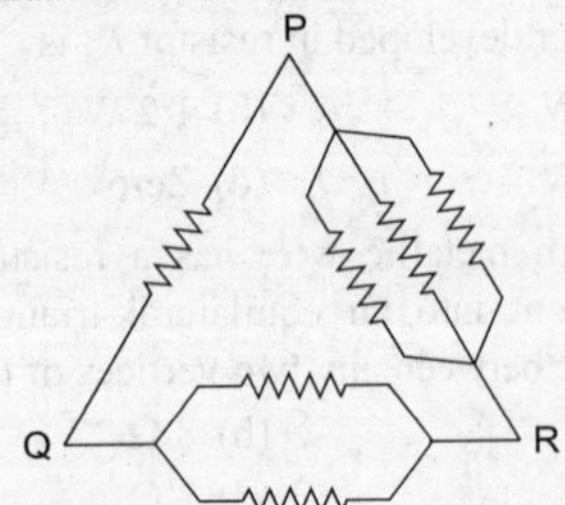

(a) P and Q

(b) Q and R

(c) P and R

(d) any two points

55. In the below circuit, the current in each resistance is

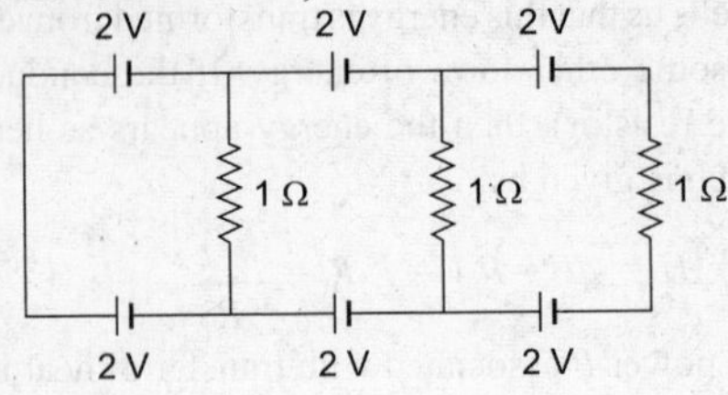

(a) 0.25 A (b) 0.5 A

(c) 0 A (d) 1 A

56. Which of the following statements is false?

(a) In a balanced Wheatstone bridge, if the cell and the galvanometer are exchanged, the null point is disturbed

(b) A rheostat can be used as a potential divider

(c) Kirchhoff's second law represents energy conservation

(d) Wheatstone bridge is the most sensitive when all the four resistances are of the same order of magnitude

57. For the circuit shown, with $R_1 = 1.0$ Ω, $R_2 = 2.0$ Ω, $E_1 = 2$ V and $E_2 = E_3 = 4$ V, the potential difference between the points 'a' and 'b' is approximately (in V):

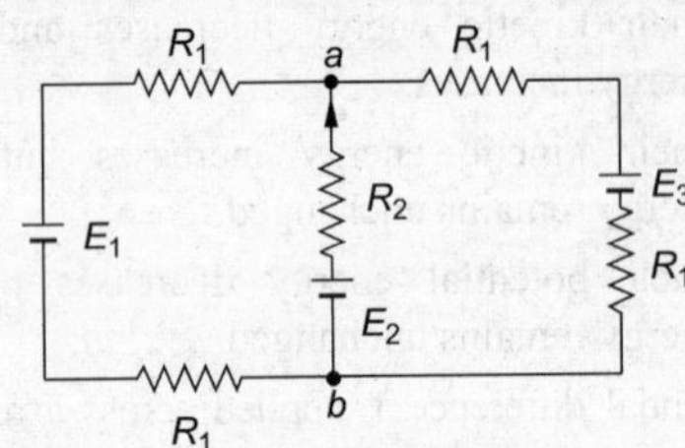

(a) 3.3 (b) 2.7

(c) 3.7 (d) 2.3

58. In the given circuit the cells have zero internal resistance. The currents (in amperes) passing through resistance R_1 and R_2 respectively, are :

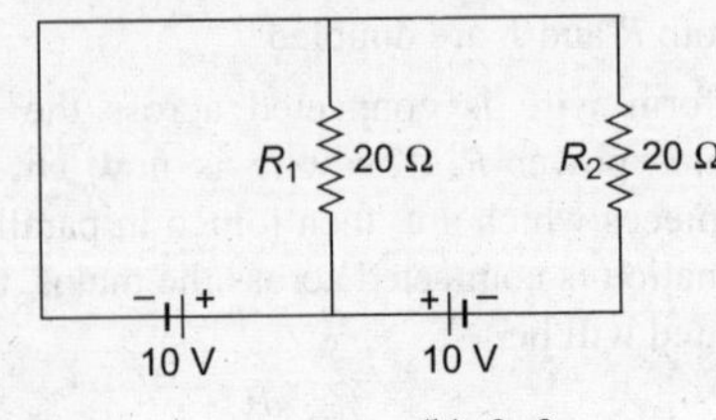

(a) 1, 2 (b) 2, 2

(c) 0.5, 0 (d) 0, 1

59. Two batteries with e.m.f 12V and 13V are connected in parallel across a load resistor of 10Ω. The internal resistance of the two batteries are 1Ω and 2Ω respectively. The voltage across the load lies between:

(a) 11.4V and 11.5V (b) 11.7V and 11.8V
(c) 11.6V and 11.7V (d) 11.5V and 11.6V

60. In the circuit shown below, the current in the 1Ω resistor is

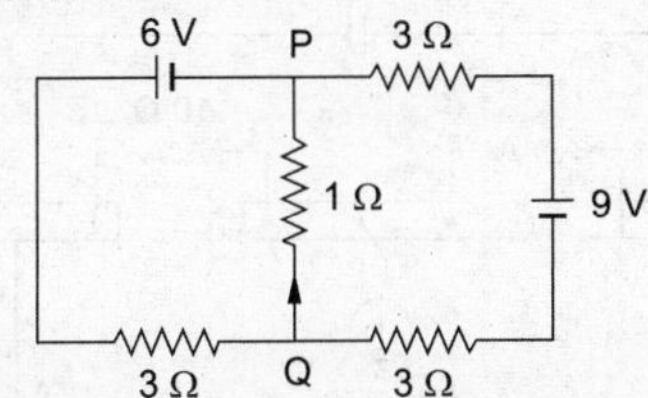

(a) 1.3 A, from P to Q (b) 0.13 A, from Q to P
(c) 0 A (d) 0.13 A, form P to Q

61. Find out the value of current through 2 Ω resistance for the given circuit.

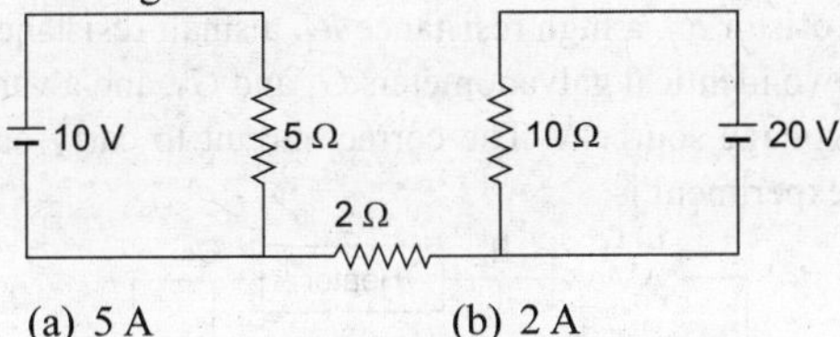

(a) 5 A (b) 2 A
(c) zero (d) 4 A

62. In a large building, there are 15 bulbs of 40 W, 5 bulbs of 100 W, 5 fans of 80 W and 1 heater of 1 kW. The voltage of the electric mains is 220 V. The minimum capacity of the main fuse of the building will be

(a) 8 A (b) 10 A
(c) 12 A (d) 14 A

63. The supply voltage in a room is 120 V. The resistance of the lead wires is 6 Ω. A 60 W bulb is already switched on. What is the decrease of voltage across the bulb when a 240 W heater is switched on in parallel to the bulb?

(a) zero (b) 2.9 V
(c) 13.3 V (d) 10.4 V

64. Incandescent bulbs are designed by keeping in mind that the resistance of their filament increases with the increase in temperature. If at room temperature, 100 W, 60 W and 40 W bulbs have filament resistances R_{100}, R_{60} and R_{40}, respectively, the relation between these resistances is

(a) $\dfrac{1}{R_{100}} = \dfrac{1}{R_{40}} + \dfrac{1}{R_{60}}$ (b) $R_{100} = R_{40} + R_{60}$

(c) $R_{100} > R_{60} > R_{40}$ (d) $\dfrac{1}{R_{100}} > \dfrac{1}{R_{60}} > \dfrac{1}{R_{40}}$

65. Figure shows three resistor configurations R_1, R_2 and R_3 connected to 3 V battery. If the power dissipated by the configuration R_1, R_2 and R_3 is P_1, P_2 and P_3, respectively, then

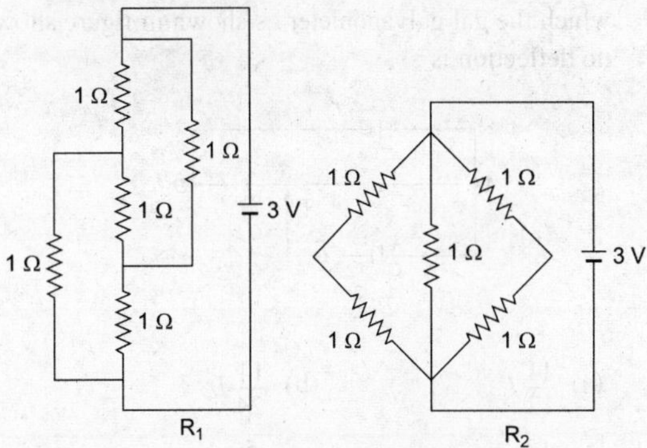

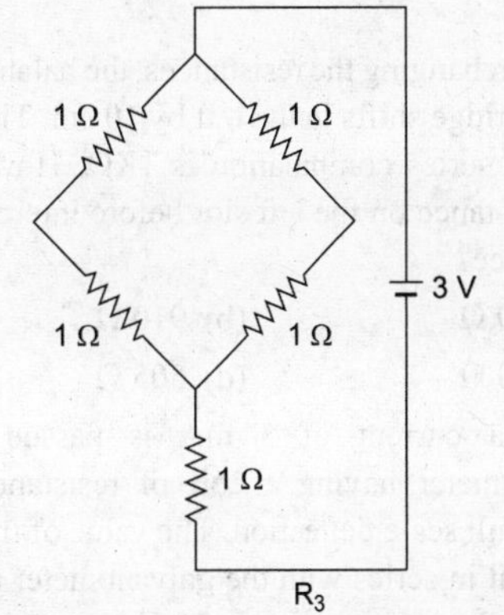

(a) $P_1 > P_2 > P_3$ (b) $P_1 > P_3 > P_2$
(c) $P_2 > P_1 > P_3$ (d) $P_3 > P_2 > P_1$

66. Two bars of radius r and $2r$ are kept in contact as shown. An electric current I is passed through the bars. Which one of the following is correct?

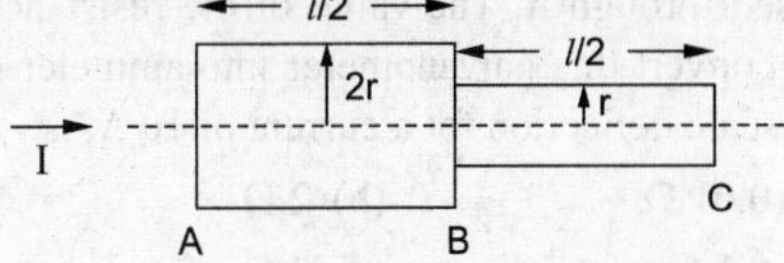

(a) Heat produced in bar BC is 4 times the heat produced in bar AB
(b) Electric field in both halves is equal
(c) Current density across AB is double that of across BC
(d) Potential difference across AB is 4 times that of across BC

67. A rigid container with thermally insulated walls contains a coil of resistance 100 Ω, carrying current 1 A. Charge in internal energy after 5 min will be

(a) zero (b) 10 kJ
(c) 20 kJ (d) 30 kJ

68. A potentiometer wire AB having length L and resistance $12r$ is joined to a cell D of emf ε and internal resistance r. A cell C having emf $\varepsilon/2$ and internal resistance $3r$ is connected. The length AJ at which the gal galvanometer as shown in figure shows no deflection is :

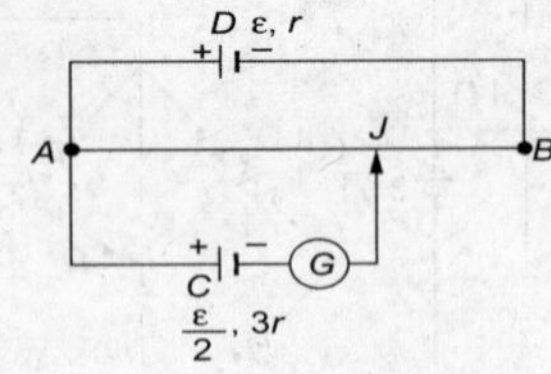

(a) $\frac{11}{12}L$ (b) $\frac{11}{24}L$

(c) $\frac{13}{24}L$ (d) $\frac{5}{12}L$

69. On interchanging the resistances, the balance point of a meter bridge shifts to the left by 10 cm. The resistance of their series combination is 1KΩ. How much was the resistance on the left slot before interchanging the resistance?

(a) 550 Ω (b) 910 Ω

(c) 990 Ω (d) 505 Ω

70. When a current of 5 mA is passed through a galvanometer having a coil of resistance 15 Ω, it shows full scale deflection. The value of the resistance to be put in series with the galvanometer to convert it into a voltmeter of range 0–10 V is

(a) 2.045×10^3 Ω (b) 2.535×10^3 Ω

(c) 4.005×10^3 Ω (d) 1.985×10^3 Ω

71. A galvanometer having a coil resistance of 100 Ω gives a full scale deflection when a current 1 mA is passed through it. The value of the resistance which can convert this galvanometer into ammeter giving a full scale deflection for a current of 10 A, is

(a) 0.01 Ω (b) 2 Ω

(c) 0.1 Ω (d) 3 Ω

72. During an experiment with a meter bridge, the galvanometer shows a null point when the jockey is pressed at 40.0 cm using a standard resistance of 90 Ω, as show in the scale used in the meter bridge is 1mm. The unknown resistance is

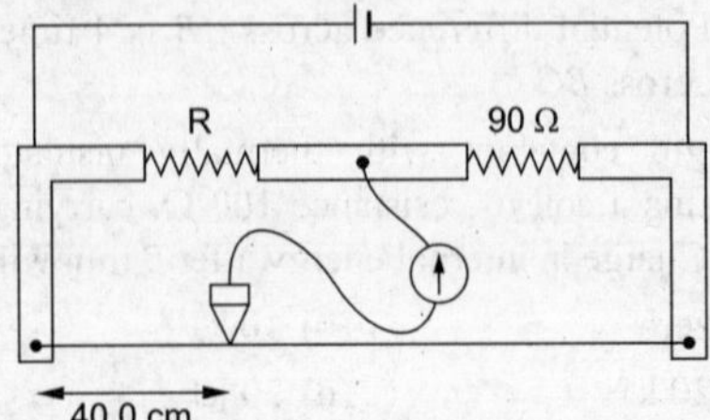

(a) 60 ± 0.15 Ω (b) 135 ± 0.56 Ω

(c) 60 ± 0.25 Ω (d) 135 ± 0.23 Ω

73. A meter bridge is set-up as shown in figure, to determine an unknown resistance X using a standard 10 Ω resistor. The galvanometer shows null point when tapping-key is at 52 cm mark. The end-corrections are 1 cm and 2 cm respectively for the ends A and B. The determined value of X is

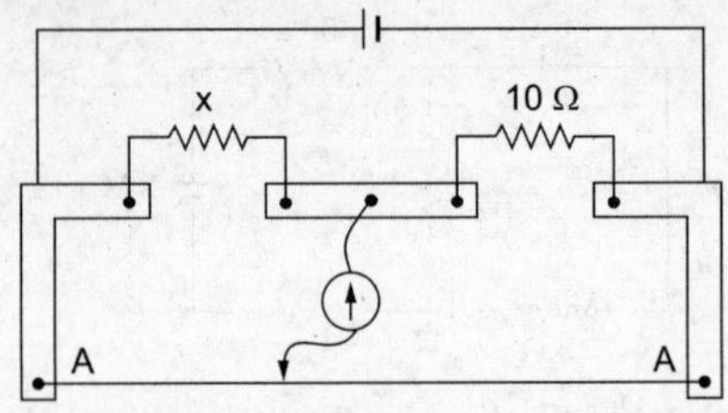

(a) 10.2 Ω (b) 10.6 Ω

(c) 10.8 Ω (d) 11.1 Ω

74. To verify Ohm's law, a student is provided with a test resistor R_T, a high resistance R_1, a small resistance R_2, two identical galvanometers G_1 and G_2, and a variable voltage source V. The correct circuit to carry out the experiment is

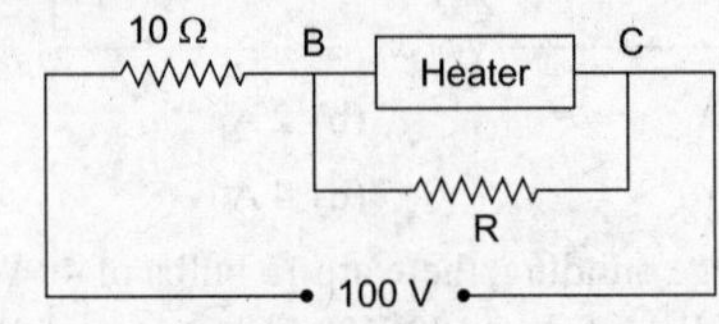

(a)

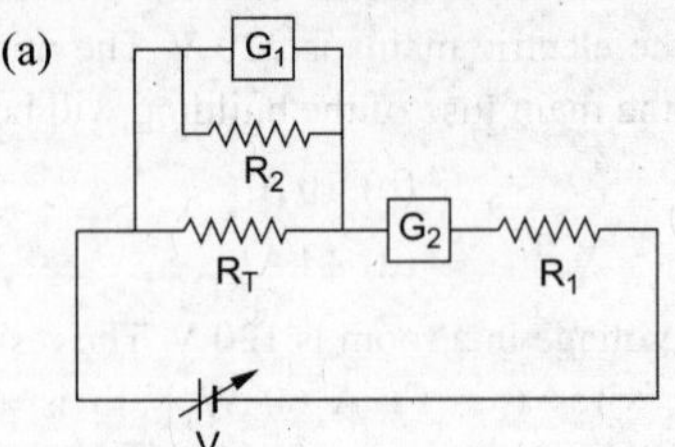

(b)

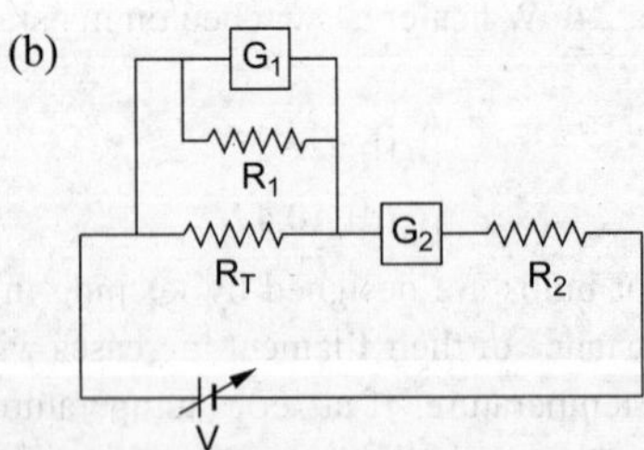

(c)

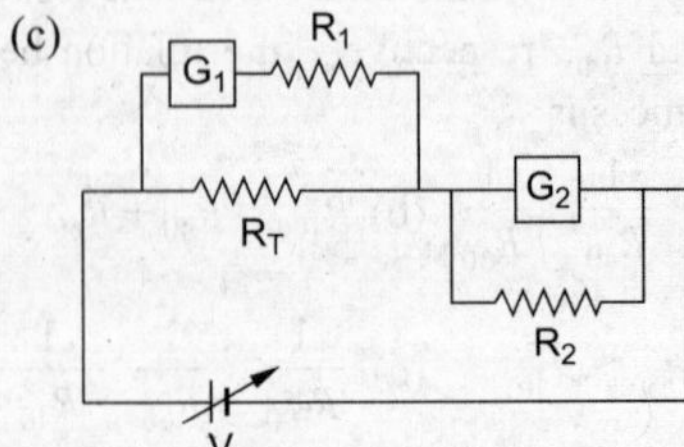

(d) 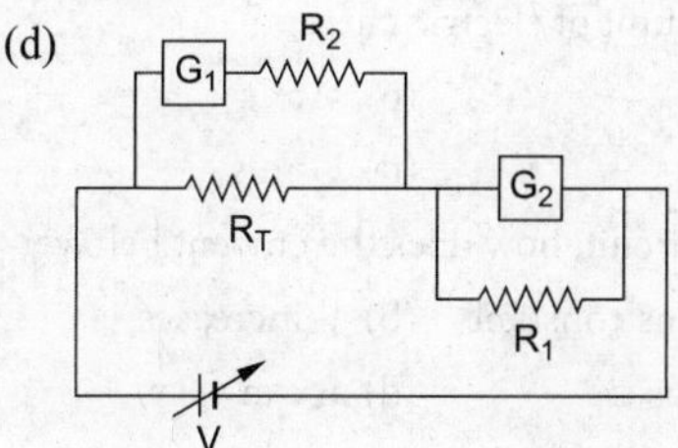

75. A resistance of 2 Ω is connected across one gap of a meter-bridge (the length of the wire is 100 cm) and an unknown resistance, greater than 2 Ω, is connected across the other gap. When these resistances are interchanged, the balance point shifts by 20 cm. Neglecting any corrections, the unknown resistance is

(a) 3 Ω (b) 4 Ω
(c) 5 Ω (d) 6 Ω

76. A moving coil galvanometer of resistance 100 Ω is used as an ammeter using a resistance of 0.1 Ω. The maximum deflection current in the galvanometer is μA. Find the current in the circuit, so that the ammeter shows maximum deflection.

(a) 100.1 mA (b) 1000.1 mA
(c) 10.01 mA (d) 1.01 mA

77. For the post office box arrangement to determine the value of unknown resistance, the unknown resistance should be connected between.

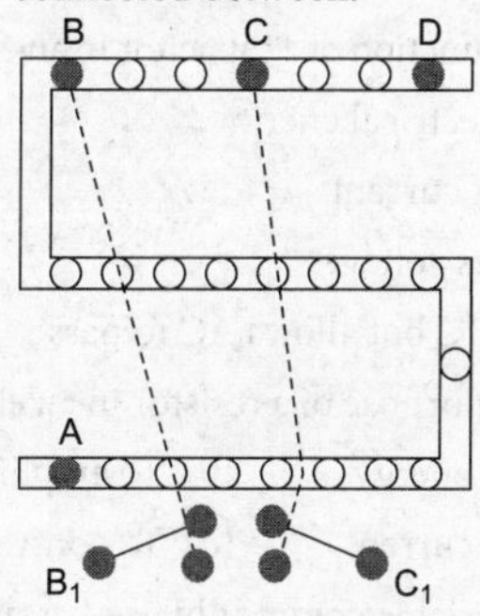

(a) *B* and *C* (b) *C* and *D*
(c) *A* and *D* (d) B_1 and C_1

78. *A* 200 Ω resistor has a certain color code. If one replaces the red color by green in the code, the new resistance will be :

(a) 300 Ω (b) 100 Ω
(c) 400 Ω (d) 500 Ω

79. A 2 W carbon resistor is color coded with green, black, red and brown respectively. The maximum current which can be passed through this resistor is :

(a) 20 mA (b) 100 mA
(c) 0.4 mA (d) 63 mA

80. What is the unit of electric current?

(a) Volt (b) Watt
(c) Ampere (d) Ohm

81. Which material is a good conductor of electricity?

(a) Rubber (b) Glass
(c) Copper (d) Wood

82. What is the SI unit of electric potential difference?

(a) Ampere (b) Volt
(c) Watt (d) Ohm

83. In a series circuit, what happens to the current when more resistors are added?

(a) Increases (b) Decreases
(c) Remains the same (d) Becomes zero

84. What is the relationship between voltage, current, and resistance in Ohm's Law?

(a) V = IR (b) I = VR
(c) R = IV (d) V = I/R

85. Which of the following is a unit of electrical power?

(a) Joule (b) Newton
(c) Watt (d) Volt

86. What is the direction of conventional current flow in a circuit?

(a) From positive to negative
(b) From negative to positive
(c) Both directions simultaneously
(d) It depends on the circuit

87. Which component stores electrical energy in a circuit?

(a) Resistor (b) Capacitor
(c) Inductor (d) Diode

88. What is the resistance of an ideal conductor?

(a) Infinite (b) Zero
(c) Variable (d) Constant

89. What does a transformer do in an electrical circuit?

(a) Converts AC to DC (b) Changes voltage
(c) Stores energy (d) Regulates current

90. Which type of current flows in household circuits?

(a) Alternating current (AC)
(b) Direct current (DC)
(c) Both AC and DC
(d) None of the above

91. What is the SI unit of electric charge?

(a) Ampere-hour (b) Coulomb
(c) Farad (d) Tesla

92. Which law describes the relationship between the voltage across a conductor and the current flowing through it, given constant temperature?

(a) Kirchhoff's Law (b) Ohm's Law
(c) Faraday's Law (d) Lenz's Law

93. What is the purpose of a fuse in an electrical circuit?
(a) To increase resistance
(b) To regulate current
(c) To interrupt excessive current
(d) To store electrical energy

94. What is the function of a diode in an electrical circuit?
(a) Amplify signals (b) Store energy
(c) Control current flow (d) Convert AC to DC

95. What is the fundamental particle carrying a negative charge in an atom?
(a) Proton (b) Neutron
(c) Electron (d) Nucleus

96. What is the SI unit of electric charge?
(a) Coulomb (b) Ampere
(c) Volt (d) Ohm

97. What is the term for the opposition that a material offers to the flow of electric current?
(a) Voltage (b) Resistance
(c) Capacitance (d) Conductance

98. In which type of circuit does the current have only one pathway to follow?
(a) Parallel circuit (b) Series circuit
(c) Complex circuit (d) Combination circuit

99. What does DC stand for in electricity?
(a) Direct Current (b) Dual Current
(c) Dynamic Current (d) Digital Current

100. Which device is used to measure electric current in a circuit?
(a) Voltmeter (b) Ammeter
(c) Ohmmeter (d) Multimeter

101. What is the term for a closed path that allows electric current to flow?
(a) Breaker (b) Conductor
(c) Insulator (d) Resistor

102. Which law states that the total current entering a junction is equal to the total current leaving the junction in a circuit?
(a) Ohm's Law (b) Kirchhoff's Voltage Law
(c) Faraday's Law (d) Kirchhoff's Current Law

103. What is the term for the rate at which electrical energy is used or produced?
(a) Voltage (b) Current
(c) Power (d) Resistance

104. Which component is commonly used to store electrical energy in a circuit?
(a) Resistor (b) Capacitor
(c) Inductor (d) Diode

105. What is the unit of electric current?
(a) Volts (b) Watts
(c) Ampere (d) Ohms

106. In a series circuit, how does the current behave?
(a) It remains constant (b) It increases
(c) It decreases (d) It can vary

107. What is the relationship between voltage (V), current (I), and resistance (R) in an electrical circuit?
(a) V = IR (b) I = V/R
(c) R = V/I (d) All of the above

108. What is the purpose of a diode in an electrical circuit?
(a) To control current
(b) To amplify signals
(c) To regulate voltage
(d) To allow current flow in one direction

109. How is power (P) in an electrical circuit calculated?
(a) P = IV (b) P = I^2R
(c) P = V^2/R (d) All of the above

110. What happens to the total resistance in a parallel circuit as more resistors are added?
(a) It increases (b) It decreases
(c) It remains the same (d) Cannot be determined

111. What is the function of a capacitor in an electrical circuit?
(a) Stores electrical energy
(b) Controls current
(c) Regulates voltage
(d) Blocks DC but allows AC to pass

112. What is the purpose of a resistor in an electrical circuit?
(a) To store energy (b) To amplify signals
(c) To limit current (d) To control voltage

113. Which material is commonly used as a semiconductor in electronic devices?
(a) Copper (b) Aluminum
(c) Silicon (d) Iron

114. What is the role of a transformer in an electrical circuit?
(a) To convert DC to AC
(b) To regulate voltage
(c) To store energy
(d) To control current

115. What is the basic building block of digital circuits?
(a) Resistor
(b) Transistor
(c) Capacitor
(d) Inductor

116. What does the term "IC" stand for in the context of electronic circuits?
(a) Integrated Capacitor
(b) Insulated Conductor
(c) Integrated Circuit
(d) Inductive Coupling

117. In a NAND gate, what is the output when both inputs are high?
(a) High (b) Low
(c) Indeterminate (d) Floating

118. What is the purpose of a flip-flop in digital circuits?
(a) To amplify signals
(b) To store binary information
(c) To regulate voltage
(d) To control current

119. What is the function of an operational amplifier (op-amp)?
(a) Voltage regulation
(b) Signal amplification
(c) Current control
(d) Frequency modulation

120. What does the term "CMOS" refer to in electronic circuits?
(a) Capacitor-MOSFET
(b) Central Modulation Oscillator
(c) Complementary Metal-Oxide-Semiconductor
(d) Current Mode Oscillation System

121. What is the primary function of a diode in electronic circuits?
(a) Signal amplification
(b) Voltage regulation
(c) Current rectification
(d) Frequency modulation

122. What is the purpose of a resistor network in an electronic circuit?
(a) Voltage amplification
(b) Current regulation
(c) Signal processing
(d) Voltage division

123. What is the role of a comparator in electronic circuits?
(a) Signal amplification
(b) Voltage regulation
(c) Comparing two input signals
(d) Current control

124. In a digital-to-analog converter (DA(c), what does the binary input control?
(a) Frequency
(b) Voltage
(c) Current
(d) Phase

125. What is the purpose of a fuse in an electrical circuit?
(a) To increase current flow
(b) To regulate voltage
(c) To protect against overcurrent
(d) To control resistance

126. What happens in a short circuit?
(a) Current follows a longer path
(b) Resistance decreases
(c) Voltage increases
(d) Current takes an unintended low-resistance path

127. Which material is commonly used as a fuse element?
(a) Copper
(b) Aluminum
(c) Silver
(d) Tin-lead alloy

128. What is the main function of a circuit breaker?
(a) To regulate voltage
(b) To interrupt the circuit in case of overcurrent
(c) To increase resistance
(d) To control capacitance

129. How does a circuit breaker differ from a fuse?
(a) A fuse is reusable, while a circuit breaker is not.
(b) A circuit breaker is reusable, while a fuse is not.
(c) Both are reusable.
(d) Both are not reusable.

130. What is the unit of electrical resistance?
(a) Volt
(b) Ampere
(c) Ohm
(d) Watt

131. In a series circuit, how does the total resistance compare to the individual resistances?
(a) It is equal to the sum of the individual resistances.
(b) It is less than the sum of the individual resistances.
(c) It is greater than the sum of the individual resistances.
(d) It is independent of the individual resistances.

Answers

1. (c)	**2.** (b)	**3.** (c)	**4.** (b)	**5.** (d)	**6.** (a)	**7.** (a)	**8.** (a)	**9.** (a)	**10.** (c)
11. (a)	**12.** (a)	**13.** (c)	**14.** (d)	**15.** (a)	**16.** (b)	**17.** (c)	**18.** (a)	**19.** (d)	**20.** (b)
21. (d)	**22.** (a)	**23.** (a)	**24.** (b)	**25.** (a)	**26.** (d)	**27.** (c)	**28.** (b)	**29.** (c)	**30.** (b,c,d)
31. (a,c,d)	**32.** (d)	**33.** (a)	**34.** (c)	**35.** (c)	**36.** (a)	**37.** (b)	**38.** (d)	**39.** (b,c)	**40.** (d)
41. (a)	**42.** (d)	**43.** (d)	**44.** (c)	**45.** (c)	**46.** (a)	**47.** (d)	**48.** (c)	**49.** (d)	**50.** (a)
51. (b)	**52.** (c)	**53.** (c)	**54.** (a)	**55.** (c)	**56.** (a)	**57.** (a)	**58.** (c)	**59.** (d)	**60.** (b)
61. (c)	**62.** (c)	**63.** (d)	**64.** (d)	**65.** (c)	**66.** (a)	**67.** (d)	**68.** (c)	**69.** (a)	**70.** (d)
71. (a)	**72.** (c)	**73.** (b)	**74.** (c)	**75.** (a)	**76.** (a)	**77.** (c)	**78.** (d)	**79.** (a)	**80.** (c)
81. (c)	**82.** (b)	**83.** (b)	**84.** (a)	**85.** (c)	**86.** (a)	**87.** (b)	**88.** (b)	**89.** (b)	**90.** (a)
91. (b)	**92.** (b)	**93.** (c)	**94.** (c)	**95.** (c)	**96.** (a)	**97.** (b)	**98.** (b)	**99.** (a)	**100.** (b)
101. (b)	**102.** (d)	**103.** (c)	**104.** (b)	**105.** (c)	**106.** (a)	**107.** (d)	**108.** (d)	**109.** (d)	**110.** (b)
111. (a)	**112.** (c)	**113.** (c)	**114.** (b)	**115.** (b)	**116.** (c)	**117.** (b)	**118.** (b)	**119.** (b)	**120.** (c)
121. (c)	**122.** (d)	**123.** (c)	**124.** (b)	**125.** (c)	**126.** (d)	**127.** (a)	**128.** (b)	**129.** (b)	**130.** (c)
131. (a)									

Explanations

1. Mass of the substance deposited at the cathode

$$m = zit = z\left(\frac{W}{V}\right)t$$

$$= 0.367 \times 10^{-6} \times \frac{100\times10^3}{125} \times 60$$

$$= 17.6 \times 10^{-3}\text{ kg}$$

2. Mass, $m = Zit = m = \frac{ZVt}{R}$

or $m \propto Vt$

$\therefore$ $\frac{m_1}{m_2} \propto \frac{V_1t_1}{V_2t_2}$

Given, $m_1 = 2$ g, $V_1 = 12$ V, $t_1 = 30$ min, $V_2 = 6$ V

and $t_2 = 45$ min

$$\frac{2}{m_2} = \frac{12\times30}{6\times45}$$

$\Rightarrow$ $m_2 = 1.5$ g

The mass of copper deposited = 1.5 g

3. According to Faraday's law of electrolysis,

$$m = zit$$

$\therefore$ $\frac{m_{Zn}}{m_{Cu}} = \frac{z_{Zn}}{z_{Cu}}$

$\therefore$ $\frac{0.13}{m_{Cu}} = \frac{32.5}{31.5}$

$m_{Cu} = 0.126$g

5. Given relation,

$$E = 40t - \frac{t^2}{20}$$

Neutral point exist where $\frac{dE}{dt}$ will be zero.

$\therefore$ $\frac{dE}{dt} = 40 - \frac{2t}{20}$

or $40 - \frac{2t}{20} = 0$

or $\frac{t}{10} = 40$

$\Rightarrow$ $t = 400°$C

6. For a thermocouple $T_i = 2T_n - T_0$

$$T_i = 2 \times 300 - 10$$

$$T_i = 600 - 10 = 590°\text{C}$$

7. Thermo-emf of the thermocouple = – 25 μV/°C

Let θ be the smallest temperature difference.

Therefore, after connecting the thermocouple with the galvanometer, thermo-emf

$$E = (25\mu\text{V/°C}) \times \theta(°\text{C})$$

$$= 25\theta \times 10^{-6}\text{ V}$$

Potential drop developed across the galvanometer

$$= iR = 10^{-5} \times 40 = 4 \times 10^{-4}\text{ V}$$

$\therefore$ $4\times10^{-4} = 25\theta \times 10^{-6}$

$\therefore$ $\theta = \frac{4}{25}\times10^2 = 16°$C

8. No change in neutral temperature but temperature of inversion is $t_i = 2t_n - t_c$

$$540 = 2t_n - 0°$$

$$270°C = t_n$$

$$t_i = 2 \times 270 - 10 = 540 - 10 = 530°C$$

9. Resistance required in series is

$$R = \frac{V}{I_g} - G = \frac{nV}{\left(\frac{V}{G}\right)} - G = (n-1)G$$

$$\therefore \quad R_{PQ} = \frac{2Rr}{R+r}$$

10. In parallel potential difference across each bulb is same equal to applied voltage of 500 V. Which is more than permissible voltage. So, both bulbs will get fused.

11. Number of units $= \dfrac{P\text{ (in watt)} \times t \text{ (in hour)}}{1000}$

Number of units $= \dfrac{2 \times 10^3 \times 1 \times 30}{1000} = 60$ unit

12. Consider upper segment above PQ.

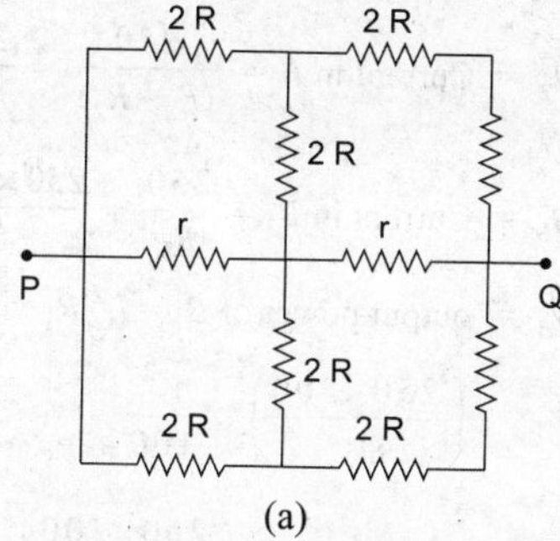

(a)

It is a balanced Wheatstone bridge. The central resistance $2R$ becomes ineffective. Similarly in the lower segment, the central resistance $2R$ becomes ineffective. The equivalent circuit is shown in the figure.

$$\therefore \quad \frac{I}{R_{PQ}} = \frac{I}{4R} + \frac{1}{2r} + \frac{1}{4R}$$

(b)

or
$$\frac{I}{R_{PQ}} = \frac{r + 2R + r}{4Rr}$$

$$R_{PQ} = \frac{4Rr}{2(R+r)} = \frac{2Rr}{R+r}$$

13. Since current I is independent of the value of resistance R_6, it is clear that R_1, R_2, R_3, and R_4 are the resistances of the arms of a balanced Wheatstone bridge.

$$\therefore \quad R_1 R_4 = R_2 R_3$$

14.
$I = neAv_d$ where

v_d = drift speed,

A = cross-sectional area.

As A is different at different sections, since the conductor is non-uniform, v_d is different.

Again electric field $E = \dfrac{I}{\sigma A}$.

E does not remain constant as A varies from section to section of a non-uniform conductor.

Hence current is the only quantity that remains constant along the length of the conductor.

15. This method is Kelvin's method of determining resistance of galvanometer by Wheatstone bridge circuit. Deflection in galvanometer G is same with switch S open or closed. It means that there is no current through S. This happens when the potentials at the two ends of S are same. This is the condition of balanced Wheatstone bridge.

$$\therefore \quad I_P = I_Q \text{ and } I_R = I_G$$

16. Initially,

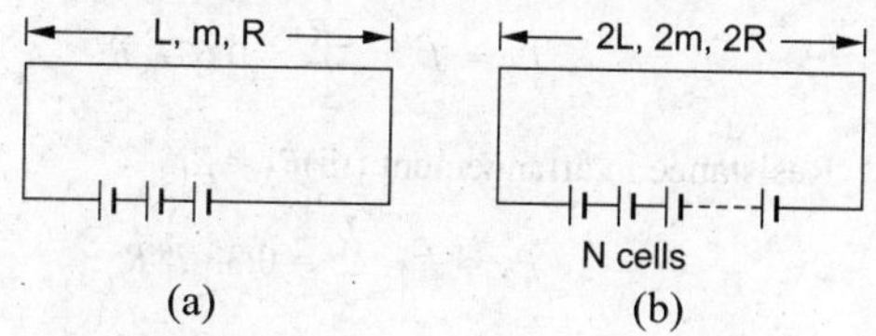

Let, resistance of wire = R

Mass of wire = m

Number of cells = 3

Time for flow of current = t

Change of temperature = ΔT

Electrical energy $= \dfrac{(3V)^2 t}{R}$

Heat energy = $ms\,\Delta T$

$$\therefore \quad ms\,\Delta T = \frac{9V^2 t}{R} \quad \text{...(i)}$$

Finally,

Electrical energy $= \dfrac{(NV)^2 t}{2R}$

Heat energy = $m's\,\Delta T = (2m)s\,\Delta T$

$$\therefore \quad \frac{N^2V^2t}{2R} = 2ms\,\Delta T = 2 \times \frac{9V^2t}{R}$$

$$\therefore \quad N^2 = 36$$

or
$$N = 6.$$

17. In the steady state condition, no current flows through the capacitor C along the branch BE.

Apply Kirchhoff's law to the closed mesh $ACDFA$,

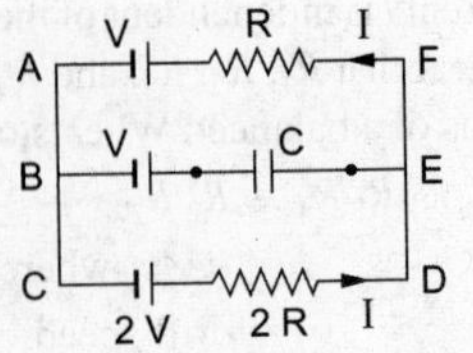

$2V - I(2R) - I(R) - V = 0$ or $V = 3\,IR$

or $$I = \frac{V}{3R} \quad ...(i)$$

Apply Kirchhoff's law to the mesh *ABEFA*,

$V + V_C - IR - V = 0$ or $V_C = IR = \left(\frac{V}{3R}\right) R = \frac{V}{3}$

$\therefore$ Potential difference across capacitor $V_C = \frac{V}{3}$.

18. Current is same through each combination.

Power dissipation = I^2R

Resistance in arrangement $IR_1 = 3R$

$\therefore$ Power in arrangement $IP_1 = I^2(3R) = 3I^2R$

Resistance in arrangement II $R_2 = \frac{2R}{3}$

$$\therefore \quad P_2 = I^2 \times \frac{2R}{3} = 0.67I^2R.$$

Resistance in arrangement (iii)$R_3 = R/3$

$$\therefore \quad P_3 = I^2 \times \frac{R}{3} = 0.33\,I^2R.$$

Similarly $P_4 = I^2 \times 3R/2 = 1.5\,I^2R$

$\therefore \quad P_1 : P_2 : P_3 : P_4 = 3 : 0.67 : 0.33 : 1.5$

$\therefore \quad$ III < II < IV < I

19. R_0 = Resistance at 0°C

$$1\Omega = R_0(1 + 27\alpha)$$

and $$2\Omega = R_0(1 + T\alpha)$$

$$\frac{2}{1} = \frac{1 + T\alpha}{1 + 27\alpha}$$

or $$T = 854°\text{C} = 1127\text{ K}$$

20. $$V_{AB} = I_2(4 + 6)$$

$\therefore$ $$V_{AB} = 10\,I_2$$

Also $$V_{AB} = I_1(5)$$

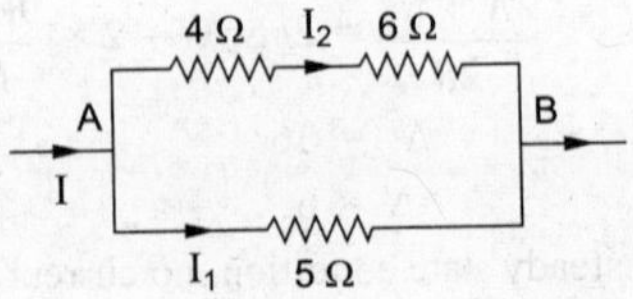

$\therefore$ $$5I_1 = 10I_2$$

or $$I_1 = 2I_2 \quad ...(i)$$

Let $$H = \frac{\text{Heat generated}}{\text{second}} = I^2R$$

$$\therefore \quad \frac{H_4}{H_5} = \frac{I_2^2 \times 4}{I_1^2 \times 5}$$

$$\frac{H_4}{10} = \frac{I_2^2 \times 4}{(2I_2)^2 \times 5}$$

or $$H_4 = \frac{10 \times 4}{4 \times 5} = 2\,\frac{\text{cal}}{\text{sec}}$$

21. A bulb is essentially a resistance $R = \frac{V^2}{P}$ where P denotes the power of the bulb.

$\therefore$ Resistance of $B_1(R_1) = V^2/100$

Resistance of $B_2(R_2) = V^2/60$

Resistance of $B_3(R_3) = V^2/60$

$$\therefore \quad I_1 = \text{Current in } B_1 = \frac{250}{(R_1 + R_2)} = \frac{250 \times 300}{8V^2}$$

$$I_2 = \text{Current in } B_2 = \frac{250}{(R_1 + R_2)} = \frac{250 \times 300}{8V^2}$$

$$I_3 = \text{Current in } B_3 = \frac{250}{R_3} = \frac{250 \times 60}{V^2}$$

$$\therefore \quad W_1 = \text{output power of } B_1 = I_1^2 R_1$$

$$\therefore \quad W_1 = \left(\frac{250 \times 300}{8V^2}\right)^2 \times \frac{V^2}{100}$$

$$W_2 = I_2^2 R_2 \text{ or } W_2 = \left(\frac{250 \times 300}{8V^2}\right)^2 \times \frac{V^2}{60}$$

$$W_3 = I_3^2 R_3 \text{ or } W_3 = \left(\frac{250 \times 60}{V^2}\right)^2 \times \frac{V^2}{60}$$

$\therefore W_1 : W_2 : W_3 = 15 : 25 : 64$ or $W_1 < W_2 < W_3$.

22. Ammeter is connected in series with the resistance-net and voltmeter is connected in parallel with the resistance net for verification of Ohm's law.

Set up (a) can be used for the purpose.

23. For null deflection of galvanometer in a metre- bridge experiment,

$$\frac{R_1}{R_2} = \frac{R_{AC}}{R_{CB}} \text{ or } \frac{R_1}{R_2} = \frac{x}{(100 - x)}$$

Since R_1/R_2 remains constant, $x(100 - x)$ also remains constant. The value of x remains as such.

$\therefore$ Length of $AC = x$.

24. Maximum power is delivered if external resistance = internal resistance.

Here internal resistance of battery = 4 Ω.

$\therefore$ External resistance should also be 4 Ω ...(i)

Network of resistances, connected across the battery, is actually a Wheatstone bridge in balanced condition. The equivalent circuits are shown below:

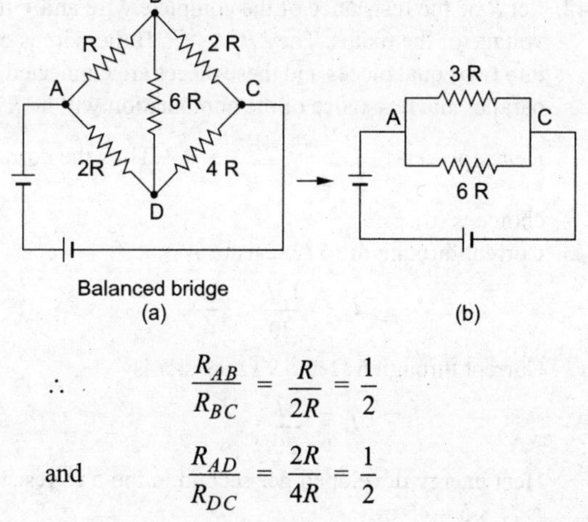

Balanced bridge
(a)
(b)

$$\therefore \quad \frac{R_{AB}}{R_{BC}} = \frac{R}{2R} = \frac{1}{2}$$

$$\text{and} \quad \frac{R_{AD}}{R_{DC}} = \frac{2R}{4R} = \frac{1}{2}$$

$$\therefore \quad \frac{R_{AB}}{R_{BC}} = \frac{R_{AD}}{R_{DC}}$$

Wheatstone bridge is therefore balanced. Hence the resistance of arm *BD* becomes ineffective.

Now *ABC* ($3R\Omega$) and *ADC* ($6R\Omega$) are in parallel

$$\therefore \quad R_{eq} = \frac{(3R)(6R)}{3R+6R} = \frac{3R \times 6R}{9R} = 2R \quad \text{...(ii)}$$

For maximum power, $2R = 4\Omega$

$\therefore R = 2\Omega$.

25. The minimum potential difference across the given galvanometer is

$$V = IR$$
$$V = 10^{-5} \times 40$$
$$V = 400\ \mu V$$

For each 25 μV thermo emf the temperature difference measured is 1°C.

For 400 μV temperature difference is 16°C

So, measured temperature difference detected by galvanometer is 16°C.

26. For a given volume, the resistance of the wire is expressed as

$$R = \frac{\rho l^2}{\text{Volume}} \Rightarrow R \propto l^2$$

$$\frac{R_2}{R_1} = \left(\frac{2l}{l}\right)^2 = 4 \Rightarrow \frac{R_2}{R_1} - 1 = 4 - 1$$

$$\frac{R_2 - R_1}{R_1} = 3$$

So, the change in resistance of wire will be 300%.

27. $$E = a\theta + b\theta^2$$

Given $$\frac{a}{b} = 700°\text{C}$$

$$\frac{dE}{d\theta} = a + 2b\theta$$

At neutral temperature, $\frac{dE}{d\theta} = 0$

$$\theta_n = \frac{-a}{2b} = \frac{-700}{2} = -350°\text{C}$$

As this temperature is below the temperature of cold Junction, hence no neutral temperature is possible for this thermocouple.

28. Power dissipation for a given value of voltage is

$$P = \frac{V^2}{R}$$

$$\frac{P_2}{P_1} = \frac{R_1}{R_2}$$

When the coil is cut into two halves; then the value of resistance for each half is $\frac{R}{2}$. When these two halves are put in parallel then

$$R_{\text{eff}} = \frac{R}{4}$$

$$\frac{P_2}{P_1} = \frac{R_1}{R_2} = \frac{R}{(R/4)} = 4$$

29.

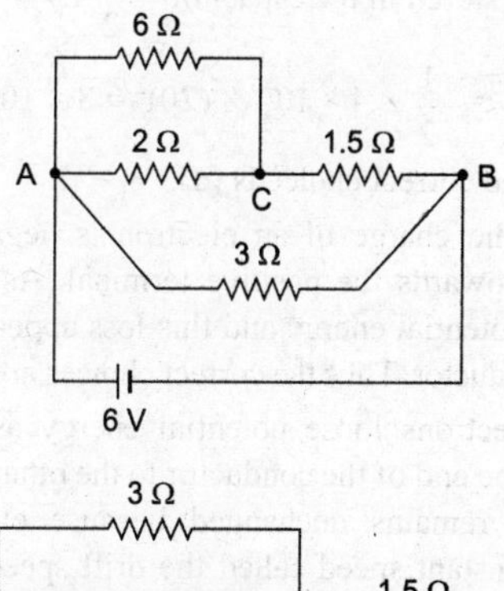

On redrawing the diagram, we get

$$I = \frac{6}{1.5} = 4\text{ A}$$

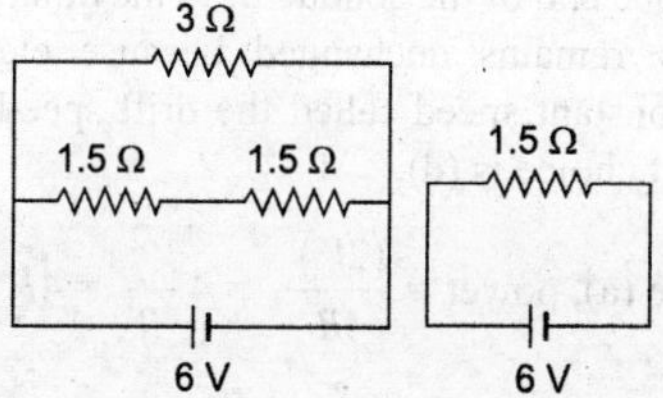

30. The correct choices are (b), (c) and (d). The free electrons in a metal are never at rest. At room temperature, they move randomly in all directions at speeds of the order of 10^5 ms^{-1}, even when no potential difference is applied across the conductor.

31. The correct choices are (a), (c) and (d).

32. The correct choices is (d). Drift speed and resistance change along the length of the conductor due to varying cross-section. Electric field is given by

$$E = -\frac{dV}{dx}$$

Since the resistance is changing along the length of the conductor dV/dx will change and hence electric field also changes along the length of the conductor.

33. Since $I = 1$ A, the charge passing through any cross-section of wire in 1 second is C. In 1.6 s, the charge transferred is $q = 1.6$ C. Now, $q = Ne$. Hence

$$N = \frac{q}{e} = \frac{1.6\text{C}}{1.6\times10^{-19}\text{C}}$$

$$= 10^{19} \text{ electrons}$$

Hence the correct choice is (a).

34. $v_d = \dfrac{I}{neA} = \dfrac{1.6}{10^{28}\times1.6\times10^{-19}\times10^{-7}}\ 10^{-2}\ \text{ms}^{-1} =$ 10 mms^{-1}, which is choice (c).

35. Applying Kirchhoff's junction rule to junction A, we have $i_1 = 2 + 1 = 3$ A, which is choice (c).

36. At junction B, $i_2 + 1 = 2$ or $i_2 = 1$ A, which is choice (a).

37. At junction D, $i_1 = i_2 + i_3$

$\Rightarrow i_3 = i_1 - i_2 = 3 - 1 = 2$ A.

So the correct choice is (b).

38. Potential drop along $AEDB$ is given by

$$V = 5\,i_1 + 1\,i_1 + 2\,i_2 = 15 + 3 + 2 = 20 \text{ V}$$

$\therefore$ Potential difference across the capacitor $C = 20$ V

Energy stored in the capacitor $= \frac{1}{2}CV^2$

$$= \frac{1}{2}\times 4\times10^{-6}\times(20)^2 = 8\times10^{-4}\text{J}$$

Thus the correct choice is (d).

39. Since the charge of an electron is negative, it will move towards the positive terminal. As it moves, it loses potential energy and this loss appears as heat in the conductor. Thus the correct choices are (b) and (c).

40. The electrons loose potential energy as they move from one end of the conductor to the other. The kinetic energy remains unchanged because electrons drift at a constant speed called the drift speed. Hence the correct choice is (d).

41. In case (a), power $= \dfrac{(2V)^2}{R} = 4\dfrac{V^2}{R} = 4P$

In case (b), power $= \dfrac{V^2}{2R} = \dfrac{P}{2}$

In case (c), power $= I^2(2R) = 2I^2R = 2P$

In case (d), power $= \dfrac{(2V)^2}{2R} = 2\dfrac{V^2}{R} = 2P$

42. Let R be the resistance of the complete wire and V the voltage of the mains. They $P = V^2/R$. If the wire is cut into two equal pieces and these pieces are connected in parallel, the resistance of the combination will be $R/4$.

Hence power $= \dfrac{V^2}{R/4} = \dfrac{4V^2}{R} = 4P$. Thus the correct choice is (d).

43. Current through the 5 Ω resistor is

$$I_2 = \frac{15I}{20} = \frac{3I}{4}$$

Current through 6 Ω and 9 Ω resistor is

$$I_1 = \frac{5I}{20} = \frac{I}{4}$$

Heat energy developed per second in the 5 Ω resistor is $I_2^2 \times 5 = 45$ or

$$\left(\frac{3I}{4}\right)^2 \times 5 = 45 \Rightarrow I = 4\text{ A}.$$

So the correct choice is (d).

44. Power developed in the 2 Ω resistor $= I^2\times 2 = (4)^2\times 2 = 32$ W, which is choice (c).

45. Potential difference across the 6 Ω resistor $= I_1\times 6 = \dfrac{I}{4}\times 6 = \dfrac{4}{4}\times 6 = 6$ V, which is choice (c).

When switch S_1 is closed, the capacitor is charged to the voltage of the battery. Energy stored in the capacitor is

$$U = \frac{1}{2}CV^2 = \frac{1}{2}\times 500\times10^{-6}\times(120)^2 = 3.6\text{ J}.$$

When S_1 is opened and switch S_2 is closed, no current flows through R_4. Hence power developed in $R_4 = 0$, i.e., $P_4 = 0$. Let I_1 be the current through the 4 Ω resistor at an instant of time t. This current divides into I_2 flowing through R_2 and I_3 flowing through R_3 such that $I_1 = I_2 + I_3$. Since the potential difference across R_2 and R_3 is the same, we have, $I_2R_2 = I_3R_3$ or $6I_2 = 12\,I_3$ or $I_2 = 2I_3$. But $I_1 = I_2 + I_3$. Therefore,

$$I_1 = I_3 + I_3 \quad\text{or}\quad I_3 = \frac{I_1}{3}.$$

Similarly $\quad I_2 = \dfrac{2I_1}{3}$

Thus, $\quad I_1 : I_2 : I_3 = I_1 : \dfrac{2I_1}{3} : \dfrac{I_1}{3}$

$$= 1 : \frac{2}{3} : \frac{1}{3} = 3 : 2 : 1$$

Now $P = I^2R$. Therefore,

$$= P_1 : P_2 : P_3 : I_1^2R_1 : I_2^2R_2 : I_3^2R_3$$

$$= (3)^2\times 4 : (2)^2\times 6 : (1)^2\times 12$$

$$= 36 : 24 : 12 = 3 : 2 : 1$$

Thus energy $U = 3.6$ J stored in the capacitor is distributed among resistors R_1, R_2 and R_3 in the ratio 3 : 2 : 1.

46. $P_1 = \dfrac{3.6 \times 3}{6} = 1.8$ W, which is choice (a).

47. $P_2 = \dfrac{3.6 \times 2}{6} = 1.2$ W, which is choice (d).

48. $P_3 = \dfrac{3.6 \times 1}{6} = 0.6$ W, which is choice (c).

49. As resistance of each side is 6 Ω.

So 12Ω and 6Ω will be parallel

So resistance between any two corners $\dfrac{6 \times 12}{18} = 4\Omega$

50. $$\frac{1}{R_{eq}} = \frac{1}{R_{Al}} + \frac{1}{R_{Fe}} = \left(\frac{A_{Al}}{\rho_{Al}} + \frac{A_{Fe}}{\rho_{Fe}}\right)\frac{1}{\ell}$$

$$= \left[\frac{(7^2 - 2^2)}{2.7} + \frac{2^2}{10}\right]\frac{10^{-6}}{10^{-8}} \times \frac{1}{50 \times 10^{-3}}$$

Simplify above we get,

$$R = \frac{1875}{64} \times 10^{-6}\ \Omega = \frac{1875}{64}\ \mu\Omega$$

51. As, we know that $i = neAv_d$

So $$\frac{V}{R} = neAv_d$$

or $$\frac{V}{\left(\dfrac{\rho l}{A}\right)} = neAv_d$$

$\therefore$ $$\rho = \frac{V}{nelv_d} = \text{resistivity of the wire}$$

On putting the values we have

$$\rho = \frac{5}{(8 \times 10^{28})(1.6 \times 10^{-19})(0.1)(2.5 \times 10^{-4})}$$

$\approx 1.6 \times 10^{-5}$ Ω-m

52. From law of resistance we have

$$R = \frac{\rho(L)}{A} = \frac{\rho L}{tL} = \frac{\rho}{t}$$

i.e., R is independent of L.

Thus, the correct option is (c)

53. As resistance of PQ $\quad R_{PQ} = \dfrac{5}{11}r$,

Resistance of QR $\quad R_{QR} = \dfrac{4}{11}r$

and resistance of PR $\quad R_{PR} = \dfrac{3}{11}r$

$\therefore$ R_{PQ} is maximum.

Therefore, the correct option is (a).

54. Since the potential drop across each resistor is zero, so the current through each of resistor is zero.

55. If we exchange the battery and galvanometer, then in a balanced Wheatstone bridge, there is no effect on position of null point.

56.

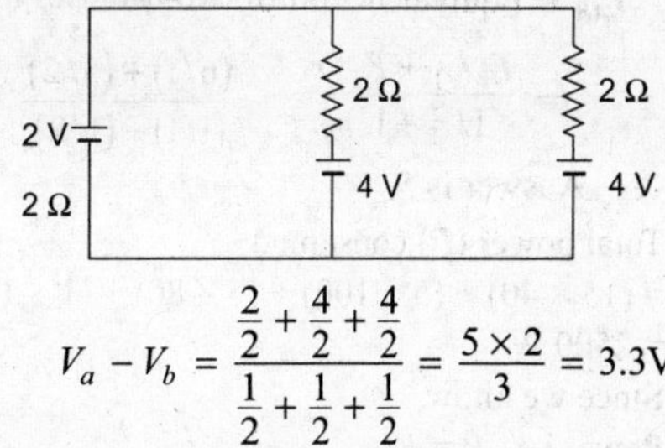

$$V_a - V_b = \frac{\dfrac{2}{2} + \dfrac{4}{2} + \dfrac{4}{2}}{\dfrac{1}{2} + \dfrac{1}{2} + \dfrac{1}{2}} = \frac{5 \times 2}{3} = 3.3\text{V}$$

57. Potential drop across R_1 is 10 V,

Current in $R_1 = 0.5$ A, Current in $R_2 = 0$ A

58.

As $$E_{eq} = \frac{\dfrac{12}{1} + \dfrac{13}{2}}{\dfrac{1}{1} + \dfrac{1}{2}} = \frac{\dfrac{37}{2}}{\dfrac{3}{2}} = \frac{37}{3}$$

$$Y_{eq} = \frac{2}{3}$$

$$I = \frac{\dfrac{37}{3}}{\dfrac{2}{3} + 10} = \frac{\dfrac{37}{3}}{\dfrac{32}{3}} = \frac{37}{32}$$

Voltage across load = IR = $\left(\dfrac{37}{32}\right)(10) = 11.56$ V.

59.

Using Kirchhoff's loop law in loops 1 and 2 in the directions shown in figure we get

$$6 - 3(i_1 + i_2) - i_2 = 0 \quad \text{...(i)}$$

and $$9 - 2i_1 + i_2 - 3i_1 = 0 \quad \text{...(ii)}$$

Solving Eqs. (i) and (ii) we get,

$$i_2 = 0.13\text{ A}$$

Thus, the current in 1 Ω resistor is 0.13 A from Q to P.

60. Current in the respective loop will remain confined in the loop itself.

Thus, current through 2 Ω resistance = 0

$\therefore$ Correct answer is (c).

61. V_{AB} = Equivalent emf of two batteries in parallel.

$$= \frac{E_1/r_1 + E_2/r_2}{1/r_1 + 1/r_2} = \frac{(6/1)+(3/2)}{(1/1)+(1/2)} = 5\text{ V}$$

$\therefore$ Answer is 5.

62. Total power (P) consumed

$= (15 \times 40) + (5 \times 100) + (5 \times 80) + (1 \times 1000)$

$= 2500$ W

Since we know,

Power i.e., $P = VI$

$$\Rightarrow \quad I = \frac{2500}{220}\text{A} = \frac{125}{11} = 11.3\text{ A}$$

Minimum capacity should be 12 A.

63. As, $\quad P = \dfrac{V^2}{R}$

where, P = power dissipates in the circuit,

V = applied voltage,

R = net resistance of the circuit

$$R = \frac{120 \times 120}{60} = 240\ \Omega \quad \text{[resistance of bulb]}$$

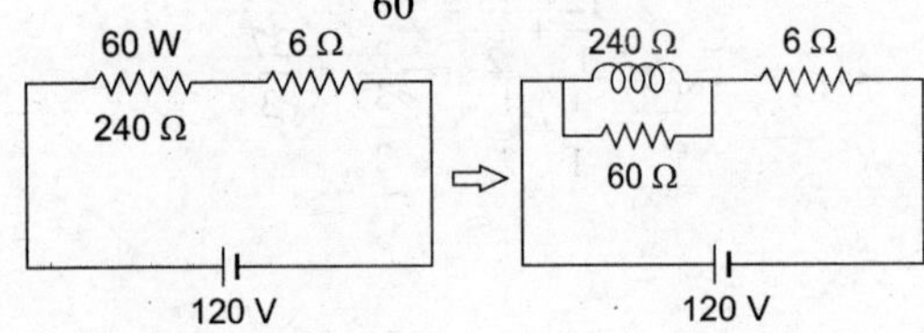

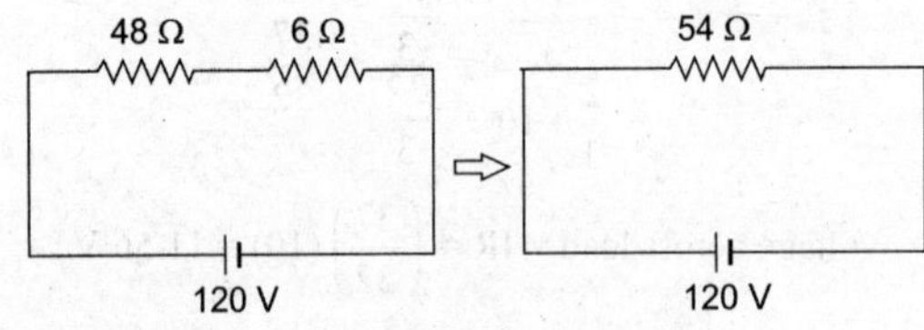

Here $\quad R_{eq} = 240 + 6 = 246\ \Omega$

$$\Rightarrow \text{So} \quad i_1 = \frac{V}{R_{eq}} = \frac{120}{246}$$

[before connecting heater]

$$\text{As} \quad R = \frac{V^2}{P} = \frac{120 \times 120}{240}$$

$\Rightarrow \quad R = 60\ \Omega \quad$ [resistance of heater]

So, tfrom figure, we have

$$V_1 = \frac{240}{246} \times 120 = 117.073\text{ V} \quad [\because V = IR]$$

$$\Rightarrow \quad i_2 = \frac{V}{R_2} = \frac{120}{54}$$

$$V_2 = \frac{48}{54} \times 120 = 106.66\text{ V}$$

$$V_1 - V_2 = 10.41\text{ V}$$

64. $R = \dfrac{V^2}{P}$ so $R \propto \dfrac{1}{P}$

Therefore $\quad \dfrac{1}{R_{100}} > \dfrac{1}{R_{60}} > \dfrac{1}{R_{40}}$

Thus, the correct option is (d).

65. Using formula $P = \dfrac{V^2}{R}$, $R_1 = 1\ \Omega$, $R_2 = 0.5\ \Omega$

and $\quad R_3 = 2\ \Omega$

$V_1 = V_2 = V_3 = 3$ V

$$\therefore \quad P_1 = \frac{(3)^2}{1} = 9\text{ W}$$

$$P_2 = \frac{(3)^2}{0.5} = 18\text{ W}$$

$$\text{and} \quad P_3 = \frac{(3)^2}{2} = 4.5\text{ W}$$

$\therefore \quad P_2 > P_1 > P_3$

$\therefore$ Correct option is (c).

66. Current flowing through both the bars is equal.

Now, the heat produced is given by

$$H = I^2Rt$$

or $\quad H \propto R$

$$\text{or} \quad \frac{H_{AB}}{H_{BC}} = \frac{R_{AB}}{R_{BC}} = \frac{(1/2r)^2}{(1/r)^2} \quad \left(\text{as } R \propto \frac{1}{A} \propto \frac{1}{r^2}\right)$$

$$= \frac{1}{4}$$

or $\quad H_{BC} = 4\,H_{AB}$

67. $W = 0$. Hence, from first law of thermodynamics,

$$\Delta U = \Delta Q = i^2Rt = (1)^2\,(100)\,(5 \times 60)\text{ J} = 30\text{ kJ}.$$

$\therefore$ Correct answer is (d).

68. Potential gradient across wire is $\dfrac{12E}{13L}$

For null deflection $\dfrac{12E}{13L} \times l = E/2 \quad l = \dfrac{13L}{24}$

69.

R
1000–R
G
l
100–l

Let resistances are R and $1000 - R$

$$\text{For case-I} \quad \frac{R}{l} = \frac{1000 - R}{100 - l} \quad \text{...(i)}$$

$$\text{For case-II} \quad \frac{1000 - R}{l - 10} = \frac{R}{110 - l} \quad \text{...(ii)}$$

Multiplying equation (i) and (ii) we have,

$$\frac{R(1000 - R)}{l(l - 10)} = \frac{(1000 - R)R}{(100 - l)(110 - l)}$$

$$\Rightarrow \quad l^2 - 10\,l = 11000 + l^2 - 210\,l$$

$$\Rightarrow \quad 200\,l = 11000$$

$$\Rightarrow \quad l = 55 \text{ cm}$$

Putting in equation (i) we have,

$$\frac{R}{55} = \frac{1000 - R}{45}$$

$$\Rightarrow \quad 45\,R = 55000 - 55\,R$$

$$\Rightarrow \quad R = 550\,\Omega$$

70. For a Voltmeter,

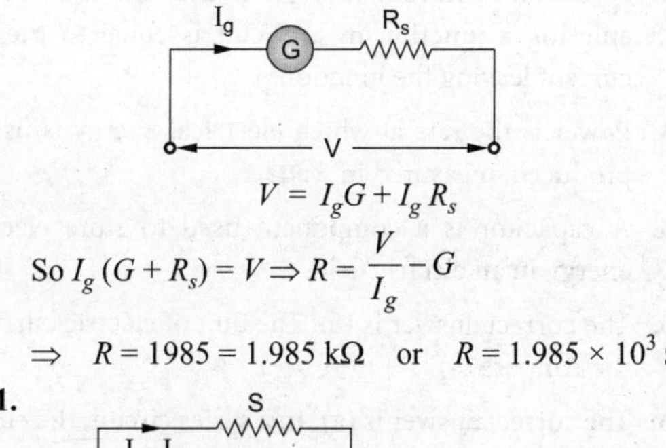

$$V = I_g G + I_g R_s$$

So $I_g\,(G + R_s) = V \Rightarrow R = \dfrac{V}{I_g} - G$

$\Rightarrow \quad R = 1985 = 1.985\ \text{k}\Omega \quad \text{or} \quad R = 1.985 \times 10^3\ \Omega$

71.

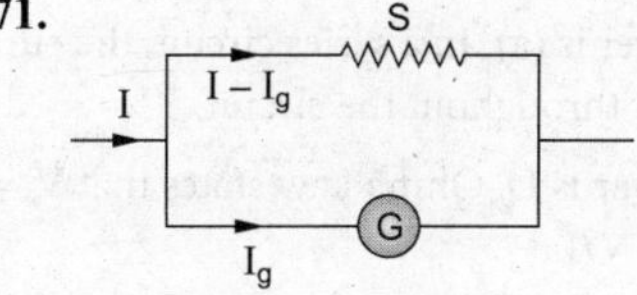

In parallel, current distributes in inverse ratio of resistance.

As $\quad I_g G = (I - I_g)S$

Hence, $\quad \dfrac{I - I_g}{I_g} = \dfrac{G}{S}$

So $\quad S = \dfrac{GI_g}{I - I_g}$

Since I_g is very small, so that

$$S = \frac{GI_g}{I}$$

$$b = \frac{(100)(1\times10^{-3})}{10} = 0.01\,\Omega$$

72. For balanced meter bridge

$$\frac{X}{R} = \frac{l}{(100 - l)} \quad (\text{where, } R = 90\,\Omega\,)$$

$$\therefore \quad \frac{X}{90} = \frac{40}{100 - 40}$$

$$\therefore \quad X = 60\,\Omega$$

$$\Rightarrow \quad X = R\frac{l}{(100 - l)}$$

$$\Rightarrow \quad \frac{\Delta X}{X} = \frac{\Delta l}{l} + \frac{\Delta l}{100 - l} = \frac{0.1}{40} + \frac{0.1}{60}$$

$$\Delta X = 0.25$$

So, $\quad X = (60 \pm 0.25)\,\Omega$

73. Applying the concept of balanced Wheatstone bridge, we get,

$$\frac{P}{Q} = \frac{R}{S}$$

$$\therefore \quad \frac{X}{(52+1)} = \frac{10}{(48+2)}$$

$$\therefore \quad X = \frac{10\times53}{50}$$

$$= 10.6\,\Omega$$

$\therefore$ Correct option is (b).

74. We will require a voltmeter, an ammeter, a test resistor and a variable battery to verify Ohm's law.

Voltmeter which is made by connecting a high resistance with a galvanometer is connected in parallel with the test resistor.

Further, an ammeter which is formed by connecting a low resistance in parallel with galvanometer is required to measure the current through test resistor.

The correct option is (c).

75. $\quad R > 2\,\Omega$

$\Rightarrow \quad 100 - x > x$

2 Ω R G ← x → ← 100 − x →

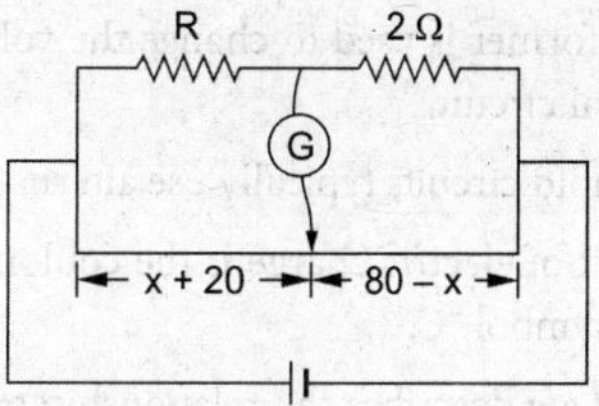

Using $\quad \dfrac{P}{Q} = \dfrac{R}{S}$

We get $\quad \dfrac{2}{R} = \dfrac{x}{100 - x}$ ...(i)

$\dfrac{R}{2} = \dfrac{x + 20}{80 - x}$ ...(ii)

On solving Eqs.(i) and (ii), we get, $R = 3\,\Omega$

$\therefore$ Correct option is (a).

76. $\quad V_{ab} = i_g.G = (i - i_g)S$

$$\Rightarrow \quad i = \left(1 + \frac{G}{S}\right) i_g$$

On putting the given i values, we get

$$i = 100.1 \text{ mA}$$

Therefore, if X is increasing R, should also increase.

$\therefore$ Correct answer is (a).

77. BC, CD and BA are known resistances.

The unknown resistance is connected between A and D.

Hence, the correct option is (c).

78. In the given resistance 200 Ω, 2 stands for red. If it is replaced by green, then the resistance becomes 500 Ω. As 5 stands for green, so multiple will be 10^5.

79. Resistance $= 50 \times 10^2 \pm 1\%$ $i_{max} = 20$ mA

80. The unit of electric current is the ampere, represented by the symbol "A."

81. Copper is a good conductor of electricity due to its high electrical conductivity.

82. The unit of electric potential difference is the volt, represented by the symbol "V."

83. In a series circuit, adding more resistors increases the total resistance, leading to a decrease in current.

84. Ohm's Law states that voltage (V) is equal to the product of current (I) and resistance (R), expressed as V = IR.

85. The unit of electrical power is the watt, represented by the symbol "W."

86. Conventional current flows from the positive terminal to the negative terminal.

87. A capacitor stores electrical energy in an electric field.

88. An ideal conductor has zero resistance.

89. A transformer is used to change the voltage level in an electrical circuit.

90. Household circuits typically use alternating current.

91. The unit of electric charge is the coulomb, represented by the symbol "C."

92. Ohm's Law describes the relationship between voltage, current, and resistance in a conductor.

93. A fuse is a safety device that interrupts the flow of excessive current to protect the circuit.

94. A diode allows current to flow in one direction and blocks it in the opposite direction, controlling the flow of current in a circuit.

95. Electrons are negatively charged subatomic particles orbiting the nucleus of an atom.

96. The coulomb is the unit of electric charge, representing the amount of charge transported by a current of one ampere in one second.

97. Resistance is the measure of opposition to the flow of electric current in a material.

98. In a series circuit, the current has only one pathway to follow.

99. DC stands for Direct Current, where the electric charge flows in one direction.

100. An ammeter is used to measure electric current in a circuit.

101. A conductor is a material that allows the flow of electric current.

102. Kirchhoff's Current Law states that the total current entering a junction in a circuit is equal to the total current leaving the junction.

103. Power is the rate at which electrical energy is used or produced, measured in watts.

104. A capacitor is a component used to store electrical energy in an electric field.

105. The correct answer is (c). The unit of electric current is the Ampere (a).

106. The correct answer is (a). In a series circuit, the current remains constant throughout the circuit.

107. The correct answer is D. Ohm's Law states that V = IR, I = V/R, and R = V/I.

108. The correct answer is (d). A diode allows current to flow in one direction and blocks it in the opposite direction.

109. The correct answer is (d). Power can be calculated using P = IV, P = I^2R, and P = V^2/R.

110. The correct answer is (b). In a parallel circuit, as more resistors are added, the total resistance decreases.

111. The correct answer is (a). A capacitor stores electrical energy in an electric field.

112. The correct answer is (c). A resistor is used to limit the flow of current in a circuit.

113. The correct answer is (c). Silicon is commonly used as a semiconductor in electronic devices.

114. The correct answer is (b). A transformer is used to regulate voltage in an electrical circuit.

115. The correct answer is (b). The transistor is the basic building block of digital circuits, acting as a switch or amplifier.

116. The correct answer is (c). "IC" stands for Integrated Circuit, which is a miniaturized assembly of electronic components.

117. The correct answer is (b). In a NAND gate, the output is low only when both inputs are high.

118. The correct answer is (b). A flip-flop is used to store binary information in digital circuits.

119. The correct answer is (b). An operational amplifier is used for signal amplification in electronic circuits.

120. The correct answer is (c). "CMOS" stands for Complementary Metal-Oxide-Semiconductor, a technology used in integrated circuits.

121. The correct answer is (c). A diode is primarily used for rectifying current in electronic circuits.

122. The correct answer is (d). A resistor network is used for voltage division in electronic circuits.

123. The correct answer is (c). A comparator is used to compare two input signals in electronic circuits.

124. The correct answer is (b). In a DAC, the binary input controls the output voltage.

125. A fuse is designed to protect against overcurrent by breaking the circuit when the current exceeds a specified value.

126. In a short circuit, current takes an unintended low-resistance path, bypassing the normal load.

127. Copper is a common material for fuse elements due to its low melting point and good conductivity.

128. The main function of a circuit breaker is to interrupt the circuit in case of overcurrent, providing protection against short circuits and overloads.

129. A circuit breaker is reusable, as it can be reset after tripping, while a fuse typically needs to be replaced after it blows.

130. The unit of electrical resistance is ohm (Ω).

131. In a series circuit, the total resistance is equal to the sum of the individual resistances.

8

CHAPTER

Machine & Its Types

MACHINE

A machine is a device or apparatus that uses energy or power to perform a specific task or work. Machines are designed to make tasks easier, more efficient, or possible in the first place.

Parts of Machine

Machine parts are individual components or elements that make up a machine and contribute to its overall functionality. They can vary depending on the type of machine and its intended purpose. Here are some common machine parts:

1. **Motor :** The motor is an essential part of many machines, providing power and generating mechanical motion.
2. **Bearings :** Bearings reduce friction and facilitate smooth movement between two moving parts, such as shafts or axles.
3. **Gears :** Gears transmit motion and power between rotating shafts. They can change the speed, torque, and direction of rotation.
4. **Belts and Pulleys :** Belts and pulleys are used to transfer power from one shaft to another when the two shafts are not in direct contact.
5. **Shafts :** Shafts are long, cylindrical components that transmit torque and rotational motion between various machine parts.
6. **Springs :** Springs store mechanical energy and release it when needed, providing suspension, cushioning, or tension in a machine.
7. **Valves :** Valves control the flow of fluids or gases within a machine, regulating the movement and pressure of the medium.
8. **Cylinders :** Cylinders convert fluid or air pressure into linear motion, often used in hydraulic or pneumatic systems.
9. **Control panels :** Control panels consist of switches, buttons, displays, and other interfaces that allow users to operate and control the machine.
10. **Sensors :** Sensors detect and measure physical quantities such as temperature, pressure, position, or speed, providing feedback and enabling automation in machines.
11. **Circuit boards :** Circuit boards, also known as PCBs (Printed Circuit Boards), contain electronic components and conductive pathways that control electrical functions within a machine.
12. **Housings and enclosures :** Housings and enclosures provide protection and support for the internal components of a machine, ensuring safety and durability.
13. **Actuators :** Actuators convert electrical, hydraulic, or pneumatic energy into mechanical motion, enabling machines to perform specific tasks or movements.
14. **Filters :** Filters remove contaminants or unwanted particles from fluids or gases flowing through a machine, ensuring clean and efficient operation.
15. **Control valves :** Control valves regulate the flow rate, pressure, or direction of a fluid or gas within a machine, allowing precise control over its operation.

Types of Machines :

They can be simple, consisting of a few basic parts, and complex, involving intricate mechanisms and systems.

Simple Machines

Simple machines are fundamental mechanical devices that have few or no moving parts and are used to perform work. They are the building blocks of more complex machines and are based on basic principles of physics.

There are six main types of simple machines :

I. Lever : "Lever" is a term that can have different meanings depending on the context.

A lever is a rigid bar that pivots around a fixed point called a fulcrum. It can be used to amplify force or change the direction of the force applied. Examples of levers include seesaws, crowbars, and scissors.

Here are a few common uses of the word "lever":

1. **Mechanical device :** A lever is a simple machine consisting of a rigid bar or beam that is used to transmit and amplify force. It typically has a fulcrum or pivot point, an effort or input force, and a load or output force. Levers are used in various applications, such as in tools, machines, and mechanisms.
2. **Financial Term :** In finance and investing, a lever refers to the use of borrowed funds (debt) to increase the potential return of an investment. This practice is known as leverage, and it can amplify both gains and losses. Using leverage involves taking on additional risk, as the investor is liable for the borrowed funds.
3. **Strategic Advantage :** In a broader sense, the term "lever" can also refer to a strategic advantage or tool that can be used to achieve a desired outcome. For example, in business or negotiations, someone may have a lever or leverage over another party if they possess information, resources, or influence that can be used to exert pressure or gain an advantage.

Types of Lever

In the context of mechanical devices, levers can be classified into three different types based on the relative positions of the fulcrum, effort (input force), and load (output force). These types are :

1. **First-class lever :** In a first-class lever, the fulcrum is positioned between the effort and the load. This means that the effort and the load are on opposite sides of the fulcrum..

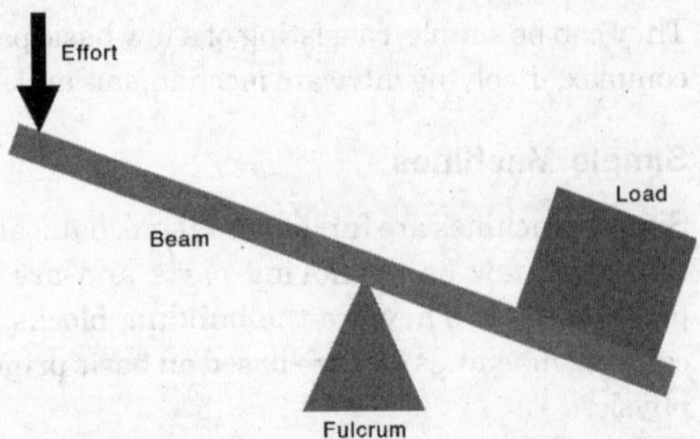

Examples of first-class levers include a see-saw, scissors, and a crowbar.

2. **Second-class lever :** In a second-class lever, the load is positioned between the fulcrum and the effort. This means that the load and the effort are on opposite sides of the fulcrum.

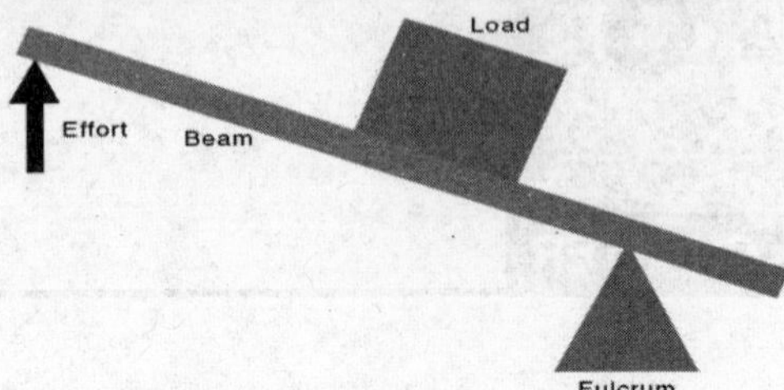

Examples of second-class levers include a wheel barrow and a nutcracker.

3. **Third-class lever :** In a third-class lever, the effort is positioned between the fulcrum and the load. This means that the effort and the load are on the same side of the fulcrum, with the effort closer to the fulcrum.

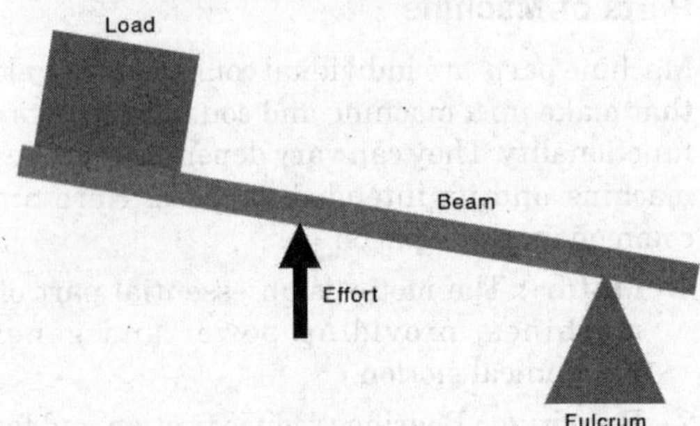

Examples of third-class levers include tweezers, tongs, and a baseball bat.

Applications and uses of Lever

Because of their high mechanical advantage, levers are used in many applications in everyday life. Here are some of them.

- Lifting and moving objects using a wheelbarrow
- Removing nails using a claw hammer
- Lifting small particles using a tweezers
- Cutting or separating materials using scissors
- Stripping wires using pliers or wire cutter

Besides, many parts of the human body function like a lever. The joints behave like a fulcrum, and the bones act as a beam.

II. Pulley : A pulley is a simple machine consisting of a wheel with a groove along its edge and a rope or cable that runs along the groove. Pulleys are used to change the direction or magnitude of a force and can be found in various applications, such as lifting heavy objects or transmitting power.

A pulley consists of a wheel with a groove and a rope or cable. It is used to change the direction of force and can also provide a mechanical advantage by allowing a person to lift heavy loads with less effort. Examples of pulleys include flagpole pulleys and cranes.

There are three main types of pulleys based on their configuration and functionality :

1. **Fixed Pulley :** A fixed pulley is attached to a fixed point, such as a beam or a ceiling. It changes only the direction of the force applied and does not provide any mechanical advantage. The load is lifted by pulling down on the rope, and the effort force required is equal to the weight of the load. Fixed pulleys are commonly used in flagpoles and blinds.
2. **Movable Pulley :** A movable pulley is attached to the load being lifted and moves with it. When using a movable pulley, the load is suspended from a fixed point, and the effort force is applied in the opposite direction. This type of pulley reduces the amount of force required to lift the load. The mechanical advantage of a movable pulley is equal to 2, meaning the effort force is half the weight of the load. Movable pulleys are often used in block and tackle systems for lifting heavy objects.
3. **Compound Pulley :** A compound pulley combines multiple fixed and movable pulleys to provide an increased mechanical advantage. In a compound pulley system, the rope is threaded through several pulleys in a way that allows the effort force to be divided over multiple segments of the rope. This arrangement enables a significant reduction in the force required to lift heavy loads. Compound pulleys are commonly used in cranes and hoists.

III. Wheel and axle : The wheel and axle is another simple machine that consists of a circular wheel attached to a cylindrical axle. The wheel and axle work together to transmit force and motion and the wheel is the larger, outer part that rotates around the axle, which is the smaller, central part.

Wheel and axles consist of a circular object (the wheel) that rotates around a shaft (the axle). It is used to transmit force or torque and to change the direction of force. Examples include wheels on vehicles, gears, and doorknobs.

There are three main types of wheel and axle based on their application and design :

1. **Ordinary Wheel and Axle :** In the ordinary wheel and axle configuration, the wheel and axle have a uniform diameter throughout their length. This type of wheel and axle is commonly found in everyday objects such as car wheels, bicycle wheels, and doorknobs. When force is applied to the wheel, it rotates around the axle, enabling the movement or transmission of force.
2. **Steering Wheel and Axle :** The steering wheel and axle configuration is specifically designed for steering vehicles. In this type, the steering wheel is connected to the axle through a mechanism such as a steering column. When the steering wheel is turned, it causes the axle to rotate, which in turn controls the direction of the vehicle's wheels.
3. **Capstan :** A capstan is a specialized type of wheel and axle used for winding ropes or cables. It consists of a cylindrical drum (the axle) around which a rope or cable is wound, and a handle or lever attached to the drum. Capstans are commonly used on ships for tasks like raising anchors or hoisting sails. By turning the handle or lever, force is applied to the drum, causing the rope to wind or unwind.

The wheel and axle is a versatile simple machine that can be found in numerous applications, ranging from transportation to mechanical systems. It provides a mechanical advantage by increasing the distance over which a force can be applied, making it easier to move or lift heavy objects.

IV. Inclined plane : An inclined plane is a simple machine that consists of a flat surface set at an angle to the horizontal plane. It allows objects to be moved up or down with less force than would be required to lift them vertically. The inclined plane is one of the six classical simple machines, and it can be found in various forms and applications.

An inclined plane is a sloping surface that allows objects to be raised or lowered with less force. It reduces the amount of work required by increasing the distance over which the force is applied. Examples include ramps, staircases, and slides.

Here are some common types of inclined planes:

1. **Ramp :** A ramp is a type of inclined plane that is commonly used for loading and unloading objects from a higher level to a lower level. It provides a sloping surface that allows for easier movement of heavy objects, such as when loading furniture into a moving truck.

2. **Wedge :** A wedge is a double-inclined plane that is thick at one end and tapers to a thin edge at the other. It is often used for splitting or cutting objects. Examples of wedges include axes, knives, and chisels. The sharp edge of the wedge concentrates the force over a smaller area, making it easier to penetrate or separate materials.

3. **Screw :** Although it may not be immediately apparent, a screw is actually a type of inclined plane wrapped around a cylinder. It consists of an inclined plane (the thread) spiraling up the shaft. Screws are used for fastening objects together, and they convert rotational motion into linear motion. Examples of screws include those used in woodworking, as well as in machinery and construction.

   These are three common types of inclined planes. Each type serves a specific purpose and offers mechanical advantages in different applications.

Features of Simple Machines:

1. **Few Moving Parts :** Simple machines are characterized by their simplicity, often consisting of only a few moving parts. They are designed to perform basic functions using minimal components.
2. **Basic Mechanisms :** Simple machines are based on fundamental mechanical principles, such as levers, inclined planes, wheels and axles, pulleys, wedges, and screws. Each type of simple machine operates on a specific mechanism to achieve a particular purpose.
3. **Mechanical Advantage :** Simple machines provide a mechanical advantage, allowing the user to accomplish tasks with less force or effort. They leverage forces to make work easier, either by amplifying force or by changing the direction of the force applied.
4. **Versatility :** Simple machines have a wide range of applications and can be used individually or in combination to create more complex systems. They can be found in everyday objects and activities, as well as in various industries.

Importance of Simple Machines :

1. **Efficiency :** Simple machines provide mechanical advantage, allowing us to accomplish tasks more easily and with less effort. They help increase efficiency in performing work by reducing the amount of force required or by enabling us to apply force in a more favorable direction.
2. **Basic Understanding of Mechanics :** Simple machines serve as the building blocks for understanding more complex principles of physics and mechanics. By studying and applying the concepts of levers, inclined planes, pulleys, and other simple machines, we gain a fundamental understanding of how forces, motion, and energy work.
3. **Everyday Applications :** Simple machines are present in numerous everyday objects and activities. From using scissors and opening doors to riding a bicycle or using a wheelbarrow, we rely on simple machines to make our daily tasks easier and more efficient.
4. **Education and Learning :** Simple machines are often used as educational tools to teach students about fundamental mechanical concepts and principles. They offer hands-on learning experiences and help develop problem-solving skills and critical thinking.

Complex Machines

Complex machines are composed of multiple simple machines and often involve intricate mechanisms and systems. They are designed to perform more sophisticated tasks and typically require an energy source or power input to function. Examples of complex machines include:

- **Automobiles :** Cars are complex machines that combine multiple simple machines like wheels and axles, levers in the braking system, pulleys in the engine, and inclined planes in the transmission.
- **Industrial Machinery :** Various complex machines are used in manufacturing and industrial processes, such as conveyor belts, robotic arms, CNC machines, and assembly lines. These machines involve a combination of mechanical, electrical, and computer systems.
- **Aircraft :** Aircraft are complex machines that incorporate numerous mechanical systems, such as engines, landing gear, control surfaces, and hydraulic or pneumatic systems.
- **Computers :** Computers are complex machines that consist of intricate electronic circuits and components, including processors, memory modules, hard drives, and input/output devices.
- **Medical Equipment :** Complex machines in the medical field include MRI scanners, X-ray machines, surgical robots, and dialysis machines, which involve advanced mechanical, electrical, and imaging systems.

  Complex machines are designed to perform specialized functions, achieve high precision, automate tasks, or accomplish complex operations that would be difficult or impossible with simple machines alone.

Features of Complex Machines :

1. **Multiple Components :** Complex machines are characterized by their intricate design, often involving numerous components and subsystems. They are composed of interconnected parts that work together to perform complex tasks.
2. **Advanced Mechanisms :** Complex machines employ a combination of simple machines, mechanical systems, electrical components, computer systems, and other technologies to achieve their functions. They may incorporate complex mechanisms like gears, linkages, actuators, sensors, and control systems.
3. **Specialized Functions :** Complex machines are designed to perform specific tasks or functions that require advanced capabilities. They are often developed for specialized applications in industries such as manufacturing, healthcare, transportation, and aerospace.
4. **Power Source :** Complex machines typically require an energy source or power input to operate. This can be in the form of electricity, hydraulic power, pneumatic power, thermal energy, chemical reactions, or a combination of these sources.
5. **Precision and Control :** Complex machines are designed for high precision and control. They often incorporate advanced sensors, feedback systems, and algorithms to ensure accurate operation, safety, and optimization of performance.
6. **Automation and Integration :** Many complex machines are automated or computer-controlled, reducing the need for human intervention. They can be integrated into larger systems or networks, enabling communication, data exchange, and coordination with other machines or devices.

Importance of Complex Machines:

1. **Specialized Functions :** Complex machines are designed to perform specific and often intricate tasks that would be difficult or impossible with simple machines alone. They enable us to achieve high precision, automation, and advanced operations in various industries.
2. **Industrial Production and Manufacturing :** Complex machines are at the heart of modern manufacturing processes. They enable large-scale production, increase productivity, and improve the quality and consistency of manufactured goods. Complex machines like CNC machines, robotic arms, and conveyor systems revolutionize industrial production.
3. **Technological Advancements :** Complex machines drive technological advancements in fields such as transportation, aerospace, healthcare, and telecomm-unications. They enable the development of advanced vehicles, medical equipment, communication systems, and more.
4. **Research and Innovation :** Complex machines are essential for conducting research and experime-ntation in various scientific and engineering disciplines. They allow scientists and engineers to study complex phenomena, simulate real-world scenarios, and push the boundaries of knowledge and innovation.
5. **Enhancing Human Capabilities :** Complex machines can augment human capabilities, enabling us to perform tasks beyond our natural abilities. Examples include exoskeletons that enhance strength and mobility, surgical robots that assist in precision surgeries, and advanced imaging equipment that aids in medical diagnoses.

Objective Type Questions

1. Which of the following is not a class of lever?

(a) First-class lever
(b) Second-class lever
(c) Third-class lever
(d) Fourth-class lever

2. In a first-class lever, where is the fulcrum located in relation to the effort and load?

(a) Between the effort and load
(b) At one end of the lever
(c) At the midpoint of the lever
(d) It can be anywhere along the lever

3. Which of the following is an example of a second-class lever?

(a) Pliers (b) Wheelbarrow
(c) Baseball bat (d) Crowbar

4. Which class of lever provides the greatest mechanical advantage?

(a) First-class lever
(b) Second-class lever
(c) Third-class lever
(d) They all provide the same mechanical advantage

5. In a third-class lever, where is the effort located in relation to the fulcrum and load?

(a) Between the fulcrum and load
(b) At one end of the lever
(c) At the midpoint of the lever
(d) It can be anywhere along the lever

6. Which of the following is an example of a first-class lever?

(a) Nutcracker (b) Shovel
(c) Fishing rod (d) Wheelbarrow

7. Which class of lever provides the least mechanical advantage?

(a) First-class lever
(b) Second-class lever
(c) Third-class lever
(d) They all provide the same mechanical advantage

8. Which of the following is an example of a third-class lever?

(a) Scissors (b) Bottle opener
(c) See-saw (d) Tweezers

9. A lever is in equilibrium when :

(a) The effort arm is longer than the load arm
(b) The load arm is longer than the effort arm
(c) The effort and load are equal
(d) The fulcrum is located at the midpoint

10. Which class of lever is most commonly found in the human body?

(a) First-class lever (b) Second-class lever
(c) Third-class lever (d) Fourth-class lever

11. Which class of lever allows for the greatest range of motion?

(a) First-class lever (b) Second-class lever
(c) Third-class lever (d) Fourth-class lever

12. Which of the following is an example of a first-class lever in the human body?

(a) Elbow joint
(b) Hip joint
(c) Ankle joint
(d) Shoulder joint

13. A lever with a mechanical advantage greater than 1:

(a) Increases the effort required
(b) Increases the load it can lift
(c) Decreases the distance the load can be moved
(d) Decreases the distance the effort has to travel

14. Which class of lever is commonly used to pry open objects?

(a) First-class lever
(b) Second-class lever
(c) Third-class lever
(d) Fourth-class lever

15. The length of the effort arm compared to the length of the load arm determines the:

(a) Mechanical advantage
(b) Distance the load can be moved
(c) Efficiency of the lever
(d) Weight of the load

16. Which class of lever is a pair of scissors?

(a) First-class lever
(b) Second-class lever
(c) Third-class lever
(d) Fourth-class lever

17. Which of the following is an example of a second-class lever in the human body?

(a) Bicep curl
(b) Knee extension
(c) Sitting down in a chair
(d) Opening and closing your hand

18. Which class of lever is a catapult?

(a) First-class lever (b) Second-class lever
(c) Third-class lever (d) Fourth-class lever

19. A lever with a mechanical advantage of less than 1:

(a) Increases the effort required
(b) Increases the load it can lift
(c) Decreases the distance the load can be moved
(d) Decreases the distance the effort has to travel

20. Which class of lever is a push-up exercise?

(a) First-class lever (b) Second-class lever
(c) Third-class lever (d) Fourth-class lever

21. Which of the following is not a common application of levers?

(a) Opening a door (b) Lifting weights
(c) Rowing a boat (d) Cooking food

22. Levers are commonly used in which field?

(a) Engineering
(b) Medicine
(c) Agriculture
(d) All of the above

23. The primary advantage of using levers is:

(a) Increased speed
(b) Increased force
(c) Increased distance
(d) Increased precision

24. Levers can be used to:

(a) Transfer motion
(b) Change the direction of motion
(c) Increase or decrease force
(d) All of the above

25. Which feature of a lever determines its mechanical advantage?

(a) Length of the lever
(b) Weight of the load
(c) Position of the fulcrum
(d) Material of the lever

26. A longer effort arm in a lever will result in:

(a) Increased mechanical advantage
(b) Decreased mechanical advantage
(c) No change in mechanical advantage
(d) Mechanical advantage depends on the load arm

27. Which type of lever has the fulcrum located between the effort and the load?

(a) First-class lever
(b) Second-class lever
(c) Third-class lever
(d) Fourth-class lever

28. Which class of lever is commonly used in wheel barrows?

(a) First-class lever (b) Second-class lever
(c) Third-class lever (d) Fourth-class lever

29. Which class of lever provides speed and range of motion but sacrifices force?

(a) First-class lever (b) Second-class lever
(c) Third-class lever (d) Fourth-class lever

30. Which class of lever is commonly used in tweezers?

(a) First-class lever (b) Second-class lever
(c) Third-class lever (d) Fourth-class lever

31. Which class of lever is commonly used in scissors?

(a) First-class lever (b) Second-class lever
(c) Third-class lever (d) Fourth-class lever

32. Levers are used in construction machinery for:

(a) Lifting heavy objects
(b) Digging trenches
(c) Excavating soil
(d) All of the above

33. Which class of lever is commonly used in nutcrackers?

(a) First-class lever
(b) Second-class lever
(c) Third-class lever
(d) Fourth-class lever

34. Which feature of a lever affects the ease of control and stability?

(a) Length of the lever
(b) Weight of the load
(c) Position of the fulcrum
(d) Material of the lever

35. Which class of lever is commonly used in fishing rods?
(a) First-class lever (b) Second-class lever
(c) Third-class lever (d) Fourth-class lever

36. Which class of lever is commonly used in tongs?
(a) First-class lever (b) Second-class lever
(c) Third-class lever (d) Fourth-class lever

37. Levers are used in gym equipment for:
(a) Weightlifting (b) Leg presses
(c) Rowing machines (d) All of the above

38. The concept of levers is based on which fundamental principle of physics?
(a) Newton's first law of motion
(b) Newton's second law of motion
(c) Archimedes' principle
(d) Pascal's principle

39. Which class of lever is commonly used in a stapler?
(a) First-class lever (b) Second-class lever
(c) Third-class lever (d) Fourth-class lever

40. Which class of lever is commonly used in a crowbar?
(a) First-class lever (b) Second-class lever
(c) Third-class lever (d) Fourth-class lever

41. What type of simple machine is a shovel?
(a) Lever (b) Wheel and axle
(c) Inclined plane (d) Pulley

42. How does a lever make work easier?
(a) By increasing force
(b) By increasing speed
(c) By changing direction
(d) By amplifying the effort applied

43. Which of the following is an example of a complex machine?
(a) Screw (b) Wheelbarrow
(c) Pulley (d) Wedge

44. What type of simple machine is a pair of scissors?
(a) Screw (b) Inclined plane
(c) Lever (d) Wedge

45. How does a pulley make work easier?
(a) By increasing force
(b) By increasing speed
(c) By changing direction
(d) By reducing friction

46. What type of simple machine is a screw?
(a) Inclined plane (b) Wheel and axle
(c) Lever (d) Wedge

47. How does an inclined plane make work easier?
(a) By increasing force
(b) By increasing speed
(c) By changing direction
(d) By reducing effort over a longer distance

48. Which of the following is an example of a complex machine?
(a) Hammer (b) Wedge
(c) Scissors (d) Pulley

49. What type of simple machine is a wheel and axle?
(a) Screw (b) Inclined plane
(c) Lever (d) Wheel and axle

50. How does a wedge make work easier?
(a) By increasing force
(b) By increasing speed
(c) By changing direction
(d) By splitting or separating objects

51. How does a pulley make work easier?
(a) By increasing force
(b) By increasing speed
(c) By changing direction
(d) By reducing friction

52. Which of the following is an example of a complex machine?
(a) Screwdriver (b) Scissors
(c) Hammer (d) Wrench

53. What type of simple machine is a seesaw?
(a) Screw (b) Inclined plane
(c) Lever (d) Pulley

54. How does an inclined plane make work easier?
(a) By increasing force
(b) By increasing speed
(c) By changing direction
(d) By reducing effort over a longer distance

55. Which of the following is an example of a complex machine?
(a) Screw (b) Wedge
(c) Crane (d) Pulley

56. What type of simple machine is a ramp?
(a) Screw (b) Inclined plane
(c) Lever (d) Wheel and axle

57. How does a lever make work easier?
(a) By increasing force
(b) By increasing speed
(c) By changing direction
(d) By amplifying the effort applied

58. Which of the following is an example of a complex machine?
(a) Screw (b) Wheel and axle
(c) Hammer (d) Scissors

59. What type of simple machine is a screw?
(a) Wedge (b) Inclined plane
(c) Lever (d) Pulley

60. How does a wedge make work easier?
(a) By increasing force
(b) By increasing speed
(c) By changing direction
(d) By splitting or separating objects

61. Which of the following is an example of a complex machine?
(a) Scissors (b) Lever
(c) Wheelbarrow (d) Inclined plane

62. What type of simple machine is a nutcracker?
(a) Screw (b) Wedge
(c) Lever (d) Pulley

63. How does a pulley system with multiple pulleys make work easier?
(a) By increasing force
(b) By increasing speed
(c) By changing direction
(d) By providing mechanical advantage

64. Which of the following is an example of a complex machine?
(a) Screwdriver (b) Wedge
(c) Bicycle (d) Wheel and axle

65. What type of simple machine is a doorknob?
(a) Screw (b) Wedge
(c) Lever (d) Wheel and axle

66. How does a lever system with a longer lever arm make work easier?
(a) By increasingforce
(b) By increasing speed
(c) By changing direction
(d) By providing mechanical advantage

67. Which of the following is an example of a complex machine?
(a) Screw (b) Wedge
(c) Elevator (d) Pulley

68. What type of simple machine is a pair of tweezers?
(a) Screw (b) Wedge
(c) Lever (d) Pulley

69. How does an inclined plane with a steeper slope make work harder?
(a) By increasing force
(b) By increasing speed
(c) By changing direction
(d) By requiring more effort over a shorter distance

70. Which of the following is an example of a complex machine?
(a) Screw (b) Wedge
(c) Bicycle (d) Hammer

71. What type of simple machine is a screwdriver?
(a) Screw (b) Wedge
(c) Lever (d) Pulley

72. How does a pulley with a greater number of ropes make work easier?
(a) By increasing force
(b) By increasing speed
(c) By changing direction
(d) By distributing the load

73. Which of the following is an example of a complex machine?
(a) Screw (b) Wedge
(c) Scissors (d) Pulley

74. What type of simple machine is a jar lid?
(a) Screw (b) Wedge
(c) Lever (d) Pulley

75. How does a lever system with the fulcrum closer to the load make work easier?
(a) By increasing force
(b) By increasing speed
(c) By changing direction
(d) By providing mechanical advantage

76. Which of the following is an example of a complex machine?
(a) Screwdriver (b) Wedge
(c) Crane (d) Wheel and axle

76. What type of simple machine is a pair of pliers?

(a) Screw (b) Wedge
(c) Lever (d) Pulley

78. How does an inclined plane with a longer length make work easier?

(a) By increasing force
(b) By increasing speed
(c) By changing direction
(d) By reducing effort over a longer distance

79. Which of the following is an example of a complex machine?

(a) Screw (b) Wedge
(c) Bicycle (d) Wheelbarrow

80. What type of simple machine is a faucet valve?

(a) Screw (b) Wedge
(c) Lever (d) Pulley

81. How does a wheel and axle make work easier?

(a) By increasing force
(b) By increasing speed
(c) By changing direction
(d) By reducing friction

82. Which of the following is an example of a complex machine?

(a) Screw (b) Wedge
(c) Hammer (d) Pulley

Answers

1. (d)	**2.** (c)	**3.** (b)	**4.** (b)	**5.** (a)	**6.** (c)	**7.** (c)	**8.** (d)	**9.** (c)	**10.** (c)
11. (c)	**12.** (d)	**13.** (b)	**14.** (b)	**15.** (a)	**16.** (c)	**17.** (b)	**18.** (a)	**19.** (a)	**20.** (c)
21. (d)	**22.** (d)	**23.** (b)	**24.** (d)	**25.** (c)	**26.** (a)	**27.** (a)	**28.** (b)	**29.** (c)	**30.** (c)
31. (a)	**32.** (d)	**33.** (a)	**34.** (c)	**35.** (c)	**36.** (c)	**37.** (d)	**38.** (b)	**39.** (a)	**40.** (a)
41. (c)	**42.** (d)	**43.** (b)	**44.** (c)	**45.** (c)	**46.** (a)	**47.** (d)	**48.** (c)	**49.** (d)	**50.** (d)
51. (c)	**52.** (b)	**53.** (c)	**54.** (d)	**55.** (c)	**56.** (b)	**57.** (d)	**58.** (d)	**59.** (b)	**60.** (d)
61. (c)	**62.** (c)	**63.** (d)	**64.** (c)	**65.** (d)	**66.** (d)	**67.** (c)	**68.** (c)	**69.** (a)	**70.** (c)
71. (c)	**72.** (d)	**73.** (c)	**74.** (a)	**75.** (d)	**76.** (c)	**77.** (c)	**78.** (d)	**79.** (d)	**80.** (a)
81. (b)	**82.** (c)								

Explanations

1. There are only three classes of levers, namely, first-class, second-class, and third-class levers.
2. In a first-class lever, the fulcrum is located at the midpoint, with the effort applied on one side and the load on the other side.
3. In a second-class lever, the load is located between the fulcrum and the effort. In a wheelbarrow, the wheel serves as the fulcrum, the load is placed in the container, and the effort is applied to the handles.
4. Second-class levers provide the greatest mechanical advantage because the load is positioned between the fulcrum and the effort, allowing for efficient force multiplication.
5. In a third-class lever, the effort is applied between the fulcrum and the load, with the fulcrum closer to the load than the effort.
6. In a first-class lever, the fulcrum is located in the middle, with the effort applied at one end and the load (fish) being lifted at the other end.
7. Third-class levers provide the least mechanical advantage because the effort is applied closer to the fulcrum than the load, resulting in a lower force multiplication.
8. In a pair of tweezers, the effort is applied between the fulcrum (the hinge) and the load (the object being picked up).
9. In order for a lever to be in equilibrium, the effort and load forces must be balanced, meaning they are equal in magnitude.
10. Third-class levers are the most common type found in the human body, such as the system of bones, muscles, and joints that create a lever mechanism.
11. Third-class levers provide a greater range of motion because the effort is applied closer to the fulcrum than the load, allowing for increased speed and mobility.
12. The shoulder joint acts as a first-class lever, with the fulcrum at the joint, the effort provided by muscles, and the load being the weight or resistance being moved.
13. A lever with a mechanical advantage greater than 1 allows for a smaller effort force to lift a larger load.
14. Second-class levers are commonly used for prying actions, such as using a crowbar to lift a heavy object by applying effort at one end and the load at the other end.
15. The ratio of the effort arm length to the load arm length determines the mechanical advantage of a lever.
16. A pair of scissors is an example of a third-class lever, where the effort is applied between the fulcrum (the pivot) and the load (the material being cut).
17. The knee joint acts as a second-class lever in the human body, with the effort provided by the quadriceps muscles, the fulcrum at the knee joint, and the load being the weight of the lower leg.
18. A catapult is an example of a first-class lever, where the fulcrum is located between the effort (the tension in the catapult's arm) and the load (the projectile being launched).
19. A lever with a mechanical advantage of less than 1 means that the load arm is longer than the effort arm, requiring a larger effort force to lift a smaller load.
20. A push-up exercise is an example of a third-class lever, where the effort is applied by the muscles between the hands (fulcrum)and the feet (load on the ground.
21. While levers are not directly involved in cooking food, they are commonly used in tasks such as opening doors, lifting weights, and rowing boats.
22. Levers are widely used in various fields, including engineering, medicine (e.g., for prosthetics), and agriculture (e.g., in machinery).
23. Levers allow for the multiplication of force, enabling the lifting of heavier loads or the application of greater force with less effort.
24. Levers are versatile tools that can transfer motion, change the direction of motion, and modify the amount of force applied.
25. The mechanical advantage of a lever is determined by the position of the fulcrum, which affects the ratio of the effort arm to the load arm.
26. A longer effort arm in a lever increases the lever's mechanical advantage, as it allows for more leverage and force multiplication.
27. In a first-class lever, the fulcrum is positioned between the effort and the load, allowing for a variety of applications.
28. Wheel barrows typically use a second-class lever design, with the load between the fulcrum (wheel) and the effort (handles).
29. Third-class levers sacrifice force in exchange for speed and a wider range of motion, making them suitable for tasks requiring agility.
30. Tweezers operate as third-class levers, with the effort (squeezing the handles) between the fulcrum (pivot point)and the load (object being picked).

31. Scissors operate as first-class levers, where the fulcrum is located at the pivot point, and the effort and load are on opposite sides.

32. Construction machinery, such as cranes, excavators, and backhoes, utilize levers to lift heavy objects, dig trenches, and excavate soil.

33. Nutcrackers operate as first-class levers, with the fulcrum at the pivot point and the effort applied at one end to crack the nut.

34. The position of the fulcrum in a lever affects the ease of control and stability, as it determines the distribution of forces and torques.

35. Fishing rods function as third-class levers, where the effort is applied through the angler's hand, between the fulcrum (reel) and the load (fish).

36. Tongs operate as third-class levers, with the effort applied between the fulcrum (hinge) and the load (object being gripped).

37. Gym equipment often incorporates levers for various exercises, such as weightlifting machines, leg presses, and rowing machines.

38. Levers operate based on Newton's second law of motion, which states that force is equal to mass multiplied by acceleration. Levers allow for the application of force to overcome resistance.

39. A stapler operates as a first-class lever, where the fulcrum is located at the pivot point, and the effort (squeezing the handles)is applied on one side to drive the staple into the paper.

40. A crowbar is an example of a first-class lever, where the fulcrum is positioned between the effort (applied force on one end and the load (object being pried).

41. A shovel has a flat, sloping surface that allows for the lifting and moving of materials, making it an inclined plane.

42. A lever is a simple machine that uses a rigid bar and a fulcrum to multiply the force applied, making it easier to move or lift heavy objects.

43. A wheelbarrow is an example of a complex machine as it combines multiple simple machines like a lever, wheel and axle, and an inclined plane.

44. Scissors consist of two levers connected at a fulcrum, making them an example of a lever.

45. A pulley is a simple machine that uses a wheel with a grooved rim and a rope or chain to lift or move objects. It changes the direction of the force applied, making it easier to lift heavy objects.

46. A screw is an inclined plane wrapped around a cylinder, making it a type of inclined plane.

47. An inclined plane is a simple machine that allows objects to be moved from a lower to a higher level with less force, but over a longer distance.

48. Scissors are considered a complex machine because they consist of two levers (blades) connected at a fulcrum.

49. A wheel and axle is a simple machine that consists of a wheel attached to a smaller axle. It allows for the transmission of force and rotation.

50. A wedge is a simple machine with a thick end and a thin, sharp end. It is used to split or separate objects apart with less force.

51. A pulley is a simple machine that uses a wheel with a grooved rim and a rope or chain to lift or move objects. It makes work easier by changing the direction of the force required to lift the object.

52. Complex machines are made up of multiple simple machines working together. Among the given options, scissors are an example of a complex machine, as they consist of two levers (blades) connected at a fulcrum.

53. A seesaw is an example of a lever, which is a simple machine. It consists of a long beam (board) that pivots on a fulcrum, with two people sitting on opposite ends.

54. An inclined plane is a simple machine that is a sloping surface used to move objects between different heights. It makes work easier by reducing the effort required to lift an object over a longer distance.

55. Among the given options, a crane is an example of a complex machine. It consists of various simple machines such as pulleys, levers, and gears working together to lift heavy loads.

56. A ramp is an example of an inclined plane, which is a simple machine. It is a flat, sloping surface that allows objects to be moved from a lower level to a higher level with less force.

57. A lever is a simple machine that consists of a rigid bar that pivots around a fixed point called a fulcrum. It makes work easier by amplifying the effort applied, allowing heavy objects to be moved with less force.

58. Among the given options, scissors are an example of a complex machine. They consist of two levers (blades) connected at a fulcrum, allowing for cutting or shearing actions.

59. A screw is an example of an inclined plane wrapped around a cylinder. Therefore, it is considered a type of inclined plane and is classified as a simple machine.

60. A wedge is a simple machine that has a thick end and a thin, sharp end. It makes work easier by splitting or separating objects apart with less force.

61. Among the given options, a wheelbarrow is an example of a complex machine. It combines various simple machines, such as levers and wheels, to facilitate the movement of heavy loads.

62. A nutcracker is an example of a lever, which is a simple machine. It consists of two arms connected by a fulcrum, allowing for the application of force to crack nuts.

63. A pulley system with multiple pulleys makes work easier by providing mechanical advantage. It allows for the distribution of the load among multiple ropes, reducing the effort required to lift heavy objects.

64. Among the given options, a bicycle is an example of a complex machine. It incorporates various simple machines, including levers, wheels and axles, pulleys, and gears, to enable motion and transportation.

65. A doorknob is an example of a wheel and axle, which is a simple machine. It consists of a wheel (the knob) attached to an axle (the spindle), allowing for the rotation and opening/closing of the door.

66. A lever system with a longer lever arm makes work easier by providing mechanical advantage. The longer lever arm allows for the application of force at a greater distance from the fulcrum, resulting in a greater mechanical advantage and requiring less force to perform the same task.

67. Among the given options, an elevator is an example of a complex machine. It involves the integration of multiple simple machines, including pulleys, levers, and gears, to move people or objects between different levels or floors.

68. A pair of tweezers is an example of a lever, which is a simple machine. It consists of two arms connected at a fulcrum, allowing for the precise grasping and manipulation of small objects.

69. An inclined plane with a steeper slope makes work harder by requiring more force to overcome gravity and move an object up the slope. It increases the vertical height that needs to be overcome, resulting in a higher required force.

70. Among the given options, a bicycle is an example of a complex machine. It incorporates various simple machines, including levers, wheels and axles, pulleys, and gears, to enable motion and transportation.

71. A screwdriver is an example of a lever, which is a simple machine. It consists of a long handle (lever arm)that can be rotated to apply torque to a screw, enabling tightening or loosening.

72. A pulley with a greater number of ropes makes work easier by distributing the load among multiple ropes. This reduces the force required to lift the load, as it is distributed among multiple strands.

73. Among the given options, scissors are an example of a complex machine. They consist of two levers (blades) connected at a fulcrum, allowing for cutting or shearing actions.

74. A jar lid is an example of a screw, which is a simple machine. It consists of an inclined plane wrapped around a cylinder, allowing for the tightening or loosening of the lid.

75. A lever system with the fulcrum closer to the load makes work easier by providing mechanical advantage. The closer the fulcrum is to the load, the greater the mechanical advantage, requiring less for to lift or move the load.

76. Among the given options, a crane is an example of a complex machine. It incorporates multiple simple machines, such as pulleys, levers, and gears, to enable the lifting and movement of heavy loads.

77. A pair of pliers is an example of a lever, which is a simple machine. It consists of two arms connected at a fulcrum, allowing for the application of force to grip, hold, or manipulate objects.

78. An inclined plane with a longer length makes work easier by reducing the effort required to move an object over a longer distance. It allows for a smaller applied force over a greater distance to achieve the same displacement.

79. Among the given options, a wheelbarrow is an example of a complex machine. It combines various simple machines, such as levers and wheels, to facilitate the movement of heavy loads.

80. A faucet valve is an example of a screw, which is a simple machine. It uses an inclined plane wrapped around a cylinder to control the flow of water, allowing for opening or closing the valve.

81. A wheel and axle is a simple machine that consists of a wheel (a circular object) attached to an axle (a cylindrical rod. It makes work easier by increasing speed or mechanical advantage when rotational motion is involved.

82. Among the given options, a hammer is an example of a complex machine. It combines a lever (handle) and a wedge (the head) to exert force and drive nails or perform other tasks.

9 CHAPTER Occupational Health and Safety

OCCUPATIONAL HEALTH AND SAFETY (OHS)

Occupational health and safety (OHS) refers to the practices and procedures implemented in the workplace to ensure the physical, mental, and social well-being of employees and to prevent work-related injuries, illnesses, and accidents. OHS encompasses a broad range of measures and regulations designed to create a safe and healthy working environment for all workers.

Some key aspects of occupational health and safety:

1. Risk Assessment: Employers are responsible for identifying and assessing potential hazards in the workplace. This involves examining the work environment, equipment, and tasks performed to determine any risks to employee safety and health.
2. Hazard Prevention and Control: Once hazards are identified, steps should be taken to eliminate or control them. This can involve implementing safety protocols, providing personal protective equipment (PPE), modifying equipment or processes, and creating safe work practices.
3. Training and Education: Employers are required to provide proper training and education to employees to ensure they understand the hazards and know how to work safely. This includes training on specific tasks, emergency procedures, proper use of equipment, and recognizing and reporting potential hazards.
4. Health Promotion: Occupational health and safety is not limited to physical safety; it also involves promoting overall employee health and well-being. This may include initiatives such as wellness programs, ergonomic assessments, mental health support, and promoting work-life balance.
5. Compliance with Regulations: Employers must comply with relevant local, national, and international regulations and standards related to occupational health and safety. These regulations often cover areas such as workplace design, ventilation, hazardous substance handling, noise control, and emergency preparedness.
6. Incident Reporting and Investigation: When accidents, injuries, or near-miss incidents occur in the workplace, they should be reported and thoroughly investigated to determine the cause and prevent future occurrences. This helps identify underlying issues and implement corrective measures.
7. Continuous Improvement: Occupational health and safety is an ongoing process that requires regular evaluation and improvement. Employers should encourage feedback from employees, conduct safety audits, and implement measures to address any identified shortcomings.

Importance of occupational health and safety

Occupational health and safety (OHS) is of paramount importance in any workplace. It refers to the measures and practices put in place to ensure the well-being, health, and safety of employees, as well as the prevention of accidents, injuries, and illnesses in the workplace. Here are some key reasons why occupational health and safety is crucial:

1. Protecting workers' lives and well-being: The primary objective of OHS is to safeguard the lives and physical well-being of employees. By implementing safety protocols, providing appropriate training, and maintaining a hazard-free work environment, employers can reduce the risk of accidents, injuries, and illnesses among their workforce.
2. Reducing workplace accidents and injuries: Occupational accidents and injuries not only cause physical harm to employees but also lead to financial losses for companies. By prioritizing safety measures, companies can significantly reduce the number of accidents, resulting in fewer injuries, medical expenses, and legal liabilities.
3. Enhancing productivity and efficiency: A safe and healthy work environment positively impacts productivity and efficiency. When employees feel safe, they are more focused, motivated, and productive. Moreover, fewer accidents mean fewer disruptions in workflow and decreased downtime due to injuries.
4. Compliance with legal requirements: Governments across the world have established regulations and

standards to ensure occupational health and safety in workplaces. Complying with these regulations is not only a legal requirement but also demonstrates a company's commitment to its employees' well-being. Failure to comply with OHS laws can lead to legal consequences, penalties, and damage to a company's reputation.

5. Boosting employee morale and engagement: When employees see that their employer values their safety and well-being, it fosters a positive work environment and boosts morale. Employees are more likely to be engaged, satisfied, and loyal to a company that prioritizes their health and safety. This, in turn, leads to increased employee retention and a more positive company culture.
6. Attracting and retaining talent: In today's competitive job market, potential employees consider occupational health and safety as a crucial factor when evaluating job opportunities. Companies that have a strong OHS program in place are more likely to attract top talent and retain skilled employees who prioritize their well-being.
7. Reputation and public image: Companies that prioritize occupational health and safety earn a positive reputation in the industry and among the public. Demonstrating a commitment to employee safety can enhance the company's public image, attract customers, investors, and partners who value ethical and responsible business practices.

Cost of occupational injury:

The cost of occupational injuries can vary depending on various factors such as the severity of the injury, the industry, the country, and the specific circumstances surrounding the incident. Here are some of the costs associated with occupational injuries:

1. Direct Costs: These are the immediate costs incurred as a result of an occupational injury. They typically include medical expenses, emergency response costs, hospitalization, surgeries, and medication. The direct costs also include the cost of rehabilitation and physical therapy required for the injured worker.

Here are some examples of direct costs:

- Raw materials: The cost of purchasing the materials and components that are directly used in the production of a product.
- Labor costs: Wages, salaries, and benefits of employees directly involved in the production or delivery of a product or service.
- Manufacturing equipment: The cost of machinery and equipment specifically used in the manufacturing process.
- Packaging materials: Expenses for packaging materials that are directly used for a product, such as boxes, labels, or containers.
- Direct labor: Wages and benefits paid to employees who work directly on a specific project or provide direct services to clients.
- Subcontractor costs: Payments made to external contractors or vendors who are hired to perform specific tasks or provide specialized services.
- Sales commissions: Commissions or incentives paid to sales personnel for selling specific products or services.
- Shipping and transportation: The cost of shipping and transporting goods or materials directly associated with a product or project.
- Direct utilities: Expenses for utilities directly related to the production process, such as electricity, water, or fuel used in manufacturing.
- Prototype development: Costs incurred during the development and creation of a prototype or sample product.

2. Indirect Costs: Indirect costs are the long-term or hidden costs that arise from occupational injuries. These costs are not as visible as direct costs but can be significant. They include lost productivity due to the absence of the injured worker, training and hiring replacement workers, reduced efficiency during the injured worker's recovery period, and administrative costs associated with workers' compensation claims.

Here are some examples of indirect costs:

- Rent and utilities: The cost of leasing or renting office space, as well as expenses for electricity, water, heating, and other utilities.
- Administrative salaries: Salaries and benefits for employees who provide administrative support, such as human resources, accounting, and management personnel.
- Office supplies and equipment: Expenses for purchasing and maintaining office supplies, computers, printers, furniture, and other necessary equipment.
- Insurance: Costs associated with various insurance policies, including general liability insurance, property insurance, workers' compensation insurance, and professional liability insurance.
- Depreciation: The reduction in value of assets over time, such as buildings, vehicles, or machinery, as they are used in the business.
- Maintenance and repairs: Expenses for routine maintenance and repairs of equipment, machinery, and facilities.
- Communication and technology: Costs related to internet services, phone systems, software licenses, and other communication and technology infrastructure.
- Training and development: Expenses for employee training programs, workshops, seminars, and professional development activities.
- Marketing and advertising: Costs associated with promoting products or services, including advertising campaigns, marketing materials, and online marketing efforts.

- Legal and professional fees: Payments made to attorneys, accountants, consultants, and other professional service providers for legal advice, tax preparation, auditing, or other specialized services.

3. Workers' Compensation: Many countries have workers' compensation programs in place to provide benefits to workers who suffer occupational injuries. The costs of workers' compensation insurance premiums are borne by employers and are based on factors such as the industry's risk level and the employer's safety record.
4. Legal Costs: In cases where an occupational injury leads to legal disputes, there may be additional costs associated with legal representation, court fees, and potential settlements or judgments.
5. Intangible Costs: Occupational injuries can also have intangible costs that are difficult to quantify. These include pain and suffering endured by the injured worker, emotional distress, damage to the company's reputation, and decreased employee morale.

Cost of occupational disease:

The cost of occupational diseases can be significant and have various impacts on individuals, employers, and society as a whole. Here are some factors to consider when assessing the cost of occupational diseases:

1. Healthcare Expenses: Occupational diseases often require medical treatment, including doctor visits, diagnostic tests, medication, and specialized care. The cost of healthcare can be substantial, particularly for chronic or long-term conditions.
2. Lost Productivity: When workers become ill due to occupational diseases, they may need time off work or be unable to perform their job duties effectively. Lost productivity can result in reduced output, decreased efficiency, and the need for temporary or permanent replacements, which can all have financial implications for employers.
3. Workers' Compensation: Many countries have workers' compensation systems in place to provide financial support to employees who suffer from occupational diseases. This includes covering medical expenses, providing disability benefits, and compensating for lost wages. Employers often bear the cost of workers' compensation insurance premiums, which can increase with higher rates of occupational diseases.
4. Legal Costs: In some cases, occupational diseases may lead to legal disputes, such as claims for compensation or lawsuits against employers. These legal processes can involve legal fees, settlements, and court costs, adding to the overall cost of the disease.
5. Rehabilitation and Disability Support: Depending on the severity of the occupational disease, affected individuals may require rehabilitation services or ongoing support to manage their condition and reintegrate into the workforce. These services can involve additional expenses.
6. Social and Economic Impact: Occupational diseases can have broader societal and economic consequences. They can lead to decreased productivity at a national level, increased strain on healthcare systems, and higher social welfare costs if individuals are unable to work and require financial support.

Poor working conditions impact on worker health and safety:

Poor working conditions can indeed have a significant impact on worker health and safety. When employees are subjected to unfavorable working conditions, it can lead to a range of negative consequences for their well-being. Here are some ways in which poor working conditions can affect worker health and safety:

1. Physical health hazards: Inadequate ventilation, exposure to harmful substances or toxins, noise pollution, improper ergonomics, and lack of personal protective equipment (PPE) can all contribute to physical health issues. These conditions may lead to respiratory problems, hearing loss, musculoskeletal disorders, skin irritations, and other occupational illnesses.
2. Accidents and injuries: Poorly maintained equipment, insufficient training, lack of safety protocols, and overcrowded or cluttered workspaces can increase the risk of accidents and injuries. Workers may be exposed to hazards such as falls, machinery accidents, electrical shocks, or being struck by falling objects.
3. Mental and emotional well-being: Unfavorable working conditions, including long working hours, excessive workload, lack of support or recognition, poor management, and workplace harassment, can take a toll on employees' mental and emotional health. It may lead to stress, anxiety, depression, burnout, and decreased job satisfaction.
4. Occupational diseases: Some industries expose workers to specific risks that can result in occupational diseases. For example, workers in construction, mining, or manufacturing may be at risk of developing lung diseases due to asbestos exposure, or those working with chemicals may experience long-term health effects.
5. Fatigue and sleep disturbances: Extended working hours, night shifts, irregular schedules, and high-stress environments can disrupt sleep patterns and lead to fatigue. Fatigue not only affects worker performance but also increases the likelihood of accidents and errors.
6. Lack of work-life balance: Poor working conditions can make it challenging for employees to maintain a healthy work-life balance. Long hours, inflexible schedules, and excessive work demands can result in heightened stress levels, strained relationships, and reduced time for self-care or leisure activities.

Challenges and issues related to occupational health and safety:

There are some common challenges and issues related to occupational health and safety such as:

1. Work-related accidents and injuries: Many industries and occupations pose inherent risks to workers, leading to accidents and injuries. These can include slips, trips,

falls, exposure to hazardous substances, machinery accidents, and more. The extent of these incidents varies across sectors, but they contribute to lost productivity, increased medical costs, and human suffering.

2. Occupational diseases: Workers may be exposed to various occupational hazards, such as chemicals, noise, radiation, or biological agents, which can lead to long-term health issues or occupational diseases. Examples include respiratory conditions, skin disorders, hearing loss, occupational cancers, and musculoskeletal disorders.
3. Psychological and psychosocial issues: Occupational health and safety concerns extend beyond physical hazards. Psychological factors such as stress, long working hours, bullying, and workplace violence can have a significant impact on employee well-being and mental health. These issues can lead to decreased productivity, absenteeism, and turnover.
4. Compliance and enforcement: Ensuring compliance with occupational health and safety regulations can be challenging for employers and regulatory agencies. Some organizations may prioritize productivity over safety, leading to inadequate safety measures or non-compliance with regulations. Additionally, enforcement efforts and resources may vary across jurisdictions, resulting in inconsistent adherence to OHS standards.
5. Emerging risks: As workplaces evolve with technological advancements and new industries, new risks to occupational health and safety may emerge. For example, the increasing use of automation, robotics, and artificial intelligence may introduce unique hazards that require specialized safety measures and training.

Identifying the cause of an accident in occupational health and safety:

Identifying the cause of an accident in the context of occupational health and safety also involves a systematic investigation. Here are the key steps typically followed in such investigations:

1. Ensure immediate safety: The first priority is to ensure the safety and well-being of the individuals involved in the accident and to prevent further harm or injuries. This may involve providing medical assistance, securing the area, and addressing any immediate hazards.
2. Form an investigation team: A team or an individual is assigned the responsibility of conducting the accident investigation. This team should ideally have relevant expertise and knowledge in occupational health and safety.
3. Collect information: Gather all available information related to the accident. This includes incident reports, witness statements, photographs, video footage, equipment data, and any other relevant documentation. If applicable, review safety policies, procedures, and training records.
4. Interview involved parties: Interview the individuals directly involved in the accident, such as the injured employees or witnesses. Collect their accounts of the incident, focusing on the sequence of events, activities being performed, equipment used, and any potential hazards they observed.
5. Examine the accident scene: Visit and thoroughly examine the accident scene. Look for physical evidence, such as equipment damage, environmental conditions, layout, lighting, or any other factors that may have contributed to the accident.
6. Identify underlying factors: Analyze the information collected to identify the underlying causes and contributing factors of the accident. These factors can include unsafe work practices, inadequate training, equipment failure, lack of maintenance, communication issues, or deficiencies in safety procedures.
7. Conduct root cause analysis: Use various tools and techniques, such as the "5 Whys" method or Fishbone (Ishikawa) diagrams, to delve deeper into the factors identified in the previous step. This helps identify the underlying root causes that led to the accident.
8. Determine preventive measures: Based on the identified root causes, develop recommendations for corrective actions and preventive measures to mitigate the risk of similar accidents in the future. These recommendations may include improvements in training, policies, procedures, equipment maintenance, or communication systems.
9. Document and communicate findings: Prepare a detailed report that outlines the investigation process, findings, and recommendations. This report should be shared with relevant stakeholders, such as management, supervisors, and workers' representatives. It can serve as a learning tool for improving occupational health and safety practices within the organization.

The range of hazards in occupational health and safety:

Occupational health and safety hazards encompass a wide range of risks that workers may face in their work environments. These hazards can vary depending on the nature of the job, industry, and specific workplace conditions. Here are some common categories of hazards in occupational health and safety:

1. Physical Hazards: These hazards involve conditions or factors that can cause physical harm to workers. They include:
    - Noise: Excessive noise levels that can lead to hearing loss or communication difficulties.
    - Vibration: Prolonged exposure to vibration from tools or machinery, leading to musculoskeletal disorders.
    - Temperature Extremes: Extreme heat or cold that can cause heatstroke, hypothermia, or frostbite.
    - Radiation: Exposure to ionizing radiation, such as X-rays or radioactive materials, leading to health issues.

- Ergonomic Hazards: Poorly designed workstations or repetitive tasks that can cause musculoskeletal disorders.

2. Chemical Hazards: These hazards arise from exposure to harmful substances in the workplace. Examples include:
   - Toxic Chemicals: Exposure to substances like solvents, pesticides, or heavy metals that can cause acute or chronic health effects.
   - Carcinogens: Substances that have the potential to cause cancer, such as asbestos or certain chemicals.
   - Irritants: Chemicals that can cause irritation or damage to the skin, eyes, or respiratory system.
3. Biological Hazards: These hazards involve exposure to biological agents such as viruses, bacteria, fungi, or parasites. Examples include:
   - Infectious Diseases: Exposure to pathogens in healthcare settings or laboratories.
   - Animal-borne Diseases: Risks associated with working with animals, including zoonotic diseases.
   - Allergens: Substances that can cause allergic reactions, such as pollen, mold, or certain chemicals.
4. Psychosocial Hazards: These hazards are related to the psychological and social aspects of work that can impact mental well-being. They include:
   - Work-related Stress: High workloads, long hours, or job insecurity that can lead to stress and burnout.
   - Workplace Violence: Threats, harassment, or physical violence from co-workers, customers, or the public.
   - Bullying: Persistent mistreatment, intimidation, or humiliation by colleagues or supervisors.
   - Organizational Culture: Poor communication, lack of support, or inadequate leadership leading to low job satisfaction.
5. Safety Hazards: These hazards pertain to conditions that can directly cause accidents, injuries, or fatalities. They include:
   - Falls: Working at heights without proper fall protection or tripping hazards.
   - Machinery Hazards: Unguarded machinery, faulty equipment, or lack of safety procedures.
   - Electrical Hazards: Exposed wiring, improper grounding, or electrical shocks.
   - Fire and Explosions: Inadequate fire prevention measures or handling of flammable materials.

Key features of a national policy in occupational safety and health:

A national policy in occupational safety and health is designed to protect workers and promote a safe working environment. While specific policies may vary from country to country, here are some key features commonly found in such policies:

1. Legal Framework: A national policy typically includes a legal framework that sets out the rights and responsibilities of employers, employees, and regulatory authorities. It may include laws, regulations, and standards related to workplace safety and health.
2. Hazard Identification and Risk Assessment: The policy emphasizes the importance of identifying workplace hazards and assessing the associated risks. It encourages employers to conduct regular inspections and risk assessments to identify potential dangers and implement appropriate control measures.
3. Prevention and Control Measures: The policy emphasizes preventive measures to eliminate or minimize workplace hazards. It promotes the use of engineering controls, administrative controls, and personal protective equipment (PPE) to mitigate risks. It may also encourage employers to implement safety management systems and provide training to employees on hazard recognition and control.
4. Occupational Health Services: The policy may advocate for the establishment of occupational health services to promote the well-being of workers. This may include access to medical examinations, health surveillance, counseling, and rehabilitation services. The policy may also emphasize the importance of promoting mental health in the workplace.
5. Worker Participation and Consultation: The policy recognizes the importance of worker involvement in decision-making processes related to occupational safety and health. It encourages employers to establish mechanisms for workers to participate in identifying hazards, assessing risks, and developing safety policies. It may also promote the establishment of worker safety committees or representatives.
6. Training and Education: The policy highlights the need for training and education programs to increase awareness and knowledge of occupational safety and health among employers, employees, and other relevant stakeholders. It may emphasize the development of training materials, guidelines, and certification programs.
7. Enforcement and Compliance: The policy establishes mechanisms for enforcement and compliance with occupational safety and health regulations. It may outline penalties and sanctions for non-compliance and the roles and responsibilities of regulatory bodies responsible for inspections, investigations, and enforcement.
8. Research and Data Collection: The policy may encourage research and data collection to improve understanding of occupational safety and health issues. It may promote the collection and analysis of occupational injury and illness data to identify trends, emerging risks, and areas requiring further attention.
9. International Cooperation: The policy may recognize the importance of international cooperation and collaboration in addressing occupational safety and health issues. It may encourage participation in international initiatives, sharing of best practices, and alignment with international standards and guidelines.
10. Continuous Improvement: The policy emphasizes the need for continuous improvement in occupational safety and health. It may require regular reviews and updates of policies and regulations based on changing technologies, work practices, and emerging risks. It may also promote the sharing of lessons learned and best practices within and across industries.

National Occupational health and safety system model

The national occupational health and safety (OHS) system model refers to the framework or structure implemented by a country to promote and regulate workplace health and safety. While specific details and components of the model can vary between countries, there are certain common elements typically found in an effective OHS system.

Here is a general outline of the elements of a national OHS system model:

1. **Legislative Framework**: A comprehensive set of laws and regulations is established to provide the legal basis for occupational health and safety. These laws define the rights and responsibilities of employers, employees, and other stakeholders, and they cover various aspects of workplace safety, such as hazard identification, risk assessment, and control measures.
2. **Regulatory Authorities**: Government agencies or bodies are designated to oversee and enforce the OHS laws and regulations. These authorities are responsible for monitoring compliance, conducting inspections, investigating accidents, and issuing penalties or sanctions for non-compliance.
3. **Occupational Health and Safety Standards**: Specific standards are developed and enforced to address various occupational hazards and risks. These standards may include requirements for safe working conditions, equipment, machinery, processes, and protective measures. They serve as guidelines for employers and employees to ensure compliance with OHS regulations.
4. **Hazard Identification and Risk Assessment**: Employers are required to identify potential hazards in the workplace and assess the associated risks. This process involves evaluating the likelihood and severity of harm resulting from exposure to hazards and taking necessary steps to eliminate or control those risks.
5. **Training and Education**: Employers are responsible for providing appropriate training and education to employees regarding workplace hazards, safe work practices, and emergency procedures. This ensures that workers are aware of the risks they may encounter and are equipped with the knowledge and skills to protect themselves and their colleagues.
6. **Consultation and Participation**: The OHS system promotes worker participation and consultation in decision-making processes that affect their health and safety. Employers are encouraged to involve employees and their representatives in OHS committees, safety meetings, and the development of policies and procedures.
7. **Incident Reporting and Investigation**: A system for reporting and investigating workplace incidents, accidents, and near misses is established. This helps identify the causes of incidents, implement corrective actions, and prevent future occurrences. Employers are required to maintain records of incidents and report serious accidents to the regulatory authorities.
8. **Enforcement and Compliance**: Regulatory authorities have the power to enforce OHS regulations through inspections, audits, and penalties for non-compliance. This ensures that employers fulfill their responsibilities and provides a deterrent against unsafe practices.
9. **Continuous Improvement**: The OHS system encourages ongoing improvement through periodic reviews, evaluations, and feedback mechanisms. Lessons learned from incidents and changes in technology or work processes are used to update standards and regulations, ensuring that the OHS system remains effective and up to date.

Fundamental principles of occupational health and safety model:

According to Convention No. 187, to be functional and effective in addressing the OSH needs of both employers and workers, a national system must include at the least the following key elements:

- Laws, regulations, collective agreements where appropriate, and any other relevant instruments on occupational safety and health;
- An authority or authorities responsible for occupational safety and health, designated in accordance with national law and practice;
- Mechanisms for ensuring compliance with national laws and regulations, including systems of inspection;
- Arrangements to promote, at the level of the undertaking, cooperation between management, workers and their representatives as an essential element of workplace-related prevention measures;
- A national tripartite body on occupational safety and health;
- Information and advisory services on occupational safety and health and Research on occupational safety and health;
- The provision of occupational health services in accordance with national law and practice, provision of OSH training;
- Mechanisms for the collection and analysis of data on occupational accidents and diseases, taking into account relevant ILO instruments;
- Provisions for collaboration with relevant insurance and compensation schemes covering occupational accidents and diseases;
- support mechanisms for a progressive improvement of occupational safety and health conditions in micro-, small and medium-sized enterprises and in the informal economy;

Other additional elements are also required to complete a system adequate to deal with so complex an area as occupational safety and health. A national OSH system designed to incorporate all these elements is illustrated in below figure:

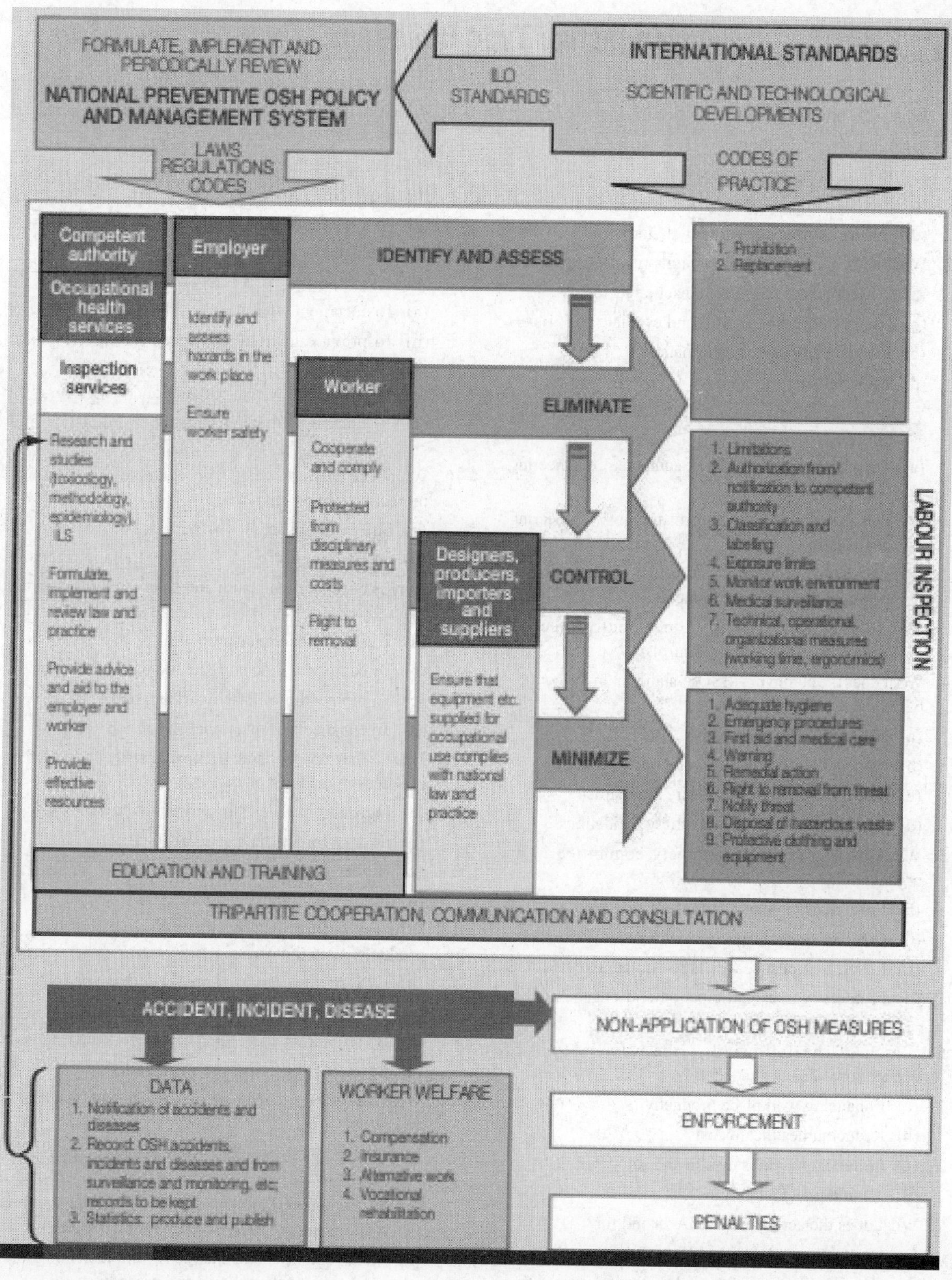
FORMULATE, IMPLEMENT AND PERIODICALLY REVIEW
NATIONAL PREVENTIVE OSH POLICY AND MANAGEMENT SYSTEM
ILO STANDARDS
INTERNATIONAL STANDARDS
SCIENTIFIC AND TECHNOLOGICAL DEVELOPMENTS
LAWS REGULATIONS CODES
CODES OF PRACTICE
Competent authority
Occupational health services
Inspection services
Research and studies (toxicology, methodology, epidemiology), ILS
Formulate, implement and review law and practice
Provide advice and aid to the employer and worker
Provide effective resources
Employer
Identify and assess hazards in the work place
Ensure worker safety
IDENTIFY AND ASSESS
Worker
Cooperate and comply
Protected from disciplinary measures and costs
Right to removal
Designers, producers, importers and suppliers
Ensure that equipment etc. supplied for occupational use complies with national law and practice
ELIMINATE
CONTROL
MINIMIZE
1. Prohibition
2. Replacement
1. Limitations
2. Authorization from/ notification to competent authority
3. Classification and labeling
4. Exposure limits
5. Monitor work environment
6. Medical surveillance
7. Technical, operational, organizational measures (working time, ergonomics)
1. Adequate hygiene
2. Emergency procedures
3. First aid and medical care
4. Warning
5. Remedial action
6. Right to removal from threat
7. Notify threat
8. Disposal of hazardous waste
9. Protective clothing and equipment
LABOUR INSPECTION
EDUCATION AND TRAINING
TRIPARTITE COOPERATION, COMMUNICATION AND CONSULTATION
ACCIDENT, INCIDENT, DISEASE
NON-APPLICATION OF OSH MEASURES
ENFORCEMENT
PENALTIES
DATA
1. Notification of accidents and diseases
2. Record: OSH accidents, incidents and diseases and from surveillance and monitoring, etc; records to be kept
3. Statistics: produce and publish
WORKER WELFARE
1. Compensation
2. Insurance
3. Alternative work
4. Vocational rehabilitation

Objective Type Questions

1. What is the primary goal of occupational health and safety?
   (a) Increase productivity
   (b) Reduce costs
   (c) Protect workers from work-related hazards
   (d) Ensure compliance with regulations
2. What is the purpose of conducting a risk assessment?
   (a) Determine the financial impact of accidents
   (b) Identify potential hazards and evaluate their risks
   (c) Evaluate employee performance
   (d) Allocate safety equipment
3. What is the hierarchy of controls in occupational health and safety?
   (a) Training, personal protective equipment, engineering controls
   (b) Personal protective equipment, training, engineering controls
   (c) Engineering controls, administrative controls, personal protective equipment
   (d) Administrative controls, personal protective equipment, engineering controls
4. What does the acronym "MSDS" stand for in the context of occupational health and safety?
   (a) Material Safety Data Sheet
   (b) Management System Development Strategy
   (c) Mandatory Safety Disclosure Standards
   (d) Occupational Health and Safety Guidelines
5. What is the purpose of a safety committee in an organization?
   (a) Enforce disciplinary actions for safety violations
   (b) Conduct safety inspections and audits
   (c) Ensure compliance with environmental regulations
   (d) Promote worker participation and engagement in safety matters
6. Which of the following is the primary goal of occupational health and safety?
   (a) Enhancing workplace productivity
   (b) Reducing healthcare costs
   (c) Protecting workers' health and safety
   (d) Avoiding legal liabilities
7. What does the acronym "OSHA" stand for?
   (a) Occupational Safety and Hazard Assessment
   (b) Organization for Safety and Health Administration
   (c) Occupational Safety and Health Act
   (d) Occupational Security and Health Association
8. Which of the following is an example of a physical hazard in the workplace?
   (a) Workplace bullying
   (b) Exposure to toxic chemicals
   (c) Poor ergonomic design of workstations
   (d) Inadequate training programs
9. What is the purpose of a safety data sheet (SDS)?
   (a) To document workplace accidents and near misses
   (b) To provide instructions for emergency response procedures
   (c) To track employee attendance and work hours
   (d) To ensure proper equipment maintenance and inspection
10. Which of the following is an example of a personal protective equipment (PPE)?
    (a) Fire extinguisher (b) First aid kit
    (c) Safety goggles (d) Safety training manual
11. Why is occupational health and safety important in the workplace?
    (a) To reduce insurance premiums
    (b) To comply with legal regulations
    (c) To protect the well-being of workers
    (d) To enhance organizational reputation
12. What is the impact of poor occupational health and safety practices in the workplace?
    (a) Increased absenteeism and turnover
    (b) Decreased customer satisfaction
    (c) Higher profit margins
    (d) Improved employee morale
13. How can occupational health and safety contribute to productivity in the workplace?
    (a) By reducing employee breaks and rest periods
    (b) By minimizing workplace distractions
    (c) By promoting a safe and healthy work environment
    (d) By increasing employee work hours
14. What role does management play in occupational health and safety?
    (a) Management is solely responsible for employee health and safety.
    (b) Management should provide safety equipment, but workers are responsible for their own safety.
    (c) Management is responsible for implementing and enforcing safety policies and procedures.
    (d) Management is responsible for conducting regular safety inspections.

15. How does occupational health and safety contribute to cost savings for organizations?
   (a) By reducing workers' salaries
   (b) By minimizing the need for employee benefits
   (c) By lowering insurance premiums and healthcare costs
   (d) By increasing productivity and profits
16. Why is it important to prioritize occupational health and safety in the workplace?
   (a) To improve employee morale
   (b) To reduce legal liabilities
   (c) To enhance productivity
   (d) All of the above
17. What is the primary reason for implementing occupational health and safety programs?
   (a) Compliance with legal regulations
   (b) Cost savings for the organization
   (c) Preservation of workers' well-being
   (d) Improvement of workplace aesthetics
18. How can occupational health and safety contribute to employee retention?
   (a) By increasing salary packages
   (b) By providing career advancement opportunities
   (c) By creating a safe and healthy work environment
   (d) By implementing strict disciplinary measures
19. What is the impact of occupational health and safety on organizational reputation?
   (a) Positive impact on brand image
   (b) Decreased customer loyalty
   (c) Increased competition in the market
   (d) Improved financial performance
20. Why is training an essential component of occupational health and safety programs?
   (a) To meet legal requirements
   (b) To develop employees' skills and knowledge
   (c) To reduce insurance premiums
   (d) To minimize workplace accidents caused by employees
21. How does occupational health and safety impact worker productivity?
   (a) By reducing employee work hours
   (b) By minimizing workplace stress
   (c) By increasing workload expectations
   (d) By enforcing strict performance evaluations
22. What is the role of employees in occupational health and safety?
   (a) To enforce safety rules and regulations
   (b) To report hazards and incidents
   (c) To conduct workplace inspections
   (d) To monitor compliance with legal standards
23. How can occupational health and safety programs contribute to cost savings for organizations?
   (a) By reducing employee salaries
   (b) By eliminating employee benefits
   (c) By lowering insurance premiums
   (d) By increasing revenue through higher sales
24. Why is risk assessment an important aspect of occupational health and safety?
   (a) To identify potential hazards and their associated risks
   (b) To implement strict disciplinary measures
   (c) To improve employee motivation and engagement
   (d) To increase revenue through cost-cutting measures
25. How does occupational health and safety contribute to legal compliance?
   (a) By minimizing workplace accidents
   (b) By providing emergency response plans
   (c) By enforcing disciplinary actions
   (d) By conducting regular safety audits
26. Which of the following is a potential cost associated with occupational injuries and diseases?
   (a) Medical treatment expenses
   (b) Lost productivity
   (c) Legal fees and fines
   (d) All of the above
27. Which of the following factors contributes to the cost of occupational injuries and diseases?
   (a) Workers' compensation claims
   (b) Absenteeism and presenteeism
   (c) Increased insurance premiums
   (d) All of the above
28. What is the significance of indirect costs related to occupational injuries and diseases?
   (a) They are easier to quantify than direct costs.
   (b) They include medical expenses and rehabilitation costs.
   (c) They are not directly associated with the injured worker.
   (d) They account for lost productivity and increased training costs.
29. How can occupational injuries and diseases impact an organization's productivity?
   (a) By increasing absenteeism and turnover rates
   (b) By decreasing healthcare expenses
   (c) By improving employee morale
   (d) By reducing insurance premiums

30. How can organizations mitigate the costs of occupational injuries and diseases?
(a) Implementing effective workplace safety measures
(b) Providing comprehensive employee training on safety protocols
(c) Encouraging a culture of reporting near misses and hazards
(d) All of the above

31. Which of the following is a potential health risk associated with poor working conditions?
(a) Musculoskeletal disorders
(b) Improved immune system
(c) Increased energy levels
(d) Enhanced mental well-being

32. Which of the following is a potential safety hazard resulting from poor working conditions?
(a) Fire safety measures
(b) Safety training programs
(c) Adequate lighting
(d) Slippery floors

33. How can poor ventilation impact worker health?
(a) Improved air quality
(b) Reduced respiratory issues
(c) Increased exposure to harmful substances
(d) Enhanced concentration

34. How can excessive noise in the workplace affect worker well-being?
(a) Improved hearing ability
(b) Reduced stress levels
(c) Increased risk of hearing loss
(d) Enhanced communication skills

35. What is the potential consequence of inadequate personal protective equipment (PPE)?
(a) Enhanced workplace aesthetics
(b) Reduced risk of injuries
(c) Increased exposure to hazards
(d) Improved productivity

36. What is the impact of poor working conditions on worker health and safety?
(a) Increased risk of accidents and injuries
(b) Improved productivity and job satisfaction
(c) Decreased absenteeism and turnover
(d) Enhanced employee engagement and motivation

37. How can poor working conditions affect worker health?
(a) Improved physical fitness and well-being
(b) Reduced stress levels and improved mental health
(c) Increased vulnerability to occupational diseases
(d) Enhanced work-life balance and job satisfaction

38. How can poor working conditions impact worker safety?
(a) Enhanced safety protocols and procedures
(b) Reduced risk of accidents and injuries
(c) Increased likelihood of workplace hazards
(d) Improved emergency response systems

39. What are the potential consequences of poor working conditions on worker health?
(a) Improved employee morale and job satisfaction
(b) Decreased healthcare costs for the organization
(c) Increased sick leaves and medical expenses
(d) Enhanced teamwork and collaboration

40. How can poor working conditions impact worker morale and job satisfaction?
(a) Increased job security and stability
(b) Improved work-life balance and flexibility
(c) Decreased job satisfaction and motivation
(d) Enhanced career growth opportunities

41. What is a common challenge related to occupational health and safety?
(a) Lack of awareness and training
(b) Excessive regulations and restrictions
(c) High cost of implementing safety measures
(d) Limited access to healthcare facilities

42. What is a potential issue regarding occupational health and safety regulations?
(a) Insufficient enforcement mechanisms
(b) Excessive leniency in penalties
(c) Lack of flexibility in compliance requirements
(d) Limited scope of covered industries

43. What is a significant challenge in promoting occupational health and safety in small businesses?
(a) Limited financial resources
(b) Lack of governmental support
(c) Decreased employee motivation
(d) Inadequate regulatory framework

44. What is a common issue related to occupational health and safety in high-risk industries?
(a) Excessive employee turnover
(b) Inadequate safety equipment availability
(c) Insufficient training programs
(d) Lack of emergency response plans

45. What is a potential challenge related to occupational health and safety in remote or mobile work settings?
(a) Lack of communication and coordination
(b) Decreased work flexibility and autonomy
(c) Inadequate access to healthcare facilities
(d) Reduced exposure to workplace hazards

46. What is a common issue associated with occupational health and safety for temporary or contract workers?
(a) Lower risk of workplace accidents
(b) Lack of safety training and orientation
(c) Higher job security and stability
(d) Inclusion in regular employee benefits

47. What is a challenge related to occupational health and safety for multinational corporations operating in different countries?
(a) Consistency in regulatory compliance
(b) Lower risk of workplace hazards
(c) Standardization of safety protocols
(d) Access to universal healthcare

48. What is an issue associated with occupational health and safety in physically demanding occupations?
(a) Excessive employee benefits
(b) Inadequate rest breaks and recovery time
(c) Reduced risk of musculoskeletal disorders
(d) Availability of ergonomic workstations

49. What is a challenge related to occupational health and safety in the agricultural sector?
(a) Advanced technology implementation
(b) Limited exposure to hazardous substances
(c) Lack of awareness about pesticide safety
(d) Availability of comprehensive insurance coverage

50. What is a potential challenge associated with occupational health and safety for night shift workers?
(a) Increased social interactions and support
(b) Availability of well-lit workspaces
(c) Higher risk of fatigue and sleep disorders
(d) Greater access to recreational facilities

51. Which of the following is an example of a physical hazard in the workplace?
(a) Exposure to toxic chemicals
(b) Repetitive motion injuries
(c) Noise pollution
(d) Poor lighting conditions

52. What is the primary concern when dealing with chemical hazards in the workplace?
(a) Ergonomic injuries
(b) Fires and explosions
(c) Noise-induced hearing loss
(d) Heat stress

53. Which of the following is an example of a biological hazard?
(a) Chemical spills (b) Slippery floors
(c) Bacterial infections (d) Heavy machinery

54. What type of hazard is associated with prolonged computer use and repetitive tasks?
(a) Physical hazard (b) Chemical hazard
(c) Ergonomic hazard (d) Biological hazard

55. Which of the following is an example of a psychosocial hazard?
(a) Fall from height (b) Exposure to toxic fumes
(c) Workplace violence (d) Electric shock

56. What is the primary concern with radiation hazards in the workplace?
(a) Exposure to ionizing radiation
(b) Electrocution risks
(c) Noise-induced hearing loss
(d) Slips, trips, and falls

57. Which of the following is an example of a fire hazard?
(a) Noise pollution (b) Chemical spills
(c) Confined spaces (d) Faulty electrical wiring

58. What is the primary concern when dealing with heat-related hazards?
(a) Exposure to hazardous substances
(b) Musculoskeletal injuries
(c) Falls from heights
(d) Heat exhaustion or heat stroke

59. Which of the following is an example of a mechanical hazard?
(a) Exposure to loud noises
(b) Inhalation of toxic gases
(c) Fall from a ladder
(d) Exposure to infectious diseases

60. What type of hazard is associated with inadequate ventilation or poor air quality in the workplace?
(a) Physical hazard (b) Biological hazard
(c) Chemical hazard (d) Radiological hazard

61. What is the key feature of a national policy in occupational safety and health?
(a) Voluntary compliance
(b) Mandatory regulations
(c) Employee training programs
(d) Workplace inspections

62. Which of the following is a key feature of a national policy in occupational safety and health?
(a) Continuous improvement
(b) Ad hoc decision-making
(c) Minimal oversight
(d) Reactive measures

63. What is a key feature of a national policy in occupational safety and health related to worker participation?

(a) Employee empowerment
(b) Solely management decision-making
(c) Limited worker involvement
(d) Lack of communication channels

64. Which of the following is a key feature of a national policy in occupational safety and health regarding risk assessment?

(a) Reactive response
(b) Absence of risk evaluation
(c) Proactive risk assessment
(d) Minimal risk control measures

65. What is a key feature of a national policy in occupational safety and health related to enforcement?

(a) Lack of penalties for non-compliance
(b) Inconsistent enforcement measures
(c) Encouragement of self-regulation
(d) Strong enforcement mechanisms

66. Which of the following is a key feature of a national policy in occupational safety and health regarding training and education?

(a) Limited access to training programs
(b) Exclusion of employers from training
(c) Emphasis on continuous training
(d) Lack of awareness campaigns

67. What is a key feature of a national policy in occupational safety and health related to monitoring and evaluation?

(a) Irregular evaluation processes
(b) Limited data collection
(c) Reactive approach to monitoring
(d) Regular monitoring and evaluation

68. Which of the following is a key feature of a national policy in occupational safety and health regarding research and development?

(a) Absence of research initiatives
(b) Inadequate funding for research
(c) Collaboration with academic institutions
(d) Lack of technological advancements

69. What is a key feature of a national policy in occupational safety and health related to communication and awareness?

(a) Limited dissemination of information
(b) Exclusion of stakeholders from communication
(c) Promotion of open communication channels
(d) Lack of awareness campaigns

70. Which of the following is a key feature of a national policy in occupational safety and health regarding international cooperation?

(a) Isolationist approach
(b) Limited collaboration with other countries
(c) Adherence to international standards
(d) Lack of information sharing

71. What does the National Occupational Health and Safety (OHS) system model aim to achieve?

(a) Promote employee wellness
(b) Ensure workplace safety and health
(c) Increase productivity
(d) All of the above

72. Which of the following is NOT a key element of the National OHS system model?

(a) Hazard identification and risk assessment
(b) Employee training and education
(c) Incident reporting and investigation
(d) Performance appraisal and rewards

73. What is the purpose of hazard identification and risk assessment in the National OHS system model?

(a) To eliminate all workplace hazards
(b) To assess the severity of workplace hazards
(c) To identify and assess workplace hazards
(d) To mitigate the impact of workplace hazards

74. Which of the following is an example of a control measure in the National OHS system model?

(a) Providing personal protective equipment (PPE)
(b) Conducting regular safety inspections
(c) Training employees on emergency procedures
(d) All of the above

75. What is the role of employee training and education in the National OHS system model?

(a) To ensure compliance with OHS regulations
(b) To develop specialized OHS expertise
(c) To increase employee awareness and knowledge
(d) To establish communication channels

76. What is the purpose of incident reporting and investigation in the National OHS system model?

(a) To assign blame to individuals responsible for incidents
(b) To meet legal reporting requirements
(c) To identify the root causes of incidents and implement corrective actions
(d) To minimize insurance costs for the organization

77. Which of the following is a key principle of the National OHS system model?
(a) Continuous improvement
(b) Employee discipline
(c) Cost reduction
(d) Short-term focus

78. What is the role of management commitment in the National OHS system model?
(a) To allocate resources for OHS initiatives
(b) To develop OHS policies and procedures
(c) To lead by example in promoting safety culture
(d) All of the above

79. What is the purpose of OHS performance measurement in the National OHS system model?
(a) To compare organizations' safety performance
(b) To identify areas for improvement
(c) To comply with regulatory requirements
(d) All of the above

80. Which entity is responsible for the development and implementation of the National OHS system model?
(a) International Labor Organization (ILO)
(b) World Health Organization (WHO)
(c) National OHS authority or agency
(d) Occupational Safety and Health Administration (OSHA)

81. Which principle of the occupational health and safety model emphasizes the responsibility of employers to provide a safe working environment?
(a) Risk assessment
(b) Hierarchy of controls
(c) Prevention through design
(d) Employer commitment and responsibility

82. Which principle of the occupational health and safety model focuses on identifying and evaluating potential hazards in the workplace?
(a) Risk assessment
(b) Worker participation
(c) Incident investigation
(d) Hierarchy of controls

83. Which principle of the occupational health and safety model promotes the involvement of workers in decision-making processes related to health and safety?
(a) Worker participation
(b) Prevention through design
(c) Continuous improvement
(d) Incident investigation

84. Which principle of the occupational health and safety model emphasizes the need to eliminate or minimize hazards through the use of engineering controls?
(a) Hierarchy of controls
(b) Risk assessment
(c) Prevention through design
(d) Incident investigation

85. Which principle of the occupational health and safety model focuses on investigating and analyzing incidents to prevent their recurrence?
(a) Incident investigation
(b) Continuous improvement
(c) Worker participation
(d) Employer commitment and responsibility

86. Which principle of the occupational health and safety model promotes the integration of health and safety considerations into the design and redesign of work processes, systems, and equipment?
(a) Prevention through design
(b) Continuous improvement
(c) Risk assessment
(d) Hierarchy of controls

87. Which principle of the occupational health and safety model emphasizes the need for ongoing evaluation and enhancement of health and safety practices?
(a) Continuous improvement
(b) Risk assessment
(c) Worker participation
(d) Incident investigation

88. Which principle of the occupational health and safety model emphasizes the use of administrative controls, such as training and procedures, to reduce risks?
(a) Hierarchy of controls
(b) Prevention through design
(c) Worker participation
(d) Incident investigation

89. Which principle of the occupational health and safety model emphasizes the need to provide workers with information and training to enable them to work safely?
(a) Worker participation
(b) Continuous improvement
(c) Risk assessment
(d) Employer commitment and responsibility

90. Which principle of the occupational health and safety model focuses on the collaboration between employers, workers, and other stakeholders to achieve and maintain a safe work environment?
(a) Worker participation
(b) Prevention through design
(c) Incident investigation
(d) Continuous improvement

Answers

1. (c)	**2.** (b)	**3.** (c)	**4.** (a)	**5.** (d)	**6.** (c)	**7.** (c)	**8.** (b)	**9.** (b)	**10.** (c)
11. (c)	**12.** (a)	**13.** (c)	**14.** (c)	**15.** (c)	**16.** (d)	**17.** (c)	**18.** (c)	**19.** (a)	**20.** (b)
21. (b)	**22.** (b)	**23.** (c)	**24.** (a)	**25.** (a)	**26.** (d)	**27.** (d)	**28.** (d)	**29.** (a)	**30.** (d)
31. (a)	**32.** (d)	**33.** (c)	**34.** (c)	**35.** (c)	**36.** (a)	**37.** (c)	**38.** (c)	**39.** (c)	**40.** (c)
41. (a)	**42.** (a)	**43.** (a)	**44.** (b)	**45.** (a)	**46.** (b)	**47.** (a)	**48.** (b)	**49.** (c)	**50.** (c)
51. (d)	**52.** (b)	**53.** (c)	**54.** (c)	**55.** (c)	**56.** (a)	**57.** (d)	**58.** (d)	**59.** (c)	**60.** (c)
61. (b)	**62.** (a)	**63.** (a)	**64.** (c)	**65.** (d)	**66.** (c)	**67.** (d)	**68.** (c)	**69.** (c)	**70.** (c)
71. (d)	**72.** (d)	**73.** (c)	**74.** (d)	**75.** (c)	**76.** (c)	**77.** (a)	**78.** (d)	**79.** (d)	**80.** (c)
81. (d)	**82.** (a)	**83.** (a)	**84.** (a)	**85.** (a)	**86.** (a)	**87.** (a)	**88.** (a)	**89.** (d)	**90.** (a)

Explanations

1. The primary goal of occupational health and safety is to ensure the well-being and safety of workers by identifying and mitigating workplace hazards, preventing occupational injuries and illnesses, and promoting a safe working environment. So, the correct answer is (c) Protect workers from work-related hazards.
2. Conducting a risk assessment involves systematically identifying workplace hazards, evaluating the associated risks, and determining appropriate control measures to minimize or eliminate those risks. It helps in preventing accidents and injuries by proactively addressing potential hazards. So, the correct answer is (b) Identify potential hazards and evaluate their risks.
3. The hierarchy of controls is a framework used to prioritize and implement measures for hazard control. It starts with engineering controls, which involve modifying the workplace or equipment to remove or reduce hazards. If engineering controls are not feasible or sufficient, administrative controls such as work procedures and policies are implemented. Personal protective equipment (PPE) is the last line of defense and is used when other controls are not adequate to mitigate the risks. So, the correct answer is (c) Engineering controls, administrative controls, and personal protective equipment.
4. An MSDS (or SDS - Safety Data Sheet) is a document that provides detailed information about potentially hazardous substances or chemicals used in the workplace. It includes information about physical properties, health effects, handling precautions, and emergency response procedures, helping workers and employers understand and manage the risks associated with the substances.
5. A safety committee is a group composed of workers and management representatives who collaborate to identify and address safety concerns in the workplace. The committee promotes communication, involvement, and consultation with workers, fostering a proactive safety culture and improving overall occupational health and safety performance. So, the correct answer is (d) Promote worker participation and engagement in safety matters.
6. While enhancing workplace productivity, reducing healthcare costs, and avoiding legal liabilities are important secondary goals, the primary goal of occupational health and safety is to ensure the well-being and safety of workers in the workplace. So, the correct answer is (c) Protecting workers' health and safety.
7. OSHA stands for Occupational Safety and Health Act, which is a federal law in the United States that establishes and regulates workplace health and safety standards.
8. Physical hazards refer to hazards that can cause harm through physical contact or exposure, such as noise, radiation, temperature extremes, and exposure to toxic substances. Workplace bullying, poor ergonomic design, and inadequate training programs are examples of other types of hazards (psychological, ergonomic, and training-related, respectively). So, the correct answer is (b) Exposure to toxic chemicals.
9. A safety data sheet (SDS) is a document that provides detailed information about hazardous chemicals, including their properties, handling procedures, storage requirements, and emergency response measures. So, the correct answer is (b) To provide instructions for emergency response procedures.

10. Personal protective equipment (PPE) refers to equipment or clothing designed to protect workers from hazards in the workplace. Safety goggles are a type of PPE that protects the eyes from flying debris, chemicals, or other potential eye hazards. Fire extinguishers, first aid kits, and safety training manuals are not considered PPE.

11. While reducing insurance premiums, complying with legal regulations, and enhancing organizational reputation are potential benefits of occupational health and safety, the primary and most important reason for its importance is to ensure the health, safety, and well-being of workers. So, the correct answer is (c) To protect the well-being of workers.

12. Poor occupational health and safety practices can result in higher rates of workplace injuries, illnesses, and accidents, which can lead to increased absenteeism and turnover as employees may need time off for recovery or may seek employment elsewhere due to safety concerns. Decreased customer satisfaction, higher profit margins, and improved employee morale are not directly associated with poor occupational health and safety practices. So, the correct answer is (a) Increased absenteeism and turnover.

13. Occupational health and safety measures create a work environment that is free from hazards, promotes employee well-being, and reduces the risk of accidents and injuries. When employees feel safe and healthy, they are more likely to be engaged, motivated, and productive. Reducing breaks, minimizing distractions, and increasing work hours are not effective or ethical ways to enhance productivity. So, the correct answer is (c) By promoting a safe and healthy work environment.

14. While employees also have a responsibility to follow safety protocols, management plays a crucial role in establishing a safe work environment, providing necessary safety equipment, training employees, and enforcing safety policies. Conducting regular safety inspections is part of management's responsibility, but it is not the sole role they play in occupational health and safety. So, the correct answer is (c) Management is responsible for implementing and enforcing safety policies and procedures.

15. Effective occupational health and safety practices can lead to a reduction in workplace accidents and illnesses, resulting in lower insurance premiums and healthcare costs for organizations. While occupational health and safety can indirectly contribute to productivity and profits, reducing workers' salaries and minimizing employee benefits are not ethical or effective strategies in promoting a safe and healthy work environment. So, the correct answer is (c) By lowering insurance premiums and healthcare costs.

16. Prioritizing occupational health and safety in the workplace has multiple benefits, including improving employee morale, reducing legal liabilities, and enhancing productivity. A safe and healthy work environment leads to higher employee satisfaction, lower risk of accidents and lawsuits, and increased efficiency and effectiveness.

17. While compliance with legal regulations, cost savings, and workplace aesthetics can be additional benefits, the primary reason for implementing occupational health and safety programs is to protect the well-being and safety of workers. It ensures that employees can perform their tasks without unnecessary risks to their health and safety. So, the correct answer is (c) Preservation of workers' well-being.

18. Occupational health and safety programs contribute to employee retention by fostering a workplace culture that values the well-being of employees. When workers feel safe and secure, they are more likely to stay with the organization. While salary, career advancement, and discipline play a role in retention, they are not directly related to occupational health and safety. So, the correct answer is (c) By creating a safe and healthy work environment.

19. Occupational health and safety practices demonstrate an organization's commitment to the well-being of its employees, which can enhance its brand image and reputation. It showcases the organization as a responsible employer and can attract customers, investors, and talented employees. Decreased customer loyalty, increased competition, and improved financial performance are not direct outcomes of occupational health and safety practices. So, the correct answer is (a) Positive impact on brand image.

20. Training is crucial in occupational health and safety programs to equip employees with the necessary skills and knowledge to identify and mitigate workplace hazards. While meeting legal requirements, reducing insurance premiums, and minimizing accidents are important, the primary goal of training is to empower employees to contribute to a safe work environment. So, the correct answer is (b) To develop employees' skills and knowledge.

21. Occupational health and safety measures contribute to worker productivity by creating a safe and healthy work environment that reduces stress and potential hazards. When employees feel safe, supported, and motivated, their productivity levels tend to increase. Reducing work hours, increasing workload expectations, and implementing strict performance evaluations are not effective or ethical means to enhance productivity. So, the correct answer is (b) By minimizing workplace stress.

22. While employees should be aware of safety rules and regulations and comply with them, their primary role in occupational health and safety is to report hazards and incidents to the appropriate channels. This helps in identifying risks, addressing concerns, and improving safety measures. Enforcing safety rules, conducting inspections, and monitoring compliance are typically the responsibility of management and designated safety personnel. So, The correct answer is (b) To report hazards and incidents.

23. Effective occupational health and safety programs can lead to a decrease in workplace accidents and illnesses, resulting in lower insurance premiums for organizations. While occupational health and safety can indirectly contribute to revenue through increased productivity and employee well-being, reducing employee salaries and eliminating benefits are not ethical or effective means of cost savings. So, the correct answer is (c) By lowering insurance premiums.

24. Risk assessment is a systematic process of identifying, evaluating, and controlling workplace hazards. It helps in understanding the potential risks to employee health and safety, allowing organizations to implement appropriate preventive measures. While disciplinary measures, employee motivation, and cost-cutting measures can be influenced by risk assessment, the primary purpose is to identify hazards. So, the correct answer is (a) To identify potential hazards and their associated risks.

25. Occupational health and safety measures, such as hazard identification, risk assessment, safety training, and the provision of appropriate equipment, help in minimizing workplace accidents and injuries. By preventing accidents, organizations can comply with legal regulations and requirements. While emergency response plans, disciplinary actions, and safety audits are essential components of occupational health and safety, they are not directly related to legal compliance. So, the correct answer is (a) By minimizing workplace accidents.

26. Occupational injuries and diseases can lead to various costs. Medical treatment expenses arise from providing necessary healthcare and rehabilitation services to injured or ill workers. Lost productivity refers to the decreased efficiency or absence of affected workers, resulting in reduced output and increased workload on other employees. Legal fees and fines may be incurred if an employer is found responsible for a workplace injury or illness due to negligence or non-compliance with safety regulations.

27. Workers' compensation claims are filed by employees seeking compensation for work-related injuries or illnesses. These claims can result in financial payouts and increased insurance costs for employers. Absenteeism occurs when workers are absent from work due to injuries or illnesses, leading to decreased productivity and increased costs. Presenteeism refers to the situation when workers come to work despite being unwell or injured, which can result in reduced productivity and potential exacerbation of the condition.

28. Indirect costs are the intangible expenses associated with occupational injuries and diseases that are not directly linked to the injured or ill worker. They include factors such as lost productivity due to absence or reduced efficiency, the need for temporary or permanent replacement workers, and expenses related to training new employees. Indirect costs are often more challenging to quantify compared to direct costs like medical expenses, but they can have a significant impact on an organization's overall financial burden. So, the correct answer is (d) They account for lost productivity and increased training costs.

29. Occupational injuries and diseases can lead to increased absenteeism as injured or ill workers may need time off to recover. Additionally, a high incidence of workplace injuries can contribute to higher turnover rates, as employees may become dissatisfied with safety conditions or perceive their workplace as unsafe. These factors can have a detrimental impact on productivity, as the organization may experience reduced workforce capacity and the need for frequent recruitment and training of new employees. So, the correct answer is (a) By increasing absenteeism and turnover rates.

30. Organizations can reduce the costs associated with occupational injuries and diseases by implementing effective workplace safety measures, such as installing safety equipment, conducting regular safety inspections, and enforcing safety protocols. Providing comprehensive training to employees on safety procedures and hazard recognition can help prevent accidents and injuries. Encouraging a culture of reporting near misses and hazards allows for early identification and rectification of potential risks, further minimizing the occurrence of injuries and illnesses in the workplace.

31. Poor working conditions such as repetitive movements, awkward postures, and lack of ergonomics can contribute to musculoskeletal disorders like back pain, carpal tunnel syndrome, and tendonitis.

32. Poor working conditions, such as inadequate housekeeping or failure to address spills and leaks, can lead to slippery floors, increasing the risk of slip and fall accidents in the workplace.

33. Poor ventilation can lead to the accumulation of hazardous substances, pollutants, and contaminants in the air, exposing workers to respiratory problems, allergies, and other health issues. So, the correct answer is (c) Increased exposure to harmful substances.

34. Excessive noise levels in the workplace can damage workers' hearing over time, leading to hearing loss and related health problems. It is important to implement measures like hearing protection and noise control to mitigate this risk. So, the correct answer is (c) Increased risk of hearing loss.

35. Inadequate or insufficient PPE can expose workers to various workplace hazards such as chemical splashes, impact injuries, and respiratory issues. Properly fitting and appropriate PPE is essential for safeguarding worker health and safety. So, the correct answer is (c) Increased exposure to hazards.

36. Poor working conditions, such as inadequate safety measures, lack of proper training, or faulty equipment, can significantly increase the likelihood of accidents and injuries in the workplace. Workers may be exposed to hazardous substances, unsafe machinery, or insufficient safety protocols, leading to an elevated risk of harm. So, the correct answer is (a) Increased risk of accidents and injuries.

37. Poor working conditions can expose workers to various health hazards, such as toxic chemicals, excessive noise, repetitive motion injuries, or inadequate ventilation. These factors can contribute to the development of occupational diseases, including respiratory problems, musculoskeletal disorders, and mental health issues. So, the correct answer is (c) Increased vulnerability to occupational diseases.

38. Poor working conditions often mean a lack of proper safety protocols, inadequate training, or insufficient maintenance of equipment and infrastructure. These factors increase the chances of workplace hazards, such as slips, falls, machinery malfunctions, or electrical accidents, jeopardizing the safety of workers. So, the correct answer is (c) Increased likelihood of workplace hazards.

39. Poor working conditions can lead to a decline in worker health, resulting in higher rates of sick leaves, medical expenses, and reduced productivity. Workers may require medical treatment, rehabilitation, or time off work to recover from work-related injuries or illnesses, imposing financial burdens on both the individual and the organization. So, the correct answer is (c) Increased sick leaves and medical expenses.

40. Poor working conditions, characterized by factors such as excessive work hours, lack of recognition, unsafe environment, or poor management, can significantly impact worker morale and job satisfaction. Workers may feel demotivated, undervalued, and dissatisfied with their work, leading to decreased productivity and higher turnover rates. So, the correct answer is (c) Decreased job satisfaction and motivation.

41. Many workers and employers may not have sufficient knowledge or understanding of occupational health and safety practices. This lack of awareness can lead to unsafe work conditions, inadequate safety protocols, and increased risk of accidents and injuries.

42. Occupational health and safety regulations may exist, but their effectiveness depends on proper enforcement. If enforcement mechanisms are weak or inadequate, employers may not prioritize compliance, leading to ongoing hazards and unsafe working conditions. So, the correct answer is (a) Insufficient enforcement mechanisms.

43. Small businesses often face financial constraints, making it challenging to invest in occupational health and safety measures. They may struggle to allocate funds for training, safety equipment, or workplace modifications, increasing the risk of accidents and injuries. So, the correct answer is (a) Limited financial resources.

44. High-risk industries, such as construction or manufacturing, require specialized safety equipment to protect workers from potential hazards. However, the availability or accessibility of such equipment can be limited, exposing workers to unnecessary risks. So, the correct answer is (b) Inadequate safety equipment availability.

45. In remote or mobile work settings, maintaining effective communication and coordination regarding occupational health and safety measures can be challenging. Workers may be geographically dispersed, making it difficult to ensure consistent adherence to safety protocols and provide immediate assistance in case of emergencies. So, the correct answer is (a) Lack of communication and coordination.

46. Temporary or contract workers often have limited exposure to comprehensive safety training and orientation programs. Due to the temporary nature of their employment, employers may overlook investing time and resources in ensuring their safety, leading to increased vulnerability to workplace accidents. So, the correct answer is (b) Lack of safety training and orientation.

47. Multinational corporations must navigate different occupational health and safety regulations across various countries. Ensuring consistent compliance with varying standards and requirements can be complex and requires dedicated efforts to prioritize the safety of workers across different geographical locations. So, the correct answer is (a) Consistency in regulatory compliance.

48. Physically demanding occupations often involve repetitive tasks or prolonged periods of physical exertion. Inadequate rest breaks and insufficient recovery time can contribute to fatigue, overexertion, and an increased risk of injuries or accidents. So, the correct answer is (b) Inadequate rest breaks and recovery time.

49. In the agricultural sector, workers often handle pesticides and other chemicals without proper training or awareness of safety protocols. This lack of knowledge can lead to pesticide exposure, posing risks to both the workers' health and the surrounding environment. So, the correct answer is (c) Lack of awareness about pesticide safety.

50. Night shift work disrupts the body's natural circadian rhythm, leading to increased fatigue and a higher risk of sleep disorders among workers. These conditions can impair concentration, reaction times, and decision-making abilities, elevating the likelihood of workplace accidents and injuries.

51. Physical hazards refer to conditions or factors within the work environment that can cause harm through physical contact or exposure. Poor lighting conditions can lead to trips, falls, and other accidents.

52. Chemical hazards involve the presence of substances that can cause harm through skin contact, inhalation, or ingestion. Certain chemicals can be flammable or reactive, posing a risk of fires and explosions.
53. Biological hazards involve exposure to living organisms or their byproducts that can cause harm, such as bacteria, viruses, fungi, or parasites. In the workplace, this can include exposure to infectious diseases.
54. Ergonomic hazards relate to factors that can lead to musculoskeletal disorders and injuries, such as repetitive tasks, poor posture, inadequate workstations, or improper lifting techniques.
55. Psychosocial hazards involve factors that affect the psychological well-being of workers, including workplace violence, stress, bullying, harassment, and inadequate social support.
56. Radiation hazards involve exposure to ionizing or non-ionizing radiation, which can cause harm to the body's cells, leading to health issues such as cancer or genetic mutations.
57. Fire hazards refer to conditions or factors that can ignite fires or contribute to their spread. Faulty electrical wiring can lead to short circuits and electrical fires.
58. Heat-related hazards involve exposure to high temperatures or extreme heat, which can cause heat-related illnesses, such as heat exhaustion or heat stroke.
59. Mechanical hazards are physical factors associated with machinery, tools, or equipment that can cause harm through contact, entanglement, or impact, such as falls, caught-in/between accidents, or machinery malfunctions.
60. Inadequate ventilation or poor air quality can lead to the accumulation of harmful chemical substances or irritants in the air, posing a risk to the health and well-being of workers.
61. A key feature of a national policy in occupational safety and health is the establishment of mandatory regulations. These regulations set specific standards and requirements that employers must follow to ensure a safe and healthy working environment for their employees.
62. A national policy in occupational safety and health should promote continuous improvement in workplace safety and health conditions. This involves regularly assessing and revising policies and practices to adapt to changing hazards and technologies, with the goal of achieving higher levels of safety and reducing the risk of workplace accidents and illnesses.
63. A key feature of a national policy in occupational safety and health is the promotion of worker participation and empowerment. This involves creating mechanisms and platforms for workers to actively participate in decision-making processes, share their knowledge and concerns, and contribute to the development and implementation of safety and health measures in the workplace.
64. A national policy in occupational safety and health should emphasize proactive risk assessment. This involves identifying and evaluating potential hazards and risks in the workplace before they result in accidents or illnesses. Through risk assessment, appropriate control measures can be implemented to mitigate or eliminate hazards, ensuring the safety and well-being of workers.
65. A key feature of a national policy in occupational safety and health is the establishment of strong enforcement mechanisms. This includes the implementation of penalties and sanctions for non-compliance with safety and health regulations, as well as the provision of adequate resources for inspections and monitoring to ensure employers adhere to the prescribed standards.
66. A national policy in occupational safety and health should emphasize the importance of continuous training and education for both employers and employees. This includes providing access to training programs, promoting ongoing learning opportunities, and ensuring that individuals have the necessary knowledge and skills to identify and manage workplace hazards effectively.
67. A key feature of a national policy in occupational safety and health is the establishment of regular monitoring and evaluation processes. This involves collecting data, conducting inspections, and assessing the effectiveness of safety and health measures to identify areas for improvement and ensure the policy's objectives are being met.
68. A national policy in occupational safety and health should promote collaboration with academic institutions and research organizations to encourage research and development activities. This can lead to the discovery of innovative approaches, technologies, and best practices that enhance workplace safety and health.
69. A key feature of a national policy in occupational safety and health is the promotion of open communication channels. This includes disseminating information about safety and health practices, regulations, and initiatives to stakeholders, facilitating dialogue between employers and workers, and promoting awareness campaigns to foster a culture of safety in the workplace.
70. A key feature of a national policy in occupational safety and health is the adherence to international standards and cooperation with other countries. This involves aligning national regulations with international guidelines, participating in international forums and initiatives, and sharing best practices to ensure a global approach to workplace safety and health.
71. The National OHS system model aims to promote employee wellness, ensure workplace safety and health, and increase productivity by providing a framework for managing occupational health and safety in the workplace.

72. While employee performance appraisal and rewards are important aspects of overall management, they are not considered key elements of the National OHS system model. The other options listed are key elements that contribute to an effective OHS system. So, the correct answer is (d) Performance appraisal and rewards.

73. Hazard identification and risk assessment are crucial steps in the National OHS system model as they help in identifying potential hazards and evaluating their associated risks in order to implement appropriate control measures. So, the correct answer is (c) To identify and assess workplace hazards.

74. Providing personal protective equipment, conducting regular safety inspections, and training employees on emergency procedures are all examples of control measures that can be implemented to prevent or minimize workplace hazards.

75. Employee training and education play a vital role in the National OHS system model by enhancing employees' understanding of workplace hazards, safe work practices, and their responsibilities in maintaining a safe and healthy work environment. So, the correct answer is (c) To increase employee awareness and knowledge.

76. To identify the root causes of incidents and implement corrective actions. Incident reporting and investigation are essential in the National OHS system model to understand why incidents occurred, identify underlying factors, and implement measures to prevent similar incidents in the future.

77. Continuous improvement is a key principle of the National OHS system model, emphasizing the need for ongoing evaluation, monitoring, and enhancement of occupational health and safety practices to achieve better outcomes over time.

78. Management commitment in the National OHS system model involves allocating resources, developing policies and procedures, and leading by example to create a positive safety culture and ensure that OHS initiatives are effectively implemented.

79. OHS performance measurement in the National OHS system model serves multiple purposes, including benchmarking safety performance, identifying areas for improvement, and ensuring compliance with regulatory requirements.

80. The development and implementation of the National OHS system model typically fall under the jurisdiction of the national OHS authority or agency in each respective country. While international organizations like the ILO and WHO may provide guidance and support, the national authority or agency takes the lead in establishing the model within their jurisdiction

81. Employer commitment and responsibility principle emphasizes that employers have a duty to provide a safe workplace and protect the health and safety of their employees.

82. Risk assessment principle involves the systematic identification and evaluation of workplace hazards to determine the level of risk they pose to workers' health and safety.

83. Worker participation principle recognizes that involving workers in health and safety decision-making leads to better outcomes, as they possess valuable insights and experiences regarding the work environment.

84. Hierarchy of controls principle suggests that hazards should be eliminated or minimized at their source through engineering controls, such as installing safety guards or implementing ventilation systems.

85. Incident investigation principle involves conducting thorough investigations into workplace incidents to determine their root causes and implement measures to prevent similar incidents in the future.

86. Prevention through design principle encourages the consideration of health and safety aspects during the design and redesign stages of work processes, systems, and equipment to minimize hazards and risks.

87. Continuous improvement principle highlights the importance of regularly reviewing and improving health and safety practices to adapt to changes in the workplace and enhance overall safety performance.

88. Principle suggests that when it is not feasible to eliminate hazards through engineering controls, administrative controls should be implemented, such as training programs, standard operating procedures, and work permits.

89. Employer commitment and responsibility principle highlights the employer's responsibility to provide workers with the necessary information, training, and resources to perform their work safely and protect their health.

90. Worker participation principle emphasizes the importance of fostering collaboration and active involvement of all stakeholders to create a safe and healthy work environment.

CHAPTER 10

Environment Education & Engineering

ENVIRONMENTAL EDUCATION

Environmental education (EE) is a process that allows individuals to develop the knowledge, values, skills, experiences, and commitment to make informed decisions and take responsible actions for the environment. It is a lifelong learning process that begins early in life and continues throughout adulthood. EE can be formal or informal. Formal EE takes place in schools, colleges, and universities, while informal EE occurs in community centers, museums, and nature centers. EE can also take place outdoors, through activities such as hiking, camping, and fishing.

The goals of EE are to :

- Increase public awareness and knowledge about environmental issues.
- Promote sustainable lifestyles.
- Develop citizens who are informed and engaged in environmental decision-making.
- Empower individuals to take action to protect the environment.

EE is essential for creating a sustainable future. By educating people about the environment, we can help them make choices that protect the planet for future generations.

Benefits to Environmental Education :

Environmental education (EE) is a process that allows individuals to develop the knowledge, values, skills, experiences, and commitment to make informed decisions and take responsible actions for the environment. It is a lifelong learning process that begins early in life and continues throughout adulthood.

There are many benefits to environmental education. Some of the most important benefits include:

- Increased awareness and understanding of environmental issues and challenges. EE can help people understand the interconnectedness of all living things and the impact of human activities on the environment.
- Improved critical thinking and problem-solving skills. EE can help people develop the skills to analyze environmental problems, identify potential solutions, and make informed decisions about environmental issues.
- Enhanced social and emotional development. EE can help people develop a sense of empathy and compassion for the environment and other living things.
- Increased sense of responsibility for the environment. EE can help people develop a sense of stewardship for the environment and a commitment to taking action to protect it.
- Greater participation in environmental stewardship activities. EE can encourage people to get involved in environmental activities, such as volunteering for environmental organizations or participating in community cleanup projects.
- Improved mental and physical health. Spending time in nature has been shown to have a number of positive benefits for mental and physical health, such as reducing stress levels, improving mood, and boosting the immune system.

Components of Environment Education

Environmental education (EE) is a process that allows individuals to develop the knowledge, values, skills, experiences, and commitment to make informed decisions and take responsible actions for the environment. It is a lifelong learning process that begins early in life and continues throughout adulthood.

There are three main components of EE:

- Awareness and sensitivity to the environment and environmental challenges. This includes understanding the interconnectedness of all living things and the impact of human activities on the environment.

- Knowledge and understanding of the environment and environmental challenges. This includes learning about the natural world, environmental issues, and the principles of sustainability.
- Attitudes of concern for the environment and motivation to improve or maintain environmental quality. This includes developing a sense of stewardship for the environment and a commitment to taking action to protect it.

All three of these components are essential for effective EE. Without awareness and sensitivity, individuals may not be motivated to learn about environmental issues or take action to protect the environment. Without knowledge and understanding, individuals may not be able to make informed decisions about environmental issues. And without attitudes of concern, individuals may not be motivated to take action to protect the environment, even if they have the knowledge and skills to do so.

EE can be delivered in a variety of ways, including:

- **Formal education :** This includes teaching about environmental issues in schools, colleges, and universities.
- **Non-formal education :** This includes teaching about environmental issues through community centers, museums, and nature centers.
- **Informal education :** This includes learning about environmental issues through everyday experiences, such as hiking, camping, and fishing.

EE can also be delivered to a variety of audiences, including :

- **Children :** EE can help children develop a lifelong love of the environment and a sense of responsibility for protecting it.
- **Adults :** EE can help adults learn about environmental issues and take action to protect the environment.
- **Communities :** EE can help communities develop sustainable practices and protect their local environment.
- **Businesses :** EE can help businesses reduce their environmental impact and become more sustainable.

EE is a powerful tool for addressing environmental challenges. By educating people about the environment, we can help them make choices that protect the planet for future generations.

Concept of environment education:

Environmental education is a holistic, interdisciplinary field that focuses on raising awareness, understanding, and appreciation of the environment. It encompasses a wide range of topics related to the natural world, ecosystems, sustainability, and the intricate relationships between humans and their environment.

Key aspects of environmental education include :

1. **Awareness and Knowledge :** Educating individuals about the environment, ecosystems, biodiversity, climate change, natural resources, pollution, and other relevant topics. This involves understanding the interconnections between various environmental factors.
2. **Promoting Environmental Stewardship :** Encouraging individuals to become responsible and active stewards of the environment. This includes fostering a sense of responsibility and care for the natural world.
3. **Sustainability and Conservation :** Highlighting the importance of sustainable practices and conservation efforts to protect natural resources, reduce environmental degradation, and preserve ecosystems for future generations.
4. **Interdisciplinary Approach :** Environmental education often draws on knowledge from various disciplines such as biology, ecology, chemistry, geology, sociology, economics, and more to provide a comprehensive understanding of environmental issues.
5. **Hands-On Learning :** It often involves practical, experiential learning methods such as field trips, hands-on activities, and outdoor experiences to facilitate a deeper understanding of environmental concepts.
6. **Critical Thinking and Problem-Solving :** Encouraging individuals to think critically about environmental issues, analyze problems, and come up with solutions to address them.
7. **Policy and Advocacy :** Empowering individuals to engage in policy discussions and advocate for environmental policies and practices that support sustainability and conservation.

The scope of environmental education (EE):

The scope of Environmental Education (EE) is broad and multifaceted, encompassing various aspects related to the environment, sustainability, and the interconnectedness of ecosystems. Its primary goal is to foster an understanding of environmental issues, promote the development of critical thinking skills, and encourage responsible and informed decision-making about environmental concerns. The scope of EE typically includes the following areas :

1. **Awareness and Understanding :** Educating individuals about the environment, its ecosystems, biodiversity, natural resources, and the impact of human activities on the environment.
2. **Sustainability :** Promoting the concept of sustainability, that is involves the responsible use of resources to meet the need of the present without compromising the ability of future generations to meet their own needs.
3. **Conservation and Preservation :** Highlighting the importance of preserving natural habitats, protecting endangered species, and conserving biodiversity.
4. **Environmental Ethics:** Encouraging the development of ethical principles that guide responsible behavior towards the environment.
5. **Climate Change Education :** Addressing the causes and effects of climate change, as well as strategies for mitigation and adaptation.
6. **Waste Management and Recycling :** Educating about proper waste disposal, recycling practices, and the reduction of waste to minimize environmental impact.
7. **Environmental Policies and Governance:** Understanding local and global environmental policies, regulations, and governance structures to advocate for sustainable practices and policies.
8. **Outdoor Education and Experiential Learning :** Providing hands-on experiences in nature to foster a deeper connection with the environment and promote active learning.
9. **Interdisciplinary Approach :** Incorporating various disciplines such as science, social studies, geography, economics, and ethics to provide a comprehensive understanding of environmental issues.
10. **Community Engagement and Action :** Encouraging individuals and communities to take action, participate in environmental initiatives, and become advocates for positive environmental change. The scope of EE is not limited to formal education systems; it extends to informal education, community programs, advocacy, and policy-making. It aims to empower individuals to become environmentally literate, take informed actions, and contribute to the sustainable development of society.

ENVIRONMENTAL ENGINEERING

Environmental education is an important part of environmental engineering. It helps to teach people about the environment and how to protect it.

Components of Environmental Engineering

I. Water Resources

Water resources engineers design and manage systems for the collection, treatment and distribution of water. In the context of environmental engineering, Water Supply is the process of providing clean and safe drinking water to a community or population.

Water is extremely useful to man, providing him luxuries and conterts, in addition to fulfilling his basic necessities of life. It has been estimated that two third of human body is constituted of water.

Sutiable system should be designed for collecting, transporting , and treating water.

Public Water Supply Scheme

Essential elements.

(1) *Intake and reservoir* : To collect water.

(2) *Water treatment plant* : Screening, sedimentations, filteration, disinfection units etc.

(3) *Elevated tanks and stand pipes* : It provide storage to meet peak demands occuring for limited periods.

(4) *Valves* : It control the flow of water in the pipe system.

(5) *Hydrants* : It provide a connection with the water in the main for fighting fires, flushing streeets etc.

(6) *Distribution system* : mains, submains, and branch lines which carry the water to the streets.

(7) *Servies* : It carry the water to the individual house etc.

Water Demand

In fact the first requirement is to consider the demand, and the second requirement is to find sources to fulfil that demand.

Types of water demands.

(1) Domestic water demand 55% to 60% of total water consumption.

(2) Industrial water demand 50 lpcd :

(3) Institutional and commercial water demand – 20 lpcd

(4) Demand for public uses – 10 lpcd

(5) Fire demand; – 1 lpcd

(6) Water required to compensate losses in wastes and thefts–55 lpcd

As per is 1172-1983 as well as National building code, the domestic consumption under normal conditions in an Indian city is expected to be around 135 letre/head/day

Table : Break up of 135 lpcd

Use	*Consumption in litres per capita per day*
Drinking	5
Cooking	5
Bathing	55
Washing of clothes	20
Washing of utensils	10
Washing and cleaning of houses and residences	10
Flushing of latrines, etc.	30
Total	135

(2) *Industrial water demand – 50 lpcd :*

The ordinary per capital consumption for industrial needs of a city is generally taken as 50 litres/capita/day.

(3) On an average, per capita demand of 20 l/h/d is usually considered to be enough to meet such commercial and institutional water requirements, although this demand may be as high as 50 l/h/d for highly commercialised cities.

(4) Demand for public uses is generally taken as 10 l/h/day.

(5) *Fire demand* :

- Fire hydrants are usually fitted in the water mains at about 100 to 150 metres apart.
- The per capita fire demand is thus generally ignored while computing the total per capita water requirement of a city.
- Kilo litre of water required = $100\sqrt{P}$ when population exceeding 50,000

  where, P = population in thousand.
- Rate of fire demand is worked out on the basis of certain empirical formula.

Kuichling's formula

$$Q = 3182\sqrt{P}$$

where, P = Population in thousand.

Freeman's formula

Amount of water required in litres/min,

$$Q = 1136\left[\frac{1}{10}+10\right]$$

For a central congested high value city

$$Q = 4637\sqrt{P}\,[1-0.01\sqrt{P}\,]$$

(6) *Wastes and thefts*, etc.

Per Capita Demand

q = Total yearly water requirement of the city in litres/365 × Design population

For an Indian city, as per recommendation of IS. code, per capita demand, q = 270 l/h/d.

Factors affecting per capita demand.

(1) Size of the city

(2) Climate conditions

(3) Types of gentry and habits of people.

(4) Industrial and commercial activities.

(5) Quality of water supplies.

(6) Pressure in the distribution system.

(7) Development of sewerage facilities

(8) System of supply.

(9) Cost of water

(10) Policy of metering and Method of charging.

Variation in the demand

(1) Maximum daily consumptions

= 180% of the annual average daily demand

= 1.8 × Average daily demand

$= 1.8q$

(2) Maximum hourly consumption= 150 % of the average houry demand of the month day.

$$= \frac{150}{100} \times \frac{\text{Maximum daily demand}}{24}$$

$$= \frac{150}{100} \times \frac{1.8q}{24}$$

$$= \frac{1.8 \times 1.5}{24}\,q$$

$$= 2.7\left(\frac{q}{24}\right)$$

= 2.7 × Annual average hourly demand

(3) Maximum hourly demand of maximum day = $2.7\,q$

(4) Goodrich's formula

$$P = 180 + t^{-0.10}$$

where, P = % of the annual average draft for the time t in days.

t = time in days from $\frac{1}{24}$ to 365

When t = 1 day (for daily variations), then

$$P = 180 \times (1)^{-0.10} = 180$$

$$\therefore \frac{\text{Maximum daily demand}}{\text{Average daily demand}} = 180\%$$

When $t = 7$ days (for weekly variations), then

$$P = 180 \times (7)^{-0.10} = 148\ \%$$

$$\therefore \quad \frac{\text{Maximum weekly demand}}{\text{Average weekly demand}} = 148\%$$

$$\text{Similarly,} \quad \frac{\text{Maximum monthly demand}}{\text{Average monthly demand}} = 128\%$$

(5) The pipe mains carrying water from the source to the reservior is designed for the maximum daily demand.

(6) Distribution system is designed for maximum hourly demand 5.5

(7) The filters and other units of the treatment plant are desinged for a 2 times the average daily demand.

(8) Coincident demand : The maximum daily demand when added to fire demands for working out total demand is known as *coincident demand*.

Water Supply Schemes

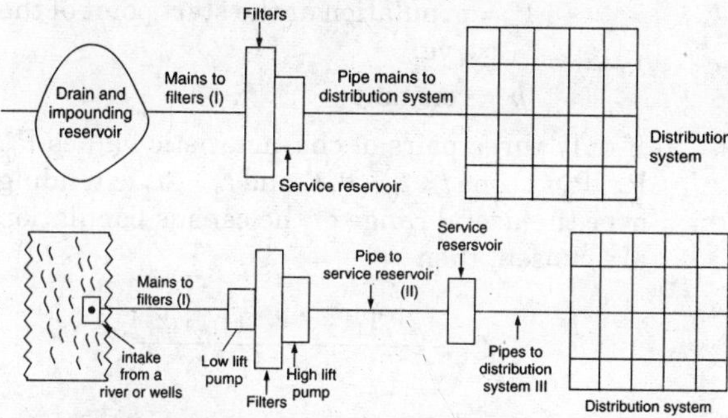

- In case of dams and reservoirs—Generally no needs of pumps.
- In case a river is used as a source, is required dumping equipment is required

Design Periods

The future period or the number of years for which a provision is made in designing the capacities of the various components of the water supply scheme is known as **design period.**

Water supply projects, under normal circumstances, may be designed for a design period of 30 years. This 30 years is to be counted after the completion of the project.

POPULATION FORECASTS

Factor affecting population growth.

(1) Birth

(2) Deaths

(3) Migrations

Besides these some other factors like wars, nature havoc and disasters may also bring about sharp reduction in the pupulations.

Population forecasting methods

(1) Arithmatical increase method.

$$P_n = [P_0 + n\bar{x}]$$

where, P_n = forcasted population after n decades from the present

P_0 = population at present (*i.e.* last known census)

n = number of decades between present and future

$\bar{x}$ = average population increase in the known decades

(2) Geometrical increase method or Uniform increase method.

In arithmatic method, no compounding is done but, in geometric method comounding is done every decade.

$$P_n = P_o\left(1 + \frac{r}{100}\right)^n$$

where, P_o = initial population

P_n = future population after n decades

r = assumed growth rate (%)

Computation of assumed growth rate (r) from the past known population data.

$$r = \sqrt[t]{\frac{P_2}{P_1}} - 1$$

where, P_1 = intial known population

P_2 = final known population

t = number of decades between P_1 and P_2

Note : Arithmetic mean,

$$r = \frac{r_1 + r_2 + r_3 + \ldots\ldots\ r_t}{t}$$

Geometric mean,

$$r = \sqrt[t]{r_1 + r_2 + r_3 \ldots\ldots\ r_t}$$

where, $r_1, r_2, r_3 \ldots\ldots\ r_t$ are % growth rates of the several known decades of past.

Arithmetic mean is slightly higher than geometric mean

Also r can be calculated as

$$r = \text{increase}\ \frac{\text{in population}}{\text{original population}} \times 100$$

Note : In geometric method computing is done every decade

(3) Incremental increase method or Method of varying increment.

$$P_n = P_o + n\bar{x} + \frac{n(n+1)}{2}\bar{y}$$

where, P_n = population after n decades from present

P_o = present population

$\bar{x}$ = average increase of population of known decades.

$\bar{y}$ = average of incremental increase of the known decades.

- Population obtained by
  Arithmatic increase method < Incremental increase method < Geometrical increment method.
- Incremental method gives quite satisfactory results.
- For newyounger cities expanding at faster rates → Geometrical increment method is applied.
- For old cities → Arithmetic method is better.
- Incremental method is applied for any type of city.

(4) Decreasing rate method.

This method is applicable only in cases where the rate of growth shows a downward manner.

In this method, the average decreases in the percentage increases is worked out, and is then substracted from the latest percentage increase for each successive decade.

(5) Simple graphical method.

In this method, a graph is plotted from the available data, between time and population. The curve is then smoothly extended upto the desired year.

(6) Comparative graphical method.

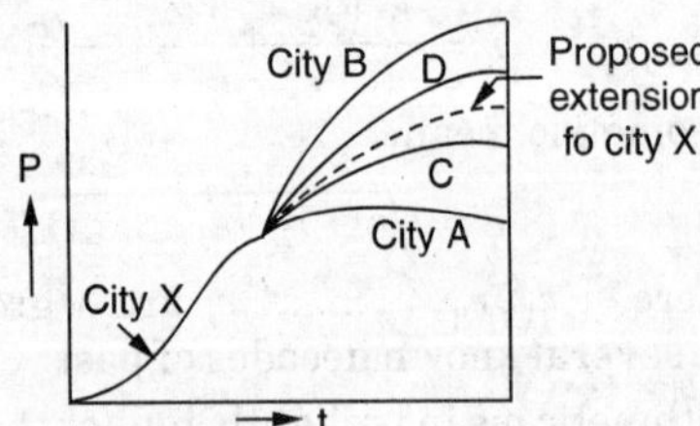

(7) Master plan method.

It is very easy to access precisely the design population, because the master plan will give us as to when and where the given number of houses, industries and commercial establishment would be developed.

(8) Apportionment method or Ratio Method.

The local population and the country population for the last four or five decades is obtained from the census method.

(9) Logistic curve method.

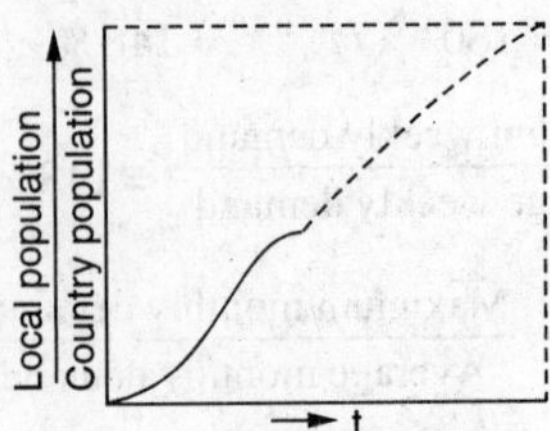

Equation of the logistic curve is

$$P = \frac{P_s}{1 + m \log_e^{-1}(nt)}$$

where, P = population at any time t from the origin A

P_s = saturated population

$m = \frac{P_s P_0}{P_0}$ (a constant)

$n = kp_s$ (another constant)

P_0 = population at the start point of the curve.

k = constant

- If only three pairs of characteristic values P_0, P_1, P_2 at time $t = t_0 = 0, t_1$ and $t_2 = 2t_1$ extending over the useful range of the census population are chosen, then

$$P_s = \frac{2P_0P_1P_2 - P_1^2 (P_0 + P_2)}{P_0P_2 - P_1^2}$$

$$m = \frac{P_s - P_0}{P_0}$$

$$n = \frac{1}{t_1} \log_e \left[\frac{P_0 (P_s - P_1)}{P_1 (P_s - P_0)}\right]$$

Note :

(i) Methods 1 to 5 are based on the assumption that factors and conditions which were responsible for population increase in the past and continue even in the future also, with the intensity. This is a vague assumption.

(ii) Methods 6 to 9 are advanced and time consuing methods which gives fair results.

(iii) None of these methods is exact, and they are all based on the laws of probability, and thus, only approximate estimation for possible future population can be made.

Sources of Water

After calculating the demand of water, the main job is to search the source of water.

Classification of sources of water available on earth.

(1) Surface sources.

(i) Ponds and lakes

(ii) Streams and rivers

(iii) Storage reservoirs; impounding reservior

(iv) Ocean, generally not used for water supplies

(2) Sub-surface sources or Underground sources.

(i) Spring

(ii) Infiltration galleries

(iii) Infiltration wells

(iv) Wells and tube-wells.

- The yield which correspond to the worst or most critical year on record is called **firm yield** or **safe yield**.

Hydrologic Principles.

- The precipitation and evaporation continues forever, and thereby a balance is maintained between the two. This process is known as **hydrological cycle**.
- The evaporated water comes back to the surface of the earth is in its various forms like rain, show, hail, mist, sleet etc. is known as **precipitation**
- A major part of the precipitation occurs in the form of rain, and a minor part occurs in the form of snow.

Types of Precipitations.

(i) Cyclonic precipitation :

It is caused by the lifting of the air mass due to the pressure difference. If low pressure occurs in an area, air will flow horizontal from the surrounding area, causing the air in the low pressure area to lift. The precipitation that results, is called *non-frontal cyclonic precipitation.* If one air mass lifts over another air mass, then the precipitation is called **frontal or cyclonic precipitation**.

- The boundry between these two air masses of different temperatures and densities is known as a **front** or a **frontal surface**.
- The large whirling mass of air, at the centre of which the barometric pressure is low, is known as a **cyclone**.

(ii) Convective precipitation :

Convective precipitation is due to the upward movement of air that is warmer than its surroundings. Precipitation occurs of high intensity and short duration.

(iii) Orographic precipitation :

Orographic precipitation is the most important precipitation which is responsible for most of the heavy rains in India. Orographic precipitation is caused by air masses which strike some natural topographic barriers like mountains, and cannot move forward, and hence rise up, causing condentation and precipitation.

Note : The usual mechanism by which the air is cooled to cause precipitation is the lifting of the air mass.

Rainfall and it's Distribution

Rainfall interception (P_i).

The rain interrupted by buildings and trees.

Ground rainfall (P_g).

Total rainfall = $P—P_i$

Infiltration (F).

The ground rainfall infiltrated by the soil.

Infiltration capacity (f).

The maximum rate at which the soil in a given condition can absorp water is known as **infiltration capacity.**

Depression storage (S_d).

None of it appear as surface runoff.

Rainfall excess (P_e).

P_e = rainfall rate (P)-infiltration capacity (f)

Measurement of Railfall

Two types of raingauges are used :

(1) Non-recording type rain gauge

(only collect the rain)

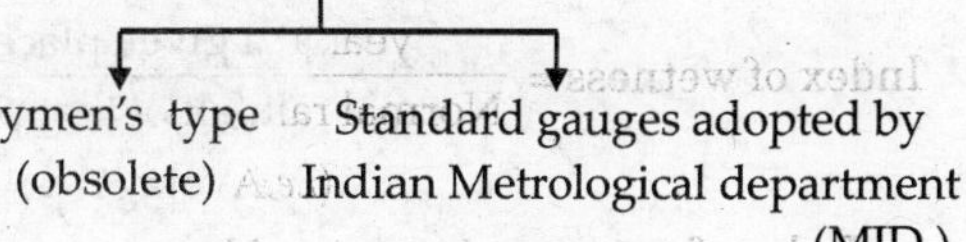

(2) Recording type rain gauge.

It gets rcorded automatically on a graph paper. This gauge thus produces a record of cumulative rain Vs. time in the form of graph, which is known as the **mass curve of rainfall.**

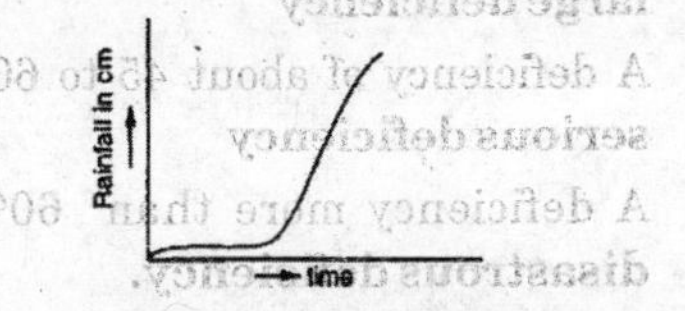

It is also known as *integrating raingauges or continuous rain-gauges.*

Type of recording raingauges :

(i) Tipping bucket type–operated through telecommounication system.

(ii) Weighing type

(iii) Floating type, etc. (most widely used in India).

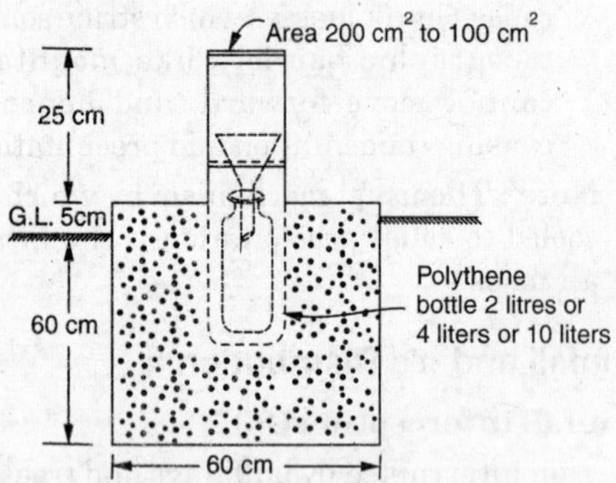

Fig. Standard non-recording raingauge.

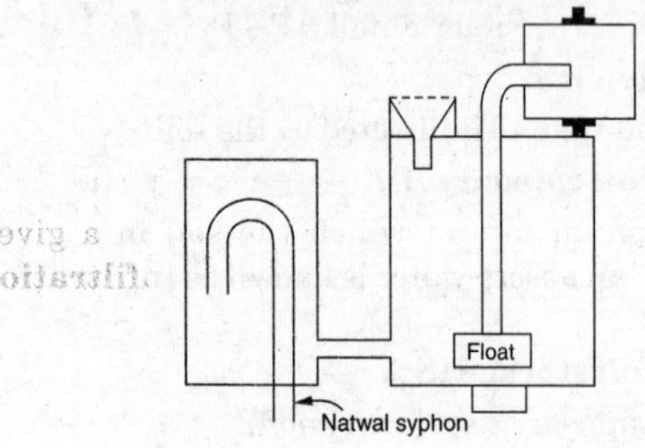

Fig. Float type automatic raingauge.

The rotating drum completes one revolution in 24 hours or sometimes in 7 days.

$$\text{Average annual rainfall} = \frac{\text{Annual rainfall at a given station should be recorded over a number of years (35 years)}}{\text{Number of years}}$$

Index of wetness.

$$\text{Index of wetness} = \frac{\text{Actual rainfall in a given year at a given place}}{\text{Normal rainfall of that place (i.e. Average)}}$$

- Index of wetness, gives us an idea of the wetness of the year.
- 60% index of wetness means a rain deficiency of 40%.
- A deficiency of about 30 to 45% is known as **large deficiency**
- A deficiency of about 45 to 60% is known as **serious deficiency**
- A deficiency more than 60% is known as **disastrous deficiency.**

The year in which the rainfall is less than the average annual, is called a **bad year** or a **sub normal year**; and the year in which the rainfall is more than the average, is called a **good year**. If the rainfall in a particular year is a approximately equal to the annual average value, then it is known as a **normal year**.

The average annual rainfall of a given place is very useful for planning water supply schemes at that place, because it direct gives us an idea of the probable amount of water that may be available at that place.

Estimating Run-off and yield of a Basin

(1) English formula :

$Q_y = 0.85\,P_y - 304$ for hilly cantchment

$Q_y = P_y\left[\frac{P_y - 17.8}{254}\right]$ for plane catchment

(Used in South India.)

where, Q_y = yearly runoff in cm depth over the basin

P_y = yearly precipitation or annual rainfall in cm.

(2) Khosla's Formula :

$$Q_y = P_y - 0.4813\,T_m \; (T_m > 4.5°C)$$

(3) $Q_y = KP_y$

where, K = impervious factor.

This runoff is helpful in evaluating the amount of water available in the river over long periods. They are, therefore, useful for estimating the storage capacity of the reservoir, and this fixed the height. of the dam required to be constructed for that storage. These determinations are hence useful when storage reservoir is to be used as a source of water. However, when a river or a stream is to be directly used as a source of water, we must determine the day to day quantities of flow in that river or stream.

Surface Sources of Water Supplies

(1) Ponds and Lakes : If size of the depression is comparatively small, it may be termed as a **pond**, and when the size of depression is larger, it many be termed as a **lake**.

Due to the smaller quantity of water available from them, lakes are not considered as principal source of water supplies.

(2) Streams and Rivers : Small stream channels feed their waters to the lakes or rivers.

Rivers are the most important sources of water supply schemes.

(i) Perennial river : water is available throughout the year.

(ii) Non-perennial rivers : The quality of water obtained from these rivers is not reliable.

(3) Storage Reservoirs : A water supply scheme drawing water directly from a river or a stream may fail to satisfy the consumers demands during extremely low flows. To avoid such problem we construct a dam across a river for storage of water. The artificial lake is formed on the up stream side is known as **storage reservoir.**

- The subject of design and planning of dams and reservoirs is a big topic in itself, and is generally dealt under the subject of irrgation.
- Surface waters are, however, generally soft and less corrosive than ground waters. On the whole it can be stated that the surface supplies are generally contaminated and cannot be used without treatment.

Subsurface or Underground Water Sources

Sometimes, the ground water is brought to the surface by some natural processes like **springs**, and sometimes the water is tapped by artificial means by constructing wells, tubewells, infiltration galleries etc. Since the ground water is largely tapped in our country for water supplies and there is a scope for its development in future also.

Factors affecting the selection of a particular source of water:

(i) Quantity of available water.

(ii) Quality of available water.

(iii) Distance of the source of supply.

(iv) General topography of the interveing area.

(v) Elevation of the source of supply.

- The dead storage zone in a reservior is provided for storage of sand and silt.
- $$\text{Trap efficiency} = \frac{\text{Total sediment deposited in the reservoir}}{\text{Total sediment flowing in the river.}}$$
- With the redution in the reservoir capacity, the quantum of sediment trapped by it decreases.

Development of Ground Water

Geological factors governing the occurrance of ground water.

Possibility of occurrance of the underground water mainly depends upon two properties of the underground soil

(i) Porosity of the soil

(ii) Permeability of the soil.

Rock Formations

Porosity values of some rock formations.

Granite, Quartzite	—	1.5%
Slate, Shale	—	4 %
Limestone	—	5 to 10 %
Sandstone	—	10 to 15 %
Sand and Gravel	—	20 to 30 %
Only gravel	—	25%
Only sand	—	35%
Clay and Soil	—	45%

Permeability and transmissibility.

- The porosity of the rock is defined the maximum amount of water that can be stored in the rock. This porosity, however, in itself, does not ensure the storage of underground water, because the water can enter into a rock only if the rock permits the flow of water through it.
- A rock which is porous, may or may not be permeable.
- The capability of the entire soil of full width and depth is represented by **permeability**; while that of the soil of unit width and full depth is known as **transmissibility**.
- The permeability is measured in terms of coefficient of permeability.

Zones of Underground Water

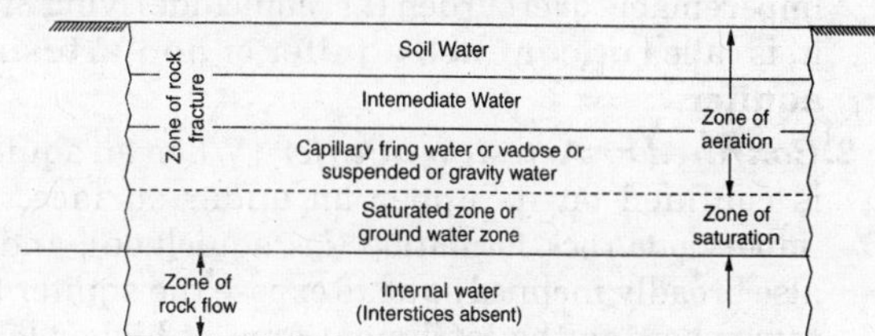

In the zone of saturation, water exists within the interstices and is known as *ground water*. This is the most important zone for a ground water hydrolic engineering because it has to tap out this water. Water in this zone is under hydrostatic pressure.

$$Q = ki\,A$$
$$V = ki$$

where, V is discharge velocity not the actual velocity (V_a) through the soil medium.

$$A_v V_a = A \times V$$

where, A_v = cross-sectional area of void

$$V = \frac{A_v}{A} V_a$$
$$V = \eta\, V_a$$
$$V_a = \frac{V}{n} = \frac{ki}{n}$$

Intrinsic permeability or specific permeability,

$$k_o = \frac{kv}{g} = k\left(\frac{\mu}{\gamma w}\right)$$

Relation between coefficient of permonability (k) and coefficient of transmissibility (T).

$$T = kd$$

where, d = mean particle size of porous medium.

Drainage of Ground Water

It means extracting the water from below the water lable through well, infiltration galleries, springs, etc.

$$\text{Porosity} = \text{Specifie yield} + \text{Specific retention}$$

$$= \frac{\text{Volume of water obtained by gravity drainage}}{\text{total weight of the material drained}} + \frac{\text{volume of water held against gravity drainage}}{\text{total weight of the material drained}}$$

- Large particles of soils like coarse gravels, the specific retention would be small and it would result in large specific yields.
- Water bearing formation of coars gravel would supply large quantities of water to wells, whereas clay formations, although saturated and of high porosity, would be of little value in this respect.

Aquifers

Types of aquifers.

1. ***Unconfined or non-artesian aquifers :*** The top most water bearing stratum having no confined imperemable overburden (*i.e.* aquiclude) lying over it, is called **unconfined aquifer** or **non-artesian aquifer.**
2. ***Confined or Artesian aquifer :*** When an aquifer is confined on its upper an under surface, by impervious rock formation (*i.e.* aquiclude), and is also broadly inclined so as to expose the aquifer for somewhere to the catchment area at higher level for the creation of sufficient hydraulic head, it is called a **confined aquifer** or **an artesion aquifer**.

Perched aquifer

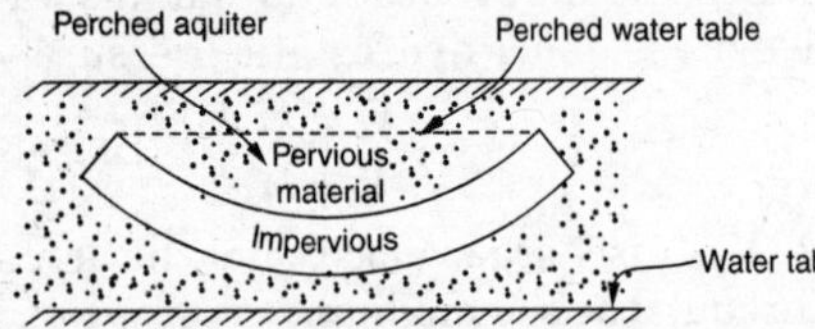

Aquifuse : It is that geological formation which is, neither porous nor permeable.

e.g. granite rock

Aquitard : It is that geological formation, which does not yield water problems to wells due to its lesser permeability. The yield from such a formation is, thus insignificant.

e.g., sandy clay.

Aquiclude : It is highly porous, containing large quantities of water, but essentially impervious.

e.g. clay layer.

Storage co-efficient (A) : It is defined as the volume of water that an aquifer release or storage per unit surface area of the aquifer per unit change in the component of head normal to that surface. The storage co-efficient (A) for an artesian aquifer is equal to the volume of water released from the aquifer of full height and unit area when the piezometricf surface declines by unity.

Ground Water Specific Yield

It is the ratio of volume of water obtained by gravity-drainage to the total volume of the sub-soil.

$$\text{Specific yield} = \frac{\text{Volume of water obtained by gravity drainage}}{\text{Total volume of the sub-soil}} \times 100$$

$$\text{Specific retention} = \frac{\text{Volume of water held against gravity drainage}}{\text{Total volume of the material}} \times 100$$

$$\text{Porosity} = \text{Specific yield} + \text{specific retention}$$

Ground Water Velocity

Slichter's formula :

$$v = \frac{k'SD^2}{\mu}$$

where, v = velocity of ground water in m/day

k' = constant (approx. 400)

s = slope of hydraulic gradient line

D = effective size of the particle in aquifer (in mm)

μ = dynamic viscosity

Hazen's formula:

$$v = \frac{k''SD^2}{60}(1.8T + 42)$$

where, K" = constant (approx. 1000)

T = temperature (in °C)

Specific yield of well in recuperating test

It can be determined from the following formula:

$$\frac{C'}{A} = \frac{2.3}{T}\log_{10}\frac{S_1}{S_2}$$

where, S_1 = depression head in the well immediately after the pumping was stopped.

S_2 = depression head in well at time '*T*' after the pumping was stopped.

T = time after which S_2 was measured

$\frac{C'}{A}$ = specific yield.

$$\text{Discharge, } Q = \left(\frac{C'}{A}\right) \cdot AS$$

where, A = cross-sectional area of well

Yield of a well,

$$Q = \frac{\pi \rho k}{2.3} \frac{(H^2 - h^2)}{\log_{10} R/r} m^3/\text{day}$$

$$= \frac{\pi \rho k \times 1000}{2.3 \times 24 \times 60} \frac{H^2 - h^2}{\log_{10}(R/r)} \text{ litres/minute}$$

$$= \frac{k_m(H^2 - h^2)}{\log_{10}(R/r)} lpm$$

where, $k_m = \frac{\pi p k \times 1000}{2.3 \times 24 \times 60}$ is known as transmission constant of the acquifer.

The above formula is known as **Thiem's formula.**

Yield of tubewell when equilibrium conditions have not reached can be determined using following formula :

$$s = \frac{Q}{4\pi\mu}\left[\log e\left(\frac{4T\mu}{r^2 A}\right) - 0.5772\right]$$

where, s = draw down in observation well after time T.

r = radial distance of the observation well from the main well.

Q = yield or constant discharge pumped out from the well.

A = coefficient of storage of measured drawdown.

μ = coefficient of transmissibility.

$$s_1 - s_2 = \frac{2.3Q}{4\pi\mu}\log_{10}\left(\frac{T_2}{T_1}\right)$$

Forms of Underground Sources :

(1) Infiltration galleries

(2) Infiltration wells

(3) Springs

(4) Wells including tubewells.

INTAKE FOR COLLECTING SURFACE WATER

The basic function of the intake structure is to help in safely withdrawing water from the source over a predetermined range of pool levels and then to discharge this water into the withdrawal condict, through which it flows upto the water treatment plant.

Site selection of intake depends on

(i) availability of water is all seasons

(ii) quality and quantity of water

(iii) away from the pollution

(iv) nearer to the city

(v) upstream side of the river

(vi) costs and reliability

Types of Intakes

(1) Simple submerged intakes:

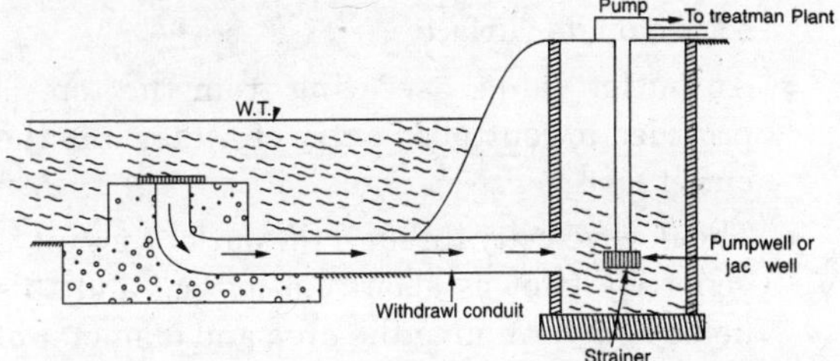

These intakes are not used on bigger projects on river and reservoir, as their main disadvantage is the fact that they are not easily accessible for cleaning, repairing, etc.

(2) Intake tower.

(i) Wet intake towers } Standing in the river or reservoir

(ii) Dry intake towers.

The essential difference between a dry intake tower and a wet intake tower is that, in a wet intake tower, the water enters from the entry ports into the tower and then it enters into the conduit pipe through separate gate conrolled opening; but in a dry intake tower, the water is directly drawn into the withdrawal conduit through the gated entry ports.

(3) Medium sized intake wells (River intake) :

(i) **Medium sized river intake :** The water from the intake chamber is taken through a withdrawal conduit (called intake conduit) to a sump well, from where it is lifted and taken to the treatment plant.

(ii) Canal intake well

Design criteria :

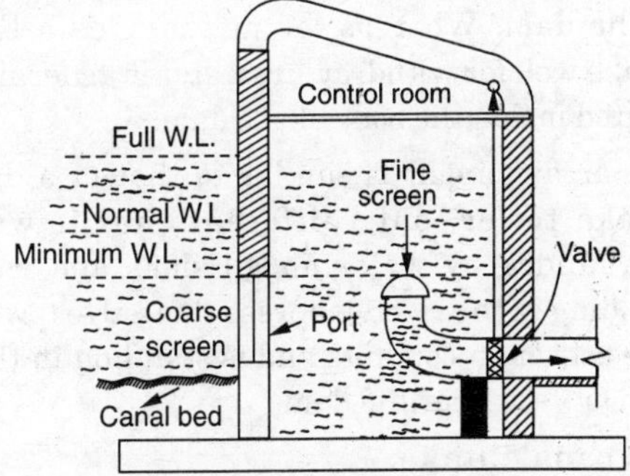

Fig. Canal intake well

- The entry of water in the intake well takes through a coarse screen, the top of which is generally provided at minimum water level in the canal, and bottom is about 0.45 m above the canal bed to avoid entry of bed load.

- An additions fine screen is provided at the inlet end of the withdrawal conduit. This inlet end of bell mouth shape with perforation of fine screen on its surface.
- An outlet value, operating from the top, is provided to controlled entry of water into the outlet pipe.
- The flow velocity through the outlet conduit is generally kept as about 1.5 m/sec., and this helps in determining the area and diameter of the withdrawal conduit.
- The area of coarse screen is designed by limiting the flow velocity to as low as 0.15 m/ sec or so. The flow velocity through the bell mouth inlet is limited to about 0.3 m/sec. or so.
- The head loss in the intake conduit upto treatment works, can be determined by using Darcy Weisback formula

$$H_L = \frac{f' L V^2}{2gd}$$

or by using Hazen William's formula.

$$V = 0.85\, C_H + R^{0.63}\, S^{0.54}$$

where, $S = \frac{H_L}{L}$ = slope of the energy line

C_H = 130 for C.I. pipe.

(4) Intake for sluiceways of dam :

In case a reservoir developed by constructing a dam, it is a common practice to fetch water through the sluiceways from inside the dam.

- In case of earthen dams, the intake for withdrawing water into the sluiceway of the dam, is generally located near the upstream toe of the dam. Whereas for masonry dam the intake well for withdrawing water is generally located inside the body of the dam.
- The arrangement is similar to that of a dry intake tower, only different that it was surrounded by water on all sides and was standing in the river, whereas this valve tower is fed through conduits and is standing in the dam or very near the dam.

Design of canal intake.

(1) Q and then assume D.T. and get volume of intake.

(2) Design of coarse screen.

(3) Design of bell mouth entry.

(4) Design of intake conduit.

(5) Head loss.

Conduits for Transporting Water

Types of conduits.

(1) Gravity conduits.

(*i*) Canal (often used for irrigation)

(*ii*) Flumes

(*iii*) Aquaducts (are closed, rectangular, circular or horse shoe sections). They are generally designed as $\frac{1}{2}$ to $\frac{3}{4}$th full.

- In gravity conduit, the hydraulic gradient line will concide with the water surface and will be parallel to the bed of the conduit.
- These conduits cannot, therefore, go up and down hills and valleys as desired by existing topography of the area.
- From hydraulic point of view, a circular section provides the maximum hydraulic mean depth or maximum area per unit of wetted perimeter $\left(i.e.\ R = \frac{A}{P}\right)$ and is, therefore, the most efficient. Moreover, since the perimeter per unit of cross section is less the construction cost or material required is also the least. But circular sections cannot be easily supported on ground and, therefore seldom used.
- A rectangular shape is hydraulically inefficient and requires more material for construction, but is more stable to support on the ground, and therefore widely used.
- Horse shoe shape may be used with great advantage.
- The bed or the invert of the conduit in pressure flows is thus independent of the grade of the hydraulic gradient line which really governs the flow velocities.

(2) Pressure conduits (Pressure above the atmospheric pressure)

- The pressure pipes can, therefore, follow the natural, available ground surface and can freely go up and down hills or can dip beneath valleys or mountains, sometimes even rising above the H.G. Lines and thusrequiring lesser length of conduit.

Water borne diseases and their control

Water borne diseases are those diseases which spread primarily through contaminated water.

(1) Disease caused by bacterial infections.

(*i*) Typhoid fever and paratyphoid fever (caused by salmonella typhi becteria)

(*ii*) Cholera (caused by vibrio-cholera bacteria)

(*iii*) Bacillary dysentery (caused by shiga bacillus or flexner bacillus.

(2) Disease caused by viral infections.

(i) Infectious hepatitis or infectious jaundice (caused by hepatitis virus).

(ii) Poliomyelitis (caused by polio virus).

(iii) Gastroentritis.

(3) Disease caused by protozoal infections.

Amoebic dysentery (caused by entamoeba hystolytic germ).

WATER QUALITY STANDARDS FOR DRINKING WATER

S.No.	Type of Characterstic	Type of imputrity	Permissible limit	Absolute maximum limit	Remark
1.	Physical	Turbidity	5	25	On silica scale
		Colour	5	50	Colour number on cobalt scale
		Taste & odour	1	3	Threshold odour number
2.	Chemical	pH value	7—8.5	6.5—9.2	
		Hardness	75 mg./l.	110 mg./l.	Hardness expenssed as $CaCO_3$
		Total solids	500 mg./l.	1500 mg./l.	As per WHO standards
		Magnesiun & Sodium	500	1000 mg./l.	As per WHO standards
		Chlorides	200	600 mg./l.	As per WHO standards
		Sulphates	200	400 mg./l.	As per WHO standards
		Calcium	75	200 mg./l.	As per WHO standards
		Zinc	5	15 mg./l.	As per WHO standards
		Copper	1	1.5 mg./l.	As per WHO standards
		Iron	0.3	1.0	As per WHO standards
		Maganese	0.1	0.5	As per WHO standards
		Arsenic	Nil	0.2	As per WHO standards
		Lead	Nil	0.1	As per WHO standards
		Selenium	Nil	0.05	As per WHO standards
		Chromium	Nil	0.05	As per WHO standards
		Phenolic compounds as phenole	0.001	0.002	As per WHO standards
		Cynide	Nil	0.01	As per WHO standards
		Fluoride	0.5 mg./l.	1.5 mg./l.	As per WHO standards
		Cadmium	–	0.05 mg/l	As per WHO standards
3.	Biological and Micro-organic		Coliform bacteria	Nil colony per 100 ml. or MPN of B coli is limited to 1 per 100 ml.	1 coliform
4.	Radiological	α-emitters	Nil	1 μμc/litre.	W.H.O. standard
	β-emitters		Nil	10 μμc/litres.	W.H.O. standard

- Water used in pulp or paper industries, must be free from iron, maganese, and hardness.
- Water required for breweries, distilleries, and bakeries should preferably be hard.
- For steel rolling mills, the chloride content of water must be less than 150 mg./l.
- The water (prevention and control of pollution) Act enacted by the Indian Parliament in 1974.

Methods of Purfication of Water

(i) Plain Sedimentation

Principle behind sedimentation is to reduce the flow velocity by providing tank called settling tank, or **clarifier** or **sedimentation basin**.

Detention period : Theoretical average time for which the water is detained in the tank is called the detention period.

Settling velocity of spherical particle :

$$V_s = \frac{g}{18}(G-1)\frac{d^2}{\nu} \quad \text{for } d < 0.1 \text{ mm.} \quad [Re < 0.5]$$

where, V_s = velocity of settlement of particle
d = diameter of the particle
G = specific gravity of the particle
v = kinematic viscosity of water

$$R_e = \text{Reynold number} = \frac{V_s d}{\upsilon}$$

Since, viscosity depend upon the temperature, the above equation can be modified as

$$V_s = 418\,(G-1)\,d^2\left(\frac{3T+70}{100}\right)$$

for $d < 0.1$ mm.

where, T = temperature of water in degree centigrades
V_s = velocity of settlement in mm/sec
d = diameter of the particle in mm.

$$V_s = 1.8\sqrt{gd\,(G-1)}$$

for $d > 1.0$ mm (turbulent settling)

In transition zone, settling velocity is given by Hazen as :

$$V_s = 418\,(G-1)\,d\left(\frac{3T+70}{100}\right)$$

when d lies between 0.1 mm. and 1 mm

The above formula represent the theoretical setling velocities of discrete spherical particles. The actual settling velocities in the sedimentation basins, will be much less than that calculated by these formulae, because of :

(i) non-sphericity of the particles
(ii) upward displacement of the fluid caused by the settling of other particles
(iii) convection currents.

Note : A plain sedimentation tank under normal conditions may remove as much as 70% of the suspended impurities present in water.

Types of sedimentation tank.

(i) Intermittenly function sedimentation tank : not preferred these day.
(ii) Continuously function sedimentation tank.

The velocity is so adjusted that the time taken by the particle to travel from one end to another is slightly more than the time required for settling of that particle.

Design of confinuous flow type of sedimentation tank

(i) **Flow velocity:** $V = \dfrac{Q}{BH}$

where, Q = discharge entering the basin
B = width of the basin
H = depth of water in the tank.

(ii) **Permissible velocity (V_s) :** $\dfrac{V}{V_s} = \dfrac{L}{H}$

$$\Rightarrow V_s = \frac{VH}{L} = \frac{Q}{BH}\times\frac{H}{L} = \frac{Q}{BL}$$

$$\Rightarrow V_s = \frac{Q}{BL}$$

It shows that all those particles having a settling velocity equal to or greater than $\dfrac{Q}{BL}$ will settle down and be removed.

(iii) **Overflow rate :**

Discharge per unit of plan area (surface area), i.e. the $\dfrac{Q}{BL}$ is a very important term for the design of continuous flow type settling tanks; and is known as the **overflow rate** or the **surface loading** or the **overflow velocity**.

For plain sedimentation tanks overflow velocity = 500 – 700 litres/hr./m^2 of plan area

For plain sedimentation tanks using coagulants as aids overflow velocity = 1000 – 1250 litres/hr./m^2. of plan area.

Smaller particles will also settle down, if the overflow rate is reduced.

(iv) **Depth of sedimentation tank :** Usual values of depth ranges between 3.0 to 4.5 m.

(v) **Detention period or Retention period (*t*) :**

It is the average time for which the water is detained in the tank.

Detention time for rectangular tank,

$$t = \frac{\text{Volume of the tank}}{\text{Rate of flow}} \quad i.e.\ t = \frac{BLH}{Q}$$

Detention time for a circular tank,

$$t = \frac{d^2(0.011d + 0.785H)}{Q}$$

where, d = diameter of the tank.
H = side water depth.

For plain sedimentation, detention time = 4 to 8 hr.

When the coagulants are used, detention time = 2 to 4 hr.

(vi) **Dimensions of the tank :** B $\approx$ 10 to 12 m.

Length of the tank is not generally allowed to exceed four times the width.

(vi) Normally kept flow velocity at about 0.3 m/min.

(vii) In actual practice, certain amount of short circuting always exist and therefore, the actual average time which a batch of water takes in passing through a settling tank, is called the **flowing through period**.

$$\text{Displacement efficiency} = \frac{\text{Flowing through period}}{\text{Detention period}} \approx 0.25 \text{ to } 0.5$$

(viii) **Sludge zone :** For tanks without mechanical sludge removal equipment, an additional minimum depth of about 0.8 to 1.2 m. should be provides for storage of sediment, and is called the **sludge zone**.

(ii) Sendimentation Aided with coagulation

Certain chemical compounds called **coagulants** are added to the water, which on thorough mixing from a gelatenous precipitate called **'floc'**. The very fine mud particles and the colloidal matter present in water get attracted and absorbed in these flocs, forming the bigger sized floculated particles. The process of addition and mixing of the chemicals (*i.e,* the coagulants) is called the **coagulation**. The coagulated water is then made to pass through the sedimentation tank, where the floculated particles settle down and, are, thus removed. The coagulation before sedimentation is almost universally adopted in all the major water treatment plants, and is followed by rapid sand filtration.

Chemicals used for coagulation.

(i) **Aluminium sulphate :**

$$\underset{}{Al_2(SO_4)\cdot 18H_2O} + \underset{\text{Bicarbonte alkalinity}}{3\,Ca(HCO_3)_2} \longrightarrow 3\,CaSO_4 + \underset{\text{(floc)}}{2Al(OH)_3\downarrow} + 6CO_2\uparrow + \underset{\text{present in raw water}}{18\,H_2O}$$

- Average normal does is about 17 mg./l. (5 mg/l – 55 mg/l.)
- If raw water supplies are not sufficiently alkaline, then the external alkalies like lime *i.e.* $Ca(OH)_2$ or soda ash ($Na_2\,CO_3$) are generally added.

(i) $Al_2(SO_4)_3\cdot 18H_2O + 3\,Ca(OH)_2 \rightarrow 3\,CaSO_4 + Al(OH)_3\downarrow + 18\,H_2O$

(ii) $Al_2(SO_4)_3\cdot 18H_2O + 3\,Na_2\,CO_3 \rightarrow 3\,Na_2\,SO_4 + 2Al(OH)_3\downarrow + 3\,CO_2\uparrow + 15\,H_2O$

- Aluminium sulphate is very effective coagulant, and is now extensively used throughout the world.

(ii) **Ferrous sulphate (copperas) ($FeSO_4\cdot 7H_2O$) :**

(a) *When copper as is added earlier to lime* :

$FeSO_4\cdot 7H_2O + Ca(HCO_3)_2 \rightarrow Fe(HCO_3)_2 + CaSO_4 + 7H_2O$

$Fe(HCO_3)_2 + 2\,Ca(OH)_2 \rightarrow Fe(OH)_2 + 2\,CaCO_3 + 2H_2O$

$4\,Fe(OH)_2 + O_2 + 2H_2O \rightarrow 4\,Fe(OH)_3\downarrow$ (Ferric hydroxide precipitate)

(b) *When lime is added first* :

$FeSO_4\cdot 7H_2O + Ca(OH)_2 \rightarrow CaSO_4 + Fe(OH)_2 + 7H_2O$

$$4Fe(OH)_2 + O_2 + 2H_2O \rightarrow \underset{\text{(floc)}}{4Fe(OH)_3\downarrow}$$

Copperas are used when the raw waters are not coloured and high pH (8 to 10).

(iii) **Chlorinated copperas**

$$6\,(FeSO_4\cdot 7H_2O) + 3Cl_2 \rightarrow \underset{\text{Ferric sulphate}}{2Fe_2(SO_4)_3} + \underset{\text{Ferric chloride}}{2\,FeCl_3} + 42\,H_2O$$

know as chlorinated copperas

$Fe(SO_4)_3 + 3\,Ca(OH)_2 \rightarrow 3\,CaSO_4 + 2Fe(OH)_3\downarrow$

$2FeCl_3 + 3Ca(OH)_2 \rightarrow 3CaCl_2 + 2Fe(OH)_3\downarrow$

It remove colour and effective in low & high pH range.

(iv) **Sodium Aluminate ($Na_2H_2O_4$) :**

$$Na\,Al_2\,O_4 + Ca\,(HCO_3)_2 \rightarrow \underset{\text{Cal. aluminate}}{CaAl_2\,O_4\downarrow} + Na_2\,CO_3 + CO_2\uparrow + H_2O$$

$Na_2\,Al_2\,O_4 + CaCl_2 \rightarrow CaAl_2\,O_4\downarrow + 2NaCl$

$Na_2\,Al_2\,O_4 + CaSO_4 \rightarrow CaAl_2\,O_4\downarrow + Na_2SO_4$

Iron salts are used as coagulants more frequently for treating sewage, and alum is used more frequently for treating raw water.

Parts of a coagulation sedimentation plant

(i) Feeding device:

These are of two types:

(a) Dry feeding

(b) Wet feeding.

Feeding depends on following factors

(a) Characteristics of coagulant and convenience.

(b) Amount of coagulant

(c) Cost of coagulant and size of plan

Note. Large plants use wet feeding and smaller plants use dry feeding, unless objected to by characteristics of coagulant.

(ii) Mixing devices:

Centrifugal pumps, compressed air, mixing basins etc.

Mixing Basings.

(a) With baffle walls

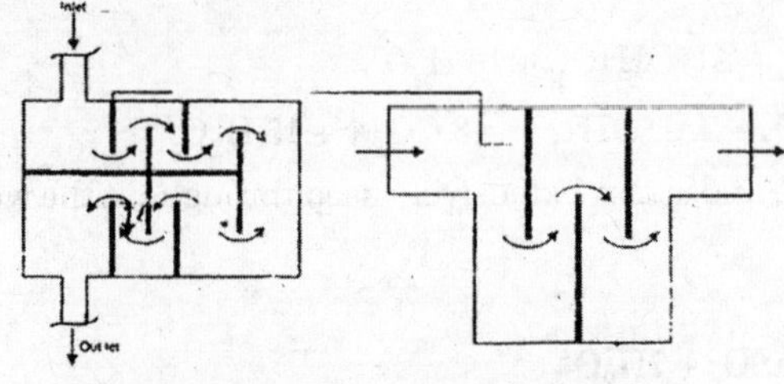

Fig. Mixing basin with baffel Walls

Design criteria

Velocity of flow in channels

= 1.15 to 0.045 m/sec.

Detention peirod = 20-50 min.

Hence length of flow is known.

Clear opening between end of each baffle and the tank wall should be kept about 1.5 × distance between baffles.

Minimum value = 60 cm

Note:

- Around the end baffles should not be used when the computed depth < 1m.
- In over and under baffles; depth is normally kept (2 to 3) × distance between baffles.
- In basins, loss of head ≈ 3.2 × velocity head in channel
- Baffle type mixing basins are not used in modern day or on large plants.

(b) With Mechanical devices:

These use Flash mixer

Impeller¢s speed = 100–120 rpm.

Detention period = 2-3 minutes.

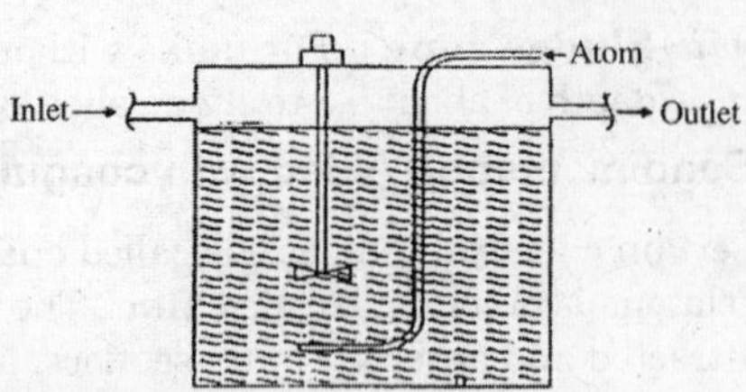

(iii) Flocculator:

Paddles rotated at speed of 2-3 rpm.

Detention period = 30 to 60 minutes (ave. 40 min.)

Clear distance between paddles and wall is about 15 to 30 cm.

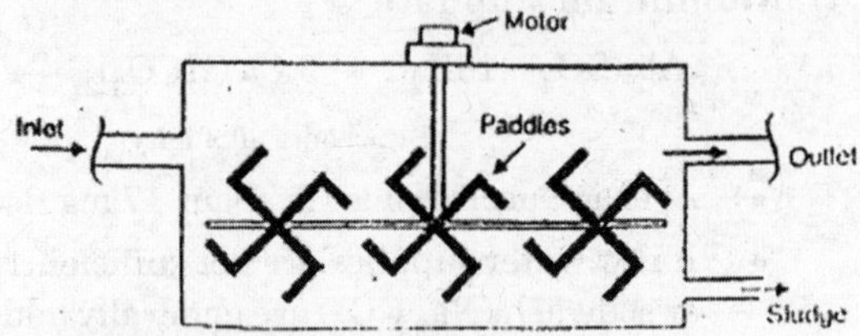

(iv) Sedimentation tank:

The complete process of coagulation sedimentation may help in removing turbidities upto as low values as 10-20 mg./l. It may also help in reducing the bacteria from the water, and thus to reduce the B-coli index by as much as 70%.

Large plant uses wet feeding while smaller plants uses dry feeding.

Detention period = 2 – 4 hrs.

Overflow rate = 1000 – 1250 lit/hr./m^2

Combined co-agulation-cum-sedimentation tank:

Detention period = 15 – 40. in floc-chamber

= 2-4 hrs. in settling tank.

Optimum coagulant quantities determination:

Jar test is made. Large number of jars are used for good results.

The amount of coagulant in jar which produces a good floc with the least amount of co-agulant, indicates optimum dosage.

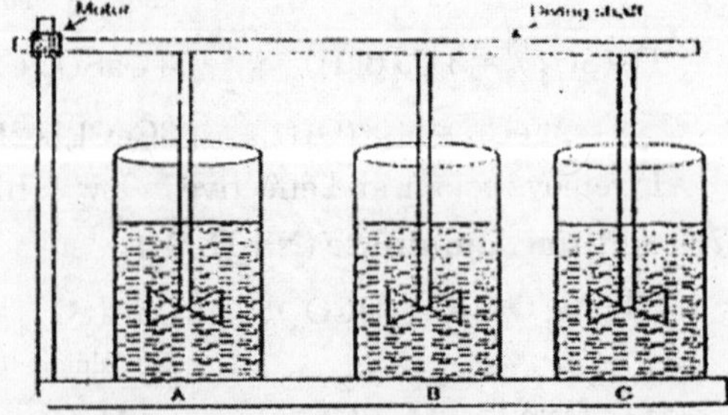

Fig. Jar Test

Production of sludge:

Alum, which s cheifly used has been found to be generating sludge equal to 0.24 times of its own weight.

Dry sludge produced in mg/day = Q in lit/day [suspended solids removed in mg/l + 0.24 × Alum does in mg/l + misc. chemicals added like carbon, clay, polymer in mg/l]

Dewatering and Disposal of sludge from water treatment plants :

Wet or watery sludge is produced in a water treatment plant in its following units :

(*i*) Sedimentation flocculation tank or clariflocculator

(*ii*) Filters

Methods for disposing of wastes obtained from above plants :

(*i*) Ponding in artificial or natural lagoons

(*ii*) Sand drying bed

(*iii*) Gravity thickners

(*iv*) High speed centrifuges

The dewatered sludge is finally disposed off either by incineration or by burial in trenches.

(iii) Filtration of Water

The process of passing the water through the beds of granular materials is know as **Filtration**. Filtration may help in removing colour, odour, turbidity and pathogenic bacteria from the water.

Types of filters.

(*i*) **Slow sand filters.**

Construction of slow sand filters : Parts of slow sund filter are :

(*a*) **Enclosure tank or basin :**

Depth of tank = 2.5 to 3.5 m.

Plan area of the tank = 100 to 2000 m^2

(*b*) **Filter media :**

Sand layers go to 110 cm. in depth.

(*c*) **Base material :**

30 to 75 cm. thick gravels of different sizes placed in layers.

(*d*) Under drainage system.

(*e*) Inlet and outlet arrangements.

(*f*) Other appurtenances.

(*ii*) **Rapid sand filters or mechanical sand filters.**

These filters employ coarse sand, with effective size as 0.5 mm or so. On an average, these filters may yield as high as 30 times the yield given by the slow sand filters. Water from the clariflocculator are used in these filters, and filtered water is treated with disinfectants, so as to obtain potable supplies.

Construction of rapid gravity filters : *Parts of rapid sand filter*:

(*a*) **Enclosure tank or basin :**

Depth of tank = 2.5 to 3.5 m.

Plan area of tank = 10 to 50 m^2 for each unit.

(*b*) Number of units at a filter plant, $N = 1.22\sqrt{Q}$

where, Q = plant capacity in million litres per day.

(*c*) *Filter media* : sand layer 60 to 90 cm. in depth.

(*d*) *Base material* : gravel layer 60 to 90 cm. thick gravels of different sizes placed in layers.

(*e*) Under drainage system

(*f*) Other appurtenances.

Working and Cleaning of Rapid gravity filters :

The amount of water required for washing a rapid gravity filter may very from 21.5% of the total amount of water filtered. The rapid gravity filters get clogged very frequently and have to be washed every 24 to 48 hours.

The rapid gravity filters are conventionally cleaned by back washing.

Rate of Filtration or Rate of loading for Rapid gravity filters.

3000 to 6000 litres/hr/m^2 of filter area.

Rate of filtration of pressure filter :

6000 to 15000 l/h/m^2 of filter media.

3000 to 6000 litres/hr/m^2 of filter area.

- The pressure filter are less efficient than the rapid gravity filter.
- Pressure filters are generally not used for treating municipal surface supplies.
- Pressure filters are used for small plants such as for individual industrial supplies, not adopted for treating large scale municipal supplies.
- Slow sand filters remove larger percentage of impurities and bacteria as compare to rapid sand filters but slow sand filters are obsolete these days due to slow rate of filtration.
- In the modern treatment plants, rapid sand gravity filters are now a days almost universally adopted. The water from the coagulation sedimentation plant is directly fed into the rapid sand gravity filters, and the resultant supplies are disinfected for complete killing of germs and colour removal.

Comparison of slow sand and Rapid sand filters :

S.No.	*Item*	*Slow sand filters*	*Rapid gravity filters*
1.	Pre treatment requirements	Effluents either from plain sedimentation tanks or raw waters without any treatment are generally fed into them; and coagulation is not at all required.	Coagulation, flocculation, and sedimentation is a must.
2.	Base material	The gravel base supports the sand. It varies from 3 to 65 mm in size and 30 to 75 cm. in depth.	The gravel base supports the sand and also distributes the wash water uniformly on the surface of sand. It varies from 3 to 40 mm. in size and its depth is slightly more, *i.e.* about 60 to 90 cm.
3.	Filter sand	The effective size (D_{10}) of filter sand ranges between 0.2 to 0.4 mm. and uniformity co-efficient between 1.8 to 2.5 or 3.0. The grain size distribution is generally uniform throughout the depth of filter media, except that top 10 to 15 cm. may be laid of finer variety.	The effective filter sand ranges between 0.35 to as and unformity co-efficient between 1.2 to 1.8. The sand is laid in layers with smallest grain size at top and coarsest grain size at the bottom.
4.	Underdrainage system	Laid in order to receive filtered water.	Laid in order to receive filtered water and also to pass water for back washing at a very high rate.
5.	Size of each unit	Large such as (30 m to 60 m). The area varying from 100 to 2000 sq. m. or more.	Small, such as 5m × 8m. The area varying from 10 to 80 sq. m.
6.	Rate of filtration	Small such as 100 to 200 lit./hr./m² of filter area.	Large such as 3000 to 6000 lit./hr./m². of filter area.
7.	Economy	High intial cost of both land and material but low cost of operation and maintenance.	Low initial cost, but higher cost of operation and maintenance overall , it is cheaper and economical.
8.	Depreciation cost	Relatively low.	Relatively high.
9.	Efficiency	Very efficient in removing bacteria (98 to 99%) but less efficient in removing colour. Overall turbidity removal in these filters using plain sedimentation is also low. They cannot handle turbid water containing turbidities more than 50 mg/l.	Less efficient in removing bacteria (80 to 90%) but very efficient in removing colour. The overall turbidity removal in these fill using coagulation sedimentation, is also high. They can threrefore, handle very turbid waters.
10.	Flexibility	Not flexible for meeting variations in demand.	Quite flexible for meeting reasonable variations in demand.
11.	Suitability and adaptability	May be adopted for treating smaller village supplies or for individual industrial supplies. They are absolete these day.	They are widely and almost univers adopted for treating public supplies especially at all major cities and town.
12.	Post treatment requirement, if any	Almost pure water is obtained. However; it may be disinfected slightly to make it completely safe. Other miscellaneous may or may not be required.	Disinfection is must and some other miscellaneous treatment may be given, if needed.
13.	Ease in construction	Simple	Complicated, as under drainage is properly designed.
14.	Skilled supervision, if required	Not required.	Essential.
15.	Method of cleaning	*(a)* Scrapping and removing the top 1.5 to 3 cm. thick layer and washing down by hoses. *(b)* Laborious method.	*(a)* Agitating the sand grains and back washing with or without compressed air. *(b)* Short and easy methode.
16.	Period of cleaning	Cleaned at intervels of 1 to 3 months.	Cleaned frequently at intervals of 1 to 3 days.
17.	Loss of head	Approximately 10 cm is the initial loss, and 0.8 to 1.2 m is the final limit when cleaning is required	Approximately 0.3m is the initial loss, and 2.5 to 3.5 m. is the final limit when cleaning is required.
18.	Quantity of wash water required	0.2 to 0.6% of the total water filtered.	1 to 5% of the total water filters.

(iv) Disinfection or Sterilisation

Chlorine has been found to be the best and the most ideal disinfectant and is now invariably used throughout the world. Disinfection means killing of only the discase producing bacteria, whereas sterilisation means killing of are the bacteria of all types. Disinfection, chlorination and sterilisation are used as synonymous to each other.

Minor methods of disinfection.

(i) **Boiling of water :** It can only kill the existing germs but cannot take care of the future possible contaminaions, hence it is not used for disinfecting public supplies. However, during water borne epidemics, public is advised to drink water only after boiling.

(ii) **Treatment with excess lime :** Lime is generally used as a water purification plant for softening (i.e. reducing hardness), but excess lime may kill the bacteria also.

- The excess lime when added to water, in fact, raises the pH value of water.
- This method is quite practical for complete removal of bacteria, yet needs the removal of excess lime from the water before it can be supplied to the general public (called recarbonation). Moreover,it cannot protect the water from the possible dangers of recontamination, and hence not used these days.

(iii) **Treatment with Ozone :**

$$3O_2 \xrightarrow[\text{arc voltage}]{\text{under high electric}} 2O_3$$

$$O_3 \rightarrow O_2 + O_{\text{nascent oxygen}}$$

- The nascent oxygen, so produced, is a powerful oxidising agent and removes the organic matter as well as the bacteria from the water.
- Ozone being unstable, nothing remain in water, by the time it reaches the distribution system.
- Ozone remove colour, taste and odour from water, in addition to removing the bacteria from it.
- The Ozonised water becomes tasty and pleasant unlike the chlorinated water which becomes bitter to tongue.

(iv) **Treatment with Pottasium permanganate ($KMnO_4$) :**

It is used for disinfecting well water supplies in village; which are generaly contaminated with lesser amount of bacteria. It also produce taste.

If the pink colour disappears, it shows that organic matter is present in water.

(v) **Treatment with iodine and bromine**

(vi) **Treatment with ultraviolet rays :** suitable for swimming pool water

(vii) **Treatment with silver :** called Eleipa-katadyn process.

(v) Chlorination

The teratment of waterby chlorine water is called **chlorination.**

$$Cl_2 + H_2O \xrightarrow{pH > 5} \underset{\text{Hypochlorous acid}}{HOCl} + HCl$$

$$HOCl \underset{pH < 7}{\overset{pH > 8}{\rightleftharpoons}} H^+ + OCl^- \text{ (Hypochlorite ions)}$$

Free available chlorine.

The sum of hypochlorous acid, hypochlorite ions, and molecular chlorine existing in a sample of water is termed as **free available chlorine**.

Out of these form of free available chlorine, the hypochlorous acid is the most destructive, being about 80 times more effective than OCl. For this reason, the pH value of water during chlorination is generally maintained slightly less than 7, so as to keep the dissociation of HOCl to minimum and thereby keeping more HOCl in solution compared to OCl ions.

- Moreover, the chlorine will immedialqtely react with ammonia present in water to form various chloramines, as given below :

$$NH_3 + HOCl \xrightarrow{pH > 7.5} \underset{\text{Monochloramine}}{NH_2Cl} + H_2O$$

$$NH_2Cl + HOCl \xrightarrow{pH\ 5\ to\ 6.5} \underset{\text{Di-chloramine}}{NHCl_2} + H_2O$$

$$NHCl_2 + HOCl \xrightarrow{pH < 4} \underset{\text{Nitrogen. Trichloramine}}{NCl_3} + H_2O$$

In usual chlorine treatment, when pH is kept slightly less than 7, $NHCl_2$ is the most predominant.

- If all NH_3 is consumed by added Cl_2, then it would persist as free **chlorine**.
- Chloramine is less effective than free chlorine.
- Correct sequence of formation of residual chlorine compound is NH_2Cl, $NHCl_2$, HOCl, OCl

Dose of chlorine : The amount of Chlorine used in reducing organic and inogranic impurities is called the **chlorine demand of water**. After the Cl_2demand is fulfilled, Chlorine will appear as free chlorine residual (hypochlorites). This residue Chlorine will serve as disinfectant to kill pathogens.

Chlorine dose required for killing isolated virus.

Types of virus to be killed	Quantity of free chlorine required in mg/l with about 30 minutes contact period for water of pH lower than 7 or so.
Poliomyelitis virus	0.1
Hepatitis virus	0.4
Cysts of E. histolytica, *i.e.* organism causing ameobic dysentery.	3.0 or even lower.
Tuberculosis organisms	3.0
Coxsaickie Virus	Very huge does varying from 21 to 138 mg/l

Forms in which chlorine can be applied.

***(i)* As free chlorine :**

In the form of liquid chlorine or as chlorine gas. ($HOCl$, OCl^-)

***(ii)* As combined chlorine :**

(a) Use of hypochlorites or bleaching powder (not used these days)

$$Ca(OCl)_2 \xrightleftharpoons{H_2O} \underset{\text{Hypochlorite ions}}{Ca^{++} + 2OCl^-}$$

$$OCl^- + H^+ \underset{pH>8}{\overset{pH<7}{\rightleftharpoons}} \underset{\text{Hypochlorans acid}}{HOCl}$$

This process is known as *hypochlorination.* The hypochlorite ions as well as hypochlorous acid both causing disinfection of water.

(b) Use of chloramines or use of chlorine with ammonia

(c) Use of chloramine dioxide :

Disinfecting power is 2½ times stronger than chlorine but is very useful.

Types of Chlorination

***(i)* Plain chlorination :** It indicates that only chlorine treatment and no other treatment has been given to the raw water.

The used quantity of chlorine requred is about 0.5 mg/l or more

***(ii)* Pre-chlorination :** Pre-chlorination is the process of applying chlorine to the water before filtration or rather before sedimentation.

The normal doses are as 5 to 10 mg/l so that 0.1 to 0.5 mg/l of residual chlorine comes to the filter plant.

***(iii)* Post-chlorination :** It is the process of applying chlorine after filtration and before enter the distribution sytem. The dosage of chlorine should be such as to leave a residual chlorine of start 0.1 to 0.2 mg/l after a contact period of about 20 minutes. This residual will ensure the disinfection of water, if at all any future recontamination occurs in the distribution system.

***(iv)* Double chlorination :** It indicates that water has been chlorinated twice. The prechlorination and post-chlorination are generally used in double chlorination. Post chlorination, however, is generally always used, while the pre-chlorination is also used when the waters are highly turbid and contaminated.

***(v)* Break-point chlorination :**

- Some Cl_2 is consumed for killing bacteria and thus the amount of residual Cl_2 shall be slightly less than that added as shown by the curve AB.

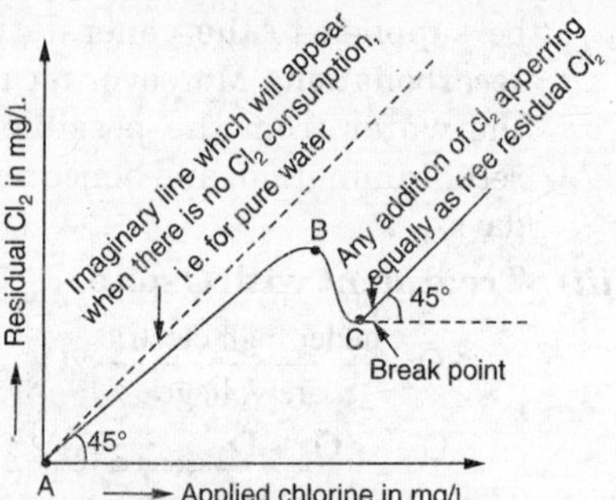

Fig:- Break point Chlorination

- If the addition of Cl_2 is continued beyond the point B, the organic matter present in water gets oxidised and therefore, the residual Cl_2 content suddenly falls down as shown by curve BC.
- Break point chlorination is a term which gives us an idea of the extent of chlorine added to water, beyond which any further addition of chlorine will appear as free residual chlorine.
- The D.P.D. test will indicate the quantum of total residual chlorine **"combined"** as well as **"free"**.
- The point C is the point beyond which any further addition of Cl_2 will appear equally as free chlorine. This point **"C"** is called the **break point**. The addition of Cl_2 beyond break point is called **break point chlorination**.
- It is a general practice to add Cl_2 beyond break point, and thus to ensure a residual of 0.2 to 0.3 mg/l of free chlorine.

(vi) **Super chlorination :** It indicates the addition of excessive amount of chlorine (*i.e.*,5 to 15 mg./l.) to the water. This may be required in some special cases of highly polluted water, or during epidemics of water borne diseases.

- The huge quantity of Cl_2 is added in super chlorination is such as to give about 1 to 2 mg./l. of residual beyond the break point in the treated water.
- Sometimes, even higher doses may be used and the resultant water is dechlorinated after the end of the desired contact period, by using dechlorinating agent. This ensures the removal of bad tastes and odour caused by the presence of excess chlorine. Since residual Cl_2 is zero, so again chlorinate the water by a dose of about 0.1 to 0.2 mg./l.

(vii) **Dechlorination :** It means removing of chlorine from water. The dechlorination may be carried out by adding **certain chemicals** to water or by **simple aerating the water**. These chemicals are called **dechlorinating agents**.

Some common dechlorinating agents :

(a) Sulphur dioxide gas (SO_2);
(b) Activated carbon;
(c) Sodium thiosulphate (Na_2, S_2, O_3), cheapest dechlorinating agent
(d) Sodium metabisulphate ($Na_2S_2O_5$);
(e) Sodium sulphite (Na_2SO_3);
(f) Sodium bisulphite ($NaH\ SO_3$); and
(g) Ammonia (NH_4OH).

Testing of chlorine residuals.

(i) Orthotolidine test *(ii)* D.P.D. test
(iii) Chlorotex test *(iv)* Starch iodine test.

(vi) Water Softening

The reduction or removal of hardness from water is known as water softening.

Methods of removing temporary hardness.

(i) **Boiling :** When water is boiled, it leads to the peccipitation of $CalO_3$, which can be sedimented out in settling tank. But boiling cannot remove hardness caused by magnesium as $MgCO_3$ is fairly soluble in water

$$Ca(HCO_3)_2 \xrightarrow[+CO_2H_2O]{Heat} CaCO_3 \downarrow \text{insoluble}$$

(ii) **Addition of lime :**

$$MgCO_3 + Ca(OH)_2 \rightarrow \underset{\text{(insoluble)}}{Mg(OH)_2\downarrow} + \underset{\text{(insoluble)}}{CaCO_3\downarrow}$$

$$Mg(HCO_3)_2 + Ca(OH)_2 \rightarrow Ca(HCO_3) + Mg(OH)_2\downarrow$$

$$Ca(HCO_3) + Ca(OH)_2 \rightarrow 2CaCO_3\downarrow + 2H_2O$$

The calcuim carbonate and magenisum hydroxide are precipitated, and can be removed in the seidmentation tank.

Method of removing permanent hardness

Following three methods, which are commonly adopted for softening waters containing either permanent hardness or permanent as well as temporary hardness both

(i) **Lime-Soda process :** In this process lime $[Ca(OH)_2]$ and soda ash $[Na_2CO_3]$ are added to the hard water, which react with the Ca and Mg salts, to form insoluble precipitates of $CaCO_3$ and $Mg(OH)_2$ These precipitates can be sedimented out in sedimentation tank.

$$Ca(HCO_3)_2 + Ca(OH)_2 \rightarrow 2CaCO_3\downarrow + 2H_2O$$

(a) $Mg(HCO_3)_2 + Ca(OH)_2 \rightarrow Ca(HCO_3)_2 + Mg(OH)_2\downarrow$

(b) $MgCO_3 + Ca(OH)_2 \rightarrow Ca(OH)_2 + CaCO_3\downarrow$

$$MgCl_2 + Ca(OH)_2 \rightarrow Mg(OH)_2\downarrow + CaCl_2$$

$$MgSO_4 + Ca(OH)_2 \rightarrow Mg(OH)_2\downarrow + CaSO_4$$

$$CO_2 + Ca(OH)_2 \rightarrow CaCO_3\downarrow + H_2O$$

(free dissolved CO_2)

$$CaCl_2 + Na_2CO_3(\text{Soda}) \rightarrow CaCO_3\downarrow + 2NaCl$$

$$CaSO_4 + Na_2CO_3 \rightarrow CaCO_3 + Na_2SO_4\downarrow$$

- After sedimentation of $Ca\ CO_3$ and $Mg(OH)_2$, a little quantity may remain as finely divided particles and may cause trouble by getting deposited on the filter or in the pipes of the distribution system. To present this, water be recarbonated by passing CO_2 gas through it if leaves the sedimentation tank.

$$CaCO_3\downarrow + CO_2 + H_2O \rightarrow \underset{\text{soluble cal. bicarbonate.}}{Ca(HCO_3)_2}$$

$$Mg(OH)_2 + CO_2 \rightarrow MgCO_3 + H_2O$$

$$MgCO_3 + CO_2 + H_2O \rightarrow Mg(HCO_3)_2$$

- Many of the hard water contain the carbonate hardnes and very low amounts of non-carbonate hardness.
- For treating all such waters, lime is often the only chemical required.
- The equipment required for lime soda treatment is similar to that required for chemical coagulation.
- The effluents from the recarbonation plant are finally passed through a rapid gravity filter.

Dry sludge produced in mg/l = $[Ca_R + 0.58\ Mg_R + Li_A]$

where, Ca_R = calcium hardness removed in mg./l. (expressed as $(CaCO_3)$

Mg_R = magnesium hardness removed in mg./l. (expressed as $CaCO_3$)

Li_A = lime added in mg./l. (expressed as $Ca\ CO_3$)

Alkalinity : It may be defined as the quantity of ions in water that will react to neutralise the hydrogen ion (H^+).

Alkalinity = $[HCO_3] + [2CO_3^{--} + [OH^-] - [H^+]$

where, [ ] refers the concentration in moles/L.

- The carbonate hardness can be considered to be equal to the alkalinity, provided there is no sodium alkalinity in water.
- It follows that if non-carbonate hardness is present in water, then its carbonate hardness will be equal to its alkalinity, since sodium alkalinity will be zero.
- When pH > 11.5, the entire alkalinity is in the form of CO_3^{--} and OH^-.
  When 7.5 < pH < 8.3 the entire alkalinity is in the form of HCO^-_3.
  When pH < 4.5 the entire alkalinity is in the form Carbonic acid H_2CO_3.

(*ii*) Zeolite process or Base-exchange or Cation-exchange process.

- General formula of zolites are $Na_2O\ Al_2O_3\ x\ SiO_2\ y\ H_2O$. The usual value of x is 2 or more and that of y of ranging amounts.
- During softening operation, the sodium ions of the zeolite get replaced by the calcium and magnesium ions present in hard waters. The Co and Mg zeolite can be regenerated into active sodium zeolite by titrating it with 5 – 10% solution of sodium chloride.
- Zeolite softeners may be either gravity or pressure filters; pressure filter type zeolite softeners being more common. The rate of filteration through a zeolite softener is about 300 l/minute/m^2 *i.e.* 18000 l./h./m^2.
- The zeolite process will result in a water of zero hardness, which generally is not suitable for public supplies. Therefore, only a portion of the water passing through the treatment plant is to be softenq and then mixed with unsoftened water to obtain the desired water quality.

Comparison of Lime-Soda and Zeolite processes of softening water supplies :

	Item	*Lime Soda Process*	*Zeolite Process*
1.	Size of plant	Bulky and Large	Compact and small.
2.	Skilled supervision if required.	Careful and skilled supervision is necessary for obtaining results.	Automatic and easy to operate.
3.	Sludge troubles, if any.	Large quantity of sludge is formed.	No sludge is formed.
4.	Post treatment if needed.	Recarbonation is a must after sedimentation and filtration.	No such post treatment is required.
5.	Results obtained	It can produce water of hardness not less than about 50 mg./l. Therefore, useful for public supplies only.	Water of zero hardness can be obtained.
6.	Removal of colour due to iron and manganese.	Can remove the colour due to iron and manganese, but only to a very small extent.	Can remove the colour due to Fe & Mn, although very costly for treating such waters, because the exhausted Mn and Fe zeolite cannot be regenerated.
7.	Effects on bacteria	The increased causticity may help in killing pathgenic bacteria.	No such advantage is offered by this process.
8.	pH of the treated water	Increases the pH value of water, which reduces the corrosion of distribution pipes.	pH value of the water is not affected.
9.	Economy.	Process is economical and can be easily combined with usual water treatment methods at slight extra cost.	Process is costlier.
10.	Hardness which can be treated	Excessively hard waters can be treated.	Raw waters with hardness greater than 800 mg./l. cannot be easily and economically treated.
11.	Allowable turbidity in raw waters.	Highly turbid and acidic water can be treated.	Highly turbid waters are difficult to be treated.

(*iii*) Demineralisation process for removing hardness: It means removing the minerals from the water. This demineralised water, sometimes called *de-ionised water*, is as pure as distilled water, and is very suitable for industrial purposes.

This complete removal of minerals present in water can be carried out by first passing the water through a bed of cation exchange resins, and then through a bed of anion exchange resins.

(vii) Miscellaneous Treatments

The flouride content of the water should neither be less as to cause dental caries (early tooth decay) in children, during the calcination of their permanent teeth, nor it should be too high as to cause fauorisis (discolouration of teeth) and even deformation of bones (in extreme cases).

(i) **Removal of colours, odours and tastes from water.**

(a) Aeration : Under the process of aeration, water is brought in intimate contact with air, so as to absorb oxygen and to remove CO_2 gas. It may also help in killing bacteria, removing H_2S gas, iron and manganese to a certain extent, from the treated water.

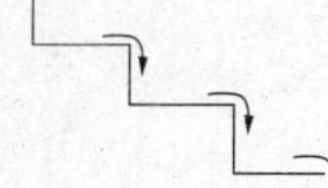

The aeration of water can be carried out in one of the following ways :

- By using spray nozzles
- By permitting water to trickle over cascades;
- By air diffusion;
- By using trickling beds : More efficient than casades.

(b) Treatment with activated carbon : It posses the property of absorbing and attracting impurities, such as gases, liquids and finely divided solids. It is widely used for removing testes and odours from public supplies. It is very useful for removing phenol type impurities.

- The activated carbon is available under various potential trade names, such as **Darco**, Nuchar etc. It is available in granular as well as powder forms.
- The activated carbon is mostly used in the powdered form and may be added to the water either before or after the coagulation, but before filtration.
- Activated carbon may also be used in the granular form as a filter media.

Advantage of activated carbon :

- It reduces the chlorine demand of treated water.
- It removes the organic matter present in water.
- It removes the tastes, odours and colours caused by the presence of Fe, Mn, phenols, excess chlorine, H_2S etc.
- It's overdose is not harmful.

(c) Treatment with copper sulphate ($CuSO_4 \cdot 7H_2O$) : Algae control compound.

The solution of $CuSO_4$ may be prepared and added just at the entry of water into the distribution system.

(d) Treatment with oxidising agents : The oxidising agents commonly used are $KMnO_4$, Cl_2, O_3 etc.

(ii) **Removal of iron and manganese from water.**

When present without combination with organic matter, they can be easily removed by aeration. On the other hand, when iron and maganese are present in combination with organic matter, it becomes difficult to break the bond between them and removal.

Manganese can be removed by activated alumina.

(iii) **Fluoridation and Defluoridation of water.**

Fluoridation : The process of adding fluoride compounds is called fluoridation.

Compounds used are : Sodium fluoride (NaF) (mostly used), sodium silico fluoride (Na_2SiF_2), hydrofluosilic acid (H_2SiF_6) etc.

Defluoridation : The process of removal of fluorine is called defluoridation process.

Process used are :

Lime soda process, cation exchange etc.

Fluorides is removed by manganese zeolite.

(iv) **Removal of radiotivity from water.**

(a) By phosphate coagulation method;

(b) By electrolysis method;

(c) By adding of clay materials to water; and

(d) By adding of metallic dusts of water.

(v) **Desalination of brackish water.**

The process of removing salts such as NaCl from water is known as **desalination**.

- Scarcity of water – Hongkong (import from other country)
- Desalination is a very costly process.
- National Chemical Laboratory (Poona), and Central Arid zones Research Institute (Jodhpur) are busy on this subject.

Methods of desalination :

(a) Desalination by evaporation and distillation

(b) Electrodialysis method

(c) Reverse osmosis method

(d) Freezing process

(e) Solar distillation method

(f) Other methods.

II. AIR POLLUTION

Air pollution is defined as "the presence in the outdoor atmosphere of one or more contaminants, such as dust, fumes, gas, mist, odour, smoke or vapour, in quantities, of characteristics, and of duration such as to injurious to human, plant or animal life or to property, or which unreasonably interferas with the comfortable enjoyment of life and property".

Composition of dry air at MSL in percentage.

Nitrogen	78.08
Oxygen	20.94
Argon	0.9340
Carbon dioxide	0.0315
Neon	0.0018
Helium	0.0005
Methane	0.0001 to 0.00015
Krypton	0.00011
Nitrous oxide	0.00005
Hydrogen	0.00005
Xenon	0.000008

Aerosol

Aerosol is a dispersion of solid or liquid particles of microscopic size in gaseous media, such as smoke, fog or mist.

Dust

Dust is a loose term applied to solid particles larger than colloidal particles and capable of temporary suspension in air or other gases. Dusts do not tend to flocculate except under electrostatic forces; they do not diffuse but settle under the influence of gravity. (Size : 1 – 200 μm)

Droplet

A droplet is a small liquid particle of such size and density as to fall under still conditions but which may remain suspended under turbulent conditions.

Fly-ash

Fly-ash is the finely divided particles of ash entrained in fuel gases arising from the combustion of fuel. The term is generally applied to the gas-borne ash from boilers using pulverised fuel (coal) firing.

Fog

Fog is a loose term applied to liquid dispersed aerosols in air by condensation.

Fume

Fume is the solid particles generated by condensation from the gaseous state, generally after volatization from melted substances, and often accompanied by a chemical reaction such as oxidation.

(Size: 0.1 to 1 μm)

Mist

Mist is a loose term applied to dispersions of liquid particles in atmosphere, the dispersion large size. (Size: 5 – 100 μm)

Particle

A particle is a small discrete mass of solid or liquid matter.

Smoke

Smoke is finely divided aerosol particles resulting from incomplete combustion. It consists mainly of carbon and other combustible material.

(Size: 0.01 to 1 μm)

Soot

Soot is collection of particles of carbon impregnated with 'tar' formed in the incomplete combustion of carbonaceous material.

Vapour

Vapour is the gaseous form of matter which normally exists in a liquid or solid state.

Classification of Air Pollution

Air pollution exists in three distinct categories

(1) Personal air pollution.

This refers to exposure of an individual to dust, fumes and gases. For example, when a person indulges in cigarette, cigar or pipe smoking.

(2) Occupational air pollution.

This represents the type of exposure of individuals to potentially harmful concentration of aerosols, vapours and gases in their working environment.

(3) Community air pollution.

This represents the most complex of the three varieties since it involves pollution from a variety of sources and contaminants and factors which cause adverse social, economic and health effects. Not only does community air pollution affect many individuals, but it can also exert a significant impact on man's total environment including plants, animals, property and the weather itself.

Sources of Air Pollution

There are two main sources of air pollution.

(1) Natural air pollution sources.

The atomosphere is polluted due to following natural causes.

(i) Wind-blown dust
(ii) Somke, fly-ash, gases from forest fires
(iii) Micro-organisms
(iv) Gases and odours from swamps and marshes
(v) Fog
(vi) Volcanic ash and gases

Pollutants from various natural sources :

- Pollutant Natural sources
- SO_2 Volcanoes
- H_2S Volcanoes, biological action in swamp areas
- CO Forest fires, ocean
- NO-NO_2 Bacterial action in soil
- NH_3 Biological decay
- Hydrocarbons
- (CH_4, etc.) Biological processes
- CO_2 Biological decay, release from oceans
- O_3 Oxygen and ozone in stratosphere and their downward transport

(2) Man-Made Sources.

Sources of pollution due to man's activities.

Source	*Category*	*Examples*	*Pollutants*
Dust-producing process	Crushing, grinding, screening Demolition Milling	Road mix plants Construction work Grain elevators	Mineral and organic particulates
Combustion	Fuel burning	Home oven, power plants	Oxides of sulphur, oxides of nitrogen.
	Motor vehicles	Cars, buses and trucks	Carbon monoxide, Smoke, flyash, organic vapour, metal oxide, particles and odours
	Refuse burning	Open burning of refuse	
Manufacturing processes	Metallurgical plant	Smelters, steel mills, non-ferrous industries, etc. of sulphur.	Metal fumes, lead, arsenic and zinc fluorides and oxides
Chemical plants	Petroleum refineries, pulp mills, fertiliser plants, cement mills	H_2S, oxides of sulphur, fluorides, organic vapour, particles, odours	
Agricultural activities	Crop spraying, dusting dusting	Pest and weed control	Organic phosphates, chlorinated hydrocarbons, arsenic, lead
	Field burning		Smokes, fly-ash and soot
Nuclear energy activities	Ore preparations	Crushing, grinding, screening	Uranium and dust beryllium
	Nuclear fissions Nuclear device testing	Nuclear reactors Atmospheric explosions	Agron-41 Radioactive fallous

Effects of Air Pollution

(1) Effect on vegetation : Vegetation exposed to atmosphere containing heavy amounts of sulphur dioxide is severly damaged. It is also affected by ozone and nitrogen dioxide.

(2) Effect on human beings and animals : People suffer from respiratory diseases when exposed to atmosphere in which the concentration of sulphur dioxide is in excess of safe limits, and their visibility is affected when exposed to higher temperature. The death rate of people suffering with cardiac or pulmonary diseases, when exposed to atmosphere contaminated with sulphur dioxide, is found to be higher.

Due to incomplete combustion of fuels from petrol engines, industrial operations, etc., carbon monoxide is liberated. When air containing CO is inhaled, the CO combines with the haemoglobin of the blood, depriving the tissues of oxygen. It has been found that when the carbonyl haemoglobin saturation level of blood is about 20%, it harms the heart and also impairs tissues restricting the oxygen. When in excess of 10%, it is found to cause headaches.

When the nitrogen dioxide level in the air is above tolerable limits, respiratory illness among children has been observed.

When oxygen content in the air is above 500 mg/m^3 and photochemical action is high, people have been found to have asthmatic attacks. Irritation of throat, nose or eyes are some other minor problems experienced in these conditions.

In general, air pollution decreases visibility. It is also found that it makes the town or city more cloudy, more foggy and is subjected to more acid rains.

(3) Effect on materials.

Air pollutants affect materials in the following ways and cause economic losses

(*i*) Abrasion

(*ii*) Deposition of materials

(*iii*) Direct chemical attack

(*iv*) Indirect chemical attack

(*v*) Corrosion

Effects of air pollution on materials.

S.No	*Material*	*Air Pollutants*	*Effect on materials*
1.	Metals	SO_2, acids, gases	Tarnishing of surface, loss of metal, etc.
2.	Paints	SO_2, H_2S and particulates	Discolouration
3.	Textiles	SO_2, acid, gases	Reduction in tensile strength
4.	Ceramics	–do–	Discolouration

AIR-POLLUTION CONTROL

The following methods are useful in controlling air pollution

(1) Control of air pollution by zoning.

In this method adopt the zoning system at the planning stage itself. A separate zone or area is set aside for industries thereby reducing the ill effects of air pollution on the urban dwellers.

The zoning of the industries is done based on the type of industries, their functions, etc. Every city has its own zoning rules.

Zoning of the industries may be based on

(*i*) Functions : These include industries such as linkages for industry, sidings, etc.

(*ii*) Performance : Here the industries are classified according to their nuisance value.

(*a*) Traffic congestion

(*b*) Abnoxious and hazardous

(*c*) Industrial nuisance such a smoke, noise, dust, odour, etc.

Separate areas may be earmarked according to their performance as stated.

In India, the zoning system varies from city to city. For instance, in Industrial Estate of Bangalore, three zones are provided for light, medium and large industries. Further, large industries are not encouraged. In Delhi also large industries are not permitted.

(2) Air-pollution control at the source.

The air-pollution problems can be minimised at the source by the following four ways:

(*i*) Raw material substitution : If one raw material results in a pollution problem while a substitute material does not, obviously the substitute would be more desirable. The raw material may contain an ingredient which is not essential but is a pollution source. If the non-essential ingredients can be removed prior to processing the raw material, the pollution pzotential can be minimised.

e.g. use low-sulphur fuels to replace high-sulphur fuels.

(*ii*) Process modifications. Pollution reduction can frequently be achieved by new or modified processes.

e.g. use of exhaust hoods and ducts over several types of industrial ovens has allowed the recovery of valuable solvents that could have become air pollutants.

(*iii*) Equipment alterations.

Equipment alterations such as the use of floating roof tanks rather than vented tanks can cut down on evaporation losses. Newer types of equipment are less pollution-prone.

e.g. basic oxygen furnaces that are replacing the open-hearth furnaces in the steel industry, pose less of a pollution problem.

(*iv*) **Removal of pollutants at source:** Sometime costly control equipment is necessary to remove pollutants from the main gas stream. In such cases it is simpler to remove pollutants at the source. It is normally more economical to remove these pollutants while they are present in relatively higher concentrations rather than at some point away from the source where the pollutants are diluted by gases from other processes or air.

(3) Controlling Air Pollution by Devices.

Due to different process in industries, various type of gases are liberated alongwith particulates. To arrest these entering the atmosphere, control devices are used depending on the collection capacity and processes used by the particular industry.

Types of devices used for dust collections based on the method of their removal.

(*i*) Internal separators.

These devices separate the dust in the gases. These are manufactured in various shapes and sizes.

Following types are commonly used :

(*a*) ***Gravity-settling chamber.*** This consists of a chamber in which the dust is separated from the gas by reducing the velocity of the gas.

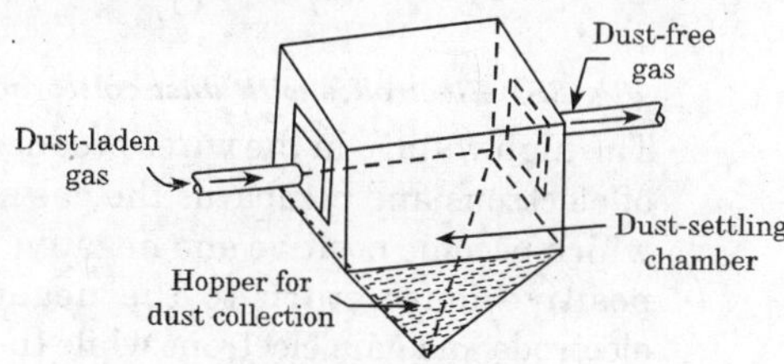

Fig. ***Gravity settling chamber***

Due to this, the dust particles settle down in the chamber. As the size of the chamber for very low velocities of the gas required is very large and cost is prohibitive, the velocity in the chamber is generally kept between 0.3 to 3.0 m/sec. By this the coarser particles are removed. The gravity-settling chamber are capable of removing only the large particles of size 25 to 50 μm dia.

(*b*) ***Cyclone:*** When a gas travels in a double vertex, the particles contained in the it are separated. The cyclone works on this principle.

The gas is first allowed to spiral down at the inner surface and then it spirals upwards at the central portion of the cyclone. Due to inertia, the dust particles tend to settle on the surface of the cyclone wall. From here they are led away to the receiver.

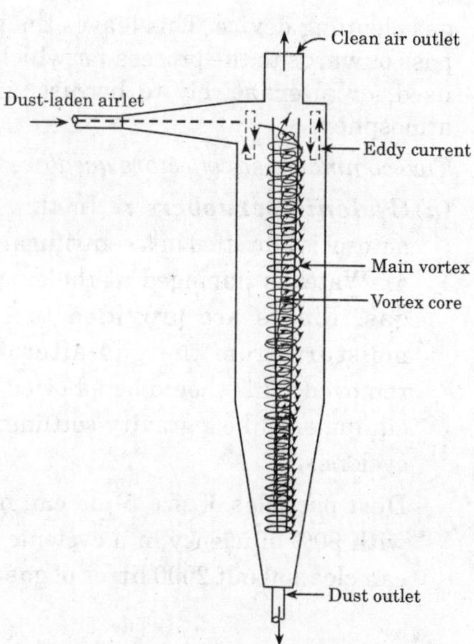

Cyclones are very efficient and can handle a number of operations. They are suitable for removing particles of size of 10–40 μm.

(*c*) ***Fabric filters :*** Here, the gas with the dust is allowed to pass through a fabric (cloth) to which the dust gets attached. If the gas is flowing at low velocity and contains considerable amount of larger particulates, these settle down by sedimentation. Fine particles are also attached to the fabric due to electrostatic charges.

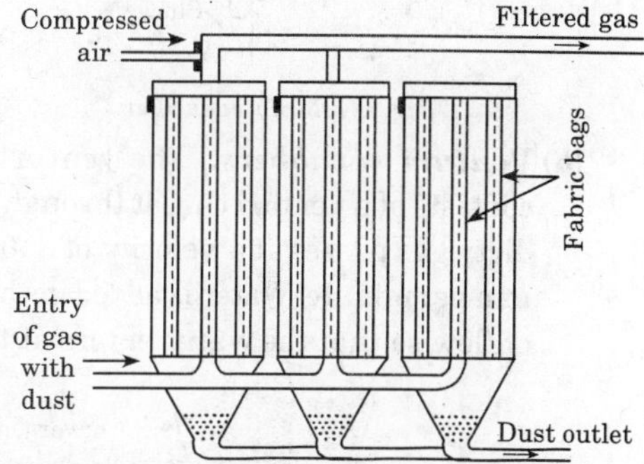

These bags are fitted with hopper at bottom. The gas enters from the bottom through the hopper. The heavy particles settle down in the hopper due to gravity. Finer particles are deposited on the fabric of the bag. For clearing the bags, compressed air is blown in the reverse direction.

(*ii*) Wet-collection devices:

Wet washers and scrubbers are devices using mixed phases of gas and liquid. The object of the scrubber or washing device is to transfer suspended particulate matter in the gas to the scrubbing liquid which can readily removed by the gas cleaning device. This leaves the gas clean to pass onwards to the process for which it is being used, or alternatively to be discharged to the atmosphere.

Two common wet-collectors used are :

(a) Cyclonic scrubbers : In this device, the aerosol is admitted in a centrifugal fashion (Fig 4). Water is impinged at the entrance of the gas. Plates are provided to remove the moisture from the gas after the dust is removed. This should be followed by a control equipment like a gravity-settling chamber or cyclones.

Dust particles of size 5 μm can be separated with 90% efficiency in a cyclonic scrubber. It can clean about 2000 litres of gas per minute.

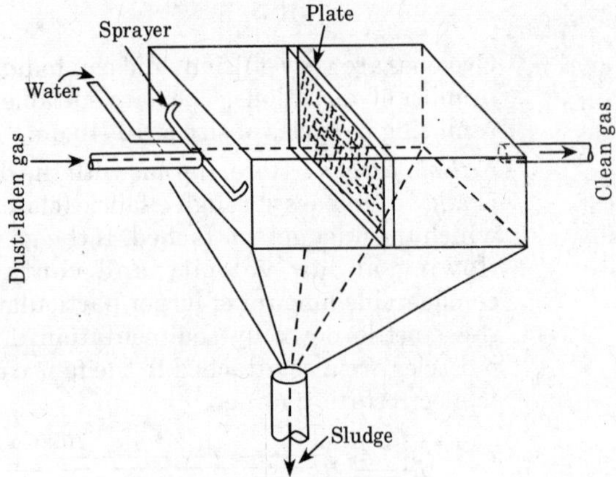

Fig. Cyclonic scrubber

(b) Venturi scrubbers. The venturi scrubber consists of a venturi throat through which the dirty gas passes at a velocity of 3400 to 12600 mm per minute. Water is added in the direction of flow so that the water enters at the throat.

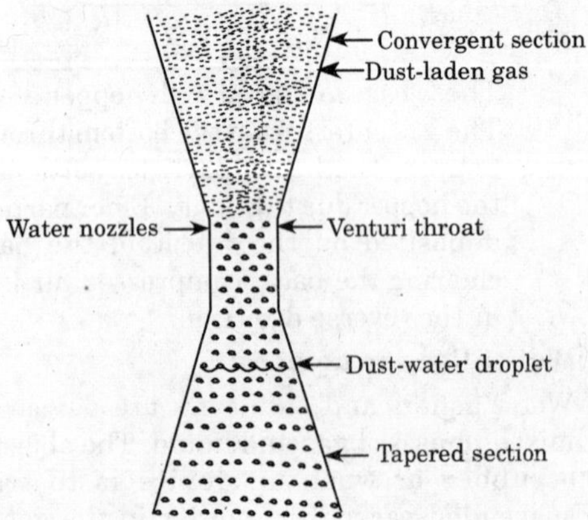

Fig. Venturi scrubber

The venturi scrubber can clean about 4000 litres of gas per minute. The efficiency is about 99% and can clean very fine particles.

If the moisture has to be removed from the gas, a cyclonic separator is used after the venturi scrubber.

(iii) Electrostatic precipitator.

The electrostatic precipitator is a device by which the dust in a gas is removed by electrostatic attractions.

The gas is allowed to enter the electrostatic precipitator through narrow vertical gas passages which are formed by parallel rows of grounded collecting electrodes. Insulated high-voltage wires of about 40-50 kV are placed in the centre of each passage. The dirty gas thus passes between the high-voltage wires and the grounded plates.

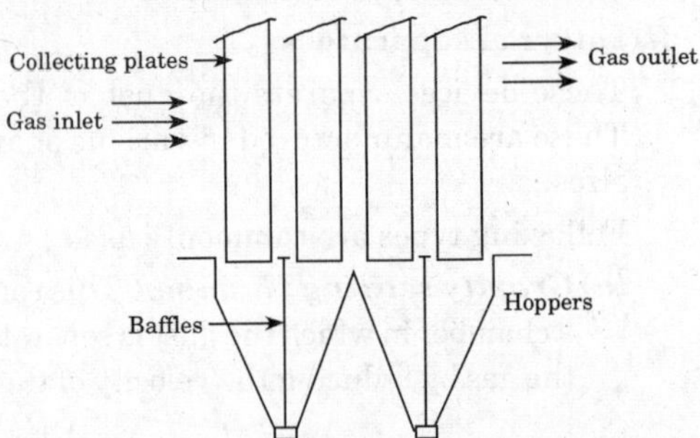

Fig. ESP Electrodes with dust collecting hoppers

The high voltage in the wires produces billions of electrons and bombards the gas molecules, which become positive and negative ions. The positive ions return to the negative wire electrode and gain electrons while the negative ions combine with the dust particles and make them negative ions.

The negatively charged dust particles collect at the positively charged plates.

When the thickness of the dust layer increases to more than 6 mm, the electrical attraction becomes weak. A sharp gap is given which causes the dust layer to separate and fall down into the hopper.

The electrostatic precipitator has an efficiency of 99.9% and can clean up to 150,000 litres of gas per minute at a temperature of 600° C.

(4) Air pollution control by stacks.

When small quantities of air pollutants are released at a source, these can be absorbed without producing noticeable pollution. However, if the quantity of pollutants released is large, and the air has a limited capacity, the pollution becomes high. If the pollutants are carried away to some distance or taken to high altitudes, they are reduced in concentration by diffusion and dilution. The pollutants are taken to high altitudes by means of stacks.

Diffusion of pollutant in air depends on the following factors :

(*i*) Atmospheric temperature

(*ii*) Speed and direction of wind

The height and diameter of stack required is designed to keep the ground level concentration within permissible limits. The concentration at ground level varies inversely with the square of the stack height and is maximum at a distance of 5-10 m stack height.

Some authors suggest the following

(a) The height of the stack must be 2.5 times the height of the surrounding buildings and

(b) The velocity of the exit gases should not be more than 20 m/sec.

(5) Air pollution control by vegetation.

To reduce the spreading of air pollutant emanating from industrial sources, growing green vegetation around the industry has been recommended by many scientists. Studies (Waren 1973, Fleming 1967) indicate that there are large differences among species vis-a-vis the response to air pollutants. Hence cultivation of pollution resistant species represents the best possibility of reducing injury by air pollutants. The degree of resistance depends on type of pollutant.

III. Noise Pollution

Noise is a characteristic of an environment, and is usually defined as unwanted sound. The unwanted sound certainly produces several undesirable effects on our body health, and it can therefore, be called a pollutant.

Noise can also be defined as that unwanted sound pollutant which produces undesirable physiological and psychological effects in an individual, by interfering with one's social activities like work, rest, recreation, sleep, etc.

It is a generalised fact that noise of sufficient intensity and duration can induce health problems like temporary and some-times permanent hearing loss, besides causing several other diseases like general annoyance, irritation, disturbance, headaches, insomnia, fatigue, mental torture, nausea, high blood pressure, high pulse rate, greater perspiration, etc.*

Chracteristics of Sound and its Measurement.

We know that sound is produced in the environment by alternating pressure changes in the air, and is caused by the vibrations of solid objects or separation of fluids, as they pass over, around, or through holes in solid objects. These vibrations cause the surrounding air to undergo compression, then rarefaction, again compression, then rarefaction, and so on. Such alternating compression and rarefaction of the surrounding air produces sound waves which propagate in the form of sinusoidal path, as shown in Fig. (a) and (b).

Fig. *(a)* shown the time between the successive peaks or troughs of oscillation is called **the period** (P), and its inverse, which represents the number of times a peak arrives in one second, is called the **frequency** *(f)*. Hence

$$P = \frac{1}{f}$$

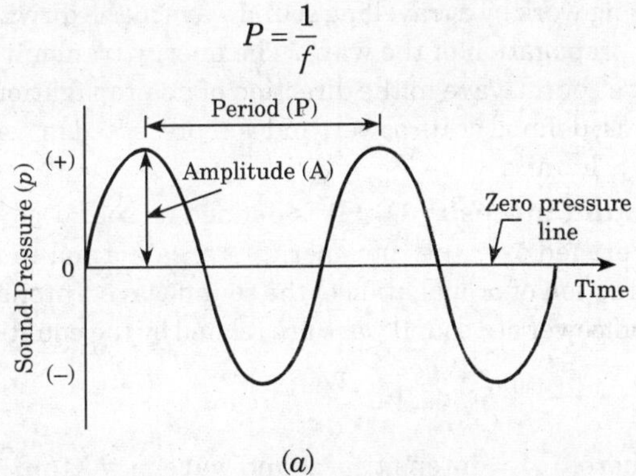

(a)

Fig. *(b)* shows the distance between successive peaks or troughs is called the **wave length** (λ), which is related to frequencey *(f)* by the relation

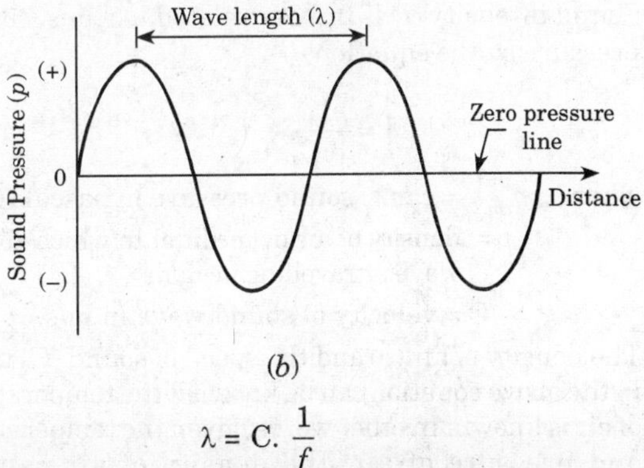

(b)

$$\lambda = C. \frac{1}{f}$$

where C = velocity of the sound wave.

The amplitude (A) of the wave is the height of the peak sound pressure measured above or below the zero pressure line. The equivalent pressure of such a sine wave is represented by root mean square pressure (p_{rms}) as

$$p_{rms} = \sqrt{p_{(t)}^2} = \sqrt{\frac{1}{T} \cdot \int_0^T p_{(t)}^2 dt}$$

where $p_{(t)}$ = pressure at any time t.

The r.m.s. sound pressure is, thus, obtained by adding the squares of amplitude values at small time intervals, and dividing the total by the averaging time, and finally taking the square root of the total. This works out equal $\frac{A}{\sqrt{2}}$ for a regular sine wave.

The sound pressure (p_{rms}) is further related to atmospheric pressure and barometric pressure by the equation

Sound pressure

= Total atmospheric pressure — barometric pressure

Power of sound (W) : It is defined as the rate of doing work by a travelling sound wave in the direction of propagation of the wave. The energy transmitted by a sound wave in the direction of its propagation is thus, defined as its power, and is represented in watts in S.I. units.

Sound intensity (I) : It is defined as sound power averaged over the time, per unit area normal to the direction of propagation of the sound wave. Intensity and power of a sound wave are related by the equation.

$$I = \frac{W}{a}$$

where, I = intensity of sound wave in watt/m^2

W = power of sound wave in watts

a = unit area perpendicular to the direction of wave motion.

Sound intensity (I) is further related to r.m.s. sound pressure by the equation

$$I = \frac{p_{rms}^2}{\rho . C}$$

where, p_{rms} = r.m.s. sound pressure in pascals (Pa)

ρ = density of air or medium in which sound wave is travelling in kg/m^3

C = velocity of sound wave in m/s.

The density of air (ρ) and the speed of sound (C) used in the above equation can be known if the temperature of air is known. In other words, given the temperature and pressure of air, the density of air can be determined from the standard tables; and the speed of sound in air at 101.325 kPa may be determined by the equation

$$C = 20.05\sqrt{T}$$

where, T = absolute temperature in kelvin (K) and C is in m/s.

Levels of Noise :

The sound pressure of the faintest sound that can be heard by a normal healthy individual is about 20 micro-pascal (μ - Pa), and the loudest sound produced by a Saturn rocket at the lift off stage is about 200 Pa. This astronomical variation in sound pressure (varying from 20 μ - Pa to 200 Pa) is usually avoided by expressing sound pressure on a scale based on the log of the ratio of the measured sound pressure and a reference standard pressure. Measurements on this scale are called **levels.**

sound level, $L = \log_{10} \frac{Q}{Q_0}$ (bels)

where, Q = measured quantity of sound pressure, or sound power, or sound intensity

Q_o = reference standard quantity of sound pressure, or sound power, or sound intensity, as case may be

L = sound level in bels (B)

The unit of sound level is turns out to be a rather large unit, a smaller unit of **decibels (dB)** is generally used.

$$1 \text{ dB} = \frac{1}{10} \text{B}$$

Hence, when sound level is expressed in decibels, the above equation reduces to

$$L = 10. \log_{10} \frac{Q}{Q_o} \quad (dB)$$

- The reference standard quantity Q_0 in the above equation is taken to be equal to 20 μ Pa, when sound pressure is measured.

  Sound pressure level,

  $$L_p = 10 . \log_{10} \left(\frac{p_{rms}}{20\mu Pa}\right)^{2*}$$

  or $$L_p = 20 \log_{10} \left(\frac{p_{rms}}{20\mu Pa}\right)$$

  The sound pressure levels so measured are reported as dB *re* : 20 μ*Pa*.

- Similarly, the reference standard quantity Q_0 in the above equation is taken to be equal to 10^{-12} watts, when sound power is measured.

  Sound power level,

  $$L_w = 10 \log_{10} \left(\frac{W}{10^{-12}}\right)$$

  The sound power levels so computed are reported as dB *re* : 10^{-12} W.

- Similarly, the reference standard quantity Q_0 is taken to be equal to $10^{-12}\ \frac{W}{m^2}$, when sound intensity level is measured.

  Sound intensity level,

$$L_I = 10 \log_{10}\left(\frac{I}{10^{-12}}\right)$$

Out of the three terms given above, *sound pressure level* on reference scale of 20 μ*Pa*, is usually adopted to express sound levels in decibels.

Averaging Sound Pressure Levels :

The average value of the various recorded sound pressure levels (L_p) at a particular place over a given period cannot be computed by simple averaging due to log scale involved in their values.

Average pressure level,

$$\bar{L}_p = 20 \log \frac{1}{N} \sum_{n=1}^{n=N} (10)^{L_n/20}$$

where, $\bar{L}_p$ = Average sound pressure level in dB re: 20μ*Pa*

N = Number of measurement readings.

L_n = *n*th sound pressure level in dB *re*. 20 μ*Pa*.

n = 1, 2, 3......... N.

Types of Sound :

(*i*) **Continuous noise :** It is an uninterrupted sound level that varies less than 5 dB during the entire period of observation. A running fan is an example of such a sound.

(*ii*) **Intermittent noise :** It is a noise which continues for more than 1 second and is then interrupted for more than 1 second. A drilling machine used by a dentist produces such type of sound.

(*iii*) **Impulse noise :** It is characterised by a change of sound pressure of atleast 40 dB within 0.5 second with a duration of less than one second. The noise produced from firing of a weapon would fall in this category.

Noise Rating Systems :

A noise may consist of different types of sounds with different pressure levels operating for different time intervals. The frequencies of these sounds may also vary. The combined resultant noise will infact be responsible for determining the human response and degree of annoyance caused by it. The combined impact of different sound pressures lasting for different periods is therefore attempted to be worked out by using some statistical measures, such as L_N and L_{eq} systems.

L_N Concept :

The parameter L_N is a statistical measure indicating how frequently a particular sound level is exceeded. The value of L_N will represent the sound pressure level that will exceed for N% of the gauging time. When L_N is plotted against N (where N = 1, 2, 3, ... 100%), a cumulative distribution curve, is obtained.

L_{eq} Concept :

L_{eq} is defined as the constant noise level, which, over a given time, expands the same amount of energy, as is expanded by the fluctuating levels over the same time. This value is expressed by the equation:

$$L_{eq} = 10 \log \sum_{i=1}^{i=n} (10)^{\frac{L_i}{10}} \times t_i$$

where, *n* = total number of sound samples

L_i = noise level of any *i*th sample

t_i = time duration of *i*th sample, expressed as fraction of total sample time.

The *equivalent noise level* (L_{eq}) constitutes an important parameter for evaluating the impact of fluctuating noises of all kinds, such as from aircraft, street and road traffic, rail traffic, industrial machines, sports stadiums, play grounds, etc.

Moreover, the duration in hours, over which L_{eq} is worked out for a given site, is further mentioned in bracket, such as $L_{eq(8)}$ which means that L_{eq} is based on 8-hour measurement; when, however, no such time is mentioned, then L_{eq} always corresponds to one hour measurement.

Noise Level Standards

The prescribed noise standards generally put a limit either on L_{eq} or L_N values. Different such limiting values are then prescribed for different areas.

e.g. example, VIP and serene areas will impose lower limiting values as compared to those for commercial or industrial areas within a city. The usually prescribed limiting L_{eq} values for different areas of a city is of the order of 40 to 70 decibels.

Table (*a*) and (*b*) show two sets of noise standards, which have been laid down in USA. The first standards developed by *U.S. Federal Highway Administration* are the levels prescribed for newly planned highways through different types of areas. These levels are above those that would be absolutely harmless, but are below those of many existing highways.

Table (*a*). Noise standards laid down by U.S. federal highway administration for highways in new delopments

Land use category	*Exterior design noise level dB(A)**		*Description of land use category*
	L_{eq} or L_{10}		
A	57	60	VIP and other protected areas, where serenity and quietness is to be maintained
B	67	70	Residence, hotels, schools, hospitals, picnic areas, play grounds, parks, etc.
C	72	75	Developed lands and properties not included in A and B category, such as commercial and industrial areas.
D	No limit	No limit	Undeveloped lands
E	52 (interior)	55 (interior)	Public meeting halls, schools, libraries, churches, hospitals, etc.
*Either L_{eq} or L_{10}, based on 1 hour samples, is to be used.			

Table *b*. has been evolved by U.S. *Environmental Protection Agency* and shows the limiting noise levels for different types of areas for indoor as well as outdoor noises, that should be maintained for adequately safeguarding public health over long periods (accounting annual average levels in L_{eq} values).

Table (*b*). Average yearly energy Levels (L_{eq}) identified as requisite to protect public health and welfare with an adequate margin of safety.

Types of areas	*Measure*	*Indoor*		*To protect against both effects (b)*	*Outdoor*		
		Activity interference	*Hearing loss consideration*		*Activity interference*	*Hearing loss consideration*	*To protect against both effects (b)*
(1)	(2)	(3)	(4)	(5)	(6)	(7)	(8)
Residential with out side space and farm residences	L_{dn} $L_{eq}(24)$	45	70	45	55	70	55
Residential with no outside space	L_{dn} $L_{eq}(24)$	45	70	45			
Commercial	$L_{eq}(24)$	(*a*)	70	70(*c*)	(*a*)	70	70(*c*)
Inside transportation	$L_{eq}(24)$	(*a*)	70	(*a*)			
Industrial	$L_{eq(24)}(d)$	(*a*)	70	70(*c*)	(*a*)	70	70(*c*)
Hospitals	L_{dn} $L_{eq(24)}$	45	70	45	55	70	55
Educational area	$L_{eq(24)}$ $L_{eq(24)}(d)$	45	70	45	55	70	55
Recreational areas	$L_{eq(24)}$	(*a*)	70	70(c)	(*a*)	70	70(*c*)
Farm land and general unpopulated land	$L_{eq(24)}$				(*a*)	70	70(*c*)

Codes:

(*a*) Since different types of activites appear to be associated with different levels, identification of a maximum level for activity interference may be difficult except in those circumstances where speech communication is a critical activity.

(*b*) Based on lowest level.

(*c*) Based only on hearing loss.

(*d*) An $L_{eq(8)}$ of 75 *d*B may be identified in these situations so long as the exposure over the remaining 16 hour per day is low enough to result in negligible contribution to the 24-hour average, that is, no greater than an L_{eq} of 60 *d*B.

- Explanation of identified level for hearing loss. The exposure period that results in hearing loss at the identified level is a period of 40 years.

Table (*c*). Acceptable noise levels for residential areas, as per I.S. code.

S. No.	*Acceptable outdoor noise levels in residential areas*		*S. No.*	*Acceptable indoor levels for various types of buildings*	
	Location	*Noise levels dB(A)*		*Location*	*Noise levels dB(A)*
1.	Rural areas	25 – 35	1.	Radio and TV studios	25 – 30
2.	Suburban areas	30 – 40	2.	Music rooms	30 – 35
3.	Urban Residential areas	35 – 45	3.	Hospitals, class rooms, auditoria	35 – 40
4.	Residential and business urban areas	40 – 50	4.	Apartments, hotels, homes Conference rooms, small offices	35 – 40
5.	City areas	45 – 55	5.	Court rooms, private offices, libraries	45 – 50
6.	Industrial areas	50 – 60	6.	Large public offices, banks, stores, etc.	45 – 50
			7.	Restaurants	50 – 55

The acceptable outdoor noise levels in different types of residential areas, as well as the acceptable indoor noise levels for various types of buildings, as recommended by *Indian standard code* IS: 4954 – 1968, are given in table *c*.

In order to legally enforce control on noise levels, the GOI has notified **the Noise Pollution (Regulation and Control) Rules 2000,** under *the Environment (Protection) Act, 1986,* Under these Rules, Ambient Air Quality Standards in respect of Noise, have been specified in respect of different types of areas uses (such as industrial area, commercial area, residential area and silence zones), as shown in Table (*d*)

Table (*d*). Ambient air quality standards in respect of noise.

Area Code	*Category of Area / Zone*	*Limits in dB (A) Leq*	
		Day Time	*Night Time*
A	Industrial Area	75	70
B	Commercial Area	65	55
C	Residential Area	55	45
D	Silence Zone	50	40

Note:

1. Day time shall mean from 6.00 a.m. to 10.00 p.m.
2. Night time shall mean from 10.00 p.m. to 6.00 a.m.

3. Silence zone is an area comprising not less than 100 metres around hospitals, educational institutions, courts, religious places or any other area which is declared as such by the competent authority.
4. Mixed categories of areas may be declared as one of the four above mentioned categories by the competent authority.

Sources of Noise and their Noise Levels :

Outdoor noise is usually produced by the following sources:

(1) *Traffic* including air traffic, road traffic, and sea-shore and inland water traffic

(2) *Industries*

(3) *Other miscellaneous activities*

Traffic Noise :

The amount and type of noise produced by traffic is largely dependent upon the type of traffic.

Table *(e)*. Noise levels of different sources of traffic.

S.No.	*Source of Noise*	*Noise level in dB*
1.	Air traffic	
	(i) Jet aircraft at take off stage at about 300m	100 – 110
	(ii) Propeller type aircraft at take off stage at about 300 m	90 – 100
2.	Rail traffic (at about 30 m)	90 – 110
3.	Heavy road traffic (highway)	80 – 90
4.	Medium road traffic (main streets)	70 – 80
5.	Light road traffic (side streets)	60 – 70

Table *(f)*. GOI noise standards for different types of vehicles.

S. No.	*Type of vehicles*	*Noise level in dB*
1	Two wheelers	80
2	Cars	82
3	Passenger or commercial vehicles	
	(i) upto 4 MT (Tonnes)	85
	(ii) between 4 MT to 12 MT	89
	(iii) More than 12 MT	91

Industrial Noise :

Noise is the essential by-product of industry; its intensity and nature being dependent upon the type of the industry. Industrial noises are usually produced by rotating, reciprocating or any other types of machinery, or by high pressure high velocity gases, liquids or vapour involved in the industrial processes. The usual noise level of the industries is of the order of 60 to 95 decibels.

Noise Produced by Other Sources :

Several other human activities, such as blarring of loud-speakers and sirens, shouting of hawkers, playing of children, general life and activity, ringing of temple and church bells, etc. do produce noises of different levels, tones and spectra.

Noise Abatement and Control :

Exposure of mankind to the day by day increasing noise. Nuisance must be reduced and abated, if its adverse effects on human health are to be controlled. The society must therefore be protected from the harmful effects of noise by devising and implementing ways and means for the abatement of noises.

There are certain noises which can be kept under control by legal laws and ordinances, and there are others which have to be damped and attenuated by the use of good technology and town planning. For example, the noises produced by motor vehicles can be controlled to some extent by proper maintenance of vehicles, which can be ensured only by prescribing maximum permissible noise levels for different types of automobiles, through Motor Vehicles Act. Similarly, Industrial noises, can be brought under the control of Factories Act by specifying maximum permissible noise levels and other checks. Similarly, public blarring of loud-speakers and playing of radio sets at loud levels can be prevented by general legal laws of public nuisance or laws specifically made for noise pollution. Yet however, there exist several other noises which have become part and parcel of our modern life. All such noises are to be reduced by better design technology to be used in the modern day gadgets like fans, air-conditioners, washing machines, refrigeratiors, mixers and grinders, etc.

Another very important method for abating noise effects on mankind is to use proper town planning techniques, and thus, to ensure construction of houses and offices away from the major sources of noise. Proper segregation, zoning and separation of residential complexes from the commercial and industrial ones, by means of physical barriers, roads, railway lines, parks or green belts, do constitute an important aspect of such good town-planning.

The noises produced by automobiles and trains, being the biggest noise nuisance in a modern city life, can be abated by construction of walls on both sides of roads and railway lines. Raising of such obstructions and barriers in between the noise sources (automobiles) and residences, may considerably reduce the noise levels reaching the residences. Attenuation of up to 15 decibels is possible in this manner.

When $D \geq R$ and $R >> H$, the noise reduction may also be calculated by the equation:

$$\text{Noise reduction (dB)} = 10 \log_{10}\left(\frac{20\,H^2}{\lambda R}\right)$$

where, H = height of the barrier wall.

λ = wavelength of sound.

D = distance between barrier and the receiving point.

Raising of thick and high vegetation and tree growing along sides of roads and railway lines, offers offer cheaper barriers to cause such noise reductions.

Locating the noisy sources on the downwind side of the residences, may be another important consideration in good town planning, because noise will then travel farther in the downwind direction away from the residences.

Noise levels in residential buildings can be reduced to some extent by offsetting the building from the main or street roads by a suitable distance. The farther is this distance, the better will be the attenuation, because the intensity of noise gets reduced with increase in distance.

Objective Type Questions

1. The chlorine demand of a water sample was found to be 0.5 mg/lt. The amount of bleaching powder containing 30% available chloride to be added to treat one litre of such a water sample is
   (a) 1.67 (b) 1.92
   (c) 1.01 (d) 1.36

2. A water treatment work treats 6000 m^3 of water per day. If it consumes 20 kg chlorine per day, then chlorine desage would be
   (a) 2.33 mg/lit (b) 5 mg/lit
   (c) 4 mg/lit (d) 3.33 mg/lit

3. A city supply of 16000 cubic metres of water per day treated with chlorine with dosage of 0.6 ppm. For this purpose the requirement of 30% bleaching powder per day would be
   (a) 32 kg (b) 16 kg
   (c) 18 kg (d) 22 kg

4. If the average daily consumption of a city is 100,000 m^3, the maximum daily consumption on peak hourly demand will be
   (a) 100, 000 m^3 (b) 150,000 m^3
   (c) 180,000 m^3 (d) 270,000 m^3

5. The polluted water is one which
   (a) contains pathogenic bacteria
   (b) consists of undesirable substances rendening it unfit for drinking and domestic use.
   (c) is safe and suitable for drinking and domestic use.
   (d) is contaminated.

6. The population of a town in three consecutive years are 5000, 7000 and 8400 respectively. The population of the town in the fourth consecutive year according to geometrical increase method is
   (a) 9500 (b) 9800
   (c) 10100 (d) 10920

7. If the total hardness of water is greater than its total alkalinity, the carbonate hardness will be equal to
   (a) total alkalinity
   (b) total hardness
   (c) total hardness–total alkalinity
   (d) non-carbonate hardness

8. The dissolved oxygen level in natural unpolluted waters, at normal temperature is found to be of the order of
   (a) 1 mg/litre (b) 10 mg/litre
   (c) 100 mg/litre (d) 1000 mg/litre

9. The most common cause of acidity in water is
   (a) carbon dioxide (b) oxygen
   (c) hydrogen (d) nitrogen

10. Standard EDTA (Ethylene Diamine Tetra Acetic Acid) solution is used to determine the
    (a) hardness in water
    (b) turbidity in water
    (c) dissolved oxygen in water
    (d) residual chlorine in water

11. The process in which the chlorination is done beyond the break point is
    (a) pre chlorination
    (b) post chlorination
    (c) super chlorination
    (d) break point chlorination

12. The rate of filtration of pressure filters is
    (a) less than that of slow sand filters
    (b) in between the filtration rate of slow sand filters and rapid sand filters
    (c) greater than that of rapid sand filters
    (d) equal to that of slow sand filters

13. The effective size of sand particles used in slow sand filters is
    (a) 0.25 to 0.35 mm (b) 0.35 to 0.60 mm
    (c) 0.60 to 1.00 mm (d) 1.00 to 1.80 mm

14. Which of the following methods of analysis of water distribution system is most suitable for long and narrow pipe system ?
    (a) Circle method
    (b) Equivalent pipe method
    (c) Hardy cross method
    (d) Electrical analysis method

15. The type of valve which is provided to control the flow of water in the distribution system at street corners and where the pipe lines intersect is
    (a) check valve (b) sluice valve
    (c) safety valve (d) scour valve

16. If the diameter of the main pipe is taken less than economic diameter, then

1. head loss will be high
2. cost of pipe will be less
3. cost of pumping will be less of these statements.

(*a*) only 1 is correct
(*b*) 1 and 2 are correct
(*c*) 1 and 3 are correct
(*d*) 1, 2 and 3 are correct

17. What is the primary purpose of the Basel Convention?

(*a*) Protecting wetlands
(*b*) Managing hazardous waste
(*c*) Regulating air quality
(*d*) Conserving marine biodiversity

18. Two samples of water A and B have pH values of 4.4 and 6.4 respectively. How many times more acidic sample A is than sample B ?

(*a*) 0 (*b*) 50
(*c*) 100 (*d*) 200

19. When the coefficient of rugosity is increased from 0.01 to 0.02, the gradient of a pipe of a given diameter to carry the same flow at the same velocity will be

(*a*) increased by 4 times
(*b*) increased by 2 times
(*c*) decreased by $\sqrt{2}$ times
(*d*) decreased by 4 times

20. A city supply of 1500 cubic metres of water per day is treated with a chlorine dosage of 0.5 ppm. For this purpose, the requirement of 25% bleaching powder per day would be

(*a*) 300 kg (*b*) 75 kg
(*c*) 30 kg (*d*) 7.5 kg

21. Figure given below shows roughly, the daily mass curves of supply to and demand from an elevated service reservoir (ESR).

The minimum required capacity of the reservoir is given by

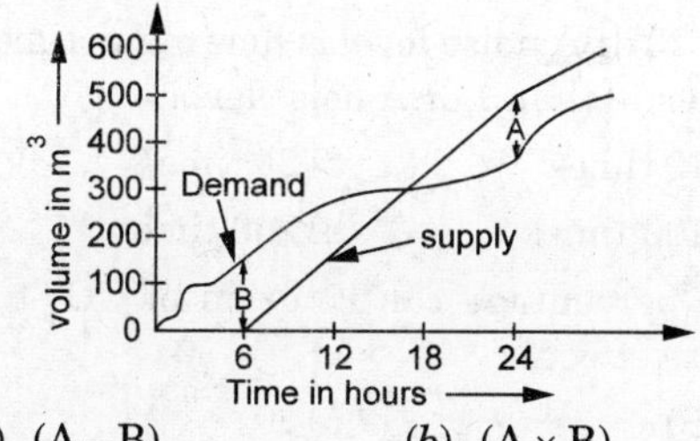

(*a*) (A – B) (*b*) (A × B)
(*c*) (A + B) (*d*) Larger of A or B

22. The water supply to a house begins with the connection of the service pipe with the municipal water mains. The connection comprises

1. Stop cock
2. Goose neck
3. Ferrule
4. Water meter

The correct sequence of these connections is

(*a*) 1, 2, 3, 4 (*b*) 3, 1, 2, 4
(*c*) 3, 2, 1, 4 (*d*) 1, 2, 4, 3

23. The chlorine demand of a water sample was found to be 0.2 mg/l. The amount of bleaching powder containing 30% available chlorine to be added to treat one litre of such a water sample is

(*a*) 0.67 mg (*b*) 0.06 mg
(*c*) 1.33 mg (*d*) 0.14 mg

24. When two identical centrifugal pumps are operating in series on a common rising main, then

(*a*) the pressure in the rising main will be nearly doubled, while the discharge will remain the same.
(*b*) the discharge will be nearly doubled, while the pressure remains the same.
(*c*) discharge as well as the pressure in the rising main will be doubled.
(*d*) discharge as well as the pressure in the rising main will increase but not become double.

25. An aeration basin with a volume of 400 m^3 contains mixed liquor with suspended solid concentration of 1000 mg/l. The amount of mixed liquor suspended solids in the tank is

(*a*) 500 kg (*b*) 250 kg
(*c*) 600 kg (*d*) 400 kg

26. Under natural conditions of flow an unpolluted river would contain

(*a*) more dissolved oxygen in summer than in winter
(*b*) less dissolved oxygen in summer than in winter
(*c*) more or less the same amount of dissolved oxygen in winter and summer.
(*d*) the least amount of dissolved oxygen during the floods.

27. Traps are used in household drainage system to

(*a*) prevent entry of foul gases in the house
(*b*) restrict the flow of water
(*c*) provide a partial vacuum
(*d*) trap the solid wastes

28. Two reservoirs at different levels are connected by two parallel pipes of diameter 2d and d. The ratio of the flows in the two pipes (large smaller) is

(*a*) $\sqrt{2}:1$ (*b*) 2 : 1

(*c*) 4 : 1 (*d*) $4\sqrt{2}:1$

29. Area method of land filling is most suitable when

(*a*) area is unsuitable for excavation of trenches.

(*b*) adequate depth of cover material is available at the site.

(*c*) the water table is near the surface

(*d*) natural or artificial depressions exist in the vicinity.

30. If the total hardness and alkalinity of a sample of water are 300 mg/l and 100 mg/l($CaCo_3$ scale) respectively, then its carbonate and non-carbonate hardness (in units of mg/l) will be respectively

(*a*) 100 and 200 (*b*) 400 and 300

(*c*) 100 and 400 (*d*) 400 and zero

31. What is carbon footprint?

(*a*) measure of radioactivity from a fossil

(*b*) environmental impact because of used cells and batteries

(*c*) total sets of green house gas emissions by organization, individual etc.

(*d*) amount of carbon content in the organic compounds

32. Thermochemical decomposition of organic materials at high temperatures, in the absence of oxygen is called

(*a*) Pyrolysis (*b*) Thermolysis

(*c*) Caramelization (*d*) Catagenesis

33. Acid rain is caused by presence of which of the following gases in the atmosphere

(*a*) Nitrogen and oxygen

(*b*) Sulfur dioxide and Nitrogen oxide

(*c*) Carbon dioxide and Carbon-mono-oxide

(*d*) Ozone and argon

34. One of the main reason for depletion of ozone layer in the Earth's atmosphere is

(*a*) Green house gases

(*b*) Colloidal impurities

(*c*) CFC and halons

(*d*) Rockets and satellite launching vehicles

35. What is the value of total hardness acceptable in potable water as per Indian Standards?

(*a*) 0.3 (*b*) 3

(*c*) 30 (*d*) 300

36. Preventing rain water to run-off and its accumulation and deposition for re-use on site is called

(*a*) rain water collection

(*b*) micro-dams

(*c*) micro-accumulation

(*d*) rain water harvesting

37. Which of the following is biodegradable pollutant?

(*a*) DDT (*b*) BHC

(*c*) Cotton cloth (*d*) Mercury

38. BOD (Bio Chemical Oxygen Demand) of safe drinking water must be :

(*a*) 0 (*b*) 50 ppm

(*c*) 100 ppm (*d*) 200 ppm

39. Large scale deforestation decreases :

(*a*) Soil Erosion (*b*) Rain fall

(*c*) Drought (*d*) Global warming

40. The prescribed per capita water demand for small cities and towns is

(*a*) 135 litres per capita per day

(*b*) 200 litres per capita per day

(*c*) 150 litres per capita per day

(*d*) 180 litres per capita per day

41. In small water supplies such as army troops, private plants and swimming pools, the most common disinfectants used are

(*a*) chlorine dioxide and potassium permanganate

(*b*) ozone and uv rays

(*c*) iodine and bromine

(*d*) chlorine and bromine

42. The air pollution control device, cyclone is used for the removal of

(*a*) 100 μm particles (*b*) 10 μm particles

(*c*) 50 μm particles (*d*) 2.5 μm particles

43. The 20 dBA noise level is how many times more powerful than 1 dBA noise level?

(*a*) 10 times (*b*) 20 times

(*c*) 100 times (*d*) 200 times

44. The percentage contribution of CO_2 to green house effect is

(*a*) 50 (*b*) 30

(*c*) 18 (*d*) 10

45. Per capita water demand is
(*a*) average amount of daily water required by one person
(*b*) monthly average amount of daily water required by one person
(*c*) annual average amount of daily water required by one person
(*d*) weekly average amount of daily water required by one person

46. The permissible/desirable drinking water standard for total hardness is
(*a*) 200 mg/l (*b*) 300 mg/l
(*c*) 250 mg/l (*d*) 500 mg/l

47. In BOD_5 determination of sewage, the initial dissolved oxygen is measured to be 8.3 mg/l. However, after 5 day incubation at 20 °C temperature, the dissolved oxygen is found to be 2.3 mg/l. If the dilution factor is 1:60, the BOD_5 of the sewage would be
(*a*) 360 mg/l
(*b*) 260 mg/l
(*c*) cannot be determined
(*d*) 6.0 mg/l

48. The suspended solids present in surface water can be determined by
(*a*) gravimetric test
(*b*) colourimetric test
(*c*) titrimetric test
(*d*) spectrophotometric test

49. Length to width ratio of rectangular sedimentation tank should be
(*a*) 3 : 4 (*b*) 3 : 1
(*c*) 4 : 1 (*d*) 1 : 5

50. In PERT analysis, event means
(*a*) Start or finish of a task
(*b*) Time taken for a task
(*c*) End of an activity
(*d*) Work involved in the project

51. In potable water, the dissolved oxygen is stipulated as-
(*a*) <6μg/l (*b*) >6μg/l
(*c*) <6mg/l (*d*) >6mg/l

52. In reference to Acid rain, what is correct statement
(*a*) The pH value is below 5.6
(*b*) It occurs due to presence of sulphuric acid or nitric acid in the atmosphere
(*c*) Maximum acid is due to strong Carbonic Acid
(*d*) Acid rain affects ecosystem

53. The working principle of turbidimeter is based on
(*a*) reflection of light (*b*) refraction of light
(*c*) scattering of light (*d*) adsorption of light

54. The major source of carcinogenic hydrocarbon, benzo (*a*) pyrene present in urban atmosphere is
(*a*) construction activities
(*b*) road traffic
(*c*) bursting of crackers
(*d*) domestic burning

55. The prescribed permissible noise level, Leq for commercial area at day time is
(*a*) 75 dBA (*b*) 50 dBA
(*c*) 55 dBA (*d*) 65 dBA

56. The global warming is caused by green house gases, which are
(*a*) CO, N_2O, CH_4 and CFC
(*b*) CO_2, NO_2, CH_4 and H_2O
(*c*) CO_2, N_2O, CH_4 and H_2O
(*d*) CO_2, NO_2, CH_4 and CFC

57. Which of the following roles fly ash does not play in concrete
(*a*) Improving the workability
(*b*) Accelerating the strength gain
(*c*) Delaying the setting time of concrete
(*d*) Helps in long-term strength gain

58. One turbidity unit NTU is equal to
(*a*) 1.0 mg/l farmazin (*b*) 1.0 meq/l SiO_2
(*c*) 1.0 mg/l SiO_2 (*d*) 1.0 meq/l kaolin

59. The prescribed permissible noise level, Leq for residential area at day time is
(*a*) 65 dBA (*b*) 45 dBA
(*c*) 50 dBA (*d*) 55 dBA

60. Which of the following is not used as a supplementary cementations material?
(*a*) Fly ash (*b*) Gypsum
(*c*) Rice husk ash (*d*) Silica fume

61. According to IS 456, if the maximum aggregate size is increased from 20 mm to 40 mm, the minimum cement content requirement changes (in kg/cum) by
(*a*) –20 (*b*) 20
(*c*) –30 (*d*) 30

62. The turbidity in surface water is due to presence of
(*a*) dissolved organics
(*b*) colloidal material
(*c*) dissolved in organics
(*d*) dissolved colors

63. The prescribed permissible noise level, for residential area at night time is

(*a*) 45 dBA (*b*) 50 dBA

(*c*) 40 dBA (*d*) 55 dBA

64. The continuous exposure of high concentration of reparable suspended particulate matter may cause

(*a*) eye irritation

(*b*) kidney damage

(*c*) failure of respiratory system

(*d*) cardiac disease

65. The prescribed permissible noise level, Leq for commercial area at night time is

(*a*) 45 dBA (*b*) 65 dBA

(*c*) 50 dBA (*d*) 55 dBA

66. The pH of acid rain should always be less than

(*a*) 5.6 even after precipitation

(*b*) 7.0 after precipitation

(*c*) 6.5 after precipitation

(*d*) 4.2 after precipitation

67. The exposure of gaseous pollutant sulphur dioxide may cause

(*a*) bronchitis and pulmonary emphysema

(*b*) lungs failure and kidney damage

(*c*) gastrointestinal problem

(*d*) the irritation in alveoli of the lungs

68. The machine 'A' and machine 'B' produce equal noise levels, i.e., 60 dBA each. The summation of these two noise levels is

(*a*) 100 dBA (*b*) 66 dBA

(*c*) 63 dBA (*d*) 55 dBA

69. In stratosphere, the temperature increases with altitude due to presence of

(*a*) radicals (*b*) chlorofluorocarbons

(*c*) HCFCs (*d*) Ozone

70. Nuclear density guage can be used for all the following purposes, except

(*a*) Moisture content

(*b*) Wet density

(*c*) Dry density

(*d*) Standard penetration reading

71. What is the main goal of environmental education?

(*a*) To teach people about the environment.

(*b*) To help people protect the environment.

(*c*) To make people aware of the benefits of environmental protection.

(*d*) All of the above.

72. What are the three main components of environmental education?

(*a*) Knowledge, skills, and attitudes.

(*b*) Science, technology, and engineering.

(*c*) Economics, politics, and social justice.

(*d*) All of the above.

73. What are some examples of environmental education activities?

(*a*) Reading books about the environment.

(*b*) Visiting a nature center or museum.

(*c*) Participating in a community clean-up project.

(*d*) All of the above.

74. What are some of the benefits of environmental education?

(*a*) It can help people make informed decisions about their environmental impact.

(*b*) It can help people develop a sense of stewardship for the environment.

(*c*) It can help people build a stronger connection to nature.

(*d*) All of the above.

75. What is the role of environmental education in sustainability?

(*a*) It can help people understand the limits of the planet's resources.

(*b*) It can help people develop ways to live more sustainably.

(*c*) It can help people create a more sustainable future.

(*d*) All of the above.

76. Which of the following is NOT a goal of environmental education?

(*a*) To increase environmental awareness

(*b*) To teach people about environmental problems

(*c*) To promote sustainable lifestyles

(*d*) To make money

77. Which of the following is one of the three main components of environmental education?

(*a*) Knowledge (*b*) Skills

(*c*) Attitudes (*d*) All of the above

78. What is one of the most important things that environmental education can teach us?

(*a*) That we are all connected to the environment

(*b*) That our actions have a ripple effect on the planet

(*c*) That we need to take responsibility for our environmental impact

(*d*) All of the above

79. What is one way that environmental education can be used to promote sustainability?

(*a*) By teaching people about the importance of recycling and composting

(*b*) By encouraging people to conserve water and energy

(*c*) By promoting the use of public transportation

(*d*) All of the above

80. How can we make environmental education more accessible to everyone?

(*a*) By making it more affordable

(*b*) By making it more inclusive

(*c*) By making it more engaging

(*d*) All of the above

81. What is one of the most important challenges facing environmental education?

(*a*) Reaching a wide audience

(*b*) Making it effective

(*c*) Measuring its impact

(*d*) All of the above

82. What is one way that we can make environmental education more effective?

(*a*) By using real-world examples

(*b*) By making it hands-on

(*c*) By making it relevant to students' lives

(*d*) All of the above

83. How can we measure the impact of environmental education?

(*a*) By tracking students' knowledge and understanding of the environment

(*b*) By assessing students' attitudes towards the environment

(*c*) By measuring students' behavior towards the environment

(*d*) All of the above

84. What is one way that we can make environmental education more inclusive?

(*a*) By using culturally relevant materials

(*b*) By providing translations in multiple languages

(*c*) By making it accessible to people with disabilities

(*d*) All of the above

85. What is one way that we can make environmental education more engaging?

(*a*) By using games and activities

(*b*) By using technology

(*c*) By taking students on field trips

(*d*) All of the above

86. What is the primary goal of environmental education?

(*a*) To instill fear about environmental problems

(*b*) To teach people how to live in harmony with nature

(*c*) To provide scientific knowledge about the environment

(*d*) To promote specific environmental solutions

87. Which of the following is NOT a key component of environmental education?

(*a*) Awareness and sensitivity to the environment

(*b*) Knowledge and understanding of environmental issues

(*c*) Skills to identify and solve environmental problems

(*d*) Emotional detachment from the environment

88. What is the role of environmental education in promoting sustainable development?

(*a*) It provides scientific data for decision-making.

(*b*) It raises awareness about environmental consequences.

(*c*) It empowers individuals to make sustainable choices.

(*d*) It dictates specific environmental policies.

89. How can environmental education be made more effective in addressing environmental challenges?

(*a*) By focusing on academic knowledge and memorization

(*b*) By emphasizing hands-on experiences and real-world applications

(*c*) By adopting a one-size-fits-all approach

(*d*) By tailoring education to specific contexts and communities

90. What is the importance of incorporating cultural perspectives into environmental education?

(*a*) It promotes a universal understanding of environmental issues.

(*b*) It recognizes the diverse relationships between cultures and the environment.

(*c*) It establishes a single set of environmental values and practices.

(*d*) It prioritizes Western scientific knowledge over traditional ecological knowledge.

91. How can environmental education promote environmental justice?

(*a*) By focusing on individual actions and behaviors

(*b*) By addressing the disproportionate impact of environmental issues on marginalized communities

(c) By promoting economic development at the expense of environmental protection

(d) By blaming individuals for environmental problems without addressing systemic issues

92. What is the role of environmental education in promoting sustainable consumption patterns?

(a) It encourages the consumption of more goods and services.

(b) It promotes responsible consumer choices and reduces environmental impact.

(c) It emphasizes the need for economic growth over environmental protection.

(d) It prioritizes the production of environmentally harmful goods.

93. How can environmental education foster a sense of stewardship for the environment?

(a) By instilling fear and guilt about environmental problems

(b) By promoting a sense of responsibility and connection to nature

(c) By imposing strict regulations and restrictions

(d) By emphasizing individual consumer choices without addressing broader systemic issues

94. What is the primary objective of environmental engineering?

(a) Resource extraction

(b) Pollution prevention

(c) Energy production

(d) Urban planning

95. Which of the following is a greenhouse gas?

(a) Oxygen (O2) (b) Carbon dioxide (CO2)

(c) Nitrogen (N2) (d) Hydrogen (H2)

96. What is the purpose of a wastewater treatment plant?

(a) Energy production

(b) Water conservation

(c) Treating and purifying sewage

(d) Agricultural irrigation

97. What is the primary function of a landfill?

(a) Water storage (b) Waste disposal

(c) Air purification (d) Energy generation

98. Which air pollutant is a major contributor to acid rain?

(a) Carbon monoxide (CO)

(b) Sulfur dioxide (SO2)

(c) Nitrogen oxides (NOx)

(d) Particulate matter (PM)

99. What is the purpose of an environmental impact assessment (EIA)?

(a) Identifying endangered species

(b) Assessing the potential environmental effects of a project

(c) Monitoring air quality

(d) Analyzing geological formations

100. Which of the following is a renewable energy source?

(a) Coal (b) Natural gas

(c) Solar power (d) Nuclear energy

101. What is the primary purpose of the Clean Water Act?

(a) Regulating air quality

(b) Protecting water resources

(c) Controlling noise pollution

(d) Managing hazardous waste

102. Which of the following is a characteristic of sustainable development?

(a) Depleting natural resources

(b) Meeting current needs without compromising future generations

(c) Maximizing short-term profits

(d) Ignoring social equity

103. What is the primary role of wetlands in environmental engineering?

(a) Waste disposal (b) Flood control

(c) Habitat for wildlife (d) Industrial production

104. What is the main source of indoor air pollution in homes?

(a) Radon

(b) Carbon monoxide

(c) Volatile organic compounds (VOCs)

(d) Mold

105. Which of the following is a non-point source of water pollution?

(a) Industrial discharge pipe

(b) Wastewater treatment plant

(c) Urban stormwater runoff

(d) Sewage outfall

106. What is the purpose of a septic system?

(a) Electricity generation

(b) Solid waste disposal

(c) Wastewater treatment for individual homes

(d) Flood control

107. Which process is commonly used for groundwater remediation?

(a) Incineration (b) Bioremediation

(c) Desalination (d) Composting

108. What is the primary purpose of the Montreal Protocol?

(*a*) Banning nuclear weapons testing

(*b*) Protecting the ozone layer

(*c*) Regulating greenhouse gas emissions

(*d*) Managing marine pollution

109. What is the primary goal of the Kyoto Protocol?

(*a*) Reducing carbon dioxide emissions

(*b*) Protecting biodiversity

(*c*) Addressing deforestation

(*d*) Controlling marine pollution

110. Which air pollutant is associated with respiratory problems and asthma?

(*a*) Carbon dioxide (CO2)

(*b*) Ozone (O3)

(*c*) Nitrogen dioxide (NO2)

(*d*) Methane (CH4)

111. What is the primary function of a bioswale in stormwater management?

(*a*) Electricity generation

(*b*) Flood control

(*c*) Treating wastewater

(*d*) Filtering and slowing stormwater runoff

112. Which of the following is a sustainable transportation option?

(*a*) Single-occupancy vehicles

(*b*) Electric scooters

(*c*) Diesel-powered buses

(*d*) Large SUVs

Answers

1. (*a*)	**2.** (*d*)	**3.** (*a*)	**4.** (*d*)	**5.** (*b*)	**6.** (*d*)	**7.** (*a*)	**8.** (*b*)	**9.** (*a*)	**10.** (*a*)
11. (*d*)	**12.** (*c*)	**13.** (*a*)	**14.** (*b*)	**15.** (*b*)	**16.** (*b*)	**17.** (*b*)	**18.** (*c*)	**19.** (*a*)	**20.** (*c*)
21. (*b*)	**22.** (*c*)	**23.** (*a*)	**24.** (*a*)	**25.** (*d*)	**26.** (*b*)	**27.** (*a*)	**28.** (*d*)	**29.** (*c*)	**30.** (*d*)
31. (*c*)	**32.** (*a*)	**33.** (*b*)	**34.** (*c*)	**35.** (*d*)	**36.** (*d*)	**37.** (*c*)	**38.** (*a*)	**39.** (*b*)	**40.** (*a*)
41. (*c*)	**42.** (*b*)	**43.** (*c*)	**44.** (*a*)	**45.** (*c*)	**46.** (*b*)	**47.** (*c*)	**48.** (*a*)	**49.** (*b*)	**50.** (*a*)
51. (*a*)	**52.** (*b*)	**53.** (*c*)	**54.** (*b*)	**55.** (*d*)	**56.** (*c*)	**57.** (*b*)	**58.** (*c*)	**59.** (*d*)	**60.** (*b*)
61. (*c*)	**62.** (*b*)	**63.** (*a*)	**64.** (*c*)	**65.** (*d*)	**66.** (*a*)	**67.** (*a*)	**68.** (*c*)	**69.** (*d*)	**70.** (*d*)
71. (*d*)	**72.** (*a*)	**73.** (*d*)	**74.** (*d*)	**75.** (*d*)	**76.** (*d*)	**77.** (*d*)	**78.** (*d*)	**79.** (*d*)	**80.** (*d*)
81. (*d*)	**82.** (*d*)	**83.** (*d*)	**84.** (*d*)	**85.** (*d*)	**86.** (*b*)	**87.** (*d*)	**88.** (*c*)	**89.** (*b*)	**90.** (*b*)
91. (*b*)	**92.** (*b*)	**93.** (*b*)	**94.** (*b*)	**95.** (*b*)	**96.** (*c*)	**97.** (*b*)	**98.** (*b*)	**99.** (*b*)	**100.** (*c*)
101. (*b*)	**102.** (*b*)	**103.** (*c*)	**104.** (*c*)	**105.** (*c*)	**106.** (*c*)	**107.** (*b*)	**108.** (*b*)	**109.** (*a*)	**110.** (*c*)
111. (*d*)	**112.** (*b*)								

Explanations

1. 1 mg m of bleaching powder contains – 0.3 mgm of chlorine

1 mg m of chlorine will be = $\frac{1}{0.3}$ mgm of bleaching

$\therefore$ 0.5 mg m of chlorine will be = $\frac{1}{0.3} \times [0.5] = \mathbf{1.667}$

2. Chlorine dosage = $\left[\frac{20\times10^6}{6000}\right]\frac{mgm}{\text{lit}}$

= **3.33 mg m/lit**

3. Chlorine required= $16000 \times 10^3 \times 0.6 = 9.6$ kg

$\therefore$ Amount of bleaching powder required

$= \left[\frac{9.6}{0.3}\right] = \mathbf{32\ kg}$

4. The maximum daily consumption on peak hourly day or maximum day

= 2.7 × (Average demand)

= 2.7 × 100,000

= **2.70,000 m^3**

5. It contains undesirable substance and unfit for domestic use.

6. Average of percentage increase in previous year = $\frac{40+20}{2}$ = 30%

Population next year = $8400 + \frac{30}{100} \times 8400 = \mathbf{10920}$

7. The carbonate hardness is equal to total hardness if total hardness is equal to or less than total alkalinity.

The non carbonate harness = Total hardness – total alkanity.

8. Minimum required for aquatic life is 4 ppm

10. Hardness of water removed by zeolite process ; while bicarbonate hardness can be removed by boiling.

11. *Methods by which chlorination may be done :*

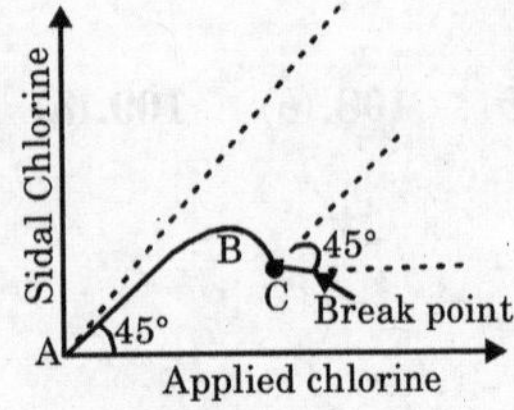

(*a*) Plain chlorination (*b*) Prechlorination
(*c*) Post chlorination (*d*) Double chlorination
(*e*) Break point chlorination
(*f*) Super chlorination (*g*) Dechlorination

12. It works on high pressure with pressure slightly above rapid sand filters.

13. In slow sand filters, rate of filtration is very slow and one of the major reason being its minute size. For rapid sand filters, the effective size of sand particles used is 0.35 to 0.60 mm.

14. In equivalent pipe system, first of all different small loops are replaced by single equivalent pipes having the same discharging capacities and causing the same head loss.

15. Sluice valves are usually placed at corners summits (3 – 5 km) interval.

16. If diameter is less than economic diameter, then cost of pipe will be less but head loss will be high. Hence cost of pumping will be more.

17. The Basel Convention aims to control the transboundary movement and disposal of hazardous waste.

18. Difference of pH = 6.4 – 4.4 = 2

Quantum of acidity = $(10)^2$ = 100 times more acidic

19. Velocity $\propto$ [R^2]

i.e. increased by 4 times.

20. Amount of chlorine required daily

$= \left[\frac{0.5 \times 15000 \times 10^3}{10^6}\right] = 7.5$ kg

Amount of bleaching powder required daily

$= \frac{7.5 \times 100}{25} = \mathbf{30\ kg}$

22.

Domestic water meter
Stop lock
Ferrule connection
goosenech
Water Supply
wiped joint

26. Dissolved oxygen in an unpolluted river will be equal to saturation D.O. which reduces with increase in temperature. Since temperature is more in summer than winter, an unpolluted river would contain less D.O. in summer than in winter.

31. A carbon footprint is historically defined as the total emissions caused by an individual, event, organisation, or product, expressed as carbon dioxide equivalent.

32. Pyrolysis is the thermal decomposition of materials at elevated temperatures in an inert atmosphere. It involves the change of chemical composition and is irreversible. The word is coined from the Greek-derived elements pyro "fire" and lysis "separating".

33. Sox and NOx are responsible for acid rain.

34. Chlorofluorocarbons (CFCs) and other halogenated **ozone depleting** substances (ODS) are mainly responsible for man-made chemical **ozone depletion**. The total amount of effective halogens (chlorine and bromine) in the stratosphere can be calculated and are known as the equivalent effective stratospheric chlorine (EESC).

35. 300 mg/l is the acceptable standard.

36. **Rainwater** harvesting is **the accumulation** and storage of **rainwater** for **reuse** on-**site**, rather than allowing it to **run off**.

37. Biodegradable pollutants: Those pollutants which can be broken down into simpler, harmless, substances in nature in due course of time (by the action of micro-organisms like certain bacteria) are called biodegradable pollutants. Cotton cloth is biodegradable pollutant.

38. A **water** supply with a **BOD** level of 1-2 ppm is considered to be very clean.

A **water** supply with a **BOD** level of 3-5 ppm is considered moderately **clean**. In **water** with a **BOD** level of 6-9 ppm, the **water** is considered somewhat polluted because there is usually organic matter present and bacteria are decomposing this waste.

39. Large scale deforestation decreases rain fall. **Drop in rainfall** occurs because **deforestation reduces** the natural recycling of moisture from soils, through vegetation, and into the atmosphere, from where it returns as□**rainfall**.

40. The prescribed per capita water demand for small cities and towns is 135 litres per capita per day.

41. The most common disinfectants are iodine and bromine. **Bromine** does not oxidize ammonia or other nitrogen substances. Hypobromous acid reacts with sunlight. When the pH value is between 7 and 8,5 dibromoamine is **the most common** form of **bromine**. Dibromoamine is almost as effective as free chlorine in killing microorganisms.

42. The most frequently used **Air Pollution Control Devices** for controlling **air pollution** emissions are Fabric filters (also called bag houses), **Cyclones** (or Multi **cyclones**), Wet scrubbers, Electrostatic Precipitator. Cyclone removes 10 mm particles.

43. On the **decibel** scale, the smallest audible **sound** (near total silence) is 1 dB. **Asound** 10 **times more powerful** is 10 dB. A **sound** 100 **times more powerful than** near total silence is **20** dB. A **sound** 1,000 **times more powerful than** near total silence is 30 dB.

44. They estimated that water vapor accounts for about 50% of Earth's greenhouse effect, with clouds contributing 25%, carbon dioxide 20%, and the minor greenhouse gases and aerosols accounting for the remaining 5%. In the study, the reference **model** atmosphere is for 1980 conditions.

45. Generally, it **means** the average amount of **water** each person in a particular area uses on a daily basis, expressed as "gallons **per capita per** day."

46. 300 mg/l is the permissible limit of the hardness.

47. Cannot be determined.

48. **Gravimetric analysis** is a technique through which the amount of an analyte (the ion being analyzed) can be determined through the measurement of mass.**Gravimetric** analyses depend on comparing the masses of two compounds containing the analyte.

49. A typical long **rectangular** tank have **length** ranging from 2 to 4 times their **width**.

50. *PERT event*: a point that marks the start or completion of one or more activities. It consumes no time and uses no resources. When it marks the completion of one or more activities, it is not "reached" (does not occur) until *all* of the activities leading to that event have been completed.

51. <6μg/l

52. pH value is generally less than 4 and it occurs due to presence of sulphuric and nitric acid.

53. The Turbidity meter uses the principle of Nephelometry. As light of a known intensity is passed through a sample some of the light will be scattered by particles in the sample. A detector is placed at 90° to the sample to collect the scattered light. The intensity of the scattered light is compared to that of the source. This value is reported as a Nephelometric Turbidity Unit, or NTU. The meter is calibrated with Formazine standards of a known NTU.

54. Road traffic is the major source of carcinogenic hydrocarbon present in urban atmosphere.

55. The prescribed permissible noise level, Leq for commercial area at day time is 65 dBA.

According to Central Pollution Control Board,

Area Code	Category of Area	Limits in dB(A), Leq	
		Day time	Night time
A	Industrial area	75	70
B	Commercial area	65	55
C	Residential area	55	45
D	Silence Zone	50	40

56. Green house gases are the gas mixed in the atmosphere that absorbs the infrared radiation emitted by the earth's surface.

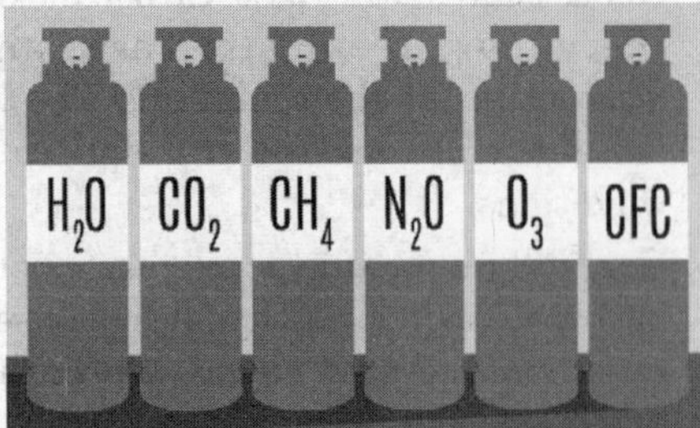

We are not accustomed to these gases because neither nitrogen nor oxygen, the two most abundant gases of the atmosphere (78% and 21%, respectively), that many of us have heard of, have this ability to intercept infrared radiation.

57. Fly ash never improves strength of concrete. The advantages of using fly ash far outweigh the disadvantages. The most important benefit is reduced permeability to water and aggressive chemicals. Properly cured concrete made with fly ash creates a denser product because the size of the pores are reduced.

58. One turbidity unit NTU is equal to 1.0 mg/l SiO2.

59. The prescribed permissible noise level, Leq is 55 dBA.

According to Central Pollution Control Board,

Area Code	Category of Area	Limits in dB(A),	
		Day	Night
A	Industrial area	75	70
B	Commercial area	65	55
C	Residential area	55	45
D	Silence Zone	50	40

60. Gypsum is not used as a supplementary cementations material.

61. Turbidity in surface water is due to colloidal material.

63. The prescribed permissible noise level, Leq is 45 dBA.

According to Central Pollution Control Board,

Area Code	Category of Area	Limits in dB(A), Leq	
		Day time	Night time
A	Industrial area	75	70
B	Commercial area	65	55
C	Residential area	55	45
D	Silence Zone	50	40

64. Continuous exposure to suspended particles are harmful to the lungs and can cause failure of respiratory system.

65. The prescribed permissible noise level, Leq for commercial area at night time is 55 dBA.

According to Central Pollution Control Board,

Area Code	Category of Area	Limits in dB(A), Leq	
		Day time	Night time
A	Industrial area	75	70
B	Commercial area	65	55
C	Residential area	55	45
D	Silence Zone	50	40

66. pH of acid rain should always be less than 5.6 even after precipitation.

67. The exposure of gaseous pollutant sulphur dioxide may cause bronchitis and pulmonary emphysema.

69. In the stratosphere, temperature increases with altitude. The reason is that the direct heat source for the stratosphere is the Sun. A layer of ozone molecules absorbs solar radiation, which heats the stratosphere. The amount of ozone present in the ozone layer is tiny, only a few molecules per million air molecules.

70. Nuclear density gauge can be used for all the following purposes except standard penetration reading.

71. The main goal of environmental education is to help people understand and appreciate the environment, and to take action to protect it.

72. Environmental education should provide people with the knowledge they need to understand the environment, the skills they need to take action to protect it, and the attitudes they need to support environmental protection.

73. There are many different ways to learn about the environment. Environmental education activities can be formal or informal, and they can take place at home, in school, or in the community.

74. Environmental education can have a positive impact on individuals, communities, and the planet.

75. Environmental education is essential for achieving sustainability. It can help people understand the challenges we face, and it can help us find solutions to those challenges.

76. Environmental education is not a business venture. Its primary goal is to educate people about the environment and to promote sustainable practices.

77. Environmental education should provide people with the knowledge they need to understand the environment, the skills they need to take action to protect it, and the attitudes they need to support environmental protection.

78. Environmental education can teach us many important things about the environment and our relationship to it. By understanding the interconnectedness of all living things, we can learn to make more sustainable choices that will benefit the planet.

79. Environmental education can play a vital role in promoting sustainability by teaching people about the importance of environmental protection and by providing them with the tools they need to make sustainable choices.

80. Environmental education should be accessible to everyone, regardless of their age, background, or income level. By making it more affordable, inclusive, and engaging, we can ensure that everyone has the opportunity to learn about the environment and to make a positive impact on the planet.

81. Environmental education faces a number of challenges, including reaching a wide audience, making it effective, and measuring its impact. However, these challenges can be overcome with careful planning and implementation.

82. Environmental education is most effective when it is relevant to students' lives and when it provides them with opportunities to learn through experience.

83. The impact of environmental education can be measured in a number of ways, including tracking students' knowledge, attitudes, and behavior.

84. Environmental education should be inclusive and accessible to everyone, regardless of their background or ability.

85. Environmental education can be made more engaging by using a variety of teaching methods and techniques. By making it fun and interactive, we can encourage students.

86. Environmental education aims to foster a deeper understanding of the environment and our relationship to it, encouraging individuals to make informed decisions and adopt sustainable practices to protect and conserve natural resources.

87. While environmental education provides knowledge and skills, it also seeks to cultivate a sense of empathy and connection to the natural world, motivating individuals to take action and advocate for environmental protection.

88. Environmental education plays a crucial role in sustainable development by equipping individuals with the knowledge, skills, and values to make informed decisions that minimize their environmental impact and contribute to a more sustainable future.

89. Effective environmental education goes beyond classroom lectures and rote learning. It provides opportunities for students to engage with the environment through field trips, experiments, and community projects, fostering a deeper understanding and appreciation for the natural world.

90. Environmental education should be inclusive and culturally sensitive, acknowledging the unique perspectives, knowledge, and practices that different cultures have developed in their interactions with the natural world.

91. Environmental education should recognize and address the unequal distribution of environmental burdens, empowering communities to advocate for environmental justice and equitable access to a healthy environment.

92. Environmental education empowers individuals to make informed decisions about their consumption habits, encouraging them to reduce waste, choose sustainable products, and adopt eco-friendly practices.

93. Environmental education cultivates a sense of stewardship by fostering understanding, empathy, and appreciation for the natural world, encouraging individuals to take proactive steps to protect and conserve the environment for future generations.

94. Environmental engineering focuses on preventing and controlling pollution to protect the environment and human health.

95. CO2 is a significant greenhouse gas contributing to climate change.

96. Wastewater treatment plants remove contaminants from sewage before releasing it into the environment.

97. Landfills are designated areas for the disposal of solid waste.

98. SO2 emissions can lead to the formation of acid rain.

99. EIAs help identify and mitigate potential environmental impacts of development projects.

100. Solar power is derived from the sun and is considered a renewable energy source.

101. The Clean Water Act is aimed at regulating and protecting water quality in the United States.

102. Sustainable development seeks to balance economic, social, and environmental goals.

103. Wetlands play a crucial role in supporting biodiversity and providing habitat for various species.

104. VOCs released from household products can contribute to indoor air pollution.

105. Non-point sources are diffuse and arise from various sources, such as runoff from streets and agricultural fields.

106. Septic systems treat and dispose of household wastewater on-site.

107. Bioremediation involves using microorganisms to break down and remove contaminants from the environment.

108. The Montreal Protocol aims to phase out the production and consumption of ozone-depleting substances.

109. The Kyoto Protocol is an international treaty focused on mitigating climate change by reducing greenhouse gas emissions.

110. NO2 is a common air pollutant that can irritate the respiratory system.

111. Bioswales are designed to capture and treat stormwater, promoting infiltration and reducing runoff.

112. Electric scooters are a more sustainable transportation option compared to traditional gasoline-powered vehicles.

Basics of Computers and Applications

PERSONAL COMPUTERS

Personal computers can be categorized by size and portability as :

1. Desktop computers
2. Laptop or notebooks
3. Personal Digital Assistants (PDAs)
4. Portable computers
5. Tablet computers
6. Wearable computers

Uses.

Personal computers are normally operated by one user at a time to perform such general purpose tasks as word processing, Internet browsing, Internet faxing, e-mail and other digital messaging , multimedia playback, computer game play, computer programming, etc. The user of modern personal computer may have significant knowledge of the operating environment and application programs, but is not necessarily interested in programming not even able to write programs for the computer. Therefore, most software written primarily for personal computers tends to be designed with simplicity of use, or "user-friendliness" in mind. However, the software industry continuously provide a wide range of new products for use in personal computers, targeted at both the expert and the non-expert user.

COMPUTER COMPONENTS

1. Computer case with power supply (usually sold together)
2. Motherboard
3. Processor with fan (usually sold together)
4. At least one memory card
5. Mass storage
6. Keyboard and mouse for input
7. Monitor for output

The motherboard connects everthing together. The memory card(s), graphics card and processor are mounted directly onto the motherboard (the processor in a socket an the memory and graphics cards in an expansion slot). The mass storage is connected to it with cables. Same for keyboard and mouse, except that they are external and connect to the back plate. The monitor is also connected to the back plate, except not (usually) directly to the motherboard, but to a connector in the graphics card.

Mass storage.

It can be

(*i*) Hard disk

(*ii*) Floppy drive or zip drive (both with media)

(*iii*) Optical drive (CD or DVD)

The operating system (e.g., Microsoft Windows, Linux or many others) can be located on either of these, but typically it son one of the hard disks. Alive CD is also possible, but very slow and used for either installation of the OS or problem solving.

A *typical* computer also has

(*i*) Sound card (*ii*) Network card

(*iii*) Modern and possibly router

Common additions, connected on the outside (peripherals).

Printer; Scanner; Webcam; Speakers; Microphone; Headset; Card reader; Gaming devices such as a joystick Several functions (implemented by chipsets) can be integrated into the motherboard, such as typically USB and network, but also graphics and sound. But even if these are present, a separate card can be added if what is available isn't sufficient.

The graphics and sound card can have a break out box to keep the analog parts away from the electromagnetic radiation inside the computer case. For really large amounts of data, a tape drive can be used or (extra) hard disks can be put together in an external case.

These components can usually be put together with little knowledge, to build a computer. If something shouldn't go somewhere, it usually doesn't fit (this used to not always be the case in the past) and if it does fit it can usually do little harm.

Most personal computers are standardized to the point that purchased software is expected to run with little or no customization for the particular computer. Many PCs are also user-upgradeable, especially desktop and workstation class computers. Devices such as main memory, mass storage, even the motherboard and central processing unit may be easily replaced by an end user. This upgradeability is, however, not idefinite due to rapid changes in the personal computer industry, A PC that was considered top-of-the-line five or six years prior may be impractical to upgrade due to changes in industry standards. Such a computer usually must be totally replaced once it's no longer suitable for its purpose. This upgrade and replacement cycle is partially related to new releases of the primary mass-market operated system, which tends to drive the acquisition of new hardware and tends of obsolete previously serviceable hardware (see planned obsolescence).

The hardware capabilities of personal computers can sometimes be extended by the addition of expansion cards connected via an expansion bus. Some standard peripheral buses often used for adding expansion cards in personal computers as of 2005 are PCI, AGP (a high-speed PCI bus dedicated to graphics adapters), and PCI Express. Most personal computers as of 2005 have multiple physical PCI expansion slots. Many also include an AGP bus and expansion slot or a PCI Express bus and one or more explansion slots, but few PCs contain both buses.

Motherboard

The motherboard (or mainboard) is the primary circuit board within a personal computer. Many other components connect directly or indirectly to the motherboard. Motherboards usually contain one or more CPUs, supporting circuitry - usually integrated circuits (ICs) providing the interface between the CPU memory and input/output peripheral circuits, main memory, and facilities for initial setup of the computer immediately after being powered on (often called boot firmware or, in IBM PC compatible computers, a BIOS). In many portable and embedded personal computers, the motherboard houses nearly all of the PC's core components. Often a motherboard will also contain one or more peripheral buses and physical connectors for expansion purposes. Sometimes a secondary daughter board is connected with the motherboard to provide further expandibility or to satisfy space constraints.

Main Memory

A PC's main memory (i.e., its primary store) is fast storage that is directly accessible by the CPU, and is used to store the currently executing program and immidiately needed data. PCs use semiconductor Random Access Memory (RAM) of various kinds such as DRAM or SRAM as their primary storage. Which exact kind depends on cost/performance issues at any particular time. Main memory is much faster than mass storage devices like hard disks or optical discs, but is usually volatile, meaning it does not retain its contents (instructions or data) in the absence of power, and is much more expensive for a given capacity than is most mass storage. Main memory is generally not suitable for long-term or archival data storage.

Mass storage devices store programs and data even when the power is off; they do require power to perform read/write functions during usage. Although semiconductor flash memory has dropped in cost, the prevailing form of mass storage in personal computers is still the electromechanical hard disk.

The disk drives use a sealed Head/Disk Assembly (HDA) which was first introduced by IBM's "Winchester" disk system. The use of a sealed assembly allowed the use of the positive air pressure to drive out particles from the surface of the disk, which improves reliability.

Video Card

The video card- otherwise called a graphics card, graphics adapter or video adapter - processors and renders the graphics output from the computer to the computer display, also called the Visual Display Unit (VDU), and is an essential part of the modern computer.

MICROPROCESSOR

A microprocessor is a multipurpose programmable logic device that reads binary instructions from a storage device called memory, accepts binary data as input and process data according to those instructions and provides results as output. A typical programmable machine can be represent with three components : microprocessor, memory, and I/O.

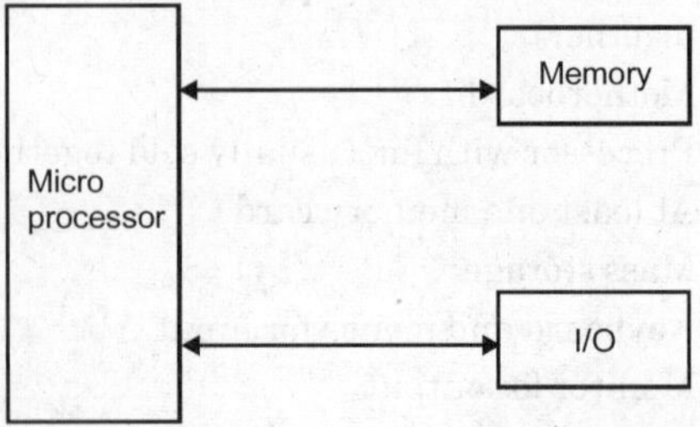

These three components work together or interact with each other to perform a given task, thus they comprise a system

Hardware

The physical components of this system are called hardware.

Software

A set of instructions written for the microprocessor to perform a task is called *a program* and a group of programs is called software.

APPLICATIONS.

The microprocessor applications are classified primarily in two categories

(*i*) In Re-programmable systems.

Such as microcomputers, the microprocessor is used for computing and data processing. These systems, include general purpose microprocessor capable of handling large data. Mass storage device (disks), and peripherals such as I/O device (printer).

(*ii*) Embedded system.

In embedded systems, the microprocessor is part of a final product and is not available for reprogrammable to the end user. A copying machine is a typical example of an embedded system. The microprocessors used in these systems are generally categorised as

(*a*) Microcontrollers that include all the components like microprocessor, memory and I/O.

(*b*) Integrated microprocessor that include various devices such as timers and various types of I/O on a chip.

(*c*) General purpose microprocessor with discrete components such as microprocessor, memory and I/O.

Embedded systems can also be increased as products that use microprocessor to perform their operations they are called as microprocessor based products.

e.g. washing machines, dish washers, automobile dashboard controls, traffic light controllers, and automatic testing instruments.

BINARY DIGIT.

The microprocessor operates in binary digits 0 and 1, also known as bits. Bit is an abbreviation for the term binary digit. Those digits are represented in terms of electrical voltages in the machine : generally 0 represents one voltage level and 1 represents another. The digits 0 and 1 are also synonyms with low and high respectively.

Each microprocessor recognizes and processes a group of bits called the word and microprocessor are classified according to their word length.

Memory

Memory is like the pages of a notebook with space for a fixed number of binary numbers on each line. However these pages are generally made of semi-conductor material. Each line in 8 bit register that can store 8 bit binary bits, and several of these registers are arranged in a sequence called memory.

Input/Output

The user can enter instructions and data into memory through devices such as keyboard or simple switches. These devices are called input devices.

The microprocessor reads instructions from the memory and processes the data according to those instructions. The result can be displayed by a device such as seven segment LED (light emitting diodes) or printed by a printer. These devices are called output devices.

MICROPROCESSOR AS A CPU

The central processing unit (CPU) consists of the Arithmetic Logic Unit (ALU) and Control Unit (CU). The CPU contains various registers to store data, ALU to perform Arithmetic and logical, operations, instruction decoders, counters and control lines. The CPU reads instructions from the memory and perform the tasks specified. It communicates with input/output devices either to accept or to send data. These devices are also known as peripherals. The CPU is the primary and central player in communicating with devices such as memory, input and output. However, the timing of the communication process is controlled by the group of circuit called control unit. CPU on single chip called microprocessor.

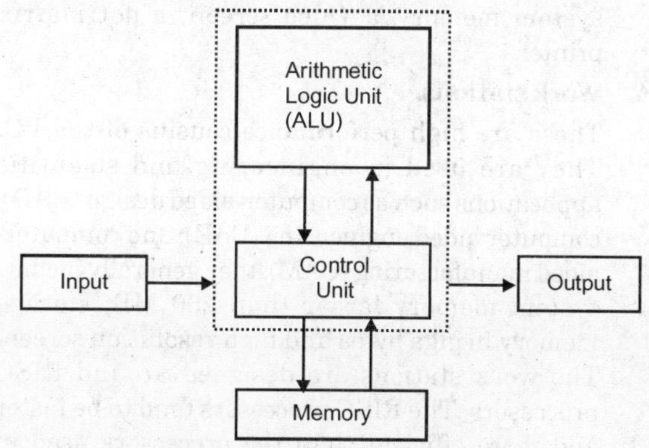

Fig. (a) Traditional block diagram of

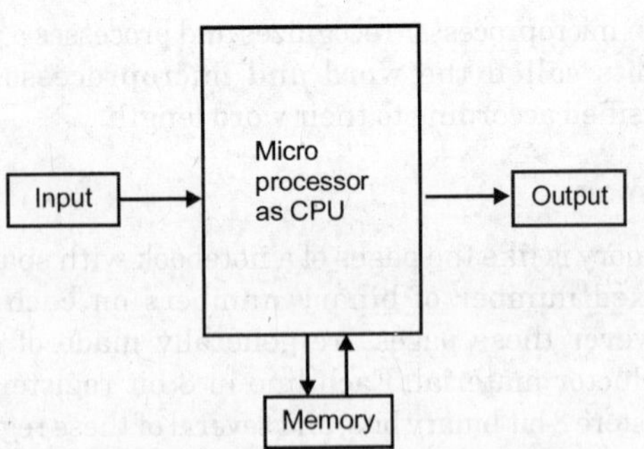

Fig. (b) Block diagram of a computer with the a computer microprocessor as CPU

1. **bit microprocessor.**
   The Intel 4004 was the first 4 bit programmable device that was primarily used in calculators.
2. **bit microprocessor.**
   The intel 8008 is 8 bit microprocessor, which was in turn superseded by the Intel 8080. Intel 8080 widely used in control applications, and small computers also were designed using the 8080 as the CPU. Within a few years after the emergence of the 8080, the Motorola 6800 and Zilog Z80 and Intel 8085 microprocessor were developed as improvements
3. **16 bit microprocessor.** 8086/88
4. **32 bit microprocessor.** 80380/486 and Pentium
5. **64 bit microprocessor.** Motorola 68000 series

MICROCOMPUTERS

Microcomputer is classified in four groups.

1. **Personnel computers.**
   These microcomputers are single user systems and being used for variety of purposes, such as payroll, business accounts, word processing, legal and medical record keeping, personnel finance and instructions. A typical configuration includes a 16 or 32 bit microprocessor, 2 to 4 MB (megabyte) of system memory, a video screen, a dot matrix printer.
2. **Work stations.**
   These are high performance cousins of the PC. They are used in engineering and scientific applications such as computer-aided design (CAD), computer aided engineering (CAE), and computer-aided manufacturing (CAM), they generally include system memory larger than 200 MB, storage memory in giga bytes and high resolution screen. The work stations are designed around RISC processors. The RISC processors tend to be faster and more efficient than the processors used in personnel computer.
3. **Single board microcomputers.**
   These microcomputers are primarily used in college, laboratories and industries for instructional purposes or to evaluate the performance of a given microprocessor. They can also be part of some larger systems. Typically these microcomputers include 8 or 16 bit microprocessor.

   e.g. These computers include such systems as Intel SDK85, SDK86, Motorola Evaluation kits, these are generally used to write and execute assembly language programs and to perform interfacing experiments
4. **Single chip microcomputers (micro-controllers)**
   These microcomputers are designed on a single chip, which typically includes a chip of 64 bytes of R/W memory from 4K to 2K bytes of ROM and several single lines to connect I/Os. These are complete microcomputers on a chip, they are also known as microcontrollers. These are used primarily for such functions as controlling appliances and traffic lights. *e.g.* Zilog Z8, Intel MCS51 and 96 series, and Motorola 68H C11.

COMPUTER LANGUAGES. Nibble

It is a group of four bits

Mnemonic : A combination of letters to suggest the operation of an instruction.

Compiler : A program that translates english like words of high language in the machine language of a computer. A complier reads a given program, called a source code and then translates the program into the machine language which is called an object code.

Assembler : A computer program that translates an assembly language program from mnemonics to the binary machine code of a computer.

Monitor program : A program that interprets the input from a keyboard and converts the input into its binary equivalent.

COMPUTER SYSTEM.

8085 Programming Model.

The 8085 programming model includes six registers, one accumulator and one flag register. It has two 16 bit register the stack pointer and the program counter.

Registers : The 8085 has six general purpose registers to store 8 bit data. These are identical as B, C, D, E, H and L. They can be combined as Registers pairs BC, DE, and HL to perform some 16 bit operations. The programmer can use these registers to store or copy data into the registers by using data copy instructions.

Accumulator A	(8)	Flag Register	
B	(8)	C	(8)
D	(8)	E	(8)
H	(8)	L	(8)
Stack pointer		(SP)	(16)
Program counter		(PC)	(16)

Data Bus — 8 Lines — Bidirectional

Address Bus — Lines — Unidirectional

Fig. (a) Programming model

D_7	D_6	D_5	D_4	D_3	D_2	D_1	D_0
S	Z		AC		P		CY

Fig. (b) Flab Register

Accumulator

The Accumulator is an 8 bit register that is part of the arithmetic/logic unit (ALU). This register is used to store 8 bit data and to perform arithmetic/logic unit (ALU). This register is used to store 8-bit data and to perform arithmetic and logical operations. The result of an operation is stored in the accumulator. The accumulator is also identified as register A.

FLAGS

The ALU includes five flip-flops, which are set or reset after an operation according to data conditions of the result in the accumulator and other registers. They are called zero (Z), carry (CY); sign (S), parity (P) and Auxiliary carry (AC) flags.

The most commonly used flags are zero, carry, and sign. The microprocessor uses these flags to test data conditions.

After an addition of two numbers, if the sum in the accumulator is larger than eight bits, the flip-flop used to indicate a carry called carry flag (CY) is set to one. When an arithmetic operation is zero the flip flop called the zero (Z) flag is set to one.

The flags have critical importance in the decision making process of the microprocessor. The conditions (set or reset) of the flags are tested through software instructions.

PROGRAM COUNTER (PC).

This 16 bit register deals with sequencing the execution of instruction. This register is a memory pointer. Memory locations have 16 bit addresses, and that is why this is a 16-bit register. The microprocessor uses this register to sequence the execution of the instructions. The function of the program counter is to point to the memory addresses from which the next byte is to be fetched. When a byte (machine code) is being fetched, the program counter is incremented by one to point to the next memory location.

STACK POINTER (SP)

The stack pointer is also a 16 bit register used as memory pointer. It points to a memory location in R/W memory, called the stack. The beginning of stack is defined by loading a 16-bit address in the stack pointer.

OPCODE FORMAT

In the design of the 8085 microprocessor chip, all operations, registers and status flags are identified with a specific code.

All internal registers are identified as follows :

Code	Registers	Code	Register pairs
000	B	00	BC
001	C	01	DE
010	D	10	HL
011	E	11	A F or S P
100	F		
101	G		
110	Reserved for Memory Related Operation		
111	A		

INSTRUCTION CODES

An instruction code is a group of bits that instruct the computer to perform a specific operation. It is usually divided into parts, each having its own particular interpretation. The most basic part of an instruction codes is its operation part.

Operation Code

The operation code of an instruction is a group of bits that define such operations as add, subtract, multiply, shift and complement. The number of bits required for the operation code of an instruction depends on the total number of operations available in the computer. The operation code must consist of atleast n bits for a given 2^n (or less) distinct operations.

OP Code.

What task to be performed, called the operation code (OPcode).

Operand.

When data to be operated on called the operand. The operand (or data) can be specified in various ways. It may include 8-bit or (16 bit) data, an internal register, a memory location, or 8 bit (or 16 bit) address. In some instructions, the operand is implicit.

ADDRESSING MODES

The control unit of a computer is designed to go through an instruction cycle that is divided into three major phases.

(i) Fetch the instruction from memory

(ii) Decode the instruction

(iii) Execute the instruction

Implied mode : All register reference instructions that use an accumulator are implied mode instructions. Zero address instructions in a stack-organized computer are implied mode instructions since the operands are implied to be on top of the stack.

Immediate mode : The operand is specified in the instruction itself. In other words, an immediate mode instruction has an operand field rather than an address field. The operand field contains the actual operand to be used in conjunction with the operation specified in the instructions.

Register mode : In this mode the operands are in registers, that reside within the CPU. The particular register is selected from a register field in the instruction. A K bit field can specify any one of 2^k registers.

Register indirect mode : In this mode the instruction specifies a register in the CPU, whose content gives the address of the operand in memory. The advantage of a register indirect mode instruction is that the address field of the instruction uses fewer bits to select a register than would have been required to specify a memory address directly,

Auto Increment or Decrement mode : This is similar to register indirect mode except that the register is incremented or decremented after or before its value is used to access memory. When the address stored in the register refers to a table of data in memory, it is necessary to increment and decrement the registers after every access to the table

Direct addressing mode : In this mode the effective address is equal to the address part of the instruction. The operand resides in memory and its address is given directly by the address field of the instruction.

Indirect addressing mode : In this mode the address field of the instruction gives the address where the effective address is stored in memory.

Effective address = address part of instruction
+ content of CPU register

Input And Output System

Input/output devices are the means through which the MPU communicates with the outside world. The MPU accepts binary data as input from devices such as keyboards and A/D converters and send data to output devices such as LEDs or printers. There are two different methods by which I/O devices can be identified. One uses an 8 bit address and the other uses a 16 bit address.

PERIPHERAL MAPPED I/O

In this type of I/O, the MPU uses eight address lines to identify an input or an output device; this is known as peripheral mapped I/O. The eight address lines can have 256 (2^8 combinations) addresses; thus the MPU can identify 256 input devices and 256 output devices with addresses ranging from 00H to FFH input and output devices are differentiated by the control signals. The MPU uses the I/O Read Control Signal for input devices and the I/O Write Control Signal for output devices. The entire range of I/O addresses from 00 to FF is known as an I/O map, and individual addresses are referred to as I/O devices addresses 8 I/O port numbers.

MEMORY MAPPED I/O (I/O WITH 16 BIT ADDRESSES).

I/O is connected as if it is memory register. This is known as memory mapped I/O. The MPU uses the same control signal (Memory Read or Memory Write) and instructions as those of memory. In some microprocessor such as motorola 6800, all I/O have 16 bit addresses. I/Os and memory share the same memory map (64K). In memory mapped I/O, the MPU follows the same steps as if it is accessing a memory register.

INPUT DEVICES

These include a mouse, track ball, space ball, joystick, digitizers, dials and button boxes. Some other input devices used in particular applications are data glove, touch panels, image scanners and voice systems.

1. **Keyboards :** An alphanumeric keyboard on a graphics system is used primarily as a device for entering text strings. The keyboard is an efficient device for inputting such non graphics data as picture labels associated with graphics display. Keyboards can also be provided with feature to facilitate entry of screen coordinates, menu selectors or graphics functions.
2. **Mouse :** A mouse is small hand held box used to position the screen cursor. Wheels or rollers on the button of the mouse can be used to record the amount and direction of movements. Another method for detecting mouse motion is with an optical sensor. For these systems, the mouse is moved over a special mouse pad that has grid of horizontal and vertical lines. The optical sensor detects movements across the lines in the grid. Since mouse can be picked up and put down at another position without change in cursor movement. It is used for making relative changes in the position of the screen cursor. One, two or three buttons are usually included on the top of the mouse for signalling the execution of some operation, such as recording cursor position or invoking a function. Most general purpose graphics system now included a mouse and keyboard as major input devices.
3. **Track Ball and Space Ball :**A track ball is a ball that can be rotated with the fingers or palm of the hand to produce screen-cursor movement, potentiometers attached to the ball measure the amount and direction of rotation. Trackballs are often mounted on keyboards or other devices such as the mouse.

   While a track ball is two dimensional posting device, a space ball provides six degree of freedom. Unlike the track ball, space ball does not actually move. Strain gauges measure the amount of pressure applied to the spaceball to provide input for spatial positioning and orientation as the ball is pushed or pulled in various directions. Space balls are used for three-dimensional positioning and selection operations in virtual reality systems, modelling, animation, CAD, and other applications.
4. **Joysticks :** A joystick consists of a small, vertical lever called stick mounted on a base that is used to steer and screen cursor around. Most joysticks select screen position with actual stick movement. Others respond to pressure on the stick. Some joysticks are mounted on keyboard, others function as stand alone units. Potentiometer mounted at the base of joystick measures the amount of movement, and springs return the stick to the center position when it is released one or more buttons can be programmed to act as input switches to signal certain actions once a screen position has been selected.
5. **Data Glove :** Data glove that can be used to grasp a "virtual" object. The glove is constructed with a series of sensors that detect hand and finger motions. Electromagnetic coupling between transmitting antennas and receiving antennas is used to provide information about the position and orientation of the hand. The transmitting and receiving antennas can each be structured as a set of three mutually perpendicular coils, forming a three dimensional cartesian co-ordinate system.
6. **Digitizers :** A common device for drawing, painting or interactively selecting co-ordinate positions on an object is a digitizer. These devices can be used to input co-ordinate values in either a two dimensional or three dimensional space. Typically, a digitizer is used to scan over a drawing or object and to input a set of discrete co-ordinate positions, which can be joined with straight-line segments to approximate the curve or surface shapes. One type of digitizer is the graphics tablet, also referred to as a data tablet which is used to input two dimensional coordinates by activating a hand cursor or styles at selected positions on a flat surface.
7. **Image Scanners :** Drawing, graphs, color and black and white photos or text can be stored for computer processing with an image scanner by passing an optical scanning mechanism over the information to be stored. The gradations of gray scale or color are then recorded and stored in an array. Once we have the internal representation of a picture, we can apply transformations to rotate, scale or crop the picture to a particular screen area. We can also apply various image processing methods to modify the array representation of the picture. For scanned text input, various editing operations can be performed on stored documents. Some scanners are able to scan either graphical representation or text, and they come in a variety of sizes and capabilities.
8. **Touch Panels :** Touch panels allow displayed objects or screen positions to be selected with the touch of a finger. A typical application of touch panels is for the selection of processing options that are represented with graphical icons. Some

systems, such as the plasma panels are designed with touch screens. Other system can be adapted for touch input by fitting a transparent device with a touch-sensing mechanism over the video monitor screen. Touch input can be recorded using optical, electrical or acoustical methods.

9. Light Pens.

Light pen is pencil-shaped devices are used to select screen positions by detecting the light coming from points on the CRT screen. They are sensitive to the short burst of light emitted from the phosphor coating at the instant the electron beam strikes a particular point. Other light sources, such as the background light in the room, are usually not detected by a light pen.

PRINTERS

Printers produce output by either impact or non-impact methods. Impact printers press formed character faces against an inked ribbon onto the paper. A line printer is an example of impact device with the type faces mounted on bands, chains, drums or wheels. Non-impact printers and plotters use laser techniques, inkjet sprays, xerographic processes as used in photocopying machine, electrostatic methods and electrothermal methods to get images on to paper.

Character impact printers often have a dot matrix print head containing a rectangular array of protruding wire pins, with the number of pens depending on the quality of the printer.

In a laser device, laser beam creates a charge distribution on a rotating drum coating with a photoelectric material, such as selenium. Toner is applied to the drum and then transferred to paper.

Inkjet methods produce output by squirting ink in horizontal rows across a roll of paper wrapped on a drum. The electrically charged ink stream *is* deflected by an electric field to produce dot matrix patterns. A desktop inkjet plotter with resolution of 360 dots per inch.

An electrostatic device places a negative charge on the paper, one complete row at a time along the length of the paper. Then the paper is exposed to a toner. The toner is positively charged and so it is attracted to the negatively charged, areas, where it adheres to produce the specified output. Electrothermal methods use heat in a dot matrix print head to output patterns on heat sensitive paper. We can get limited color output on an impact printer by using different colored ribbons. Non impact devices use various techniques to combine three color pigments (cyan, magneta and yellow) to produce a range of color patterns.

Parallel printers use :

(*a*) RS-232C interface

(*b*) Centronics interface

(*c*) Handshake mode

Storage Unit

It consists of main memory and secondary memory.

Main Memory :

1. A flip-flop made of electronic semiconductor devices is used to fabricate a memory cell. These memory cells organized as a Random Access Memory (RAM). Each cell has a capability to store one bit of information. A main memory or store of a computer is organized using a large number of cells. Each cell stores a binary digit.
2. A memory cell, which does not loose the bit stored in it when no power is supplied to the cell, is known as a non-volatile cell.
3. A word is a group of bits, which are stored and retrieved as a unit. A memory system is organized to store a number of words.
4. A Byte consists of 8 bits. A word may store one or more bytes.
5. The storage capacity of a memory is the number of bytes it can store.
6. The address of the location from where a word is to be retrieved or to be stored is entered in a Memory Address Register (MAR).
7. The data retrieved from memory or to be stored in memory are placed in a Memory Data Register (MDR).
8. The time taken to write a word is known as the Write time.
9. The time to retrieve information is called the Access time of the memory.
10. The time taken to access a word in a memory is independent of the address of the word and hence it is know as a Random Access Memory (RAM).
    - The main memory used to store programs and data in a computer is a RAM.
11. A RAM may be fabricated with permanently stored information, which cannot be erased. Such a memory is called a Read Only Memory (ROM).
    - For more specialized uses, a user can store his won special functions or programs in a ROM. Such ROM's are called Programmable ROM (PROM).
12. A serial access memory is organized by arranging memory cells in a linear sequence.

- Information is retrieved or stored in such a memory by using a read/write head.
- Data is presented serially for writing and is retrieved serially during read.

Secondary / Auxiliary storage devices : Magnetic surface recording devices used in computers as Hard disks, Floppy disks, CD-ROMs and Magnetic tapes.

1. **Floppy Disk Drive (FDD) :** In this device, the medium used to record the data is called as floppy disk. It is a flexible circular disk of diameter 3.5 inches made of plastic coated with a magnetic material. This is housed in a square plastic jacket. Data recorded on a floppy disk is read and stored in a computer's memory by a device called a floppy disk is read and stored in a computer's memory by a device called a floppy disk drive (FDD). A floppy disk is inserted in a slot of the FDD. Floppy Disks with various capacities are as follow:
   - $5^{1/4}$ drive- 360KB, 1.2MB (1 KB= 2^{10} = 1024 bytes)
   - $3^{1/2}$ drive- 1.44 Mb, 2.88 MB (1MB= 2^{20} bytes)
2. **Compact Disk Drive (CDD) :** CD-ROM (Compact Disk Read Only Memory) used a laser beam to record and read data along spiral tracks on a 51/4 disk. A disk can store around 650 MB of information. CD-ROMs are normally used to store massive text data. Recently CD writers have come in the market. Using a CD writer, lot of information can be written on CD-ROM and stored for future reference.
3. **Hard Disk Drive (HDD) :** Unlike a floppy disk that is flexible and removable, the hard disk used in the PC is permanently fixed. The data transfer rate between the CPU and hard disk is much higher as compared to the between the CPU and the floppy disk drive. The CPU can use the hard disk to load programs and data as well as to store data.

CLASSIFICATION OF COMPUTERS

Computers come in sizes from tiny to monstrous, in both appearance and power. The size of a computer that a person or an organization needs depends on the computing requirements.

Supercomputers : The mightiest computers-and, of course, the most expensive-are known as supercomputers. Supercomputers process billions of instructions per second. One uses supercomputers for tasks that require mammoth data manipulation, such as worldwide weather forecasting and weapons research.

Mainframes : In the jargon of the computer trade, large computers are called mainframes. Mainframes are capable of processing data at very high speeds-millions of instructions per second-and have access to billions of characters of data. Their principal use of it is for processing vast amounts of data quickly, some of the obvious customers are banks, insurance companies, and manufacturers.

Personal Computers : Personal computers are often called PCs. A PC usually comes with a tower that holds the main circuit boards and disk drives of the computer, and a collection of peripherals, such as a keyboard, mouse, and monitor. The term "PC" often means machines that are compatible to IBM other than a Macintosh.

Personal Computers (PC) and MAC : A PC is based on a microprocessor originally made by the Intel Company (Intel's Pentium) with other companies such as AMD. The computers made by Macintoshes which uses, PowerPC processor, made by Motorola are referred as Mac. Also, the operating system software that runs these two kinds of computers is different. PCs usually use an Operating System made by Microsoft, i.e., Windows. Macintoshes use operating system, called Mac OS, made by Apple.

Notebook Computers : A computer that fits in a briefcase?. Notebook computers, also known as Laptop computers, are portable and popular with travelers who need a computer that can go with them. Most notebooks accept diskettes or network connections, so it is easy to move data from one computer to another.

INTERNET

The **Internet** is a global system of interconnected computer networks that use the standard Internet Protocol Suite (TCP/IP) to serve billions of users worldwide. It is a *network of networks* that consists of millions of private, public, academic, business, and government networks, of local to global scope, that are linked by a broad array of electronic, wireless and optical networking technologies. The Internet carries a vast range of information resources and services, such as the inter-linked hypertext documents of the World Wide Web (WWW) and the infrastructure to support electronic mail.

NETWORKS

A **computer network**, often simply referred to as a network, is a collection of computers and devices interconnected by communications channels that facilitate communications and allows sharing of resources and information among interconnected devices. **Computer networking** or **Data communications (Datacom)** is the engineering discipline concerned with the computer networks.

The three types of networks are:

(*i*) the Internet

(*ii*) the intranet

(*iii*) the extranet.

Examples of different network methods are :

1. Local area network (LAN), which is usually a small network constrained to a small geographic area. An example of a LAN would be a computer network within a building.
2. Metropolitan area network (MAN), which is used for medium size area. examples for a city or a state.
3. Wide area network (WAN) that is usually a larger network that covers a large geographic area.
4. Wireless LANs and WANs (WLAN & WWAN) are the wireless equivalent of the LAN and WAN.

IP ADDRESS

An **Internet Protocol address** (**IP address**) is a numerical label assigned to each device (e.g., computer, printer) participating in a computer network that uses the Internet Protocol for communication.[1] An IP address serves two principal functions: host or network interface identification and location addressing. Its role has been characterized as follows: "*A name indicates what we seek. An address indicates where it is. A route indicates how to get there.*

Important Devices Used in Network

1. **Modem :** A **modem** (**mo**dulator-**dem**odulator) is a device that modulates an analog carrier signal to encode digital information, and also demodulates such a carrier signal to decode the transmitted information. The goal is to produce a signal that can be transmitted easily and decoded to reproduce the original digital data. Modems can be used over any means of transmitting analog signals, from light emitting diodes to radio.
2. **Router :** A **router** is a device that forwards data packets across computer networks. Routers perform the data "traffic directing" functions on the Internet. A router is connected to two or more data lines from different networks. When data comes in on one of the lines, the router reads the address information in the packet to determine its ultimate destination.
3. **Bridge :** A **network bridge** connects multiple network segments. **Bridging** is a forwarding technique used in packet-switched computer networks. Unlike routing, bridging makes no assumptions about where in a network a particular address is located. Instead, it depends on flooding and examination of source addresses in received packet headers to locate unknown devices. Once a device has been located, its location is recorded in a table where the MAC address is stored so as to preclude the need for further broadcasting.
4. **Hub : hub** is a device for connecting multiple twisted pair or fiber optic Ethernet devices together and making them act as a single segment. The device is a form of multiport repeater.
5. **Repeater :** A **repeater** is an electronic device that receives a signal and retransmits it at a higher level and/or higher power, or onto the other side of an obstruction, so that the signal can cover longer distances.
6. **Server :** A **server computer** is a computer, or series of computers, that link other computers or electronic devices together. They often provide essential services across a network, either to private users inside a large organization or to public users via the internet. For example, when you enter a query in a search engine, the query is sent from your computer over the internet to the servers that store all the relevant web pages. The results are sent back by the server to your computer.

EMAIL

Electronic mail, commonly called **email** or **e-mail**, is a method of exchanging digital messages from an author to one or more recipients. Modern email operates across the Internet or other computer networks. Some early email systems required that the author and the recipient both be online at the same time, *a la* instant messaging. Today's email systems are based on a store-and-forward model. Email servers accept, forward, deliver and store messages. Neither the users nor their computers are required to be online simultaneously; they need connect only briefly, typically to an email server, for as long as it takes to send or receive messages.

EMAIL ADDREES

An **email address** identifies an email box to which email messages are delivered. An example format of an email address is lewis @ example .com which is read as *lewis at example dot net*. It has two parts. The part before the @ sign is the *local-part* of the address, often the username of the recipient *lewis* and the part after the @ sign is a *domain name i.e.* example.com to which the email message will be sent.

MS OFFICE

Microsoft Office is a proprietary commercial office suite of inter-related desktop applications, servers and services for the Microsoft Windows and Mac OS X operating systems, introduced by Microsoft in 1989. Initially a marketing term for a bundled set of applications, the first version of Office contained Microsoft Word, Microsoft Excel, and Microsoft PowerPoint.

WORD

Microsoft Word is a word processor and was previously considered to be the main program in Office. Its proprietary DOC format is considered a *de facto* standard, although Word 2007 can also use a new XML-based, Microsoft Office-optimized format called .DOCX which has been standardized by Ecma International as Office Open XML and its SP2 update will support ODF and PDF. Word is also available in some editions of Microsoft Works. It is available for the Windows and Mac platforms. The first version of Word, released in the autumn of 1983, was for the MS-DOS operating system and had the distinction of introducing the mouse to a broad population. Word 1.0 could be purchased with a bundled mouse, though none was required. Following the precedents of LisaWrite and MacWrite, Word for Macintosh attempted to add closer WYSIWYG features into its package. Word for Mac was released in 1985. Word for Mac was the first graphical version of Microsoft Word. Despite its bugginess, it became one of the most popular Mac applications.

EXCEL

Microsoft Excel is a spreadsheet program which originally competed with the dominant Lotus 1-2-3, but eventually outsold it. It is available for the Windows and Mac platforms. Microsoft released the first version of Excel for the Mac in 1985, and the first Windows version (numbered 2.05 to line up with the Mac and bundled with a standalone Windows run-time environment) in November 1987.

OUTLOOK

Microsoft Outlook (not to be confused with Outlook Express) is a personal information manager and e-mail communication software. The replacement for Windows Messaging, Microsoft Mail and Schedule+ starting in Office 97, it includes an e-mail client, calendar, task manager and address book.

On the Mac, Microsoft offered several versions of Outlook in the late 1990s, but only for use with Microsoft Exchange Server. In Office 2001, it introduced an alternative application with a slightly different feature set called Microsoft Entourage. It reintroduced Outlook in Office 2011, replacing Entourage.

POWERPOINT

Microsoft PowerPoint is a popular presentation program for Windows and Mac. It is used to create slideshows, composed of text, graphics, movies and other objects, which can be displayed on-screen and navigated through by the presenter or printed out on transparencies or slides.

Objective Type Questions

1. Which of the following is the fastest ?
  (*a*) CPU
  (*b*) magnetic tapes and disks
  (*c*) video terminal
  (*d*) sensors, mechanical controllers

2. The input unit of a computer
  (*a*) feeds data to the CPU or memory
  (*b*) retrieves data from CPU
  (*c*) directs all other units
  (*d*) all of these

3. Offline device is
  (*a*) a device which is not connected to CPU
  (*b*) a device which is connected to CPU
  (*c*) a direct access storage device
  (*d*) an I/O device

4. Which of the following is a set of general purpose internal registers ?
  (*a*) Stack (*b*) Scratchpad
  (*c*) Address register (*d*) Status register

5. A single bus structure is primarily found in
  (*a*) main frames
  (*b*) super computers
  (*c*) high performance machines
  (*d*) mini-and micro-computers

6. Which of the following registers is used to keep track of address of the memory location where the next instruction is located ?
  (*a*) Memory Address Register
  (*b*) Memory Data Register
  (*c*) Instruction Register
  (*d*) Program Counter

7. Which of the following registers is loaded with the contents of the memory location pointed by the PC ?
  (*a*) Memory Address Register
  (*b*) Memory Data Register
  (*c*) Instruction Register
  (*c*) Program counter

8. In a generic microprocessor, instruction cycle time is
  (*a*) shorter than machine cycle time
  (*b*) larger than machine cycle time
  (*c*) exactly double the machine cycle time
  (*d*) exactly the same as the machine cycle time

9. Program Status Word (PSW) contains various (different) status of
  (*a*) CPU (*b*) ALU
  (*c*) program (*d*) registers

10. When an interrupt occurs, CPU saves the value of———in a stack,
  (*a*) accumulator
  (*b*) program status word (PSW) only
  (*c*) Instruction Address Counter (IAC)only
  (*d*) both PWS and IAC

11. Bus Arbitration is
  (*a*) clearing the bus
  (*b*) latching information on the bus
  (*c*) deciding the controller of the bus
  (*d*) controlling the bus

12. Control Memory Address Register is present in
  (*a*) ALU
  (*b*) Instruction Register Unit
  (*c*) Control Unit
  (*d*) Disk Control Interface Unit

13. Which of the following is not one of the three primary functions that on-line direct access system can serve?
  (*a*) inquiry (*b*) backup
  (*c*) update (*d*) programming

14. Which of the following is not true of punched cards as data entry media?
  (*a*) They can be used as turn around documents
  (*b*) They are inexpensive
  (*c*) Input is slow compared with other media
  (*d*) They are easily damaged

15. Magnetic tape can serve as
  (*a*) input media
  (*b*) output media
  (*c*) secondary storage media
  (*d*) all of these

16. In the context of Information Technology, OCR means
  (*a*) Optical Character Recognition
  (*b*) Octagonal Cyclic Recharge
  (*c*) Octadecimal Cyclic Regeneration
  (*d*) Optical Character Regeneration

17. In Boolean algebra $\overline{(1+1\cdot 0+0)} = ?$

(a) 0 (b) 1

(c) 2 (d) –1

18. Which of the followingis not an I/O device of the computer?

(a) Keyboard (b) Joy stick

(c) ALU (d) Printer

19. What is floating point with reference to computers?

(a) It is a software subroutine around which other subroutines are built

(b) It is a representation of real numbers to facilitate computing

(c) It is the main algebraic formula of the software

(d) It is the voltage point given to various operating units of the computer

20. A system of digital rules for exchange and processing of data between various devices is called

(a) software programme

(b) algorithm

(c) protocol

(d) information processing

21. A theoretical computer with infinite type and memory, used in analysis of problems of computation, is called

(a) Tape calculator

(b) Babbage machine

(c) Turing machine

(d) Theoretical machine

22. ASCII coding allocated binary codes to English alphabets and symbols for computer use. More recently a new standard has been adopted which allocates code to almost all the languages of the world and also to symbols covering more than a lakh characters. The new standard is called

(a) CCS

(b) Unicode

(c) Standard CCS code

(d) Universal CCS code

23. For using passwords on the Internet a software is used so that the password is not intercepted easily. It is called

(a) Coding

(b) Malware

(c) Virus

(d) Encryption

24. A software, coding of which is available freely on Internet and is open for users for further use and improvement and which is generally developed in a collaborative manner is called

(a) open source software

(b) unlicensed software

(c) free software

(d) community software

25. Which of the following are machine level languages?

(a) C++ (b) Java

(c) Python (d) None of these

26. Which of the following statements is incorrect?

(a) Microsoft windows is GUI

(b) Linux is GUI

(c) More than 5000 kB data can be stored in a DVD

(d) A 1 TB flash drive can store 2 million files each of size 1 MB

27. The terms ALU, CPU, I/O devices pertain to

(a) computers

(b) environmental engineering

(c) diesel engine

(d) engineering drawing and orthogonal projections

28. In a computing device 'MHz' is mentioned in the specifications. It refers to

(a) size of memory

(b) speed of computation

(c) clock speed

(d) none of the above

29. The value of binary 1111 is :

(a) 2^3 (b) $2^3 - 1$

(c) 24 (d) $2^4 - 1$

30. The term 'Operating System' means :

(a) A set of programmes which controls computer working

(b) The way a computer operator works

(c) Conversion of high level language into machine level language

(d) None of these

31. Which of these is NOT an Operating System?

(a) Android (b) iOS

(c) Linux (d) Power point

32. A software user interface feature that allows the user to view something very similar to the end result while the document is being created is called-

(a) Format creator (b) Format fidelity
(c) WYSIWYG (d) WYGIWYS

33. In a computer system there are softwares and languages at various levels, like High level Language (HL), Machine Language (ML), Compiler (C). Which of the following is the correct indicative representation from user (U) to the computer (COMP)?

(a) $U \rightleftharpoons HL \rightleftharpoons C \rightleftharpoons ML \rightleftharpoons Comp$
(b) $U \rightleftharpoons C \rightleftharpoons ML \rightleftharpoons HL \rightleftharpoons Comp$
(c) $U \rightleftharpoons C \rightleftharpoons HL \rightleftharpoons ML \rightleftharpoons Comp$
(d) $U \rightleftharpoons ML \rightleftharpoons HL \rightleftharpoons C \rightleftharpoons Comp$

34. Which of these devices performs the function of both input device and output device for a computer?

(a) Joy Stick (b) Mouse
(c) Modem (d) Printer

35. Who wrote/invented the Linux software?

(a) Microsoft (b) Apple INC
(c) IBM (d) None of these

36. A technique of anonymous communication over a computer network using encryption of messages and splitting between the nodes, is called-

(a) Spice routing (b) Onion routing
(c) Cabbage routing (d) Flower routing

37. Processing speed of computer is measured in-

(a) MIPS(Million Instruction Per Second)
(b) MHz of clock
(c) Both (a) and (b)
(d) None of these

38. To close a presentation and quit PowerPoint, one must click the close button on the :

(a) menu bar (b) title bar
(c) standard tool bar (d) common tasks toolbar

39. Expression + + i is equivalent in 'C' to :

(a) i = i + 1 (b) i = i + 2
(c) i = 2i (d) None of these

40. Which of the following rational relation operations in 'C means "not equal to" ?

(a) # (b) ==
(c) ! = (d) < =

41. Microsoft Windows is a/an :

(a) Word-processing program
(b) Database program
(c) Operating system
(d) Graphics program

42. ___________will translate the complete program at once from a High Level Language to the Machine Language.

(a) Compiler (b) Joy stick
(c) Ports (d) Light pen

43. The word function that corrects text as we type is referred to as :

(a) Auto insert (b) Auto correct
(c) Auto summarize (d) Track changes

44. Primary Storage, in computer terminology, refers to :

(a) Hard Disc Drive
(b) Random Access Memory (RAM)
(c) Read Only Memory (ROM)
(d) The storage device where the operating system is stored

45. What does an electronic spreadsheet consist of ?

(a) Rows (b) Columns
(c) Cells (d) All of the above

Answers

1. (*a*)	**2.** (*a*)	**3.** (*a*)	**4.** (*b*)	**5.** (*d*)	**6.** (*d*)	**7.** (*c*)	**8.** (*b*)	**9.** (*a*)	**10.** (*d*)
11. (*c*)	**12.** (*c*)	**13.** (*d*)	**14.** (*b*)	**15.** (*d*)	**16.** (*a*)	**17.** (*a*)	**18.** (*c*)	**19.** (*b*)	**20.** (*c*)
21. (*c*)	**22.** (*b*)	**23.** (*d*)	**24.** (*a*)	**25.** (*d*)	**26.** (*d*)	**27.** (*a*)	**28.** (*c*)	**29.** (*d*)	**30.** (*a*)
31. (*d*)	**32.** (*c*)	**33.** (*a*)	**34.** (*c*)	**35.** (*d*)	**36.** (*c*)	**37.** (*b*)	**38.** (*b*)	**39.** (*b*)	**40.** (*c*)
41. (*c*)	**42.** (*a*)	**43.** (*b*)	**44.** (*b*)	**45.** (*d*)					

Explanations

16. Optical Character Reader is full form of OCR, which can read a character and convert its bitmap image to equivalent ASCII codes.

17. It is equivalent to 0.1 = 0

18. Arithmetic Logical Unit is not an Input device while all the other three are.

19. Floating point numbers are used in computers to represent real numbers. Since real numbers can not be accurately represented in computers through binary numbers.

20. Protocols are rules developed for exchanging and processing of data between various devices. Examples include HTTP, IP, FTTP etc.

21. Turing machine is a mathematical model of a hypothetical computing machine which can use a predefined set of rules to determine a result from a set of input variables.

22. The new standard which allocates codes to almost all languages and symbols, totaling more than a lakh is called Unicode. It makes transfer and reuse of translated data etc. very easy. Also it represents each character with 16 bits.

23. To protect passwords etc. Encryption is used which is coding each data point in a particular pattern which is not easy to decode.

24. Open source softwares like Unix have their source code freely available and these are developed through collaboration of coders from across the world. Many developers as a principle use only open source softwares.

25. All the languages mentioned here are high level languages, in which it is easier to write code.

26. 1 TB flash drive can store approximately 1 million file sizes each of 1 MB.

27. All these devices are related to computers. CPU is Central Processing Unit, while ALU is Arithmetic and Logical unit, while I/O is Input Output devices.

28. MHz is used to measure the number of operations that can be done by the CPU in 1 second. So it refers to clock speed.

29. 1111 of binary is $2^4 - 1$. It is $2^3 + 2^2 + 2^1 + 2^0$

30. An operating system (OS) is system software that manages computer hardware and software resources and provides common services for computer programs.

31. Powerpoint is not an operating system but an application to make presentation slides.

32. When users can see something very similar to end result while document creation, it is called WYSIWYG.

33. It is the correct representation where user gives input in high level language, it is then compiled and becomes machine language which is computed and the output is similarly provided to the user.

34. The modem is an input and an output device. It is used for sending and receiving information and data over telephone lines.

35. LINUX software was invented by Linus Torvalds while studying computer science at University of Helsinki in 1991.

37. Processing speed is measured in MHz. Nowadays it is even measured in GHz i.e. Giga Hertz. Basically it represents how many operations can be processed in 1 second.

38. To close applications such as Powerpoint, MS-word etc. one must click the close button on the title bar which is at the top right hand corner.

39. ++I in C means i = i + 2. This was a way developed to write smaller lines in code.

40. != means not equal to in C.

41. Microsoft Windows is the world's most popular commercial operating system for PCs.

42. Compilers are used to translate entire programs from High level language to machine language, so that computer can understand and execute it.

43. When we type text, Auto correct feature corrects the word's spelling or any other portion of the text.

44. Primary storage, also known as main storage or memory, is the area in a computer in which data is stored for quick access by the computer's processor. The terms random access memory (RAM) and memory are often used as synonyms for primary or main storage.

45. An electronic spreadsheet like MS-Excel consists of Cells which are arranged in Rows and Columns. So all are present.

Electronics

Basic Electronics

INTRINSIC SEMICONDUCTORS

In a pure semiconductor, an atom behaves as if there are 8 electrons in its valence shell (because of formation of covalent bonds) and the entire material behaves as an insulator at low temperature. A semiconductor atom needs energy of order of 1.1 eV which is easily available at room temperature. Due to thermal agitation of crystal structure, electrons from a few covalent bonds come out and the bond form which an electron comes out has a vacancy called **Hole** (of positive nature). This hole can be filled by some other electron from some other covalent bond. As the electrons from some other covalent bond moves to fill this vacancy a hole is created at its place. In other words we can say that hole has shifted its position from one covalent bond to another as an electron does this in an attempt to fill the hole.*Since, a hole moves in a direction opposite to that of an electron so a hole is treated as a positive charged carrier.*

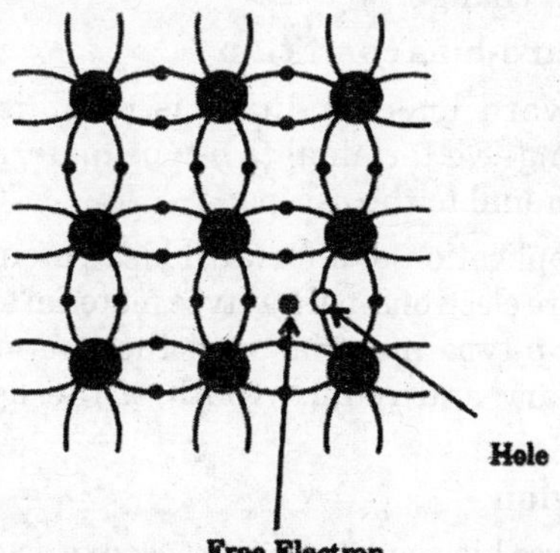

So, at room temperature a pure semiconductor will have electrons and holes wandering in random directions. These electrons and holes are called **intrinsic carriers** and such a semiconductor is called **intrinsic type semiconductor.**

EXTRINSIC SEMICONDUCTOR

P-type semiconductors

Consider a silicon crystal to which a trivalent impurity say Indium is added. The four silicon atoms surrounding the In atom, can share one electron each with the In atom which has got three valence electrons. In an attempt to have 8 electrons in valence shell, In atom borrows one of the nearly covalent bonds of electron. Thus, valence shell of the In atom possesses 8 electrons but a borrowed. Thus, for every trivalent impurity atom added, an extra hole will be created. As the trivalent impurity atoms accept electrons from the silicon crystal, it is called **acceptor impurity.**

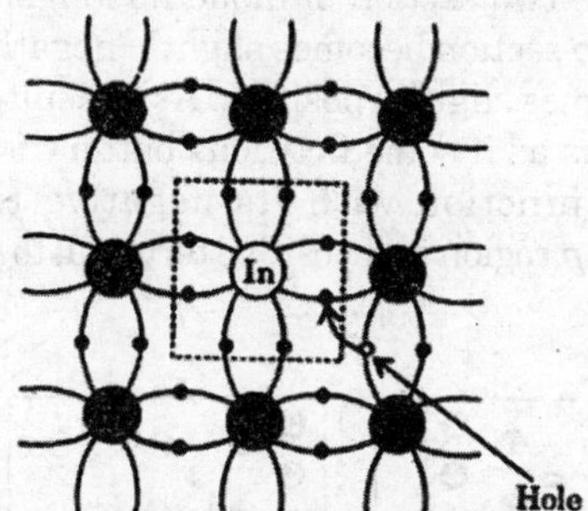

Si-crystal so obtained is called *p-type* as it contains excess free holes. Each hole is equivalent to positive charge. The holes so created are extrinsic carriers and the p-type Si-crystal obtained is called p-type extrinsic semiconductor.

n-Type Semiconductors

When the arsenic impurity atoms are added to the silicon crystal in a small ratio ($1 : 10^6$), its atoms replace the silicon atoms here and there. The four electrons out of the five valence electrons of As atom take part in covalent bonding with four silicon atoms surrounding it. The fifth electron is set free. Obviously, the extra free electrons created in the crystal will be as many as the number of the pentavalent impurity atoms added. Since the pentavalent impurity increases the number of free electrons, it is called **donor impurity.** The silicon crystal so obtained is termed as n-type Si crystal. The electrons so set free in the silicon crystal are called **extrinsic carriers** and the n-type Si crystal is called n-type

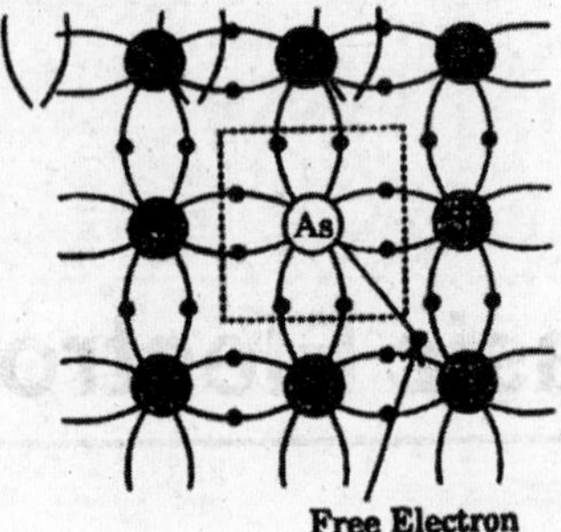

Free Electron

Due to thermal agitation, the pure Si crystal possesses a new electrons and holes. So, n-type Si crystal will have a large number of free electrons (majority charge carriers) and a small number of hole (minority charge carriers).

pn JUNCTION DIODE or Crystal Diode or Diode

It is formed when a p type semiconductor is joined with an n type semiconductor. The surface of contact of p and n is called **junction.** Due to combination a diffusion of electrons from n type to p type semiconductor and so on is expected as a result of which a depletion region (free from any type of charge carries) is formed. because of diffusion of holes and electrons the two section of diode no longer remain neutral, i.e. p section becomes slightly negative and n section becomes slightly positive. As a result of this it appears to us as if some fictitious battery is applied across the junction with its negative terminal connected to p region and positive terminal to n region.

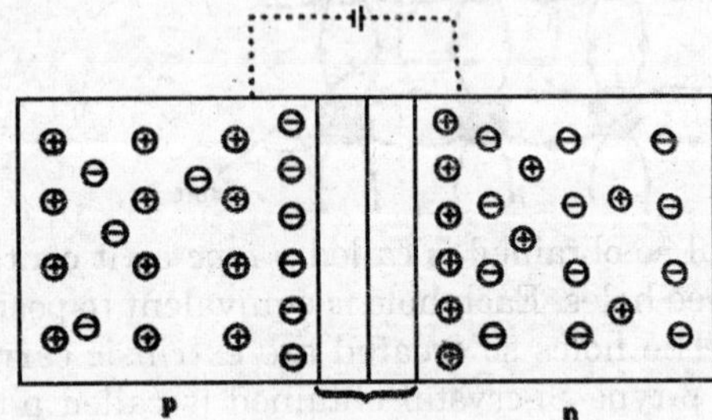

Depletion Region

Potential difference developed across the junction due to migration of majority charge carriers is called *potential barrier.* The potential barrier is of 0.7 V for Silicon and 0.3 for Germanium.

FORWARD BIAS

When an external DC source is connected such that p is conneced to positive terminal and n to the negative terminal, then diode is said to be **forward biased.**

In this case the majority charge carriers cross the junction thus making the depletion region thin and diode conducts and offers low resistance path to the flow of current.

SEMICONDUCTOR-DIODE

The semiconductor diode is formed by simply bringing n and p-type materials together (constructed from same base Ge or Si).

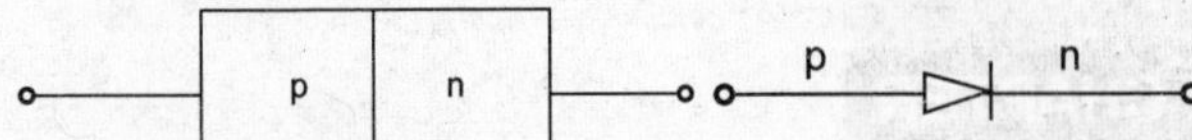

At the instant two materials are *joined,* the electron and holes in the region of junction will combine resulting in a lack of carriers in the region near the junction.

This region of uncovered positive and negative ions is called *depletion region* due to the depletion of carriers in this region.

BIASING OF DIODES.

(i) **No bias (V_D = 0).**

In the absence of an applied bias voltage, the net flow of charge in any one direction for a semiconductor is zero.

(ii) **Reverse bias condition (V_D < 0 V).**

If an external voltage V is applied across the p-n-junction such that positive terminal to n-type and negative terminal to p-type material, then depletion layer will be increased. This widening of depletion layer will establish too great a barrier for the majority carrier to overcome

However the number of minority carrier that find themselves entering the depletion region will not change.

(iii) **Forward-bias condition**

A forward bias condition is established by applying +ve terminal to p-type material and -ve terminal to the n-type.

The application of a forward bias potential will pressure electrons in the n-type material and holes in the p-type material with the ions near the boundary and reduce width of the depletion region.

Zener Region

When reverse bias voltage is increased to a very high value, then a point is reached where the I_S will suddenly goes to a very high value. And this reverse bias potential is represented by symbol V_z. As V_D increase in reverse direction, velocity of the minority carriers responsible for the reverse saturation current will also increase the velocity and kinetic energy of minority carrier - with collision with other atoms. The ionisation process occur hence avalanche break down occur. The maximum reverse-bias potential that can be applied before entering the zener region is called *peak inverse voltage.*

TYPES OF DIODES

1. **Zener diodes**

   In zener region, the characteristic drops in an almost vertical manner at a reverse bias potential denoted V_z. For zener diode ,direction of conduction of current is reversed to that of simple diode. Si is preferred in manufacturing of zener diode due to higher temperature and current capability.

2. **Light emitting diode (L.E.D) :** When a junction diode is forward biased, energy is released at junction in the form of light due to recombination of electrons and holes. In case of Si or Ge diodes, the energy ereleased in the infra-red region.

   In the junction diode made of GaAs, InP etc energy is released in visible region suchn a junction diode is called **light emitting diode (LED).** Its symbol

   Solar cell : Solar cell is a device for converting solar energy into electrical energy. A junction diode in which one of the P or N sections is made very thin (so that the light energy falling on diode is not greatly asorbed before reaching the junction) can be used to convert light energy into electric energy; such diode is called as sola cell.

   Its symbol is .

3. **Tunnel diode.**

   An *pn* junction diode has an impurity concentration of about 1 part in 10^8. With this amount of doping the width of the depletion region which constitutes a potential barrier at the junction, is of the order of a micron. This potential barrier restrains the flow of carriers from the side of the function where they constitute majority carriers to the side where they constitute minority carriers. If the concentration of impurity atoms is greatly increased say to 1 part in 10^3 the device characteristicsare completely changed.

SOME SPECIAL DIODES

Photodiode : A kimctopm diode made from "light or photo sensitive semiconductor" is called *photo diode.* Its sysmbol is When light of energy "hv" falls on the photodiode (here hv > energy gap) more electrons move from valence band to conduction band, and due to this current in circuit of photodiode in reverse bias, increases. As light intensity is increased, the current goes on increasing so photo diode is used, to detect light intensity.

JUNCTION DIODE AS A RECTIFIER

A rectifier is used for converting A.C. to D.C.

A diode conducts in Forward Bias and a diode does not conduct in Reverse Bias.

Half Wave Rectifier

It rectifies only one half of AC input.

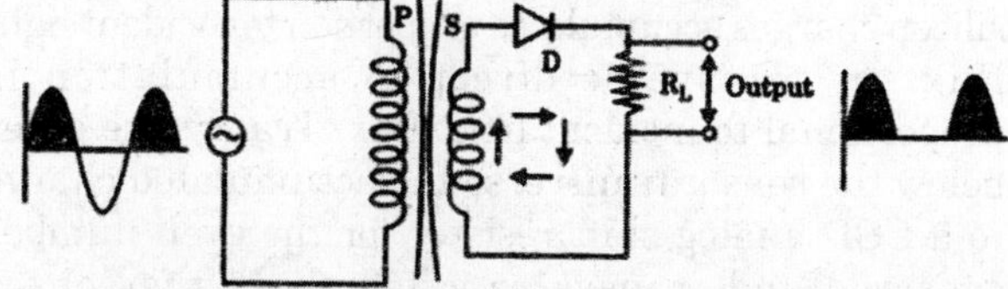

Full wave rectifier.

It has got 2 diodes, D_1 and D_2. When D_2 conducts, D_1 does not conduct. When D_1 conducts, D_2 does not conduct. It rectifies both halves of AC input and this output is also called a **pulsating D.C.**

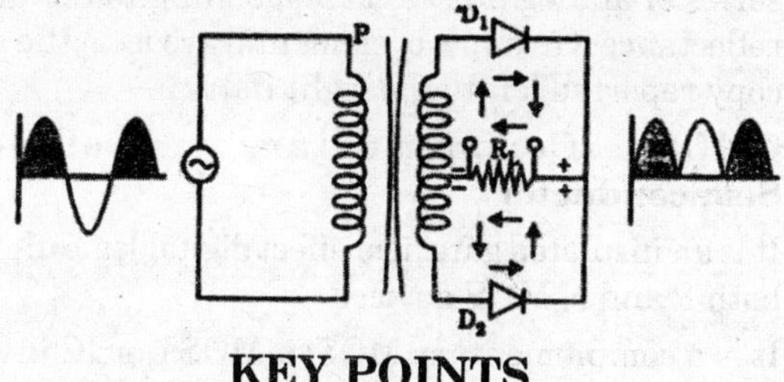

KEY POINTS

Arc Rectifier

It is a rectifier in which an arc struck between electrodes is so controlled as to be during the current wave direction in one only,

e.g. Metal rectifier.

A style of rectifier similar in principle to (thermionic rectifier except that the cathode is heated by the current itself and not by an external source.

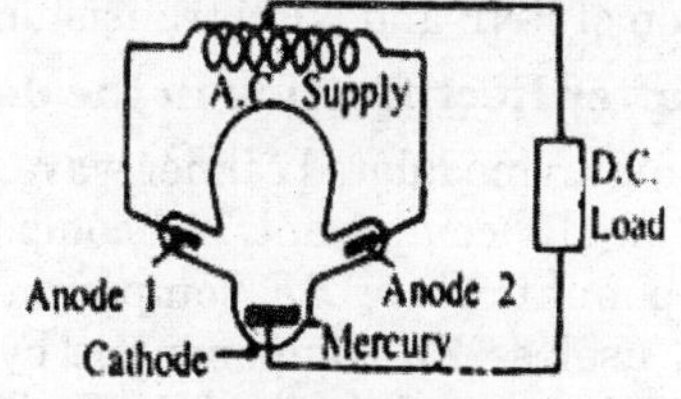

ARC Rectifier

CCD Filter

It is a circuit in which ability of a charge-coupled device to provide a precise predetermined delay time to an analog signal is utilized in order to produce a desired signal--processing function.

CCD Sensor

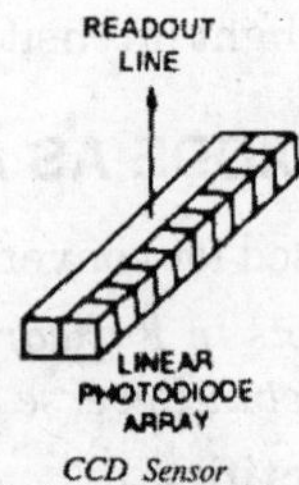

CCD Sensor

CCD as a linear image sensor uses silicon sensor (1,728 of them for group 3). While light is incident on the silicon charges accumulates proportion to incident light flux. In transverse direction accumulation is proportional to incident light flux. Transverse gates below the sensor transverse the accumulated charge to a CCD analog shift resister for the even number sensored and transverse gates above the sensor transverse charge to another CCD analog shift register for the odd number sensor. Clocking signals cause these charges to move down their respective analogue shift register where they emerge alternatively into preamplifier the output of which is a discrete time series of analog pulses corresponding to the diffused reflectance. On a row of elemental areas on the subject copy reported left to the right in turn.

CMOS (Complementary metal oxide Semiconductor)

It is an insulated gate field effect digital logic unit using both P and N MOS devices.

It is a complementary MOS; a MOST or IC involving both P-channel and N-Channel MOS-FETs.

Code

It is a combination of binary digits that represents information such as letters, numbers or symbols.

Code Converter

It is an electronic digital circuit which converts one type of coded information into another coded form.

CTL (Complementary Transistor Logic)

It is a logic system using emitter coupled circuits with a combination of PNP and NPN transistors.

Filtration after Rectification in the detection

After rectifying an modulated carrier wave, the output contains AF and RF components. AF component is the useful component while RF component becomes useless. So, useless RF component is by-passed to ground by filtration and the useful AF component is led to the following amplifier stage.

Solid state diode

It rectify a modulated RF signal. A solid stale diode is the simplest type of detector, which rectifies positive or negative half cycles of a modulated carrier wave as per circuit requirements. A capacitor connected across the load resistor is used to by-pass RF component of the rectifier output.

Simple crystal receiver

During early stage of electronic development, carborundum or galena crystals were used for detection. The radio receiver employing a crystal detector was called *crystal receiver*.

Diode

It is an electronic device that has only two electrodes. There are various types of diodes, their voltage characteristics determining their application. Diodes are most commonly used as rectifiers.

Diode Forward Voltage

The voltage across the electrodes of a diode when current flows. The current increases exponentially with voltage and therefore voltage is substantially constant over the range of currents in common use. A typical value is about 0-7 volts at 10 milliamps, making diodes very useful. The diode may also function as a voltage reference diode when it is used to provide a reference voltage, equal to the diode forward voltage, across its terminals.

Diode Transistor Logic (DTL)

It is a class of integrated logic circuits comprising of each input coming from a diode and the output taken from the collector of an inverting transistor.

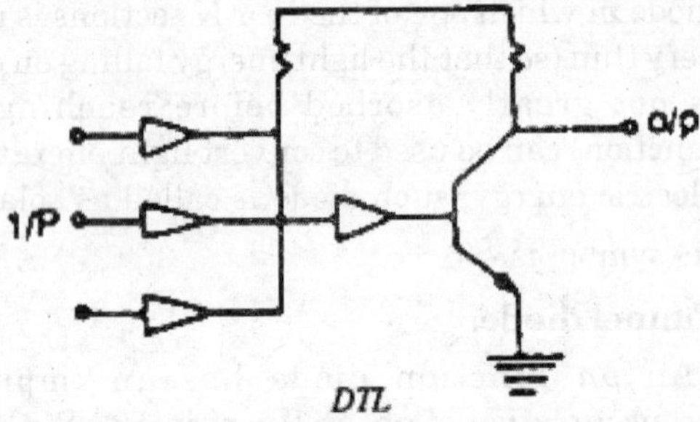

DTL

It is a family of integrated logic circuits in which each input signal comes through a diode and the output is taken from the collector of an inverting transistor. The basic circuit is NAND gate.

Dot Generator

It is a test generator used with a television receiver to adjust convergence of the picture tube. A pattern of evenly spaced dots or small squares is produced on a dark background and dynamic focussing is adjusted until a satisfactory image is formed on the screen.

Dot Interlace Scanning

It is a method of scanning, in which picture elements are explored in a regular but non sequential order.

Drift

It is deviation of the operating frequency of a crystal oscillator from its nominal value, generally owing to temperature variations. Drift often occurs during warm up or when device is nearing end of its useful life.

Dual-in-line package

It is a type of integrated circuit package.

Duplex

It is a process for bidirectional transmission of data along transmission line.

Electronic Device

A device which utilizes properties of electrons for ions moving in a vacuum, gas, or semiconductor. Timer is basically an oscillator generating very low frequency output. It is used for time control purposes in electric motors, photographic enlargers, electric heaters, radar etc.

Photo tube

It is a special type of vacuum diode which consists of a photo sensitive cathode and an anode. In this tube, a beam of light causes electrons emission from photo sensitive cathode. It is used in light operated counters and relays.

Photo resistor LDR (Light Dependent Resistor)

It is made of selenium and it is used in electronic counters.

Servo control

In this of control system, rotational portion of a motor is controlled by the '*feedback*' derived from its own output.

Transducer or Sensor

It is a device which is capable to convert one form of energy into another form or which is capable to produce equivalent variations in one form of energy by energy variations in the other form.

e.g., microphone, loudspeaker, pickup, LDR, fuel gauge etc.

Alarm

It is a warning device. An alarm employs a sensor and an electric alarm (bell). There are various types of alarms,

e.g., fire alarm burglar alarm, water level alarm, flood alarm etc.

UJT Unijunction transistor

It consists of a single PN junction with two leads connected to the N region and one to the P region. Resistance between the two bases is kept 5 to 10k ohms. It is used in low frequency oscillators and timers.

SCR (Silicon Controlled Rectifier)

It is a three electrode diode. It has a cathode, anode and gate. It can conduct 30 to 100 amperes of current when its anode is made positive with respect its cathode as well as an energizing positive pulse is applied to its gate. It is used in switching circuits, regulated power supplies etc.

DIAC

It is a two electrode three layer bi-directional diode. It is used as trigger, dipper, speed controller for universal motors and in thermos controlled devices.

TRIAC

It is an equivalent to two SCRs joined together in parallel. It is used in time relays etc.

MOSFET or (Metal oxide semiconductor field effect transistor)

It is an improved type of FET in which gate voltage doesn't affect very much conduction of current through the transistor. It is used in digital circuits.

LASER

It is an electromagnetic wave having a frequency of the range of 5×10^5 MHz.

These waves are used in surgery, radar, welding, long distance communications etc.

ELECTRONIC TEST INSTRUMENTS

These are equipments and devices that use electronics to perform various test and checks for reliability and maintainability.

CRO (Cathode Ray Oscilloscope)

It is an electronic equipment designed for visual display of various electrical wave forms.

General purpose oscilloscope

Specifications:

Band width – DC to 50 MHz

Sensitivity – 5 m V/Div. to 0.1 mV/Div.

Time base – 0.5 sec/Div. to 0.1 u sec/Div.

Trigger – Auto normal TV line and frame

CRT – 8 × 10 cm rectangular

Emission

It is liberation of electrons or electromagnetic radiation from the surface of a metal solid or liquid. It has many types depending on cause which makes the electrons to leave the surface like-high potential or heat (called *thermionic emission*).

Emitter

Short for emitter region. It is that part of a bipolar junction transistor from which carriers flow, through the emitter junction into the base. The electrode attached to this is emitter electrode.

Emitter Coupled Logic or current mode logic

It is a group of integrated logic circuits coupled but their emitters. High Speed non saturating logic family.

Emitter Follower

It is a transistor amplifier using common collector mode of operation. The output is derived from the emitter. The transistor is biased such that it is non saturated and conducting mode. Then it has a constant value relative to base at all times and emitter follows the signal applied to the base. Voltage gain is nearly unity, but the current gain is high. It is used as buffer with high input impedance and low output impedance.

Encoder

It is a digital circuit which converts the information/ data into coded form.

End-around Carry

It is the final carry that is added to the result in 1's or 9's complement addition.

Energy Levels

It is the possible values of energy of an atom or molecule. Quantum theory dictates that only certain fixed values are possible and these may only change by an integral multiple of some fixed amount. An electron orbiting the nucleus of the hydrogen atom may only occupy certain orbits of different energy. These allowed states of energy of the atom are called *electronic energy level*. The *ground state* is the lowest possible energy level and higher states being called *excited states*. Total energy of an atom is composed of kinetic energy, as it translates kinetic energy through space.

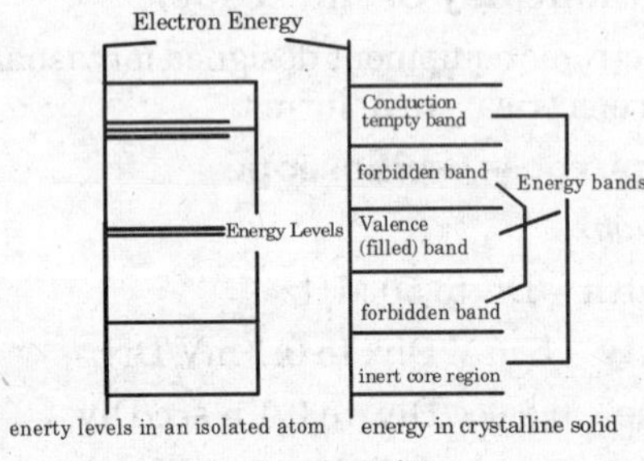

Energy Levels

Feedback

It is the process of feeding back a fraction of output energy of an energy changing device to input. The circuit that sends back the fractional energy is beta circuit and the circuit that generates output signal is '*mu circuit*.'

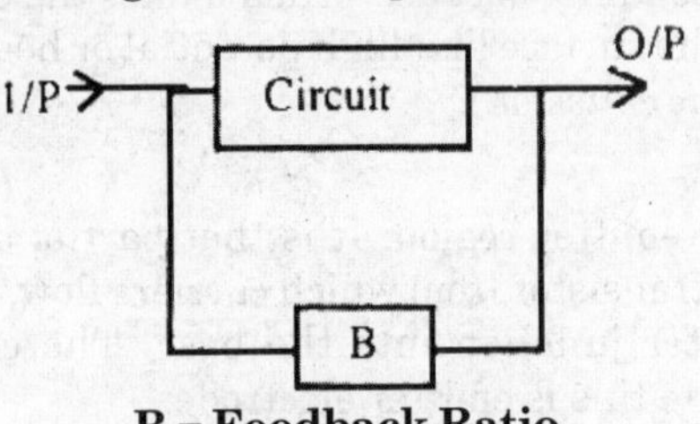

B = Feedback Ratio

Feedback Current

This is a form of feedback in which a fraction of current of the output load is fed back to the input.

Fermi Dirac

It is a system of quantum statics that is used to describe the behaviour of solids in terms of a free electron model. In this model, the most weakly bound electrons of the constituent atoms are considered to behave as a gas subject to certain conditions. The maximum electronic energy level that is occupied by an electron is a solid at a temperature of absolute zero. At higher temperatures, some electrons are excited into higher energy states. Then fermi level corresponds to the value of energy at which the Fermi-Dirac distribution function has a value given by Fermi Dirac function.

Fermi-dirac Function

It is a function expressing probability P(e) of finding occupying an energy level (E) by an electron.

This is given by :

$$P(E) = 1 + \exp (E - E_t)/kT \text{ joules}$$

where, E_t = fermi level

K = Boltzman constant

T = absolute temperature.

Field Effect Transistor (FET)

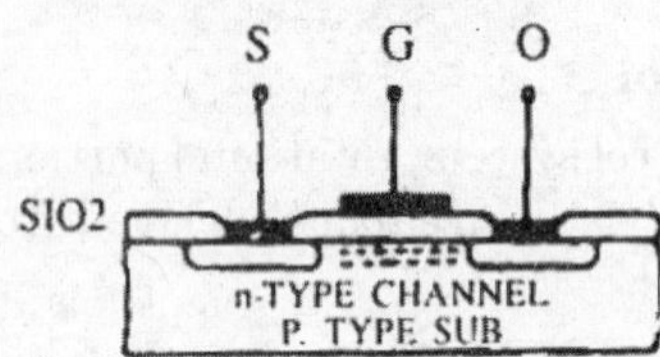

It is a majority carrier multi-electrode semiconductor device in which current flows through a narrow conducting channel between two electrodes and conduction through channel is modulated by an electric field applied through third electrode. *Three electrodes corresponding to three regions are*

(*i*) Source

(*ii*) Gate

(*iii*) Drain

Narrow channel connects source and drain while modulating signal is applied to gate.

Application of suitable bias to the device enables carriers to flow across the channel. FET is a unipolar device since charge carrier are majority device unlike a transistor which is a bipolar device. In both P channel and N channel, FETs are used.

FET Insulated Gate

This is a type of FET where channel is formed by the action of gate voltage. FET is formed by a wafer of semiconductor material that has two highly doped regions of opposite polarity diffused into it to form source and drain. Then insulating layer is formed on the surface between these regions and conductor deposited on top to form gate.

It is also called MISFET, MIST (Metal insulator silicon FET).

MOSFET, MOST (Metal oxide silicon FET).

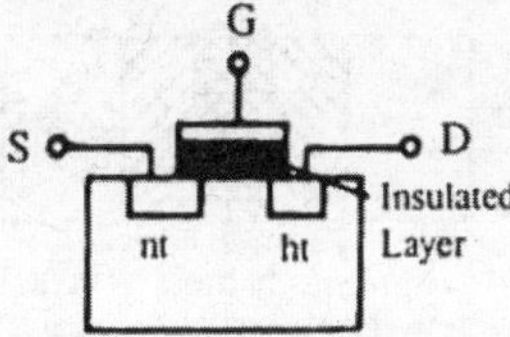

FET Junction

This FET employes conducting channel which is a part of the structure of device. It is also called JFET. It consists of a wafer of semiconductor flanked by two highly doped layers of opposite conductivity type *n* or *p*, forming source, drain and gate regions.

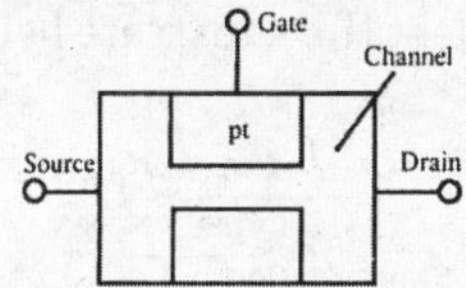

Pick's Law

The law is applied to achieve desired impurity profile in a particular specimen of semiconductor. The law states that *flows of atoms takes place from region of high concentration to low concentration if a concentration gradient of mobile impurity atoms exists in a semiconductor.*

At normal temperature impurity atoms are immobile until heated to a high temperature. A concentration gradient is formed by heating the semiconductor wafer in a gaseous atmosphere of impurity atoms, so that a high concentration exists at the surface. Under such conditions the impurity atoms diffuse into semiconductor according to Pick's law.

Film Resistor

It is a type of resistor, that uses a thin layer of resistive material deposited on an insulating core. For low power applications, film resistors are more stable than composition resistors and except for very high precision requirements, are smaller and less expensive than accurate wire-wound resistors.

Band Pass Filter (BPF)

It provides low attenuation to range of frequency signals having frequencies between lower cutoff frequency of filter and upper cutoff frequency of the filter. Frequencies rest outside this upper and lower limit are attenuated heavily.

Filter Butterworth :

This is a bandpass filter with output characteristics as shown where they have flat response in pass band.

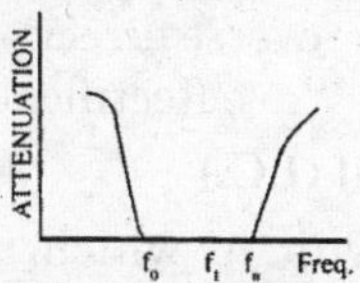

Filter Chebyshev (Tchebysheve).

This is bandpass filter with output characteristics as shown, where these have some variations sort of ripple in pass band but have more rapid increase of attenuation in unwanted bands, thus giving a sharper cutoff profile.

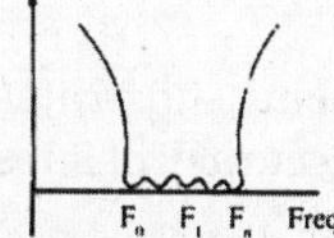

High Pass Filter (HPF)

It provides low attenuation to all frequency signals having frequency higher than the cut off frequency of filter. Frequencies below the cutoff are attenuated heavily.

Filter Passive

These filters employ impedance arranged in series and/ or short (L.C networks).

Glitch

It is a current or voltage spike of short duration usually unwanted.

Grid

It is an electrode that has an open structure, such as a mesh or a plate with a hole in it, thus allowing an electron beam to pass through it.

The nationwide high voltage transmission line system that interconnects many electricity power stations. It transmits voltages of up to 400 kilovolts. Voltages as high as 735 kV are used in some countries anything made essentially of parallel wires or bars in one plane. Particularly a wire screen or auxiliary anode between hot cathode and the plate anode in a Thermionic valve.

Gunn diode

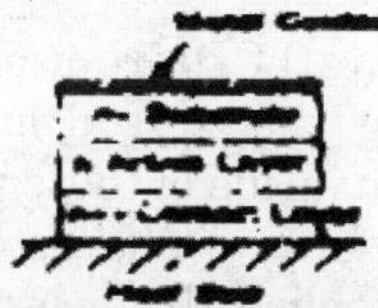

It is a negative-resistance microwave device that operates by means of Gunn effect. It is a diode formed from a sample of low resistivity n-type gallium arsenide that produces coherent microwave oscillations when a large electric field is applied across it.

Half - wave Rectification

It is the rectification, in which half-waves of the alternating current in one direction only are made use of while those in the reverse direction are suppressed. It is also called One Wave Rectification.

Integrated Circuit (I.C.)

It is a type of circuit in which all the parts are integrated on a single silicon chip of very small size.

Isolation Diode :

These diodes form by collector substrate junctions in bipolar integrated circuits to maintain isolation between parts of integrated circuit junctions by reverse biasing the junction.

Lapping

It is a method of reducing substrate/slice thickness for applications where accuracy of substrate thickness is critical like in case.

e.g., MMICs (Monolithic Microwave Integrated Circuits).

Liquid Crystal

It is an organic liquid consisting of long-chain molecules that line up under the influence of an applied electric field to give a quasi-crystalline structure of the liquid.

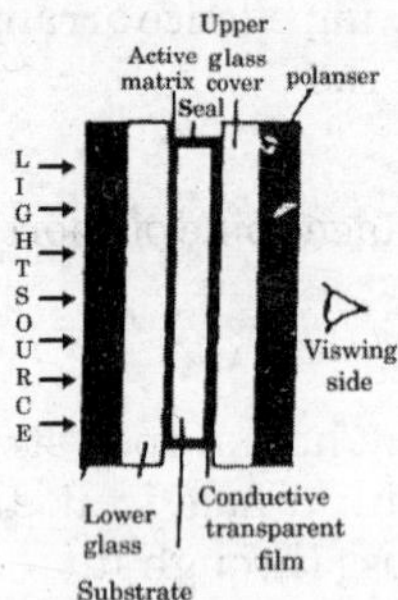

A change in the applied field causes a change in the reflectivity indices.

Liquid Crystal Display (LCD)

It is a type of passive display that uses liquid crystal display liquid crystals.

e.g., seven-segment numerical display of digital watches and pocket calculators.

LX

Liquid-crystal displays (LCD) are displays which consist of a very thin layer of liquid crystal fluid sealed between two glass plates. On inside of these plates, electrodes are etched in the form of characters. When in an electric field LX is applied, the molecular alignment of the fluid is disturbed. Due to difference in reflection, activated characters become visible.

Pin

It is connection point for logic integrated module.

PIN Diode

It consists of a layer of intrinsic semiconductor sandwiched between narrow layer of P and N semiconductor. Diode is used for microwave power switching, limiting and modulation. The intrinsic layer is lightly doped.

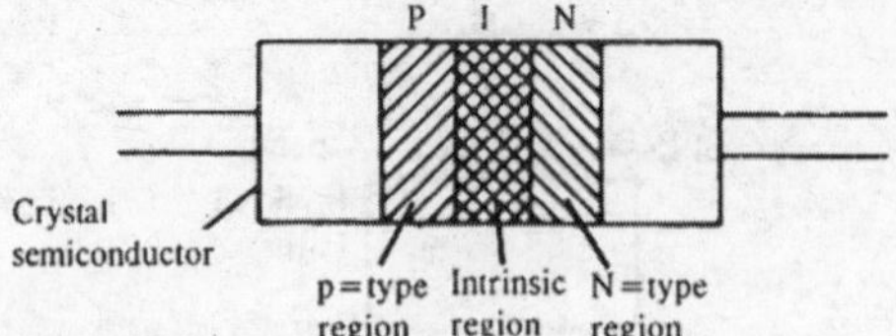

Planar process

It is method of fabricating semiconductor junction devices, in which a layer of silicon dioxide is grown on silicon substrate of required conductivity. Then photolithography is applied for etching oxide layer which then acts as mask. The junction between two semiconductors meet the substrate below oxide layer.

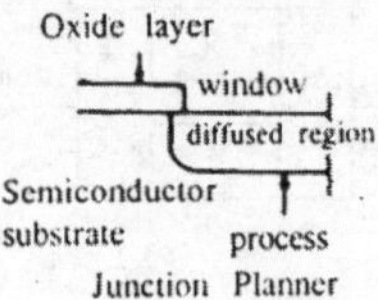

PN Junction

It is a two-terminal, solid state junction made from a semiconductor that has been treated to conduct current more readily in one direction than in the other. This treatment results in a p-type semiconductor at one end and an n-type semiconductor at the other end. PN junction forms the basis of most solid state devices, such as diodes, transistors, and silicon controlled rectifiers.

Pn pn Device

It is a three junction semiconductor device normally silicon with alternative p-type and n-type layers. The device has bistable current-voltage characteristic. It is used for power-switching purposes.

p	n	p	n

pnp Transistor

It is a semiconductor device where collector and emitter are made from p-type semiconductor material while the base is made from n-type material. In normal operation, emitter is positive with respect to the base while collector is negative with respect to the base.

RECTIFICATION

It is conversion of an Alternating current into a Unidirectional current.

RECTIFIERS

Types of rectifiers are :

1. Diode valve rectifier

Diode valve is a two electrode vacuum tube which consists of a cathode and an anode. When cathode is heated up by passing a current through its filament, it starts to emit electrons. Anode attracts emitted electrons if it is made positive with respect to cathode. If AC is applied to anode, then a current will flow for each positive half cycle only. In this way, AC will be converted into DC. Silicon diode is better tor the rectification of AC.

2. Metal rectifier:

As, $\quad$ mechanical pressure = $\dfrac{\text{Force}}{\text{Area}}$,

similarly $\quad$ electric pressure = $\dfrac{\text{Potential}}{\text{Area}}$.

So, electric current can flow easily from a sharp edged point towards a flat surface even across a thin layer of an insulation.

Type of Metal rectifiers:

(*i*) Selenium rectifier

(*ii*) Copper oxide rectifier

3. Solid state Rectifiers:

Half-wave and Full-wave rectifier

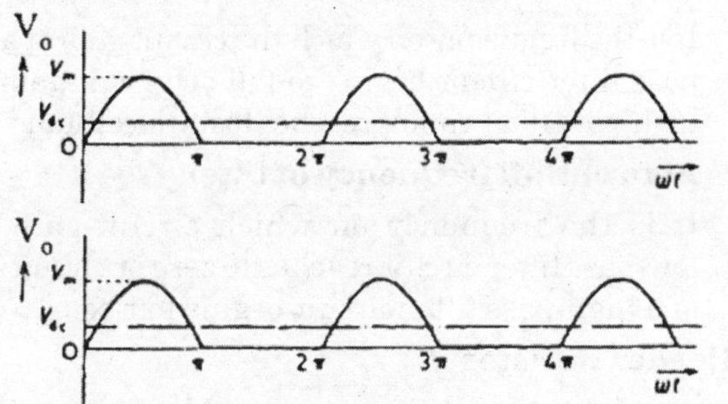

Output voltage from half wave rectifier

Half-wave rectifier circuit :

It provides DC output for positive half cycles only.

Maximum rectification efficiency of a half wave rectifier is 40.6%.

Ripple factor for a half wave rectifier is 1.21.

Full-wave rectifier:

It provides DC output for both half cycles of AC.

Advantages:

Advantages of full-wave rectifier circuit as compared to half-wave rectifier are follows:

(*i*) High efficiency.

(*ii*) Ordinary filter circuit is sufficient.

(*iii*) Provides more output current.

Bridge Rectifier

It is a transformer less full-wave rectifier. It requires 4 diodes.

Advantages:

Advantages of a bridge rectifier over full-wave rectifier are as follows:

Full-wave rectifier (two diodes type) requires a transformer with centre-tapped secondary, whereas, bridge rectifier does not require such transformer.

Battery Eliminator

It is an AC operated power supply unit which eliminates necessity of a battery for the operation of an electronic equipment.

Inverters

It is the device or circuit meant for the conversion of DC into AC. An inverter may both of dynamic or static type. Vibrator is a dynamic inverter while a solid state circuit meant for the purpose is called a static inverter.

Power supply unit

It is a sort of equipment which converts and modifies given input supply in accordance to the supply requirements of an electronic or electrical equipment.

Voltage Doubler

It is a rectifier circuit which doubles voltage supplied to it as well.

Types of Voltage doublers

1. **Half-wave voltage doubler**
2. **Full-wave voltage doubler**
3. **Voltage multiplier.**

A rectifier circuit which can be made to multiply the given input voltage of three, four, five, six-times by employing the require number of diodes accordingly is called a voltage multiplier.

Ripple frequency

It is frequency of pulses present in the rectified output. It is equal to frequency of AC supplied as input to the rectifier circuit.

Ripple frequencies of full-wave wave rectifiers is 100 Hz.

Ripple frequency of half-wave rectifier is 50 Hz.

Pulsating DC

It is the DC in which output current of a rectifier varies between maximum and zero values in the positive direction.

Static Inverter

It is a low frequency (400 Hz) oscillator which is associated with amplifiers and other controlling circuits.

Plate AC voltage

It is the maximum AC voltage which can be applied safely across a diode.

Peak inverse voltage

It is the maximum AC voltage which can be applied safely across a diode in its non conducting state.

Peak plate current and Load current

Maximum amount of current which can flow through a rectifier is called its '*peak plate current*'.

Maximum amount of DC which can be supplied by a rectifier to the load is called *load current*.

FILTER CIRCUIT

It is a circuit which is capable of selecting desired type of current out of a mixture of two or more types of currents.

Elements of a Filter circuit

1. **Choke**

   It presents a high impedance to AC and a very low impedance to DC.

2. **Capacitor**

   DC can't pass through a capacitor, whereas impedance of a capacitor decreases by increasing frequency of AC supplied to it.

3. **Resistor**

   Basically, a resistor has no filtration property, but if it is used in series of a choke or capacitor, it increases circuit impedance.

4. **Crystal**

Classification of Filter circuits

1. **According to work.**

   (*i*) **Low-pass filter:**

   It is the circuit which allows low frequency currents (upto 100 Hz) and obstructs currents of all frequencies above a pre-decided valve. It consists of a choke connected in series or a capacitor connected in parallel to the given input.

   (*ii*) **High pass filter**

   It is the circuit which allows currents of higher frequencies above a predecided value and obstructs currents of all frequencies lesser than that value. It consists of a capacitor connected in series or a choke connected in parallel to the given input.

   (*iii*) **Band-pass filter**

   The circuit which allows currents of a narrow band of frequencies and obstructs currents of all other frequencies. It consists of a series resonant circuit connected in series or a parallel resonant circuit connected in parallel to the given input.

   (*iv*) **Band-stop filter**

   It is the circuit which obstructs currents of a narrow band of frequencies and allows currents of all other frequencies. It consists of a series resonant circuit connected in parallel or a parallel resonant circuit connected in series to the given input.

2. **Classification filter circuits according to the input component**

   (*i*) **Choke input filter:**

   It is the circuit in which input filter element is a choke. *Voltage regulation* of this type of circuit is better than any other type of circuit.

   (*ii*) **Capacitor input filter:**

   It is the circuit in which input filter element is a capacitor. *Voltage regulation* of the circuit is poor than that of a choke input filter.

   (*iii*) **Crystal input filter**

   It is the circuit in which a crystal (quartz etc.) is used as the input filter element. Crystal has a property of vibrating at an exact frequency for which same is designed hence it is used as a filter element also in communication receivers.

3. **Classification filter as per circuit design**

   (*i*) Simple single element circuit

   (*ii*) L-Type

   (*iii*) T-type

   (*iv*) H-type

   (*v*) Multi section filters.

   In these circuits, the filter elements are connected in L, T, II, 2x etc. pattern.

Cut-off Frequency of Filter

1. **Alpha cut-off frequency of a filter**

   It is the frequency on which the circuit gain of a low-pass filter circuit begins to fall or circuit-gain of a high-pass filter circuit reaches to its maximum value.

2. **Beta cut-off frequency of filter**

   It is the frequency on which circuit-gain of a low-pass filter circuit reaches to zero or circuit-gain of a high-pass filter circuit begins to rise.

Bleeder Resistor

It is a high value resistor connected across a diode's output is called bleeder resistor.

Advantages:

Advantages of employing a bleeder resistor in a filter circuit are as follows:

(*i*) It provides a discharging path to the filter capacitors in case no load is connected to the diode.

(*ii*) It improves voltage regulation.

(*iii*) It can be used as an output voltage divider.

Rectification Efficiency

It is be defined as the percentage of input ac power that is converted into useful dc output power *i.e,*

$$\eta = \frac{\text{d.c. power output}}{\text{a.c. power input}} \times 100$$

Ripple Factor

It is a measure of purity of DC output of a rectifier. It can be defined as

$$r = \frac{\text{rms value of the wave components}}{\text{average of DC value}}$$

Semiconductor

It is a small component having an electrical conductivity between high conductivity of metals and low conductivity of insulators. It has resistivity in the range of conductors and insulators and having a negative temperature coefficient of resistance. The conductivity increases not only with temperature but is also affected very considerably by the presence of impurities in the crystal lattice. Semiconductors are used in wide variety of solid-state devices including transistors, integrated circuits, diodes, photodiodes, and light emitting diodes.

Principal semiconductors

(*i*) Germanium diode.

It is a very sensitive diode and a forward bias of 0.1 volt is sufficient to conduct a forward current through out it.

(*ii*) Silicon diode.

It requires a minimum forward bias of 0.7 volts for the conduction of forward current through it.

Germanium and silicon are the principal semiconductors.

Characteristics of a semiconductor

(*i*) It has a crystalline structure.

(*ii*) Its conductivity is greatly affected by light rays of high intensity, ultra-violet rays and infra-red rays.

(*iii*) Its conductivity varies in accordance to the temperature variations.

Intrinsic and Extrinsic Semiconductors.

Intrinsic semiconductor

Semiconductor material in its pure form is called *intrinsic*

Extrinsic semiconductor : Semiconductor material added with other element is called *extrinsic* semiconductors, such as 'N type' and 'P type' materials.

(*a*) P-type material : When a trivalent element (such as indium, gallium) is added to tetravalent semiconductor (germanium or silicon) then a deficit of an electron is produced for each impurity atom; such type of material is called *'P-type' material*.

(*b*) N-type material : When a pentavalent element (such as arsenic, antimony) is added to tetravalent semiconductor, then a surplus electron is produced by each impurity atom; such type of material is called *'N-type' material*.

Acceptor atom

It is 'hole' producing impurity atom 'hole' is *empty space* for an electron.

Donor atom

It is *'free electron'* producing atom.

Doping

It is the act of adding up an element as an impurity to a semiconductor

P-N JUNCTION

Only P-type or N-type material acts as a common conductor, but when two small pieces of P and N-type materials are joined together by heat treatment, then junction so formed is called a *P-N junction*.

A P-N junction diode is capable to work as a rectifier, i.e. it can convert AC into DC.

Biasing

A P-N junction can be biased in forward and reverse states,

(*i*) **Forward biased :** When P terminal is connected to the positive and N terminal to the negative end of a battery, the junction is said to be forward biassed.

(*ii*) **Reverse biased :** P terminal is connected to the negative and N terminal to the positive end of a battery, the junction is said to be reverse biased.

Leakage current

Effective conduction of current lakes place in *'forward bias'* state, a small amount of current flows in reverse direction also. The conduction of leakage current is the result of recombination of free-electrons with holes.

Knee voltage

It is the minimum forward bias voltage required for conduction of current across a P-N junction.

Fabrication.

P-N junction diodes are fabricated in following two ways

(*i*) Grown junction method

In this method, say P-type material is melted and then allowed to cool slowly, so that molten material may take a crystalline shape. The crystals so developed are slightly lifted out and an impurity of N-type material is added to the molten material. In this way, lower portion of the crystal becomes of N-type while upper portion of the same remains of P-type.

(*ii*) Fused junction method :

In this method, few particles of indium are fused into a small and thin N-type crystal at 500-600°C. Thus a P-type dot is formed in the N-type material.

Effect of heat.

An increase in the temperature of a P-N diode gives a corresponding rise to the leakage current. Therefore, operating temperature of a P-N diode should be kept low for its long life.

Zener diode

It is a silicon diode having a lower value of inverse voltage (break down voltage) It has a property that its leakage current increases suddenly by increasing the reverse bias. It is used in voltage regulator circuits.

Break down voltage of a zener diode

Magnitude of inverse voltage ai which 'zener current' or 'avalanche current' starts to flow across a zener diode is called its *'break down voltage'* or *'safe inverse voltage'*.

Tunnel diode

P-N junction of a tunnel diode is designed in such a way that the electrons passing through the junction have to manage any how to cross the junction. It is used in amplifiers and oscillator circuits.

LED

It is a gallium-arsenide (Ga.As) diode which has a property of emitting light when its forward bias increases above a predecided voltage value.

Varactor diode

It is a P-N junction diode which is designed to work at high frequencies. Its internal capacitance varies in accordance to the signal applied, hence it is used for amplification, frequency multiplication and switching purposes.

Silicon Controlled Rectifier

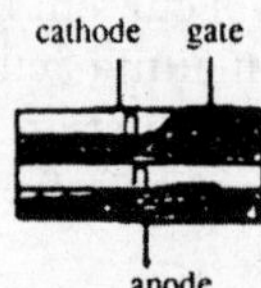

It is three junction three terminal semiconductor diode used for switching moderate power devices. It can be switched ON by a voltage pulse at gate at anode voltage less than the break over voltage. For turning OFF the device, a voltage pulse is applied to a second gate electrode.

Small Scale Integration (SSI)

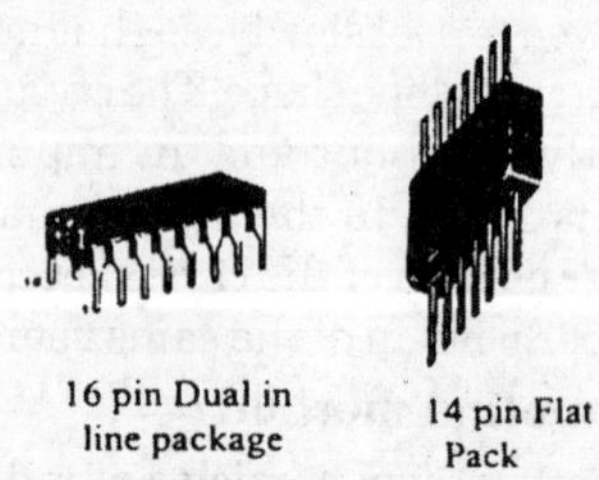

The least complex digital ICs are placed in small scale integration category. These are circuits with upto 12 equivalent gate circuits on a single chip.

Transistor

It is solid state equivalent of a triode valve. A solid state, current-gain device having a collector, base and emitter terminals. It is made by using both p-and n-type materials. It is are available in either PNP or NPN configurations. It is also called a *bipolar transistor*. It is a multielectrode semiconductor device in which current flowing between two specified electrodes is modulated by the voltage or current applied to one or more specified electrodes. The semiconductor material is usually silicon.

It transistor is called a solid state device because of its construction within a single crystal piece.

Valve

It is a unidirectional device. It is also *vacuum tube* because it is made in a perfectly evacuated glass tube.

Triode valve

It is a three electrode valve. Electrodes are

(*i*) Cathode,

(*ii*) Control grid

(*iii*) Anode (or plate).

Transistors over Vacuum tubes

(*i*) Transistor's have low working temperature (20-250°C)

(*ii*) Transistor's have limited power handling capability.

Thermal runway

If a transistor is subjected to a temperature of 800°C or above, it becomes nearly a conductor (in general). This phenomenon is called *thermal runway*.

Unipolar transistor

A transistor in which conduction of current is a result of movement or drift of only one type of charge carrier is called *unipolar transistor.*

Comparison of silicon transistors and Germanium transistors

(*i*) Silicon transistors are capable to work at a higher temperature with respect to germanium transistors,

(*ii*) Silicon transistors are capable to carry large current with respect to germanium transistors.

PNP and NPN Transistors

(*i*) **PNP transistor:** It consists of two P-regions and a thin N-region between them.

It transistor drifting of holes from emitter to collector is responsible for conduction of current in a PNP transistor.

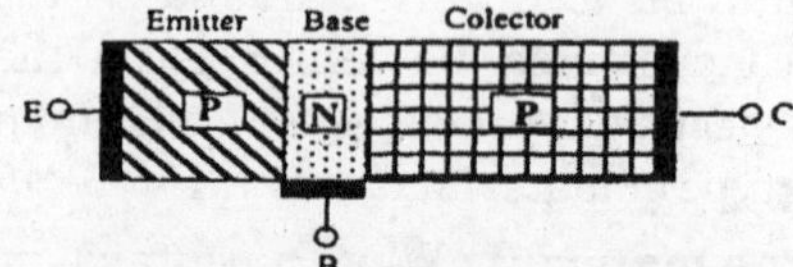

PNP-Type Junction Diode

(*ii*) **NPN:** Consequently, the flow of electrons from collector to emitter constitutes the current in PNP transistors consists of two N-regions and a thin P-region between them.

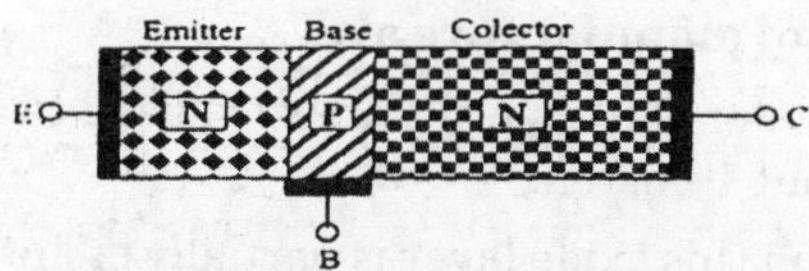

NPN-Type Junction Diode

The movement of free electrons from emitter to collector is responsible for the conduction of current in NPN transistor.

Effect of base bias variations

Magnitude of base bias voltage controls the number of charge carriers moving or drifting across the transistor. Therefore, a transistor is used for producing amplification, oscillations, modulation etc.

Methods of Manufacturing Transistors

There are three principal methods of fabricating transistors:

(*i*) **Junction of method :** In this method, small quantities of indium are doped into two opposite sides of a N-type wafer at about 500-6000°C temperature for making a PNP transistor. Similarly for making an NPN transistor, arsenic is doped into two opposite sides of a P-type water. This type of transistors are also called *alloy junction transistors*.

(*ii*) **Point contact method :** In this method, two sharply pointed indium-steel pins are fused in N-type pallet at about 500-6000°C temperature for making a PNP transistor. Similarly, for making an NPN transistor two arsenic steel pins are fused in a P-type pallet. A thin portion remained between two pins acts as 'base.'

(*iii*) **Diffused junction method:** In this method, small pits are made in P or N-type material by the pits by thermal action. This type of transistors are also called *epitaxial* or *homotaxial transistors*.

Point contact transistors have High value of current gain '*alpha*' (greater than one). These are capable to work at a frequency of 100 MHz above, and to carry more current.

These are capable to handle hundreds of watts of electrical power and can carry 10 or more amperes of current when installed with a suitable '*heat sink*'.

Heat sink is a metallic heat radiator mounted around a transistor (especially collector of the transistor).

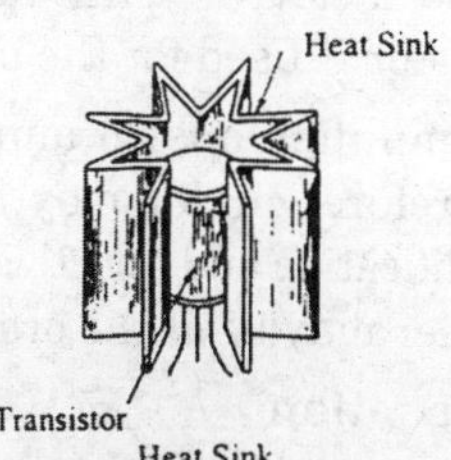

Transistor Characteristics

These are studied by plotting IE-VE and IC-VC curves.

(*i*) **IE-VE curves :** It show that emitter current depends on the emitter voltage and the collector voltage has a very little effect on the emitter current and hence transistor has a low input impedance.

(*ii*) **IC-VC curves :** It show that a transistor attains a high collector current at a low collector voltage and hence the transistor has a high output impedance.

Current gain Alpha (α)

It is ratio of the collector current variations to the emitter current variations on no-load and constant voltages

$$\alpha = \frac{I_C}{I_E}$$

where, IC = collector current variations

IC = emitter current variations

Note : Both current variations should be measured in the same units.

***(ii)* Beta (β)**

It is ratio of the collector current variations to the base current variations on no load and constant voltages.

$$\beta = \frac{I_C}{I_B}$$

where, I_B = base current variations.

Relation between α and β

$$\beta = \frac{\alpha}{1-\alpha} \text{ or } \alpha = \frac{\beta}{1+\beta}$$

Alpha cut-off frequency

The frequency at which gain of a transistor is reduced to *10.1%* of its gain at low frequency is called *alpha cut-off frequency of the transistor*.

Voltage gain of a transistor

It is ratio of the output voltage to the input voltage

$$\text{V.G.} = \frac{V_0}{V_i} = \frac{\text{Output voltage}}{\text{Input voltage}}$$

Power gain of a transistor

It is ratio of the output power to the input power

$$\text{P.G.} = \frac{\text{Output power}}{\text{Input power}} = \frac{P_0}{P_i}$$

Three Basic configurations of Transistors

There are three basic configurations of transistors:

1. **Common base (CB) configuration**

   It is the transistor circuit in which base is kept common to the input and output circuits.

   Characteristics

   (*i*) Low input impedance (50 to 500 ohms).

   (*ii*) High output impedance (1 to 10 mega ohms)

   (*iii*) Current gain alpha = less than unity.

2. **Common emitter (CE) configuration**

   It is the transistor circuit is which emitter is kept common to the input and output circuits.

Characteristics

(*i*) High input impedance (500 to 5000 ohms)

(*ii*) Low output impedance (50 to 500 kilo ohms)

(*iii*) Currem gain, β is = upto 98

(*iv*) Power gain uplo 5000 or 37 dB.

(*v*) 180° out of phase output.

3. Common collector circuits (CC) configuration

It is the transistor circuit in which collector is kept common to the input and output circuits.

It is also called emitter follower

Characteristics

(*i*) High input impedance (150 to 600 kilo ohms)

(*ii*) Low output impedance (100 to 1000 ohms)

(*iii*) Current gain, β = 99

(*iv*) Voltage and power gain is equal to or less than unity.

Tetrode Transistor

It has four terminals:

(*i*) Emitter (*ii*) base-1

(*iii*) base-2 (*iv*) collector

Addition of fourth electrode base-2 enables it to work satisfactorily at high frequencies even.

FET (Field Effect Transistor)

It is a solid state device in which conduction of current is controlled by an electrostatic field. Its electrodes are called *source, drain and gate.*

Transistor Data

It is a reference book which contains following information regarding characteristics of transistors :

(*i*) Maximum collector-emitter voltage

(*ii*) Maximum collector current

(*iii*) Leakage current

(*iv*) Input output impedances

(*v*) Current gain and power gain

(*vi*) Alpha cut off frequency

(*vii*) Power dissipation

(*viii*) Working temperature

(*ix*) Collector-base voltage and capacitance

(*x*) Base current etc.

Transistor Manufacture

Many transistors or other elements, together with their interconnecting links, are made on a single chip to turn it into an IC, I usual method of manufacturer of monolithic ICs (mono= single, Iithos = stone, in this case silicon) has many similarities in technique with the making of a single silicon (planar) transistor.

Stages of manufacture are:

(*i*) A wafer of n-type silicon is oxidized to a depth of about 1 micron.

(*ii*) Then this oxide layer is partially etched off.

(*iii*) The wafer is exposed to a vapor of the acceptor element boron. This element diffused into the wafer to a predetermined depth (creating a p-type zone). The wafer surface is at the same time de-oxidized.

(*iv*) Then a part of the newly de-oxidized surface is etched away again.

(*v*) Then wafer is exposed to a vapor of the donor element phosphorus. This diffuses in (to create an n-type zone) the surface is again de-oxidized.

(*vi*) More etching away of the oxide surface follows, to separate what have become the base and emitter regions on the surface of the wafer.

(*vii*) Metal contacts are alloyed on to the etched areas,

TRF (Tuned Radio Frequency) receiver

It is a radio receiver in which detection is accomplished on a tuned radio frequency (without any frequency conversion).

Changing wave bands of a radio receiver

Wave bands of a radio receiver are changed by following means of:

(*i*) Rotary (*ii*) Slide

(*iii*) Push button 3r (*iv*) Piano type switch.

(*i*) Rotary switch : It consists of a long spindle on which a number of contractors of '*poles*' are mounted to establish contact with stator points or 'ways' type rotary switches. 4P-3W, 6P-3W, 6P-5W and 6P-8W b

(*ii*) Slide switch : A slide switch has 4 or 6 poles which can slide aver, 2, 3 or 5 ways.

(*iii*) Push button or piano type switch : It consists of '*contractor leaves*' and '*pins*'. '*Poles*' are made, by joining pole-pins and other pins act as '*ways*'.

IF amplifier

It is the amplifier which amplifiers at a definite radio frequency (with a narrow pass hand). A high gain pentode/transistor is used for the purpose.

Since an IF amplifier has to amplify at a definite frequency, therefore, circuit may designed to obtain maximum amplification and selectivity. The voltage gain of an IF amplifier may be of the order of 500 to 5000.

Ultradyne Reception

It is a system of radio reception, similar to the superheterodyne system, in which intermediate. Frequency is obtained from auxiliary oscillation superimposed upon anode circuit of the first valve.

UPS (Uninterrupted Power Supply)

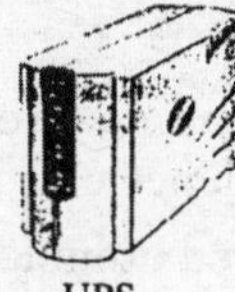

UPS

It is a device used to supply in case of power failure. It comes in various VA ratings and stand by times.

Uranium (U)

It is a radioactive element. It's a atomic number is 92. Naturally occurring uranium is a mixture of 99.28%2"U, 0.71 %-*U, and 0.0058%-^{235}U. The nucleus of ^{235}U is capable of absorbing a neutron and thereupon undergoing fission into two highly radioactive fragments that fly apart with great energy, releasing neutrons. A chain reaction is possible because fission is induced by one neutron but release more than one neutron.

Vaccum Triode

It is the device which has ability to amplify small electrical signals (audio signals)

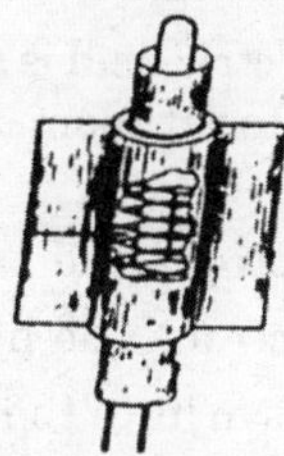

Variable speed Scanning

Beam in the transmitter owing to interconnect ion of the deflecting circuits and as apparent illumination of the screen depends upon the beam, the picture is reproduced. In method of scanning in cathode-ray television, speed of deflection of the scanning beam is governed by the optical density of the object (in this case a film). Beam in the receiver is of constant intensity and copies motion of the object.

Zener Breakdown

It is a type of breakdown observed in a reverse biased p-n junction that has very high doping concentration on both-sides of the junction. The build-in-field is high and the depletion layer narrow as a result of high level of doping.

Zener Diodes

These diodes are designed to operate in the break down region without damage. It is specified by its break down voltage and maximum power dissipation.

Circuit symbol of a zener diode

Z Modulation of CRT

Intensity of beam is modulated by an external signal.

Zone Levelling

It is method of *zone refining* in order to distribute impurities evenly throughout the bulk of the material.

Zone purification is the application of zone refining in order to reduce concentration of an impurity in a material.

Standard Values of Commercially Available Resistors tolerance ± 10%

ohms (Ω)		kilo ohms kΩ		Mega ohms MΩ
1.0	33	1.0	33	1.0
1.2	39	1.2	39	1.2
1.5	47	1.5	47	1.5
1.8	56	1.8	56	1.3
2.2	68	2.2	68	2.2
2.7	82	2.7	82	2.7
3.3	100	3.3	100	3.3
3.9	120	3.9	120	3.9
4.7	150	4.7	150	4.7
5.6	180	5.6	180	5.6
6.8	220	6.8	220	6.8
8.2	270	8.2	270	8.2
10	330	10	330	10
12	390	12	390	12
15	470	15	470	15
18	560	18	560	18
22	680	22	680	22
27	820	27	820	—

Conductivity and Resistivity

Classification	Material	Conductivity (S/m)	Resistivity (Ohm)
Conductors	Silver	6.25×10^7	1.6×10^{-8}
	Copper	5.88×10^7	1.7×10^{-8}
	Aluminium	3.85×10^7	2.6×10^{-8}
Semi-conductors	Germanium	1.54	6.5×10^{-1}
	Silicon	5.0×10^{-4}	2.0×10^3
Insulators	Porcelain	3.33×10^{-10}	3.0×10^9
	Glass	5.88×10^{-12}	1.7 × 1011
	Hard rubber	1×10^{-16}	$1 - 10^{16}$

Some Derived Units

Physical	Quantity	Name of SI Unit	Symbol
Electric	Capacitance	Farad	F = A S/V
Electric	Charge	Coulomb	C = As
Electric	Conductance	Siemen (mho ν)	S = A/V
Electric	resistance	ohm	Ω = V/A
Electric	potential	Volt	V=W/A
Force		Newton	N = Kg m/s^2
Frequency		hertz	Hz=cycles/s
Inductance		henry	H = V S/A
Magnetic	flux	Weber	Wb = Vs
Magnetic	flux density	Tesla	T=Wb/m^2
Power		Watt	W=J/s
Pressure		Pascal	Pa = N/m
Work,	energy, heat	Joule	J = Nm

Objective Type Questions

1. One electron volt equals
   (*a*) 1.6×10^{19} joule (*b*) 1.6×10^{16} joule
   (*c*) 9.1×10^{-31} joule (*d*) 91.1×10^{16} joule
2. At room temperature, resistivity of pure germanium expressed in ohm-cum is
   (*a*) 0.45 (*b*) 4.5
   (*c*) 45 (*d*) 450
3. At room temperature resistivity of pure silicon expressed in ohm-cm is
   (*a*) 2,300 (*b*) 23,000
   (*c*) 230,000 (*d*) 450
4. Resistivity range of semiconductors in ohm-meter is
   (*a*) 10^{-5} to 10^{5} (*b*) 10^{-5} to 10^{10}
   (*c*) 10^{-3} to 10^{3} (*d*) 10^{-1} to 10^{6}
5. Resistivity of a semiconductor depends on
   (*a*) the length of the semiconductor specimen
   (*b*) cross-sectional area of the semiconductor specimen
   (*c*) volume of the semiconductor specimen
   (*d*) the atomic nature of the semiconductor
6. Resistivity measurements are often used to determine
   (*a*) carrier mobility
   (*b*) carrier concentration in intrinsic semiconductor
   (*c*) carrier concentration in extrinsic semiconductor
   (*d*) life time of polycrystalline materials
7. An intrinsic semiconductor at absolute zero temperature
   (*a*) has only a few holes and a few electrons
   (*b*) has very large number of holes and electrons
   (*c*) behaves like a good conductor
   (*d*) behaves like a good insulator
8. A germanium atom contains
   (*a*) four valence electrons
   (*b*) six valence electrons
   (*c*) four protons
   (*d*) six protons
9. In Ge, an electron in the conduction band
   (*a*) is bound to its parent atom
   (*b*) has a higher energy than an electron in the valence band
   (*c*) has zero charge
   (*d*) is located near the top of the crystal
10. In Ge, when atoms are held together by the sharing of valence electrons
    (*a*) each shared atom leaves a hole
    (*b*) valence electrons are free to move away from the nucleus
    (*c*) velence electrons form irreversible covalent bands
    (*d*) valence electrons form reversible covalent bands
11. A hole is the vacancy created when
    (*a*) a free electron moves on application of electric field
    (*b*) an electron breaks its covalent band
    (*c*) an atomic core moves
    (*d*) an electron reverts from conduction band to valence band
12. When an electric field is applied to an intrinsic semiconductor at room temperature say from left to right
    (*a*) both electrons and holes drift to the right
    (*b*) both electrons and holes drift to the left
    (*c*) electrons drift to the right while the holes drift to the left
    (*d*) electrons drift to the left while holes drift to the right
13. Energy required to break a covalent in semiconductor is
    (*a*) always equal to 1.6 eV
    (*b*) greater in Ge than in Si
    (*c*) equal to the width of the forbidden energy gap
    (*d*) is the sae in Ge as in Si
14. At absolute zero, all the valence electrons in an intrinsic semiconductor are
    (*a*) in the conduction band
    (*b*) in the forbidden band
    (*c*) in the valence band
    (*d*) reduced to zero in number
15. Germanium
    (*a*) can not be purified by zone refining method
    (*b*) is usualy purified by the floating zone method
    (*c*) is more easily purified than silicon
    (*d*) has melting temperature higher than silicon

16. In a semiconductor, rate of diffusion of charge carriers
(*a*) depends on the concentration gradient and the mobility
(*b*) depends on the concentration gradient alone
(*c*) depends on the mobility alone
(*d*) is independent of concentration gradient and the mobility

17. Adjacent atoms in the crystalline structure of a semiconductor like germanium form
(*a*) ionic bands (*b*) metallic bands
(*c*) molecular bands (*d*) covalent bands

18. When a pure semiconductor is heated
(*a*) its resistance increases
(*b*) its resistance decreases
(*c*) its atomic structure changes
(*d*) it becomes metal

19. Valence electrons are
(*a*) found in the nucleus
(*b*) the inner core electrons of an atom
(*c*) the outer orbit electrons
(*d*) always free electrons

20. Pure semiconductors are poor conductor because
(*a*) they have no valence electrons
(*b*) all valence electrons are in electron-pairs
(*c*) they have a number of holes
(*d*) there are fewer electrons than protons

21. Hole in a lattice in defined as
(*a*) free proton
(*b*) free neutron
(*c*) vacancy created by removal of electron from covalent band
(*d*) acceptor ion

22. In a pure semiconductor, electric current is due to
(*a*) holes alone
(*b*) electrons alone
(*c*) both holes and electrons
(*d*) valence electrons alone

23. Forbidden energy gap between valence band and conduction band is least in the case of
(*a*) mica (*b*) pure silicon
(*c*) pure germanium (*d*) impure silicon

24. Temperature coefficient of resistance in a pure semiconductor is
(*a*) zero
(*b*) positive
(*c*) negative
(*d*) dependent on size of specimen

25. Forbidden energy gap in semiconductors is of the order of
(*a*) 7 eV (*b*) 1 eV
(*c*) 0.1 eV (*d*) 0.05 eV

26. At 0°K, the forbidden energy gap in germanium is
(*a*) 0.785 eV (*b*) 1.21eV
(*c*) 0.72 eV (*d*) 1.1 eV

27. At 300°K, the forbidden energy gap in germanium is
(*a*) 0.785 eV (*b*) 1.21 eV
(*c*) 0.72 eV (*d*) 1.1 eV

28. At 0°K, the forbidden energy gap in silicon is
(*a*) 0.785 eV (*b*) 1.21 eV
(*c*) 0.72 eV (*d*) 1.1 eV

29. A 300°K, the forbidden energy gap in silicon is
(*a*) 0.785 eV (*b*) 1.21 eV
(*c*) 0.72 eV (*d*) 1.1 eV

30. The diffusion length of a carrier depends on
(*a*) shape of the semiconductor
(*b*) life time of the carriers alone
(*c*) mobility and life time of the carriers
(*d*) mobility of the carriers alone

31. Donor impurity atom in a semiconductor result in new
(*a*) wide energy band
(*b*) narrow energy band
(*c*) discrete energy level just below conduction level
(*d*) discrete energy level just above valence level

32. Acceptor impurity atoms in a semiconductor result in new
(*a*) wide energy band
(*b*) narrow energy band
(*c*) discrete energy level just below conduction level
(*d*) discrete energy level just above valence level

33. If donor concentration N_D equals acceptor concentration N_A, resulting semiconductor is
(*a*) n-type
(*b*) p-type
(*c*) intrinsic
(*d*) may be p or n type depending on temperature

34. In n-type germanium with boron impurity, the ionisation energy is about
(*a*) 0.001 eV (*b*) 0.01 eV
(*c*) 0.1 eV (*d*) 1 eV

35. Mobility of free electrons in germanium at 300°k expressed in cm^2/V-s is
(*a*) 1800 (*b*) 3800
(*c*) 1300 (*d*) 500

36. Mobility of free electrons in silicon at 300°k expressed in cm^2/V-s is

(*a*) 500 (*b*) 1300
(*c*) 1800 (*d*) 3800

37. Mobility of holes in germanium of 300°k expressed in cm^2/V-s is

(*a*) 500 (*b*) 1300
(*c*) 1800 (*d*) 3800

38. Mobility of holes in silicon at 300°k expressed in cm^2/V-s is

(*a*) 500 (*b*) 1300
(*c*) 1800 (*d*) 3800

39. In n-type germanium with assenic impurity, the ionisaiton energy is about

(*a*) 0.001 eV (*b*) 0.01 eV
(*c*) 0.1 eV (*d*) 1 eV

40. In silicon at room temperature, concentration of thermally generated electrons/cm^3 is of the order of

(*a*) 10^8 (*b*) 10^{10}
(*c*) 10^{13} (*d*) 10^{15}

41. In germanium at room temperature, concentration of thermally generated electrons/cm^3 is of the order of

(*a*) 10^{11} (*b*) 10^{13}
(*c*) 10^{15} (*d*) 10^7

42. In Ge or Si, light doping corresponds to impurity of following magnitude

(*a*) 1 in 10^8 (*b*) 1 in 10^6
(*c*) 1 in 10^5 (*d*) 1 in 10^4

43. In Ge or Si, medium doping corresponds to impurity of the following order

(*a*) 1 part in 10^8 (*b*) 1 part in 10^6
(*c*) 1 part in 10^5 (*d*) 1 part in 10^4

44. In Ge or Si, heavy doping approximately corresponds to impurity of magnitude

(*a*) 1 part in 10^8 (*b*) 1 part in 10^6
(*c*) 1 part in 10^5 (*d*) 1 part in 10^4

45. When germanium is doped with pentavalent impurity, the resulting material is

(*a*) p-type semiconductor
(*b*) n-type semiconductor
(*c*) intrinsic semiconductor
(*d*) no longer a semiconductor

46. When germanium is doped with trivalent impurity, the resulting material is

(*a*) p-type semiconductor
(*b*) n-type semiconductor
(*c*) intrinsic semiconductor
(*d*) no longer a semiconductor

47. A p-type semiconductor is

(*a*) positively charged
(*b*) negatively charged
(*c*) electrically neutral
(*d*) not used in semiconductor devices

48. An n-type semiconductor is

(*a*) positively charged
(*b*) negatively charged
(*c*) electrically neutral
(*d*) not used in semiconductor devices

49. In p-type semiconductor

(*a*) $n = p$ (*b*) $p < n$
(*c*) $p << n$ (*d*) $p >> n$

50. In n-type semiconductor

(*a*) $n = p$ (*b*) $n < p$
(*c*) $n >> p$ (*d*) $n << p$

where n and p are densities of free electrons & holes respectively.

51. Through repeated zone refining, the residual impurity in a semiconductor is of the order of

(*a*) 1 part in 10^3 (*b*) 1 part in 10^5
(*c*) 1 part in 10^7 (*d*) 1 part in 10^{11}

52. Mobility of electron in a semiconductor

(*a*) decreases as the temperature increases
(*b*) increases as the temperature increases
(*c*) has no effect on conductivity
(*d*) is independent of temperature

53. Mobility of charge carrier in a semiconductor depends on

(*a*) recombination rate
(*b*) temperature of the semiconductor
(*c*) resistivity of the semiconductor
(*d*) charge per carrier

54. Movement of charge carriers from an area of high carrier concentration to an area of low carrier concentration is called

(*a*) drift (*b*) diffusion
(*c*) recombination (*d*) gradient

55. Change of carrier concentration along the length of a semiconductor is called

(*a*) mobility
(*b*) diffusion
(*c*) concetration gradient
(*d*) drift

56. When a free electron is recaptured by a hole, the process is called

(*a*) recombination (*b*) diffusion
(*c*) drift (*d*) restoration

57. In a semiconductor, movement of charge carriers under influence of an electric field is called

(*a*) diffusion (*b*) drift
(*c*) mobility (*d*) conductivity

58. Imperfections in the crystal structure result in

(*a*) increased conductivity
(*b*) decreased conductivity
(*c*) increased mobility
(*d*) decreased mobility

59. In pure silicon, major part of the drift current is due to free electrons because

(*a*) there are more free electrons than holes
(*b*) free electrons are in the valence band
(*c*) mobility of electrons is greater than the mobility of holes
(*d*) diffusion constant of electrons is greater than that of holes

60. At room temperature intrinsic carrier concentration is higher in germanium than in silicon because

(*a*) carrier mobilities are higher Ge than in Si
(*b*) energy gap in Ge is smaller than that in Si
(*c*) Atomic number of Ge is larger than in Si
(*d*) Atomic weight of Ge is larger than in Si

61. In preparing a semiconductor material for use in semiconductor devices the first step involved is

(*a*) crystal growth (*b*) chemical purification
(*c*) crystal pulling (*d*) zone refining

62. Final purification of germanium or silicon is generally accomplished by

(*a*) chemical purification (*b*) crystal pulling
(*c*) zone refining (*d*) epitaxial growth

63. One reason why purification of silicon is difficult is that

(*a*) its melting temperature is high
(*b*) its surface tension is high
(*c*) it does not form a single crystal
(*d*) its resistivity is high

64. Seed crystal used in crystal growth is a

(*a*) small crystal formed by epitaxial growth
(*b*) single crystal with a specific orientation
(*c*) single crystal containing donor impurity
(*d*) single crystal containing acceptor impurity

65. Semiconductor may be made n-type by adding donor impurity

(*a*) during zone refining
(*b*) during chemical purification
(*c*) during crystal pulling
(*d*) before purification process

66. Epitaxial growth is best suited for growing

(*a*) polycrystalline silicon
(*b*) very thin single crystal layer on a substrate
(*c*) single crystals several inches in size
(*d*) single crystals several mm in size

67. Germanium epitaxial film may be doped by

(*a*) using hydrogen as carrier
(*b*) adding doping impurity in the melt
(*c*) introducing the doping impurity in vapour form along with the germanium compound vapour
(*d*) using chlorine to form the vapour compound

68. In the four point probe method of determining resistivity

(*a*) one probe point must inject monority carriers
(*b*) current flows in only a small area of the sample
(*c*) curent source is connected to the two inner probes
(*d*) the sample must be extrinsic

69. A requirement of four point probe method of determining resistivity is

(*a*) curent must be low
(*b*) current must be high
(*c*) cross-section along the sample must be constant
(*d*) currrent source is connected to two inner probes

70. Merit of four point probe method of determining resistivity is that

(*a*) it needs very small current
(*b*) it gives the average resistivity of the sample
(*c*) it gives the resistivity at a localized region of the sample
(*d*) it injects excess minority carriers

71. A normal atom is one which

(*a*) has equal number of electrons and protons
(*b*) always has four valence electrons
(*c*) always has an atomic core with charge of + 4q
(*d*) always shares its electrons with other atoms

72. The n-types impurity

(*a*) must have only three valence electrons
(*b*) creates excess holes
(*c*) creates excess electrons
(*d*) can be added to Ge but not Si

73. The conduction band is

(*a*) always located at the top of the crystal
(*b*) the same as forbidden energy gap
(*c*) a range of energies coresponding to the energies of free electrons
(*d*) not an allowed energy band

74. If arsenic impurity is added to germanium
(*a*) it creates more holes
(*b*) it causes free-electron density to excess hole density
(*c*) it causes increase in resistance of Ge sample
(*d*) it results in new energy level just above valence level

75. If indium impurity is added to germanium
(*a*) it creates excess electrons
(*b*) it results in hole density to exceed free electron density
(*c*) it causes increase in resistance of Ge sample
(*d*) it results in a new energy level just below conduction level

76. A hole shifts its position basically due to
(*a*) a valence electron from a neighbouring atom joinging the hole to fill the vacancy
(*b*) breaking of covalent band
(*c*) movement of atomic core
(*d*) increase in temperature

77. In n-type semiconductor
(*a*) holes form the mojority carrier
(*b*) electrons form the mojority carriers
(*c*) impurity is trivalent
(*d*) free electron density equals the hole density

78. In p-type semiconductor
(*a*) holes form the mon ority carrier
(*b*) free electrons form the minority carriers
(*c*) hole density equals free electron density
(*d*) impurity is pentavalent

79. Drift current in germanium is caused by
(*a*) thermal agitation of crystal lattice
(*b*) concentration gradient of charge carriers
(*c*) applied electric field
(*d*) incidence of light

80. Donor impurity in germanium results in
(*a*) increased forbidden energy gap
(*b*) reduced forbidden energy gap
(*c*) a narrow energy band slightly below conduction level
(*d*) new discrete energy level slightly below cunduction level

81. Acceptor inpurity atoms in silicon result in
(*a*) increased forbidden energy gap
(*b*) reduced forbidden energy gap
(*c*) new discrete energy level slightly below conduction band
(*d*) new discrete energy level slightly above valence level

82. The transition region in an open circuited p-n junction contains
(*a*) free electrons only
(*b*) holes only
(*c*) both free electrons and holes
(*d*) uncovered immobile impurity ions

83. In a pn diode, hole diffuse from p-region to n-region because
(*a*) there is higher concentration of holes in the p-region
(*b*) holes are positively charged
(*c*) holes are urged to move by the barrier potential
(*d*) the free-electron in the n-region attract the holes

84. In an unbiased pn junction, the junction current at equilibrium is
(*a*) due to diffusion of majority carriers
(*b*) due to diffusion of minority carriers
(*c*) zero due to equal and opposite currents crossing the junction
(*d*) zero because no charges cross the junction

85. In an unbiased pn junction, zero current implies that
(*a*) the potential barier has disappeared
(*b*) number of holes diffusing from p-side to n-side equals the number of electrons diffusing fron n-side to p-side
(*c*) no carriers cross the junction
(*d*) total current crossing the junction from p-side to n-side equals the total current crossing the junction from n-side to p-side

86. In the energy band diagram of an open circuited pn junction, the energy band of n region has shifted relative to that of p-region
(*a*) downward by E_o (*b*) upward by E_o
(*c*) downward by $E_o/2$ (*d*) upward by $E_o/2$
where E_o *equals* $q\,V_o$

87. In a pn diode, with the increase of reverse bias, the reverse current
(*a*) increases
(*b*) decreases
(*c*) remains constant
(*d*) may increase or decrease depending on the doping

88. A reverse based pn junction has
(*a*) net hole current
(*b*) net electron current
(*c*) extremely small constant reverse current
(*d*) very large current

89. In a Ge diode, reverse saturation current I_o is of the order of

(*a*) 1 pA (*b*) 1 nA

(*c*) 1μA (*d*) 1 mA

90. In a silicon diode, the reverse saturation current is of the order of

(*a*) 1pA (*b*) 1nA

(*c*) 1 μA (*d*) 1mA

91. In Ge diode, the cutin voltage is about

(*a*) 0.2 volt (*b*) 0.6 volt

(*c*) 1.1 volt (*d*) 2 volt

92. In Si diode, the cutin voltage is about

(*a*) 0.2 volt (*b*) 0.6 volt

(*c*) 1.1 volt (*d*) 1.75 volt

93. In a pn diode, for constant value of current at room temperature dV/dT varies approximately at the rate of

(*a*) – 2.5 m V/deg C

(*b*) – 25 mV/deg C

(*c*) + 2.5 mV/deg C

(*d*) + 25 mV/deg C

94. Ge diode at room temperature for forward current of 26 mA has dynamic resistance of about

(*a*) 0.1 Ω (*b*) 1 Ω

(*c*) 10 Ω (*d*) 1000 Ω

95. The reverse bias on pn junction

(*a*) pushes the electrons and holes aways from the junction

(*b*) has no effect on the holes and electrons

(*c*) attracts holes and electrons towards the junction

(*d*) increases the reverse current

96. In a forward biased pn diode

(*a*) forward current is zero

(*b*) only holes cross the junction from p side to n side

(*c*) only electrons cross the junction from n-side to p-side

(*d*) both holes on the p-side and electron on the n-side cross the junction to the opposite sides.

97. In a pnp transistor operating in the active region, the concentraiton of minority carrier holes in the n-region at collector junction J_c is

(*a*) zero

(*b*) thermal equilibrium value p_{no} of emitter

(*c*) thermal equilibrium concentration of hole in collector region

(*d*) same as at J_E

98. As the magnitude of the collector junction reverse bias increases, the effective base width

(*a*) increases

(*b*) decreases

(*c*) remains unaltered

(*d*) first increases and later becomes constant

99. In an npn diffused junction transistor, the p-type base region is formed on the n-type collector region through process of

(*a*) alloying

(*b*) epitaxial

(*c*) change in the nature of doping during crystal growth

(*d*) diffusion of p-type impurity

100. In a pnp transistor operating in the active region; in the base region, the main stream of current is

(*a*) drift of holes

(*b*) diffusion of holes

(*c*) drfit of electrons

(*d*) diffusion of electrons

101. In a Ge BJT, for usual value of the collector current, the transistor α is of the order of

(*a*) 0.99 (*b*) 0.9

(*c*) 0.5 (*d*) 50

102. In a pnp Ge transistor, the cutin voltage is about

(*a*) –0.01 volt (*b*) –0.1 volt

(*c*) –0.5 volt (*d*) –5 volt

103. In a pnp Si transistor, the cutin voltage is about

(*a*) –0.01 volt (*b*) –0.1 volt

(*c*) –0.5 volt (*d*) –5 volt

104. In a BJT, as the conductivity of the base region increases, the punch through voltage

(*a*) remains unaltered

(*b*) increases

(*c*) decreases

(*d*) may increase or decrease depending on bias at J_E

105. The dynamic emitter resistance of a BJT operating in the active region is of the order of

(*a*) 0.01 Ω (*b*) 1 Ω

(*c*) 100 Ω (*d*) 10 kΩ

106. In active region operation of a transistor

(*a*) both junctions are reverse biased

(*b*) both junctions are forward biased

(*c*) Emitter junction is forward biased while collector junction is reverse biased

(*d*) Emitter junction is reverse biased while collector junction is forward biased

107. In cutoff region operation of a transistor
(*a*) both J_E and J_C are forward biased
(*b*) both J_E and J_C are reverse biased
(*c*) J_E is forward biased while J_C is reverse biased
(*d*) J_E is reverse biased while J_C is forward biased
where J_E *and* J_C *are respectively the emitter and collector junctions*

108. In saturation region operation of a transistor
(*a*) both J_E and J_C are forward biased
(*b*) both J_E and J_C are reverse biased
(*c*) J_E is forward biased while J_C is reverse biased
(*d*) J_E is reverse biased while J_C is forward biased

109. For active region operation of a pnp transistor
(*a*) Emitter is positive with respect to base
(*b*) Emitter is negative with respect to base
(*c*) Emitter is at the same voltage as base
(*d*) Base is at the same voltage as collector

110. For active region operation of npn transistor
(*a*) Emitter is positive with respect to base
(*b*) Emitter is negative with respect to base
(*c*) Emitter is at the same voltage as base
(*d*) Base is at the same voltage as collector

111. In a BJT, the base spreading resistance is of the order of
(*a*) 10Ω (*b*) 100Ω
(*c*) 1Ω (*d*) 1 kΩ

112. The value of voltage V_{BE}, cutoff in a pnp silicon transistor approximately equals
(*a*) 0 (*b*) 0.1 volt
(*c*) 0.2 volt (*d*) 0.5 volt

113. The value of V_{BE}, cutoff in a pnp Ge transistor approximately equals
(*a*) 0 (*b*) 0.1 volt
(*c*) 0.2 volt (*d*) 0.5 volt

114. MOS transistor
(*a*) has only one pn junction
(*b*) conducts when sufficient voltage is applied to the gate electrode
(*c*) has only two electrodes
(*d*) has gate electrode in direct contact with the silicon

115. In inverted operation of a transistor
(*a*) both junctions are reverse biased
(*b*) both junctions are forward biased
(*c*) emitter junction is reverse biased while collector junction is forward biased
(*d*) emitter junction is forward biased while collector junction is reverse biased

116. Most of the small signal transistors are
(*a*) npn silicon transistor in plastic package
(*b*) pnp silicon transistor in plastic package
(*c*) npn germanium transistor in metallic case
(*d*) pnp germanium gransistor in metallic case

117. Transistor is usually encapsuled in
(*a*) graphite powder (*b*) enamel paint
(*c*) epoxy resin (*d*) all the above

118. Encapsulation of transistor is done to
(*a*) provide mechanical ruggedness
(*b*) prevent photo-electric effects
(*c*) prevent electrical interference
(*d*) to case heat radiation

119. Power transistors are invariably provided with
(*a*) heat sink (*b*) metallic casing
(*c*) soldered connections (*d*) fan for heat removal

120. Heat sink removes heat from a power transistor mainly by
(*a*) radiation 0(*b*) conduction
(*c*) nature convection (*d*) forced convection

121. With both junctions reverse biased the transistor operates in
(*a*) active region (*b*) cutoff region
(*c*) saturation region (*d*) inverted region

122. In an npn transistor operating in the active region the main current crossing the collector junction from base side is
(*a*) hole drift current
(*b*) hole diffusion current
(*c*) electron diffusion current
(*d*) electron drift current

123. A transistor with emitter junction forward biased and collector junction reverse biased is said to operate in
(*a*) active region (*b*) saturation region
(*c*) cutoff region (*d*) inverted region

124. In a transistor, current I_{CBO}
(*a*) increase with increase of temperature
(*b*) decrease with increase of temperature
(*c*) is normally greater for Si transistor than Ge transistor
(*d*) mainly depends on the emitter base junction bias

125. In a transistor current I_{CBO} flow in
(*a*) base and emiter leads
(*b*) collector and emitter leads
(*c*) base and collector leads
(*d*) emitter, base and collector leads

126. In an npn transistor, the function of emitter is
(*a*) to inject holes into base
(*b*) to inject electrons into the base
(*c*) to inject electrons into the collector
(*d*) to inject holes into the collector

127. Pinch off voltage V_p for an FET is the drain voltage at which
(*a*) significant drain current starts flowing
(*b*) drain current becomes zero
(*c*) all free charges get removed from the channel
(*d*) avalanche break down takes place

128. In a JFET, beyond the pinch off voltage, as the drain voltage increases; the drain current
(*a*) remains almost constant
(*b*) decreases
(*c*) increases
(*d*) may increase or decrease

129. n-channel FETs are superior to p-channel FETs because
(*a*) they have lower switching time
(*b*) they have lower pinch off voltage
(*c*) they have higher input impedance
(*d*) mobility of charge carrier electron in n-channel FET is greater than the mobility of charge carrier hole in p-channel FET

130. The charge carriers in a p-channel FET are
(*a*) electrons alone
(*b*) holes alone
(*c*) both electrons and holes
(*d*) may be either electrons or holes

131. The charge carriers in an n-channel FET are
(*a*) electrons alone
(*b*) holes alone
(*c*) both electrons and holes
(*d*) may be either electrons or holes

132. When the gate-to-source voltage V_{GS} of an n-channel JET is made more and more negative, the drain current
(*a*) increases
(*b*) decreases
(*c*) remains unchanged
(*d*) may increase or decrease

133. When the gate to source voltage V_{GS} of a p-channel JFET is made more positive, the drain current
(*a*) increases
(*b*) decreases
(*c*) remains constant
(*d*) may increase or decrease

134. The input resistance of a JFET is of the order of
(*a*) 1 kΩ (*b*) 10 kΩ
(*c*) 10 MΩ (*d*) 100 MΩ

135. The main drawback of a JFET is its
(*a*) high input impedance
(*b*) low input impedance
(*c*) higher noise
(*d*) lower gain

136. Inter electrode capacitances in an FET are of the order of
(*a*) 1 pF (*b*) 100 pF
(*c*) 0.1 μF (*d*) 1 μF

137. The dynamic drain resistance of a JFET is of the order of
(*a*) 1 kΩ (*b*) 10 kΩ
(*c*) 500 MΩ (*d*) 100 MΩ

138. The dynamic drain resistance of MOSFET is of the order of
(*a*) 10 kΩ (*b*) 500 kΩ
(*c*) 5 MΩ (*d*) 100 MΩ

139. The magnitude of the threshold voltage V_T for enhancement MOSFET is of the order of
(*a*) 4 volts (*b*) 10 volts
(*c*) 40 volts (*d*) 100 volts

140. Out of the four devices mentioned below, the fastest switching device is
(*a*) JFET (*b*) BJT
(*c*) MOSFET (*d*) Triode

141. The JFET can operate in
(*a*) depletion mode only
(*b*) enhancement mode only
(*c*) either depletion or enhancement mode at a time
(*d*) both depletion and enhancement modes simultaneously

142. The input gate current of FET is
(*a*) a few amperes
(*b*) a few milli-amperes
(*c*) a few micro-amperes
(*d*) negligibly small

143. Which of the following transistor is affected by static electricity
(*a*) npn transistor (*b*) JFET
(*c*) UJT (*d*) MOSFET

144. Which of the following device has the highest input impedance
(*a*) CE BJT (*b*) CC BJT
(*c*) JFET (*d*) MOSFET

145. A field-effect transistor (FET)

(*a*) has three pn junctions

(*b*) uses a forward biased junction

(*c*) depends on the variation of a magnetic field for its operation

(*d*) depends on the variation of a reverse voltage its operation

146. The operation of a JFET involves

(*a*) flow of minority carriers alone

(*b*) flow of majority carriers alone

(*c*) flow of both minority and majority carriers

(*d*) use of a magnetic field

147. FET

(*a*) has a very high input impedance

(*b*) depends on minority carrier flow

(*c*) uses a forward biased junction

(*d*) uses a high concentration emitter junction

148. A pnpn device having no gate is called

(*a*) UJT (*b*) Triac

(*c*) Schockley diode (*d*) SCR

149. A pnpn diode is

(*a*) a negative resistance device

(*b*) a voltage controllable device

(*c*) a controlled rectifier

(*d*) a current controlled negative resistance device

150. In a pnpn diode, breakover condition is marked by

(*a*) a sudden decrease in current

(*b*) a sudden increase in current

(*c*) diode getting burnt off

(*d*) a sudden glow taking place

151. Holding current in a pnpn diode is the

(*a*) maximum operating current

(*b*) normal operating current

(*c*) current corresponding to breakover voltage

(*d*) minimum current to keep the device ON.

152. A pnpn diode

(*a*) is always made of silicon

(*b*) is always made of germanium

(*c*) may be made of either silicon or germanium

(*d*) may be made of any semiconductor

153. The pnpn diode

(*a*) is unilateral device

(*b*) is a bilateral device

(*c*) may function either as a unilateral or as a bilateral device

(*d*) functions as a bilateral device depending on the ambient temp.

154. In a pnpn diode, breakover takes place when

(*a*) $(\alpha_1 + \alpha_2) = 0.5$

(*b*) $(\alpha_1 + \alpha_2) = 0.9$

(*c*) $(\alpha_1 + \alpha_2) = 1.0$

(*d*) $\alpha_1 = \alpha_2$, where α_1 and α_2 refer to the constituent transistors

155. In a pnpn diode, the phenomenon of rate effect depends on

(*a*) rate of change of temperature

(*b*) rate of change of applied voltage

(*c*) avalanche breakdown

(*d*) negative resistance in the forward voltage condition

156. A bilateral pnpn diode switch

(*a*) consists of two pnpn diodes in parallel but in opposite order

(*b*) is a 3 layer semiconductor device

(*c*) is a unilateral device

(*d*) is a bilateral device

157. Over temperature range of –60° to +150°C, sensitor has temperature coefficient of resistance of about

(*a*) –0.5% per deg C (*b*) –0.2% per deg C

(*c*) +0.7% per deg C (*d*) + 2.0% per deg C

158. For Ge at room temperature, critical wavelength for photoconduction is

(*a*) 1.13 micron (*b*) 1.73 micron

(*c*) 11.3 micron (*d*) 17.3 micron

159. For Si at room temperature, critical wavelength for photoconduction is

(*a*) 1.13 micron (*b*) 1.73 micron

(*c*) 11.3 micron (*d*) 17.3 micron

160. Photoconductive cell most popularly used for visible light spectrum uses

(*a*) Ge (*b*) Si

(*c*) GA As (*d*) Cadmium sulphide

161. In a photodiode, light is focussed to fall on

(*a*) p region only (*b*) n-region only

(*c*) full p and n regions (*d*) junction region only

162. Response time of PIN photodiode is of the order of

(*a*) 0.1 ns (*b*) 1 ns

(*c*) 10 ns (*d*) 1 milli-sec

163. In phototransistor, light is focussed to fall on

(*a*) emitter-to-base junction

(*b*) collector-to-base junction

(*c*) base region only

(*d*) all the three regions of the transistor

164. An npn phototransistor has typical sensitivity of the order of

(*a*) 25 μA/mW/cm² (*b*) 250 μA/mW/cm²

(*c*) 2.5 mA/mW/cm² (*d*) 250 mA/mW/cm²

165. Photovoltaic emf of a Ge photovoltaic cell is of the order of
(*a*) 0.1 volt (*b*) 0.5 volt
(*c*) 1.1 volt (*d*) 1.72 volt

166. Photovoltaic emf of a Si photovoltaic cell is of the order of
(*a*) 0.1 volt (*b*) 0.5 volt
(*c*) 1.1 volt (*d*) 1.72 volt

167. Conversion efficiency of a silicon solar cell is about
(*a*) 5% (*b*) 10%
(*c*) 14% (*d*) 25%

168. A semiconductor photo-diode uses
(*a*) photo-emissive effect
(*b*) photovoltaic effect
(*c*) photoconductive effect
(*d*) none of these

169. LED gives off visible light from
(*a*) region of depletion layer
(*b*) p region alone
(*c*) n region alone
(*d*) both p and n regions

170. LEDs have response time of the order of
(*a*) 0.1 ns (*b*) 1 ns
(*c*) 100 ns (*d*) 1 μs

171. In LED, when excited electrons revert from conduction band to valence band, the phenomenon utilized is
(*a*) radioative recombination
(*b*) formation of photons
(*c*) energy transfer from one electron to other
(*d*) none of these

172. LEDs fabricated from Ga As emit radiation in
(*a*) ultraviolet region
(*b*) infrared region
(*c*) visible range
(*d*) none of these

173. LEDs fabricated from Ga As P emit radiation in
(*a*) ultraviolet region
(*b*) infrared region
(*c*) visible region
(*d*) none of these

174. In a tunnel diode, impurity concentration is of the order of
(*a*) 1 in 10^3 (*b*) 1 in 10^5
(*c*) 1 in 10^7 (*d*) 1 in 10^9

175. In a tunnel diode, depletion layer width is of the order of
(*a*) 100 Å (*b*) 0.1 micron
(*c*) 1 micron (*d*) 5 micron

176. Tunnel diode
(*a*) uses very heavy doping resulting in extremely small depletion layer width
(*b*) is a point contact diode with a very high value of reverse resistance
(*c*) has a small hole in its centre permitting tunnelling
(*d*) none of these

177. Tunnel diode is a pn diode with
(*a*) very high doping in p region
(*b*) very high doping in n region
(*c*) very high doping in both p and n regions
(*d*) low doping in both p and n region

178. Most important application of tunnel diode is
(*a*) as rectifier
(*b*) as switching device in digital circuits
(*c*) as voltage controllable device
(*d*) as oscillator

179. Avalanche break down results basically due to
(*a*) impact ionization
(*b*) strong electric field across the junction
(*c*) emission of electrons
(*d*) rise in temperature

180. Avalanche breakdown results at applied
(*a*) forward bias exceeding about 6 volt
(*b*) forward bias below 6 volts
(*c*) reverse bias exceeding about 6 volt
(*d*) reverse bias below 6 volts

181. Zener breakdwon results basically due to
(*a*) impact ionization
(*b*) strong electric field across the junction
(*c*) emission of electrons
(*d*) high thermal energy of the electrons

182. Zener breakdown results at applied
(*a*) forward bias exceeding about 6 volt
(*b*) forward bias below 6 volts
(*c*) reverse bias exceeding about 6 volt
(*d*) reverse bias below 6 volts

183. In a breakdown diode, the temperature coefficient of breakdown voltage Vz
(*a*) is always positive
(*b*) is always negative
(*c*) is always zero
(*d*) may be positive or negative

184. On increasing the current through the zener diode by a factor of 2, the voltage across the diode
(*a*) gets doubled
(*b*) becomes half
(*c*) remains almost unchanged
(*d*) becomes 4 times as large

185. The dynamic resistance of a zener diode
(*a*) increases with increase of its current
(*b*) decreases with increase of its current
(*c*) is almost independent of current
(*d*) may increase or decrease with increase of current

186. Two identical breakdown diodes on being connected in series have breakdown voltage of
(*a*) 20 volts (*b*) 10 volts
(*c*) 40 volts (*d*) 6 volts

187. Two breakdown diodes A and B have breakdown voltage ratings of 5.8 volts and 24 volts respectively. Then
(*a*) A is zener diode and B is avalanche diode
(*b*) A is avalanche diode and B is zener diode
(*c*) both are zener diodes
(*d*) both are avalanche diodes

188. The temperature coefficient of breakdown diode is defined as
(*a*) rate of change of breakdown voltage with temperature
(*b*) rate of change of dynamic resistance with temperature
(*c*) rate of change of power handling capacity with temperature
(*d*) rate of change of diode current with temperature

189. Zener breakdown diodes have breakdown voltage which
(*a*) has positive temperature coefficient
(*b*) has negative temperature coefficient
(*c*) is independent of temperature
(*d*) none of these

190. Avalanche breakdown diodes have breakdown voltage
(*a*) having positive temperature coefficient
(*b*) having negative temperature coefficient
(*c*) independent of temperature
(*d*) none of these

191. At 25°C, a zener diode is rated at 2 watts. Its 8 power rating at 50°C will be
(*a*) 2 watts
(*b*) 1 watt
(*c*) greater than 2 watts
(*d*) much greater than 2 watts

192. In Schottky barrier diode, conduction is
(*a*) entirely by electrons
(*b*) entirely by holes
(*c*) mainly by holes but partly by electrons
(*d*) mainly by electrons but partly by holes

193. Maximum value of temperature coefficient of Vz in a breakdown diode is
(*a*) ±0.1 per cent/deg C (*b*) ±0.5 per cent/deg C
(*c*) +0.2 per cent/deg C (*d*) – 0.2 per cent/deg C

194. Unijunction transistor
(*a*) has only one pn junction
(*b*) has two pn junctions
(*c*) is a unipolar device
(*d*) is a bulk semiconductor device

195. In a UJT, instrinsic stand off ratio η is typically
(*a*) 0.2 (*b*) 0.4
(*c*) 0.7 (*d*) 0.99

196. A diode which utilizes cumulative multiplication of carriers through field induced impact ionization
(*a*) tunnel diode
(*b*) varactor diode
(*c*) avalanche diode
(*d*) zener breakdown diode

197. LCD consumes power of the order of
(*a*) a few microwatts
(*b*) a few milliwatts
(*c*) hundreds of milliwatts
(*d*) a few watts

198. LCDs have response time of the order of
(*a*) a few ns
(*b*) tens of ns
(*c*) a few milliseconds
(*d*) hundred of milliseconds

199. Transferred electron mechanism involved in Gunn diode consists in transfer of electrons
(*a*) from valence band to conduction band
(*b*) from valence band to satellite valley
(*c*) from central valley to satellite valley
(*d*) from satellite valleys to central valley

200. Performance of the following diode is not based on its negative resistance characteristic
(*a*) Gunn diode (*b*) IMPATT diode
(*c*) Tunnel diode (*d*) LSA diode

201. Transferred-electron bulk effect occurs in
(*a*) germanium (*b*) silicon
(*c*) gallium assenide (*d*) antimony

202. The main advantage of TRAPATT diode over IMPATT diode is its

(*a*) higher output

(*b*) higher efficiency

(*c*) lower noise

(*d*) capability to operate at higher frequencies

203. A zener diode is used for

(*a*) Voltage regulation

(*b*) Rectification

(*c*) Noise suppression

(*d*) Blocking a.c.

204. An SCR is a device having

(*a*) three layers with four junctions.

(*b*) three layers with two junctions.

(*c*) four layers with three junctions.

(*d*) two layers with three junctions.

205. Semi-conductor diode time constant is equal to

(*a*) value of majority carrier life time

(*b*) life time of minority carrier

(*c*) difussion capacitance time constant

(*d*) zero

206. To prepare a 'P' type semiconducting material the impurities to be added to silicon are

(*a*) Boron, Gallium

(*b*) Arsenic, Antimony

(*c*) Gallium, Phosphorous

(*d*) Gallium, Arsenic

207. FET is a good signal chopper because it

(*a*) exhibits no offset voltage at zero drain current

(*b*) occupies less space in integrated form

(*c*) has got high input impedance.

(*d*) is less noisy

208. In Bipolar Junction transistors, type of configuration which will give both voltage gain and current gain is

(*a*) CC (*b*) CB

(*c*) CE (*d*) None of these

209. $V^D - I^D$ characteristics of an FET are similar to that of

(*a*) Triode (*b*) Pentode

(*c*) Tertode (*d*) None of these

210. Transformer utilization factor for a Bridge Rectifier is given as

(*a*) 0.287 (*b*) 0.50

(*c*) 0.693 (*d*) 0.812

211. In every practical oscillatorm loop gain is

(*a*) slightly larger than unity

(*b*) slightly larger than ten

(*c*) infinity

(*d*) zero

212. Photoemission multipliers make use of

(*a*) Secondary emission

(*b*) Thermionic emission

(*c*) High emission

(*d*) Photoemission

213. By passing a triangular wave through a differentiating circuit the output wave shape is

(*a*) Spikes (*b*) Squarewave

(*c*) Sawtooth (*d*) Sinewave

214. Clipper circuits are used to obtain which one of the following waveforms?

(*a*) Sharper (*b*) Rectified

(*c*) Fast rising (*d*) Smaller amplitude

215. Zener diodes semiconductors are

(*a*) Lightly doped (*b*) Heavily doped

(*c*) Medium doped (*d*) Not at all doped

216. When a junction is formed between a metal and a semiconductor, the depletion layer is

(*a*) more on the side of the metal

(*b*) equal on both sides

(*c*) less on the side of the metal

(*d*) less on semiconductor side

217. Zener diodes are used in

(*a*) Rectifiers (*b*) Inverters

(*c*) Demodulator (*d*) Voltage regulators

218. A silicon transistor at a temperature of 25°C has leakage current I_{CBO} of 10 microamps. If temperature rises to 55°C leakage current would be

(*a*) 300 microamps (*b*) 80 microamps

(*c*) 22 microamps (*d*) 10 microamps

219. The value of voltage across the diode in figure given below is

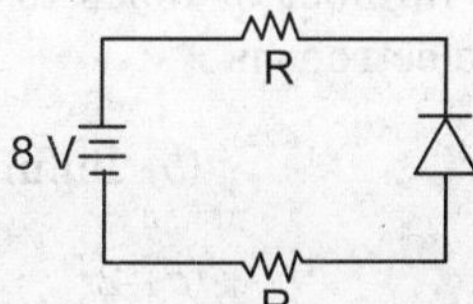

(*a*) Zero volt

(*b*) 4 V

(*c*) 8 V

(*d*) Depends upon the value of R

220. The temperature co-efficient of an intrinsic semiconductor is
(*a*) Zero
(*b*) Positive
(*c*) Negative
(*d*) Like that of metals

221. A FET is essentially a
(*a*) Current driven device
(*b*) Voltage driven device
(*c*) Power driven source
(*d*) Solar device

222. A transistor has a current gain of 0.99 in common base mode. Its current gain in common emitter mode is
(*a*) 0.99 (*b*) 99
(*c*) 10.1 (*d*) 100

223. In the given circuilt the function of the diode D is

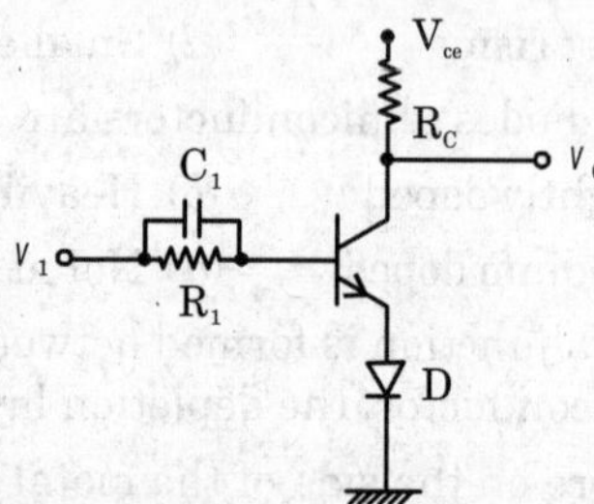

(*a*) To protect the base-emitte junction
(*b*) To hold the output voltage to a constant value
(*c*) To bias the transistor
(*d*) To clip the output voltage

224. FETs are
(*a*) Either unipolar or bipolar
(*b*) None of these
(*c*) Unipolar devices
(*d*) Bipolar devices

225. Which of the following materials is semiconductor
(*a*) Chromium (*b*) Selenium
(*c*) Bismuth (*d*) Silica

226. Under thermal equilibrium semi-conductor the ratio of the number of holes to the number of conduction electrons is
(*a*) $\frac{1}{2}$ (*b*) Iinfinity
(*c*) 1 (*d*) 2

227. The switching transistor as shown, carries in the collector side an rms current of 8 mA. If the frequency of rectangular pulse train v_i is 50 Hz, then on-time of the transistor is

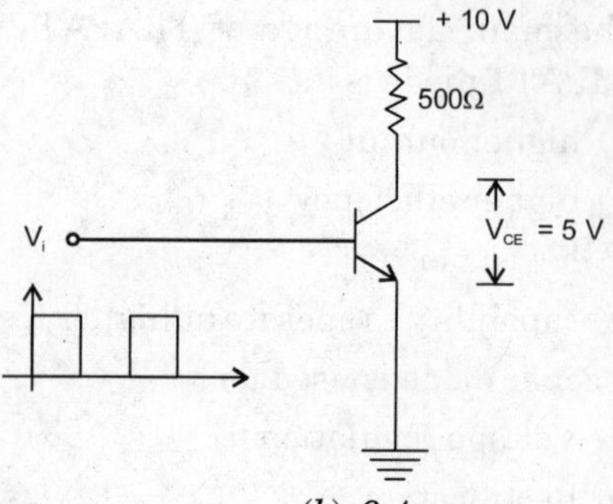

(*a*) 20 ms (*b*) 6.4 ms
(*c*) 12.8 ms (*d*) 16 ms

228. In electronic circuits, for blocking the DC component of a voltage signal, a/an ________ is connected is series with the voltage source.
(*a*) capacitor (*b*) diode
(*c*) resistor (*d*) inductor

229. For n-type semiconductor, the doping material is
(*a*) tetravalent (*b*) pentavalent
(*c*) trivalent (*d*) bivalent

230. Silicon content in iron lamination is kept within 5% as it
(*a*) makes the material brittle
(*b*) reduces the curie point
(*c*) increases hysteresis loss
(*d*) increases cost

231. If the transistor having V_{CE} = 5 V, V_{BE} = 0.7 has β = 45, value of R is

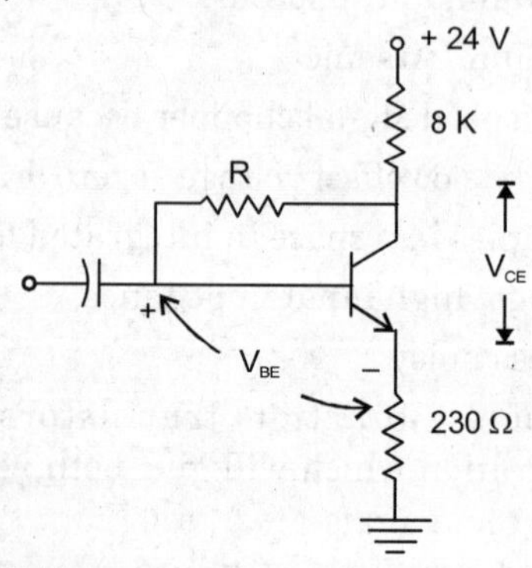

(*a*) 85.64 k
(*b*) 63.14 k
(*c*) 72.15 k
(*d*) 91.18 k

232. In a semiconductor, the resistivity
(*a*) depends on temperature
(*b*) depends on voltage
(*c*) depends on current through it
(*d*) None of the above

233. The given circuit represents a

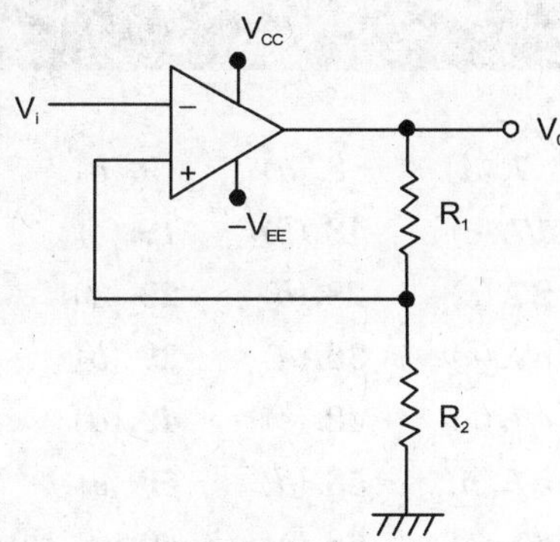

(*a*) monostable multivibrator
(*b*) astable multivibrator
(*c*) Schmitt trigger
(*d*) bistable multivibrator

234. The input resistance of a FET is of the order of
(*a*) 100 Ω (*b*) 10 kΩ
(*c*) 1 mΩ (*d*) 100 MΩ

235. In a CE (common emitter) transistor, V_{CC} = 12 V and the zero signal collector current is 1 mA. Determine the operating point when collector load (R_C) is 6 kΩ.
(*a*) 6 V, 1 mA
(*b*) 6 V, 2 mA
(*c*) 12 V, 1 mA
(*d*) 12 V, 2 mA

236. The potential barrier existing across pn junction
(*a*) prevents flow of minority carriers
(*b*) prevents flow of majority carriers
(*c*) prevents total recombination of holes and electrons
(*d*) prevents neutralisation of acceptor and donor ions

237. The Ebers - Moll model is applicable to :
(*a*) JFET
(*b*) BJT
(*c*) NMOS transistor
(*d*) UJT

238. The current in reverse bias in P - N junction diode may be :
(*a*) between 2A and 5A
(*b*) few micro or nano amperes
(*c*) few milli amperes
(*d*) between 0.2 A and 2A

239. Which of the following is non-linear circuit parameter ?
(*a*) Transistor (*b*) Inductance
(*c*) Condenser (*d*) Wire wound resistor

240. For average values of load current, current chopping occurs more frequently in :
(*a*) VCB's (*b*) OCB's
(*c*) ACB's (*d*) SF_6CB's

241. A BJT is said to be operating in the saturation region, if :
(*a*) Both the junctions are forward biased
(*b*) both the junctions are reverse biased
(*c*) B – E junction is reverse biased and B – C junction is forward biased
(*d*) B – E junction is forward biased and B – C junction is reverse biased

242. Which semiconductor device behaves like two SCR's ?
(*a*) Triac (*b*) MOSFET
(*c*) JFET (*d*) UJT

243. In Bipolar Junction transistors, the type of configuration which will give both voltage gain and current gain is:
(*a*) CC (*b*) None of the options
(*c*) CB (*d*) CE

244. With the positive probe on an NPN base, an ohmmeter reading between the other transistor terminals should be?
(*a*) Infinite (*b*) Open
(*c*) Low resistance (*d*) High resistance

245. Silicon has a preference in IC technology because?
(*a*) it is an indirect semiconductor
(*b*) it is an elemental semiconductor
(*c*) it is a covalent semiconductor
(*d*) of the availability of nature oxide SiO

246. To prepare a P type semiconducting material the impurities to be added to silicon are?
(*a*) Boron, Gallium
(*b*) Arsenic, Antimony
(*c*) Gallium, Arsenic
(*d*) Gallium, Phosphorous

247. An amplifier has a gain of 10,000 expressed in decibels the gain is?
(*a*) 10 (*b*) 40
(*c*) 100 (*d*) 80

Answers

1. (*b*)	**2.** (*c*)	**3.** (*c*)	**4.** (*c*)	**5.** (*d*)	**6.** (*c*)	**7.** (*d*)	**8.** (*a*)	**9.** (*b*)	**10.** (*d*)
11. (*b*)	**12.** (*d*)	**13.** (*c*)	**14.** (*c*)	**15.** (*c*)	**16.** (*a*)	**17.** (*c*)	**18.** (*b*)	**19.** (*c*)	**20.** (*b*)
21. (*c*)	**22.** (*c*)	**23.** (*b*)	**24.** (*c*)	**25.** (*b*)	**26.** (*a*)	**27.** (*c*)	**28.** (*b*)	**29.** (*d*)	**30.** (*c*)
31. (*c*)	**32.** (*d*)	**33.** (*c*)	**34.** (*b*)	**35.** (*b*)	**36.** (*b*)	**37.** (*c*)	**38.** (*a*)	**39.** (*b*)	**40.** (*b*)
41. (*b*)	**42.** (*a*)	**43.** (*c*)	**44.** (*c*)	**45.** (*b*)	**46.** (*a*)	**47.** (*c*)	**48.** (*c*)	**49.** (*d*)	**50.** (*c*)
51. (*c*)	**52.** (*a*)	**53.** (*b*)	**54.** (*b*)	**55.** (*c*)	**56.** (*a*)	**57.** (*b*)	**58.** (*d*)	**59.** (*c*)	**60.** (*b*)
61. (*b*)	**62.** (*c*)	**63.** (*a*)	**64.** (*b*)	**65.** (*c*)	**66.** (*b*)	**67.** (*c*)	**68.** (*c*)	**69.** (*a*)	**70.** (*c*)
71. (*a*)	**72.** (*c*)	**73.** (*c*)	**74.** (*b*)	**75.** (*b*)	**76.** (*a*)	**77.** (*b*)	**78.** (*b*)	**79.** (*c*)	**80.** (*d*)
81. (*d*)	**82.** (*a*)	**83.** (*c*)	**84.** (*d*)	**85.** (*b*)	**86.** (*c*)	**87.** (*c*)	**88.** (*c*)	**89.** (*b*)	**90.** (*b*)
91. (*b*)	**92.** (*a*)	**93.** (*b*)	**94.** (*a*)	**95.** (*d*)	**96.** (*a*)	**97.** (*b*)	**98.** (*d*)	**99.**(*b*)	**100.** (*a*)
101. (*b*)	**102.** (*c*)	**103.** (*c*)	**104.** (*b*)	**105.** (*b*)	**106.** (*b*)	**107.** (*a*)	**108.** (*a*)	**109.** (*b*)	**110.** (*d*)
111. (*a*)	**112.** (*b*)	**113.** (*c*)	**114.** (*c*)	**115.** (*a*)	**116.** (*c*)	**117.** (*a*)	**118.** (*a*)	**119.** (*c*)	**120.** (*b*)
121. (*c*)	**122.** (*a*)	**123.** (*a*)	**124.** (*c*)	**125.** (*b*)	**126.** (*c*)	**127.** (*c*)	**128.** (*d*)	**129.** (*b*)	**130.** (*a*)
131. (*b*)	**132.** (*a*)	**133.** (*d*)	**134.** (*d*)	**135.** (*c*)	**136.** (*c*)	**137.** (*a*)	**138.** (*a*)	**139.** (*c*)	**140.** (*a*)
141. (*d*)	**142.** (*d*)	**143.** (*d*)	**144.** (*d*)	**145.** (*b*)	**146.** (*a*)	**147.** (*c*)	**148.** (*d*)	**149.** (*b*)	**150.** (*d*)
151. (*a*)	**152.** (*a*)	**153.** (*c*)	**154.** (*b*)	**155.** (*a*)	**156.** (*c*)	**157.** (*b*)	**158.** (*a*)	**159.** (*d*)	**160.** (*d*)
161. (*b*)	**162.** (*b*)	**163.** (*c*)	**164.** (*b*)	**165.** (*a*)	**166.** (*c*)	**167.** (*c*)	**168.** (*a*)	**169.** (*b*)	**170.** (*a*)
171. (*c*)	**172.** (*c*)	**173.** (*c*)	**174.** (*a*)	**175.** (*b*)	**176.** (*c*)	**177.** (*b*)	**178.** (*a*)	**179.** (*c*)	**180.** (*b*)
181. (*d*)	**182.** (*d*)	**183.** (*c*)	**184.** (*c*)	**185.** (*b*)	**186.** (*a*)	**187.** (*a*)	**188.** (*a*)	**189.** (*b*)	**190.** (*c*)
191. (*a*)	**192.** (*a*)	**193.** (*a*)	**194.** (*c*)	**195.** (*c*)	**196.** (*a*)	**197.** (*d*)	**198.** (*c*)	**199.** (*d*)	**200.** (*c*)
201. (*b*)	**202.** (*b*)	**203.** (*a*)	**204.** (*c*)	**205.** (*a*)	**206.** (*a*)	**207.** (*a*)	**208.** (*c*)	**209.** (*b*)	**210.** (*d*)
211. (*a*)	**212.** (*a*)	**213.** (*a*)	**214.** (*d*)	**215.** (*b*)	**216.** (*c*)	**217.** (*d*)	**218.** (*b*)	**219.** (*c*)	**220.** (*c*)
221. (*b*)	**222.** (*b*)	**223.** (*a*)	**224.** (*c*)	**225.** (*b*)	**226.** (*c*)	**227.** (*c*)	**228.** (*a*)	**229.** (*b*)	**230.** (*a*)
231. (*a*)	**232.** (*a*)	**233.** (*c*)	**234.** (*d*)	**235.** (*a*)	**236.** (*c*)	**237.** (*b*)	**238.** (*b*)	**239.** (*a*)	**240.** (*a*)
241. (*a*)	**242.** (*a*)	**243.** (*d*)	**244.** (*c*)	**245.** (*d*)	**246.** (*a*)	**247.** (*b*)			

Explanations

219. Here the voltage across the diode in the given figure is

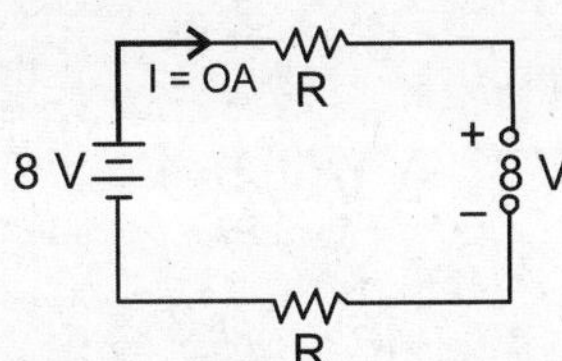

Given, diode is reverse baised as there will be no current in the circuit. So the value of voltage across the diode is 8V.

223.

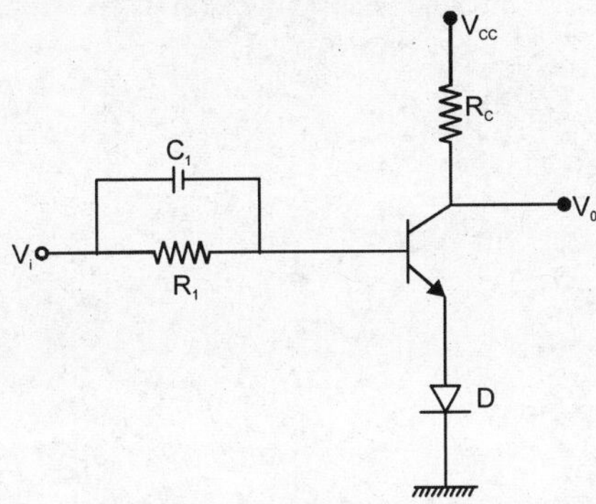

Function of the diode is to protect the base-emitter junction.

224. FETs are unipolar devices.

225. Selenium is a semiconductor.

226. At thermal equilbrium number of holes is equal to number of conduction electrons.

228. For blocking the DC component of a voltage signal a capacitor is connected in series with the voltage source.

229. For n type semi conductor, the doping material is pentavalent.

230. Silicon content in Iron lamination is kept within 5% as it makes the material briffle.

232. In a semiconductor, the resistivity depends on temperature.

233. The given circuit represents schmitt trigger.

234. Input resistance of a FET is of the order of 100 MΩ

243. CE will give both voltage gain and current gain.

247. $$\text{Gain} = 10 \log_{10} 10^4 = 40 \text{ dB}$$

2

CHAPTER

Communication Systems

MODULATION

In continuous wave (C W) modulation, a sinusoidal signal $A_c \cos(\omega_c t + \phi)$ is used to represent a carrier signal and a modulated carrier, therefore can be expressed as

$$x_c(t) = A(t) \cos[\omega_c t + \phi(t)]$$

where ω_c = carrier frequency
$A(t)$ = instantaneous amplitude
$\phi(t)$ = phase angle of the carrier.

Amplitude Modulation (AM)

In AM, instantaneous amplitude, *i.e.* $A(t)$ is linearly related to the message signal $m(t)$ and the modulated carrier is represented as

$$x_c(t) = A(t). \cos \omega_c t$$

There are many types of AM depending upon the nature of spectral relationship between $A(t)$ and $m(t)$.

Ordinary Amplitude Modulation

In this modulation, modulated signal is generated by adding a large carrier signal to the DSB signal, and expressed as

$$x_{AM}(t) = m(t) \cdot \cos \omega_c t + A \cos \omega_c t$$
$$= [A + m(t)] \cdot \cos \omega_c t$$

Figure below shows AM signal in both time domain and frequency domain.

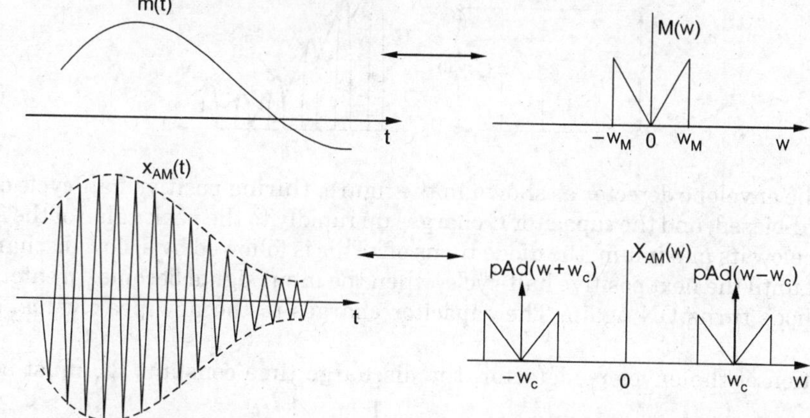

Demodulation of AM Signals

If amplitude of carrier wave is large enough, then envelope of the modulated waveform is directly proportional to $m(t)$ and in that case demodulation depends only upon the detection of the envelope of a modulated carrier and independent of the phase or frequency of the carrier.

The condition for demodulation of AM by an envelope detector is

$$A + m(t) > 0 \quad \text{for all } t$$

or

$$A \geq |\min\{m(t)\}|$$

where $\min\{m(t)\}$ = minimum value of $m(t)$.

If A is not large enough, then envelope of $x_{AM}(t)$ is not always proportional to $m(t)$, as shown in the figure below.

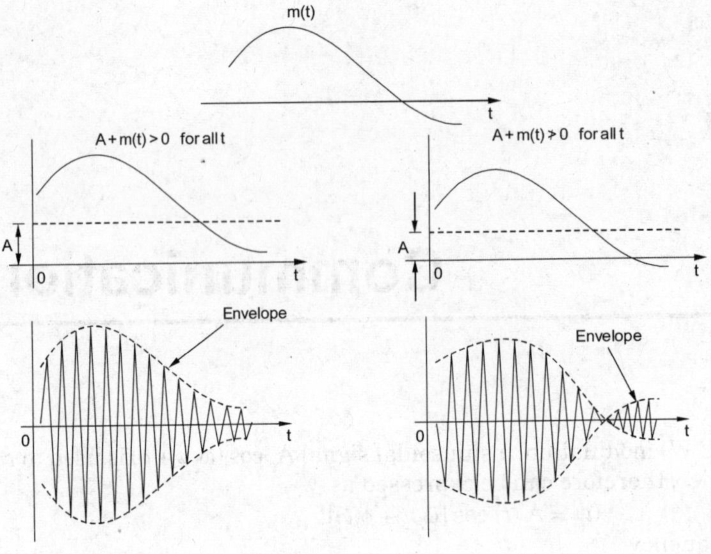

Modulation Index

For AM, *modulation index,* $\mu = \dfrac{|\min\{m(t)\}|}{A}$

For demodulation of AM by an envelope detector, $\mu \le 1$

When $\mu > 1$, the carrier is called *overmodulated*, resulting in envelope distortion.

Envelope Detector

The demodulation of an AM wave can be carried out by a simple and highly efficient *envelope detector* which actually consists of a diode and resistor-capacitor filter.

For the proper function of envelope detector, it being desired that AM wave should be narrow-band and for this carrier frequency should be large compared to the message bandwidth. The percentage modulation must be less than 100 percent.

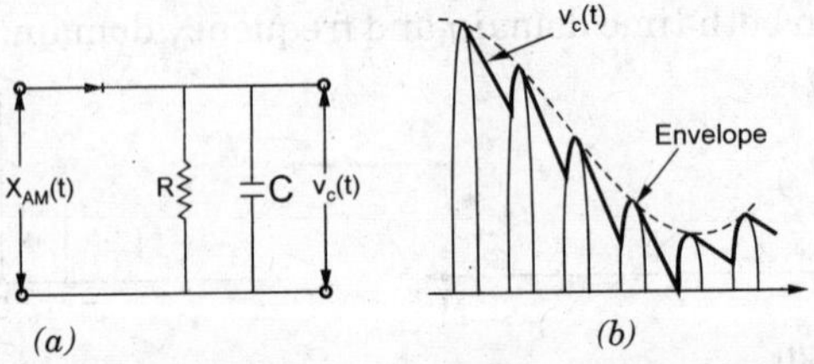

(a) (b)

The operation of the envelope detector as shown in the figure. During positive half-cycle of the input signal, the diode is forward-biased, and the capacitor C charges up rapidly to the peak value of the input signal. As the input signal falls below its maximum, the diode turns off. This is followed by a slow discharge of the capacitor through resistor R until the next positive half-cycle, when the input signal becomes greater than the capacitor voltage and the diode turns ON again. The capacitor charges to the new peak value, and the process is repeated.

For proper operation of the envelope detector, the discharge time constant RC must be chosen properly.

In practice, satisfactory operation requires that $\dfrac{1}{f_c} \ll \dfrac{1}{f_M}$

where f_M = message signal bandwidth.

For the detector output to follow the envelope at

all times : $$RC \le \frac{1}{\omega_m}\cdot\sqrt{\frac{1-\mu^2}{\mu}}$$

any time t_o : $$\frac{1}{RC} \ge \omega_m\left(\frac{\mu \sin \omega_m t_0}{1+\mu \cos \omega_m t_0}\right)$$

TYPES OF MODULATION.

1. Double-Sideband Modulation (DSB)

In DSB modulation, A (t) [instantaneous amplitude] is directly proportional to the message signal $m(t)$

$$x_{DSB}(t) = m(t).\cos\omega_c t$$

$$X_{DSB}(\omega) = \frac{1}{2}M(\omega - \omega_c) + \frac{1}{2}M(\omega + \omega_c)$$

Generation of DSB signals.

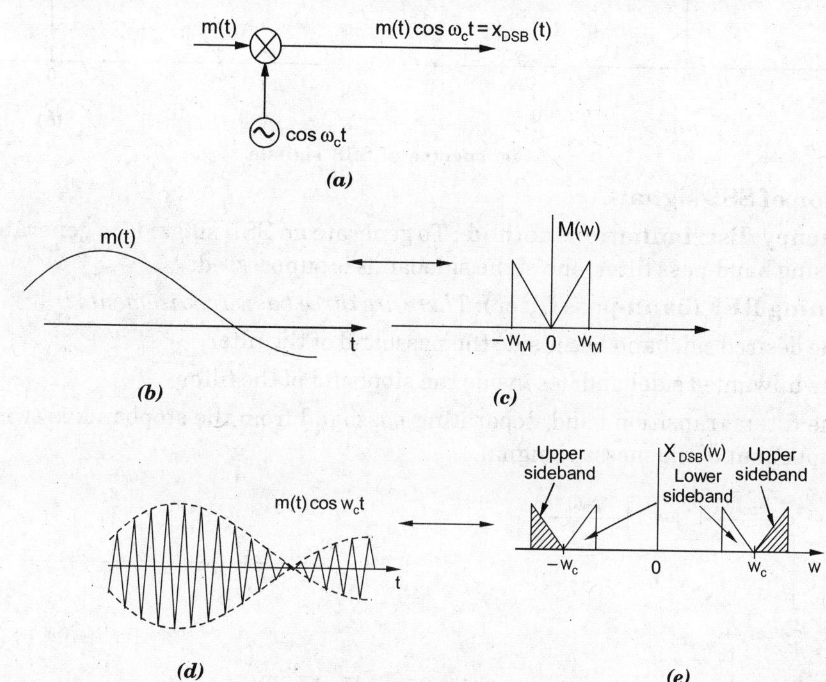

Fig. DSB modulation process

The time domain waveforms are shown in Figs. (b) and (c) and their corresponding frequency-domain representation is shown in Figs. (d) and (e). The spectral range covered by the message signal is called *baseband*, and therefore message signal is called *baseband signal.*

As seen from the spectrum, transmission bandwidth required for DSB modulation is 2ω. Since in this type of modulation, there is no identifiable carrier contains, therefore, it is also called *Double-sideband Suppressed Carrier (DSB-SC) modulation.*

Also, carrier frequency ω_c is much greater than ω_M, i.e. $\omega_c >> \omega_M$.

Demodulation of DSB singals.

The baseband signal $m(t)$ can be recovered from a, DSB-SC wave by first multiplying it with a locally generated sinusoidal wave and then low-pass filtering the product. Here, it is being assumed that local signal is exactly in the phase and frequency synchronism with the incoming carrier. This type of modulation is called *synchronous detection or coherent detection*, as shown in the figure below.

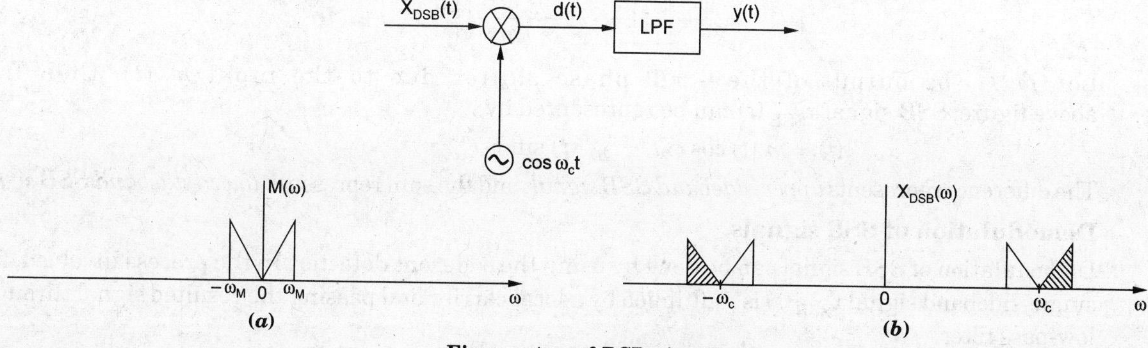

Fig spectra of DSB signals

2. Single-Sideband Modulation (SSB)

In this type of modulation, modulated wave consists of either upper sideband or the lower sideband, since any of them contains complete information about the message signal. This modulation is well suited for the transmission of voice signals by virtue of the energy gap that exists in the spectrum of the voice signals between zero and few hundred hertzs. This modulation require reduced bandwith requirement and minimum transmitted power but cost and complexity of its implementation.

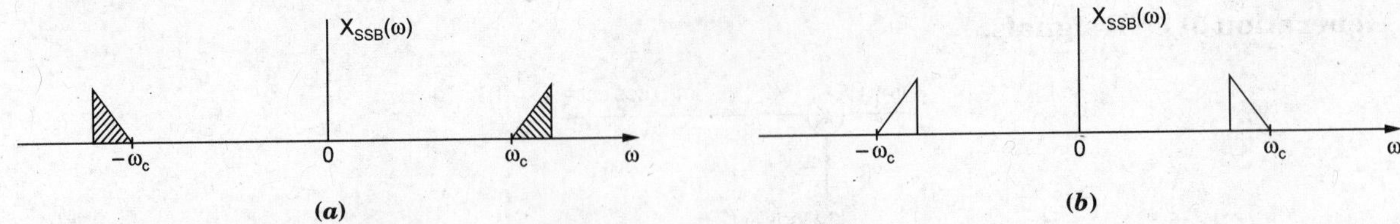

(a) *(b)*

Fig. spectra of SSB signals.

Generation of SSB signals.

(i) **Frequency discrimination method :** To generate an SSB singal is to generate first a DSB signal and then using band-pass filter, one of the sidebands is suppressed.

Designing BPF (band-pass filter): *There are three basic requirements :*

(a) The desired sideband lies inside the passband of the filter.

(b) The unwanted sideband lies inside the stopband of the filter

(c) The filters transition band, separating passband from the stopband, is twice the lowest frequency component of the message signal.

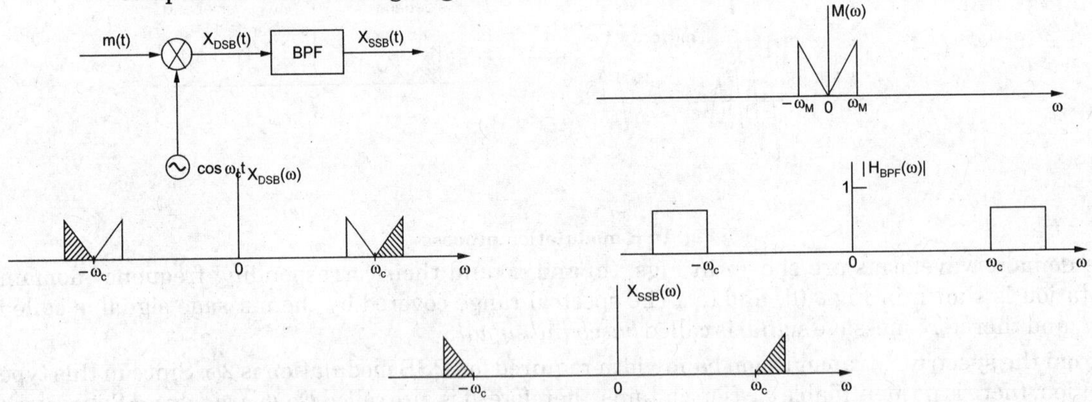

(ii) **Phase-shift method :** In this method two $\pi/2$ phase shifter has been incorporated to delay the phase of every frequency component by $\pi/2$.

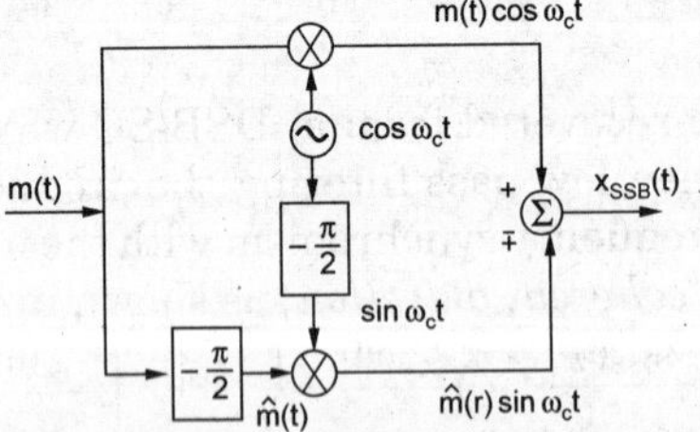

Let $\hat{m}(t)$ be output of the $-\pi/2$ phase shifter due to the input $m(t)$, then from above figure, SSB signal $x_{SSB}(t)$ can be represented by

$$x_{SSB}(t) = m(t) \cos \omega_c t \mp \hat{m}(t) \sin \omega_c t$$

The difference represents *upper-sideband SSB signal*, and the sum represents *lower-sideband SSB signal.*

Demodulation of SSB signals.

Demodulation of SSB signal can be done by using the coherent detector. In the process involved, first single-sideband signal $x_{SSB}(t)$ is multiplied by a local carrier and passing the resulted signal through a low-pass filter.

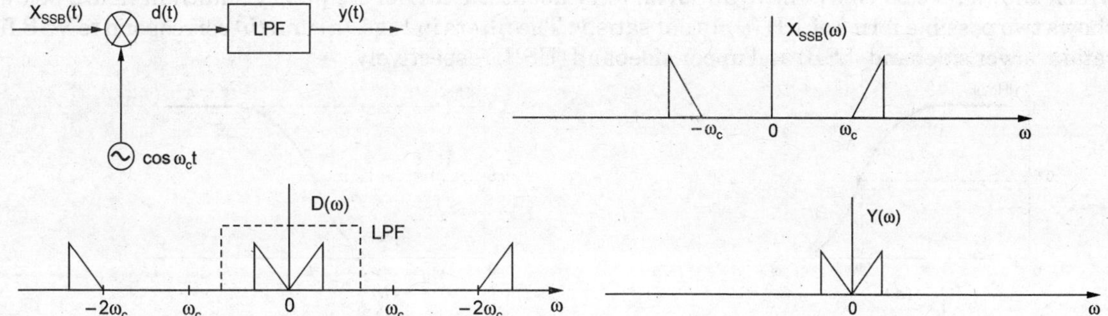

3. Vestigial-Sideband (VSB) Modulation

In this type of modulation, one sideband is passed almost completely and just a trace of other sideband is retained. Hence, channel bandwidth required is in excess of the message bandwidth by an amount equal to width of the vestigial sideband.

This type of modulation is used in television signal transmission that contains significant components at extremely low frequencies.

The typical bandwidth required to transmit a VSB signal is 1.25 times to that of SSB.

Generation of VSB singals.

A VSB signal can be generated by passing a DSB signal through a sideband shaping filter as shown in Figs. *(a)*, *(b)* and *(c)*. It shows spectrum of a VSB signal in relation to that of the message signal *m(t)*.

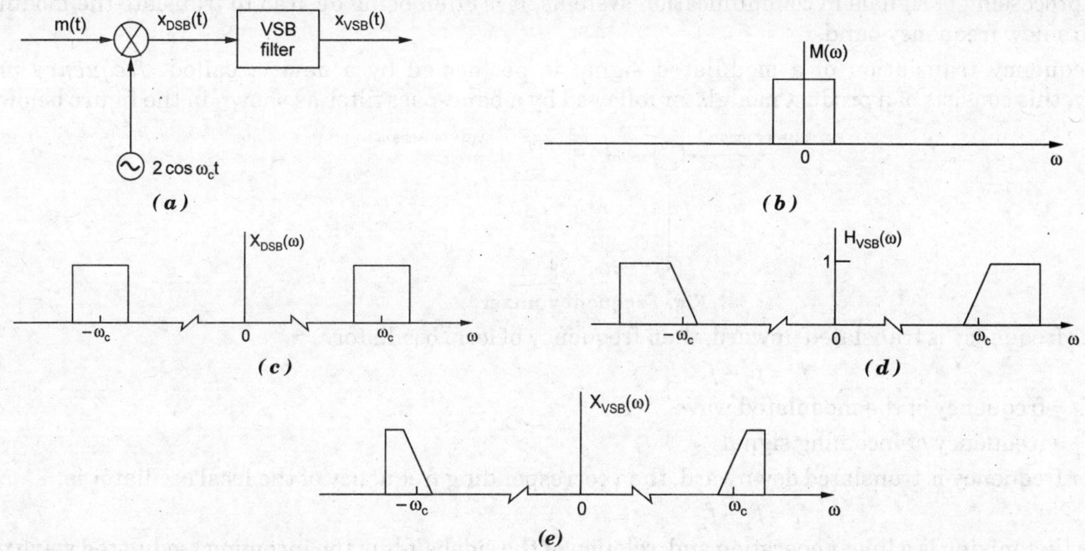

(a) *(b)* *(c)* *(d)* *(e)*

VSB filter characteristics.

For VSB signals, $m(t)$ can be recovered by synchronous or coherent demodulation. This determines the requirements of the frequency response $H(\omega)$.

It can be shown that for distortionless recovery of $m(t)$, it is required that

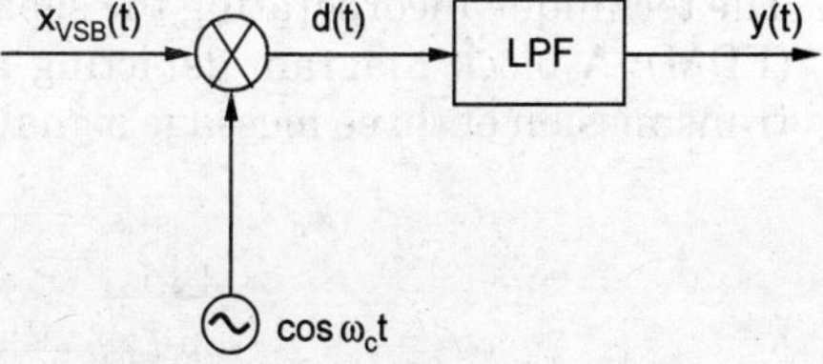

$$H(\omega + \omega_c) + H(\omega - \omega_c) = \text{constant} \quad \text{for } |\omega| \leq \omega_M$$

where ω_M = maximum frequency of $m(t)$.

Now letting the constant in be $2H(\omega_c)$, we get

$$H(\omega - \omega_c) - H(\omega_c) = -[H(\omega + \omega_c) - H(\omega_c)]$$

which shows that H (ω) will have antisymmetry about the carrier frequency shown in figure below. Figures shows two possible forms of | H (ω) | that satisfy. The filters in Figs. *(a)* and *(b)* correspond to VSB filters that retain lower sideband (LSB) and upper sideband (USB) respectively.

Demodulation of VSB signals.

Figure below shows demodulation of the VSB signal by the synchronous detector of VSB demodulator.

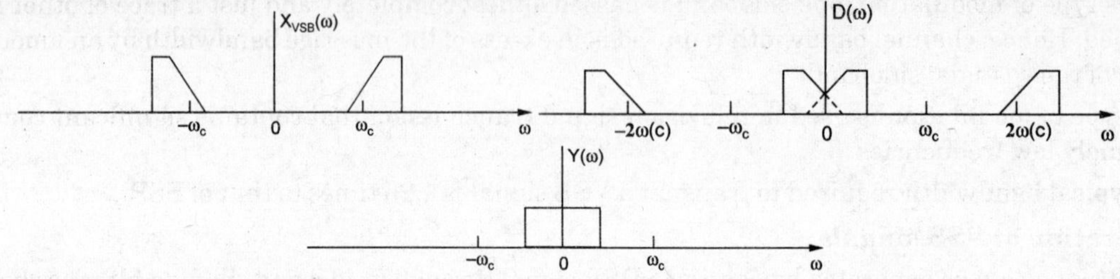

FREQUENCY TRANSLATION

During processing of signals in communication systems, it is often being desired to translate the modulated signal to a new frequency band.

This frequency translation of a modulated signal is performed by a device, called *frequency mixer.* Actually, this consists of a product modulator followed by a band-pass filter as shown in the figure below.

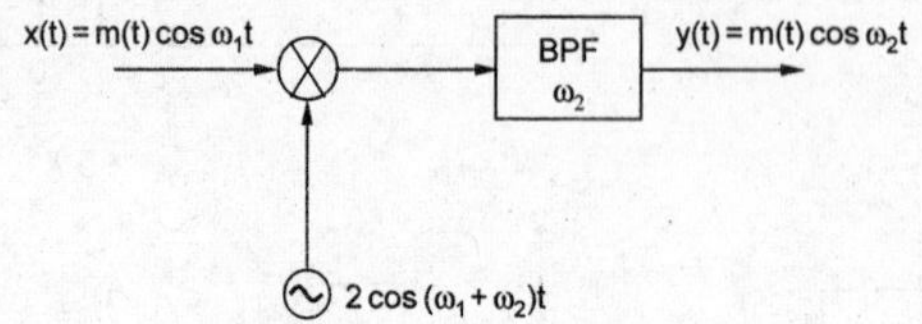

Fig. Frequency mixer.

If carrier frequency is translated upward, then frequency of local oscillator,

$$f_l = f_2 - f_1$$

where f_2 = frequency of the modulated wave

f_1 = frequency of incoming signal.

If carrier frequency is translated downward, then corresponding frequency of the local oscillator is

$$f_l = f_1 - f_2$$

It shows that mixing is a linear operation and relation of the sidebands of the incoming modulated wave to the carrier is completely preserved at the output.

FREQUENCY–DIVISION MULTIPLEXING

The technique incorporating the separation of signals in frequency, is called *frequency-division multiplexing* (FDM). A block diagram depicting an FDM system is shown in the figure below with the simultaneous transmission of three message signals.

Spectra of the message signals and sum of the modulated carriers are shown in the figure. DSB modulation is used in illustrating the spectra of figure. Any type of modulation can be used in FDM as long as the carrier spacing is sufficient to avoid spectral overlap. At the receiving end of the channel, three modulated signals are separated by bandpass filters (BPFs) and then demodulated.

FDM is used in telephone system, telemetry, commercial broadcast, television, and communication networks. Commercial AM broadcast stations use carrier frequency spaced 10 kHz apart in the frequency range from 540 to 1600 kHz. This separation is not sufficient to avoid spectral overlap for AM with a reasonably high-fidelity (50 Hz to 15 kHz) audio signal. Therefore, AM stations on adjacent carrier frequencies are placed geographical far apart to minimize interference.

ANGLE-MODULATION

In angle modulation, spectral components of the modulated waveform are not related in any simple fashion to the message spectrum. In addition, superposition does not apply to angle-modulated signal, *i.e.,* this modulation is non-linear modulation. Again, bandwidth of the angle-modulation signal is much greater than the message bandwidth.

For angle modulation, modulated carrier is represented by

$$x_c(t) = A\cos[\omega_c t + \phi(t)]$$

where A and ω_c are constants and the phase angle $\phi(t)$ is a function of message signal $m(t)$.

Rewriting above equation as $x_c(t) = A\cos\theta(t)$

where $\theta(t) = \omega_c t + \phi(t)$

Defining instantaneous radian frequency of $x_c(t)$, denoted by ω_i, as

$$\omega_i = \frac{d\theta(t)}{dt} = \omega_c + \frac{d\phi(t)}{dt}$$

When $\phi(t)$ = constant, then $\omega_i = \omega_c$

The function $\phi(t)$ and $\frac{\phi(t)}{dt}$ are called *instantaneous phase deviation* and *instantaneous frequency deviation* of $x_c(t)$.

Now, $\Delta\omega = |\omega_i - \omega_c|_{max}$

This quantity is called *maximum (or peak) radian frequency deviation of the angle-modulated signal.*

Types of Angle Modulation

1. **Phase Modulation (PM).**

   In phase modulation, instantaneous phase deviation of the carrier is proportional to the message signal, *i.e.*

   $$\phi(t) = k_p m(t)$$

   where k_p = phase deviation constant, expressed in radians per unit of $m(t)$.

2. **Frequency Modulation (FM).**

   In frequency modulation, instantaneous frequency deviation of the carrier is proportional to the message signal, *i.e.*

   $$\frac{d\phi(t)}{dt} = k_f m(t)$$

   or $$\phi(t) = k_f \int_{t_0}^{t} m(\lambda)\,d\lambda + \phi(t_0)$$

   where, k_f = frequency deviation constant, expressed in radians per second per unit of $m(t)$

   $\phi(t_0)$ = initial phase angle at $t = t_0$.

   It is usually assumed that $t_0 = -\infty$ and $\phi(-\infty) = 0$.

   We can express the angle-modulated signal as

   $$x_{PM}(t) = A\cos[\omega_c t + k_p m(t)]$$

   $$x_{FM}(t) = A\cos\left[\omega_c t + k_f \int_{-\infty}^{t} m(\lambda)\,d\lambda\right]$$

But we know, $\omega_i = \omega_c + \dfrac{d\phi(t)}{dt}$

For PM, $\omega_i = \omega_c + k_p \cdot \dfrac{dm(t)}{dt}$

For FM, $\omega_i = \omega_c + k_f \cdot m(t)$

Hence in PM, instantaneous frequency ω_i varies linearly with the derivative of the modulating signal and in FM, ω_i varies linearly with the modulating signal.

Modulation Index

In the message signal $m(t)$ is a pure sinusoidal, *i.e.*

$$m(t) = \begin{cases} a_m \sin\omega_m t & \text{for PM} \\ a_m \cos\omega_m t & \text{for FM} \end{cases}$$

Then for PM, instantaneous phase deviation,

$$\phi(t) = k_p\, m(t)$$

or
$$\phi(t) = k_p\, a_m \cdot \sin\omega_m t$$

or
$$\phi(t) = \beta \sin\omega_m t$$

where
$$\beta = k_p a_m \qquad \text{... (i)}$$

And for FM, instantaneous phase deviation,

$$\phi(t) = k_f \int_{t_0}^{t} m(\lambda)\, d\lambda + \phi(t_0) = \frac{a_m k_f \sin\omega_m t}{\omega_m} = \beta \sin\omega_m t$$

where
$$\beta = \frac{k_f\, a_m}{\omega_m} \qquad \text{... (ii)}$$

The parameter defined in equations (*i*) and (*ii*) is called *modulation index* and is maximum value of phase deviation for both PM and FM. It is pertinent to be noted that β is defined only for sinusoidal modulation and expressed as,

$$\beta = \frac{\Delta\omega}{\omega_m}$$

where, $\Delta\omega$ = maximum frequency deviation

Bandwidth of Angle-Modulated Signals

1. **Sinusoidal Modulation.**

In angle-modulated signal with sinusoidal modulation, 98 percent of the normalized total signal power is contained in the bandwidth,

$$W_B \approx 2(\beta + 1)\,\omega_m$$

When $\beta << 1$, signal is an NB angle-modulated signal and its bandwidth is approximately equal to $2\omega_m$. Usually $\beta = 0.2$ is used to satisfy this criterion.

2. **Arbitrary Modulation.**

For an angle-modulated signal with an arbitrary modulating signal $m(t)$ band-limited to ω_M radians/sec

Deviation ratio, $$D = \frac{\text{maximum frequency deviation}}{\text{bandwidth of } m(t)} = \frac{\Delta\omega}{\omega_M}$$

$$W_B \text{ (bandwidth)} \approx 2(D + 1)\,\omega M$$

For $D << 1$, $W_B \approx 2\,\omega_M$

and signal is narrowband (NB) angle-modulated signal.

For $D >> 1$, $W_B \approx 2\,D\omega_M = 2\Delta\omega$

i.e. twice the peak frequency deviation and signal is wideband (WB) angle-modulated signal.

Wide-Band Angle-Modulated Signals.

Two methods are employed usually to generate (WB) wide-band angle-modulated signals.

1. **Indirect method.**

   In this method, an narrow-band angle-modulated signal is produced first and then converted to a wide-band angle-modulated signal by using frequency multipliers. The frequency multiplier multiplies the argument of the input sinusoid by n.

   Thus, if input of a frequency multiplier is

   $$x(t) = A \cos [\omega_c t + \phi(t)]$$

   then output of the frequency multiplier is

   $$y(t) = A \cos [n\omega_c t + n\,\phi(t)]$$

   Use of frequency multiplication normally increases the carrier frequency to an impractically high value. To avoid this, a frequency conversion (using a mixer or DSB modulator) is necessary to shift the spectrum.

2. **Direct method.**

   In direct method of generating FM signal, modulating signal directly controls the carrier frequency. A common method used for generating FM directly is to vary the inductance or capacitance of a tuned electric oscillator. Any oscillator whose frequency is controlled by the modulating signal voltage is called *voltage controlled oscillator* (VCO). The main advantage of direct FM is that large frequency deviations are possible and thus less frequency multiplication is required. The major disadvantage is that the carrier frequency tends to drift and so additional circuitry is required for frequency stablization.

DEMODULATION OF ANGLE-MODULATED SIGNALS.

Frequency demodulation is done by using a popular device called *frequency discriminator,* whose instantaneous amplitude is directly proportional to the instantaeous frequency of the input FM signal. Basically, frequency discriminator consists of a *slope circuit* followed by an *envelope detector.* An ideal slope circuit is characterized by a transfer function, that is purely imaginary, varying linearly with frequency inside a prescribed frequency interval.

PULSE-CODE MODULATION (PCM)

In this a message signal is represented by a sequence of coded pulses, which is accomplished by representing the signal in discrete form in both time and amplitude. The basic operations involved are sampling, quantizing and encoding. The low-pass filter prior to sampling is included to prevent aliasing of the message signal. The quantizing and encoding operations are usually performed in the same circuit, which is called *analog-to-digital converter*. The basic operations in the receiver are regeneration of unpaired signals, decoding and reconstruction of the train of quantized samples as shown in Fig. *(c)*. Regeneration along the transmission path also occurs at the intermediate points as it being necessary. If time-division-multiplexing is employed, then proper synchronization between receiver and transmitter is needed.

Fig *(a)* Transmitter

Fig *(b)* Transmission path

Fig *(c)* Receiver

Band-limited signals

It is a signal $m(t)$ for which Fourier transform of $m(t)$ is zero above a certain frequency ω_M,

$$m(t) \leftrightarrow M(\omega) = 0 \text{ for } |\omega| > \omega_M = 2\pi f_M \quad \text{... (i)}$$

SAMPLING.

Sampling theorem

If a signal *m(t)* is a real-valued band-limited signal fulfilling condition given in equation (*i*), then $m(t)$ can be uniquely determined from its values $m(nT_s)$ sampled at uniform intervals $T_s\left[\le \frac{1}{12 f_m}\right]$.

Then
$$m(t) = \sum_{n=-\infty}^{\infty} m(nT_s) \frac{\sin \omega_M (t - nT_s)}{\omega_M (t - nT_s)}$$

where T_s is called *sampling period* and its reciprocal $f_s = 1/T_s$ is called *sampling rate*.

Thus, sampling theorem states that, *a band-limited signal which has no frequency components higher than* f_M *Hz can be recovered completely from a set of samples taken at the rate of* f_s ($\ge 2 f_M$) *samples per second.*

The above sampling theorem is often called *uniform sampling theorem* for baseband or low-pass signals.

The minimum sampling rate, $2f_M$ samples per second, is called *Nyquist rate*; its reciprocal $1/(2f_M)$ (measured in seconds) is called *Nyquist interval*.

Type of Sampling

1. Instantaneous sampling.

Sampling of an arbitrary signal $m(t)$ instantaneously and at a uniform rate results in an infinite sequence of samples $\{m(nT_s)\}$, where n have all possible integer values. This ideal form of sampling is called *instantaneous sampling.*

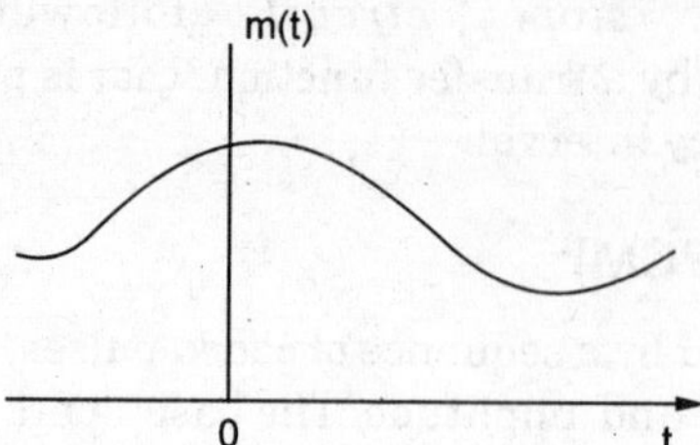

Ideal sampled signal :

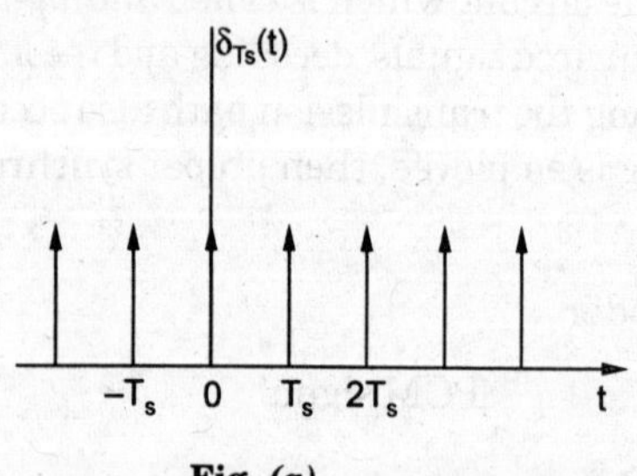

Fig (a)

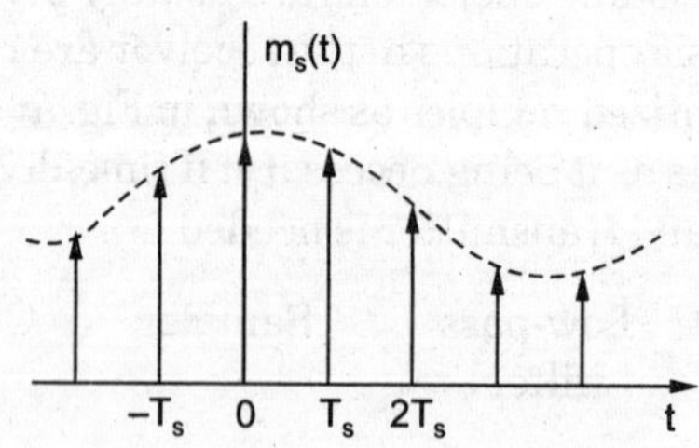

Fig (b)

Multiplication of $m(t)$ by a unit impulse train $\delta_T(t)$ as shown in Fig. (*a*), we get

$$m_s(t) = m(t)\, \delta T_s(t) = m(t) \sum_{n=-\infty}^{\infty} \delta(t - nT_s) = \sum_{n=-\infty}^{\infty} m(t)\, \delta(t - nT_s)$$

Now, using the property, $x(t)\,\delta(t - t_0) = x(t_0) \cdot \delta(t - t_0)$

we have
$$m_s(t) = \sum_{n=-\infty}^{\infty} m(nT_s)\, \delta(t - nT_s)$$

The signal shown is Fig. (*b*), is called *ideal sampled signal.*

2. Practical sampling.

A more practical way to sample band-limited analog sampling is done by employing high-speed switching circuits, as shown in Fig. *(c)* and resulting sampled signal is shown in Fig. *(d)*.

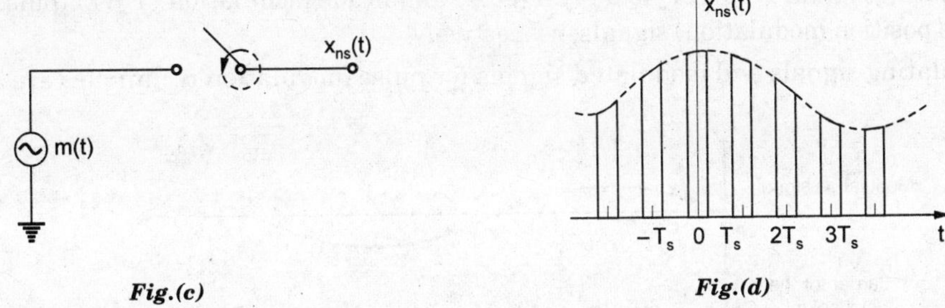

Fig.(c) ***Fig.(d)***

Sampled signal $x_{ns}(t) = m(t)\, x_p(t)$

where $x_p(t)$ is periodic train of rectangular pulses with period T_s, and each rectangular pulse in $x_p(t)$ having width d and unit amplitude.

Since top of each pulse in $x_{nx}(t)$ retains the shape of its corresponding analog signal, it is also called *natural sampling*. The condition for the message $m(t)$ to be recovered from the natural sampled signal $x_{nx}(t)$ is that, sampling rate is equal to or greater than twice the highest message frequency.

3. Flat-top sampling.

For flat-top sampling, a sample-and-hold circuit employed is shown below.

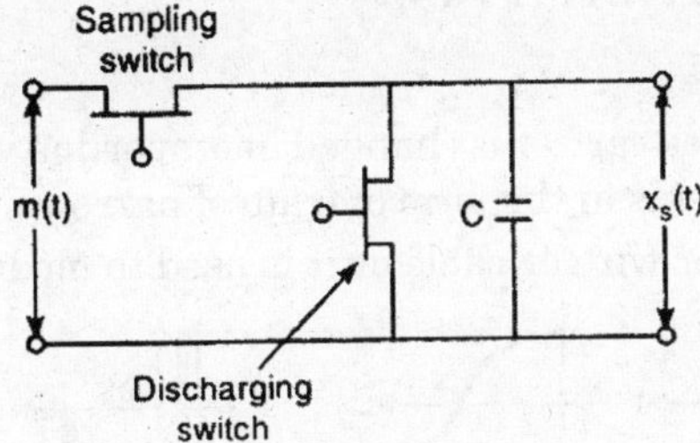

This circuit produces a flat-top sampled signal. Flat-top sampling is equivalent to passing an ideal sampled signal through a filter having the frequency response

$$H(\omega) = \frac{d \sin(\omega_d / 2)}{\omega_d / 2}.$$

The high-frequency roll-off characteristic of H (ω) acts as a low-pass filter and therefore attenuates the upper portion of the message spectrum. This loss of high-frequency content is called *aperature effect.*

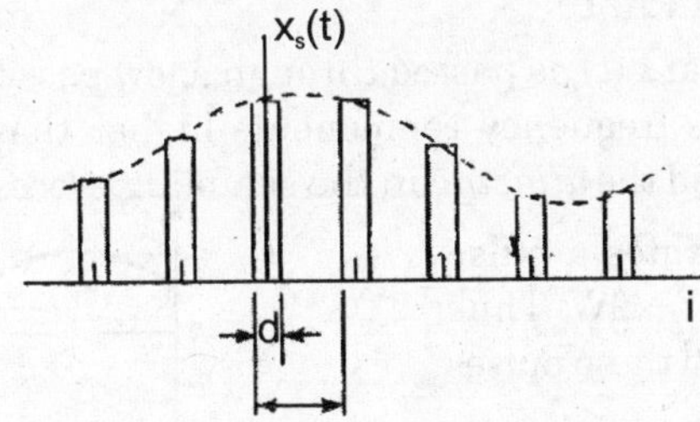

The effect is more pronounced if larger pulse duration of aperature d is used, Practically if $d/T_s \le 0.1$, then aperature effect can be neglected.

ANALOG PULSE MODULATION SYSTEMS

In the *pulse modulation* systems, the carrier is a train of discrete pulses rather than a sinewave. Any one characteristics of this pulse train, i.e. amplitude, width or position can be changed in proportion with the amplitude of modulating signal. This will yield PAM (pulse amplitude modulation), PWM (pulse width modulation) or PPM (pulse position modulation) signals, respectively.

The carriers, modulating signals and modulated signals for pulse modulation techniques are as shown in the figures below.

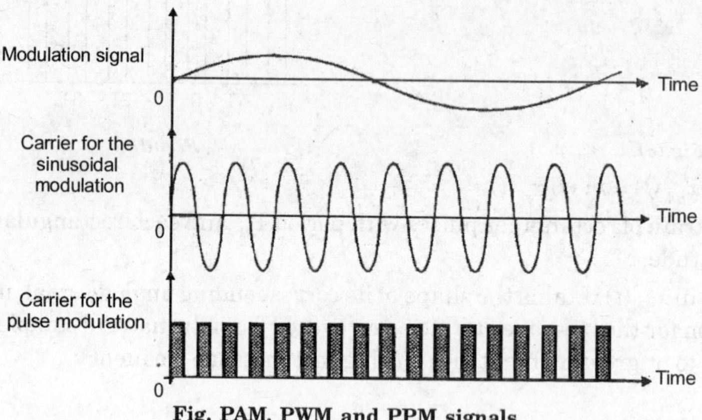

Fig. PAM, PWM and PPM signals

PULSE AMPLITUDE MODULATION (PAM).

Naturally sampled PAM

In the PAM system, amplitude of pulsed carrier is changed in proportion with the instantaneous amplitude of the modulating signal x (t). The carrier is in the form of train of narrow pulses as shown in figure.

The PAM signal is then sent by either wire or cable or it is used to modulate another carrier.

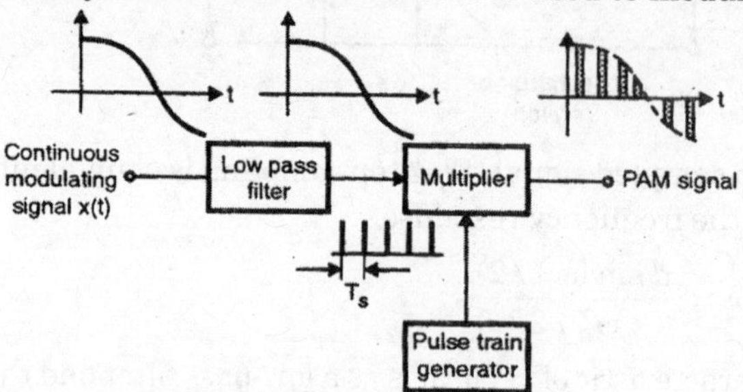

Fig. Generation of PAM

Generation of naturally sampled PAM

(i) The continuous modulating signal x (t), is passed through a low pass filter. The LPF will bandlimit this signal to W. That means all the frequency components higher than the frequency W are removed. Bandlimiting is necessary to avoid the *aliasing* in the sampling process.

(ii) The pulse train generator generates a pulse train at a frequency f_s, such that $f_s > 2W$. Thus the Nyquist criteria is satisfied. All these pulses are of equal widths.

(iii) The uniform *sampling* takes place in the multiplier block to generate PAM signal as shown in figure below. The samples are placed T_s seconds away from each other.

(iv) The *information* in the modulating signal is contained in the *Amplitude variations* of the pulsed carrier. Therefore this system is similar to the AM system.

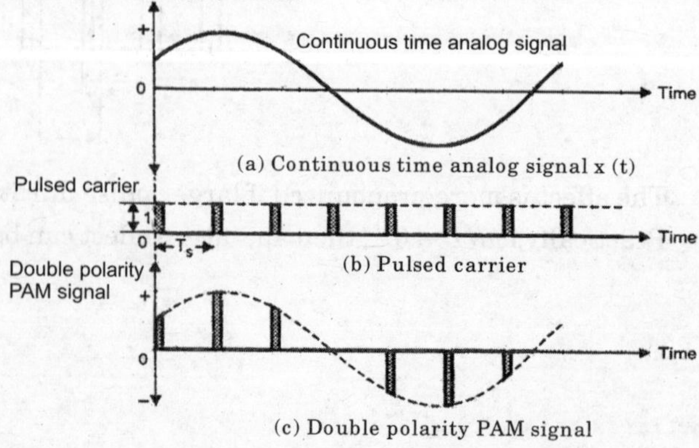

(a) Continuous time analog signal x (t)

(b) Pulsed carrier

(c) Double polarity PAM signal

Types of PAM

There are two types of PAM systems.

(*i*) Double polarity PAM

(*ii*) **Single polarity PAM** : In single polarity PAM, a fixed dc level is added to the continuous signal *x* (*t*). Due to this, modulated pulses are always positive. The waveforms of single polarity PAM are as shown in Fig (*b*) below

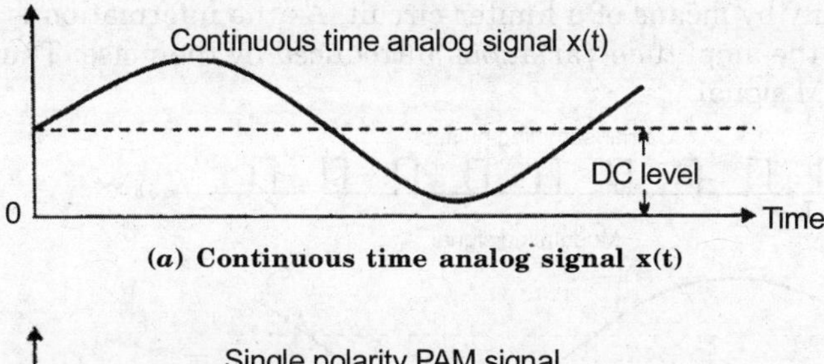

(*a*) **Continuous time analog signal x(t)**

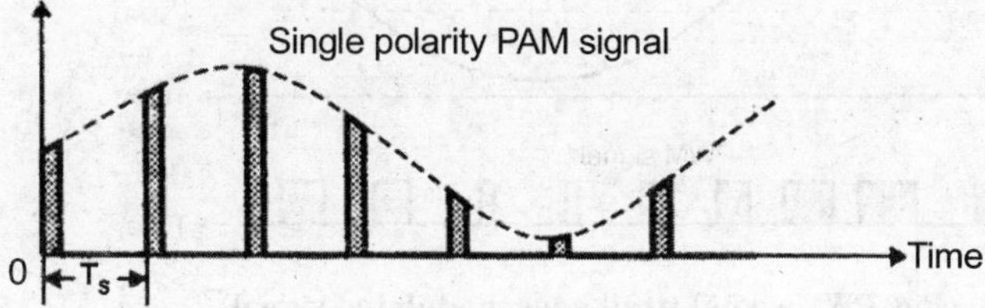

(*b*) **Single polarity PAM signal**

Detection of PAM

The PAM signal can be detected (demodulated) by passing it through a low pass filter. The low pass filter cutoff frequency is adjusted to W so that all the high frequency components are removed and the original modulating signal is recovered back. The PAM detection and corresponding waveforms are as shown in the figure below.

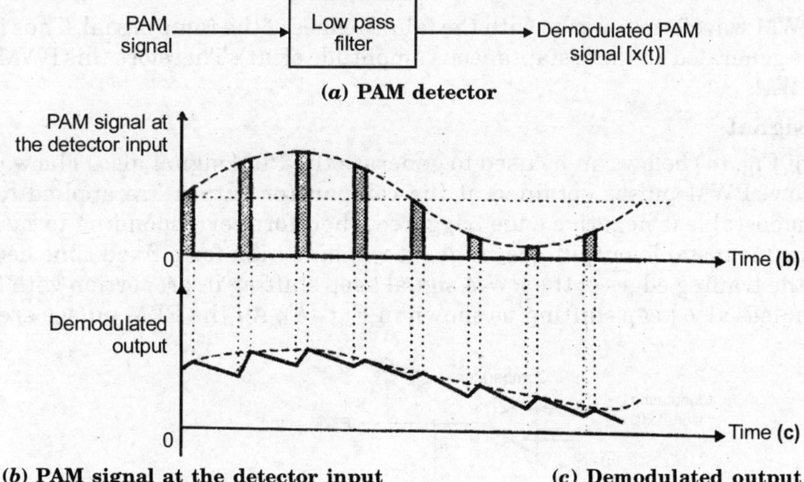

(*a*) **PAM detector**

(*b*) **PAM signal at the detector input** (*c*) **Demodulated output**

Advantages of PAM

Simplicity of generation and detection.

Disadvantages of PAM

(*i*) The amplitude of PAM signal changes according to the amplitude of modulating signal x (t). Therefore like AM, PAM signal gets affected due to the additive noise. The added noise then cannot be removed easily.

(*ii*) The transmission bandwidth is much larger than the maximum frequency content in x_s (t).

(*iii*) Due to changes in amplitudes of PAM pulses, the transmitted power does not remain constant.

PULSE WIDTH MODULATION (PWM) AND PULSE POSITION MODULATION (PPM).

In PWM, width of the modulated pulses varies in proportion with the amplitude of modulating signal. The waveforms of PWM are as shown in the figure below.

As seen from the waveforms, amplitude and frequency of the PWM wave remains constant and only width changes. Thus *information* is contained in the width variation. This is similar to FM. As the noise is normally *additive* noise, it changes amplitude of the PWM signal. At the receiver, it is possible to remove these unwanted amplitude variation very easily by means of a limiter circuit. As the information is contained in the width variation, it is unaffected by the amplitude variations introduced by the noise. Thus PWM system is more immune to noise than the PAM signal.

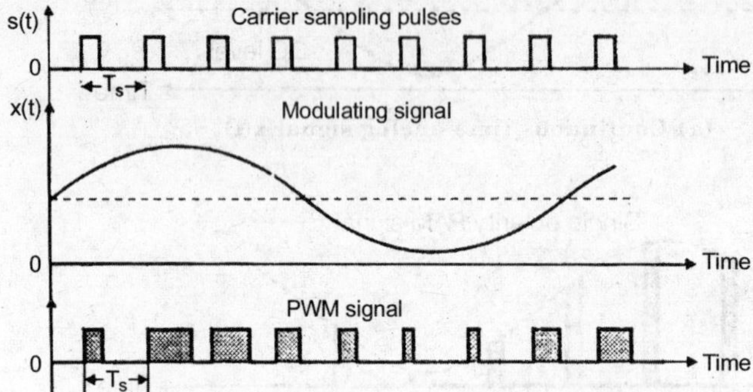

Fig. PWM signal (trail edge modulated signal)

Generation of PWM and PPM signals

The block diagram of Fig. (*a*) can be used for the generation of PWM as well as PPM. A sawtooth generates a sawtooth signal of frequency f_s, therefore sawtooth signal in this case is a sampling signal. It is applied to the inverting terminal of a comparator. The modulating signal *x*(*t*) is applied to the non-inverting terminal of the same comparator.

The comparator output will remain high as long as instantaneous amplitude x(t) is higher than that of the ramp signal. This gives rise to a PWM signal at the comparator output as shown in Fig. (b).

Leading edges of the PWM waveform coincide with the falling edges of the ramp signal. Thus leading edges of PWM signal are always generated on the instantaneous amplitude of x(t). Therefore this PWM signal is called *trail edge modulated PWM*.

Generation of PPM signal

The PWM generator of Fig. (*a*) below can be used to generate the PPM signal also. The waveforms are as shown in Fig. (*b*) below. PWM pulses obtained at the comparator output are applied to a monostable multivibrator. This monostable is negative edge triggered, therefore corresponding to each trailing edge of the PWM signal, the monostable output goes high. It remains high for a fixed time decided by its RC components. Thus as the trailing edges of the PWM signal keep shifting in proportion with the modulating signal *x*(*t*), the PPM pulses also keep shifting as shown in Fig. (*b*). All the PPM pulses are of same width and amplitude.

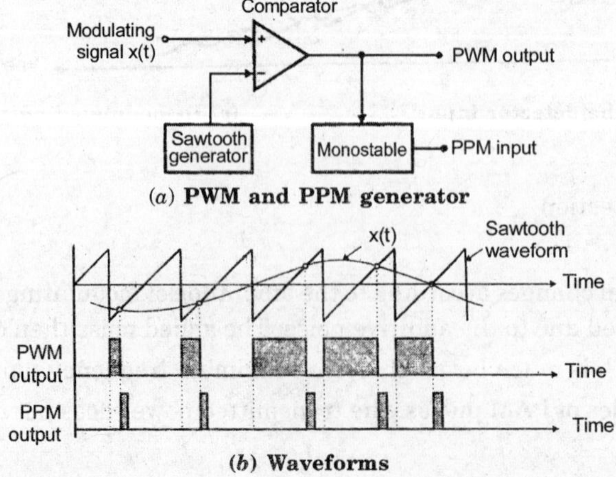

(*a*) **PWM and PPM generator**

(*b*) **Waveforms**

Advantages of PWM

(i) Less effect of noise, i.e. very good noise immunity.

(ii) Synchronization between transmitter and receiver is not essential (which is essential in PPM).

(iii) It is possible to reconstruct PWM signal from a noise contaminated PWM. Thus it is possible to separate out signal from noise (which is not possible in PAM).

Disadvantages of PWM

(i) Due to variable pulse width, pulses have variable power contents. So transmitter must be powerful enough to handle maximum width pulse, though average power transmitted can be as low as 50% of this maximum power.

(ii) In order to avoid any waveform distortion, bandwidth required for the PWM communication is large as compared to band width of PAM.

Advantages of PPM

(i) Due to constant amplitude of PPM pulses, information is not contained in the amplitude. Hence noise added to PPM signal does not distort the information. Thus it has good noise immunity.

(ii) It is possible to reconstruct PPM signal from the noise contaminated PPM signal. This is also possible in PWM but not possible in PAM.

(iii) Due to constant amplitude of pulses, transmitted power always remains constant. It does not change as it used to, in PWM.

Disadvantages of PPM

(i) As position of the PPM pulses is varied with respect to a reference pulse, a transmitter has to send synchronizing pulses to operate timing circuits in the receiver. Without them the demodulation won't be possible to achieve.

(ii) Large bandwidth is required to ensure transmission of undistorted pulses.

COMPARISON OF PAM, PWM AND PPM SYSTEMS.

Sr. No.	Parameter	PAM	PWM	PPM
1.	Type of carrier	Train of pulses	Train of pulses	Train of pulses
2.	Variable characteristic of the pulsed carrier	Amplitude	Width	Position
3.	Bandwidth requirement	Low	High	High
4.	Noise immunity	Low	High	High
5.	Information is contained in-	Amplitude variations	Width variation	Position variation
6.	Transmitted power	Varies with amplitude of pulses	Varies with variation in width	Remains constant
7.	Need to transmit synchronizing pulses	Not needed	Not needed	Necessary
8.	Complexity of generation and detection	Complex	Easy	Complex
9.	Similarity with other modulation systems	Similar to AM	Similar to FM	Similar to PM
10.	Output waveforms			

QUANTIZING

Uniform Quantizing

In the figure below, it is assumed that amplitude of $m(t)$ is confined to the range $(-m_p, m_p)$. This range is divided in L zones, each having step size Δ.

$$\Delta = \frac{2m_p}{L}$$

A sample amplitude value is approximated by the midpoint of the interval in which it lies. The input – ouput characteristics of a uniform quantizer is shown in the figure below.

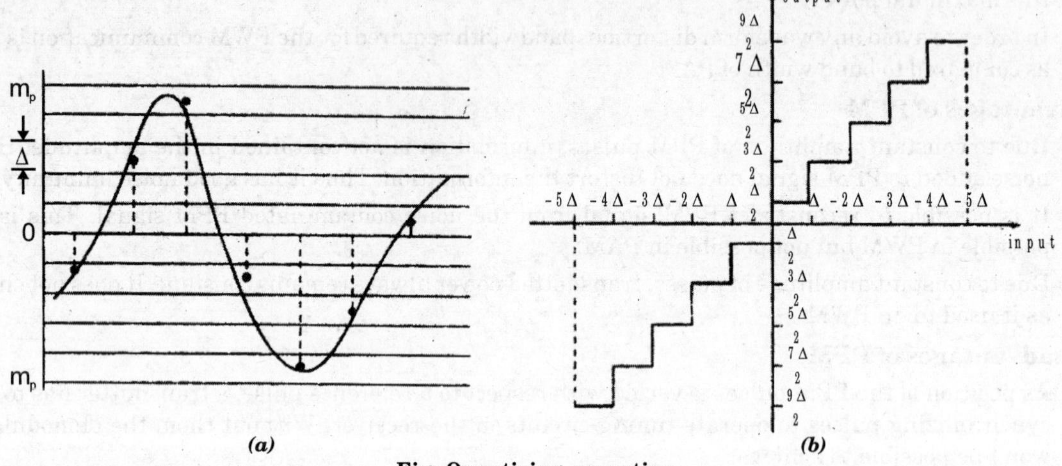

Fig. Quantizing operation

Quantizing Noise

The difference between input and output signals of the quantizer becomes *quantizing error*, or *quantizing noise*.

The quantizing error q_e varies randomly within interval, $\frac{-\Delta}{2} \le q_e \le \frac{\Delta}{2}$

After assuming that the error is equally likely to lie anywhere in the range $(-\Delta/2, \Delta/2)$,

$$\text{mean-square quantizing error, } \langle q_e^2 \rangle = \frac{1}{\Delta}\int_{-\Delta/2}^{\Delta/2} q_e^2 \, dq_e = \frac{\Delta^2}{12}$$

Also,
$$\langle q_e^2 \rangle = \frac{m_p^2}{3L^2}$$

ENCODING

It involves the process of representing any discrete set of values in a particular arrangement of discrete events, *i.e.* quantized samples translates into a code number.

There are several *line codes* that can be used for the electrical representation of binary symbols 1 and 0, as follows.

1. Unipolar Non Return-to-Zero (NRZ) signaling

Symbol 1 is represented by transmitting a pulse of constant amplitude for the duration of the bit interval, and symbol 0 is represented by no pulse. NRZ indicates that the assigned amplitude level is maintained throughout the entire bit interval.

2. Bipolar NRZ signaling

Symbols 1 and 0 are represented by pulses of equal positive and negative amplitudes. In either case, the assigned pulse amplitude level is maintained throughout the bit interval.

3. Unipolar Return-to-Zero (RZ) signaling

Symbol 1 is represented by a positive pulse that returns to zero before the end of the bit interval, and symbol 0 is represented by the absence of pulse.

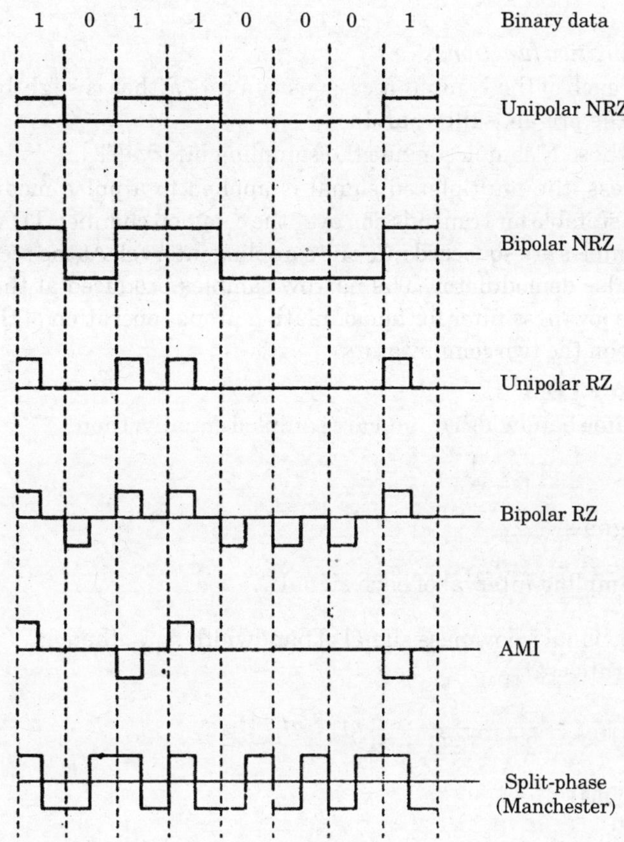

4. **Bipolar RZ signaling**
   Positive and negative pulses of equal amplitude are used for symbols 1 and 0, respectively. In either case, the pulse returns to 0 before the end of the bit interval.
5. **Alternative Mark Inversion (AMI) RZ signaling**
   Positive and negative pulses (of equal amplitude) are used alternately for symbol 1, and no pulse is used for symbol 0. In either case the pulse returns to 0 before the end of the bit interval.
6. **Split-phase (Manchester) signaling**
   Symbol 1 is represented by a positive pulse followed by a negative pulse, with both pulses being of equal amplitude and half-bit duration; for symbol 0, the polarities of these pulses are reversed.

TIME-DIVISION MULTIPLEXING (TDM)

This multiplexing is commonly used for the transmission of several different signals through a single channel.

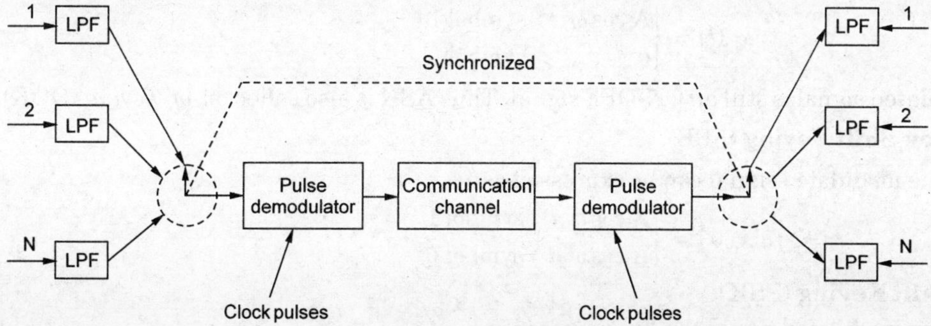

Each input signal is first restricted in bandwidth by a low-pass filter, to remove frequencies that are non-essential for adequate signal representation. The low-pass filter outputs are then applied to a commutator, which is usually implemented using electronic switching circuity. Each signal is sampled at the Nyquist rate or higher.

Functions of Commutator

Commutator performs following two functions :

(*i*) Take a narrow sample of each of the N input messages at a rate f_s that is slightly higher than 2W, where W is cut-off frequency of the pre-alias filter, and

(*ii*) Sequentially inter leave these N samples inside the sampling interval T_s.

Following commutation process, the multiplexed signal is applied to a pulse modulator, which transform multiplexed signal into a form suitable for transmission over the common channel. TDM introduces a bandwidth expansion factor N, since N samples are squeezed into one sampling interval. At the receiving end, the composite signal is demultiplexed by pulse demodulator. The narrow samples produced at the pulse demodulator are distributed to the appropriate low-pass filter for demodulation proper operation of this system depends upon proper synchronization between the two commutators.

Bandwidth requirements for TDM

If all input signals have the same bandwidth f_m and are sampled equally, then

$$T = \frac{T_s}{n}$$

where n = number of input signals

$$T_s = \frac{1}{f_s} \leq \frac{1}{2f_m} \text{ is the sampling interval of each signal.}$$

If resultant time-multiplexed signal is low-pass signal of bandwidth f_{TDM}, then

minimum sampling rate $= 2f_{TDM}$

Thus
$$f_{TDM} = \frac{1}{2T} = \frac{n}{2T_s} = \frac{1}{2} nf_s \geq nf_m \text{ Hz.}$$

DELTA MODULATION (DM)

In this an incoming message signal is oversampled to increase correlation between adjacent samples of the signal. This rate is much higher than the Nyquist rate.

In its basic form, DM provides a staircase approximation to the oversampled version of the message signal,

DIGITAL CARRIER MODULATION TECHNIQUES

In binary modulation schemes, modulation process corresponds to switching (or keying) the amplitude, frequency, or phase of the CW carrier between either of two values corresponding to binary symbols 0 and 1.

Types of Digital Carrier Modulation

There are three types of digital modulation :

1. **Amplitude-Shift Keying (ASK).**

   In ASK, the modulated signal can be expressed as

$$x_c(t) = \begin{cases} A \cos \omega_c t & \text{symbol 1} \\ 0 & \text{symbol 0} \end{cases}$$

   The modulated signal is still an ON-OFF signal. Thus ASK is also called *on-off keying* (OOK).

2. **Frequency-Shift Keying (FSK).**

   In FSK, the modulated signal can be expressed as

$$x_c(t) = \begin{cases} A \cos \omega_1 t & \text{symbol 1} \\ A \cos \omega_2 t & \text{symbol 0} \end{cases}$$

3. **Phase-Shift Keying (PSK).**

   In PSK, the modulated signal can be expressed as

$$x_c(t) = \begin{cases} A \cos \omega_c t & \text{symbol 1} \\ A \cos (\omega_c t + \pi) & \text{symbol 0} \end{cases}$$

   Figure given shows these digital modulation schemes for the case in which the data bits are represented by the bipolar NRZ waveform.

DATA COMMUNICATION

Transmission Modes

1. Simplex mode.

It defines a one-way communication between two nodes, one ,which is always a sender and the other which is always a receiver.

2. Half - duplex.

In this mode, only one station can send at a time

3. Full- duplex.

This allows both nodes to send and receive simultaneously.

Network Topology

S.No.	Type	Advantages
1.	Mesh	Privacy
2.	Star	Robustness
3.	Tree	Isolating and prioritizing communications between different computers
4.	Bus	Ease of installation
5.	Ring	Simple fault isolation

S.No.	Type	Disadvantage
1.	Mesh	Large amount of cabling makes it expensive
2.	Star	Need for an extra intermediate device
3.	Tree	Difficult reconfiguration and fault isolation
4.	Bus	No privacy

LINE CONFIGURATION.

It defines the way two or more devices are connected to a link. Topology is a way two or more links are connected to form a network. Both are used to describe a relationship between communicating devices.

Types of Line Configuration

1. Point -to-point
2. Point-to- multipoint

Advantage of a multipoint over a point-to-point configuration is ease of installation and low expenses.

PEER-TO-PEER NETWORKS.

Characteristics

(1) No server (hardware and software) needed

(2) Used in small networks of 10 or less users

(3) No centralization of resources or management

(4) Management of resources is maintained by each user

(5) Poor security

Hardware components needed to connect computers together to make Peer-To-Peer network.

(1) Cable

(2) Hub

(3) Network Interface Care (NIC)

Disadvantages.

(1) Poor security

(2) No central location for file saving

(3) Limited to 10 users or less

(4) Limited number of connections to share resources

(5) poor performance under heavy load

(6) no centralized management

MODES OF TRANSMITTING BINARY DATA ON A LINK.

1. **Serial Transmission**

In serial mode, all bits are transmitted over only one communication line and one bit follows another

Methods of Serial Transmission.

(*i*) Asynchronous transmission : In synchronous transmission, no timing is needed at the byte level, because information is teceived and transmitted by agreed upon patterns.

(*ii*) Synchronous transmission : In synchronous transmission, timing is very important. This method is used for high speed communication.

2. **Parallel Teransmission**

In parallel mode, bits are grouped together and transmitted parallely over separate communication lines.

Disadvantage : Cost of multiple parallel lines is the main disadvantage of parallel mode of communication

MODULATOR AND DEMODULATOR.

M*odulator* converts a digital signal to an analog signal using ASK, FSK, PSK and QAM modulation techniques. *Demodulator* converts an analog signal to a digital signal.

PROTOCOLS.

The sets of rule is called protocol.

There are different protocol.

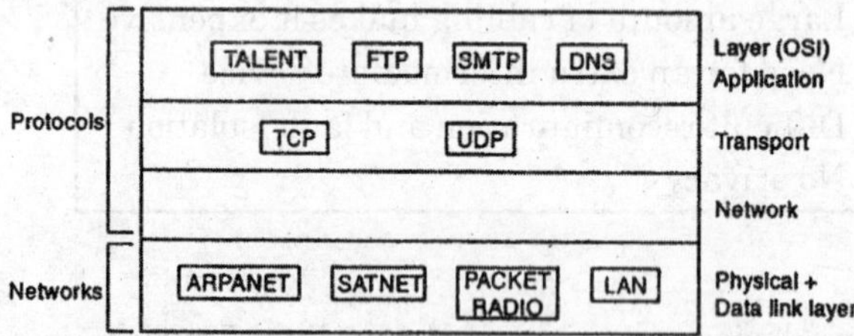

Protocol Architecture

The protocol architecture is the set of protocols that implement the service architecture.

Set of tasks performed by a Protocol layer

In a computer network, each layer may perform one or more of the following set of tasks:

(1) ***Error control.*** This makes the logical channel between the layers in two peer network element more reliable.

(2) ***Flow control.*** This avoids overwhelming a slower peer with PDUs ro packets.

(3) ***Segmentation and reassembly.*** At transmitting side, it divides large data chunks into smaller pieces and at the receiving side reassembles the smaller pieces into the original large chunk.

(4) ***Multiplexing.*** This allows several higher level sessions to share a single lower level connection.]

(5) ***Connection setup and tear down.***

OPTICAL COMMUNICATION

This communication is through carrier optical signals. Easily accessible optical frequencies lie in the range 10^{12} to 10^{16} Hz. It is very high as compared to the radio frequencies (10^6 to 10^8 Hz) or microwaves (10^9 to 10^{11} Hz). A large number of *channels* and higher bandwidth transmission is possible with high frequency carriers. Hence, optical communication is better.

Advantages

Advantages of optical communication over the conventional two-wire or cable electronic are follows :

(1) Wide channel bandwidth and large channel carrying capacity.

Because of the use of higher frequencies ~ 10^{14} Hz as compared to the electronic communication links.

(2) Low transmission losses.

In optical fibres losses per km are less.

(3) Signal security and not accessible to interference :

Optical signal is confined to the inside of fibre and cannot be tempered easily. So secret information like banking, defence etc. is more secure.

Basic Optical Communication Link

The simplest optical transmission link is a point-to-point link having a transmitter at one end and a receiver at the other end as shown in the figure.

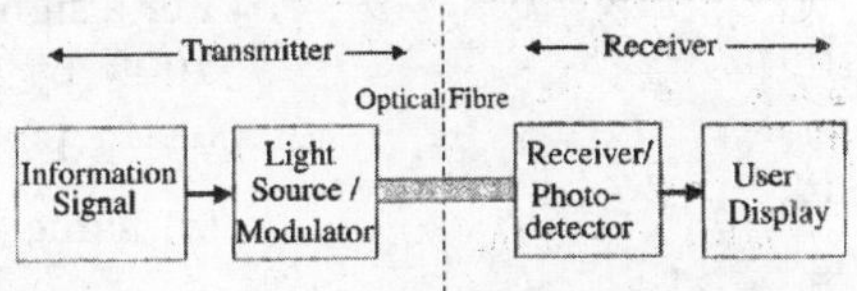

Fig. Point-to-point optical communication link.

Important components of an optical communication link :

(1) Optical source and modulator

(2) Optical signal detector or photodetector

(3) Optical fibre cable through which optical signal is transmitted

Optical Sources for Communication Links

Semiconductor Light Emitting Diodes (LED) and diode lasers are preferred light sources because

(i) these give adequate power.

(ii) diode laser light is monochromatic and coherent. Therefore, they can easily be obtained as parallel beams spread over a narrow cone or angle. These are preferred for very large distance transmission.

(iii) LED also gives near monochromatic light (not as much as in diode laser). This near monochromaticity is sufficient for applications over small distances. LED is low cost device as compared to diode laser.

(iv) dimensional characteristics of both diode laser and LED are compatible with those of the optical fibre, which means that coupling of fibres with light source will be easier.

(v) light from LED or diode laser can be varied or modulated by varying the applied voltage or current throught the device which is essentially the information to be transmitted.

OPTICAL DETECTORS.

The optical signal reaching the receiving end has to be detected by a detector which converts light into electrical signal so that the transmitted information may be decoded.

The optical detector should have

(i) size compatible with the fibre

(ii) high sensitivity at the desired optical wavelength

(iii) high response time for fast speed data transmission/reception.

OPTICAL FIBRE.

In a point-to-point communication link using electrical signal, we use a conducting wire or a cable and the signal current is *guided* through the conductor cable wire.

The optical fibres make use of the principle of total internal reflection.

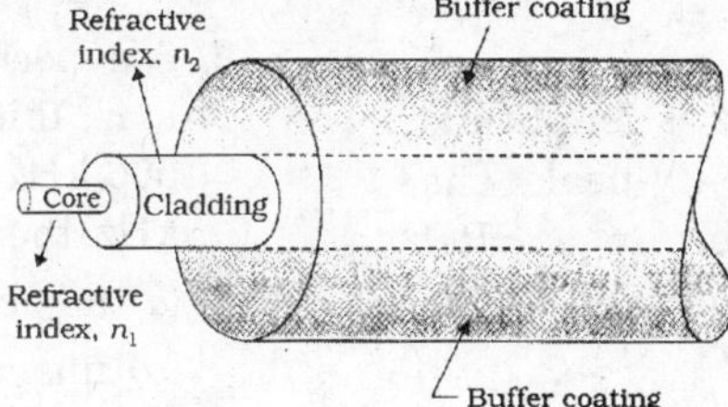

Fig. Single optical fibre structure.

A typical optical fibre, as shown in figure consists of a **core** of glass/silica/plastic with approximate diameter of 10 to 100 μm with refractive index n_1. The plastic core has high loss and hence glass cores are preferred.

The core is surrounded by a glass or a plastic **cladding** with refractive index n_2 such that $n_2 < n_1$.

Difference, $\Delta n = n_1 - n_2$ is typically very small of the order of 10^{-3}.

The refractive index of cladding can change either abruptly from n_1 to n_2 (a *step-index fibre,*) or gradually (*graded-index fibre*)

For providing safety and strength, a **buffer** plastic coating or housing encapsulates the *core-cladding* of the fibres.

Objective Type Questions

1. Leak type bias is used in a plate modulated class C amplifier to
(*a*) increase the bandwidth
(*b*) prevent excessive grid current
(*c*) prevent tuned circuit damping
(*d*) prevent over modulation

2. Frequency frogging is used in carrier system to
(*a*) conserve frequencies
(*b*) reduce distortion
(*c*) reduce cross talk
(*d*) none of these

3. A 1000 kHz carrier is simultaneously modulated with 300 Hz and 2 kHz audio sine waves. The frequency which will not be present in the output is
(*a*) 998 kHz
(*b*) 999.7 kHz
(*c*) 1000.3 kHz
(*d*) 700 kHz

4. A carrier is simultaneously modulated by two sine waves with modulation indicates of 0.3 and 0.4. If modulated power is 10 kW, then total modulated power will be
(*a*) 12.5 kW (*b*) 10 kW
(*c*) 10.125 kW (*d*) 10.5 kW

5. The saving in power in a DSBSC system modulated at 80% is
(*a*) Nil (*b*) 80%
(*c*) 75.76% (*d*) 50%

6. A RF carrier of 12 kV at 1 MHz is amplitude modulated by a 1 kHz signal of 6 kV peak. The modulation pattern is observed on a CRO calibrated suitably. The voltage indicated will be
(*a*) 1.8 kV (*b*) 1.001 kV
(*c*) 18 V (*d*) 36 kV

7. The d.c. voltage on a plate modulated class C amplifier is 8 kV and the peak modulation voltage is 4 kV. The peak RF voltage delivered to the load is
(*a*) 32 kV (*b*) 12 kV
(*c*) 0.5 kV (*d*) 24 kV

8. For a signal amplitude modulated to a depth of 100% by a sinusoidal signal, the power is..... as the power of unmodulated carrier.
(*a*) same (*b*) $\sqrt{2}$ times
(*c*) 1.5 times (*d*) twice

9. The minimum value of m_f for an FM system required to produce a noticeable improvement in S/N ratio over a comparable AM system with $m = 1$ is
(*a*) $\sqrt{3}$ (*b*) $\sqrt{2}$
(*c*) $1\frac{1}{\sqrt{2}}$ (*d*) $\frac{1}{\sqrt{3}}$

10. Consider the following statements:
1. Bandwidth of the A.M. wave depends on the bandwidth of the modulating signal.
2. Bandwidth of the A.M. wave depends on the modulation Index.
3. Bandwidth of F.M. wave, for all practical purposes, depends on the amplitude of the carrier.

Of these statements the correct statements are
(*a*) 1 and 2 (*b*) 1 and 3
(*c*) 1 and 4 (*d*) 2 and 4

11. Which of the following pairs are correctly matched?
(*a*) Medium – wave radio propagation ....AM
(*b*) Television ....VSB
(*c*) Short – wave radio – progagation ....AM
(*d*) All of these

12. A superheterodyne receiver has an IF of 465 kHz. If it is tuned to a station broadcasting at 500 kHz and its oscillator is operating at 965 kHz, then the 1430 kHz frequency would be the
(*a*) adjacent channel frequency
(*b*) image frequency
(*c*) gyrofrequency
(*d*) maximum usable frequency

13. One of main functions of the RF amplifiers in a superheterodyne receiver is to
(*a*) provide improved tracking
(*b*) permit better adjacent channel rejection
(*c*) increase tuning range of the receiver
(*d*) improve reflection of the image frequency

14. The sound signal in TV broadcast is modulated in
(a) SSB (b) VSB
(c) FM (d) DSB–SC

15. In a low level modulation AM system, the amplifier following the modulated stage can be
(a) linear amplifiers
(b) harmonic generators
(c) class C power amplifiers
(d) class B untuned amplifiers

16. In the generation of modulated signal, a varactor diode can be used for
(a) FM generation only
(b) AM generation only
(c) PM generation only
(d) both AM and PM generation

17. The choice of the product RC is an envelope detector using a diode and an R–C circuit is governed by
(a) both lowest and the highest modulation frequencies
(b) only depth of modulation
(c) depth of modulation and the lowest modulation frequency
(d) depth of modulation and the highest modulation frequency

18. If radiated power of AM transmitter is 10 kW, then power in the carrier for modulation index of 0.6 is nearly
(a) 8.24 kW (b) 8.47 kW
(c) 9.26 kW (d) 9.6 kW

19. In a low-level AM system, the amplifier which follows the modulated stage must be the
(a) linear device (b) harmonic device
(c) class–C amplifier (d) non–linear device

20. A radio station works at 800 kHz and uses AM. If this is a public broadcast system, it should transmit using
(a) parabolic reflector to transmit all round
(b) turnstile antenna for the required band
(c) half-wave long horizontal wire
(d) a vertical antenna less than quarter for practical reasons

21. Match List-I with List-II and select the correct answer using the codes given below the Lists.

List-I	List-II
A. AM Broadcast	1. Tropospheric waves
B. FM Broadcast	2. 535 kHz – 1600 kHz
C. TV Broadcast	3. Repeater tower
D. Point-to-point communication	4. VSB modulation
	5. Multipath phenomenon

Codes :

	A	B	C	D
(a)	1	2	3	4
(b)	2	3	4	5
(c)	3	4	5	1
(d)	2	1	4	3

22. 12 signals each band-limited to 5 kHz are to be transmitted over a signal channel by frequency division multiplexing. If AM-SSB modulation guard band of 1 kHz is used, then the bandwidth of the multiplexed signal will be
(a) 51 kHz (b) 61 kHz
(c) 71 kHz (d) 81 kHz

23. In a superheterodyne receiver, the IF is 455 kHz. If it is tuned to 1200 kHz, then image frequency will be
(a) 1655 kHz (b) 2110 kHz
(c) 745 kHz (d) 910 kHz

24. A DSB-SC signal is to be generated with a carrier frequency f_c = 1 MHz using a non-linear device with the input-output characteristic

$$v_0 = a_0 v_i + a_1 v_i^3$$

where a_0 and a_1 are constants. The output of the non-linear device can be filtered by an appropriate band-pass filter.

Let $v_i = A_c^i \cos(2\pi f_c^i t) + m(t)$

where $m(t)$ is the message signal.

Then the value of f_c^i (in MHz) is
(a) 1.0 (b) 0.333
(c) 0.5 (d) 3.0

25. The envelope detector is a/an
(a) synchronous detector
(b) asynchronous detector
(c) product demodulator
(d) coherent detector

26. Which one of the following statements regarding the following signal is correct?

$$x(t) = 5 \sin (2\pi \times 10^3 t) \sin (2\pi \times 10^6 t)$$

(*a*) Upper side band frequency is 1001000
(*b*) Lower side band frequency is 999000
(*c*) $x(t)$ is a DSB – SC signal
(*d*) All of these

27. If large amounts of power are required, a pushpull amplifier is designed for operation as

(*a*) class – A (*b*) class – B
(*c*) class – AB (*d*) class – C

28. Match List-I with List-II and select the correct answer using the codes given below the Lists.

List-I	List-II
A. If noise	1. Ganged tuning
B. Image frequency	2. Spurious response
C. Station selector	3. Leaky filter capacitor
D. Excessive hum	4. Mixer stage

Codes :

	A	B	C	D
(*a*)	3	2	1	4
(*b*)	1	2	3	4
(*c*)	2	3	1	4
(*d*)	4	2	1	3

29. A block diagram for a superheat receiver for AM signal is shown in the figure.

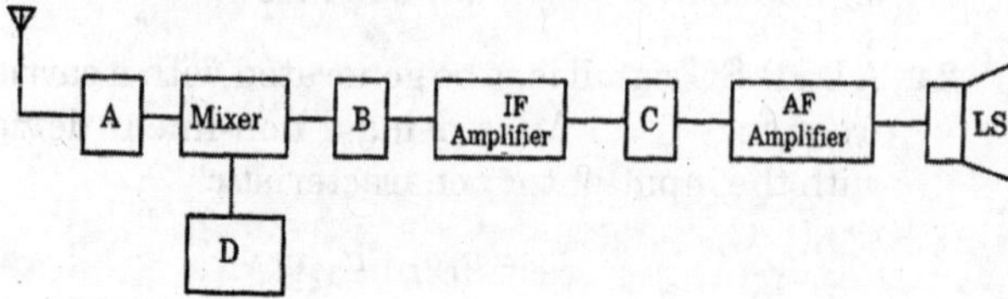

Match the following and select the correct answer from the codes given below:

Column-I	Column-II
A. Block A	1. Local oscillator
B. Block B	2. AM detector
C. Block C	3. First AF Amplifier
D. Block D	4. RF Amplifier

Codes :

	A	B	C	D
(*a*)	1	2	3	4
(*b*)	2	4	1	3
(*c*)	3	4	1	2
(*d*)	4	3	2	1

30. If a signal band limited to f_m is sampled at a rate less than $2f_m$, then constructed signal will be

(*a*) distortionless
(*b*) small in amplitude
(*c*) having higher frequency suppressed
(*d*) distorted

31. A 60 Hz carrier is amplitude modulated by the speech band of 300 to 3000 Hz. The range of upper side bands will be

(*a*) 60.3 to 63 kHz
(*b*) 60 to 59.7 kHz
(*c*) 57 to 59.7 kHz
(*d*) 56.7 to 56.3 kHz

32. The function of padders in ratio receivers is to

(*a*) improve sensitivity
(*b*) reduce image frequency rejection
(*c*) reduce noise
(*d*) improve tracking

33. Double spotting in superheterodyne receivers is caused by

(*a*) poor front-end rejection
(*b*) misalignment of receiver
(*c*) detuning of one or more IF stages
(*d*) non-functioning of AGC

34. The threshold effect in demodulators is

(*a*) exhibited by all demodulators when the input signal to noise ratio is low
(*b*) the rapid fall on output signal to noise ratio when the input signal to noise ratio falls below a particular value
(*c*) the property exhibited by all AM suppressed carrier coherent demodulators
(*d*) the property exhibited by correlation receivers.

35. An FM signal with modulation index m_f is passed through a frequency tripler. The modulation index of the output signal will be

(*a*) m_f
(*b*) $3\ m_f$
(*c*) $9\ m_f$
(*d*) $27\ m_f$

36. An FM radio receiver is tuned to a 90.6 MHz broadcast station. It will receive an image frequency of

(*a*) 110 MHz (*b*) 112 MHz
(*c*) 114 MHz (*d*) 120 MHz

37. A FM signal is being broadcast in the 88.108 MHz band having a carrir swing of 125 kHz. The modulation index is

(*a*) 100 % (*b*) 83%
(*c*) 67% (*d*) 50%

38. An FM signal with a deviation δ is passed through a mixer and has its frequency reduced fivefold. The deviation in the output of the mixer is

(*a*) 5δ (*b*) intermediate
(*c*) $\frac{\delta}{5}$ (*d*) δ

39. Two carriers 40 MHz and 80 MHz respectively are frequency modulated by a signal of frequency 4 kHz, such that the band-widths of the FM signal in the two cases are the same. The peak value deviation in the two cases are in the ratio of

(*a*) 1 : 4 (*b*) 1 : 2
(*c*) 1 : 1 (*d*) 2 : 1

40. If FM sound broadcasting system, the maximum frequency deviation is usually

(*a*) 15 kHz (*b*) 75 kHz
(*c*) 200 kHz (*d*) 5.2 MHz

41. Pre-emphasis in FM systems involves

(*a*) compression of the modulating signal
(*b*) expansion of the modulating signal
(*c*) amplification of lower frequency components of the modulating signal
(*d*) amplification of higher frequency components of the modulating signal

42. As the modulation index of an FM signal with sinusoidal modulation is increased from zero to three, the power in the carrier component will

(*a*) increase continuously
(*b*) decrease continuously
(*c*) first increase, attain a maximum and then decrease
(*d*) first decrease, become zero and then increase

43. The ratio $\frac{\left(\frac{S}{N}\right)_{WBFM}}{\left(\frac{S}{N}\right)_{AM}}$ for 100% amplitude modulation with identical total transmitted power (m_f is modulated index of FM) is

(*a*) $\frac{9}{2}m_f^2$ (*b*) $\frac{3}{2}m_f^2$
(*c*) $\frac{3}{2}m_f^3$ (*d*) $\frac{9}{2}m_f^3$

44. If an angle–modulated signal is expressed by

$f_a(t) = \cos(2 \times 10^8\,\pi t + 75 \sin 2 \times 10^3\,\pi t)$

then peak frequency deviation of the carrier is

(*a*) 1 kHz (*b*) 7.5 kHz
(*c*) 75 kHz (*d*) 100 kHz

45. MCVF telegraphy uses

(*a*) SSB techniques
(*b*) pulse modulation
(*c*) out–of–band signalling
(*d*) FM

46. A signal $m(t) = 5 \cos 2\pi\, 100t$ frequency modulates a carrier. The resulting FM signal is

$10 \cos\{(2\pi\, 10^5\, t) + 15 \sin(2\pi\, 100t)\}$

The approximate bandwidth of the FM would be

(*a*) 0.1 kHz (*b*) 1 kHz
(*c*) 3.2 kHz (*d*) 100 kHz

47. If the transmission bandwidth is doubled in FM, then the SNR is

(*a*) also doubled
(*b*) improved four-fold
(*c*) decreased by one fourth
(*d*) unaffected

48. The typical squeich circuit

(*a*) cutt off an audio-amplifier when the carrier is absent
(*b*) eliminates the RF interference when the signal is weak
(*c*) cutt off an IF amplifier when the AGC is maximum
(*d*) cutt off an IF amplifier when the AGC is minimum

49. What changes would be necessary in block C if FM signals are to be received?

(*a*) This block becomes redundant
(*b*) A FM detector would be required
(*c*) A high frequency signal generator
(*d*) An additional local oscillator will be needed

50. If IF signal frequency is 470 kHz, what will be the frequency of block D when frequency of incoming signal is 1.15 MHz?

(*a*) 1.15 MHz
(*b*) 1.620 MHz
(*c*) 2.090 MHz
(*d*) $\sqrt{2.09}$ MHz

51. A telephone channel has badwidth B of 3 kHz and SNR$\left(\frac{S}{\eta B}\right)$ of 30 dB. It is connected to a teletype machine having 32 different symbols. The symbol rate required for errorless transmission is nearly
(*a*) 1800 symbols/s
(*b*) 3000 symbols/s
(*c*) 5000 symbols/s
(*d*) 6000 symbols/s

52. Quadrature multiplexing is
(*a*) same as FEM
(*b*) same as TDM
(*c*) a combination of FDM and TDM
(*d*) the scheme where same carrier frequency is used for two different signals

53. The ramp signal $m(t) = at$ is applied to a delta modulator with sampling period T, step size δ. Slope overload distortion would occur if
(*a*) $\delta < a$
(*b*) $\delta > a$
(*c*) $\delta < aT$
(*d*) $\delta > aT$

54. In a PCM system each quantisation level is encoded into 8 bits. The signal to quantisation noise ratio is equal to
(*a*) $\frac{1}{12}\left(\frac{1}{256}\right)^2$ (*b*) 48 dB
(*c*) 64 dB (*d*) 256 dB

55. A band-pass signal has significant frequency components in the range of 1.5 MHz to 2 MHz. If the signal is to be reconstructed from its sample, then minimum sampling frequency will be
(*a*) 1 MHz
(*b*) 2 MHz
(*c*) 3.5 MHz
(*d*) 4 MHz

56. A 8 *k*Hz communication channel has an SNR of 30 dB. If the channel bandwidth is doubled, keeping the signal power constant, then SNR for the modified channel will
(*a*) 27 dB
(*b*) 30 dB
(*c*) 33 db
(*d*) 60 dB

57. In a communication system, each message (1 or 0) is transmitted three times in order to reduce the probability of error. The detection is based on the majority rule at the receiver. If P_e is the probability of bit error, then probability of error for this communication system will be
(*a*) $2P_e^3 - 2P_e^3$ (*b*) $1 - P_e^2 - P_e^3$
(*c*) P_e^3 (*d*) $P_e^2(1 - P_e)$

58. Nyquist sampling rate for the signal

$$g(t) = 10 \cos (50 \pi t) \cos^2 (150 \pi t)$$

where '*t*' is in seconds, is
(*a*) 150 samples per second
(*b*) 200 samples per second
(*c*) 300 samples per second
(*d*) 350 samples per second

59. For a given data rate, the bandwidth required with *m*-ary transmission is smaller than that for binary transmission by
(*a*) $\log_2 m$ (*b*) $\frac{\log_2 m}{m}$
(*c*) $\frac{2}{\log_2 m}$ (*d*) $\frac{\log_2 m}{2}$

60. Modems are used for data transmission telephone lines to
(*a*) increase the transmission capacity
(*b*) improve noise performance
(*c*) incorporate error control coding
(*d*) eliminate dc component in the transmitted signal

61. Four voice signals, each limited to 4 kHz and sampled at Nyquist rate, are converted into binary PCM signal using 256 quantisation levels. The bit transmission rate for the time-division multiplexed signal will be
(*a*) 8 kbps (*b*) 64 kbps
(*c*) 256 kbps (*d*) 512 kbps

62. Frequency shift keying is used mostly in
(*a*) radio transmission
(*b*) telegraphy
(*c*) telephony
(*d*) none of these

63. In a PCM, the amplitude levels are transmitted in a 7 unit code. The sampling is done at the rate of 10 Hz. The bandwidth should be
(*a*) 5 kHz (*b*) 35 kHz
(*c*) 70 kHz (*d*) 5 MHz

64. An image uses 512 × 512 picture elements. Each of the picture elements can take any of the 8 distinguishable intensity levels. The maximum entropy in the above image will be

(*a*) 2097152 bits

(*b*) 786432 bits

(*c*) 648 bits

(*d*) 144 bits

65. The power spectral density of white noise

(*a*) varies as square root of frequency

(*b*) varies as inverse of frequency

(*c*) varies as square of frequency

(*d*) is constant with frequency

66. A correlation receiver consists of

(*a*) a multiplier and an integrator

(*b*) an integrator only

(*c*) a multiplier only

(*d*) an adder and integrator

67. The rate at which information can be passed through a telecommunication channel depends on the

(*a*) a carrier frequency

(*b*) bandwidth

(*c*) transmission loss

(*d*) transmitter power

68. A source has two symbols x_1 and x_2 with probabilities P_1 and P_2 respectively. If a new source, with four symbols is generated from the above source, then the new symbol probabilities will be (ε is a number such that $0 < \varepsilon < 1$)

(*a*) P_1, P_2, P_1, P_2

(*b*) P_1, P_1, P_2, P_2

(*c*) $(1-\varepsilon) P_1, (1-\varepsilon) P_2, \varepsilon P_1, \varepsilon P_2$

(*d*) $\frac{P_1}{4}, \frac{P_2}{4}, \frac{P_1}{4}, \frac{P_2}{4}$

69. The purpose of source coding is to

(*a*) increase the information transmission rate

(*b*) decrease the information transmission rate

(*c*) decrease the $\frac{S}{N}$ ratio

(*d*) decrease the probability of error.

70. Match List-I with List-II and select the correct answer by using the codes given below the lists.

List-I	List-II
A. Resistance	1. Current Noise
B. Diode	2. Partition Noise
C. Triode	3. Shot Noise
D. *pn* junction	4. Atmospheric Noise
	5. Johnson Noise

Codes :

	A	B	C	D
(*a*)	1	3	4	5
(*b*)	5	3	2	1
(*c*)	5	3	2	4
(*d*)	1	5	3	2

71. An amplifier operating over the frequency range of 18 to 20 MHz has a 10 kΩ input resistance. The RMS noise voltage at the input to the amplifier at ambient temperature of 27°C is (Assume the Boltzman constant value as 1.38×10^{-23} J/K)

(*a*) 18.2 microvolts

(*b*) 17.2 microvolts

(*c*) 16.2 microvolts

(*d*) 14.2 microvolts

72. If a carrier modulated by a digital bit stream had one of the possible phases of 0, 90, 180 and 270 degrees, then the modulation is called

(*a*) BPSK

(*b*) QPSK

(*c*) QAM

(*d*) MSK

73. Preset equalisation follows the same processes as adaptive equalisation except that the equalisation is set prior to transmission and then updated during breaks in transmission using

(*a*) special test sequences

(*b*) block codes

(*c*) BCD

(*d*) correlators

74. The bit rate of a digital communication system is 34 M bit/s. The modulation scheme is QPSK. The baud rate of the system is

(*a*) 68 M bit/s

(*b*) 34 M bit/s

(*c*) 17 M bit/s

(*d*) 8.5 M bit/s

75. The use of non-uniform quantisation leads to
(*a*) reduction in transmission bandwidth
(*b*) increase in maximum SNR
(*c*) increase in SNR for low level signals
(*d*) simplification of quantisation process

76. The baud rate is
(*a*) always equal to the bit transfer rate
(*b*) equal to twice the bandwidth of an ideal channel
(*c*) not equal to the signalling rate
(*d*) equal to one – half the bandwidth of ideal channel

77. In a 100 line exchange with 10 first selectors, the number of line finder required
(*a*) is 10
(*b*) is 100
(*c*) would depend upon the traffic flow
(*d*) is busy - hour calling rate

78. In a carrier the telephone system, a group occupies a frequency band of
(*a*) 36 to 48 kHz (*b*) 60 to 108 kHz
(*c*) 92 to 140 kHz (*d*) 140 to 172 kHz

79. In a DM (delta modulation) system, the granular (idling) noise occurs when
(*a*) modulation signal increases rapidly
(*b*) pulse rate decreases
(*c*) modulating signal remains constant
(*d*) pulse amplitude decreases

80. The capacity of an analog communication channel with 4 kHz bandwidth and 15 dB SNR is approximately
(*a*) 20,000 bps (*b*) 16,000 bps
(*c*) 10,000 bps (*d*) 8,000 bps

81. PAM signals can be demodulated by using a
(*a*) low pass filter (LPF) alone
(*b*) a Schmitt trigger followed by a LPF
(*c*) a differentiator followed by a LPF
(*d*) a clipper circuit followed by a LPF

82. For 10-bit PCM system, signal to quantisation noise ratio is 62 dB. If the number of bits is increased by 2, then the signal to quantisation noise will
(*a*) increase by 6 dB
(*b*) increase by 12 dB
(*c*) decrease by 6 dB
(*d*) decrease by 12 dB

83. For a given data rate, bandwidth β_p of a BPSK signal and the bandwidth β_0 of the OOK signal are related as
(*a*) $\beta_p = \frac{\beta_o}{2}$ (*b*) $\beta_p = 2\,\beta_o$
(*c*) $\beta_p = \frac{\beta_o}{4}$ (*d*) $\beta_p = \beta_o$

84. In a certain '12 channel TDM' system, it is found that channel No.3 and channel No. 8 are connected to the same input signal. This technique
(*a*) wastes the channel capacity
(*b*) takes care of different sampling rates
(*c*) is required when different bandwidth signals are to be transmitted
(*d*) reduces noise

85. If binary PSK modulation is used for transmission, the required minimum bandwidth is 9600 Hz. To reduce the transmission bandwidth to 2400 Hz, the modulation scheme to be adopted should be
(*a*) quadrature phase–shift keying
(*b*) minimum shift keying
(*c*) 16–ary quadrature amplitude modulation
(*d*) 8–ray PSK

86. If in a particular digital communication application, the receiver designed is an optimum coherent receiver, the channel noise is white and bits are transmitted using rectangular pulses, then which one of the following statements would be INCONSISTENT?
The receiver is
(*a*) a correlator receiver
(*b*) matched filter receiver
(*c*) an integrate and dump receiver
(*d*) sample, hold and dump receiver

87. Four signals each band-limited to 5 kHz are sampled at twice the Nyquist rate. The resulting PAM samples are transmitted over a single channel after time division multiplexing. The theoretical minimum transmissions bandwidth of the channel should be equal to
(*a*) 5 kHz
(*b*) 20 kHz
(*c*) 40 kHz
(*d*) 80 kHz

88. Generally, a transversal type equaliser with 5 taps can take care of distorted signal due to intersymbol interference in the received signal at

(*a*) 4 sampling instants
(*b*) 5 sampling instants
(*c*) 9 sampling instants
(*d*) 10 sampling instants

89. Shannon's law relates

(*a*) antenna gain to bandwidth
(*b*) frequency to antenna gain
(*c*) antenna gain to transmission
(*d*) information carrying capacity to S/N ratio.

90. A zero memory source generates two messages with probabilities 0.8 and 0.2. These are coded an 1 and 0.2. The code effeciency is

(*a*) 0.2 (*b*) 0.5
(*c*) 0.7 (*d*) 1.0

91. Match List-I with List-II and select the correct answer using the codes given below the Lists.

List-I	List-II
A. Frequency modulation	1. Envelope detection
B. Double sideband suppressed signal carrier	2. Companding
C. PCM	3. Balanced modulator
D. Amplitude modulation	4. Pre-emphasis and deemphasis

Codes:

	A	B	C	D
(*a*)	1	2	3	4
(*b*)	1	2	4	3
(*c*)	4	3	1	2
(*d*)	4	3	2	1

92. The information capacity (bits/sec) of a channel with bandwidth W and transmission time T is given by

(*a*) $C \propto WT$ (*b*) $C = \frac{W}{T}$
(*c*) $C = \frac{T}{W}$ (*d*) $C = \frac{W^2}{T}$

93. Which of the following are useful in comparing the noise performance of receivers?

(*a*) Input noise voltage
(*b*) Equivalent noise resistance
(*c*) Noise temperature
(*d*) All of these

94. A comparison of frequency division and time division multiplexing systems shows that

(*a*) FDM requires a lower bandwidth, but TDM has greater noise immunity
(*b*) FDM has greater noise immunity and requires lower bandwidth than TDM
(*c*) FDM requires channel synchronisation, while TDM has greater noise immunity
(*d*) FDM requires more multiplexing while TDM requires band pass filter

95. Match List-I with List-II and select the correct answer using the codes given below the Lists.

List-I	List-II
A. Detection of a periodic signal in noise	1. Increase in band width
B. Recovery of a band-limited signal from its uniformly sampled values	2. Slope overload error
C. Finer quantization of signals	3. Nyquist's rate
D. Delta modulation	4. Cross correlation

Codes:

	A	B	C	D
(*a*)	4	3	1	2
(*b*)	3	4	2	1
(*c*)	4	3	2	1
(*d*)	4	2	1	3

96. In a PCM system, the number of quantization levels are 16 and the maximum signal frequency is 4 kHz. The bit transmission rate is

(*a*) 64 K bits/sec (*b*) 16 K bits/sec
(*c*) 32 K bits/sec (*d*) 32 bits/sec

97. In PCM if the transmission path is very long, then

(*a*) repeater stations are used
(*b*) pulse width may be increased
(*c*) pulse amplitude is increased
(*d*) pulse spacing is reduced

98. A signal having unformly disturbed amplitude in the interval (–V, + V) is to be encoded using PCM with uniform quantization. The signal to quantizing noise ratio is determined by the

(*a*) dynamic range of the signal
(*b*) sampling rate
(*c*) number of quantizing levels
(*d*) power spectrum of signal

99. In PCM, the biggest advantage as compared to AM is

(*a*) larger bandwidth

(*b*) larger noise

(*c*) inability to handle analog signals

(*d*) incompatibility with time division multiplex system

100. In delta modulation which of the following drawbacks are existing?

1. Slope overload
2. Serration noise
3. Granular noise

Of these, the correct answer is

(*a*) 1 and 2 only

(*b*) 2 and 3 only

(*c*) 1 and 3 only

(*d*) 1, 2 and 3

101. A binary system linking teletypewriters to a computer operates at a mean frequency of 1080 Hz shifting to 980 Hz when a one is transmitted and to 1180 Hz for a zero. The maximum permitted data rate for this system is

(*a*) 200 bits/second (*b*) 200 baud

(*c*) 100 baud (*d*) 1080 bits/second

102. Which of the following requires a synchronizing signal?

(*a*) Singal channel PPM system

(*b*) PAM

(*c*) PDM

(*d*) All of these

103. The signal to quantisation noise ratio in a PCM system depends upon

(*a*) sampling rate

(*b*) number of quantisation levels

(*c*) message signal width

(*d*) none of these

104. PCM systems requires regenerative repeaters over long distances. The correct sequence of the operations which such a repeater performs is

(*a*) timing, equalization and decision making

(*b*) equalization, timing and decision making

(*c*) timing, thresholding (decision) and equalization

(*d*) thresholding, timing and equalization

105. A TDM link has 20 signal channels and each channel is sampled 8000 times/sec. Each sample is represented by seven binary bits and contains an additional bit for synchronization. The total bit rate for the TDM link is

(*a*) 1180 M bits/sec

(*b*) 1280 K bits/sec

(*c*) 1180 K bits/sec

(*d*) 1280 M bits/sec

106. A message signal band limited to 5 kHz is sampled at the minimum rate as dictated by the sampling theorem. The number of quantisation levels is 64. If samples are encoded in binary form, then transmission rate is

(*a*) 60 kbps (*b*) 50 kbps

(*c*) 32 kbps (*d*) 10 kbps

107. In an ADM transmission system, the output signal amplitudes for 1's and 0's are

(*a*) fixed and the repetition rate is also fixed

(*b*) fixed but the repetition rate is variable

(*c*) variable and the repetition rate is also variable

(*d*) variable but the repetition rate is fixed

108. A binary symmetrical channel transmitting 1's and 0's with equal probability has an error rate of 10^{-2}. Then channel transmission rate (in bits/symbol) will be

(*a*) 0.99

(*b*) 0.919

(*c*) 0.95

(*d*) 1

109. A communication system is used to transmit one of 16 possible signals. Assume that transmission is accomplished by encoding the signals into binary digits. Further assume that signals are equally likely to occur. If each binary digit requires 1 μ sec for transmission, then how much information (in bits) is transmitted by the system in 8 microseconds?

(*a*) 8 (*b*) 16

(*c*) 4 (*d*) 2

110. The noise figure of a receiver is 1.6. Its equivalent noise temperature is

(*a*) 464.00 K

(*b*) 174.00 K

(*c*) 108.75 K

(*d*) 181.25 K

111. An earth station employs a 1 kW high power amplifier (HPA) and a 20 m Cassegrain antenna whose transmitted gain is 65 dB at a free wavelength of 21 cm. If loss of the wavelength that connects HPA to the feed is dB, then earth station EIRP is

(*a*) 29 dB m

(*b*) 59 dB m

(*c*) 49 dB m

(*d*) 124 dB m

112. Match List-I (Microwave band) with List-II (Frequency used in satellite communication) and select the correct answer by using the codes given below the Lists:

List -I	List -II
A. C–band	1. 12 GHz to 14 GHz
B. Ku–band	2. 24 GHz to 26 GHz
C. Ka–band	3. 20 GHz to 30 GHz
	4. 4 GHz to 6 GHz

Codes :

	A	B	C
(*a*)	4	2	1
(*b*)	2	1	3
(*c*)	4	1	3
(*d*)	3	4	2

113. If an antenna has 40 Ω antenna resistance and 60 Ω radiation resistance, then efficiency of the antenna will be

(*a*) 30% (*b*) 40%

(*c*) 50% (*d*) 60%

114. For a microstrip with a substrate of dielectric constant ε, the value of effective dielectric contant ε_e will be such that

(*a*) $\frac{\varepsilon}{2} < \varepsilon_e < \varepsilon$ (*b*) $\frac{(\varepsilon+1)}{2} < \varepsilon_e < \varepsilon$

(*c*) $1 < \varepsilon_e < \frac{(\varepsilon+1)}{2}$ (*d*) $\frac{(\varepsilon-1)}{2} < \varepsilon_e < \frac{(\varepsilon+1)}{2}$

115. The insertion loss of the Device Under Test (DUT) shown in the given figure is

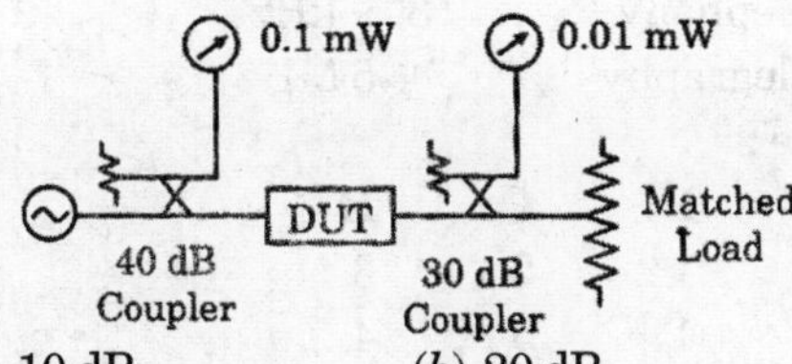

(*a*) 10 dB (*b*) 20 dB

(*c*) 30 dB (*d*) 40 dB

116. In the standing wave detector method for measuring a slightly mismatched load impedence, the distance from the load position to the nearest voltage minimum towards the generator is one-eight the guide wavelength. The load is a/an

(*a*) capacitive impedance

(*b*) inductive impedance

(*c*) pure capacitance

(*d*) pure inductance

117. Consider the following parameters:

1. Loss in the media
2. Permeability of the media
3. Frequency of the wave
4. Velocity of the wave

Which of these parameters are responsible for the change of phase of a propagating electromagnetic wave?

(*a*) 1, 2 and 3

(*b*) 2, 3 and 4

(*c*) 1, 3 and 4

(*d*) 1 and 4

118. As a result of reflections from a plane conducting wall, electromagnetic waves acquire an apparent velocity greater than the velocity of light in space. This is called

(*a*) velocity of propagation

(*b*) normal velocity

(*c*) group velocity

(*d*) phase velocity

119. While determining antenna height for terrestrial microwaves links, the effect of refraction from the atmosphere is taken care of by considering effective curvature of the earth to be

(*a*) $\frac{2}{3}$ times the radius of the earth

(*b*) $\frac{3}{4}$ times the radius of the earth

(*c*) $\frac{4}{3}$ times the radius of the earth

(*d*) $\frac{3}{2}$ times the radius of the earth

120. Input impedance of a S.C. loss-less line of length $\frac{\lambda}{8}$ is

(*a*) zero (*b*) resistive

(*c*) inductive (*d*) capacitive

121. Consider the following statements:

A duplexer is used in a radar system to

1. protect the receiver when high power signal is transmitted.
2. enable the use of a common antenna for transmission and reception.
3. allow the antenna to only receive when the signal is arriving.
4. avoid noise interference in the radar system.

Of these statements, the correct statements are

(*a*) 1 and 2 (*b*) 3 and 4

(*c*) 1 and 4 (*d*) 2 and 4

122. In radar systems, the term *'rat-race'* is used in connection with

(*a*) modulator

(*b*) pulse characteristics

(*c*) receiver bandwidth

(*d*) duplexer

123. The type of radar that is used to eliminate clutter in navigational application is

(*a*) Pulse radar

(*b*) Tracking radar

(*c*) MTI radar

(*d*) Monopulse radar

124. Which one of the following is capable of giving the highest data speed?

(*a*) Coaxial cable link

(*b*) Microwave LOS link

(*c*) Microwave satellite system

(*d*) Optical fibre system

125. Match List-I (Component) with List-II (Dominant DE Mode) and select the correct answer by using the codes given below the Lists:

List -I	List -II
A. Rectangular wave guide	1. TE_{101}
B. Circular wave guide	2. TE_{10}
C. Rectangular cavity	3. TE_{111}
	4. TE_{11}

Codes :

	A	B	C
(*a*)	4	2	1
(*b*)	2	1	3
(*c*)	3	4	1
(*d*)	2	3	1

126. Approximate thickness of the radome wall should be

(*a*) λ (*b*) $\frac{\lambda}{2}$

(*c*) $\frac{\lambda}{4}$ (*d*) $\frac{\lambda}{8}$

127. Given that $\int_0^{\pi} \sin^4 \theta \, d\theta = \frac{3\pi}{8}$. If radiation intensity of an antenna is proportional to $\sin^2 \theta$, where θ is elevation angle, then antenna directivity will be

(*a*) $\frac{8}{3\pi}$ (*b*) $\frac{16}{3\pi}$

(*c*) $\frac{4\pi}{3}$ (*d*) $\frac{3\pi}{8}$

128. Cassegrain feed is used with a parabolic reflector to

(*a*) increase gain of the system

(*b*) increase beamwidth of the system

(*c*) reduce size of the main reflector

(*d*) allow the feed to be placed at a convenient point

129. Satellites used for international communication are called

(*a*) cossat (*b*) domsat

(*c*) marisat (*d*) intelsat

130. In ionosphere, if incidence angle is 60°, then maximum unstable frequency will be

(*a*) $2 f_c$ (*b*) f_c

(*c*) $\frac{2}{\sqrt{3}} f_c$ (*d*) $\sqrt{3} f_c$

131. Line of sight transmission is used in

(*a*) radio frequency below 1 MHz

(*b*) VHF only

(*c*) sound signals only

(*d*) VHF and UHF

132. Match List-I with List-II and select the correct answer by using the codes given below the lists.

List-I	List-II
A. Television	1. 1 kHz
B. Radio	2. 3 kHz
C. Telephony	3. 9 kHz
D. Telegraphy	4. 5 MHz

Codes :

	A	B	C	D
(*a*)	4	1	2	3
(*b*)	2	1	3	4
(*c*)	4	3	2	1
(*d*)	1	2	3	4

133. Which one of the following relations is correct for luminance signal with Red (R), Green (G) and Blue (B) components?

(*a*) Y = 0.59 R + 0.30 G + 0.11 B

(*b*) Y = 0.11 R + 0.30 G + 0.59 B

(*c*) Y = 0.29 R + 0.11 G + 0.60 B

(*d*) Y = 0.30 R + 0.59 G + 0.11 B

134. In a satellite communication to obtain circular polarization, the antenna preferred will be

(*a*) Parabolic antenna

(*b*) Horn antenna

(*c*) Log periodic antenna

(*d*) Helical antenna

135. In an optical fibre, refractive index of the cladding material should be

(*a*) nearly unity

(*b*) very low

(*c*) less than that of the core

(*d*) more than that of the core

136. Fibres have Numerical Aperture (N.A.) in the region of 0.15 to 0.4 Fibres with higher N.A. values generally exhibit

(*a*) reduced losses

(*b*) high bandwidth

(*c*) reduced losses and low bandwidth

(*d*) greater losses and low bandwidth

137. If target cross-section is changing, then best system for accurate tacking is

(*a*) lobe switching (*b*) sequential lobing

(*c*) conical scanning (*d*) nono-pulse

138. Two isotropic antennas are separated by a distance of two wave lengths. If both the antennas are with currents of equal phase and magnitude, then number of lobes in the radiation pattern in the horizontal plane is

(*a*) 2 (*b*) 4

(*c*) 6 (*d*) 8

139. What is the Numerical Aperture of an optical fiber when its critical angle is 30°?

(*a*) 0.5 (*b*) 0.704

(*c*) 0.866 (*d*) 0.2

140. If antenna diameter in a radar is increased by a factor of 4, then maximum range will be increased by a factor of

(*a*) $\sqrt{2}$ (*b*) 2

(*c*) 4 (*d*) 8

141. The frequency of resonance of water vapour in the atmosphere is

(*a*) 10.225 GHz (*b*) 12.850 GHz

(*c*) 17.500 GHz (*d*) 60.000 GHz

142. The intrinsic impedance of free space

(*a*) is independent of frequency

(*b*) decreases with increase of frequency

(*c*) increases with increase of frequency

(*d*) varies as square root of frequency

143. Match the following and select the correct answer from the codes given below:

Column-I (Display)	Column-II (Applications)
A. Type A	1. For elevation of a target
B. Type B	2. Range and azimuth bearing
C. Type C	3. Giving information about other ships around
D. Type D	4. Range estimation

Codes :

	A	B	C	D
(*a*)	1	2	3	4
(*b*)	4	3	2	1
(*c*)	4	1	3	4
(*d*)	2	4	1	3

144. Match the following and select the correct answer from the codes given below:

Column-I (Navigational Aid)	Column-II (Frequency)
A. Loran – C	1. 100 kHz continuous wave
B. Omega	2. 300 kHz
C. Consol	3. 100 kHz pulsed
D. Decca navigator	4. 10.2 kHz
	5. 400 MHz

Codes :

	A	B	C	D
(*a*)	1	2	4	5
(*b*)	5	1	3	2
(*c*)	4	1	5	4
(*d*)	3	4	2	1

145. Cassegrain feed used with a parabolic reflector
(*a*) increases gain of the system
(*b*) increases beamwidth of the system
(*c*) reduces size of the main reflector
(*d*) allows feed to be placed at a convenient point

146. Frequencies is UHF range propagate by means of
(*a*) ground waves (*b*) sky waves
(*c*) space waves (*d*) surface waves

147. Diffraction of electromagnetic waves
(*a*) is caused by reflection from the ground
(*b*) rises only with spherical wave fronts
(*c*) will occur when the waves pass through a large slot
(*d*) may occur around the edge of a sharp obstacle

148. If peak transmitted power in a radar system is increased by a factor of 81, then maximum range will be increased by a factor of
(*a*) 3 (*b*) 9
(*c*) 27 (*d*) 81

149. A radar have a maximum range of 120 km. The maximum allowable pulse repetition frequency (in pulses per second) for unambiguous reception will be
(*a*) 1250 (*b*) 330
(*c*) 2500 (*d*) 8330

150. Consider the following statements:
Hyperbolic system of navigation is associated with
1. time of arrival of the echo pulse from the time of transmission of the signal to measure distance.
2. time of arrival to two signals from two transmitters at the receiver located in the craft.
3. Doppler shift in the frequency.
4. the master station operating independently and the distant slave stations being synchronised with the master station by ground waves.

Of these statements, correct statements are
(*a*) 1, 2 and 3
(*b*) 1 and 2
(*c*) 1 and 3
(*d*) 2 and 4

151. The resolution of a TV picture is determined by
(*a*) video amplification factor
(*b*) video bandwidth
(*c*) number of frames scanned
(*d*) output of the video detector

152. Radiation pattern of the antenna used in VHF omnidirectional range (VOR) is
(*a*) pencil beam
(*b*) omnidirectional
(*c*) cardioid
(*d*) elliptical

153. Earth–coverage satellite antennas from synchronous altitudes have a beamwidth of
(*a*) 1.73° (*b*) 7.3°
(*c*) 17.3° (*d*) 34.6°

154. The full-duplex round-trip delay through a synchronous satellite is approximately
(*a*) 300 msec
(*b*) 550 msec
(*c*) 600 msec
(*d*) 800 msec

155. Consider the following statements:
Traffic load on a telephone network depends on the
1. rate of calls initiated by each subscriber.
2. number of subscribers on the network.
3. average duration of each call.

Of these statements
(*a*) 2 and 3 are correct
(*b*) 1 and 2 are correct
(*c*) 1 and 3 are correct
(*d*) 1, 2 and 3 are correct

156. Which of the following pairs of types of wave propagation and associated property are correctly matched?
1. Surface wave .... Vertical polarization.
2. Duct propagation .... Superrefraction.
3. Sky wave .... Critical frequency.

Select the correct answer using the codes given below codes:
(*a*) 1, 2 and 3 (*b*) 1 and 2
(*c*) 1 and 3 (*d*) 2 and 3

157. In satellite communication, highly directional antennas are used to
(*a*) direct the spot beam to a particular region of space on Earth
(*b*) strengthen the beam to overcome the cosmic noise
(*c*) make corrections in change of polarization of the beam
(*d*) select a particular channel in transmission and reception

158. Four main types of telephone exchanges are in use in India. The correct order in which they appeared in our country, is
(*a*) manual, electronic, strowger, cross-bar
(*b*) strowger, manual, electronic, cross-bar
(*c*) manual, strowger, cross-bar, electronic
(*d*) manual, cross-bar, strowger, electronic

159. If minimum range is to be doubled in a radar, then peak power has to be increased by a factor of
(*a*) two (*b*) four
(*c*) eight (*d*) sixteen

160. The instrument landing system has which of the following components?
1. Goniometer 2. Marker beacons
3. Ad cock antenna 4. Localizer
5. Glide slop
Select the correct answer using the codes given below:
(*a*) 2, 4 and 5 (*b*) 1, 2, 4 and 5
(*c*) 1, 2, 3 and 5 (*d*) 2, 3, 4 and 5

161. The blind speed of an MTI radar can be avoided by changing
(*a*) carrier frequency
(*b*) pulse repetition frequency
(*c*) antenna rotation rate
(*d*) transmitted power

162. Match List-I with List-II and select the correct answer by using the codes given below the lists.

List-I (System)	List-II (Order of wavelength)
A. Optical fibre communication	1. 10^4 pm
B. Local television system	2. 10^2 pm
C. FM broadcasting	3. 10^0 pm
D. Satellite	4. 10^{-2} pm
	5. 10^{-6} pm

Codes :

	A	B	C	D
(*a*)	5	3	3	4
(*b*)	1	3	4	5
(*c*)	2	2	3	5
(*d*)	1	2	5	4

163. In an air line, adjacent maximum are found at 12.5 cm and 37.5 cm. The operating frequency is
(*a*) 1.5 GHz (*b*) 600 MHz
(*c*) 300 MHz (*d*) 1.2 GHz

164. Equalising pulses in TV are sent during
(*a*) horizontal blanking
(*b*) vertical blanking
(*c*) serrations (slots)
(*d*) horizontal retrace

165. In optical communications, the losses in optical fibres can be caused by
(*a*) impurities
(*b*) microbending
(*c*) attenuation in glass
(*d*) all of these

166. A TV station works at 300 MHz and radiates 100 kW of power. This signal received at a distance of 200 km will be
(*a*) a few μV/m due to attenuation by atmosphere
(*b*) 1 – 5 mV due to ionospheric reflection
(*c*) nil since propagation is line of sight
(*d*) nil because signal fades completely at 300 MHz

167. For a parabolic reflector antenna with diameter of 3 m, the far field pattern measurement at 10 GHz should be carried out at a distance of at least
(*a*) 200 m
(*b*) 300 m
(*c*) 400 m
(*d*) 600 m

168. In Troposcatter links, diversity system is used to
(*a*) increase bandwidth
(*b*) increase directivity of the antenna
(*c*) prevent noise effects
(*d*) detect signal in the presence of fading

169. If a sky wave with a frequency of 50 MHz is incident on the D–region at an angle of 30°, then angle of refraction is
(*a*) 15°
(*b*) 60°
(*c*) 30°
(*d*) 5.5°

170. An altimeter is basically a/an
(*a*) CW radar
(*b*) FM radar
(*c*) Doppler radar
(*d*) device to indicate the direction at height

171. Antenna elevation angle at the ground station for satellite communication is always kept above 5° to

(*a*) minimise sky noise temperature

(*b*) reduce effect of oxygen and water vapour absorption on the antenna noise temperature

(*c*) minimise slant range

(*d*) increase visibility of the satellite

172. Random satellite moves in

(*a*) random paths

(*b*) polar orbits

(*c*) geostationary orbits

(*d*) equatorial plane

173. A received signal in a Radar system occupies an IF bandwidth of 12 MHz. If the transmitted signal was a pulsed carrier of 10 GHz with duty ratio 1 : 0.5 @ 400 Hz, then received signal power will contain

(*a*) frequency component at 400 Hz

(*b*) frequency spread over the whole IF bandwidth

(*c*) dc or average value of the IF

(*d*) RF signals at 10 GHz and 12 MHz

174. In radar system, if peak transmitted power is increased by a factor of 16 and the antenna diameter is increased by a factor of 2, then maximum range will increase by a factor of

(*a*) 16 (*b*) 8

(*c*) 4 (*d*) $\sqrt{8}$

175. A glass fibre has refractive indices n_1 of 1.5 and n_2 of 1. Assuming $c = 3 \times 10^8$ m/s, the multipath time dispersion will be

(*a*) 2.5 ns/m (*b*) 2.5 μs/m

(*c*) 5 ns/m (*d*) 5 μs/m

176. The electric field at a point from a transmitter radiating a certain power is 2.5 mV/m. If the transmitter power is doubled, then yield strength at that point will be about

(*a*) 2.5 mV/m (*b*) 3.5 mV/m

(*c*) 5 mV/m (*d*) 10 mV/m

177. Consider the following statements :

Losses in optical fibres are caused by

1. impurities in the fibre material
2. microbending
3. splicing
4. step index profile

Of these statements, correct statements are

(*a*) 1, 3 and 4

(*b*) 2, 3 and 4

(*c*) 1, 2 and 3

(*d*) 1, 2 and 4

178. Which one of the following is caused by reflection from stratified atmosphere or from the surface or load conditions along the path?

(*a*) Multipath fading

(*b*) Selective fading

(*c*) Duofading

(*d*) Reflection fading

179. Radiation from a helical antenna is

(*a*) plane-polarised

(*b*) partially plane polarised

(*c*) circularly polarised

(*d*) elliptically polarised

180. Match List-I (type of antenna) with List-II (communication system using such an antenna) and select the correct answer using the codes given below the Lists.

List-I	List-II
A. Turnstile	1. RADAR
B. Yagi	2. TV transmission
C. Dish	3. MW broadcasting
D. Vertical mast	4. TV reception

Codes :

	A	B	C	D
(*a*)	4	2	3	1
(*b*)	2	4	1	3
(*c*)	2	4	3	1
(*d*)	4	2	1	3

181. Radiation efficiency of an antenna is defined as the ratio of

(*a*) total power radiated by an antenna to the net power accepted by the antenna from the connected transmitter

(*b*) the frequency at which minimum power is radiated to the frequency at which maximum power is radiated

(*c*) total power accepted from the transmitter to total power generated by the transmitter

(*d*) power in main lobe to that in the side lobe

182. In broadcast television, the number of scanning per frame is chosen to be an odd number to

(*a*) reduce required bandwidth
(*b*) improve picture resolution
(*c*) reduce peak power requirement
(*d*) make interlacing easier

183. In TV system, equalizing pulses are sent during

(*a*) horizontal blanking
(*b*) vertical blinking
(*c*) serrations
(*d*) horizontal retrace

184. In a satellite, to obtain circular polarization, the antenna used is

(*a*) parabolic antenna
(*b*) horn-antenna
(*c*) log-periodic antenna
(*d*) helical antenna

185. In TV system, equalizing pulses are sent during

(*a*) horizontal blanking
(*b*) vertical blanking
(*c*) serrations
(*d*) horizontal retrace

186. The intrinsic impedance of free space is

(*a*) 1 ohm
(*b*) 13.3 ohms
(*c*) 377 ohms
(*d*) 3×10^6 ohms

187. A video signal is observed as shown below:

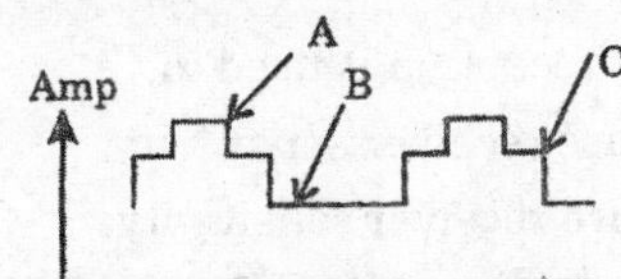

The correct matching for A, B and C is

	A	B	C
(*a*)	Horizontal Sync	Camera signal	Blanking
(*b*)	Blanking	Camera signal	Vertical Syn
(*c*)	Syno	Camera signal	Blanking
(*d*)	Blanking	Camera signal	Sync

188. If distance between target and radar is reduced to half, then power received is increased by

(*a*) $\frac{1}{16}$ (*b*) $\frac{1}{4}$
(*c*) 4 times (*d*) 16 times

189. Consider following communication systems :

1. Telephony
2. Radio communication
3. Microwave communication
4. Optical communication

The correct sequence of these systems from the point of view of increasing order of base band channels each one of them can accommodate is

(*a*) 2, 4, 3, 1 (*b*) 3, 4, 1, 2
(*c*) 1, 2, 3, 4 (*d*) 4, 2, 1, 3

190. In push button keypad dialling in telephony, touching a button generates a tone which is a

(*a*) combination of two frequencies
(*b*) single frequency
(*c*) chirp tone
(*d*) sequence of pulses

191. The configuration used by a line communcation system capable of transmitting a data at the rate of 1000 MB/s is

(*a*) open line system
(*b*) optical fibre system
(*c*) coaxial wire system
(*d*) twisted wire system

192. The loading of telephone line by inductances at uniform intervals is done to

(*a*) reduce attenuation
(*b*) eliminate high frequencies
(*c*) reduce near end cross talk
(*d*) reduce far end cross talk

193. The attenuation in a telephone cable is 1 dB per km and the transmitted voltage is 1V. The voltage received 1000 km away is

(*a*) 10^{-100} V (*b*) 10^{-50} V
(*c*) 10^{-3} V (*d*) 10^{-4}V

194. Bandwidth of colour television transmission of the order of

(*a*) 100 kHz (*b*) 1 MHz
(*c*) 6 MHz (*d*) 10 MHz

195. If antenna diameter in a radar system is increased by a factor of 9, then maximum range will increase by a factor of

(*a*) $\sqrt{3}$ (*b*) 3
(*c*) 9 (*d*) 81

196. The pulse repetition frequency in a radar system is determined primarily from
(*a*) transmitter power
(*b*) signal/noise ratio
(*c*) minimum range at which targets are expected
(*d*) maximum range at which targets are expected

197. For a given bandwidth of the receiver in a radar system, high discrimination between targets is achieved, when
(*a*) PRF is high
(*b*) receiver sensitivity is high
(*c*) pulsewidth is increased
(*d*) diameter of the antenna aperture is increased

198. The correct sequence of frequency bands in order of increasing available peak power is
(*a*) C-band, X-band, L-band, S-band
(*b*) X-band, C-band, S-band, L-band
(*c*) X-band, S-band, C-band, L-band
(*d*) S-band, X-band, C-band, L-band

199. Consider the following statements relating to communication satellite systems:
1. Geosynchronous orbits of the satellites are in the earth's meridional plane
2. It is not necessary to incroporate a very low noise amplifier in the satellite as the noise temperature of the satellite antenna will be high.
3. Total delay on one round trip is about one quarter of a second which is near the limit of satisfactory two-way telephone communication.

Of these statements, the correct statements are
(*a*) 1, 2 and 3 (*b*) 1 and 2
(*c*) 2 and 3 (*d*) 1 and 3

200. Match List-I with List-II and select the correct answer using the codes given below the Lists.

List-I	**List-II**
A. Gonimeter	1. Based on phase difference between signals of two stations
B. Radio Compass	2. Based on time interval between signal of two stations
C. LORAN – A	3. Provides three-dimensional data in a zimuth elevation and range
D. DECCA	4. Automatic direction finder
	5. Couples fixed loop antennas and receiver.

Codes :

	A	B	C	D
(*a*)	5	4	2	1
(*b*)	5	3	2	4
(*c*)	1	5	3	2
(*d*)	2	4	5	1

201. The most probable band width of a transponder in a satellite communication system is
(*a*) 100 kHz (*b*) 1 MHz
(*c*) 36 MHz (*d*) 10 GHz

202. Telephone traffic is specified in terms of
(*a*) average waiting time
(*b*) peak waiting time
(*c*) grade of service
(*d*) Erlangs

203. The amplifiers which are inserted at intervals to amplify the signal and compensate for transmission loss on the cable are called
(*a*) line amplifiers
(*b*) equalizing amplifiers
(*c*) compandors
(*d*) repeaters

204. Transmission of signals in a terrestrial microwave system is achieved through
(*a*) reflection from the ionosphere
(*b*) line-of-sight mode
(*c*) reflection from the ground
(*d*) diffraction from the stratosphere

205. Diversity reception is used to
(*a*) increase receiver sensitivity
(*b*) improve receiver sensitivity
(*c*) overcome degrading effect of fading
(*d*) overcome degrading effect of receiver detuning

206. Besides video, which of the following signals are found in the output of a normal television video detector?
1. Sync
2. Sweep
3. Sound (modulated signal)

Select the correct answer using the codes given below:
(*a*) 1, 2 and 3 (*b*) 1 and 3
(*c*) 1 and 2 (*d*) 2 and 3

207. The signal(s) applied to the yoke of a picture tube from the vertical amplifier output include(s)

(*a*) a saw-tooth voltage

(*b*) a saw-tooth current

(*c*) amplified vertical sync pulses

(*d*) blanking pulses

208. The maximum unambiguous range in a radar system depends on

(*a*) maximum power of the transmitter

(*b*) pulse repetition frequency

(*c*) width of the transmitted pulse

(*d*) sensitivity of the radar receiver

209. Which one due to the following is referred to as the '*night effect*' in radio direction finding?

(*a*) Error due to additional propagation paths

(*b*) Site errors due to reflection of energy from nearby objects

(*c*) Errors due to bats flying

(*d*) Errors due to fog

210. The entropy of a message source generating four messages with probabilities 0.5, 0.25, 0.125 and 0.125 is

(*a*) 1.0 bit/message (*b*) 1.75 bits/message

(*c*) 3.32 bits/message (*d*) 5.93 bits/message

211. To permit selection of 1 out of 16 equiprobable events, the number of bits required is

(*a*) 2 (*b*) $\log_{10} 16$

(*c*) 8 (*d*) 4

212. Which one of the following types of noise gains importance at high frequency?

(*a*) Shot noise

(*b*) Random noise

(*c*) Impulse noise

(*d*) Transit–time noise

213. When the channel is noisy, producing a conditional probability of error p = 0.5; then channel capacity and entropy function would berespectively

(*a*) 1 and 1 (*b*) 1 and 0.5

(*c*) 0.5 and 1 (*d*) zero and 1

214. In a signal error correcting Hamming code, the number of message bits in a block is 26. The number of check bits in the block would be

(*a*) 3 (*b*) 4

(*c*) 5 (*d*) 7

215. A communication channel with additive white Gaussian noise, has a bandwidth of 4 kHz and an SNR of 15. Its channel capacity is

(*a*) 1.6 kbps (*b*) 16 kbps

(*c*) 32 kbps (*d*) 256 kbps

216. The noise figure of an amplifier is 3 dB. Its noise temperature will be about

(*a*) 145 K (*b*) 290 K

(*c*) 580 K (*d*) 870 K

217. A discrete zero memory information source has 40 symbols and each symbol is equally likely. The minimum number of bits required to code the source with uniform length code and the entropy of the source are respectively

(*a*) 5, 5.03 (*b*) 6, 5.83

(*c*) 5, 6.64 (*d*) 6, 5.32

218. If each stage had a gain of 10 dB, and noise figure of 10 dB, then the overall noise figure of a two-stage cascade amplifier will be

(*a*) 10 (*b*) 1.09

(*c*) 1.0 (*d*) 10.9

219. Noise voltage varies in a resistor as

(*a*) $4\ KTR_B$ (*b*) $\sqrt{4\ KTR_B}$

(*c*) $\sqrt{2eI_p\beta}$ (*d*) $\sqrt{2eI_p\beta.R}$

220. Which one of the following functions qualifies to be an autocorrelation function of a revalued time signal?

(*a*) $\sin(\omega\tau)$ (*b*) $\exp(-\tau)$

(*c*) $\delta(\tau)$ (*d*) $u(\tau)$

221. The autocorrelation function of white noise is

(*a*) a delta function

(*b*) a constant

(*c*) gaussian

(*d*) $\exp(-|\tau|)$ with usual notation

222. A source generates four messages. The entropy of the surce will be maximum, when

(*a*) all probabilities are equal

(*b*) one of the probabilities equals 1.0 and others are zero

(*c*) the probabilities are $\frac{1}{2}, \frac{1}{4}, \frac{1}{8}$

(*d*) two of the probabilities are $\frac{1}{2}$ each and others are zero

223. The spectral density of white noise is
(*a*) exponential
(*b*) uniform
(*c*) Poisson
(*d*) Gaussian

224. A source generates four equiprobable symbols. If source coding is adopted, then average length of code for 100 percent efficiency is
(*a*) 6 bits per symbol
(*b*) 4 bits per symbol
(*c*) 3 bits per symbol
(*d*) 2 bits per symbol

225. The probability density function of the envelope of narrow band noise is
(*a*) Uniform (*b*) Gaussian
(*c*) Rayleigh (*d*) Rician

226. Fourier transform of a Gaussian time pulse is
(*a*) uniform (*b*) a pair of impulses
(*c*) Gaussian (*d*) Rayleigh

227. The channel capacity under the Gaussian noise environment for a discrete memoryless channel with a bandwidth of 4 MHz and SNR of 31 is
(*a*) 20 Mbps (*b*) 4 Mbps
(*c*) 8 kbps (*d*) 4 kbps

Answers

1. (*b*) **2.** (*c*) **3.** (*d*) **4.** (*a*) **5.** (*c*) **6.** (*d*) **7.** (*d*) **8.** (*c*) **9.** (*d*) **10.** (*b*)
11. (*d*) **12.** (*b*) **13.** (*d*) **14.** (*c*) **15.** (*c*) **16.** (*a*) **17.** (*d*) **18.** (*b*) **19.** (*a*) **20.** (*d*)
21. (*b*) **22.** (*b*) **23.** (*c*) **24.** (*c*) **25.** (*c*) **26.** (*d*) **27.** (*b*) **28.** (*d*) **29.** (*d*) **30.** (*d*)
31. (*a*) **32.** (*d*) **33.** (*a*) **34.** (*b*) **35.** (*b*) **36.** (*b*) **37.** (*b*) **38.** (*d*) **39.** (*b*) **40.** (*b*)
41. (*d*) **42.** (*b*) **43.** (*b*) **44.** (*c*) **45.** (*a*) **46.** (*c*) **47.** (*c*) **48.** (*a*) **49.** (*b*) **50.** (*b*)
51. (*d*) **52.** (*d*) **53.** (*c*) **54.** (*b*) **55.** (*a*) **56.** (*a*) **57.** (*a*) **58.** (*a*) **59.** (*a*) **60.** (*a*)
61. (*c*) **62.** (*b*) **63.** (*b*) **64.** (*b*) **65.** (*d*) **66.** (*a*) **67.** (*b*) **68.** (*c*) **69.** (*d*) **70.** (*b*)
71. (*a*) **72.** (*b*) **73.** (*b*) **74.** (*a*) **75.** (*c*) **76.** (*b*) **77.** (*a*) **78.** (*a*) **79.** (*c*) **80.** (*a*)
81. (*d*) **82.** (*b*) **83.** (*d*) **84.** (*b*) **85.** (*c*) **86.** (*b*) **87.** (*d*) **88.** (*a*) **89.** (*d*) **90.** (*c*)
91. (*d*) **92.** (*d*) **93.** (*d*) **94.** (*c*) **95.** (*a*) **96.** (*b*) **97.** (*a*) **98.** (*b*) **99.** (*a*) **100.** (*b*)
101. (*b*) **102.** (*a*) **103.** (*c*) **104.** (*a*) **105.** (*c*) **106.** (*a*) **107.** (*d*) **108.** (*c*) **109.** (*b*) **110.** (*b*)
111. (*b*) **112.** (*c*) **113.** (*d*) **114.** (*a*) **115.** (*b*) **116.** (*b*) **117.** (*b*) **118.** (*d*) **119.** (*c*) **120.** (*c*)
121. (*a*) **122.** (*d*) **123.** (*c*) **124.** (*d*) **125.** (*c*) **126.** (*b*) **127.** (*d*) **128.** (*d*) **129.** (*d*) **130.** (*a*)
131. (*d*) **132.** (*c*) **133.** (*d*) **134.** (*d*) **135.** (*c*) **136.** (*d*) **137.** (*d*) **138.** (*d*) **139.** (*a*) **140.** (*c*)
141. (*c*) **142.** (*a*) **143.** (*c*) **144.** (*d*) **145.** (*d*) **146.** (*c*) **147.** (*d*) **148.** (*a*) **149.** (*a*) **150.** (*d*)
151. (*c*) **152.** (*a*) **153.** (*c*) **154.** (*a*) **155.** (*d*) **156.** (*d*) **157.** (*a*) **158.** (*c*) **159.** (*d*) **160.** (*c*)
161. (*b*) **162.** (*a*) **163.** (*b*) **164.** (*b*) **165.** (*d*) **166.** (*c*) **167.** (*d*) **168.** (*d*) **169.** (*b*) **170.** (*b*)
171. (*d*) **172.** (*b*) **173.** (*b*) **174.** (*c*) **175.** (*c*) **176.** (*a*) **177.** (*b*) **178.** (*a*) **179.** (*c*) **180.** (*c*)
181. (*a*) **182.** (*d*) **183.** (*b*) **184.** (*d*) **185.** (*b*) **186.** (*c*) **187.** (*c*) **188.** (*d*) **189.** (*d*) **190.** (*a*)
191. (*b*) **192.** (*a*) **193.** (*b*) **194.** (*c*) **195.** (*c*) **196.** (*d*) **197.** (*a*) **198.** (*c*) **199.** (*d*) **200.** (*a*)
201. (*d*) **202.** (*d*) **203.** (*d*) **204.** (*b*) **205.** (*c*) **206.** (*d*) **207.** (*b*) **208.** (*b*) **209.** (*c*) **210.** (*b*)
211. (*d*) **212.** (*d*) **213.** (*d*) **214.** (*c*) **215.** (*b*) **216.** (*b*) **217.** (*d*) **218.** (*d*) **219.** (*b*) **220.** (*c*)
221. (*a*) **222.** (*a*) **223.** (*b*) **224.** (*b*) **225.** (*b*) **226.** (*c*) **227.** (*a*)

Explanations

3. $f_c = 1000$ kHz

Following frequencies will be present in the modulated wave:

1000 ± 0.3 kHz, 1000 kHz, 1000 ± 2kHz

Hence 700 kHz will not be present in the modulated output

4. $m_t = \sqrt{m_1^2 + m_2^2}$

$= \sqrt{(0.3)^2 + (0.4)^2} = \sqrt{0.25}$

∴ Total modulated power,

$$P_t = 10\left(1+\frac{m^2}{2}\right)$$

$$= 10\left(1+\frac{(0.5)^2}{2}\right)$$

$= 10\,(1.125)$

$= 11.25$ kW

5. $P_{SB} = \frac{m^2}{2}P_c = \frac{0.8^2}{2}P_c = \frac{64}{2}P_c = 0.32P_c$

Total power, $P_t = P_c(1 + \frac{m^2}{2}) = 1.32P_c$

$$\text{Saving} = \frac{132P_c - 0.32P_c}{1.32P_c} \times 100 = 75.76\%$$

6. Voltage observed on CRO (peak to peak)

$= (12 + 6) \times 2 = 36\ kV$

12. IF = 465 kHz = f_i

$f_s = 500$ kHz

Image frequency = $f_s + 2f_i$

$= 500 + 465 \times 2$

$= 1430\ k$ Hz

18. We know $P_t = P_c\left(1+\frac{m^2}{2}\right)$

∴ $10 = P_c\left(1+\frac{0.6^2}{2}\right)$

⇒ $P_c = 8.4746$ kW

23. Given: $f_i = 455$ kHz

$f_s = 1200$ kHz

∴ Image frequency = $f_s + 2f_i$

$= 1200 + 2 \times 455$

$= 2110$ kHz

31. Upper side band = 60 + 0.3 to 60 + 3

= 60.3 to 63 kHz

35. $M_f = \frac{\Delta f}{f_m}$

Now when FM single is passed through frequency tripler, then new modulation

$$m_f = \frac{3\,\Delta f}{f_m} = 3\,m_f$$

44. $m = 75 = \frac{\delta}{f_m}$

$$f_m = \frac{2\times 10^3\pi}{2\pi} = 10/3$$

∴ $\delta = 75 \times 10^3 = 75$ kHz

46. $m = \frac{\delta}{f_m} = 15$

$$f_m = \frac{2\pi\,100}{2\pi} = 100 \text{ Hz}$$

∴ $\delta = 15 \times 1000 = 1500$ Hz

∴ Approximate bandwidth

$= 2\,(f_m + \delta f)$

$= 2\,(100 + 1500) = 3200$ Hz

$= 3.2$ kHz

51. $30 = 10 \log S/N$

⇒ $\log_{10}\frac{S}{N} = 3$

⇒ $S/N = 10^3 = 1000$

Now capacity of the channel

$= \delta f \log_{32}(1 + S/N)$

$= 3000 \log_{32}(1 + 1000)$

$$= 3000\frac{\log_{10}1001}{\log_{10}32}$$

= 5980 symbols/sec

56. $\delta f = 8000$ H_z

SNR = 30 dB

$= \text{antilog}_{10}\frac{30}{10}$

$= 1000$

Now when bandwidth signal remains same but noise will change as per

$P_n = KT\delta f$

∴ $(S/N)_2 = \frac{1000}{2} = 500$

$(S/N)_{2dB} = 10 \log 500 = 27.00$ dB

58. $g(t) = 10\cos(50\pi t)\cos(150\pi t)$

Nyquist rate $= f_n$

where, f_n = highest frequency component

$$2\pi f_n = 150\pi$$
$$f = 75$$

$\therefore$ Nyquist rate $= 2 \times 75$

= 150 samples per second

71. $V_n = \sqrt{4KT\delta f\,T}$

$$= \sqrt{4 \times 1.38 \times 10^{-23} \times (273 + 27) \times 2 \times 10^6 \times 10 \times 10^3}$$

$$= \sqrt{33120 \times 10^{-14}}$$

$= 181.989 \times 10^{-7}$

$= 18.2\mu V$

80. $C = \delta f \log_2 (1 + S/N)$

$$S/N = \text{antilog}\frac{15}{10} = 31.62$$

$\therefore$ $C = 400 \log_2 31.62$

$$\therefore \frac{4000\log_{10} 31.62}{\log_{10} 2} = 19931.56$$

≈ 20000 *bps*

96. $N = 16$

$\delta f = 4000$

$C = 4000 \log_2 16$

$= 4000 \times 4 = 16000$ *bps*

= 16 kbps

106. $C = 2 \times 5000 \log_2 64$

$= 1000 \times 6$

= 6000 bps

= 60 kbps

110. $F = 1.6$

$T_{eq} = T_0 (F - 1)$

$T_0 = 290°$ K

$T_{eq} = 290 \times (1.6 - 1)$

$= 290 \times 0.6 = 174°$ K

113. $$\text{Efficiency} = \frac{R_{red}}{R_{red} + R_a} = \frac{60}{60 + 40}$$

$= 0.60 = 60\%$

148. R maximum range $\propto P^{1/4}$

$$\frac{R_2}{R_1} = (81)^{1/4} = 3$$

$$R_2 = 3R_1$$

149. $$\text{Run ambiguous} = \frac{c}{2f_p}$$

$$f_p = \frac{3 \times 10^8}{2 \times 120 \times 10^3} = \frac{3 \times 10^5}{240}$$

$= 1.25 \times 10^3$

= 1250 Hz

174. R maximum range $\propto d \propto P^{1/4}$

$$\frac{R_2}{R_1} = \frac{D_2 P_2^{1/4}}{D_1 P_1^{1/4}} = \frac{2D_1 \times (16P_1)^{1/4}}{D_1 P_1^{1/4}}$$

$= 2 \times 2 = 4$

196. R maximum range $\propto$ D

$$\therefore \frac{R_1}{R_2} = \frac{D}{D} = 9$$

215. $C = 400 \log_2 (1 + S/N)$

$$S/N = \text{antilog}\frac{15}{10} = 31.623$$

$\therefore$ $C = 4000 \log_2 (1 + 31.623)$

$$= \frac{4000\log_{10} 32.623}{\log_{10} 2}$$

= 20.11 kbps

216. $T_{eq} = T_0 (F - 1)$

$T_0 = 290$ K

$$F = \text{antilog}\frac{3}{10} = 1.9952623$$

$\therefore$ $T_{eq} = 290\,(1.9952623 - 1) = 288.63°$K

227. $C = \delta f \log_2 (1 + S/N)$

$$S/N = \text{antilog}\frac{31}{10} = 1359$$

$\therefore$ $C = 4 \times 10^6 \log_2 (1 + 1259)$

$$= \frac{4 \times 10^6 \log_{10} 1260}{\log_{10} 2}$$

$= 41.1968 \times 10^6$

3 CHAPTER

Radio Communication and Radar Systems

RADIO COMMUNICATION SYSTEMS

Radio communication systems are systems that use radio waves to transmit and receive information between two or more locations. These systems are widely used for various purposes, including broadcasting, two-way communication, wireless networking, and remote control of devices.

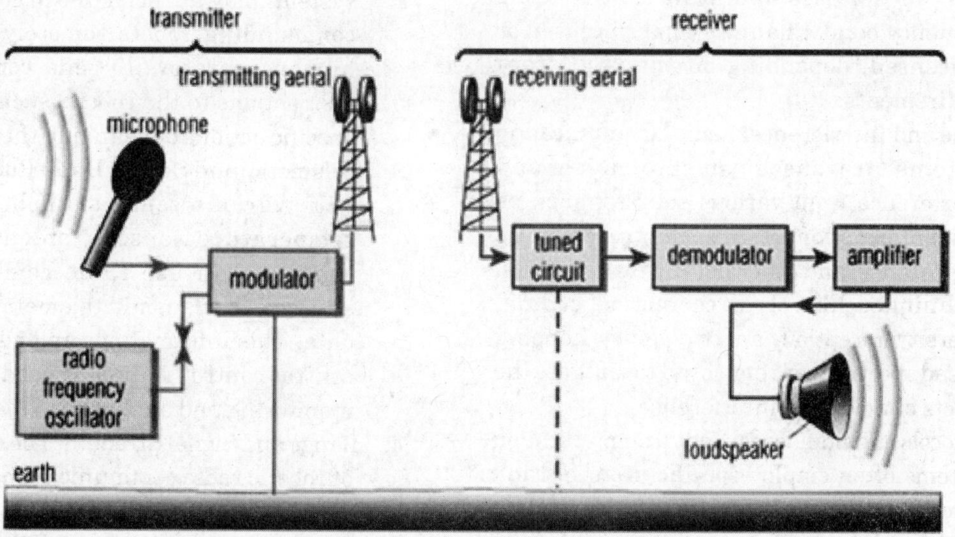

There are some key components and concepts related to radio communication systems:

1. Transmitter: The transmitter is a device that converts electrical signals into radio waves for transmission. It modulates the carrier wave by superimposing the information signal onto it. The modulated carrier wave is then amplified and transmitted through an antenna.
2. Receiver: The receiver is a device that captures radio waves from the air using an antenna. It demodulates the received signal to extract the original information and amplifies it for further processing and decoding.
3. Antenna: An antenna is an essential component of a radio communication system. It converts electrical signals into radio waves for transmission or vice versa for reception. Antennas come in various shapes and sizes, depending on the frequency and application.
4. Frequency: Radio waves are characterized by their frequency, which is the number of complete cycles of the wave that occur per second. The unit of frequency is hertz (Hz). Different frequency bands are allocated for different purposes, such as AM radio, FM radio, television, cellular communications, and Wi-Fi.

5. Modulation: Modulation is the process of impressing the information signal onto a carrier wave for transmission. The carrier wave's properties, such as amplitude, frequency, or phase, are modified to carry the information. Common modulation techniques include amplitude modulation (AM), frequency modulation (FM), and phase modulation (PM).
6. Demodulation: Demodulation is the process of extracting the original information signal from the modulated carrier wave at the receiver. The receiver detects and interprets the changes in the carrier wave's properties to recover the transmitted information.
7. Channels: In radio communication, channels refer to specific frequencies or frequency ranges assigned for different uses. Channels help avoid interference between different users or services operating in the same frequency band. Channels can be licensed or unlicensed, depending on the regulatory requirements.
8. Noise and Interference: Radio communication systems are susceptible to noise and interference from various sources, such as atmospheric conditions, electromagnetic interference, and other nearby transmitters. Techniques like error correction coding, diversity reception, and frequency hopping spread spectrum are employed to mitigate the effects of noise and interference.
9. Protocols and Standards: Radio communication systems often employ specific protocols and standards to ensure compatibility and efficient data exchange. For example, cellular communication systems use protocols like GSM, CDMA, or LTE, while Wi-Fi networks utilize standards such as IEEE 802.11.
10. Applications: Radio communication systems have a wide range of applications. They are used in broadcasting, including AM and FM radio, as well as television. Two-way communication systems, like walkie-talkies and amateur radios, rely on radio waves. Wireless networking technologies, such as Wi-Fi and Bluetooth, enable data transmission between devices. Additionally, radio systems are employed in navigation systems, satellite communication, emergency services, and more.

Robotic Radio Communications Systems:

Robotic radio communications systems refer to the use of radio technology for communication between robotic devices or between robots and humans. These systems utilize radio waves to transmit and receive data, commands, and other information necessary for the operation and control of robotic systems.

There are some key points about robotic radio communications systems:

1. Wireless Communication: Robotic radio communications systems enable wireless communication between robots, allowing them to exchange information without the need for physical connections. Radio waves, which are a form of electromagnetic radiation, are used to transmit and receive signals.

   Example: Zigbee, Radio wave, etc.
2. Control and Command: Radio communications systems play a crucial role in controlling and commanding robots remotely. They allow human operators to send commands and instructions to the robots, such as initiating specific actions or changing their behavior.
3. Telemetry and Sensor Data: Robots equipped with various sensors, such as cameras, temperature sensors, or environmental sensors, can use radio communications systems to transmit telemetry and sensor data. This information can be sent back to a central control station or used for real-time monitoring and analysis.
4. Range and Signal Strength: The effective range of robotic radio communications systems can vary depending on factors such as the frequency used, the power of the transmitter, and the presence of obstacles or interference. Longer-range systems may use lower frequencies, such as those in the UHF (Ultra High Frequency) or VHF (Very High Frequency) bands, while shorter-range systems may operate in higher frequency bands, such as the 2.4 GHz or 5.8 GHz bands.
5. Interference and Security: Radio communications systems can be susceptible to interference from other devices operating in the same frequency range. Measures like frequency hopping or encryption can be employed to minimize the risk of unauthorized access or data interception.

6. Multi-Robot Systems: Robotic radio communications systems are essential for coordinating and synchronizing the actions of multiple robots operating together. Communication protocols and algorithms are used to ensure efficient communication and collaboration between the robots.
7. Application Areas: Robotic radio communications systems find applications in various fields, including industrial automation, unmanned aerial vehicles (UAVs) or drones, space exploration, search and rescue operations, and more.

Zigbee Communications Systems:

Zigbee is a wireless communication technology that can be utilized. Zigbee is a low-power, low-data-rate wireless protocol specifically designed for applications such as home automation, industrial control, and sensor networks. Here's how Zigbee can be integrated into robotic radio communications systems:

1. Zigbee Network Topology: Zigbee operates in a mesh network topology, where multiple devices form a network by connecting to each other. In a robotic system, robots equipped with Zigbee radios can communicate with each other in a peer-to-peer manner or through a central coordinator device.
2. Low Power Consumption: Zigbee devices are designed for low power consumption, which is advantageous for robotic systems that require efficient energy usage. This feature enables extended battery life or reduced power requirements for robotic devices.
3. Short-Range Communication: Zigbee operates in the 2.4 GHz frequency band and has a typical range of up to 10-100 meters, depending on the environment and the power output of the devices. This makes it suitable for short-range communication within a robotic system.
4. Reliable and Robust Communication: Zigbee utilizes the IEEE 802.15.4 standard and employs a robust communication protocol. It includes mechanisms for automatic channel selection, interference avoidance, and retransmission of lost packets, ensuring reliable communication even in noisy or congested environments.
5. Mesh Networking: Zigbee's mesh networking capability allows robots to communicate with each other via multiple hop paths. This feature enhances the reliability and coverage of the communication network, as data can be routed through intermediate devices to reach the intended recipient.
6. Scalability: Zigbee supports a large number of devices within a single network. This scalability feature is beneficial for robotic systems that involve multiple robots operating simultaneously, as they can all communicate with each other using Zigbee.
7. Interoperability: Zigbee is an industry-standard wireless protocol, which means that devices from different manufacturers that support Zigbee can communicate with each other seamlessly. This interoperability enables the integration of various Zigbee-enabled robotic devices and components within a system.

RADIO WAVE

Robotic radio communications systems utilize radio waves for wireless communication between robots or between robots and humans. Radio waves are a form of electromagnetic radiation that can be transmitted and received to convey information. Here are some key aspects of radio waves in robotic radio communications systems:

1. Frequency Bands: Radio waves used in robotic radio communications systems operate within specific frequency bands allocated for various purposes. Common frequency bands include the Ultra High Frequency (UHF), Very High Frequency (VHF), Industrial, Scientific, and Medical (ISM) bands, among others. The selection of a specific frequency band depends on factors such as range, interference, and regulatory requirements.
2. Transmitters and Receivers: Robotic radio communications systems consist of transmitters and receivers. The transmitter converts electrical signals carrying information into radio waves and broadcasts them into the surrounding environment. The receiver captures the radio waves and converts them back into electrical signals for interpretation by the receiving device.

3. Modulation Techniques: Modulation is used to encode information onto radio waves. Common modulation techniques include amplitude modulation (AM), frequency modulation (FM), and phase modulation (PM). The choice of modulation technique depends on factors such as data rate, bandwidth requirements, and noise resilience.
4. Range and Line-of-Sight: The range of radio waves in robotic radio communications systems can vary depending on factors like the frequency used, transmit power, and the presence of obstacles or interference. Line-of-sight communication refers to direct communication between devices without obstructions. In non-line-of-sight scenarios, radio waves may undergo reflections, diffraction, or scattering to reach the receiver.
5. Signal Strength and Signal-to-Noise Ratio: Signal strength refers to the power of the received radio waves at the receiver. A higher signal strength generally results in better communication quality. The signal-to-noise ratio (SNR) compares the power of the desired signal to the power of background noise and interference. Higher SNR values indicate clearer and more reliable communication.
6. Antennas: Antennas are essential components in robotic radio communications systems. They are used to transmit and receive radio waves efficiently. The design of the antennas affects factors like radiation pattern, gain (directivity), and polarization. Different antenna types, such as dipole antennas, patch antennas, or directional antennas, can be employed based on the application requirements.
7. Interference and Regulation: Radio waves are susceptible to interference from other devices operating in the same frequency band. Interference sources include other radios, electrical equipment, or environmental factors. Regulatory bodies define rules and regulations to allocate and manage the use of radio frequency bands to minimize interference and ensure efficient spectrum utilization.

Radio wave propagation

Radio wave propagation refers to the behavior and transmission characteristics of radio waves as they travel through the atmosphere or other media. Understanding radio wave propagation is crucial for designing and optimizing robotic radio communications systems.

There are several factors that affect radio wave propagation:

1. Line of sight: Radio waves travel in straight lines and require a clear path between the transmitter and receiver. In the absence of obstacles, this is known as line-of-sight propagation. Line-of-sight communication provides the strongest signal strength and is commonly used for short-range wireless communication.
2. Reflection: Radio waves can bounce off surfaces like buildings, mountains, and the ground. This phenomenon is known as reflection. Reflection can help extend the range of radio communication by redirecting the waves towards the receiver. However, it can also cause multipath interference, where multiple reflections reach the receiver at slightly different times, leading to signal distortion.
3. Diffraction: When radio waves encounter an obstacle, such as a building or a hill, they can bend around the obstacle. This phenomenon is called diffraction. Diffraction allows radio waves to reach areas beyond the line of sight by bending around obstructions.
4. Scattering: Scattering occurs when radio waves encounter objects that are smaller than the wavelength of the wave. The waves are redirected in various directions, resulting in a weakened and scattered signal. Scattering is more pronounced at higher frequencies.
5. Absorption: Radio waves can be absorbed by various objects and materials, including buildings, trees, and the atmosphere itself. The absorption of radio waves leads to signal attenuation and reduces the range of communication.
6. Atmospheric conditions: The state of the atmosphere can significantly influence radio wave propagation. Factors such as temperature, humidity, and atmospheric pressure can affect the speed and direction of radio waves. Atmospheric conditions can also cause phenomena like refraction, where radio waves bend due to variations in the density of the atmosphere.

RADAR

Radar, which stands for "Radio Detection and Ranging," is a system used to detect, locate, and track objects using radio waves. It operates by emitting radio waves and then measuring the time it takes for the waves to reflect off an object and return to the radar system. Based on this information, the radar can determine the distance, direction, and speed of the object. In other words Radar is a technology that uses electromagnetic waves to detect and locate objects at various distances. It is widely used in applications such as aviation, maritime navigation, weather forecasting, military operations, and traffic control.

Block Diagram of Radar System

The figure below shows the block diagram representation of radar:

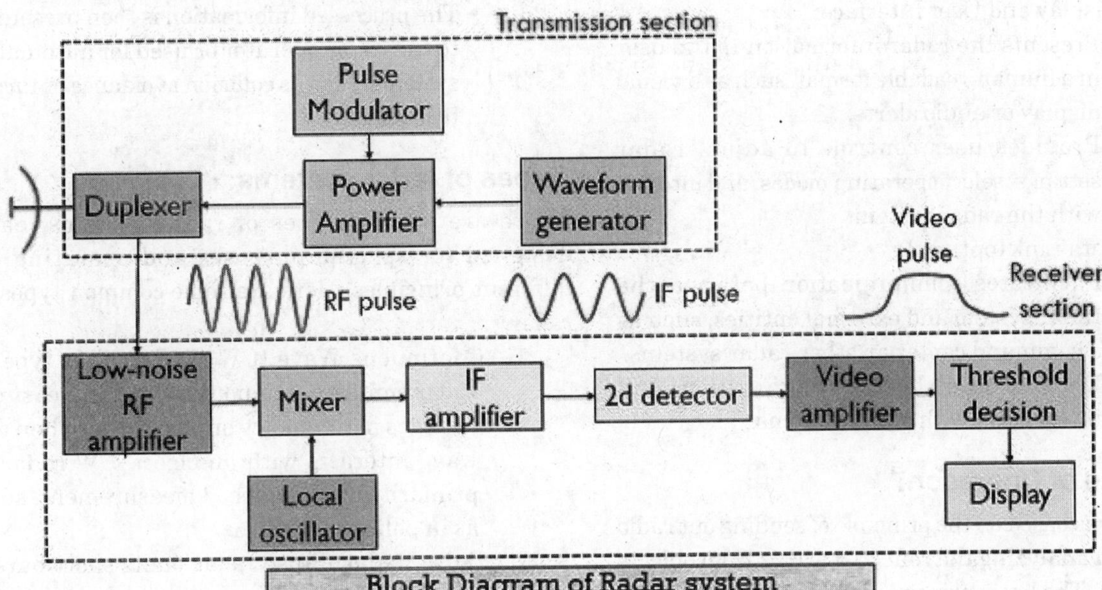

Block Diagram of Radar system

A block diagram of a radar system illustrates the major components and their interconnections. While the specific configuration may vary depending on the type and application of the radar system, here is a generalized block diagram:

1. Transmitter:
   - Modulator: Generates high-power RF pulses by modulating a carrier signal with the radar waveform.
   - Power Amplifier: Amplifies the modulated signal to a level suitable for transmission.
   - Oscillator: Provides the stable frequency reference for the radar system.
2. Antenna:
   - Transmits the high-power RF pulses generated by the transmitter into space.
   - Receives the echoes or reflections of the transmitted pulses from the targets.
3. Duplexer:
   - Allows the antenna to switch between the transmit and receive modes.
   - Protects the sensitive receiver components from the high-power transmitted pulses.
4. Receiver:
   - Low-Noise Amplifier (LNA): Amplifies the weak received signals while introducing minimal noise.
   - Mixer: Mixes the received signals with a local oscillator signal to convert the frequency.
   - Intermediate Frequency (IF) Amplifier: Amplifies the converted signals at a lower frequency.
   - Detector: Extracts the target information from the amplified IF signals.
   - Analog-to-Digital Converter (ADC): Converts the analog target information into digital form for further processing.
5. Signal Processor:
   - Pulse Compression: Uses signal processing techniques to enhance the radar's range resolution by compressing the transmitted pulses.

- Doppler Processing: Analyzes the frequency shift in the received signals to determine the target's radial velocity.
- Target Detection and Tracking: Applies algorithms to detect and track the targets based on the processed radar echoes.
- Data Processing: Performs various data analysis and interpretation tasks, such as target identification, classification, and imaging.

6. Display and User Interface:
   - Presents the radar information to the user in a human-readable format, such as a visual display or audio alerts.
   - Provides user controls to adjust radar settings, select operating modes, and interact with the radar system.
7. Data Link (optional):
   - Facilitates communication between the radar system and external entities, such as a command center or other radar systems.
   - Enables data sharing, coordination, and integration with other systems.

Principle of Operation:

Radar works based on the principle of sending out radio waves and analyzing the reflected waves from objects in its path. The basic principle behind radar is simple - extremely short bursts of radio energy (traveling at the speed of light) are transmitted, reflected off a target and then returned as an echo. Radar makes use of a phenomenon we have all observed, that of the echo principle.

Working Process of Radar:

Simplified step-by-step process of how radar operates:

- The radar system emits a short-duration pulse of electromagnetic waves through the antenna.
- These waves travel at the speed of light and spread out in a cone-shaped pattern as they move away from the antenna.
- When the waves encounter an object in their path, a portion of the energy is reflected back towards the radar system.
- The radar antenna receives the reflected waves.
- The receiver amplifies the weak signals received by the antenna.
- Signal processing algorithms analyze the received signals to determine the time delay between the transmitted and received pulses.
- Using the time delay, the distance to the object can be calculated by multiplying the time delay by the speed of light.
- By continuously transmitting pulses and analyzing the echoes, radar can track the movement of objects, measure their speed, and estimate their size and shape.
- The processed information is then presented to the radar operator or used for automated systems, such as collision avoidance or target tracking.

Types of radar systems:

There are several types of radar systems, each designed for specific purposes and operating on different principles. Here are some common types of radar:

1. Continuous Wave (CW) Radar: This type of radar emits a continuous wave and measures changes in frequency or phase shift when the wave interacts with an object. CW radar is primarily used for speed measurement, such as in police radar guns.
2. Pulse Radar: Pulse radar emits short bursts or pulses of radio waves and measures the time it takes for the pulse to travel to the target and back. The radar system then analyzes the received pulses to determine the distance and other characteristics of the target.
3. Doppler Radar: Doppler radar measures the Doppler shift in the frequency of the radio waves reflected by moving objects. It can determine the speed and direction of moving targets, making it useful for weather monitoring, air traffic control, and vehicle speed detection.
4. Synthetic Aperture Radar (SAR): SAR systems use the motion of the radar antenna or platform to synthesize a large virtual antenna, producing high-resolution images of the Earth's surface. SAR is commonly used in remote sensing applications, such as mapping, topographic analysis, and surveillance.
5. Phased Array Radar: Phased array radar uses an array of antenna elements to electronically steer and shape the radar beam without

physically moving the antenna. This allows for rapid scanning, precise control of the radar beam, and the ability to track multiple targets simultaneously.

6. Weather Radar: Weather radar is specifically designed to detect and track weather phenomena, including precipitation, storms, and other atmospheric conditions. It provides valuable information for meteorological forecasting and severe weather monitoring.

RADAR EQUATION

The radar equation is a fundamental equation in radar theory that relates the power received by a radar system to the transmitted power, the characteristics of the radar system, and the properties of the target and the propagation medium. The radar equation is expressed as follows:

$$P_r = P_d A_e = \frac{P_t \cdot G_t \sigma G_r \lambda^2}{\left(4\pi R^2\right)^2 L \cdot 4\pi} A_e$$

$$= \frac{P_t G^2 \sigma \lambda^2}{(4\pi)^3 R^4 L} A_e$$

$$P_r = P_t = \frac{G^2 \lambda^2 \sigma}{(4\pi)^3 R^4 L} A_e$$

Where:

1. Transmitted Power (P_t): This represents the power transmitted by the radar system. It depends on the capabilities of the radar transmitter and is usually specified by the radar system design or operating requirements.
2. Transmitter Antenna Gain (G_t): It is the measure of the directional focus of the transmitted energy. The gain describes how much the antenna concentrates the transmitted power in a particular direction. A higher gain means more focused radiation in the desired direction.
3. Receiver Antenna Gain (G_r): It represents the ability of the receiving antenna to capture the incoming signal from the target. Similar to the transmitter antenna gain, a higher receiver antenna gain improves the radar system's sensitivity to weak return signals.
4. Wavelength (λ): It is the physical length of one complete cycle of the transmitted electromagnetic wave. The wavelength is inversely proportional to the frequency of the signal. In the radar equation, the wavelength is squared (λ^2) to account for the spreading of the transmitted energy as it propagates through space.
5. Radar Cross-Section (σ): It is a measure of how much radar energy is reflected by the target. The radar cross-section depends on the target's size, shape, and material properties. A larger radar cross-section indicates a stronger reflected signal, making the target easier to detect.
6. Effective Aperture (A_e): It represents the ability of the receiving antenna to gather the incoming power. The effective aperture is related to the physical size and directivity of the receiving antenna.
7. Distance to the Target (R): It is the range between the radar system and the target. The radar equation includes the inverse fourth power of the distance (R^4) to account for the spreading of the transmitted energy over a larger area as the distance increases.
8. Total Path Loss Factor (L): This factor includes all the losses that occur during the propagation of the electromagnetic wave from the radar system to the target and back to the receiver. It accounts for factors such as free-space loss, atmospheric absorption, target reflection losses, and losses due to obstacles in the propagation path.

RADAR ANTENNA

Radar antennas play a crucial role in the transmission and reception of radio waves in radar systems.

A radar antenna is a device used in radar systems to transmit and receive electromagnetic waves. It serves as a crucial interface between the radar system and the surrounding environment, allowing the system to detect, locate, and track objects by emitting radio waves and analyzing their reflections.

The primary functions of a radar antenna are:

1. Transmission: The radar antenna emits electromagnetic waves, typically in the form of radio frequency (RF) pulses, into the surrounding space. These waves propagate outward and interact with objects in their path.

2. Reception: The radar antenna collects the electromagnetic waves that have reflected off objects in the environment. It captures these return signals, which contain information about the objects' position, distance, velocity, and other characteristics.
3. Beam-forming: In many radar systems, the antenna plays a role in shaping and directing the emitted and received electromagnetic waves. It can focus the radiation into a specific direction, adjust the beam width, and steer the beam electronically without requiring physical movement.
4. Signal Processing: The antenna feeds the collected signals to the radar receiver, which amplifies and processes the received electromagnetic waves. The received signals are then analyzed to extract useful information about the detected objects.

Radar antennas come in various types, such as parabolic reflector antennas, horn antennas, phased array antennas, and more.

Each type has its own design, characteristics, and applications, tailored to specific radar requirements, such as range, coverage, resolution, and agility.

1. Parabolic Reflector Antenna:
   - Structure: It consists of a curved metal surface in the shape of a paraboloid. The curved surface reflects incoming or outgoing electromagnetic waves towards a focal point.
   - Function: The parabolic reflector focuses the waves into a narrow beam, providing high gain and directivity. It captures the signals in the focal region and directs them to the radar receiver or transmits them towards the target.
   - Applications: Parabolic reflector antennas are commonly used in radar systems that require long-range detection, such as air surveillance radar, space tracking radar, and long-range weather radar.
2. Horn Antenna:
   - Structure: A horn antenna is a flared or tapered waveguide with an open end. It can be conical or pyramidal in shape.
   - Function: Horn antennas emit or receive electromagnetic waves by launching them into the open end of the waveguide. They have a wide radiation pattern and can provide broad coverage.
   - Applications: Horn antennas are used in radar systems where wide coverage angles are required, such as weather radar, marine radar, and some types of airborne radar.
3. Phased Array Antenna:
   - Structure: A phased array antenna consists of an array of individual radiating elements, each with its own phase shifter and usually connected to a common feed network.
   - Function: By adjusting the phase and amplitude of the signals across the array elements, the antenna can electronically steer the radar beam without any mechanical movement. Phased array antennas provide rapid beam scanning and agile beam control.
   - Applications: Phased array antennas are extensively used in radar systems that require agile beam steering, such as air traffic control radar, military surveillance radar, and weather radar.
4. Planar Array Antenna:
   - Structure: Planar array antennas consist of multiple radiating elements arranged in a flat or planar configuration, often on a printed circuit board or a planar substrate.
   - Function: These elements, which can be patch antennas or microstrip antennas, work together to emit or receive electromagnetic waves. Planar arrays offer compact size, ease of integration, and can be designed for specific radiation patterns.
   - Applications: Planar array antennas are commonly used in radar systems with size constraints, such as automotive radar, short-range surveillance radar, and some types of portable radar systems.
5. Slot Antenna:
   - Structure: A slot antenna is a narrow, elongated opening or slot in a conducting surface, such as a metal plate or waveguide wall.
   - Function: The slot radiates or receives electromagnetic waves through the slot opening. Slot antennas can provide wide bandwidth and low-profile design advantages.
   - Applications: Slot antennas are often used in radar systems operating at microwave frequencies. They find applications in radar systems for airborne platforms, ground-based radar, and some types of imaging radar.

6. Dipole Antenna:
   - Structure: A dipole antenna consists of two conductive elements of equal length, typically straight and aligned in opposite directions.
   - Function: The dipole antenna radiates or receives electromagnetic waves along its axis. It can be oriented vertically or horizontally, depending on the polarization requirements.
   - Applications: Dipole antennas are commonly used in radar systems operating in the lower frequency bands, such as VHF and UHF radar. They are utilized in applications like air traffic control, weather radar, and ground-based surveillance radar.

Ranging & target tracking in Radar systems:

Radar systems play a crucial role in various applications, including navigation, aviation, weather monitoring, and military operations. Let's explore how radar systems relate to ranging and target tracking:

1. Ranging in Radar Systems: Radar systems utilize ranging techniques to measure the distance between the radar sensor and the target object. By transmitting a radio wave signal and analyzing the time it takes for the signal to travel to the target and back, radar systems can estimate the range or distance. This process is commonly known as "radar ranging" or "range measurement" and is essential for determining the position of the target.
2. Target Tracking in Radar Systems: Target tracking is a vital task in radar systems. Once a target is detected, the radar system aims to continuously estimate and predict its position, velocity, and other relevant attributes over time. Tracking algorithms in radar systems help maintain an updated and accurate representation of the target's state despite uncertainties and measurement noise. These algorithms utilize filtering techniques such as Kalman filters or particle filters to fuse measurements from the radar system and predict the target's future trajectory.

Target detection and radar resolution in radar system:

Target detection and radar resolution are two important aspects of radar systems that determine their ability to detect and accurately identify objects. Let's explore each of these concepts:

1. Target Detection: Target detection refers to the capability of a radar system to detect the presence of objects or targets in its surveillance area. The primary goal of radar is to identify and locate targets by analyzing the echoes or reflected signals received from them.

   The detectability of a target depends on several factors, including the radar's power and sensitivity, the size and radar cross section (RCS) of the target, the distance between the radar and the target, and the noise level in the environment.

   To improve target detection, radar systems often use techniques such as:
   - High transmit power: Increasing the power of the transmitted radar signal can enhance the detection range and increase the probability of detecting smaller targets.
   - Low noise receivers: Using sensitive receivers with low noise levels allows the radar system to detect weak echoes from distant or low RCS targets.
   - Signal processing: Sophisticated signal processing techniques, such as pulse compression, matched filtering, and adaptive filtering, can improve the signal-to-noise ratio and enhance target detection in noisy or cluttered environments.
2. Radar Resolution: Radar resolution refers to the ability of a radar system to distinguish and separate multiple targets that are located close to each other in range, azimuth, or elevation. Resolution is important to accurately identify and track individual targets in crowded scenarios.

   Resolution is determined by several factors, including the radar's operating frequency, antenna size, beam width, and signal processing capabilities. The two main types of resolution are range resolution and angular resolution:
   - Range Resolution: Range resolution determines the ability to resolve targets located at different distances from the radar. It is determined by the pulse width or duration of the radar signal. A shorter pulse width allows for better range resolution, enabling the radar to distinguish between closely spaced targets.
   - Angular Resolution: Angular resolution refers to the ability to resolve targets that are located close to each other in the radar's

field of view. It is determined by the beam-width of the radar antenna. A narrower beam-width leads to better angular resolution, enabling the radar to accurately determine the direction of targets.

Improving radar resolution can involve techniques such as:

- Narrower beam-width: Using antennas with narrower beam-widths allows for better angular resolution, enabling the radar system to distinguish between closely spaced targets.
- Multiple antenna systems: Employing multiple antennas, such as phased array antennas or antenna arrays, can enhance resolution by providing spatial diversity and enabling beam-forming techniques.
- High-frequency operation: Operating at higher frequencies can improve resolution, as shorter wavelengths allow for finer spatial discrimination.

Both target detection and radar resolution are important considerations in radar system design, as they impact the system's capability to detect and identify targets accurately and distinguish them from noise and clutter. Advanced radar systems employ a combination of sophisticated hardware and signal processing algorithms to optimize these capabilities for various applications, including surveillance, tracking, and object recognition.

ROC Curves and Radar Cross Section (RCS) in Radar systems:

1. ROC Curves in Radar Systems: ROC curves are not directly related to radar systems themselves, but they can be used to evaluate and assess the performance of target detection algorithms or classifiers employed in radar systems. Radar systems often employ signal processing and classification algorithms to distinguish between desired targets (e.g., aircraft) and clutter or interference (e.g., birds, weather phenomena). The output of these algorithms can be evaluated using ROC curves to understand their trade-off between true positive rate (detection probability) and false positive rate (false alarm rate).
2. Radar Cross Section (RCS) is a measure of the reflectivity or "visibility" of an object to radar waves. It quantifies the amount of electromagnetic energy that is scattered back towards the radar system when it illuminates a target. RCS is an important concept in radar engineering, as it directly affects the detection and tracking capabilities of radar systems.

When radar waves encounter an object, they can be reflected, scattered, absorbed, or transmitted through the object. The RCS of an object depends on its size, shape, composition, and the wavelength of the radar waves. Objects with larger physical dimensions or complex shapes tend to have a higher RCS, making them more easily detectable by radar systems.

To reduce the RCS of an object, various techniques can be employed, including:

- Stealth technology: Stealth technology aims to minimize the RCS of an object, making it less visible to radar. This involves designing the object with specific angles and shapes to deflect radar waves away from the radar system or absorb them. Additionally, radar-absorbent materials can be used to reduce the amount of reflected energy.
- Radar absorbing materials: Special coatings or materials can be applied to surfaces to absorb radar waves and reduce their reflection. These materials often consist of conductive and absorptive substances that convert the incoming electromagnetic energy into heat.
- Radar cross section shaping: The shape of an object can be optimized to reduce its RCS. Smooth, rounded surfaces and angles that minimize the reflection of radar waves can be employed. Additionally, the use of faceted surfaces can help scatter radar waves in different directions, reducing the overall RCS.
- Radar cross section reduction techniques: Various techniques can be used to reduce the RCS of specific parts of an object, such as covering joints and seams, using radar-absorbent materials in critical areas, or incorporating radar-absorbing structures.

Reducing the RCS of an object is particularly important for military aircraft, naval vessels, and other applications where stealth and reduced detectability are desired. By minimizing the RCS, these objects can avoid detection or appear as smaller, less significant targets on radar screens, increasing their survivability and mission effectiveness.

SATELLITE

A satellite is an object that orbits around a larger celestial body, such as a planet or a star. Satellites can be natural, like moons orbiting planets, or artificial, which are human-made objects launched into space. In this context, I will provide more details about artificial satellites.

Types of Satellites:

- Communication Satellites: These satellites are used for transmitting and receiving signals for various forms of communication, such as television, radio, telephone, and internet.
- Weather Satellites: Weather satellites monitor and collect data about the Earth's weather patterns, including cloud formations, temperature, humidity, and precipitation.
- Navigation Satellites: Navigation satellites, like the Global Positioning System (GPS) satellites, provide accurate positioning, navigation, and timing information to users on the ground.
- Remote Sensing Satellites: These satellites capture images and collect data about the Earth's surface, atmosphere, and oceans. They are used for applications like mapping, agriculture, environmental monitoring, and disaster management.
- Scientific Satellites: Scientific satellites are designed to conduct various scientific experiments and observations. They study space phenomena, celestial bodies, and the universe to enhance our understanding of astronomy, astrophysics, and cosmology.
- Military and Spy Satellites: These satellites are used for military purposes, including reconnaissance, surveillance, and intelligence gathering.

Components of Satellite:

- Payload: The payload is the primary purpose or equipment carried by the satellite, such as cameras for imaging satellites, transponders for communication satellites, or sensors for scientific satellites.
- Power System: Satellites use solar panels to convert sunlight into electrical energy, which is stored in onboard batteries for use when the satellite is in the Earth's shadow or during periods of high power demand.
- Propulsion System: Some satellites have propulsion systems to control their orbit or make adjustments. They typically use small thrusters or ion engines for propulsion.
- Antenna Systems: Antennas are used for transmitting and receiving signals to communicate with ground stations or other satellites.
- Control and Guidance System: Satellites have onboard computers, sensors, and control systems to maintain their orientation, stability, and pointing accuracy.
- Structure: The satellite's structure provides support and protection to its internal components. It is designed to withstand the harsh conditions of space, including extreme temperatures, vacuum, and radiation.
- Telemetry, Tracking, and Command (TT&C): These systems enable communication between the satellite and ground control stations. They allow operators to monitor the satellite's health, send commands, and receive data.

Launch Satellite:

Launching a satellite involves a complex process that requires careful planning and coordination. Here are the general steps involved in launching a satellite:

1. Mission Planning: Define the purpose and objectives of the satellite mission. Determine the type of satellite, its payload, and the desired orbit.
2. Design and Construction: Develop the satellite based on the mission requirements. This includes designing the spacecraft, payload integration, and testing.
3. Launch Vehicle Selection: Choose a suitable launch vehicle based on the satellite's weight, size, and desired orbit. Consider factors such as cost, availability, and performance.
4. Launch Site Selection: Identify a suitable launch site with the necessary infrastructure and capabilities for the planned launch. Factors like proximity to the desired orbit and geopolitical considerations may influence the selection.
5. Pre-launch Preparations: Conduct various pre-launch activities, including final testing, integration of the satellite with the launch vehicle, and fueling the rocket.
6. Launch Window: Identify an appropriate launch window based on factors such as orbital dynamics, weather conditions, and range availability. This ensures a favorable launch opportunity.

7. Countdown and Launch: Execute the countdown sequence, which involves final checks, propellant loading, and various system tests. Once all systems are verified to be functioning correctly, the launch vehicle ignites its engines and lifts off from the launch pad, carrying the satellite into space.
8. Separation: After reaching the desired orbit, the satellite is separated from the launch vehicle. This can be a critical moment, as the satellite must be deployed correctly to ensure its functionality.
9. In-Orbit Operations: Once separated, the satellite undergoes a series of checks to ensure its systems are functioning properly. It is then commissioned for its specific mission, which may involve activating various payloads and conducting calibration procedures.
10. Mission Operations: The satellite's mission operations team takes over control and monitoring of the satellite from the ground station. They ensure the satellite remains in its intended orbit, perform necessary adjustments, and collect and analyze data from the satellite's instruments.

Satellites are launched into space using various methods; including rockets, space shuttles, or other launch vehicles. Once in space, they are placed into specific orbits based on their intended mission.

Satellite Orbit Earth

Satellites can orbit the Earth in various types of orbits depending on their mission requirements. Here are some commonly used satellite orbits:

1. Low Earth Orbit (LEO): Satellites in LEO typically orbit the Earth at altitudes ranging from a few hundred kilometers to around 2,000 kilometers (approximately 120 to 1,240 miles). LEO orbits offer several advantages, including lower latency for communication, shorter orbital periods, and better resolution for Earth observation. Examples of satellites in LEO include the International Space Station (ISS), imaging satellites, and some communication satellites.
2. Medium Earth Orbit (MEO): Satellites in MEO are positioned at higher altitudes than LEO, typically ranging from a few thousand to around 20,000 kilometers (approximately 1,240 to 12,427 miles). MEO orbits are commonly used for navigation systems like the Global Positioning System (GPS). The higher altitude provides wider coverage, but the longer distance from Earth results in slightly higher signal latency.
3. Geostationary Orbit (GEO): Satellites in GEO are located at an altitude of approximately 36,000 kilometers (22,236 miles) above the Earth's equator. In this orbit, satellites rotate at the same speed as the Earth's rotation, which allows them to remain fixed in a specific position relative to the ground. This characteristic makes GEO satellites ideal for communication and broadcasting purposes since they can maintain continuous coverage over a specific area. Many television and communication satellites, including those used for satellite TV and internet services, are placed in GEO.
4. Highly Elliptical Orbit (HEO): Satellites in HEO have elliptical orbits with high eccentricity, meaning their paths take them far from the Earth at their apogee (highest point) and closer at their perigee (lowest point). HEO orbits are often used for specific purposes such as communication in polar regions or for surveillance missions requiring extended coverage over specific areas.
5. Polar Orbit: Satellites in polar orbits pass over or near the Earth's geographic poles. These orbits provide comprehensive coverage of the Earth's surface over multiple passes. Polar orbiting satellites are commonly used for scientific research, weather observation, and Earth imaging. They offer a global perspective and can capture images of the entire planet over time.

The selection of the orbit depends on factors like mission requirements, coverage area, communication range, and desired orbital parameters.

Important of satellites

Satellites play a crucial role in various aspects of our modern world. Here are some important contributions and benefits of satellites:

- Communication: Satellites enable global communication by facilitating long-distance telephone calls, internet connectivity, television broadcasting, and data transmission. They make it possible to connect people and businesses across continents and oceans, providing reliable and instant communication services.

- Navigation and Global Positioning: Satellite-based navigation systems, such as the Global Positioning System (GPS), have become integral to daily life. GPS allows precise positioning, navigation, and timing services for various applications, including personal devices, transportation (aircraft, ships, and automobiles), logistics, emergency services, and surveying.
- Weather Forecasting and Monitoring: Weather satellites provide critical data for monitoring and predicting weather patterns. They capture images, measure atmospheric conditions, and collect data about cloud formations, temperature, humidity, precipitation, and other parameters. This information helps meteorologists issue accurate weather forecasts and warnings, aiding in disaster preparedness and mitigation efforts.
- Earth Observation and Environmental Monitoring: Satellites equipped with advanced sensors and imaging technology capture high-resolution images and collect data about the Earth's surface, atmosphere, and oceans. This data is used for mapping, urban planning, agriculture, environmental monitoring, natural resource management, climate studies, and disaster management. It provides valuable insights into changes in land use, deforestation, pollution levels, and the impact of climate change.
- Scientific Research and Exploration: Satellites contribute significantly to scientific research and exploration. They help astronomers study space phenomena, celestial bodies, and the universe, advancing our understanding of astronomy, astrophysics, and cosmology. Satellites also aid in space exploration missions, providing data on other planets, moons, asteroids, and comets.
- Disaster Management and Emergency Response: Satellites play a vital role in disaster management by monitoring natural disasters, tracking their progression, and assessing damages. They provide real-time images and data to emergency response teams, aiding in rescue and relief operations. Satellites also support communication and coordination during emergencies when ground-based infrastructure may be damaged or inaccessible.
- Defense and Security: Satellites are essential for military and defense purposes. They provide intelligence gathering, surveillance, reconnaissance, and secure communication capabilities. Military satellites contribute to national security by monitoring potential threats, facilitating military operations, and enhancing situational awareness.
- Connectivity and Bridge the Digital Divide: Satellites are instrumental in bridging the digital divide by providing internet connectivity to remote and underserved areas. They can reach regions where terrestrial infrastructure is limited or economically unviable. Satellite internet services help expand access to education, healthcare, e-commerce, and information resources, empowering communities and driving socio-economic development.

Applications of Satellites:

- Communication: Satellites enable global communication by facilitating telephone calls, internet connectivity, television broadcasting, and data transmission.
- Navigation: Satellite-based navigation systems, like GPS, allow precise positioning, navigation, and timing services for various applications, including personal devices, transportation, and military operations.
- Earth Observation: Satellites capture high-resolution images and collect data about the Earth's surface, atmosphere, and oceans, aiding in mapping, agriculture, weather forecasting, and environmental monitoring.
- Scientific Research: Satellites help scientists study space phenomena, celestial bodies, and the universe, advancing our knowledge in fields like astronomy, astrophysics, and cosmology.
- Disaster Management: Satellites assist in monitoring natural disasters, tracking their progression, assessing damages, and coordinating rescue and relief operations.
- Military and Defense: Satellites play a vital role in military operations, providing intelligence, surveillance, reconnaissance, and secure communication capabilities.

SUBMARINE TELEGRAPHY

Submarine telegraphy, also known as submarine cables or undersea cables, refers to the transmission of telegraph signals through cables laid on the seabed. It is a method of long-distance communication that predates modern telecommunications technologies like satellite communications and fiber optics.

Historically, submarine telegraphy played a crucial role in international communication during the 19th and early 20th centuries. The first successful submarine telegraph cable was laid across the English Channel in 1851, connecting England and France. This accomplishment paved the way for the expansion of submarine telegraphy across the world's oceans.

Submarine telegraph cables consist of insulated copper or, more recently, fiber optic strands bundled together and protected by various layers of armor and insulation. These cables are typically several centimeters thick and can span thousands of kilometers across the ocean floor.

The process of laying submarine telegraph cables involves specialized ships equipped with cable-laying machinery. The ships deploy the cable from large storage drums and carefully lower it to the seabed. The cable is then guided along a predetermined route, taking into account the ocean's depth, underwater terrain, and potential hazards.

Once the cable is in place, telegraph signals are transmitted by electrically encoding the message into a series of electrical pulses. These pulses travel through the copper or fiber optic strands within the cable. At regular intervals, repeaters or amplifiers are placed along the cable to boost the signals and compensate for any loss of strength or quality during transmission.

Upon reaching the destination, the signals are received, decoded, and converted back into readable messages. Submarine telegraphy allowed for rapid long-distance communication between continents and played a significant role in international commerce, diplomacy, and news transmission during its heyday.

While submarine telegraphy is no longer the primary method of intercontinental communication, it laid the groundwork for modern undersea communication systems. Today, fiber optic cables, which transmit data as pulses of light, are widely used for undersea telecommunications. These modern submarine cables carry vast amounts of internet and telecommunications traffic, connecting continents and enabling global connectivity.

Selecting submarine cable routes:

Selecting submarine cable routes involves careful planning and consideration of various factors to ensure efficient and reliable connectivity. Here are some key steps and factors to consider when selecting submarine cable routes:

1. Identify connectivity requirements: Determine the specific needs and objectives of the submarine cable project. Consider factors such as capacity requirements, geographic coverage, latency, and redundancy.
2. Conduct feasibility studies: Evaluate the feasibility of potential routes based on factors like ocean depth, seabed conditions, geophysical hazards (e.g., earthquakes, volcanoes), marine protected areas, and shipping lanes. Conduct surveys and studies to gather data on these aspects.
3. Assess geopolitical considerations: Consider geopolitical factors such as international borders, political stability, and legal frameworks in the countries or regions through which the cable will pass. Evaluate potential risks and ensure compliance with international regulations.
4. Evaluate landing points: Identify suitable landing points for the cable at both ends. Consider factors such as accessibility, proximity to population centers, existing telecommunication infrastructure, and environmental impact.
5. Consider route diversity and redundancy: Aim for route diversity to minimize the risk of single points of failure. Assess the availability of alternative routes and select paths that provide redundancy in case of cable damage or outages.
6. Analyze technical aspects: Evaluate technical aspects such as cable length, transmission technologies, fiber count, and future scalability. Consider the capacity of the cable to meet anticipated demands and technological advancements.
7. Assess commercial viability: Consider the commercial viability of the cable route, including market demand, potential customers, and financial feasibility. Evaluate the business case for the project and assess potential return on investment.

8. Engage stakeholders: Collaborate with relevant stakeholders, including governments, telecommunication companies, investors, and regulatory authorities. Seek input and approvals from involved parties and ensure compliance with legal and regulatory requirements.
9. Environmental impact assessment: Conduct an environmental impact assessment to evaluate the potential effects of the cable installation on marine ecosystems and other environmental factors. Mitigate any potential negative impacts and ensure compliance with environmental regulations.
10. Financial considerations: Consider the costs associated with cable installation, maintenance, and operation. Evaluate the long-term financial sustainability of the project, including potential revenue streams and cost recovery mechanisms.

Morse code:

Morse code is a method of transmitting text information as a series of on-off tones, lights, or clicks that can be understood by a skilled listener or observer. It was developed by Samuel Morse and Alfred Vail in the early 1830s as a means of long-distance communication using telegraph systems.

In Morse code, each letter of the alphabet, along with numbers and a few special characters, is represented by unique sequences of short and long signals, which are commonly referred to as "dots" and "dashes." A dot represents a short signal, while a dash represents a longer signal. These signals are combined to form the code for each character.

Here is a table showing the Morse code representations for letters, numbers, and some special characters:

A: .- N: -. 0: ----- B: -... O: --- 1: .---- C: -.-. P: .--. 2: ..--- D: -.. Q: --.- 3: ...-- E: .

R: .-. 4: ....- F: ..-. S: ... 5: ..... G: --. T: - 6: -.... H: .... U: ..- 7: --... I: .. V: ...- 8: ---.. J: .---

W: .-- 9: ----. K: -. - X: -..-

L: .-.. Y: -.--

M: -- Z: --..

For example, the word "HELLO" in Morse code would be represented as ".... . .-.. .-.. ---".

Morse code can be transmitted using various methods, such as sound signals (such as beeps or clicks), visual signals (such as flashing lights or flags), or even written forms (dots and dashes on paper). It has been widely used in the past for long-distance communication, particularly in telegraph systems, and it still finds some applications today, such as in amateur radio communication or military operations.

Objective Type Questions

1. Which of the following is an advantage of using radio waves for communication?
   (a) High data transfer rates
   (b) Long-range coverage
   (c) Immunity to interference
   (d) Low equipment cost
2. What is the purpose of modulation in radio communication?
   (a) To amplify the signal
   (b) To convert digital signals into analog signals
   (c) To encrypt the signal
   (d) To eliminate interference
3. Which of the following is the most commonly used modulation technique in modern wireless communication systems?
   (a) Amplitude modulation (AM)
   (b) Frequency modulation (FM)
   (c) Phase modulation (PM)
   (d) Quadrature amplitude modulation (QAM)
4. What is the purpose of a repeater in radio communication?
   (a) To amplify the received signal
   (b) To convert analog signals to digital signals
   (c) To provide encryption for secure communication
   (d) To establish a direct connection between two devices
5. Which of the following is a disadvantage of analog modulation techniques?
   (a) Susceptibility to noise and interference
   (b) Limited frequency range
   (c) Incompatibility with digital systems
   (d) High power consumption
6. What is the purpose of a demodulator in radio communication?
   (a) To amplify the received signal
   (b) To convert analog signals to digital signals
   (c) To extract the original information from the modulated signal
   (d) To establish a direct connection between two devices
7. Which of the following is a characteristic of simplex communication?
   (a) Two-way communication between two devices
   (b) Simultaneous transmission and reception on the same frequency
   (c) Communication over two separate frequencies
   (d) Communication using digital signals only
8. Which of the following is an example of a half-duplex communication system?
   (a) Walkie-talkie
   (b) Mobile phone
   (c) Satellite TV receiver
   (d) Wi-Fi router
9. Which of the following is a common frequency band used for Wi-Fi communication?
   (a) 900 MHz (b) 2.4 GHz
   (c) 5 GHz (d) 20 GHz
10. Which of the following is a disadvantage of using radio waves for communication in urban areas?
    (a) Limited bandwidth availability
    (b) High cost of equipment
    (c) Low data transfer rates
    (d) Short-range coverage due to signal blockage
11. Which of the following is a key advantage of using robotic radio communication systems?
    (a) Enhanced mobility
    (b) Increased payload capacity
    (c) Improved sensing capabilities
    (d) Reduced power consumption
12. What is the purpose of a radio transceiver in a robotic communication system?
    (a) To receive and transmit radio signals
    (b) To control the robotic movements
    (c) To process sensor data
    (d) To store communication logs
13. Which of the following frequency bands is commonly used for robotic radio communication systems?
    (a) VHF (Very High Frequency)
    (b) UHF (Ultra High Frequency)
    (c) SHF (Super High Frequency)
    (d) EHF (Extremely High Frequency)
14. What is the role of an antenna in robotic radio communication systems?
    (a) To process sensor data
    (b) To store communication logs
    (c) To amplify radio signals
    (d) To transmit and receive radio signals

15. Which of the following is a disadvantage of using radio waves for robotic communication in certain environments?

(a) Limited bandwidth availability

(b) High latency

(c) Susceptibility to interference

(d) Excessive power consumption

16. What is the purpose of a repeater in robotic radio communication systems?

(a) To amplify radio signals

(b) To control robotic movements

(c) To encrypt communication

(d) To increase battery life

17. Which of the following is a common wireless communication protocol used in robotic systems?

(a) Bluetooth

(b) Wi-Fi

(c) Zigbee

(d) NFC (Near Field Communication)

18. What is the purpose of error correction techniques in robotic radio communication systems?

(a) To reduce power consumption

(b) To improve data transfer rates

(c) To enhance signal propagation

(d) To correct transmission errors

19. Which of the following is an example of a robot-to-robot communication scenario?

(a) Robot vacuum cleaner receiving commands from a smartphone app

(b) Drone transmitting live video feed to a remote controller

(c) Robotic arms in a manufacturing line exchanging sensor data

(d) Self-driving car communicating with traffic lights

20. What is the role of modulation in robotic radio communication systems?

(a) To amplify radio signals

(b) To encode data onto a carrier wave

(c) To control robotic movements

(d) To encrypt communication

21. Which of the following describes the nature of radio waves?

(a) Electromagnetic waves

(b) Mechanical waves

(c) Sound waves

(d) Ultrasonic waves

22. Which of the following statements about radio wave propagation is correct?

(a) Radio waves can propagate through a vacuum.

(b) Radio waves require a physical medium for propagation.

(c) Radio waves can propagate only through water.

(d) Radio waves cannot penetrate obstacles.

23. What is the range of frequencies typically used by Zigbee communication?

(a) Low-frequency range

(b) Medium-frequency range

(c) High-frequency range

(d) Ultra-high-frequency range

24. Which of the following statements about Zigbee communication is true?

(a) Zigbee operates on a single hop communication model.

(b) Zigbee communication supports long-range transmission.

(c) Zigbee uses a high amount of power for transmission.

(d) Zigbee is primarily used for high-bandwidth applications.

25. How does Zigbee handle network topologies in a mesh network?

(a) Zigbee uses a star topology.

(b) Zigbee uses a bus topology.

(c) Zigbee uses a ring topology.

(d) Zigbee uses a mesh topology.

26. What is the typical range of Zigbee communication in an indoor environment?

(a) Few meters

(b) Few tens of meters

(c) Few hundreds of meters

(d) Few kilometers

27. Which of the following is a benefit of using Zigbee in robotic communication systems?

(a) High data transfer rates

(b) Long-range coverage

(c) Low power consumption

(d) Immunity to interference

28. Which of the following components is essential for robotic radio communication systems using Zigbee?

(a) Modulator (b) Antenna

(c) Power amplifier (d) Demodulator

29. Which of the following is an advantage of using a mesh network in robotic radio communication systems?
(a) Reduced latency
(b) Increased data transfer rates
(c) Extended network coverage
(d) Lower power consumption

30. What is the purpose of error checking and correction techniques in robotic radio communication systems?
(a) To reduce latency
(b) To increase network scalability
(c) To improve signal strength
(d) To ensure reliable data transmission

31. What does RADAR stand for?
(a) Radio Analog Detection and Ranging
(b) Radio Angle Detection and Ranging
(c) Radio Automated Detection and Ranging
(d) Radio Detection and Ranging

32. Which physical phenomenon is used by RADAR to detect objects?
(a) Reflection (b) Refraction
(c) Diffraction (d) Interference

33. Which of the following is a common application of RADAR?
(a) Weather forecasting
(b) Wi-Fi communication
(c) Optical fiber transmission
(d) Satellite navigation

34. Which property of radio waves allows RADAR to determine the range of objects?
(a) Amplitude (b) Frequency
(c) Phase (d) Wavelength

35. Which of the following RADAR systems is commonly used for air traffic control?
(a) Pulsed RADAR
(b) Continuous Wave RADAR
(c) Synthetic Aperture RADAR
(d) Passive RADAR

36. What is the purpose of the Doppler effect in RADAR?
(a) To measure the direction of an object
(b) To determine the range of an object
(c) To calculate the velocity of an object
(d) To identify the shape of an object

37. Which RADAR system is capable of generating high-resolution images of the Earth's surface?
(a) Weather RADAR
(b) Airborne RADAR
(c) Spaceborne RADAR
(d) Ground Penetrating RADAR

38. Which of the following is an advantage of using RADAR over other sensing technologies, such as LiDAR or cameras?
(a) Higher accuracy in measuring range
(b) Ability to see through obstacles
(c) Lower power consumption
(d) Greater color depth in imaging

39. Which parameter of a RADAR system determines its resolution?
(a) Frequency
(b) Bandwidth
(c) Pulse duration
(d) Antenna size

40. Which of the following is an example of an active RADAR system?
(a) Radio telescope
(b) Infrared camera
(c) Sonar
(d) Ground Penetrating RADAR

41. Which type of radar system is primarily used for weather monitoring and tracking precipitation?
(a) Airborne radar
(b) Ground-penetrating radar
(c) Weather radar
(d) Synthetic Aperture Radar (SAR)

42. Which type of radar system is commonly used in air traffic control to track and manage aircraft movement?
(a) Marine radar
(b) Ground-based radar
(c) Space-based radar
(d) Airborne radar

43. Which type of radar system is designed to provide high-resolution images of the Earth's surface using satellite-based technology?
(a) Weather radar
(b) Synthetic Aperture Radar (SAR)
(c) Ground-penetrating radar
(d) Airborne radar

44. Which type of radar system is used to detect and track objects in the ocean, such as ships and submarines?

(a) Airborne radar (b) Space-based radar

(c) Marine radar (d) Ground-based radar

45. Which type of radar system is employed for detecting and tracking moving objects, such as vehicles or aircraft, using continuous wave transmission?

(a) Continuous Wave (CW) radar

(b) Pulse-Doppler radar

(c) Ground-penetrating radar

(d) Weather radar

46. Which type of radar system is specifically designed for imaging subsurface features, such as buried objects or geological structures?

(a) Synthetic Aperture Radar (SAR)

(b) Weather radar

(c) Ground-penetrating radar

(d) Airborne radar

47. Which type of radar system is used for monitoring and controlling the speed of vehicles on roadways?

(a) Weather radar (b) Pulse-Doppler radar

(c) Police radar (d) Airborne radar

48. Which type of radar system is used for remote sensing and monitoring of the Earth's surface from satellites or aircraft?

(a) Airborne radar

(b) Synthetic Aperture Radar (SAR)

(c) Weather radar

(d) Ground-based radar

49. Which type of radar system is used for measuring the distance between two objects by measuring the time delay of the reflected signal?

(a) Continuous Wave (CW) radar

(b) Pulse-Doppler radar

(c) Altimeter radar

(d) Airborne radar

50. Which type of radar system is used in military applications to detect and track ballistic missiles or enemy aircraft?

(a) Weather radar (b) Marine radar

(c) Airborne radar (d) Surveillance radar

51. What does the Radar Equation describe?

(a) The power loss of radar signals during transmission

(b) The relationship between radar range and target size

(c) The Doppler shift of radar signals due to target velocity

(d) The relationship between radar signal power and received signal strength

52. Which factor affects the power density of the radar signal at the target in the Radar Equation?

(a) Transmit power of the radar

(b) Range from the radar to the target

(c) Radar cross-section of the target

(d) Gain of the radar antenna

53. What is the unit of measure for the radar cross-section (RCS) in the Radar Equation?

(a) Watts per square meter (W/m^2)

(b) Meters per second (m/s)

(c) Decibels (dB)

(d) Square meters (m^2)

54. Which term represents the losses in the Radar Equation due to atmospheric absorption and scattering?

(a) Receiver bandwidth

(b) Target range

(c) Antenna gain

(d) Propagation factor

55. Which factor affects the received signal power in the Radar Equation due to signal spreading over a larger area as the range increases?

(a) Antenna gain

(b) Radar cross-section of the target

(c) Target range

(d) Receiver bandwidth

56. How does an increase in the radar antenna gain affect the received signal power in the Radar Equation?

(a) It increases the received signal power.

(b) It decreases the received signal power.

(c) It has no effect on the received signal power.

(d) It affects the range, not the received signal power.

57. Which factor affects the received signal power due to losses in the receiver system, such as noise and impedance mismatch?

(a) Radar cross-section of the target

(b) Target range

(c) Antenna gain

(d) Receiver bandwidth

58. What term in the Radar Equation represents the ratio of the received signal power to the noise power in the receiver system?
(a) Propagation factor
(b) Receiver bandwidth
(c) Signal-to-noise ratio (SNR)
(d) Antenna gain

59. Which factor affects the received signal power due to the target's ability to reflect radar signals?
(a) Radar cross-section of the target
(b) Target range
(c) Antenna gain
(d) Transmit power of the radar

60. What is the general purpose of the Radar Equation?
(a) To calculate the velocity of a moving target
(b) To determine the target's position in 3D space
(c) To estimate the size and shape of the target
(d) To assess the performance and capabilities of a radar system

61. Which of the following is a primary function of a radar antenna?
(a) To generate radio waves
(b) To receive radio waves
(c) To process radar signals
(d) To amplify radar signals

62. Which type of antenna is commonly used in radar applications to provide a narrow beamwidth and high gain?
(a) Yagi antenna
(b) Parabolic dish antenna
(c) Whip antenna
(d) Loop antenna

63. Which property of an antenna determines its directivity or ability to concentrate energy in a specific direction?
(a) Gain (b) Beamwidth
(c) Polarization (d) Efficiency

64. Which type of polarization is commonly used in radar antennas to minimize the effects of signal fading due to multipath interference?
(a) Horizontal polarization
(b) Vertical polarization
(c) Circular polarization
(d) Elliptical polarization

65. Which characteristic of an antenna determines the angle at which the radar beam is emitted or received?
(a) Gain (b) Beamwidth
(c) Polarization (d) Directivity

66. Which type of antenna array is composed of multiple antenna elements arranged in a linear configuration?
(a) Planar array (b) Circular array
(c) Linear array (d) Phased array

67. Which property of an antenna refers to its ability to handle power without excessive losses?
(a) Efficiency (b) Bandwidth
(c) Impedance (d) Directivity

68. Which type of antenna is commonly used in portable or handheld radar devices?
(a) Parabolic dish antenna
(b) Whip antenna
(c) Horn antenna
(d) Log-periodic antenna

69. Which of the following factors can affect the radiation pattern and performance of a radar antenna?
(a) Weather conditions
(b) Target size
(c) Antenna material
(d) Power supply voltage

70. Which type of antenna is commonly used in radar altimeters for measuring the height above the ground?
(a) Parabolic dish antenna
(b) Whip antenna
(c) Horn antenna
(d) Slot antenna

71. What is the primary purpose of ranging in Radar systems?
(a) To determine the position of a target
(b) To measure the distance to a target
(c) To track the velocity of a target
(d) To identify the type of target

72. Which of the following techniques is commonly used for range measurement in Radar systems?
(a) Time of Arrival (TOA)
(b) Frequency Modulation (FM)
(c) Doppler Effect
(d) Pulse Compression

73. Which factor affects the accuracy of range measurement in Radar systems?

(a) Target size
(b) Target velocity
(c) Radar antenna gain
(d) Signal-to-noise ratio

74. What is target tracking in Radar systems?

(a) Measuring the target's range and velocity
(b) Identifying the target type
(c) Locating the target in 3D space
(d) Continuously monitoring the target's position and motion

75. Which technique is commonly used for target tracking in Radar systems to estimate the target's velocity?

(a) Doppler Effect
(b) Time of Arrival (TOA)
(c) Pulse Compression
(d) Frequency Modulation (FM)

76. Which term describes the ability of a Radar system to track multiple targets simultaneously?

(a) Monopulse tracking
(b) Sequential lobing
(c) Track-While-Scan (TWS)
(d) Pulse-Doppler tracking

77. Which technique is commonly used for angle measurement in Radar systems?

(a) Frequency Modulation (FM)
(b) Pulse Compression
(c) Monopulse tracking
(d) Time of Arrival (TOA)

78. What is the primary purpose of pulse repetition frequency (PRF) in Radar systems?

(a) To control the transmitted signal power
(b) To measure the target's range
(c) To determine the target's velocity
(d) To avoid range ambiguities

79. Which tracking mode allows a Radar system to maintain continuous track on a target while scanning the environment for new targets?

(a) Track-While-Scan (TWS)
(b) Sequential lobing
(c) Conical scanning
(d) Frequency Modulation (FM) tracking

80. What is the primary benefit of target tracking in Radar systems?

(a) Improved accuracy in range measurement
(b) Enhanced detection of small targets
(c) Ability to predict the target's future position
(d) Minimization of false alarms

81. What is the primary purpose of target detection in Radar systems?

(a) To measure the range to a target
(b) To identify the type of target
(c) To determine the target's velocity
(d) To detect the presence of a target

82. Which term describes the minimum detectable signal level required for reliable target detection in Radar systems?

(a) Sensitivity
(b) Signal-to-Noise Ratio (SNR)
(c) Antenna gain
(d) Bandwidth

83. Which factor affects the detection range of a Radar system?

(a) Target velocity
(b) Target size
(c) Radar cross-section of the target
(d) Target's material composition

84. Which of the following techniques is commonly used in Radar systems to mitigate the impact of noise and improve target detection?

(a) Pulse Compression
(b) Monopulse tracking
(c) Doppler Effect
(d) Frequency Modulation (FM)

85. What is the primary purpose of radar resolution in Radar systems?

(a) To determine the target's range
(b) To measure the target's size
(c) To estimate the target's velocity
(d) To distinguish between closely spaced targets

86. Which term describes the ability of a Radar system to distinguish between two closely spaced targets?

(a) Range resolution
(b) Angular resolution
(c) Doppler resolution
(d) Cross-range resolution

87. Which factor affects the range resolution of a Radar system?
(a) Target size
(b) Pulse duration
(c) Antenna gain
(d) Doppler frequency shift

88. Which term describes the ability of a Radar system to differentiate between two targets that are close together in angle?
(a) Range resolution
(b) Angular resolution
(c) Doppler resolution
(d) Cross-range resolution

89. Which factor affects the angular resolution of a Radar system?
(a) Target size
(b) Antenna gain
(c) Beamwidth
(d) Doppler frequency shift

90. What is the main benefit of improved resolution in Radar systems?
(a) Increased target detection range
(b) Enhanced accuracy in range measurement
(c) Improved tracking of moving targets
(d) Better identification of target characteristics

91. What does ROC stand for in the context of Radar systems?
(a) Radar Observation Control
(b) Range of Coverage
(c) Receiver Operation Characteristics
(d) Radar Object Classification

92. What is the primary purpose of an ROC curve in Radar systems?
(a) To analyze the radar transmitter's power output
(b) To determine the accuracy of radar measurements
(c) To evaluate the performance of radar detection
(d) To measure the range resolution of a radar system

93. What does the true positive rate represent in an ROC curve?
(a) The probability of correctly detecting targets
(b) The probability of incorrectly detecting clutter
(c) The probability of correctly identifying target characteristics
(d) The probability of incorrectly identifying background noise

94. What does the false positive rate represent in an ROC curve?
(a) The probability of correctly detecting targets
(b) The probability of incorrectly detecting clutter
(c) The probability of correctly identifying target characteristics
(d) The probability of incorrectly identifying background noise

95. Which term describes the measure of a target's ability to reflect radar signals?
(a) Target scattering coefficient
(b) Radar object classification
(c) Receiver operation characteristics
(d) Radar Cross Section (RCS)

96. Which of the following factors affects the RCS of a target?
(a) Target velocity
(b) Target range
(c) Target size and shape
(d) Target material composition

97. Which of the following targets would typically have a higher RCS value?
(a) Small, spherical target
(b) Large, flat target
(c) Small, irregularly shaped target
(d) Large, cylindrical target

98. How does the RCS of a target affect its detectability by a radar system?
(a) Higher RCS increases detectability
(b) Higher RCS decreases detectability
(c) RCS has no effect on detectability
(d) RCS affects the target's range, not detectability

99. Which factor, other than target size and shape, can affect the RCS of a target?
(a) Target velocity
(b) Target range
(c) Target material composition
(d) Target altitude

100. How can the RCS of a target be reduced for stealth or low observable applications?
(a) By increasing the target's velocity
(b) By reducing the target's range
(c) By altering the target's shape and surface characteristics
(d) By increasing the target's altitude

101. What is a satellite?
(a) A celestial body that orbits a planet
(b) A man-made object that orbits a celestial body
(c) A space station for human habitation
(d) A type of telescope used for astronomical observations

102. What is the primary purpose of communication satellites?
(a) Observing the Earth's surface for scientific research
(b) Conducting astronomical observations
(c) Providing wireless communication services
(d) Studying the composition of the atmosphere

103. Which of the following is an example of a natural satellite?
(a) The Hubble Space Telescope
(b) The International Space Station (ISS)
(c) The Moon
(d) The Mars Rover

104. Which satellite orbits the Earth at the same rotational speed as the Earth's rotation, appearing stationary from the ground?
(a) Polar satellite
(b) Geostationary satellite
(c) Low Earth Orbit (LEO) satellite
(d) Sun-synchronous satellite

105. What is the purpose of weather satellites?
(a) To study the composition of distant stars
(b) To observe and monitor weather patterns on Earth
(c) To study the geological features of other planets
(d) To search for signs of extraterrestrial life

106. Which of the following satellite orbits typically provides global coverage?
(a) Polar orbit
(b) Low Earth Orbit (LEO)
(c) Medium Earth Orbit (MEO)
(d) Highly Elliptical Orbit (HEO)

107. Which satellite component is responsible for generating electrical power?
(a) Antenna
(b) Transmitter
(c) Receiver
(d) Solar panels

108. Which type of satellite is used to collect data for mapping and environmental monitoring purposes?
(a) Communications satellite
(b) Navigation satellite
(c) Earth observation satellite
(d) Scientific research satellite

109. Which satellite component is responsible for controlling the satellite's orientation and stability in space?
(a) Transponder
(b) Solar panels
(c) Attitude control system
(d) Payload

110. Which satellite component is responsible for receiving signals from the ground and transmitting them back to Earth?
(a) Solar panels
(b) Antenna
(c) Transmitter
(d) Receiver

111. Which type of satellite is primarily used for communication purposes?
(a) Weather satellite
(b) Navigation satellite
(c) Communication satellite
(d) Earth observation satellite

112. Which type of satellite is used for studying the Earth's weather patterns and climate?
(a) Weather satellite
(b) Navigation satellite
(c) Communication satellite
(d) Earth observation satellite

113. Which type of satellite is used for determining accurate positioning and navigation on Earth?
(a) Weather satellite
(b) Navigation satellite
(c) Communication satellite
(d) Earth observation satellite

114. Which type of satellite is used for capturing images and data about the Earth's surface and environment?
(a) Weather satellite
(b) Navigation satellite
(c) Communication satellite
(d) Earth observation satellite

115. Which component of a satellite is responsible for generating electrical power?
(a) Antenna (b) Transmitter
(c) Receiver (d) Solar panels

116. Which component of a satellite is responsible for controlling the satellite's orientation and stability in space?
(a) Transponder
(b) Solar panels
(c) Attitude control system
(d) Payload

117. Which component of a satellite is responsible for receiving signals from the ground and transmitting them back to Earth?
(a) Solar panels (b) Antenna
(c) Transmitter (d) Receiver

118. Which component of a satellite is responsible for processing and amplifying signals received from the ground?
(a) Solar panels (b) Antenna
(c) Transmitter (d) Receiver

119. Which component of a satellite is responsible for storing and transmitting data or signals?
(a) Transponder
(b) Solar panels
(c) Attitude control system
(d) Payload

120. Which component of a satellite is responsible for carrying scientific instruments, sensors, or equipment for specific missions?
(a) Transponder
(b) Solar panels
(c) Attitude control system
(d) Payload

121. Which country successfully launched the first artificial satellite, Sputnik 1?
(a) United States
(b) China
(c) Russia (Soviet Union)
(d) Germany

122. Which type of vehicle is commonly used to launch satellites into space?
(a) Space shuttle
(b) Airplane
(c) Rocket
(d) Helicopter

123. What is the term for the altitude above the Earth's surface at which a satellite orbits?
(a) Geostationary (b) Suborbital
(c) Atmospheric (d) Altitude

124. Which type of satellite orbit is characterized by a fixed position relative to the Earth's surface?
(a) Low Earth Orbit (LEO)
(b) Geostationary Orbit (GEO)
(c) Medium Earth Orbit (MEO)
(d) Polar Orbit

125. Which type of satellite orbit is commonly used for global navigation systems like GPS?
(a) Low Earth Orbit (LEO)
(b) Geostationary Orbit (GEO)
(c) Medium Earth Orbit (MEO)
(d) Polar Orbit

126. Which type of satellite orbit is used for remote sensing and Earth observation satellites?
(a) Low Earth Orbit (LEO)
(b) Geostationary Orbit (GEO)
(c) Medium Earth Orbit (MEO)
(d) Polar Orbit

127. Which type of satellite orbit passes over or near the Earth's geographic poles?
(a) Low Earth Orbit (LEO)
(b) Geostationary Orbit (GEO)
(c) Medium Earth Orbit (MEO)
(d) Polar Orbit

128. What is the term for the speed required for a satellite to maintain a stable orbit around the Earth?
(a) Launch velocity (b) Escape velocity
(c) Orbital velocity (d) Terminal velocity

129. Which factor affects the duration of a satellite's orbital lifetime?
(a) Satellite's weight
(b) Satellite's size
(c) Atmospheric drag
(d) Launch location

130. What is the term for the process of intentionally deorbiting a satellite at the end of its operational life?
(a) Reentry
(b) Decommissioning
(c) Termination
(d) Disposal

131. What is the primary advantage of using satellites for communication purposes?

(a) Wide coverage area

(b) Low cost

(c) High bandwidth

(d) Low latency

132. Which application heavily relies on satellites for accurate navigation and positioning services?

(a) Weather forecasting

(b) Television broadcasting

(c) Internet connectivity

(d) Global positioning systems (GPS)

133. How do weather satellites contribute to meteorology and weather forecasting?

(a) By monitoring space weather events

(b) By studying climate change patterns

(c) By tracking atmospheric pollution levels

(d) By observing weather systems and cloud formations

134. What is the primary purpose of Earth observation satellites?

(a) Tracking celestial objects

(b) Studying the Earth's climate

(c) Monitoring natural disasters

(d) Exploring other planets

135. Which application utilizes satellites for collecting and relaying data from remote sensing instruments?

(a) Agricultural monitoring

(b) Air traffic control

(c) Financial transactions

(d) Power generation

136. How do satellites contribute to the field of environmental monitoring?

(a) By analyzing space debris

(b) By studying distant galaxies

(c) By tracking climate change indicators

(d) By monitoring seismic activity

137. What is the significance of satellite-based internet connectivity in remote and underserved areas?

(a) Enabling faster-than-light communication

(b) Facilitating seamless streaming services

(c) Bridging the digital divide

(d) Supporting online gaming networks

138. How do satellites contribute to disaster management and emergency response efforts?

(a) By predicting earthquakes

(b) By providing early warnings for tsunamis

(c) By coordinating search and rescue operations

(d) By assessing building code violations

139. What is the primary application of satellite imagery in mapping and urban planning?

(a) Monitoring wildlife populations

(b) Assessing air quality levels

(c) Identifying land-use patterns

(d) Measuring seismic activity

140. How do satellites contribute to scientific research and space exploration?

(a) By monitoring the Sun's activities

(b) By studying distant galaxies

(c) By collecting data on cosmic radiation

(d) By aiding in spacecraft navigation

141. What is submarine telegraphy?

(a) The transmission of signals through underwater cables

(b) Communication using flags and visual signals on ships

(c) Wireless communication between submarines

(d) Sending Morse code messages through satellite links

142. When did the first successful submarine telegraph cable connection between continents occur?

(a) 1800s (b) 1900s

(c) 2000s (d) 1700s

143. Which cable system facilitated the first transatlantic telegraph communication?

(a) TAT-1

(b) TPC-5

(c) HAW-5

(d) Atlantic Telegraph Cable

144. What was the transmission medium used in early submarine telegraphy systems?

(a) Fiber optics (b) Copper wires

(c) Radio waves (d) Electrical currents

145. Which material was commonly used to insulate early submarine telegraph cables?

(a) Rubber

(b) Plastic

(c) Glass

(d) Gutta-percha

146. What was the major challenge faced during the early days of submarine telegraphy?
(a) Signal interference from radio waves
(b) Limited cable length and signal degradation
(c) Insufficient power supply for cable transmission
(d) Difficulty in laying and repairing submarine cables

147. What role did cable ships play in the development of submarine telegraphy?
(a) Laying and repairing submarine telegraph cables
(b) Transmitting signals wirelessly
(c) Developing encryption techniques for secure communication
(d) Conducting underwater research and exploration

148. How were messages typically transmitted in early submarine telegraphy systems?
(a) Using Morse code
(b) Sending voice signals
(c) Transmitting digital data packets
(d) Utilizing semaphore signals

149. Which major event accelerated the adoption of submarine telegraphy on a global scale?
(a) Industrial Revolution
(b) World War I
(c) Invention of radio
(d) Space race

150. How has submarine telegraphy evolved over time?
(a) Transition to wireless communication systems
(b) Introduction of fiber optic cables
(c) Integration with satellite communication
(d) All of the above

151. What is the primary consideration when selecting submarine cable routes?
(a) Cost
(b) Cable length
(c) Geological features
(d) Maintenance requirements

152. Which factor is important in minimizing signal loss and maintaining data transmission quality in submarine cables?
(a) Cable diameter
(b) Cable material
(c) Cable route length
(d) Cable route directness

153. Which consideration is important to ensure the security and protection of submarine cables?
(a) Avoiding marine life habitats
(b) Selecting routes away from fishing areas
(c) Assessing potential damage from anchors and fishing gear
(d) Choosing routes with high internet demand

154. What role does international law play in selecting submarine cable routes?
(a) It determines the cost of the cable installation.
(b) It defines the allowed cable lengths.
(c) It regulates cable ownership and operation.
(d) It governs the selection of landing points.

155. Which consideration is crucial for selecting submarine cable routes in areas prone to natural disasters?
(a) Avoiding tectonic plate boundaries
(b) Selecting routes near population centers
(c) Assessing seismic activity and vulnerability
(d) Choosing routes with favorable ocean currents

156. Which factor is important for selecting submarine cable routes in regions with heavy maritime traffic?
(a) Avoiding shipping lanes
(b) Selecting routes near major ports
(c) Choosing routes with high internet demand
(d) Assessing underwater geological features

157. Which consideration is important for selecting submarine cable routes in regions with extreme temperature variations?
(a) Cable insulation thickness
(b) Cable burial depth
(c) Availability of repair vessels
(d) Cable route directness

158. What is the importance of selecting cable routes with favorable ocean currents?
(a) It reduces the risk of cable entanglement with marine life.
(b) It minimizes signal loss and attenuation.
(c) It facilitates cable laying and maintenance operations.
(d) It increases the lifespan of the submarine cables.

159. Which factor is important in selecting cable routes for intercontinental connectivity?
(a) Availability of landing stations
(b) Cable length
(c) Cable burial depth
(d) Geological stability

160. What is the benefit of selecting direct cable routes for long-distance submarine cables?
(a) Reduced latency and improved signal quality
(b) Lower cost of cable installation
(c) Enhanced protection against cable damage
(d) Increased cable capacity and bandwidth

161. What is Morse code?
(a) A binary code used in computers
(b) A system of communication using dots and dashes
(c) A musical notation system
(d) A programming language

162. Who is credited with inventing Morse code?
(a) Samuel Morse
(b) Alexander Graham Bell
(c) Thomas Edison
(d) Nikola Tesla

163. What is the basic unit of time in Morse code?
(a) Dash (b) Dot
(c) Letter (d) Word

164. Which Morse code symbol represents the letter "A"?
(a) -. (b) –
(c) . (d) ..

165. What does the Morse code symbol "---" represent?
(a) The letter "O" (b) The letter "S"
(c) The letter "T" (d) The letter "N"

166. How is the space between letters represented in Morse code?
(a) A single dot
(b) Three dots
(c) A dash
(d) A gap equal to three dots

167. Which Morse code symbol represents the number "5"?
(a) .--. (b) .----
(c) ..... (d) ....-

168. Which Morse code symbol represents the question mark "?"
(a) .-.. (b) ..--
(c) ..-.- (d) ..--..

169. What does the Morse code symbol "-.-.-." represent?
(a) The letter "R" (b) The letter "K"
(c) The letter "C" (d) The letter "X"

170. How is the end of a Morse code message typically represented?
(a) The word "END" in Morse code
(b) A series of dots
(c) A long dash
(d) A short pause

Answers

1. (*b*)	**2.** (*b*)	**3.** (*d*)	**4.** (*a*)	**5.** (*a*)	**6.** (*c*)	**7.** (*b*)	**8.** (*a*)	**9.** (*b*)	**10.** (*d*)
11. (*a*)	**12.** (*a*)	**13.** (*b*)	**14.** (*d*)	**15.** (*c*)	**16.** (*a*)	**17.** (*c*)	**18.** (*d*)	**19.** (*c*)	**20.** (*b*)
21. (*a*)	**22.** (*a*)	**23.** (*a*)	**24.** (*a*)	**25.** (*d*)	**26.** (*b*)	**27.** (*c*)	**28.** (*b*)	**29.** (*c*)	**30.** (*d*)
31. (*d*)	**32.** (*a*)	**33.** (*a*)	**34.** (*d*)	**35.** (*a*)	**36.** (*c*)	**37.** (*c*)	**38.** (*b*)	**39.** (*c*)	**40.** (*d*)
41. (*c*)	**42.** (*b*)	**43.** (*b*)	**44.** (*c*)	**45.** (*a*)	**46.** (*c*)	**47.** (*c*)	**48.** (*b*)	**49.** (*c*)	**50.** (*d*)
51. (*d*)	**52.** (*a*)	**53.** (*d*)	**54.** (*d*)	**55.** (*c*)	**56.** (*a*)	**57.** (*d*)	**58.** (*c*)	**59.** (*a*)	**60.** (*d*)
61. (*b*)	**62.** (*b*)	**63.** (*a*)	**64.** (*c*)	**65.** (*b*)	**66.** (*c*)	**67.** (*a*)	**68.** (*b*)	**69.** (*a*)	**70.** (*d*)
71. (*b*)	**72.** (*a*)	**73.** (*d*)	**74.** (*d*)	**75.** (*a*)	**76.** (*c*)	**77.** (*c*)	**78.** (*d*)	**79.** (*a*)	**80.** (*c*)
81. (*d*)	**82.** (*a*)	**83.** (*c*)	**84.** (*a*)	**85.** (*d*)	**86.** (*a*)	**87.** (*b*)	**88.** (*b*)	**89.** (*c*)	**90.** (*d*)
91. (*c*)	**92.** (*c*)	**93.** (*a*)	**94.** (*b*)	**95.** (*d*)	**96.** (*c*)	**97.** (*b*)	**98.** (*a*)	**99.** (*c*)	**100.** (*c*)
101. (*b*)	**102.** (*c*)	**103.** (*c*)	**104.** (*b*)	**105.** (*b*)	**106.** (*c*)	**107.** (*d*)	**108.** (*c*)	**109.** (*c*)	**110.** (*b*)
111. (*c*)	**112.** (*a*)	**113.** (*b*)	**114.** (*d*)	**115.** (*d*)	**116.** (*c*)	**117.** (*b*)	**118.** (*d*)	**119.** (*a*)	**120.** (*d*)
121. (*c*)	**122.** (*c*)	**123.** (*d*)	**124.** (*b*)	**125.** (*c*)	**126.** (*a*)	**127.** (*d*)	**128.** (*c*)	**129.** (*c*)	**130.** (*b*)
131. (*a*)	**132.** (*d*)	**133.** (*d*)	**134.** (*c*)	**135.** (*a*)	**136.** (*c*)	**137.** (*c*)	**138.** (*c*)	**139.** (*c*)	**140.** (*d*)
141. (*a*)	**142.** (*a*)	**143.** (*d*)	**144.** (*b*)	**145.** (*d*)	**146.** (*b*)	**147.** (*a*)	**148.** (*a*)	**149.** (*a*)	**150.** (*d*)
151. (*c*)	**152.** (*c*)	**153.** (*c*)	**154.** (*c*)	**155.** (*c*)	**156.** (*a*)	**157.** (*a*)	**158.** (*c*)	**159.** (*a*)	**160.** (*a*)
161. (*b*)	**162.** (*a*)	**163.** (*b*)	**164.** (*c*)	**165.** (*a*)	**166.** (*d*)	**167.** (*c*)	**168.** (*d*)	**169.** (*c*)	**170.** (*b*)

Explanations

1. Long-range coverage. Radio waves have the ability to propagate over long distances, making them suitable for long-range communication. While radio communication can provide high data transfer rates, immunity to interference, and cost-effective solutions, none of these options are as directly related to the advantage of long-range coverage.

   Hence, the correct answer is option (b).

2. To convert digital signals into analog signals. Modulation is the process of impressing information onto a carrier wave, typically by varying its amplitude, frequency, or phase. In radio communication, modulation is used to convert digital signals (which are typically in binary form) into analog signals that can be transmitted over the airwaves.

   Hence, the correct answer is option (b).

3. Quadrature amplitude modulation (QAM). QAM is widely used in modern wireless communication systems because it allows for high data transfer rates by encoding multiple bits per symbol. Both AM and FM are analog modulation techniques, while QAM is a digital modulation technique.

   Hence, the correct answer is option (d).

4. To amplify the received signal. A repeater receives a weak or deteriorated signal and retransmits it with increased power, allowing it to cover a larger distance. Repeaters do not convert analog signals

to digital signals, provide encryption, or establish direct connections between devices.

Hence, the correct answer is option (a).

5. Susceptibility to noise and interference. Analog modulation techniques, such as AM and FM, are more vulnerable to noise and interference compared to digital modulation techniques. They can experience signal degradation and reduced quality due to external factors.

Hence, the correct answer is option (a).

6. To extract the original information from the modulated signal. A demodulator, also known as a detector, is used to recover the original information from a modulated signal. It extracts the modulating signal from the carrier wave, allowing for the retrieval of the transmitted data.

Hence, the correct answer is option (c).

7. Simultaneous transmission and reception on the same frequency. Simplex communication refers to a communication mode where data can only flow in one direction at a time. In simplex communication, transmission and reception occur on the same frequency, but not simultaneously. Two-way communication between two devices is referred to as duplex communication.

Hence, the correct answer is option (b).

8. Walkie-talkie. In a half-duplex communication system, communication can occur in both directions, but not simultaneously. Walkie-talkies typically operate in half-duplex mode, allowing users to take turns transmitting and receiving messages.

Hence, the correct answer is option (a).

9. 2.4 GHz. The 2.4 GHz frequency band is commonly used for Wi-Fi communication. It provides good signal propagation and is compatible with a wide range of Wi-Fi devices. While other frequency bands like 5 GHz are also used for Wi-Fi, 2.4 GHz is the most widely adopted.

Hence, the correct answer is option (b).

10. Short-range coverage due to signal blockage. In urban areas, the presence of buildings, structures, and other obstacles can obstruct and attenuate radio signals, reducing their effective range. Limited bandwidth availability, high equipment cost, and low data transfer rates are not directly related to the disadvantage of signal blockage in urban areas.

Hence, the correct answer is option (d).

11. Enhanced mobility. Robotic radio communication systems allow for wireless communication between robots and their control systems, providing them with the ability to move freely and operate at a distance. While the other options may also have their merits, enhanced mobility is the primary advantage of using robotic radio communication systems.

Hence, the correct answer is option (a).

12. To receive and transmit radio signals. A radio transceiver in a robotic communication system is responsible for both receiving and transmitting radio signals. It enables bidirectional communication between the robot and its control system.

Hence, the correct answer is option (a).

13. UHF (Ultra High Frequency). The UHF frequency band, typically ranging from 300 MHz to 3 GHz, is commonly used for robotic radio communication systems. It offers a good balance between signal propagation and data transfer rates.

Hence, the correct answer is option (b).

14. To transmit and receive radio signals. An antenna in a robotic radio communication system is responsible for transmitting and receiving radio signals. It acts as a conduit for the electromagnetic waves, allowing the robot to communicate wirelessly.

Hence, the correct answer is option (d).

15. Susceptibility to interference. Radio waves used for robotic communication can be vulnerable to interference from other devices or environmental factors, leading to signal degradation or loss. While the other options may also pose challenges in certain scenarios, susceptibility to interference is a specific disadvantage of radio waves.

Hence, the correct answer is option (c).

16. To amplify radio signals. A repeater in robotic radio communication systems receives weak or deteriorated signals and retransmits them with increased power, effectively extending the communication range. It does not control robotic movements, encrypt communication, or impact battery life.

Hence, the correct answer is option (a).

17. Zigbee. Zigbee is a commonly used wireless communication protocol in robotic systems, especially for applications requiring low-power, short-range communication. Bluetooth, Wi-Fi, and NFC are also used in certain robotic applications, but Zigbee is specifically known for its suitability in robotics.

Hence, the correct answer is option (c).

18. To correct transmission errors. Error correction techniques are employed in robotic radio communication systems to detect and correct errors that may occur during transmission. These techniques ensure reliable and accurate data communication between the robot and its control system.

Hence, the correct answer is option (d).

19. Robotic arms in a manufacturing line exchanging sensor data. In this scenario, the robotic arms are communicating with each other, exchanging sensor data or coordinating their actions to perform a task. The other options involve communication between a robot and a human or external devices.

Hence, the correct answer is option (c).

20. To encode data onto a carrier wave. Modulation in robotic radio communication systems involves encoding the digital data onto a carrier wave, allowing it to be transmitted wirelessly. Modulation techniques, such as amplitude modulation or frequency modulation, are used to achieve this data encoding.

Hence, the correct answer is option (b).

21. Electromagnetic waves. Radio waves are a form of electromagnetic waves that can propagate through space without the need for a medium. They are part of the electromagnetic spectrum, which includes other waves such as visible light, microwaves, and X-rays.

Hence, the correct answer is option (a).

22. Radio waves can propagate through a vacuum. Unlike sound waves, radio waves do not require a physical medium and can travel through a vacuum, such as space. They can also propagate through air, water, and other substances, but their ability to penetrate obstacles may vary depending on the frequency and nature of the obstacles.

Hence, the correct answer is option (a).

23. Low-frequency range. Zigbee communication typically operates in the 2.4 GHz frequency band, which is considered a low-frequency range. This frequency band offers good signal penetration and is suitable for short-range wireless communication in various applications, including robotics, home automation, and industrial control systems.

Hence, the correct answer is option (a).

24. Zigbee operates on a single hop communication model. Zigbee communication follows a single hop model, where devices directly communicate with each other within a limited range. Zigbee is designed for low-power, low-data-rate applications, making it suitable for applications where energy efficiency and scalability are important.

Hence, the correct answer is option (a).

25. Zigbee uses a mesh topology. Zigbee networks are typically organized in a mesh topology, where devices can communicate with each other directly or through intermediate devices (routers) to extend the network coverage. This allows for reliable and robust communication, as multiple paths are available for data transmission.

Hence, the correct answer is option (d).

26. Hence, the correct answer is option (b).

Few tens of meters. In an indoor environment, the typical range of Zigbee communication is a few tens of meters. The exact range can vary depending on factors such as the presence of obstacles, signal interference, and the transmit power of the devices. Zigbee's focus is on short-range communication within a localized area.

27. Low power consumption. Zigbee communication is designed for low-power applications, making it suitable for robotic systems that operate on limited power resources. While Zigbee offers moderate data transfer rates and is less susceptible to interference compared to some other wireless technologies, its primary advantage lies in its low power consumption.

Hence, the correct answer is option (c).

28. Antenna. In robotic radio communication systems using Zigbee, an antenna is an essential component. The antenna is responsible for transmitting and receiving Zigbee signals, facilitating wireless communication between the robot and its control system. The other options, such as modulator, demodulator, and power amplifier, may be involved in the overall system but are not specific to Zigbee.

Hence, the correct answer is option (b).

29. Extended network coverage. Using a mesh network in robotic radio communication systems allows for extended network coverage as devices can communicate with each other through multiple paths, leveraging the routers present in the network. While a mesh network offers advantages such as fault tolerance and self-healing capabilities, extended network coverage is directly associated with its use.

Hence, the correct answer is option (c).

30. To ensure reliable data transmission. Error checking and correction techniques in robotic radio communication systems are employed to detect and correct transmission errors. These techniques help ensure that the data transmitted between the robot and its control system is accurate and reliable, reducing the chances of data corruption or loss.

Hence, the correct answer is option (d).

31. Radio Detection and Ranging. RADAR is an acronym for Radio Detection and Ranging. It is a technology that uses radio waves to detect and determine the range, angle, and velocity of objects.

Hence, the correct answer is option (d).

32. Reflection. RADAR relies on the principle of reflection, where radio waves are transmitted towards an object, and the reflected waves are detected. By analyzing the time delay and properties of the reflected waves, RADAR can determine the presence and characteristics of objects.

Hence, the correct answer is option (a).

33. Weather forecasting. RADAR is widely used in weather forecasting to detect and track precipitation, storm systems, and other atmospheric phenomena. While RADAR technology has diverse applications, weather forecasting is one of its prominent uses.

Hence, the correct answer is option (a).

34. Wavelength. RADAR can determine the range of objects based on the time taken for the radio waves to travel to the object and back. This is achieved by measuring the time delay between the transmitted and received waves. The wavelength of the radio waves is used to calculate the range.

Hence, the correct answer is option (d).

35. Pulsed RADAR. Pulsed RADAR is commonly used for air traffic control as it allows for accurate range measurement and detection of moving targets. Continuous Wave RADAR is used for applications such as speed guns, while Synthetic Aperture RADAR and Passive RADAR have different specialized uses.

Hence, the correct answer is option (a).

36. To calculate the velocity of an object. The Doppler effect is used in RADAR to determine the velocity of a moving object. By measuring the frequency shift between the transmitted and received waves, RADAR can calculate the relative speed of the object.

Hence, the correct answer is option (c).

37. Spaceborne RADAR. Spaceborne RADAR systems, such as Synthetic Aperture RADAR (SAR), are used to generate high-resolution images of the Earth's surface. By combining multiple radar measurements taken from space, SAR can create detailed images for various applications, including mapping and monitoring.

Hence, the correct answer is option (c).

38. Ability to see through obstacles. One of the advantages of RADAR over other sensing technologies is its ability to penetrate certain obstacles, such as fog, rain, or foliage. RADAR can detect objects behind obstructions, making it useful in various applications, including navigation and object detection.

Hence, the correct answer is option (b).

39. Pulse duration. The resolution of a RADAR system is determined by the pulse duration, which is the time interval during which the radar transmits a pulse. A shorter pulse duration leads to better range resolution and the ability to distinguish between closely spaced objects.

Hence, the correct answer is option (c).

40. Ground Penetrating RADAR. Ground Penetrating RADAR is an example of an active RADAR system as it emits radio waves and analyzes the reflected signals to determine subsurface features. Radio telescopes, infrared cameras, and sonar are passive sensing technologies that rely on the detection of external signals.

Hence, the correct answer is option (d).

41. Weather radar. Weather radar systems are specifically designed for monitoring and tracking weather phenomena, such as precipitation, storms, and severe weather conditions. These radar systems provide valuable information for weather forecasting and monitoring purposes.

Hence, the correct answer is option (c).

42. Ground-based radar. Ground-based radar systems are extensively used in air traffic control to monitor the position, altitude, and movement of aircraft. These radar systems help ensure safe and efficient air traffic management.

Hence, the correct answer is option (b).

43. Synthetic Aperture Radar (SAR). SAR systems use radar technology mounted on satellites or aircraft to capture high-resolution images of the Earth's surface. SAR allows for detailed mapping, environmental monitoring, and surveillance applications.

Hence, the correct answer is option (b).

44. Marine radar. Marine radar systems are specifically designed for maritime applications. They are used to detect and track objects on the water, including ships, boats, and submarines. These radar systems aid in navigation, collision avoidance, and maritime security.

    Hence, the correct answer is option (c).

45. Continuous Wave (CW) radar. CW radar systems use continuous transmission of radio waves to detect and track moving objects. They rely on the Doppler effect to measure the velocity of the targets and are commonly used in speed guns, traffic control, and motion detection applications.

    Hence, the correct answer is option (a).

46. Ground-penetrating radar. Ground-penetrating radar (GPR) systems emit radio waves into the ground and measure the reflections to create subsurface images. GPR is used in archaeological surveys, utility detection, and geological studies.

    Hence, the correct answer is option (c).

47. Police radar. Police radar systems are employed by law enforcement agencies to monitor and enforce speed limits on roadways. These radar systems measure the velocity of moving vehicles and assist in traffic law enforcement.

    Hence, the correct answer is option (c).

48. Synthetic Aperture Radar (SAR). SAR systems mounted on satellites or aircraft are extensively used for remote sensing and Earth observation purposes. They provide detailed images of the Earth's surface, aiding in applications such as land cover mapping, disaster monitoring, and environmental studies.

    Hence, the correct answer is option (b).

49. Altimeter radar. Altimeter radar systems are specifically designed to measure the altitude or height of an object above a reference point. They calculate the distance based on the time taken for the radar signal to travel to the object and back.

    Hence, the correct answer is option (c).

50. Surveillance radar. Surveillance radar systems are used for military applications to detect, track, and monitor airborne objects such as ballistic missiles, enemy aircraft, or unmanned aerial vehicles (UAVs). These radar systems aid in situational awareness and defense capabilities.

    Hence, the correct answer is option (d).

51. The relationship between radar signal power and received signal strength. The Radar Equation mathematically describes the relationship between the power of the transmitted radar signal, the properties of the radar system, the characteristics of the target, and the received signal strength.

    Hence, the correct answer is option (d).

52. Transmit power of the radar. The power density of the radar signal at the target is directly influenced by the transmit power of the radar system. A higher transmit power leads to a stronger signal at the target.

    Hence, the correct answer is option (a).

53. Square meters (m^2). The radar cross-section (RCS) is a measure of the target's ability to reflect radar signals and is expressed in square meters (m^2). It represents the effective area that the target presents to the radar system.

    Hence, the correct answer is option (d).

54. Propagation factor. The propagation factor in the Radar Equation accounts for the losses in the radar signal due to atmospheric absorption, scattering, and other factors that affect the signal's propagation from the radar to the target.

    Hence, the correct answer is option (d).

55. Target range. As the target range increases, the radar signal spreads over a larger area, resulting in a decrease in the received signal power. The Radar Equation considers this effect by including the range factor in the equation.

    Hence, the correct answer is option (c).

56. It increases the received signal power. An increase in the radar antenna gain improves the sensitivity of the radar system, allowing it to capture a stronger signal from the target. This results in an increase in the received signal power according to the Radar Equation.

    Hence, the correct answer is option (a).

57. Receiver bandwidth. The receiver bandwidth accounts for losses in the receiver system, such as noise and impedance mismatch, which can reduce the quality of the received signal. A wider receiver bandwidth can improve the received signal power.

    Hence, the correct answer is option (d).

58. Signal-to-noise ratio (SNR). The signal-to-noise ratio (SNR) represents the ratio of the received signal power to the noise power in the receiver system. A higher SNR indicates a stronger signal relative to the noise, resulting in better detection and performance.

    Hence, the correct answer is option (c).

59. Radar cross-section of the target. The radar cross-section (RCS) of the target influences the received signal power. A larger RCS indicates that the target reflects more radar signals, resulting in a stronger received signal power according to the Radar Equation.

Hence, the correct answer is option (a).

60. To assess the performance and capabilities of a radar system. The Radar Equation provides a mathematical model that allows engineers and radar operators to evaluate and optimize the performance of radar systems. It helps estimate the received signal power, assess detection capabilities, and compare different radar system configurations.

Hence, the correct answer is option (d).

61. To receive radio waves. The primary function of a radar antenna is to receive radio waves reflected by targets in the environment. The antenna captures the incoming signals and transfers them to the radar system for processing.

Hence, the correct answer is option (b).

62. Parabolic dish antenna. Parabolic dish antennas are commonly used in radar applications due to their ability to provide high gain and a narrow beamwidth. The shape of the dish focuses the radio waves into a concentrated beam, enabling long-range and directional radar coverage.

Hence, the correct answer is option (b).

63. Gain. Gain is a measure of an antenna's ability to concentrate energy in a specific direction. A higher gain indicates greater directivity, allowing the antenna to focus the emitted or received signals in a narrower beam, providing increased sensitivity and range.

Hence, the correct answer is option (a).

64. Circular polarization. Circular polarization is commonly used in radar antennas to minimize the effects of signal fading caused by multipath interference. Circularly polarized waves can rotate their polarization as they reflect off objects, reducing the impact of signal cancellation or degradation.

Hence, the correct answer is option (c).

65. Beamwidth. Beamwidth is a measure of the angular coverage of the radar beam emitted or received by an antenna. It determines the angle at which the radar beam is concentrated, and a narrower beamwidth corresponds to a more focused and directional antenna.

Hence, the correct answer is option (b).

66. Linear array. A linear array consists of multiple antenna elements arranged in a line. It allows for beam steering in a specific direction by varying the phase and amplitude of the signals fed to the individual elements.

Hence, the correct answer is option (c).

67. Efficiency. Efficiency is a measure of an antenna's ability to handle power without significant losses. An efficient antenna minimizes power dissipation and maximizes power transfer between the antenna and the transmission or reception system.

Hence, the correct answer is option (a).

68. Whip antenna. Whip antennas, also known as rod antennas, are commonly used in portable or handheld radar devices due to their compact size and ease of use. They are typically composed of a flexible metal rod and provide omnidirectional coverage.

Hence, the correct answer is option (b).

69. Weather conditions. Weather conditions, such as rain, fog, or atmospheric disturbances, can affect the propagation of radio waves and influence the radiation pattern and performance of a radar antenna. These factors can introduce signal attenuation, scattering, or interference.

Hence, the correct answer is option (a).

70. Slot antenna. Slot antennas are commonly used in radar altimeters for measuring the height above the ground. They consist of a narrow slot cut into a conducting surface and provide a relatively wide beamwidth for altitude measurement purposes.

Hence, the correct answer is option (d).

71. To measure the distance to a target. Ranging in Radar systems refers to the process of measuring the distance between the Radar system and a target. It provides crucial information about the target's range, allowing for effective detection and tracking.

Hence, the correct answer is option (b).

72. Time of Arrival (TOA). Time of Arrival (TOA) is a common technique used for range measurement in Radar systems. It involves measuring the time taken for a transmitted pulse to travel to the target and return. By knowing the speed of propagation, the range can be calculated.

Hence, the correct answer is option (a).

73. Signal-to-noise ratio. The accuracy of range measurement in Radar systems is influenced by the Signal-to-Noise Ratio (SNR). A higher SNR provides a stronger and clearer received signal, resulting in improved accuracy in range estimation.

Hence, the correct answer is option (d).

74. Continuously monitoring the target's position and motion. Target tracking in Radar systems involves continuously monitoring the position, velocity, and other parameters of a target over time. It allows for the estimation of target trajectory and facilitates reliable tracking of moving targets.

Hence, the correct answer is option (d).

75. Doppler Effect. The Doppler Effect is commonly used for target tracking in Radar systems to estimate the target's velocity. It analyzes the change in frequency of the reflected signal due to the relative motion between the Radar system and the target.

Hence, the correct answer is option (a).

76. Track-While-Scan (TWS). Track-While-Scan (TWS) is a technique used in Radar systems to simultaneously track multiple targets. It involves continuously scanning the environment while maintaining track on detected targets, allowing for efficient tracking of multiple objects.

Hence, the correct answer is option (c).

77. Monopulse tracking. Monopulse tracking is a technique used in Radar systems for accurate angle measurement of targets. It relies on multiple antenna beams with overlapping coverage to determine the target's direction or angle relative to the Radar system.

Hence, the correct answer is option (c).

78. To avoid range ambiguities. Pulse Repetition Frequency (PRF) in Radar systems is primarily used to avoid range ambiguities. By selecting an appropriate PRF, the Radar system can prevent overlapping or confusion of target echoes at different ranges.

Hence, the correct answer is option (d).

79. Track-While-Scan (TWS). Track-While-Scan (TWS) is a tracking mode in Radar systems that enables the system to maintain continuous track on a target while simultaneously scanning the environment for new targets. It ensures uninterrupted monitoring of the tracked target while searching for additional targets.

Hence, the correct answer is option (a).

80. Ability to predict the target's future position. Target tracking in Radar systems allows for the prediction of a target's future position based on its current motion. This information is crucial for tasks such as interception, collision avoidance, and target engagement.

Hence, the correct answer is option (c).

81. To detect the presence of a target. Target detection in Radar systems refers to the process of identifying the existence of a target within the radar coverage area. It is essential for initiating further analysis, tracking, and decision-making.

Hence, the correct answer is option (d).

82. Sensitivity. Sensitivity in Radar systems refers to the minimum detectable signal level necessary for reliable target detection. A higher sensitivity allows for the detection of weaker signals and enhances the system's ability to identify targets.

Hence, the correct answer is option (a).

83. Radar cross-section of the target. The detection range of a Radar system is primarily influenced by the radar cross-section (RCS) of the target. A larger RCS corresponds to a stronger reflected signal, enabling detection at longer ranges.

Hence, the correct answer is option (c).

84. Pulse Compression. Pulse Compression is a technique commonly used in Radar systems to improve target detection by reducing the impact of noise. It involves transmitting a long coded pulse and processing the received echo to enhance the signal-to-noise ratio.

Hence, the correct answer is option (a).

85. To distinguish between closely spaced targets. Radar resolution in Radar systems refers to the system's ability to differentiate between two or more targets that are closely spaced in range or angle. It enables target discrimination and identification in complex scenarios.

Hence, the correct answer is option (d).

86. Range resolution. Range resolution in Radar systems refers to the system's ability to distinguish between two targets that are close together along the range axis. It is determined by the duration of the radar pulse and affects the system's ability to resolve targets in the radial direction.

Hence, the correct answer is option (a).

87. Pulse duration. The range resolution of a Radar system is primarily influenced by the pulse duration. A shorter pulse duration leads to better range resolution, allowing the system to differentiate between targets that are closely spaced along the range axis.

Hence, the correct answer is option (b).

88. Angular resolution. Angular resolution in Radar systems refers to the system's ability to distinguish between two targets that are close together in angle. It depends on the beamwidth of the radar antenna and affects the system's ability to resolve targets in the azimuth or elevation direction.
Hence, the correct answer is option (b).

89. Beamwidth. The angular resolution of a Radar system is primarily influenced by the beamwidth of the radar antenna. A narrower beamwidth results in better angular resolution, enabling the system to differentiate between targets that are close together in angle.
Hence, the correct answer is option (c).

90. Better identification of target characteristics. Improved resolution in Radar systems facilitates better identification of target characteristics, such as size, shape, and composition. It enables the system to extract more detailed information about the targets, enhancing situational awareness and decision-making.
Hence, the correct answer is option (d).

91. Receiver Operation Characteristics. ROC stands for Receiver Operation Characteristics and refers to a graphical representation that shows the performance of a radar receiver system at different detection thresholds.
Hence, the correct answer is option (c).

92. To evaluate the performance of radar detection. An ROC curve in Radar systems is used to assess the performance of radar detection by plotting the true positive rate against the false positive rate at different detection thresholds. It helps determine the trade-off between detection accuracy and false alarms.
Hence, the correct answer is option (c).

93. The probability of correctly detecting targets. The true positive rate in an ROC curve represents the probability of correctly detecting targets or true positives. It indicates the effectiveness of the radar system in detecting actual targets.
Hence, the correct answer is option (a).

94. The probability of incorrectly detecting clutter. The false positive rate in an ROC curve represents the probability of incorrectly detecting clutter or false positives. It reflects the tendency of the radar system to generate false alarms.
Hence, the correct answer is option (b).

95. Radar Cross Section (RCS). Radar Cross Section (RCS) is a measure of a target's ability to reflect radar signals. It quantifies the effective area that the target presents to the radar system and is used to assess the target's detectability.
Hence, the correct answer is option (d).

96. Target size and shape. The RCS of a target is primarily influenced by its size and shape. Targets with larger effective areas or complex shapes tend to have higher RCS values, making them more detectable by radar systems.
Hence, the correct answer is option (c).

97. Large, flat target. A large, flat target tends to have a higher RCS value compared to a small, spherical or irregularly shaped target. The larger effective area and reflection characteristics of the flat surface contribute to a stronger radar reflection.
Hence, the correct answer is option (b).

98. Higher RCS increases detectability. A higher RCS indicates a target's stronger reflection of radar signals, which improves its detectability by a radar system. Targets with larger RCS values are more likely to produce detectable echoes.
Hence, the correct answer is option (a).

99. Target material composition. In addition to target size and shape, the material composition of a target can also affect its RCS. Different materials have varying reflection properties, leading to differences in the RCS for targets made of different substances.
Hence, the correct answer is option (c).

100. By altering the target's shape and surface characteristics. To reduce the RCS for stealth or low observable applications, targets are designed with specific shapes and surface treatments that minimize radar reflections and scattering. These design features help to reduce the detectability of the target by radar systems.
Hence, the correct answer is option (c).

101. A man-made object that orbits a celestial body. In the context of space exploration, a satellite refers to a man-made object that is intentionally placed into orbit around a celestial body, such as the Earth or another planet.
Hence, the correct answer is option (b).

102. Providing wireless communication services. Communication satellites are primarily designed and deployed to facilitate various forms of wireless communication, including television broadcasting, internet connectivity, telephone services, and data transmission.
Hence, the correct answer is option (c).

103. The Moon. The Moon is an example of a natural satellite. It is a celestial body that orbits around the Earth, and it plays a significant role in Earth's tides and other natural phenomena.
Hence, the correct answer is option (c).

104. Geostationary satellite. A geostationary satellite is positioned at a specific altitude above the

Earth's equator, and it orbits the Earth at the same rotational speed as the Earth's rotation. As a result, it appears stationary from the ground, making it ideal for communication and broadcasting purposes.

Hence, the correct answer is option (b).

105. To observe and monitor weather patterns on Earth. Weather satellites are specifically designed to observe and collect data on Earth's weather patterns, including cloud formations, atmospheric conditions, temperature variations, and other meteorological phenomena.

Hence, the correct answer is option (b).

106. Medium Earth Orbit (MEO). Satellites in a Medium Earth Orbit (MEO) are positioned at an intermediate altitude, allowing them to provide global coverage as they circle the Earth. Global Navigation Satellite Systems (GNSS), such as the GPS, use MEO satellites.

Hence, the correct answer is option (c).

107. Solar panels. Solar panels, typically mounted on the outer surface of the satellite, are used to capture sunlight and convert it into electrical power. This power is essential for the operation of various systems and instruments onboard the satellite.

Hence, the correct answer is option (d).

108. Earth observation satellite. Earth observation satellites are designed to collect data about the Earth's surface, atmosphere, and environment. They are used for purposes such as mapping, monitoring weather patterns, studying climate change, and managing natural resources.

Hence, the correct answer is option (c).

109. Attitude control system. The attitude control system of a satellite is responsible for maintaining the satellite's orientation and stability in space. It consists of various mechanisms, such as reaction wheels, thrusters, and gyroscopes, which adjust the satellite's attitude and position as required.

Hence, the correct answer is option (c).

110. Antenna. The antenna is the satellite component responsible for receiving signals from the ground and transmitting them back to Earth. It serves as the interface between the satellite and the outside world, facilitating communication and data transmission.

Hence, the correct answer is option (b).

111. Communication satellite. Communication satellites are specifically designed and deployed to facilitate various forms of wireless communication, including television broadcasting, internet connectivity, telephone services, and data transmission.

Hence, the correct answer is option (c).

112. Weather satellite. Weather satellites are specifically designed to observe and collect data on Earth's weather patterns, including cloud formations, atmospheric conditions, temperature variations, and other meteorological phenomena.

Hence, the correct answer is option (a).

113. Navigation satellite. Navigation satellites, such as the GPS (Global Positioning System), are designed to provide accurate positioning and navigation information for various applications, including aviation, maritime navigation, surveying, and personal navigation devices.

Hence, the correct answer is option (b).

114. Earth observation satellite. Earth observation satellites are specifically designed to capture images and collect data about the Earth's surface, atmosphere, vegetation, ocean currents, and other environmental features. This information is used for various purposes, including mapping, resource management, and environmental monitoring.

Hence, the correct answer is option (d).

115. Solar panels. Solar panels, typically mounted on the outer surface of the satellite, are used to capture sunlight and convert it into electrical power. This power is essential for the operation of various systems and instruments onboard the satellite.

Hence, the correct answer is option (d).

116. Attitude control system. The attitude control system of a satellite is responsible for maintaining the satellite's orientation and stability in space. It consists of various mechanisms, such as reaction wheels, thrusters, and gyroscopes, which adjust the satellite's attitude and position as required.

Hence, the correct answer is option (c).

117. Antenna. The antenna is the satellite component responsible for receiving signals from the ground and transmitting them back to Earth. It serves as the interface between the satellite and the outside world, facilitating communication and data transmission.

Hence, the correct answer is option (b).

118. Receiver. The receiver is the satellite component responsible for processing and amplifying signals received from the ground. It converts the received signals into a usable form and prepares them for further processing or transmission.

Hence, the correct answer is option (d).

119. Transponder. A transponder is a satellite component responsible for receiving, amplifying, and retransmitting signals or data. It plays a crucial role in communication satellites by relaying signals between different locations on Earth.

Hence, the correct answer is option (a).

120. Payload. The payload of a satellite refers to the scientific instruments, sensors, or equipment carried onboard for specific missions or purposes. It could include cameras, spectrometers, radar systems, or any other instruments required to fulfill the satellite's objectives.

Hence, the correct answer is option (d).

121. Russia (Soviet Union). Sputnik 1, the first artificial satellite, was successfully launched by the Soviet Union on October 4, 1957.

Hence, the correct answer is option (c).

122. Rocket. Rockets are commonly used to launch satellites into space. They provide the necessary thrust to overcome Earth's gravity and propel the satellites into orbit.

Hence, the correct answer is option (c).

123. Altitude. Altitude refers to the distance above the Earth's surface at which a satellite orbits. It is usually measured in kilometers or miles.

Hence, the correct answer is option (d).

124. Geostationary Orbit (GEO). Geostationary Orbit is characterized by a fixed position relative to the Earth's surface, meaning that the satellite appears stationary in the sky when viewed from a specific location on Earth.

Hence, the correct answer is option (b).

125. Medium Earth Orbit (MEO). Medium Earth Orbit is commonly used for global navigation systems like GPS. Satellites in MEO provide global coverage and orbit at intermediate altitudes.

Hence, the correct answer is option (c).

126. Low Earth Orbit (LEO). Low Earth Orbit is commonly used for remote sensing and Earth observation satellites. Satellites in LEO orbit at relatively low altitudes and provide detailed imaging and data collection of the Earth's surface.

Hence, the correct answer is option (a).

127. Polar Orbit. Polar Orbit is characterized by a path that passes over or near the Earth's geographic poles. Satellites in Polar Orbit provide global coverage by effectively covering the entire Earth's surface.

Hence, the correct answer is option (d).

128. Orbital velocity. Orbital velocity is the speed required for a satellite to maintain a stable orbit around the Earth. It depends on the satellite's altitude and is typically several kilometers per second.

Hence, the correct answer is option (c).

129. Atmospheric drag. The duration of a satellite's orbital lifetime is affected by atmospheric drag. The presence of the Earth's atmosphere creates friction that gradually slows down the satellite and can cause it to re-enter the Earth's atmosphere.

Hence, the correct answer is option (c).

130. Decommissioning. Decommissioning is the process of intentionally deorbiting a satellite at the end of its operational life. This is done to ensure the satellite's controlled reentry into the Earth's atmosphere and prevent it from becoming space debris.

Hence, the correct answer is option (b).

131. Wide coverage area. Satellites provide wide coverage areas, allowing communication services to reach remote and rural areas that are otherwise difficult to connect through terrestrial infrastructure.

Hence, the correct answer is option (a).

132. Global positioning systems (GPS). Satellites play a critical role in providing accurate navigation and positioning services through systems like GPS, which have applications in various fields such as transportation, surveying, and personal navigation.

Hence, the correct answer is option (d).

133. By observing weather systems and cloud formations. Weather satellites capture images and collect data about Earth's weather systems, cloud formations, and atmospheric conditions, enabling meteorologists to study and forecast weather patterns.

Hence, the correct answer is option (d).

134. Monitoring natural disasters. Earth observation satellites are primarily used to monitor and gather data on natural disasters such as hurricanes, wildfires, floods, and earthquakes, aiding in disaster management and response efforts.

Hence, the correct answer is option (c).

135. Agricultural monitoring. Satellites equipped with remote sensing instruments collect data on crop health, soil moisture, and vegetation patterns, supporting agricultural monitoring and management for increased productivity and resource efficiency.

Hence, the correct answer is option (a).

136. By tracking climate change indicators. Satellites play a crucial role in monitoring climate change indicators such as sea surface temperature, ice melt, deforestation, and carbon dioxide levels, providing essential data for environmental research and policymaking.

Hence, the correct answer is option (c).

137. Bridging the digital divide. Satellite-based internet connectivity helps bridge the digital divide by providing reliable and high-speed internet access to remote and underserved areas that lack terrestrial infrastructure, empowering communities with information and communication capabilities.

Hence, the correct answer is option (c).

138. By coordinating search and rescue operations. Satellites provide crucial support in disaster management by facilitating communication, coordinating search and rescue operations, assessing damages, and monitoring affected areas to aid in emergency response efforts.

Hence, the correct answer is option (c).

139. Identifying land-use patterns. Satellite imagery plays a key role in mapping and urban planning by providing accurate and up-to-date information on land-use patterns, urban growth, infrastructure planning, and environmental impacts.

Hence, the correct answer is option (c).

140. By aiding in spacecraft navigation. Satellites are instrumental in space exploration and scientific research by providing precise navigation and positioning data for spacecraft, facilitating their safe travel and exploration of celestial bodies.

Hence, the correct answer is option (d).

141. The transmission of signals through underwater cables. Submarine telegraphy refers to the communication method that involves transmitting signals, typically in the form of electrical impulses or Morse code, through specially designed cables laid on the seabed.

Hence, the correct answer is option (a).

142. 1800s. The first successful submarine telegraph cable connection between continents occurred in the 1800s. The historic transatlantic telegraph cable was laid in 1858, connecting Europe and North America.

Hence, the correct answer is option (a).

143. Atlantic Telegraph Cable. The first transatlantic telegraph communication was made possible by the Atlantic Telegraph Cable. It was a submarine cable system laid across the Atlantic Ocean, enabling telegraph communication between Europe and North America.

Hence, the correct answer is option (d).

144. Copper wires. Early submarine telegraphy systems utilized copper wires as the transmission medium. These wires were insulated and protected, allowing electrical signals to be transmitted over long distances beneath the sea.

Hence, the correct answer is option (b).

145. Gutta-percha. Gutta-percha, a natural latex derived from trees, was commonly used as an insulating material for early submarine telegraph cables. It provided effective electrical insulation and protected the copper conductors from seawater corrosion.

Hence, the correct answer is option (d).

146. Limited cable length and signal degradation. During the early days of submarine telegraphy, one of the major challenges was limited cable length and signal degradation over long distances. Signals transmitted through the cables experienced attenuation and distortion, requiring signal amplification and repeater stations.

Hence, the correct answer is option (b).

147. Laying and repairing submarine telegraph cables. Cable ships played a crucial role in the development of submarine telegraphy by laying and repairing the submarine telegraph cables. These specialized ships carried the necessary equipment and personnel for cable installation and maintenance.

Hence, the correct answer is option (a).

148. Using Morse code. Messages in early submarine telegraphy systems were typically transmitted using Morse code. Morse code consists of a series of dots and dashes that represent letters and numbers, allowing messages to be encoded and decoded.

Hence, the correct answer is option (a).

149. Industrial Revolution. The Industrial Revolution, with its advancements in technology and infrastructure, greatly accelerated the adoption of submarine telegraphy on a global scale. It allowed for the rapid expansion of telegraph networks and increased connectivity between countries.

Hence, the correct answer is option (a).

150. All of the above. Submarine telegraphy has evolved significantly over time. It transitioned from copper cables to fiber optic cables, which offer higher data transmission capacity. Additionally, wireless communication systems and satellite integration have expanded the options for long-distance communication.

Hence, the correct answer is option (d).

151. Geological features. When selecting submarine cable routes, one of the primary considerations is the geological features of the seafloor. Factors such as depth, slope, presence of canyons or underwater mountains, and geological stability play a crucial role in determining the viability and durability of the cable route.

Hence, the correct answer is option (c).

152. Cable route length. Signal loss and data transmission quality in submarine cables are affected by the length of the cable route. Longer routes introduce more opportunities for signal degradation, attenuation, and latency. Therefore, selecting a shorter cable route helps minimize these issues.

Hence, the correct answer is option (c).

153. Assessing potential damage from anchors and fishing gear. Ensuring the security and protection of submarine cables involves considering potential damage from anchors, fishing gear, and other human activities. Cable routes should be selected to minimize the risk of accidental or intentional damage to the cables.

Hence, the correct answer is option (c).

154. It regulates cable ownership and operation. International law plays a role in regulating the ownership and operation of submarine cables. It provides guidelines and regulations to ensure fair and equitable use of the cables, but it does not dictate the specific selection of cable routes.

Hence, the correct answer is option (c).

155. Assessing seismic activity and vulnerability. In areas prone to natural disasters, such as earthquakes or tsunamis, it is essential to assess the seismic activity and vulnerability of the region when selecting submarine cable routes. This helps minimize the risk of cable damage and disruption due to natural events.

Hence, the correct answer is option (c).

156. Avoiding shipping lanes. In regions with heavy maritime traffic, it is important to select submarine cable routes that avoid shipping lanes. This helps reduce the risk of accidental damage to the cables by ships or their anchors.

Hence, the correct answer is option (a).

157. Cable insulation thickness. In regions with extreme temperature variations, selecting the appropriate cable insulation thickness is crucial. The insulation helps protect the cable from temperature-related stresses and ensures the integrity of the transmission under varying environmental conditions.

Hence, the correct answer is option (a).

158. It facilitates cable laying and maintenance operations. Selecting cable routes with favorable ocean currents helps facilitate cable laying and maintenance operations. Favorable currents can assist in the deployment and positioning of the cables, reducing installation and maintenance challenges.

Hence, the correct answer is option (c).

159. Availability of landing stations. When selecting cable routes for intercontinental connectivity, the availability of landing stations plays a significant role. Landing stations serve as the connection points between submarine cables and terrestrial networks, enabling seamless data transmission across continents.

Hence, the correct answer is option (a).

160. Reduced latency and improved signal quality. Selecting direct cable routes for long-distance submarine cables helps reduce latency, as it minimizes the distance traveled by the signals. This results in improved signal quality and faster data transmission.

Hence, the correct answer is option (a).

161. A system of communication using dots and dashes. Morse code is a system of communication that represents letters, numbers, and punctuation using combinations of short and long signals, often referred to as dots and dashes.

Hence, the correct answer is option (b).

162. Samuel Morse. Samuel Morse, an American inventor, along with his assistant Alfred Vail, is credited with inventing Morse code in the early 1830s. Morse code was initially developed to be used with the telegraph system.

Hence, the correct answer is option (a).

163. Dot. In Morse code, a dot represents the basic unit of time. A dash, on the other hand, is equal to three times the duration of a dot.

Hence, the correct answer is option (b).

164. . (dot). The letter "A" in Morse code is represented by a single dot.

Hence, the correct answer is option (c).

165. The letter "O". The Morse code symbol "---" represents the letter "O".

Hence, the correct answer is option (a).

166. A gap equal to three dots. The space between letters in Morse code is represented by a gap that is equal to the duration of three dots.

Hence, the correct answer is option (d).

167. ..... The number "5" in Morse code is represented by five consecutive dots.

Hence, the correct answer is option (c).

168. ..--.. The question mark "?" in Morse code is represented by the sequence "..--..".

Hence, the correct answer is option (d).

169. The letter "C". The Morse code symbol "-.-.-." represents the letter "C".

Hence, the correct answer is option (c).

170. A series of dots. The end of a Morse code message is typically represented by a series of dots, signaling the completion of the transmission.

Hence, the correct answer is option (b).

4

CHAPTER

Microprocessor and Microcontroller

The microprocessor(s) is the central processing unit (CPU) of a computer. It is the heart of the computer. This chapter describes Intel 8085 as it is one of the most popular 8-bit microprocessors.

INTEL 8085 MICROPROCESSOR ARCHITECTURE

Intel 8085 is an 8-bit, NMOS microprocessor. It is a 40 pin I.C. package fabricated on a single LSI chip. The Intel 8085 uses a single + 5V d.c. supply for its operation. Its clock speed is about 3 MHz. The clock cycle is of 320 ns. It has 80 basic instructions and 246 opcodes. Figure.1 shows the block diagram of Intel 8085. It consists of three main sections: an arithmetic and logic unit, a timing and control unit and a set of registers. These sections are described in the following sections.

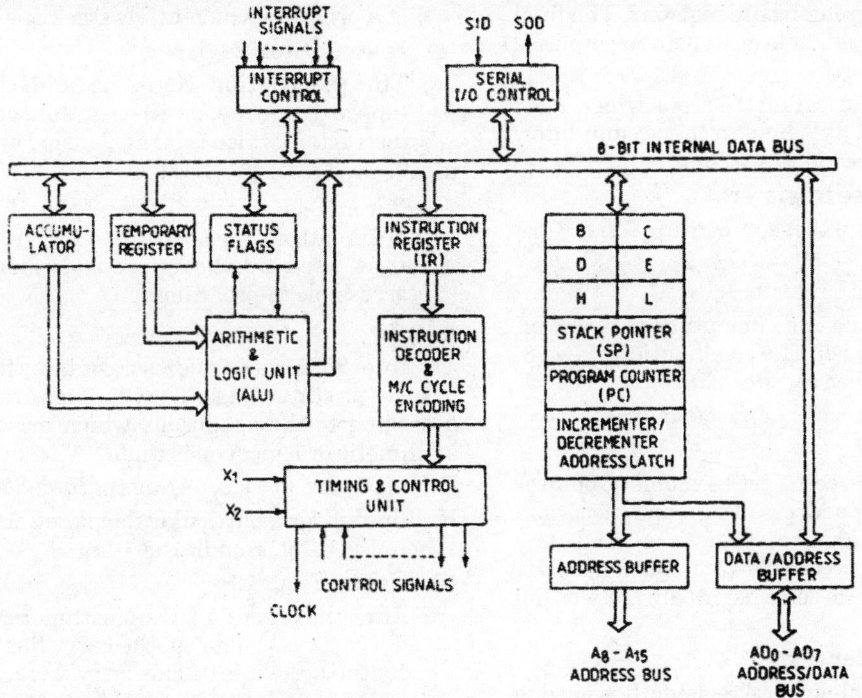

Block diagram of Intel 8085.

ALU (Arithmetic Logic Unit)

It performs the following arithmetic and logical operations:

(*i*) Addition

(*ii*) Subtraction

(*iii*) Logical AND

(*iv*) Logical OR

(*v*) Logical EXCLUSIVE-OR

(*vi*) Complement (logical NOT)

(*vii*) Increment (add 1)

(*viii*) Decrement (subtract 1)

(*ix*) Left shift, Rotate left, Rotate right

(*x*) Clear etc.

Timing and Control Unit

The timing and control unit is a section of the CPU. It generates timing and control signals which are necessary for the execution of instructions. It controls data flow between CPU and peripherals (including memory). It provides status, control and timing signals which are required for the operation of memory and I/O devices. It controls the entire operations of the microprocessor and peripherals connected to it. Thus it is seen that the control unit of the CPU acts as the brain of the computer system.

Registers

Figure.1 shows the various registers of Intel 8085. These registers are used by the microprocessor for temporary storage and manipulation of data and instructions. Data remains in the registers till they are sent to the memory or I/O devices.

Intel 8085 microprocessor has the following registers.

***(i)* Accumulator (ACC)**

It is an 8-bit register associated with the ALU. The register 'A' in the 8085 is an accumulator. It is used to hold one of the operands of an arithmetic or logical operation. It serves as one input to the ALU. The other operand for an arithmetic or logical operation may be stored either in the memory or in one of the general-purpose registers. The final result of an arithmetic or logical operation is placed in the accumulator.

There are some logical instructions which need only one operand. It is held in the accumulator. The result is placed in the accumulator.

***(ii)* General-Purpose Registers**

The 8085 microprocessor contains six 8-bit general-purpose registers:

B, C, D, E, H and L register.

To hold 16-bit data a combination of two 8-bit registers can be used. The combination of two 8-bit registers is called *register-pair*.

The valid register pairs in the 8085 are :

B-C, D-E, and H-L.

The H-L pair is used to act as memory pointer holding the 16-bit address of a memory location. The general-purpose registers and the accumulator are accessible to programmer. He can store data in these registers during writing his program.

***(iii)* Program Counter (PC)**

It is a 16-bit special-purpose register. It is used to hold the memory address of the next instruction to be executed. It keeps the track of memory addresses of the instructions in a program while they are being executed. The microprocessor increments the content of the program counter during the execution of an instruction so that it points to the address of the next instruction in the program at the end of the execution of an instruction.

***(iv)* Stack Pointer (SP)**

It is a 16-bit special function register. The stack is a sequence of memory locations set aside by a programmer to store/retrieve the contents of accumulator, flags, program counter and general-purpose registers during the execution of a program. Any portion of the memory can be used as stack. Since the stack works on LIFO (last-in-first-out) principle, its operation is faster compared normal store/retrieve of memory locations. During the execution of a program sometimes it becomes necessary to save the contents of some registers which are needed for some other operations in the subsequent steps of the program. The contents of such registers are saved in the stack. Then the registers are used for some other operations. After completing the needed operations the contents which were saved in the stack are brought back to the registers. The contents of only those registers are saved, which are needed in the later past of the program. The stack pointer (SP) controls addressing of the stack. The SP holds the address of the top element of data stored in the stack.

The stack is defined and the stack pointer is initialized by the programmer at the beginning of a program which needs stack operation.

***(v)* Instruction Register**

The instruction register holds the opcode (operation code or instruction code) of the instruction which is being decoded and executed.

***(vi)* Temporary Register**

It is an 8-bit register associated with the ALU. It holds data during an arithmetic/logical operation. It is used by the microprocessor. It is not accessible to programme.

Flags

The Intel 8085 microprocessor contains five flip-flops to serve as status flags. The flip-flops are set or reset according to the conditions which arise during an arithmetic or logical operation.

Following are five status flags of Intel 8085 :

If a flip-flop for a particular flag is set, it indicates 1. When it is reset, it indicates 0.

***(i)* Carry Flag (CS)**

After the execution of an arithmetic instruction if a carry is produced, the carry flag CS is set to 1, otherwise it is 0. The carry flag is set or reset in case of addition as well as subtraction. After the addition of two 8-bit numbers, if the sum is larger than 8 bits, a carry is produced; and the carry flag is set to 1. In case of subtraction, if borrow occurs, the carry flag is set to 1. The carry flag holds carry out of the most significant bit resulting from the execution of an arithmetic operation.

***(ii)* Parity Flag (P)**

The parity status flag P is set to 1, if the result of an arithmetic or logical operation contains even number of 1s. It is reset i.e., it is 0, if the result contains odd number of 1s.

***(iii)* Auxiliary Carry Flag (AC)**

The auxiliary carry flag AC holds carry out of the bit number 3 to the bit number 3 resulting from the execution of an arithmetic operation. The counting of bits starts from 0, and hence, the Bit No. 3 is actually the fourth bit from the least significant bit.

***(iv)* Zero Flag (Z)**

The zero status flag Z is set to 1, if the result of an arithmetic or logical operation is 0. If the result is not zero, the flag is set to 0.

***(v)* Sign Flag (S)**

The sign flag S is set to 1, if the result of an arithmetic or logical operation is negative. If the result is positive, the sign flag is set to 0.

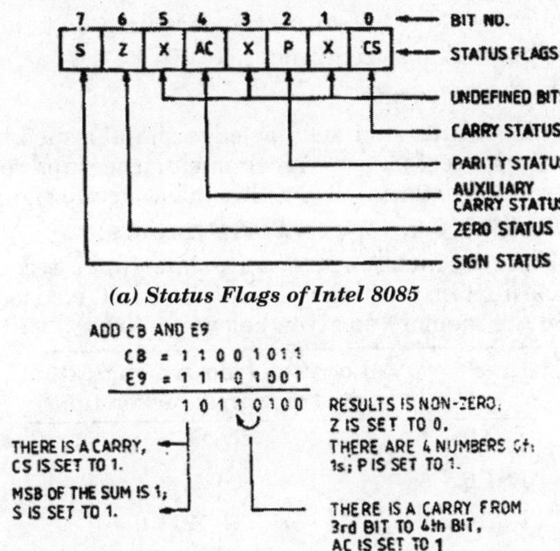

(a) Status Flags of Intel 8085

(b) Status Flags for ADD operation

shows the status flags of ADD operation. Take an example of the instruction ADD B. The execution of the instruction ADD B will add the content of the register B to the content of the accumulator. Suppose, the contents of the accumulator and register B are CB and E9 respectively. Now CB and E9 are added and the result is 01, B4. As the accumulator is an 8-bit register B4 remains in the accumulator and there is a carry. The various status flags are shown in Fig (b).

PSW (Program Status Word)

In Fig. (a), five bits indicate the five status flags and three bits are undefined. The combination of these 8 bits is called *Program Status Word (PSW)*. PSW and the accumulator are treated as a 16-bit unit for stack operation.

Data and Address Bus

The Intel 8085 is an 8-bit microprocessor. Its data bus is 8-bit wide so it can transmit 8-bit data in parallel from or to the microporcessor. The Intel 8085 requires a 16-bit wide address bus as the memory address are of 16 bits. The 8 most significant bits of the address are transmitted by the address bus, A-bus (pins A_8 to A_{15}). The 8 least significant bits of the address are transmitted by address/data bus, AD-bus (pins $AD_0 - AD_7$). The address/data bus transmits data and address at different moments. At a particular moment it transmits either data or address. Thus the AD-bus operates in time shared mode. This technique is known as multiplexing. First of all 16-bit memory address is transmitted by the microprocessor; the 8 MSBs of the address bus becomes 16-bit wide. Then the 8 LSBs of the address is latched either into the memory or external latch so that the complete 16-bit address remains available for further operation. The 8-bit AD-bus now becomes free, and it is available for data transmission. 2^{16} (= 65536 = 64 K, where 1 K = 1024) memory locations can be addressed directly by Intel 8085. Each memory location contains 1 byte of data.

Pin Configuration

$A_8 - A_{15}$ (Output)

These are address bus and are used for the most significant bits of the memory address or 8 bits of I/O address.

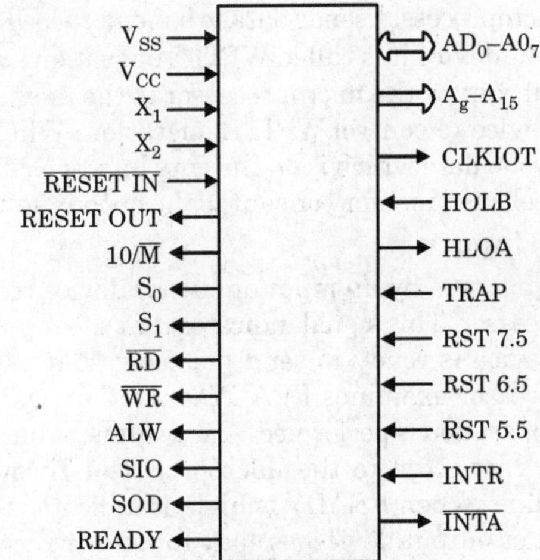

Schematic Diagram of Intel 8085

$AD_0 - AD_7$ (Input/Output)

These are time multiplexed address/data bus i.e., they serve dual purpose. They are used for the least significant 8 bits of the memory address or I/O address during the first clock cycle of a machine cycle. Again they are used for data during second and third clock cycles.

ALE (Output)

It is an address latch enable signal. It goes high during first clock of a machine cycle and enables the lower 8 bits of the address to be latched either into the memory or external latch.

IO/$\overline{M}$ (Output)

It is a status signal which distinguishes whether the address is for memory or I/O. When it goes high the address on the address bus is for an I/O device. When it goes low the address on the address bus is for a memory location.

S_0, S_1 (Output)

These are status signals sent by the microprocessor to distinguish various types of operations given in Table 1.

Table.1 Status Codes for Intel 8085

S_1	S_0	*Operations*
0	0	HALT
0	1	WRITE
1	0	READ
1	1	FETCH

$\overline{RD}$ (Output)

When microprocessor reads data or codes from a memory location or an input device, it is called *READ operation*. $\overline{RD}$ is a signal sent by the microprocessor to the memory input device to control READ operation. When it goes low, the selected memory or input device is read.

$\overline{WR}$ (Output)

When microprocessor sends data to a memory location or an input device it is called WRITE operation. $\overline{WR}$ is a signal sent by the microprocessor to the memory/ output device to control WRITE operation. When it goes low, the data which is on the data bus, is written into the selected memory or sent to the output device.

READY (Input)

It is a signal sent by an input or output device to the microprocessor. This signal indicates that the input or output device is ready to send or receive data. The microprocessor examines READY signal before data transfer operation is performed. A slow input or output device is connected to the microprocessor through READY line. When READY is high, it indicates that the input or output device is ready to send or receive data. When READY is low, the microprocessor waits till READY becomes high. The microprocessor examines the status of READY signal in the second clock cycle of the machine cycle.

HOLD (Input)

When another device of the computer system, requires address and data buses for data transfer, it sends HOLD signal to the microprocessor. After receiving the HOLD request the microprocessor sends out a HLDA (HOLD Acknowledge) signal to the device. Then the microprocessor leaves the control over the buses as soon as the current machine cycle is completed. Internal processing may continue. The microprocessor regains the control over the buses after the HOLD signal is removed.

HLDA (Output)

It is a HOLD acknowlege signal sent out by the microprocessor after receiving the HOLD signal. It is sent to the device which has issued the HOLD signal. After the removal of the HOLD signal, the HOLD goes low, and thereafter the microprocessor takes over the buses.

INTR (Input)

It is an interrupt signal sent by an external device to the microprocessor. Through this line an external device informs microprocessor that it is ready to transfer data or to initiate certain operation. The 8085 microprocessor has 5 interrupt lines. The INTR is one of them. When it goes high, the microprocessor suspends the execution of its normal sequence of instructions. After completing the current instruction at hand, it attends the interrupting device. The microprocessor issues an interrupt acknowledge signal $\overline{INTA}$. Then it transfers data or takes any other action as required.

$\overline{INTA}$ (Output)

It is an interrupt acknowledge signal issued by the microprocessor after receiving an interrupt request from an external device. It is a low active signal.

RST 5.5, 6.5, 7.5 and TRAP (inputs)

These are interrupts. When an interrupt is recognised the next instruction is executed from a fixed location in the memory as given below.

Line	Location from which next instruction is picked up
TRAP	0024
RST 5.5	002C
RST 6.5	0034
RST 7.5	003C

RST 7.5, RST 6.5 and RST 5.5 are the restart interrupts. Each of them has a programmable mask. The TRAP has the highest priority among interrupts. It is a nonmaskable interrupt. It is a unaffected by any mask or interrupt enable.

Order of priority of interrupts :

TRAP (highest priority)
RST 7.5
RST 6.5
RST 5.5
INTR (lowest priority).

RESET IN (Input)

It resets the program counter to zero. It also resets interrupt enable and HLDA flip-flops. It does not affect any other flag or register except the instruction register. The CPU is held in reset condition as long as RESET is applied.

RESET OUT (Output)

It indicates that the CPU is being reset.

X_1, X_2 (Input)

These are terminals to be connected to an external crystal oscillator which drives an internal circuitry of the microprocessor to produce a suitable clock for the operation of microprocessor.

CLK (Output)

It is a clock output for user, which can be used for other digital ICs. Its frequency is same at which processor operates.

SID (Input)

It is data line for serial input. The data on this line is located into the 7th bit of the accumulator when RIM instruction is executed.

SOD (Output)

It is a data line for serial output. The 7th bit of the accumulator is output on SOD line when SIM instruction is executed.

V_{CC} + 5 volts supply

V_{SS} ground reference

INSTRUCTION

To perform a task in a particular microprocessor system, programmer has to know the instructions supported by microprocessor used in the microprocessor system.

Instruction Classification

Based on nature of function of the instructions, instructions provided by 8085 can be classified into five different groups.

1. **Data Transfer Operations**

   The data transfer instructions load given data into register, copy data from register to register, copy data from register to memory location, and vice versa. In other words, data transfer instructions copy data from source to destination. Source can be data or contents of register or contents of memory location whereas destination can be register or memory location. These instructions do not affect the flag register of the processor.

2. **Arithmetic Operations**

   (i) **Addition :** Any 8-bit number, or contents of a register, or contents of a memory location can be added to the contents of the accumulator and resulted sum is stored in the accumulator. The resulted carry bit is stored in the carry flag. In 8085, no two other registers can be added directly, i.e. contents of B and C registers cannot be added directly. To add two 16-bit numbers the 8085 provides DAD instruction. It adds the data within the register pair to the contents of the HL register pair and resulted sum is stored in the **HL register pair.**

   (ii) **Subtraction :** Any 8-bit number, or the contents of a register, or the contents of a memory location can be subtracted from the contents of the accumulator and the result is stored in the accumulator. The resulted borrow bit is stored in the carry flag. In 8085, no two other registers can be subtracted directly.

   (iii) **Increment decrement :** The 8085 has increment and decrement instructions to increment and decrement the contents of any register, memory location or register pair by 1.

3. **Logical Operations**

   (i) **Logical :** Using logical instructions, any 8-bit number, or the contents of a register, or of a memory location can be logically ANDed, ORed, or Exclusive-ORed with the contents of the accumulator and the result is stored in the accumulator. The result also affects the flags according to definition of flags. e.g. zero result sets the zero flag.

   (ii) **Rotate :** These instructions allow shifting of each bit in the accumulator either left or right by 1 bit position.

   (iii) **Compare :** Any 8-bit number, or the contents of a register, or the contents of a memory location can be compared for equality, greater than, or less than, with the contents of the accumulator.

   (iv) **Complement :** The result of accumulator can be complemented with this instruction. It replaces all 0s by 1s and all 1s by 0s.

4. **Branching Operations**

   These instructions allow the 8085 to change the sequence of the program, either unconditionally or under certain test conditions. *These instructions include*

   (i) Jump Instructions

   (ii) Subroutine call and return instructions

   (iii) Restart instructions.

5. **Stack, Input/Output and Machine Control Operations.**

   These instructions control following :

   (i) ***Stack instructions:*** These allow the transfer of data from register pair to stack memory and from stack memory to the register pair.

   (ii) ***Input/output instruction:*** These allow the transfer of 8-bit data to input/output port.

   (iii) ***Machine instructions:*** These control the machine operations such as interrupt, halt, or do nothing.

Elements of Instruction

Each instruction of the 8085 microprocessor has specific information fields. These information fields of instructions are called *elements of instruction*.

(1) Operation Code

The operation code field in the instruction specifies the operation to be performed. The operation is specified by binary code, hence the name operation code or simply opcode.

e.g. 8085 processor operation code for ADD B instruction is 80H.

(2) Source/destination Operand

The source/destination operand field directly specifies the source/destination operand for the instruction. In 8085, the instruction MOV A,B has B register contents as a source operand and A register contents as a destination operand because this instruction copies the contents of register B to register A.

(3) Source Operand Address

The operation specified by the instruction may require one or more operands. The source operand may be in the 8085 register or in the memory. Many times the instruction specifies the address of the source operand so that operand(s) can be accessed and operated by the 8085 according to the instruction.

In 8085, source operand address for instruction ADD M is given by HL register pair.

(*i*) **Destination operand address :** The operation executed by the 8085 may produce result. Most the times the result is stored in one of the operand. Such operand is known as destination operand. The instruction which produce result specifies the destination operand address. In 8085, the destination operand address for instruction INR M is given by HL register pair because INR M instruction increments the contents of memory location specified by HL register pair and stores the result in the same memory location.

(*ii*) **Next instruction address :** The next instruction address tells the 8085 from where to fetch the next instruction after completion of execution of current instruction. For BRANCH instructions the address of the next instruction is specified within the instruction. However, for other instructions, the next instruction to be fetched immediately follows the current instructions.

e.g. in 8085, instruction after INR B follows it. The instruction JMP 2000H specifies the next instruction address as 2000H.

Instruction Formats

The 8085 instruction set consists of one, two and three byte instructions.

(1) One byte instruction

The first byte is always the opcode

FORMAT : Opcode

1 byte

e.g. MOV A, B whose opcode is 78H which is one byte. The instruction copies the contents of B register in A register.

(2) Two byte instruction

In two-byte instructions the second byte is usually data

FORMAT : Opcode Operand

2 bytes

e.g. MVI B, 02H. The opcode for this instruction is 06H and is always followed by a byte data (02H in this case). This instruction is a two byte instruction which copies immediate data into B register.

(3) Three byte instruction

In three byte instructions, the last two bytes present address or 16-bit data.

FORMAT : Opcode Operand Operand

3 bytes

e.g. JMP 6200H. The opcode for this instruction is C3H and is always followed by 16 bit address (6200H in this case). This instruction is a three byte instruction which loads 16 bit address into program counter.

OP CODE FORMATS

The 8085 microprocessor has 8-bit opcodes. The opcode is unique for each instruction and contains the information about operation, register to be used, memory to be used etc. The 8085 identifies all operations, register and flags with a specific code.

e.g. All internal registers are identified as shown below in the Tables 2 and 3.

Table 2

Registers	Code
B	0 0 0
C	0 0 1
D	0 1 0
E	0 1 1
H	1 0 0
L	1 0 1
M (Memory)	1 1 0
A	1 1 1

Table 3

Registers Pairs	Code
BC	0 0
DE	0 1
HL	1 0
AF or SP	1 1

There are different codes for each operation. Some operation codes are identified as follows :

Sr. No.	Function	Operation code							
		B_7	B_6	B_5	B_4	B_3	B_2	B_1	B_0
1	MVI r, data	0	0	D	D	D	1	1	0
2	LXI rp, data	0	0	D	D	0	0	0	1
3	MOV rd, rs	0	1	D	D	D	S	S	S

Note : DDD defines destination register, SSS defines source register and DD defines register pair.

Design of opcodes for some instruction using information given in the above tables

Example 1.

Instruction	: MVI B Operation
	: Move immediate 8-bit data
Operation code	: 00 D D D 110
Register code	: 0 0 0
∴ Opcode	: 0000 0110 = 06H

Example 2.

Instruction	: MVI A Operation
	: Move immediate 8-bit data
Operation code	: 00 D D D 110
Register code	: 1 1 1
∴ Opcode	: 0011 1110 = 3EH

Example 3.

Instruction	: LXI B Operation
	: Load immediate 16-bit data
Operation code	: 00 D D 0001
Register code	: 0 0
∴ Opcode	: 0000 0001 = 01H

Example 4.

Instruction	: LXI D Operation
	: Load immediate 16-bit data
Operation code	: 00 D D 0001
Register code	: 0 1
∴ Opcode	: 0001 0001 = 11H

Example 5.

Instruction	: MOV A, B Operation
	: Copy data from source register to destination register
Operation code	: 01 D D D SSS
Register code	: 1 1 1 000
∴ Opcode	: 0111 1000 = 78H

Example 6.

Instruction	: MOV E, L Operation
	; Copy data from source register to destination register
Operation code	: 01 D D D SSS
Register code	: 0 1 1 101
∴ Opcode	: 0101 1101 = 5DH

DATA FORMATS

The operand is another name for data.

FORMS OF DATA FORMAT

(1) Addresses.

It is a 16-bit unsigned integer number used to refer a memory location.

(2) Numbers/Logical data

The 8085 supports following numeric data types.

***(i)* Signed integer :** A signed integer number is either a positive number or a negative number. In 8085, 8-bits are assigned for signed integer, in which most significant bit is used for sign and remaining seven bits are used for magnitude. Sign bit 0 indicates positive number whereas sign bit 1 indicates negative number.

***(ii)* Unsigned integer :** The 8085 microprocessor supports 8-bit unsigned integer.

***(iii)* BCD :** The term BCD number stands for binary coded decimal number. It uses ten digits from 0 through 9. The 8-bit register of 8085 can store two digit BCD number.

(3) Characters

The 8085 uses ASCII code to represent characters. It is a 7-bit alphanumeric code that represents decimal numbers, English alphabets, and other special characters.

Assembly Language Program

Define a program statement as *write an assembly language program to add two numbers.*

Three tasks are involved in this program :

(1) Load two hex numbers

(2) Add numbers

(3) Store the result in the memory

These tasks can be symbolically presented as flow chart, as shown in the Fig.5

Start → Load two hex numbers → Add numbers → Store the result → Stop

Next job is to find the suitable 8085 assembly language instruction/s for each task.

These instructions are as follows :

Task 1 Instruction :

```
MVI A , 20H     ; Load 20H as a first
                ; number in register A
MVI B, 40H      ; Load 40 H as a second
                  number
                ; in register B
```

Task 2 Instruction :

```
ADD B           ; Add two numbers and save
                ; result in register A
```

Task 3 Instruction :

```
STA 2200H       ; Store the result in memory
                ; location 2000H
HLT             ; Stop the program execution
```

To execute three tasks in a sequence in writing corresponding instructions in the same sequence constitutes an assembly language program.

Assembly Language Program to Machine Language Program

Once the assembly language program is ready, it is necessary to convert it in the machine language program. This is done by referring proper hex code for each assembly instruction from the 8085 instruction set manual. This process is called *hand assembly* and the resulted machine language program is also called *Hex code.*

Hex code for program

Mnemonics	Hex code		
MVI A, 20H	3EH	←	Opcode
	20 H	←	Operand
MVI B, 40H	06H	←	Opcode
	40H	←	Operand
ADD B	80H	←	Opcode
STA 2200H	32 H	←	Opcode
	00H	←	Operand (lower byte of address)
	22H	←	Operand (higher byte of address)
HLT	76H	←	Opcode

Storing Hex code in the Memory

Once the hex code is ready, it has to be loaded in the memory of specially designed microprocessor system (Microprocessor training kit) for execution. To perform this task, the address range of read/write memory in the system should be known. Assume that the read/ write memory ranges from 2000H to 22FFH. The microprocessor training kit has keypad to enter the hex code in the memory. It provides a special routines (monitor program) to enter a hex code byte by byte and execute the program.

Typical steps for storing hex code in the memory from address 2000H :

(1) Reset microprocessor system by pressing the RESET key.

(2) Enter into store mode by pressing SET key.

(3) Enter address of the memory 2000H, where the first hex code (starting address of the program) is to be stored using hex keys.

(4) Enter hex code using hex keys.

(5) Increment memory address by 1 using INC key.

(6) Repeat steps 4 and 5 until the last hex code.

Executing the Program

The microprocessor training kit provides a procedure to execute the program. To activate the procedure we have to enter the starting address of the program. To enter this address we have to go into execute mode by pressing GO key and enter the starting address using hex keys. Once the starting address is entered, the program can be executed by pressing EXECUTE key. The EXECUTE key procedure loads the starting address of the program, into the program counter and program control is transferred from monitor program to our program.

After this microprocessor reads one hex code at a time, and when it fetches the complete instruction, it executes that instruction. Then it fetches the next instruction and this process continues until the last instruction in the program is executed.

ADDRESSING MODES

Part of the programming flexibility for each microprocessor is the number and different kind of ways the programmer can refer to data stored in the memory. The different ways that a microprocessor can access data are called *addressing modes.*

The 8085 has following 5 addressing modes

1. Immediate Addressing Mode

In this mode, 8 or 16 bit data can be specified as a part of instruction. In 8085, the instructions having 'I' letter fall under this category. 'I' indicates immediate addressing mode.

Example

MVI A, 20H ; Moves 8 bit immediate data (20H) into accumultor

MVI M, 30H ; Moves 8 bit immediate data (30 H) into the memory location ; pointed by HL register pair

LXI SP, 2700H ; Moves 16 bit immediate data (2700H) into SP

LXI D, 10FFH; Moves 16 bit immediate data (10FFH) into DE register pair ; (D = 10H and E = FFH)

2. Register Addressing Mode

It specifies the source operand, destination operand, or both to be contained in an 8085 registers. This results in faster execution, since it is not necessary to access memory locations for operands.

Example

MVI A, 20H ; Moves 8 bit immediate data

MOV A, B ; Moves the contents of register B into the accumulator

SPHL ; Moves the contents of HL register pair into stack pointer.

ADD C ; Adds the contents of register C into the contents of ; accumulator and stores result in the accumulator

3. Direct Addressing Mode

It specifies the 16 bit address of the operand within the instruction itself. The second and third bytes of instruction contain this 16 bit address.

Example :

MVI A, 20H ; Moves 8 bit immediate data
LDA 2000H ; Loads the 8 bit contents of memory location
; 2000H into the accumulator
SHLD 3000H ; Stores HL register pair into two consecutive memory
; locations. Lower byte, i.e. the contents of L register into
; memory location 3000H and higher byte, i.e. the contents
; of H register into memory location 3001 H

4. **Indirect Addressing Mode**

In this mode,. the memory address where the operand located is specified by the contents of a register pair.

Examsple :

LDAX B ; Loads the accumulator with the contents of memory
; location pointed by BC register pair
MOVM,A ; Stores the contents of accumulator into the memory
; location pointed by HL register pair.

5. **Implied Addressing Mode**

In this mode, opcode specifies the address of the operands.

Example :

CMA : Complements contents of accumulator
RAL : Rotates the contents of accumu-lator left through carry.

8085 INSTRUCTION SET

Based on the nature of functions the instruction carry out, 8085 instruction set can be classified into five different groups :

(1) Data Transfer Group (2) Arithmetic Group
(3) Branch Group (4) Logic Group
(5) Stack Input/Output and Machine Control Group

Notations used in the Instructions

Notation	Meaning
M	Memory location pointed by HL register pair
R	8-bit register
Reg.pair	16-bit register pair
Rd	Destination Register, Rs – Source Register
addr	16-bit address/8-bit address

Data Transfer Group

The data transfer group instructions load the given data into register, copy data from register to register, and copy data from register to memory location and vice versa. This group consists of following set of instruction. These instructions do not affect any flag in the flag register.

(1)MOV: Move–Copy from Source to Destination

Opcode	MOV	MOV	MOV
Operand	Rd. Rs	M, Rs	Rd, M
Operation	$[r_1] \leftarrow [r_2]$	$[[H-L]] \leftarrow [r]$	$[r] \leftarrow [[H-L]]$
Bytes	1	2	1
M-Cycles	1	2	2
T-States	4	7	7

Description : This instruction copies contents of the source register into destination register; contents of the source register are not altered. If one of the operands is a memory location, it is specified by the contents of HL registers.

Flags: No flags are affected.

Example. Assume the contents of registers HL are 20H and 50H, respectively. Memory location 2050H contains 9FH. Transfer contents of the memory location to register B.

Instruction: MOV B,M

Register contents before instruction:

B	XX	XX	C
D	XX	XX	E
H	20	50	L

Memory contents: 2050 → 9F

Register contents after instruction:

B	9F	XX	C
D	XX	XX	E
H	20	50	L

(2) MVI: Move Immediate 8-Bit

Opcode	MVI	
Operand	Reg., Data	Mem., Data
Operation	$[r] \leftarrow$ data	$[[H-L]] \leftarrow$ data
Bytes	2	2
M-Cycles	2	3
T-States	7	10

Description : The 8-bit data is stored in the destination register or memory. If operand is a memory location, it is specified by the contents of HL registers.

Flags : No flags are affected.

Example : Load 92H in register B.

Instruction : MVI B, 92H Hex Code: 06 92

This instruction loads 92H in register B.

(3) LXI: Load Register Pair Immediate

Opcode	LXI
Operand	Reg. pair, 16-bit data
Operation	$[rp] \leftarrow$ data 16 bits
Bytes	3
M-Cycles	3
T-States	10

Description: The instruction loads 16-bit data in the register pair designated in the operand. This is a 3-byte instruction; the second byte specifies the low-order byte and the third byte specifies the high-order byte.

Flags: No flags are affected.

(4) STA: Store Accumulator Direct

Opcode STA
Operand 16-bit
Operation [addr] ← [A]
Bytes 3
M-Cycles 4
T-States 13

Description : The contents of the accumulator are copied to a memory location specified by the operand. This is a 3-byte instruction; the second byte specifies the low-order address and the third byte specifies the high-order address.

Flags : No flags are affected.

Example : Assume the accumulator contains 9FH. Load the accumulator into memory location 2050H.

Instruction :

STA 2050H Hex Code: 32 50 20

Register contents before instruction	Memory contents after instruction
A [9F XX]	2050 [9F]

(5) LDA: Load Accumulator Direct

Opcode LDA
Operand 16-bit address
Operation [A] ← [addr]
Bytes 3
M-Cycles 4
T-States 13

Description : The contents of a memory location, specified by a 16-bit address in the operand, are copied to the accumulator. The contents of the source are not altered. This is a 3-byte instruction; the second byte specifies the low-order address and the third byte specifies the high-order address.

Flags : No flags are affected.

Example : Assume memory location 2050H contains byte F8H. Load the accumulator with the contents of location 2050H.

Instruction :

LDA 2050H Hex Code : 3A 50 20
(note the reverse order)

A [F8 X] 2050 F8

(6) LHLD : Load H and L Registers Direct

Opcode LHLD
Operand 16-bit address
Operation [L] ← [addr], [H] ← [add r + 1)
Bytes 3
M-Cycles 5
T-States 16

Description : The instruction copies the contents of the memory location pointed out by the 16-bit address in register L and copies the contents of the next memory location in register H. The contents of source memory locations are not altered.

Flags: No flags are affected.

Example : Assume memory location 2050H contains 90H and 2051H contains 01H. Transfer memory contents to registers HL.

Instruction:

LHLD 2050H Hex Code: 2A 50 20

Memory contents before instruction	Register contents after instruction
2050 90	
2051 01	H→ 01H → L →90 H

(7) SHLD: Store H and L Registers Direct.

Opcode SHLD address
Operand 16-bit
Operation [addr] ← [L] , [add r + 1] ← H]
Bytes 3
M-Cycles 5
T-States 16

Description : The contents of register L are stored in the memory location specified by the 16-bit address in the operand, and the contents of H register are stored in the next memory location by incrementing the operand. The contents of registers HL are not altered. This is a 3-byte instruction; the second byte specifies the low-order address and the third byte specifies the high-order address.

Flags: No flags are altered.

Example: Assume the H and L registers contain 01H and FFH, respectively. Store the contents at memory locations 2050H and 2051H.

Instruction:

SHLD Hex Code: 22 50 20

Register contents before instruction	Memory and register contents after instruction	
H → 01 H	2050 FF	H → 01H
L → FF H	2051 01	L → FFH

(8) STAX: Store Accumulator Indirect

Opcode STAX
Operand B/D reg. Pair
Operation [[rp]] ← [A]
Bytes 1

M-Cycles 2

T-States 7

Description : The contents of the accumulator are copied into the memory location specified by the contents of the operand (register pair). The contents of the accumulator are not altered.

Flags : No flags are affected.

Example : Assume contents of the accumulator are F9H and contents of registers B and C are 20H and 50H, respectively. Store the accumulator contents in memory location 2050H.

Instruction :

STAX B Hex Code: 02

Register contents before instruction — Register and memory contents after instruction

A	F9	XX	F	2050	F9	A	F9	XX	F
B	20	50	C			B	20	50	C

Comments: This instruction performs the same function as MOV A, M except this instruction uses the contents of BC or DE as memory pointers.

(9) LDAX: Load Accumulator Indirect

Opcode	LDAX Pair
Operand	B/D reg.
Operation	[A] ← [[rp]]
Bytes	1
M-Cycles	2
T-States	7

Description : The contents of the designated register pair point to a memory location. This instruction copies the contents of that memory location into the accumulator. The contents of either the register pair or the memory location are not altered.

Flags : No flags are affected.

Example : Assume the contents of register B = 20H, C = 50H, and memory location 2050 H = 9FH. Transfer contents of the memory location 2050H to the accumulator.

Instruction :

LDAX B Hex Code: 0A

Register contents before instruction — Memory contents — Register contents after instruction

A	XX	XX	F			A	9F	XX	F
B	20	50	C	⟶ 2050	9F	B	20	50	C

(10) XCHG: Exchange H and L with D and E

Opcode	XCHG
Operand	None
Operation	[H – L] « [D – E]
Bytes	1
M-Cycles	1
T-States	4

Description : The contents of register H are exchanged with the contents of register D, and contents of register L are exchanged with the contents of register E.

Flags : No flags are affected.

Arithmetic Group.

This group consists of following set of instructions.

(1) ADD : Add Register to Accumulator

Opcode	ADD	
Operand	Reg.	Memory
Operation	[A] ← [A] + [r]	[A] ← [[H – L]]
Bytes	1	1
M-Cycles	1	2
T-States	4	7

Description : The contents of the operand (register or memory) are added to the contents of the accumulator and the result is stored in the accumulator. If operand is a memory location, that is indicated by the 16-bit address in the HL register.

Flags : All flags are modified to reflect the result of the addition.

Example : Register B has 51H and the accumulator has 47H. Add contents of register B to the contents of the accumulator.

Instruction : ADD B Hex Code : 80

Register contents before instruction — Addition — Register contents after instruction

									S	Z	AC	P	CY	
A	47	X	F	47H	=	0100 0111	A	98	1	0	0	0	0	F
B	51	X	C	51H	=	0101 0001	B	51	X					C
				98H	=	1001 1000								

Flags : S = 1, Z = 0, AC = 0

P = 0, CY = 0

(2) ADI : Add Immediate to Accumulator

Opcode ADI
Operand 8-bit data
Operation [A] ¬ [A] + data
Bytes 2
M-Cycles 2
T-States 7
Hex Codes C6

Description : The 8-bit data (operand) are added to the contents of the accumulator, and the result is placed in the accumulator.

Flags : All flags are modified to reflect the result of the addition.

(3) ADC : Add Register to Accumulator with Carry

Opcode	ADC	
Operand	Reg. MM	
Operation	[A] ← [A] + [r] + CS	
Bytes	1	1
M-Cycles	1	2
T-States	4	7

Description : The contents of the operand (register or memory) and the Carry flag and added to the contents of the accumulator and the result is placed in the accumulator. The contents of the operand are not altered; however, the previous Carry flag is reset.

Flags : All flags are modified to reflect the result of the addition.

(4) ACI: Add Immediate to Accumulator with Carry

Opcode ACI data
Operand 8-bit
Operation [A] ← [A] + data + [CS]
Bytes 2
M-Cycles 2
T-States 7

Description : The 8-bit data (operand) and the Carry flag are added to the contents of the accumulator, and the result is stored in the accumulator.

Flags : All flags are modified to reflect the result of the addition.

(5) DAD : Add Register Pair to H and L Registers

Opcode DAD
Operand Reg. pair
Operation [H – L] ← [H – L] + [rp]
Bytes 1
M-Cycles 3
T-States 10

Description : The 16-bit contents of the specified register pair are added to the contents of the HL register and the sum is saved in the HL register. The contents of the source register pair are not altered.

Flags : If the result is larger than 16 bits the CY flag is set. No other flags are affected.

Example : Assume register pair HL contains 0242H. Multiply the contents by 2.

Instruction :

DAD H	Hex Code : 29	
Before instruction	DAD operation	After instruction
H → 02 H	0242	H → 04 H
L → 42 H	+ 0242	L → 84 H
	0484	

SUBTRACT.

This group consists of following set of instructions.

1. SUB: Subtract Register or Memory from Accumulator

Opcode SUB
Operand Reg. Mem.
Operation [A] ← [A] – [r] [A] ← [A] – [H – L]
Bytes 1
M-Cycles 1
T-States 4

Description : The contents of the register or the memory location specified by the operand are subtracted from the contents of the accumulator, and the results are placed in the accumulator. The contents of the source are not altered.

Flags : All flags are affected to reflect the result of the subtraction.

2. SUI: Subtract Immediate from Accumulator

Opcode SUI
Operand 8-bit data
Operation [A] ← [A] – data
Bytes 2
M-Cycles 2
T-States 7

Description : The 8-bit data (the operand) are subtracted from the contents of the accumulator, and the results are placed in the accumulator.

Flags : All flags are modified to reflect the results of the subtraction.

3. SBB: Subtract Source and Borrow from Accumulator

Opcode	SBB	
Operand	Reg.	Mem.
Operation	[A] ← [A]– [r]– C[s]	[A]← [A] – [[H – L]] – [CS]
Bytes	1	1
M-Cycles	1	2
T-States	4	7

Description : The contents of the operand (register or memory) and the borrow flag are subtracted from the contents of the accumulator and the results are placed in the accumulator.

The contents of the operand are not altered; however, the previous Borrow flag is reset.

Flags : All flags are altered to reflect the result of the subtraction.

4. **SBI: Subtract Immediate with Borrow**

Opcode SBI

Operand 8-bit data

Operation [A] ← [A] – data – [CS]

Bytes 2

M-Cycles 2

T-States 7

Description : The 8-bit data (operand) and the borrow are subtracted from the contents of the accumulator, and the results are placed in the accumulator.

Flags : All flags are altered to reflect the result of the operation.

DAA : DECIMAL ADJUST ACCUMULATOR.

This instruction adjusts accumulator to packed BCD (Binary Coded Decimal) after adding two BCD numbers.

Instruction works as follows :

1. If value of the low-order four bits ($D_3 - D_0$) in the accumulator is greater than 9 or if auxiliary carry flag is set, then instruction adds 6 (06) to the low-order four bits.
2. If value of the high-order four bits ($D_7 - D_4$) in the accumulator is greater than 9 or if carry flag is set, then instruction adds 6(60) to the high-order four bits.

INCREMENT AND DECREMENT .

This group consists of the following set of instructions.

(1) INR r : Increment specified register

Operation : [r] ← [r + 1]

Opcode	**Operand**	**Bytes**
INRr	Regi. add.	1

Description : This instruction increments the contents of specified register by 1. The result is stored in the same register. The register r is 8-bit general purpose register such as A, B, C, D, E, H and L.

Flags : All flags except carry flag are affected

Example : B = 10H

INR B : This instruction will increment the contents of B register (10H) ; by one and stores the result (10 +1 =11H) in the same i.e. B register

Before instruction		**After instruction**
B 10 H	INR B	B 11

(2) INR M : Increment data in memory

Operation : [[H – L]] ← [[H – L]] + 1

Description : This instruction increments the contents of memory location pointed by HL register pair by 1. The result is stored at the same memory location. the HL register pair is used as a memory pointer.

Flags : All flags except carry flag are affected

Example : HL = 2050H, (2050H) = 30H

This instruction will increment the contents of memory location pointed by HL register pair, 2050H, i.e. data 30H by one. It will store the result (30 + 1 = 31H) at the same place.

(3) INX : Increment Register Pair by 1

Opcode INX

Operand Reg. pair

Operation [rp] ← [rp] + 1

Byes 1

M-Cycles 1

T-States 6

Description : The contents of the specified register pair are incremented by 1. The instruction views the contents of the two registers as a 16-bit number.

Flags : No flags are affected.

Example : Register pair HL contains 9FFFH. Specify the contents of the entire register if it is incremented by 1.

Instruction :

INX H Hex Code: 23

After adding 1 to the contents of the HL pair the answer is

H | A0 00 | L

(4) DCR r : Decrement specified register

Operation : [r] ← [r – 1]

Description : This instruction decrements the contents of the specified register by one. It stores the result in the same register. The register r is 8-bit general purpose register such as A, B, C, D, E, H and L.

Opcode	**Operand**	**Bytes**
DCR r	Register addressing	1

Flags : All flags except carry flag are affected

Example : E = 20H

This instruction will decrement the contents of E register (20 H) by one. It will store the result (20 – 1 = 1 FH) in the same, i.e. E register.

Before Execution		After Execution
E = 20	HDCR	EE = 1 F – H

(5) DCR ML : Decrement data in memory

Operation : [[H – L]] ← [[H – L]] – 1

Description : This instruction decrements the contents of memory location pointed by HL register pair by 1. The HL register pair is used as a memory pointer. The result is stored in the same memory location.

Opcode	**Operand**	**Bytes**
DCRM	Reg. indirect addressing	1

Flags : All flags except carry flag are affected

E xample : HL = 2050 H, (2050H) = 21 H

This instruction will decrement the contents of memory location pointed by HL register pair, 2050H, i.e. data 21H by one. It will store the result (21 – 1 = 20H) in the same memory.

Before Execution

H	20	L	50

Address	Data
204FH	
2050H	21
2051H	

DCR M

After Execution

H	20	L	50

Address	Data
204FH	
2050H	20
2051H	

(6) DCX : Decrement Register Pair by 1

Opcode	**Operand**	**Operation**	**Bytes**	**M-Cycles**	**T-States**
DCX	Reg. pair	[rp] ← [rp] – 1	1	1	6

Description : The contents of the specified register pair are decremented by 1. This instruction views the contents of two registers as a 16-bit number.

Flags : No flags are affected.

Example : Register pair DE contains 2000H. Specify the contents of the entire register if it is decremented by 1.

Instruction : DCX D

Before Execution

D	20
E	00

After Execution

D	1F
E	FF

Branch Group

The branch group instructions allow the microprocessor to change the sequence of a program, either unconditionally or under certain test conditions. This group include :

- Jump instructions
- Call and Return instructions
- Restart instructions

In this section only jump instructions are explained. The call, return, and restart instructions are associated with the subroutine technique and also require stack operation, hence are discussed in the stack group of instructions

JUMP.

This group consists of the following set of instructions.

(1) JMP addr : Jump unconditionally to the address

Operation : [PC] ← addr

Description : This instruction loads the PC with the address given within the instruction and resumes the program execution from this location.

Number of bytes : 3 bytes

First byte : Opcode of JMP

Second byte : Low order byte of the address

Third byte : High order byte of the address

Addressing mode : Immediate addressing

Flags : Flags are not affected

Example : JMP 2000H

This instruction will load PC with 2000H and processor will fetch next instruction from this address.

(2) Jump conditions addr : Jump condition to the address

Operation : If condition is true PC ← addr, else PC ← PC + 3

Description : This instruction causes a jump to an address given in the instruction if the desired condition occurs in the program before the execution of the instruction. The table below shows the possible conditions for jumps.

Table conditional jumps

Instruction code	**Description**	**Condition for jump**
JC	Jump on carry	CY = 1
JNC	Jump on not carry	CY = 0
JP	Jump on positive	S = 0
JM	Jump on minus	S = 1
JPE	Jump on parity even	P =1
JPO	Jump on parity odd	P = 0
JZ	Jump on zero	Z = 1
JNZ	Jump on not zero	Z = 0

Number of byte : 3 bytes

First byte : Opcode of Jcondition

Second byte : Low order byte of the address

Third byte : High order byte of the address

Addressing mode : Immediate addressing

Flags : Flags are not affected. Flags are checked

Example : Carry flag = 1

JC 2000H : This instruction will cause a jump to an address 2000H , i.e. program counter will load with 2000H since CF = 1

Before Execution After Execution

JC 2000H

(3) PCHL : Load HL contents into program counter

Operation : [PC] ← [HL], [PCH] ← [H], [PCL] ← [L]

Description : This instruction loads the contents of HL register pair into the program counter. Thus the program control is transferred to the location whose address is in HL register pair.

Addressing mode : Register addressing

Flags : Flags are not affected

Example : HL = 6000H

This instruction will load 6000H into the program counter

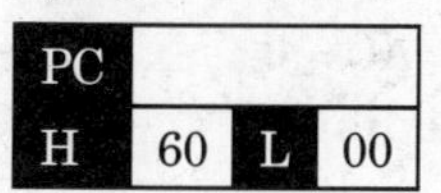

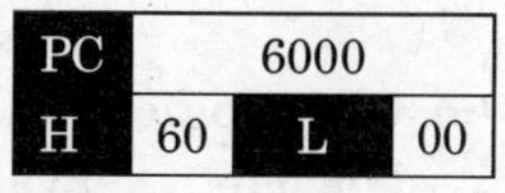

Note : This is effectively one byte unconditional jump instruction, provided that address of the jump is stored in HL register pair

Logic Group

Logic group instructions perform logic operations such as AND, OR and XOR, compare data between registers or between register and memory, rotate and complement data in registers.

This group consists of following set of instructions.

(1) ANA : Logical AND with Accumulator

Opcode	ANA	
Operand	Reg.	Mem
Bytes	1	1
M-Cycles	1	2
T-States	4	7

Description : The contents of the accumulator are logically ANDed with the contents of the operand (register or memory), and the result is placed in the accumulator. If the operand is a memory location, its address is specified by the contents of HL registers.

Flags: S, Z, P are modified to reflect the result of the operation CY is reset. In 8085, AC is set, and in 8080A AC is the result of ORing bits D_3 of the operands.

Example : The contents of the accumulator and the register D are 54H and 82H respectively. Logically AND the contents of register D with the contents of the accumulator. Show the flags and the contents of each register after ANDing.

Instruction : ANA D Hex Code : A2

Register contents before instruction — Logical AND — Register contents after instruction

AC P CY S Z

A 54 X F 54H = 0 1 0 1 0 1 0 0 A 00

D 82 X E 82H = 1 0 0 0 0 0 1 0 D 82

0 0 0 0 0 0 0 0

Flags : S = 0, Z = 1, P = 1

AC = 1, CY = 0

(for 8080A, AC = 0)

(2) ANI: AND Immediate with Accumulator

Opcode	**Operand**	**Bytes**	**M-Cycles**	**T-States**
ANI	8-bit data	2	2	7

Description : The contents of the accumulator are logically ANDed with the 8-bit data (operand) and the results are placed in the accumulator.

Flags : S, Z, P are modified to reflect the results of the operation. CY is reset. In 8085, AC is set.

Example : AND data byte 97H with the contents of the accumulator, which contains A3H.

Instruction: ANI 97H Hex Code: E6 97

Logical AND:

(A) A3H = 1 0 1 0 0 0 1 1

AND

(Data) 97H = 1 0 0 1 0 1 1 1

1 0 0 0 0 0 1 1 A 83

S	Z	AC	P	CY
1	0	1	0	0

(3) XRA: Exclusive OR with Accumulator

Opcode	XRA	
Operand		Reg. Mem
Operation	[A] ← [A] ∀ [r]	[A] ← [A] ∀ [[H – L]]
Bytes	1	1
M-Cycles	1	2
T-States	4	7

Description : The contents of the operand (register or memory) are Exclusive ORed with the contents of the accumulator, and the results are placed in the accumulator. The contents of the operand are not altered.

Flags : Z, S, P are altered to reflect the results of the operation. CY and AC are reset.

(4) XRI: Exclusive OR Immediate with Accumulator

Opcode	XRI
Operand	8-bit data
Operation	[A] ← [A] ∀ data
Bytes	2
M-Cycles	2
T-States	7

Description : The 8-bit data (operand) are Exclusive ORed with the contents of the accumulator, and the results are placed in the accumulator.

Flags : Z, S, P are altered to reflect the results of the operation. CY and AC are set to zero.

Example : Assume the contents of the accumulator are 8FH. Exclusive OR the contents of the accumulator with A2H.

Instruction: XRI, A2H

8FH	= 1000 1111
A2H	= 1010 0010
Exclusive OR:	0010 1101
Flags:	S = 0, Z = 0, P = 1, CY = 0, AC = 0

(5) ORA: Logically OR with Accumulator

Opcode		ORA
Operand	Reg.	Mem.
Operation	[A] ← [A] ∀ [r]	[A] ← [A] ∀ [[H – L]]
Bytes	1	1
M-cycles	1	2
T-States	4	7

Description : The contents of the accumulator are logically ORed with the contents of the operand (register or memory), and the results are placed in the accumulator. If the operand is a memory location, its address is specified by the contents of HL registers.

Flags : Z, S, P are modified to reflect the results of the operation. AC and CY are reset.

Example : Assume the accumulator has data byte 03H and register C holds byte 81H. Combine the bits of register C with the accumulator bits.

Instruction : ORA C

Register contents before instruction	Logical OR	Register contents after instruction
A 03	03H = 0000 0011	A 82
C 81	81H = 1000 0001	C 81
	82H = 1000 0010	
	S = 1, Z = 0, P = 1	
	Flags: CY = 0, AC = 0	

(6) ORI: Logically OR Immediate

Opcode	ORI
Operand	8-bit data
Operation	[A] ← [A] ∀ data
Bytes	2
M-Cycles	2
T-States	7
Hex code	F6

Description : The contents of the accumulator are logically ORed with 8-bit data in the operand and the results are placed in the accumulator.

Flags : S, Z, P are modified to reflect the results of the operation. CY and AC are reset.

(7) CMP: Compare with Accumulator

Opcode	CMP	
Operand	Reg. Mem.	
Operation	[A] – [r]	[A] – [[H – L]
Bytes 1	1	
M-Cycles	1	2
T-States	4	7

Description : The contents of the operand (register or memory) are compared with the contents of the accumulator. Both contents are preserved and the comparison is shown by setting the flags as follows :

(a) If (A) < (Reg/Mem) : Carry flag is set and Zero flag is reset.

(b) If (A) = (Reg/Mem) : Zero flag is set and Carry flag is reset.

(c) If (A) > (Reg/Mem) : Carry and Zero flags are reset.

The comparison of two bytes is performed by subtracting the contents of the operand from the contents of the accumulator; however, neither contents are modified.

Flags : S, P, AC are also modified in addition to Z and CY to reflect the results of the operation.

Example : Register B contains data byte 62H and the accumulator contains data byte 57H. Compare the contents of register B with those of the accumulator.

Instruction : CMP B

Before instruction		After instruction	
A	57	A	57
B	62	B	62

Flags : S = 1, Z = 0, AC = 1
P = 1, CY = 1

Results after executing the instruction :

(i) No contents are changed.

(ii) Carry flag is set becuase (A) < (B).

(iii) S, Z, P, AC flags will also be modified as listed above.

(8) CPI : Compare Immediate with Accumulator

Opcode	CPI
Operand	8-bit
Operation	[A] – data
Bytes	2
M-Cycles	2
T-States	7

Description : The second byte (8-bit data) is compared with the contents of the accumulator. The values being compared remain unchanged and the results of the comparison are indicated by setting the flags as follows.

(a) If (A) < Data : Carry flag is set and Zero flag is reset.

(b) If (A) = Data : Zero flag is set and Carry flag is reset.

(c) If (A) > Data : Carry and Zero flags are reset.

The comparison of two bytes is performed by subtracting the data byte from the contents of the accumulator, however, neither contents are modified.

Flags: S, P, AC are also modified in addition to Z and CY to reflect the result of the operation.

Example: Assume the accumulator contains data byte C2H.Compare 98H with the accumulator contents.

Instruction : CPI 98H Hex Code : FE 98

Results after executing the instruction :

(i) The accumulator contents remain unchanged.

(ii) Z and CY flags are reset because (A) > Data.

(iii) Other flags : S = 0, AC = 0, P = 0.

(9) CMC: Complement Carry

Opcode	CMC
Operand	None
Operation	$[CS] \leftarrow [\overline{CD}]$
Bytes	1
M-Cycles	1
T-States	4

Description : The Carry flag is complemented.

Flags : The Carry flag is modified, no other flags are affected.

(10) CMA : Complement Accumulator

Opcode	CMA
Operand	None
Operation	$[A] \leftarrow [\overline{A}]$
Bytes	1
M-Cycles	1
T-States	4

Description : The contents of the accumulator are complemented.

Flags : No flags are affected.

Example: Complement the accumulator, which has data byte 89H.

Instruction : CMA

Before instruction

A 1 0 0 0 1 0 0 1 = 89H

After instruction

A 0 1 1 1 0 1 1 0 = 76H

ROTATE

(1) RLC: Rotate Accumulator Left

Opcode	RLC
Operand	None
Operation	$[A_{n+1}] \leftarrow A_n$, $[A_0] \leftarrow [A_7]$, $[CY] \leftarrow [A_7]$
Bytes	1
M-Cycles	1
T-States	4

Description : Each binary bit of the accumulator is rotated left by one position. Bit D_7 is placed in the position of D_0 as well as in the Carry flag.

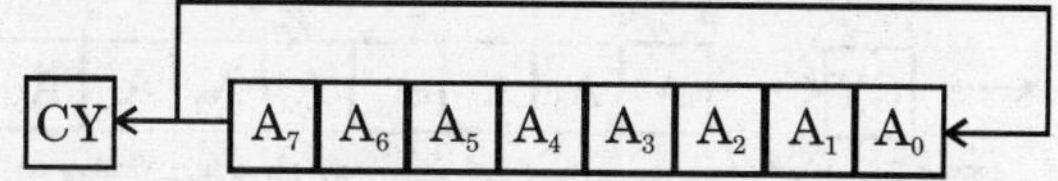

Flags : CY is modified according to bit D7, S, Z, P, AC are not affected.

Example: Rotate the contents of the accumulator left, assuming it contains A7H and the Carry flag is reset to 0.

Instruction: RCL

Accumulator contents before instruction

D7 D6 D5 D4 D3 D2 D1 D0 — 1 0 1 0 0 1 1 1 — CY 0

Accumulator contents

1 0 1 0 0 1 1 1 — CY 1

Comments: The contents of bit D_7 are placed in bit D_0, and the Carry flag is modified accordingly. However, the contents of the Carry are not placed in bit D_0 as in instruction RAL.

(2) RRC: Rotate Accumulator Right

Opcode RRC
Operand None
Operation $[A_7] \leftarrow [A_0]$, $[cy] \leftarrow [A_0]$, $[A_n] \leftarrow [A_{n+1}]$
Bytes 1
M-Cycles 1
T-States 4

Description : Each binary bit of the accumulator is rotated right by one position. Bit D_0 is placed in the position of D_7 as well as in the Carry flag.

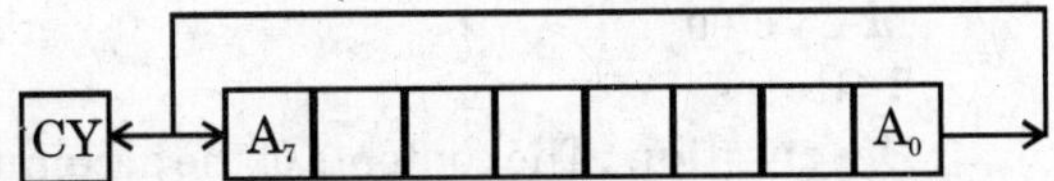

Flags : CY is modified according to bit D_0, S, Z, P, AC are not affected.

Example : Rotate the contents of the accumulator right, if it contains A7H and the Carry flag is reset to 0.

Instruction: RRC Hex Code: 0F

Accumulator contents before instruction

Accumulator contents after instruction

(3) RAL: Rotate Accumulator Left through Carry

Opcode RAL
Operand None
Operation $[A_{n+1}] \leftarrow [A_n]$, $[CY]] \leftarrow [A_7]$, $[A_0] \leftarrow [CY]$
Bytes 1
M-Cycles 1
T-States 4

Description : Each binary bit of the accumulator is rotated left by one position through the Carry flag. Bit D_7 is placed in the bit in the Carry flag and the Carry flag is placed in the least significant D_0.

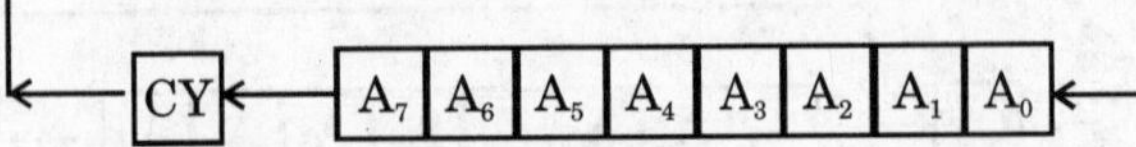

Flags : CY is modified according to bit D_7, S, Z, AC, P are not affected.

Example : Rotate the contents of the accumulator through Carry, assuming the accumulator has A7H and the Carry flag is reset.

Instruction: RAL

Accumulator contents before instruction

Accumulator contents after instruction

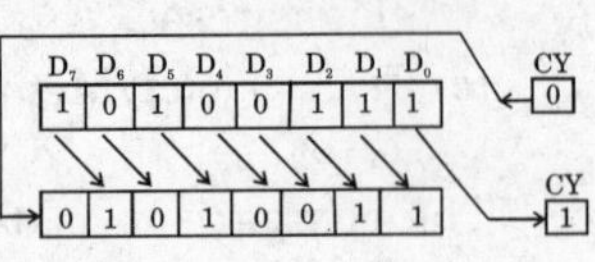

(4) RAR: Rotate Accumulator Right through Carry

Opcode RAR
Operand None
O peration $[A_n] \leftarrow [A_{n+1}]$, $[CY] \leftarrow [A_0]$, $[A_7] \leftarrow [CY]$
Bytes 1
M-Cycles 1
T-States 4

Description: Each binary bit of the accumulator is rotated right by one position through the Carry flag. Bit D_0 is placed in the Carry flag and the bit in the Carry flag is placed in the most significant position, D_7.

Flags : CY is modified according to bit D_0, S, Z, P, AC are not affected.

Example : Rotate the contents of the accumulator assuming it contains A7H and the Carry flag is reset to 0.

Instruction: RAR

Accumulator contents before instruction

Accumulator contents after instruction

Stack Operations, Input/Output and Machine Control Group.

Stack Operations

This group consists of following set of instructions.

(1) LXI SP, Data and SPHL : Initializes Stack Pointer.

Before execution of any stack related instruction, stack pointer must be initialized with a valid memory address.

The stack pointer can be initialized by two ways :

(*i*) Direct way : LXI SP, data (16) ; Loads 16-bit data into SP

(*ii*) Indirect way : LXI H, data (16) ; Load the 16-bit data into HL

SPHL ; Load the contents of HL into SP

Normally, the stack pointer is initialized by the direct way. When a programmer wishes to set the stack pointer to a value that has been computed by the program, indirect way is used. The computed value is placed in H and L and the contents of HL register pair then moved into the stack pointer.

SPHL : Move data from HL to stack pointer.

Operation : [SP] ← [HL]

Description : This instruction copies the contents of HL register pair into the stack pointer. The contents of H register are copied to higher order byte of stack pointer and contents of L register are copied to the lower byte of pair then moved into the stack pointer.

Opcode	SPHL
Operand	Reg.addressing
Bytes	1
M-cycles	1
T-states	6

Flags : Flags are not affected.

Example : SP = 2700 H ; HL = 2500 H

This instruction will copy 2500H into stack pointer. So after execution of instruction stack pointer contents will be 2500 H.

Before Execution

SP	2700
HL	2500

After Execution

SP	2500
HL	2500

Note.

(*i*) The stack pointer can be initialized anywhere in the read/write memory map. However, as a general practice, the stack pointer is initialized at the highest Read/Write memory location so that it will be less likely to interfere with a program.

(*ii*) Since the 8085A's stack pointer is decremented before data is written to the stack, the stack pointer can actually be initialized to a value one higher than the highest read/write memory location available.

(2) PUSH and POP.

When programmer realizes the shortage of the registers, he stores present contents of the registers in the stack with the help of PUSH instruction and then uses registers for other function. After completion of other function programmer loads previous contents of the register from the stack with the help of POP instruction.

PUSH operation.

In PUSH operation, 16-bit data is stored on the stack. This 16-bit data is stored in two steps. In the first step, stack pointer is decremented by one and then the higher byte of the 16-bit data is stored at the memory location pointed by stack pointer. In the second step, stack pointer is again decremented by one and then lower byte of the 16-bit data is stored at the memory location pointed by stack pointer.

Steps involved in PUSH Operation

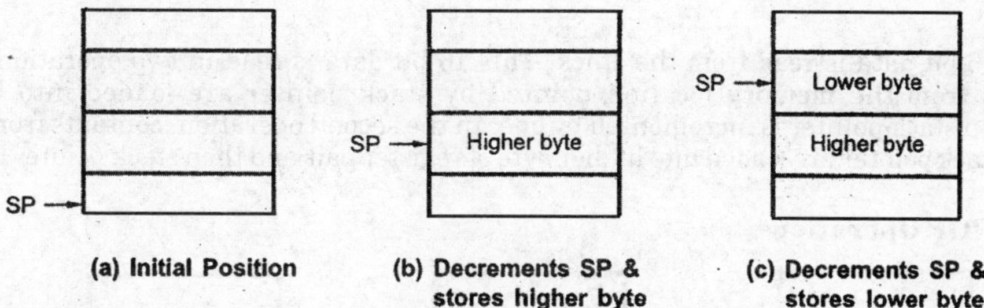

(a) Initial Position **(b) Decrements SP & stores higher byte** **(c) Decrements SP & stores lower byte**

PUSH instructions :

(*i*) PUSH rp : Stores the contents specified register pair on the stack.

Operation : [SP] ← [SP – 1], [SP] ← rpH, [SP] ← [SP – 1], [SP] ← rpL.

Description : This instruction decrements stack pointer by one and copies the higher byte of the register pair into the memory location pointed by stack pointer. It then decrements the stack pointer again by one and copies the lower byte of the register pair into the memory location pointed by stack pointer. The rp is 16- bit register pair such as BC, DE, HL. Only higher order register is to be specified within the instruction.

Opcode	**Operand**	**Bytes**	**M-cycles**
PUSH rp	Reg. indirect addressing	1	3

Flags : Flags are not affected.

Example : SP = 2000H ; DE = 1050H

PUSH D : This instruction will decrement the stack pointer (2000H) by one (SP = 1FFFH) and copies the contents of D register (10H) into the memory location 1FFFH. It then decrements the stack pointer again by one (SP = 1FFEH) and copies the contents of E register (50H) into the memory location 1FFEH.

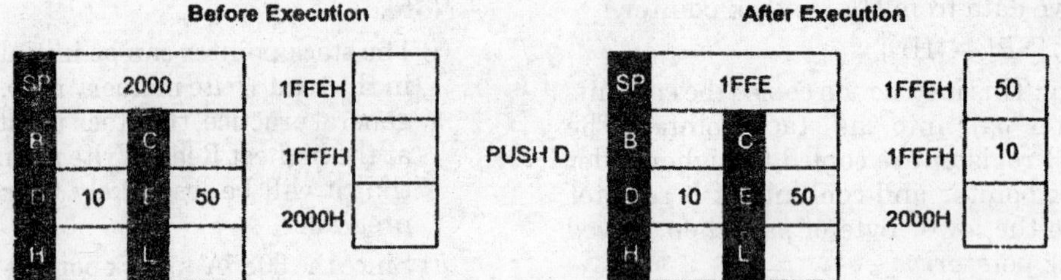

(ii) PUSH PSW : Stores the contents of program status word and accumulator on the stack.

Operation : [SP] ← [SP – 1]

[SP] ← [A]

[SP] ← [SP – 1]

[SP] ← Flag register

Description : This instruction decrements stack pointer by one and copies the accumulator contents into the memory location pointed by stack pointer. It then decrements the stack pointer again by one and copies the flag register into the memory location pointed by the stack pointer.

Opcode	Operand	Bytes	M-cycles	T-states
PUSH PSW	Reg. indirect addressing	1	3	12

Flags : Flags are not affected.

Example : [SP] = 2000H, [A] = 20H, Flag register = 80H

This instruction decrements the stack pointer (SP = 2000H) by one (SP = 1FFFH) and copies the contents of the accumulator (20H) into the memory location 1FFFH. It then decrements the stack pointer again by one (SP = 1FFEH) and copies the contents of the flag register (80H) into the memory location 1FFEH.

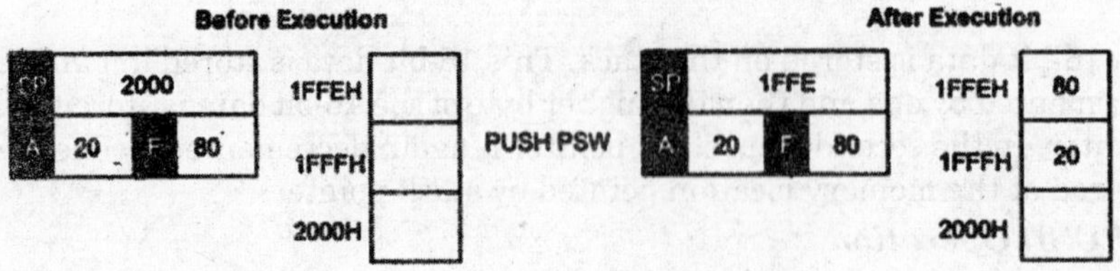

POP operation.

In POP operation, 16-bit data is read from the stack. This 16-bit data is read in two operations. In the first operation, contents from the memory location pointed by stack pointer are loaded into lower byte of register pair and then stack pointer is incremented by one. In the second operation, contents from the memory location pointed by stack pointer are loaded into higher byte of register pair and then stack pointer is incremented by one.

Step Involved in POP Operation

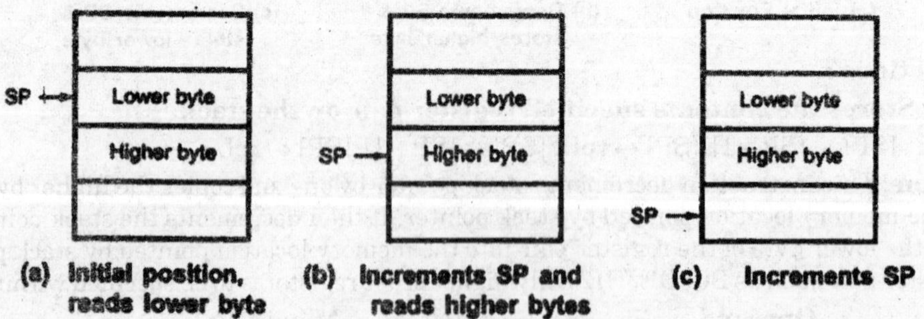

(a) Initial position, reads lower byte (b) Increments SP and reads higher bytes (c) Increments SP

POP instructions.

(i) POP rp : Loads specified register pair with 16-bit data from the stack.

Operation : rpL ← [SP]

[SP] ← [SP] + 1

rpH ← [[SP]], [SP] ← [SP + 1]

Description : This instruction copies the contents of memory location pointed by the stack pointer into the lower byte of the specified register pair and increments the stack pointer by one. It then copies the contents of memory location pointed by stack pointer into the higher byte of the specified register pair and increments the stack pointer again by one. The rp is 16-bit register pair such as BC, DE, HL. Only higher order register is to be specified within the instruction.

Opcode	Operand	Bytes	M-cycles	T-states
POP rp	Reg. indirect addressing	1	3	10

Flags : Flags are not affected.

Example : [SP] = 2000H, [2000H] = 30H, [2001H] = 50H **POP B**

This instruction will copy the contents of memory location pointed by stack pointer, 2000H (*i.e.* data 30H) into the C register. It will then increment the stack pointer by one, 2001H and will copy the contents of memory location pointed by stack pointer, 2001H (*i.e.* data 50H) into B register, and increment the stack pointer again by one.

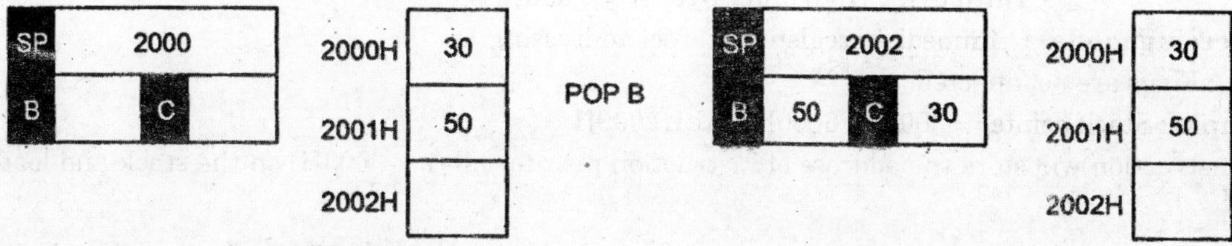

***(ii)* POP PSW :** Loads program status word and accumulator with 16-bit from the stack.

Operation : Flag register ← [[SP]]

[SP] ← [SP] + 1

A ← [[SP]]

[SP] ← [SP] + 1

Description : This instruction copies the contents of memory location pointed by the stack pointer into the flag register and increments the stack pointer by one. It then copies the contents of memory location pointed by stack pointer into the accumulator and increments the stack pointer again by one.

Opcode	Operand	Bytes	M-cycles	T-states
POP PSW	Reg. indirect addressing	1	3	10

Flags : All flags are affected.

Example : [SP] = 2000H, [2000H] = 30H, [2001H] = 50H

This instruction will copy the contents of memory location pointed by the stack pointer, 2000H (i.e. data 30H) into the flag register. It will then increment the stack pointer by one, 2001H and will copy the contents of memory location pointed by stack pointer into the accumulator and increment the stack pointer again by one.

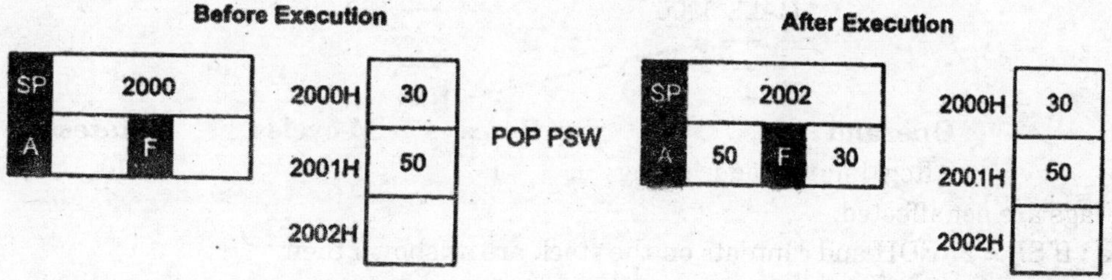

(3) CALL

This group consists of the following set of instructions.

***(i)* CALL addr.**

Call unconditionally a subroutine whose starting address is given within instruction

Operation : $[[SP]-1] \leftarrow PC_H$

$[[SP]-2] \leftarrow PC_L$

$[SP] \leftarrow [SP]-2$

$[PC] \leftarrow addr$

Description : The CALL instruction is used to transfer program control to a subprogram or subroutine. This instruction pushes the current PC contents onto the stack and loads the given address into the PC. Thus the program control is transferred to the address given in the instruction. Stack pointer is decremented by two.

When the subroutine is called, the program control is transferred from calling program to the subroutine. After execution of subroutine it is necessary to transfer program control back to the calling program. To do this processor must remember the address of the instruction next to the CALL instruction. Processor saves this address on the stack when the CALL instruction is executed.

Note : The stack is a part of read/write memory set aside for storing intermediate results and addresses.

Number of Bytes : 3 bytes

First byte : Opcode of CALL.

Second byte : Low order byte of the address.

Third byte : High order byte of the address.

Addressing mode : Immediate register indirect addressing.

Flags : Flags are not affected.

Example : Stack pointer = 3000 H. 6000H CALL 2000H

This instruction will store the address of instruction next to call (i.e. 6003H) on the stack and load PC with 2000H.

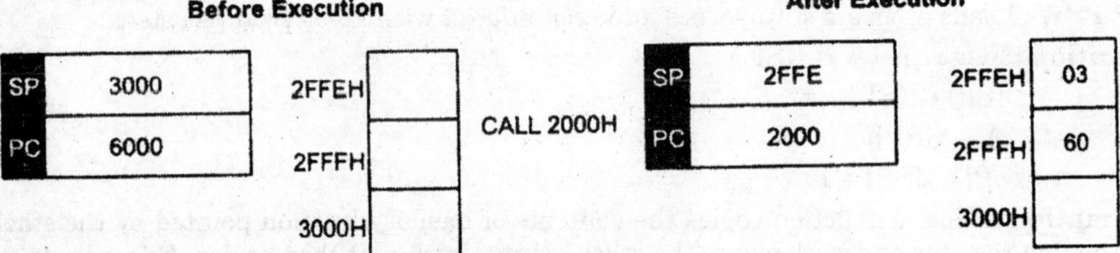

RET : Return from the subroutine unconditionally.

Operation : $[PC_L] \leftarrow [[SP]]$

$[PC_H] \leftarrow [[SP] + 1]$

$[SP] \leftarrow [SP] + 2$

Description : This instruction pops the return addr (address of the instruction next to CALL in the main program) from the stack and loads program counter with this return address. Thus transfers program control to the instruction next to call in the main program.

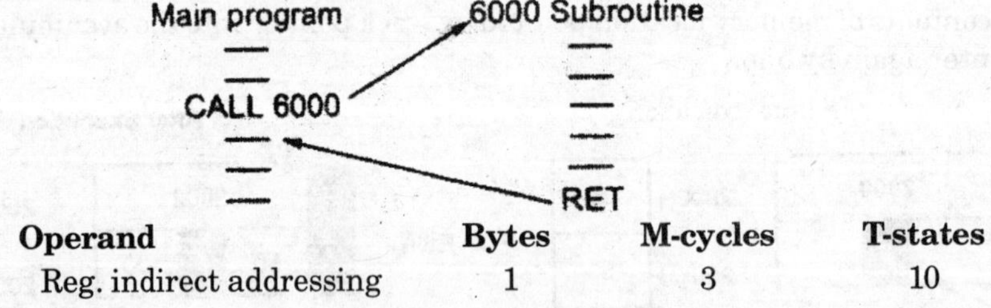

Opcode	**Operand**	**Bytes**	**M-cycles**	**T-states**
RET	Reg. indirect addressing	1	3	10

Flags : Flags are not affected.

Example : If SP = 27 FDH and contents on the stack are as shown then

SP → 27FD 00

27FE 62

27FF

This instruction will load PC with 6200H and it will transfer program control to the address 6200H. It will also increment the stack pointer by two.

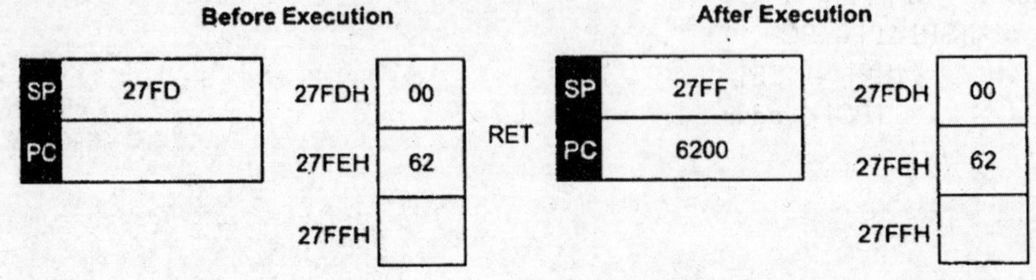

Conditional call and Return instructions :

In addition to the unconditional CALL and RET instructions, the 8085A instruction set includes eight conditional CALL instructions and eight conditional RET instructions. These conditions are checked by reading the status of respective flags. If the condition associated with the conditional CALL is not met, the instruction following the CALL is executed. If the condition is met, the program counter contents are saved on the stack, and the address contained in the CALL instruction is loaded into program counter. The number of machine cycles and T-states required by a conditional CALL depends on whether or not the condition is satisfied. When the condition is not satisfied, two machine cycles with a total of nine T-state are required to fetch, decode and execute the instruction. When the condition is satisfied, five machine cycles with 18 T-states are required.

***(ii)*Condition addr.**

Call the subroutine conditionally at given addr.

Operation : If condition true [[SP]–1] ← $[PC_H]$

[[SP]–2] ← $[PC_L]$

[PC] ← addr

else [PC] ← [PC] + 3 ↓[SP] ← [SP] – 2

Description : This instruction calls the subroutine at the given address if a specified condition is satisfied. Before call it stores the address of instruction next to the call on the stack and decrements stack pointer by two. The table shows the possible conditions for calls.

Table : Conditional calls

Instruction code	Description	Condition for CALL
CC	Call on carry	CY = 1
CNC	Call on not carry	CY = 0
CP	Call on positive	S = 0
CM	Call on minus	S = 1
CPE	Call on parity even	P = 1
CPO	Call on parity odd	P = 0
CZ	Call on zero	Z = 1
CNZ	Call on not zero	Z = 0

Bytes : 3 bytes

First byte : Opcode at Ccondition.

Second byte : Low order byte of the address.

Third byte : High order byte of the address.

Addressing mode : Immediate register indirect addressing.

Flags : Flags are not affected. Flags are checked.

Example : Carry flag = 1, stack pointer = 4000H

2000H CC 3000H ; This instruction will store the address of the next instruction i.e. 2003H on the stack and load the program counter with 3000H.

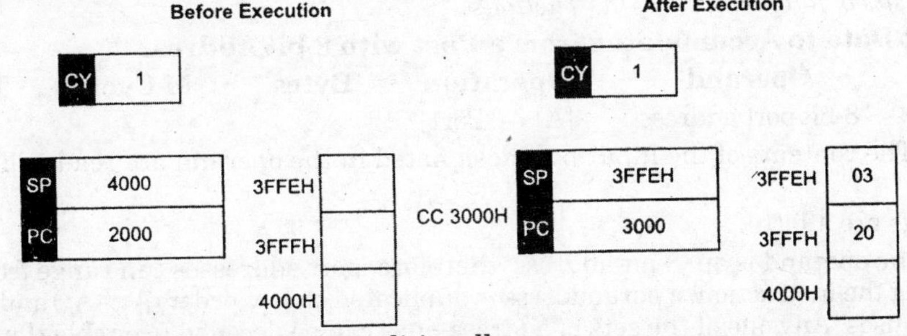

Rcondition : Return from the subroutine conditionally.

Operation : If condition is true

$[PC_L]$ ← [[SP]]

$[PC_H]$ ← [[SP] + 1]

[SP] ← [SP] + 2

else

[PC] ← [PC] + 1

Description : This instruction returns the control to the main program if the specified condition is satisfied. Table shows the possible conditions for return.

Table : Conditions for return

Instruction code	Description	Condition for RET
RC	Return on carry	CY = 1
RNC	Return on not carry	CY = 0
RP	Return on positive	S = 0
RM	Return on minus	S = 1
RPE	Return on parity even	P = 1
RPO	Return on parity odd	P = 0
RZ	Return on zero	Z = 1
RNZ	Return on not zero	Z = 0

Opcode	Operand	Byte
Rcondition	Reg. indirect addressing	1

Flags : Flags are not affected.

(4) RST : RESTART

This group consists of following set of instruction

(i) RST: Restart

Opcode	Bytes	M-Cycles	T-States
R S T n	1	3	12

Opcode/Operand	Binary Code	Hex Code	Restart Address (H)
RST 0	11 000 111	C7	0000
RST 1	11 001 111	CF	0008
RST 2	11 010 111	D7	0010
RST 3	11 011 111	DF	0018
RST 4	11 100 111	E7	0020
RST 5	11 101 111	EF	0028
RST 6	11 110 111	F7	0030
RST 7	11 111 111	FF	0038

Operation : [[SP] – 1] ← [P C H], [[SP] – 2] ← [PCL], [SP] ← [SP] – 2, [PC] ← 8n

Description : The RST instructions are equivalent to 1-byte call instructions to one of the eight memory locations on page 0. The instructions are generally used in conjunction with interrupts and inserted using external hardware. However, these can be used as software instructions in a program to transfer program execution to one of the eight locations.

Flags : No flags are affected.

***(ii)* Input/ouput.**

This group consits of following set of instructions.

***(a)* IN : Input Data to Accumulator from a Port with 8-bit Address**

Opcode	Operand	Operation	Bytes	M-Cycles	T-States
IN	8-bit port address	[A] ← [Port]	2	3	10

Description The contents of the input port designated in the operand are read and loaded into the accumulator.

Flags : No flags are affected.

Comments: The operand is an 8-bit address; therefore, port addresses can range from 00H to FFH. While executing the instruction, a port address is duplicated on low-order ($A_7 - A_0$) and high-order ($A_{15} - A_8$) address buses. Any one of the sets of address lines can be decoded to enable the input port.

***(b)* OUT : Output Data from Accumulator to a Port with 8-bit Address**

Opcode	Operand	Operation	Bytes	M-Cycles	T-States
OUT	8-bit port address	[Port] ← [A]	2	3	10

Description : The contents of the accumulator are copied into the output port specified by the operand.

Flags : No flags are affected.

(c) XTHL : Exchange H and L with Top of Stack

Opcode	Operand	Bytes	M-Cycles	T-States
XTHL	None	1	5	16

Description : The contents of the L register are exchanged with the stack location pointed out by the contents of the stack pointer register. The contents of the H register are exchanged with the next stack location [SP] + 1 ; however, the contents of the stack pointer register are not altered.

Flags : No flags are affected.

Example : The contents of various registers and stack locations are as shown:

				Stacks	
H	A2	57	L	2095	38
SP	2095			2096	67

Illustrate the contents of these registers after instruction XTHL

Register contents after XTHL				Stacks	
H	67	38	L	2095	57
SP	2095			2096	A2

(iii) Machine control.

This group consists of following set of instructions

(a) EI: Enable Interrupts

Opcode	Operand	Bytes	M-Cycles	T-States
EI	None	1	1	4

Description : The Interrupt enable flip-flop is set and all interrupts are enabled.

Flags : No flags are affected.

Comments : After a system reset or the acknowledgment of an interrupt, the Interrupt Enable flip-flop is reset, thus disabling the interrupts. This instruction is necessary to reenable the interrupts (except TRAP).

(b) DI: Disable Interrupts

Opcode	Operand	Bytes	M-Cycles	T-States
DI	None	1	1	4

Description The Interrupt enable flip-flop is reset and all the interrupts except the TRAP (8085) are disabled.

Flags : No flags are affected.

Comments : This instruction is commonly used when the execution of a code sequence cannot be interrupted. For example, in critical time delays, this instruction is used at the beginning of the code and the interrupts are enabled at the end of the code. The 8085 TRAP cannot be disabled.

(c) HLT: Halt and Enter Wait State

Opcode	Operand	Bytes	M-Cycles	T-States
HLT	None	1	2 or more	5 or more

Description : The MPU finishes executing the current instruction and halts any further execution. The MPU enters the Halt Acknowledge machine cycle and Wait states are inserted in every clock period. The address and the data bus are placed in the high impedance state. The contents of the registers are unaffected during the HLT state. An interrupt or reset is necessary to exit from the Halt state.

Flags : No flags are affected

(d) SIM: Set Interrupt Mask

Opcode	Operand	Bytes	M-Cycles	T-States
SIM	None	1	1	4

Description : This is multipurpose instruction and used to implement the 8085 interrupts (RST 7.5, 6.5, and 5.5) and serial data output.

The instruction interprets the accumulator contents as follows :

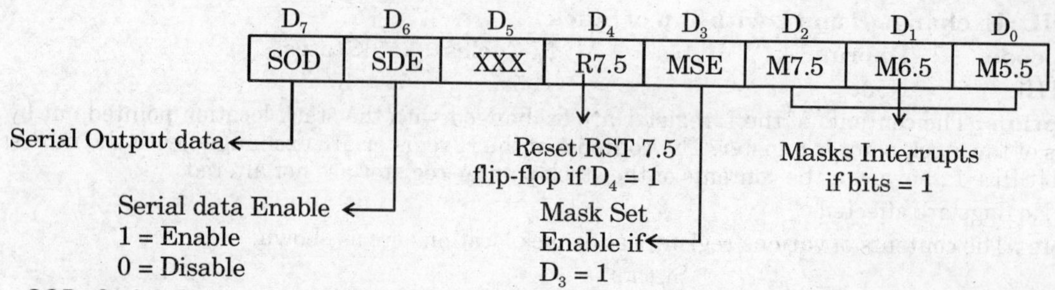

- SOD–Serial Output Data: Bit D_7 of the accumulator is latched into the SOD output line and made available to a serial peripheral if bit $D_6 = 1$.
- SDE–Serial Data Enable: If this bit = 1, it enables the serial output. To implement serial output, this bit needs to be enabled.
- XXX–Don't Care
- R7.5–Reset RST 7.5: If this bit = 1, RST 7.5 flip-flop is reset. This is additional control to reset RST 7.5.
- MSE–Mask Set Enable: If this bit is high, it enables the functions of bis D_2, D_1, D_0. This is a master control over all the interrupt masking bits. If this bit is low, bits D_2, D_1, and D_0 do not have any effect on the masks.
  - M7.5–D_2 = 0, RST 7.5 is enabled
    = 1, RST 7.5 is masked or disabled
  - M6.5–D1 = 0, RST 6.5 is enabled
    = 1, RST 6.5 is masked or disabled
  - M5.5–D0 = 0, RST 5.5 is enabled
    = 1, RST 5.5 is masked or disabled

(*e*) RIM: Read Interrupt Mask

Opcode	**Operand**	**Bytes**	**M-Cycles**	**T-States**
RIM	None	1	1	4

Description : This is a multipurpose instruction used to read the status of interrupts 7.5, 7.5, 5.5 and to read serial data input bit. The instruction loads eight bits in the accumulator with the following interpretations:

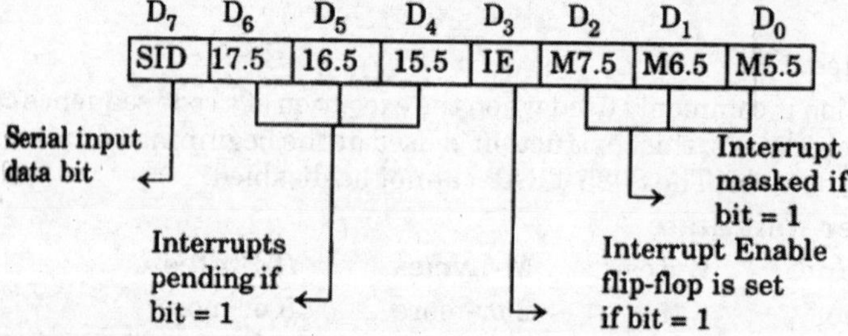

Flags : No flags are affected.

Example : After the execution of instruction RIM, the accumulator contained 49H. Explain the accumulator contents.

(A):

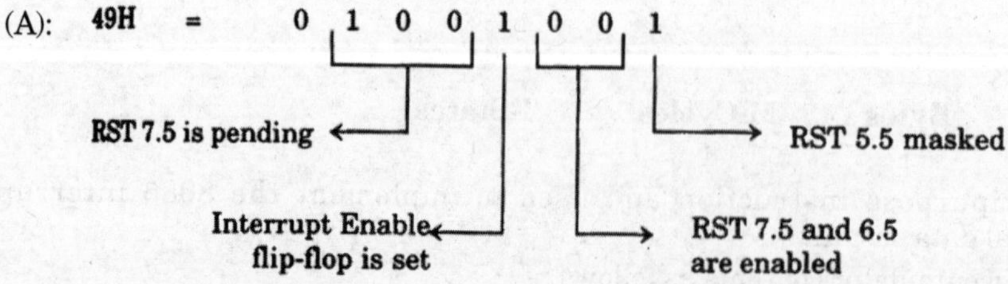

MEMORY INTERFACING

Memory interfacing circuit is used to access memory quite frequently to read instruction codes and data stored in memory. These read/write operations are monitored by control signals. The microprocessor activates these signals when it wants to read from and write into memory.

Memory Structure and its Requirements

Read/write memories consist of an array of registers, in which each register has unique address. The size of the memory is N × M as shown in Fig.6, where N is number of registers and M is word length, in number of bits.

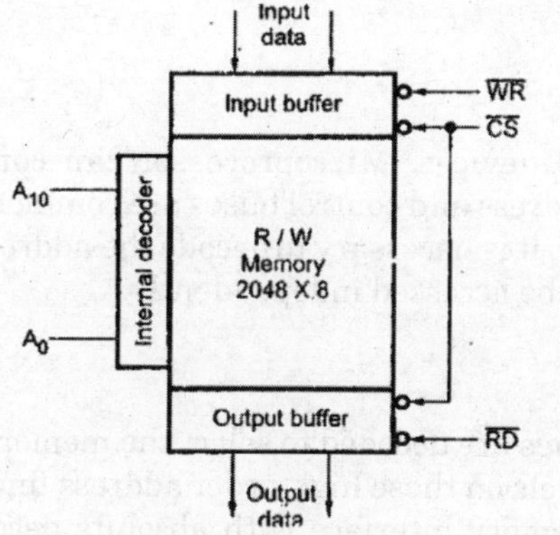

Logic diagram for RAM

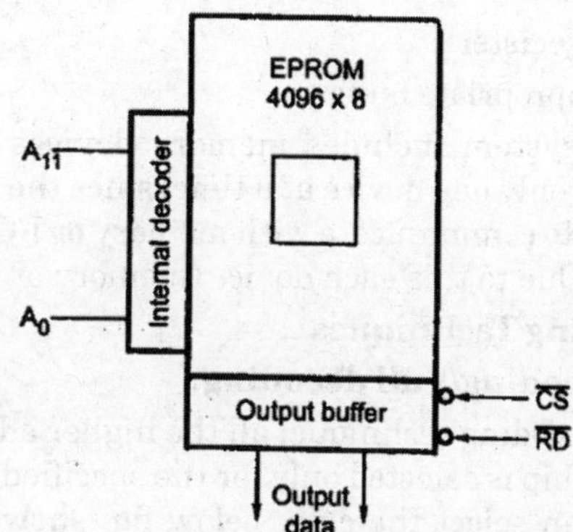

Logic diagram for EPROM

e.g : If memory is having 12 address lines and 8 data lines, then

Number of registers/memory locations = $2^N = 2^{12} = 4096$.

Word length = M bit = 8 bit

e.g : If memory has 8192 memory locations, then it has 13 address lines.

The Table below summarizes the memory capacity and address lines required for memory interfacing.

Memory Capacity	Address Lines Required
1K = 1024 memory locations	10
2K = 2048 memory locations	11
4K = 4096 memory locations	12
8K = 8192 memory locations	13
16K = 16384 memory locations	14
32K = 32768 memory locations	15
64K = 65536 memory locations	16

As shown in Fig.(a) memory chip has 11 address lines A_{10}-A_0, one chip select ($\overline{CS}$), and two control lines. Read ($\overline{RD}$) to enable output buffer and write ($\overline{WR}$) to enable the input buffer. The internal decoder is used to decode address lines. Fig.(b) shows logic diagram of a typical EPROM (Erasable Programmable Read-Only Memory) with 4096 (4K) registers. It has 12 address lines A_{11}-A_0, one chip select ($\overline{CS}$), one read control signal. Since EPROM is a read only memory, it does not require the ($\overline{WR}$) signal.

Basic Concepts in Memory Interfacing

Microprocessor 8085 can access 64Kbytes memory since address bus is 16-bit. But it is not always necessary to use full 64Kbytes address space. Total memory size depends upon the application.

Generally EPROM (or EPROMs) is used as a program memory and RAM (or RAMs) as a data memory. When both, EPROM and RAM are used, then total address space 64Kbytes is shared by them.

Capacity of program memory and data memory depends on the application.

It is not always necessary to select 1 EPROM and 1 RAM. We can have multiple EPROMs and multiple RAMs as per the requirement of application.

e.g. We have to implement 32 Kbytes of program memory and 4Kbytes EPROMs are available. In this case, we can connect 8 EPROMs in parallel (4 Kbytes × 8 = 32 Kbytes) with different chip select for each EPROM. We can place EPROM/RAM anywhere in full 64 Kbytes address space. But program memory (EPROM) should be located from address 0000H since reset address of 8085 microprocessor is 0000H.

It is not always necessary to locate EPROM and RAM in consecutive memory addresses. For example: If the mapping of EPROM is from 0000H to 0FFFH, it is not must to locate RAM from 1000H. We can locate it anywhere between 1000H and FFFFH. Where to locate memory component totally depends on the application.

Requirements of Memory Interfacing

(1) Select the chip

(2) Identify the register

(3) Enable the appropriate buffer.

Microprocessor system includes memory devices and I/O devices. Microprocessor can communicate (read/write) with only one device at a time, since the data, address and control buses are common for all the devices. In order to communicate with memory or I/O devices, it is necessary to decode the address from the microprocessor. Due to this each device (memory or I/O) can be accessed independently.

Address Decoding Techniques

(1) Absolute decoding/Full decoding.

In absolute decoding technique, all the higher address lines are decoded to select the memory chip, and the memory chip is selected only for the specified logic levels on these high-order address lines; no other logic levels can select the chip. below fig. shows the memory interface with absolute decoding. This addressing technique is normally used in large memory systems.

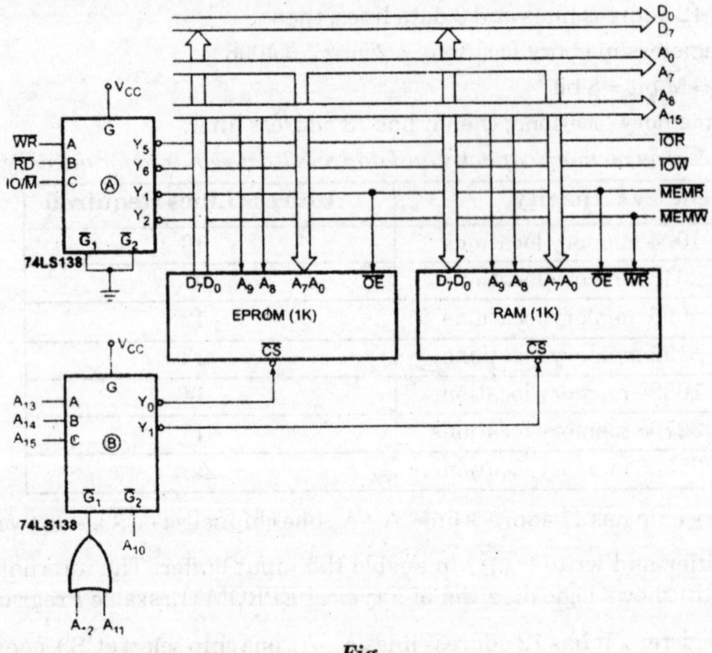

Fig.

Memory Map :

Memory ICs	A_{15}	A_{14}	A_{13}	A_{12}	A_{11}	A_{10}	A_9	A_8	A_7	A_6	A_5	A_4	A_3	A_2	A_1	A_0	Address
Starting address of EPROM	0	0	0	0	0	0	0	0	0	0	0	0	0	0	0	0	0000H
End address of EPROM	0	0	0	0	0	0	1	1	1	1	1	1	1	1	1	1	03FFH
Starting Address of RAM	0	0	1	0	0	0	0	0	0	0	0	0	0	0	0	0	2000H
End address of RAM	0	0	1	0	0	0	1	1	1	1	1	1	1	1	1	1	23FFH

(2) Linear decoding/Partial decoding.

In small systems, hardware for the decoding logic can be eliminated by using individual high-order address lines to select memory chips. This is referred to as linear decoding. Fig.9 shows the addressing of RAM with linear decoding technique. This technique is also called *partial decoding.* It reduces the cost of decoding circuit, but it has a drawback of multiple addresses (shadow addresses).

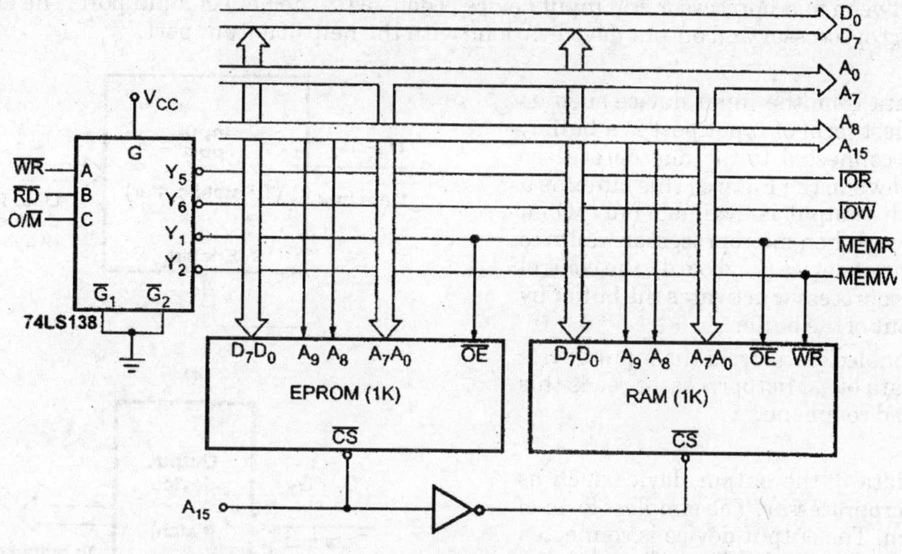

Fig.

above Fig. shows addressing of RAM with linear decoding technique. A_{15} address line, is directly connected to the chip select signal of EPROM and after inversion it is connected to the chip select signal of the RAM. Therefore, when status of A_{15} line is 'zero', EPROM gets selected and when status of A_{15} line is 'one', RAM gets selected. Status of the other address lines is not considered, since those address lines are not used for generation of chip select signals.

Memory map:

Memory ICs	A_{15}	A_{14}	A_{13}	A_{12}	A_{11}	A_{10}	A_9	A_8	A_7	A_6	A_5	A_4	A_3	A_2	A_1	A_0	Address
Starting address of EPROM	0	x	x	x	x	x	0	0	0	0	0	0	0	0	0	0	0000H
End address of EPROM	0	x	x	x	x	x	1	1	1	1	1	1	1	1	1	1	03FFH
Starting Address of RAM	1	x	x	x	x	x	0	0	0	0	0	0	0	0	0	0	8000H
End address of RAM	1	x	x	x	x	x	1	1	1	1	1	1	1	1	1	1	83FFH

Comparison Between full address decoding and Partial address decoding

Full address decoding	Partial address decoding
1. All higher address lines are decoded to select the memory or I/O device	1. Few higher address lines are decoded to select the memory or I/O device.
2. More hardware is required to design decoding logic.	2. Hardware required to design decoding logic is less and sometimes it can be eliminated.
3. Higher cost for decoding circuit.	3. Less cost for decoding circuit.
4. No multiple addresses.	4. It has a disadvantage of multiple addresses (shadow addresses).
5. Used in large systems.	5. Used in small systems.

I/O INTERFACING

The transfer of data between keyboard and microprocessor, and microprocessor and display device is called *input / output data transfer* or *I / O data transfer*.

Basic Interfacing Concepts

The data transfer between microprocessor and input device is done with the help of input port. The data transfer between microprocessor and output device is done with the help of output port.

Input port.

It is used to read data from the input device such as keyboard. The simplest form of input port is a buffer. The input device is connected to the microprocessor through buffer as shown in the Figure. This buffer is a tri-state buffer and its output is available only when enable signal is active. When microprocessor wants to read data from the input device (keyboard), the control signals from the microprocessor activates the buffer by asserting enable input of the buffer.

Once the buffer is enabled, data drom the input device is available on the data bus. Microprocessor reads this data by initiating read command.

Output port.

It is used to send data to the output device such as display from the microprocessor. The simplest form of output port is a latch. The output device is connected to the microprocessor through latch, as shown in the Figure. When microprocessor wants to send data to the output divice, it puts the data on the data bus and activates the clock signal of the latch, latching the data from the data bus at the output of latch. It is then available at the output of latch for the output device.

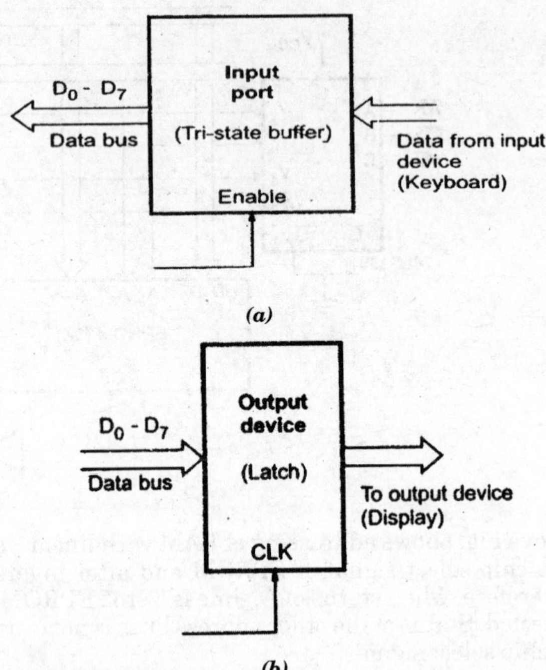

I/O Interfacing Techniques

Most of the microprocessors support isolated I/O system. It partitions memory from I/O, via software, by having instructions that specifically access (address) memory, and others that specifically access I/O. When these instructions are decoded by the microprocmessor, an appropriate control signal is generated to activate either memory or I/O operation. In 8085, IO/$\overline{M}$ signal is used for this purpose. The 8085 outputs a logic '1' on the IO/$\overline{M}$ line for an I/O operation and a logic '0' for memory operation. In 8085, it is possible to connect 64 Kbyte memory and 256 I/O ports in the system since 8085 sends 16 bit address for memory and 8-bit address for I/O.

I / O devices can be interfaced to an 8085A system in two ways :

(1) I/O Mapped I/O

In this, the 8085 uses IO/$\overline{M}$ signal to distinguish between I/O read/write and memory read/write operations. The 8085 has separate instructions IN and OUT for I/O data transfer. When 8085 executes IN or OUT instruction, it places device address (port number) on the demultiplexed low order address bus as well as the high order address bus. In other words, we can say that higher order address bus duplicates the contents of demultiplexed low-order address bus, when 8085 microprocessor executes an IN or OUT instruction.

Instruction IN inputs data from an input device (such as keyboard) into the accumulator and the instruction OUT sends contents of the accumulator to an output device such as LED display. These are two byte instructions. The second byte of the instruction specifies the address or port number of an I/O device. As it is a byte, the address or port number can be any of the 256 combinations of eight bits, from 00H to FFH. Therefore, the 8085 can communicate with 256 different I/O devices. When we want to interface an I/O device, it is necessary to assign a device address or a port number.

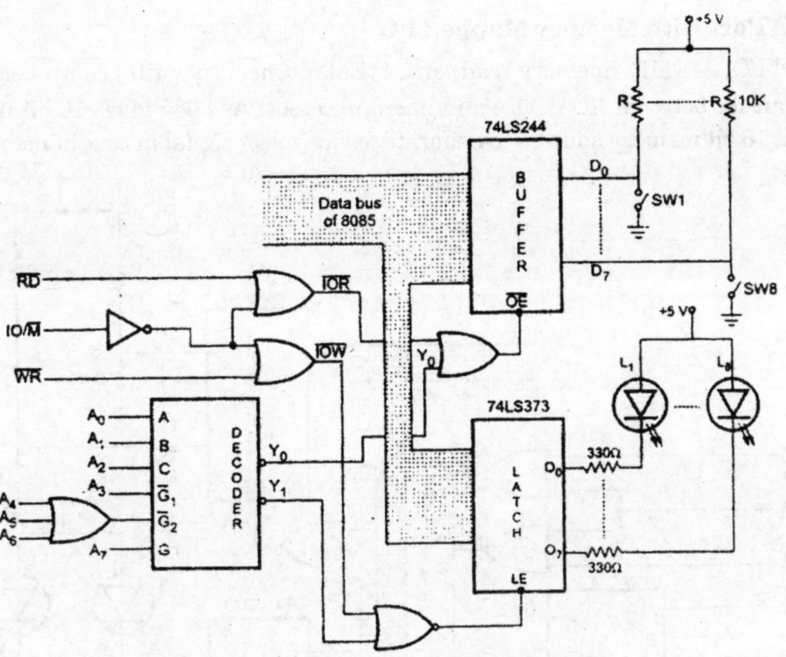

Fig. I/O interfacing Using I/O Mapped I/O

(2) Memory Mapped I/O

In memory mapped I/O, the I/O devices are assigned and identified by 16 bit addresses. The memory related instructions transfer the data between an I/O device and the microprocessor, as long as I/O port is assigned to the memory address space rather than to the I/O address space. The register associated with the I/O port is simply treated as a memory location. Thus I/O device becomes a part of the system's memory map and hence its name. In memory-mapped I/O every instruction that refers to a memory location can control I/O. The source and destination of the data is limited with I/O mapped I/O, since for an IN instruction the destination register is always the accumulator, and for the OUT instruction the source register is always the accumulator. However, for memory mapped I/O there are number of sources and destinations.

Instructions		**Interpretation for memory mapped I/O**
MOV r, M	:	Input from a port to specified register.
LDA addr	:	Input from a port to accumulator.
LHLD addr	:	Input from two ports to HL register pair.
ADD M	:	Port contents are added into accumulator
	:	contents and result is stored in the accumulator.
ANA M	:	Port contents are logically ANDed with the accumulator contents and result is stored in the accumulator.
ORA M	:	Port contents are logically ORed with the accumulator contents and result is stored in the accumulator.
XRA M	:	Port contents are logically XORed with the accumulator contents and result is stored in the accumulator.
CMP M	:	Compares the port contents with the accumulator contents and updates the flag register contents accordingly.
MOV M,r	:	Outputs specified register contents to the port.
STA addr	:	Outputs accumulator contents to the port.
SHLD addr	:	Outputs HL register contents to two ports.
MVI M, data	:	Outputs immediate data to the port.

Interfacing of I/O Port with Memory Mapped I/O

In memory mapped I/O, $\overline{MEMR}$ (memory read) and $\overline{MEMW}$ (memory write) control signals are required to control the data transfer between I/O device and microprocessor. As 8085 gives 16 bit memory address, it is necessary to decode 16 bit memory address to generate device select signal in case of memory mapped I/O.

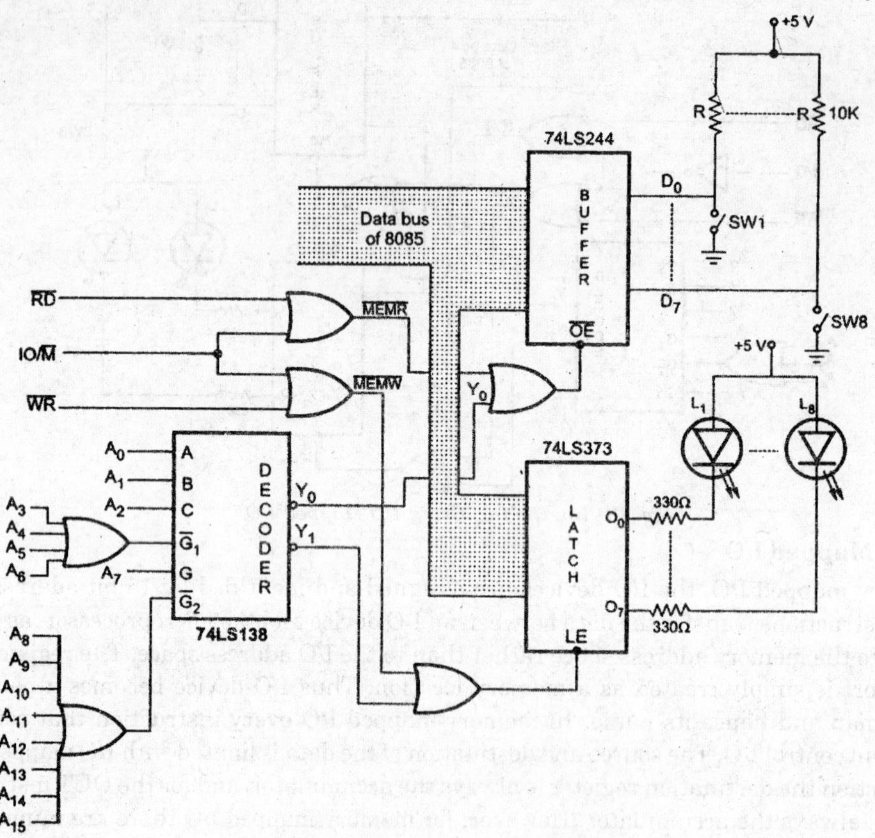

Fig. I/O interfacing using memory mapped I/O

Comparison between Memory Mapped I/O and I/O Mapped I/O

Memory mapped I/O	I/O maped I/O
1. In this device address is 16 bit. Thus A_0 to A_{15} lines are used to generate device address.	1. In this I/O device address is 8 bit. Thus A_0 to A_7 or A_8 to A_{15} lines are used to generate device address.
2. $\overline{MEMR}$ and $\overline{MEMW}$ control signals are used to control read and write I/O operations.	2. $\overline{IOR}$ and $\overline{IOW}$ control signals are used to control read and write I/O operations.
3. Instructions available are LDA addr, STA addr, LDAX rp, STAX rp, MOV M,R, MOV R,M ADD, M, CMP M etc.	3. Instructions available are IN and OUT.
4. Data transfer is between any register and I/O. device	4. Data transfer is between accumulator and I/O device.
5. Maximum number of I/O devices are 65536 (theoretically).	5. Maximum number of I/O devices are 256.
6. Exection speed using LDA addr, STA addr is 13 T-state & 7T-states for MOV M, r and MOV r, M instructions.	6. Execution speed is 10 T-states.
7. Decoding 16 bit address may require more hard ware.	7. Decoding 8 bit address will require less hardware.

MICROCONTROLLER

A microcontroller is a computer. All computers -- whether we are talking about a personal desktop computeror a large mainframe computer or a microcontroller -- have several things in common:

"All computers have a CPU (central processing unit) that executes programs. If you are sitting at a desktop computer right now reading this article, the CPU in that machine is executing a program that implements the Web browser that is displaying this page.

"The CPU loads the program from somewhere. On your desktop machine, the browser program is loaded from the hard disk.

"The computer has some RAM (random-access memory) where it can store "variables."

"And the computer has some input and output devices so it can talk to people. On your desktop machine, the keyboard and mouse are input devices and the monitor and printer are output devices. A hard disk is an I/O device -- it handles both input and output.

The desktop computer you are using is a "general purpose computer" that can run any of thousands of programs. Microcontrollers are "special purpose computers." Microcontrollers do one thing well. There are a number of other common characteristics that define microcontrollers. If a computer matches a majority of these characteristics, then you can call it a "microcontroller":

Objective Type Questions

1. In microprocessor
   (*a*) program is stored in memory and data is stored in registers
   (*b*) program is stored in registers and data is stored in memory
   (*c*) both program and data are stored in memory
   (*d*) both program and data are stored in registers
2. A microprocessor contains
   (*a*) most of the control and arithmetic logic functions of a computer
   (*b*) most of the RAM
   (*c*) most of the ROM
   (*d*) peripheral drivers
3. An instruction cycle is made up of
   (*a*) one or more execute cycles
   (*b*) one or more fetch cycles
   (*c*) one opcode and one execute cycle
   (*d*) none of these
4. In a 8-bit microprocessor, the fetch cycle required to fetch a 8 byte instruction will be
   (*a*) 1
   (*b*) 2
   (*c*) 3
   (*d*) depends on computer design
5. The register which contains the instruction to be executed is called
   (*a*) instruction register
   (*b*) index register
   (*c*) memory address register
   (*d*) memory data register
6. The register which keeps track of the execution of a program and which contains the memory address of the instruction currently being executed is called
   (*a*) index register
   (*b*) memory address register
   (*c*) program counter
   (*d*) instruction register
7. The register which holds address of the location to or from which data are to be transferred is known as
   (*a*) index register
   (*b*) instruction register
   (*c*) memory address register
   (*d*) memory data register
8. The register which contains the data to be written into or read out of the addressed location is known as
   (*a*) index register
   (*b*) memory address register
   (*c*) memory data register
   (*d*) program counter
9. The process of fetching and executing instructions one at a time in the order of increasing addresses is known as
   (*a*) instruction execution
   (*b*) straight line sequencing
   (*c*) instruction fetching
   (*d*) random sequencing
10. The flow and timing of data to and from the microprocessor is regulated by
    (*a*) control pins (*b*) address pins
    (*c*) data pins (*d*) power pins
11. A microprocessor with 12 address lines is capable of addressing
    (*a*) 1024 locations
    (*b*) 2028 locations
    (*c*) 4096 locations
    (*d*) 64 K locations
12. The stack pointer in the 8085 microprocessor is a
    (*a*) 16 bit register which points to stack memory locations
    (*b*) 16 bit accumulator
    (*c*) memory location in the stack
    (*d*) flag register used for the stack

13. Which of the following enables peripherals to pass a signal down the bus to the next device on the bus during polling of the device?

(*a*) DMA (*b*) interrupt vectoring

(*c*) daisy chain (*d*) cycle stealing

14. An opcode

(*a*) translates a mnemonic

(*b*) instructs the CPU

(*c*) stores data

(*d*) all of these

15. The register whose contents may be added to or subtracted from the operand address prior to or during the execution of an instruction is known as

(*a*) index register (*b*) control register

(*c*) address register (*d*) none of these

56. What is the state of the signal at X?

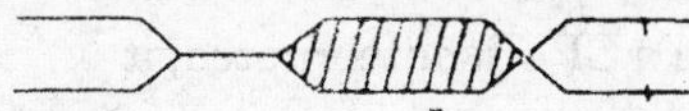

(*a*) Don't know

(*b*) Floating

(*c*) Changing their states

(*d*) All high

57. Which of the following actions detect locations, and remove mistakes from a programme routine?

(*a*) Erase

(*b*) Debug

(*c*) Diagnose

(*d*) Emulate

58. Direct–Memory Access Channel (DMA) facilitates data to move into and out of the system

(*a*) on first-come first-serve basis

(*b*) with equal time delay

(*c*) without sub – routine

(*d*) without programme intervention

59. Every processor must necessarily have

(*a*) data bus

(*b*) data bus and address bus

(*c*) control bus

(*d*) data bus, a control bus and an address bus

60. A microprocessor with a 12–bit address bus will be able to access

(*a*) 1 kilobyte of memory

(*b*) 4 kilobytes of memory

(*c*) 8 kilobytes of memory

(*d*) 0.4 kilobytes of memory

61. Which of the following flag conditions are not available in 8085 processor?

(*a*) Zero flag (*b*) Parity flag

(*c*) Overflow flag (*d*) Auxiliary carry flag

62. The frequency of the driving network connected between pin 1 and 2 of a 8085 chip must be

(*a*) twice of the desired clock frequency

(*b*) equal to the desired clock frequency

(*c*) four times the desired clock frequency

(*d*) none of these

63. READY signal in 8085 is useful when the CPU communicates with

(*a*) a slow peripheral device

(*b*) a fast peripheral device

(*c*) a DMA controller chip

(*d*) a PPI chip

64. A DAD H instruction is same as

(*a*) shifting each bit one position to the left

(*b*) shifting each bit one position to the right

(*c*) shifting each bit one position to the left with a zero inserted in 1st position

(*d*) shifting each bit one position to the right with a zero inserted in 1st position

65. Return from a subroutine is affected by

(*a*) a jump instruction

(*b*) an RST instruction

(*c*) a RET instruction

(*d*) a hardware interrupt signal

66. PSW stands for

(*a*) accumulator contents

(*b*) flag byte

(*c*) accumulator and the flag byte

(*d*) accumulator and temporary register byte

67. During a DMA transfer, the processor (check the incorrect statement)

(*a*) continues its normal operations

(*b*) suspends its normal operations

(*c*) needs to initiate read (write) command

(*d*) needs to check if the input/output device is ready for data transfer

68. In 8085, interrupts excepts TRAP are disabled (check the incorrect statement) by

(*a*) a DI instruction

(*b*) a system reset

(*c*) acknowledgement of a previous interrupt

(*d*) none of these

69. A high on RESET OUT line signifies that

(*a*) all the registers of the CPU are being reset

(*b*) all the registers and counters are being reset

(*c*) all the registers and counters are being reset and in addition this signal can be used to reset external support chips

(*d*) processing can begin when this signal goes high

70. Normally a microprocessor cycles between

(*a*) Fetch and Halt states

(*b*) Fetch and Interrupt states

(*c*) Fetch and Execute states

(*d*) Halt and Execute states

71. After completing the execution, microprocessor return to

(*a*) Halt state (*b*) Fetch state

(*c*) Execute state (*d*) Interrupt state

72. The chip select access time for reading ROM contents is

(*a*) the delay between application of proper chip select signal and the stable output address

(*b*) the delay between the previous valid output data and the next change in address

(*c*) the time for which the output data remains valid when the device is no longer selected

(*d*) maximum time for which the valid address can be changed

73. A microprocessor, on arrival of RESET signal returns, from HALT state to

(*a*) execute

(*b*) fetch

(*c*) interrupt

(*d*) none of these

74. The decoding circuit has been used to generate active low chip. Signal for a microprocessor peripheral (address line are designated as A 0 to A7 for I/O address)

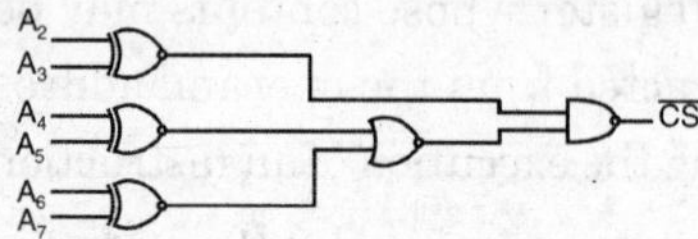

(*a*) 60H to 63 H (*b*) A 4 to A 7 H

(*c*) 71H to 73 H (*d*) 70 H to 73 H

75. When a CPU is interrupted, it

(*a*) stops execution of instructions

(*b*) acknowledges interrupt and branches to a subroutine

(*c*) acknowledges interrupt and continues

(*d*) acknowledges interrupt and waits for the next instruction from the interrupting device

76. An 'Assembler' for a micro-processor is used for

(*a*) assembly of processors in a production line

(*b*) creation of new programmes using different modules

(*c*) translation of a program from assembly language to machine language

(*d*) translation of a higher level language into English text

77. A single instruction to clear the lower four bits of the accumulator in 8085 assembly language is

(*a*) XRI OFH (*b*) ANI FOH

(*c*) XRI FOH (*d*) ANI OFH

78. Which of the following statements is true?

(*a*) ROM is a Read/ Write memory

(*b*) PC points to the last instruction that was executed

(*c*) Stack works on the principle of LIFO

(*d*) All instructions affect the flags

79. Which of the following is an example of a spooled device?

(*a*) A line printer used to print the output of a number of jobs

(*b*) A terminal used to enter input data to a running program

(*c*) A secondary storage device in a virtual memory system

(*d*) A graphic display device

80. A ROM is used to store the table for multiplication of two 8-bit unsigned integers. The size of ROM required is

(*a*) 256 × 16

(*b*) 16K × 8

(*c*) 4K × 16

(*d*) 64K × 16

81. Number of machine cycles required for RET instruction in 8085 microprocessor is

(*a*) 1 (*b*) 2

(*c*) 3 (*d*) 5

82. An instruction used to set the carry flag in a computer can be classified as

(*a*) data transfer

(*b*) arithmetic

(*c*) logical

(*d*) program control

83. In an 8085 microprocesser system, the RST instruction will cause an interrupt

(*a*) only if an interrupt service routine is not being executed

(*b*) only if a bit in the interrupt mask is made 0

(*c*) only if interrupts have been enabled by an EI instruction

(*d*) none of these

84. An I/O processor control the flow of information between

(*a*) cache memory and I/O devices

(*b*) main memory and I/O devices

(*c*) two I/O devices

(*d*) cache and main memories

85. If instruction RST is written in a program the problem will jump to location

(*a*) 0020 H

(*b*) 0024 H

(*c*) 0028 H

(*d*) 002 CH

86. The data bus in 8080A/8085 microprocessor is a group of

(*a*) eight bidirectional lines that are used to transfer 8 bits between the microprocessor and its I/O and memory

(*b*) eight lines used to transfer data among the registers

(*c*) eight unidirectional lines that are used for I/O devices

(*d*) sixteen bidirectional lines that are used for data transfer between the microprocessor and memory

87. The TRAP is one of the interrupts available in INTEL 8085. Which one of the following statements is true of TRAP?

(*a*) It is level triggered

(*b*) It is negative edge triggered

(*c*) It is positive edge triggered

(*d*) It is both positive edge triggered and level triggered

88. An advantage of memory interfacing is that

(*a*) a larger memory is obtained

(*b*) effective speed of the memory is increased

(*c*) the cost of the memory is reduced

(*d*) a non-volatile memory is obtained

89. A personal computer has typically

(*a*) 5 to 10 kilobytes of main memory

(*b*) 10 to 100 kilobytes of main memory

(*c*) 100 to 256 kilobytes of main memory

(*d*) 256 kilobytes to 1 megabyte of main memory.

90. Consider the following set of instructions :

STC

CMC

MOV A,B

RAL

MOV B,A

This set of instructions

(*a*) doubles the number in Register by B

(*b*) divides the number in Register by 2

(*c*) multiples B by A

(*d*) adds A and B

91. Which of the following cycle is required to fetch and execute information?

(*a*) Clock cycle (*b*) Tri cycle

(*c*) Introduction cycle (*d*) Memory cycle

92. The three buses associated with three-bus system are I/O bus, memory bus and the

(*a*) address bus

(*b*) unibus

(*c*) direct memory access bus

(*d*) data bus

93. The bus which is used to transfer data from main memory to peripheral device is the

(*a*) data bus (*b*) input bus

(*c*) DMA bus (*d*) output bus

94. Which of the following statements is not applicable to serial transmission of data?

(*a*) One bit at a time

(*b*) Faster method of trans-mission

(*c*) LSB transferred first

(*d*) Only one wire used

95. An interrupt which can be temporarily ignored by the counter is known as

(*a*) vectored interrupt

(*b*) non-maskable interrupt

(*c*) maskable interrupt

(*d*) low priority interrupt

96. An interrupt in which the external device supplies its address as well as the interrupt request is known as

(*a*) vectored interrupt

(*b*) maskable interrupt

(*c*) non-maskable interrupt

(*d*) designated interrupt

97. When used with I/O devices, the term intelligent implies

(*a*) a colour output capability

(*b*) speech processing capability

(*c*) high speed printing capability

(*d*) features to support offline and online tasks

98. A microprocessor is also referred to as

(*a*) the chip that does some calculations for the computer

(*b*) the computer on a chip

(*c*) the chip that is responsible for data transfer

(*d*) none of these

99. A microprocessor is called an n-bit microprocessor depending on

(*a*) register's length

(*b*) size of internal data bus

(*c*) size of external data bus

(*d*) none of these

100. Two operands can be checked for equality using

(*a*) OR-operation

(*b*) AND-operation

(*c*) X-OR operation

(*d*) none of these

101. Setting contents of a register to zero can be efficiently done by

(*a*) Mov immediate instruction using zero as immediate data

(*b*) AND immediate instruction using zero as immediate data

(*c*) XORing register with itself

(*d*) none of these

102. Stack memory is used

(*a*) to provide additional memory to the base memory

(*b*) to save return addresses of a subroutine

(*c*) to save the status of the microprocessor

(*d*) none of these

103. 8085 microprocessor is a

(*a*) zero address microprocessor

(*b*) one address microprocessor

(*c*) two address microprocessor

(*d*) none of these

104. SHIFT LEFT instruction causes all bits shifted from one position to the left with rightmost bit set to zero. The effect is to

(*a*) multiply by 2

(*b*) divide by 2

(*c*) SET the most significant bit

(*d*) none of these

105. The selection of a microprocessor for an application is done keeping in mind

(*a*) speed compatibility of microprocessor with perip-herals

(*b*) the time critical behaviour of the application

(*c*) the size of program required to implement certain functions

(*d*) all of these

106. Which of the following signal is used when a microprocessor wants to address the memory?

(*a*) $IO/\overline{M}$

(*b*) Status signals

(*c*) ALE

(*d*) HOLD and HLDA

107. Which of the following signal is used when a peripheral device request the microprocess to have a DMA operation?

(*a*) $IO/\overline{M}$

(*b*) READY

(*c*) HOLD and HLDA

(*d*) $\overline{RD}$ and $\overline{WR}$

108. Program Counter is used to

(*a*) store address of the next instruction to be executed

(*b*) store temporary data to be used in arithmetic operations

(*c*) store the status of the microprocessor

(*d*) none of these

109. The synchronization between microprocessor and memory is done by

(*a*) ALE signal (*b*) HOLD signal

(*c*) READY signal (*d*) none of these

110. Intel 8080A and 8085A differ in

(*a*) number of address lines

(*b*) number of data signal

(*c*) instruction set

(*d*) number of interrupt

111. In 8085 Program Status Word consists of

(*a*) accumulator contents

(*b*) flags

(*c*) both accumulator and flag

(*d*) status bits

112. Intel 8080A and Motorola 6800 microprocessor differ in

(*a*) number of address lines

(*b*) number of data lines

(*c*) instruction set

(*d*) instruction set and operating frequency

113. As compared to 16-bit microprocessor, 8 bit micro-processor are limited in

(*a*) speed

(*b*) directly addressable memory

(*c*) data handling capability

(*d*) all of these

114. WAIT states are used

(*a*) to give slow devices additional time to put out valid data

(*b*) to insert a deliberate delay

(*c*) during I/O operation

(*d*) none of these

115. Intel 8085A and 8086A differ in

(*a*) number of address lines

(*b*) number of data lines

(*c*) operating frequency

(*d*) all of these

116. The advantage of using segment registers in 8086 and above microprocessors are that they

(*a*) allow the memory capacity to be 1 megabyte even though the addresses associated with the individual instructions are only 16 bits wide

(*b*) allow the instruction, data or stack portion of a program to be more than 64K bytes long by using more than one code, data or stack segment

(*c*) facilitate the use of separate memory area for a program, its data and the stack

(*d*) all of these

117. The set of commands which give directions to the assembler during the assembly process but are not translated into machine instructions are called

(*a*) mnemonics (*b*) directives

(*c*) identifiers (*d*) operands

118. The microprocessor contains ROM chip which contains

(*a*) control function

(*b*) arithmetic functions

(*c*) instructions to execute data

(*d*) memory functions

119. The process of causing an unplanned branching operation to occur, usually initiated by external system is called

(*a*) debugging

(*b*) masking

(*c*) interrupt

(*d*) iteration

120. An instruction register is storage for

(*a*) location of data in memory

(*b*) location of instruction in memory

(*c*) binary code for the operation to be performed

(*d*) address of the next instruction to be executed

Answers

1. (*a*)	**2.** (*a*)	**3.** (*a*)	**4.** (*d*)	**5.** (*b*)	**6.** (*c*)	**7.** (*c*)	**8.** (*c*)	**9.** (*b*)	**10.** (*a*)
11. (*c*)	**12.** (*a*)	**13.** (*c*)	**14.** (*b*)	**15.** (*a*)	**56.** (*b*)	**57.** (*b*)	**58.** (*d*)	**59.** (*d*)	**60.** (*a*)
61. (*c*)	**62.** (*a*)	**63.** (*a*)	**64.** (*c*)	**65.** (*c*)	**66.** (*c*)	**67.** (*a*)	**68.** (*d*)	**69.** (*c*)	**70.** (*c*)
71. (*b*)	**72.** (*a*)	**73.** (*b*)	**74.** (*a*)	**75.** (*b*)	**76.** (*c*)	**77.** (*b*)	**78.** (*c*)	**79.** (*a*)	**80.** (*d*)
81. (*c*)	**82.** (*b*)	**83.** (*c*)	**84.** (*b*)	**85.** (*c*)	**86.** (*d*)	**87.** (*d*)	**88.** (*b*)	**89.** (*d*)	**90.** (*b*)
91. (*c*)	**92.** (*c*)	**93.** (*c*)	**94.** (*b*)	**95.** (*c*)	**96.** (*a*)	**97.** (*d*)	**98.** (*b*)	**99.** (*b*)	**100.** (*c*)
101. (*c*)	**102.** (*b*)	**103.** (*b*)	**104.** (*a*)	**105.** (*d*)	**106.** (*c*)	**107.** (*c*)	**108.** (*a*)	**109.** (*c*)	**110.** (*d*)
111. (*c*)	**112.** (*d*)	**113.** (*d*)	**114.** (*a*)	**115.** (*d*)	**116.** (*d*)	**117.** (*b*)	**118.** (*c*)	**119.** (*c*)	**120.** (*c*)

Explanations

OBJECTIVE TYPE QUESTIONS

1. To enable 3L × 8L decoder, three enable lines E_1 (which is connected as an output of AND-gate) should be HIGH and $\overline{E}_2$ and $\overline{E}_3$ should be active low, it means $\frac{I_0}{m}$ should be active low which is indicating that it is memory mapped I/O interfacing. So address of the device will be in 16-bits. To select output port through decoder 2nd line the status of A_{15} (I_2) A_{14}(I_1) A_{13}(I_0) = 010 and to enable decoder through E_1 enable line A_{12} = 1 and A_{11} =0 and by default as a starting address other address lines (A_{10}......A_0) shold be zero. So, overall port address is

A_{15}	A_{14}	A_{13}	A_{12}	A_{11}	A_{10}	A_9	A_8	
A_7	A_6	A_5	A_4	A_3	A_2	A_1	A_0	
0	1	0	1	0	0	0	0	0
0	0	0	0	0	0	0	= 5000H	

3. XRA A

A ← 00

MVIBF0

B ← F0

SUB B

A ← A – B

A ← A + (2's complement to B)

A = 00000000

B = 11110000

2's complement of B = 00010000

∴ A + B = (10)H

4. L × 1 H, 2500H : the data 2500H is loaded into HL pair

MOV A,M : the content of memory location whose address is in HL pair, is moved to accumulator.

So finally input data from device is moved to accumulator.

5. Given (SP) = 2700H

(PC) = 2100H

(HL) = 0000H

2100H : DAD SP : it adds the contents of stack pointer (SP) to the content of HL pair and store the result in HL pair.

∴ 2700H + 0000H = 2700H stored in HL pair

2101H : PCHL ; the content of HL pair are transfered to program counter.

So now PC has 2700H and contents of SP remains unchanged

∴ (PC) = 2700H

(SP) = 2700H

6. Interrupt is sampled after every machine cycle and Bus request pin is sampled after every instruction cycle.

7. DCRL will be executed 255 times till it content of L becomes zero.

Then, for every decrement of content of H, DCRL will again be executed by 256 times. (When L is decremented by 1 and becomes FFH). This will be repeated by 254 times.

Hence, no. of execution of DCRL

$$= 254 \times 256 + 255 = 65279$$

8. The address of the memory location is stored in DE register pair. But INR M command will increase the content of the memory location M. But this command will execute only on HL pair. So we have to exchange the address of Memory location in HL pair from DE pair first.

■■

5

CHAPTER

Data Communication and Network

REFERENCE MODELS.

This model is called the ISO OSI (Open Systems Intercommunication) Reference model because it deals with connecting open systems that is systems that are open for communication with other system.

Physical layer.

The physical layer is concerned with transmitting raw bits over a communication channel. The design issues have to do with making sure that when one side sends a 1 bit, it is received by the other side as a 1 bit, not as a 0 bit. Typical questions here are how many volts should be represented to one and how many volts for a 0.

Data link layer.

The main task of the data link layer is to take a raw transmission facility and transform it into a line that appears free of undetected transmission error to the network layer.

Network layer.

The network layer is concerned as the operation of the subnet. A key design issue is determining how packets are routed from sources to destination. Routes can be based on static table that are "wired into" into the network and rarely changed. They can also be determined at the start of each conversation.

When a packet has to travel from one network to another to get to its destination, many problems can arise like, the addressing used by the 2nd network may be different from the 1st one.

Transport layer.

The basic function of the transport layer is to accept data from the sessions layer, split it up into smaller units if need be, pass these to the network layer and ensures that pieces all arrive correctly at the other end.

Session layer.

The session layer allows users on different machines to establish session between them. A session allows ordinary data transport, as does the transport layer, but it also provides enhanced services useful in some applications. A session might be used to allow a user to log into remote time sharing system or to transfer a file between two machines.

One of the services of the session layer is to manage dialogue control. Sessions can allow traffic to go in both directions at the same time and any one direction at a time.

Presentation layer.

The presentation layer performs certain function that are requested sufficiently often to warrant finding a general solution for them, rather than letting each user solve the problems in particular unlike all the lower layers, which are just interested to moving into reliably from here to there, the presentation layer is concerned with the syntax and semantics of the information transmitted.

Application layer.

The application layer contains a variety of protocols that are commonly needed. For example, there are hundreds of incompatible terminal type in the world. Consider the plight of full screen editor that is supposed to work over a network with many different terminal types, each with different screen layouts escape sequences for inserting and deleting text, moving the cursor etc.

TCP/IP REFERENCE MODEL

It four layers.

1. **Internet layer :**It is a packet switching network based on a connectionless internet work layer. This layer called the internet layer is the linchpin that holds the whole architecture together. Its job is to permit hosts to inject packets into any network and have them travel independently to the destination. The internet layer defines an official packets format and protocol called IP (Internet Protocol). The job of the internet layer is to deliver IP packets where they are supposed to go. Packet routing is clearly the major issue here as is avoiding congestion.

2. **Transport layer :**The layer above the internet layer in the TCP/IP model is called the transport layer. It is designed to allow peer entities on the source and destination, the same as in the OSI transport layer. Two end to end protocols have been defined here.
   - TCP (transmission control protocol) is reliable connection oriented protocol that allows a byte stream originating on one machine to be delivered without error on any other machine in the internet. It machine in the internet. It fragments the incoming byte stream into discrete messages and passes each one onto the internet layer.
   - The second protocol in this layer, UDP (user datagram protocol) is an unreliable connection less protocol for applications that do no want TCP's sequencing or flow control.
3. **Application Layer**

   (i) **E mail.** The ability to compose, send, and receive electronic mail has been around since the early days of the ARPANET and is popular. Many people get dozens of messages a day and consider it their primary way of interacting with the outside world, far out distancing the telephone and snail mail.

   (ii) **News.** News groups are specialised forms in which users with a common interest can exchange messages, thousands of news groups exist on technical and non technical topics, include computers, science, recreation and politics. Each news group has its own etiquette, style and customs.

   (iii) **Remote log in.** Using the telnet R log in or other programs, users anywhere on the Internet can log into any other machine on which they have an account.

   (iv) **File transfer.** Using the FTP program it is possible to copy files from one machine on the internet to another. Vast numbers of articles, databases and other information are available this way.
4. **Host-to-Network layer :** The host has to connect to the network using some protocol so it can send IP packets over it. This protocol is not defined and varies from host to host and network to network.

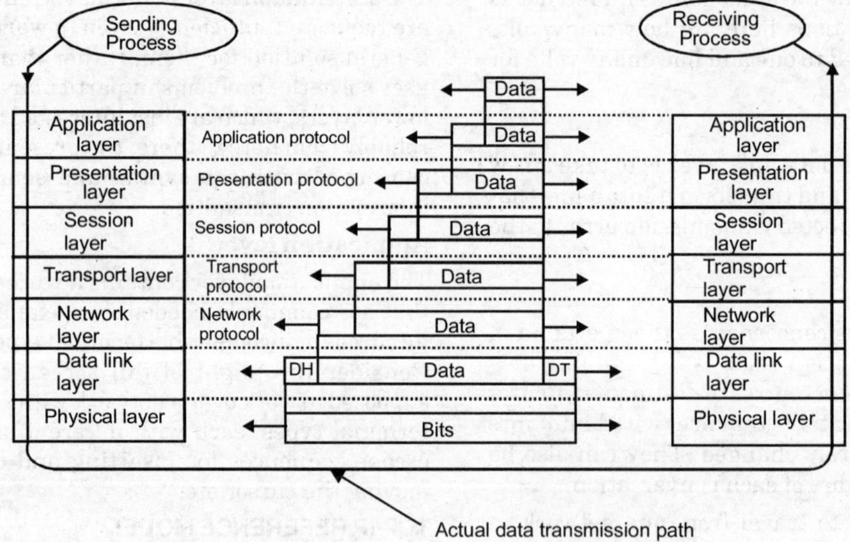

XDS 940.

XDS 940 operating system was designed at the university of California at Berkeley. Like the atlas system, it used paging for memory management. Unlike the Atlas system, XDS 940 was a time shared system. Paging was only used for relocation, it was not used for demand paging.

The virtual memory of any user process was only 16 K words, whereas the physical memory was 64 K words. Pages were 2K words each page table kept in registers. Since physical memory was larger than virtual memory.

X. 25 NETWORKS.

- Many other public networks especially outside the United States, follow a standard called X.25.
- Physical layer protocol called X.21 specifies the physical electrical and procedural interface between the host and the networks. Very few public networks actually support this standard because it requires digital rather than analog signalling on the telephone lines.
- X.25 is connection oriented and supports both switched virtual act and permanent. A switched

virtual act is located when one computer sends a packet to the network asking to make a call to a remote computer. X.25 provides flow control to make sure a fast sender cannot swamp a slow or busy receiver.

- A black box is called a PAD. (Packet Assembler Disassembler) is described in a document known as X3. A standard protocol has been defined between the terminal and the PAD called X.28, another standard protocol exists between PAD and the network call X.29
- Together these three recommendations are often called triple X

IP ADDRESSES

All IP addresses are 32 bits long and are used in the source address and destination address fields of IP packets.

- Network address, which are 32-bit numbers are usually written in dotted decimal notation.
- The lowest IP address is 0.0.0.0 and the highest is 255.255.255.255.
- The value 0 means this network or this host.
- The value 1 is used as a broadcast address to mean all hosts on the indicated network.
- The address consisting of all 1's allows broadcasting on the local network typically a LAN.
- Finally all address of the form 127 . xx.yy.zz are reserved for loop back testing.
- Network user Address = 1 – 4
- Area code of network user address = 5 – 7
- Terminal no of network user Address = 8 – 12
- How energy digits identify the country = 1 – 3

DATA COMMUNICATION

MANCHESTER ENCODING

None of the versions of 802.3 use straight binary encoding with 0 volts for a 0 bit and 5 volts for a 1 bit because it leads to ambiguities. If one station sends the bit string 0001000, others might falsely interpret it as 10000000 or 01000000 because they cannot tell the difference an idle sender (0 volts) and a 0 bit (0 volts)

What is needed is a way for receivers to unambiguously determine the start, end or middle of each bit without reference to an external clock. *Two such approaches are*

(*i*) *Manchester encoding*

(*ii*) *Differential Manchester encoding.*

With Manchester encoding, each bit period is divided into two equal intervals.

A binary 1 bit is sent by having voltage set high during first interval and low in the second one.

A binary 0 is just the reverse :
first low and then high.

This scheme ensures that every bit period has a transition in the middle, making it easy for the receiver to synchronize with the sender.

The disadvantage of Manchester encoding is that it requires twice as much bandwidth as straight binary encoding, because the pulses are half the width.

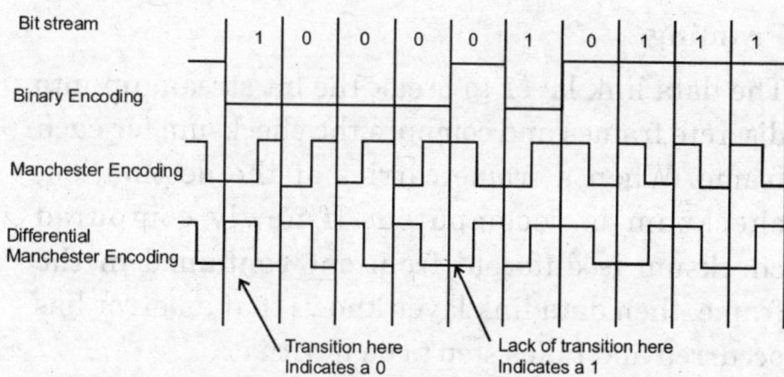

Fig. (a) Binary encoding (b) Manchester encoding (c) Differential Manchester encoding

Differential Manchester encoding.

It is variation of basic Manchester encoding. In it, a 1 bit indicated by the absence of a transition at the start of the interval. A 0 bit it indicated by the presence of a transition at the start of the interval.

In both cases, there is a tansition in the middle as well. The differential scheme requires more complex equipment out offers better noise immunity. All 802.3 baseband systems use Manchester encoding due to its simplicity. The high signal is + 0.85 volts and the low signal is –0.85 volts, giving a DC value of 0 volts.

802.3 MAC SUBLAYER PROTOCOL

In 802.3 (IEEE, 1985a) frame structure each frame starts with a *preamble* of 7 bytes, each containing the bit pattern 10101010. The Manchester encoding of this pattern produces a 10-MHz square waves for 5.6 μ sec to allow the receiver's clock to synchronize with the sender's. Next comes a *start of frame* byte containing 10101011 to denote the start of the frame itself.

Frame contains two addresses:

(*i*) one of the destination

(*ii*) one of the source.

The standard allows 2-byte addresses, but the parameters defined for the 10-Mbps baseband standard use only the 6-byte addresses. The high-order bit of the destination address is a 0 for ordinary addresses and 1 for group addresses. Group addresses allow multiple stations to listen to a single address.

When a frame is sent to a group address, all the stations in the group receive it. Sending to a group of stations is called *multicast*.

The address consisting of all 1 bits is reserved for **broadcast**. A frame containing all 1s in the destination field is delivered to all stations on the network.

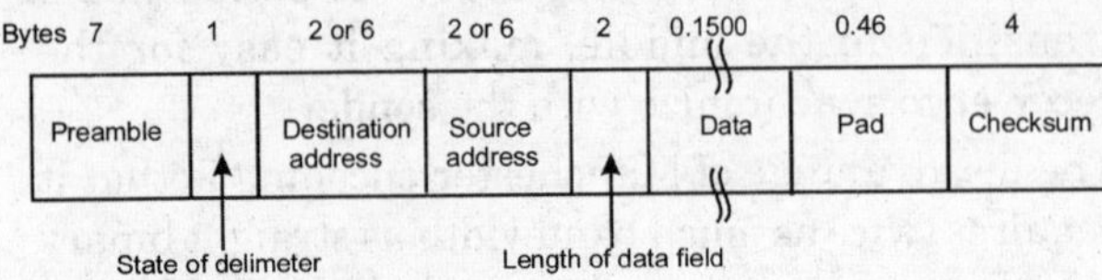

DATA LINK LAYER

Framing.

The data link layer to break the bit stream up into discrete frames and compute the checksum for each frame. When a frame carries at the destination, checksum is recomputed. If newly computed checksum is different from one contained in the frame, then data link layer knows that an error has occurred and takes step to deal with it.

Breaking the bit stream up into frames is more difficult than it at first appears. One way to achieve this framing is to insert time gaps between frames much like the spaces between words in ordinary text.

Framing methods.

(*i*) Using a field in the header to specify the number of characters in the frame.

(*ii*) Gets around the problem of resynchronisation after an error by having each frame start with the ASCII character sequence DLE STX and end with the sequence DLE ETX.

DLE = Data Link Escape

STX = Start of Text

ETX = End of Text

Character stuffing.

The data link layer on the receiving end removes the DLE before the data are given to network layer. This technique is called **character stuffing**. Thus a framing DLE STX or DLE ETX can be distinguished from one in the data by the absence or presence of a single DLE. DLE in the data are always doubled.

(*a*) | DLE | STX | A | DLE | B | DLE | ETX |

(*b*)

| DLE | STX | A | DLE | DLE | B | DLE | ETX |

(*c*) 

(*a*) Data sent by the network layer.

(*b*) Data after being character stuffed by the data link layer.

(*c*) Data passed to the network layer on the receiving side.

Bit stuffing.

Each frame begins and ends with a special bit pattern, 01111110, called a **flag byte**. Whenever the sender data link layer encounters five consecutive ones in the data, it automatically stuff a 0 bit into the outgoing bit stream. The bit stuffing is analogous to character stuffing, in which a DLE is stuffed into the outgoing in the data.

When receiver sees five consecutive incoming 1 bits, followed by 0 bit, it automatically destuff the 0 bit

(*a*) 01101 11111111111111 10010

(*b*) 01101 1111011111011111010010

(*c*) 0110111111111111111110010

(*a*) The original data

(*b*) The data as they appear on the line after stuffing.

(*c*) The data as they are stored in the receiver memory after destuffing.

Error correcting codes.

To correct *d* errors, a distance 2d + 1 code is needed because that way the legal codewords are so for a part that even with d changes, the original codeword is closer than any other codeword.

Error detecting codes.

To detect *d* errors, *d* + 1 code is needed because with such a code there is no possibility that *d* single-bit errors can change a valid codeword.

Hamming distance.

The number of bit positions is which two codewords differ is called the *Hamming distance*. The error-detecting and error correcting properties of a code depend on its Hamming distance.

e.g. 1101 001 and 10110001

It is possible to determine how many corresponding bits differ. In this case, 3 bits differ, just exclusive or the few codewords and count the 1 bits in the result.

HDLC (High-level data link control).

A group of closely related protocol that are a bit old but are still heavily used in networks. They are all derived from the data link protocol use in IBM's SNA called *SDLC (Synchronous Data Link Control Protocol*).

SDLC, modified to ADCCP (Advanced Data Communication Control Procedure) by ANSI. ISO modified it to become HDLS (High Data Link Control)

SLIP (Serial Line IP).

SLIP is the older of the two protocols. It was devised by Rick Adams in 1984 to connect sun workstation to the internet over a dial up line using a modem. The protocol which is described in RFC 1055, is very simple. The workstation just sends raw IP packet over the line with a special flag byte (OXCO) at the end of framing.

Characteristics.

(*i*) It is widely used. SLIP has some serious problems.

(*ii*) It does not do any error detection or connection, so it is up to higher layers to detect and recover from lost damaged or merged frames.

(*iii*) Second SLIP supports only IP.

(*iv*) Each side must know the other IP address in advance, neither address can be dynamically assigned during setup.

(*v*) SLIP does not provide any form of authentication, so neither party knows whom its is really talking to.

Polynomial code.

It is also known as *cyclic redundancy code or CRC code*. Polynomial codes are based upon treating bit strings as representations of polynomials with coefficients of 0 and 1 only. A K bit frame is regarded as the coefficient list for a polynomial with *K* terms ranging from x^{K-1} to x^0. Such a polynomial is said to be of degree K – 1. The higher order bit is the coefficient of x^{K-1}.

e.g. 110001 has 6 bits and thus represent 8 a six term polynomial with coefficients

110001: $x^5 + x^4 + x^0$,.

Polynomial arithmetic is done modulo 2, according to the rules of algebraic field theory. Both addition and substraction are identical to EX-OR.

e.g.

10011011	11110000
+11001010	+10101111
01010001	01011111

Error detection.

To detect errors following steps are involved

(*i*) Let r be the degree of G(x) (generator polynomials). Append *r* zero bits at the end of the M (x) [message bits]. This corresponds to x^r M (x).

(*ii*) Divide x^r M (x) by G (x) using modulo 2 division.

(*iii*) Subtract the remainder from x^r M (x) using modulo 2 subtraction. The result is the check summed frame to be transmitted.

MULTIPLEXING.

Multiplexing is the set of techniques that allows the simultaneous transmission of multiple signals across a single data link.

In a multiplexed system, n lines shares the bandwidth of one link.

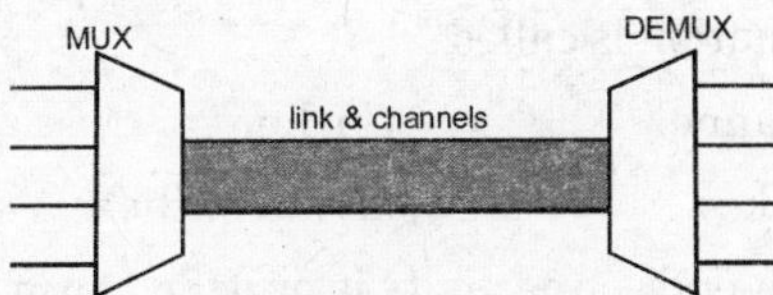

Remaining portion of data communication are induced in the computer networks.

LOCAL AREA NETWORK

A local area network (LAN) is usually privately owned and links the devices in a single campos. It is designed to allow resources to be shared between personal computers or workstations.

Objective Type Questions

1. The probability that a single bit will be in error on a typical public telephone line using 4800 bps modem is 10^{-3}. If no error detection mechanism is used, the residual error rate for a communication line using 9-bit frames is approximately equal to
   (*a*) 0.003 (*b*) 0.009
   (*c*) 0.991 (*d*) 0.999
2. If digital data rate of 9600 bps is encoded using 8-level phase shift keying (PSK) method, the modulation rate is
   (*a*) 1200 bauds (*b*) 3200 bauds
   (*c*) 4800 bauds (*d*) 9600 bauds
3. Communications software package enable users to access services such as
   (*a*) electronic mail
   (*b*) electronic bulletin boards
   (*c*) video channels
   (*d*) both (*a*) and (*b*)
4. The physical path that is used for sending information is called
   (*a*) channel (*b*) line
   (*c*) link (*d*) all of these
5. End-to-end connectivity is provided form host-to-host in
   (*a*) Network layer (*b*) Session layer
   (*c*) Network layer (*d*) Transport layer
6. Baseband is
   (*a*) transmission of signals without modulation
   (*b*) a signal all of whose energy is contained within a finite frequency range
   (*c*) simultaneous transmission of data to a number of stations
   (*d*) all of these
7. Internet address can be used to refer to networks as well as individual hosts. By convention, the network address has hosted with all bits
   (*a*) 0
   (*b*) 1
   (*c*) combination of 0 and 1
   (*d*) none of these
8. ARP (Address Resolution Protocol) is
   (*a*) a protocol used to dynamically bind IP Address to a low-level physical hardware address
   (*b*) a high level protocol for transferring files from one machine to another
   (*c*) a protocol used to monitor computers
   (*d*) a protocol that handles error and control messages
9. Which of the following protocol is used for transferring electronic mail messages from one machine to another ?
   (*a*) FTP (*b*) SNMP
   (*c*) SMTP (*d*) RFC
10. The Internet Control Message Protocol (ICMP)
    (*a*) allows gateways to send error a control messages to other gateways or hosts
    (*b*) provides communication between the Internet Protocol Software on one machine and the Internet Protocol Software on another
    (*c*) only reports error conditions to the original source, the source must relate error to individual application programs and take action to correct the problem
    (*d*) all of these
11. A machine that connects two or more electronic mail systems and transfers mail messages among them is called
    (*a*) Gateways (*b*) Mail gateway
    (*c*) Bridges (*d*) User Agent
12. Protocol converters are
    (*a*) the same as multiplexers
    (*b*) the same as TDMs
    (*c*) usually operated in Paris
    (*d*) usually not operated in Paris
13. Full-capability dialled backup of a multipoint full-duplex 4800 bps private line having 4 remote drops requires
    (*a*) 4 cells
    (*b*) either 4 or 8 cells
    (*c*) 8 cells
    (*d*) Can't tell

14. In serial communication employing 8 data bits, a parity bit and 2 stop bits, the minimum band rate required to sustain a transfer rate of 300 characters per second is

(*a*) 2400 band (*b*) 19200 band
(*c*) 4800 band (*d*) 1200 band

15. A packet-switching network

(*a*) is free
(*b*) can reduce the cost of using an information utility
(*c*) allows communications channel to be shared among more than one user
(*d*) both (*b*) and (*c*)

16. Which opening a TCP connection, the initial sequence number is to be derived using a time-of-day (ToD) clock that keeps running even when the host is down. The low order 32 bits of the counter of the ToD clock is to be used for the initial sequence numbers. The clock counter increments once per millisecond. The maximum packet lifetime is given to be 64s.

Which one of the choices given below is closest to the minimum permissible rate at which sequence numbers used for packets of a connection can increase ?

(*a*) 0.015/s (*b*) 0.064/s
(*c*) 0.135/s (*d*) 0.327/s

17. The economics of computing dictates

(*a*) sharing peripherals and data
(*b*) giving processors to people who need processing time and instantaneous response
(*c*) both (*a*) and (*b*)
(*d*) all of these

18. Local area networks can transmit

(*a*) faster than telecommunications over public telephone lines
(*b*) slower than telecommunications over public telephone lines
(*c*) using twisted-pair wiring or coaxial cables
(*d*) both (*a*) and (*c*)

19. The application layer of a network

(*a*) establishes, maintains and terminates virtual circuits
(*b*) defines user's port into the network
(*c*) consists of software being run on the computer connected to the network
(*d*) none of these

20. A software that allows a personal computer to pretend it, as a terminal is

(*a*) auto-dialling
(*b*) bulletin board
(*c*) modem
(*d*) terminal emulation

21. Which of the following assertions is FALSE about the Internet Protocol (IP) ?

(*a*) It is possible for a computer to have multiple IP addresses
(*b*) IP packets from the same source to the same destination can take different routes in the network
(*c*) IP ensures that a packet is discarded if it is unable to reach its destination within a given number of hops
(*d*) The packet source cannot set the route of an outgoing packets; the route is determined only by the routing tables in the routers on the way

22. The address resolution protocol (*A*RP) is used for

(*a*) Finding the IP address from the DNS
(*b*) Finding the IP address of the default gateway
(*c*) Finding the IP address that corresponds to a MAC address
(*d*) Finding the MAC address that corresponds to an IP address

23. In a network of LANs connected by bridges, packets are sent from one LAN to another through intermediate bridges. Since more than one path may exist between two LANs, packets may have to be routed through multiple bridges. Why is the spanning tree algorithm used for bridge-routing?

(*a*) For shortest path routing between LANs
(*b*) For avoiding loops in the routing paths
(*c*) For fault tolerance
(*d*) For minimizing collisions

24. An organization has a class B network and wishes to form subnets for 64 departments. The subnet mask would be

(*a*) 255.255.0.0
(*b*) 255.255.64.0
(*c*) 255.255.128.0
(*d*) 255.255.252.0

25. In a packet switching network, packets are routed from source to destination along a single path having two intermediate nodes. If the message size is 24 bytes and each packet contains a header of 3 bytes, then the optimum packet size is

(a) 4 (b) 6
(c) 7 (d) 9

26. In the slow start phase of the TCP congestion control algorithm, the size of the congestion window

(a) does not increase
(b) increases linearly
(c) increases quadratically
(d) increases exponentially

27. If a class B network on the Internet has a subnet mask of 255.255.248.0, what is the maximum number of hosts per subnet?

(a) 1022 (b) 1023
(c) 2046 (d) 2047

28. A client process P needs to make a TCP connection to a server process S. Consider the following situation: the server process S executes a socket (), a bind () and a listen () system call in that order, following which it is preempted. Subsequently, the client process P executes a socket () system call followed by connect () system call to connect to the server proccess S. The server process has not executed any accept () system call. Which one of the following events could take place?

(a) connect () system call returns successfully
(b) connect () system call blocks
(c) connect () system call returns an error
(d) connect () system call results in a core dump

29. What is an aim purpose of a data link content monitor?

(a) To detect problems in protocols
(b) To determine the type of transmission used in data link
(c) To determine the type of switching used in data link
(d) To determine the flow of data

30. The amount of uncertainty in a system of symbol is called

(a) bandwidth (b) entropy
(c) loss (d) quantum

31. How many digits of the DNIC (data network identification code) identify the country?

(a) first three (b) first four
(c) first five (d) first six

32. Which data communication method is used to send data over a serial communication link?

(a) Simplex (b) Half duplex
(c) Full Duplex (d) All of these

33. The amount of uncertainty in a system of symbol is called

(a) Bandwidth (b) Entropy
(c) Loss (d) Quantum

34. What is the main difference between synchronous and asynchronous transmission?

(a) The bandwidth required is different.
(b) The pulse height is different.
(c) The clocking is derived from the data in synchronous transmission.
(d) The clocking is mixed with data in asynchronous transmission.

35. The synchronous modems are more expensive than the asynchronous modems because

(a) they must contain clock recovery circuits
(b) production volume is larger
(c) they must operate on a larger bandwidth
(d) they are larger

36. When transmitting odd-parity coded symbols, the number of zeros in each symbol is

(a) odd (b) even
(c) unknown (d) none of these

37. Which of the following is possible in a token passing bus network?

(a) Unlimited number of stations
(b) Unlimited distance
(c) In-service expansion
(d) "Multiple time-division channels

38. What is the number of separate protocol layers at the serial interface gateway specified by the X.25 standard?

(a) 2 (b) 3
(c) 4 (d) 1

39. In OSI network architecture; the routing is performed by

(a) data link layer (b) network layer
(c) transport layer (d) session layer

40. In the current frequency assignments, how many frequency bands are there for the uplink frequencies ?

(*a*) 16 (*b*) 8
(*c*) 4 (*d*) 2

41. If each character in an XMODEM block has an ASCII value of 50, what would be the value of the checksum added to the block ?

(*a*) 50 (*b*) 23
(*c*) 41 (*d*) 25

42. The second YMODEM block used to transport a 1100 byte file would use data field of

(*a*) 1024 characters (*b*) 100 characters
(*c*) 128 characters (*d*) 64 characters

43. An example of a sliding windows protocol is

(*a*) XMODEM (*b*) YMODEM
(*c*) YMODEM-G (*d*) WXMODEM

44. How many messages can be outstanding (unacknowledged) on a BiSney link?

(*a*) 1 (*b*) 2
(*c*) 4 (*d*) 8

45. The escape character that identifies control characters in BiSync Transparency mode is

(*a*) ESC (*b*) SYN
(*c*) DLE (*d*) RVI

46. One primary difference between DDCMP and SDLC is

(*a*) DDCMP does not have a transparent mode
(*b*) SDLC does not use a CRC
(*c*) DDCMP has a message header
(*d*) DDCMP does not require special hardware to find the beginning of a message

47. To effectively use a compression performing modem set the serial port rate

(*a*) equal to the modem operating rate
(*b*) higher than the modem operating rate
(*c*) lower than the modem operating rate
(*d*) to automatic speed detect

48. Which of the following transmission systems provides the highest data rate to an individual device ?

(*a*) Voiceband modem (*b*) Local area network
(*c*) Computer bus (*d*) Digital PBX

49. Which of the following systems provides the longest digital transmission distance ?

(*a*) Voiceband modem (*b*) Local area network
(*c*) Computer bus (*d*) Digital PBX

50. Which of the following options is not a useful property of a Manchester line code for an Ethernet?

(*a*) Continuous energy
(*b*) Continuous clock transitions
(*c*) No DC component
(*d*) No signal change at a 1 to 0 transition

51. The purpose of the preamble in an Ethernet is

(*a*) clock synchronization
(*b*) error checking
(*c*) collision avoidance
(*d*) broadcast

52. Which of the following features is not possible in a token passing loop network ?

(*a*) Unlimited number of stations
(*b*) Unlimited distances
(*c*) Multiple time division
(*d*) In-service expansion

53. Which of the following items cannot be provided in a broadband LAN ?

(*a*) Frequency agile modems
(*b*) Closed-circuit TV
(*c*) Voice circuits
(*d*) Fibre-optic-transmission

54. In OSI network architecture, the routing is performed by

(*a*) network layer (*b*) data link layer
(*c*) transport layer (*d*) session layer

55. Which of the following is considered a broad band communication channel ?

(*a*) Coaxial code (*b*) Fibre optic cable
(*c*) Microwave (*d*) All of these

56. The transmission signal coding method of T1 carrier is called

(*a*) Bipolar (*b*) NRZ
(*c*) Manchester (*d*) Binary

57. Which one of the following uses UDP as the transport protocol ?

(*a*) HTTP (*b*) Telnet
(*c*) DNS (*d*) SMTP

58. An organization has a class B network and wishes to form subnets for 64 departments. The subnet mask would be

(*a*) 255.255.0.0 (*b*) 255.255.64.0
(*c*) 255.255.128.0 (*d*) 255.255.252.0

Answers

1. (*b*)	**2.** (*b*)	**3.** (*d*)	**4.** (*d*)	**5.** (*d*)	**6.** (*a*)	**7.** (*a*)	**8.** (*a*)	**9.** (*c*)	**10.** (*a*)
11. (*b*)	**12.** (*d*)	**13.** (*c*)	**14.** (*c*)	**15.** (*d*)	**16.** (*b*)	**17.** (*c*)	**18.** (*d*)	**19.** (*c*)	**20.** (*d*)
21. (*a*)	**22.** (*d*)	**23.** (*b*)	**24.** (*d*)	**25.** (*d*)	**26.** (*d*)	**27.** (*c*)	**28.** (*c*)	**29.** (*a*)	**30.** (*b*)
31. (*a*)	**32.** (*c*)	**33.** (*b*)	**34.** (*c*)	**35.** (*a*)	**36.** (*c*)	**37.** (*c*)	**38.** (*b*)	**39.** (*b*)	**40.** (*c*)
41. (*d*)	**42.** (*c*)	**43.** (*d*)	**44.** (*a*)	**45.** (*c*)	**46.** (*d*)	**47.** (*b*)	**48.** (*c*)	**49.** (*a*)	**50.** (*d*)
51. (*a*)	**52.** (*d*)	**53.** (*d*)	**54.** (*a*)	**55.** (*d*)	**56.** (*a*)	**57.** (*c*)	**58.** (*d*)		

Explanations

16. *Sequence number* : Frame from a sending station are numbered sequentially we need to set a limit.

21. Every computer has a fixed IP addresses.

22. The Address Resolution Protocol (ARP), allows a host to find the MAC (Physical) address of a target host on the same physical network, given only the targets IP address.

23. The spanning tree approach is a mechanism in which bridges automatically develop a routing table and update that table in response to changing topology. The algorithm consists of three mechanisms.

1. Frame Forwarding
2. Address Learning
3. Loop resolution

24. Since, we have to support 64 department

so our first

1 1 1 1 1 1 0 0

= 252

25. Consider optimum packet size which required minimum number of packet and does not waste any space.

Here consider each packet header because they are all work on packet switching network.

3 bytes is header size;

9 – 3 = 6 is data size

24/6 = 4 are the required packet

For case 1 : 24 packets are required

For case 2 : 8 packets are required

For case 3 : 6 packets are required

26. Congestion window increases exponentially.

27. Starting address : 255. 255. 248. 0

End address : 255. 255. 255. 254.

28. As there is no accept() at server side, the connect() at client could not get anything that can respond to its requests, so error occurs.

57. DNS uses UDP as the transport protocal.

58. Since, we have to support 64 department

so our first

1 1 1 1 1 1 0 0

= 252

■■

6 CHAPTER Analog Electronics

DIODES

CHARACTERISTICS OF DIODES.

Volt-ampere Characteristic

For a *p-n* junction, current I is related to the voltage V by the equation

$$I = I_o\left(\varepsilon^{\frac{V}{\eta V_T}} - 1\right) \quad ...(i)$$

At rated current, $\eta = 1$; Ge

$\eta = 2$; Si

A positive value of I means that current flows from the *p* to the *n* side. The diode is forward-baised if V is positive, indicating that *p* side of the junction is positive with respect to the *n* side.

Volt equivalent of temperature, $V_T \equiv \dfrac{T}{11{,}600}$ ...(*ii*)

At room temperature (T = 300°K), $V_T = 0.026$ V = 26 *m*V.

Form of volt-ampere characteristic described by equation (*i*) is shown in Fig. (*a*) of reverse bias. When voltage V is positive and several times V_T, then unity in the parentheses of equation (*ii*) may be neglected.

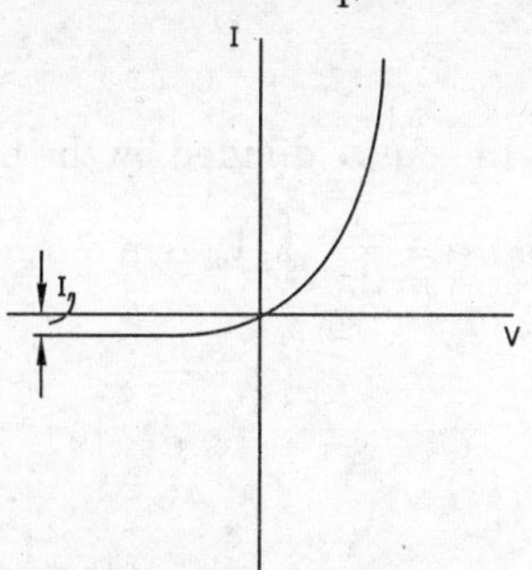

Fig. (a) Volt-ampere characteristic of an ideal p-n diode

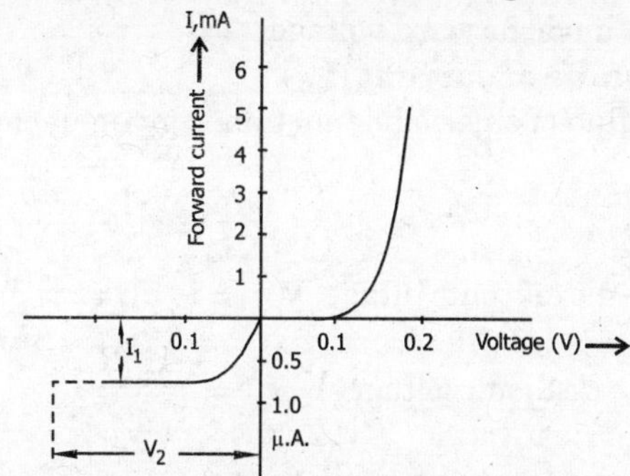

Fig. (b) Volt-ampere characteristic for a germanium diode redrawn to show the order of magnitude of currents.

Note : Volt-ampere characteristic shown in Fig. (*b*) has a forward-current scale in milliamperes and a reverse scale in microamperes.

Dashed portion of the curve of Fig. (*b*) indicates that, at a reverse-biasing voltage V_Z, diode characteristic exhibits an abrupt and marked departure from equation (*i*). At this critical voltage a large reverse current flows, and diode is said to be in the breakdown region.

Avalanche Multiplication

Two mechanisms of diode breakdown for increasing reverse voltage are recognized.

Consider the following situation :

A thermally generated carrier (part of the reverse saturation current) falls down the junction barrier and acquires energy from the applied potential. This carrier collides with a crystal ion and imparts sufficient energy to disrupt a covalent bond. In addition to the original carrier, a new electron-hole pair is generated. These carriers may also pick up sufficient energy from the applied field, collide with another crystal ion, and create still another electron-hole pair. Thus each new carrier may, in turn, produce additional carriers through collision and the action of disrupting bonds. This cumulative process is called *avalanche multiplication*. It results in large reverse currents, and the diode is said to be in the region of *avalanche breakdown*.

Zener Breakdown

Even if the initially available carriers do not acquire sufficient energy to disrupt bonds, it is possible to initiate breakdown through a direct rupture of the bonds. Because of the existence of the electric field at the junction, a sufficient strong force may be exerted on a bound electron by the field to tear it out of its covalent bond. The new hole-electron pair which is created increases the reverse current. This process, called *Zener breakdown*, does not involve collisions of carriers with the crystal ions (as does avalanche multiplication).

The field intensity ε increases as the impurity concentration increases, for a fixed applied voltage. It is found that Zener breakdown occurs at a field of approximately 2×10^7 V/*m*. This value is reached at voltages below about 6 V for heavily doped diodes. For lighter doped diodes the breakdown voltage is higher, and avalanche multiplication is the predominant effect. The term Zener is commonly used for the avalanche, or breakdown, diode even at higher voltages. Silicon diodes operated in avalanche breakdown are available with maintaining voltages from several volts to several hundred volts and with power up to 50 W.

RECTIFIER CIRCUITS

It is used to convert an ac voltage into a dc voltage.

Types of Rectifier Circuits.

1. **Half wave Rectifier.**

This rectifier conducts current only during positive half cycle of input ac supply. Therefore current flows in one direction in each cycle.

Fig. curcuit diagrom

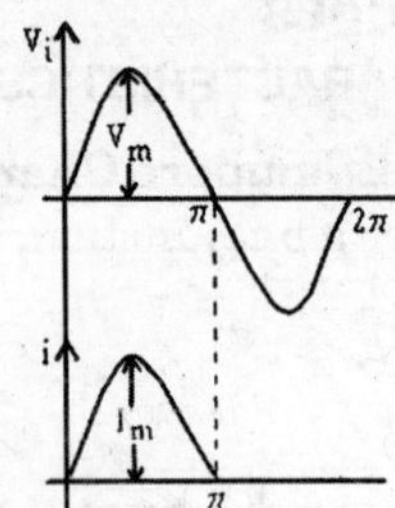

Fig. waveform

Let input to the rectifier is, $V_i = V_m \sin\alpha$

where, $\alpha = \omega t$

Average value (dc value) of sinusoidal input is zero

At the rectifier output, output current

$$i = I_m \sin\alpha, \text{ if } 0 \le \alpha < \pi$$

$$i = 0, \quad \text{if } \pi \le \alpha \le 2\pi$$

$$\text{Maximum value of current, } I_m = \frac{V_m}{R_L + R_f}$$

where, R_f = diode forward voltage

Average value of current (I_{dc}):

Average value of a periodic function is given by area of one cycle of the curve divided by the base.

$$I_{dc} = \frac{1}{2\pi}\int_0^{2\pi} i.d\alpha = \frac{1}{2\pi}\int_0^{2\pi} I_m \sin\alpha\, d\alpha = \frac{1}{2\pi}\int_0^{\pi} I_m \sin\alpha\, d\alpha = \frac{I_m}{\pi}$$

$$\text{d.c. output voltage, } V_{dc} = I_{dc} R_L = \frac{I_m.R_L}{\pi}$$

$$\text{Average } dc \text{ diode voltage, } V'_{dc} = \frac{-I_m.R_L}{\pi}$$

r.m.s value of load current (I_{rms}): $I_{rms} = \dfrac{I_m}{2}$

$$\text{where, } I_{rms} = \left(\frac{1}{2\pi}\int_0^{2\pi} i^2 d\alpha\right)^{1/2}$$

$$\textit{Efficiency, } \frac{P_{dc}}{P_{in}} = \frac{0.406}{(1 + R_0/R_L)}$$

where, $R_0 = R_b$ + transformer secondary resistance.

$$\textit{Form factor, } K_f = \frac{I_{L(ac)}}{I_{L(dc)}} = \frac{I_m/2}{I_m/\pi} = \frac{\pi}{2} = 1.57$$

$$\textit{Ripple factor, } r = \sqrt{K_f^2 - 1} = 1.21$$

Peak Inverse Voltage (PIV) rating for diode $\ge V_m$

Transformer Utilization Factor (T.U.F.) = $\frac{\text{d.c. power delivered to the load}}{\text{ac rating of transformer secondary}} = 0.287$

Voltage regulation (V_R): $V_R = \frac{V_{NL} - V_{FL}}{V_{FL}} \times 100$

Here, $V_{FL} = V_{NL} \times \frac{R_L}{R_L + R_0}$ and $V_R = \frac{R_0}{R_L}$

d.c. output voltage, $V_{dc} = \frac{V_m}{\pi} - I_{dc}.R_f$

$\therefore$ % Regulation $= \frac{V_{NL} - V_{FL}}{V_{NL}} \times 100 = \frac{V_m/\pi - I_{dc}.R_L}{I_{dc}.R_L} \times 100$

2. Full wave Rectifier

In this current flows through the load in the same direction for both half cycles of input ac voltage. This is done by two diodes working alternately.

Let input to the rectifier is, $V_i = V_m \sin \alpha$

where, $\alpha = \omega t$

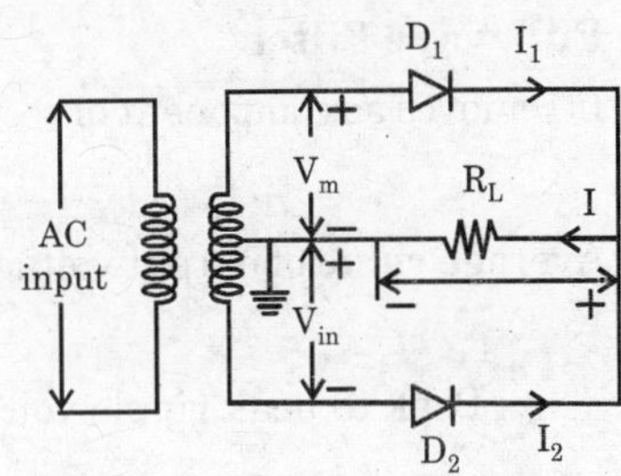

Fig. Circuit diagram

Maximum current at output of rectifier, $I_m = \frac{V_m}{R_f + R_L}$

Average dc current, $I_{dc} = \frac{2I_m}{\pi}$

Direct current in each tube $= \frac{I_{dc}}{2}$

Average dc diode voltage, $V_{dc} = I_{dc}.R_L = \frac{2I_m}{\pi} R_L$

r.m.s. value of load current, $I_{rms} = \frac{I_m}{\sqrt{2}}$

Efficiency, $\frac{P_{dc}}{P_{in}} = \frac{0.812}{(1 + R_0/R_L)}$

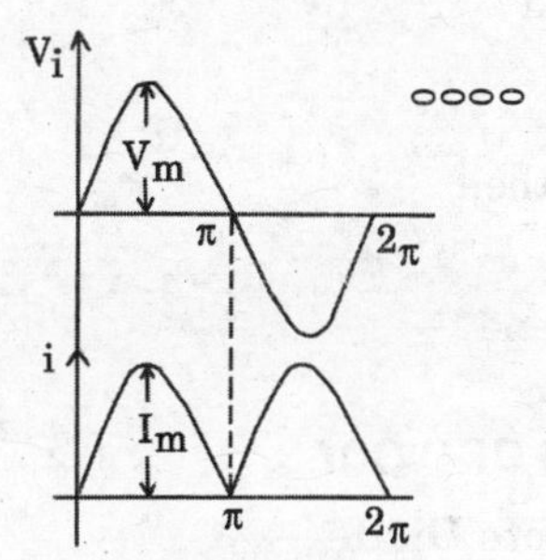

Fig. waveform

where, $R_0 = R_b$ + transformer secondary resistance.

Form factor, $K_f = \frac{V_{ac}}{V_{dc}} = \frac{\pi}{2\sqrt{2}} = 1.11$

Ripple Factor, $r = \sqrt{K_f^2 - 1} = 0.481$

Peak Inverse Voltage (PIV) rating for diode > $2V_m$

Transformer Utilization Factor:

T.U.F. = $\frac{\text{d.c. power delivered to the load}}{\text{ac rating of transformer secondary}} = 0.693$

Voltage regulation, $V_R = \frac{R_0}{R_L}$

d.c. output voltage, $V_{dc} = \frac{2V_m}{\pi} - I_{dc}.R_f$

Disadvantage:

(*i*) It is difficult to located center tap on transformer.

(*ii*) Diode used must have high PIV.

3. Bridge Rectifier

In this requirement of center tapped transformer is eliminated.

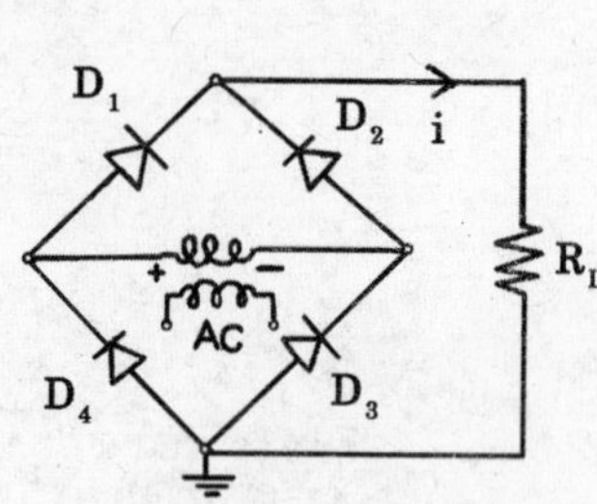

Fig. Circuit diagram

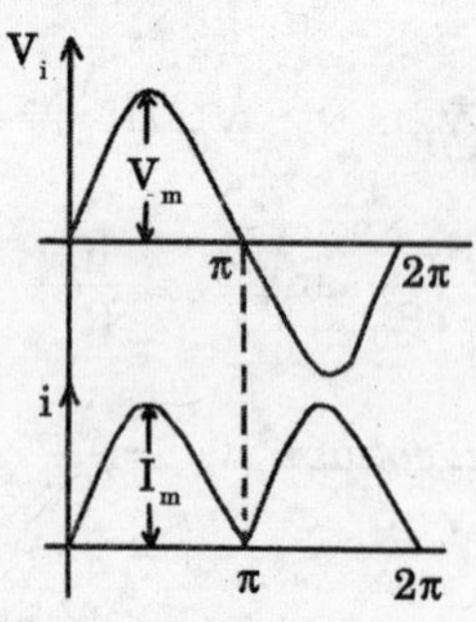

Fig. Waveform

In a bridge rectifier

(i) four diodes are used.

(ii) less size of transformer is required.

(iii) PIV $\geq V_m$

4. Full wave Filter.

It removes ac component of rectifier output but allows dc component to reach the load.

Average value of output voltage, $V_{dc} = V_m - \frac{V_r}{2}$

Peak to peak ripple voltage, $V_r = \frac{I_{dc} T_2}{C}$

where, T_2 = total non conducting time.

If $$T_2 = \frac{T}{2} = \frac{1}{2f},$$

then $$V_r\,(p.p) = \frac{I_{dc}}{2fC}$$

and $$V_{dc} = V_m - \frac{I_{dc}}{4fC}$$

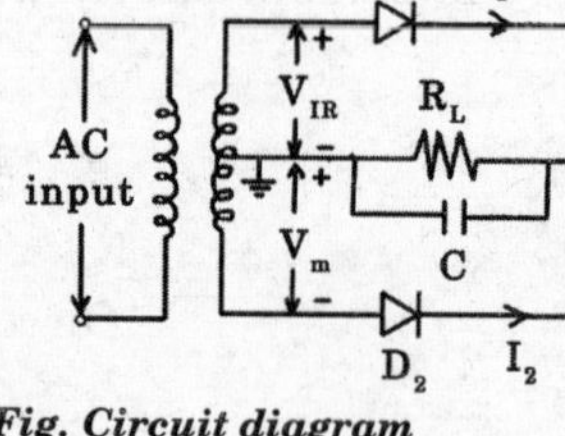

Fig. Circuit diagram

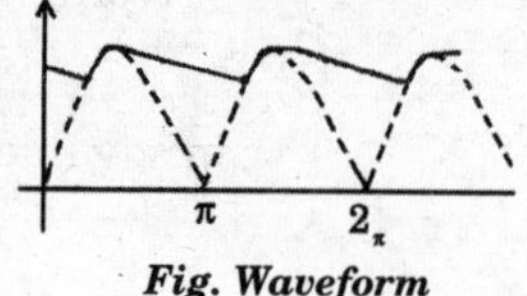

Fig. Waveform

TYPES OF DIODES.

1. Photo Diode

It is a two terminal device which operates on reverse bias. It has a small transparent window which allows light to strike the PN junction. When there is dark current it means no radiations.

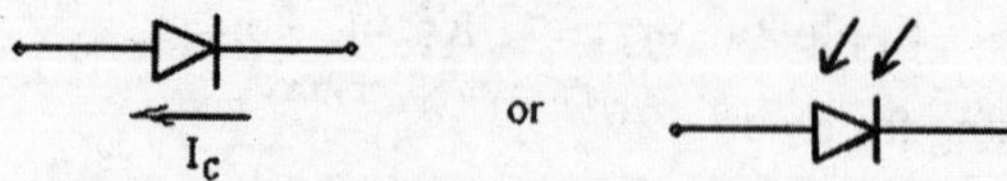

In reverse bias condition in the absence of light, reverse current through diode is very small like ordinary diode. But when light falls on the junction, a large amount of current flows and diode is forward biased.

Applications :

(i) Photo detection

(ii) Demodulation

(iii) Logic circuits

(iv) Switching

(v) Optical communication system

(vi) Character recognition etc.

Note : Photo-voltaic cell is a special application of Photo Diode.

2. LED (Light Emitting Diode)

It is PN junction which emits light when forward biased.

Only difference between LED and PN junction diode is of the material used for manufacturing LEDs.

Material	Light emitted
(*i*) Gallium Arsenide (GaAs)	Infrared radiation
(*ii*) Gallium arsenide phosphide (GaAsP)	Red or yellow
(*iii*) Gallium phosphide (GaP)	Red or green
(*iv*) Gallium nitride	Blue light

Applications :

(*i*) In 7 or 16 segment display.

(*ii*) Indicating ON/OFF condition in power switch or setreo amplifiers.

(*iii*) In optical switching applications.

(*iv*) In the field of optical communication to transfer energy from one circuit to another circuit.

(*v*) For image sensing circuits.

(*vi*) Infrared LEDs has application in burgler alarm system.

3. Pin Diode

It consists of heavily doped p and n regions separated by an intrinsic (i.e. undoped) region. Intrinsic region offers high resistance to the current through it.

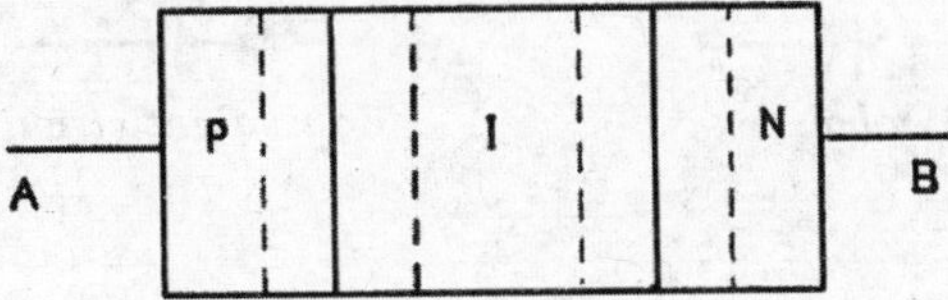

Characteristics :

(*i*) Works as an ordinary diode at frequencies upto 100 MHz.

(*ii*) Used in switching of microwaves

(*iii*) Above 100 MHz, it seizes operation of rectifier and behaves as a switch or resistance.

(*iv*) In reverse bias, it acts as a capacitor.

Three conditions in PIN Diode.

(*i*) Unbiased: When PIN diode is unbiased, there is a diffusion of electron across the junction due to different concentrations of atoms in the P and N regions. Depletion layer is produced across P and N junctions, with less penetration in the intrinsic region.

(*ii*) Forward Bias: With this condition, PIN diode works as a variable resistance and resistance decreases with increase in forward bias.

Fig. Forward bias equivalent circuit

(*iii*) Reverse Bias: In this condition, PIN diode works as a fixed capacitor because depletion width becomes constant after some voltage.

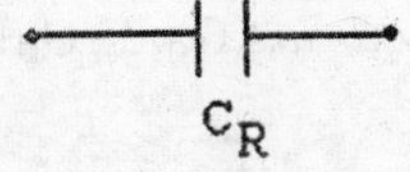

Fig. Equivalent circuit in reverse bias

Applications:

(*i*) As a d.c. controlled microwave switch.

(*ii*) In attenuator because its resistance can be controlled by the current.

Advantages of PIN over Normal PN junction diode.

(*i*) Capacitance between P and N regions decreases because of increased separation between them. Hence it can be used of very high frequencies.

(*ii*) Weak signal can also be processed.

4. Varactor diode

It utilize inherent capacitance of depletion layer. It is basically used in reverse bias because variation in depletion width can be achieved by reverse voltage.

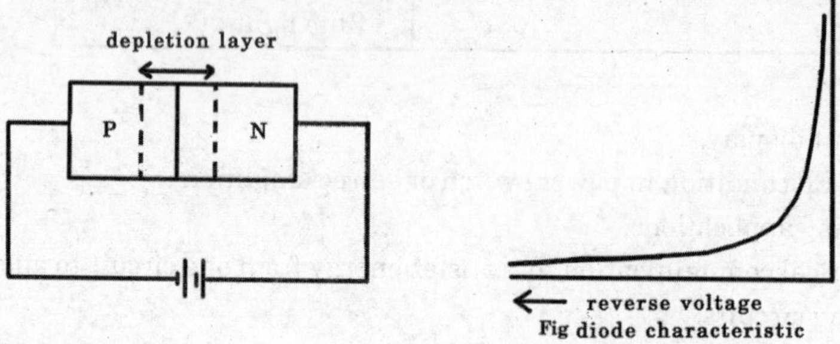

Fig diode characteristic

Characteristics :

Capacitance parameters are controlled by *method of doping* in the depletion layer or size and geometry of the diode.

Hyper abrupt profile provides better tuning range of about 10 : 1 compared to 4 : 1 of abrupt doping profile.

Symbol *Equivalent circuit*

Applications:

(*i*) As a variable capacitor.

(*ii*) Tuning circuit in radio and television receiver.

(*iii*) Frequency modulator.

5. Step recovery Diode

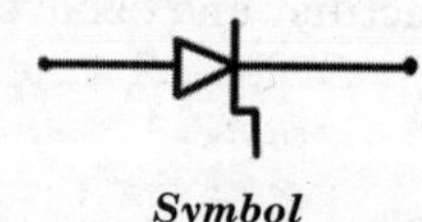

Symbol

Characteristics :

(*i*) It is a special form of varactor diode.

(*ii*) Diode works in forward bias.

(*iii*) When it is forward biased, snap off energy is stored by this and their capacitors. In reverse bias, it releases this energy.

(*iv*) Diode uses diffusion constant.

(*v*) It is used to generate harmonics.

(*vi*) It is used as a frequency modulator.

6. Gunn Diode

It is a wide band amplifier. Properties of diode does not depends upon junction but depends on *bulk of materials*. Gunn Diode cannot be used as a diode.

Materials used for construction of Gunn Diode are GaAs, GaP, InP, CdTe etc.

VI characteristics :

Due to negative resistance region in Gunn diode, population inversion occurs. It is observed only in n-type materials. In this, electron jumps from completely filled band to the partially filled band.

It starts in 3.3 kV/m.

Population inversion depends on length of the crystal, and gradient of the electric field intensity.

Gunn diode is used as an amplifier and oscillator.

7. Impatt avalanche transit time Diode

- It operates in reverse bias.
- Impact avalanche and transit time results in negative resistance region.
- Voltage and current have 180° phase difference in which 90° is contributed by avalanche and 90° by transit time.
- Avalanche is possible at 400 kV/cm.
- IMPATT diode is a $(p^+ - n - n^+)$ junction
- Maximum difference between maximum current and maximum voltage is 180°.
- It is a narrow band amplifier.

BIPOLAR JUNCTION TRANSISTOR (BJT)

A bipolar juction transistor is a three-layer device (*npn* or *pnp*) with two junctions and can provide circuit properties of both a current-controlled source (employed for signal amplification) and a switch (employed for digital signal processing).

Construction

A *pnp* BJT is fabricated by sandwiching a thin *n*-type region between two *p*-type regions as shown in Fig. (*a*), while an *npn* BJT has an *p*-type region placed between two *n*-type regions Fig. (*b*).

Elements of a BJT

(*i*) **Base :** It is the sandwiched layer.

(*ii*) **Emitter :** It acts as the source of mobile carriers.

(*iii*) **Collector :** It extracts the carriers to transport energy to the external circuit, while control of carriers flow from the emitter to the collector is accomplished in the base.

Symbols

Direction of the arrow on E-terminal indicates direction of conventional current flow.

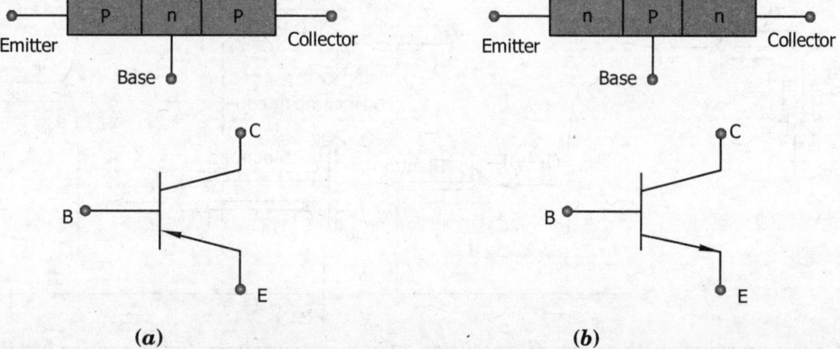

Fig. BJT schematics and circuit symbols

Operation

In the operation of a BJT, the emitter requires higher doping densities as it is called upon to serve as a source of mobile charges. Again in most applications, the collector region handles more power than the emitter and so it must be provided with significantly larger area than that of the emitter.

It is easier to describe the operation of a BJT using the *pnp* configuration. Fig. (*a*) represents a thin horizontal slice through a *pnp* transistor. The mode of operation which results in a controlled source, called *active region*, is achieved by forward biasing emitter-base *pn* junction and reverse biasing base-collector junction as shown in the Fig. (*c*).

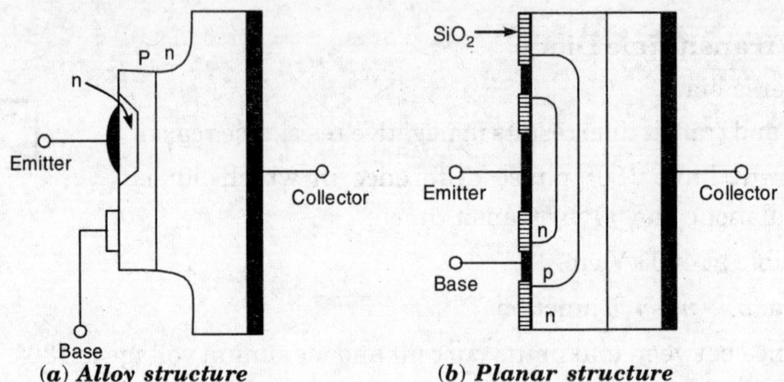

(a) Alloy structure ***(b) Planar structure***

Fig. Operation of npn bipolar transistors

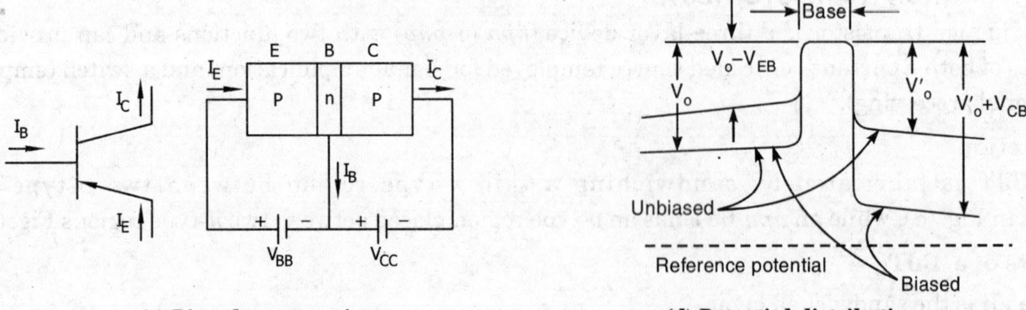

(c) Biased pnp transistor ***(d) Potential distribution***

The corresponding potential distribution is shown in Fig. *(d)*. This distribution in the emitter is different from that in the collector because of their different doping densities.

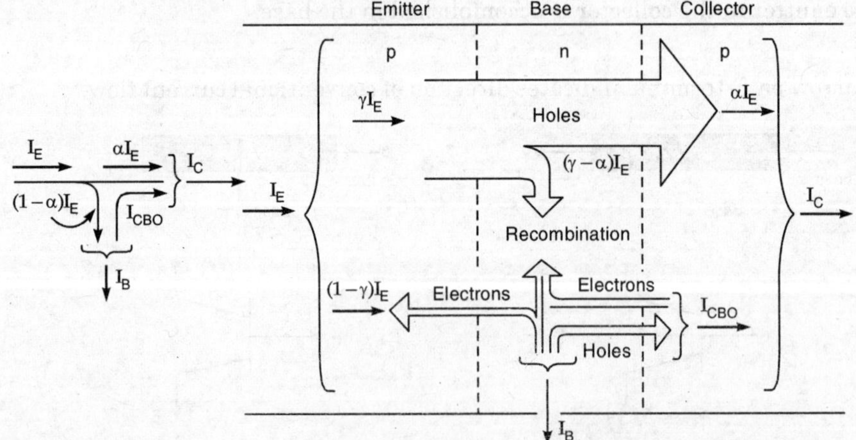

Fig. (e) Carrier motion in the normal operation of a pnp transistor (with proper biasing)

The operation of a *pnp* transistor is explained with the help of Fig. (*e*). Because of forward biasing, the emitter injects a large number of holes into the base region, where these become *minority carriers*. In the base region, holes diffuse towards the collector-base junction and are swept into the collector because of high field intensity associated with reverse bias. Thus emitter current injected into the base increases minority carrier density in the base on which depends value of the reverse minority collector current. So input emitter current controls output collector current making the BJT act as a current controlled current source. However, a fraction of the holes injected into the base recombine with the electrons (which are majority carriers in the base). To replenish this loss of electrons due to recombination, an electron current flows into the base from the base terminal.

Besides the holes injected from the emitter, thermally generated holes in the base and electrons in the collector also cross collector-base junction contributing to the collector current.

Thus collector current consists of two components :

(*i*) due to injected holes at the emitter base junction

(*ii*) attributed to thermally generated carriers (which constitute reverse saturation current) crossing the collector base junction.

Since both holes and electrons contribute to the device current, hence device is called *bipolar*. Also, assume that potential is constant within each region and no conduction (drift) currents exist. Hence all the currents in the transistor are diffusion currents.

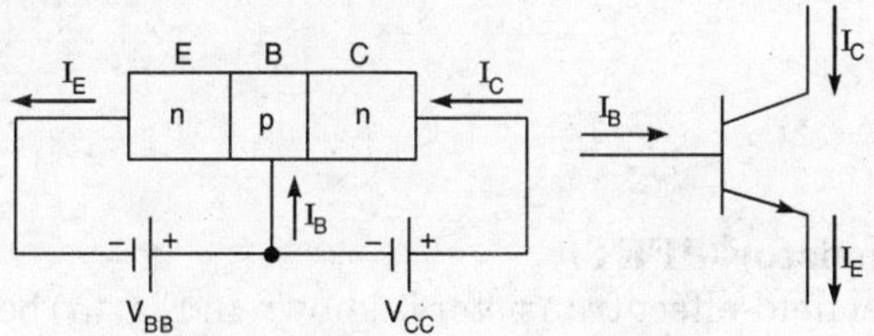

Fig. (f) Biased npn transistor

Fig. (*f*) shows a similarly biased *npn* transistor. Electrons now flow into emitter and out of collector and also a hole current flows into base to provide for recombination in the base. Reverse saturation current is contributed by minority electrons crossing from base to collector and minority holes from collector to base.

Now develop a quantitative model to describe the transistor operation.

As in Fig. (*e*), α is fraction of emitter current which leaves the collector (*pnp*) (or enters the collector (*npn*)) and I_{CBO} is the reverse saturation current in the reverse biased base-collector junction.

I_{CBO} could be witnessed as a separate entity by opening the emitter connection, *i.e.* $I_E = 0$

From Fig. (*f*) (left) $\quad I_C = \alpha I_E + I_{CBO}$

and $\quad I_B = (1 - \alpha) I_E - I_{CBO}$

$\therefore \quad I_C + I_B = I_E$

Hence $$I_C = \left(\frac{\alpha}{1-\alpha}\right) I_B + \left(\frac{1}{1-\alpha}\right) I_{CBO}$$

Above equations are fundamental BJT transistor relations and apply for both *pnp* and *npn* transistors with the conventional current directions as indicated respectively in Fig. *(c)* and Fig. (*e*).

As carriers injected into the base (thin slice) stay there for very short duration before being swept off to the collector region, recombination current is very small and the ratio α is as high as 0.98-0.998.

OPERATING MODES.

A BJT can operate in cut-off, active and saturation modes. If both collector and emitter junctions are reverse biased, then transistor is in the cut-off mode. If collector-base junction is reverse biased and emitter-base junction is forward biased, then transistor is operating in the active region; so for this region, mathematical relationship is derived. If both junctions are forward biased, then transistor is said to be in *saturation*.

In order to understand forward biasing of the collector base junction, $V_{CB} = V_{CE} - V_{BE}$

As V_{CE} decreases, voltage across the collector-base junction becomes successively less reverse biased till it reaches the cut-in voltage of the *pn*-junction.

This occurs for $V_{CE} \approx 0.2$ V when $\quad V_{CB} = 0.2 - 0.7 = -0.5$ V (= cut-in voltage of *pn* junction)

In this region I_B no longer '*controls*' I_C, so that mathematical relationships derived for the active region are no longer valid.

Operating modes of a BJT

Operating mode	Junction Bias		Application
	Emitter-Base	**Collector-Base**	
Forward-active current	Forward	Reverse	Controlled source; amplification
Cut-off	Reverse	Reverse	Switch "OFF"
Saturation	Forward	Forward	Switch "ON"
Reverse-active (Inverted)	Reverse	Forward	Rare use

In reverse-active mode, behaviour is that of a controlled source with

$$I_E = \beta_R I_B$$

where β_R = reverse current gain.

As $\beta_R << \beta$ (forward current gain), this mode is unsuitable in general except for certain special applications in digital circuits.

FIELD-EFFECT TRANSISTORS

TYPES OF FET'S.

1. Junction Field-Effect Transistor (JFET)

The structure of an *n*-channel field-effect transistor is shown in Fig. (*a*) below. Ohmic contacts are made to the two ends of a semiconductor bar of *n*-type material (if *p*-type silicon is used, the device is referred to as a *p*-channel FET). Current is caused to flow along the length of the bar because of the voltage supply connected between the ends.

Standard FET Notations

Source (S) : It is terminal through which majority carriers enter the bar.

Drain (D) : It is terminal through which majority carriers leave the bar.

The drain-to-source voltage is called V_{DS}, and is positive if D is more positive than S.

From Fig. (*a*) below, $V_{DS} = V_{DD}$ = drain supply voltage.

Gate.

On both sides of the *n*-type bar shown below heavily doped (*p*+) regions of acceptor impurities have been formed by alloying, by diffusion, or by any other procedure available for creating *p-n* junctions, this impurity region are called *gate G*.

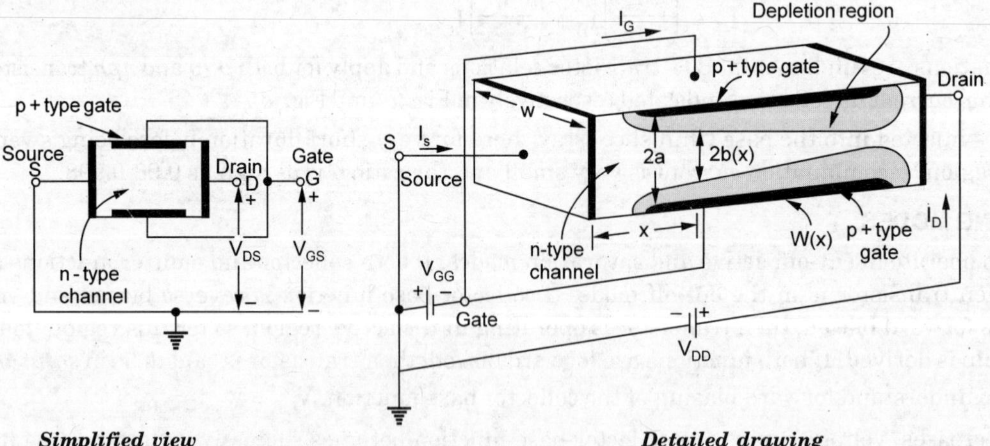

Fig. (a) Basic structure of an n-channel field-effect transistor

Between gate and the source, a voltage, $V_{GS} = -V_{GG}$ is applied in the direction to reverse-bias the *p-n* junction. Conventional current entering the bar at G is designated I_G.

Channel.

The region in Fig. (*a*) above *n*-type material between two gate regions is the channel through which majority carriers move from source to drain.

Operation.

As reverse bias across the junction increases thickness of the region of immobile uncovered charges. Conductivity of this region is normally zero because of the unavailability of current carriers. Hence effective width of the channel in Fig. (*a*) will become progressively decreased with increasing reverse bias. Accordingly, for a fixed drain-to-source voltage, the drain current will be a function of the reverse-biasing voltage across the gate junction. The term field effect is used to describe this device because the mechanism of current control is the effect of the extension, with increasing reverse bias, of the field associated with the region of uncovered charges.

Static Characteristics

Direction of the arrow at the gate of the junction FET in Fig. (*a*) indicates direction in which gate current would flow if gate junction were forward-biased. The common-source drain characteristic for a typical *n*-channel FET shown in Fig. (*a*) give I_D against V_{DS}, with V_{GS} as a parameter. To see qualitatively why characteristics have the form shown, consider, say the case for which $V_{GS} = 0$.

For $I_D = 0$, the channel between gate junctions is entirely open. In response to a small applied voltage V_{DS}, then *n*-type bar acts as a simple semiconductor resistor, and current I_D increases linearly with V_{DS}. With increasing current, ohmic voltage drop between source and the channel region reverse-biases the junction, and conducting portion of the channel begins to construct. Because of the ohmic drop along the length of thechannel itself, the constriction is not uniform, but is more pronounced at distances farther from the source, as shown in Fig. (*a*). Eventually, a voltage V_{DS} is reached at which the channel is *pinched off*. This is the voltage, not too sharply defined in Fig. (*c*), where current I_D begin to level off and approach a constant value. It is in principle not possible for the channel to close completely and thereby reduce the current I_D to zero. In such a case, the ohmic drop required to provide the necessary back bias would itself be lacking.

For an n-channel FET, I_D and V_{DS} are positive and V_{GS} is negative.

For a p-channel FET, I_D and V_{DS} are negative and V_{GS} is positive.

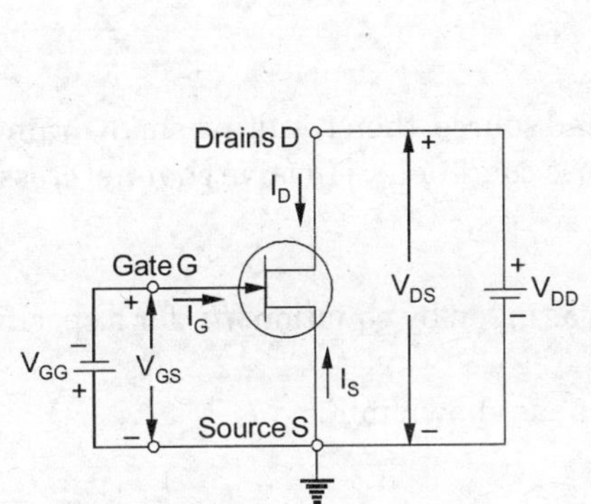

Fig. (b) Circuit symbol for an n-channel FET

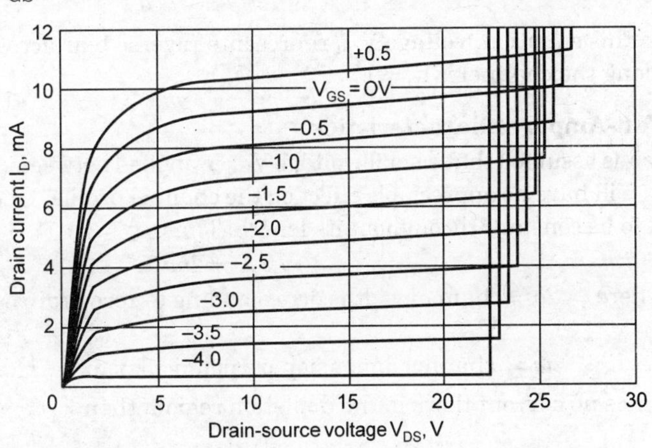

Fig. (c) Common-source drain characteristics of an n-channel field-effect transistor

If now a gate voltage V_{GS} is applied in the direction to provide additional reverse bias, pinch-off will occur for smaller values of $|V_{DS}|$, and maximum drain current will be smaller. The maximum voltage that can be applied between any two terminals of the FET is the lowest voltage that will cause Avalanche breakdown across the gate junction. From Fig. (*c*), avalanche occurs at a lower value of $|V_{DS}|$ when gate is reverse-biased than for

$V_{GS} = 0$. This is caused by the fact that reverse-bias gate voltage adds to the drain voltage, and hence increases effective voltage across the gate junction.

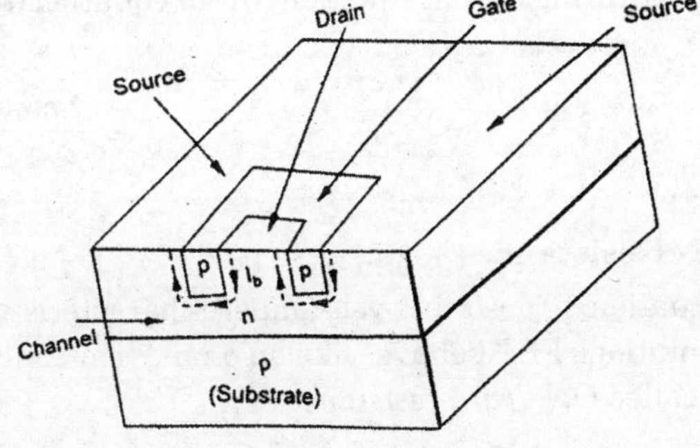

Pinch-off voltage (V_P).

Assume that *p*-type region is doped with N_A acceptors per cubic meter, *n*-type region is doped with N_D donors per cubic meter, and the junction formed is abrupt.

Moreover, if $N_A >> N_D$, $W_p << W_n$, then for the space-charge width, $W_n(x) = W(x)$ at a distance x along channel in Fig. (*a*).

$$W(x) = a - b(x) = \left\{\frac{2\varepsilon}{qN_D}[V_o - V(x)]\right\}^{1/2} \quad ...(i)$$

where ε = dielectric constant of channel material

q = magnitude of electronic charge

V_o = junction contact potential at x

$V(x)$ = applied potential across space-charge region at x and is a negative number for an applied reverse bias

$a - b(x)$ = penetration $W(x)$ of depletion region into channel at a point x along channel (Fig. *a*)

If drain current is zero, $b(x)$ and $V(x)$ are independent of x and $b(x) = b$. If in equation (*i*) $b(x) = b = 0$ is substituted and solve for V, assuming that $|V_o| << |V|$, we get pinch-off voltage V_p, diode reverse voltage that removes all the free charge from the channel.

$$\therefore \quad |V_P| = \frac{qN_D}{2\varepsilon}a^2 \quad ...(ii)$$

If we substitute V_{GS} for $V_o - V(x)$ in equation (*i*), and use equation (*ii*), we get

$$V_{GS} = \left(1 - \frac{b}{a}\right)^2 V_p \quad ...(iii)$$

In this equation, voltage V_{GS} represents reverse bias across the gate junction and is independent of distance along the channel if $I_D = 0$.

Volt-Ampere characteristics

If it is assumed that a small voltage V_{DS} is applied between drain and source, then resulting small drain current I_D will have no appreciable effect on the channel profile. Under these conditions, effective channel cross section A to be constant throughout its length. Thus

$$A = 2bw$$

where, $2b$ = channel width corresponding to zero drain current as given by equation (*iii*) for a specified V_{GS},

w = channel dimension perpendicular to the b direction, as shown in Fig. (*a*)

Since no current flows in the depletion region, then

$$\text{drain current, } I_D = AqN_D\mu_n\varepsilon = 2bwqN_D\mu_n\frac{V_{DS}}{L} \quad ...(iv)$$

where L = length of the channel.

Substituting b from equation (*iii*) in equation (*iv*), we have for small I_D,

$$I_D = \frac{2awqN_D\mu_n}{L}\left[1 - \left(\frac{V_{GS}}{V_P}\right)^{\frac{1}{2}}\right]V_{DS} \quad ...(v)$$

ON Resistance $r_{d, ON}$.

Equation (*v*) describes volt-ampere characteristics of Fig. (*c*) for very small V_{DS}, and it suggests that under these conditions FET behaves like an ohmic resistance whose value is determined by V_{GS}. Ratio V_{DS}/I_D at the origin is called *ON drain resistance* $r_{d\,ON}$.

For a JFET from equation (*v*), with $V_{GS} = 0$, $\quad r_{d, ON} = \dfrac{L}{2awqN_D\mu_n}$

Pinch-off Region.

If a substantial drain current I_D flows, the drain end of the gate is more reverse-biased than the source end, and hence the boundaries of the depletion region are not parallel to the longitudinal axis of the channel, but converge as shown in Fig. (*a*). If convergence of the depletion region is gradual, the previous one-dimensional analysis is valid in a thin slice of the channel of thickness Δx and at a distance x from the source. Subjects to this condition of the *gradual channel*, the current may be written by referring Fig. (*a*) as

$$I_D = 2b(x)wqN_D\mu_n\varepsilon_x \quad \text{...(vi)}$$

As V_{DS} increases, ε_x and I_D increase, whereas $b(x)$ decrease because the channel narrows, and hence the current density $J = I_D/2b(x)w$ increases. Complete pinch-off ($b = 0$) cannot take place because, if it did, J would become infinite, which is a physically impossible condition. If J were to increase without limit, then from equation (*vi*), so also would ε_x, provided that μ_n remains constant.

It is found that mobility is a function of electric field intensity and remains constant only for $\varepsilon_x < 10^3$ V/*cm* in *n*-type silicon.

For moderate fields, 10^3 to 10^4 V/*cm*, mobility is approximately inversely proportional to the square root of the applied field.

For still higher fields, such as are encountered at pinch-off, μ_n is inversely proportional to ε_x. In this region drift velocity of the electrons ($v_x = \mu_n\varepsilon_x$) remains constant, and Ohm's law is no longer valid.

Region before Pinch-off.

FET behaves as an ohmic resistance for small V_{DS} and as a constant-current device for large V_{DS}.

In this region, mobility is at first independent of electric field and then μ varies with $\varepsilon_x^{-\frac{1}{2}}$ for larger values of ε_x (before pinch-off).

Taking this relationship into account, it is possible to obtain an expression for I_D as a function of V_{DS} and V_{GS} which agrees quite well with experimentally determined curves.

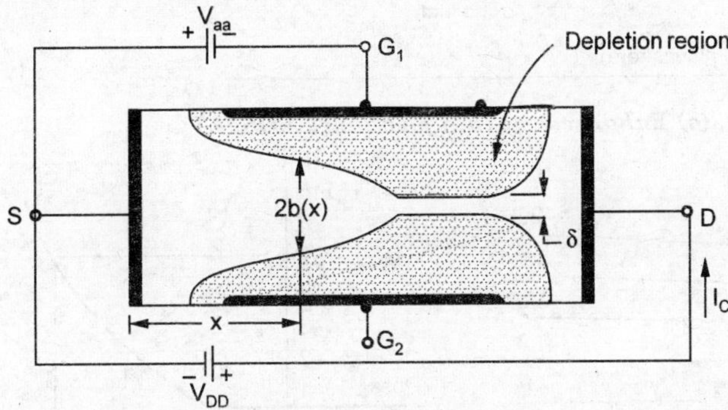

Fig. (e) After pinch-off, as V_{DS} is increased, then L′ increases but δ and I_D remain essentially constant (G_1 and G_2 are tied together)

Transfer characteristic

In amplifier applications, FET is almost always used in the region beyond pinch-off (also called *constant-current, pentode, or current-saturation region).*

Let saturation drain current be designed by I_{DS}, and its value with the gate shorted to the source ($V_{GS} = 0$) by I_{DSS}.

The relationship between I_{DS} and V_{GS}, is given by

$$I_{DS} = I_{DSS}\left(1 - \frac{V_{GS}}{V_P}\right)^2$$

Cutoff

Consider an FET operating at a fixed value of V_{DS} in the constant-current region. As V_{GS} is increased in the direction to reverse-bias the gate junction, the conducting channel will narrow.

When $V_{GS} = V_P$, the channel width is reduced to zero,and $I_{DS} = 0$. But some leakage current $I_{D,\,OFF}$ still flows even under the cutoff condition $|V_{GS}| > |V_P|$.

2. Metal-Oxide-Semiconductor FET (MOSFET)

The *p*-channel MOSFET consists of a lightly doped *n*-type substrate into which two highly doped p^+ regions are diffused, as shown in Fig. (*a*) below. These p^+ sections which will act as the source and drain, are separated by about 5 to 10 μm. A thin (1,000 to 2,000 Å) layer of insulating silicon dioxide (SiO_2) is grown over the surface of the structure, and holes are cut into the layer oxide layer, allowing contact with the source and drain. Then gate-metal area is overlaid on the oxide, covering the entire channel region. Simultaneously, metal contacts are made to the drain and source, as shown in Fig. (*a*).

The metal area of the gate, in conjunction with the insulating dielectric oxide layer and the semiconductor channel, form a parallel-plate capacitor. Because of insulating layer of silicon dioxide, this device is called the *insulated-gate field-effect transistor*. This layer results in an extremely high input resitance (10^{10} to $10^{15}\Omega$) for the MOSFET.

Enhancement MOSFET.

Apply negative voltage at the gate, an electric field will be directed perpendicularly through the oxide. This field will end on *induced* positive charges on the semiconductor site, as shown in Fig. (*a*). Positive charges, which are minority carriers in the *n*-type substrate, form an *inversion layer*. As the magnitude of the negative voltage on the gate increases, the induced positive charge in the semiconductor increases. The region beneath the oxide now has *p*-type carriers, the conductivity increases, and current flows from source to drain through the induced channel. Thus the drain current is *enhanced* by the negative gate voltage, and such a device is called *enhancement-type MOS*.

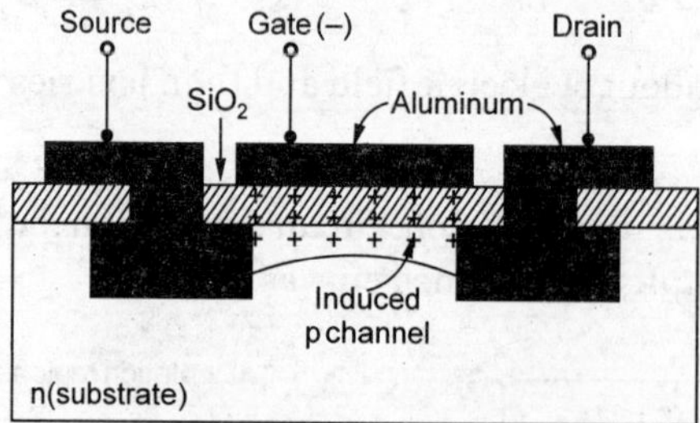

Fig. (a) Enhancement in a p-channel MOSFET

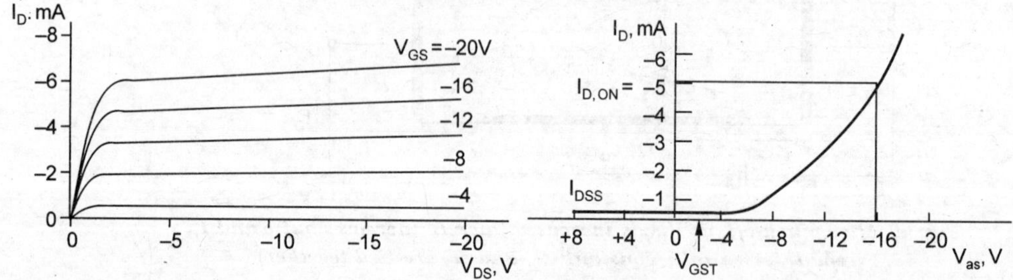

(b) Drain characteristics

(c) Transfer curve (for V_{DS} = 10 V) of a p-channel enhancement-type MOSFET

Threshold voltage.

The volt-ampere drain characteristics of a *p*-channel enhancement-mode MOSFET are given in Fig. (*b*) and its transfer curve in Fig. (*c*). The current I_{DSS} at $V_{GS} \geq 0$ is very small, of the order of a few nanoamperes. As V_{GS} is made negative, the current $|I_D|$ increases slowly at first, and then much more rapidly with an increase in $|V_{GS}|$. The manufacturer often indicates the gate-source threshold voltage V_{GST}, or V_T at which $|I_D|$ reaches some defined small value, say 10 μA. A current $I_{D,ON}$ corresponding approximately to the maximum value given on the drain characteristics, and the value of V_{GS} needed to obtain this current are also usually given on the manufacturer's specification sheets.

The value of V_T for the *p*-channel standard MOSFET is typically - 4 V, and it is common to use a power-supply voltage of – 12 V for the drain supply.

Power supply requirements.

Table below gives voltage customarily used with high-threshold and low-threshold *p*-channel MOSFETs. V_{SS} refers to the source, V_{DD} to the drain, and V_{GG} to the gate supply voltages. The subscript 1 denotes that the source is grounded and the subscript 2 designates that the drain is at ground potential.

The low-threshold MOS circuit require lower power supply voltages and this means less expensive system power supplies. In addition, the input voltage swing for turning the device ON and OFF is smaller for the lower-threshold voltage, and this means faster operation. Another feature of low-threshold MOS circuits is that they are directly compatible with bipolar ICs. They require and produce essentially the same input and output signal swings and the system deginer has the flexibility of using MOS and bipolar circuits in the same system.

Table : Power supply voltages for *p*-channel MOSFETs, in volts

	V_{SS1}	$-V_{DD1}$	$-V_{GG1}$	V_{SS2}	V_{DD2}	$-V_{GG2}$
High-threshold	0	−12	−24	+12	0	−12
Low-threshold	0	−5	−17	+5	0	−12

Depletion MOSFET.

Consider an *n*-channel structure, shown in Fig. (*d*), drain current I_{DSS} flows for zero gate-to-source voltage $V_{GS} = 0$. If gate voltage is made negative, positive charges are induced in the channel through the SiO_2 of the gate capacitor. Since current in an FET is due to majority carriers (electrons for an *n*-type material), the induced positive charges make the channel less conductive, and the drain current drops as V_{GS} is made more negative. The redistribution of charge in the channel causes an effective depletion of majority carriers, which accounts for the designation depletion MOSFET.

In Fig. (*e*) because of the voltage drop due to the drain current, the channel region nearest the drain is more depleted than is the volume near the source like that of pinch-off occurring in a JFET at the drain end of the channel. The volt-ampere characteristics of the depletion-mode MOS and the JFET are quite similar.

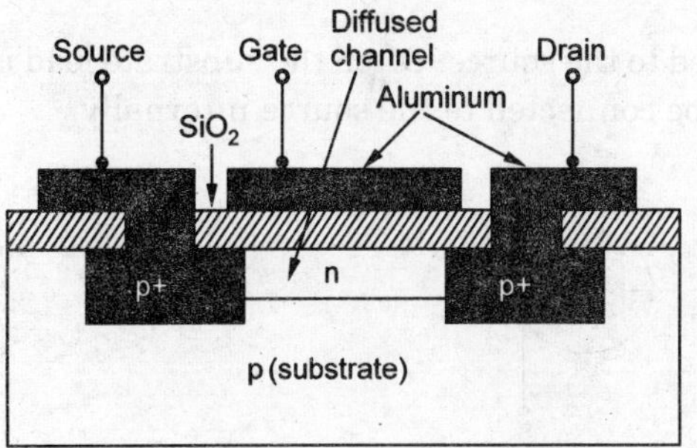

(d) n-channel depletion-type MOSFET

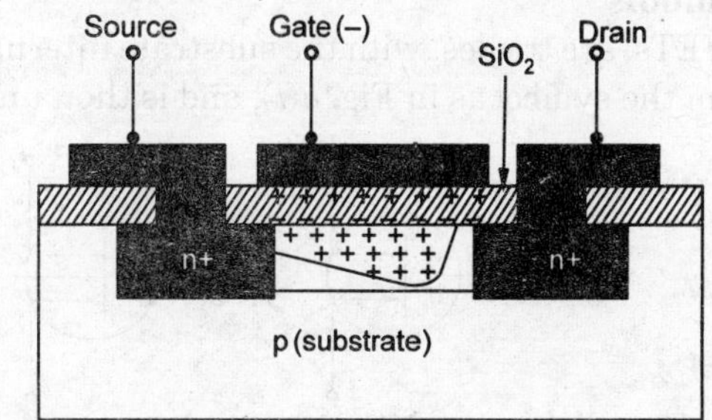

(e) Channel depletion with application of a negative gate voltage

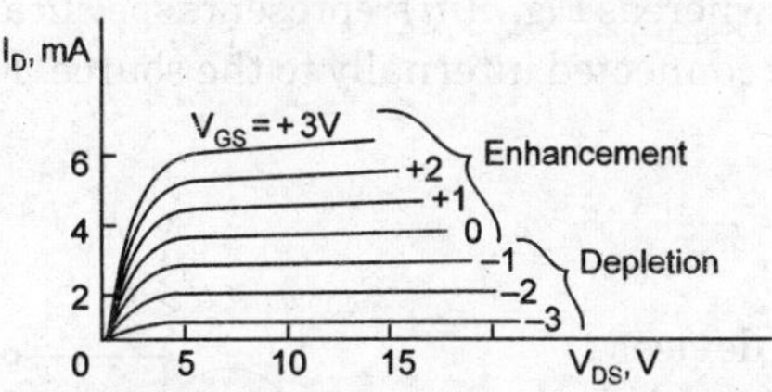

(f) Drain characteristics

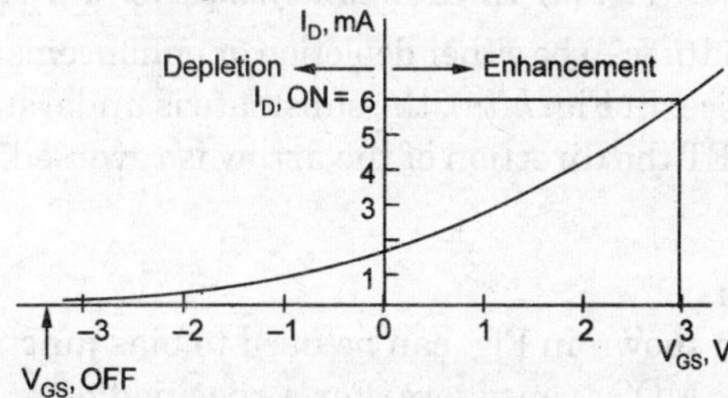

(b) Transfer curve (for V_{DS} = 10 V) for an n-channel MOSFET

A MOSFET of the depletion type just described may also be operated in an enhancement mode. It is only necessary to apply a positive gate voltage so that negative charges are induced into the *n*-type channel. In this manner the conductivity of the channel increases and the current rises above I_{DSS}. The volt-ampere characteristics of this device are indicated in Fig. (*f*) and transfer curve is given in Fig. (*g*).

Comparison of *p*- with *n*- channel FETs.

The *p*-channel enhancement FET, is very popular in MOS systems because it is much easier to produce than the *n*-channel device. Most of the contaminants in MOS fabrication are mobile ions which are positively charged and are trapped in the oxide layer between gate and the substrate. In an *n*-channel enhancement device the gate is normally positive with respect to the substrate and hence, the positively charged contaminants collect along the interface between the SiO_2 and the silicon substrate. The positive charge from this layer of ions attracts free electrons in the channel which tends to make the transistor turn on prematurely. In *p*-channel devices the positive contaminant ions are pulled to the opposite side of the oxide layer (to the aluminium-SiO_2 interface) by the negative gate voltage and there they cannot affect the channel.

The hole mobility in silicon and at normal field intensities is approximately 500 $cm^2/V\text{-}s$, and electron mobility is about 1,300 $cm^2/V\text{-}s$. Thus the *p*-channel device will have more than twice the ON resistance of an equivalent *n*-channel of the same geometry and under the same operating conditions. *i.e.*, the *p*-channel device must have more than twice the area of the *n*-channel device to achieve the same resistance. Therefore *n*-channel MOS circuits can be smaller for the same complexity than *p*-channel devices. The higher packing density of the *n*-channel MOS also makes it faster in switching applications due to the smaller junction areas. The operating speed is limited primarily by the internal RC time contants, and the capacitance is directly proportional to the junction cross sections. Due to all these reasons, *n*-channel MOS circuits are more desirable than *p*-channel circuits.

MOSFET Gate protection.

Since SiO_2 layer of the gate is extremely thin, it may easily be damaged by excessive voltage. An accumulation of charge on an open-circuited gate may result in a large enough field to punch through the dielectric. To prevent this damage some MOS devices are fabricated with a Zener diode between gate and substrate. In normal operation this diode is open and has no effect upon the circuit. However, if the voltage at the gate becomes excessive, then diode breaks down and gate potential is limited to a maximum value equal to the Zener voltage.

Circuit symbols.

Most MOSFETs, are triodes, with the substrate internally connected to the source. Often the substrate lead is omitted from the symbol as in Fig. *h*(*i*), and is then understood to be connected to the source internally.

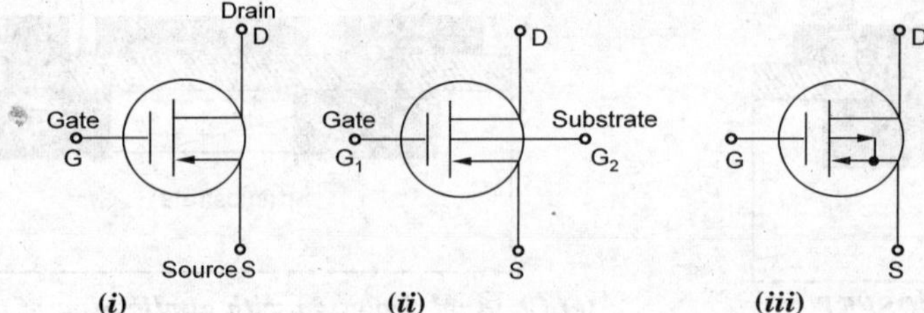

Fig. (h) Three circuit symbols for a p-channel MOSFET

Referring Figs. *h*(*i*) and (*ii*) can be either depletion or enhancement types, whereas Fig. *h*(*iii*) represents specifically an enhancement device. In Fig. *h*(*iv*), the substrate is understood to be connected internally to the source. For an n-channel MOSFET the direction of the arrow is reversed.

BIASING THE FET.

1. Source Self-bias

The configuration shown in Fig. can be used to bias junction FET devices or depletion-mode MOS transistors. For a specified drain current I_D, the corresponding gate-to-source voltage V_{GS} can be obtained applying either equation or the plotted drain or transfer characteristics. Since the gate current (and, hence, voltage drop across R_g) is negligible, the source resistance R_s can be found as the ratio of V_{GS} to the desired I_D.

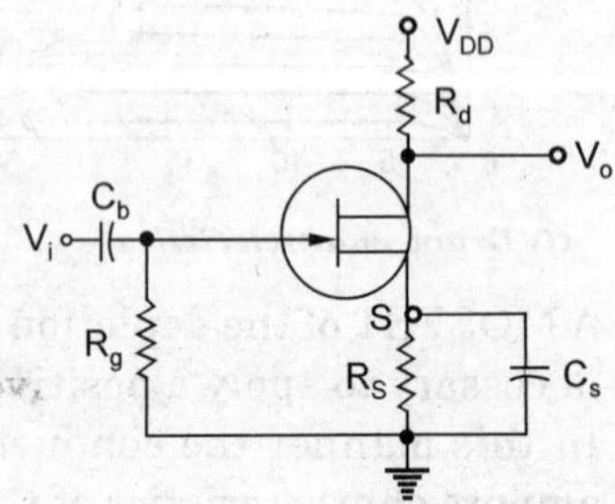

2. Biasing against Device variation

The transfer characteristics for a given type of *n*-channel FET may appear as in Fig. (*b*), where top and bottom curves are for extreme values of temperature and device variation. It is necessary to bias the device at a drain current which will not drift out of $I_D = I_A$ and $I_D = I_B$. Then bias line $V_{GS} = -I_D R_s$ must intersect the transfer characteristic between the points A nd B, as shown in Fig. (*b*). The slope of this bias line is determined by the source resistance R_s. For any transfer characteristic between two extremes shown, current I_Q is such that $I_A < I_Q < I_B$, as desired.

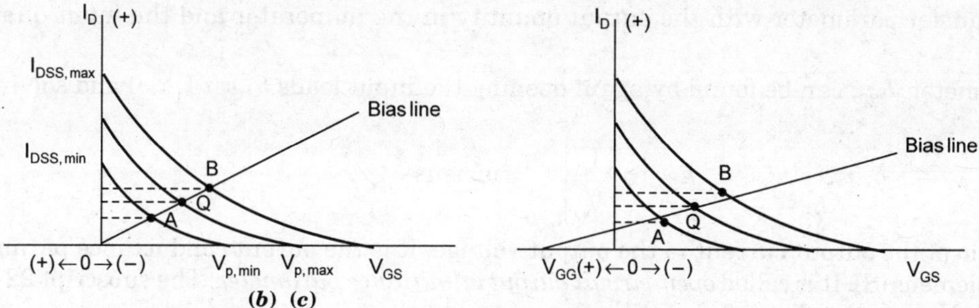

(*b*) (*c*)

Fig. Maximum and minimum transfer curves for an n-channel FET.

The drain current must lie between I_A and I_B. The bias line can be drawn though the origin for the current limits shown in Fig. (*b*), but this is not possible for the currents specified in Fig. (*c*). Consider the situation shown in Fig. (*c*), where a line drawn to pass between points A and B does not pass through the origin. This bias line satisfies the equation

$$V_{GS} = V_{GG} - I_D R_s$$

TRANSISTOR EQUIVALENT CIRCUITS

Hybrid equivalent Model

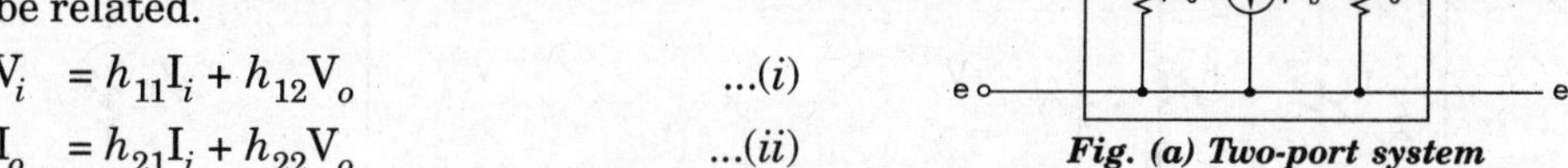

Fig. (a) Two-port system

Following set of equations is only one of a number of ways in which four variables of Fig. (*a*) can be related.

$$V_i = h_{11} I_i + h_{12} V_o \quad \text{...(i)}$$

$$I_o = h_{21} I_i + h_{22} V_o \quad \text{...(ii)}$$

The parameters relating four variables are called *h-parameters* from the word *hybrid*. The term *hybrid* was chosen because mixture of variables (V and I) in each equation results in a *hybrid* set of units of measurement for the *h*-parameters.

If we set $V_o = 0$ (short circuit output terminals), and solve for h_{11} in equation (*i*), we get

$$h_{11} = \left.\frac{V_i}{V_o}\right|_{V_o=0} \text{ ohms}$$

The ratio indicates that the parameters h_{11} is an impendance parameter with the units of ohms. Since it is the ratio of the input voltage to the input current with the output terminals shorted, it is called the short-circuit input-impedance parameter. The subscript 11 of h_{11} defines the fact that the parameter is determined by a ratio of quantities measured at the input terminals.

If I_i is set equal to zero by opening the input leads, the following will results for h_{12}.

$$h_{12} = \left.\frac{V_i}{V_o}\right|_{I_i=0} \text{ unitless}$$

The parameter h_{12}, therefore is ratio of the input voltage to the output voltage with the input current equal to zero. It has no units since it is a ratio of voltage levels and is called the open-circuit reverse transfer voltage ratio parameter. The subscript 12 of h_{12} reveals that the parameter is a transfer quantity determined by a ratio of input to output measurements. The first integer of the subscript defines the measured quantity to appear in the numerator; the second integer defines the source of the quantity to appear in the denominator. The term reverse is included because the ratio is an input voltage over an output voltage rather than the reverse ratio which is the matter of interest.

Now, if in equation (*ii*), V_o is equal to zero by again shorting then output terminals, then

$$h_{21} = \left.\frac{I_i}{I_o}\right|_{V_o=0} \text{ unitless}$$

Now we have the ratio of an output quantity to an input quantity. The term forward will now be used rather than reverse as indicated for h_{12}. The parameter h_{21} is ratio of the output current to the input current with the output terminals shorted. This parameter, like h_{12}, has no units since it is the ratio of current levels. It is formally called *short-circuit forward transfer current ratio parameter*. The subscript 21 again indicates that it is a transfer parameter with the output quantity in the numerator and the input quantity in the denominator.

The last parameter, h_{22}, can be found by again opening the input leads to set $I_1 = 0$ and solving for h_{22} in equation (*ii*)

$$h_{22} = \left.\frac{I_i}{V_o}\right|_{I_i=0} \quad \text{siemens}$$

Since it is ratio of the output current to the output voltage, it is the output conductance parameter and is measured in siemens (S). It is called *open-circuit output admittance parameter*. The subscript 22 reveals that it is determined by a ratio of output quantities.

Since each term of equation (*i*) has the unit volt, apply Kirchhoff's voltage law *in reverse* to find a circuit *fits* the equation. Performing this operation will result in the circuit of Fig. (*b*). Since the parameter h_{11} has the unit ohm, it is represented by a resistor in Fig. (*b*). The quantity h_{12} is dimentionless and therefore simply appears as a multiplying factor of the *feedback* term in the input circuit.

Since each term of equation (*ii*) has the units of current, now apply Kirchhoff's current law *in reverse* to obtain the circuit of Fig. (*c*). Since h_{22} has the units of admittance, which for the transistor model is conductance, it is represented by the resistor symbol.

Notes : resistance in ohms of this resistor is equal to reciprocal of conductance ($1/h_{22}$).

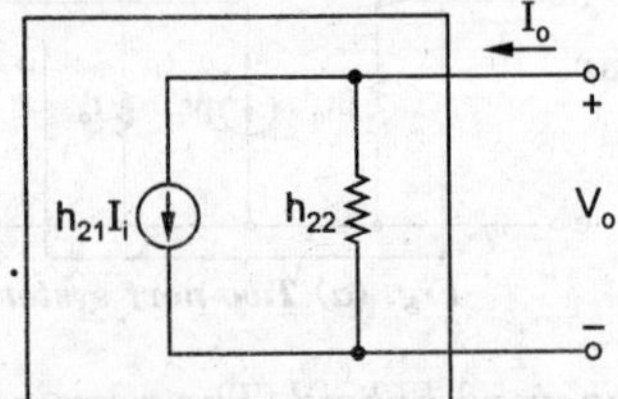

Fig. (b) Hybrid input equivalent circuit

Fig. (c) Hybrid output equivalent circuit

The complete "ac" equivalent circuit for the basic three-terminal linear device is shown in Fig. (*d*) with a new set of subscripts for the *h*-parameters.

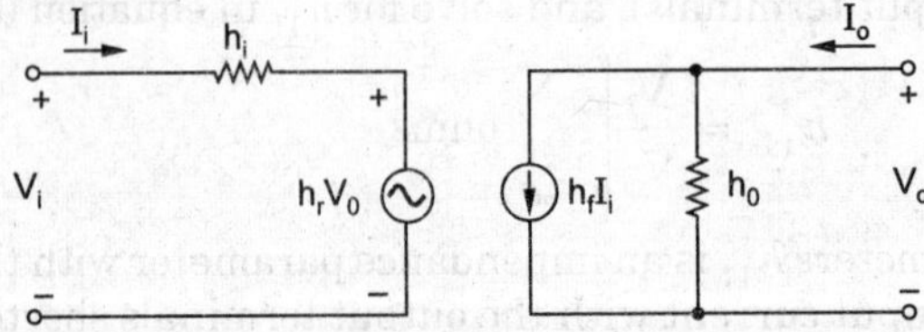

Fig. (d) Complete hybrid equivalent circuit

h-parameters are

$h_{11} \rightarrow$ input resistance $\rightarrow h_i$
$h_{12} \rightarrow$ reverse transfer voltage ratio $\rightarrow h_r$
$h_{21} \rightarrow$ forward transfer current ratio $\rightarrow h_f$
$h_{22} \rightarrow$ output conductance $\rightarrow h_o$

The circuit given in Fig. (*d*) is applicable to any linear three-terminal electronic device or system with no internal independent sources. The input and output sections of the network of Fig. (*d*) can be connected as shown in Fig. (*e*), since the potential level is the same. Essentially, therefore, the transistor model is a three-terminal two-port system. The *h*-parameters, however, will change with each configuration. To distinguish which parameter has been used or which is available, a second subscript has been added to the *h*-parameter notation. For the common-base configuration the lowercase letters *b* was added, while for the common-emitter and common-collector configurations the letter *e* and *c* were added, respectively. The hybrid equivalent network for the common-emitter configuration appears with standard notation is in shown in Fig. (*e*).

Here $I_i = I_b, I_o = I_c$,

and through Kirchhoff's current law, $I_e = I_b + I_c$.

Input voltage is now V_{be} with the output voltage V_{ce}.

For common-base configuration $I_i = I_e, I_o = I_c$

with $V_{eb} = V_i$ and $V_{cb} = V_o$

The networks of Figs. (*e*) and (*f*) are applicable for *pnp* or *npn* transistors.

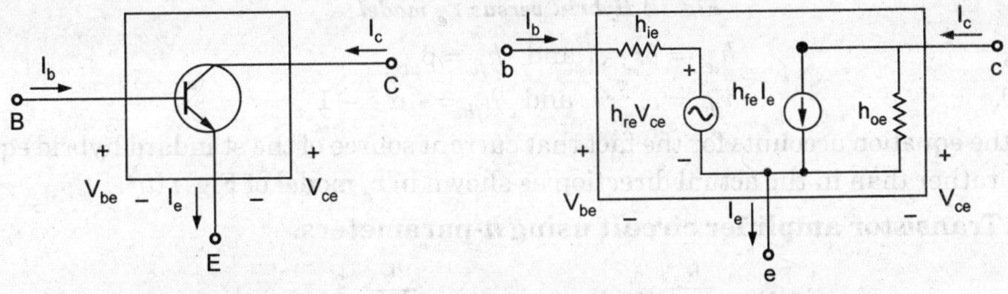

(i) Graphic symbol *(ii) Hybrid equivalent circuit*

Fig. (e) Common-emitter configuration

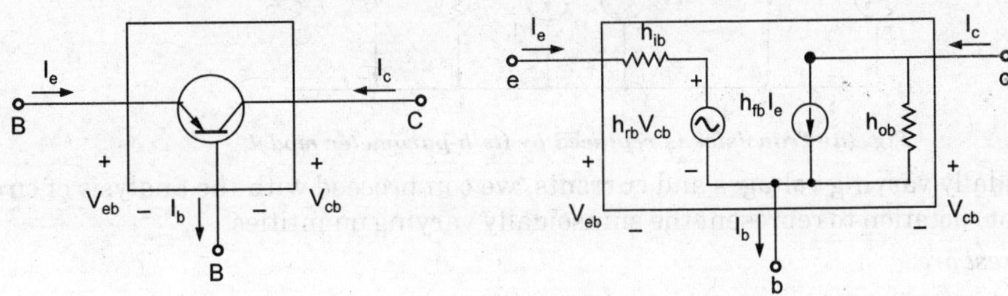

(i) Graphic symbol ***Fig. (ii) Hybrid equivalent circuit***

Fig. (f) Common-base configuration

As h_r is normally a relatively small quantity, its removal is approximated by $h_r \cong 0$ and $h_r V_o = 0$, resulting in a short-circuit equivalent for the feedback element as shown in Fig. (*g*). The resistance determined by $1/h_o$ is often large enough to be ignored in comparison to a parallel load permitting its replacement by an open-circuit equivalent for the CE and CB models, as shown in Fig. (*g*).

The resulting equivalent of Fig. (*h*) is quite similar to the general structure of the common-base and common-emitter equivalent circuits obtained with the r_e model. Infact, the hybrid equivalent and the r_e model for each configuration have been repeated in Fig. (*i*) for comparison.

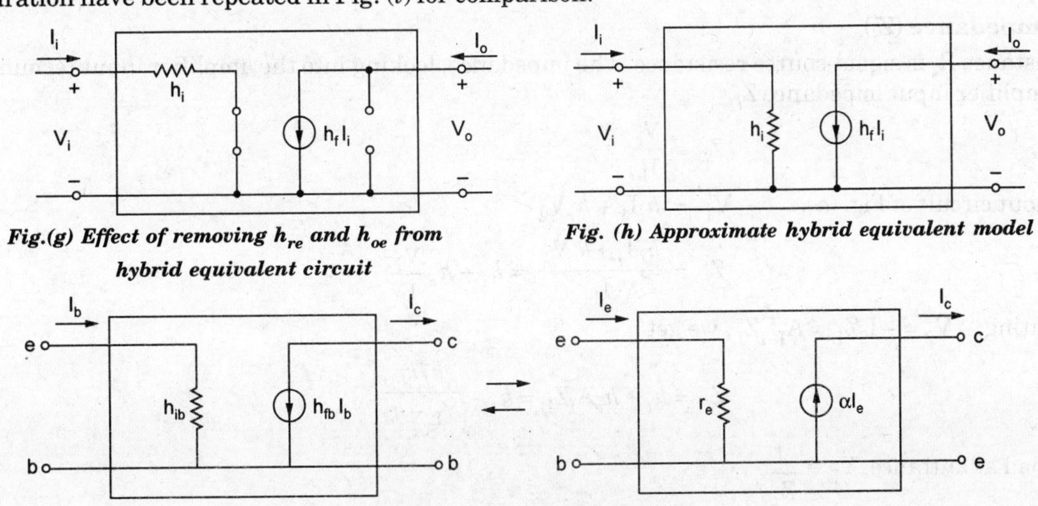

Fig.(g) Effect of removing h_{re} and h_{oe} from hybrid equivalent circuit

Fig. (h) Approximate hybrid equivalent model

(i) Common-emmitter configuration

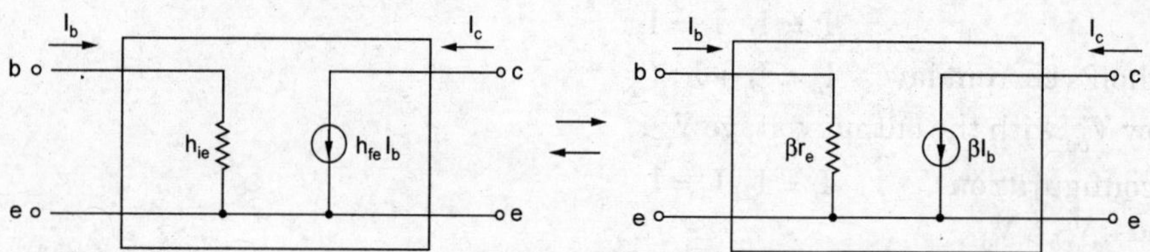

(ii) Common-base configuration

Fig. (i) Hybrid versus r_e model

From Fig. *i (i)*, $h_{ie} = \beta r_e$; and $h_{fe} = \beta_{ac}$

From Fig. *i (ii)*, $h_{ib} = r_e$; and $h_{fb} = -\alpha \cong -1$

Minus sign in the equation accounts for the fact that current source of the standard hybrid equivalent circuit is pointing down rather than in the actual direction as shown in r_e model of Fig. *i (ii)*.

Analysis of a Transistor amplifier circuit using *h*-parameters.

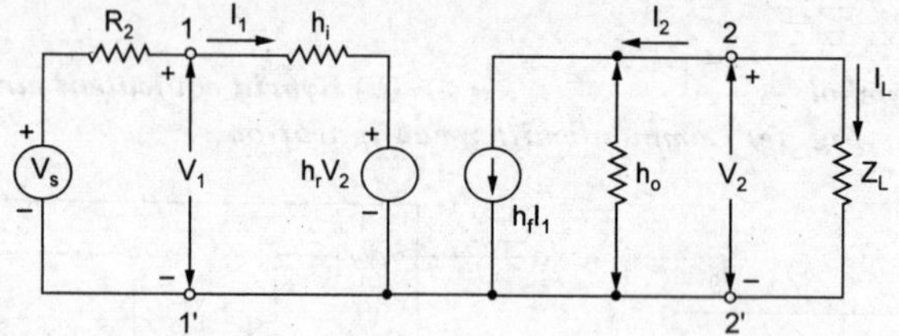

Fig. (a) Transistor is replaced by its h-parameter model

Assuming sinusoidally varying voltages and currents, we can proceed with the analysis of circuit of Fig. (*a*), using phasor (sinor) notation to represent the sinusoidally varying quantities.

Quantities of interest are

current gain, input impedance, voltage gain, and output impedance.

Current gain or Current amplification (A_I).

It is defined as the ratio of output to input currents, i.e.

$$A_I \equiv \frac{I_L}{I_1} = -\frac{I_2}{I_1}$$

From the circuit of Fig. (*a*), $I_2 = h_f I_1 + h_o V_2$

Substituting $V_2 = -I_2 Z_L$, we get $A_I = -\frac{I_2}{I_1} = -\frac{h_f}{1 + h_o Z_L}$

Input impedance (Z_i)

The resistance R_s is signal-source resistance. The impedance, looking into the amplifier input terminals (1, 1′) is the amplifier input impedance Z_i

$$Z_i \equiv \frac{V_1}{I_1}$$

From input circuit of Fig. (*a*), $V_1 = h_i I_1 + h_r V_2$

Then $Z_i = \frac{h_f I_1 + h_r V_2}{I_1} = h_i + h_r \frac{V_2}{I_1}$

Substituting, $V_2 = -I_2 Z_L = A_I I_1 Z_L$, we get

$$Z_i = h_i + h_r A_I Z_L = h_i - \frac{h_f h_r}{Y_L + h_o}$$

where load admittance, $Y_L \equiv \frac{1}{Z_L}$.

Note : *Input impedance is a function of the load impedance.*

Voltage gain or Voltage amplification (A_V)

The ratio of output voltage V_2 to input voltage V_1 gives voltage gain of the transistor

$$A_V \equiv \frac{V_2}{V_1}$$

$$\Rightarrow \quad A_V = \frac{A_I I_1 Z_L}{V_1} = \frac{A_I Z_L}{Z_i}$$

Voltage amplification (A_{Vs}) considering Account Source resistance (R_s).

$$\text{Overall voltage gain, } A_{Vs} \equiv \frac{V_2}{V_s} = \frac{V_2}{V_1}\frac{V_1}{V_s} = A_V \frac{V_1}{V_s}$$

From equivalent input circuit of the amplifier, shown in Fig. *b* (*i*),

$$V_1 = \frac{V_s Z_i}{Z_i + R_s}$$

Then
$$A_{Vs} = \frac{A_V Z_i}{Z_i + R_s} = \frac{A_I Z_L}{Z_i + R_s}$$

If $R_s = 0$, then $A_{Vs} = A_V$.

Hence A_V *is voltage gain for an ideal voltage source* (one with zero internal resistance).

In practice, the quantity A_{Vs} is more meaningful than A_V since, usually, source resistance has an appreciable effect on the overall voltage amplification.

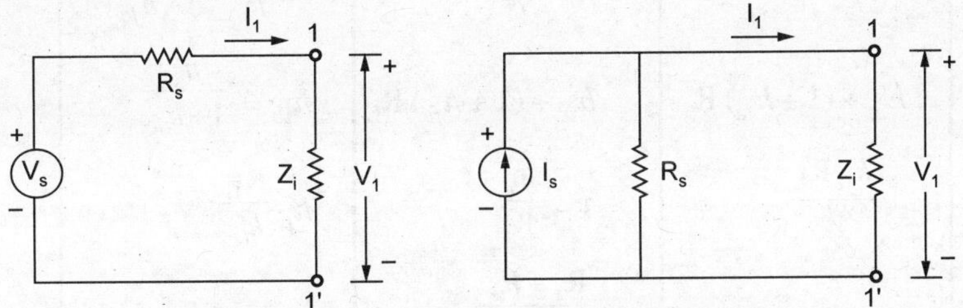

(i) Thevenin's equivalent for the source (ii) Norton's equivalent for the source

Fig. (b) Input circuit of a transistor amplifier using

Current amplification (A_{Is}) taking into Account Source resistance (R_s).

If input source is a current generator I_s in parallel with a resistance R_s, as indicated in Fig. (*b*), then

$$\text{overall current gain, } A_{Is} \equiv \frac{-I_2}{I_s} = \frac{-I_2}{I_1}\frac{I_1}{I_s} = A_I \frac{I_1}{I_s}$$

From Fig. (*b*) (*ii*),
$$I_1 = \frac{I_s R_s}{Z_i + R_s}$$

$$\therefore \quad A_{Is} = \frac{A_I R_s}{Z_i + R_s}$$

If $R_s = \infty$, then $A_{Is} = A_I$.

Hence A_I *is current gain for an ideal current source* (one with infinite source resistance).

Independent of the transistor characteristic, voltage and current gains, taking source impedance into account, are related by

$$A_{Vs} = A_{Is}\frac{Z_L}{R_s}$$

This relationship is valid if current and voltage generators have the same source resistance R_s.

Output admittance

$$\text{Output impedan ce } Z_o = \frac{1}{Y_o}$$

It is obtained by setting the source voltage V_s to zero and load impedance Z_L to infinity and by driving the output terminals from a generator V_2.

If current drawn from V_2 is I_2, then $Y_o \equiv \dfrac{I_2}{V_2}$ with $V_s = 0$ and $R_L = \infty$

Also, $$Y_o = h_f \frac{I_1}{V_2} + h_o$$

From Fig. (*b*), with $V_s = 0$

$$R_s I_1 + h_i I_1 + h_r V_2 = 0$$

$$\Rightarrow \quad \frac{I_1}{V_2} = -\frac{h_r}{h_i + R_s}$$

$$\therefore \quad Y_o = h_o - \frac{h_f h_r}{h_i + R_s}$$

The output admittance is a fucntion of the source resistance. If source impedance is resistive, as we have assumed, then Y_o is real (a conductance).

The expressions for A_V, A_{Vs}, and A_{Is} are without reference to the hybrid parameters, and hence are valid regradless of what equivalent circuit is used for the transistor. In particular, these expressions are valid at high frequencies, where h parameters are functions of frequency or where we may prefer to use another model for the transistor.

Typical *h*-parameter values :

	CE	CE with R_e	CC	CB
A_I	$-h_{fe}$	$-h_{fe}$	$1 + h_{fe}$	$-h_{fb} = \frac{h_{fe}}{1+h_{fe}}$
R_i	h_{ie}	$h_{ie} + (1 + h_{fe}) R_e$	$h_{ie} + (1 + h_{fe}) R_L$	$h_{ib} = \frac{h_{ie}}{1+h_{fe}}$
A_V	$-\frac{h_{fe}R_L}{h_{ie}}$	$-\frac{h_{fe}R_L}{R_i}$	$1 - \frac{h_{ie}}{R_i}$	$h_{fe}\frac{R_L}{h_{ie}}$
R_o	∞	∞	$\frac{R_s + h_{ie}}{1+h_{fe}}$	∞
R'_o	R_L	R_L	$R_o \parallel R_L$	R_L

Frequency response of an Amplifier.

1. Low-frequency Response

From circuit of Fig. (*a*), $$V_o(s) = V_i(s) \frac{R_1}{R_1 + \frac{1}{sC_1}} = \frac{sR_1C_1}{sR_1C_1 + 1} V_i \qquad ...(i)$$

Thus voltage transfer function at low frequencies, $A_L(s) \equiv V_o(s)/V_i(s)$, has one zero at $s = 0$ and one pole at $s = -1/R_1C_1$. f real frequencies

Here, $s = j\omega = j2\pi f$

Hence equation (*i*) becomes $$A_L(jf) = \frac{1}{1 - j\left(\frac{fc}{f}\right)},$$

where $$f_L \equiv \frac{1}{2\pi R_1 C_1}$$

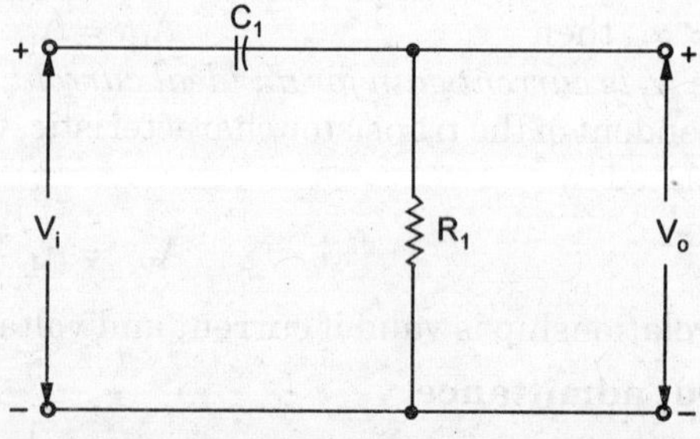

Fig. (a) High - pass RC circuit used to calculate low - frequency response of an amplifier

$$\text{Magnitude } |A_L(jf)| = \frac{1}{\sqrt{1 + \left(\frac{f_c}{f}\right)^2}},$$

$$\text{phase lead of gain, } \theta_L = \arctan\left(\frac{f_c}{f}\right)$$

At frequency $f = f_L$, $\quad A_L = \dfrac{\pi}{\sqrt{2}} = 0.707$

whereas in midband region, $f >> f_L$, $\quad A_L \rightarrow 1$.

Hence, f_L is that frequency at which gain has fallen to 0.707 times its midband value A_o. This drop in signal level corresponds to a decibel reduction of 20 log , or 3 dB. Accordingly, f_L is referred to as lower 3-dB frequency. f_L is that frequency for which resistance R_1 equals capacitive reactance .

2. High-frequency Response.

In high-frequency region, above the midband, amplifier stage can often be approximated by simple low-pass circuit of Figs. (*b*) and (*c*) given below.

In terms of complex variables, $V_o(s) = \dfrac{1/sC_2}{R_2 + \dfrac{1}{sC_2}} V_i(s) = \dfrac{1}{sR_2C_2 + 1} V_i(s)$

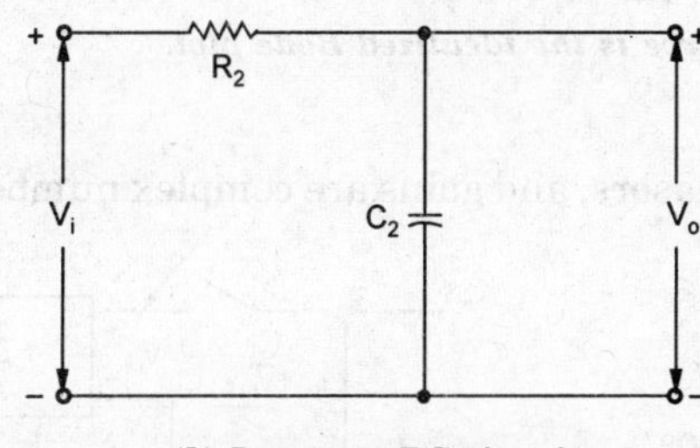

(b) Low pass RC circuit

(c) Norton's equivalent

A low-pass RC circuit used to calculate high-frequency response of an amplifier shown in Fig. (*b*).

Here $\quad I = \dfrac{V_i}{R_2}$

In this region, transfer function has a single pole of $s = -\dfrac{1}{R_2C_2}$.

For real frequencies $s = j\omega = j2\pi f$, we get $\quad |A_H(jf)| = \left|\dfrac{V_o(s)}{V_i(s)}\right|_{s=j2\pi f}$

and for phase lead angle θ_H of the gain in the high-frequency region,

$$|A_H(jf)| = \frac{1}{\sqrt{1+\left(\dfrac{f}{f_H}\right)^2}};$$

$$\theta_H = -\arctan\frac{f}{f_H}$$

where, $\quad f_H = \dfrac{1}{2\pi R_2C_2}$

Since at $f = f_H$, the gain is reduced to $\dfrac{1}{\sqrt{2}}$ times its midband value, hence f_H is called *upper 3-dB frequency*. It also represents that frequency at which resistance R_2 equals capacitive reactance $\dfrac{1}{2\pi f_H C_2}$.

θ_L and θ_H represent the angle by which output leads the input, neglecting the initial 180° phase shift through the amplifier. The frequency dependence of the gains in the high-and low-frequency range is shown in Fig. (*d*)

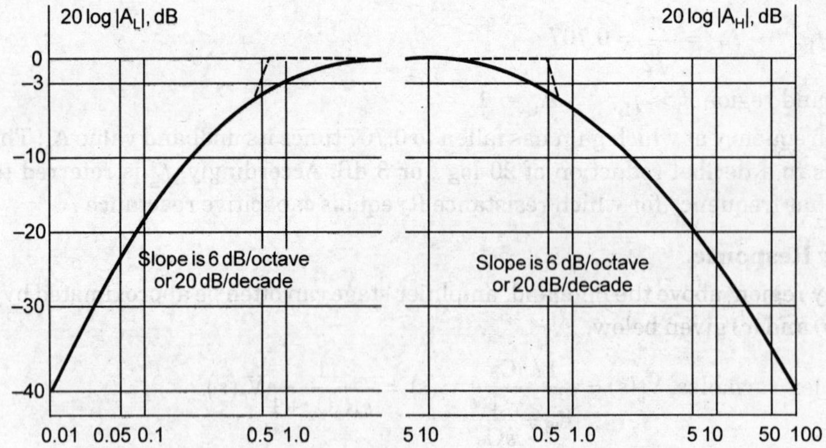

Fig. (d) Semi-log plot of the amplitude frequency-response (Bode) characteristic of an RC-coupled amplifier. The dashed curve is the idealized Bode plot.

OSCILLATORS

In general, input and output signals (sinusoidal) are phasors, and gains are complex numbers.

Overall gain is expressed as $\frac{\overline{V_o}}{\overline{V_s}} = \frac{\overline{A}}{1+\overline{\beta A}}$

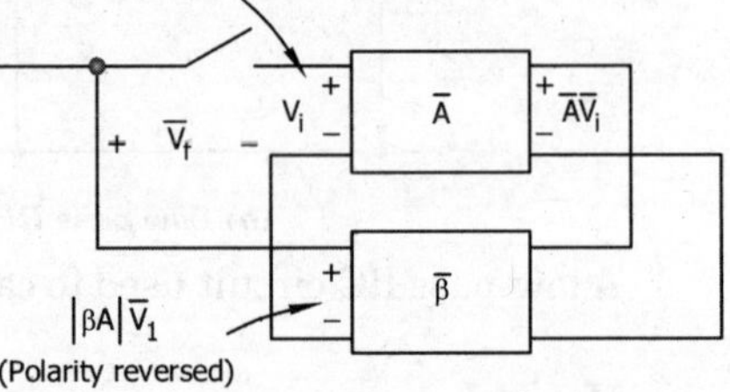

Fig. Basic oscillator scheme

At a particular frequency, phase shift of $\overline{\beta A}$ becomes 180°,

reversing polarity of feedback voltage $\overline{V_f}$.

So feedback is positive and overall gain, $\frac{\overline{V_o}}{\overline{V_s}} = \frac{\overline{A}}{1-|\overline{\beta A}|}$

For $|\overline{\beta A}| = 1$, gain $\angle\ |\overline{BA}|$ becomes infinite, i.e. input $\overline{V_s}$ needed to produce any output $\overline{V_o}$ is zero.

With the signal $\overline{V_s}$ removed, the circuit still oscillates at a frequency at which $\angle\ \overline{\beta A} = 180°$.

Condition (combined) for oscillation, $\overline{\beta A} = -1$ is called *Barkhausen condition for oscillation.*

In basic oscillator scheme shown below, as switch included in the circuit is closed, amplifier amplifies the internal noise which is fed round the loop positively and signal builds up. Theoretically in a negative feedback circuit with $\overline{\beta A} = -1$, the output would become infinite. But, signal amplitude is limited by setting in of saturation in the amplifier.

Types of Oscillators

1. Phase Shift Oscillator.

To build an oscillator circuit, phase shift in feedback path of an amplifier can be an RC network as shown. This network has a phase shift of 180° at a frequency of

$$f = \frac{1}{2\pi RC\sqrt{6}}$$

Corresponding feedback gain, $\beta = \frac{1}{29}$

Hence circuit will oscillate if A > 29.

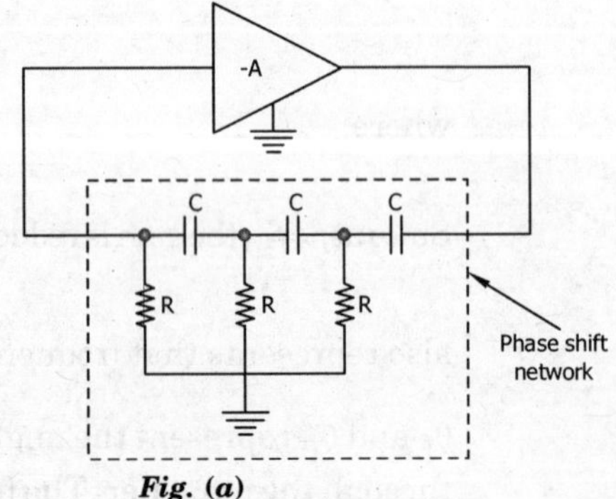

Fig. (a)

2. FET Phase Shift Oscillator.

The circuit of FET phase oscillator is shown

$$\text{Load resistance, } R_L = R_D \,||\, r_d$$

and, $\quad$ amplifier gain, $A = -g_m R_L$

Negative in the amplifier gain cause the feedback to be negative.Network phase shift of 180° causes this feedback round the loop to become positive.

At high frequencies, input capacitance of the FET contributes loading effect, and oscillation condition would need larger sufficiently gain at low frequencies.

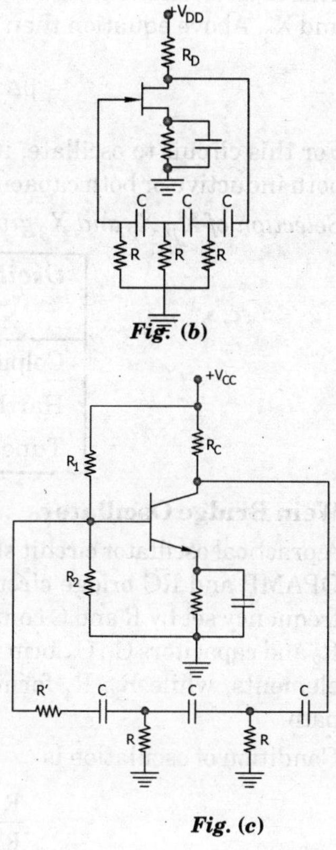

Fig. (b)

Fig. (c)

3. BJT Phase Shift Oscillator.

In this case, input resistance r_π of the BJT will load the output so it may be better to use two transistors with the second one in emitter follower connection. However, in case of a single transistor as shown in figure voltage shunt feedback is preferred.

Analysing the circuit, we have

$$f = \frac{1}{2\pi RC} \frac{1}{\sqrt{[6+4(R_C/R)]}}$$

For the loop gain to be greater than unity, current gain of the BJT must meet the condition

$$\beta \text{ (or } h_{fe}) \geq 23 + 29\left(\frac{R}{R_C}\right) + 4\left(\frac{R_C}{R}\right)$$

sign '*more than*' in this equation compensates for parameter changes in the amplifier. As transistors change charateristics with age, temperature, voltage, etc.

4. Tuned Oscillator.

The output is taken from terminals 2, 3, while input is at terminals 1, 3.

If A is open-circuit gain of the amplifier, then gain with load but without feedback is

$$\overline{A}_L = \frac{\overline{Z}_L A}{\overline{Z}_L + R_o}$$

where, R_o = output resistance of the amplifier.

$$\text{Load impedance, } \overline{Z}_L = \overline{Z}_2 \,||\, (\overline{Z}_2 + \overline{Z}_3)$$

$$\text{feedback factor, } \overline{\beta} = \frac{\overline{Z}_1}{\overline{Z}_1 + \overline{Z}_3}$$

$$\text{loop gain, } -\overline{\beta}\,\overline{A}_L = \frac{-A\overline{Z}_1\overline{Z}_2}{R_o(\overline{Z}_1 + \overline{Z}_2 + \overline{Z}_3) + \overline{Z}_2(\overline{Z}_1 + \overline{Z}_3)}$$

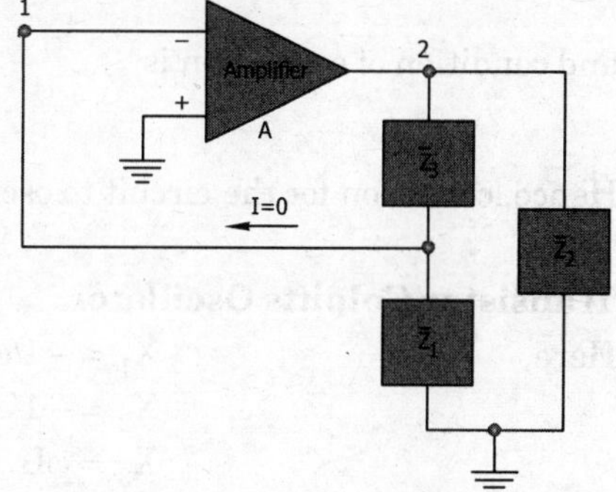

Fig. (d) Basic tuned oscillator circuit

For the oscillation to occur, we need to set $-\overline{\beta A_L} = 1$.

If we select, $\overline{Z}_1 = jX_1$, $\overline{Z}_2 = jX_2$ and $\overline{Z}_3 = jX_3$; purely reactive, then

$$-\overline{\beta A_L} = \frac{AX_1X_2}{jR_o(X_1 + X_2 + X_3) - X_2(X_1 + X_3)}$$

Loop gain in this equation can be made real by setting

$$X_1 + X_2 + X_3 = 0$$

This is also condition for the circuit to oscillate at resonance frequency of the series combination of X_1, X_2 and X_3. Above equation then simplifies to

$$-\beta A_L = \frac{-AX_1}{X_1 + X_3} = \frac{AX_1}{X_2}$$

For this circuit to oscillate, it requires $BA_L = -1$ in above equation, which means that X_1 and X_2 must be both inductive or both capacitive.

Selection of X_1, X_2 and X_3 gives the three oscillator types as shown below :

Oscillator type	***Reactive elements***		
	X_1	X_2	X_3
Colpitts	C	C	L
Hartley	L	L	C
Tuned input, tuned output	LC	LC	

5. Wein Bridge Oscillator.

A practical oscillator circuit shown in Fig.(*e*) uses an OPAMP and RC bridge circuit, with the oscillator frequency set by R and C components. Resistors R_1, R_2 and capacitors C_1, C_2 form frequency adjustement elements, while R_3, R_4 form part of the feedback path.

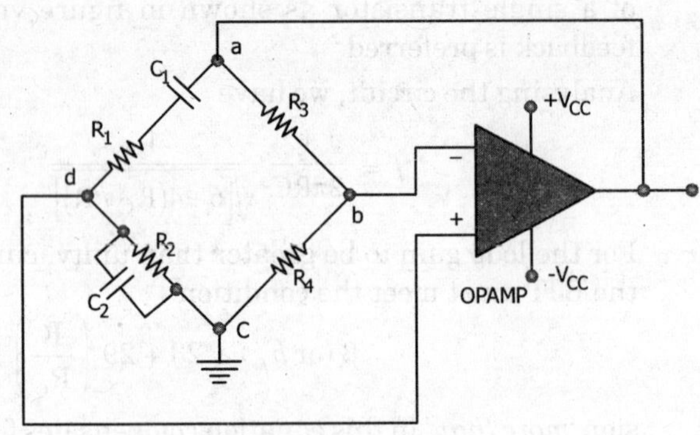

Fig. (e)

Condition of oscillation is

$$\frac{R_3}{R_4} = \frac{R_1}{R_2} + \frac{C_2}{C_1}$$

and frequency of oscillation,

$$f_o = \frac{1}{2\pi} \cdot \frac{1}{\sqrt{(R_1 R_2 C_1 C_2)}}$$

If we choose $R_1 = R_2 = R$, and $C_1 = C_2 = C$,

then resulting oscillation frequency, $f_o = \dfrac{1}{2\pi(RC)}$

and condition of oscillation is, $\dfrac{R_3}{R_4} = 2$

Hence, condition for the circuit to oscillate is, $\left(\dfrac{R_3}{R_4}\right) > 2$

6. Transistor Colpitts Oscillator.

Here,

$$X_1 = -1/\omega C_1$$
$$X_2 = -1/\omega C_2$$
$$X_3 = \omega L$$

It satisfies the condition that X_1 and X_2 are both reactive.

Then output frequency of the circuit is

$$\frac{1}{\omega_o C_1} + \frac{1}{\omega_o C_2} = \omega_o L$$

which gives $f_o = \dfrac{1}{2\pi\sqrt{(LC_{eq})}}$; $C_{eq} = \dfrac{C_1 C_2}{C_1 + C_2}$

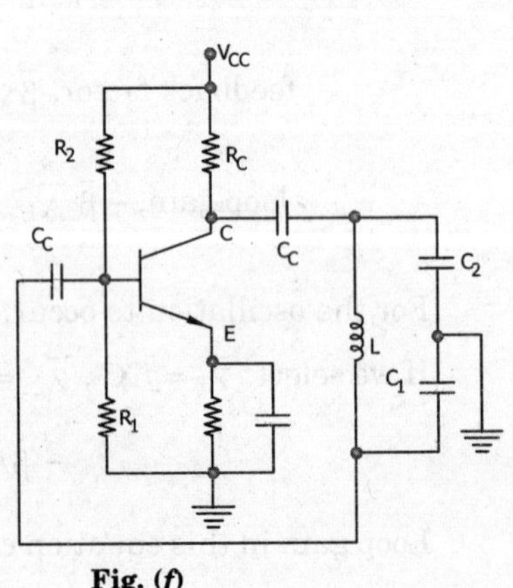

Fig. (*f*)

7. **Transistor Hartley oscillator.**

Here,
$$X_1 = \omega(L_1 + M)$$
$$X_2 = \omega(L_2 + M)$$
$$X_3 = -\frac{1}{\omega C}$$

With unity loop gain,

$$\text{oscillator frequency, } f_o = \frac{1}{2\pi\sqrt{L_{eq}C}}$$

$$L_{eq} = L_1 + L_2 + 2M$$

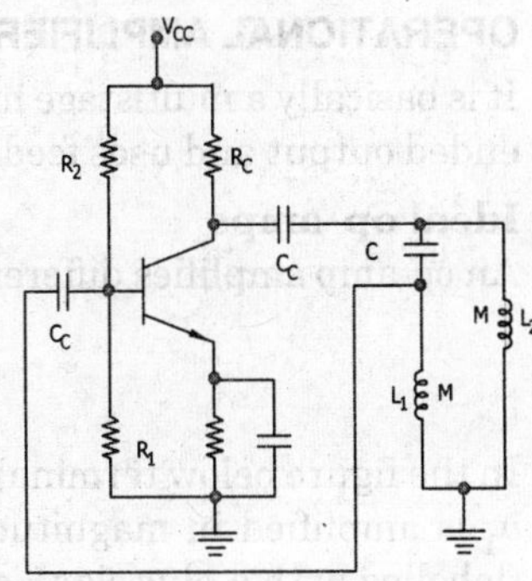

Fig. (g) Transistor Hartley oscillator

8. **Crystal oscillator.**

In piezoelectric crystal (usually quartz) which has electrodes plated on its opposite faces, when a potential is applied across these, then electric field so set up exerts forces on bound charges within the crystal. As a result, crystal responds electromechanically, i.e. it vibrates. The crystal's resonant frequency and its Q (quality factor) depends upon its dimensions, orientation of its surfaces with respect to its axis and the mechanical mounting. Crystals are available with a wide range of frequencies from a few kHz to 100 MHz and with Q factors from a few thousand to several hundred thousands. The resonant frequency of these crystals is extremely stable with respect to temperature changes and aging.

The symbol for a crystal is given in Fig. *h*(*i*) and its electric analog is drawn in Fig. *h*(*ii*).

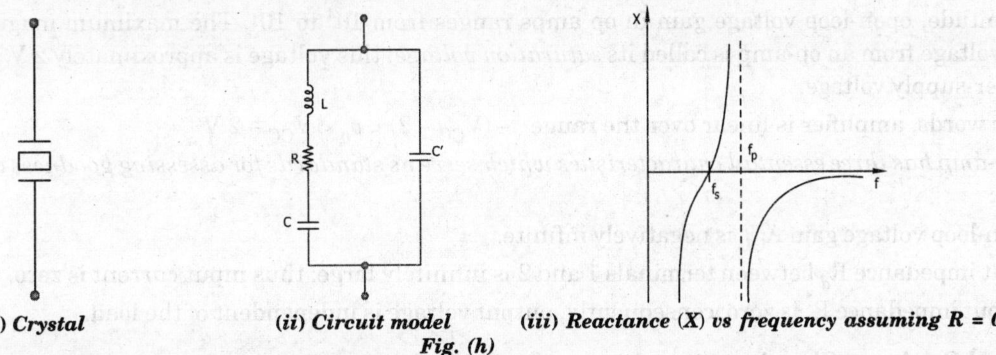

(i) Crystal *(ii) Circuit model* *(iii) Reactance (X) vs frequency assuming R = 0*

Fig. (h)

Here, L = mass of crystal (inductance)

C = compliance (reciprocal of spring constant)

R = viscous damping capacitance between electrodes

C′ = electrostatic capacitance between electrodes; C′>> C

Typical parameters of a 90 kHz crystal :

L = 137 H, C = 035 pF, R = 15 kΩ, Q = 5500, C′ = 3.5 pF

Crystal oscillator exhibits following two resonant frequencies :

$$\text{Series resonant frequency, } f_s = \frac{1}{2\pi\sqrt{(LC)}}$$

$$\text{Parallel resonant frequency, } f_p = \frac{1}{2\pi\sqrt{(LC_{eq})}}$$

$$\text{where, } C_{eq} = \left(\frac{1}{C} + \frac{1}{C'}\right)$$

As C′ >> C;
$$f_p = \frac{1}{2\pi\sqrt{(LC)}}$$

$$\therefore \quad f_p \approx f_s$$

But $f_p > f_s$ as shown in Fig. (*c*) whereas X = 0 at f_s and X = ∞ at f_p.

OPERATIONAL AMPLIFIER (Op Amp)

It is basically a multistage high gain ($A_v > 10^5$), direct coupled amplifier with two differential inputs and a single ended output and uses feedback to control the overall response characteristics of the amplifier circuit.

Ideal op–amps

An op-amp amplifies difference $v_d \equiv v_1 - v_2$ between two input signals, exhibiting open-loop voltage gain

$$A_{OL} \equiv \frac{v_o}{v_d}$$

In the figure below terminal 1 is the inverting input (labelled with a minus sign on the actual amplifier); signal v_1 is amplified in magnitude and appears phase-inverted at the output. Terminal 2 is noninverting input (labelled with a plus sign); output due to v_2 is phase-reserved.

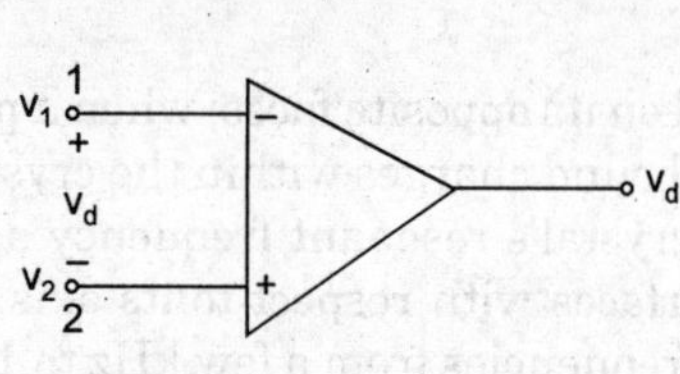

(a) Complete representation

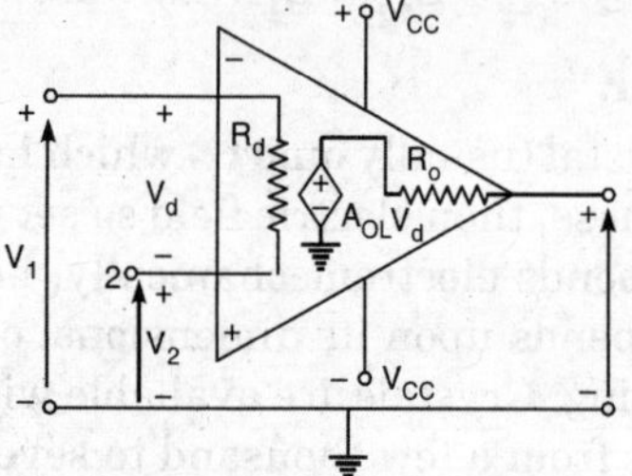

(b) Simplified representation

Fig. Operational amplifier

In magnitude, open-loop voltage gain in op amps ranges from 10^4 to 10^7. The maximum magnitude of the output voltage from an op-amp is called its *saturation voltage*; this voltage is approximately 2 V smaller than the power-supply voltage.

In other words, amplifier is linear over the range $-(V_{CC} - 2) < v_o < V_{CC} - 2$ V

Ideal op-amp has three essentail characteristics which serve as standards for assessing goodness of a practical op-amp :

(*i*) Open-loop voltage gain A_{OL} is negatively infinite.

(*ii*) Input impedance R_d between terminals 1 and 2 is infinitely large; thus input current is zero.

(*iii*) Output impedance R_o is zero; consequently, output voltage is independent of the load.

Practical Op-Amps Circuits

1. **Inverting Amplifier.**

This is the most widely used constant-gain amplifier circuit. The output is obtained by multiplying the input by a fixed or constant gain, set by the input resistor (R_1) and feedback resistor (R_f). This output also being inverted from the input and given as

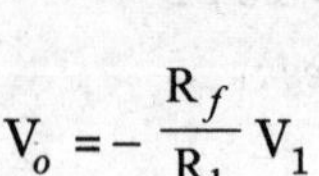

$$V_o = -\frac{R_f}{R_1} V_1$$

Fig. Inverting constant-gain multiplier

2. **Noninverting Amplifier.**

This connection of Fig. (*a*) shows a non-inverting amplifier or constant-gain multiplier. The inverting amplifier connection is more widely used because it has better frequency stability. To determine voltage gain of circuit, the equivalent representation shown in Fig. (*b*) can be used.

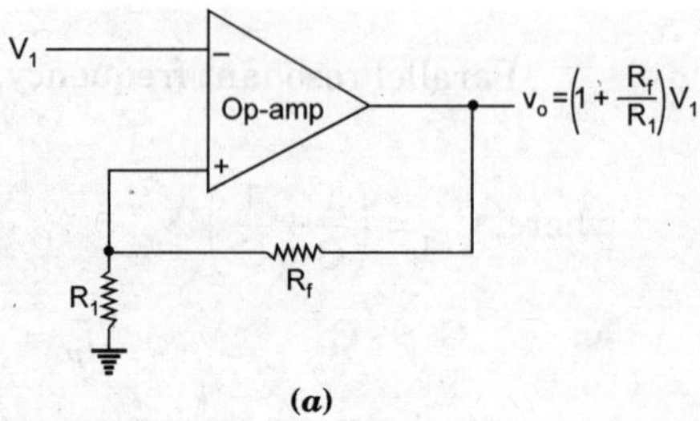

(a)

Since $V_1 \approx 0$ V, we have $V_1 = \frac{R_1}{R_1 + R_f} V_o$

which gives $$\frac{V_o}{V_1} = \frac{R_1 + R_f}{R_1}$$

$$= 1 + \frac{R_f}{R_1}$$

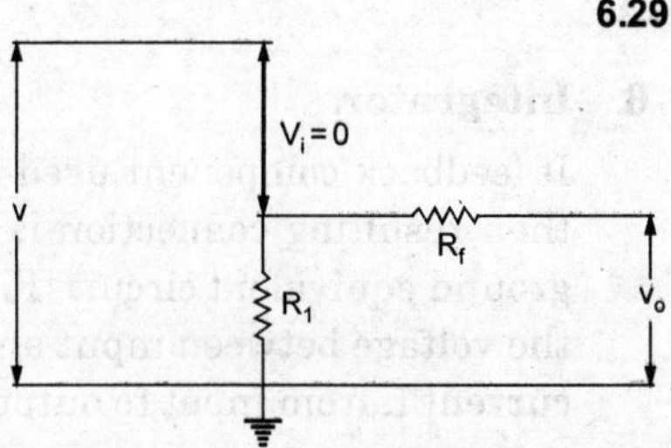

Fig. Noninverting constant-gain multiplier

3. Differential Amplifier (DA).

This amplifies the difference of the two input voltages

$$V_0 = \frac{R_2}{R_1}[V_2 - V_1]$$

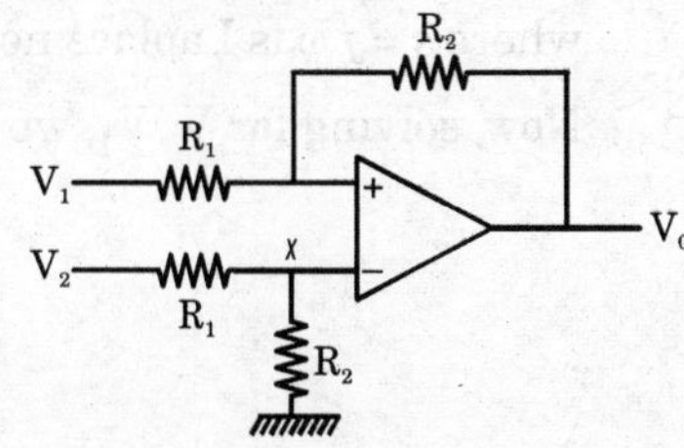

4. Unity Follower.

This unity-follower circuit, shown in Fig. (*a*), provides a gain of unity(1) with no polarity or phase reversal. From the equivalent circuit, we have $V_o = V_1$

and output has the same polarity and magnitude as the input. The circuit operates like an emitter- or source-follower circuit except that the gain is exactly unity.

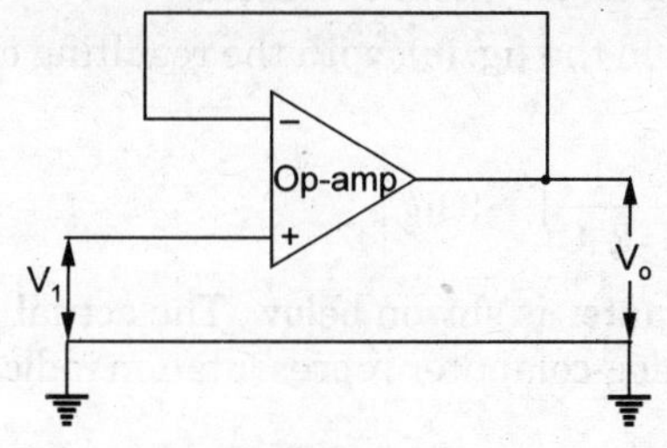

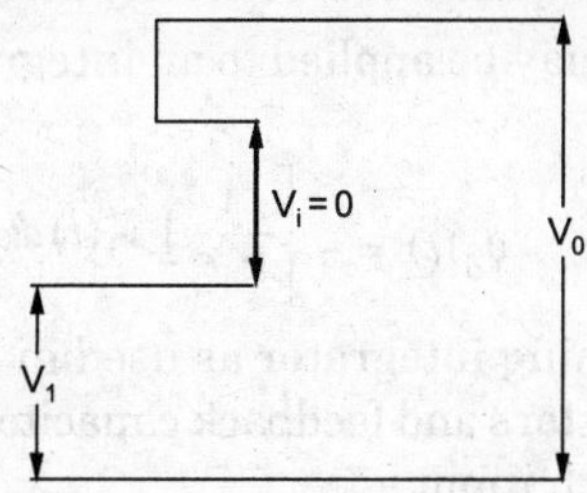

(a) Unity follower *(b) Virtual-ground equivalent circuit.*

5. Summing Amplifier.

The circuit of summing amplifier is shown in Fig. (*a*). The circuit shows a three-input summing amplifier circuit which provides a means of algebracially summing (adding) three voltages, each multiplied by a constant-gain factor.

Using equivalent representation shown in Fig. (*b*), the output voltage can be expressed in terms of the inputs as

$$V_o = -\left(\frac{R_f}{R_1}V_1 + \frac{R_f}{R_2}V_2 + \frac{R_f}{R_3}V_3\right)$$

Thus, each input adds a voltage to the output multiplied by its separate constant-gain multiplier. If more inputs are used, they each add an additional component to the output. It is probably most used among the OP-AMP circuits.

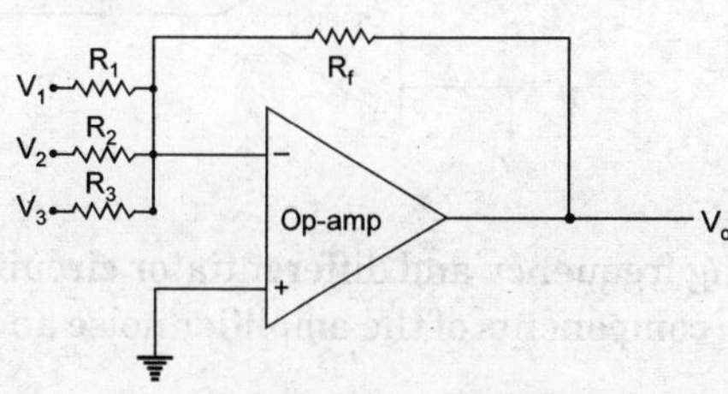

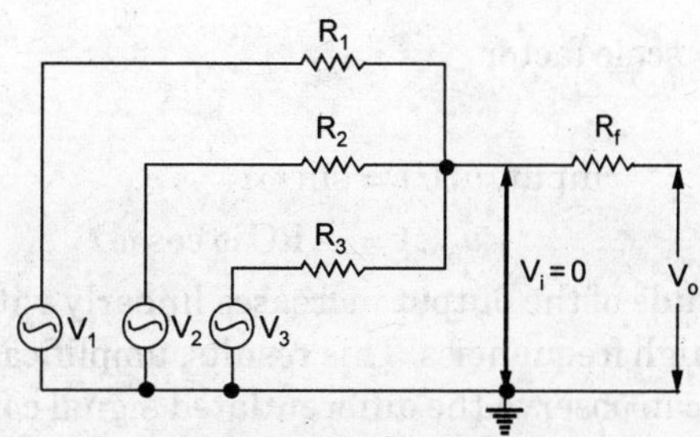

(a) Summing amplifier *(b) Virtual-ground equivalent circuit.*

6. Integrator.

If feedback component used is a capacitor, as shown in Fig. (*a*), then resulting connection is called an *intergrator*. The virtual-ground equivalent circuit [Fig. (*b*)] shows that an expression for the voltage between input and output can be derived in terms of current I, from input to output.

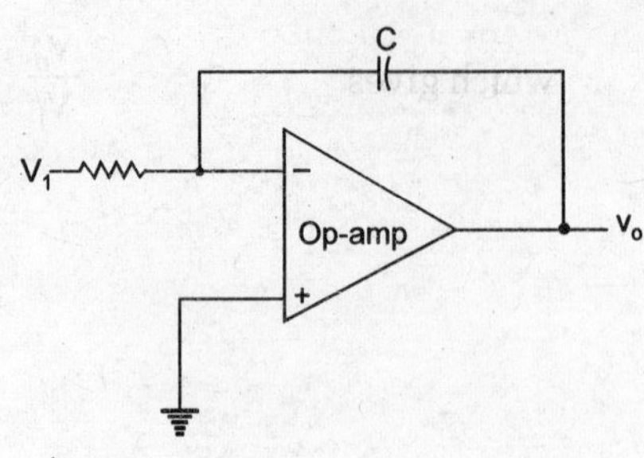

(*a*)

$$\text{Capacitive impedance, } X_C = \frac{1}{j\omega C} = \frac{1}{sC}$$

where $s = j\,\omega$ is Laplace notation.

Now, solving for V_o/V_1, we have

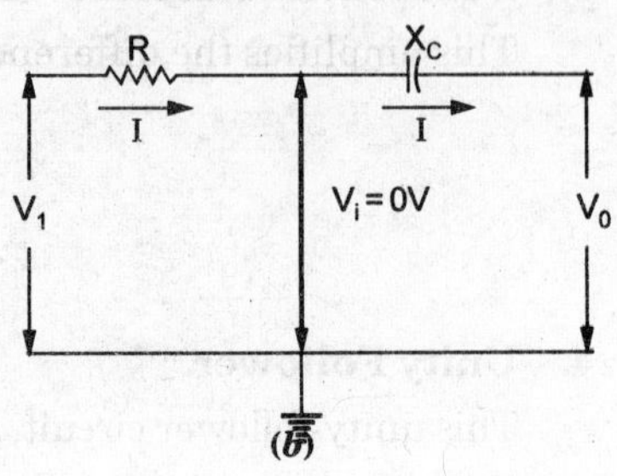

(*b*)

$$I = \frac{V_1}{R} = -\frac{V_o}{X_C} = \frac{-V_o}{\frac{1}{sC}} = -s\,CV_o$$

$$\therefore \quad \frac{V_o}{V_1} = \frac{-1}{sCR}$$

Now, expression above can be rewritten in the time domain as

$$v_o(t) = -\frac{1}{RC}\int v_1(t)\,dt$$

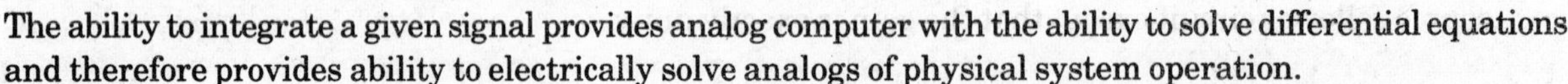

The ability to integrate a given signal provides analog computer with the ability to solve differential equations and therefore provides ability to electrically solve analogs of physical system operation.

More than one input may be applied to an integrator, as shown in the fig. (*c*), with the resulting operation given by

$$v_o(t) = -\left[\frac{1}{R_1C}\int v_1(t)\,dt + \frac{1}{R_2C}\int v_2(t)\,dt + \frac{1}{R_3C}\int v_3(t)\,dt\right]$$

As example of a summing integrator as used in an analog computer is shwon below. The actual circuit is shown with input resistors and feedback capacitor, whereas analog-computer representation indicates only the scale factor for each input.

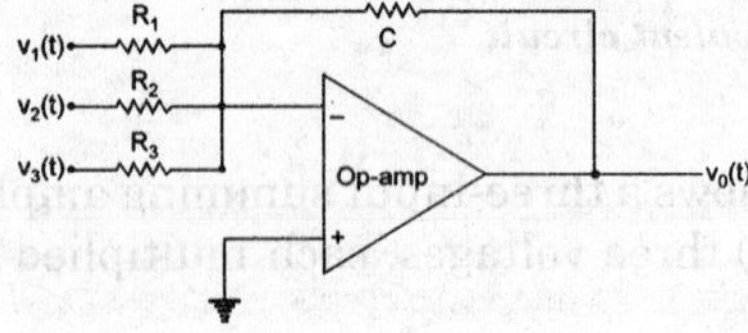

(*c*) *Summing-integrator circuit*

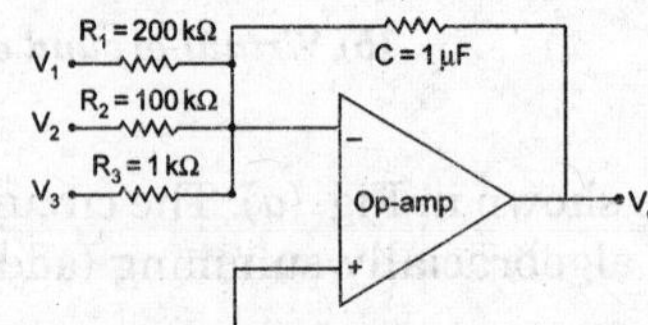

(*d*) *Component values*

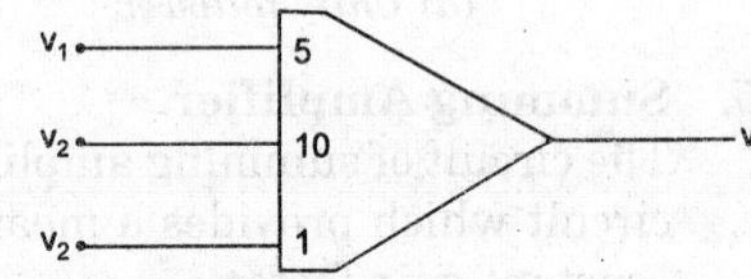

(*e*) *Analog-computer, integrator-circuit representation.*

7. Differentiator.

It provide a useful operation. The resulting relation for the circuit being

$$v_o(t) = -RC\,\frac{dv_1(t)}{dt}$$

where, –RC = scale factor

If $\quad$ input, $v_1(t) = \sin \omega t$

then, $\quad v_o(t) = -RC\,\omega \cos \omega t$

Here, magnitude of the output increases linearly with increasing frequency and differentiator circuit has high gain at high frequencies. This results, amplification of high components of the amplifier noise and the noise output can observe the differentiated signal completely.

OP-AMP SPECIFICATIONS.

1. DC offset Parameters

(i) Offset currents and voltages.

While for an ideal op-amp, output should be 0 V when input is 0 V, but in actual operation there is some offset voltage at the output. The output offset voltage is determined by the input offset voltage and gain of the amplifier.

Output offset voltage is also affected by two separate circuit conditions :

(*a*) Input offset voltage, V_{IO},

(*b*) Offset current due to difference in currents resulting at the plus (+) and minus (–) inputs.

(ii) Input offset voltages (V_{IO}).

To determine effect of this input voltage on the output, consider connection shown below.

Using $V_o = AV_i$, we can write

$$V_o = AV_i = A\left(V_{IO} - V_o \frac{R_1}{R_1 + R_f}\right)$$

$$\therefore \quad V_o = V_{IO} \frac{A}{1 + A\left[\dfrac{R_1}{R_1 + R_f}\right]} \approx V_{IO} \frac{A}{A\left[\dfrac{R_1}{(R_1 + R_f)}\right]}$$

$$\therefore \quad V_o \text{ (offset)} = V_{IO} \frac{R_1 + R_f}{R_1}$$

Fig. Operation showing effect of input offset voltage VIO

(iii) Output offset voltage due to Input offset current (I_{IO}).

An output offset voltage will also result due to any difference in dc bias currents at both inputs. Since two input transistors are never exactly matched, each will operate at a slightly different current. For a typical op-amp connection, such as that shown in Fig. 6.107, an output offset voltage can be determined as follows. Replacing the bias currents through the input resistors by the voltage drop that each develops. Now, using superposition, output voltage due to input bias current I^+_{IB} is

$$V^+_o = I^+_{IB} R_C \left(1 + \frac{R_f}{R_1}\right)$$

for a total output offset voltage of

$$V_o \text{ (offset due to } I^+_{IB} \text{ and } I^-_{IB}) = I^+_{IB} R_C \left(1 + \frac{R_f}{R_1}\right) - I^-_{IB} R_1 \frac{R_f}{R_1} \quad ...(i)$$

while output voltage due to only I^-_{IB}, denoted by V^-_o, is

$$V^-_o = I^-_{IB} R_1 \left(-\frac{R_f}{R_1}\right)$$

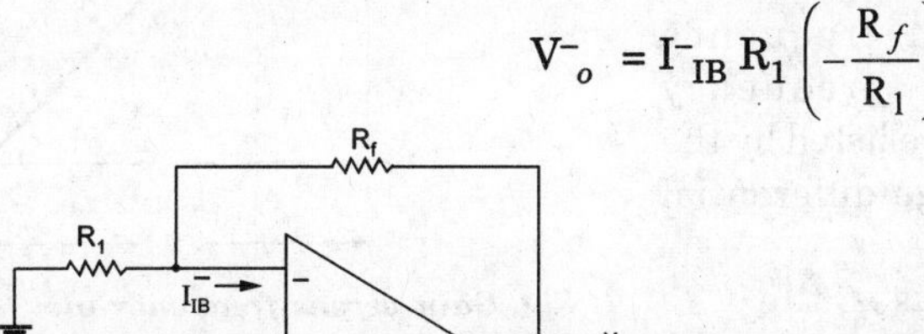

Fig. (a) OP-amp connection showing input bias currents

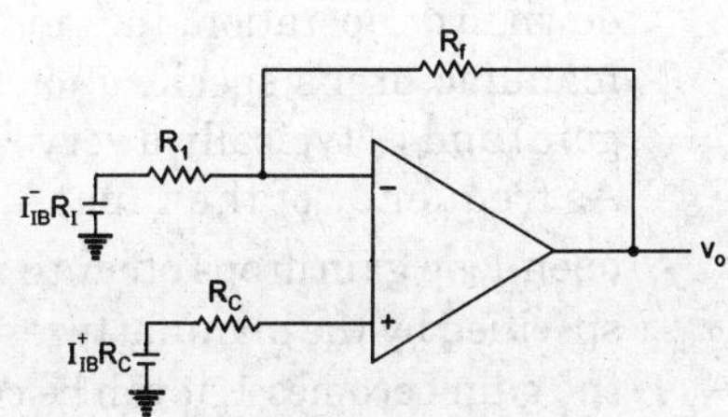

Fig. (b) Redrawn circuit of (a)

Since main consideration is the difference between input bias currents rather than each value, hence

$$\text{Offset current, } I_{IO} = I^{+}_{IB} - I^{-}_{IB}$$

Since compensating resistance R_C is usually approximately equal to the value of R_1, using $R_C = R_1$ in equation (*i*), we have

$$V_o \text{ (offset due to } I_{IO}) = I^{+}_{IB} (R_1 + R_f) - I^{-}_{IB} R_f$$

$$= I^{+}_{IB} R_1 - I^{-}_{IB}$$

$$= R_f(I^{+}_{IB} - I^{-}_{IB})$$

$$= I_{IO} R_f$$

(*iv*) Input bias current (I_{IB})

A parameter related to I_{IO} and separate input bias currents I^{+}_{IB}, I^{-}_{IB} is the average bias current defined as

$$I_{IB} = \frac{I^{+}_{IB} + I^{-}_{IB}}{2}$$

It is possible to determine separate input bias current using specified values I_{IO} and I_{IB}.

But for $I^{+}_{IB} > I^{-}_{IB}$, $I^{+}_{IB} = I_{IB} + \frac{I_{IO}}{2}$, and $I^{-}_{IB} = I_{IB} - \frac{I_{IO}}{2}$

2. Frequency Parameters

An op-amp is designed to be a high-gain, wide-bandwidth amplifier. This operation tends to be unstable (oscillate) due to positive feedback. To ensure stable operation, op-amps are built with internal compensation circuitry, which also causes the very high open-loop gain to dimish with increasing frequency. This gain reduction is called *roll-off*. In most op-amps roll-off occurs at a rate of 20 dB per decade (– 20 dB/decade) or 6 dB per octave (– 6 dB/octave).

While op-amp specfications list an open-loop voltage gain (A_{VD}), the user typically connects the op-amp using feedback resistors to reduce the circuit voltage gain to a much smaller value (closed-loop voltage gain, A_{CL}).

From this gain reduction, following circuit improvements occur :

(*a*) Amplifier voltage gain is a more stable, precise value set by the external resistors.

(*b*) Input impedance of the circuit is increased over that of the op-amp alone.

(*c*) Frequency response of the circuit is increased over that of the op-amp alone.

Parameters

(*i*) Gain–Bandwidth

Because of the internal compensation circuitry included in an op-amp, the voltage gain drops off as frequency increases. Op-amp specifications provide a descriptions of the gain versus bandwidth. Figure below provides a plot of gain versus frequency for a typical op-amp. At low frequency down to dc operation, the gain is that value listed by the manufacturer's specification A_{VD} (voltage differential gain) and is typically a very large value.

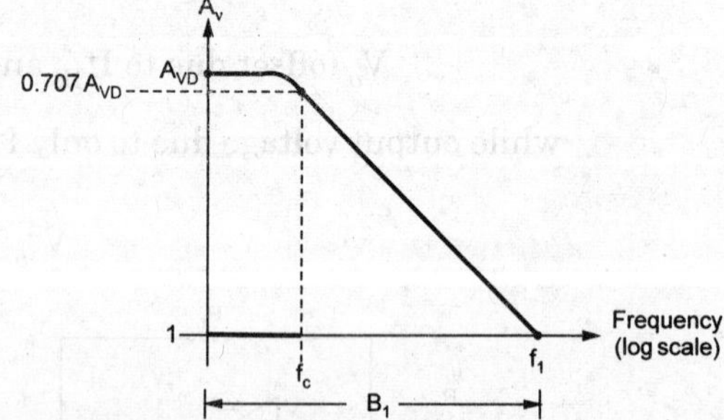

Fig. Gain versus frequency plot

As frequency of the input signal increases, the open-loop gain drops off until it finally reaches the value of 1 (unity). The frequency at this gain value is specified by the manufacturer as the unity-gain bandwidth, B_1. While this value is a frequency at which the gain becomes 1, it can be considered a bandwidth, since frequency band from 0 Hz to the unity-gain frequency is also a bandwidth. Hence we can refer to the point at which the gain reduces to 1 as the unity-gain frequency (f_1) or unity-gain bandwidth (B_1).

Another frequency which is shown in above figure, at which gain drop by 3 dB (or to 0.707 the dc gain, A_{VD}), this being the cutoff frequency of the op-amp, f_C. In fact, unity-gain frequency and cutoff frequency are related by

$$f_1 = A_{VD} f_C$$

This equation shows that unity-gain frequency may also be called *gain-bandwidth product of the op-amp.*

(ii) Slew Rate (SR)

It reflect the op-amp's ability to handle varying signals.

Slew rate = maximum rate at which amplifier output can change in volts per microsecond (V/ms)

$$SR = \frac{\Delta V_o}{\Delta t} = \tilde{N}/ms \text{ with } t \text{ in ms}$$

It provides a parameter specifying the maximum rate of change of the output voltage when driven by a large step-input signal. If output at a rate of voltage changes greater than the slew rate, then output would not be able to change fast enough and would not vary over the full range expected, resulting in signal clipping or distortion. In any case, the output would not be an amplified duplicate of the input signal if the op-amp slew rate is exceeded.

(iii) Maximum signal frequency.

Maximum frequency that an op-amp may operate at depends on both bandwidth (BW) and the slew rate (SR) parameters of the op-amp.

For a sinusoidal signal of general form, $v_o = K \sin(2\pi f t)$

Signal maximum rate of change $= 2\pi f K$ V/s

To prevent distortion at the output, rate of change must also be less than the slew rate, *i.e.*

$$2\pi f K \leq SR$$

$$\Rightarrow \quad \omega K \leq SR$$

$$\therefore \quad f \leq \frac{SR}{2\pi K} \text{ Hz}$$

$$\omega \leq \frac{SR}{K} \text{ rad/s}$$

Also, maximum frequency, f, in the above equation, is also limited by the unity-gain bandwidth.

POWER AMPLIFIER

Power amplifiers or large-signal amplifiers provide sufficient power to an output load to drive a speaker or other power device, typically a few watts to tens of watts. The main features of a large-signal amplifier are the circuits power efficiency, the maximum amount of power that the circuit is capable of handling, and the impedance matching to the output device. Figure below illustrates amplification close by small-signal amplifier and power-amplifier.

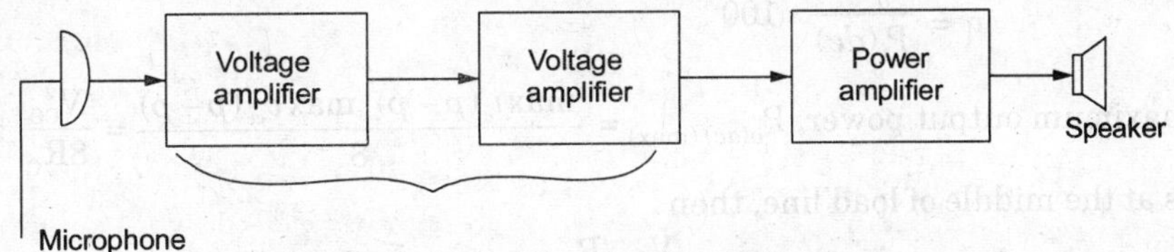

Fig. block diagram of a simple audio amplifier

In the above figure microphone produces a very small signal. The first two stages amplify this audio signal and it becomes larger in voltage level but current level remains low, thus low power level. The last stage produces a much larger signal and also sufficient power to drive the loud speaker coil. Thus a power amplifier has to handle large voltage and current swings.

One method generally employed to categorize amplifier is by class which basically represent the amount of output signal varies over one cycle of operation for a full cycle of input signal.

AMPLIFIER CLASSES.

1. Class-A power Amplifier

The amplifier circuits which falls into this category are linear as these operate in a small region in the middle of the load line.

In this amplifier, output signal is a faithful replica of the input signal. But, as Q-point is the middle of the load line, therefore half the supply voltage drops across the transistor and hence, current flowing through the transistor is half of its saturation current. These values of voltage drop and current produces a constant power loss in the transistor. Even there is a power loss in class-A amplifier when there is no signal is being amplified.

There are two configuration of class-A power amplifier :

(*i*) Series-fed class-A Amplifier

The circuit connection for this amplifier is shown in Fig. (*a*)

Fig. (a) Circuit connection

In this biasing, Q-point is fixed by V_{CC} and R_B

i.e.,
$$I_C = \beta I_B = \frac{\beta(V_{CC} - V_{BE})}{R_B}$$

and, collector-emitter voltage,

$$V_{CE} = V_{CC} - I_C R_C$$

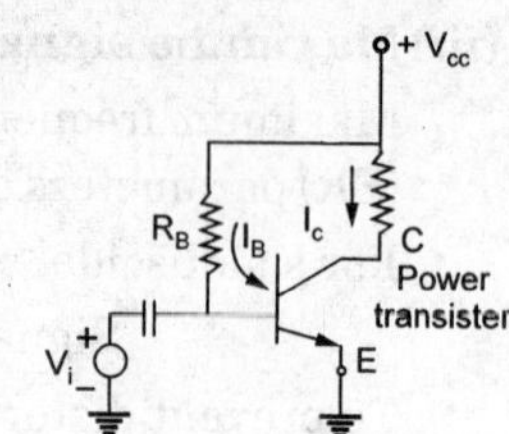

Fig. (b) Load line

In the load-line drawn in Fig. (*b*), Q-point is located. If this point is set half way between 0 and V_{CC}/R_C, then largest collector current sewing will be possible.

Input power from the voltage supply, $P_i(dc) = V_{CC} I_{CQ}$

Waveforms of I_C and V_{CC} (*ac* component) for the input base current I_b.

From Fig. (*c*), $i_c(\text{peak}) = \dfrac{V_{CC}}{2R_C}$,

$$V_{ce}(\text{peak}) = \frac{V_{CC}}{2}.$$

Hence, power delivered to the load by the transistor,

$$P_O(ac) = I_c(\text{rms}) \cdot V_{ce}(\text{rms})$$

$$= \frac{i_c(p-p)}{2\sqrt{2}} \cdot \frac{V_{cc}(p-p)}{2\sqrt{2}}$$

$$= \frac{i_c(p-p) \cdot V_{ce}(p-p)}{8}$$

Fig. (c)

∴ Efficiency of the amplifier,

$$\eta = \frac{P_o(ac)}{P_i(dc)} \times 100$$

Now, maximum output power, $P_{o(ac)\,(\text{max})} = \dfrac{\max i_e(p-p) \cdot \max v_{ce}(p-p)}{8} = \dfrac{V_{CC}^2}{8R_C}$

If Q-point is at the middle of load line, then

$$I_{CQ} = \frac{V_{CC}/R_C}{2}$$

and, $P_i(dc)(Q) = V_{CC}^2 I_{CQ} = \dfrac{V_{CC}^2}{2R_C}$

∴ **Maximum efficiency, η(max)** $= \dfrac{P_o(ac)(\text{max})}{P_i(dc)(Q)} \times 100 = \dfrac{V_{CC}^2/8R_C}{V_{CC}^2/2R_C} \times 100 = 25\%$

This is maximum efficiency of series-fed class-A amplifiers under ideal condition.

Power dissipated as heat by the transistor, $P_D = P_i(dc) - I_{CQ}{}^2 R_C - P_O(ac)$

(ii) Transformer-coupled class-A amplifier

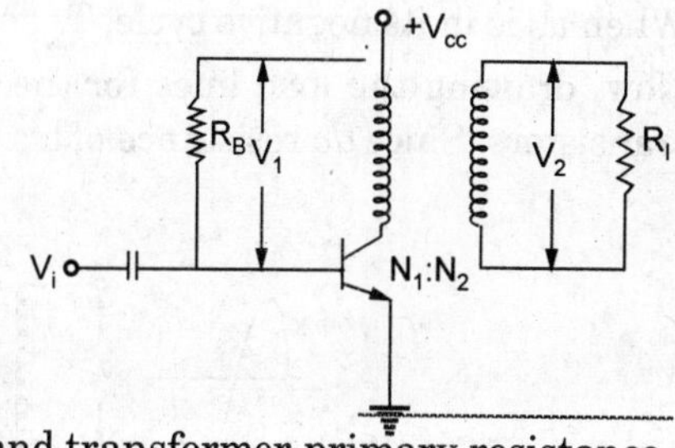

Under *dc* conditions, *dc* resistance seen on the primary side is quite low and it is indeed the resistance of the primary winding (under *dc* conditions load resistance is not seen on the primary side). It implies that almost all the supply voltage will drop across the transistor at the operating point. Hence, as shown in Fig. (*e*), *dc* load line is almost vertical.

Due to series resistance corresponding to the battery resistance and transformer primary resistance, the *dc* load line will not be vertical, but quite steep.

Now, for the *ac* signal, load resistance seen on the primary side of the transformer is

$$R'_L = \left(\frac{N_1}{N_2}\right)^2 \cdot R_L$$

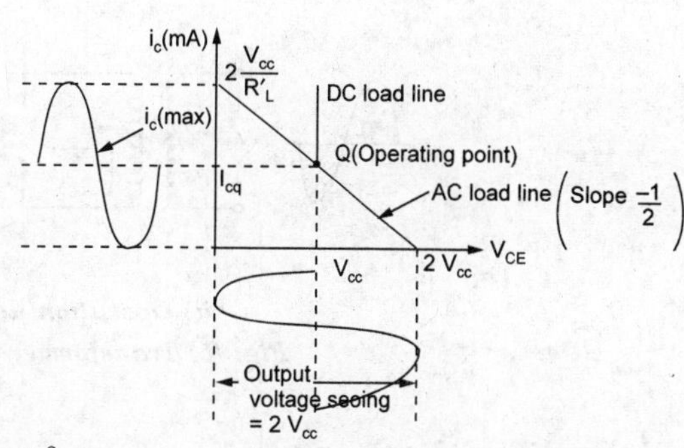

This acts as R_C of the transistor circuit of Fig. (*a*). The *ac* load line is drawn in Fig. (*e*). The value of $2V_{CC}$ on the V_{CC}-axis of the *ac* load line can be explained by the fact that transformer is an inductive circuit element so as the current I_C collapses (so the core flux also), a voltage is induced in the transformer primary in the direction to aid the supply voltage (Lenz's law), so that V_{CC} becomes $2V_{CC}$.

Now,
$$P_o(ac)(\text{max}) = \frac{(2V_{CC}/R'_L)\cdot 2V_{CC}}{8} = \frac{V_{CC}^2}{2R'_L}$$

and
$$P_i(dc)(Q) = V_{CC}\,I_{CQ} = V_{CC}\left(\frac{V_{CC}}{R'_L}\right) = \frac{V_{CC}^2}{R'_L}$$

$\therefore$
$$\eta(\text{max}) = \left(\frac{V_{CC}^2}{2R'_L}\right) \bigg/ \left(\frac{V_{CC}^2}{R'_L}\right) = 0{\cdot}5 = 50\%.$$

Here, transformer coupling raises **maximum possible efficiency of the amplifier circuit to 50%.**

2. Class-B power Amplifier

This amplifier circuit provides an output signal varying over one-half the input signal cycle.

Class B operation creates a very distorted output as reproduction of the input takes place for only 180° of the output signal swing. Biasing this amplifier at cut-off end of the load-line saves power as there is no drain in the supply during the non-conduction period as in this period transistor dc current is zero. Thus the, power efficiency of class-B is more than that of Class-A.

The transistor shown in Fig. (*a*) is biased at cut-off, *i.e.*, $I_B = 0$, $V_{CE} = V_{CC}$ and so transistor in cut-off state during half cycle of the signal and goes into conduction state during state positive half cycle of the signal. Hence, highly distorted output results. To overcome from this problem, a second device operation in class-B is added in such a way that one transistor conducts only for the negative half cycles. This mode of operation is called *push-pull operation*.

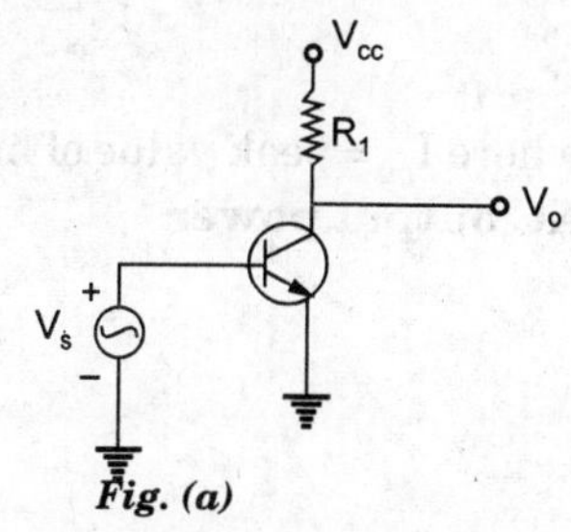

Fig. (a)

Consider transformer coupled push-pull amplifier.

When $V_S = 0$, T_1 and T_2 are both at cut-off.

When V_S is in its positive cycle, T_1 goes ON and a circuit current *i*, flows in the direction as shown.

$$\text{Load resistance, } R'_L = R_L\left(\frac{N_1/2}{N_2}\right)^2 = \left(\frac{R_L}{4}\right)\left(\frac{N_1}{N_2}\right)^2$$

When v_S is in its negative cycle, T_2 goes ON and a current i_2 flows in the direction as shown.

Now, drawing the load lines for the circuit given in Fig. (*b*) and when v_S = 0, V_{CC} appears across both the transistors. Since *dc* resistance of transformer winding being negligible, the *dc* load line is almost vertical.

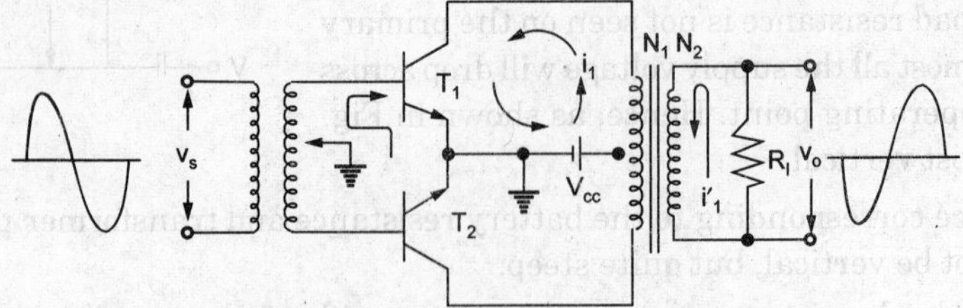

(i) Operation during positive half cycle

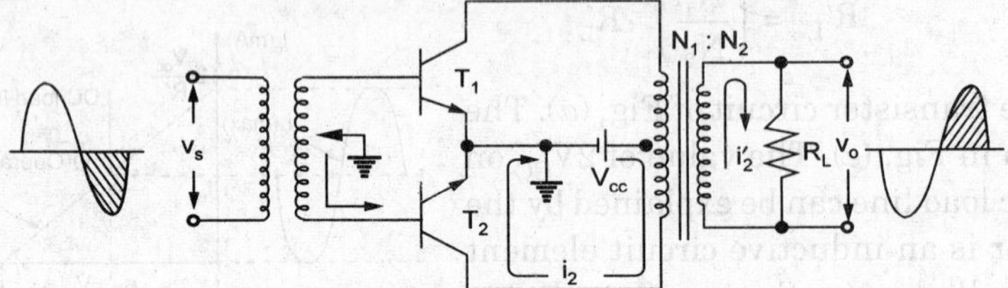

(ii) Operation during negative half cycle

Fig. (b) Transformer coupled push-pull complifier

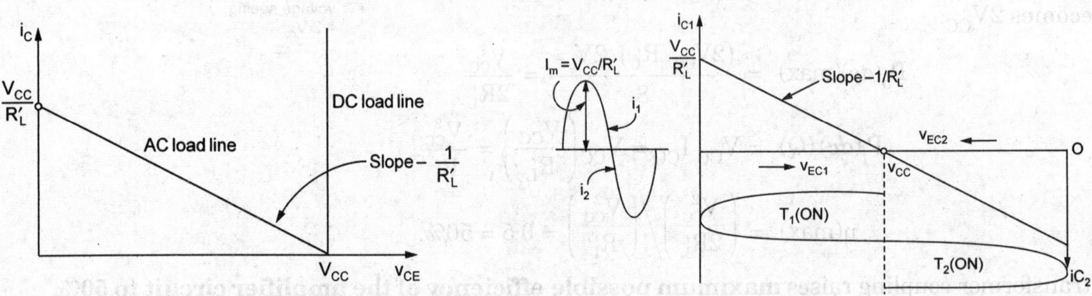

Fig. (c) Load line for push-pull complifier ***Fig. (d) Combined load line of two transistor in push-pull***

When v_S is non-zero, resistance R'_L is presented to i_1 to i_2. The current i_1 in Fig. *b* (*i*) is taken as +ve and anticlockwise current i_2 in Fig. c (*ii*) is taken as –ve.

The combination of two half cycles is shown in Fig. (*d*).

Now, direct current supplied by the battery, $I_{dc} = i_1(dc) + i_2(dc) = \dfrac{2I_m}{\pi}$

$$\therefore \qquad P_i(dc) = \frac{2V_{CC}\, I_m}{\pi}$$

where I_m = peak value of half cycle of i_c (conducted by T_1 or T_2)

AC output power

$$P_o(ac) = V_{rms} I_{rms} = \frac{I_{rms}^2}{R'_L}$$

$$I_{rms} = i_c(p-p)/(2\sqrt{2}) = I_m/\sqrt{2}$$

$$\therefore \qquad P_o(ac) = I_m^2/(R'_L/2)$$

From Fig. (*d*),
$$I_m(\max) = \frac{V_{CC}}{R'_L}$$

$$\therefore \qquad P_i(dc)(\max) = \frac{2V_{CC}^2}{\pi R'_L}$$

$$P_o(ac)(\max) = \frac{V_{CC}^2}{2R'_L}$$

$$\therefore \quad \text{Efficiency}, \eta = \frac{P_o(ac)}{P_i(dc)} = \frac{I_m^2 R_L'/2}{2V_{CC}I_m/\pi} = \frac{\pi I_m R_L'}{4V_{CC}}$$

$$\Rightarrow \quad \eta(\max) = \frac{P_o(ac)(\max)}{P_i(dc)(\max)} = \frac{\pi I_m(\max) R_L'}{4V_{CC}} = \frac{\pi}{4} \text{ or } 78{\cdot}54\%.$$

3. Class-AB power Amplifier

This amplifier is biased at a dc level above the zero base current level of class B and above one-half supply voltage level of class A. For class AB operation, the output signal during occurs between 180° to 360° and is neither class A nor class B operation as shown in Fig (*a*).

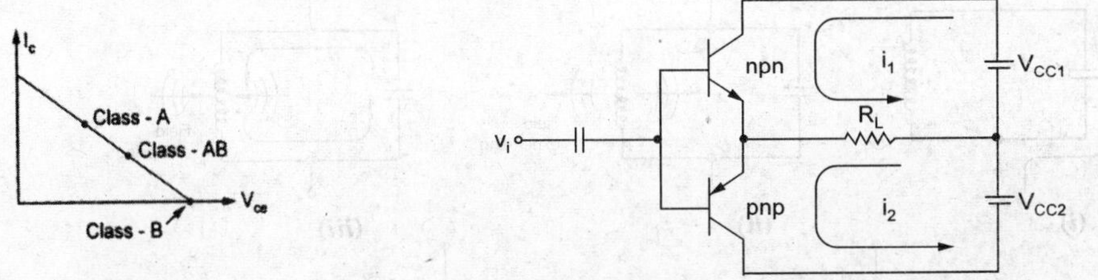

Fig (a) *Fig. (b) Complementary-symmetry circuit*

In this amplifiers, Q-point (operating point) of the transistors lies between that for class-A and class-B type amplifiers. A complementary-symmetry class-B amplifier shown in Fig. (*b*) can be made as class-AB by choosing R_1 and R_2 such that the V_{BE} of both T_1 and T_2 places each transistor away from the cut-off point *i.e.*, $V_{BE} > 0{\cdot}6V$.

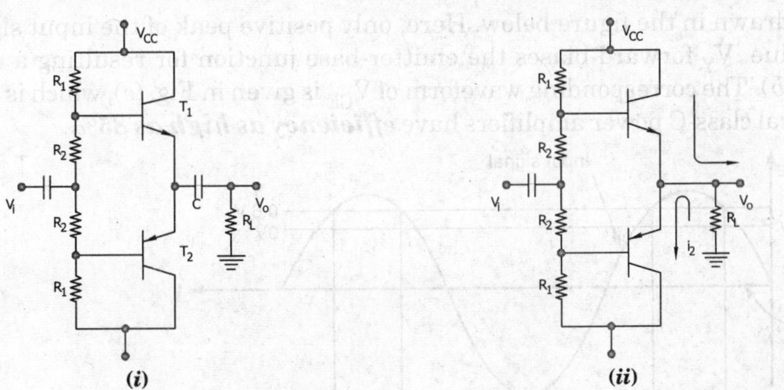

Fig. (c) Complementary-symmetry circuits with signal power supply

4. Class-C power Amplifier

The output of class C amplifier is biased for operation at less than 180° of the cycle and will operate only with a tuned circuit which provides a full cycle of operation for the tuned frequency.

Class-C amplifiers are biased deep into the cut-off. A class-C amplifier is shown in Fig. (*a*) below. The negative voltage at the base terminal reverse-biases the base emitter junction of the transistor, so that it will not conduct until the input signal overcomes this reverse bias. This occurs for only a small part of positive half cycle of input signal. Here, as shown above i_c is in the form of pulses implies that class-C amplifiers suffer from extreme distortion. Therefore, they are suitable for the audio work and are used at radio frequencies.

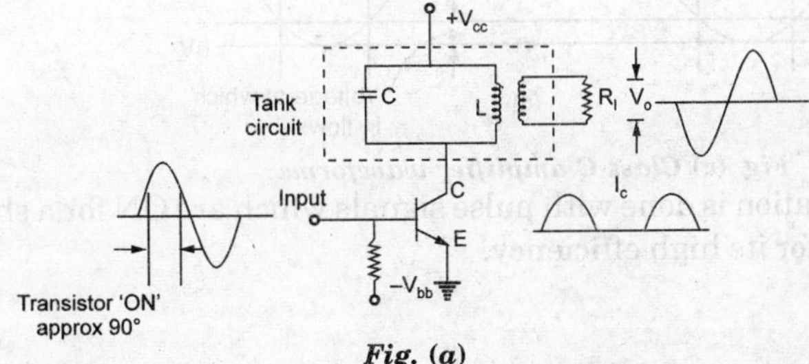

Fig. (a)

In Fig. (*b*), a tank circuit in the collector circuit of the class-C amplifier, which restores the sine wave form of the input signal at the output. But there is problem with it is that, it can not restore rectangular waveform or complex audio wave forms.

The tank circuit shown is a parallel LC oscillating circuit and is excited by collector current pulse, which sets the circuit into self oscillations. In this circuit, the energy transfers back and fourth between the capacitor and inductor, thus producing a sinusoidal waveform. Because of the small effective resistance of the tank circuit, the energy loss occurs which is being maintained by cyclic pulses of the tank. This is accomplished in class-C amplifier by the collector current pulse recharging the capacitor every cycle.

Frequency of oscillation of the tank circuit, $f = \dfrac{1}{2\pi\sqrt{LC}}$

(*i*) (*ii*) Field expending (*iii*) Field collapsing

(*iv*) Field expending (*v*) Field collapsing

Fig. (b)

The class-C waveforms are drawn in the figure below. Here, only positive peak of the input signal is seen in Fig. (*a*) above the cut-in value. V_Y forward biases the emitter-base junction for resulting a cyclic collector current pulse shown in Fig. (*b*). The corresponding waveform of V_{CE} is given in Fig. (*c*), which is sinusoidal due to tank circuit action. Practical class-C power amplifiers have ***efficiency as high as 85%.***

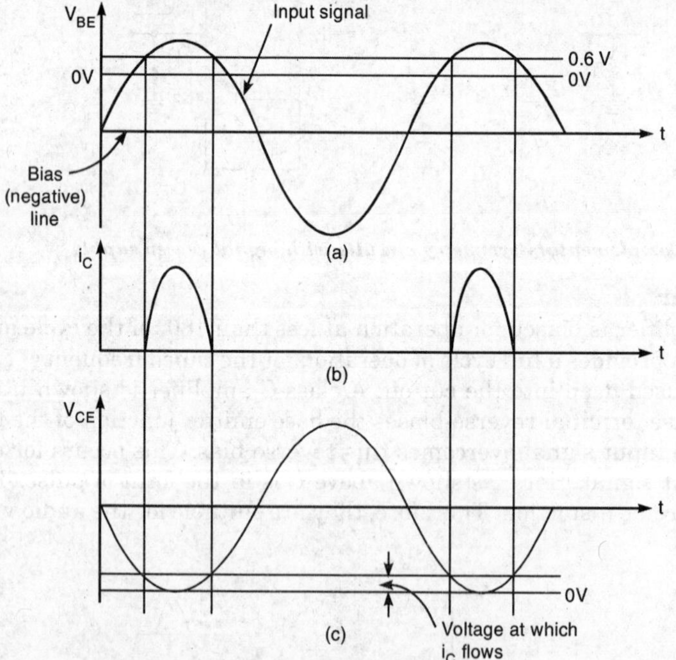

Fig. (c) Class-C amplifier waveforms

In this amplifier circuit, amplification is done with pulse signals which are ON for a short interval and OFF for a longer interval, which causes for its high efficiency.

FEEDBACK AMPLIFIERS

Types of Feedback Connections

There are four basic ways of connecting the feedback signal. Both voltage and current can be feedback to the input either in series or parallel :

(1) Voltage-series feedback [Fig. (*a*)]

(2) Voltage-shunt feedback [Fig. (*b*)]

(3) Current-series feedback [Fig. (*c*)]

(4) Current-shunt feedback [Fig. (*d*)]

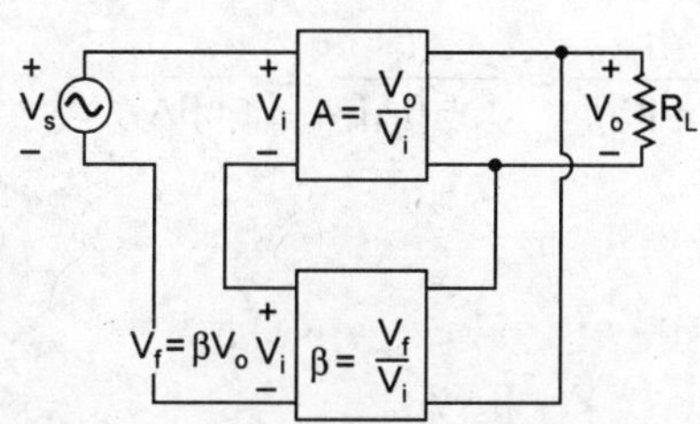

(a) Voltage-series feedback, $A_f = V_o/V_s$

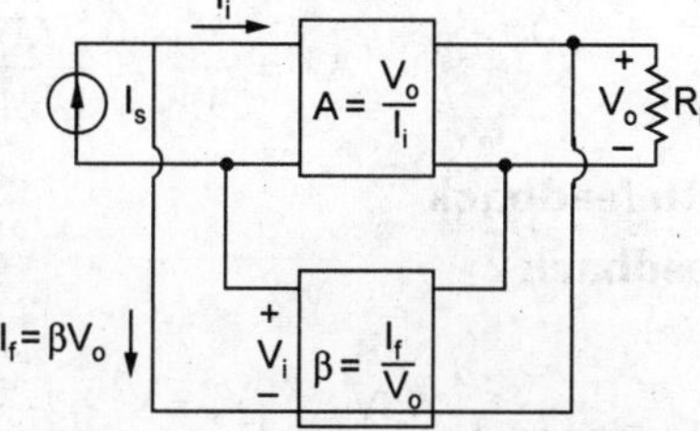

(b) Voltage-shunt feedback, $A_f = V_o/I_s$

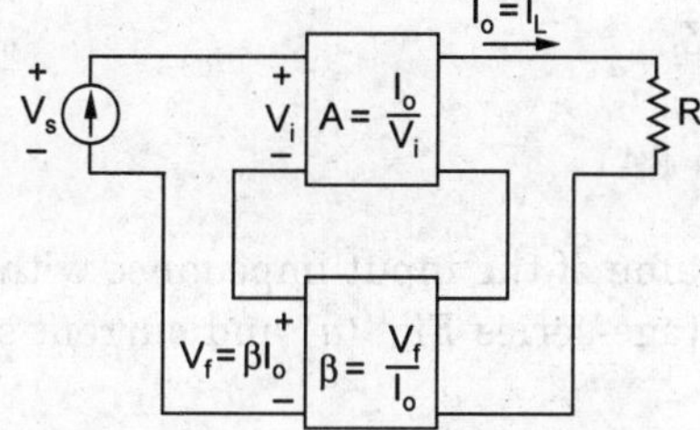

(c) Current-series feedback, = $A_f = I_o/V_s$

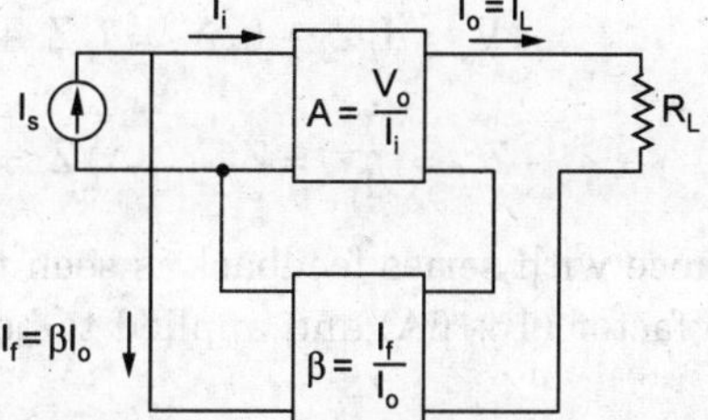

(d) Current-shunt feedback, $A_f = I_o/I_s$.

Fig. Feedback amplifier types

Voltage refers to connecting the output voltage as input to the feedback network.

Current refers to tapping off some output current through the feedback network.

Series refers to connecting the feedback signal in series with the input signal voltage.

Shunt refers to connecting the feedback signal in shunt (parallel) with an input current source.

Gain with Feedback

Examine gain of each of the feedback circuit connections of above figures. The gain without feedback, A, is that of the amplifier stage. With feedback, β, overall gain of the circuit is reduced by a factor (1 + βA).

		Voltage-Series	Voltage-Shunt	Current-Series	Current-Shunt
Gain without feedback	A	$\frac{V_o}{V_i}$	$\frac{V_o}{I_i}$	$\frac{I_o}{V_i}$	$\frac{I_o}{I_i}$
Feedback	β	$\frac{V_f}{V_o}$	$\frac{I_f}{V_o}$	$\frac{V_f}{I_o}$	$\frac{I_f}{I_o}$
Gain with feedback	A_f	$\frac{V_o}{V_s}$	$\frac{V_o}{I_s}$	$\frac{I_o}{V_s}$	$\frac{I_o}{I_s}$

(*i*) Voltage-Series Feedback :

Figure *(a)* shows voltage-series feedback connection with a part of the output voltage feedback in series with the input signal, resulting in an overall gain reduction.

If there is no feedback ($V_f = 0$), then voltage gain of the amplifier stage is

$$A = \frac{V_o}{V_s} = \frac{V_o}{V_i}$$

If a feedback signal, V_f, is connected in series with the input, then

$$V_i = V_s - V_f$$

Since $$V_o = AV_i = A(V_s - V_f) = AV_s - AV_f = AV_s - A(\beta V_o)$$

$$\therefore \quad (1+\beta A)V_o = AV_s$$

Hence overall voltage gain with feedback, $A_f = \dfrac{V_o}{V_s} = \dfrac{A}{1+\beta A}$

This equation shows that gain with feedback is the amplifier gain reduced by the factor $(1 + \beta A)$.

(*ii*) Voltage-Shunt Feedback:

For the network of Fig. (*b*), gain with feedback

$$A_f = \frac{V_o}{I_s} = \frac{AI_i}{I_i + I_f} = \frac{AI_i}{I_i + \beta V_o} = \frac{AI_i}{I_i + \beta AI_i} = \frac{A}{1+\beta A}$$

Input impedance with feedback

(*i*) Voltage-Series Feedback

It is shown in Fig. (*e*).

$$\text{input impedance, } I_i = \frac{V_i}{Z_i} = \frac{V_s - V_f}{Z_i} = \frac{V_s - \beta V_o}{Z_i} = \frac{V_s - \beta AV_i}{Z_i}$$

$$I_i Z_i = V_s - \beta AV_i$$

$$V_s = I_i Z_i + \beta AV_i = I_i Z_i + \beta AI_i Z_i$$

$$Z_{if} = \frac{V_s}{I_i} = Z_i + (\beta A) Z_i = Z_i(1 + \beta A)$$

The input impedance with series feedback is seen to be value of the input impedance without feedback multiplied by the factor $(1 + \beta A)$ and applied to both voltage-series Fig. (*a*) and current-series Fig. (*c*) configurations.

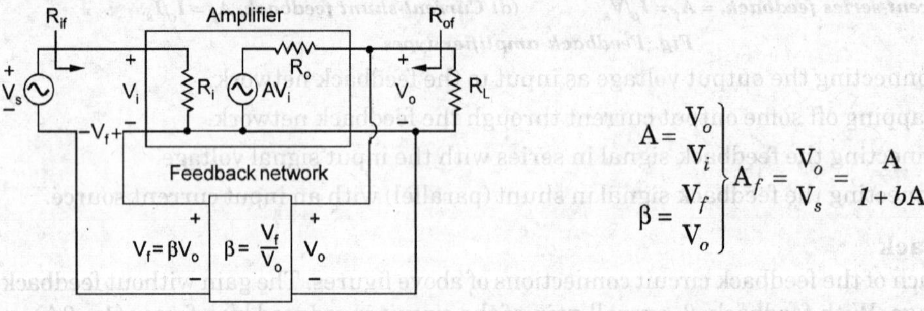

Fig. (e) Voltage-series feedback connection

(*ii*) Voltage-Shunt Feedback

Input impedance can be determined to be

$$Z_{if} = \frac{V_i}{I_s} = \frac{V_i}{I_i + I_f} = \frac{V_i}{I_i + \beta V_o} = \frac{V_i / I_i}{\dfrac{I_i}{I_i} + \dfrac{\beta V_o}{I_i}}$$

$$\Rightarrow \quad Z_{if} = \frac{Z_i}{1+\beta A}$$

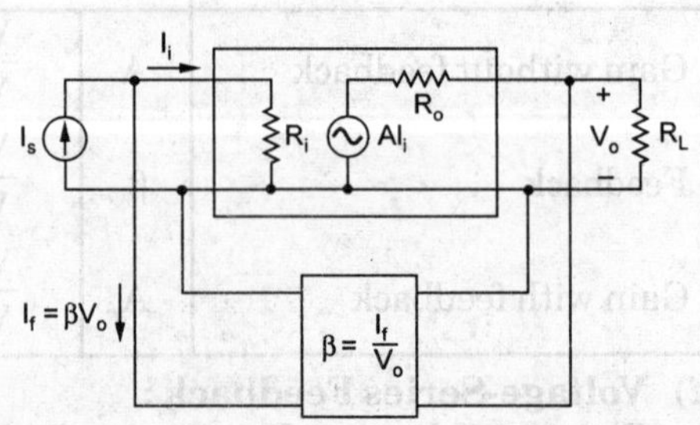

Fig. (f) Voltage-shunt feedback connection

This reduced input impedance applies to the voltage-series connection of Fig. (*a*) and voltage-shunt connection of Fig. (*b*).

Output impedance with Feedback.

The output impedance for the connections of Fig. (*a*), (*b*), (*c*), (*d*) are dependent on the use of voltage or current feedback. For voltage feedback the output impedance is decreased, while current feedback increases the output impedance.

(*i*) Voltage-Series Feedback

The voltage-series feedback circuit of Fig. (*c*) provides sufficient circuit detail to determine the output impedance with feedback. The output impedance is determined by applying a voltage, V, resulting in a current, I, with V_s shorted out ($V_s = 0$). Then

$$\text{Voltage, } V = IZ_o + AV_i$$

For $V_s = 0$, $\quad V_i = -V_f$

$$\therefore \quad V = IZ_o - AV_f = IZ_o - A(\beta V)$$

Rewriting the equation as $\quad V + \beta AV = IZ_o$

allows solving for the output resistance with feedback

$$Z_{of} = \frac{V}{I} = \frac{Z_o}{1+\beta A}$$

This equation shows that with voltage-series feedback, the output impedance is reduced from that without feedback by the factor $(1 + \beta A)$.

(*ii*) Current-Series Feedback :

The output impedance with current-series feedback can be determined by applying a signal V to the output with V_s shorted out, resulting in a current I, the ratio of V to I being the output impedance. Fig. (*g*) shows a more detailed connection with current-series feedback. For the output part of a current-series feedback connection shown in Fig. (*g*), the resulting output impedance is determined as follows :

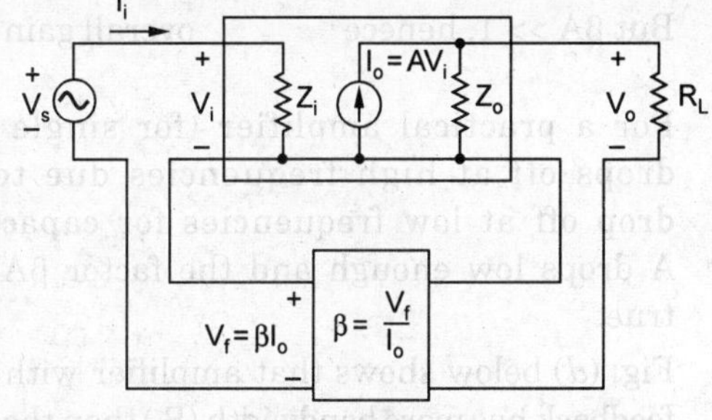

Fig. (g) Current-series feedback connection

With $\quad V_s = 0, \quad V_i = V_f$

$$I = \frac{V}{Z_o} - AV_i = \frac{V}{Z_o} - AV_f = \frac{V}{Z_o} - A\beta I$$

$$Z_o(1 + \beta A) I = V$$

$$Z_{of} = \frac{V}{I} = Z_o(1 + \beta A)$$

Effect of Feedback Connection on Input and Output Impedance

	Voltage-Series	Current-Series	Voltage-Shunt	Current-Shunt
Z_{if}	$Z_i(1 + \beta A)$ (increased)	$Z_i(1 + \beta A)$ (increased)	$\frac{Z_i}{1+\beta A}$ (decreased)	$\frac{Z_i}{1+\beta A}$ (decreased)
Z_{of}	$\frac{Z_o}{1+\beta A}$ (decreased)	$Z_o(1 + \beta A)$ (increased)	$\frac{Z_o}{1+\beta A}$ (decreased)	$Z_o(1 + \beta A)$ (increased)

CHARACTERISTICS OF FEEDBACK.

(i) Reduction in Frequency Distortion

For a negative-feedback amplifier having $\beta A >> 1$, gain with feedback, $A_f \cong \frac{1}{\beta}$

It follows that if feedback network is purely resistive, the gain with feedback is not dependent on frequency even though the basic amplifier gain is frequency dependent. Practically, frequency distortion arising because of varying amplifier gain with gain frequency is considerably reduced in a negative-voltage feedback amplifier circuit.

(ii) Reduction in Noise and Nonlinear Distortion

Signal feedback tends to hold down the amount of noise signal (such as *power-supply* hum) and non-linear distortion. The factor $(1 + \beta A)$ reduces both input noise and resulting non-linear distortion for considerable improvement. However, there is a reduction in overall gain (the price required for the improvement in circuit performance). If additional stages are used to bring the overall gain up to the level without feedback, the extra stage(s) might introduce as much noise back into the system as that reduced by the feedback amplifier. This problem can be somewhat alleviated by readjusting the gain of the feedback-amplifier circuit to obtain higher gain while also providing reduced noise signal.

(iii) Effect of Negative feedback on Gain and Bandwidth

Overall gain with negative feedback, $A_f = \frac{A}{1+\beta A} \cong \frac{A}{\beta A}$

But $\beta A >> 1$, henece overall gain $\approx \frac{1}{\beta}$

For a practical amplifier (for single low-and high-frequency breakpoints) the open-loop gain drops off at high frequencies due to active device and circuit capacitances. Gain may also drop off at low frequencies for capacitively coupled amplifier stages. Once the open-loop gain A drops low enough and the factor βA is no longer much larger than 1, $A_f \cong 1/\beta$ no longer holds true.

Fig. (*d*) below shows that amplifier with negative feedback has more bandwidth (B_f) than the amplifier without feedback (B). The feedback amplifier has a higher upper 3-dB frequency and smaller lower 3-dB frequency.

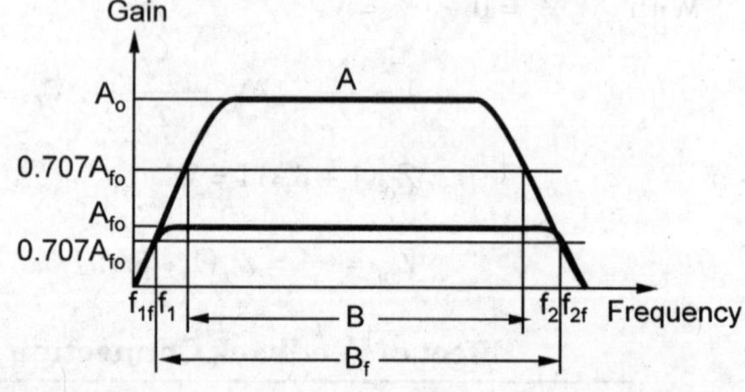

The use of feedback, while resulting in a lowering of voltage gain, has provided an increase in B and in the upper 3-dB frequency, particularly. In fact, the product of gain and frequency remains the same so that the gain–bandwidth product of the basic amplifier is the same value for the feedback amplifier. However, since the feedback amplifier has lower gain, the net operation was to trade gain for bandwidth (we use bandwidth for the upper 3-dB frequency since typically $f_2 >> f_1$).

AMPLIFIERS

Types of Amplifiers

(1) Single stage amplifiers

(2) Multistage amplifiers.

MULTISTAGE AMPLIFIERS.

When gain of a single amplifier is not sufficient to drive an output, then to obtain additional amplification, two or three stages are required. For this, output of each amplifier stage is coupled to the input of the next amplifier stage.

Coupling

Main purpose of coupling device (e.g. capacitor, transformer etc)

(*i*) To transfer AC output of one stage to the input of the next stage.

(*ii*) To isolate the DC conditions of one stage from the next stage.

Types of Multistage Amplifiers

1. RC Coupled amplifiers.

These are used as a coupling device. The capacitor connects output of one stage to the input of the next stage in order to pass ac signal while blocking the dc bias current.

In RC coupling, a coupling capacitor C_C is used to connect output of first stage to the input as of the second stage. Emitter bypass capacitor C_E offers low reactance path to the a.c. signal about it, the voltage gain of each stage is low. Coupling capacitor C_C transmits a.c. signal but blocks dc signal.

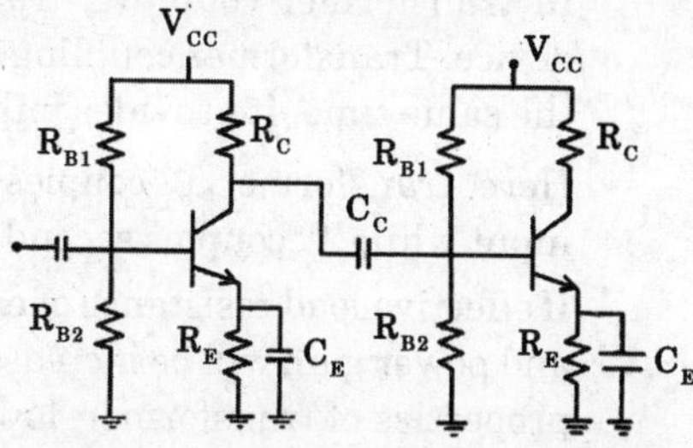

Fig. a two stage RC coupled amplifier

Behaviour of RC Coupled amplifier :

(*i*) *At low frequencies (<50 Hz):*

Reactance, $\frac{1}{\omega C_C}$ of coupling capacitor, C_C is very high and hence very small part of signal is transferred from one stage to the next. Also C_E cannot effectively shunt emitter resistance R_E because of large reactance at low frequencies. These factors cause a falling of voltage gain at low frequencies.

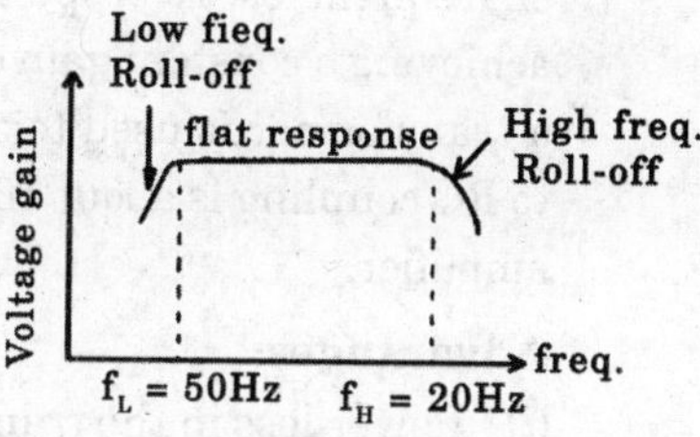

Fig.Frequency Response

(*ii*) *At high frequencies (> 20 kHz) :*

Reactance offered by C_C is very small and it behaves as a short circuit. This increases loading effects next stage and reduce the voltage gain. Also, capacitance reactances of C_E is low which increases base current which in turn reduces current amplification factor β. These factors causes a falling of voltage gain at high frequencies.

(*iii*) *At mid frequencies (between 50 Hz to 20 kHz) :*

Voltage gain of the amplifier is constant. As frequency increases in this range, reactance offered by C_C decreases which increases voltage gain. Low reactance means higher loading of first stage and hence lower gain. These two factors cancel each others effect, resulting a uniform gain at mid frequencies.

Advantages:

(*i*) It is most popular type of coupling.

(*ii*) It is least expensive multistage amplifier.

(*iii*) It has excellent audio fidelity over a wide range of frequency.

(*iv*) It provides less frequency distortion.

(*v*) It is usually employed for voltage amplification.

(*vi*) Circuit is very compact.

Disadvantages :

(*i*) Loading effect of successive stages reduce the overall gain.

(*ii*) It has tendency to become noisy.

(*iii*) It provides poor impedance matching between stages.

Applications:

(*i*) These have excellent audio fidelity over a wide range of frequency.

(*ii*) These are widely used as a voltage amplifier in initial stages of public address system.

(*iii*) These rarely used in the final stages because of its poor impedance matching.

2. Transformer Coupled Amplifier.

In transformer coupling, transformer is used as the coupling device. Transformer coupling pass the ac signal and blocks dc at the same time. It provides impedance matching.

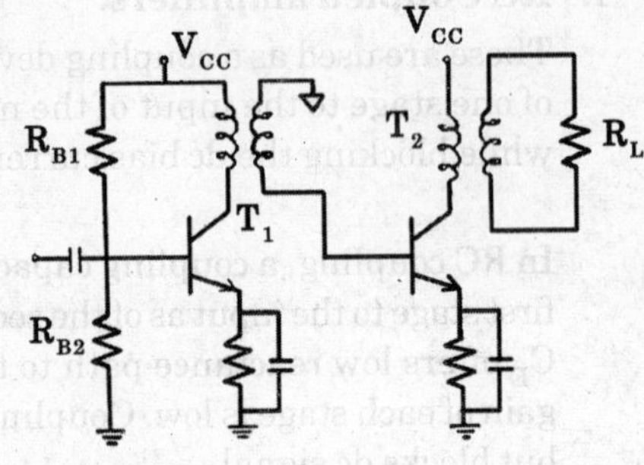

Here, transformer T_1 couples first stage output to second stage input while T_2 couples second stage output to load.

If effective load resistance of each stage is increased, then voltage and power gain will be increased. Because of impedance changing properties of transformer, low resistance of a stage (or load) can be reflected as a high load resistance to the previous stage.

Frequency Response:

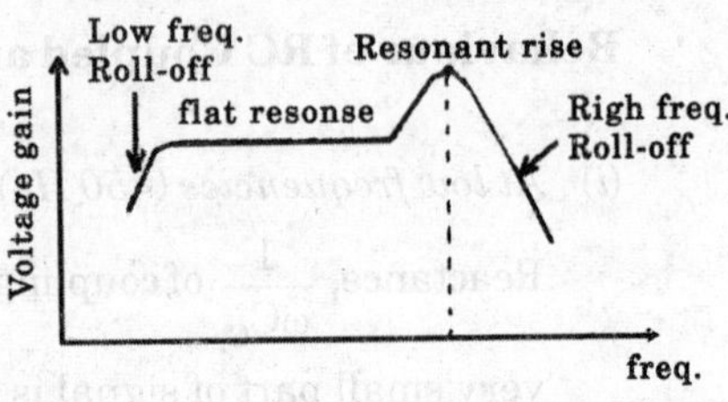

Frequency response is poor and gain is constant over small range of frequencies. A properly designed transformer, is capable of achieving a constant gain over the audio frequency range. But such a transformer is used to achieve frequency response comparable to RC coupling is about 10 to 20 times costly as that of RC coupled amplifier.

Advantages:

(*i*) Power loss in the transformer winding due to d.c. supply is zero.

(*ii*) It provides higher voltage gain than the RC coupled stage.

(*iii*) It provides excellent impedance matching.

Disadvantages:

(*i*) The coupling transformer is expensive and bulky at audio frequency.

(*ii*) Reverse frequency distortion at radio frequency.

(*iii*) It tends to produce hum in the circuit.

(*iv*) It has poor frequency response.

3. Direct Coupled Amplifiers.

In direct coupling of DC coupling, individual amplifier stage bias conditions are so designed that two stages may be directly connected without DC isolation.

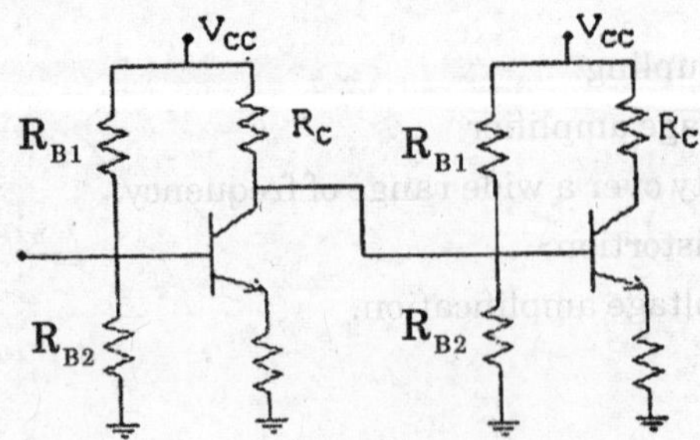

Frequency Response :

There are many applications in which extremely low frequencies are to be amplified. Other coupling devices like capacitors, transformers etc. cannot be used because of their large sizes at lower frequencies. For this, one stage is directly coupled to the next stage.

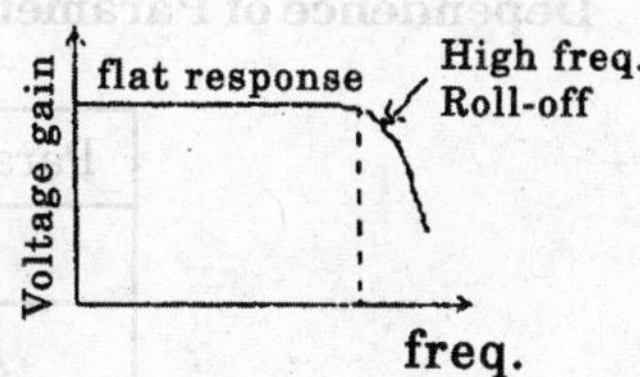

Advantages:

(*i*) Circuit arrangement is most simple.

(*ii*) Circuit cost is low.

(*iii*) It can amplify even zero frequency (dc) signals.

Disadvantages :

(*i*) It cannot amplify high frequency signals.

(*ii*) It has poor temperature stability.

Applications:

(*i*) Analog computation.

(*ii*) Power supply regulators.

(*iii*) Bio-electric measurement.

(*iv*) Linear integrated circuits.

Comparison between various Couplings

Particular	RC coupling	Transformer coupling	Direct coupling
Frequency response	Excellent in the audio frequency range	Poor	Best
Cost	Less	More	Least
Space and weight	Less	More	Least
Impedance matching	Not good	Excellent	Good
Use	For voltage amplification	For power amplification	For amplifying extremely low frequency

h-π MODEL

For analysis at high frequencies, *h*-π or Gia-coletto model is preferred.

Typical values of all parameters :

$g_m = \dfrac{I_C}{V_A} = 50$ mA/V; $\quad r_{bb} = 100\ \Omega$

$r_{bc} = \dfrac{V_T}{I_B} = 4\text{M}\Omega$; $\quad r_{be} = 1\text{k}\Omega$, $\quad r_{ce} = 80\text{k}\Omega$

$C_\mu = 3$ pF; $C_\pi = 100$ pF; C_M = negligibly small

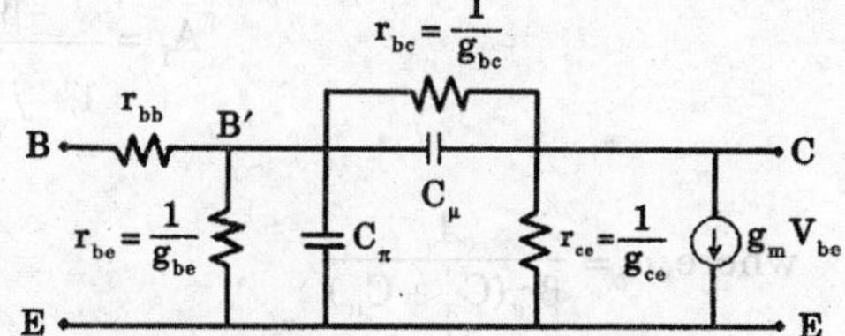

Fig. h-π model for CE configuration

If CE h-parameters at low frequencies are known, then h-π parameters are calculable from following relations:

$$\text{Transistor transconductance, } g_m = \frac{|I_C|}{V_T}$$

$$\text{Input conductance, } g_{be} = \frac{g_m}{h_{fe}} = \frac{|I_C|}{V_T h_{fe}} \quad \text{or,} \quad r'_{be} = \frac{h_{fe}}{g_m}$$

$$\text{Feedback conductance, } g_{bc} = \frac{h_{re}}{r'_{be}}, \quad \text{or,} \quad r'_{bc} = \frac{r_{be}}{h_{re}}$$

$$\text{Base spreading resistance, } r'_{bb} = h_{ie} - r'_{be}$$

$$\text{Output conductance, } g_{ce} = h_{oe} - (1 + h_{fe})g_{bc} = \frac{1}{r_{ce}}$$

Dependence of Parameters on Current, Voltage and Temperature

Parameter	Variation with increasing		
	$\lvert I_C \rvert$	$\lvert V_{CE} \rvert$	T
g_m	$\lvert I_C \rvert$	Independent	1/T
r_{bb}	Decreases	-	Increases
r_{be}	$1/\lvert I_C \rvert$	Increases	Increases
C_π	$\lvert I_C \rvert$	Decreases	
C_μ	Independent	Decreases	Independent
h_{fe}	-	Increases	Decreases
h_{ie}	$1/\lvert I_C \rvert$	Increases	Increases

CE short circuit current gain

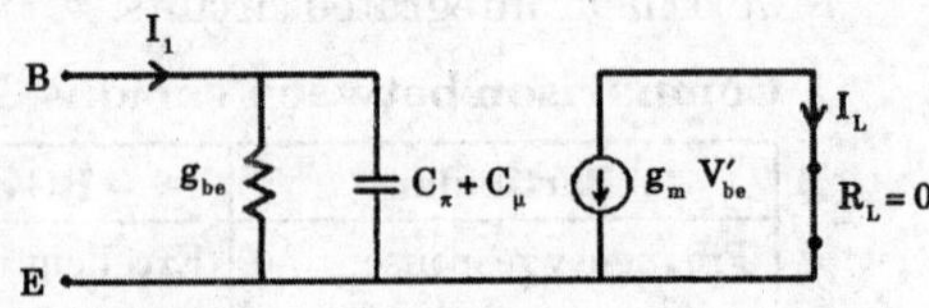

Fig. Approximate equivalent circuit

Load current, $I_L = -g_m V'_{be}$

and, $I_L = V'_{be}\left[\frac{1}{r'_{be}} + j\omega(C_\pi + C_\mu)\right]$

Under shorted condition, current gain, $A_I = \frac{I_L}{I_1} = \frac{g_m}{g'_{be} + j\omega(C_\pi + C_\mu)}$

$$A_I = \frac{-1/r_e}{1/\beta r_e + j\omega(C_\pi + C_\mu)} = \frac{-\beta}{1 + j\omega\beta r_e(C_\pi + C_\mu)} \quad \text{...(since } \beta = -h_{fe})$$

$$A_I = \frac{-\beta}{1 + j\frac{\omega}{\omega_b}}$$

where, $\omega_b = \frac{1}{\beta r_e (C_\pi + C_\mu)}$

Unit Gain-bandwidth

It is defined as frequency at which short circuit CE current gain attains unit magnitude.

Gain × B.W. = constant

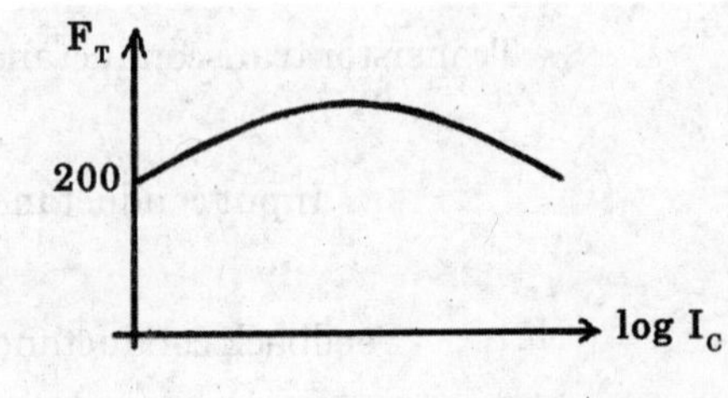

i.e. $1 \times f_T = h_{fe} f_b$

$\Rightarrow$ $f_T = h_{fe} f_b = \frac{g_m}{2\pi(C_\pi + C_\mu)} \cong \frac{g_m}{2\pi C_\pi}$

$\Rightarrow$ $C_\pi \cong \frac{g_m}{2\pi f_T}$

Capacitance, C_π = Emitter diffusion capacitance (C_{De}) + Emitter junction capacitance (C_{Te}).

But in forward bias, emitter junction capacitance (C_{Te}) is negligible, therefore

$$C_\pi \cong C_{De} = \frac{g_m w^2}{2D_B}$$

where, w = base width

D_B = diffusion constant for base.

High frequency calculation

Consider equivalent circuit of the CE amplifier, and divide capacitance C_μ using Miller effect.

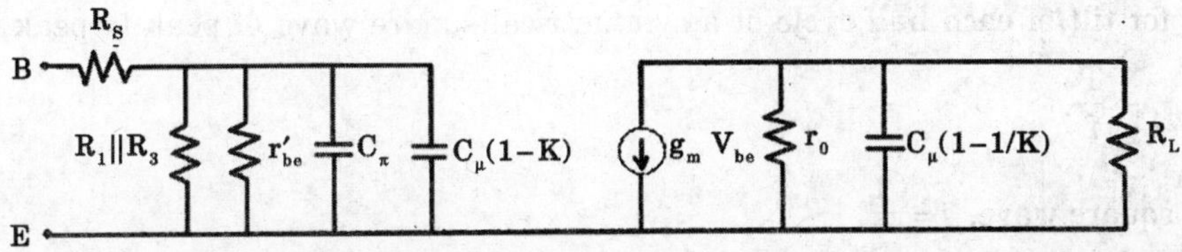

At input side, higher cut-off frequency, $f_{H1} = \dfrac{1}{2\pi R_{eq_1}[C_\pi + C_\mu(1-K)]}$

where, $R_{eq1} = R_s + R_1 \parallel R_2 \parallel r_{be,}$

At output side, higher cut off frequency, $f_{H2} = \dfrac{1}{2\pi R_{eq2} C_\mu (1-1/K)}$

where, $R_{eq2} = R_L \parallel r_0$

Beta Frequency (f_β).

It is the frequency which decides bandwidth. It is the frequency at which gain becomes 3dB down to its midband value.

$$f_\beta = \frac{g_{be}}{2\pi(C_\pi + C_\mu)}, \quad \text{and} \quad g_{be} = \frac{g_m}{\beta}$$

$$f_\beta \times \beta = f_T$$

Alpha frequency (f_α).

It is the frequency at which gain becomes zero.

$$f_\alpha = (1+\beta) f_\beta$$

i.e. $f_\alpha > f_T > f_\beta$

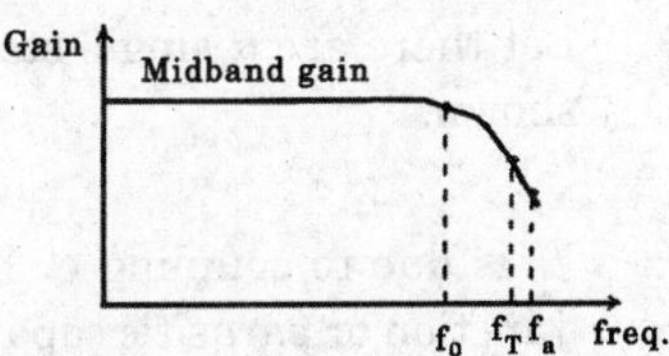

Step response of an Amplifier

Step input is the most useful waveform of all available waveforms. Response V_0 of the low pass circuit to a step input of amplitude V_i = V and time constant of low pass filter is RC

$$\text{Output, } v = V(1 - e^{-t/RC})$$

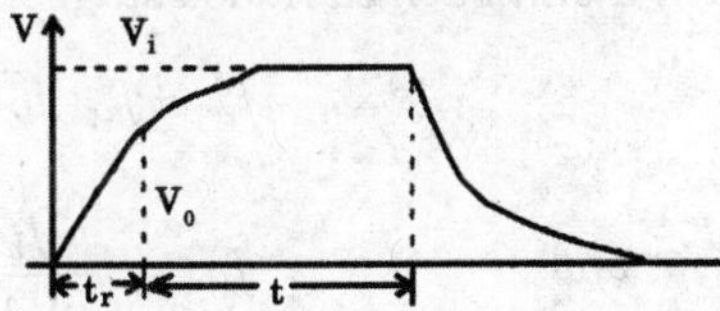

How fast the amplifier can respond to a discontinuity in the input signal is indicated by the time

$$t_r = \frac{0.35}{f_H}$$

Tilt or Sag

When a step input v_i is applied to a high pass RC circuit , output V_0 exhibits a tilt in the low frequency part

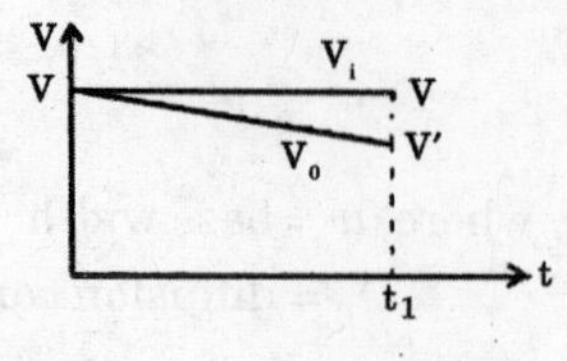

In time t_1 , percentage tilt or sag,

$$P = \frac{V - V'}{V} \times 100$$

$$= \frac{t_1}{R_1C_1} \times 100$$

This is also valid for tilt of each half cycle of a symmetrical square wave of peak to peak value of V and period T provided, $t_1 = \frac{T}{2}$.

If frequency of the square wave, $f = \frac{1}{T}$

then percent tilt, $P = \frac{T}{2R_1C_1} \times 100$

$$= \frac{1}{2fR_1C_1} \times 100 = \frac{\pi f_L}{f} \times 100$$

TYPES OF MULTISTAGE AMPLIFIERS.

1. Cascade Amplifier

Cascading is used to achieve proper amplification, in which two or three different CE stages are connected to achieve sufficient amplification.

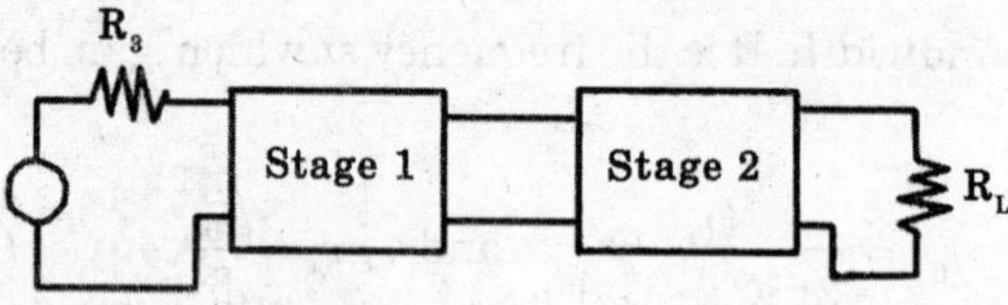

In cascade, overall voltage gain, $A_V = A_{V1} \times A_{V2}$

Let there are n single stages amplifier with lower cut off frequency f_L and higher cut off frequency f_H as shown.

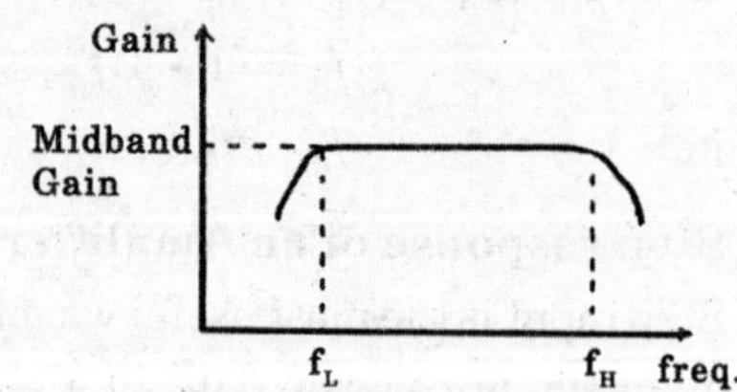

f_L is due to coupling or bypass capacitor and f_H is due to junction or parasitic capacitance.

For n such cascaded stages, overall frequency response

$$f_H^* = f_H \sqrt{2^{1/n} - 1}$$

and

$$f_L^* = \frac{f_L}{\sqrt{2^{1/n} - 1}}$$

Hence, increase in gain in multistage amplifier is at the cost of bandwidth.

For interacting stage, $\frac{1}{f_H} = 1.1\sqrt{\frac{1}{f_1^2} + \frac{1}{f_2^2} + ... + \frac{1}{f_n^2}}$

Step response.

Let rise time of isolated individual cascaded stages are, t_{r1}, t_{r2}, ... t_{rn} and input waveform rise time is t_{r0}.

$$\therefore \quad \text{Output signal rise time, } t_r = 1.1\sqrt{t_{r0}^2 + t_{r1}^2 + t_{r2}^2 + ... + t_{rn}^2}$$

If one circuit produces a tilt of P_1% and if second stage gives a tilt of P_2%, then effect of cascading a number of stages is

$$P = P_1 + P_2 + P_3 + ...$$

2. Cascode Amplifier

In a multistage amplifier if common emitter is a first stage and common base (or common collector) is a second stage, then connection is called *cascode connection*

It arrangement is designed to provide a high input impedance with low voltage gain.

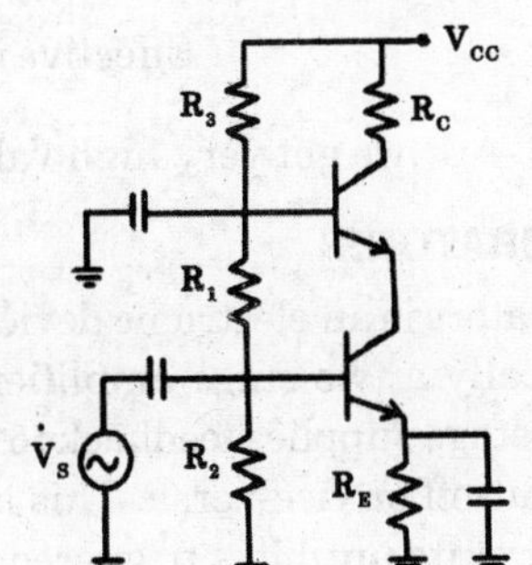

Cascode amplifier has:

(*i*) High input impedance (of CE)

(*ii*) Low output resistance (of CB)

(*iii*) Very good frequency response.

(*iv*) Reverse-open circuit voltage amplification,

$$h_r = h_{re} \times h_{rb} \cong 10^{-7}.$$

3. Darlington Pair

It is a cascade of two CC-CC configurations. Since emitter current of one transistor Q_1 is working as a base current of Q_2, hence quescent current of Q_1 is very smaller than Q_2.

In Darlington connection, composite transistor acts as a single unit with current gain proportional to the product of current gains of the individual transistors.

If transistors Q_1 and Q_2 have current gains of β_1 an β_2 respectively, then current gain of Darlington pair,

$$\beta_D = \beta_1\beta_2$$

Properties of Darlington pair

(*i*) Current gain is high.

(*ii*) Input resistance is very high.

(*iii*) Voltage gain is close to unity i.e. $A_V \cong 1$

(*iv*) Available in package form.

Drawback:

It has high leakage current and it is present because of the amplification of leakage current.

4. Bootstrapping

When darlington pair is used with biasing resistors, its input resistance decreases.

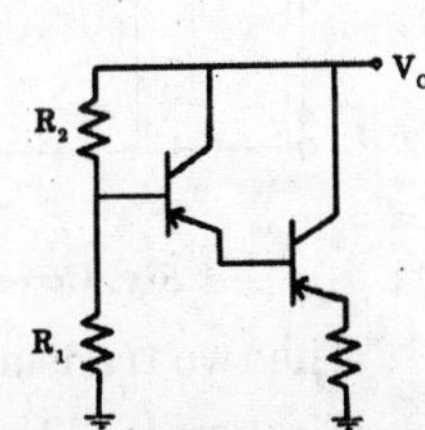

Input impedance becomes $\quad R_i' = R_i \parallel R_B$

where, $\quad R_B = R_1 \parallel R_2$ and $R_i = R_C(1+\beta)^2$

Generally $\quad R_i > R_B$ therefore, $R_i' \cong R_B$ which is low.

To overcome this biasing problem, Bootstrapping is used as shown in the figure below :

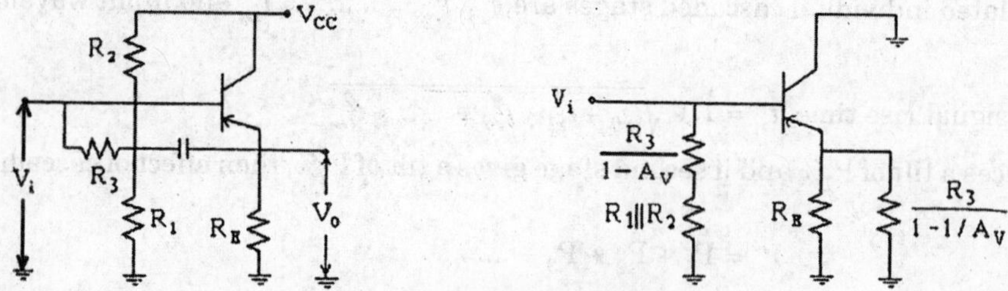

Here capacitor works as short circuit even for lowest frequency component of concern.

$$\text{Effective input impedance, } R_{eff} = \frac{R_3}{1-A_V}$$

When $A_V \to 1$,we get very high value of effective resistance.

MULTIVIBRATORS

Multivibrators is an electronic device that generates non-sinusoidal waves and behaves like a switching circuit. It is basically a two-stage amplifier with output of one supplied back to the input of another. In this, each amplifier stage supplies feedback to the other stage in such a way that one transistor is driven to saturation and other to cut-off or vice-versa. This is called *state of multivibrator.* Multivibrator may remain indefinitety in a particular state until it is triggered by same external signal is called *stable state.*

Uses.

(*i*) Generation of non-sinusoidal wave forms

(*ii*) Generation of pulses occuring periodically

(*iii*) Frequency division

(*iv*) Generation of time delays

(*v*) Storage of binary bit of information

Classification of Multivibrator

1. Astable Multivibrator

Each amplifier stage provides phase shift of 180° in the mid band so as to provide a total phase shift of 360° or 0°. It has no stable state. The two temporary states are called *quasi state.* It makes a successive transition from one quasi-state to another after a predetermined time interval, without aid of any external trigger signal. It generates a square wave of known periodic time, so it is called *free-running multivibrator*.

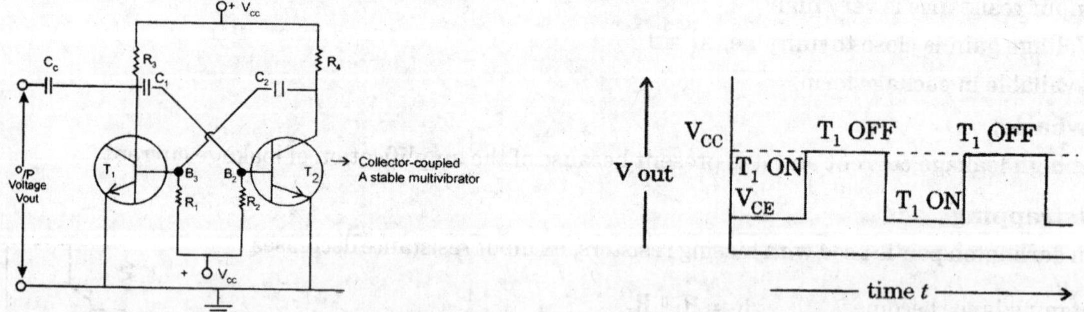

Fig. Circuit diagram of astable multivibrator *Fig. Astable multivibrator output*

The two transistor switches from one state to another with out an aid of external trigger, i.e.

First state : T_1 on and T_2 off

Second state : T_1 off and T_2 on

2. Monostable Multivibrator

It is also called a *single serving or delay multivibrator.* In this circuit, one coupling network provides ac-coupling while the other provides dc-coupling. It has one-stable state and one quasi stable state. A triggering signal is required to induce a transition from stable to quasi-stable state. The circuit remains in a quasi-state for a predetermined time after which it return back to its units at state with the requirement of external trigger.

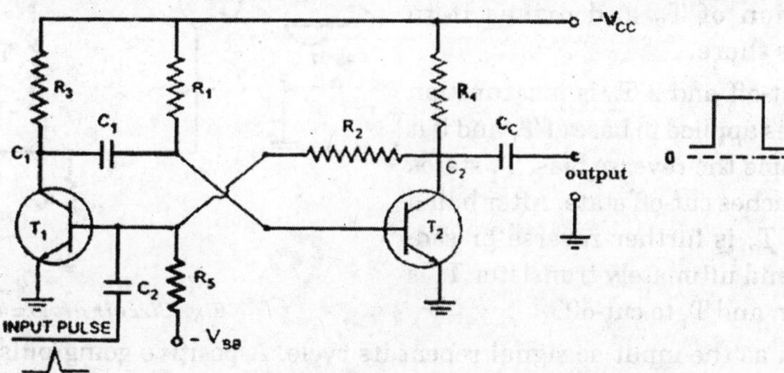

Fig. Circuit diagram of monostable multivibrator

3. Bistable Multivibrator

It has two stable state. It can stay in either of the two states indefinitely. Only an application of a suitable trigger pulse makes the circuit to change to the other stable state.

The triggering pulse causes the multivibrator to flip from one state to another and the next pulse causes it to flop back to its original state, hence it is called *flip-flop multivibrator.*

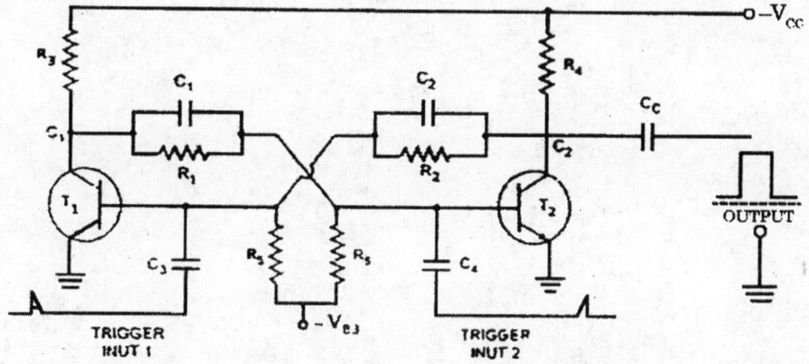

Fig. Circuit diagram of Bistable multivibrator

Schmitt trigger.

It is an important bistable multivibrator. The main difference between the two are :

(*i*) coupling from output terminal C_2 of transistor T_2 to input to T_1 is missing

(*ii*) feedback from T_2 to T_1 is achieved through R_E.

Using transistor it is an emitter-coupled binary oscillator. Schmitt trigger circuit is preferred when ever free base terminal is required.

Uses :

(*i*) As a squaring circuit because it can convert inputs of any shape into output pulses of rectangular or square wave shapes.

(*ii*) As an amplified comparator or level detector

(*iii*) As a flip-flop circuit

(*iv*) For reshaping the worn-out pulses by giving them sharp leading or trailing edges

Circuit operation :

When power supply is switched on, R_3, R_1 and R_2 across V_{CC} and $-V_{BB}$ forward biases T_2 and it starts conducting. T_1 is reverse biased due to flow of current. In R_E from T_2. Thus T_1 goes to cut-off. As a result potential of T_1 collector C_1 rises to V_{CC}. This positive going signal appears across emitter-base junction of T_2 and drives it to saturation and holds there.

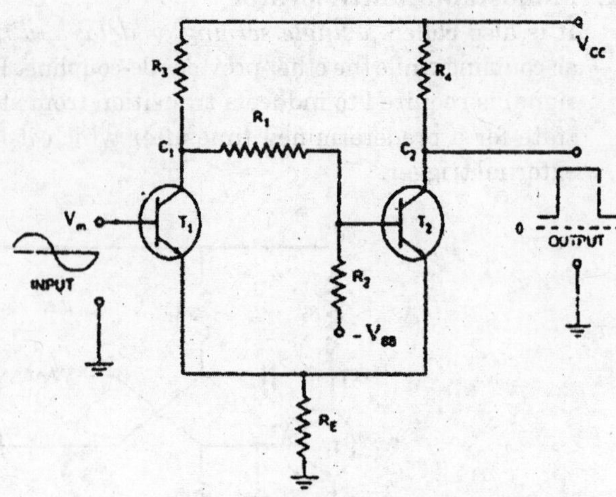

Fig. Circuit diagram of Schmitt Trigger

At this state T_1 is cut-off and 2 T_2 is insaturation when input ac signal is applied to base of T_1 and if it is sufficient to overcome the reverse bias, T_1 states conducting and T_2 reaches cut-off state. After half a cycle of input signal T_1 is further reverse biased. The process goes on and ultimately transistor T_2 is driven into saturation and T_1 to cut-off.

The cycle is repeated as the input ac signal repeat its cycle. A positive going pulse is generated at the output of schmitt trigger for each cycle.

The output pulse width depends upon the time duration for which T_2 conducts.

■■

Objective Type Questions

1. The piece-wire linear V-I characteristic of a diode is shown in the given figure. When the applied voltage is 6 V, the current through the diode will be

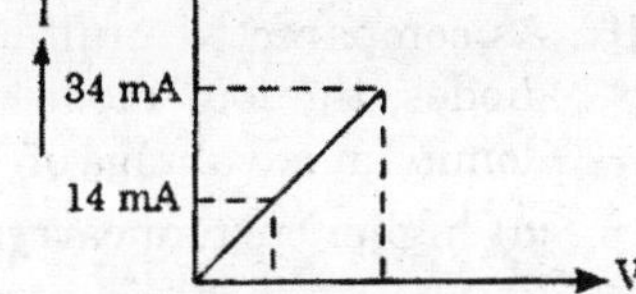

(*a*) 42 mA
(*b*) 48 mA
(*c*) 51 mA
(*d*) 54 mA

2. The circuit shown in the given figure is a

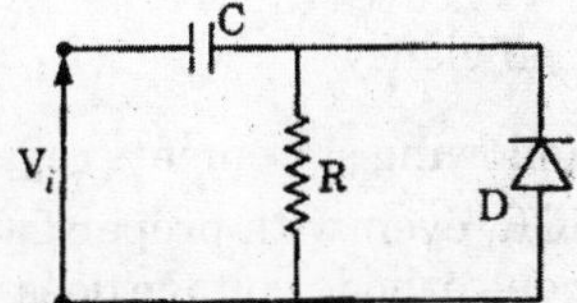

(*a*) positive clamper (*b*) negative clamper
(*c*) differentiator (*d*) positive peak clipper

3. For the circuit given in figure I assuming ideal diode, the output waveform v_0 is

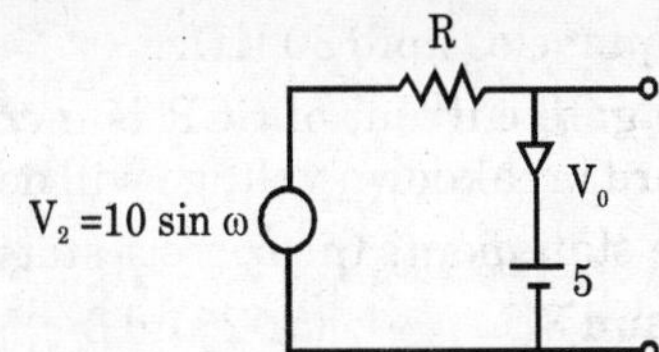

(*a*) 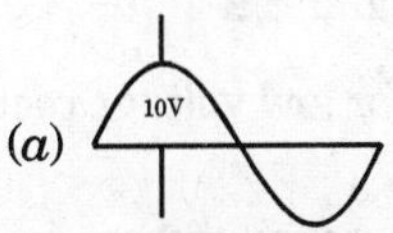

(*b*) 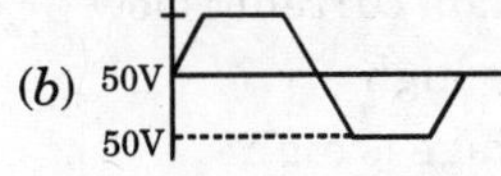

(*c*) 

(*d*) 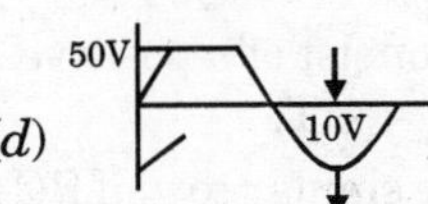

4. The depletion capacitance, C_p of an abrupt P-N junction with constant doping on either side varies with reverse bias, V_R' as

(*a*) $C_J \propto V_R$
(*b*) $C_J \propto V_R^{-1}$
(*c*) $C_J \propto V_R^{-1/2}$
(*d*) $C_J \propto V_R^{-1/3}$

5. If the input ac is 10 V rms, the maximum voltage that will appear across the diode of a half-wave rectifier with a capacitor input filter will be

(*a*) 10 V (*b*) 14 V
(*c*) 20 V (*d*) 28 V

6. In order to rectify sinusoidal signals of millivolt range (< 0.6 V)

(*a*) bridge rectifier diodes can be employed
(*b*) full-wave diode rectifier can be used
(*c*) a diode is to be inserted in the feedback loop of an OP-AMP
(*d*) a diode is to be inserted in the input of an OP-AMP

7. In switching devices, gold doping is used to

(*a*) improve bonding
(*b*) reduce storage time
(*c*) increase the mobility of carrier
(*d*) protect the terminals against corrosion

8. For an input of $V_S = 5 \sin \omega t$ (assuming ideal diode), circuit shown in the figure will behave as a

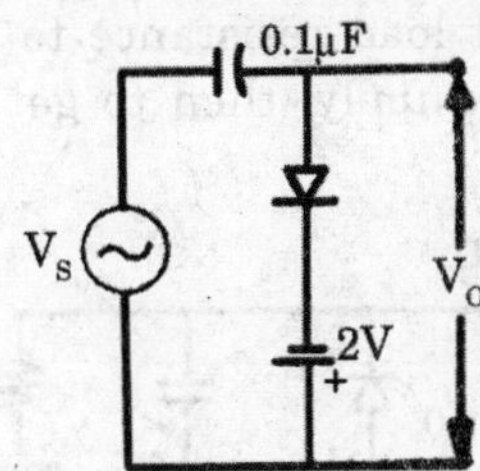

(*a*) clipper, sine wave clipped at –2 V
(*b*) clamper, sine wave clamped at –2 V
(*c*) clamper, sine wave clamped at zero volt
(*d*) clipper, sine wave clipped at 2 V

9. A three-terminal monolithic IC regulator can be used as a/an

(*a*) adjustable output voltage regulator alone
(*b*) adjustable output voltage regulator and a current regulator
(*c*) current regulator and a power switch
(*d*) current regulator alone

10. Which one of the following devices is NOT used as the controller in a stabilizer?

(*a*) Diac (*b*) Triac
(*c*) SCR (*d*) Power transistor

11. A p-n junction diode's dynamic conductance is directly proportional to

(*a*) the applied voltage

(*b*) the temperature

(*c*) its current

(*d*) the thermal voltage

12. Consider the following statement in relation to a large value of capacitor filter used in a full-wave rectifier:

It gives the

1. low conduction period for the diode rectifier
2. increased peak current rating of the diode
3. large peak inverse voltage rating of the diode

Which of these statements are correct?

(*a*) 1, 2 and 3 (*b*) 2 and 3

(*c*) 1 and 2 (*d*) 1 and 3

13. The input voltage of Zener regulator varies from 20 V to 30 V. The load current varies from 10 mA to 15 mA. If Zener voltage is 5 V, then value of series resistor will be

(*a*) 1 kΩ (*b*) 1.5 kΩ

(*c*) 1.66 kΩ (*d*) 2.5 kΩ

14. Zener diode in the circuit shown in the Fig. I has the characteristics shown in Fig. II. If R_2 is the lowest load resistance to be used in the regulated supply, then to get regulation, R_1 must be

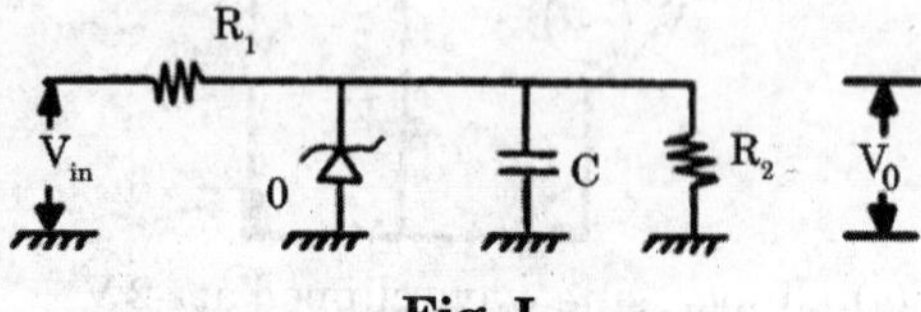

Fig. I

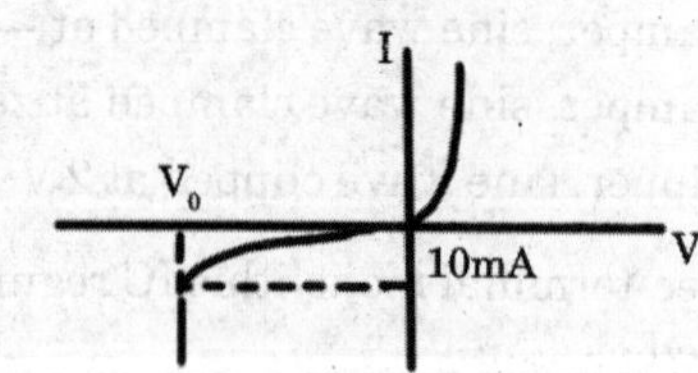

Fig. II

(*a*) greater than $\frac{V_0 + 0.01R_2}{(V_{in} - V_0)R_2}$

(*b*) greater than $\frac{(V_{in} - V_0)R_2}{V_0 + 0.01R_2}$

(*c*) less than $\frac{(V_{in} - V_0)R_2}{V_0 + 0.01R_2}$

(*d*) less than $\frac{V_0 + 0.01R_2}{(V_{in} - V_0)R_2}$

15. If V_m is the peak value of an applied voltage in a half-wave with a large capacitor across the load, then the peak inverse voltage will be

(*a*) $\frac{V_m}{2}$ (*b*) V_m

(*c*) $\sqrt{2}\, V_m$ (*d*) $2\, V_m$

16. As compared to a full-wave rectifier using the diodes, the four diode bridge rectifier has the dominant advantage of

(*a*) higher current carrying

(*b*) blower peak increase voltage requirement

(*c*) lower ripple factor

(*d*) higher efficiency

17. Consider following statements regarding SCR :

1. If the SCR, even with proper gate excitation and anode-cathode voltage does not conduct for a particular load resistance, then it would be necessary to decrease the load resistance to turn ON the SER.
2. The SCR would be turned OFF by voltage reversal of the applied anode-cathode *ac* supply of frequencies upto 30 KHz.
3. If the gate current of SCR is increased, the forward breakdown voltage will decrease.

Of these statements the correct statements are

(*a*) 1, 2 and 3 (*b*) 2 and 3

(*c*) 1 and 3 (*d*) 1 and 2

18. Silicon diode is less suited for low voltage rectifier operation because

(*a*) it can withstand high temperatures

(*b*) its reverse saturation current is low

(*c*) its cut-in voltage is high

(*d*) its breakdown voltage is high

19. For the circuit given in the figure, consider the following statements:

1. The output V_o will consist of a positive and a negative spike if RC << T.
2. The output V_o will be similar to v_1 if RC >> T.
3. The output will have a higher rise time if RC is made progressively smaller than T.

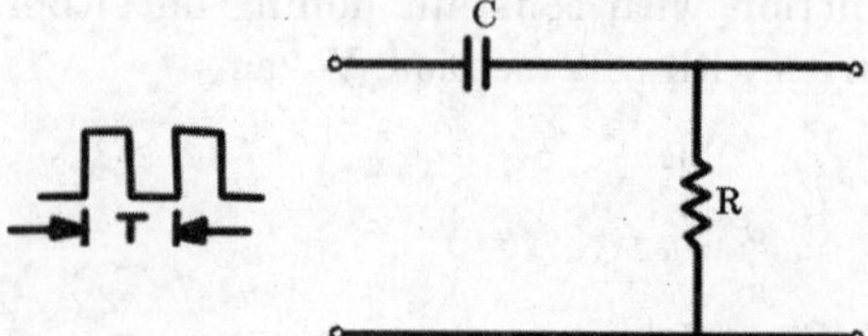

Of these statements, the correct statements are

(*a*) 1, 2 and 3 (*b*) 1 and 2

(*c*) 2 and 3 (*d*) 1 and 3

20. Schottky diodes, also called hot carrier diodes, are used in wave shaping circuits because

(*a*) they have a small recovery time

(*b*) they have a large reverse resistance

(*c*) they have a large forward current

(*d*) their peak inverse voltage is small

21. Consider the following statements regarding the circuit given in the figure, where the output voltage is constant:

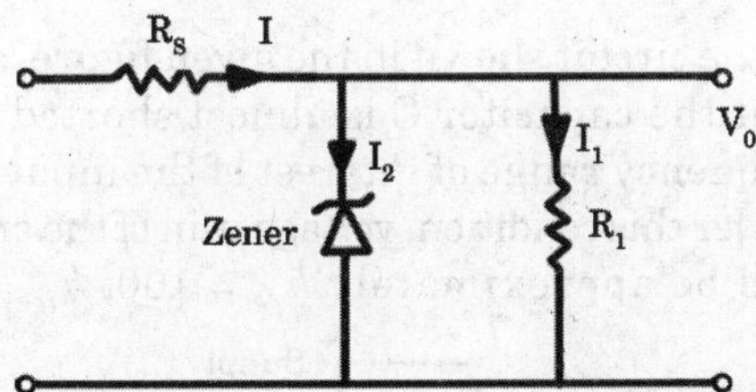

1. V_{in} > voltage at which the zener breaks down
2. I_L < difference between I and I_Z the current at which the zener breaks down
3. R_S < zener nominal resistance

Of these statements, the correct statements are

(*a*) 1, 2 and 3

(*b*) 1 and 2

(*c*) 2 and 3

(*d*) 1 and 3

22. The ideal characteristic of a stabilizer is constant

(*a*) output voltage with low internal resistance

(*b*) output current with low internal resistance

(*c*) output voltage with high internal resistance

(*d*) internal resistance with variable output voltage

23. Consider the following statements:

Thyristors can be turned off by

1. reducing the current below the holding current value.
2. applying a negative voltage to the anode of the device.
3. reducing the gate current.

Of these statements, the correct statements are

(*a*) 1 and 2

(*b*) 1 and 3

(*c*) 2 and 3

(*d*) 1, 2 and 3

24. Consider the following statements:

A power supply uses bridge rectifier with capacitor input filter. If one of the diode is defective, then

1. dc voltage will be lower than its expected value
2. ripple frequency will be lower than the expected value
3. surge current will increase manifold.

Of these statements, the correct statements are

(*a*) 1 and 2 (*b*) 1 and 3

(*c*) 2 and 3 (*d*) 1, 2 and 3

25. The snubber circuit for an S.C.R. is required as a protection against breakdown due to

(*a*) low voltage

(*b*) high voltage

(*c*) rate of change of applied forward voltage

(*d*) rate of change of current

26. The function of a bleeder resistor in a rectifier with LC filter is to

(*a*) maintain the minimum current through C

(*b*) maintain the minimum current is necessary for optimum inductor operation

(*c*) maintain maximum current through L

(*d*) charge the capacitor C to maximum value

27. A 24 V, 600 mW Zener diode is to be used for providing a 24 V stabilized supply to a variable load. Assume that for proper Zener action, a minimum of 10 mA must flow through the Zener. If the input voltage is 32 V, then value of R and the maximum load current respectively will be

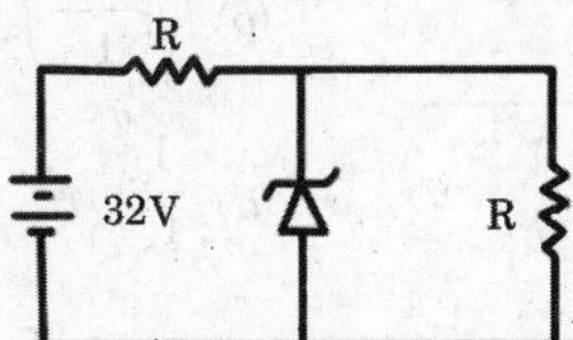

(*a*) 30 Ω, 10 mA (*b*) 400 Ω, 15 mA

(*c*) 400 Ω, 10 mA (*d*) 320 Ω, 15 mA

28. Consider the following statements:

A clamper circuit

1. adds or subtracts a dc voltage to or from a waveform.
2. does not change the shape of the waveform.
3. amplifies the waveform.

Of these statements, the correct statements are

(*a*) 1 and 2 (*b*) 1 and 3

(*c*) 2 and 3 (*d*) 1, 2 and 3

29. Consider the following statements :
Monolithic regulators can be used to
1. realize a constant voltage regulator
2. realize a constant current regulator
3. introduce flexibility in setting output voltage level.
Of these statements, the correct statements are
(a) 1 and 2 (b) 1 and 3
(c) 2 and 3 (d) 1, 2 and 3

30. In the circuit shown in the figure, if $e_1 = 2$ V, $e_2 = 5$ V, $e_3 = 1$V and E = 2V, then which one of the diodes will be conducting and what will be the e_0?

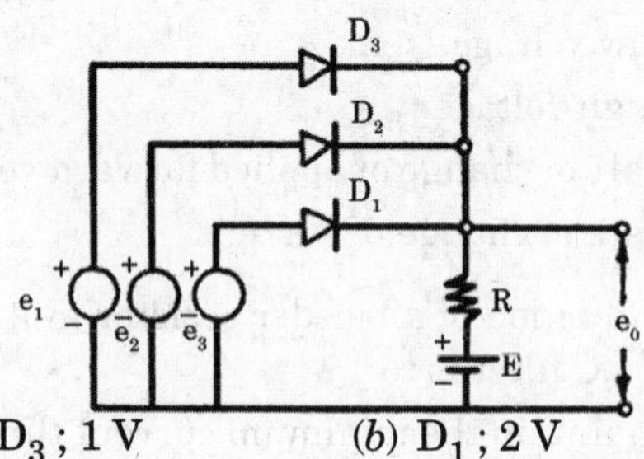

(a) D_3 ; 1 V (b) D_1 ; 2 V
(c) D_2 ; 5 V (d) D_1 ; 5 V

31. In an LC filter, the ripple factor
(a) increases with the load current
(b) increases with the load resistance
(c) remains constant with the load current
(d) has the lowest value

32. The ripple factor of a power supply is given by (symbols have the usual meaning)
(a) $\frac{P_{dc}}{P_{ac}}$ (b) $\sqrt{\left(\frac{I_{rms}}{I_{dc}}\right)^2 - 1}$
(c) $\sqrt{\left(\frac{I_{dc}}{I_{rms}}\right)^2 - 1}$ (d) $\frac{I_{dc}}{I_{rms}}$

33. A dc-to-dc converter having an efficiency of 80% delivering 16 W to a load. If the converter is generating an output of 200 V from an input of 20 V, then the current drawn from the source will be
(a) 0.1 A (b) 0.5 A
(c) 1.0 A (d) 10.0 A

34. SCR turns OFF from conducting state to blocking state on
(a) reducing gate current
(b) reversing gate voltage
(c) reducing anode current below holding current value
(d) applying ac to the gate

35. In an integrated circuit, the SiO_2 layer provides
(a) electrical connection to external circuit
(b) physical strength
(c) isolation
(d) conducting path

36. AE 139 is a
(a) tunnel diode
(b) germanium power transistor
(c) photoconductive cell
(d) silicon diode

37. In the circuit shown in the given figure, assume that the capacitor C is almost shorted for the frequency range of interest of the input signal. Under this condition, voltage gain of the amplifier will be approximately $h_{fe} = 100$, $h_{ie} = 1$k

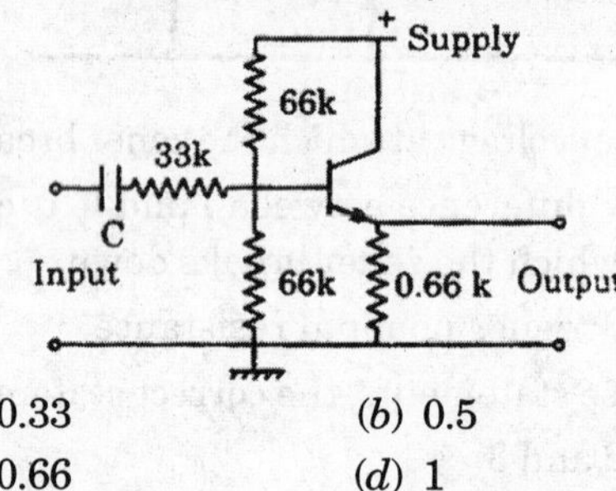

(a) 0.33 (b) 0.5
(c) 0.66 (d) 1

38. What should be the collector-emitter breakdown voltage, BV_{CEO} of the transistors used in the circuit shown in the given figure?

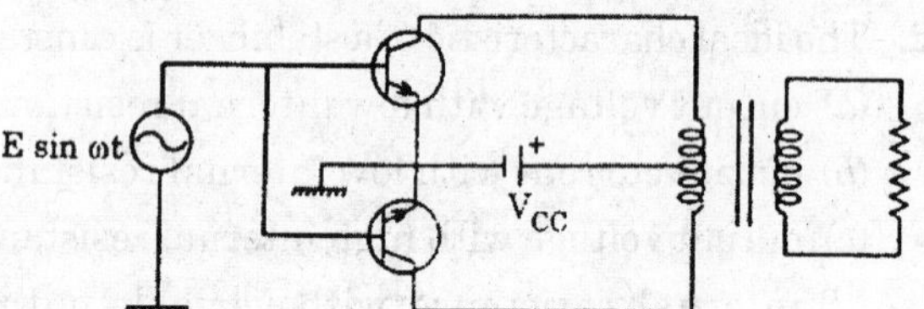

(a) $BV_{CEO} \geq V_{cc}$ (b) $BV_{CEO} \geq \frac{V_{cc}}{2}$
(c) $BV_{CEO} \geq 2V_{cc}$ (d) $BV_{CEO} \geq (V_{cc} + E)$

39. For the circuit shown in given figure, the quiescent point is

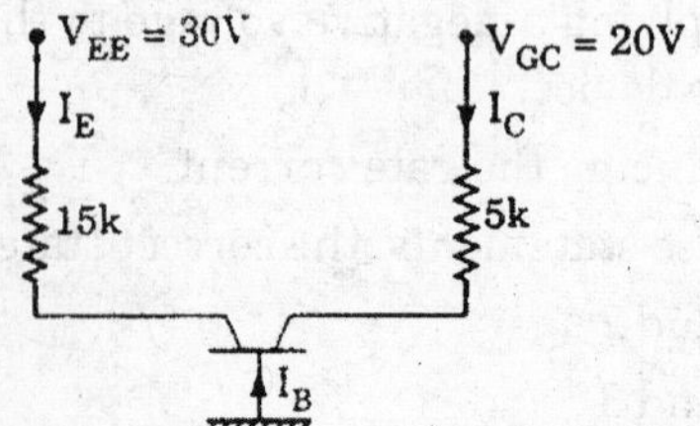

(a) 12 V, 5 mA (b) 12 V, 2 mA
(c) 10 V, 2 mA (d) 10 V, 5 mA

40. When a square wave pulse is fed to the input of the circuit shown in the given figure, then V_C the voltage across C will have the waveform

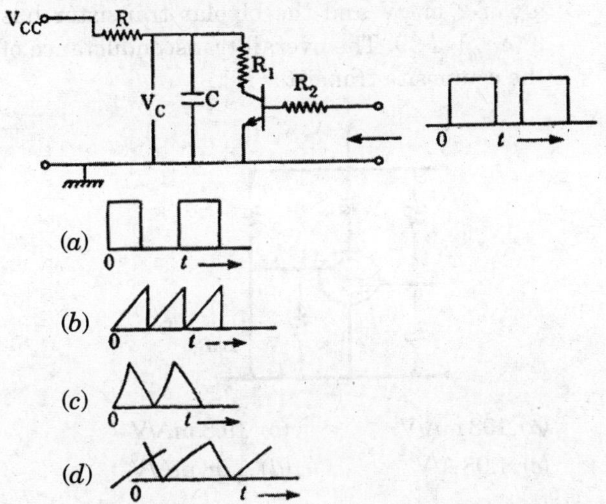

41. Which one of the following biasing will give the best performance in preventing the variation of collector current against change in ambient temperature?

(a)

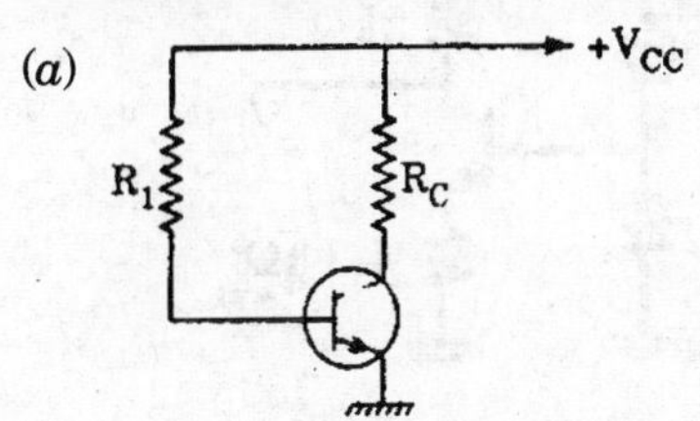

(b)

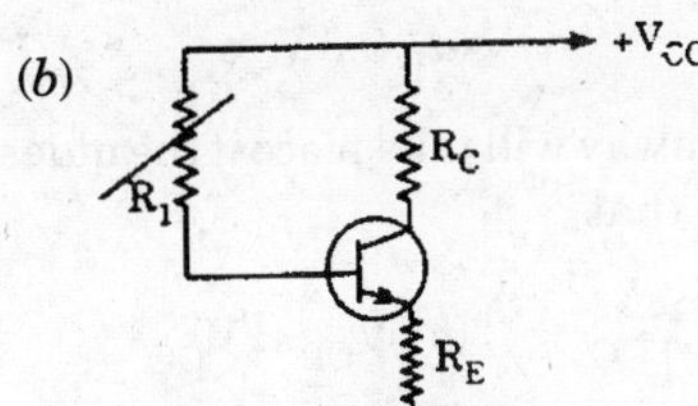

(c)

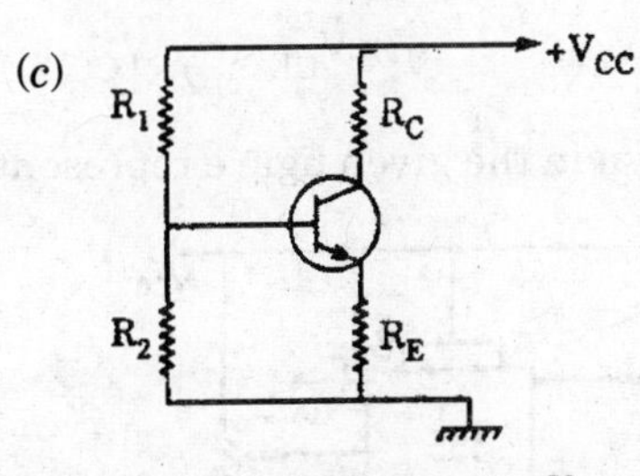

(d)

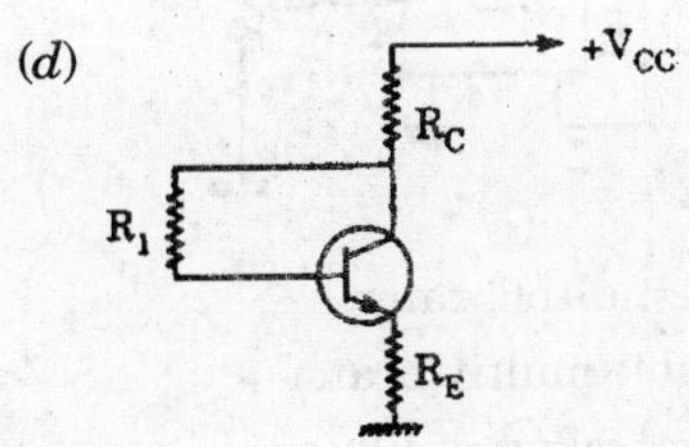

42. Consider the following circuit:

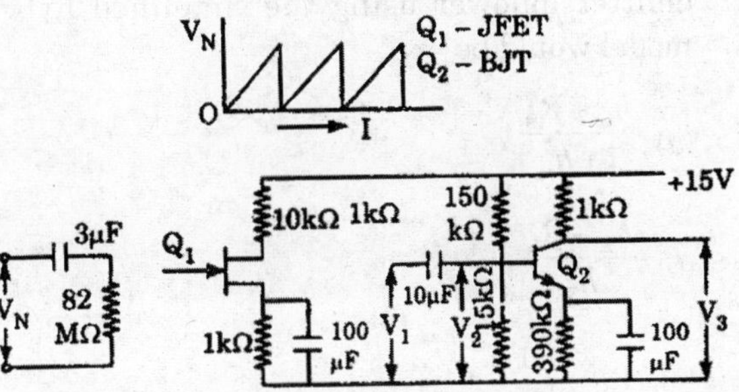

For the given input shown in the figure, which of the following pair(s) of voltage and output waveform is/are correctly matched?

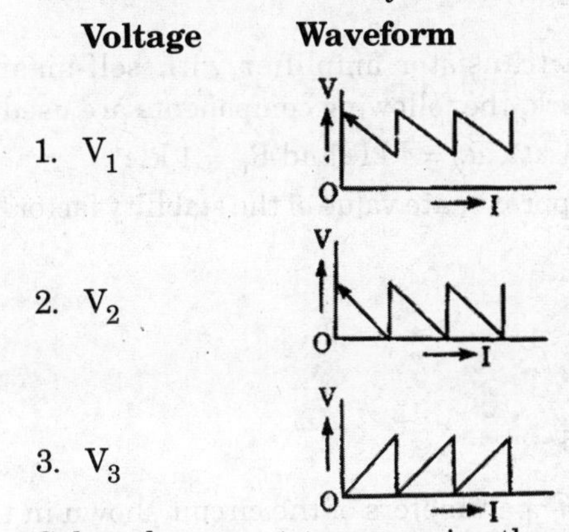

Voltage	Waveform
1. V_1	
2. V_2	
3. V_3	

Select the correct answer using the codes given below:

Codes:

(a) 2 and 3 (b) 1 and 3

(c) 1 alone (d) 1 and 3

43. In a transistor amplifier Z_{CQ} = 5A and ac collector current of 1 mA peak flows into a load of 1 kΩ. The ac power delivered to the load is

(a) 0.5 mW (b) 1 mW

(c) 6.25 mW (d) 25 mW

44. Consider the following statements:

In a series transistor regulator the regulation factor and output resistance can be improved by

1. increasing h_{fe} of the series transistor.
2. increasing h_{fe} of the shunt transistor.
3. increasing the external resistance R connected between the collector and base of the series transistor.

Of these statements, the correct statements are

(a) 1 and 2

(b) 2 and 3

(c) 1 and 3

(d) 1, 2 and 3

45. If R_S is the source resistance, the output of an emitter follower using the simplified hybrid model would be

(a) $\frac{h_{ie} + R_S}{1 + h_{fe}}$

(b) $\frac{h_{ie} + R_S}{h_{fe}}$

(c) $R_S + \frac{1}{h_{oe}}$

(d) $\frac{1}{h_{oe}}$

46. For a transistor amplifier with self-biasing network, the following components are used: $R_1 = 4\ k\Omega$, $R_2 = 4\ k\Omega$ and $R_C = 1\ k\Omega$
The approximate value of the stability factor "S" will be

(a) 4

(b) 3

(c) 2

(d) 1.5

47. The "h" parameters of the circuit shown in the figure are :
$h_{ib} = 25\ \Omega$; $h_{fb} = 0.999$ and $h_{ob} = 10^{-6}\ \Omega$.
The voltage gain is

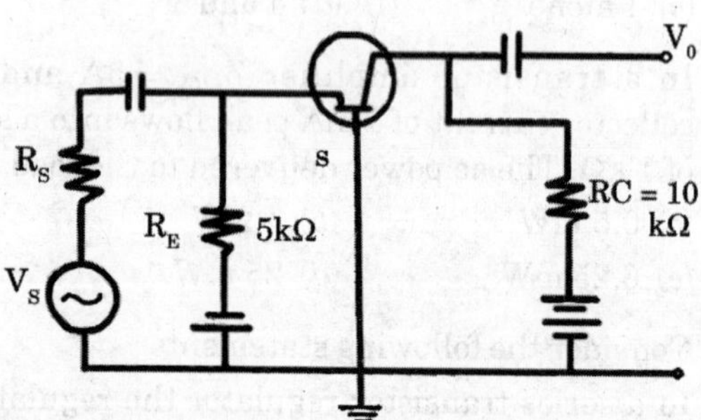

(a) 0.999 (b) 1.98

(c) 2.0 (d) 400

48. The dissipation at the collector is zero in the quiescent state and increases with excitation in the case of a

(a) Class A series - fed amplifier

(b) Class A transistor coupled amplifier

(c) Class AB amplifier

(d) Class B amplifier

49. The given figure shows a composite transistor consisting of a MOSFET and a bipolar transistor in cascode. The MOSFET has a transconductance g_m of 2 mA/V and the bipolar transistor has β (Δh_{fe}) of 99. The overall transconductance of the composite transistor is

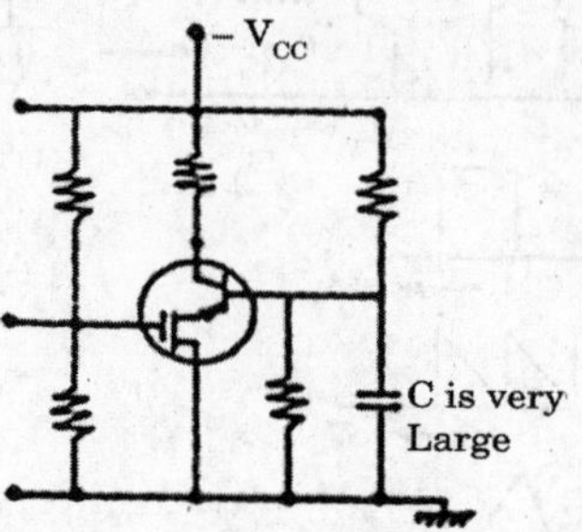

(a) 198 mA/V (b) 19.8 mA/V

(c) 1.98 A/V (d) 1.98 mA/V

50. The collector voltage, V_C of the circuit shown in the given figure is approximately

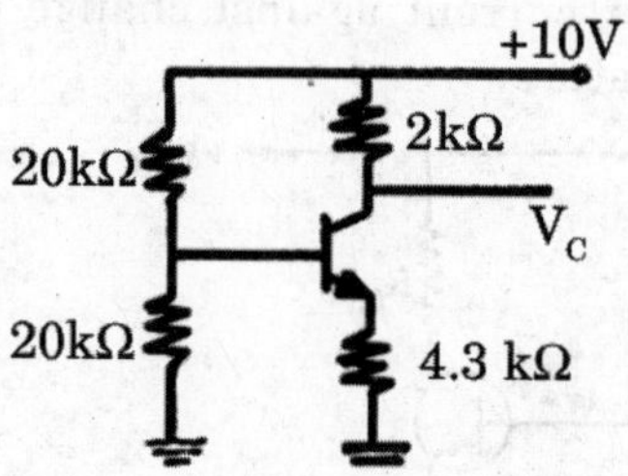

(a) 2 V (b) 4.6 V

(c) 8 V (d) 8.6 V

51. Thermal runaway will take place if the quiescent point is such that

(a) $V_{CE} > \frac{1}{2} V_{CC}$ (b) $V_{CE} < V_{CC}$

(c) $V_{CE} > 2\ V_{CC}$ (d) $V_{CE} < \frac{1}{2} V_{CC}$

52. Circuit shown in the given figure represents

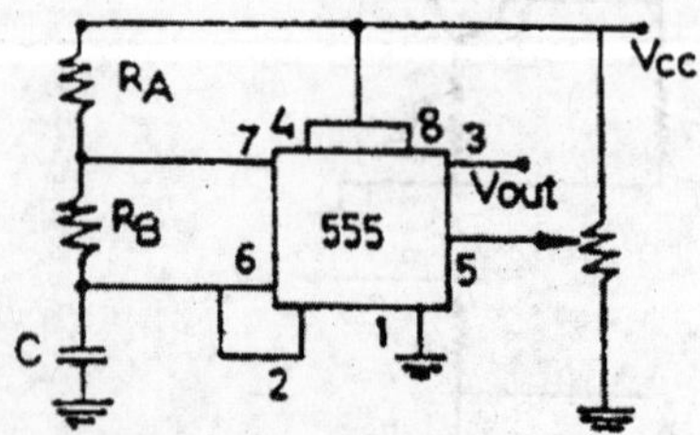

(a) an astable multivibrator

(b) a monostable multivibrator

(c) voltage controlled oscillator

(d) ramp generator

53. In the case of the circuit shown in the figure, the collector current I_C will be

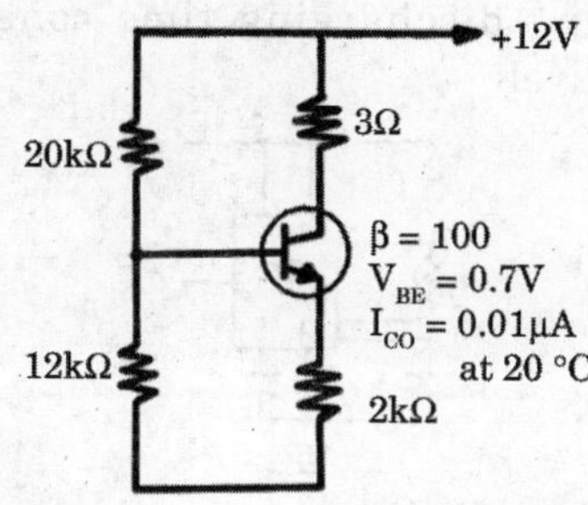

(a) 2.24 mA (b) 1.85 mA
(c) 0.375 mA (d) 0.185 mA

54. A transistor emitter base voltage (V_{EB}) of 20 m V has a collector current (I_C) of 5 mA. For V_{EB} of 30 mV, I_C is 30 mA. If V_{EB} is 40 mV, then the I_C will be

(a) 55 mA (b) 160 mA
(c) 180 mA (d) 270 mA

55. In a junction transistor, the collector cut-off current 'I_{CBO}' reduces considerably by doping the

(a) emitter with high level of impurity
(b) emitter with low level of impurity
(c) collector with high level of impurity
(d) collector with low level of impurity

56. In a junction transistor biased for operation at emitter current 'I_E' and collector current 'I_C', the transconductance 'g_m' is

(a) $\frac{KT}{qI_E}$ (b) $\frac{qI_E}{KT}$

(c) $\frac{I_C}{I_E}$ (d) $\frac{I_E}{I_C}$

57. An amplifier using BJT has two identical stages each having a lower cut-off (3 dB) frequency of 64 Hz due to coupling capacitor. The emitter bypass capacitor also provides a lower cut-off (3 dB) frequency due to emitter degeneration alone of 64 Hz. The lower (3 dB) frequency of the overall amplifier is nearly

(a) 100 Hz (b) 128 Hz
(c) 156 Hz (d) 244 Hz

58. Which one of the following sets of the circuits can be obtained by using a 555 timer?

(a) Pulse modulator and amplitude demodulator
(b) Plus modulator and astable multivibrator
(c) Amplifier demodulator and a.c. to d.c. converter
(d) a.c. to d.c. converter and astable ultivibrator

59. A wide pulse is given as input to the monostable multi-vibrator shown in figure. The collector outputs of Q_1 and Q_2 will be pulses duration

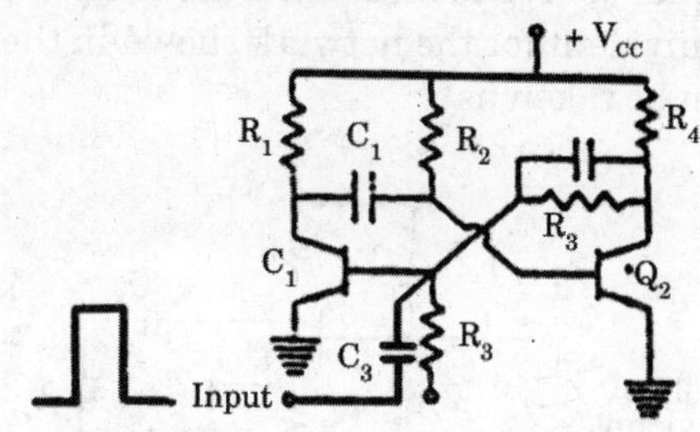

(a) $0.69\,R_1C_1$
(b) $0.69\,R_2C_1$
(c) $0.69\,R_3C_2$
(d) $0.69\,R_5C_3$

60. Which of the following circuits realizes self-bias with compensation?

1.
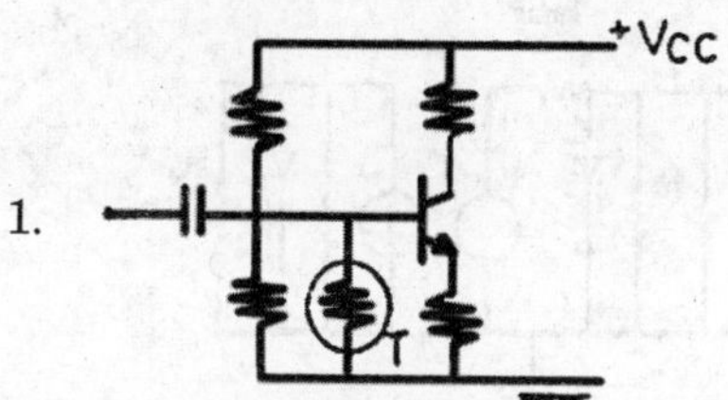

2.
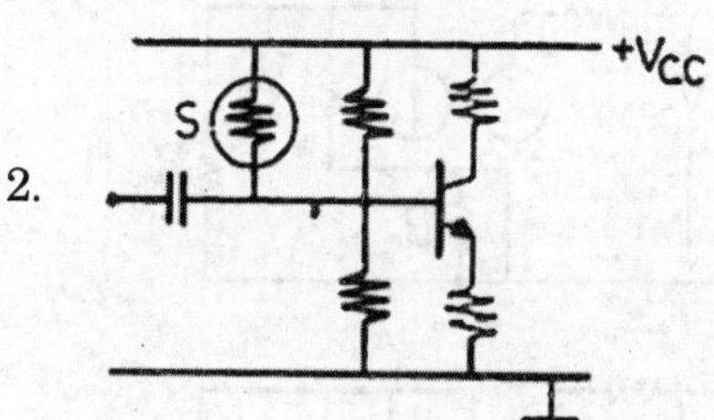

3.
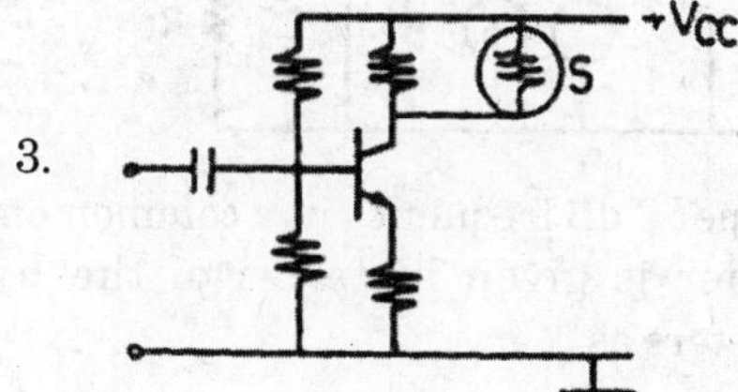

T = Thermistor; S = Sensistor.

Select the correct answer using the code given below:

Codes:

(a) 2 and 3
(b) 1 and 2
(c) 1 and 3
(d) 1, 2 and 3

61. If the values of C_1, C_2 and C_3 are so large that they behave as short circuits at the signal frequency and if the internal impedance of the signal source is zero, then the small signal ac equivalent for the network shown in the figure can be taken as

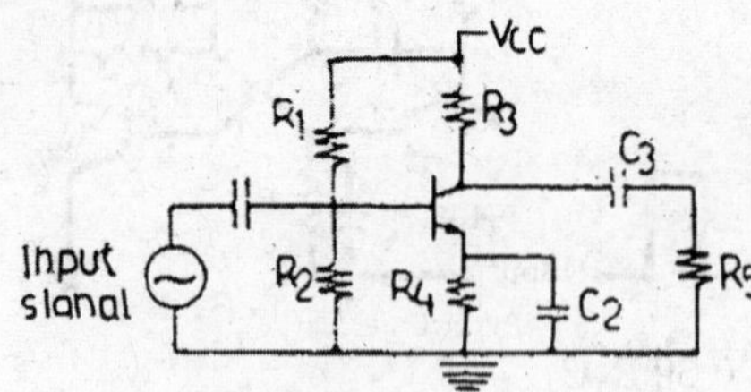

(a) 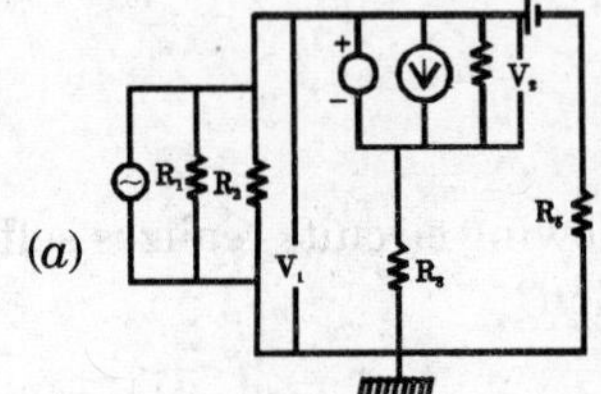

(b) 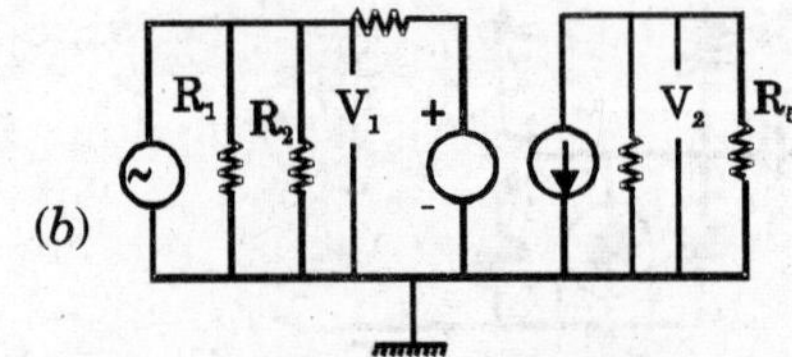

(c) 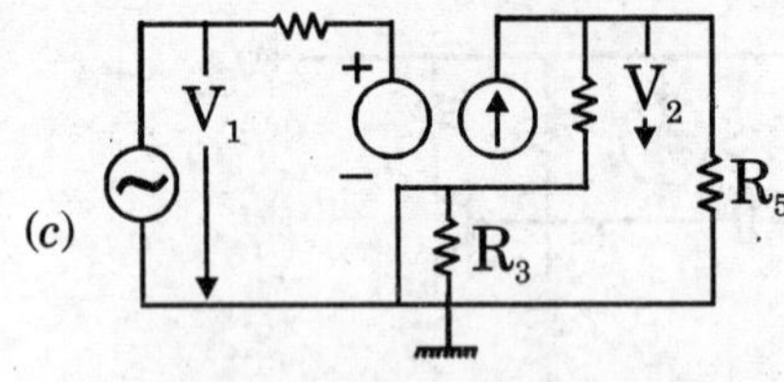

(d) 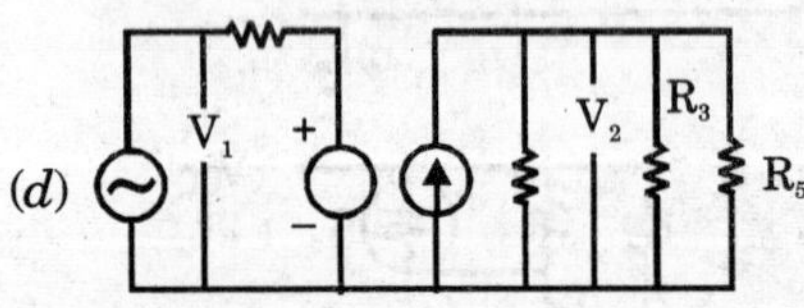

62. The upper 3 dB frequency in a common emitter amplifier is given in terms of the hybrid parameters as

(a) $\frac{gb'e}{2\pi C}$

(b) $\frac{gb'e}{C}$

(c) $\frac{h_{fe}}{gb'e}$

(d) $\frac{gm}{h_{fe}}$

63. The given figure shown the application of 555 timer circuit as an astable multivibrator. The charging discharging time constants are respectively

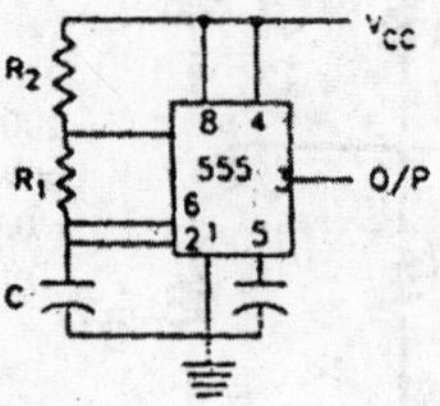

(a) R_1C and R_2C
(b) R_1C and $(R_1 + R_2)C$
(c) $(R_1C + R_2)C$ and R_1C
(d) R_2C and R_1C

64. If $\alpha = 0.995$, $I_E = 10$ mA and $I_{CO} = 0.5$ μA, then I_{CEO} will be

(a) 100 μA (b) 25 μA
(c) 10.1 mA (d) 10.5 mA

65. The approximate value of input impedance of a common emitter amplifier with emitter resistance R_e is given by

(a) $h_{ie} + A_iR_e$ (b) $h_{ie} + (1 + h_{fe})R_e$
(c) h_{ie} (d) $(1 + h_{fe})R_e$

66. Consider the following statements:
The 555 timer can be employed in
1. a monostable multivibrator
2. a bistable multivibrator
3. an stable multivibrator.
Of these statements, the correct answers are

(a) 1 and 2 (b) 1 and 3
(c) 2 and 3 (d) 1, 2 and 3

67. The circuit shown in the given figure is a

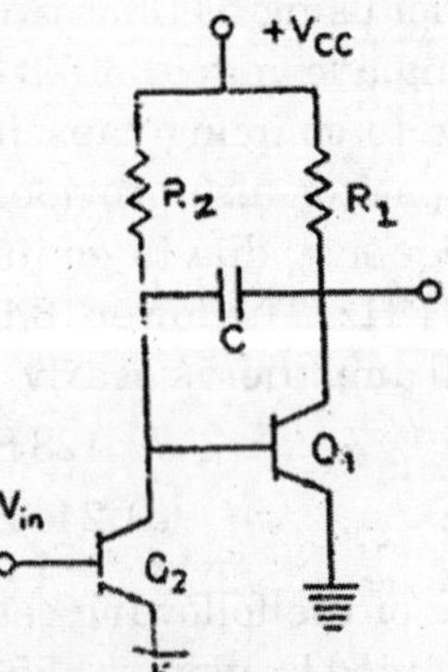

(a) monostable multivibrator
(b) frequency division circuit
(c) miller sweep circuit
(d) bootstrap sweep circuit

68. In a transistor amplifier, the reverse saturation current I_{CO}

(*a*) doubles for every 10°C rise in temperature

(*b*) doubles for every 1°C rise in temperature

(*c*) increases linearly with temperature

(*d*) doubles for every 5°C rise in temperature

69. In the circuit shown in the given figure, the approximate voltages at the transistor

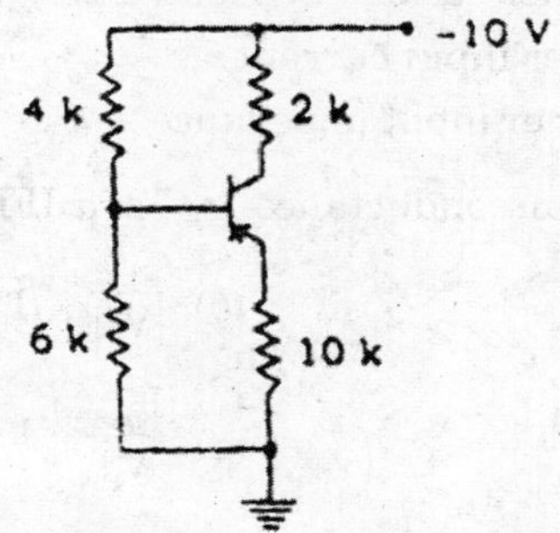

(*a*) base and emitter respectively are – 8 V and – 7.3 V

(*b*) base and collector respectively are – 8 V and – 5 V

(*c*) collector and emitter respectively are – 5 V and – 7.3 V

(*d*) base, emitter and collector respectively are –8 V, – 7.3 V and – 5 V

70. Consider the following statements:

The lower cut-off frequencies for an RC coupled CE amplifier depend on

1. input and output coupling capacitors
2. emitter bypass capacitors
3. junction capacitors

Of these statements, correct statements(s) is/are

(*a*) 1 alone (*b*) 2 alone

(*c*) 1 and 2 (*d*) 2 and 3

71. Consider the following statements:

Sziklai pair

1. is also called complementary Darlington
2. acts like single p-n-p transistor with a very high current gain
3. can be used in class B push-pull power amplifier

Of these statements, correct statements are

(*a*) 1 and 2

(*b*) 1 and 3

(*c*) 2 and 3

(*d*) 1, 2 and 3

72. If a common emitter amplifier with an emitter resistance R_e has an overall transconductance gain of 1 mA/V, a voltage gain of –4 and desensitivity of 50, then value of emitter resistance R_e would be

(*a*) 50 kΩ (*b*) 0.98 kΩ

(*c*) 50 Ω (*d*) 0.98 Ω

73. A common emitter amplifier circuit is shown in the given figure. The slope of a.c. load line is

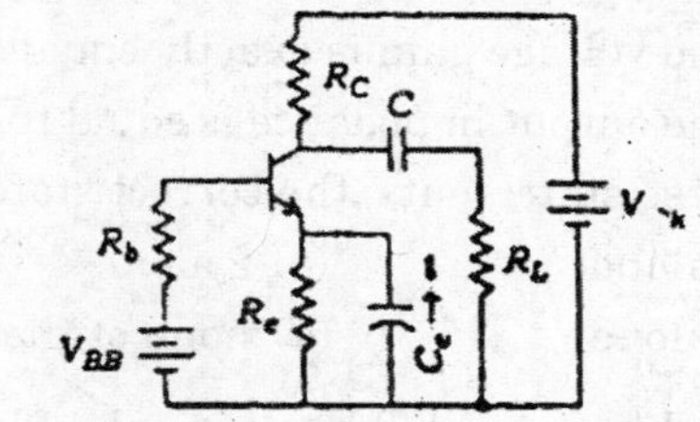

(*a*) $-\left(\frac{1}{R_L}+\frac{1}{R_C}\right)$ (*b*) $-\left(\frac{1}{R_L+R_C}\right)$

(*c*) $-\frac{1}{R_L}$ (*d*) $-\frac{1}{R_C}$

74. An amplifier circuit is shown in the given figure. The voltage gain (V_0/V_s) is

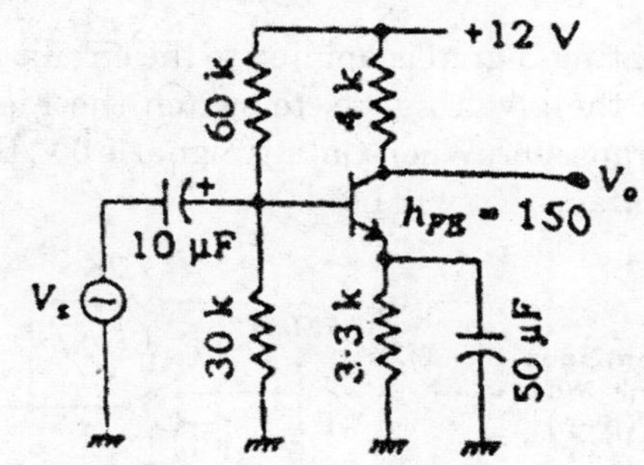

(*a*) $\frac{4}{3.3}$ (*b*) 100

(*c*) 150 (*d*) 160

75. Consider the following statements:

A totem pole configuration used in the output stage of an op-amp has the advantage *of using*

1. only *n-p-n* BJTs
2. complementry symmetrical pair of transistors
3. only one transistor

Of these statements, correct statement(s) is/are

(*a*) 1 alone

(*b*) 2 alone

(*c*) 3 alone

(*d*) 1 and 3

76. A 1 ms plus can be stretched to 1 s plus by using
(*a*) an astable multivibrator
(*b*) a monostable multivibrator
(*c*) a bistable multivibrator
(*d*) a Schmitt trigger circuit

77. Consider the following statements regarding the bootstrap biasing arrangement for a BJT emitter follower:
1. The input impedance is very high.
2. The voltage gain is exactly equal to one.
3. The output impedance is equal to zero.

Of these statements, the correct statements is
(*a*) 1 alone (*b*) 2 alone
(*c*) 3 alone (*d*) none of these

78. An n-channel JFET has a pinch-off voltage of $V_p = -5V$, $V_{DS}(max) = 20V$, and $\delta_m = 2m$ A/V. The minimum 'ON' resistance is achieved in the JEFT for
(*a*) $V_{GS} = -7V$ and $V_{DS} = 0$ V
(*b*) $V_{GS} = 7$ and $V_{DS} = 0$ V
(*c*) $V_{GS} = 0$ V and $V_{DS} = 20$ V
(*d*) $V_{GS} = -7V$ and $V_{DS} = 20$ V

79. Gating Signal is applied to the circuit as shown in the given figure, to switch the Field Effect Transistor. When Gating Signal is 0 V, the output voltage (V_o) will be

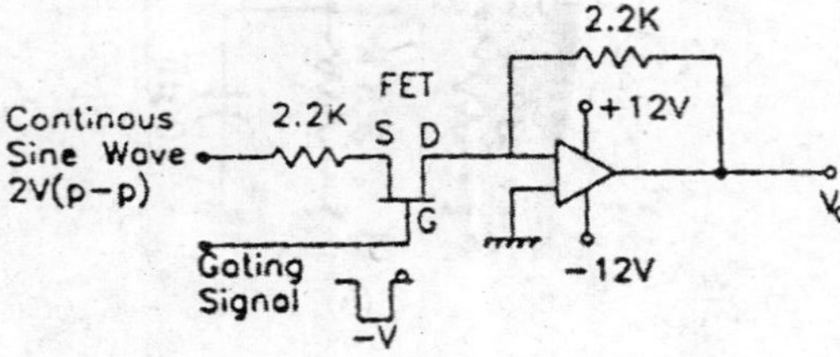

(*a*) zero
(*b*) sine wave 2 V (*p* – *p*)
(*c*) 2 V dc
(*d*) ± 12 V

80. In the biased JFET, shape of the channel is as shown in the given figure because

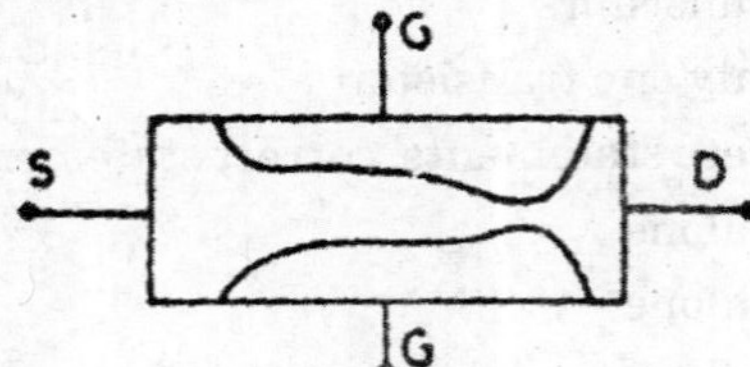

(*a*) it is property of the material used
(*b*) drain end is more reverse biased than source end
(*c*) drain end is more forward biased than source end
(*d*) impurity profile varies with the distance from source

81. An FET is a better chopper than a BJT because it has
(*a*) lower off-set voltage
(*b*) higher series ON resistance
(*c*) lower input current
(*d*) higher input impedance

82. The transconductance "g_m" of a JFET is equal to
(*a*) $-\dfrac{2I_{DSS}}{V_P}$ (*b*) $\dfrac{2}{|V_P|}\sqrt{I_{DSS}I_{DS}}$
(*c*) $-\dfrac{2I_{DS}}{V_P}$ (*d*) $\dfrac{I_{DSS}}{V_P}\left(1-\dfrac{V_{GS}}{V_P}\right)$

83. Consider the following statements:
Stagger tuning is used
1. to obtain sharp fall in the frequency response.
2. to obtain a wider pass band.
3. in the IF amplifiers of radio receivers.

Of these statements, correct statements is/are
(*a*) only 1
(*b*) 1 and 3
(*c*) only 2
(*d*) 1, 2 and 3

84. The circuit diagram shown in the figure consists of transistors in

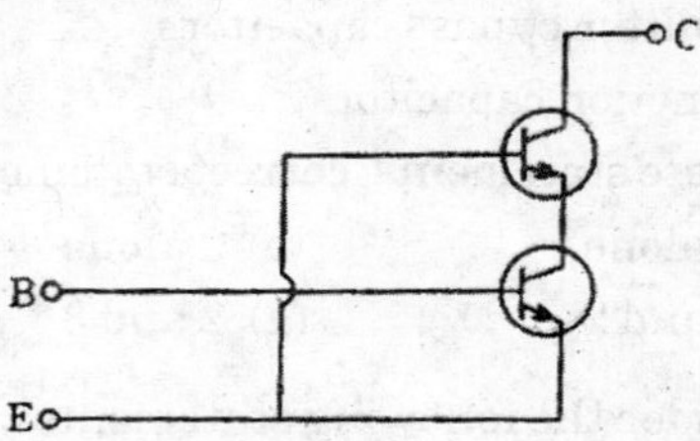

(*a*) parallel connection
(*b*) cascode connection
(*c*) darlington connection
(*d*) cascade connection

85. If an amplifier with gain of –1000 and feedback of β = – 0.1 had a gain change of 20% due to temperature, then change in gain of the feedback amplifier would be
(*a*) 10% (*b*) 5%
(*c*) 0.2% (*d*) 0.01%

86. Match List I with List II and select the correct answer using the codes given below:

List I	List II
A. Darlington concentration	1. The output current is the same in both the devices in the circuit.
B. Cascade	2. The output current of connection the first device becomes the input current of the second device.
C. Differential amplifier	3. The collect of the first device is connected to the base of the second device without using a capacitor.
D. Direct coupled amplifier	4. Output voltage depends on the relative values of the two input voltages.

Codes:

	A	B	C	D
(a)	1	2	3	4
(b)	2	1	4	3
(c)	3	4	1	2
(d)	4	3	2	1

87. In the circuit shown in the following figure, the feedback causes

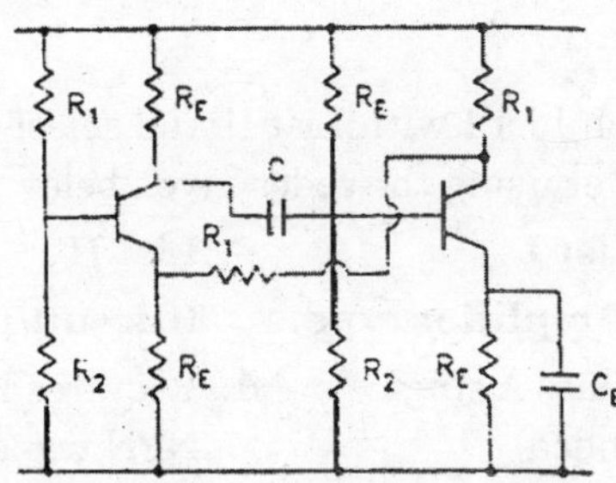

(a) an increase in both the input and output impedance
(b) an increase in the input impedance but a decrease in the output impedance
(c) a decrease in both the input and output impedance
(d) a decrease in the input impedance but an increase in the output impedance

88. The circuit shown in the given figure is

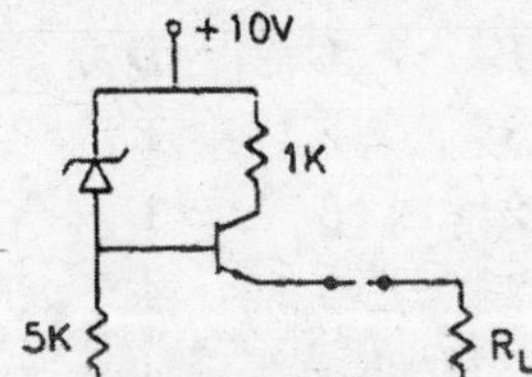

(a) constant voltage source
(b) constant current source
(c) common emitter amplifier
(d) common base amplifier

89. For the transistor amplifier in the given figure, the voltage amplification is approximately

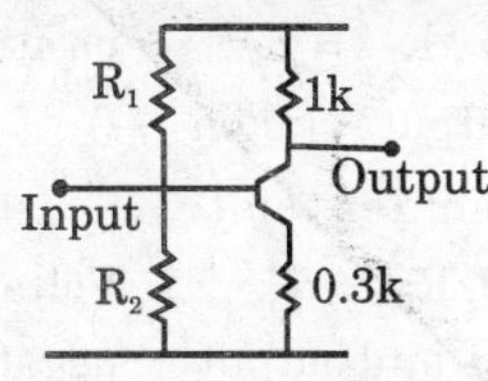

(a) 100 (b) 84
(c) 0.723 (d) – 2

90. The minimum value of h_{fe} of a transistor to be used in three sections R-C phase shift oscillator is

(a) 54.4 (b) 45.4
(c) 44.5 (d) 29

91. Match List I with List II and select the correct answer using the codes given below the lists:

List I (Name of circuit)	List II (Characteristics)
A. Tunnel diode oscillator	1. Produces high current pulses of short duration
B. UJT oscillator	2. An LC oscillator used for generation of sinewave at RF
C. Hartley oscillator	3. A negative resistance oscillator for MW frequency
D. Blocking oscillator	4. Uses negative resistance property for the generation of sawtooth waveform

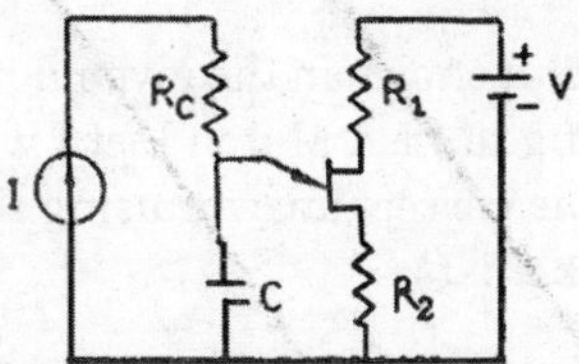

Codes:

	A	B	C	D
(a)	3	2	1	4
(b)	1	2	4	3
(c)	3	4	2	1
(d)	4	3	1	2

92. The given feedback amplifier circuit is modified according to List I and the possible feedback is as per List II. Match the two lists and select the correct answer using the codes given below the lists:

List I	List II
A. $R_C = 0, C_E = 0,$ $R_{r1} = \infty, R_{F2} = \infty$ and output is taken from emitter point	1. Curren t shunt positive feedback
B. $C_E = 0, R_{F1} = \infty,$ $R_{F2} = \infty$ and output is taken from collector point	2. Voltage series negative feedback
C. $R_{F2} = \infty$ and output is taken from collector point	3. Current series negative feedback
D. $C_E = 0, R_{F1} = \infty$ and output is taken from collector point	4. Voltage shunt negative feedback

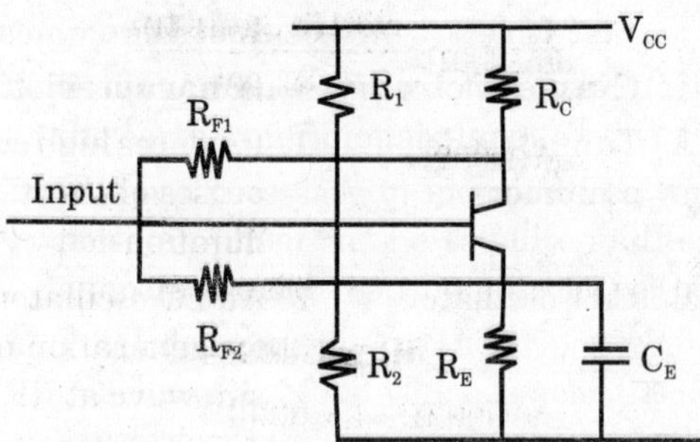

Codes:

	A	B	C	D
(a)	1	3	4	2
(b)	2	3	4	1
(c)	3	2	1	4
(d)	4	3	2	1

93. The circuit shown in the given figure is modified according to List. Match List I with List II and select the correct answer using the codes given below the lists:

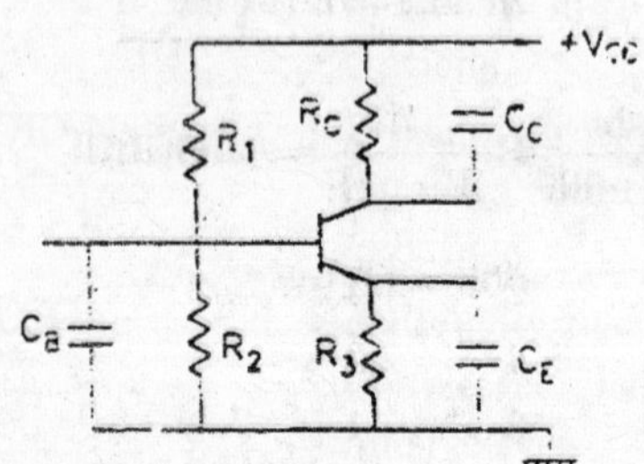

List I	List II
A. $R_B = 0, C_C = 0,$ $C_E = \infty.$ Input at base and output from collector point	1. Amplifier in CC mode with point feedback
B. $C_B = 0, C_E = 0,$ $C_E = \infty.$ Input at base point and output from emitter point	2. Amplifier in CB mode with no feedback
C. $C_B = 0, C_C = 0,$ $C_C = 0.$ Input at emitter point and output from collector point	3. Amplifier in CE mode with feedback
D. $C_B = 0, C_E = 0,$ $C_C = 0.$ Input at base point and output from collector point	4. Amplifier in CE mode with no feedback

Codes:

	A	B	C	D
(a)	1	2	3	4
(b)	4	3	2	1
(c)	4	1	2	3
(d)	2	3	4	1

94. Match List I with List II and select the correct answer using the codes given below the lists:

List I (Amplifier type)	List II (Circuit/property)
A. Class A single ended	1. Requires PNP & NPN transistor pairs
B. Class B pushpull transformer coupled	2. Prevents cross-over distortion
C. Class AB push-pull	3. Has maximum efficiency amongst these amplifiers
D. Class AB complementary symmetry	4. Has minimum efficiency amongst these amplifiers.

Codes:

	A	B	C	D
(a)	4	3	2	1
(b)	4	2	3	1
(c)	1	2	3	4
(d)	3	2	1	4

95. Match List I with List II and select the correct answer using the codes given below the lists:

List I (Name of the electronic circuit)	List II (Special characteristics)
A. Darlington amplifier	1. Low input impedance
B. Cascade amplifier (FET)	2. Low output impedance
C. Common gate amplifier	3. Low input capacitance but high R_{in}
D. Differential amplifier	4. Large common mode rejection

Codes:

	A	B	C	D
(*a*)	1	2	3	4
(*b*)	1	2	4	3
(*c*)	2	1	3	4
(*d*)	2	3	1	4

96. In a feedback series regular circuit, the output voltage is regulated by controlling

(*a*) magnitude of the input voltage
(*b*) gain of the feedback transistor
(*c*) reference voltage
(*d*) voltage drop across the series pass transistor

97. A second-order band-pass active filter can be obtained by cascading a low pass second order section having cut off frequency f_{OH} with a high pass second order section having cut-off frequency f_{OL} provided

(*a*) $f_{OH} > f_{OL}$
(*b*) $f_{OH} < f_{OL}$
(*c*) $f_{OH} = f_{OL}$
(*d*) $f_{OH} \leq \frac{1}{2} f_{OL}$

98. If a class C power amplifier has an input signal with frequency of 200 kHz and width of collector current pulses of 0.1 μs, then duty cycle of the amplifier will be

(*a*) 1%
(*b*) 2%
(*c*) 10%
(*d*) 20%

99. The given circuit has a feedback factor of

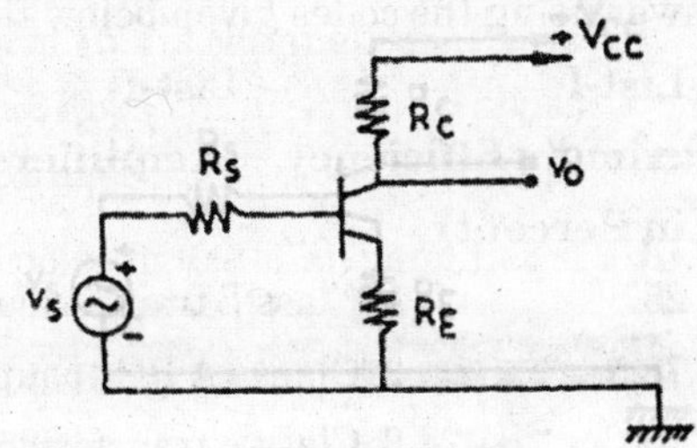

(*a*) $-\frac{R_C}{R_S}$ (*b*) $-\frac{R_E}{R_C}$

(*c*) $-\frac{R_E}{R_S}$ (*d*) $-\frac{R_C}{R_E}$

100. Hartley oscillator is used for the generation of

(*a*) very low frequency oscillation
(*b*) radio frequency oscillation
(*c*) microwave oscillation
(*d*) audio-frequency oscillation

101. An ideal constant voltage source is connected in series with an ideal constant current source. Considered together, the combination will be a

(*a*) constant voltage source
(*b*) constant current source
(*c*) constant voltage and a constant source or a constant power source
(*d*) resistance

102. In every practical oscillator, the loop is slightly larger than unity and amplitude of the oscillations is limited by the

(*a*) magnitude of the loop gain
(*b*) onset if non-linearity
(*c*) magnitude of gain of the amplifier
(*d*) feedback transmission factor

103. The essential blocks of a Phase Lock Loop (PLL) are phase detector, amplifier,

(*a*) high-pass filter and crystal controlled oscillator
(*b*) low-pass filter and crystal controlled oscillator
(*c*) high-pass filter and voltage controlled oscillator
(*d*) low-pass filter and voltage controlled oscillator

104. Match List-I with List-II and select the correct answer using the codes given below the lists:

List-I (Maximum Efficiency in Percent)	List-II (Amplifiers)
A. 25	1. Class-B transformer-coupled
B. 78.5	2. Class - A RC - coupled
C. 100	3. Class-A transformer-coupled
D. 50	4. Class - D switching mode

Codes:

	A	B	C	D
(a)	1	2	3	4
(b)	2	3	4	1
(c)	2	1	4	3
(d)	3	4	1	2

105. In the circuit shown in the given figure, the frequency of oscillation depends mainly upon

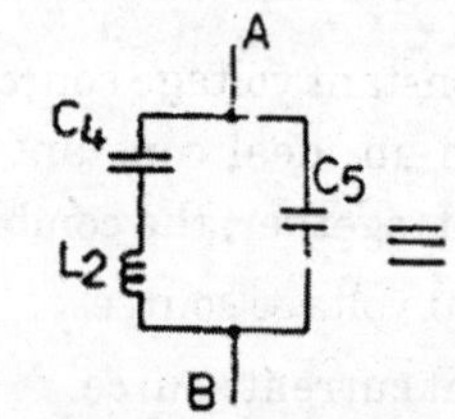

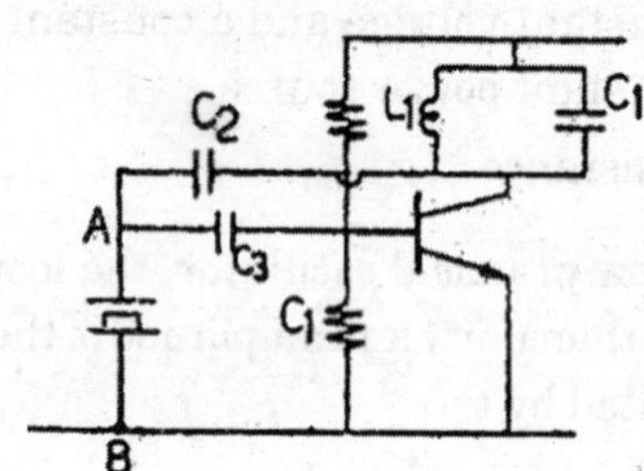

(a) L_1, C_1

(b) L_2, C_1 and C_2

(c) L_1, C_1, C_4, C_5 and L_2

(d) L_2, C_4 and C_5

106. A two-stage amplifier is required to have an upper cut-off 2 MHz and a lower cutoff frequency of 30 Hz. The upper and lower cut off frequencies of individual stage are respectively approximately

(a) 4 MHz, 60 Hz

(b) 3 MHz, 20 Hz

(c) 3 MHz, 60 Hz

(d) 4 MHz, 20 Hz

107. In the circuit shown in the given figure, transistors Q_2 and Q_3 form a push-pull amplifier. Assuming that the input signal level is large enough to drive both Q_2 and Q_3 to saturation and that the time constant $\frac{L}{R}$ is large, the waveform of the current I can be represented as

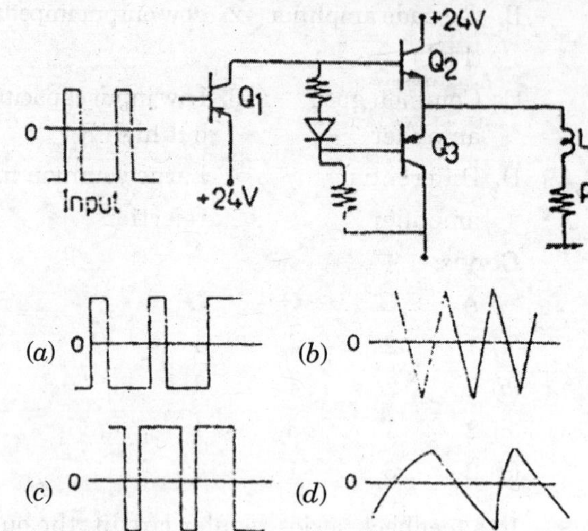

108. The gate, whose output is an RC-coupled amplifier is limited by

(a) coupling capacitors at the low-frequency end and bypass capacitors at the high-frequency end

(b) coupling capacitors at the high frequency end and bypass capacitors at the low-frequency end

(c) bypass and coupling capacitors at the low frequency end and shunt capacitors at the high frequency end

(d) shunt capacitors at the low frequency end and bypass as well as coupling capacitors at the high frequency end.

109. In the circuit of the relaxation oscillator shown in the given figure, what will be the change in the voltage waveform across capacitor, if the voltage V is doubled?

(a) The amplitude as well as the frequency of the waveform will get doubled.

(b) The amplitude will get doubled but the frequency will reduce to half its value.

(c) The amplitude will get doubled but the frequency will remain unchanged.

(d) The amplitude will remain unchanged but the frequency will get doubled.

110. It is desired to reduce total harmonic distortion of an amplifier from 85 to 2% by use of 5% feedback. What is gain of the amplifier with original distortion and with reduced distortion?

(*a*) 60, 15 (*b*) 15, 90

(*c*) 6, 1.5 (*d*) 1.5, 6

111. A class-B push-pull power amplifier uses two transistors each having a power dissipation capacity of 2 watts. The maximum power that the circuit can deliver to the load without extending the power dissipation capacity of the transistor is

(*a*) 1 watt (*b*) 2 watts

(*c*) 5 watts (*d*) 10 watts

112. Match List-I with List-II and select the correct answer using the codes given below the lists:

List-I (Amplifier Type)	List-II (Circuit/property)
A. RC coupling	1. Higher voltage gain and impedance matching
B. Inductive coupling	2. Ability to amplify dc and low frequency signals
C. Transformer coupling	3. Minimum possible non-linear distortion
D. Direct coupling	4. Low collector supply voltages can be used.

Codes:

	A	B	C	D
(*a*)	4	1	3	2
(*b*)	3	4	1	2
(*c*)	1	2	3	4
(*d*)	4	3	2	1

113. The oscillator circuit shown in the figure is has an ideal inverting amplifier. Its frequency of oscillation (in Hz) is

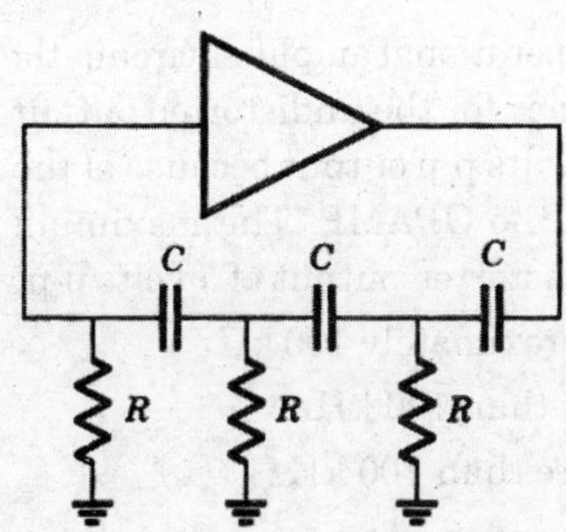

(*a*) $\dfrac{1}{(2\pi\sqrt{6}\,RC)}$ (*b*) $\dfrac{1}{(2\pi RC)}$

(*c*) $\dfrac{1}{(\sqrt{6}\,RC)}$ (*d*) $\dfrac{1}{\sqrt{6}\,(2\pi RC)}$

114. A transconductance amplifier has

(*a*) high input impedance and low output impedance

(*b*) low input impedance and high output impedance

(*c*) high input and output impedances

(*d*) low input and output impedances

115. The primary advantage of a crystal oscillator is that

(*a*) it can oscillate at any frequency

(*b*) it is given a high output voltage

(*c*) its frequency of oscillation remains almost constant

(*d*) it operates on a very low dc supply voltage

116. The transfer function of an amplifier is given by

$$A_v = \frac{V_o}{V_s} = \frac{2810}{\left(1+j\dfrac{f}{5.85\times10^5}\right)\left(1+j\dfrac{f}{5.85\times10^6}\right)}$$

The high 3-dB frequency of the amplifier will be approximately

(*a*) 5850 kHz

(*b*) 585 kHz

(*c*) 5850 Hz

(*d*) 585 Hz

117. In the case of an amplifier, the normalised voltage gain is given by

$$\frac{A_v}{A_o} = \frac{1}{1+\dfrac{R}{R}} \cdot \frac{1+j\dfrac{f}{f_o}}{1+j\dfrac{f}{f_p}}$$

where f_o is zero frequency and f_p is pole frequency. For a standard frequency response of the amplifier,

(*a*) $f_p >> f_o$

(*b*) $f_p = f_o$

(*c*) $f_p << f_o$

(*d*) $f_o = 2 f_p$

118. Consider the following statements regarding the time-base voltage of an oscilloscope:

It can be generated using

1. Miller sweep circuit.
2. boot-strap integrator circuit.
3. time-delay circuit.
4. a controlled rectifier.

Of these statements, the correct statements are

(*a*) 1, 2 and 3 (*b*) 1 and 2

(*c*) 2 and 4 (*d*) 1, 3 and 4

119. A transistor amplifier has poles at

$S_1 = -0.00245 \times 10^9$ rad/s

$S_2 = -0.0748 \times 10^9$ rad/s

$S_3 = -0.670 \times 10^9$ rad/s and

$S_4 = -4.38 \times 10^9$ rad/s

Upper 3 dB frequency of the amplifier will be

(*a*) S_1

(*b*) $S_1 + S_2 + S_3 + S_4$

(*c*) $S_1 + S_4$

(*d*) S_4

120. Wide-banding technique is employed in the

(*a*) video amplifier of a TV receiver

(*b*) IF amplifier of an FM receiver

(*c*) RF amplifier of an AM receiver

(*d*) input section of a communication receiver

121. Consider the following statements:

A class-B amplifier

1. is biased just at cut-off.
2. has a high theoretical efficiency of 78.5 % because its quiescent current is low.

Of these statements, correct statements is/are

(*a*) 2 and 3 (*b*) 1 only

(*c*) 2 only (*d*) 1 and 2

122. Which one of the following power amplifiers has the maximum efficiency?

(*a*) Class A (*b*) Class B

(*c*) Class AB (*d*) Class C

123. The voltage gains of an amplifier without feedback and with negative feedback respectively are 100 and 20. The percentage of negative feedback (β) would be

(*a*) 4%

(*b*) 5%

(*c*) 20%

(*d*) 80%

124. If the Q of a single-stage single-tuned amplifier is doubled, then its bandwidth will

(*a*) remain same

(*b*) become half

(*c*) become double

(*d*) become four times

125. In case of the circuit shown in the figure, V_{io} = 10 mV dc maximum, the maximum possible output offset voltage V_{oo} caused by the input offset voltage V_{io} with respect to ground is

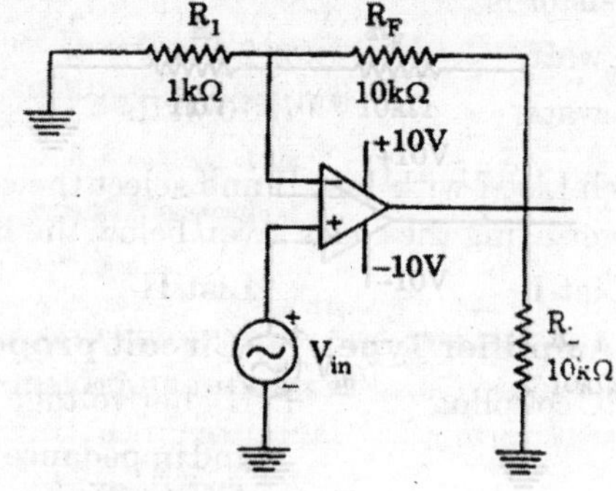

(*a*) 60 mV dc

(*b*) 110 mV dc

(*c*) 130 mV dc

(*d*) 150 mV dc

126. The approximate input impedance of the OPAMP circuit shown in the figure is

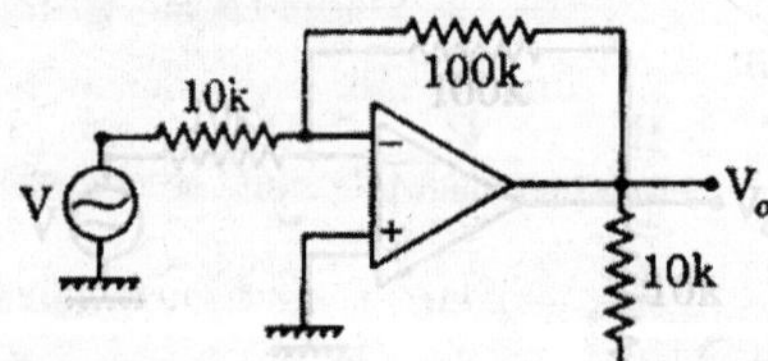

(*a*) Infinity

(*b*) 120 k

(*c*) 110 k

(*d*) 10 k

127. In an operational amplifier circuit, the maximum frequency for the undistorted output is 100 kHz for 10 volts p-p output because of the finite slew rate of the OPAMP. The maximum frequency for undistorted output of 5 volts p-p will be

(*a*) approximately 100 kHz

(*b*) less than 100 kHz

(*c*) more than 100 kHz

(*d*) none of these

128. The circuit shown in the given figure can be used as a

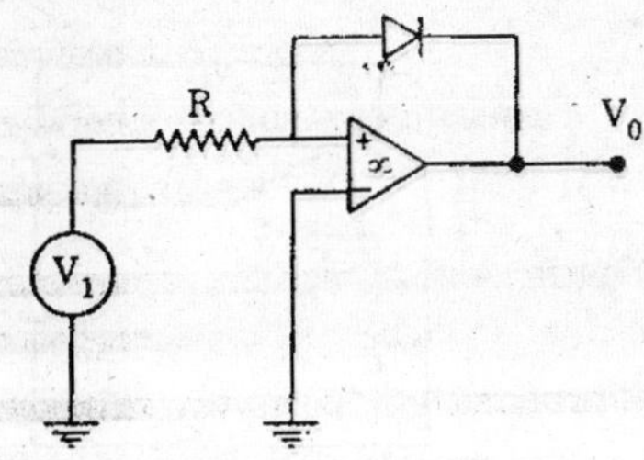

(a) rectifier
(b) voltage to frequency converter
(c) frequency to voltage converter
(d) logarithmic amplifier

129. For the circuit shown in the given figure match List I with List II and select the correct answer using the codes given below the lists:

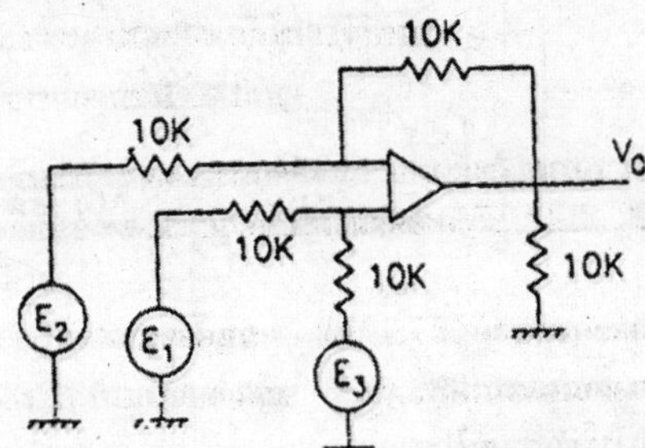

List I	List II (V_0)
A. $E_1 = -2$ V, $E_2 = -2$ V, $E_3 = 0$ V	1. 1.0 volt
B. $E_1 = -2$ V, $E_2 = -2$ V, $E_3 = 1$ V	2. Zero
C. $E_1 = 2$ V, $E_2 = -2$ V, $E_3 = 2$ V	3. 5.0 volts
D. $E_1 = 2$ V, $E_2 = 0$ V, $E_3 = 3$ V	4. 6.0 volts

Codes:

	A	B	C	D
(a)	4	3	1	2
(b)	2	1	4	3
(c)	4	3	2	1
(d)	2	1	4	3

130. Under what condition will the instrumentation amplifier circuit given in the figure possess highest CMRR?
(R_{s1} and R_{s2} are source resistances)

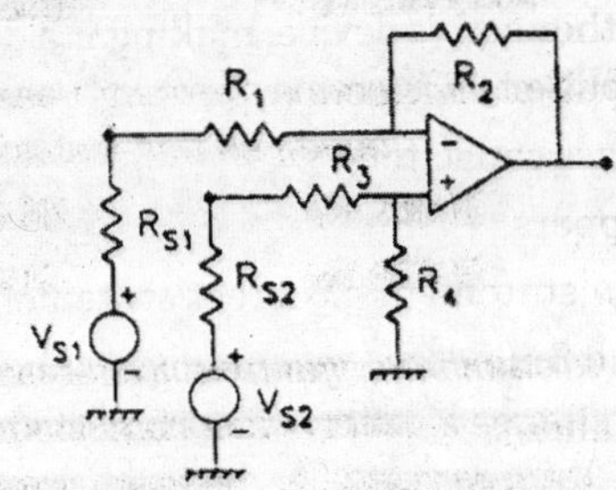

(a) $\frac{R_1}{R_2} = \frac{R_3}{R_4}$

(b) $\frac{R_{s1} + R_1}{R_2} = \frac{R_{s2} + R_3}{R_4}$

(c) $\frac{R_{s1} + R_2}{R_1} = \frac{R_{s2} + R_4}{R_3}$

(d) $\frac{R_{s1}}{R_2} = \frac{R_{s2}}{R_4}$

131. The output off-set voltage is zero for circuit given in the figure, when

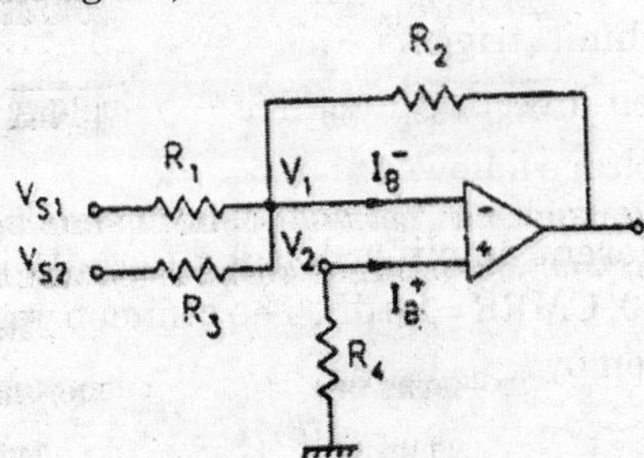

(a) $V_1 = 0$, $\bar{I}_B = \bar{I}_B^+$ and $V_1 = V_2$
(b) $V_1 = 0$, and $\bar{I}_B = \bar{I}_B^+$
(c) $\bar{I}_B = \bar{I}_B^+$ and $V_1 = V_2$
(d) $V_1 = 0$, and $V_1 = V_2$

132. The op-amp of the circuit shown in the figure has a unity gain frequency of 1 MHz. The cut-off frequency of the feedback amplifier is

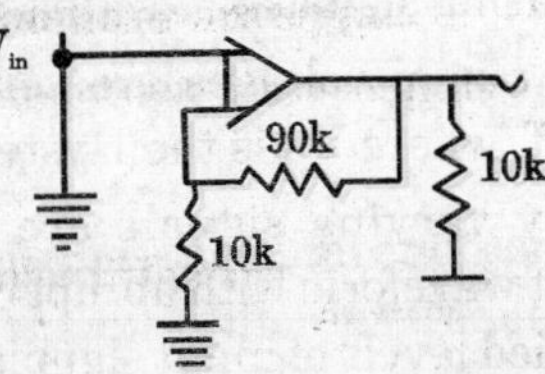

(a) 100 kHz (b) 1 MHz
(c) 10 MHz (d) 90 MHz

133. Consider the following statements:

Drift in direct coupled amplifiers may be reduced effectively by the use of

1. a diode as thermal compensating element.
2. another active device, making it a differential amplifier.
3. bypass capacitors.
4. choppers.

Of these statements, correct statements are

(*a*) 1 and 3

(*b*) 1, 2 and

(*c*) 2 and 4

(*d*) 1, 2 and 4

134. When Z′ << Z, then OP-AMP circuit shown in the given figure behaves as a/an

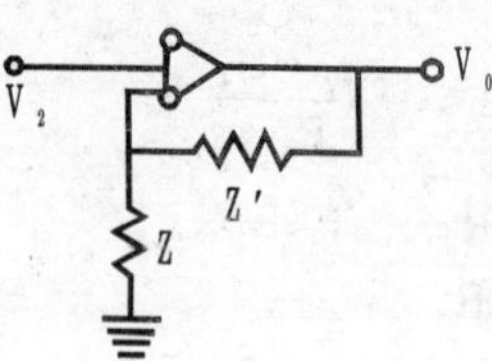

(*a*) inverting amplifier

(*b*) schmitt trigger

(*c*) non-inverting amplifier

(*d*) voltage follower

135. A different amplifier has a differential gain of 20,000, CMRR = 80 dB. The common mode gain is given by

(*a*) 2 (*b*) 1

(*c*) $\frac{1}{2}$ (*d*) 0

136. The Hysteresis phenomenon in Schmitt Trigger has, which of the following features ?

1. It is due to negative feedback.
2. In the inverted mode, circuit triggers at a higher voltage for increasing signals than for decreasing signals.
3. Noise signal voltages greater than V_H are cut-off, where V_H is the Hysteresis voltage.
4. Slowly varying signals are converted to output waveform with abrupt changes at two specified levels of input signals.

Of these statements, correct statements are

(*a*) 2 and 3 (*b*) 2 and 4

(*c*) 2, 3 and 4 (*d*) 3 and 4

137. For a sinusoidal input, the circuit shown in the figure will act as a

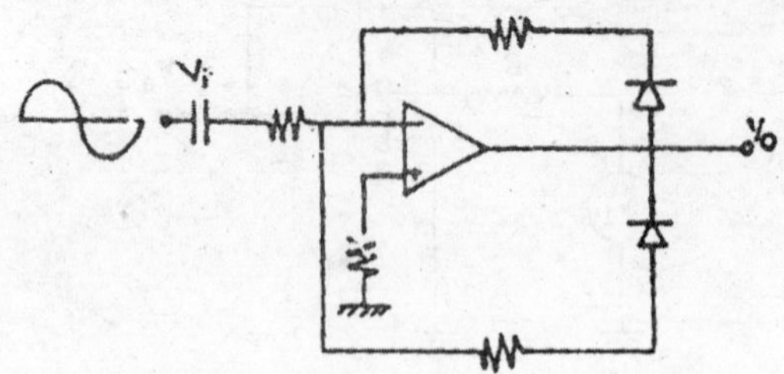

(*a*) pulse generator (*b*) full-wave rectifier

(*c*) ramp generator (*d*) voltage doubler

138. In the circuit shown in the figure

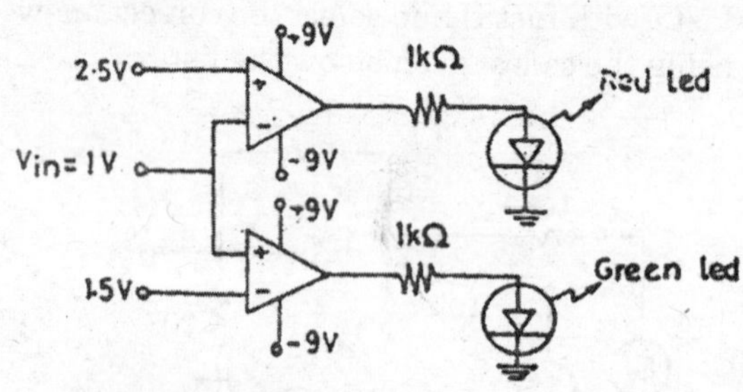

(*a*) only red will glow

(*b*) only green will glow

(*c*) both red and green will glow

(*d*) neither red nor green will glow

139. For the high-pass circuit to act as a differentiator, the time constant must be

(*a*) small

(*b*) very small in comparison to the time period of the input signal

(*c*) very high in comparison to the time period of the input signal (that is low pass circuit)

(*d*) of moderate value

140. The output voltage V_0 of the given circuit is

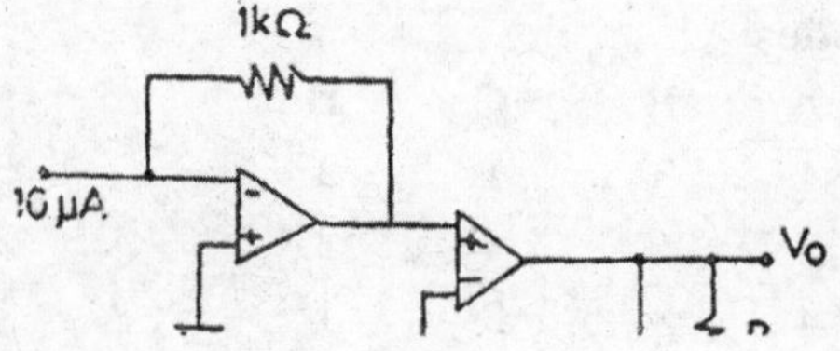

(*a*) –100 V (*b*) –100 mV

(*c*) 10 V (*d*) 10 mV

141. In the circuit shown in the given figure, the current flowing through resistance of 100 Ω would be

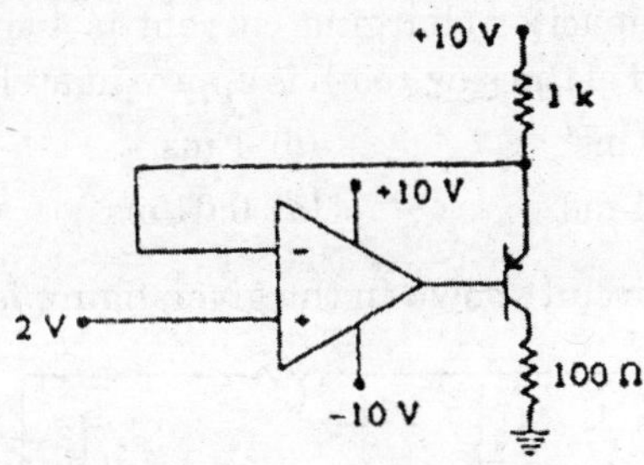

(*a*) 8 mA (*b*) 10 mA
(*c*) 20 mA (*d*) 100 mA

142. Which of the following conditions would give $V_o = 0$ in the circuit shown in the given figure?

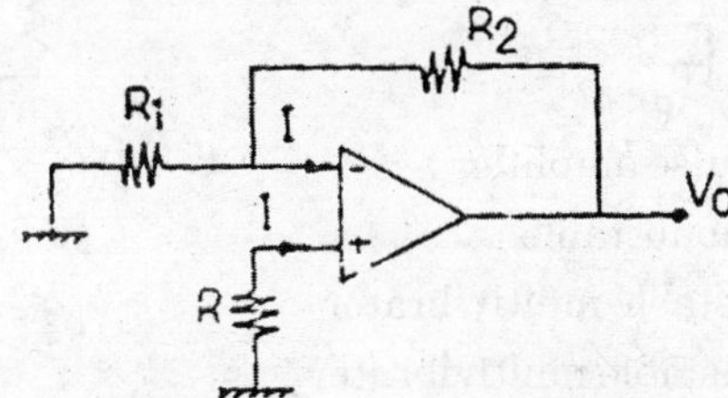

(*a*) $R = R_1 + R_2$ (*b*) $R = \frac{R_2}{R_1}$
(*c*) $R = R_2 - R_1$ (*d*) $R = R_1 \parallel R_2$

143. The overall voltage gain in the amplifier shown in the figure is

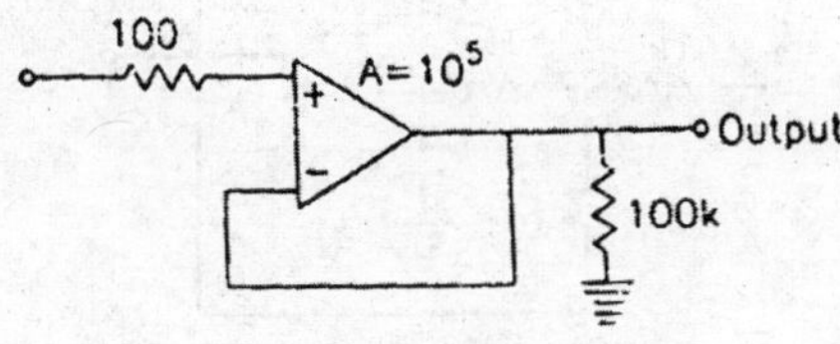

(*a*) zero (*b*) 1
(*c*) 1000 (*d*) 100000

144. In the OPAMP circuit shown in the figure below, the output would be

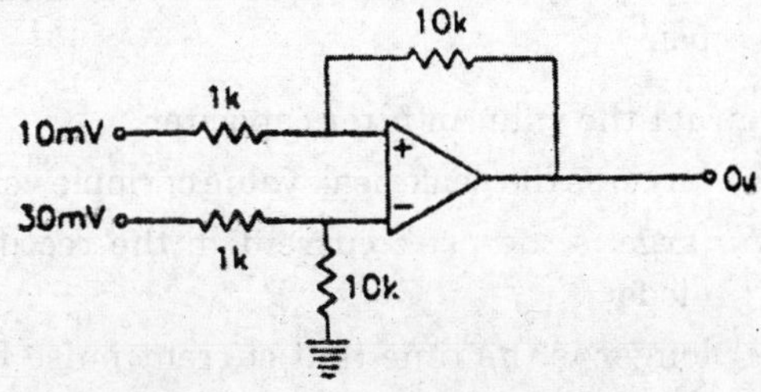

(*a*) 400 mV (*b*) 300 mV
(*c*) 200 mV (*d*) 100 mV

145. If open-loop of the OPAMP shown in the figure is 100000, then approximate output voltage (V_0) will be

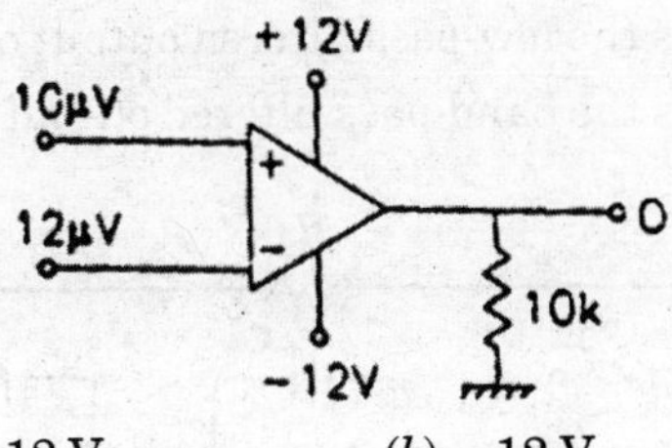

(*a*) + 12 V (*b*) – 12 V
(*c*) – 2 microvolt (*d*) – 0.2 V

146. Which of the following pairs is/are correctly matched?

Waveform	Circuitry and input signal
1. Triangular wave	Integrating circuit and square wave
2. Impulsive wave	Differentiating circuit and step signal
3. Saw-tooth wave	Differentiating circuit and triangular wave

Select the correct answer using the codes given below:

Codes:

(*a*) 2 and 3
(*b*) 1 and 2
(*c*) 1 alone
(*d*) 1 and 3

147. In an L-section filter, a bleeder resistance connected across the load

(*a*) provides good regulation for all values of load
(*b*) ensures lower PIV of the diodes
(*c*) ensures lower values of capacitance in the filter
(*d*) reduces ripple content

148. The circuit given in the figure is a

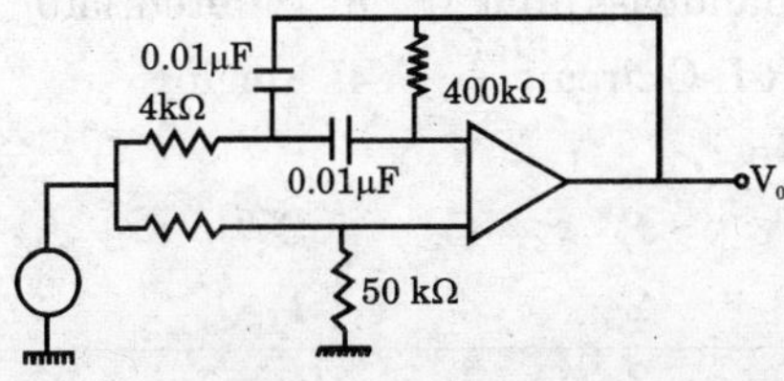

(*a*) low pass filter (*b*) high pass filter
(*c*) band pass filter (*d*) notch filter

149. Consider the following statements regarding the state variable section given in the figure.

1. V_1 is the notch filtered output of V_i
2. V_3 is the low-pass filtered output of V_i
3. V_2 is the band-pass filtered output of V_i

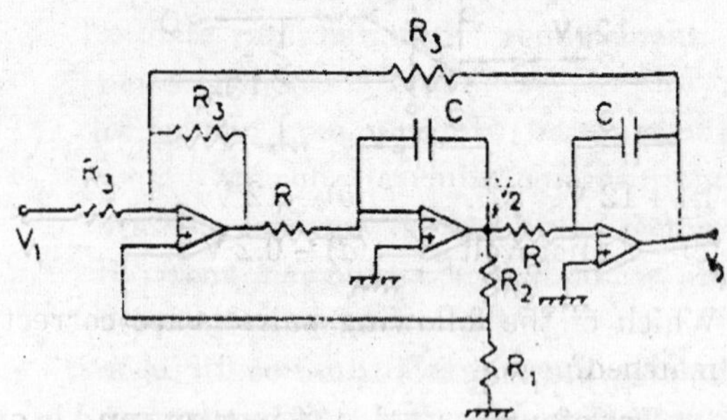

Of these statements, the correct statements are

(*a*) 1, 2 and 3
(*b*) 1 and 2
(*c*) 2 and 3
(*d*) 1 and 3

150. Which one of the following statements regarding filters is correct?

(*a*) Butterworth response has a sharp cut-off
(*b*) Chebyshev response has a flat response in the pass band
(*c*) Butterworth response has ripples in the pass band
(*d*) Chebyshev response has ripples in the pass band

151. Match List I with List II and select the correct answer using the codes given below the lists:

List I (Type of filter)	List II (Property associated with it)
A. Low pass filter	1. Tuned circuit
B. High pass filter	2. Compensated attenuator
C. Bandpass filter	3. Differentiator
D. R-L-C circuit	4. Ringing

Codes:

	A	B	C	D
(*a*)	3	2	4	1
(*b*)	2	3	1	4
(*c*)	2	3	4	1
(*d*)	2	1	3	4

152. A saw-tooth generator is built using a UJT with a constant current charged capacitor C of 1 μf driving the emitter. If voltage V_{BB} is 15 V and the capacitor charging current is 1 mA, then period of the saw-tooth is approximately

(*a*) 10 ms (*b*) 1 ms
(*c*) 0.1 ms (*d*) 0.01 ms

153. The circuit shown in the given figure is

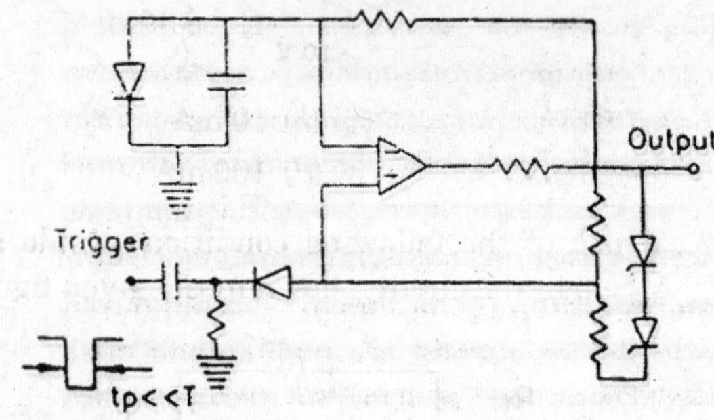

(*a*) pulse amplifier
(*b*) monostable
(*c*) astable multivibrator
(*d*) bistable multivibrator

154. The current range in a voltage regulator can be improved by

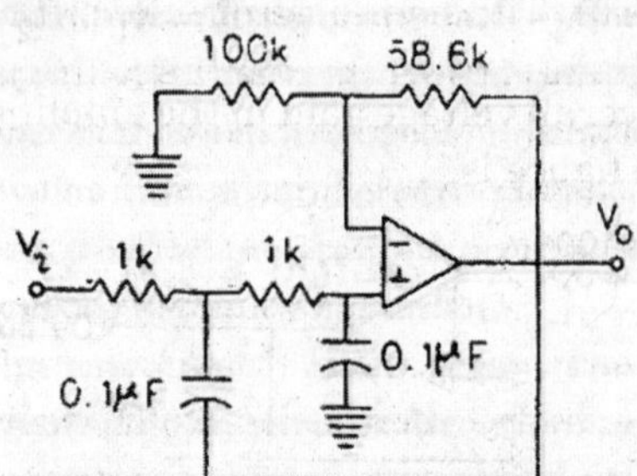

(*a*) increasing the input voltage
(*b*) decreasing the reference voltage
(*c*) putting the control potentiometer at the highest setting
(*d*) replacing the series transistor by a Darlington pair

155. Larger the value of filter capacitor

(*a*) larger is the peak-peak value of ripple voltage
(*b*) large is the peak current in the rectifying diode
(*c*) longer is the time that current pulse flows through the diode
(*d*) smaller is the dc voltage across the load

156. A second-order low-pass Butterworth active filter is shown in the given figure. What is the 3-dB cutoff frequency ω_o and the damping factor (K) of the filter?
(a) 1.6 kHz and 0.586
(b) 1.6 kHz and 0.707
(c) 10 kHz and 0.586
(d) 10 kHz and 0.707

157. For the circuit shown in the given figure, assuming ideal diodes, the output waveform V_0 will be

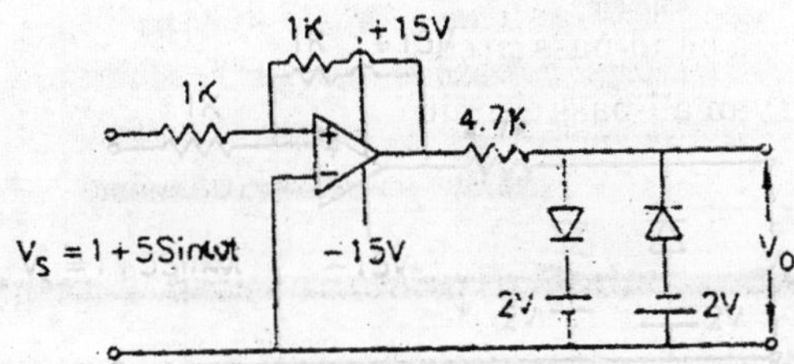

(a)
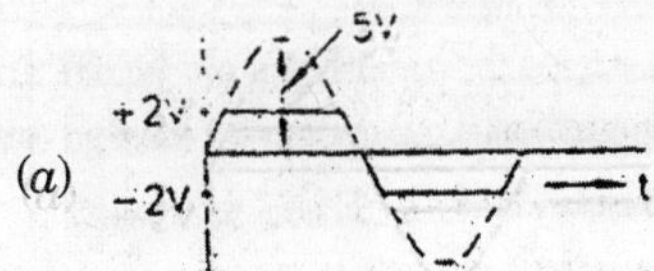

(b)
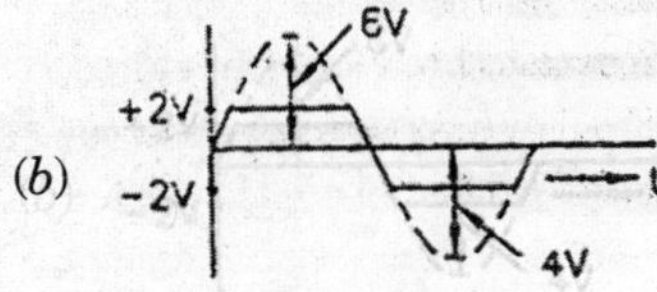

(c)
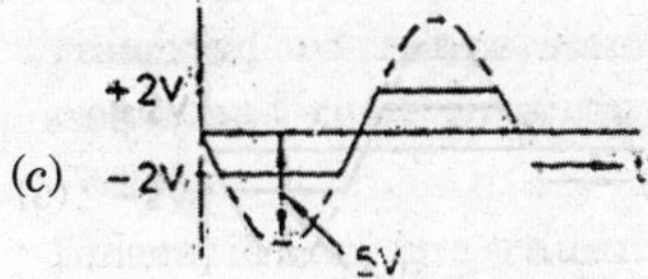

(d)
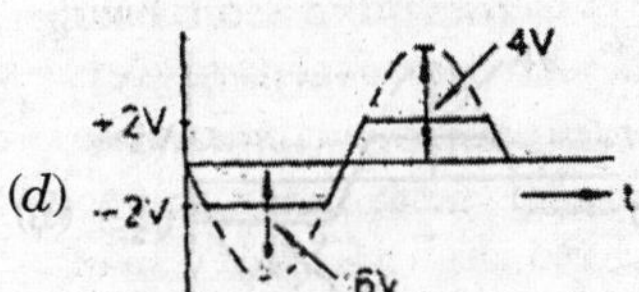

158. The circuit shown in the given figure is a/an

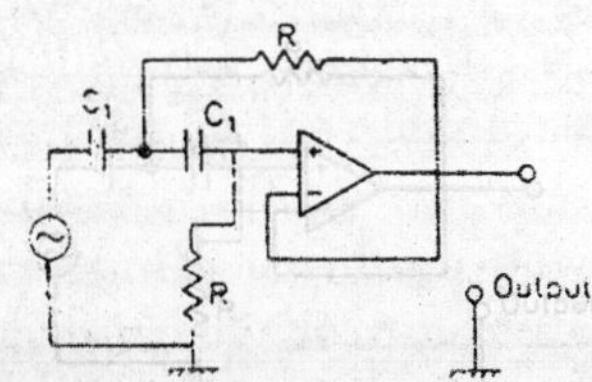

(a) amplifier
(b) oscillator
(c) high pass filter
(d) saw tooth generator

159. The op-amp circuit shown in the given figure can be used for

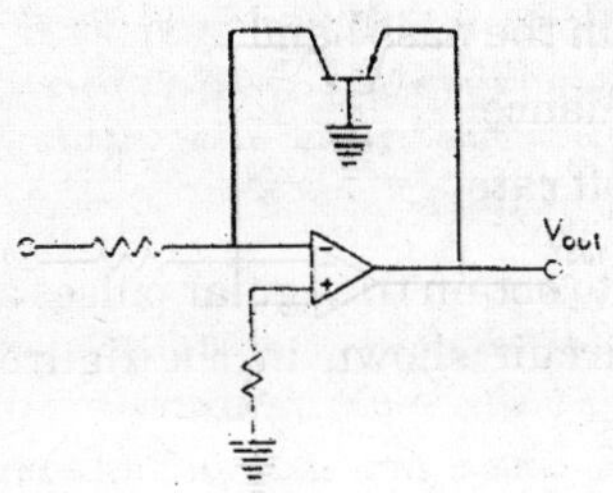

(a) addition
(b) subtraction
(c) both addition and subtraction
(d) multiplication

160. For the circuit shown in the given figure, assuming ideal op-amps, the output corresponding to the given input will be

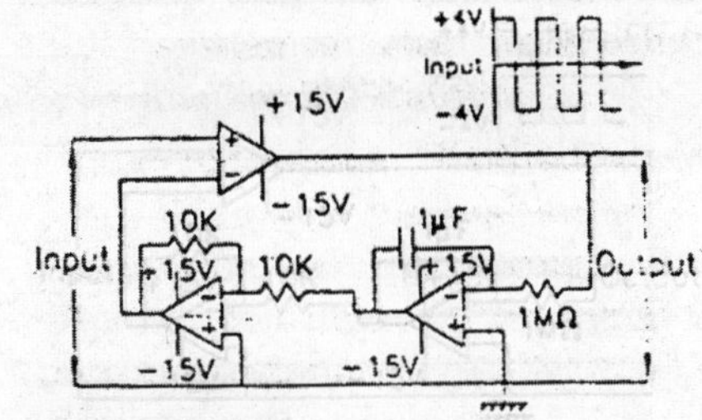

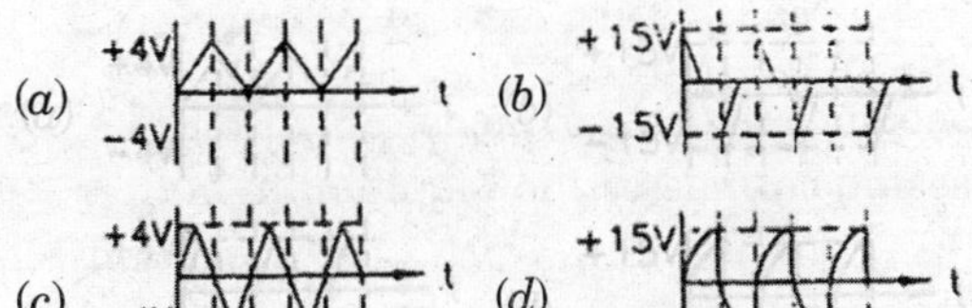

161. In a bistable multivibrator, commutating capacitors are used to
(a) increase the base storage charge
(b) provide ac coupling
(c) increase the speed of response
(d) alter the frequency of the output

162. If a capacitor C is charged by a constant current I, then the rate of change of voltage with time is given by sweep speed equal to
(a) $\frac{C}{I}$
(b) IC
(c) $\frac{I}{C}$
(d) $\frac{1}{2}\frac{I}{C}$

163. Higher order active filters are used for variable

(a) bandwidth

(b) gain in the pass-band

(c) impedance

(d) roll-off rate

164. In order to obtain triangular pulses at the output of the circuit shown in the figure, the input should be

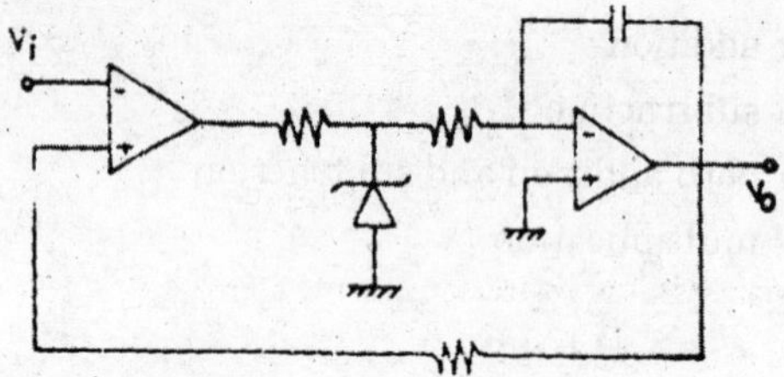

(a) grounded

(b) a square wave

(c) a triangular wave

(d) a trigger

165. The op-amp circuit shown in the given figure is

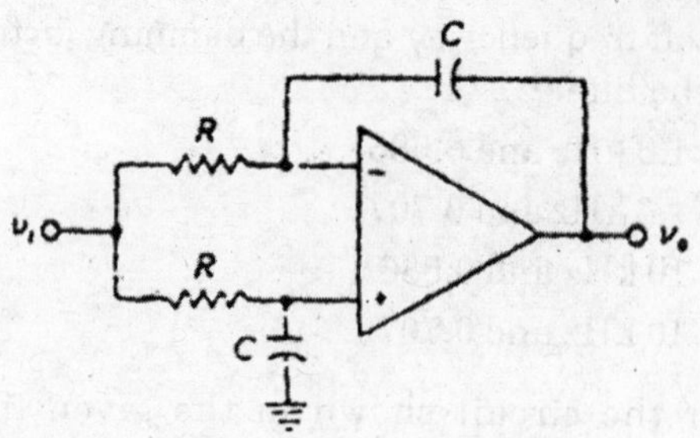

(a) a high-pass circuit

(b) a low-pass circuit

(c) a band-pass circuit

(d) an all-pass circuit

Answers

1. (*d*) 2. (*a*) 3. (*d*) 4. (*c*) 5. (*b*) 6. (*c*) 7. (*b*) 8. (*b*) 9. (*a*) 10. (*d*)
11. (*c*) 12. (*c*) 13. (*a*) 14. (*c*) 15. (*d*) 16. (*b*) 17. (*c*) 18. (*d*) 19. (*b*) 20. (*a*)
21. (*b*) 22. (*a*) 23. (*b*) 24. (*b*) 25. (*d*) 26. (*b*) 27. (*d*) 28. (*a*) 29. (*b*) 30. (*c*)
31. (*d*) 32. (*b*) 33. (*c*) 34. (*c*) 35. (*c*) 36. (*b*) 37. (*d*) 38. (*b*) 39. (*c*) 40. (*d*)
41. (*b*) 42. (*c*) 43. (*c*) 44. (*a*) 45. (*a*) 46. (*b*) 47. (*d*) 48. (*d*) 49. (*a*) 50. (*c*)
51. (*a*) 52. (*a*) 53. (*a*) 54. (*a*) 55. (*a*) 56. (*b*) 57. (*a*) 58. (*b*) 59. (*a*) 60. (*b*)
61. (*d*) 62. (*a*) 63. (*c*) 64. (*a*) 65. (*b*) 66. (*b*) 67. (*a*) 68. (*a*) 69. (*a*) 70. (*c*)
71. (*b*) 72. (*b*) 73. (*a*) 74. (*a*) 75. (*a*) 76. (*b*) 77. (*d*) 78. (*d*) 79. (*c*) 80. (*b*)
81. (*a*) 82. (*b*) 83. (*b*) 84. (*a*) 85. (*c*) 86. (*b*) 87. (*b*) 88. (*a*) 89. (*d*) 90. (*c*)
91. (*c*) 92. (*b*) 93. (*c*) 94. (*a*) 95. (*d*) 96. (*d*) 97. (*a*) 98. (*d*) 99. (*d*) 100. (*d*)
101. (*b*) 102. (*b*) 103. (*d*) 104. (*c*) 105. (*d*) 106. (*b*) 107. (*d*) 108. (*c*) 109. (*c*) 110. (*a*)
111. (*b*) 112. (*b*) 113. (*a*) 114. (*c*) 115. (*c*) 116. (*a*) 117. (*a*) 118. (*a*) 119. (*a*) 120. (*a*)
121. (*d*) 122. (*d*) 123. (*a*) 124. (*b*) 125. (*b*) 126. (*d*) 127. (*c*) 128. (*d*) 129. (*b*) 130. (*b*)
131. (*d*) 132. (*d*) 133. (*d*) 134. (*d*) 135. (*a*) 136. (*b*) 137. (*b*) 138. (*a*) 139. (*b*) 140. (*b*)
141. (*a*) 142. (*d*) 143. (*b*) 144. (*c*) 145. (*b*) 146. (*b*) 147. (*a*) 148. (*c*) 149. (*a*) 150. (*d*)
151. (*b*) 152. (*a*) 153. (*b*) 154. (*d*) 155. (*d*) 156. (*b*) 157. (*d*) 158. (*c*) 159. (*d*) 160. (*a*)
161. (*c*) 162. (*c*) 163. (*d*) 164. (*a*) 165. (*b*)

Explanations

5.

$$V_{max} = 10 \times \sqrt{2} = 14.1 \text{ V}$$

49.

$$g_m = \frac{\Delta I_0}{\Delta V_{GS}} \; ; \; \beta = \frac{\Delta I_C}{\Delta I_B}$$

Transconductance of composite transistor

$$= 2 \times 99$$
$$= 198 \text{ m A/V}$$

50.

20 kΩ, 20 kΩ, I_c, 2 kΩ, V_c, I_E, 4.3 kΩ, $I_c = I_E$

$$I_C = I_E$$

$$V_C = \frac{4.3 \times (10 - 0)}{2 + 4.3} + 0.7$$
$$= 7.5253 \text{ V}$$

53.

$$\alpha = \frac{\beta}{1+\beta}$$
$$= \frac{100}{101} = 0.999$$

$$I_C \approx I_E$$
$$I^2 - 3\,I_C - 2I_E = 0$$
$$I^2 - 3\,I_C - 2I_C = 0$$

$$\therefore \quad I_C = \frac{12}{5} = 2.4 \text{ mA}$$

64. $\alpha = 0.995$, $I_E = 10$ mA, $I_{CO} = 0.5\ \mu A$

$$I_{CEO} = \frac{I_{CO}}{1-\alpha} = \frac{0.5}{1-0.995} = 100\ \mu A$$

82. $$I_D = I_{DSS}\left[1-\frac{V_{GS}}{V_P}\right]$$

$$g_m = \frac{\Delta I_D}{\Delta V_{GS}}$$

$$= 2\, I_{D_{SS}}\left[1-\frac{V_{GS}}{V_P}\right]\left[\frac{1}{|V_P|}\right]$$

$$= \left[\frac{2\, I_{DSS}}{V_P}\right] \times \sqrt{\frac{I_D}{I_{DSS}}}$$

$$= \frac{2}{V_P}\sqrt{I_{DS}\, I_{DSS}}$$

85. $$\frac{dA_f}{A_f} = \frac{1}{1+A\beta}\,\frac{dA}{A}$$

$$= \frac{1}{1+1000\times 0.1} \times \frac{20}{100}$$

$$= \frac{0.2}{101}$$

$$\frac{dA_f}{A_f} = \frac{0.2}{101} \times 100 = 0.2\%$$

113. The feedback network is shown below.

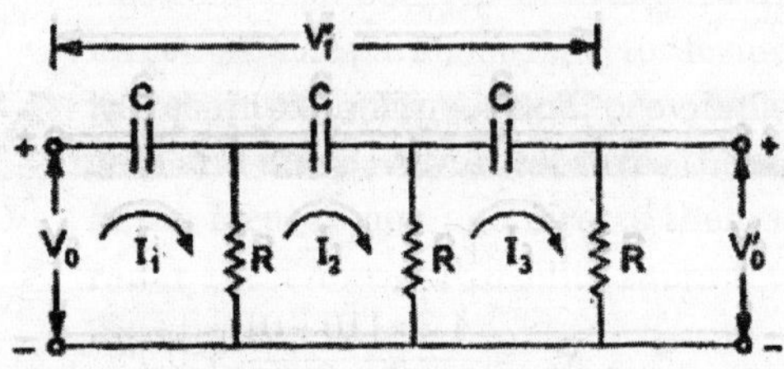

Let $X = \frac{1}{\omega C}$

then, using KVL, we have following set of linear equations

$$\begin{bmatrix} R-jX & -R & 0 \\ -R & 2R-jX & -R \\ 0 & -R & 2R-jX \end{bmatrix}\begin{bmatrix} I_1 \\ I_2 \\ I_3 \end{bmatrix} = \begin{bmatrix} V_0 \\ 0 \\ 0 \end{bmatrix}$$

Putting $\alpha = \frac{X}{R} = \frac{1}{\omega RC}$, we get

or $$R^3\begin{bmatrix} 1-i\alpha & -1 & 0 \\ -1 & 2-i\alpha & -1 \\ 0 & -1 & 2-i\alpha \end{bmatrix}\begin{bmatrix} I_1 \\ I_2 \\ I_3 \end{bmatrix} = \begin{bmatrix} V_0 \\ 0 \\ 0 \end{bmatrix}$$

Now, $$I_3 = \frac{\Delta_3}{\Delta}$$

where $$\Delta_3 = R^3\begin{vmatrix} 1-i\alpha & -1 & V_0 \\ -1 & 2-i\alpha & 0 \\ 0 & -1 & 0 \end{vmatrix}$$

and, $$\Delta = R^3\begin{vmatrix} 1-i\alpha & -1 & 0 \\ -1 & 2-i\alpha & -1 \\ 0 & -1 & 2-i\alpha \end{vmatrix}$$

then, $$I_3 = \frac{\Delta_3}{\Delta} = \frac{V_0}{1-5\alpha^2 + j(\alpha^3 - 6\alpha)}$$

and, $$\frac{V_0'}{V_0} = \frac{-I_3 R}{V_0}$$

$$= \frac{-1}{(1-5\alpha^2)+j(\alpha^3-6\alpha)}$$

For 180° phase shift, $\alpha^3 - 6\alpha = 0$

or $\alpha = \sqrt{6}$

or $\frac{1}{\omega RC} = \sqrt{6}$

or $f = \frac{1}{2\pi RC\sqrt{6}}$

123. $$A_f = \frac{A}{1+\beta A}$$

$\therefore$ $20 = \frac{100}{1+\beta\times 100}$

$\Rightarrow$ $20 + 20000\,\beta = 100$

$\Rightarrow$ $\beta = \frac{80}{2000} = 0.04$

$\therefore$ $\%\beta = 0.04 \times 100 = 4.0\%$

126. Equivalent circuit can be drawn as

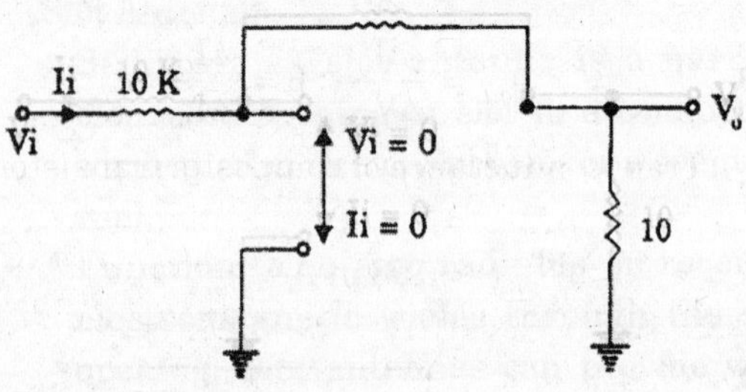

From above,

$V_i - 0 = 10\, I_i$

$\Rightarrow$ $\frac{V_i}{I_i} = 10\text{ K}$

$\therefore$ $Z_i = 10\text{ K}$

127. $\text{Resolution} = \frac{50mV}{10} = \frac{50}{10000} = \frac{1}{200}$

$$\frac{1}{2^r} = \frac{1}{200}$$

$\Rightarrow$ Minimum number of bits $n = 8$

135. $\text{CMRR} = 80\ dB$

$$\text{CMRR} = \frac{A_d}{A_c}$$

$$= (10)^{\frac{80}{20}} = 10000$$

$$A_c = \frac{20000}{10000} = 2$$

141. Equivalent circuit can be drawn as

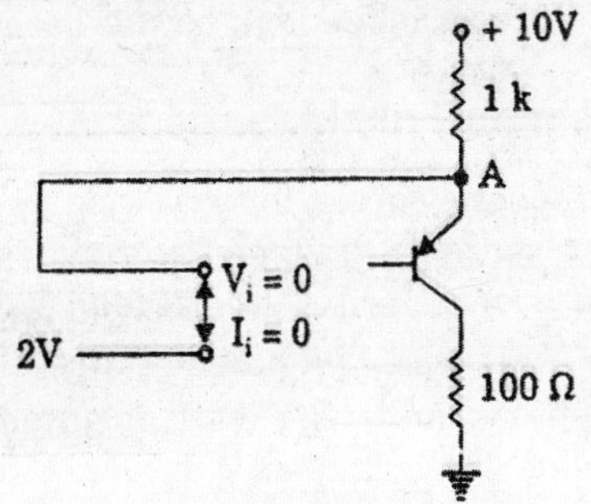

Voltage of point A = 2 V

Current through 1 K resistor $= \frac{10-2}{1}$

or $I_E = 8$ mA

$I_C \approx I_E$

$\therefore$ Current through 100 Ω = 8 mA

143. Drawing virtual ground equivalent circuit

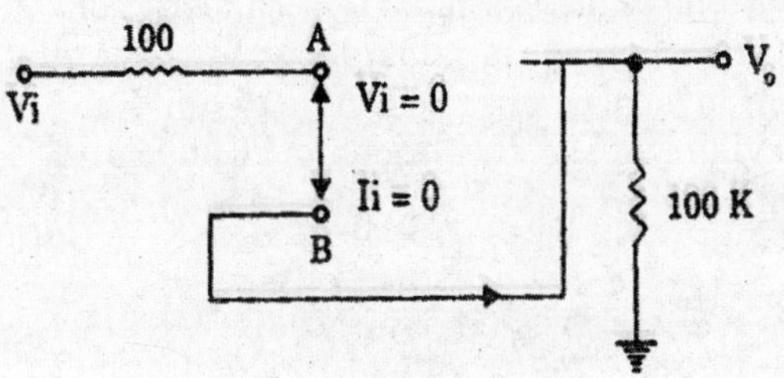

Since voltage at A and B is equal

$\therefore \quad V_i = V_A = V_B = V_0$

$\therefore \quad \text{Voltage gain} = \frac{V_o}{V_i} = 1$

144. Drawing virtual ground equivalent circuit

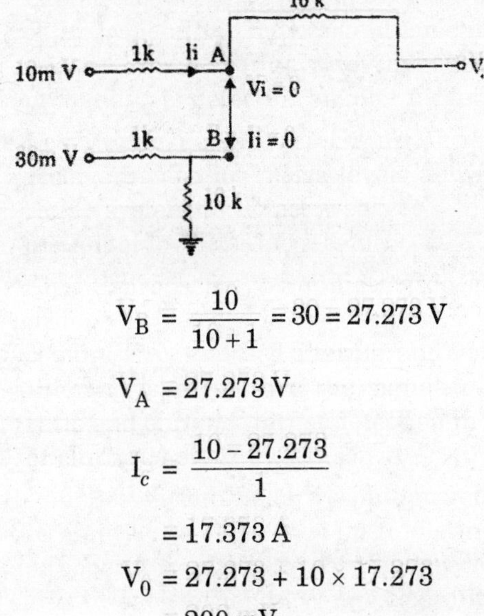

$$V_B = \frac{10}{10+1} = 30 = 27.273\ V$$

$\therefore \quad V_A = 27.273$ V

$$I_c = \frac{10 - 27.273}{1}$$

$$= 17.373\ A$$

$$V_0 = 27.273 + 10 \times 17.273$$

$$= 200\ mV$$

CHAPTER

Digital Electronic Circuits

NUMBER SYSTEM

Number Conversion

1. **Binary-to-Decimal conversion.**

   To convert a binary number to its decimal equivalent, add decimal equivalent of each position occupied by 1.

   e.g. $(101.01)_2 = 1 \times 2^2 + 0 \times 2^1 + 1 \times 2^0 + 0 \times 2^{-1} + 1 \times 2^{-2}$

   $= 2^2 + 0 + 2^0 + 0 + 2^{-2} = 4 + 1 + 0.25 = (5.25)_{10}$

   Subscript 2 and 10 respectively identify base of binary and decimal number systems.

2. **Decimal-to-Binary conversion.**

   A *double dabble* method is used for decimal-to-binary conversion, which is as follows :

   To convert a decimal number to its binary equivalent, progressively divide decimal number by 2, noting the remainders; the remainders taken in reverse order form the binary equivalent.

   To convert a decimal fraction to its binary equivalent, progressively multiply the fraction by 2, removing and noting the carries; the carries taken in forward order form the binary equivalent.

Binary Arithmetic

1. **Binary Addition**

   Rules of binary addition :

A	B	SUM	CARRY
0	0	0	0
0	1	1	0
1	0	1	0
1	1	0	1

2. **Binary subtraction**

   Rules of binary subtraction :

A	B	SUB	BORROW
0	0	0	0
0	1	1	1
1	0	1	0
1	1	0	0

   In subtraction, subtract column by column, borrowing wherever necessary from higher position.

3. **Binary Multiplication.**

   It is similar to decimal multiplication. In this, say A × B, each partial product is either 0 or A itself (*i.e.* multiplicand) as multiplication is either by 0 or by 1 respectively.

Signed Numbers

In decimal number system, '+' sign is used for denoting positive numbers and '–' sign is used for denoting negative numbers. (absence of any sign indicates that number is positive).

There are three binary signed number systems :

1. **Sign-magnitude Notation.**

   In this representation, MSB is used to represent sign (0 for positive and 1 for negative) and remaining bits are used to repersent magnitude of the number.

e.g., binary 6–bit number 011010 represents a positive number and its value is 26, whereas 111010 represents a negative number written as – 26.

2. One's complement Notation.

In a binary number, if each 0 is replaced by 1 and each 1 by 0, another binary number is obtained which is the one's complement of the first binary number. Both the numbers are complements of each other.

e.g. while $(0111)_2$ represents $(+7)_{10}$, $(1000)_2$ represents (–7).

3. Two's complement Notation.

By adding a 1 to the one's complement of a binary number we get the two's complement of that binary number.

e.g. 0101 represents + 5, whereas its 2's complement, 1011 (1's complement + 1) represents – 5.

Octal Number System

It is one of the popular number system. There are $8(2^3)$ combinations of 3-bit binary numbers. Therefore, sets of 3-bit binary numbers can be conveniently represented by octal numbers with base 8.

These numbers are 0, 1, 2, 3, 4, 5, 6 *and* 7.

e.g. $(1062 . 403)_8$ is an octal number and can be written as

$$(1062 . 403)_8 = 1 \times 8^3 + 0 \times 8^2 + 6 \times 8^1 + 2 \times 8^0 + 4 \times 8^{-1} + 0 \times 8^{-2} + 3 \times 8^{-3}$$

$$= 512 + 48 + 2 + \frac{4}{8} + \frac{3}{512} = (562 . 50586)_{10}$$

This procedure gives the decimal equivalent of an octal number.

Decimal to octal conversion is same as decimal to binary, the only difference is that here we have to divide the number by 8 in place of 2.

Octal-to-Binary and Binary-to-Octal conversion :

Octal numbers can be converted to equivalent binary numbes by replacing each digit by its 3-bit binary equivalent. Table below gives octal and binary equivalents for decimal numbers 0-7.

e.g. $(642 . 71)_8 = (110100010 . 111001)_2$

Similarly, binary numbers can be converted into equivalent octal numbers by making groups of 3-bits starting from LSB and moving towards MSB for integer part and grouping the bit next to binary point and move towards right for fractional part.

Hexadecimal Number System

Hexadecimal numbers are extensively used in association with microprocessors. There are 16 combinations of 4-bit binary numbers which can be entered in the microprocessor in the form of hexadecimal digits. The base (or radix) of hexadecimal number is 16. This means that it uses 16 symbols to represent all numbers. These are 0, 1, 2, 3, 4, 5, 6, 7, 8, 9, A, B, C, D, E, F.

Since both numbers as well as alphabets are used to represent the digits in hexadecimal number system, it is also called *alphanumeric number system.*

Various Numbering systems.

Decimal	Binary	Hexadecimal	Octal
0	0000	0	0
1	0001	1	1
2	0010	2	2
3	0011	3	3
4	0100	4	4
5	0101	5	5
6	0110	6	6
7	0111	7	7
8	1000	8	10
9	1001	9	11
10	1010	A	12
11	1011	B	13
12	1100	C	14
13	1101	D	15
14	1110	E	16
15	1111	F	17

Since 16 digits are used, weights are in powers of 16. Decimal equivalent of a hexadecimal string equals sum of all hexadecimal digits multiplied by their weights.

e.g.

$$
\begin{aligned}
(F8E.2B)_{16} &= F \times 16^2 + 8 \times 16^1 + E \times 16^0 + 2 \times 16^{-1} + B \times 16^{-2} \\
&= 15 \times 16^2 + 8 \times 16^1 + 14 \times 16^0 + 2 \times 16^{-1} + 11 \times 16^{-2} \\
&= 3840 + 128 + 14 + \frac{2}{16} + \frac{11}{256} \\
&= (3982.167968775)_{10}
\end{aligned}
$$

Conversion from decimal to hexadecimal is similar to the procedure used in binary and octal conversion except that here, 16 is used in dividing for integer part and multiplying for fractional part.

Hexadecimal-to-Binary and Binary-to-Hexadecimal Conversions

Hexadecimal numbers can be converted into equivalent binary by replacing each hexadecimal digit by its equivalent 4–bit binary number.

e.g.

$$
\begin{aligned}
(20E.CA)_{16} &= (0010\ 0000\ 1110.1100\ 1010)_2 \\
&= (001000001110.11001010)_2
\end{aligned}
$$

Binary numbers can also be converted into hexadecimal numbers by making groups of four bits starting from LSB and moving towards MSB, for integers, and then replacing each group of four bits by its hexadecimal equivalents. Sometimes, in forming 4-bit groupings, 0's may be required to complete the most significant digit group in the integer part.

e.g. $(10100110111110)_2 = (0010\ 1001\ 1011\ 1110)_2 = (29BE)_{16}$.

For fractional part, above procedure is repeated starting from the bit next to the hexadecimal point and moving towards the right.

CODES.

When numbers, letters or words are represented by a special group of symbols, then they are being encoded and group of symbols is called *code*.

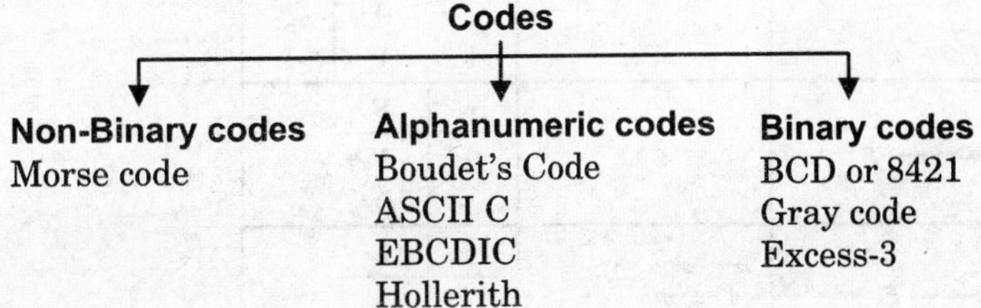

Types of Binary Codes

1. Binary Coded Decimal code (BCD code)

It is used to represent each of the 10 decimal digits as a 4 bit binary code. It is also called *8-4-2-1 code*. It is very convenient and useful code for inputs and output operations in digital circuits.

If each digit of a decimal number is represented by its binary equivalent, the result is called BCD code. Since a decimal digit can be as large as 9, four bits are required to code each digit.

e.g. consider a decimal number such as 874. Each digit is changed to its binary equivalent as follows:

8	7	4	(decimal)
↓	↓	↓	
1000	0111	0100	(BCD)

Hence, $(874)_{10} = (100001110100)_{BCD}$

2. Excess-3 code.

This is also a 4 bit code and can be derived from BCD code by adding three to each coded number.

e.g. to encode the decimal digit 4 into excess 3 code, three is added to 4 get 7.

This code is self complementing in nature, i.e. 1's complement of an Exces-3 number is the Excess-3 code for the 9's complement of the corresponding decimal number.

3. Gray code (Reflected code)

It belongs to a class of codes called *minimum change codes*. In it only one bit changes in code group when going from one step to the next. It is unweighted code. It is not used in arithmetic operation but finds application in input output devices.

In it, representation of successive numbers differs only by one bit and is therefore often used in digital systems.

Binary to gray	Gray to Binary
$G_3 = B_3$	$B_3 = G_3$
$G_2 = B_3 \oplus B_2$	$B_2 = B_3 \oplus G_2$
$G_1 = B_2 \oplus B_1$	$B_1 = B_2 \oplus G_1$
$G_0 = B_1 \oplus B_0$	$B_0 = B_1 \oplus G_0$

e.g., binary number 1101 in Gray code becomes 1011. This can be verified from the Table to generalize, the MSB of Gray code and binary code are the same. Subsequent Gray code bits are obtained by EX-Oring that bit of the binary code with its immediate higher bit.

DIGITAL LOGIC GATE

Logic gate	Graphic symbol	Algebraic function	Truth table x	y	F
AND		$F = xy$	0	0	0
			0	1	0
			1	0	0
			1	1	1
OR		$F = x+y$	0	0	0
			0	1	1
			1	0	1
			1	1	1
Inverter		$F = \overline{x}$	0		1
			1		0
Buffer		$F = x$	0		0
			1		1
NAND		$F = \overline{xy}$	0	0	1
			0	1	1
			1	0	1
NOR		$F = \overline{(x+y)}$	0	0	1
			0	1	0
			1	0	0
			1	1	0
Exclusive-OR (XOR)		$F = x\overline{y} + \overline{x}y = x \oplus y$	0	0	0
			0	1	1
			1	0	1
			1	1	0
Exclusive-NOR or equivalence		$F = xy + \overline{x}\overline{y} = x \odot y$	0	0	1
			0	1	0
			1	0	0
			1	1	1

BOOLEAN ALGEBRA

It may be defined with a set of elements, a set of operators and a number of unproved axioms or postulates. A set of elements is any collection of objects having a common property. It is a set and x and y are certain objects, then $x \in s$ denotes that x is a member of the set s, and $y \notin s$ denotes that y is not an element of s.

Basic Postulate and Theorems of Boolean Algebra

Following postulates, properties, theorems, laws of Boolean algebra form standard list for use in the course, along with the standard (for this course) identifying label in each case. Here, x, y and z represent logical variables.

Postulates:

P1*a*	$x = 1$ if $x \neq 0$	**P1*b***	$x = 0$ if $x \neq 1$
P2*a*	$0 \bullet 0 = 0$	**P2*b***	$0 + 0 = 0$
P3*a*	$1 \bullet 1 = 1$	**P3*b***	$1 + 1 = 1$
P4*a*	$1 \bullet 0 = 0$	**P4*b***	$1 + 0 = 1$
P5*a*	$1' = \bar{1} = 0$	**P5*b***	$0' = \bar{0} = 1$

Algebraic Properties

Commutativity:

P6*a*	$x \bullet y = y \bullet y$	**P6*b***	$x + y = y + x$

Associativity:

P7*a*	$x(y \bullet z) = (x \bullet y)z$	**P7*b***	$x + (y + z) = (x + y) + z$

Distributivity:

P8*a*	$x(y + z) = x \bullet y + x \bullet z$	**P8*b***	$x + y \bullet z = (x + y)(x + z)$

Theorems

T9*a*	$x \bullet 0 = 0$	**T9*b***	$x + 0 = x$
T10*a*	$x \bullet 1 = x$	**T10*b***	$x + 1 = 1$

Idempotency:

T11*a*	$x \bullet x = x$	**T11*b***	$x + x = 1$
T12*a*	$x \bullet x' = x \bullet \bar{x} = 0$	**T12*b***	$x + x' = x + \bar{x} = 1$

Double Negation Theorems:

T13*a*	$x' = \bar{\bar{x}} = x$	**T13*b***	$x = x' = \bar{\bar{x}}$

Absorption

T14*a*	$x + x \bullet y = x$	**T14*b***	$x(x + y) = x$
T14*c*	$x(\bar{x} + y) = x \bullet y$	**T14*d***	$x + \bar{x}y = x + y$

DeMorgan's Theorems

T15*a*	$\overline{x \bullet y \bullet z} = \bar{x} + \bar{y} + \bar{z}$	**T15*b***	$\overline{x + y + z} = \bar{x} \bullet \bar{y} \bullet \bar{z}$

Boolean Functions

A binary variable can take the value 0 or 1. Boolean function is an expression formed with binary variables, two binary operators OR and AND, and unary operator NOT, parentheses, and an equal sign.

For a given value of the variables, function can be either.

e.g. consider Boolean function, $F_1 = xy\bar{z}$

Function F_1 is equal to 1 if $x = 1$ and $y = 1$ and $\bar{z} = 1$; otherwise $F_1 = 0$.

Boolean function may also be represented in a truth table. To represent a function in a truth table, we a list of the 2^n combination of 1's and 0's of the n binary variables is required and a column showing the combinations for which function is equal to 1 or 0.

For given function $F_1 = xy\bar{z}$, Truth Table is shown below :

x	y	z	$F_1 = xy\bar{z}$
0	0	0	0
0	0	1	0
0	1	0	0
0	1	1	0
1	0	0	0
1	0	1	0
1	1	0	1
1	1	1	0

VK Map Method of Solving Boolean Function

This method provides a simple straight forward procedure for minimizing Boolean functions. This method may be regarded either as a pictorial form of a truth table or as an extension of the Venn diagram. The map is a diagram made up of squares. Each square represents on minterm. Since any Boolean function can be expressed as a sum of minterms, it follows that a Boolean function is recognized graphically in the map from the area enclosed by those squares whose minterms are included in the function. In fact, the map presents a visual diagram of all possible ways a function may be expressed in a standard form.

Boolean Relations

Some basic Logic gate relations, Operations.

(1) **OR operation :** $A + 0 = A$, $A + 1 = 1$

$A + A = A$, $A + \bar{A} = 1$

A, B → Y = A + B

(2) **AND operation :** $A . 0 = 0$, $A . 1 = A$

$A . A = A$, $A . \bar{A} = 0$

A, B → Y = A . B

(3) **Commutative law :** $A + B = B + A$

(4) **Associative law :** $A + (B + C) = (A + B) + C$

(5) **Distributive law :** $A . (B + C) = A . B + A . C$

(6) $A + (B . C) = (A + B) . (A + C)$

(7) $A = \bar{\bar{A}}$

De Morgan's Theorem

(*i*) $\overline{A + B} = \bar{A} . \bar{B}$

(*ii*) $\overline{A . B} = \bar{A} + \bar{B}$

To obtain inverse of any Boolean function, invert all variable and replace all OR's by AND's and vice versa.

Truth Table to prove De Morgan's theorem.

A	B	$\bar{A}$	$\bar{B}$	$\overline{A.B}$	$\bar{A} + \bar{B}$	$\overline{A+B}$	$\bar{A} . \bar{B}$
0	0	1	1	1	1	1	1
0	1	1	0	1	1	0	0
1	0	0	1	1	1	0	0
1	1	0	0	0	0	0	0

Duality Theorem

This theorem says that starting with a Boolean relation, we can derive another Boolean relation, called its *dual* by the following steps :

(1) Changing each OR sign to an AND sign

(2) Changing each AND sign to an OR sign

(3) Complementing all 0's and 1's

e.g., dual of A . 0 = 0 is written as A + 1 = 1.

Sum-of-Products/Product-of-Sums method

Switching function (Boolean function) implied by a truth table may be stated as sum-or-products (SOP) or a product-of-sums (POS).

e.g. For an EXOR truth table, Output = $\bar{A}B + A\bar{B}$ (SOP form)

and Output = $(A + B)(\bar{A} + \bar{B})$ (POS form)

Here each term contains all the inputs, *i.e.* individual Boolean variables in complemented or uncomplemented form called literals. This is the canonical or standard form. Each term in standard SOP form is called **minterm** and that each term in standard POS form is called **maxterm.** For *n* inputs there are 2^n – maxterms. Two logically different functions do not contain the same set of minterms (maxterms).

Consider example of a two input OR with truth Table given below :

Truth Table

A	B	Y	Minterm	Maxterm
0	0	0	$\bar{A}\bar{B}$	A + B
0	1	1	$\bar{A}B$	$A + \bar{B}$
1	0	1	$A\bar{B}$	$\bar{A} + B$
1	1	1	AB	$\bar{A} + \bar{B}$

Output is given by sum of minterm corresponding to 1 output.

$$Y = \bar{A}B + A\bar{B} + AB \text{ ; (SOP form)}$$

Output can written as product of those maxterms which correspond to 0 output, *i.e.*

$$Y = A + B \text{ ; (POS form)}$$

Equivalence of these expression is established below :

$$= \bar{A}B + A\bar{B} + AB$$

$$= \bar{A}B + A(\bar{B} + B)$$

$$= \bar{A}B + A = A + \bar{A}B$$

$$= (A + \bar{A})(A + B) \quad \text{(Distributive law)}$$

$$= (A + B)$$

KARNAUGH MAP.

SOP form Simplification using K-Map

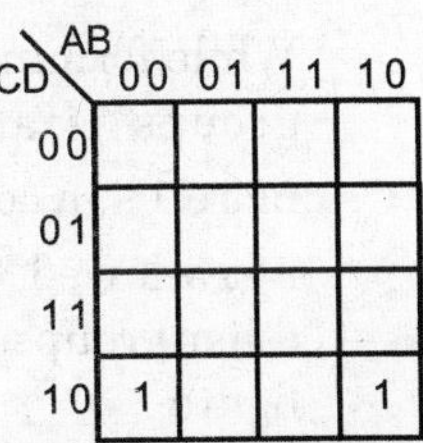

Fig. Karnaugh Map

To get simplified expression in SOP form (AND-OR configutation), corresponding to each minterm in the given function, '1' is entered in the corresponding cell of the K map.

Consider the term $\bar{B}C\bar{D}$. Enter 1 in the two cells with B = 0, C = 1 and D = 0 but A can be either 0 or 1. These entries are shown in the figure. Such entries are made for all terms of a sum-or-products expression.

Simplification proceeds by combining 1's of adjacent cells.

Two cells are said to be adjacent if

(i) these are vertically above each other or are in the top and bottom cells of a column and

(ii) these are horizontally side by side or in left and right most cells of a row.

In combining adjacent cells, these differ in one variable only because of use of the Gray code.

1's of the K-map are combined in groups of 2^i where *i* = 1, 2, . . ., *n; n* being number of variables.

Types of Combinations for Simplification

1. Pair.

The sum-of-products terms corresponding to a pair of adjacent 1's can be combined to eliminate the variable, which appears in complemented form in these terms; this results from the use of Gray code.

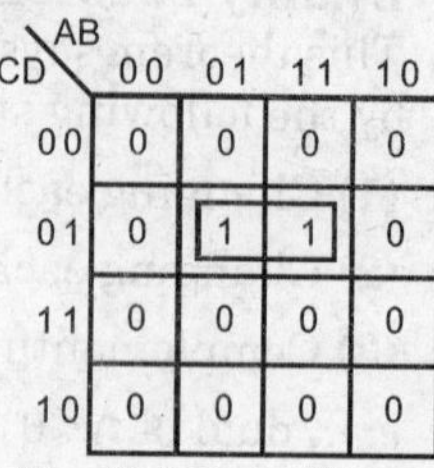

Fig. Pair on a K-map

Thus in figure, for the pair of 1's

$$Y = \overline{A}B\overline{C}D + AB\overline{C}D = B\overline{C}D(\overline{A} + A)$$
$$= B\overline{C}D; \quad \text{A is eliminated.}$$

2. Quad.

It is a group of four adjacent 1's in a K-map. It can appear in various ways as shown below. This group is called a **quad** which leads to the elimination of two variables. Thus Y's corresponding to the four quads figures are given below.

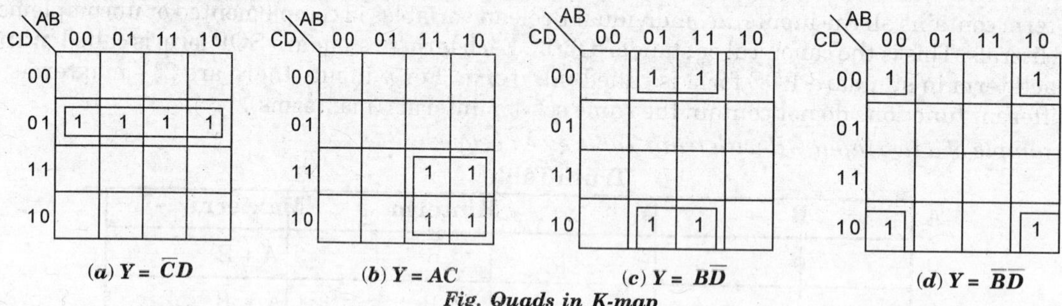

(*a*) $Y = \overline{C}D$ (*b*) $Y = AC$ (*c*) $Y = B\overline{D}$ (*d*) $Y = \overline{B}\overline{D}$

Fig. Quads in K-map

3. Octet.

It is a group of eight adjacent 1's as shown in the figure below. It leads to elimination of three variables.

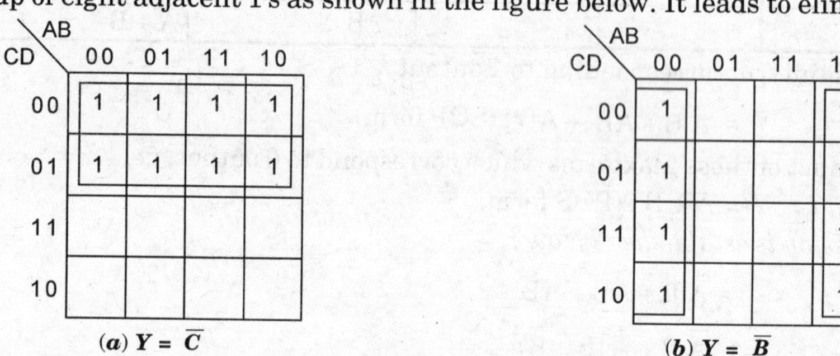

(*a*) $Y = \overline{C}$ (*b*) $Y = \overline{B}$

Fig. Octet in K-maps

In a K-map there may be more than one pair or a quad or an octet. Because of simplification afforded identification must proceed first as octet, followed by quads and then pairs. 1's which cannot be grouped must also be encircled. Then boolean equation is obtained by ORing the products corresponding to the encircled groups.

While forming groups, it is to be noted that overlapping of groups is allowed, *i.e.* two groups can have one or more 1's in common. At the same time, redundancy is not allowed, *i.e.* a group whose all 1's are overlapped by other groups. Both these grouping are shown in the given figure.

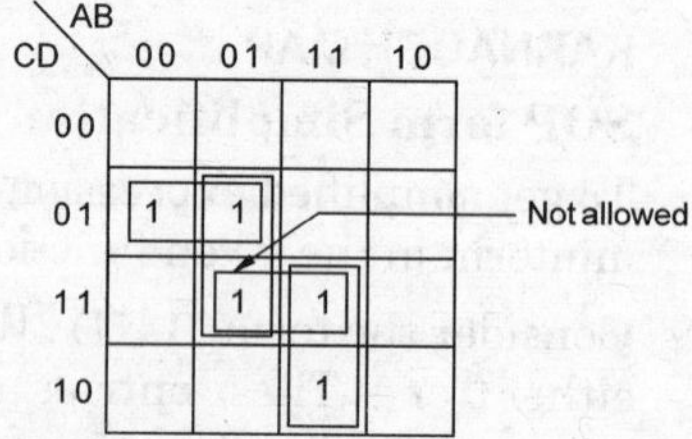

Fig. Redundant group not (allowed)

IC LOGIC FAMILIES

Digitalic Specification Terminology

Propagation Delay.

It is the amount of time lapse during propagation of pulse through a gate from input to output.

$$t_{pd} = \frac{t_{PLH} + t_{PHL}}{2}$$

where, t_{PLH} = signal delay time when the output goes form a logic 0 to a logic 1 state
t_{PHL} = signal delay time when the output goes from a logic 1 to a logic 0 state

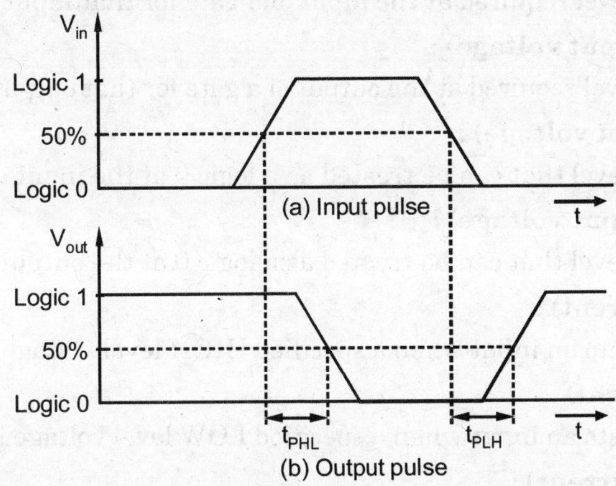

Fig. Propagation delay in an inverter

Power Dissipation (P_D).

Power dissipation of a logic gate is the power required by the gate to operate with 50% duty cycle at a specified frequency and is expressed in milliwatts.

$$\text{Power dissipation of a gate, } P_D = V_{CC} \times I_{CC}\,(\text{avg})/n$$

where, V_{CC} = gate supply voltage,
I_{CC} (avg)= average current drawn from the supply by the entire IC
n = the number of gates in the IC.

Now,
$$I_{CC}\,(\text{avg}) = \frac{I_{CCH} + I_{CCL}}{2}$$

where, I_{CCH} = current drawn by the IC when all the gates in the IC are in HIGH state
I_{CCL} = current drawn by the IC when all the gates in the IC are in LOW state.

Total power consumed by an IC is equal to product of the power dissipated by each gate and number of gates in that IC.

Fan-in.

Fan-in of a logic gate is defined as the number of inputs that the gate is designed to handle.

Fan-out.

Fan-out (also called *loading factor*) of a logic gate is defined as maximum number of standard loads that output of the gate can drive without impairing its normal operation.

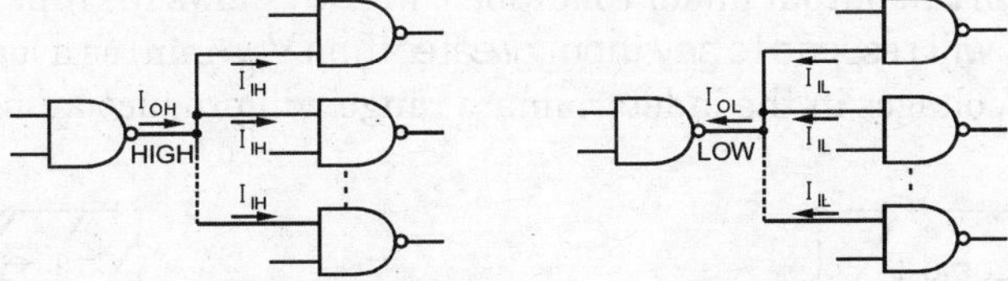

(a) Current sourcing in HIGH state *(b) Current sinking in LOW state*

Fig. High state and Low state fan-outs

Fan-out may be HIGH state fan-out, *i.e.* fan-out of the gate when its output is at logic 1, or it may be LOW state fan-output, *i.e.* fan-out of the gate when its output is at logic 0.

The fan-out of a gate affects the propagation delay time as well as saturation. The driving gate sinks current when it is in LOW state and sources current when it is in HIGH state.

$$\text{HIGH state fan-out} = \frac{I_{OH}\,(\text{max})}{I_{IH}}$$

$$\text{LOW state fan-out} = \frac{I_{OL}\,(\text{max})}{I_{IL}}$$

Voltage and Current Parameters.

(1) V_{IH} (min) (HIGH level input voltage) :

It is the minimum voltage level required at the input of a gate for that input to be treated as a logic 1.

(2) V_{OH}(min) (HIGH level output voltage) :

It is the minimum voltage level required at the output of a gate for that output to be treated as a logic 1.

(3) V_{IL} (max) (LOW level input voltage) :

It is the maximum voltage level that can be treated as a logic 0 at the input of the gate.

(4) V_{OL} (max) (LOW level output voltage) :

It is the maximum voltage level that can be treated as a logic 0 at the output of the gate.

(5) I_{IH} (HIGH level input current) :

It is the current that flows into an input when a specified HIGH level voltage is applied to that input.

(6) I_{IL} (LOW level input current) :

It is the current that flows into an input when a specified LOW level voltage is applied to that input.

(7) I_{OH} (HIGH level output current) :

It is the current that flows from an output in a logic 1 state under specified load conditions.

Figure below shows currents and voltages in the HIGH and LOW states.

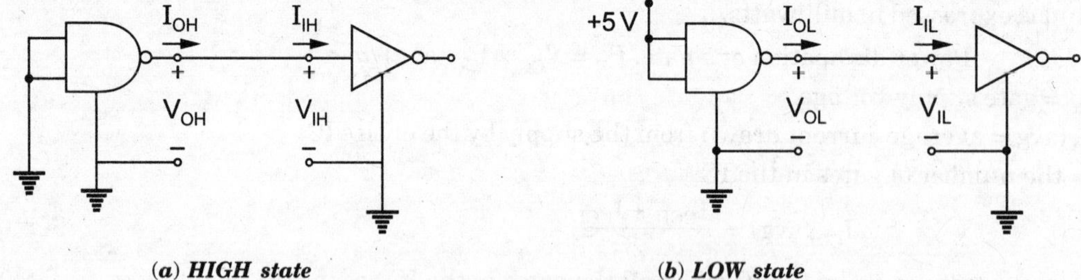

(*a*) *HIGH state* (*b*) *LOW state*

Fig. Currents and voltages in the HIGH and LOW states

Noise Margin.

Noise immunity of a logic circuit refers to the circuits ability to tolerate noise voltages at its inputs. A quantitative measure of noise immunity is called *noise margin.* Unwanted spurious signals are called *noise*. Noise may be ac noise or dc noise. A drift in the voltage levels of signals is called dc noise. The ac noise is a random pulse caused by other switching signals. Noise margin is expressed in volts and represents the maximum noise signal that can be added to the input signal of a digital circuit without causing an undersirable change in the circuit output. Fig. (*a*) shows the range of output voltages that can occur in a logic circuit. Voltages in the disallowed range should not appear at a logic circuit output under conditions. Fig. (*b*) shows the input voltage requirements of a logic circuit. The logic circuit will respond to any input greater than V_{IH} (min) as a logic 1 and to any input lower than V_{IL} (max) as a logic 0. Voltages in the indeterminate range will produce an unpredictable response and should not be used.

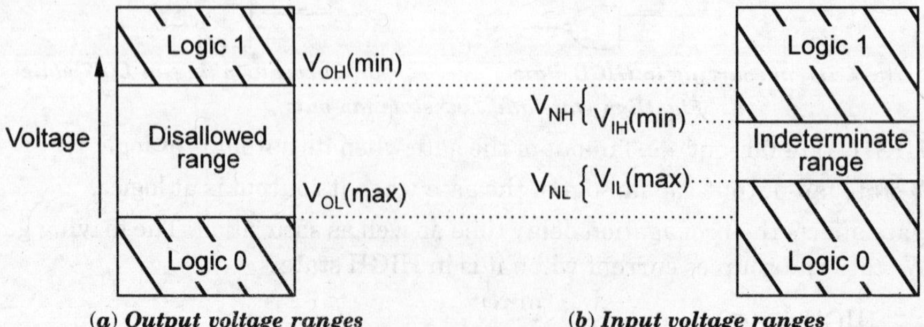

(*a*) ***Output voltage ranges*** (*b*) ***Input voltage ranges***

Fig. DC noise margins

Noise margin may be High state noise margin or Low state noise margin.

High state noise margin (NM_H), $V_{NH} = V_{OH}(\text{min}) - V_{IH}(\text{min})$

Low state noise margin (NM_L), $V_{NL} = V_{IL}(\text{max}) - V_{OL}(\text{max})$

Operating Temperatures.

For IC gates, specified range of temperature :

Commercial applications 0 to 70°C.

Industrial it 0 to 85°C

Military applications – 55°C to 125°C.

Speed Power Product.

It is obtained by multiplying gate propagation delay by the gate power dissipation. A low value of speed power product is desirable.

Let an IC family has an average propagation delay of 10 ns and an average power dissipation of 5 mW.

$\therefore$ Speed power product = 10 ns × 5 mW

= 50×10^{-12} watt-seconds

= 50 picjoulses (pJ)

I.C. FAMILIES

1. Resistor-Transistor Logic (RTL) Gate

The basic circuit of RTL digital logic family is the NOR gate as shown in the figure given below.

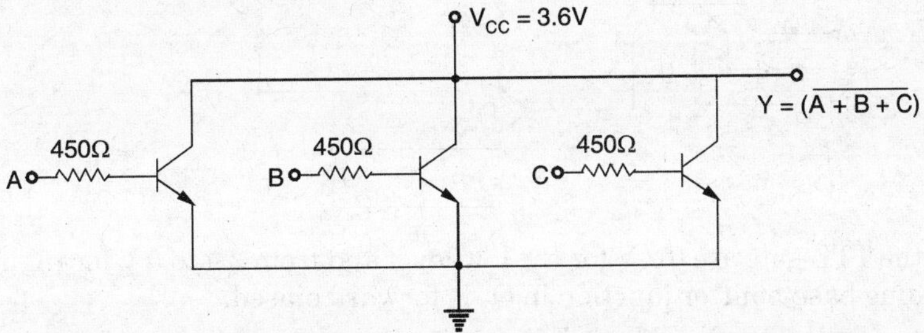

Each input is associated with one resistor and one transistor. The collectors of the transistors are tied together at the output. The voltage levels for the circuit are 0.2 V for the low level and from 1 to 3.6 V for high level. If any input of the RTL gate is high, the corresponding transistor is driven into saturation. This causes the output to be low, regardless of the state of the other transistors. If all inputs are low at 0.2 V, all transistors are cut off because V_{BE} < 0.6 V. This causes output of the circuit to be high, approaching the value of supply voltage V_{CC}.

Fan-out of the RTL gate is limited by the value of the output voltage when high. As output is loaded with input of other gate, more current is consumed by the load. This current must flow through 640 Ω resistor.

The power dissipation of RTL gate is about 10 mW and propagation delay averages 50 *ns*.

2. Diode Transistor Logic Gate

The basic circuit in the DTL digital logic family is the NAND gate as shown in the figure below.

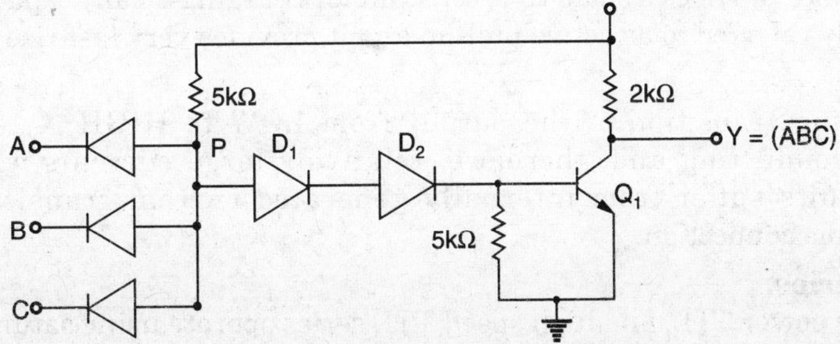

Each input is associated with one diode. The diodes and the 5 kΩ resistor form an AND gate. The transistor serves as a current amplifier while inverting the digital signal. The two voltage levels are 0.2 V for low level, and between 4 and 5 V for the high level.

The power dissipation of a DTL gate is about 8 mW and the propagation delay averages 30 *ns*. The noise margin is about 1 V and a fan-out as high as 8 is possible. The fan-out of the DTL gate is limited by the maximum current that can flow in the collector of the saturated transistor.

3. Transistor-Transistor Logic (TTL) Gate

The standard TTL gate is the first version in the TTL family. This basic gate is then designed with different resistor values to produce gates with lower power dissipation or with higher speed. The propagation delay of transistor circuit that goes into saturation depends mostly on two factors ; storage time and RC time constant. Reducing storage time decreases the propagation delay. Reducing resistor values in the circuit reduces the RC time constants and decreases the propagation delay. The speed of the gate is inversely proportional to the propagation delay.

In the low power TTL gate, the resistor values are higher than in standard gate to reduce the power dissipation, but the propagation delay is increased. In the high speed TTL gate, resistor values are lowered to reduce the propagation delay, but the power dissipation is increased.

All TTL series are available in SSI and in more complex forms as MSI and LSI components. The difference in the TTL series are not in the digital logic that they perform, but rather in the internal construction of the basic NAND gate.

The basic TTL gate is NAND gate as shown in the figure below

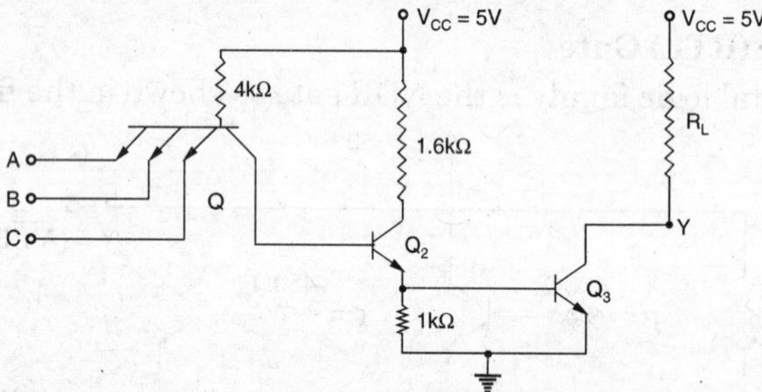

The two voltages of the TTL gate are 0.2 V for the low level and from 2.4 to 5 V for high level. If any input is low, then corresponding base-emitter junction in Q_1 is forward biased.

In any case, TTL gates in all the available series come in three different types of output configuration:

(*i*) Out - collector output

(*ii*) Totem - pole output

(*iii*) *Tri-state (or 3–State) TTL output:* It utilizes advantage of high speed of operation of the totem-pole configuration and wire ANDing of the open-collector configuration. It is called tri-state TTL, because it allows three possible output states:

HIGH, LOW, and HIGH impedance (Hi-Z).

In the Hi-Z state, both transistors in the totem-pole arrangements are turned off, so that output terminal is a HIGH impedance to ground or V_{CC}. In fact, the output is an open or floating terminal, *i.e.* LOW nor a HIGH. In practice the output terminal is not an exact open circuit, but has a resistance of several MΩ or more relative to ground and V_{CC}.

Advantage : In the output HIGH state, Q_3 acts as an emitter follower with its associated low output impedance. This low output impedance provides a small time constant for charging up any capacitive load on the output. This action is commonly referred to as active pull-up and it provides very fast rise time waveforms at TTL output.

Disadvantages : During transition of the output from LOW to HIGH, Q_4 turns off more slowly than Q_3 and Q_4 are conducting and, therefore, relatively large currents will be drawn from the supply. So, TTL circuits suffer from internally generated current transients or current spikes because of the totem-pole connection.

Schottky TTL, 74S series.

The standard TTL, low power TTL, and high speed TTL series operate using saturated switching. When a transistor is saturated, excess charge carriers will be stored in the base region and they must be removed before the transistor can be turned off. So, owing to storage time delay, the speed is reduced.

The Schottky TTL 74S series reduces this storage time delay by not allowing the transistor to go into full saturation. This is accomplished by using a Schottky barrier diode (SBD) between the base and the collector of each transistor. Virtually, all modern TTL devices incorporate this so-called Schottky clamp. The SBD has a forward voltage of only 0.25 V. The circuits in the 74S series also use smaller resistance values to improve the speed of operation. The speed of the 74S series is twice that of the 74H series. Schottky TTL has more than three times the switching speed of standard TTL, at the expense of approximately doubling the power consumption.

4. Complementary MOS (CMOS)

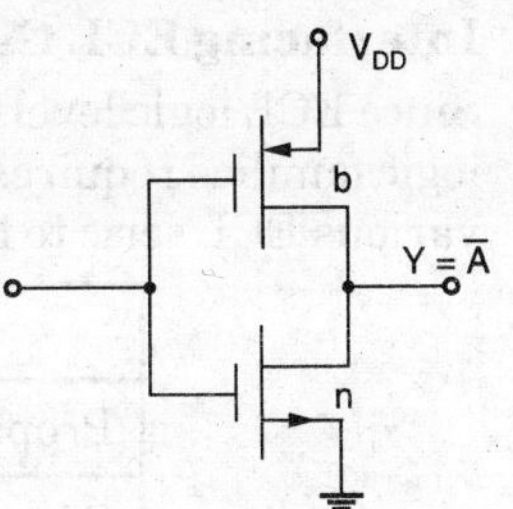

These circuits take advantage of the fact that both n - channel and p - channel devices can be fabricated on the same substrate. CMOS circuits consist of both types of MOS devices interconnected to form logic functions. The basic circuit is the inverter, which consists of one p-channel transistor and one n - transistor as shown in the figure.

The basic circuit consists of one p - channel transistor and one n - channel transistor. The source terminal of the p - channel device is at V_{DD} and the source terminal of the n-channel device is at ground. The value of V_{DD} may vary from any where from + 3 to + 18 V. The two voltage levels are 0 V for the low level and V_{DD} for the high level.

When a CMOS circuit is in a static state, its power dissipation is very low. This is because there is always an off transistor in the current path when the state of the circuit is not changing. As a result, a typical CMOS gate has a static power dissipation on the order of 0.01 mW. However when the circuit is changing state at a rate of MHz, the power dissipation increases to about 1 mW. CMOS logic is usually specified for a single power - supply operation over the range between 3 and 18 V with a typical V_{DD} value of 5 V. Operating CMOS at a larger value of supply voltage reduces the propagation delay time and improves the noise margin, but the power dissipation is increased. The propagation delay time with V_{DD} = 5 V ranges from 8 to 50 *ns*, depending on the type of CMOS used. The noise margin is usually about 40 percent of the V_{DD} supply voltage. The fan-out of CMOS gates, is 50 when operated at a frequency of less than 1 MHz. The fan-out decreases with increase in frequency of operation.

CMOS fabrication process is simpler than TTL and provides a greater packing density. This means that more circuit can be placed on a given area of silicon at a reduced cost per function. This property of CMOS, together with its low power dissipation, excellent noise community and reasonable propagation delay, makes it a strong contender for a popular standard as a digital logic family.

5. Emitter-Coupled Logic (ECL)

It is also called *current-mode logic or current-steering logic.*

It is fastest of all logic families because

(*i*) it is a non-saturated logic, in the sense that the transistors are not allowed to go into saturation. So, storage time delays are eliminated and, therefore, speed of operation is increased.

(*ii*) currents are kept high, and the output impedance is so low that circuit and stray capacitances can be quickly charged and discharged.

(*iii*) of the limited voltage swing.

ECL because of its use of BJTs that are coupled (joined) at their emitters. In ECL, the transistors are prevented from going into saturation when the input changes from LOW to HIGH, by choosing logic levels very close to each other. One disadvantage of having logic levels close to each other is that, it is difficult to achieve good noise immunity. Also, the power consumption is increased since the transistors are not saturated. But the advantage is that the current drawn from the supply is more steady and ECL gates do not experience large switching transients. The ECL family has considerably greater power consumption compared to other families.

The ECL operates on the principle of current switching, whereby a fixed bias current less than I_C(sat) is switched from one transistor's collector to another. Because of this current mode operation, this form is also referred to as current-mode logic (CML). It is also called current-steering logic (CSL), because current is steered from one device to another. The ECL family is not as popular and widely used as the TTL and MOS, except in very high frequency applications where its speed is superior.

Characteristics of ECL Gates.

(*i*) Transistors never saturate, so, speed is high with t_{pd} = 1 ns.

(*ii*) Logic levels are negative, – 0.9 V for a logic 1 and – 1.7 V for a logic 0.

(*iii*) Noise margin is less, about 250 mV, which makes ECL unreliable for use in heavy industrial environment.

(*iv*) ECL circuits produce the output and its complement, and therefore eliminate need for inverters.

(*v*) Fan-out is large because output impedance is low. It is about 25.

(*vi*) Power dissipation per gate is large, P_D = 40 mW.

(*vii*) Total current flow in ECL is more or less constant, so, no noise spikes will be internally generated.

Interfacing ECL Gates.

Since ECL logic levels are so different from those of TTL and CMOS circuits, interfacing ECL gates with other logic families requires special level shifter circuits called **level translators.** Level translators are available in various ECL seris to facilitate interfacing of ECL with other families.

	DTL	HTL	TTL	ECL	ECL	CMOS
Propagation delay (ns)	50	30	90	10	1	70
Power dissipation (mw)	10	8	55	10	5	0.01
Figure of merit (pj)	500	240	5000	100	55	0.7
Fan out	3	3	10	10	25	50
Noise margin	0.2	0.7	4	0.4	0.3	0.35 V_{DD}

	Propagation delay (ns)	Power dissipation (mw)	Figure of merit (pj)	Fan in	Fan out	Noise margin
Lowest	ECL	CMOS	RTL	RTL	RTL	I^2L
Highest	MOS	ECL	CMOS	CMOS	CMOS	ECL

COMBINATIONAL CIRCUIT

ADDERS AND SUBTRACTORS.

Symbol of XOR gate, its truth-table and K-map are given in Fig. (*a*), (*b*) and (*c*).

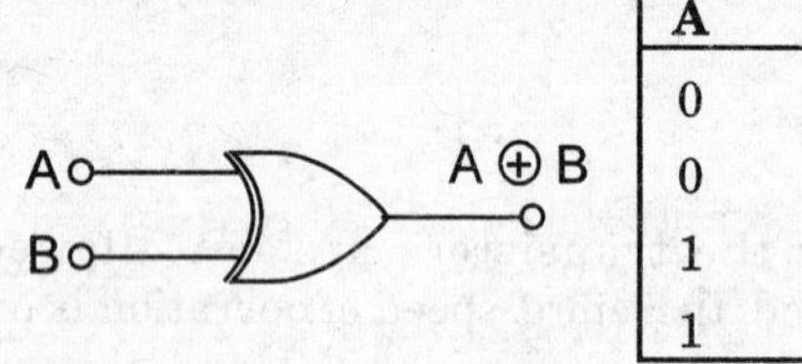

(*a*)

A	B	A⊕B
0	0	0
0	1	1
1	0	1
1	1	0

Fig. (b) Truth table

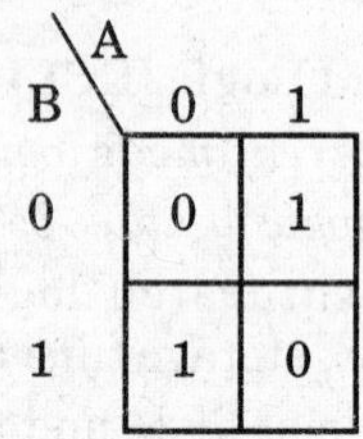

B \ A	0	1
0	0	1
1	1	0

Fig. (c) K-map

$$A \oplus B = \overline{A}B + A\overline{B}$$

$$= \overline{(A+\overline{B})(\overline{A}+B)}; \quad \text{(De Morgan's theorem)}$$

$$= \overline{A\overline{A} + AB + \overline{A}\,\overline{B} + \overline{B}B}$$

$$= \overline{AB + \overline{A}\,\overline{B}}$$

$$= \overline{AB}\,(\overline{\overline{A}\,\overline{B}})$$

$$= (A+B)\,\overline{AB}$$

XOR implementation via function of of above equation is shown in Fig. (*d*).

It needs three gates:

(*i*) OR

(*ii*) NAND

(*iii*) AND.

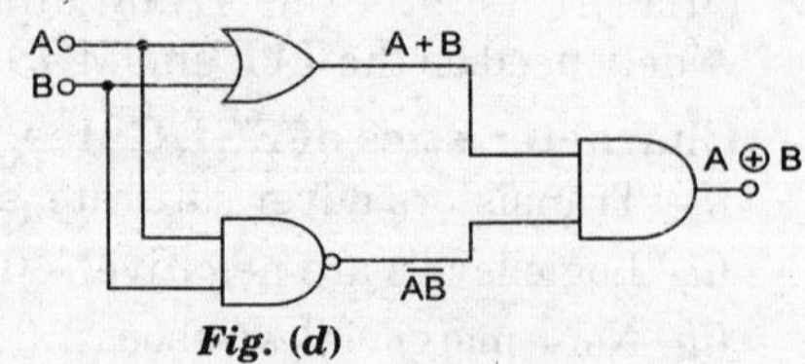

Fig. (d)

The fucntion $(\bar{A}B + A\bar{B})$ is called *inequality comparator*, because it provides an output 1 only if A and B are not equal. The inverse (complement) of inequality comparator is an equality comparator. It is functionally manipulated as

$$\overline{\bar{A}B + A\bar{B}} = (A+\bar{B})(\bar{A}+B) = AB + \bar{A}\bar{B}$$

Types of Adders and Subtractors

1. **Half Adder (HA).**

This circuit adds two binary variables, yields a carry but does not accept carry from another circuit (adder). The truth table of half adder is given in Fig. (*a*) below from which we can write

$$S = \bar{A}B + A\bar{B} = A \oplus B$$
$$C = AB$$

A	B	S	C
0	0	0	0
0	1	1	0
1	0	1	0
1	1	0	1

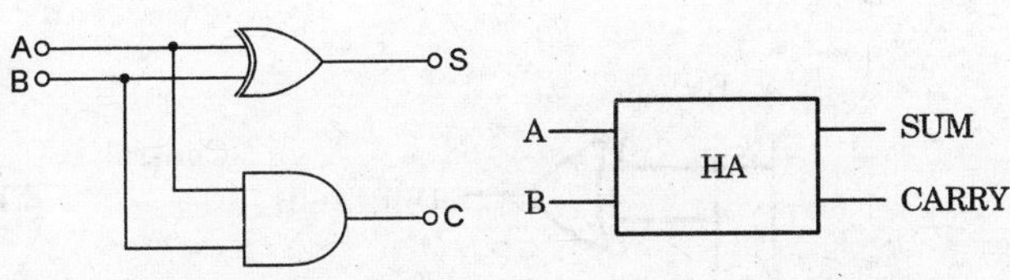

Fig.* (*a*) *Truth Table

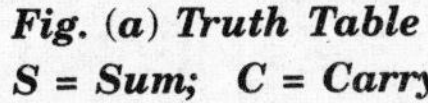

S = Sum; C = Carry

Fig.* (*b*) *Circuit using XOR

***Fig.* (*c*)**

2. **Full Adder**

This circuit can add two binary numbers, accept a carry and yield a carry. Such a circuit can easily be visualized by means of two half adders (HA) and OR.

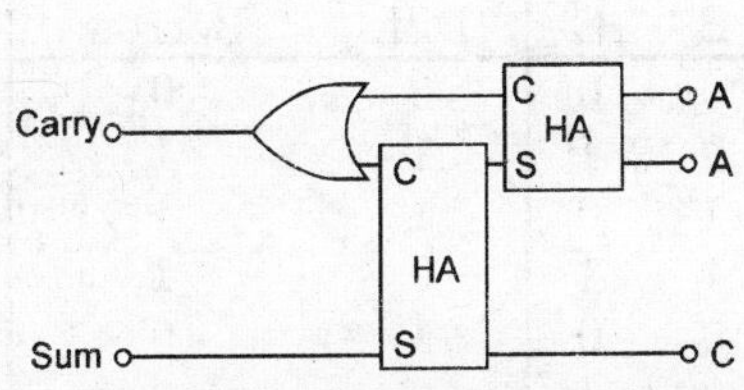

Fig. Full adder using two half address

Truth-table

A	B	C_i	S	C_0
0	0	0	0	0
0	0	1	1	0
0	1	0	1	0
0	1	1	0	1
1	0	0	1	0
1	0	1	0	1
1	1	0	0	1
1	1	1	1	1

From given truth-table, full-adder circuit can be synthesize.

Here C_i = input carry, S = sum, and C_0 = output carry.

From table, $$S = \bar{A}\bar{B}C_i + \bar{A}B\bar{C}_i + A\bar{B}\bar{C}_i + ABC_i$$

and $$C_0 = \bar{A}BC_i + A\bar{B}C_i + AB\bar{C}_i + ABC_i$$

Since, Y + Y + ... + Y = Y and adding ABC_i twice to right hand side of above equation, we can write

$$C_0 = (\bar{A}BC_i + ABC_i) + (A\bar{B}C_i + ABC_i) + (AB\bar{C}_i + ABC_i)$$

Observing that $Y + \bar{Y} = 1$

we get, $$C_0 = BC_i + AC_i + AB$$

Following identity is easily established :

$$S = \left[\left(\overline{AC_i + BC_i + AB}\right) + ABC_i\right](A + B + C_i)$$
$$= \left[\left(\overline{AC_i}\,.\,\overline{BC_i}\,.\,AB\right) + ABC_i\right](A + B + C_i)$$
$$= \left(\overline{AC_i}\,.\,\overline{BC_i}\,.\,\overline{AB}\right)(A + B + C_i) + ABC_i$$
$$= \left(\bar{A} + \bar{C}_i\right)\left(\bar{B} + \bar{C}_i\right)(\bar{A} + \bar{B})(A + B + C_i) + ABC_i$$
$$= \bar{A}\bar{B}C_i + \bar{A}B\bar{C}_i + A\bar{B}\bar{C}_i + ABC_i$$
$$= S$$

3. Half substractor

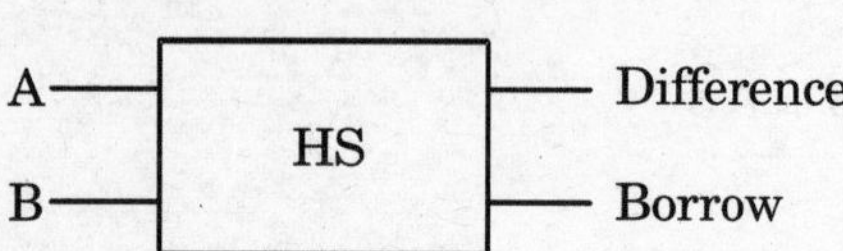

Truth Table.

A	B	D	B
0	0	0	0
0	1	1	1
1	0	1	0
1	1	0	0

Logical Expression :

Difference = $\bar{A}B + A\bar{B} = A \oplus B$

Borrow = $\bar{A}B$

Circuit diagram

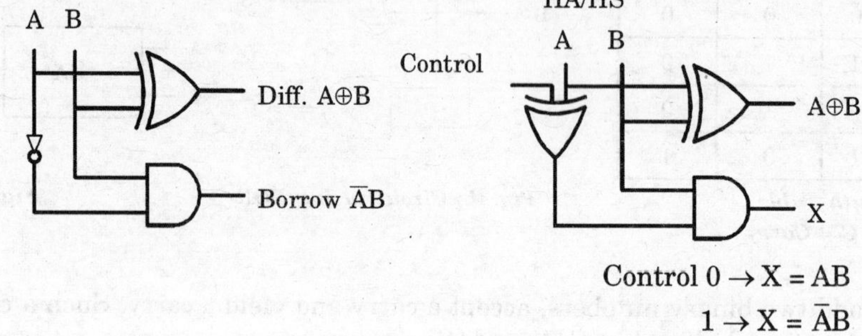

4. Full substractor.

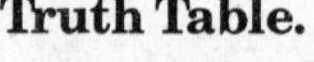

Truth Table.

A	B	C	Diff.	Borrow
0	0	0	0	0
0	0	1	1	1
0	1	0	1	1
0	1	1	0	1
1	0	0	1	0
1	0	1	0	0
1	1	0	0	0
1	1	1	1	1

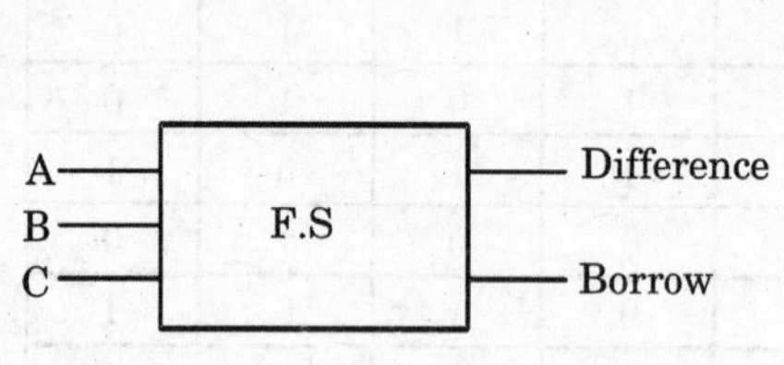

Difference = $A \oplus B \oplus C$

Borrow = $\bar{A}C + \bar{A}B + BC$

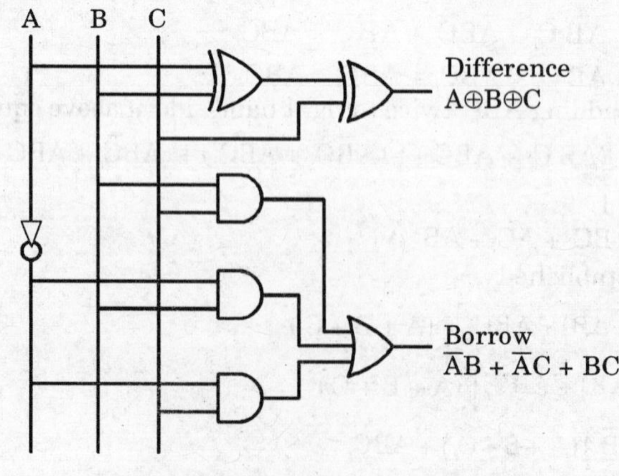

Circuit diagram

DIGITAL COMPARATOR.

A 1-bit digital comparator circuit is shown in Fig. (*a*). XOR gate with an inverter at the output acts as an equality comparator so that A = B if $y = 1$.

It follows that X = 1 implies A > B and Z = 1 means A < B.

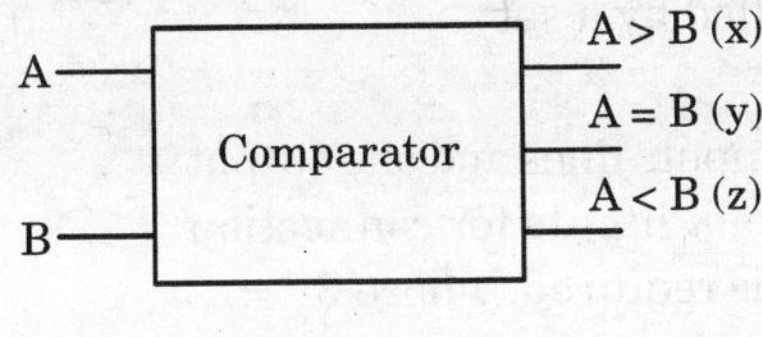

Fig. (a)

Truth table

A	B	x	y	z
0	0	0	1	0
0	1	0	0	1
1	0	1	0	0
1	1	0	1	0

Circuit diagram

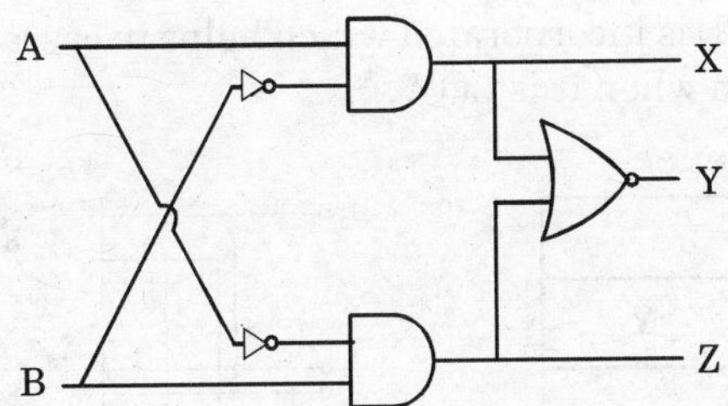

Logical expression

$X = A\overline{C}$

$Y = \overline{A}\,\overline{B} + AB = A \odot B$

$Z = \overline{A}B$

PARITY.

Odd and Even Parity

It is an arithmetic operation that is often used in a digital system for determining whether sum of the binary bits in a word is odd, which is called *odd parity*, or even which is called *even parity*.

e.g., 11000010 has odd parity while 01011100 has even parity.

Parity checker/Generator

Exclusive OR gates are ideal for checking parity of a binary number because output of this gate is 1, if and only if, one input is 1 and the other is 0. Alternatively stated, output is 1 if sum of the digits is 1, odd parity.

The concept can easily be extended to any number of inputs. Figure given below shows 4-input Exclusive-OR tree for checking parity of a 4-bit word. Input P′ can be considered as a cascading input.

In this circuit Z = 1 or Y = 0, if sum of the input bits A, B, C and D is odd.

Hence, if input P′ is grounded (P′ = 0), then P = 0 for odd parity and P = 1 for even parity.

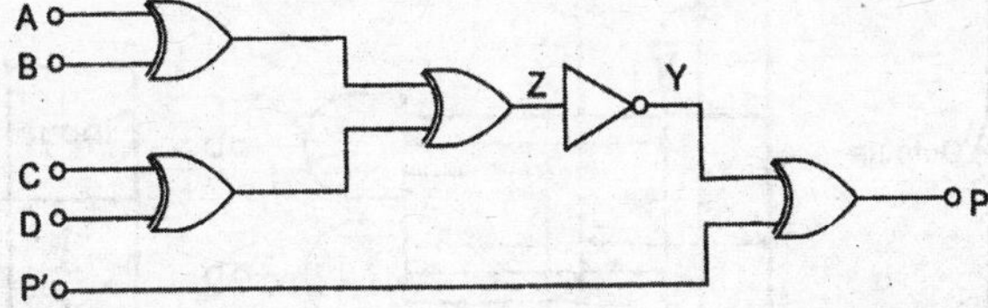

Fig. Odd parity checker/generator for a 4-bit word

Above circuit may also be used to generate a parity bit P. Independently of the parity of the 4-bit input word, parity of the 5-bit code A, B, C, D and P is odd. This statement follows from the fact that, if sum of A, B, C, and D is odd (even), then P is 0 (1) and therefore the sum of A, B, C, D and P is always odd. To get an even parity generator, delete the inverter in the circuit.

MULTIPLEXERS AND DEMULTIPLEXERS.

Multiplexer

It is a special combinational circuit which is most widely used standard circuit in digital design. Multiplexer (or data selector) is a logic circuit that gates one out of several inputs to single outputs. The input selected is controlled by a set of select inputs.

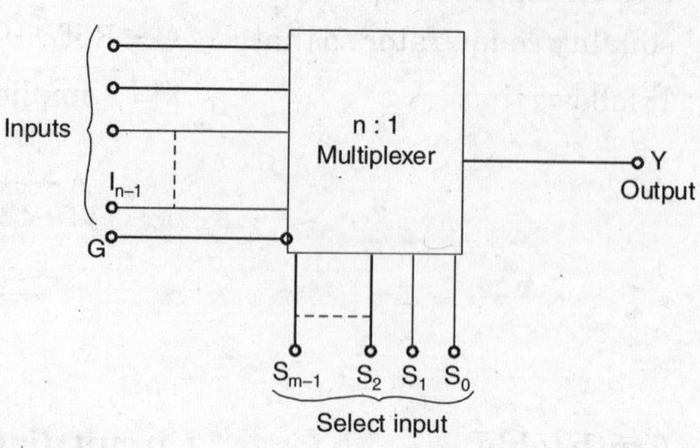

Block diagram of a multiplexer with n inputs lines and one output line (as shown) for selecting one out of n inputs for connection to the output, a set of m select inputs is required, where $2^m = n$. Depending upon the digital code applied at the select input one out of n date source is selected and transmitted to a single output channel.

Normally a strobe (or enable) input (G) is incorporated which helps in cascading and it is generally active low, which means it performs its operation when it is LOW.

Truth Table for *a* 4 : 1 multiplexer

Select Inputs	Output	
S_1	S_0	Y
0	0	I_0
0	1	I_1
1	0	I_2
1	1	I_3

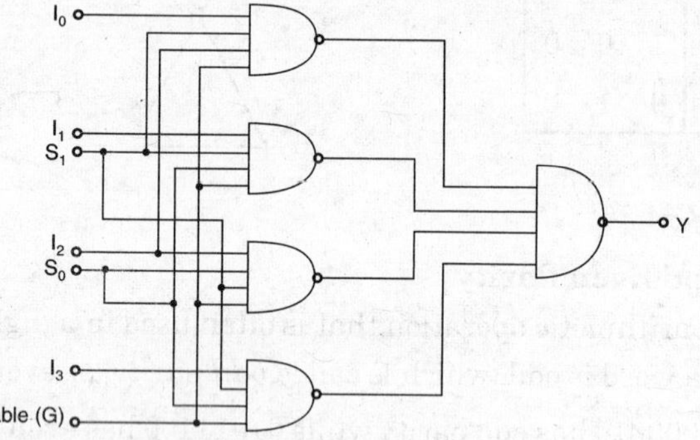

With LOW input at G, the output Y can be expressed as

$$Y = \bar{S}_1\,\bar{S}_0\,I_0 + \bar{S}_1\,S_0\,I_1 + S_1\,\bar{S}_0\,I_2 + S_1S_0I_3$$

The 4 : 1 multiplexer can be realized using NAND gates.

Demultiplexers/Decoders

It performs reverse operation of a multiplexer. It accepts a single input and distributes it over several outputs. Select input code determines to which output the data input will be transmitted.

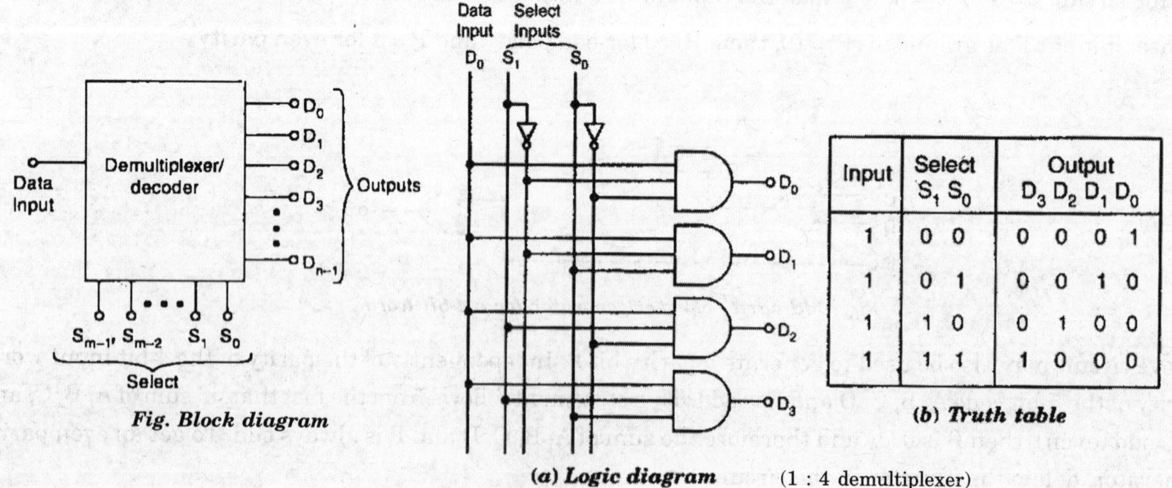

Fig. Block diagram

Input	Select S_1 S_0	Output D_3 D_2 D_1 D_0
1	0 0	0 0 0 1
1	0 1	0 0 1 0
1	1 0	0 1 0 0
1	1 1	1 0 0 0

(b) Truth table

(a) Logic diagram (1 : 4 demultiplexer)

Number of output lines is n and number of select lines is m, where $n = 2^m$.

This circuit can also be used as binary to decimal decoder with binary input applied at the select input lines and the output will be obtained on the corresponding line. The data input line is to be connected to logic 1 level. This device is very useful if multiple output combinational circuit is to be designed, because this needs minimum package count.

The output line being selected is determined by te bit combination of the select lines.

SEQUENTIAL CIRCUITS

BASIC MEMORY CELL.

A basic memory cell is a circuit that store one bit information. This one-bit memory element is called *flip-flop* or *latch*, since it latches (or locks) data in it.

A flip-flop has two outputs Q and $\overline{Q}$, that are always complements of each other.

It can exist in two stable states :

***(i)* Set state :** Q is HIGH (logic 1) and $\overline{Q}$ is LOW (logic 0)

***(ii)* Reset state :** $\overline{Q}$ is HIGH (logic 1) and Q is LOW (logic 0).

For a flip-flop to act as a memory device, it should retain the information stored in it. Thus, if it is set state it should remain set and if it is in reset state, it should remain reset.

This function can be realized by using two NAND or NOR inverters connected in a feedback loop as shown in the figure below.

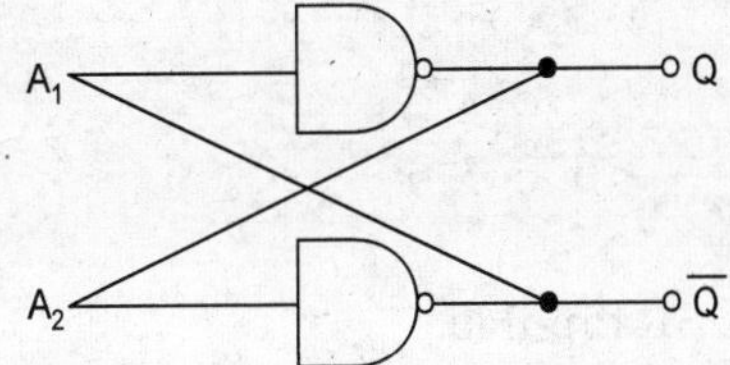

$Q = \overline{A_1} = A_2$

$\overline{Q} = \overline{A_2} = A_1$

Q	A_2	$\overline{Q}$	A_1
1	1	0	0
0	0	1	1

Fig. Basic memory cell

From truth-table,

if Q = 1, it remains 1 and $\overline{Q}$ remains 0

if Q = 0, it remains 0 and $\overline{Q}$ remains 1.

It is not possible to have both Q and $\overline{Q}$ in the same state (HIGH or LOW).

SR FLIP-FLOP.

To serve the purpose of storing desired bits in the flip-flops, two-input NAND or NOR gates are used as shown in the figure below

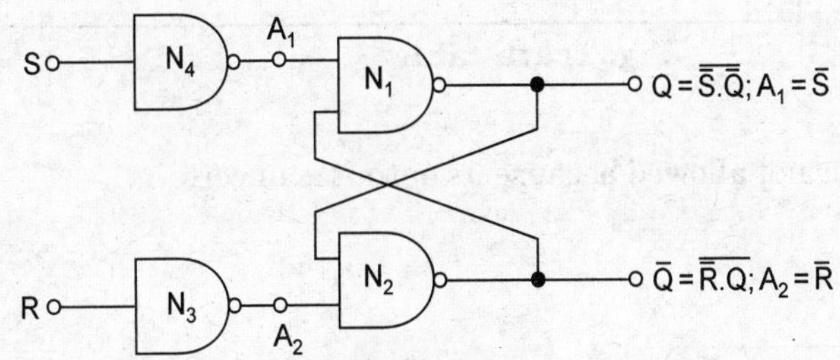

Truth-table

S	R	A_1	A_2	State
0	0	1	1	No change
0	1	1	0	Reset
1	0	0	1	Set
1	1	0	0	Race

Fig. SR flip-flop

Following observations are made from this figure and the truth-table.

Set state.

When S = 1 and R = 0, A_1 becomes 0, making Q = 1. So, $\overline{Q} = \overline{1.1} = 0$. This input condition sets the flip-flop (Q = 1, $\overline{Q}$ = 0) ; so it is called *set state.*

Reset state.

When S = 0 and R = 1, A_2 becomes 0, making $\overline{Q}$ = 1 and $Q = \overline{1.1} = 0$. This input condition resets the flip-flop (Q = 0, $\overline{Q}$ = 1); so it is called *reset state.*

No change.

When S = R = 0, $Q = \overline{1.\overline{Q}} = Q$ and $\overline{Q} = \overline{1.\overline{Q}} = \overline{Q}$. The flip-flop remains in whatever state it is in, the function is that of a basic memory cell.

Race.

When S = R = 1, A_1 and A_2 both become 0. So $Q = \overline{Q} = 1$. This is an undesired output state because if S and R now change to 0, A_1 and A_2 will be 1, both Q and $\overline{Q}$ will try to become 0. The actual state of the flip-flop depends on the relative delays of the two gates. If N_2 is faster, $\overline{Q}$ will become $\overline{1.1} = 0$ first and will make Q = 1. Similarly, if N_1 is faster, Q will become 0 first and will make $\overline{Q} = 1$. Similarly, if N_1 is faster, Q will become 0 first and will make $\overline{Q} = 1$. This is called *race condition*. Here state of the flip-flop is uncertain, so this condition is not allowed.

This circuit is called *SR flip-flop*. It is an asynchronous circuit because the output changes with changes as and when SR inputs change.

CLOCKED SR FLIP-FLOP

SR flip-flop modified to include clock (CK) pulses is shown in the figure below.

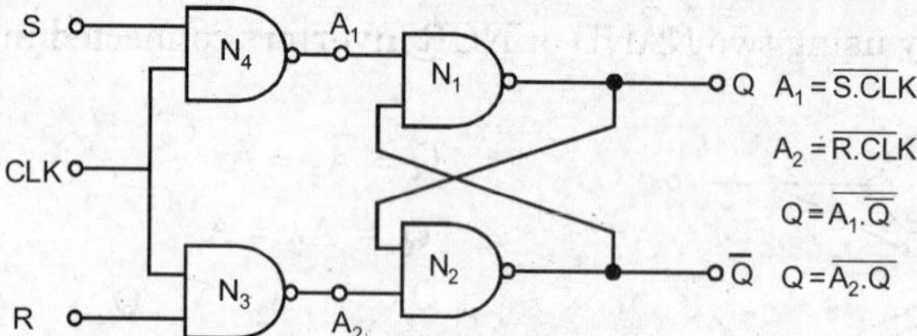

When CLK = 1, $A_1 = \overline{S}$ and $A_2 = \overline{R}$, the circuit functions like SR flip-flop.

When CLK = 0, $A_1 = A_2 = 1$, the circuit reduces to that of a basic memory cell and outputs remain unchanged (latched).

Here N_1, and N_2 form basic latch, whereas N_3 and N_4 control state of the flip-flop.

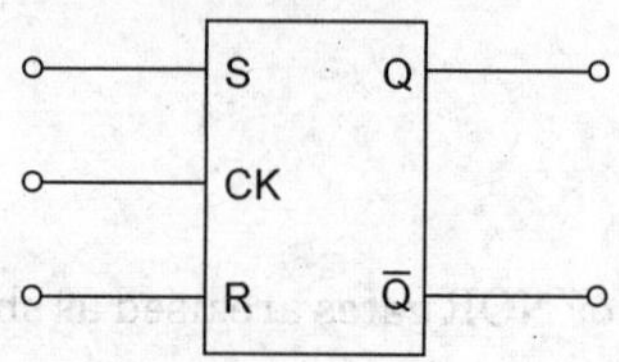

Fig. Symbol

CLK	*S*	*R*	Q_{n+1}	
1	0	0	Q_n	(SR enabled)
1	0	1	0	
1	1	0	1	
1	1	1		Not allowed
0	×	×		Qn (SR disabled)

Fig. Truth-table

JK FLIP-FLOP.

In an SR flip-flop, the input combination S = R = 1 is not allowed because its output is uncertain.

It is called *JK flip-flop* with inputs J and K.

Truth-table SR/JK Flip-flops

J	K	Q_n	Q_{n+1}	S	R	
0	0	0	0	0	0/1	Inactive
0	0	1	1	1/0	0	$Q_{n+1} = Q_n$
0	1	0	0	0	0/1	Reset state
0	1	1	0	0	1	$Q_{n+1} = 0$
1	0	0	1	1	0	Set state
1	0	1	1	1/0	0	$Q_{n+1} = 1$
1	1	0	1	1	0	Toggle state
1	1	1	0	0	1	$Q_{n+1} = \overline{Q}_n$

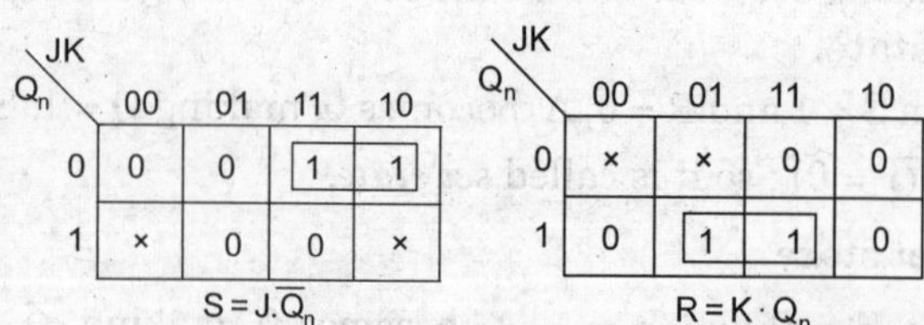

Fig. K-maps with S and R as outputs, and taking J, K and Q_n as inputs

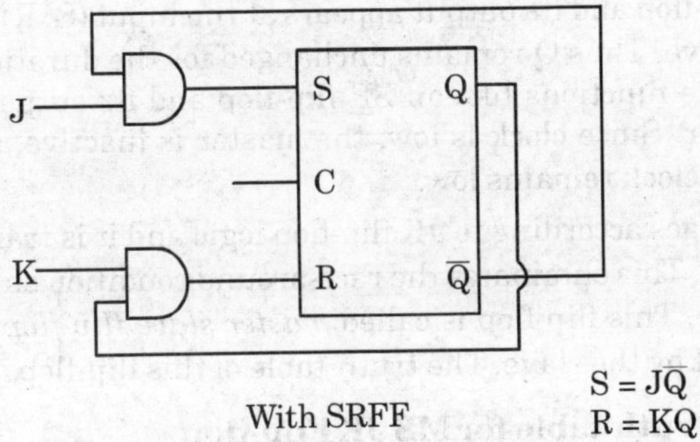

With SRFF

Based on K-map, JK–FF has been designed as shown in Fig. (*a*) and its qualified circuit diagram in Fig. (*b*) below.

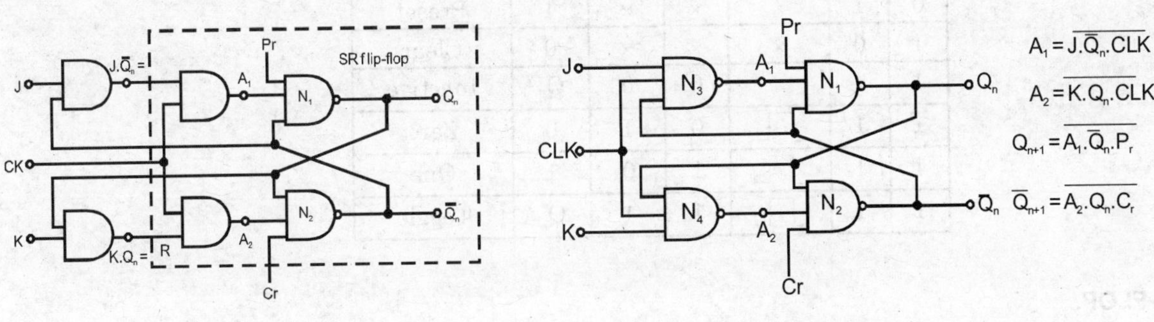

Fig. (*a*) *Fig.* (*b*)

For the level triggered JK flip-flop of Fig. (*b*), consider the case when J = K = 1, $Q_n = 0$ and a clock-pulse occurs. After a propagation delay of Δt ($<< t_p$, pulse width) equal to delay time of two NAND gates, the output will toggle to $Q_n = 1$. Since this is feedback to the inputs, the output can toggle back to $Q_n = 0$ after another delay of Δt, if clock is still high.

Thus, as long as clock pulse is present, the output will toggle at every Δt seconds. This is called *race-around*. This can be overcome by using a JK master-slave flip-flop.

Truth-table JK Flip-flop

J	K	Q_{n+1}
0	0	Q_n
0	1	0
1	0	1
1	1	$\overline{Q}_n$

JK MASTER-SLAVE FLIP-FLOP.

This flip-flop is made of two SR flip-flops. The output of the first, called *master flip-flop*, is given to the inputs of the second, called *slave flip-flop*. The output of the slave is fedback to the inputs of the master. The master is triggered by a positive clock pulse and the slave is triggered by a negative clock pulse, obtained by inverting the clock pulse applied to the master.

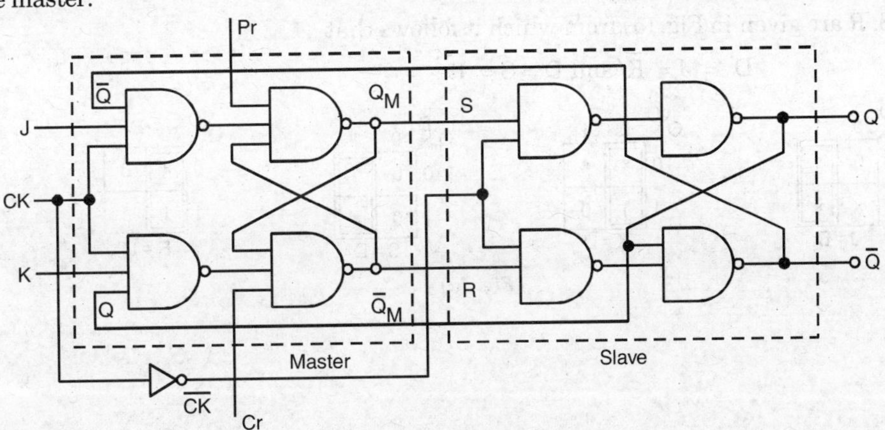

When clock is high (CK = 1, Pr = 1, Cr = 1), the master is enabled, while slave is disabled as $\overline{CK} = 0$. So, the master functions like a JK flip-flop and its output appears at the input (S, R) of the slave.

Since CK is low, the slave is inactive. Thus Q remains unchanged for the duration of the clock pulse t_p.

When the clock goes low, the slave functions like an SR flip-flop and its output changes to Q_M, which also appears at the input of the master. Since clock is low, the master is inactive, so that Q_M (and so S and R) remains unchanged as long as the clock remains low.

Thus, when clock is high, Q_M changes according to JK flip-flop logic and it is transferred to Q when the clock goes low (negative edge transition). This eliminates the race-around condition as the output remains constant for the duration of one clock pulse. This flip-flop is called *master slave flip-flop* because master decides the output, which is simply latched out by the slave. The truth-table of this flip-flop is shown in below.

Truth-table for MS JK Flip-flop

Pr	Cr	CK	J	K	Q_{n+1}	States
0	0	×	×	×	?	Not desired
0	1	×	×	×	1	Preset
1	0	×	×	×	0	Clear
1	1	×	0	0	Q_n	Inactive
1	1	⎍	0	1	0	Zero
1	1	⎍	1	0	1	One
1	1	⎍	1	1	$\overline{Q}_n$	Toggle

D FLIP-FLOP.

In a D flip-flop, output follows the input whenever flip-flop is triggered. This can be realized by means of a JK/SR flip-flop. The JK/SR inputs needs to achieve D logic are given in the truth table below.

Truth-table JKSR Flip-flop

D	Q_n	Q_{n+1}	J	K	S	R
0	0	0	0	0/1	0	0/1
0	1	0	0/1	1	0	1
1	0	1	1	0/1	1	0
1	1	1	0/1	0	0/1	0

First three columns form desired truth-table of a D flip-flop and fourth to the seventh column indicate required JK and SR inputs for the given Q_n and Q_{n+1}.

K-maps for J, K, S, R are given in Fig. (*a*) from which it follows that

$$D = J = \overline{K} \text{ and } D = S = \overline{R}$$

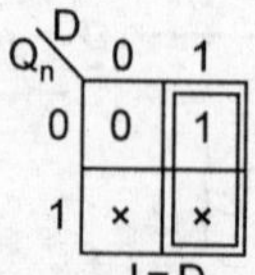

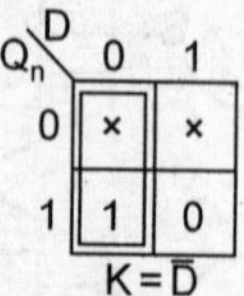

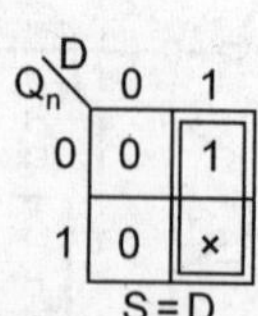

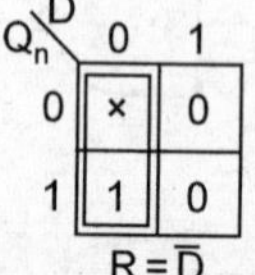

Fig. (*a*)

Using these equations the design of a D flip-flop using JK flip-flop/SR flip-flop along with its truth-table is as given in Figs. (*b*), (*c*) and (*d*) respectively. Here output follows the input, when flip-flop is triggered. If flip-flop is edge triggered, then output is same as the input, but is delayed by one clock pulse. Due to this property, D flip-flop is used as a delay device. Its function is illustrated by the waveforms of Fig. (*e*). From figure, short duration spurious pulses in the datas (D) (called *glitches*) are eliminated in the output (Q).

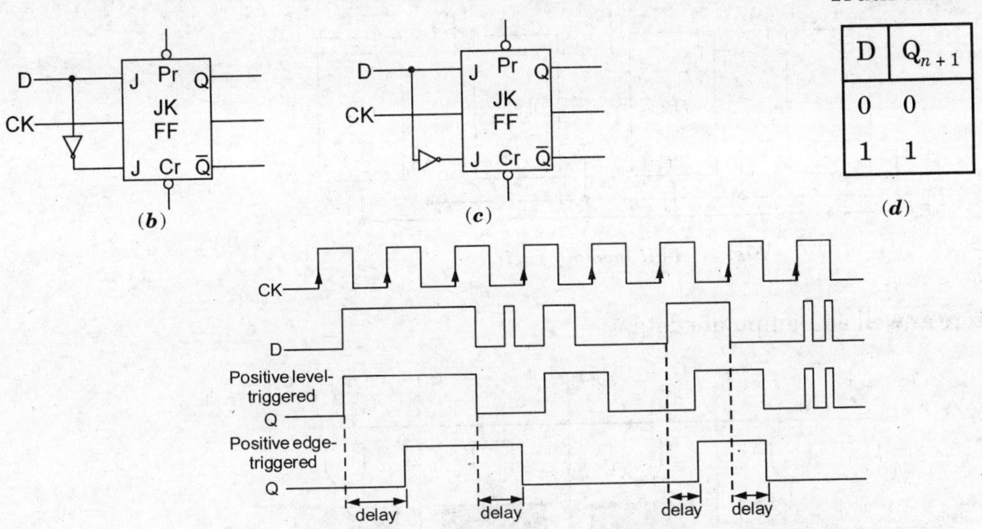

Truth-table

D	Q_{n+1}
0	0
1	1

(*d*)

Fig. **(*e*)** ***. Wave form of a D flip-flop***

T FLIP-FLOP.

Two combinations of J and K inputs of a JK flip-flop are used to make a D flip-flop. These were J = 0, K = 1 and J = 1, K = 0. The remaining two combinations can be used to make a T flip-flop. These combinations are J = K = 0 and J = K = 1. As J = K for both the inputs, this is equivalent to a single input T (0/1) connected to both J and K as shown in figure along with its truth-table. This configuration is called *T flip-flop*.

If we keep T = 1, we have a toggle switch in which $Q_{n+1} = Q_n$ whenever flip-flop is triggered. T fliop-flops are widely used as toggle switches. The function of a T flip-flop is shown by the wave forms shown below.

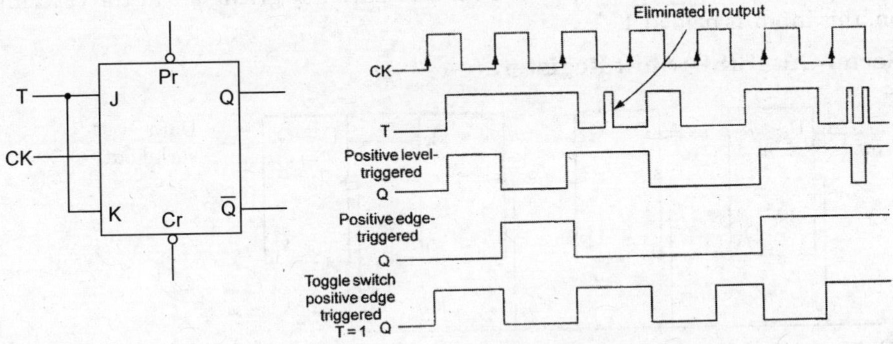

Fig. Wave forms in a T flip-flop

Various flip-flops are available as ICs and are widely used in registers, counters are memory devices. One flip-flop can be converted to another flip-flop by the procedure followed in SR to JK conversion and JK/SR to D conversion.

Excitations-Tables for various Flip-Flops

Q_n	Q_{n+1}	S	R	J	K	D	T
0	0	0	X	0	X	0	0
0	1	1	0	1	X	1	1
1	0	0	1	X	1	0	1
1	1	X	0	X	0	1	0

REGISTERS

1. Memory Registers

Memory registers store *n* bits of data using *n* flip-flops. Fig. (*a*) shows a 4-bit memory register (or buffer) composed of four D flip-flops which are triggered by a common clock. All the four flip-flops can be cleaved by giving a 0 at the CLR input. Data input (4–bits).

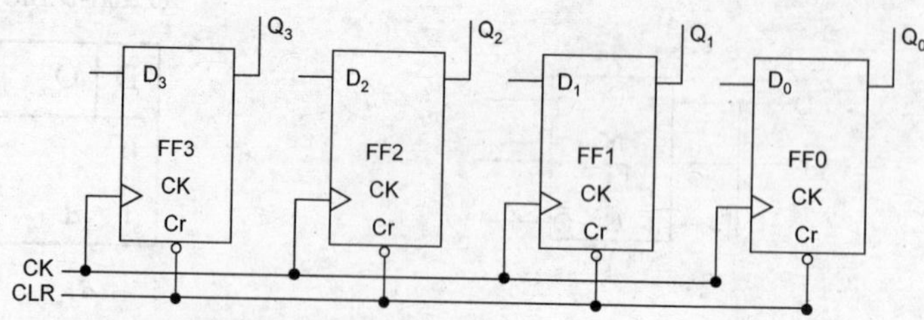

Fig. **(*a*) *4-bit memory register***

2. Shift Registers

Shift registers store as well as manipulate data.

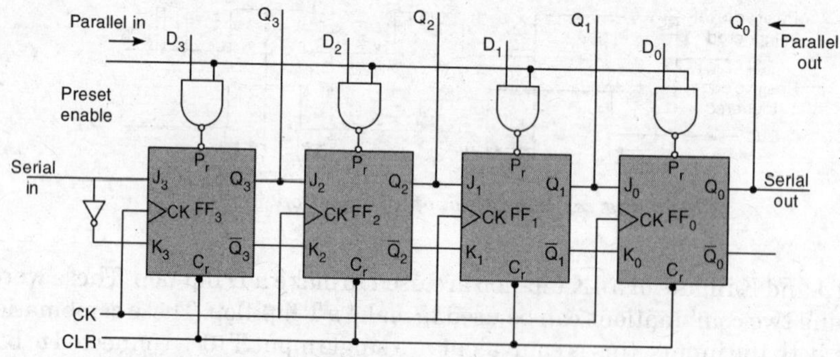

Fig. **(*b*) *4-bit shift register.***

Four JK (or SR) flip-flops are converted into D flip-flops by giving mutually complementary inputs. All the four flip-flops are triggered by a common clock and can be cleared by giving a 0 at the CLR input. During normal operation, this input is held at 1.

(*i*) Serial-In Serial-Out (SISO) Shift Register.

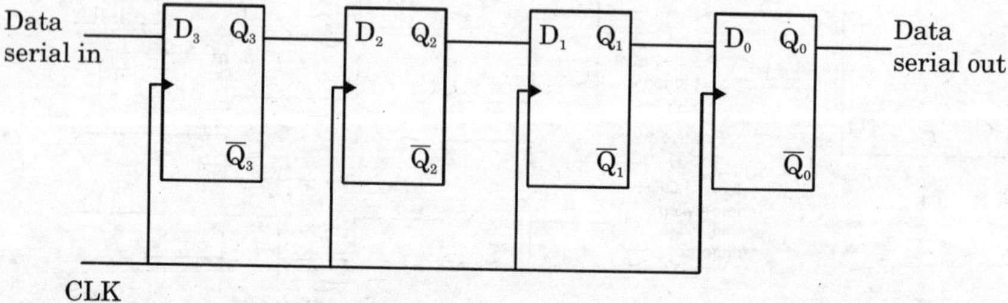

Data bits are entered serially, LSB first and MSB last. This form of data, in which bits are separated in time, is called **temporal code**. Input data is given at the serial-in input.

Let word 0101 is to be entered. The LSB 1, is given at the serial-in input, which is transferred to Q_3 when first clock pulse occurs. By similar D flip-flop logic, this 1 gets transferred to Q_2 and next bit (0 here) appears at Q_3 after the second clock pulse.

Thus, after fourth clock pulse, all the four bits are entered into the register and stored till the next clock pulse appears. Data can be read serially at the serial-out output. LSB first and MSB last, by giving three clock pulses. After fourth clock pulse all the four flip-flops get reset to 0.

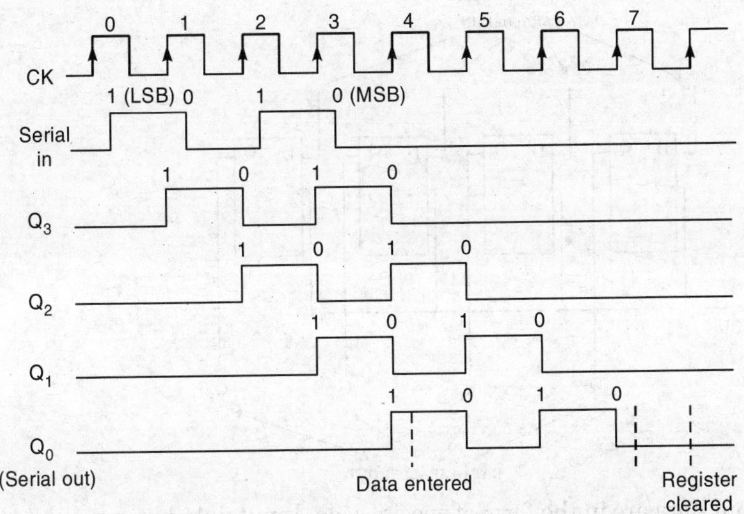

Fig. (c) Wave forms in 4-bit shift register–SISO

Clock pulse	Serial in	Q_3	Q_2	Q_1	Serial out Q_0
0	1 (LSB)	0	0	0	0
1	0	1	0	0	0
2	1	0	1	0	0
3	0 (MSB)	1	0	1	0
4	0	0	1	0	1 Data entered
5	0	0	0	1	0
6	0	0	0	0	1
7	0	0	0	0	0
8	0	0	0	0	0 Register is cleared

(*ii*) Serial-In Parallel-Out (SIPO) Shift Register.

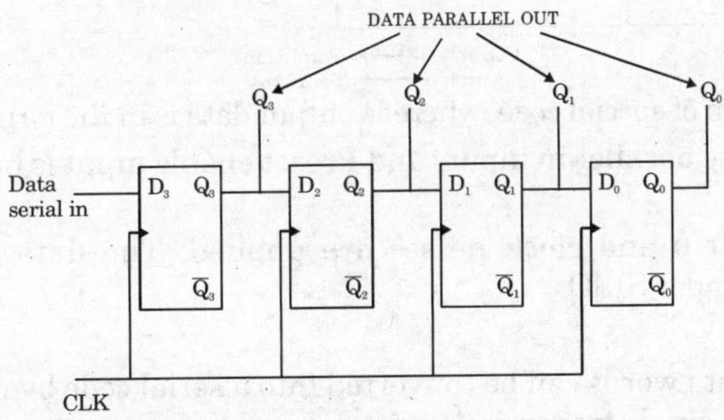

In this, input data is a temporal code and the output, is a special code, in which all the bits of a data word are read at the same time. Data is entered serially. For an n-bit register, all the n-bits are entered into the n flip-flops at the end of nth clock pulse.

Hence, we have four data bits at the Q outputs of the four flip-flops at the end of fourth clock pulse. This data can be read as a special code : Q_3 Q_2 Q_1 Q_0 at the end of the fourth clock pulse.

(iii) Parallel-In Parallel-Out (PIPO) Shift Register.

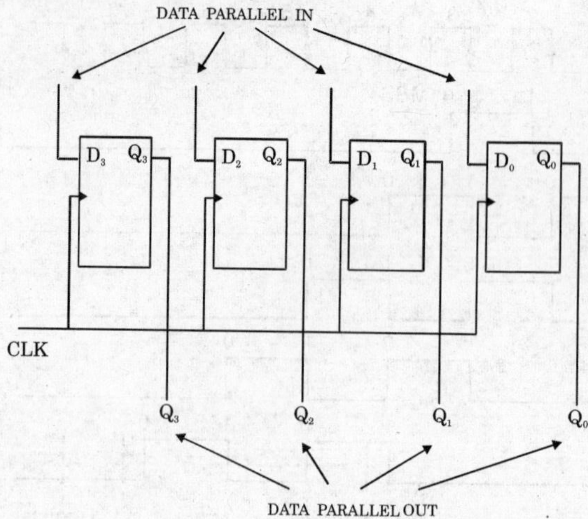

In this, input and output data are in the form of special code. Input data bits are applied at the parallel in inputs (D_3, D_2, D_1, D_0) and are read at the parallel-out outputs (Q_3, Q_2, Q_1 Q_0).

When after clearing the register, Preset enable input is made 1, NAND gates connected to the P_r inputs of the flip-flops function as inverters for the parallel-in inputs (D_t). Hence,

When D_t is 0, corresponding flip-flop has a 1 at its P_r input, which keeps the Q_i output at 0.

When D_i is 1, corresponding flip-flop has a 0 at its P_r input, which sets the Q_i output at 1.

Thus, data input at D_i appears as it is at Q_i.

Application : PIPO registers can be used as Read/Write memory registers.

(iv) Parallel-In Serial-Out (PISO) Shift Registers.

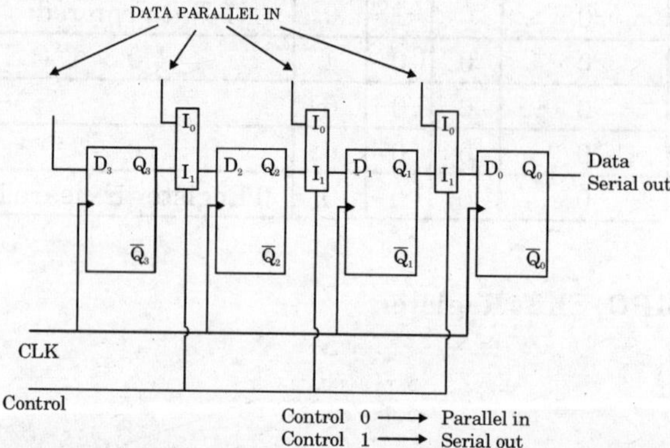

In figure, input data is in the form of special code, whereas output data is in the form of temporal code.

Input data bits are applied at the parallel-in inputs and Preset enable input is held at 1. Thus, input word is written into the register.

Now, Preset enable is held at 0 and clock pulses are applied. The data bits can be read at the serial-out output as explained under SISO.

Application :

In digital transmission, n-bit data words can be converted into a serial code by using a PISO register and then can be transmitted along a single transmission line.

(v) Bi-directional Shift Register.

SISO and PISO registers shift the n-bit data word to right by one place at the occurrence of a clock pulse. This results in a binary number which is the previous number divided by two, given that 1 is not shifted out of the LSB.

If instead of giving the outputs of FF3 to the inputs of FF2 and so on, outputs of FF0 is given to the inputs of FF1. FF1 to FF2, and FF2 to FF3, the data word can be shift to left by one bit by giving a clock pulse. This results in a binary number which is previous number multiplied by two given that 1 is not shifted out of the MSB.

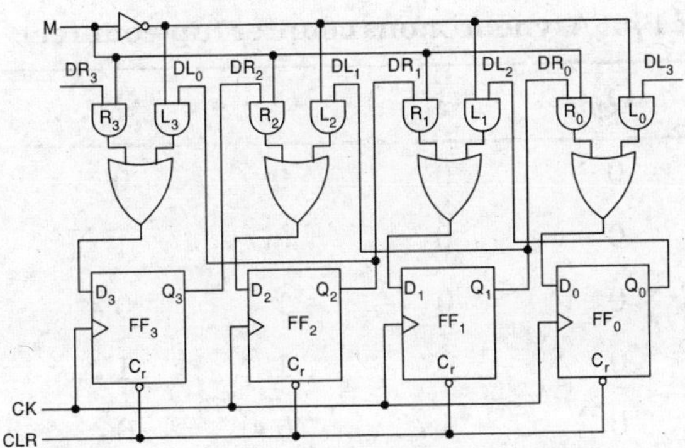

Fig. 4-bit bi-directional shift register

When M is 1, AND gates labeled as R_3, R_2, R_1, R_0 are enabled and register functions as a shift right register. When M is 0, AND gates labeled as R_i are disabled and ones labeled as L_3, L_2, L_1, L_0 are enabled. This makes register function as a *left shift register*. The data for shift right operation is entered at the Shift Right Serial-In input (DR_3). The data for shift left register is entered at the Shift Left Serial-In input (DL_3).

COUNTERS.

Binary counters are widely used digital circuits. Counter is a circuit, which counts the number of occurrences of an input. Each count, a binary number, is called *state of the counter*. Hence, a counter counting in terms of n-bits has 2^n different states. The number of different states of a counter is also called *modulus of the counter*. Thus an n-bit counter is a modulo 2^n counter.

Counter circuits are primarily constituted of flip-flops which alongwith combinational elements are used for the generation of control signals.

Types of Conters

Depending on the manner in which flip-flops are triggered, counters can be divided into two major categories :

1. Asynchronous Counter (ripple counter)
2. Synchronous Counter

In case of an asynchoronous counter, all the flip-flops are not clocked simultaneously, whereas in a synchronous counter all the flip-flops are clocked simultaneously.

If counter counts in such a way that decimal equivalent of the output increases with successive clock pulses, it is called *UP counter* and if it decreases, it is called *DOWN counter*.

A decoding circuit can be connected to the output of a counter in such a way that output of the cirtuit goes high (or low) only when counter contents are equal to a given state.

1. **Asynchronous Counters.**

   Four negative edge triggered JK flip flops are converted into T flip-flops by making J = K = 1 for all four of them. The Q output of one flip-flop is fed to the CK input of the next one.

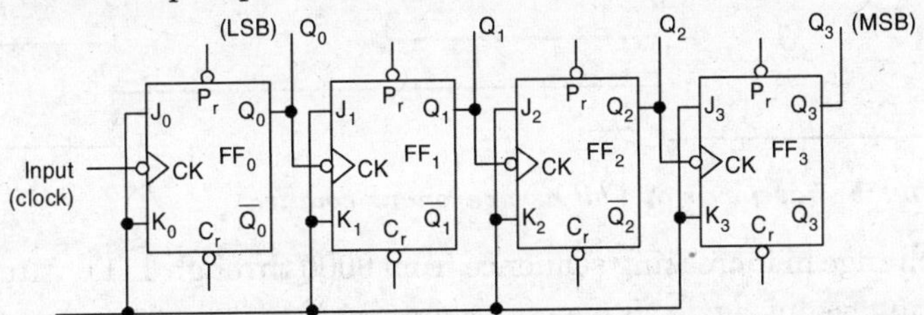

Fig. (a) 4-bit asynchronous counter

From Fig. (*a*), it can be seen that for every negative edge transition (1 to 0) of the input pulse, the output of FF0, *i.e.* Q_0 toggles. Similarly for every negative transition of Q_0, Q_1 toggles and so on for Q_2 and Q_3. This is shown in terms of truth-table and wave forms of Fig. (*b*), assuming that all the flip-flops were reset to '0' at the beginning of the input pulse. Also, it is assumed that flip-flops change state without any delays.

Truth-table of 4-bit Asynchronous counter (up-counter)

Input pulse number	Q_3	Q_2	Q_1	Q_0
0	0	0	0	0
1	0	0	0	1
2	0	0	1	0
3	0	0	1	1
4	0	1	0	0
5	0	1	0	1
6	0	1	1	0
7	0	1	1	1
8	1	0	0	0
9	1	0	0	1
10	1	0	1	0
11	1	0	1	1
12	1	1	0	0
13	1	1	0	1
14	1	1	1	0
15	1	1	1	1
0	0	0	0	0

– ve edge

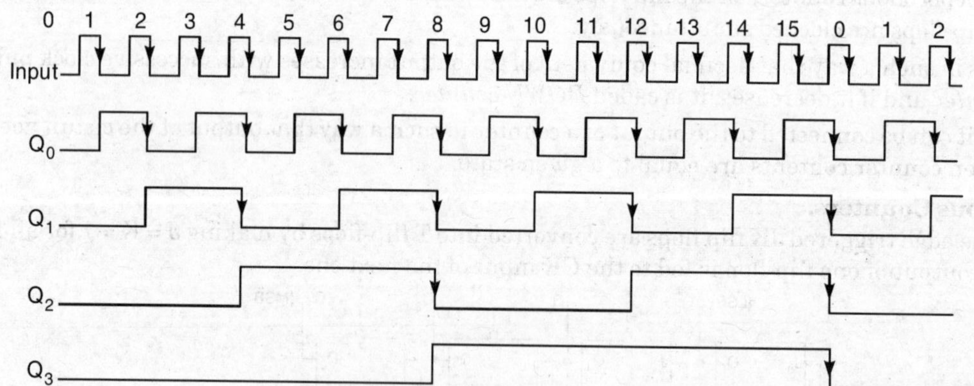

Fig. (b) Waveforms of 4-bit asynchronous counter

Thus outputs Q_3, Q_2, Q_1, Q_0 change in increasing sequence from 0000 through 1111. After 15th pulse, they are reset back to 0000 and counting begins again. It is an *up-counter* because the count sequence is increasing in order.

Instead of counting in increasing order, *we can design* a counter can be designed to count in a decreasing order. This is called a **down-counter.** In table below, if the $\overline{Q}$ output of one flip-flop is connected to the CK input of the next one, a decreasing count sequence at Q outputs is obtained. This is shown by the truth-table below. Here, flip-flops are set to '1' state in the beginning.

Truth-table of 4-bit Asynchronous Down-counter

Input pulse	$\bar{Q}_3$	$\bar{Q}_2$	$\bar{Q}_1$	$\bar{Q}_0$	Q_3	Q_2	Q_1	Q_0
0	0	0	0	0	1	1	1	1
1	0	0	0	1	1	1	1	0
2	0	0	1	0	1	1	0	1
3	0	0	1	1	1	1	0	0
4	0	1	0	0	1	0	1	1
5	0	1	0	1	1	0	1	0
6	0	1	1	0	1	0	0	1
7	0	1	1	1	1	0	0	0
8	1	0	0	0	0	1	1	1
9	1	0	0	1	0	1	1	0
10	1	0	1	0	0	1	0	1
11	1	0	1	1	0	1	0	0
12	1	1	0	0	0	0	1	1
13	1	1	0	1	0	0	1	0
14	1	1	1	0	0	0	0	1
15	1	1	1	1	0	0	0	0
0	0	0	0	0	1	1	1	1

An up/down counter with a control signal controlling the increasing/decreasing order of counting is shown in Fig. (*c*).

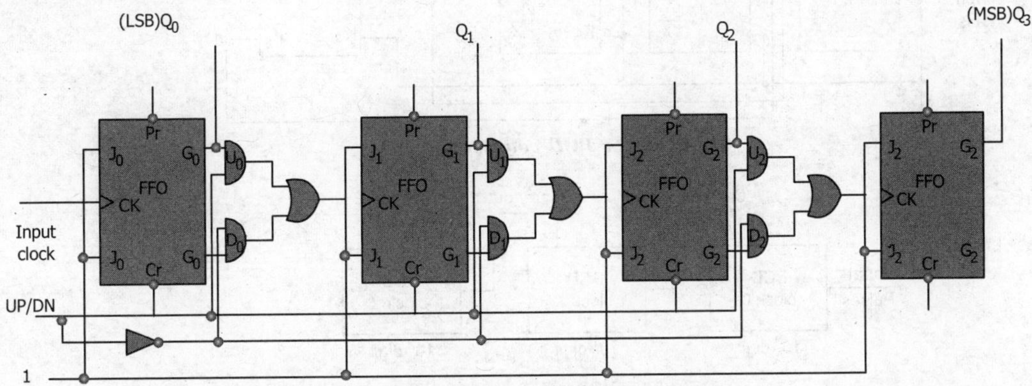

Fig. **(*c*)** ***4-bit asynchronous up/down counter***

Here, when up/down (UP/$\overline{\text{DN}}$) is 1, the D_i AND gates are disabled and Q outputs of preceding flip-flops goes to CK inputs of the next ones. Thus, it acts as an *up counter*.

When up/down (UP/$\overline{\text{DN}}$) is 0, the U_i AND gates are disabled connecting $\bar{Q}$ outputs of preceding flip-flops to CK inputs of the next ones. Thus it acts as a *down counter*.

In asynchronous counters, the effect of a negative edge in the input pulse moves from one flip-flop to the next one, or ripples through the circuit from LSB to MSB. Hence they are also called **ripple counters.**

From wave forms of Fig. (*b*), in a modulo-16 counter, the input frequency is divided by two at the output of FFO (Q_0– wave form). This is divided by four in Q_1, by eight in Q_2 and by sixteen (2^4) in Q_3. Thus an asynchronous counter can be used to generate various frequencies. A modulo-*n* asynchronous counter is also called *divide-by n* (power of 2) *counter* because input frequency gets divided by *n* at the output of the last flip-flop (MSB).

BCD Counters :

BCD (or decade) counter is a nonbinary counter which counts normally until it reaches 1001 (*i.e.* decimal 9) and then reset itself, while generating a carry, which will be used for BCD count of the next decimal digit. A typical BCD counter (using 4 flip-flops) is shown in Fig. *f* (*i*). The output states of the flip-flop (till the state 1001) are shown in the below table when next negative going edge occurs at the input, BCD counter returns to all 0's. At the same time (*i.e.,* during interval when counter goes from 9 to 0), a negative-going signal edge occurs at the CARRY output. This CARRY output can be connected to the input of another BCD counter, which will be stepped by 1 when first BCD stage goes from 9 to 0. This is shown in Fig. *f* (*ii*), where several four flip-flop BCD stages are combined to make a large counter.

Decimal count	X_3	X_2	X_1	X_0
0	0	0	0	0
1	0	0	0	1
2	0	0	1	0
3	0	0	1	1
4	0	1	0	0
5	0	1	0	1
6	0	1	1	0
7	0	1	1	1
8	1	0	0	0
9	1	0	0	1
10	1	0	1	0

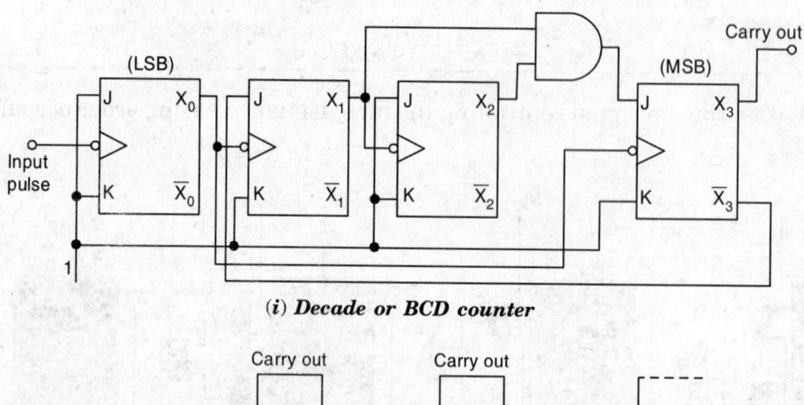

(*i*) ***Decade or BCD counter***

Carry out
Carry out
Input Pulses
BCD block 0
BCD block 1
BCD block 2
10^0 digit
10^1 digit
10^2 digit

(*ii*) ***Cascading BCD counter***

Fig. (f)

With reference to Fig. *f* (*i*) and table above from 0 to count 6, we have $X_3 = 0$, $\overline{X_3} = 1$, which keeps J of FF1 at 1. Therefore, it works as a T-FF and count ripples through up to 4.

- **At count 6 :** $X_0 = 0$, $X_1 = X_2 = 1$, AND gate output makes J = 1 at FF3 which becomes T-FF.
- **At count 7 :** $X_0 = 1$, no other change.
- **At count 8 :** $X_0 = 0$ which ripples through and so $X_1 = X_2 = 0$. and $X_3 = 1$, $\overline{X_3} = 0$.
  So J = 0. K = 1 at FF1, ready for clearing. Also AND gate output changes to 0 and so J = 0, K = 1 at FF3. Thus FF3 is also ready for clearing.
- **At count 9 :** $X_0 = 1$, no other change.
- **At count 10 :** $X_0 = 0$, $X_1 = 1$, $X_2 = 0$ and FF3 clears to $X_3 = 0$, $\overline{X_3} = 1$. Carry out is generated. The cycle is ready for "*repeat*".

Let states on the block 0 and block 1 of Fig. *f* (*ii*) are respectively 0001 and 0010. It can be easily seen that this corresponds to a count of 21.

2. Synchronous Counters.

In a synchronous counter, all the flip-flops are triggered by a common clock pulse. Thus, maximum propagation delay is equal to that of one flip-flop and any additional combinational circuitry required.

To design a modulo-16 synchronous counter, following steps should be covered. This is a typical example of synchronous counter design but a counter with any desired modulus can be designed by following steps :

(i) $16 = 2^4$, so 4 flip-flops are required. We shall use T flip-flops.

(ii) Truth-table for desired output sequence of Q_3, Q_2, Q_1, Q_0 is given below.

In the truth-table,

T-inputs are required to be 1 for the states for which corresponding Q outputs toggle and

T-inputs are required to be 0 for the states for which corresponding Q outputs remain unchanged in the next state.

A truth-table which gives excitations of flip-flops to produce a desired output is called *state table*.

Input (Clock)	Q_3	Q_2	Q_1	Q_0	T_3	T_2	T_1	T_0
0	0	0	0	0	0	0	0	1
1	0	0	0	1	0	0	1	1
2	0	0	1	0	0	0	0	1
3	0	0	1	1	0	1	1	1
4	0	1	0	0	0	0	0	1
5	0	1	0	1	0	0	1	1
6	0	1	1	0	0	0	0	1
7	0	1	1	1	1	1	1	1
8	1	0	0	0	0	0	0	1
9	1	0	0	1	0	0	1	1
10	1	0	1	0	0	0	0	1
11	1	0	1	1	0	1	1	1
12	1	1	0	0	0	0	0	1
13	1	1	0	1	0	0	1	1
14	1	1	1	0	0	0	0	1
15	1	1	1	1	1	1	1	1
0	0	0	0	0				

(iii) Here,

$$T_0 = 1,\ T_1 = Q_0$$

$$T_2 = Q_1Q_0\,(\overline{Q}_3\overline{Q}_2 + \overline{Q}_3Q_2 + Q_3\overline{Q}_2 + Q_3Q_2) = Q_1Q_0$$

$$T_3 = \overline{Q}_3Q_2Q_1Q_0 + Q_3Q_2Q_1Q_0 = Q_2\,Q_1\,Q_0$$

(iv) Hence, circuit of a modulo-16 synchronous counter is as shown below.

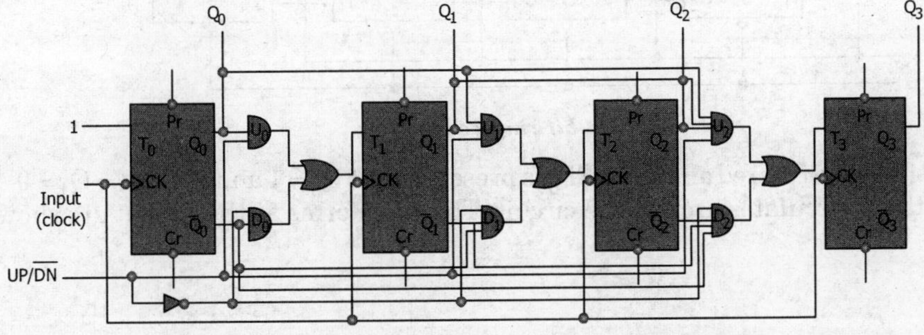

Fig. Modulo-16 synchronous counter (serial carry)

Nonbinary Counters :

There are too many ways in which a nonbinary counter can be designed to make it practical or even worthwhile to develop general procedures for designing nonbinary counters. Now design a mod-3 counter.

A mod-3 counter requires two flip-flops and would go through the three states specified in Table (*a*) below. Table (*b*) gives excitation table for JK flip-flop, using which the states of FF_0 (J_0, K_0) and FF_1 (J_1, K_0) can be filled in Table (*a*) below. Observing that a ripple counter is not possible in the present case, a synchronomous counter will be designed.

Table (*a*)

Counter states	Q_1	Q_0	J_0	K_0	J_1	K_1
0	0	0	1	×	0	×
1	0	1	×	1	1	×
2	1	0	0	×	×	1
0	0	0				

Table (*b*)

Q_n	Q_{n+1}	J	K
0	0	0	×
0	1	1	×
1	0	×	1
1	1	×	0

With reference to Table (*a*), K-maps given below can be filled from which it easily follows that

$J_0 = \overline{Q}_1$, $K_0 = 1$, $J_1 = Q_0$, $K_1 = 1$

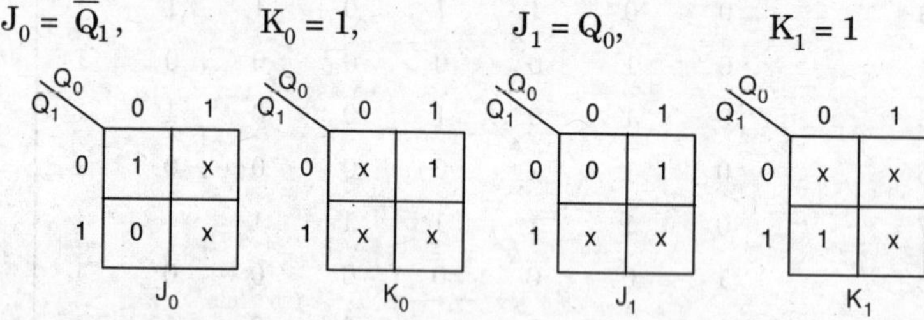

The resulting counter is drawn below.

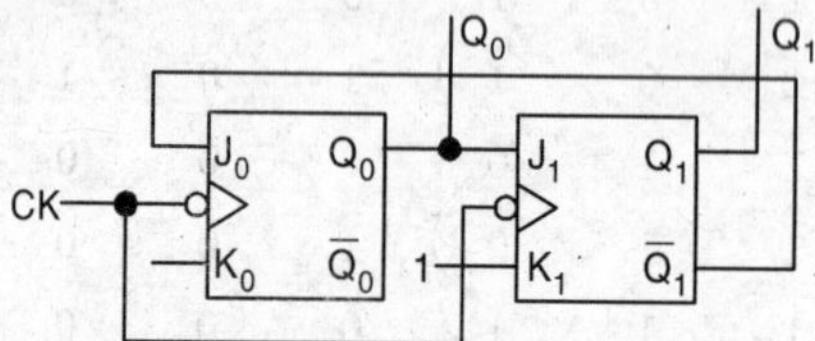

Fig. Mod-3 counter (synchronous)

Consider a 4-bit shift register. If serial output Q_0 is connected back to the serial input as shown in the figure below, then injected pulse will keep circulating. This circuit is called *ring counter*.

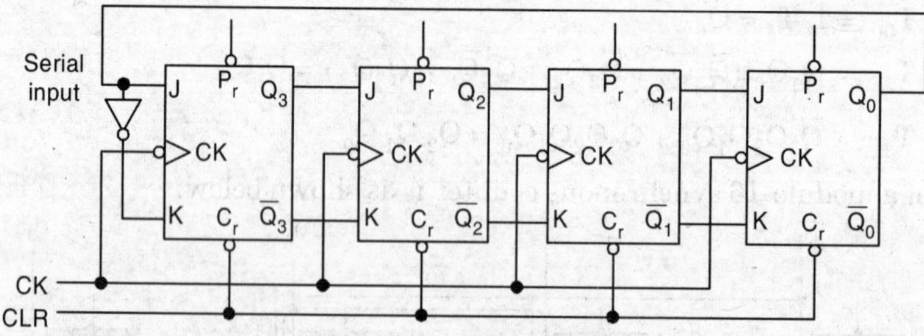

Fig. A 4-bit ring counter.

Assume that all flip-flops are cleared and than FF_0 is preset so that $Q_0 = 1$ and $Q_3 = Q_2 = Q_1 = 0$. When the clock pulses are applied, this 1 circulates around the circuit. The waveforms at the output are shown in the figure below.

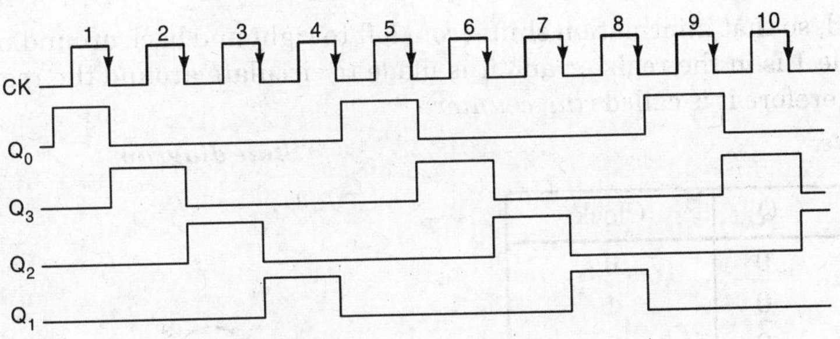

Fig. Output waveforms of ring counter

The outputs are sequential non-overlapping pulses, which are useful for control state counters and for stepper motors which require sequential pulses to rotate these from one position to the next etc. This counter can also be used to count number of pulses. These can be read by noting which flip-flop is in 1 state. No decoding circuitry is required.

If 4-bit shift register of Q_0 is connected to the serial input, then resulting circuitry is called *twisted ring counter*. If clock pulses are applied after clearing all flip flops, square waveform is obtained at the Q output as shown in the figure below.

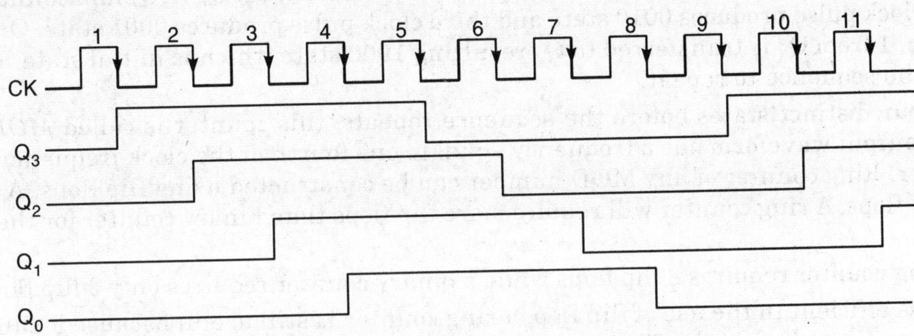

Fig. Output wave forms of twisted-ring counter

Advantages of Synchronous counters :

These offer reduced time delays as compared to asynchronous counters, hence offering higher frequencies. Moreover, since all the flip-flops simultaneously change their states, there doesn't arise a danger of false reading at any instant in the counting sequence.

Disadvantages of Synchronous counters :

(*i*) Large fan-in of combinational circuitry (AND gates) at the input of last flip-flop (whose output is MSB).

(*ii*) Large fan-out (N–1) of first flip-flop (whose output is LSB).

(*iii*) As a consequence of (*i*) and (*ii*) above, increased complexity of combinational circuitry compared to asynchronous counters.

SHIFT REGISTER COUNTER.

It can be arranged to form different types of counters. Shift register counters use feed-back, which means output of the last flip flop in the register is connected back to the first flip flop in some way.

Commonly used Shift register Counters

1. **Ring Counter.**

   The simple shift register counter is a circulating shift register connected, so that output of last flip flop shifts its value into the first flip flop. Such arrangement using D flip flop is shown below.

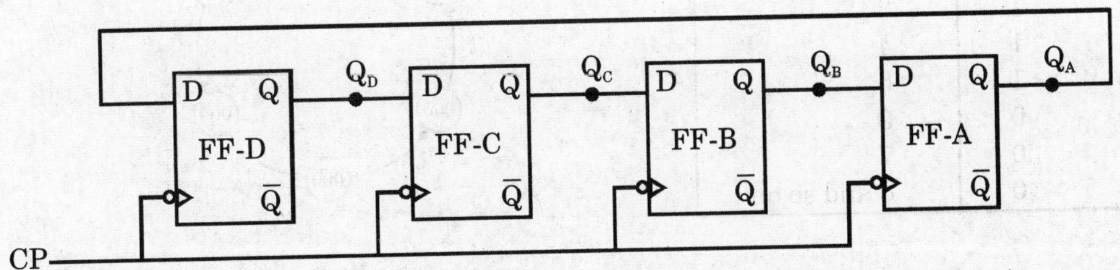

flip flops are connected, so that information shifts from left to right and back around from Q_A to Q_B. In most instances, only a single 1 is in the register and it is made to circulate around the register as long as clock pulses are applied. Therefore it is called *ring counter*.

Truth table

Q_D	Q_C	Q_B	Q_A	Clock
1	0	0	0	0
0	1	0	0	1
0	0	1	0	2
0	0	0	1	3
1	0	0	0	4
0	1	0	0	5
0	0	1	0	6
0	0	0	1	7 and so on

State diagram

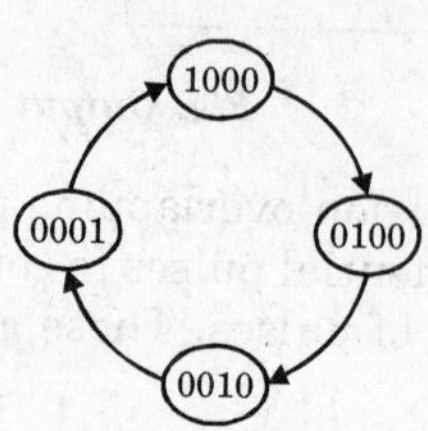

From the above table, assume a starting state of $Q_D = 1$ and $Q_C = Q_B = Q_A = 0$ which is necessary preset condition of ring shift counter. After first clock pulse 1 is shifted from Q_D to Q_C and counter is in 0100 state, second clock pulse produces 0010 state and third clock pulse produces 0001 state. On application of fourth pulse, 1 from Q_A is transferred to Q_D resulting 1000 state which is initial state. Fourth clock pulses cause the sequence to repeat.

Since it has four-distinct states before the sequence repeats, this counter is called *MOD-4 counter*. Each flip flop output waveform has a frequency equal to one fourth of the clock frequency since it is a MOD-4 counter. Ring counter of any MOD number can be constructed using flip flops. A MOD-N flip flop uses N flip flops. A ring counter will require more flip flops than binary counter for the same MOD number.

e.g. MOD-8 ring counter requires 8 flip flops while a binary counter requires only 3 flip flops.

Even if it is less efficient in the use of flip flop, a ring counter is still useful because it can be decoded without the use of decoding gates. The decoding signal for each state is obtained at the output of its corresponding flip flop.

2. Johnson Counter.

It is modification of basic ring counter, which is constructed exactly like a normal ring counter except that inverted output of the last flip flop is connected to the input of the first flip flop. Figure below shows a 3-bit Johnson counter using three D flip flops.

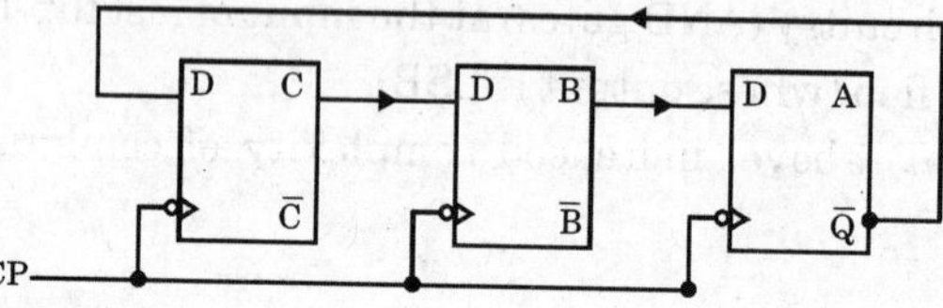

Sequence of Johnson counter:

Truth table

C	B	A	Clock
0	0	0	0
1	0	0	1
1	1	0	2
1	1	1	3
0	1	1	4
0	0	1	5
0	0	0	6
1	0	0	7
1	1	0	8 and so on

State diagram

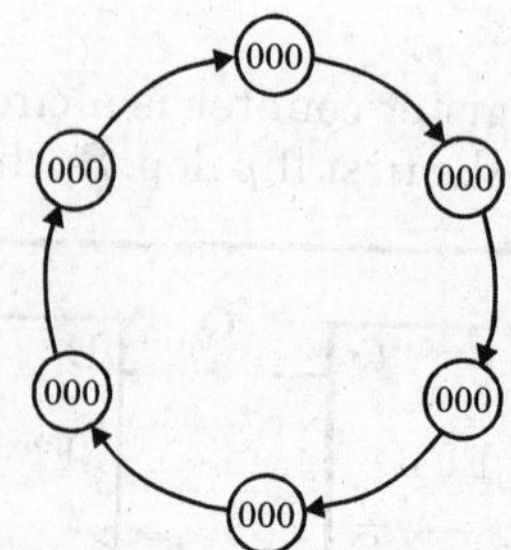

MOD number of a Johnson counter will always be equal to twice the number of flip flop e.g. if five flip flops are connected, then result is a MOD-10 Johnson counter. Each flip flop output waveform is a square wave at one tenth the clock frequency. Thus it is possible to construct a MOD-N counter by connecting N-2 flip flops in a Johnson counter arrangement.

Johnson counters represent a middle ground between ring counters and binary counters. It requires fewer-flip flops than a ring counter but more than a binary counter. It requires more decoding circuitry than a ring counter but less than binary counter.

CONVERTERS

1. Digital to Analog (D/A) Converter (DAC)

Analog output voltage V_A of an N-bit straight binary DAC converter is related to the digital equation

$$V_A = K(2^{N-1} b_{N-1} + 2^{N-2} b_{N-2} + \ldots + 2b_1 + b_0)$$

where, K = proportionality factor

$b_j = +1$ if jth bit of input 1, $= 0$ if jth bit of input is 0 $\quad \Big\} \; j = 0$ to $(N-1)$

Weighted resistor DAC.

As D/A conversion involves a weighted sum corresponding to the input to the converter, the summing circuit given below can be used as a DAC.

In this circuit, $I_i = I_{N-1} + I_{N-2} + \ldots + I_1 + I_0$

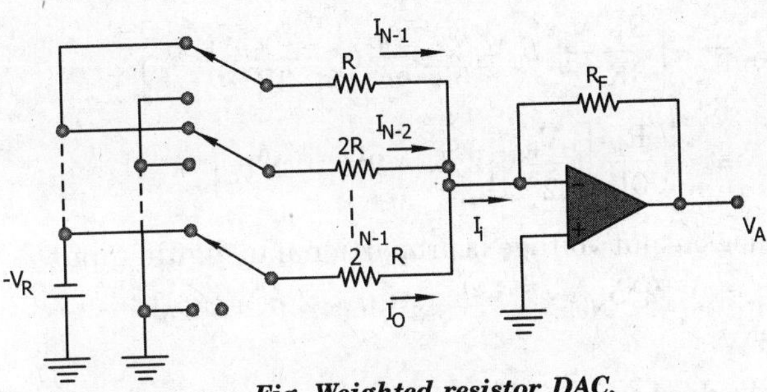

Fig. Weighted resistor DAC.

These currents can be expressed in terms of voltages as

$$I_{N-1} = V_{N-1}/R$$
$$I_{N-2} = V_{N-2}/2R$$

$$I_0 = V_0/2^{N-1} R$$

Let $\quad V(0) = 0; \quad V(1) = -V_R$

Then $\quad V_N = -b_n V_R$

The switches in the circuit are digitally controlled causing b_n to acquire values 0 or 1.

Now, $$I_i = -V_R\left[\frac{1}{R} b_{N-1} + \frac{1}{2R} b_{N-2} + \ldots + \frac{1}{2^{N-1}R} b_0\right]$$

Analog output of the circuit is given by

$$V_A = -R_F I_i$$

$$V_A = V_R\left[\frac{R_F}{R} b_{N-1} + \frac{R_F}{2R} b_{N-2} + \ldots + \frac{R_F}{2^{N-1}R} b_0\right]$$

$$= K[2^{N-1} b_{N-1} + 2^{N-1} b_{N-2} + \ldots + 2^1 b_1 + 2^0 b_0]$$

where $K = \dfrac{R_F}{2^{N-1}R}$

Hence the circuit is a DAC.

R-2R ladder Network.

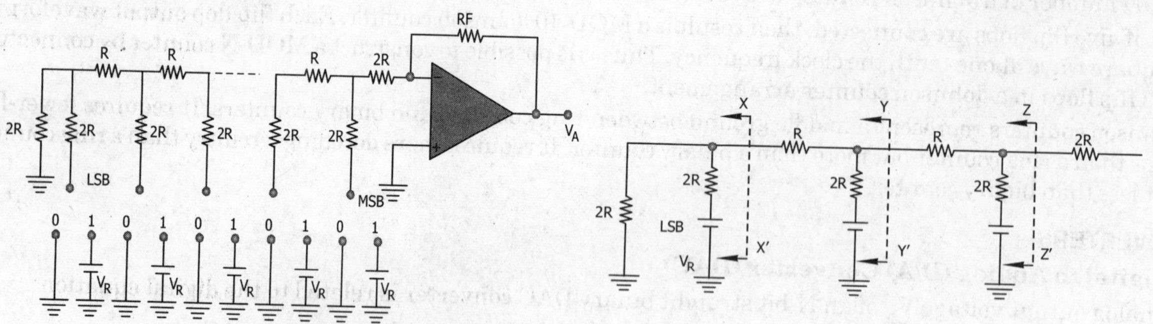

Fig. (a) R-2R ladder DAC network *Fig. (b) 3 bit R-2R ladder DAC network*

An R-2R ladder network [Fig. (*a*)] uses resistors of only two values R and 2R. The inputs to the resistor network is applied through digitally controlled switches.

In a 3 bit R – 2 R ladder DAC [Fig. (*a*)], the input is assumed as 001. Applying Thevenin's theorem at XX', YY' and ZZ', we obtain circuits of Figs. (*c*), (*d*) and (*e*) respectively. It is immediately seen that for input 001, voltage $V_R/2^3$ is applied through 3R to the inverting terminal of the OPAMP.

Similarly for the digital input of 010 and 100, equivalent voltages are $V_R/2^2$ and $V_R/2^1$ respectively with resistance 3R in each case. Therefore, equivalent circuit of Fig. (*f*) is obtained

where, voltage, $V_0 = -\left[\frac{R_F}{3R}\frac{V_R}{2^3}b_0 + \frac{R_F}{3R}\frac{V_R}{2^2}b_1 + \frac{R_F}{3R}\frac{V_R}{2^1}b_2\right]$

$$= -\left(\frac{R_F}{3R}\right)\left(\frac{V_R}{2^3}\right)\left[2^2 b_2 + 2^1 b_1 + 2^0 b_0\right]$$

The equation shows that analog output voltage is proportional to digital input.

In general for N bit DAC, $V_0 = V[2^N b_{N-1} + 2^{N-2} b_{N-2} + \ldots + 2^1 b_1 + 2^0 b_0]$

where $R_F = 3R$ and $V_R = -2^N V$

The number of resistors required for an N bit DAC is 2N in case of R–2R ladder, whereas it is only N in case weighted resistor network. But because of wide spread in the resistance values for large N, weighted resistor DAC is not widely used.

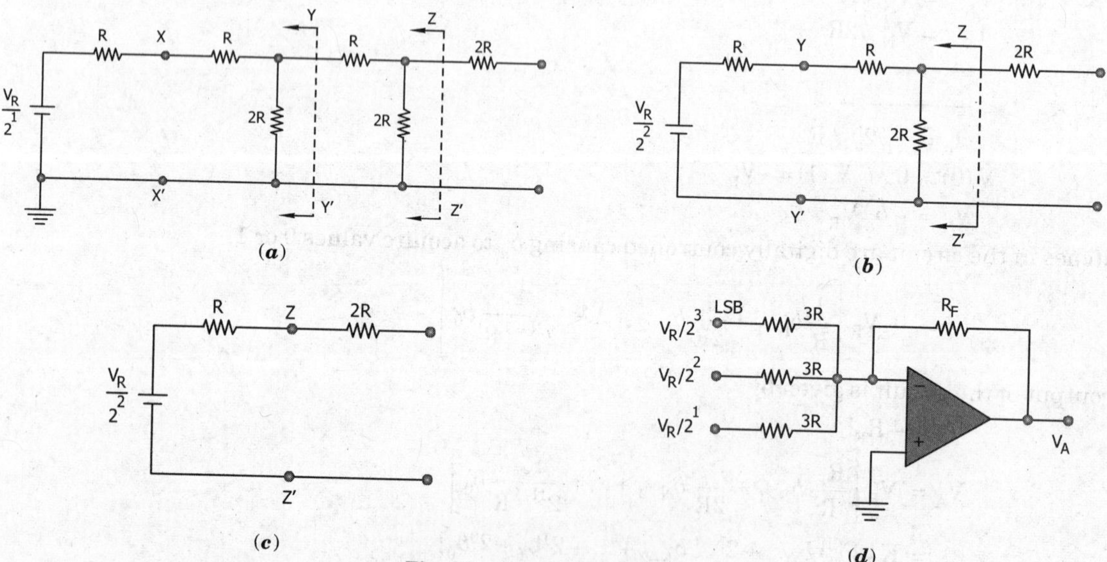

Fig. Simplification of the circuit

2. Analog to Digital (A/D) Converter (ADC)

Counting ADC.

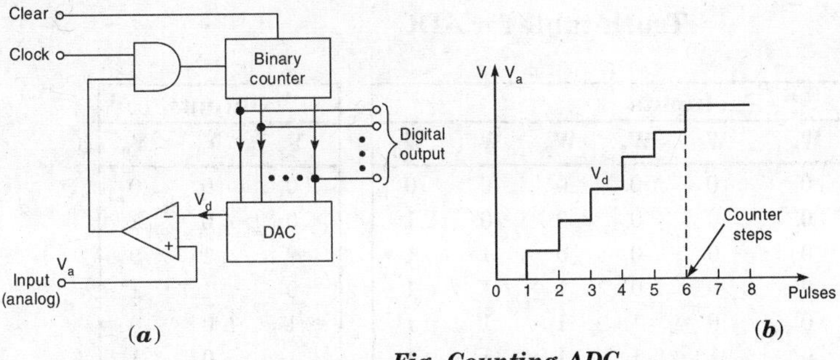

Fig. Counting ADC

The clear pulse resets the counter to the zero count. The counter then records in binary form the number of pulses from the clock line. The clock is the source of pulses equally spaced in time. Since number of pulses counted increases with time, the binary word representing this count is used as an input to the DAC, whose output is the staircase waveform shown in Fig. (*b*). The comparator has an output which is 'HIGH' and the AND gate is open for transmission of clock pulses. When V_d exceeds V_a, the comparator output goes 'LOW' and AND gate is disabled. This stops counting at the time when $V_a \approx V_d$ and the counter can be read as the digital output representing analog input voltage.

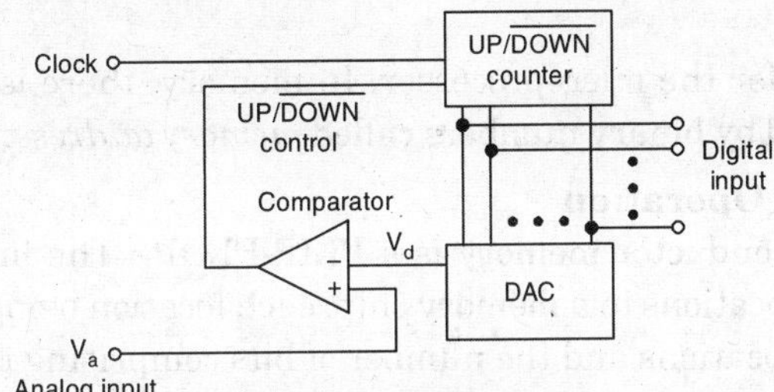

Fig. (c) A tracking ADC.

An improved version of the counting ADC called *tracking* or *servo converter* is shown in Fig. To understand operation of the system, assume initially that output of the DAC is less than the analog input V_a. Then positive comparator output causes the counter to read UP. The DAC output increases until it exceeds V_d. The UP-$\overline{\text{DOWN}}$ control line changes state, so that it now counts down and the count decreases by one count. This causes the control to change to UP and the count increases by 1 LSB. This process keeps repeating, so that digital output bounces back and forth by $\pm$ 1 LSB around the correct value.

Parallel comparator ADC.

This system is the fastest of all converters. Its operation is easily understood if reference is made to the 3–bit A/D converter as shown in the given figure.

The analog voltage is applied simultaneously to a bank of comparators with equally spaced thresholds (reference voltages). This type of processing is called *bin conversion*, because the analog input is sorted into a given voltage rangeor voltage bin determined by the thresholds to two adjacent comparators. For all comparators with thresholds above the input voltage output is LOW, while for all comparators with thresholds below the input voltage output is HIGH.

e.g. $\frac{2}{8}$ V < V_a < $\frac{3}{8}$, then W_0 = 1 and all other W's are 0.

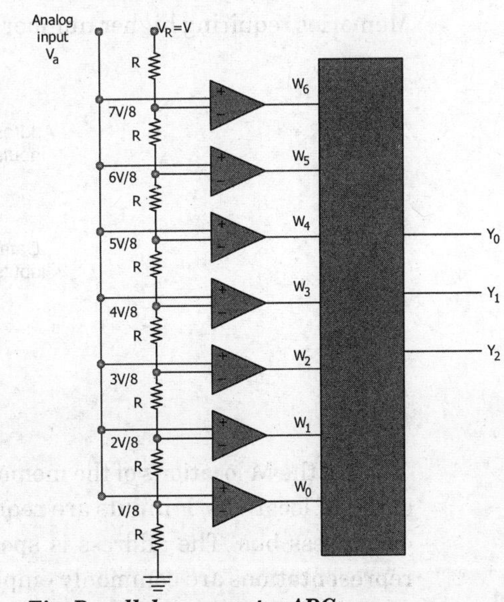

Fig. Parallel comparator ADC

ROM code converter considers these inputs as addresses and gives corresponding digital 3-bit output. The truth-table with inputs W and outputs Y is given in the table below.

Truth-table for ADC

Inputs							Outputs		
W_6	W_5	W_4	W_3	W_2	W_1	W_0	Y_2	Y_1	Y_0
0	0	0	0	0	0	0	0	0	0
0	0	0	0	0	0	1	0	0	1
0	0	0	0	0	1	1	0	1	0
0	0	0	0	1	1	1	0	1	1
0	0	0	1	1	1	1	1	0	0
0	0	1	1	1	1	1	1	0	1
0	1	1	1	1	1	1	1	1	0
1	1	1	1	1	1	1	1	1	1

Conversion line of parallel comparator ADC is limited by the speed of the comparator and ROM. The number of comparators required is $2^N - 1$, where N is number of bits. Complexity of the hardware is its major disadvantage.

MEMORY

It stores binary information for the microprocessor. In memory, there is a sequential arrangement of registers, which are identified by binary numbers called *memory address.*

Memory Organization and Operation

The basic element of a semiconductor memory is a FLIP-FLOP. The information is stored in binary form. There are a number of locations in a memory chip, each location being meant for one word of digital information. The number of locations and the number of bits comprising the work vary from memory to memory.

The size of a memory chip is specified by two numbers M and N as

$N \times N$ bits. The number M specifies the number of locations available in the memory and N is the number of bits at each location. In other words, this means that M words of N bits each can be stored in the memory.

Commonly used values of the number of words per chip are 64, 256, 512, 1024, 2048, 4096 etc.

Whereas common values for the number of words size are 1, 4 and 8 etc.

Memories requiring higher number of words and/or larger word sizes can be formed by using these chips.

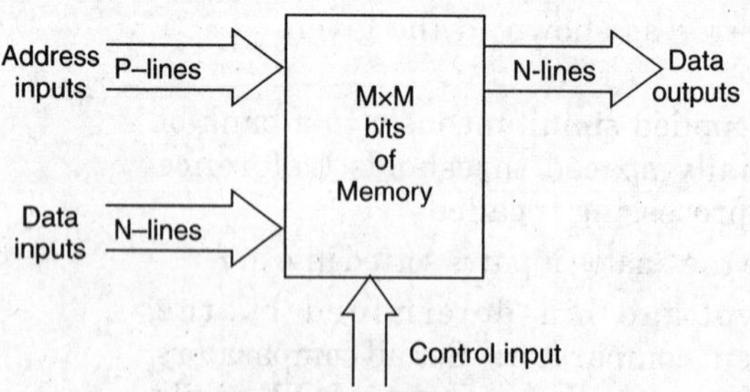

Fig. Block diagram of a memory device

Each of the M locations of the memory is defined by a unique address and therefore for accessing any one of the M locations, P inputs are required, where $2^p = M$. This set of lines is referred to as address inputs or address bus. The address is specified in the binary form. For convenience, octal and hexadecimal representations are commonly employed.

CLASSIFICATION OF MEMORY.

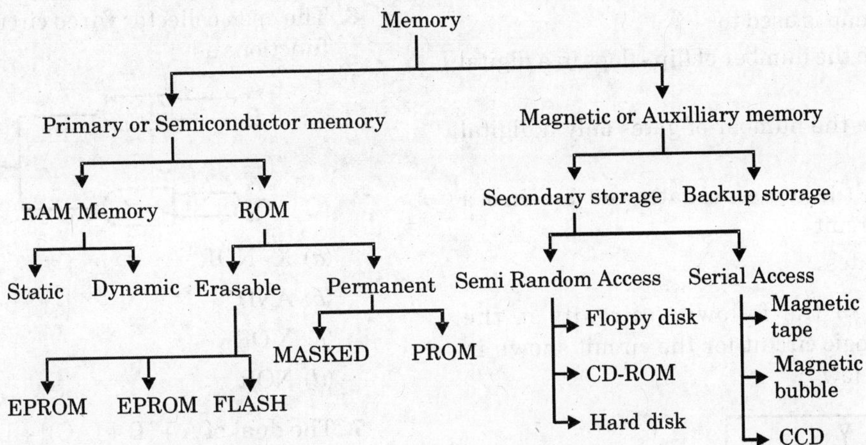

■■

Objective Type Questions

1. Karnaugh map is used to

(*a*) minimise the number of flip - flops in a digital circuit

(*b*) minimise the number of gates only a digital circuit

(*c*) minimise the number of gates and fan - in of a digital circuit

(*d*) design gates

2. Which one of the following circuits is the minimised logic circuit for the circuit shown in the figure below

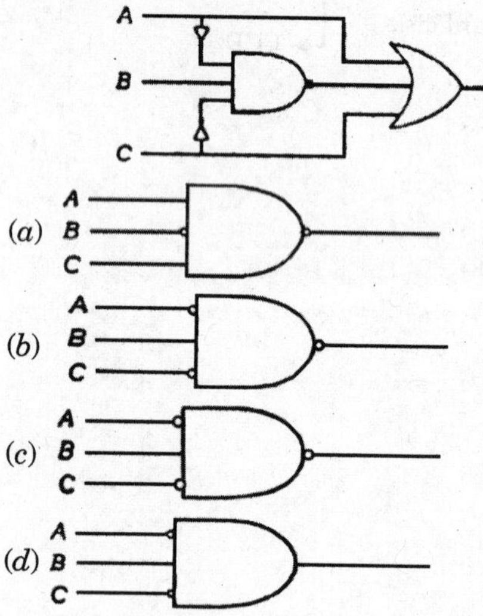

3. The circuit shown in the given figure realizes the function

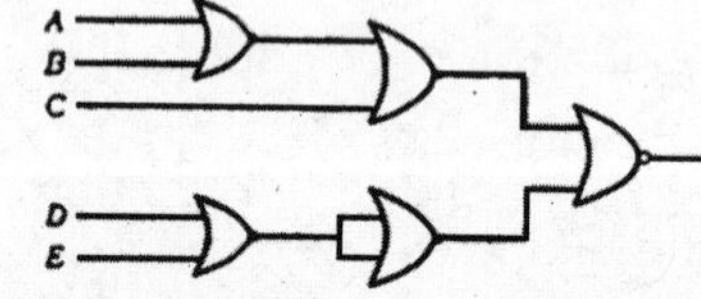

(*a*) $(\overline{A+B}+C)(\overline{D}\,\overline{E})$ (*b*) $(\overline{A+B}+C)\,\overline{E}(D)$

(*c*) $(A+\overline{B+C})\,\overline{E}(D)$ (*d*) $(A+B+\overline{C})(\overline{D}\,\overline{E})$

4. The prefix from the expression X + Y – Z is

(*a*) – + XYZ

(*b*) + – XYZ

(*c*) XYZ – +

(*d*) XYZ + –

5. Of the following, the error - correcting code is

(*a*) EBCDIC (*b*) GRAY

(*c*) Hamming (*d*) ASCII

6. The open collector wired circuits shown below functions as

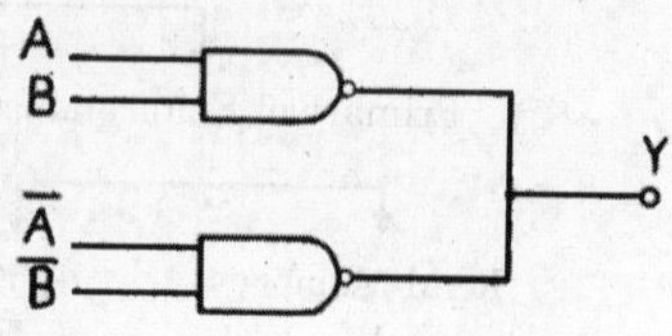

(*a*) X - NOR

(*b*) AND

(*c*) X-OR

(*d*) NOR

7. The dual of A + [B + (AC)] + D, is

(*a*) A + [B(A + C)] + D

(*b*) A [B + AC] D

(*c*) A + [B(A + C)] D

(*d*) A [B(A + C)] D

8. The minimized version for the logic circuit shown in the given figure is

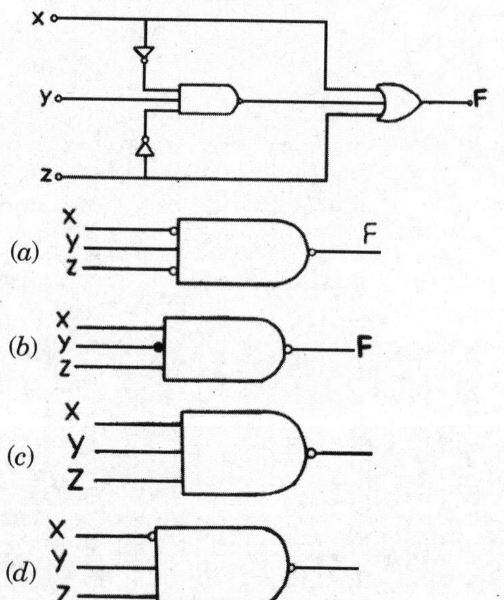

9. The "ECL" has very high switching speed because the transistors are

(*a*) switching between cut-off and saturation regions

(*b*) switching between cut-off and active regions

(*c*) switching between active and saturation regions

(*d*) all of these.

10. The circuit shown in the given figure is

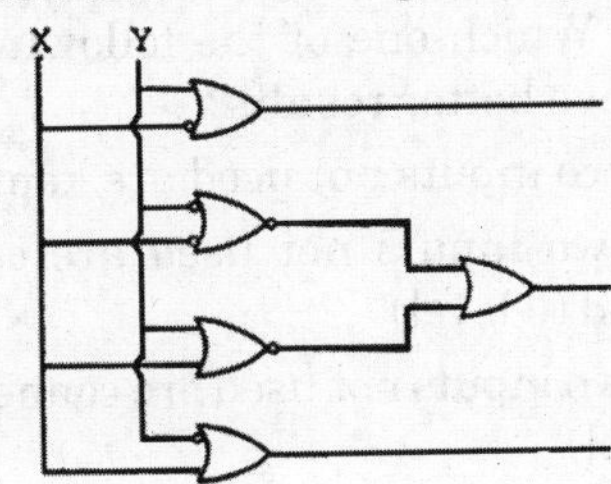

(*a*) an adder circuit

(*b*) a subtractor circuit

(*c*) a comparator circuit

(*d*) a parity generator circuit

11. In the negative logic system,

(*a*) the more negative of the two logic levels represents a logic "1" state

(*b*) the more negative of the two logic levels represents a logic "0" state

(*c*) all input and output voltage levels are negative

(*d*) the output is always complement of the intended logic function

12. If the output of a logic gate is "1" when all its inputs are at logic '0', the gate is either

(*a*) a NAND or a NOR

(*b*) an AND or an X-NOR

(*c*) an OR or a NAND

(*d*) an X-OR an X-NOR

13. For the Karnaugh map shown in the given figure, the minimum Boolean function is

yz \ x	0	1
00	1	1
01	1	
11	1	1
10	1	1

(*a*) $x'y' + z' + yz$

(*b*) $xz' + z + zy'$

(*c*) $xy + z + y'z$

(*d*) $x'z + z' + yz$

14. The voltage levels of a negative logic system must

(*a*) necessarily be negative

(*b*) be negative or positive

(*c*) necessarily be positive

(*d*) necessarily be 0 V and – 5 V

15. The given figure shows a NAND gate with input waveforms A and B

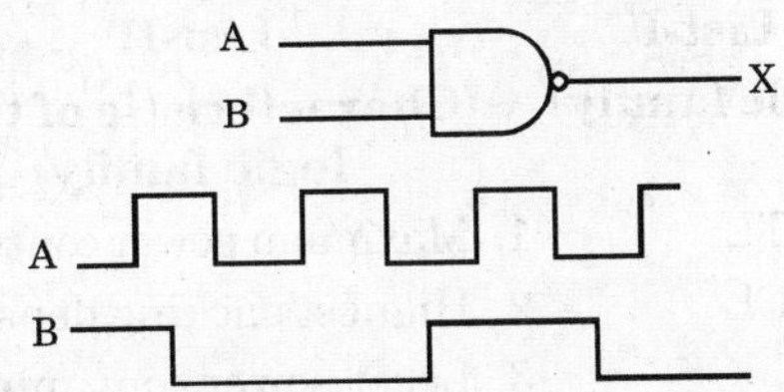

The correct output waveform X of the gate is

(*a*) 

(*b*)

(*c*)

(*d*)

16. The output Y of the given circuit is

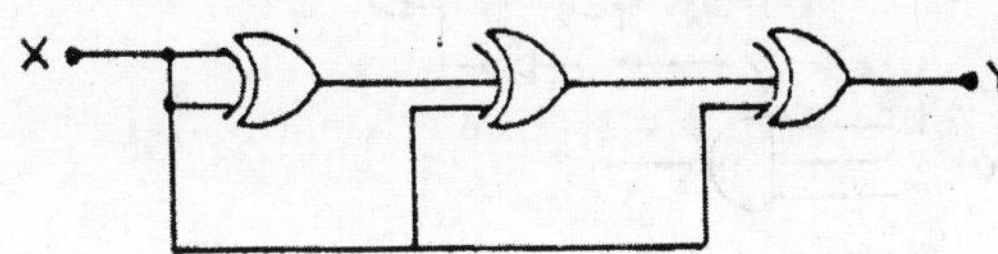

(*a*) 1

(*b*) zero

(*c*) X

(*d*) $\overline{X}$

17. The Boolean theorem $AB + \overline{A}C + BC = AB + \overline{A}C$ corresponds to

(*a*) $(A + B) . (\overline{A} + C) . (B + C) = (A + B). (\overline{A} + C)$

(*b*) $AB + \overline{A}C + BC = AB + BC$

(*c*) $AB + \overline{A}C + BC = (A + B) . (\overline{A} + C) . (B + C)$

(*d*) $(A + B) . (\overline{A} + C) . (B + C) = AB + \overline{A}C$

18. The Boolean expression for the shaded area in the given Venn diagram is

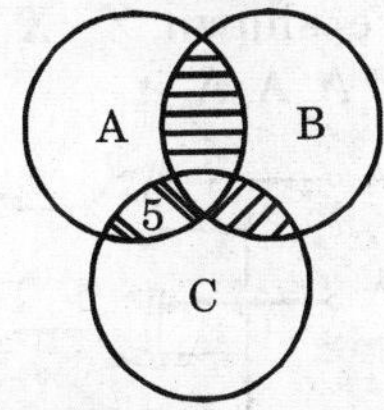

(*a*) $AB + BC + CA$

(*b*) $AB\overline{C} + \overline{A}BC + A\overline{B}C$

(*c*) $ABC + \overline{A}\,\overline{B}\,\overline{C}$

(*d*) $\overline{A}\,\overline{B}\,\overline{C} + A\overline{B}\,\overline{C}$ 5

19. Match List-I with List-II and select the correct answer by using the codes given below the lists:

List-I (Logic family)	List-II (Characteristic of the logic family)
A. TTL	1. Maximum power consumption
B. ECL	2. Highest packing density
C. NMOS	3. Least power consumption
D. CMOS	4. Saturated logic

Codes:

	A	B	C	D
(a)	1	4	2	3
(b)	1	4	3	2
(c)	4	1	2	3
(d)	4	1	3	2

20. The minimised logic circuit for the circuit shown in figure is

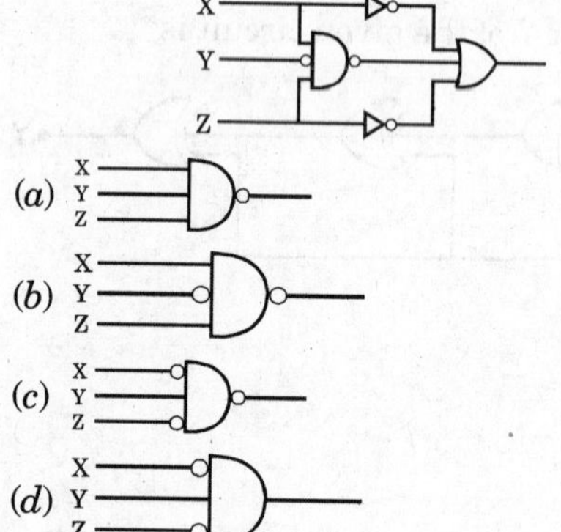

21. The minimisel expression for the given K-map is (X: don't care)

(a) $\overline{C}\ \overline{B} + BD + CD$

(b) $AB + C\overline{B} + B\overline{C}$

(c) $\overline{C}B + AC + B\overline{C}$

(d) $\overline{C}B + CD + C\overline{B}$

22. In the figure shown $X_2\ X_1\ X_0$ will be 1's complement of $A_2\ A_1\ A_0$ if

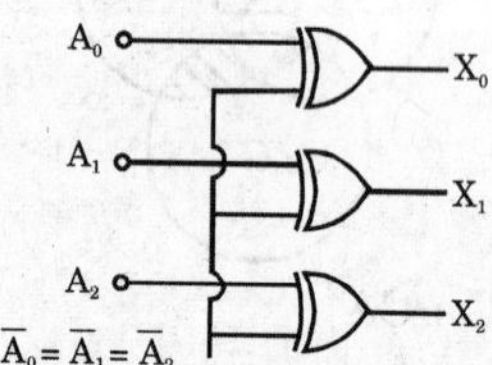

(a) $Y = 0$

(b) $Y = 1$

(c) $Y = \overline{A_0} = \overline{A_1} = \overline{A_2}$

(d) $Y = A_0 = A_1 = A_2$

23. A three-input NAND gate is to be used as an inverter. Which one of the following measures will achieve better results?

(a) The two inputs not used are kept open

(b) The two inputs not used are connected to ground (0 level)

(c) The two inputs not used are connected to logic (1 level)

(d) None of these

24. Which one of the following represents the coincidence logic?

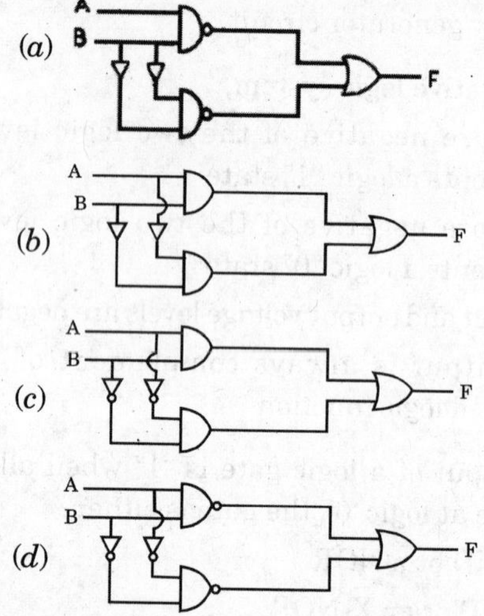

25. The output of the gate circuit shown in the given figure is

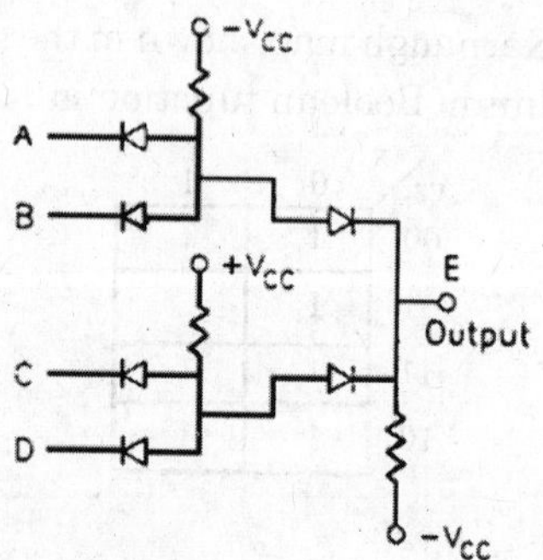

(a) $(A + B)(C + D)$ (b) $\overline{AB + CD}$

(c) $AB + CD$ (d) $\overline{(A+B)(C+D)}$

26. Which one of the following is the dual-form of the Boolean identity

$$AB + \overline{A}C = (A + C)(\overline{A} + B)?$$

(a) $AB + \overline{A}C = AC + \overline{A}B$

(b) $(A + B) + (\overline{A} + C) = (A + C)(\overline{A} + B)$

(c) $(A + B)(\overline{A} + C) = AC + \overline{A}B$

(d) $AB + \overline{A}C = AB + \overline{A}C + BC$

27. The circuit shown in the given figure is a

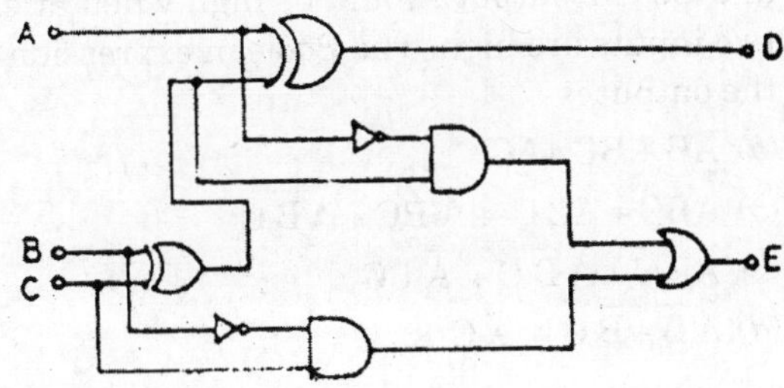

(a) full adder

(b) full subtractor

(c) shift register

(d) decade counter

28. Match List-I with List-II and select the correct answer by using the codes given below the lists:

List-I	List-II
A. 45	1. 1 0 1 1 0 1 0 0
B. 90	2. 1 1 0 1 0 0 1 0
C. 180	3. 0 1 0 1 1 0 1 0
D. 210	4. 0 0 1 0 1 1 0 1
	5. 1 0 1 0 1 0 0 0

Codes:

	A	B	C	D
(a)	3	4	5	2
(b)	4	3	1	2
(c)	4	3	5	2
(d)	3	4	2	1

29. The output Y of the circuit shown in the figure is

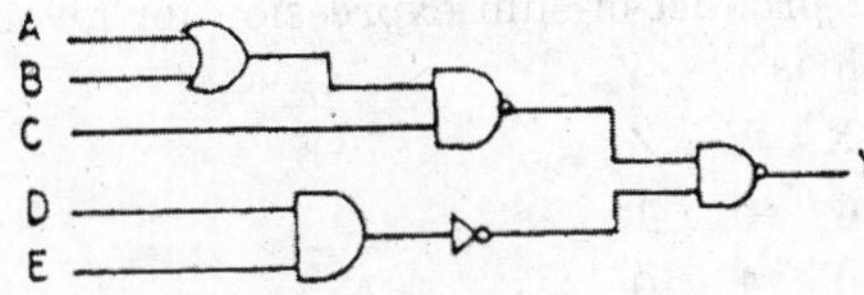

(a) (A + B)C + DE

(b) AB + C (D + E)

(c) (A + B)C + D + E

(d) (AB + C). DE

30. The circuit shown in the figure below 1 is equivalent to

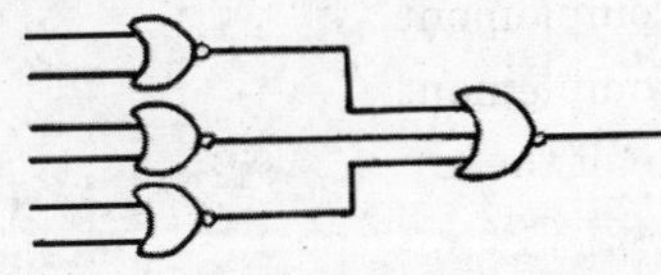

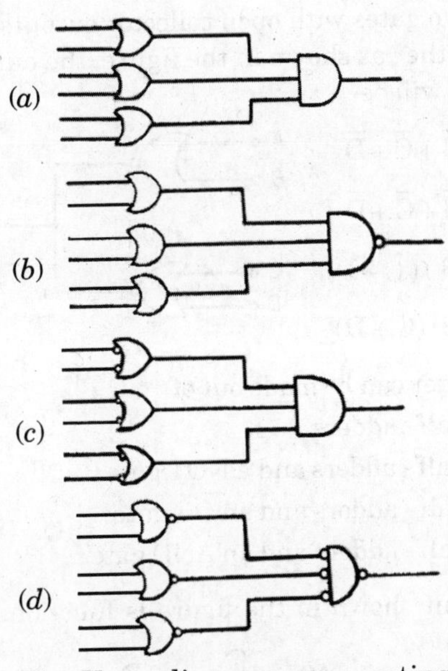

31. The Venn diagram representing the Boolean expression A + ($\overline{A}$. B) is

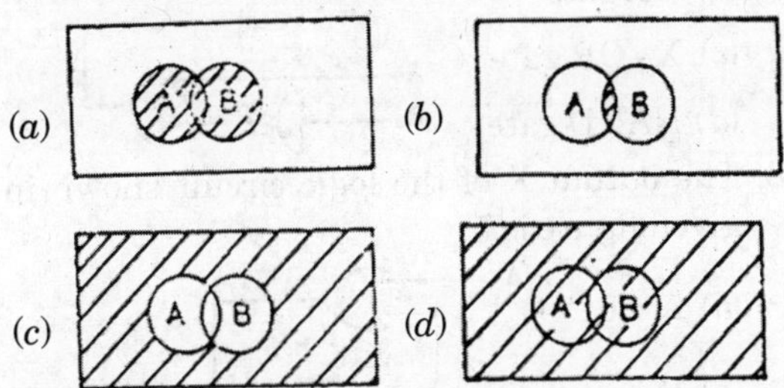

32. How many minterms (excluding redundant terms) does the minimal switching function $f(v, w, x, y, z) = x + \overline{y}\ z$ originally have?

(a) 16 (b) 20

(c) 24 (d) 32

33. While obtaining minimal sum of products expression,

(a) all don't cares are ignored

(b) all don't cares are treated as logic ones

(c) all don't cares are treated as logic zeros

(d) only such don't cares that aid minimisation are treated as logic ones.

34. The complement of the Boolean expression AB . ($\overline{B}$ C + AC) is

(a) ($\overline{A}$ + $\overline{B}$) + (B + $\overline{C}$)($\overline{A}$ + $\overline{C}$)

(b) ($\overline{A}$. $\overline{B}$) + (B C + $\overline{A}$ C)

(c) ($\overline{A}$ + $\overline{B}$) . (B + $\overline{C}$)($\overline{A}$ + $\overline{C}$)

(d) (A + B). ($\overline{B}$ + C)(A + C)

35. When two gates with open collector outputs are tied together as shown in the figure, the output obtained will be

(a) $\overline{A}+\overline{B}+\overline{C}+\overline{D}$

(b) $\overline{A}+\overline{B}+\overline{C}+\overline{D}$

(c) $(\overline{A}+\overline{B})(\overline{C}+\overline{D})$

(d) $(A+B)(C+D)$

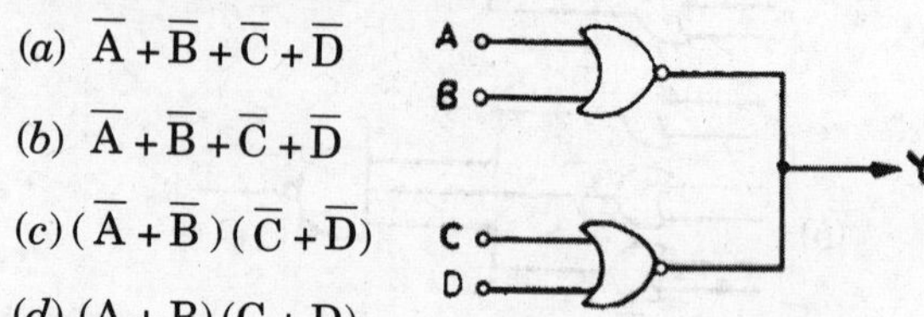

36. A full-adder can be made out of

(a) two half-adders

(b) two half-adders and a NOT gate

(c) two half-adders and an OR gate

(d) two half-adders and an AND gate

37. The circuit shown in the figure is functionally equivalent to

(a) NOR gate

(b) OR gate

(c) X-OR gate

(d) NAND gate

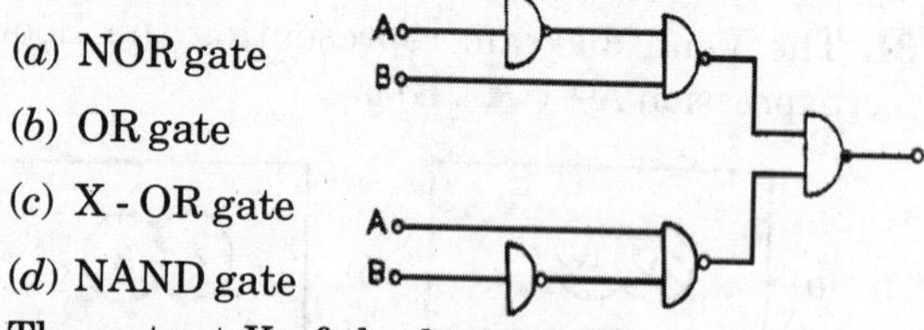

38. The output X of the logic circuit shown in the given figure is

(a) A + BC

(b) BC

(c) AB

(d) AB + C

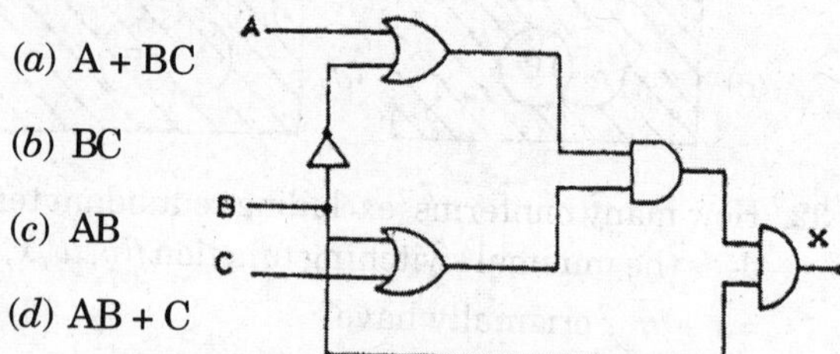

39. Consider the Karnaugh map given below:

x_3x_4 \ x_1x_2	00	01	11	10
00	1		d	d
01		1	d	1
11		d	1	
10	1	d		d

The function represented by this map can be simplified to the minimal form as

(a) $\overline{x}_1\overline{x}_2\overline{x}_4 + x_2x_4 + x_1\overline{x}_3$

(b) $\overline{x}_1\overline{x}_2\overline{x}_4 + x_2x_4 + x_1\overline{x}_2\overline{x}_3x_4$

(c) $x_2x_4 + \overline{x}_2\overline{x}_4 + x_1\overline{x}_3$

(d) $\overline{x}_1\overline{x}_2\overline{x}_4 + \overline{x}_1x_2\overline{x}_3x_4 + x_1x_2x_3x_4 + x_1\overline{x}_2\overline{x}_3x_4$

40. In a digital system, there are three inputs A, B and C. The output should be high when atleast two inputs are high. The Boolean expression for the output is

(a) AB + BC + AC

(b) $ABC + AB\overline{C} + \overline{A}BC + A\overline{B}C$

(c) $AB\overline{C} + A\overline{B}C + \overline{A}BC$

(d) $A\overline{B} + \overline{B}C + \overline{A}C$

41. The input waveform V_i and the output waveform V_0 of a Schmitt NAND are shown in the given figures.

The duty cycle of the output waveform will be

(a) 100%

(b) 85.5%

(c) 72.2%

(d) 25%

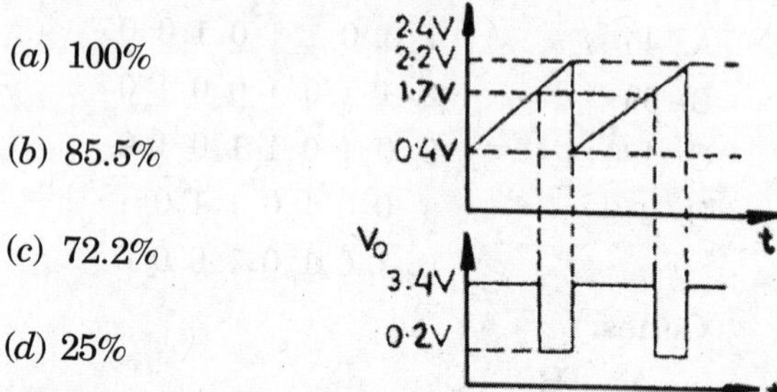

42. Y = f(A, B) = πM(0, 1, 2, 3) represents (M is Maxterm)

(a) NOR gate

(b) NAND gate

(c) OR gate

(d) a situation where output is independent of input

43. The product-of-sum expression for given truth table is

X	Y	Z
0	0	1
0	1	0
1	0	1
1	1	0

(a) $(\overline{X}\,\overline{Y})(X+Y)$ (b) $(X+\overline{Y})(\overline{X}+\overline{Y})$

(c) $(X+\overline{Y})(\overline{X}+\overline{Y})$ (d) None of these

44. Which of the following number systems has two O's?

(a) Sign plus magnitude

(b) 1's complement

(c) 2's complement

(d) None of these

45. The expression for shaded area shown below is

(*a*) $AB + BC$

(*b*) $\bar{A}\,\bar{B}\,C + A\bar{B}\,\bar{C}$

(*c*) $AB\bar{C} + \bar{A}BC$

(*d*) None of these

46. Which of the following is a coincidence logic circuit?

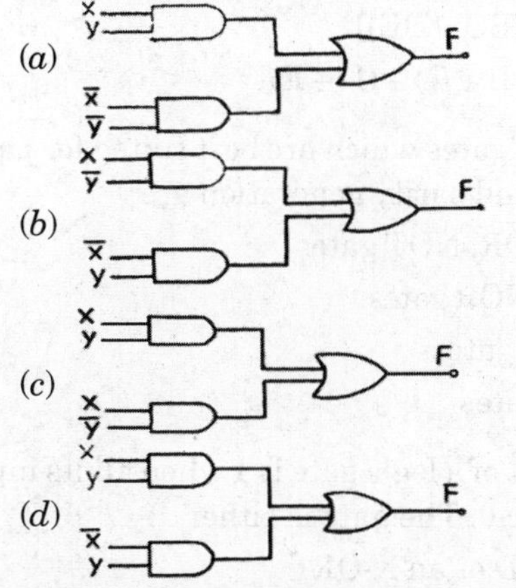

47. The circuit shown in the given figure realizes the function

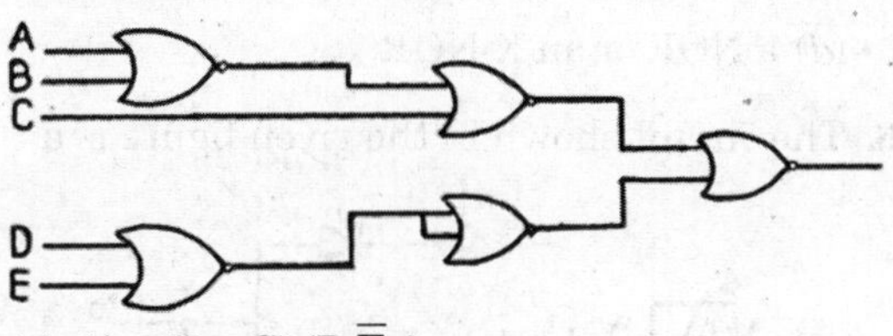

(*a*) $(A + B + C)(D\bar{E})$

(*b*) $(A + (\overline{B + C})(\bar{D}\,E)$

(*c*) $(A + B + C)(\bar{D}\bar{E})$

(*d*) $(\overline{A + B} + C)(\bar{D}\bar{E})$

48. If two numbers in excess-3 code are added and the result is less than 9, then to get equivalent binary

(*a*) 0011 is subtracted

(*b*) 0011 is added

(*c*) 0110 is subtracted

(*d*) 0110 is added

49. A 7 bit Hemming code (Even parity checker) 0001001 for a BCD digit is known to have errors. The BCD encoded digit is

(*a*) 9

(*b*) 6

(*c*) 3

(*d*) 0

50. A is even or B is true

Negative of above statement will be

(*a*) A is odd or B is false

(*b*) A is odd and B is false

(*c*) A is even and B is false

(*d*) A is even and B is false

51. The number of NAND gates required for two dimensional addressing of 256 × 8 bit ROM using 8 to 1 selectors is

(*a*) 16 (*b*) 32

(*c*) 64 (*d*) 104

52. The negative logic AND gate shown in the given figure is equivalent to a positive logic

(*a*) AND gate

(*b*) OR gate

(*c*) NAND gate

(*d*) NOR gate

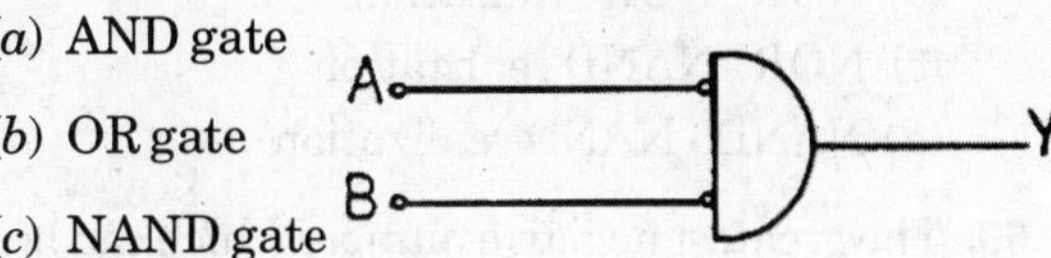

53. The minimum Boolean for the following circuit is

(*a*) AB + AC + BC

(*b*) A+BC

(*c*) A + B

(*d*) A + B + C

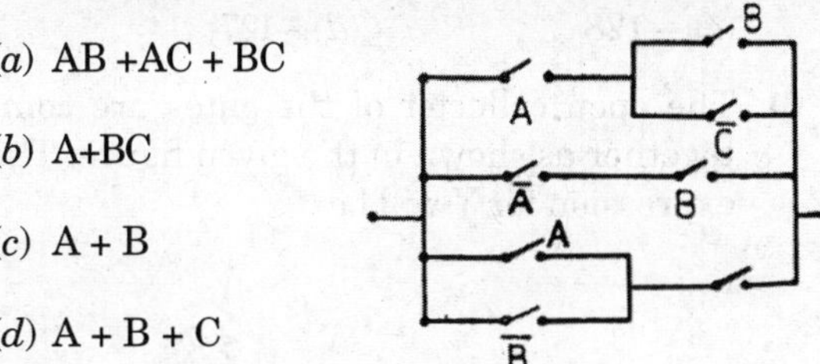

54. The number of switching functions of 3 variables is

(*a*) 8 (*b*) 64

(*c*) 128 (*d*) 256

55. When signed numbers are used in binary arithmetic, then which one of the following notation would have unique representation for zero?

(*a*) sign - magnitude (*b*) 1's complement

(*c*) 2's complement (*d*) 9's complement

56. What is Boolean expression for a gating network that will have ouput 0 only, when

X = 1, Y = 1, Z = 1;

X = 0, Y = 0, Z = 0;

X = 1, Y = 0, Z = 0 ?

(*a*) $XYZ + \bar{X}\,\bar{Y}Z + X\bar{Y}Z$

(*b*) $(XYZ) + (\bar{X} + \bar{Y} + Z) + (X + \bar{Y} + Z)$

(*c*) $(\bar{X} + \bar{Y} + Z) + (X + Y + Z)(\bar{X} + Y + Z)$

(*d*) $\bar{X}\,\bar{Y}Z + XYZ + \bar{X}YZ$

57. The number of Boolean functions which can be generated with four variables is

(*a*) 4 (*b*) 16

(*c*) 256 (*d*) 65,536

58. Which one of the following will give the sum of full-adder as output?

(*a*) Three input majority circuit

(*b*) Three bit parity checker

(*c*) Three bit comparator

(*d*) Three bit counter

59. Which one of the following is equivalent to AND - OR realization?

(*a*) NAND - NOR realization

(*b*) NOR - NOR realization

(*c*) NOR - NAND realization

(*d*) NAND - NAND realization

60. The greatest negative number which can be stored in computer that has 8-bit work length and uses 2's complement arithmetic is

(*a*) – 256 (*b*) – 255

(*c*) – 128 (*d*) –127

61. The open collector of the gates are connected together as shown in the given figure. The logic expression for Y will be

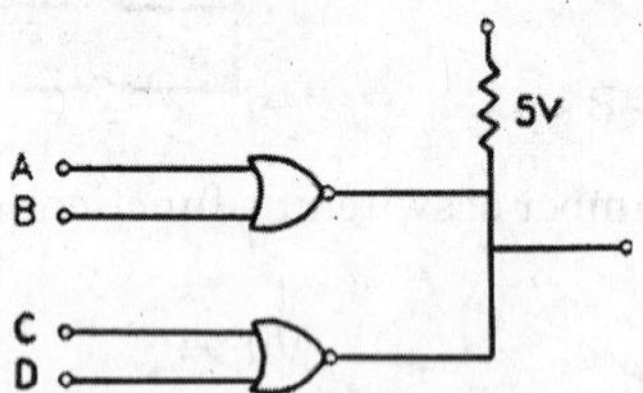

(*a*) $\overline{A + B} + \overline{C + D}$ (*b*) $\overline{A + B + C + D}$

(*c*) (A + B) (C + D) (*d*) AB + CD

62. Consider the following truth table:

A	B	C	D
0	0	0	1
0	0	1	1
0	1	0	0
0	1	1	0
1	0	0	1
1	0	1	1
1	1	0	0
1	1	1	0

The corresponding Boolean- function 'F' is

(*a*) A + B + C (*b*) $\overline{A}$ + B + C

(*c*) $\overline{A}$ (*d*) $\overline{B}$

63. The Boolean function represented by the following circuit is

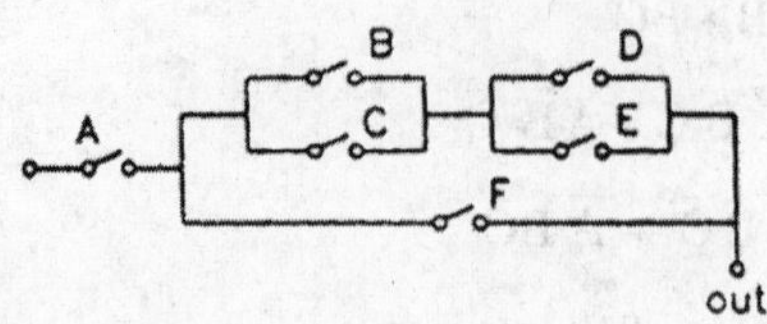

(*a*) A[F + (B + C). (D – E)]

(*b*) A[F + (B + C). DE]

(*c*) A+ [F. (BC + DE)]

(*d*) A. [F . (B + C) + (D – E)]

64. The sets of gates which are best suited for parity checking and parity generation are

(*a*) AND, OR, NOT gates

(*b*) X-OR-NOR gates

(*c*) NAND gates

(*d*) NOR gates

65. The output of a logic gate is 1 when all its inputs are at logic 0. The gate is either

(*a*) a NAND or an X-OR

(*b*) an OR or an X-OR

(*c*) an AND or an X-OR

(*d*) a NOR or an X-NOR

66. The circuit shown in the given figure is a

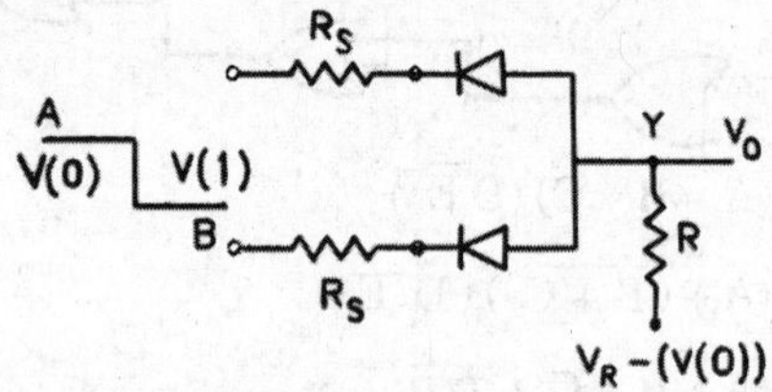

(*a*) positive logic OR circuit

(*b*) negative logic OR circuit

(*c*) positive logic NAND circuit

(*d*) negative logic NAND circuit

67. The circuit shown in the figure given below is equivalent to

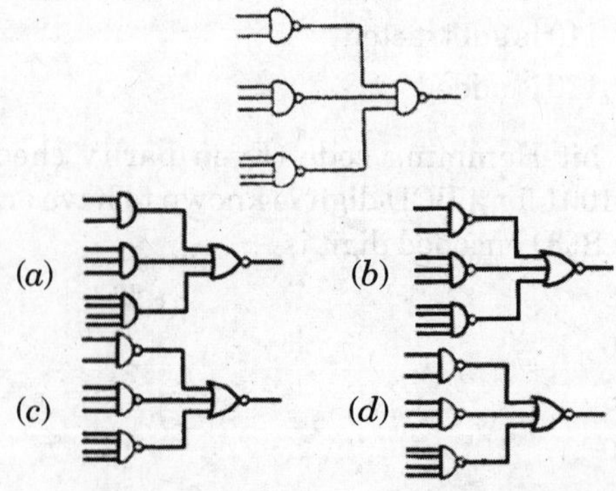

68. The simplified Boolean expression from the Karnaugh map given in the figure below is

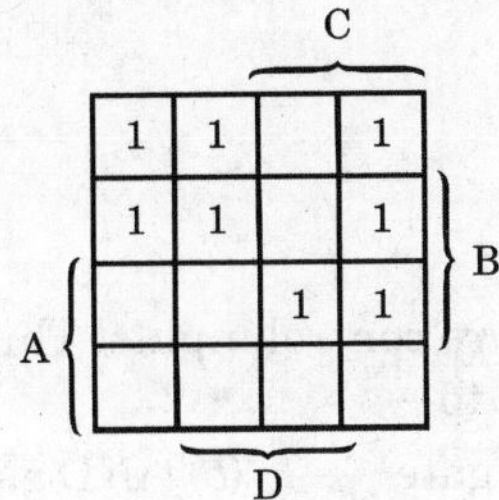

(a) $\overline{A}\,\overline{C} + \overline{A}\,\overline{D} + ABC$

(b) $\overline{AB} + \overline{AD} + ABC$

(c) $AC + ACD + ABD - BC\overline{D}$

(d) $\overline{AB} + \overline{CD} + \overline{AD}$

69. The logic circuit shown in the given figure can be minimized to

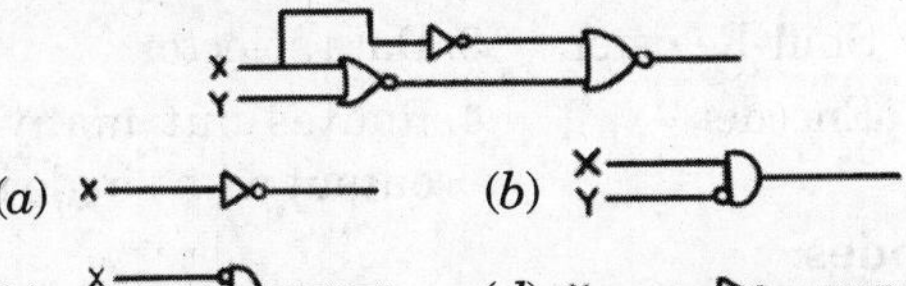

70. Which one of the following logic function is implemented by the gates when their open collector type outputs are tied together as shown in the given figure?

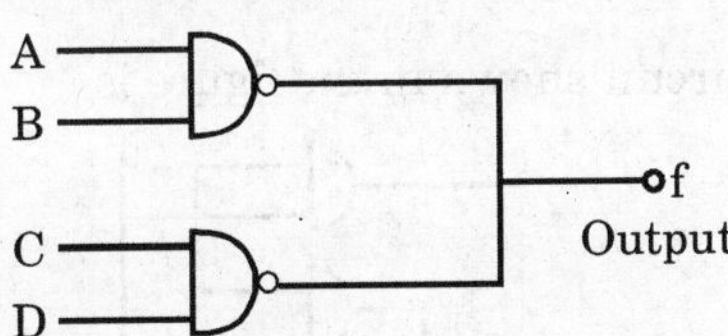

(a) $f = AB + C + D$

(b) $f = \overline{AB} + (\overline{C + D})$

(c) $f = AB + (C + D)$

(d) $f = \overline{AB + C + D}$

71. The circuit shown in the following figure realises the function

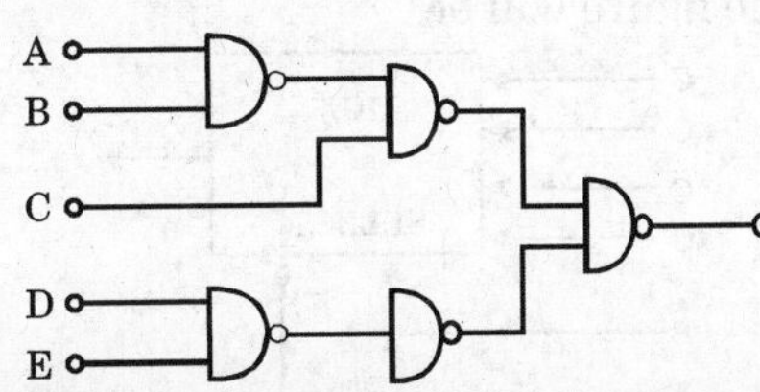

(a) $(\overline{A} + \overline{B})C + \overline{DE}$

(b) $(A + B)C + D + E$

(c) $AB + C + DE$

(d) $AB + C(D + E)$

72. The output Y for the logic circuit shown in the given figure is

(a) $A\overline{B}$

(b) $\overline{A} + \overline{B}$

(c) $\overline{A}\,\overline{B}$

(d) $A + \overline{B}$

73. F's complement of $(2BFD)_{hex}$ is

(a) E 304 (b) D 403

(c) D 402 (d) C 403

74. The number of digit 1 present in the binary representation of

$$3 \times 512 + 7 \times 64 + 5 \times 8 + 3 \text{ is}$$

(a) 8 (b) 9

(c) 10 (d) 12

75. Which one of the following is equivalent to the Boolean expression

$$Y = \overline{AB} + \overline{BC} + \overline{CA}?$$

(a) $\overline{AB + BC + CA}$

(b) $(\overline{A} + \overline{B})(\overline{B} + \overline{C})(\overline{A} + \overline{C})$

(c) $\overline{(A + B) + (B + C) + (C + A)}$

(d) $(\overline{A + B})\ (\overline{B + C})\ (\overline{C + A})$

76. Given Boolean theorem $AB + \overline{A}C + BC = AB + \overline{A}C$. Which one of the following identities is true?

(a) $(A + B) . (\overline{A} + C) . (B + C) = (A + B).(\overline{A} + C)$

(b) $AB + \overline{A}C + BC = AB + BC$

(c) $AB + \overline{A}C + BC = (A + B) . (\overline{A} + C) . (B + C)$

(d) $(A + B) . (\overline{A} + C) . (B + C) = AB + \overline{A}C$

77. The operation $x \oplus \overline{y}$ represents

(a) $x - y$ (b) $\overline{x}y + \overline{xy}$

(c) $xy + \overline{xy}$ (d) $\overline{x} - \overline{y}$

78. The term $AB + AC + B\overline{C}$ reduce to

(a) $AB + CA$ (b) $AC + BC$

(c) $AC + B\overline{C}$ (d) $AB + \overline{B}\,\overline{C}$

79. If m is the number of bits required to code N items in the binary form, then

(a) $m = \log_{10} N$

(b) $m > \log_e N$

(c) $m \geq \log_2 N$

(d) $m = 2 \log_{10} N$

80. The Boolean function F = A.B. + C.D. + E can be realised as

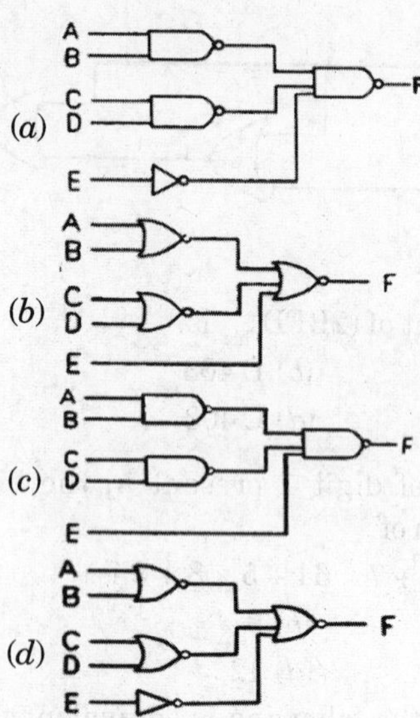

COMBINATIONAL CIRCUITS

81. The number of comparator circuits required to build a three-bit simultaneous A/D converter is

(a) 7 (b) 8
(c) 15 (d) 16

82. The number of 4-line-to-line decoders required to make an 8-line-to-256-line decoder is

(a) 16 (b) 17
(c) 32 (d) 64

83. Full adder circuit can be implemented by

(a) Multiplexers
(b) Half adders
(c) AND & OR gates
(d) Decoders

84. In a 4-bit full adder, how many half adders and OR gates are required?

(a) 8 & 4
(b) 7 & 4
(c) 7 & 3
(d) 8 & 3

85. The type of gate shown in the given figure is

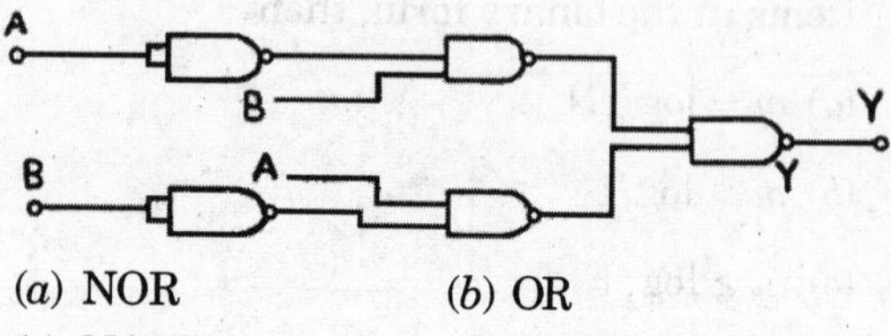

(a) NOR (b) OR
(c) NAND (d) X-OR

86. In the figure shown

X_1 HI
X_2 HI
X_3 HI
X_4 LO

S_1 and S_0 are control inputs. This multiplexer is equivalent to

(a) NAND gate (b) AND gate
(c) OR gate (d) X-NOR gate

87. Match List-I with List-II and select the correct answer by using the codes given below the lists:

List-I	List-II
A. Multiplex	1. Sequential memory
B. De-Multiplexer	2. Converts decimal number to binary
C. Shift-Register	3. Data selector
D. Encoder	4. Routes out many data output with single input.

Codes:

	A	B	C	D
(a)	3	4	1	2
(b)	4	3	1	2
(c)	3	4	2	1
(d)	1	2	3	4

88. The circuit shown in the figure is

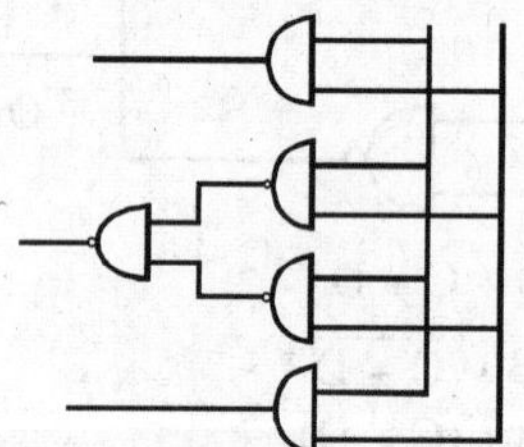

(a) an adder (b) a subtractor
(c) parity generator (d) comparator

89. The output 'F' of the multiplexer circuit shown in the figure will be

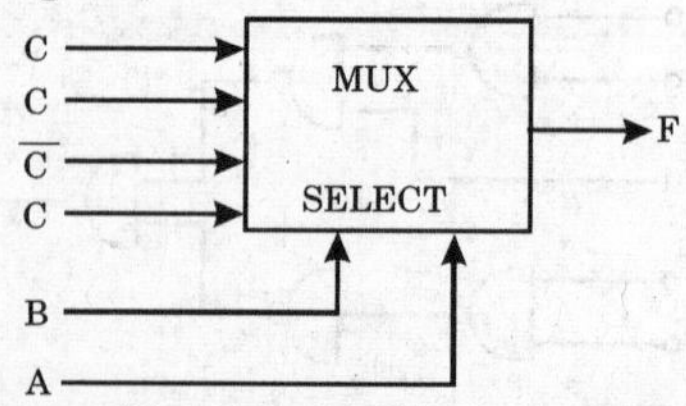

(a) $AB + B\overline{C} + \overline{C}A + \overline{B}\,\overline{C}$
(b) $A \oplus B \oplus C$
(c) $A \oplus B$
(d) $\overline{A}\,\overline{B}C + \overline{A}B\overline{C} + A\overline{B}\,\overline{C} + ABC$

90. The logic circuit realized by the circuit shown in the given figure will be

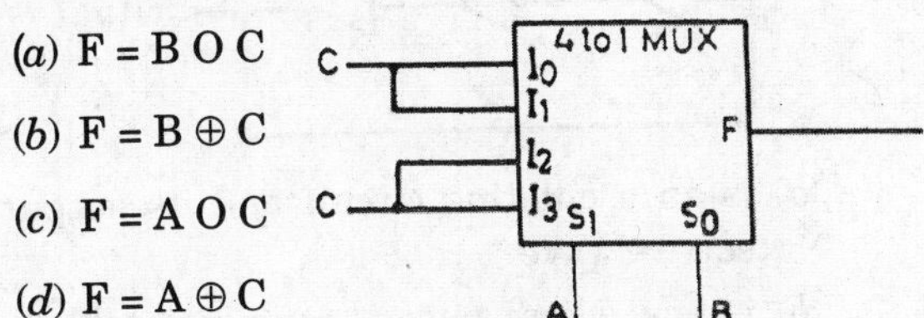

(a) F = B ⊙ C
(b) F = B ⊕ C
(c) F = A ⊙ C
(d) F = A ⊕ C

91. A carry look ahead adder is frequently used for a addition because it
(a) is faster
(b) is more accurate
(c) used fewer gates
(d) costs less

92. The logic circuit given below converts a binary code $y_1 y_2 y_3$ into

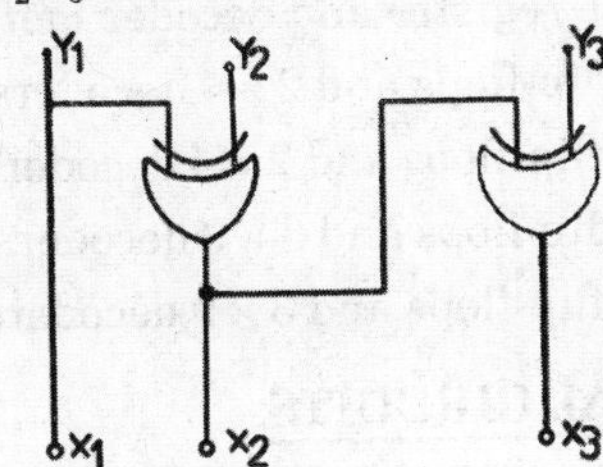

(a) Excess - 3 code
(b) Gray code
(c) BCD code
(d) Hamming code

93. A full-adder can be implemented with half-adders AND OR gates. A 4-bit parallel full adder without any initial carry requires
(a) 8 half-adders, 4-OR gates
(b) 8 half-adders, 3-OR gates
(c) 7 half-adders, 4-OR gates
(d) 7 half-adders, 3-OR gates

94. A 4-line-to-1-line multiplexer shown in Fig (a) the same as per IEEE convention is shown in Fig (b) is fed with three logic inputs A, B and C as shown. The output of the multiplexer will be

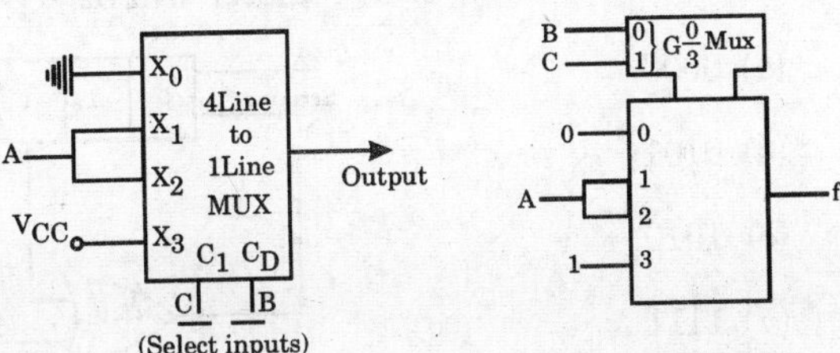

Fig (a) **Fig (b)**

(a) Σm (0, 1, 2, 4) (b) Σm (0, 3, 5,7)
(c) Σm (3, 5, 6, 7) (d) Σm (1, 2, 5, 6)

95. The output f(x, y) of the multiplexer shown in Fig (a) (the same IEEE convention is shown in Fig (b) resulting from the input logical values is

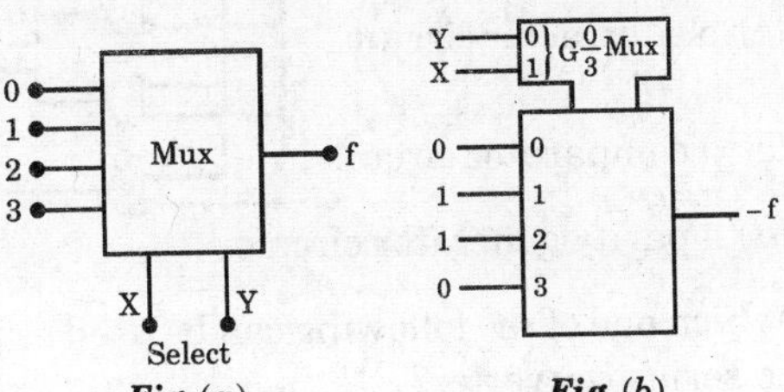

Fig (a) **Fig (b)**

(a) an XOR gate (b) a NOR gate
(c) an AND gate (d) a NAND gate

96. The following switching functions are to be implemented using a decoder:

$f_1 = \Sigma\, m\, (1, 2, 8, 10, 14)$
$f_2 = \Sigma\, m\, (2, 5, 9, 11)$
$f_3 = \Sigma\, m\, (2, 4, 5, 6, 7)$

The minimum configuration of the decoder should be
(a) 2-to-4 line (b) 3-to-8 line
(c) 4-to-16 line (d) 5-to-32 line

97. A combinational circuit is one in which the output depends on the
(a) input combination at that time
(b) input combination and the previous output
(c) input combination at that time and the previous input combination
(d) present output and the previous output

98. The output (X) waveform for the given combination circuit for the inputs at A and B (waveform shown in the figure) will be

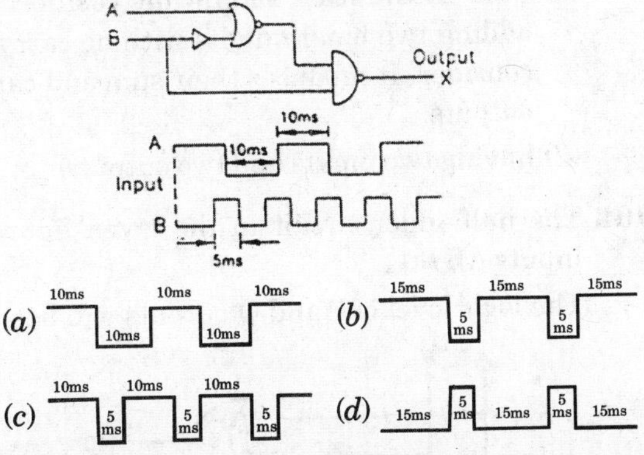

99. Two's complement of a given 3 or more bit binary number of non-zero magnitude same as the original number if all bits except the
(a) MSB are zeros (b) LSB are zeros
(c) MSB are ones (d) LSB are ones

100. The circuit shown in the given figure is

(*a*) an adder circuit

(*b*) a subtractor circuit

(*c*) a comparator circuit

(*d*) a parity generator circuit

101. Which one of the following can be used as parallel to series converter?

(*a*) Decoder (*b*) Digital counter

(*c*) Multiplexer (*d*) Demultiplexer

102. Consider the following statements:

A multiplexer

1. Selects one of the several inputs and transmits it to a single output
2. Routes the data from a single input to one of many outputs
3. Converts parallel data into serial data
4. Is a combinational circuit

Of these statements the correct statements are

(*a*) 1, 2 and 4 (*b*) 2, 3 and 4

(*c*) 1, 3 and 4 (*d*) 1, 2 and 3

103. The full-adder is defined by an adder circuit an adder circuit

(*a*) having two inputs used to add two binary digits. It produces their sum and carry as input.

(*b*) having three inputs used to add two binary digits plus a carry. It produces their sum and carry as outputs.

(*c*) used in the least significant position when adding two binary digits with no carry-in to consider. It produces their sum and carry as outputs.

(*d*) having two inputs and two outputs.

104. The half-adder circuit in the given figure has inputs AB = 11.

The logic level of P and Q outputs will be

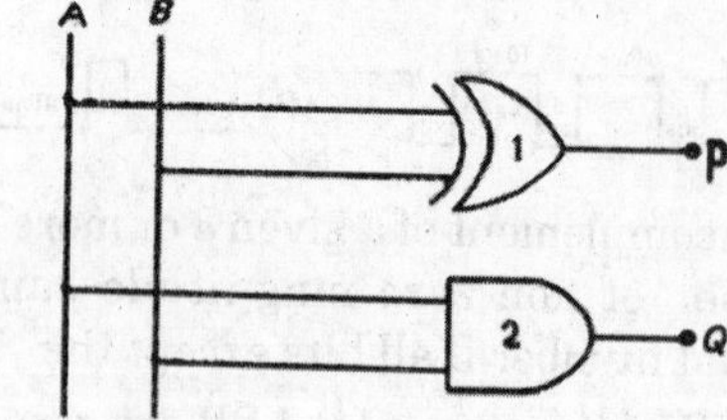

(*a*) P = 0 and Q = 0 (*b*) P = 0 and Q = 1

(*c*) P = 1 and Q = 0 (*d*) P = 1 and Q = 1

105. The circuit shown in the given figure

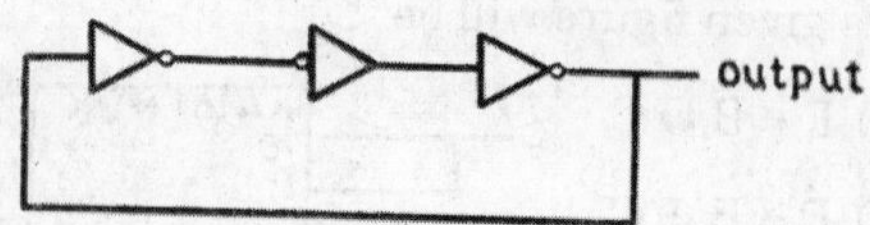

(*a*) is an oscillating circuit and its output is a square wave

(*b*) is one whose output remains stable in "1" state

(*c*) is one whose output remains stable in "0" state

(*d*) gives a single pulse of 3 times propagation delay

106. The control logic for a binary multiplier is specified by a state diagram. The state diagram has four states and two inputs. To implement it by the sequence register and decoder method

(*a*) two flip-flops and 2 × 4 decoders are needed

(*b*) four flip-flops and 2 × 4 decoders are needed

(*c*) two flip-flops and 3 × 9 decoders are needed

(*d*) four flip-flops and 3 × 9 decoders are needed

SEQUENTIAL CIRCUITS

107. A T-flip-flop function is obtained from a JK flip-flop. If the flip-flop belongs to a TTL family, the connection needed at the input must be

(*a*) J = K = 1. (*b*) J = K = 0

(*c*) J = 1 and K = 0 (*d*) J = 0 and K = 1

108. The characteristic equation of the T - flip - flop is given by

(*a*) $Q^+ = \overline{T}Q + T\overline{Q}$

(*b*) $Q^+ = T\overline{Q} + Q\overline{T}$

(*c*) $Q^+ = TQ$

(*d*) $Q^+ = T\overline{Q}$

109. The initial contents of the 4-bit serial-in-parallel-out, right-shift, shift register shown in the given figure is 0110. After three clock pulses are applied, the contents of the shift register will be

(*a*) 0000

(*b*) 0101

(*c*) 1010

(*d*) 1111

110. The race around condition exists in J-K flip flop if

(*a*) J = 0, K = 1 (*b*) J = 1, K = 0

(*c*) J = 0, K = 0 (*d*) J = 1, K = 1

111. In a JK flip-flop, the output Q_n is 1 and it does not change when a clock pulse is applied. The possible combination of J_n and K_n could be (x denotes don't care).

(*a*) x and 0 (*b*) x and 1

(*c*) 0 and x (*d*) 1 and x

112. The type of counter shown in the given figure is

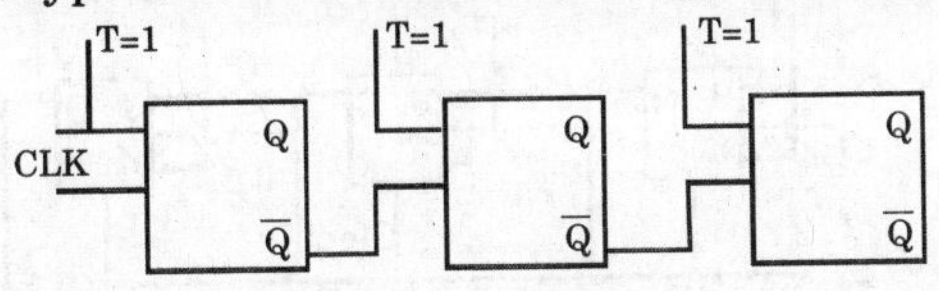

(*a*) Sychronous (*b*) Johnson

(*c*) Ring (*d*) None of these

113. In a negative edge triggered J-K flip-flop in order to the output Q state 0, 0 and 1 in the next three seccessive clock pulses, the J-K input states required would be respectively

(*a*) 00, 01 and 10 (*b*) 00, 01 and 11

(*c*) 00, 10 and 01 (*d*) 01, 10 and 11

114. The initial state of MOD-16 down counter is 0110. After 87 clock pulses, the state of counter will be

(*a*) 1011 (*b*) 0110

(*c*) 0101 (*d*) 0001

115. A three bit shift register is shown in the given figure. To have the content "000" again, the number of clock pulses required would be

(*a*) 3

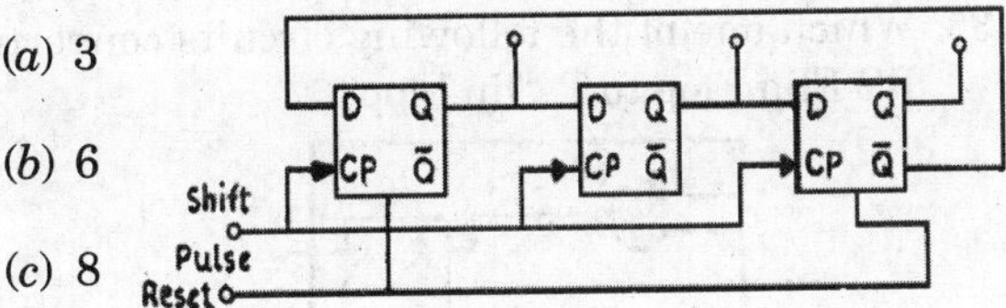

(*b*) 6

(*c*) 8

(*d*) 16

116. Symmetrical square wave of time period 100 μs can be obtained from square wave of time period 10 μs by using a

(*a*) divide by - 5 circuit

(*b*) divide by - 2 circuit

(*c*) divide by - 5 circuit followed by a divide by - 2 circuit

(*d*) BCD counter

117. A 1 μs pulse can be converted into a 1 ms pulse by using

(*a*) a monostable multivibrator

(*b*) an stable multivibrator

(*c*) a bistable miltivibrator

(*d*) a J-K flip-flop

118. An input frequency of 12 kHz is applied to the J-K flip-flops arrangement shown in the given figure. The resulting output frequency will be

(*a*) 24 kHz

(*b*) 12 kHz

(*c*) 6 kHz

(*d*) 3 kHz

119. The Q output of a J-K FLIP-FLOP is 'I'. The output does not change when a clock-pulse is applied. The inputs J and K will be respectively (where 'x' don't care state)

(*a*) 0 and x (*b*) x and 0

(*c*) 1 and 0 (*d*) 0 and 1

120. A 12-bit ADC is employed to convert an analog voltage of zero to 10 volts. The resolution of the ADC is

(*a*) 2.44 m V (*b*) 24.4 m V

(*c*) 83.3 mV (*d*) 1.2 V

121. In a 4 - bit weighted - resistor D/A converter, the resistor value corresponding to LSB is 16 kΩ. The resistor value corresponding to the MSB will be

(*a*) 1 kΩ (*b*) 2 kΩ

(*c*) 4 kΩ (*d*) 16 kΩ

122. For the design of a sequential circuit having nine states MINIMUM number of memory elements required is

(*a*) 3 (*b*) 4

(*c*) 5 (*d*) 9

123. A 4-bit binary ripple counter uses flip-flops with a propagation delay time of 25 ns each. The maximum possible time required for change of state will be

(*a*) 25 ns (*b*) 50 ns

(*c*) 75 ns (*d*) 100 ns

124. The circuit shown below is

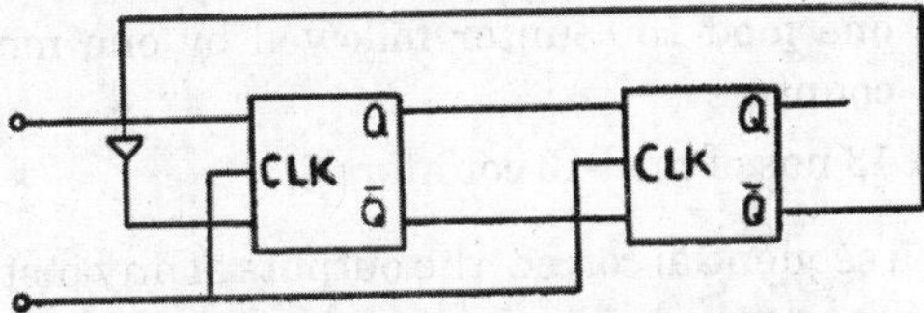

(*a*) 2 : 1 scalar (*b*) 4 : 1 scalar

(*c*) up-down counter (*d*) None of these

125. The difference between sequential and combinational circuit is that

(*a*) combinational circuits store bits

(*b*) combinational circuits have memory

(*c*) sequential circuits store bits

(*d*) sequential circuits have memory

126. Which of the following flip-flop cannot be converted to D-type (delay) flip-flop?
(a) S—R flip flop
(b) J—K flip flop
(c) Master slave flip-flop
(d) None of these

127. The characteristic of a flip-flop is
(a) the flip-flop is a bistable device with only two stable states
(b) the flip-flop has two output signals
(c) the outputs are complement of each other
(d) all of these

128. Which one of the following can be used to change data from spatial code to temporal code?
(a) Shift registers
(b) Counters
(c) A/D converters
(d) Combinational circuits

129. Which of the following statements are correct?
1. A flip-flop is used to store I-bit of information.
2. Race-around condition occurs in a J-K flip-flop to store 2-bits of information.
3. Master-slave configuration is used in flip-flops to store 2-bits of information.
4. A transparent latch consists of a D-type flip-flop.

Select the correct answer using the codes given below:
(a) 1, 2 and 3
(b) 1, 3 and 4
(c) 1, 2 and 4
(d) 2, 3 and 4

130. A divide-by-78 counter can be realized by using
(a) 6 nos of mod-13 counters
(b) 13 nos of mod-6 counters
(c) one mod-13 counter followed by one mod-6 counters
(d) 13 nos of mod-13 counters

131. In a sequential corced, the outputs at any instant of time depend
(a) only on the inputs present at that instant of time
(b) on past output as well as present inputs
(c) only on the past inputs
(d) only on the past outputs

132. A bit synchronous counter uses flip-flops with propagation delay time of 15 ns each. The maximum possible time required for change of state will be
(a) 15 ns (b) 30 ns
(c) 45 ns (d) 60 ns

133. The block diagram shown in the given figure represents

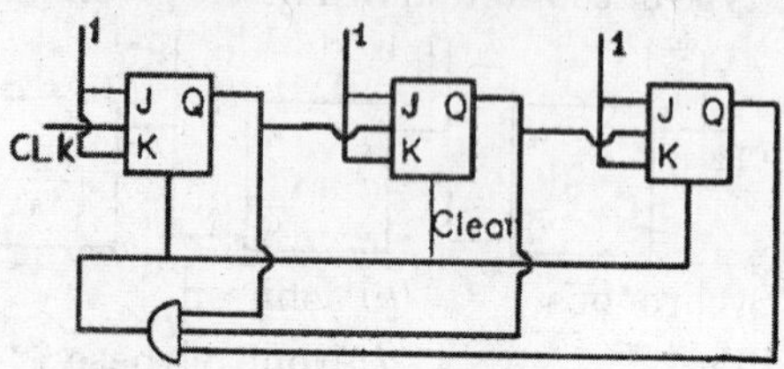

(a) modulo-3 ripple counter
(b) modulo-5 ripple counter
(c) modulo-7 ripple counter
(d) modulo-7 synchronous counter

134. If the input and signals of a block box are as given in the following figures, then the black box is a/an

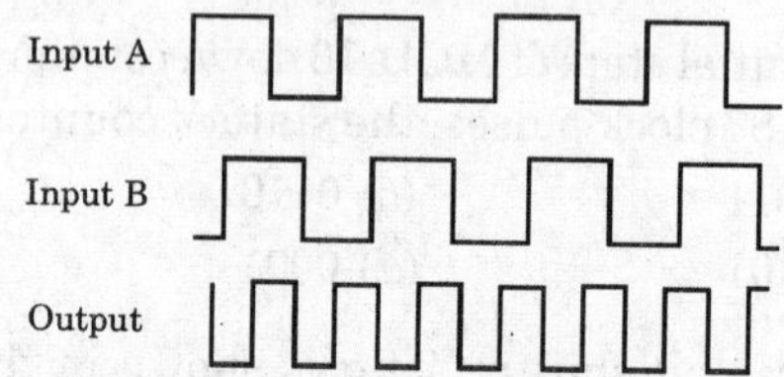

(a) coincidence circuit (b) X OR circuit
(c) JK Flip Flop (d) R-S Flip Flop

135. Which one of the following circuits converts an RS Flip Flop to T Flip Flop?

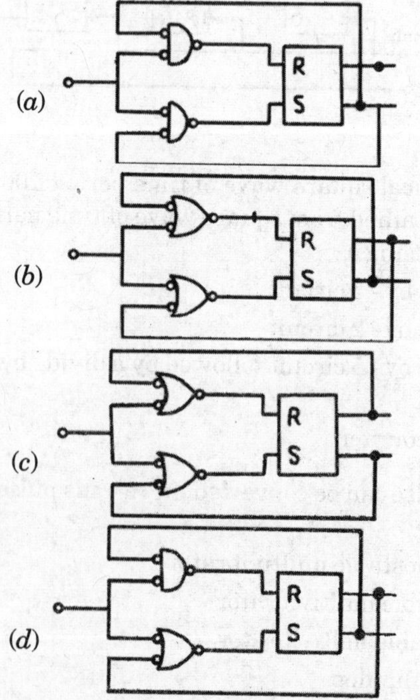

136. Given A = 1, B = 1, $Q_n = 0$ and $P_n = 1$. When the clock input (CK) is applied, then

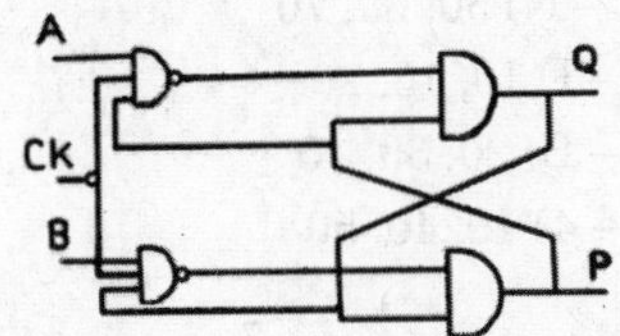

(a) $Q_{n+1} = 0, P_{n+1} = 0$

(b) $Q_{n+1} = 0, P_{n+1} = 1$

(c) $Q_{n+1} = 1, P_{n+1} = 0$

(d) $Q_{n+1} = 1, P_{n+1} = 1$

137. The characteristic necessary for a sequential circuit are

(a) It must have at least six gates.
(b) It must have some feedback.
(c) Its output should depend on some past value.
(d) Both (b) and (c)

138. Which one of the circuits given below converts a JKF/F to a TF/F?

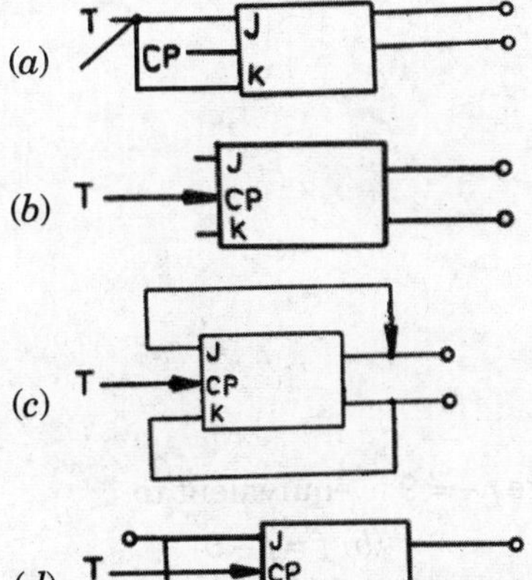

139. For the circuit shown in the given figure, the frequency of the output Q will be

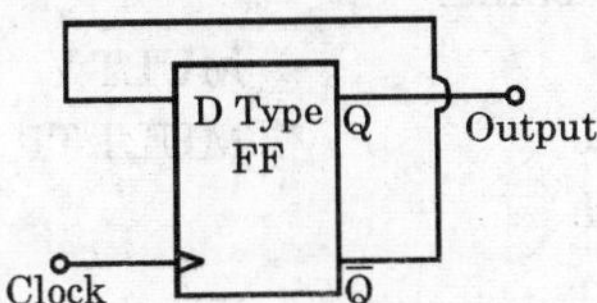

(a) twice the input frequency
(b) half the input clock frequency
(c) same as the input clock frequency
(d) inverse of the propagation delay of the EF

140. The input pulses to the different stages of the counter shown in the following figure must be of

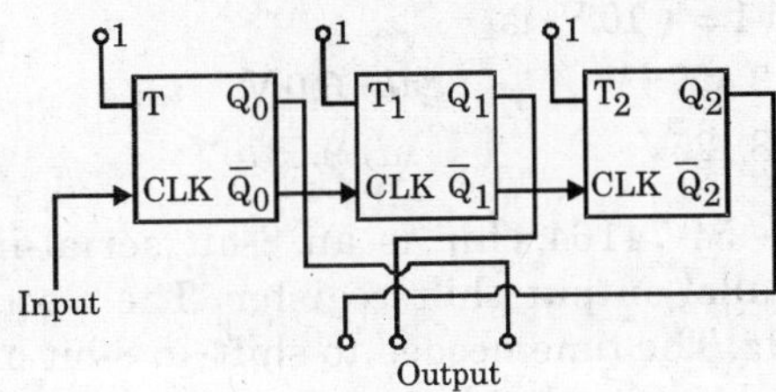

(a) constant frequency and constant width
(b) constant frequency but variable width
(c) variable frequency but constant width
(d) variable frequency as well as variable width

141. State transition table and state transition diagrams from part of design steps is the case of

(a) Combinational circuits
(b) Amplifier circuits
(c) Delay circuits
(d) Sequential circuits

142. The decoding error of the counter can be avoided by

(a) increasing propagation delay of flip-flops used in the counter
(b) using very fast logic gates
(c) using the strobe signal
(d) reducing the propagation delay of flip-flops used in the counter

143. Consider the following statements:

1. Race around condition occurs in a JK flip-flop when both inputs are one.
2. A flip-flop is used to store one bit of information.
3. A transparent latch consists in of D-type flip-flop.
4. Master-slave configuration is used in flip-flop to store two bits of information.

Of these statements, the correct statements are

(a) 1, 2 and 3 (b) 1, 3 and 4
(c) 1, 2 and 4 (d) 2, 3 and 4

144. A ring counter consisting of five flip-flop will have

(a) 5 states
(b) 10 states
(c) 32 states
(d) infinite states

145. The output voltage of a 5-bit D/A binary ladder that has a digital input of 11010 (Assuming 0 = 0 V and 1 = + 10 V) is

(*a*) 3.4375 V (*b*) 6.0 V
(*c*) 8.125V (*d*) 9.6875V

146. The 54/74164 chip is an 8-bit serial-input-parallel-output shift register. The clock is 1 MHz. The time needed to shift an 8-bit binary number into the chip is

(*a*) 1 μs (*b*) 2 μs
(*c*) 8 μs (*d*) 16 μs

MICRO PROCESSOR

147. Consider the following statements :
The horoizontal microinstruction has

1. longer control word than vertical micrinstruction
2. high degree of parallelism
3. slower execution than vertical microinstruction

Of these statements the correct statement(s) is/are

(*a*) 1 alone (*b*) 2 alone
(*c*) 1 and 2 (*d*) 2 and 3

148. The logic operation that will selectively clear bits in register A in those positions where there are 1's in the bits of register B is given by

(*a*) $A \leftarrow A + B$ (*c*) $A \leftarrow \overline{A}\ B$
(*b*) $A \leftarrow \overline{A} + \overline{B}$ (*d*) $A \leftarrow A\ \overline{B}$

149. Which of the following is loaded in the main memory by the bootstrap loader?

(*a*) System data (*b*) User program
(*c*) BIOS (*d*) Part of DOS

150. If a RAM has 34 bits in its MAR and 16 bits in its MDR, then its capacity will be

(*a*) 32 GB (*b*) 16 GB
(*c*) 32 MB (*d*) 16 MB

151. In 8068, if the content of the code segment register is 1 FAB and the content of the IP register is 10 AI, then the effective memory address is

(*a*) IFBCO (*b*) 304 C
(*c*) FDB5 (*d*) 20B51

152. Four memory chips of 16 × 4 size have their address buses connected together. This system will be of size

(*a*) 64 × 4 (*b*) 16 × 16
(*c*) 32 × 8 (*d*) 256 × 1

153. Of the following, which Arithmetic IE statements is invalid?

(*a*) IF (M – N) 50, 60, 70
(*b*) IF (A – I) 10, 15, 20
(*c*) IF (A – B) 20, 30, 40
(*d*) IF (A – 4) 40, 40, 50

154. The expression, $I = 8 + \frac{7}{4}$ will be computed as

(*a*) 3.75 (*b*) 9.75
(*c*) 9 (*d*) 3

155. The minimum decimal equivalent of the number 11C.0 is

(*a*) 183 (*b*) 194
(*c*) 268 (*d*) 269

156. $(FE35)_{16}$ XOR $(CB15)_{16}$ is equal to

(*a*) $(3320)_{16}$ (*b*) $(FE35)_{16}$
(*c*) $(FF50)_{16}$ (*d*) $(3520)_{16}$

157. If the value of x in decimal number is 3954, the value of y in decimal number computed by the given flow chart is

(*a*) 20

(*b*) 22

(*c*) 21

(*d*) 3954

158. In C language $f - = 9$ is equivalent to

(*a*) $f = -9$ (*b*) $f = f - 9$
(*c*) $f = 9 - 1$ (*d*) $-f = 9$

159. A primitive computer uses a single register. The following fragment of assembly code is written for the machine:

```
LOAD X
STORE YI
STORE TI
LOAD Z
ADD Y
ADD TI
STORE R
MULT Y
MULT TI
```

Which one of the following expressions is evaluated?

(*a*) R : (XY) + Y = Z (*b*) R : = $(XY)^2$ + Y + Z
(*c*) R : XY^2 + Y + Z (*d*) R : = XY^2 + (Y + Z)

160. For a particular type of memory, the access time and the cycle time are respectively 200 ns and 200 ns. The maximum rate at which the data can be accessed is

(*a*) 2.5×10^6/s (*b*) 5×10^6/s
(*c*) 2×10^6/s (*d*) 1×10^6/s

161. When a human being tries to approach an object, his brain acts as

(*a*) an error measuring device
(*b*) a controller
(*c*) an actuator
(*d*) an amplifier

162. The microprocessor having refresh logic for dynamic memory is

(*a*) 6502
(*b*) INTEL 8085
(*c*) Motorola MC 6800
(*d*) Z 80

163. In hexadecimal system, 7716 - 3B16 is equal to

(*a*) 3D16 (*b*) 6016
(*c*) 3C16 (*d*) 7316

164. The register which keeps track of the sequence of instruction execution is

(*a*) memory address register
(*b*) memory buffer register
(*c*) stack pointer
(*d*) program counter

165. The interface chip used for data transmission between 8086 and a 16-bit ADC is

(*a*) 8259 (*b*) 8255
(*c*) 8253 (*d*) 8251

166. Match List-I with List-II and select the correct answer by using the codes given below the lists:

List-I (Pin terminals)	**List-II (Applications)**
A. SID, SOD	1. Wait state
B. READY	2. Interrupt
C. TRAP	3. Serial data transfer
D. ALE	4. Memory or I/O read/write
	5. Address latch control

Codes:

	A	**B**	**C**	**D**
(*a*)	3	1	5	2
(*b*)	3	1	2	5
(*c*)	4	3	2	5
(*d*)	4	3	1	2

167. The software that transfers the object program from secondary memory to the main memory is called

(*a*) assember (*b*) loader
(*c*) linker (*d*) task builder

168. Which one of the following is a correct set of specifications of one side of a 360 K floppy disc?

	Number of tracks	**Number of bits/inch**	**Number of sectors**	**Number of bytes/ sector**
(*a*)	40	4000	9	512
(*b*)	80	2000	18	256
(*c*)	60	3000	9	512
(*d*)	40	1000	9	256

169. The basic memory cell of dynamic RAM consists of

(*a*) a capacitance
(*b*) a transistor
(*c*) a flip- flop
(*d*) a transistor acting as a capacitor

170. PROMs are used to store

(*a*) bulk information
(*b*) sequence information
(*c*) information to be accessed rarely
(*d*) relatively permanent information

171. The Address Bus of Intel 8085 is 16 bit and hence the memory which can be accessed by this address bus is

(*a*) 1 k Byte (*b*) 16 k Bits
(*c*) 32 k Bits (*d*) 64 Bytes

172. T_1 evaluate under a condition, $100 < m < 200$. The computer statement shall be

(*a*) IF (M. GE. 100. AND. M. LE. 200)
(*b*) IF (M. GT. 100. AND M. LT. 200)
(*c*) IF (M. LT. 100. AND. M. GT. 100)
(*d*) IF (M. LE. 200. AND M. GT. 100)

173. Which of the following relation is valid?

(*a*) M T B F = M T T F + M T T R
(*b*) M T T R + M T T F + M T B T = 1
(*c*) $\frac{1}{MTTR} + \frac{1}{MTTF} = \frac{1}{MTBF}$
(*d*) M T B F . M T T F . M T T R = 1

Where M T N F = Mean Time Between Failures
M T T F = Mean Time To Failure
M T T R = Mean Time To Repair

174. Most of the digital computers do not have floating-point hardware because

(*a*) floating point hardware is costly

(*b*) it is slower than software

(*c*) it is not possible to perform floating point addition by hardware

(*d*) of no specific reason

175. Match List-I (computer terms) with List-II (definitions) and select the correct answer using the codes given below the lists:

List-I	List-II
A. Interface	1. A measure of rate of data transmission
B. A bit	2. A binary digit
C. Baud speed	3. The common boundary between various sections and sub sections
	4. Analog to digital converter

Codes:

	A	B	C
(*a*)	3	2	1
(*b*)	3	1	2
(*c*)	2	4	1
(*d*)	4	2	3

176. If the memory chip size is 256 × 1 bits, then the number of chips required to make up 1 k (1024) bytes of memory is

(*a*) 32 (*b*) 24

(*c*) 12 (*d*) 8

177. Match List-I with List-II and select the correct answer using the codes given below the lists:

List-I (Memories)	List-II (Particular characteristic)
A. Static PL memory	1. Erasable programmable
B. CCD memory	2. Ultra high speed
C. ECL memory	3. Stores large volume of data
D. GAL memory	4. Does not need refreshing
	5. Non-volatile

Codes:

	A	B	C	D
(*a*)	4	3	2	1
(*b*)	4	2	3	1
(*c*)	5	1	2	3
(*d*)	3	5	2	1

178. Which one of the following keeps track of instruction execution sequence?

(*a*) Accumulator (*b*) Program counter

(*c*) Stack pointer (*d*) Instruction register

179. Consider the following statements associated with microprocessors:

1. Debug is synonymous with exponent.
2. Direct-Memory Access Channel (DMA) facilitates to move into and out of the system without program interruption.
3. Double precision employs double signal speed.
4. Dump means copying data from internal storage to external storage.

Of these statements, the correct statements are

(*a*) 2 and 4

(*b*) 1, 2 and 4

(*c*) 2 and 3

(*d*) 1, 3 and 4

180. The flag which is not used for branching in a microprocessor is

(*a*) Carry flag

(*b*) Auxiliary carry flag

(*c*) Overflow flag

(*d*) Parity flag

181. RAM

(*a*) is a non-volatile memory whereas ROM is a volatile memory.

(*b*) is a volatile memory whereas ROM is non-volatile memory.

(*c*) and ROM are volatile memories but in ROM data is not lost when power is switched off.

(*d*) and ROM are non-volatile memories but in RAM data is lost when power is switched off.

182. Match List-I (Memory elements) with List-II (Properties) and select the correct answer using the codes given below the lists:

List-I	List-II
A. Semiconductor memory	1. Destructive read out
B. Ferrite core memory	2. Combinational logic
C. Magnetic tape memory	3. Volatile

Codes:

	A	B	C
(*a*)	2	1	3
(*b*)	1	3	2
(*c*)	3	2	1
(*d*)	3	1	2

183. Which of the following conditional IF statements of Pascal are correct?

I. IF condition 1 THEN statement 1
Else IF condition 2 THEN
statement 2 ELSE statement 3

II. IF condition 1 THEN IF condition 2 .
THEN statement 1
ELSE statement 2
ELSE statement 3

III. IF condition 1 THEN IF condition 2
THEN statement 1
ELSE statement 2

Select the correct answser using the codes given below:

(*a*) I and II (*b*) II and III
(*c*) I and III (*d*) I, II and III

184. In an assembler, which one of the following is required for variable names in symbol table?

(*a*) Addresses (*b*) Values
(*c*) Registers (*d*) Storage

185. The operations performed on linear queues are

(*a*) testing a linear queue for underflow
(*b*) enqueue and Dequeue operation
(*c*) testing a linear queue for overflow
(*d*) all of these

186. Effective address is calculated by adding or subtracting displacement value to .

(*a*) immediate address
(*b*) relative address
(*c*) absolute address
(*d*) base address

187. The microprograms provided by a manufacturer to be used on his microgrammed computer are generally called

(*a*) software (*b*) netware
(*c*) firmwar (*d*) hardware

188. A relaxation oscillator

(*a*) has two stable states
(*b*) oscillates continuously
(*c*) relaxes indefinitely
(*d*) produces non-sinusoidal output

189. A retriggerable monshot is one which

(*a*) can be triggered only once
(*b*) has two quasi-stable states
(*c*) cannot be triggered until full pulse has been outputted
(*d*) is capable of being triggered while the output is being generated

Answers

1. (b)	2. (c)	3. (a)	4. (a)	5. (c)	6. (c)	7. (d)	8. (a)	9. (b)	10. (c)
11. (a)	12. (a)	13. (d)	14. (b)	15. (c)	16. (b)	17. (a)	18. (a)	19. (c)	20. (c)
21. (d)	22. (b)	23. (c)	24. (b)	25. (b)	26. (c)	27. (b)	28. (b)	29. (a)	30. (a)
31. (a)	32. (c)	33. (d)	34. (a)	35. (d)	36. (c)	37. (c)	38. (c)	39. (c)	40. (b)
41. (c)	42. (d)	43. (c)	44. (b)	45. (c)	46. (a)	47. (d)	48. (c)	49. (a)	50. (b)
51. (b)	52. (d)	53. (d)	54. (a)	55. (c)	56. (c)	57. (b)	58. (a)	59. (d)	60. (c)
61. (a)	62. (d)	63. (a)	64. (b)	65. (d)	66. (b)	67. (d)	68. (a)	69. (d)	70. (c)
71. (a)	72. (c)	73. (c)	74. (b)	75. (c)	76. (a)	77. (c)	78. (c)	79. (c)	80. (a)
81. (a)	82. (b)	83. (a)	84. (c)	85. (d)	86. (a)	87. (a)	88. (d)	89. (d)	90. (d)
91. (a)	92. (b)	93. (b)	94. (b)	95. (c)	96. (c)	97. (a)	98. (c)	99. (a)	100. (c)
101. (c)	102. (c)	103. (b)	104. (b)	105. (a)	106. (a)	107. (a)	108. (b)	109. (c)	110. (d)
111. (a)	112. (d)	113. (b)	114. (d)	115. (b)	116. (c)	117. (d)	118. (d)	119. (b)	120. (a)
121. (b)	122. (b)	123. (d)	124. (b)	125. (d)	126. (d)	127. (d)	128. (a)	129. (c)	130. (c)
131. (b)	132. (a)	133. (c)	134. (a)	135. (b)	136. (a)	137. (d)	138. (a)	139. (b)	140. (d)
141. (d)	142. (a)	143. (a)	144. (a)	145. (c)	146. (c)	147. (a)	148. (d)	149. (d)	150. (a)
151. (d)	152. (b)	153. (d)	154. (c)	155. (d)	156. (d)	157. (c)	158. (b)	159. (b)	160. (d)
161. (b)	162. (d)	163. (c)	164. (d)	165. (b)	166. (b)	167. (b)	168. (b)	169. (d)	170. (d)
171. (d)	172. (b)	173. (a)	174. (a)	175. (a)	176. (a)	177. (c)	178. (b)	179. (a)	180. (b)
181. (b)	182. (a)	183. (a)	184. (c)	185. (d)	186. (d)	187. (c)	188. (d)	189. (d)	

Explanations

3. $\overline{\overline{[\overline{(A+B)}+C+\overline{\overline{(D+E)}}]}} = \overline{[(A+B).\overline{C}+\overline{\overline{(D+E)}}]}$

$= [\overline{(A+B)}+C][\overline{D}\,\overline{E}]$

8. $F = X+\overline{(\overline{\overline{X}.Y.\overline{Z}})}+Z$

$= X+\overline{(X+\overline{Y}+Z)}+Z$

$= X+\overline{Y}+Z$

Its can be realized as

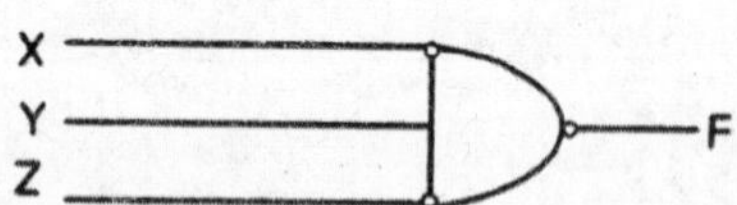

12.

A	B	X
0	0	1
0	1	0
1	0	0
1	1	0

Gate can be NAND or NOR gate

13.

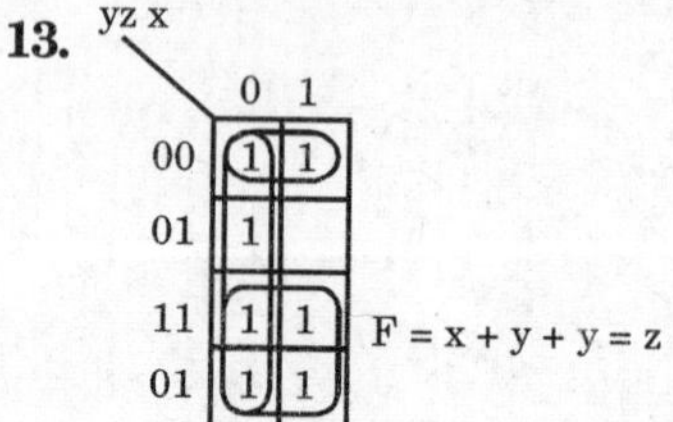

15.

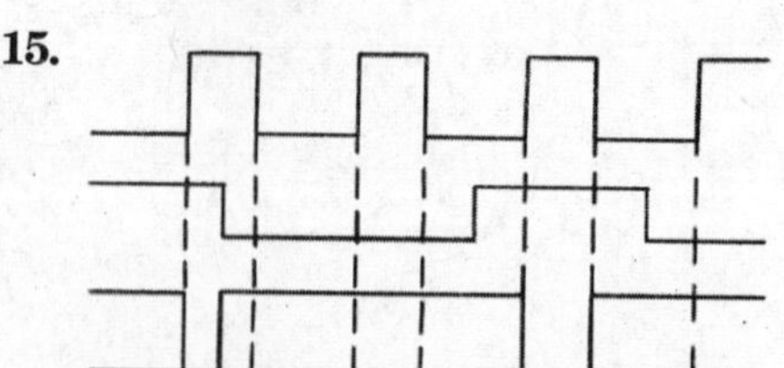

NAND gate T T

A	B	X
0	0	1
0	1	1
1	0	1
1	1	0

18.

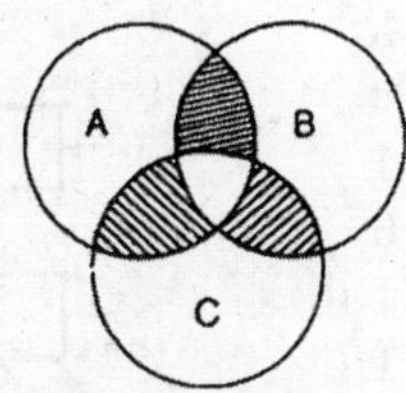

Boolean expression will be

$$AB + BC + CA$$

20. $F = \overline{x} + \left(\overline{x\,\overline{y} + z}\right) + Z$

$= \overline{x} + \overline{x} + y + \overline{z} + \overline{z}$

$= \overline{x} + y + \overline{z}$

Hence correct gate is

29. $Y = \overline{[\overline{(A+B).C}].(DE)}$

$= (A+B).C + DE$___

$= A.C + B.C + DE$

$= (A+B).C + DE$

38. $X = (A+\overline{B}).(B+C).B$

$= (A+\overline{B}).(B.B + B.C)$

$= (A+\overline{B}).(B + B.C)$

$= A.B + ABC + \overline{B}.B + \overline{B}BC$

$= AB(1+C) + 0 + 0$

$= AB$

40.

A	B	C	X
0	0	0	0
0	0	1	0
0	1	0	0
0	1	1	1
1	0	0	0
1	0	1	1
1	1	0	1
1	1	1	1

$X = \overline{A}BC + A\overline{B}C + AB\overline{C} + ABC$

43. $Z = \overline{(\overline{X}\,Y + X\,Y)}$

$= \overline{(\overline{X}\,Y)}.\overline{(X\,Y)}$

$= (X+\overline{Y}).(\overline{X}+\overline{Y})$

47. $F = \overline{[\overline{\overline{((\overline{A+B}) + C)}}.\overline{\overline{(D+F)}}]}$

$= \overline{\overline{[(\overline{A+B}+C)}}.\overline{\overline{(D+F)]}}$

$= [\overline{(A+B)} + C].(\overline{D+E})$

$= [\overline{A+B+C}].(\overline{D}\,\overline{E})$

56.

X	Y	Z	F
0	0	0	0
0	0	1	1
0	1	0	1
0	1	1	1
1	0	0	0
1	0	1	1
1	1	0	1
1	1	1	0

$F = \overline{x}\,\overline{y}\,\overline{z} + \overline{y}\,\overline{z} + x\,y\,z$

$\therefore\ F = \left(\overline{\overline{x}\,\overline{y}\,\overline{z} + \overline{y}\,\overline{z} + x\,y\,z}\right)$

$= \left(\overline{x}\,\overline{y}\,\overline{z}\right).\left(x\,\overline{y}\,\overline{z}\right).\left(\overline{xyz}\right)$

$= (x+y+z).(\overline{x}+y+z)(\overline{x}+\overline{y}+\overline{z})$

62. $F = \overline{A}\,\overline{B}C + \overline{A}\,\overline{B}\,\overline{C} + A\overline{B}\,\overline{C} + A\overline{B}C$

$= \overline{A}\,\overline{B}(C+\overline{C}) + A\overline{B}(\overline{C}+C)$

$= \overline{A}\,\overline{B} + A\overline{B}$

68.

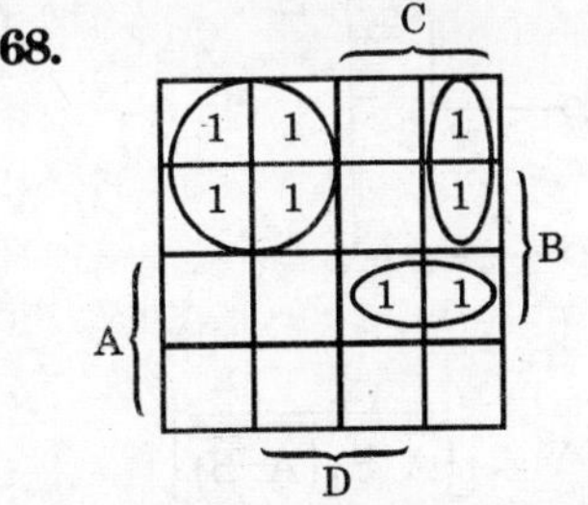

$F = \overline{A}\,\overline{C} + \overline{A}\,\overline{D} + ABC$

$= (\overline{A}+A)B = \overline{B}$

72.

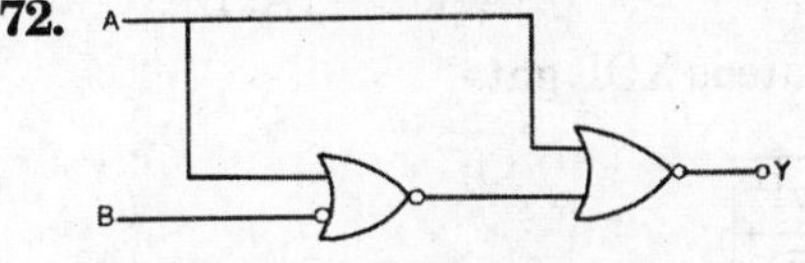

$Y = \left[\overline{A + (\overline{\overline{A+\overline{\overline{B}}}})}\right] = \overline{A}.(A+\overline{B})$

$= \overline{A}.A + \overline{A} + \overline{B} = \overline{A}\,\overline{B}$

73.

$$\begin{array}{r} \text{F F F F} \\ -\,\text{2 B F D} \\ \hline \text{D 4 0 2} \end{array}$$

$\therefore$ Fig. Complement is D 402.

75. $Y = \overline{AB} + \overline{BC} + \overline{CA}$

Taking double inversion

$Y = \left(\overline{\overline{\overline{AB} + \overline{BC} + \overline{CA}}}\right)$

$= \left[\overline{\left(\overline{\overline{AB}}\right).\left(\overline{\overline{BC}}\right).\left(\overline{\overline{CA}}\right)}\right]$

$= \left[\overline{(AB).(BC).(CA)}\right]$

78. $AB + AC + B\overline{C}$

Drawing venn Diagram

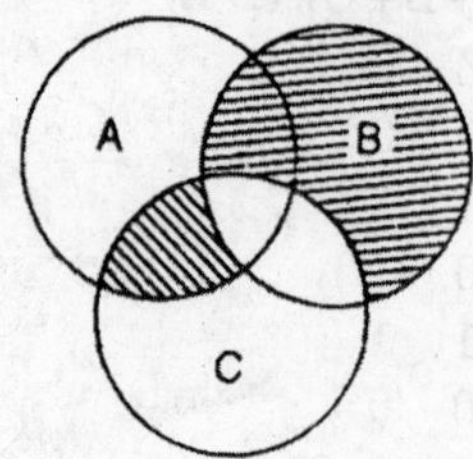

above even diagram can be reduced to $AC + B\overline{C}$.

80. $F = A \,.\, B + C\,D + E$

Taking double inversion

$$F = \left(\overline{\overline{AB + CD + E}}\right)$$

$$= \left(\overline{(\overline{AB}).(\overline{CD}).\,\overline{E}}\right)$$

Which can be realized as

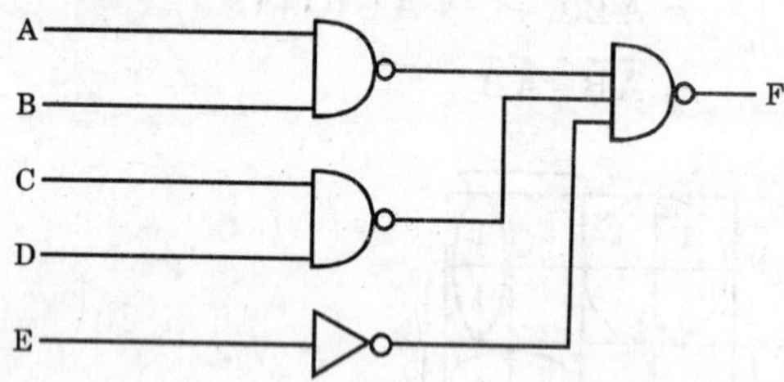

85. $$Y = \left[\overline{\overline{(\overline{A}.\,B)}\;\overline{(A.\,\overline{B})}}\right]$$

$$= \left[\overline{(A + \overline{B}).(\overline{A} + B)}\right]$$

$$= \overline{(\overline{A}.\,B)} + \overline{(A.\,\overline{B})}$$

∴ Given gate is XOR gate

86.

S_1	S_0	O/P
0	0	1
0	1	1
1	0	1
1	1	0

Hence given multiplexer is NAND gate

89.

A	B	C	F
0	0	0	0
0	1	0	0
0	1	1	1
1	0	0	1
1	0	1	0
1	1	0	0
1	1	1	1

$$\therefore\; F = \overline{A}BC + \overline{A}B\overline{C} + AB\overline{C} + ABC$$

90.

A	B	C	X
0	0	0	0
0	0	1	1
0	1	0	0
0	1	1	1
1	0	0	1
1	0	1	0
1	1	0	1
1	1	1	0

$$F = \overline{A}\overline{B}C + \overline{A}BC + A\overline{B}\overline{C} + AB\overline{C}$$

$$= \overline{A}(\overline{B} + B)C + A\overline{C}(\overline{B} + B)$$

$$= \overline{A}C + A\overline{C}$$

$$F = A \oplus C$$

107. Truth table of J K flip flop is

J	K	Q_+
0	0	Q
0	1	0
1	0	1
1	1	$\overline{Q}$

Truth table of T flip flop is

T	Q_+
0	a
1	$\overline{a}$

From truth table of J K and T flip flop it is obvious that T flip flop can be obtained from J K flip flop by making J = K = 1

118. Output frequency will be 1/4th of input frequency

$$= \frac{12}{4} = 3 \text{ kHz}$$

120. Resolution $= \frac{10}{2^{12}} = 2.44$ mV

156.

FE 35 = 1 1 1 1 1 1 1 0 0 0 1 1 0 1 0 1

CB 15 = 1 1 0 0 1 0 1 1 0 0 0 1 0 1 0 1

XOR = 0 0 1 1 0 1 0 1 0 0 1 0 0 0 0 0

$= (3520)_{16}$

XOR gate T T is

A	B	X
0	0	0
0	1	1
1	0	1
1	1	1

176. Number of chips required $= \frac{1024 \times 8}{265 \times 1} = 32$

■■